The period of the tenth and early eleventh centuries was crucial in the formation of Europe, much of whose political geography and larger-scale divisions began to take shape at this time. It was also an era of great fragmentation, and hence of differences which have been magnified by modern national historiographical traditions. The international team of authors in this volume of *The New Cambridge Medieval History* reflects these varying traditions, and provides an authoritative survey of the period in its own terms.

The volume is divided into three sections. The first covers common themes and topics such as the economy, government, and religious cultural and intellectual life. The second is devoted to the kingdoms and principalities which had emerged within the area of the former Carolingian empire, as well as the 'honorary Carolingian' region of England. The final section deals with the emergent principalities of eastern Europe and the new and established empires and statelets of the Mediterranean world.

The New Cambridge Medieval History

Volume III *c.* 900–*c.* 1024

London, Victoria and Albert Museum, the Basilewski ivory *situla*, *c.* 980, showing scenes from the Passion

THE NEW
CAMBRIDGE
MEDIEVAL HISTORY

Volume III c. 900–c. 1024

EDITED BY
TIMOTHY REUTER
Professor of Medieval History
University of Southampton

CAMBRIDGE
UNIVERSITY PRESS

PUBLISHED BY THE PRESS SYNDICATE OF THE UNIVERSITY OF CAMBRIDGE
The Pitt Building, Trumpington Street, Cambridge, United Kingdom

CAMBRIDGE UNIVERSITY PRESS
The Edinburgh Building, Cambridge CB2 2RU, United Kingdom   http://www.cup.cam.ac.uk
40 West 20th Street, New York, NY 10011-4211, USA   http://www.cup.org
10 Stamford Road, Oakleigh, Melbourne 3166, Australia

First published 1999

Printed in the United Kingdom at the University Press, Cambridge

Typeset in 10.5/12.5 pt. Garamond in QuarkXPress™   [SE]

A catalogue record for this book is available from the British Library

Library of Congress Cataloguing in publication data

ISBN 0 521 36447 7 hardback

CONTENTS

vii

MAPS

PLATES

frontispiece

London, Victoria and Albert Museum, the Basilewski ivory *situla*, *c.* 980
(photo © Victoria and Albert Museum)

between pages 230 and 231

xi

CONTRIBUTORS

GERD ALTHOFF, *Professor of Medieval History, University of Münster*

DAVID BATES, *Professor of Medieval History, University of Glasgow*

CONSTANCE BOUCHARD, *Professor of Medieval History, Kenyon College, Ohio*

ROGER COLLINS, *Edinburgh*

JEAN DUNBABIN, *Fellow of St. Anne's College, University of Oxford*

ROBERT FOSSIER, *Professor of History, University of Paris I*

PETER JOHANEK, *Professor of Regional History, University of Münster*

HUGH KENNEDY, *Reader in History, University of St Andrews*

SIMON KEYNES, *Fellow of Trinity College, University of Cambridge*

CLAUDIO LEONARDI, *Professor of Latin Philology, University of Florence*

G. A. LOUD, *Reader in History, University of Leeds*

HENRY MAYR-HARTING, *Regius Professor of Ecclesiastical History, University of Oxford*

ROSAMOND MCKITTERICK, *Professor of Medieval History, University of Cambridge*

ECKHARD MÜLLER-MERTENS, *Professor of History Emeritus, Humboldt University of Berlin*

JANET L. NELSON, *Professor of History, King's College, London*

T. S. NOONAN, *Professor of History, University of Minnesota*

MICHEL PARISSE, *Professor of Medieval History, University of Paris VIII*

TIMOTHY REUTER, *Professor of Medieval History, University of Southampton*

GIUSEPPE SERGI, *Professor of Medieval History, University of Turin*

JONATHAN SHEPARD, *Fellow of Peterhouse, University of Cambridge*

JERZY STRZELCZYK, *Professor of History, University of Poznań*

HERWIG WOLFRAM, *Director, Institut für österreichische Geschichtsforschung, University of Vienna*

JOACHIM WOLLASCH, *Professor of Medieval History Emeritus, University of Münster*

MICHAEL ZIMMERMANN, *Professor of Medieval History, University of Paris*

PREFACE

Timothy Reuter

No one can be more aware than a volume editor of the difficulties inherent in the project of a *New Cambridge Medieval History*, not least the argument that all such projects belong to a positivistic attitude to knowledge which has now rightly passed from the stage. Had the intention simply been to make a better job of providing a 'definitive account' of this particular section of the past than was done under the editorship of J. P. Whitney when volume III of the old *Cambridge Medieval History*, subtitled 'Germany and the Western Empire', was published in 1922, the project would indeed seem problematic. But periodic stock-takings are both important and necessary, especially given that approaches to the early medieval past have changed so fundamentally in the last seventy years. They allow a group of scholars to set out for a wider audience the current state of play in their own areas of specialisation, and so to provide students, teachers and the general public with a set of accounts of the subject which have all been produced at much the same time and to much the same set of instructions. The result may no doubt date, though slowly, but it is in any case no longer expected to do anything else. If the framework is still, as it was in the early years of this century, that of political history, it is a political history conceived more broadly, and, it is to be hoped, more readably, than was current in the 1920s. My introductory chapter and those of the other contributors to the opening thematic section set out some of the links between political history and other ways of practising the discipline.

The division around 1024 between this volume and its twin successors, inherited from the earlier *Cambridge Medieval History*, obviously has no immediate significance except for German, Italian and (more or less) Byzantine history, and it has been appropriately modified for the chapters on other topics. Both it and its substitutes here are divisions conceived essentially in terms of political history, but this has the positive advantage of not having to plump for either of the current rival datings on offer for the Great Medieval Shift: that from the ancient world to the medieval world (or from slavery to feudalism)

xv

around 1000; or that from 'archaic society' to the 'Old European Order' around 1050. More is said of these and other interpretative schemata in the introductory chapter.

An intellectual climate more relativistic than that which prevailed in the time of Acton, Whitney and Tanner has had the advantage for the editor that he has felt little pressure to harmonise interpretations and interpretative styles between contributions, though he hopes that there are few if any remaining discrepancies in respect of 'facts'. Indeed, it is a positive advantage that the reader should become more aware of the great range of approaches to early medieval history currently being practised in this country, on the continent and in North America. It is for this reason that the team of contributors is a fairly international one rather than being restricted to Anglophone historians. To have followed the latter course would have had many advantages, but would have risked presenting the reader with a greater appearance of homogeneity in current approaches to the subject than really exists. Intellectual stock-taking should take account not only of what is currently thought but of how and why it has come to be so thought, and in particular should emphasise rather than conceal the differences between national historiographical traditions. In the introduction I have attempted to set out some of the implications of these traditions and explore their strengths and weaknesses.

The volume is arranged in three parts. The chapters in the opening section cover themes not easily or sensibly divided up geographically. The following section has nine chapters on the polities which emerged after the break-up of the Carolingian empire, and also includes the chapter on England, which was institutionally, culturally and politically an important part of the post-Carolingian order. The final section covers non-Carolingian Europe (including Byzantium and the Islamic polities within Europe), with the chapters arranged from north-east to south-west. In order to avoid too many mini-chapters, some responsibilities have been divided between this volume and its predecessor. Volume II contains accounts of the histories of the Scandinavian peninsula and of the Celtic regions which extend into the tenth and early eleventh centuries. The present volume has a full account of Russian history from its earliest stages to 1054; the chapter planned on Jews and Jewish life in western Europe from 700 to 1050 fell victim to the death of a contributor and the impossibility of finding a replacement who could undertake to deliver within a reasonable space of time. Originally planned chapters on lordship and on warfare suffered similar fates; a little of the ground which would have been covered in these chapters is touched on in my introductory chapter, which is for that reason longer than it otherwise might have been.

Each chapter has its own bibliography of secondary sources (including works not referred to in the footnotes), but references to primary sources are made by short title to the consolidated bibliography of primary sources. The spelling of place-names follows the conventions in use by Cambridge University Press. The spelling of medieval personal names is inevitably in part a matter of prejudice and habit. The editor has on the whole preferred an Anglophone, more international and less anachronistic mode of spelling: Radulf/Rudolf rather than Ralph or Raoul, Odo rather than Eudes, Henry rather than Heinrich, Enrico or Henri. The results may on occasion be unfamiliar, but do at least have the advantage that they do not give to tenth-century people who in fact bore the same name spellings of that name which vary arbitrarily according to whereabouts in twentieth-century Europe they happen to have been studied. Traditional forms like Raoul and Eudes are cross-referenced in the index. Technical terms have largely been left in their Latin (or vernacular) forms, and they are explained on their first occurrence.

In the course of an enterprise of this kind one incurs many debts. I owe thanks to all my contributors, especially to those who responded to what were often very belated proposals for changes and cuts with consideration and courtesy, and also to those contributors who did meet the original deadline for delivery punctually and then found themselves waiting in limbo. Most, though certainly not all, of the materials for the volume were ready at the time of my move to Southampton in 1994, and although the contributors have kept their bibliographies up to date they have made only minor changes to their texts. The delays since 1994 have had a number of causes: illness; pressure of other university duties; and not least the publication of other volumes in the series, which have set precedents and so forced me to redo some editorial work I had thought finished and to undertake other work I had not anticipated having to do. The readers of this volume will not suffer as a result of the delays, but some of the contributors have, and I am grateful to them for their forbearance.

I am very grateful to Dr Sarah Hamilton (Southampton) and Dr Eleanor Screen (Peterhouse, Cambridge) for their assistance in checking references and bibliographies in the final stages of preparation. My special thanks go to Jinty Nelson, Jonathan Shepard and Chris Wickham for their friendship and for their freely granted advice and support on both the intellectual and the psychological problems involved in planning the volume and in dealing with contributors. During the whole period of preparation Rosamond McKitterick and I have exchanged much advice and information on our respective volumes, and I should like to thank her here for this and for much-needed support at various difficult points in the gestation of the volume. Last but not least I must thank William Davies and the staff at Cambridge University Press most warmly for the help they have given at all stages, and for their patience in awaiting delivery.

Timothy Reuter

ABBREVIATIONS

AASS	*Acta Sanctorum quotquot toto orbe coluntur*, ed. J. Bollandus *et al.*, Antwerp and Brussels (1634–)
Adalbert, *Reginonis Continuatio*	Adalbert of St Maximin, *Reginonis Continuatio*, ed. F. Kurze, Regino of Prüm, *Chronicon*, pp. 154–79
Adam of Bremen, *Gesta*	Adam of Bremen, *Gesta Hammaburgensis ecclesiae pontificum*, ed. B. Schmeidler, *MGH SRG* II, Hanover (1917)
Adhémar, *Chronicon*	Adhémar of Chabannes, *Chronicon*, ed. J. Chavanon, *Adémar de Chabannes, Chronique publiée d'après les manuscrits*, Paris (1897)
AfD	*Archiv für Diplomatik*
AHP	*Archivum historiae pontificae*
AHR	*American Historical Review*
AKG	*Archiv für Kulturgeschichte*
An. Boll.	*Analecta Bollandiana*
Annales ESC	*Annales: Economies, Sociétés, Civilisations*
AQ	*Ausgewählte Quellen zur deutschen Geschichte des Mittelalters (Freiherr-von-Stein-Gedächtnis-Ausgabe)*
ASC	*Anglo-Saxon Chronicle*, trans. Whitelock, *EHD*, pp. 145–245
ASE	*Anglo-Saxon England*
BAR	British Archaeological Reports
BEC	*Bibliothèque de l'Ecole des Chartes*
BHL	*Bibliotheca hagiographica latina, subsidia hagiographica* VI, Brussels (1898–1901), *Supplementum, subsidia hagiographica* XII, Brussels (1911); *Novum supplementum, subsidia hagiographica* LXX, Brussels (1986)

Bib. Mun.	Bibliothèque Municipale
BL MS	London, British Library manuscript
BMGS	*Byzantine and Modern Greek Studies*
BN lat., BN n.a. lat.	Paris, Bibliothèque Nationale, manuscrit latin; nouvelles acquisitions latines
BSl	*Byzantinoslavica*
Byz	*Byzantion*
Byzbulg	*Byzantinobulgarica*
BZ	*Byzantinische Zeitschrift*
CBA	Council for British Archaeology
CCCM	Corpus Christianorum, Continuatio mediavalis, Turnhout (1966–)
CCM	Corpus consuetudinem monasticarum, ed. K. Hallinger, Siegburg (1963–)
CCSL	Corpus Christianorum, series latina, Turnhout, (1952–)
CFHB	Corpus fontium historiae Byzantinae
Clm	Munich, Bayerische Staatsbibliothek, Codex Latinus Monacensis
D(D)	Diploma(ta), cited by number in the following editions:
D B I	Berengar I, king of Italy, *Diplomata*, ed. L. Schiaparelli, *I diplomi di Berengario I (sec. IX–X)* (Fonti per la storia d'Italia 35), Rome (1903)
D C I	Conrad I, king of east Francia, *Diplomata*, ed. T. Sickel, *Die Urkunden Konrad I., Heinrich I. und Otto I.* (MGH Dip. regum 1), Hanover (1879–84)
D C II	Conrad II, emperor, *Diplomata*, ed. H. Bresslau, *Die Urkunden Konrads II.* (MGH Dip. regum IV) Berlin (1909)
D Ch S	Charles the Simple, king of west Francia, *Acta*, ed. P. Lauer, *Recueil des actes de Charles III le Simple, roi de France, 893–923*, Paris (1949)
D H I	Henry I, king of east Francia, *Diplomata*, ed. T. Sickel, *Die Urkunden Konrad I., Heinrich I. und Otto I.* (MGH Dip. regum 1), Hanover (1879–84)
D H II	Henry II, king of east Francia and emperor, *Diplomata*, ed. H. Bresslau, H. Bloch,

	R. Holtzmann, M. Meyer and H. Wibel, (MGH Dip. regum III), Hanover (1900–3)
D Hugh	Hugh, king of Italy, *Diplomata*, ed. L. Schiaparelli, *I diplomi di Ugo e di Lotario, di Berengario II e di Adalberto (secolo X)* (Fonti per la storia d'Italia 38), Rome (1924)
D L IV	Louis IV, king of west Francia, *Acta*, ed. P. Lauer, *Recueil des actes de Louis IV, roi de France (936–954)*, Paris (1914)
D L C	Louis the Child, king of east Francia, *Diplomata*, ed. T. Schieffer, *Die Urkunden Zwentibolds und Ludwigs des Kindes* (MGH Dip. Germ. IV), Berlin (1960)
D L G	Louis (the German), king of east Francia, *Diplomata*, ed. P. Kehr, *Ludwig des Deutschen, Karlmanns und Ludwigs des Jüngeren Die Urkunden* (MGH Dip. Germ. I), Berlin (1932–4)
D Lo	Lothar, king of west Francia, *Acta*, ed. L. Halphen and F. Lot, *Recueil des actes de Lothaire et Louis V, rois de France (954–987)*, Paris (1908)
D Lothar	Lothar, king of Italy, *Diplomata*, ed. L. Schiaparelli, *I diplomi di Ugo e di Lotario, di Berengario II e di Adalberto (secolo X)* (Fonti per la storia d'Italia 38), Rome (1924)
D O I	Otto I, king of east Francia, *Diplomata*, ed. T. Sickel, *Die Urkunden Konrad I., Heinrich I., und Otto I.* (MGH Dip. regum I), 2 vols., Hanover (1879– 84)
D O II	Otto II, *Diplomata*, ed. T. Sickel, *Die Urkunden Otto des II.* (MGH Dip. regum II.1), Hanover (1888)
D O III	Otto III, *Diplomata*, ed. T. Sickel, *Die Urkunden Otto des III.* (MGH Dip. regum II.2), Hanover (1893)
D Ra	Radulf (Raoul), king of west Francia, *Acta*, ed. R.-H. Bautier and J. Dufour, *Recueil des actes de Robert Ier et de Raoul, rois de France, 922–936,* Paris (1978)
D Ro I	Robert I, king of west Francia, *Acta*, ed.

	R.-H. Bautier and J. Dufour, *Recueil des actes de Robert Ier et de Raoul, rois de France, 922–936*, Paris (1978)
D Ro II	Robert II, king of west Francia, *Acta*, ed. W. M. Newman, *Catalogue des actes de Robert II, roi de France*, Paris (1937)
DA	*Deutsches Archiv für Erforschung des Mittelalters*
DAI	Constantine VII Porphyrogenitus, *De administrando imperio*, ed. and trans. G. Moravcsik and R. J. H. Jenkins (CFHB 1 = Dumbarton Oaks Texts 1), Washington, DC (1967)
DC	Constantine VII Porphyrogenitus, *De cerimoniis aulae byzantinae*, ed. I. I. Reiske, 2 vols., Bonn (1829).
DOP	Dumbarton Oaks Papers
DOT	Dumbarton Oaks Texts
EHD	Dorothy Whitelock (ed.), *English Historical Documents 1, c. 500–1042*, 2nd edn (London, 1979)
EHR	*English Historical Review*
EME	*Early Medieval Europe*
ep(p.).	*epistola(e)*
Eparch	*The Book of The Eparch*, ed. and trans. J. Koder, *Das Eparchenbuch Leons des Weisen* (CFHB 33, Series Vindobonensis), Vienna (1991)
Flodoard, *Annales*	Flodoard, *Annales*, ed. P. Lauer, *Les annales de Flodoard publiées d'après les manuscrits*, Paris (1905)
Flodoard, *HRE*	Flodoard, *Historia Remensis ecclesiae*, ed. M. Stratmann, *MGH SS* xxxvi, Hanover (1998),
FmaSt	*Frühmittelalterliche Studien*
fol.	folio
FSI	Fonti per la storia d'Italia (Instituto storico per il medio evo) (1887–)
Fulbert, *Ep(p).*	*The Letters and Poems of Fulbert of Chartres*, ed. and trans. F. Behrends, Oxford (1976)
Gerbert, *Ep(p).*	Gerbert of Aurillac, *Epistolae*, ed. F. Weigle, *Die Briefsammlung Gerberts von Reims* (*MGH Die*

	Briefe der deutschen Kaiserzeit II), Weimar (1966)
HJb	*Historisches Jahrbuch*
HZ	*Historische Zeitschrift*
JEccH	*Journal of Ecclesiastical History*
JL	P. Jaffé, *Regesta pontificum romanorum*, 2nd edn, ed. S. Loewenfeld, with F. Kaltenbrunner and P. Ewald, Leipzig (1885–8)
JMH	*Journal of Medieval History*
Liudprand, *Antapodosis*	Liudprand of Cremona, *Antapodosis*, ed. J. Becker, *Liudprandi opera* (*MGH SRG* XLI), Hanover (1915), pp. 1–158
Liudprand, *Historia*	Liudprand of Cremona, *Liber de rebus gestis Ottonis Magni imperatoris*, ed. J. Becker, *Liudprandi opera* (*MGH SRG* XLI), Hanover (1915), pp. 159–75
Liudprand, *Relatio*	Liudprand of Cremona, *Relatio de legatione Constantinopolitana*, ed. J. Becker, *Liudprandi opera* (*MGH SRG* XLI), Hanover (1915), pp. 175–212
MA	*Le Moyen Age*
Mansi	J. D. Mansi, *Sacrorum Conciliorum nova et amplissima collectio*, Florence and Venice (1757–98)
MGH	*Monumenta Germaniae Historica*, with subseries:
AA	*Auctores antiquissimi*, 15 vols., Berlin (1877–1919)
Cap.	*Capitularia. Legum sectio* II, *Capitularia regum Francorum*, ed. A. Boretius and V. Krause, 2 vols., Hanover (1883–97)
Cap. episc.	*Capitula episcoporum*, ed. P. Brommer, Hanover (1984)
Conc.	*Concilia. Legum sectio* III, *Concilia*, II, ed. A. Werminghoff, Hanover (1906–8); III, ed. W. Hartmann, Hanover (1984); IV, ed. W. Hartmann, Hanover (1998)
Const.	*Constitutiones et acta publica imperatorum et regum inde ab a.* DCCCCXI *usque ad a.* MCXCVII *(911–1197)*, ed. L. Weiland, Hanover (1893)
Dip. Germ.	*Diplomata regum Germaniae ex stirpe Karolinorum: Die Urkunden der deutschen Karolinger* I, ed.

MGH (cont.)	P. Kehr, Berlin (1932–4); II, ed. P. Kehr, Berlin (1936–7); III, ed. P. Kehr, Berlin (1956); IV, ed. T. Schieffer, Berlin 1960)
Dip. Kar.	*Diplomata Karolinorum: Die Urkunden der Karolinger* I and III, ed. E. Mühlbacher and T. Schieffer, Hanover (1893–1908)
Dip. regum	*Diplomata regum et imperatorum Germaniae: Die Urkunden der deutschen Könige und Kaiser* I, ed. T. Sickel, Hanover (1879–84); II.1, ed. T. Sickel, Hanover (1888); II.2, ed. T. Sickel, Hanover (1893); III, ed. H. Bresslau, H. Bloch and R. Holtzmann, Hanover (1900–3); IV, ed. H. Bresslau, Berlin (1909)
Epp.	*Epistolae* III–VIII (= *Epistolae Merovingici et Karolini aevi,* Hanover (1892–1939)
Epp. sel.	*Epistolae selectae in usum scholarum,* 5 vols., Hanover (1887– 91)
Fontes	*Fontes iuris Germanici antiqui in usum scholarum ex Monumentis Germaniae Historicis separatim editi,* 13 vols., Hanover (1909–86)
Form.	*Formulae Merowingici et Karolini aevi,* ed. K. Zeumer, *Legum sectio* V, Hanover (1886)
Leges nat. Germ.	*Leges nationum Germanicarum,* ed. K. Zeumer (*Lex Visigothorum*); L. R. de Salis (*Leges Burgundionum*); F. Beyerle and R. Buchner (*Lex Ribuaria*); K. A. Eckhardt (*Pactus legis Salicae* and *Lex Salica*); E. von Schwind (*Lex Baiwariorum*), 6 vols. in 11 parts, Hanover (1892–1969)
Lib. mem.	*Libri memoriales,* and *Libri memoriales et Necrologia nova series,* Hanover (1979–)
Nec. Germ.	*Necrologia Germaniae,* 5 vols. and Suppl. Hanover (1886–1920)
Poet.	*Poetae Latini aevi Carolini,* ed. E. Dümmler, L. Traube, P. von Winterfeld and K. Strecker, 4 vols., Hanover (1881–99)
SRG	*Scriptores rerum Germanicarum in usum scholarum separatim editi,* 63 vols., Hanover (1871–1987)
SRL	*Scriptores rerum Langobardicarum et Italicarum saec. VI–IX,* ed. G. Waitz, Hanover (1878)
SRM	*Scriptores rerum Merovingicarum,* ed. B. Krusch

MGH (cont.)	and W. Levison, 7 vols., Hanover (1885–1920)
SS	*Scriptores* (in Folio), 30 vols., Hanover (1824–1924)
MIÖG	*Mitteilungen des Instituts für Österreichische Geschichtsforschung* (1922–1944, *Mitteilungen des Österreichischen Instituts für Geschichtsforschung*)
EB	*MIÖG, Ergänzungsband*
MMS	Münstersche Mittelalterschriften
MS	Manuscript
NA	*Neues Archiv der Geselleschaft für ältere deutsche Geschichtskunde*, continued as *Deutsches Archiv für Erforschung des Mittelalters*
N.F.	Neue Folge
n.s.	nova series, new series
PG	*Patrologiae cursus completus, series graeca*, ed. J.-P. Migne, 161 vols. (Paris, 1857–66)
PL	*Patrologiae cursus completus, series latina*, ed. J.-P. Migne, 221 vols., Paris (1841–64)
QFIAB	*Quellen und Forschungen aus italienischen Archiven und Bibliotheken*
Radulf Glaber, *Historiae*	Radulf Glaber, *Historiarum libri quinque*, ed. with English trans. J. France, Oxford (1989)
RB	*Revue Bénédictine*
Regino, *Chronicon*	Regino of Prüm, *Chronicon*, ed. F. Kurze, *Reginonis abbatis Prumiensis Chronicon cum continuatione Treverensi, MGH SRG* L, Hanover (1890)
RHEF	*Revue d'Histoire de l'Eglise de France*
RHF	*Académie des Inscriptions et Belles-Lettres, Recueil des historiens des Gaules et de la France*, series in folio, eds. M. Bouquet and M.-J.-J. Brial, revised by L. Delisle, 19 vols., Paris (1869–80)
RhVjb	*Rheinische Vierteljahrsblätter*
Richer, *Historiae*	Richer, *Historiae*, ed. and trans. R. Latouche, Richer, *Histoire de France (888–995)* (Classiques de l'histoire de France au moyen âge), 2 vols., Paris (1930, 1937; repr. 1960, 1964)
RISS	*Rerum italicarum scriptores*, ed. L. A. Muratori, 25 vols., Milan (1723–51); new edn, G. Carducci and V. Fiorini, Città di Castello and Bologna (1900–)

s.a.	*sub anno*
Sawyer	P. H. Sawyer, *Anglo-Saxon Charters: A Handlist*, London (1968)
Settimane	*Settimane di Studio del Centro Italiano di Studi sull'alto medioevo* (Spoleto 1955–)
Skylitzes, *Synopsis*	John Skylitzes, *Synopsis historiarum*, ed. I. Thurn (CFHB 5, Series Berolinensis), Berlin and New York (1973)
SM	*Studi Mediaevali*
StMGBO	*Studien und Mitteilungen zur Geschichte des Benediktiner-Ordens und seiner Zweige*
Thietmar, *Chronicon*	Thietmar of Merseburg, *Chronicon*, ed. R. Holtzmann (*MGH SRG N.S.* ix, Berlin (1935)
TRHS	*Transactions of the Royal Historical Society*
Vat. (lat.; pal. lat.; reg. lat.)	Bibliotheca Apostolica Vaticana, MS (latinus; palatinus latinus; reginensis latinus)
VSWG	*Vierteljahresschrift für Wirtschaftsgeschichte*
VuF	Vorträge und Forschungen, herausgegeben vom Konstanzer Arbeitskreis für mittelalterliche Geschichte
Widukind, *Res gestae Saxonicae*	*Widukindi monachi Corbeiensis rerum gestarum Saxonicarum libri III*, ed. P. Hirsch and H.-E. Lohmann (*MGH SRG* lx, Hanover (1935)
Wipo, *Gesta*	Wipo, *Gesta Chuonradi*, ed. H. Bresslau, *Wiponis opera* (*MGH SRG* lxi), Hanover (1915), pp. 3–62
ZRG	*Zeitschrift der Savigny-Stiftung für Rechtsgeschichte*
GA	*Germanistische Abteilung*
KA	*Kanonistische Abteilung*

CHAPTER I

INTRODUCTION: READING
THE TENTH CENTURY

Timothy Reuter

THE PRESENT volume covers a period in European history best described as the 'long tenth century', stretching from the 890s through to around 1020/30. Though this volume covers Byzantine history of the period and also Islamic history so far as it impinges on European territory, the emphasis in this introduction will be largely on what was or would become the Latin west. I shall try to sketch what currently seem the main concerns of historians working on the period and what are generally seen as its salient features, though any such attempt will probably date far faster than the substantive chapters which follow. The ways in which historians make and have made sense of the period as a whole have been determined by a range of inputs. Before we can look at the general trends which are currently held to characterise the period (and the extent to which they actually do) we need to examine these inputs. The most important of them is the nature, real and perceived, of the available source-materials. But two others are almost as important. The first comes from the traditional and non-traditional interpretative schemata and periodisations which the community of professional scholars has brought to bear. The second, perhaps even more important, is the fact that the members of this community for the most part work and have worked within specific historiographical traditions.

It is widely held that the long tenth century is a period more lacking in sources and reliable and precise information on 'what actually happened' than any other period of post-Roman European history, with the exception perhaps of the seventh century. It is not just the very evident brutality of much of the period that has caused it to be termed a 'dark century' (*dunkles Jahrhundert*) or an 'obscure age' (*secolo oscuro*), or an 'iron age' (with the overtone, so chilling for modern professional scholars, that words and thoughts are silenced in the face of armed force).[1] It is also the difficulty historians often encounter, for

---

[1] See Zimmermann (1971), pp. 15–21, on the history of these terms; Lestocquoy (1947), White (1955) and Lopez (1962) are early attempts at re-evaluating the period as a conscious reaction against them.

example, when trying to establish precise sequences of events or office-holders. At least in parts of the post-Carolingian core of Europe there seems to have been a decline in pragmatic literacy and a reversion to oral and symbolic means of communication. As we shall see, this was by no means a universal feature of the long tenth century; but to the extent that it did really exist it meant that human interaction often took forms which have inevitably left relatively fewer traces in the written record, and those often indirect and difficult to interpret.

Nevertheless, notions of a dark or obscure or 'iron' age are problematic. Though they go back a long way, they exercised their most formative influence during the period when a Rankean primacy of political history still dominated medievalists' consciousnesses. When there is at most one substantial narrative dealing with the high politics of a region, writing about 'what actually happened' seems even more difficult and uncertain than it is in any case, and the results thus dark or obscure. Many regions of Europe are in this position for most of the long tenth century: east Frankish/German history is unusual in having the accounts of Widukind of Corvey, Liudprand of Cremona and Adalbert of St Maximin running in parallel for much of the middle third of the tenth century.

Even this dearth of narratives is a difficulty found mainly in the west, Latin and Islamic, rather than the east, where the tenth century is no more obscure than any other period of Byzantine history and rather less than some. Outside the Mediterranean world there are indeed regions for which we have virtually no contemporary narratives at all. The emergent realms of Rus', Hungary, Bohemia and Poland, naturally, as well as the Scandinavian kingdoms, have no contemporary indigenous accounts, only later, mythologising origin histories: the *Tale of Bygone Years* or *Russian Primary Chronicle* for Rus'; the late twelfth-century Anonymus and later derivatives like Simon de Kéza and the *Chronicon pictum* for Hungarian history; the early twelfth-century court writers, Cosmas of Prague and Gallus Anonymus, for Bohemian and Polish history; Saxo Grammaticus, *Heimskringla* and its precursors for Scandinavian history. The savage positivist source-criticism of the late nineteenth and early twentieth centuries has left few historians willing to use such works as 'primary sources' except in a state of cautious desperation or for the citation of an occasional phrase to add rhetorical colour. Even when it is evident that their authors must have drawn on earlier works now lost to us, it is normally impossible to tell precisely where they are doing this, while the analysis of these works as later representations of an earlier past has in many cases barely begun. Once the information offered by these high-medieval versions of earlier pasts is seen as the product of later construction rather than the echo of past reality, the political history of these regions has to be written in a much more tentative and

uncertain fashion, drawing mainly on casual and largely decontextualised fragments of information found in narratives from the Frankish, Anglo-Saxon and
Byzantine world and in Arabic and Jewish travellers' tales. Some parts of
western Europe are almost as badly placed, most notably the kingdom of
Burgundy and the principalities of Catalonia and Toulouse, at least as far as any
reconstruction of *histoire événementielle* is concerned: few European rulers of
any period can have left as little trace in the record after reigning for nearly sixty
years as has Conrad the Pacific of Burgundy.

Yet the long tenth century is also an age of great historians, writers who offer
rich and juicy texts with a wide narrative sweep and much significant detail:
Widukind of Corvey, Adalbert of Magdeburg and Thietmar of Merseburg
working in Saxony; Flodoard and Richer in Rheims; Dudo of Saint-Quentin in
Normandy; Adhémar of Chabannes and Radulf Glaber in central France;
Liudprand of Cremona in Italy (and north of the Alps); Benedict of Soracte in
Rome; Sampiro in León. Some sections and some versions of the enigmatic
complex known collectively as the *Anglo-Saxon Chronicle*, notably the strange
compilation by the ealdorman Æthelwold written around 980, would also
qualify. There are also impressive works of more local compass, such as the
Lotharingian episcopal *gesta*, or Flodoard's lengthy and archivally based history
of the church of Rheims. Most important of all, and not only for the sheer
bulk of what survives, is the large corpus of saints' lives and miracle-
collections from this period: it was a golden age of hagiographic production.

Traditional attitudes, however, are slow to change. Modern medievalists'
relationship with 'hagiography' is revealed by the fact that whereas almost all
the major 'historiographical' works of the period are available in good modern
editions, most 'hagiography' still has to be consulted in old and often very inadequate editions. A nineteenth-century distinction between historians, who deal
in facts, and hagiographers, who deal in fictions, was perhaps appropriate to an
era of scholarship in which it was important to begin by establishing the who,
the what, the where and the when, all matters on which 'hagiographic' texts are
often imprecise or inaccurate. But it now needs to be transcended: it is by no
means clear that the distinction reflects anything significant about the intentions and practices of tenth-century authors: many 'historians' also wrote
'hagiography'.[2]

Yet few even of those conventionally thought of as historians rather than
hagiographers have left us straightforward and unproblematic texts. The acid-
bath of positivist source-criticism may have dissolved the later mythologising
histories of the European periphery almost completely, but it has also left the
smooth surfaces of writers like Widukind, Richer and Dudo deeply pitted, so

[2] Lifshitz (1994).

much so that Martin Lintzel could write about the 'problem of truth in the tenth century' (meaning the problem of having any confidence at all in the relation between our surviving accounts and the course of an increasingly inaccessible past reality 'out there'), and more recently Carlrichard Brühl has felt able to dismiss both Widukind and Richer as *romanciers*.[3] Few historians at the end of the twentieth century are still willing to offer this kind of robust empiricism without qualms; but though the aspects of these sources problematised by Lintzel and Brühl are not the only ones, they are real enough, for elements of saga, of epic, of the preacher's *exemplum*, of folk-tale, seem to greet us on many pages of these works, and they will rarely submit to a straightforward positivist unpacking of their meaning.[4]

Historians of a positivist frame of mind have traditionally contrasted the uncertain and subjective information derived from narratives with the firmer data to be won from record evidence, which in this period means from charters. Many series of royal diplomata from this period now exist in complete and satisfactory modern editions: those issued by or in the name of the rulers of east Francia/Germany, of Burgundy, of Hungary and of Italy are available complete, and those of the west Frankish rulers almost so, while as far as surviving papal letters and privileges are concerned it is for this period alone that we possess a comprehensive edition of everything surviving.[5] Even for those regions where the picture is still incomplete – Anglo-Saxon England, the Spanish peninsula, Byzantium – the gaps are being filled. Below that level the picture is less favourable. Although the period is characterised by the exercise of 'quasi-regal' power by figures with less than royal status – archbishops, bishops, dukes, margraves – the charters they issued were not numerous, and in most regions have hardly begun to be collected in modern editions;[6] an exception is the collection of the *placita* of the kingdom of Italy, accounts of judicial decisions given by a court president acting (or ostensibly acting) in the ruler's name.[7]

The bulk of non-royal charter material surviving from this period consists of what we would nowadays think of as either conveyancing records or accounts of dispute settlement. Normally such documents offer a miniature narrative of a conveyance or settlement with a list of those present at the transaction; in many areas of northern Europe they were treated, so far as we can tell, as a mere record of the transaction with no inherent legal force, though both England and Italy show that this did not have to be the case. It is precisely during the period covered by this volume that the narratives in many parts of

[3] Lintzel (1956); Brühl (1990), pp. 465–7, 589–93.   [4] Reuter (1994).

[5] Zimmermann, H. (ed.), *Papsturkunden 896–1046*.

[6] Kienast (1968) provides a convenient guide to the charters produced for secular princes; there is a complete edition for Normandy in *Recueil des actes des ducs de Normandie*.

[7] Manaresi, C. (ed.), *I placiti del 'Regnum Italiae'*.

Europe, especially in France, become less miniature and more detailed, and it has indeed been argued that such loquacity has misled historians into thinking that the things they describe in such detail were really new around the millennium rather than simply coming to be recorded for the first time.[8] Both their geographical distribution and the quality of the editions they have received are very uneven. The archives of the Mediterranean regions – Italy, both north and south, and parts of Spain (especially Catalonia and Castile) – are very full, if not always very fully known or exploited. In northern Europe such collections of material as have survived have normally done so in the form of cartularies put together by religious institutions, often in the century and a half after the period covered by this volume, when such institutions were taking steps to put their property ownership and administration on a more ordered and rational basis, and so to arrange selected and edited versions of their archives in book form. Large and unmediated archival deposits are rare, the large tenth- and eleventh-century archives of Cluny being an unusual exception.[9] In particular, many of the north European centres active in producing archival material in the eighth and ninth centuries, from Redon to St Gallen, either ceased to do so altogether in the tenth century or else did so at a greatly reduced rate.

Little of this material has been edited both comprehensively and recently. Nor has its nature always been properly appreciated by historians. The history of diplomatic has been one of a preoccupation with distinguishing the genuine from the false. The question of authenticity is an appropriate and important point from which to start when dealing with royal and papal charters, because such documents, at least in theory, were in themselves adequate to guarantee the claims contained in them, and this made them worth forging, both at the time and later. But it does not go far enough, even for them. Every charter tells a story, and even if we can establish that the charter is indeed what it purports to be, the authenticity of the charter in a formal legal sense is in itself no guarantee of the authenticity or completeness or meaningfulness in a historical sense of the story which it tells. Most such stories are indeed manifestly incomplete, and historians have barely begun to study the narrative strategies of charter-writers and of those who commissioned their activities. This is all the more significant with the advent, already noted, of a much more garrulous style of charter-writing, including plaints (*querimoniae*) and concords (*convenientiae*) which set out the whole history of a dispute. The fact that these miniature histories are found embedded in what look like legal documents does not make them any less subjective or their interpretation any less problematic.

In some, though not all parts of Latin Europe there was a temporary downturn in charter production in the early part of this period, though the view of the

---

[8] Barthélemy (1992a).   [9] *Recueil des chartes de l'abbaye de Cluny.*

period as an 'obscure age' has itself obscured the fact that this downturn was reversed almost everywhere by the later tenth century, to be followed by steady growth. But there was a quite genuine and long-lasting downturn in legislative activity almost everywhere in Latin Europe; it was one of the most evident contrasts between the Latin west on the one hand and Byzantine or Islamic political culture on the other, for those few contemporaries who were familiar with both.[10] For most of the west during this period little or no legislation survives, even in those regions where rulers appear to have been powerful and impressive figures, and this is not to be attributed to large-scale losses of what once existed. The Carolingian capitulary tradition had virtually died out by the end of the ninth century (after 884 in west Francia, after 898 in Italy, after 852 in east Francia). The Ottonians and their entourages knew what capitularies were, but confined themselves to very occasional *ad hoc* edicts.[11] Collections of Carolingian capitularies, notably that of Ansegis, continued to be copied in the tenth and early eleventh centuries, both in west and in east Francia in particular, but it is far from clear what use might have been made of such manuscripts in practical life.[12] Anglo-Saxon England is the great western European exception to the tenth-century legislative drought; here, collections of Carolingian capitularies transmitted from the continent provided some of the inspiration which enabled the kingdom to catch up with, absorb and develop the lessons of Carolingian government in a long series of law-codes, notably those of Æthelstan, Æthelred and Cnut.[13] Paler forms of imitation of the Carolingians can be seen in the laws of Stephen of Hungary from the early eleventh century.[14] The Byzantine development was, as one might expect, smoother and more continuous: the tenth-century rulers continued to legislate as a matter of course, without break or decline.[15]

The church also legislated less: councils, where they did meet, were more likely to leave only protocols of judicial decisions or charters solemnised by the fortuitous presence of numerous imposing witnesses than they were to produce legislation in the form of canons.[16] Equally, the great Carolingian tradition of episcopal capitularies had comparatively weak echoes in the practice of tenth-century bishops.[17] This picture of inactivity is particularly true of the

---

[10] See Nelson's analysis of John of Gorze's account of his visit to the Cordovan court, below, pp. 126–8.

[11] *MGH Const* I, no. 8, p. 17; D H II 370.

[12] Mordek (1995); Ansegis, *Collectio capitularium*, ed. Schmitz, pp. 189–90.

[13] Edited in *Die Gesetze der Angelsachsen*, ed. Liebermann; on the Carolingian sources for such legislation see Wormald (1978), pp. 71–4.   [14] Stephen, King of Hungary, *Laws*.

[15] See Shepard, below, pp. 553–4; on the contrast with the west in this respect see Leyser (1994b), pp. 160–1.

[16] This is the conclusion of Schröder (1980) for west Francia; the situation elsewhere was similar if less extreme.

[17] *Capitula episcoporum* III contains a few tenth-century specimens; the overall distribution of texts and manuscripts is to be surveyed in vol IV, which has not yet appeared.

early tenth century; from around 950 onwards there was something of a recovery. Although this recovery was hardly a rapid one anywhere, the great sequence of reforming councils initiated by Leo IX's councils at Rheims and Mainz in 1049 was not preceded by a long legislative drought in the way that the otherwise comparable revival of conciliar activity in the early Carolingian period had been.[18] Our picture is still an imperfect one, for though such secular laws as have survived, in Byzantium and in the west, have generally been well edited, conciliar legislation is only now receiving the attention it deserves.[19] In particular, we lack a comprehensive edition of the texts produced by those councils at which the 'legislation' of the Peace and Truce of God movements was promulgated.[20] But we also lack a modern edition of almost any of the collections of canon law regularly used in the long tenth century, or of the great collection produced at the end of it by Burchard of Worms, which largely superseded these earlier collections.[21]

Almost all of the surviving letter-collections of the period (and not many tenth-century letters have been preserved outside collections) can be seen in a context of canon law. It is not an accident that the most important ones are associated with important reforming clerics – Rather of Verona and Liège, Gerbert of Rheims, Fulbert of Chartres, Dunstan of Canterbury – and that they contain many letters dealing with practical matters of church law.[22] Letters should not be seen in this context alone, however. The impulse to preserve them in collections, which would become stronger and more widespread in the course of the eleventh and twelfth centuries, was not simply a product of the period's concern with *memoria* and of a desire to preserve the memory of the people with whom they were associated. It also stemmed from the need for models to be used in the training of clerics: significantly, Dunstan, Gerbert and Fulbert were teachers as well as lawyers. The Latin poetry of the period was also located in this rhetorical-didactic tradition: an art of the schools rather than of the court, which it had been at least to some extent in the preceding period.[23] Here again we have a contrast between the Latin west and the court-centred cultures of Byzantium and Islam.

As with the earlier medieval centuries, one feels that the material remains of

---

[18] Hartmann (1989) pp. 47–50.

[19] *Concilia aevi Saxonici 916–1001*, I: *916–961*; for commentary see Schröder (1980), Vollrath (1985), Wolter (1988), and the chapters in the forthcoming *History of Medieval Canon Law* edited by Wilfried Hartmann and Kenneth Pennington.

[20] See Hoffmann (1964) for details of the printed sources; much of the manuscript work remains to be done.

[21] Hoffmann and Pokorny (1991) is now the starting point for any work on Burchard's collection.

[22] Rather of Verona, *Epistolae*; Gerbert of Aurillac, *Epistolae*; Fulbert of Chartres, *The Letters and Poems*; *Memorials of Saint Dunstan*, pp. 354–438. The connection is most evident in the case of Fulbert: see, e.g., *epp*. 28, 36, 56, 71.   [23] Godman (1987).

the long tenth century ought to have made more impact on historians' consciousnesses and interpretations than in practice they have done. Excavation
has played a major part in reshaping post-Carolingian urban history, not least
through the very detailed investigation of Viking York and Dublin; Peter
Johanek's chapter shows how this has affected our view of the period. Our
view of post-Carolingian settlement patterns owes in general much less to
archaeology: this is certainly true of villages, which, as Robert Fossier argues
below (in common with many other though by no means all scholars), first
start to take on definitive form and permanent location in this period. It is
perhaps less true of the dwellings of the dominant aristocratic strata of post-
Carolingian society, also seen as 'settling down' in the course of the long tenth
century, but although the development of the aristocratic dwelling, often a fortified site, has been extensively studied and has been linked to shifts in family
structure in this period, we are still far from having a clear view of where and
how the non-urban aristocracies of northern Europe lived.[24] Historians of the
tenth century should undoubtedly pay more attention to archaeology than they
have, though the absence of substantial syntheses and the gaps in the publication of excavations as well as the divergences between national archaeological
traditions (even more marked than the historiographical divergences to be
examined shortly) will continue to make this difficult in the foreseeable future.

Some kinds of material remains have escaped historians' general neglect of
non-written sources, most notably those traditionally studied by art historians:
painting, sculpture, goldsmithery and ivorywork, architecture. The study of
manuscripts, both as material objects and as repositories of images, has
received at least as much attention as the study of the written sources of the
period. So have the surviving remains of metalwork and wood- and ivory-
carvings, in the form of book-covers and other carved panels, of liturgical
combs, and above all of reliquaries and items of regalia. Much of this record is
lost, however, and some of its context is irrecoverable. Virtually no secular
buildings and very few ecclesiastical ones have survived unchanged and intact
from the tenth century. The wall-paintings and tapestries which once decorated them, and which would probably have told us even more about the
culture and self-image of the period than do illuminated manuscripts, have
vanished almost without trace, except for an occasional survival like the church
of St George on the Reichenau with its almost intact cycle of wall-paintings.
Ecclesiastical vestments have survived in quite substantial numbers, but the
tapestries recording the deeds of kings and aristocrats are known only from a
handful of casual written references. Many of these kinds of material survival
have attracted the attention of cultural and political historians as well as of his-

---

[24] See below, pp. 18–19.

torians of art, because they fall or can be seen as falling into the category of 'signs of lordship and symbols of state', to use a phrase invented by the German medievalist Percy Ernst Schramm. Like their counterpart in written sources, the (often anecdotalised) record of symbolic action, they have seemed to offer a way in to the mindset of the period's elites which might otherwise be closed to us by the sheer inarticulacy of more direct evidence.[25]

The source-materials available for the study of a period are far from defining the ways in which that period will be studied. Claudio Leonardi begins his chapter on intellectual life by remarking that the era between the late Carolingian scholars and *litterati* and the early scholastics of the later eleventh century is often thought of either as post-Carolingian or as pre-Gregorian, and is thus denied an identity of its own.[26] Analagous remarks could be made about the prevailing interpretation of other aspects of the period. There is, of course, some justification for such terminology and the interpretative schemata which lie behind it. Much of tenth-century Europe – though hardly the Byzantine and Islamic spheres – saw itself as in a sense post-Carolingian: it simultaneously perpetuated and looked back nostalgically to an order once glorious, now in decline. The heirs of the direct successor-states looked back to a supposedly golden age of Frankish unity, which seemed all the more golden for the absence of any clear and precise memories of it. Carolingian nostalgia was at its strongest in regions where the Carolingians had been largely absent, like the south of France, and it grew once real Carolingians were no longer around: it was Otto III, not Otto I, who took the first steps towards the canonisation of Charlemagne.[27] The post-Carolingian core of Europe retained a residual sense of pan-Frankishness long after kingdoms (not, as yet, nations), had started to develop their own sense of identity. In the large arc to the north and east of the former Frankish empire, from England through to Hungary, it was as much the written and unwritten myth of the Carolingian polity as experience of the contemporary hegemonial power, the Ottonians, that provided a model for development, whether in the form of imitation capitularies in the Wessex of Edgar and Æthelred or in the adaptation of *Lex Baiuuariorum* to serve as the basis for early Hungarian law. Equally, although the 'Gregorian' and 'pre-Gregorian' terminology may have been subjected to powerful attacks in recent years it can hardly be escaped altogether.[28] The apparent universality of the charges laid by the church reformers and historians of the mid- and late eleventh century and echoed by historians of the nineteenth and twentieth at least gives a degree of unification to our perceptions of tenth- and early eleventh-century Europe, united by sin, by

[25] For the work of Schramm see Bak (1973); for work on political ritual see Althoff (1990); Koziol (1992); Althoff (1997).   [26] Below, p. 187.

[27] Folz (1950), pp. 47–114; Remensnyder (1995).   [28] Tellenbach (1985, 1993).

ecclesiastical abuse, and by attempts by a small radical minority to overcome
these failings.

Two other models currently offer broader versions of the divisions just
mentioned. Much German-language historiography – and formerly French
historiography as well, as witness Marc Bloch's distinction between the first
and the second feudal age – sees the mid-eleventh century as having marked a
crucial change from an 'archaic' society to that 'old European order' which prevailed from the late eleventh to the late eighteenth century.[29] This may be seen
as a more secular and sociological rewriting of the schema 'pre-' and 'post-
Gregorian': church reform was on this view merely symptomatic of more
general changes in the eleventh century towards greater rationality and greater
social differentiation.[30]

An alternative view, which would stress political more than other kinds of
development, is to see the period as initiating, as far as Latin-speaking western
Europe is concerned, a very long era during which Europe would be shaped by
competing dynastically oriented territories, many of them the ancestors of the
modern nation-state, even though that term is hardly applicable to the tenth
century. Geoffrey Barraclough defined the long tenth century as the 'crucible
of Europe', the period in which large-scale supra-regional empires finally disappeared, to be replaced by the smaller kingdoms familiar from later European
history.[31] Certainly much of Europe's political geography can be seen to have
begun in this period, a fact which was taken as the basis of a large international
conference in 1968 on the 'origins of nation-states' in this period.[32] Yet even as
an interpretation of political history alone it fits some parts of Europe much
better than it does others. It clearly works well for the northern and eastern
parts of Europe, where present-day polities very evidently emerged from prehistory in a recognisable form in the course of the tenth century. German
medieval historiography has also devoted much attention to the 'beginnings of
German history', which are now generally placed in the course of the long
tenth century rather than the ninth, even if they are no longer defined in terms
of a significant date like 911 or 919 or 936.[33]

Yet it is German medievalists who have sought to establish the 'beginnings
of French history' and place them in the same period;[34] it is far less of a defining moment for French historians, for whom something recognisable as
France had already been around for some time by the tenth century. Indeed it is
in the French historiographical tradition that a quite opposite view has been
developed. Rather than the 'birth of Europe' rhetoric, this offers the tenth

---

[29] Brunner (1968); Gerhard (1981) For Bloch's distinction see Bloch (1961), pp. 59–71.

[30] Murray (1978), esp pp. 25–137.

[31] Barraclough (1976); cf. also the titles of Calmette (1941), Fossier (1982) and Fried (1991).

[32] Manteuffel (1968).   [33] Brühl (1990); Ehlers (1994).   [34] Ehlers (1985).

century as the last century of an old order, one which was not merely post-Carolingian, but post-Roman. The reasons which have been given for taking such a view have varied. Some scholars have wanted to stress a continuity of the late antique legal and political order through to the late tenth century.[35] Others, Marxisant or neo- Marxisant, have stressed an underlying shift in the mode of production and hence the dominant social formation from slavery to serfdom (and hence, in the Marxist sense of the terminology, from slavehold-ing to feudalism).[36] Others have seen the tenth century as ending in a new frag-mentation (*encellulement*) of society, a world in which interaction at a distance had almost ceased to exist, in which the horizon did not extend much beyond the view from the castle wall.[37]

With considerations like these we have already arrived at the third kind of input mentioned at the outset, and it is not only for the reasons just discussed that the interpretative schemata on offer for tenth-century history depend on the historiographical tradition in which a historian is working. There is a common European tradition, but its regional variations are very marked. In particular, the master narratives dominant in the various European countries and regions mean that there is no comprehensive European consensus on which aspects of the period are to be seen as significant. To some extent there is also a problem of language: both the technical terms and the underlying con-ceptual apparatus in use vary from national tradition to national tradition, and there are as yet few guides to these which will allow the historian to carry out reliable translation. It may well be that an increasing awareness of other tradi-tions and of the work being done within them will create a more genuinely European view of tenth-century history within the coming generation; some of what we currently perceive as real differences in the past may turn out to be mere differences of perception, the products of divergent terminology and historiographical tradition.

It is noteworthy how many of the periodisations and implicit or explicit underlying models are drawn from French history, and in an English-lan-guage history it is worth stressing the point. Not only have French medieval-ists been given to offering such theories more than most; both the Anglo-Norman and Anglo-Angevin connections of English medieval history and the foreign-language teaching traditions dominant in the Anglolexic world have created a 'Francocentric' approach: French medieval history has

---

[35] Durliat (1990); Magnou-Nortier (1981, 1982, 1984); for a critique see Wickham (1993) The same peri-odisation is found, more impressionistically justified, in Sullivan (1989).

[36] Bois (1989); Bonnassie (1991).

[37] Fossier (1982), pp. 288–601, esp. pp. 288–90; also below, pp. 45–53. For the relationship between *encellulement* and *incastellamento*, its Italian relative, see the historiographical account in Wickham (1986), pp. xxiii–xxvi; for critiques of the concept see Leyser (1994c) and Campbell (1990).

often been taken metonymically in Britain and America for the whole of
tenth- and early eleventh-century Europe. More important still is the way in
which an impressive series of regional studies, beginning with and in many
cases inspired by Duby's classic study of the Mâconnais, have fleshed out in
often very substantial detail the transformation of various parts of France in
the post-Carolingian era.[38] We have a better picture of the tenth century on
the ground for west Francia than for any other part of Europe, not necessarily because the supply of sources is inherently superior, but because many of
its regions have been systematically studied in a way in which tenth-century
Bavaria or Umbria have not yet been (it would be possible to do so, and
indeed French historians have themselves exported the approach beyond the
boundaries of west Francia).[39] This is, arguably, accident: the original *Annales*
idea of 'total history' has simply turned out to be more easy to realise by historians of the high middle ages than by historians of later periods in the time
available for the production of theses. If this is so, it has been a very significant accident.

The positions and traditions of Italian and Spanish medievalists show great
similarities. The tenth century is one of extreme localisation: meaningful generalisations about or general histories of the Italian or Spanish peninsulas are
difficult, if not impossible. Moreover, the master narratives of Italian and
Spanish historiography make the tenth century a period of marking time:
waiting for the communes, or for the *reconquista*, and so looking for the antecedents of these things. The tenth century hardly works for either Italy or Spain
as the end of an old or the beginning of a new era. Although it is possible to
talk about the first half of the tenth century as one in which Italy was ruled by
'national' kings, this is only acceptable nowadays when accompanied by a heavy
coating of inverted commas. Nor is the tenth century a significant one for
Spanish self-perception. On the one hand, the crucial period for the survival of
the kingdom of León-Asturias and its taking firm root was the ninth, not the
tenth century. On the other hand, Spanish political geography was not definitively shaped until much later. Castile, which would ultimately play Wessex to
most of the rest of the peninsula, was still an insecure border region in this
period. There has also been much to do. Professional history-writing has not
been so long established or so well funded as in the lands north of Alps and
Pyrenees, and there is still an immense amount of positivist establish-the-facts
spadework to be done for this period. It is significant, therefore, that Italian
and Spanish historians have been heavily influenced in recent years by the concerns of French medievalists. Two large and highly influential studies, those of

---

[38] Duby (1952); most of the others are listed in Poly and Bournazel (1991), English translation, pp.
365–6.
[39] E.g. Toubert (1973a, 1973b); Bonnassie (1975, 1976); Taviani-Carozzi (1991); Menand (1993).

Pierre Toubert on Latium and of Pierre Bonnassie on Catalonia, have been particularly important in setting agendas.[40]

As is explained in the preface, the present volume is ordered by reference to the tenth century's Carolingian past: the chapters on the 'post-Carolingian core' are grouped before those on what from this point of view was the periphery, though neither the Byzantines nor the Islamic rulers of Spain would have seen themselves in this light. But other groupings are possible: if the French, Italian and Spanish histories of this period appear highly regionalised and fragmented, German, English and eastern European histories appear much less so, though the reasons are different in each case. German medievalists have been little troubled by ideas of revolution, feudal or otherwise; for them the decisive break in European history comes in the second half of the eleventh century, with the end of Ottonian and Salian rule, church reform, crusades and the emergence of early scholasticism. Germany in the tenth century was as regionalised as France or Italy or England, but the master narrative for its history is still perceived as that of the history of kings. Although this has been rewritten in the last generation with considerable sophistication and surprising detail, it is still hardly linked at all to developments in social and economic history.[41] The kinds of tenth-century developments which have impressed French, Italian and Spanish medievalists – fortified aristocratic residences, the growth of private jurisdiction, an increase in violence, the shift from slavery to serfdom – can also be registered in the German long tenth century, but they are not seen as having such significant consequences either for the course of events or for the development of the polity.

Such conservatism should not be taken to mean stasis. A generation ago the historiography of the German long tenth century did indeed not seem particularly lively. The sources were both well edited and of known limitations, and it was generally felt that, except perhaps for the ideology of rulership, where there was evidently still mileage in continuing the lines of investigation opened up by Schramm, Erdmann and Kantorowicz, there was little new to be said. If today that no longer seems true, then this is not because of major discoveries of source-material, or because the subject has received significant impulses from outside: the debates on periodisation and revolutions have hardly touched German historians at all. In retrospect, the shift can be seen to have been begun by Helmut Beumann's study of Widukind of Corvey;[42] what this triggered off over the next forty years was an increased sense of the need to

---

[40] See note 39.

[41] The largest recent survey, Fried (1994), goes further in attempting such an approach than any previous survey; see also Fried (1991) It may be a sign of change that Fried's neo-Lamprechtian approach was not challenged, though other aspects of his work were: see Althoff (1995) and Fried (1995).

[42] Beumann (1950).

read the great works of Ottonian historiography in their own terms. An almost literary 'close reading' (though this owed little to literary scholarship and nothing at all to post-structuralist views of the world, which have affected German medievalists hardly at all) replaced what had become the increasingly desperate interwar attempts to unpack these texts in a purely positivist manner, to try to force them to reveal 'how it really was'. At the same time, our understanding of the nuts and bolts of the east Frankish/German kingdom was transformed by detailed prosopographic investigations and by meticulous reconstructions of the rulers' itineraries.[43]

England in the long tenth century was clearly as regionalised a society as anything on the other side of the Channel. Indeed, it was in this period that England came into being as anything more than an aspiration and perhaps on occasions as a virtual community, and the process was not yet fully completed by the early eleventh century.[44] Yet its historiography firmly resists a regionalising perspective; it is not that no such perspective has been offered, but rather that there is no real place for it within the dominant discourse.[45] It might be thought that the main reason for this is the sheer paucity of source-material: the number of indisputably genuine tenth-century charters of all types from the whole of Anglo-Saxon England hardly exceeds. the number of surviving genuine diplomata issued by Otto I alone, and is a mere fraction of the number surviving from the single if admittedly atypically rich archive of Cluny. The richly symbolic accounts of east or west Frankish politics found in contemporary narratives also have no surviving counterpart from Anglo-Saxon England. More significant, though, is the influence of a dominant master-narrative, one of English history as a success story made possible by the early development of a strong centralising state. Recent historiography has fought hard to push back the beginnings of this development beyond its traditional starting point in the generations following the Norman Conquest, and a plausible case can be (and has been) made for a 'Carolingian' phase of English history between Alfred and Edgar, one in which military success, unification, legislation and the development of what by early medieval standards was a fairly homogenous set of local institutions went hand in hand.[46] Yet where an older generation of historians saw England as first dragged kicking and screaming into Europe, and hence into modernity, as a result of the Norman Conquest, the new view has rewritten tenth- and eleventh-century English history at one level whilst preserving its isolation from continental developments at another. No kind of mutation or revolution, feudal or otherwise, troubles the island, nor apparently

---

[43] For the methodology and bibliography see Müller-Mertens, chapter 9 below; see also Fleckenstein (1966) and Leyser (1982b).　　[44] Wormald (1994).

[45] For examples of regional studies see Stafford (1985), Gelling (1992), Yorke (1995).

[46] See Campbell (1994), for the fullest recent statement of the view.

do such things as the development of fortified residences or the freezing of previously fluid settlement patterns, which remain by and large the concern of archaeologists.[47]

If the sources for English history in the long tenth century seem thin compared with the wealth of the Mediterranean regions or even the plenty of the former Frankish kingdoms north of the Alps, they are rich compared with those available for eastern and northern Europe. The histories of Rus' and of the eastern European proto-states, 'Poland', 'Bohemia' and 'Hungary', are probably the most contestable and contested of all those covered in this volume.[48] This is partly the inevitable product of fragmentary information, often late in date and highly ambiguous in its interpretation. But it is also, at least for eastern Europe, a product of twentieth-century uncertainties. The new states of the post-Versailles settlement have simply not enjoyed a continuous existence over the last eighty years, unthreatened from without and consensually accepted from within, and under such conditions it is not surprising that historians of these regions have been slow to take up the methodological novelties increasingly taken for granted further west. The histories of tenth-century Poland, Hungary or Russia are as difficult to 'read' as those of sixth-century Gaul or Britain – if anything, more so, since the written information we have is almost all external as well as being late. But they are not so distant in time and significance as are, for example, the sixth-century Saxon kingdoms in England; and interpretations of the fragmentary evidence are not as detached from present-day reality and significance as they are for western European historians, who inhabit societies whose sense of national identity does not require a consensual view of a very distant past.

There remain the anomalous (from a western European perspective) historiographical traditions of Byzantine history and European Islamic history.[49] Though Byzantine history has a particular significance for Greeks and Russians as the history of a 'virtual precursor', it is a more international discipline than any of the areas of 'national' history so far studied. At the same time, the high demands it makes on its scholars' linguistic and technical skills have a double effect: few of its specialists have had the time or energy to become genuinely familiar with the history of western Europe (or even a part of it) on the same level, while western medievalists have equally had to rely on others as guides (as has the author of this chapter). None of the trajectories which apply to the west really fit Byzantine history, for which the long tenth century between 886 and 1025 is as much a golden age as an age of iron, in recent interpretations not only politically and culturally, but also economically.

---

[47] Hodges (1991) offers an outsider's perspective on this.

[48] For organisational reasons, the history of the Scandinavian lands was covered in *NCMH* II; see the preface.   [49] See chapters 22–5 (Jonathan Shepard) and 27 (Hugh Kennedy) below.

Similar considerations apply to the histories of the Spanish caliphate and the Islamic amirs in Sicily in this period, except that here the problem is compounded by the fragmentary (and often late) nature of the source-material, and by the politico-cultural significance of these regions, peripheries of a larger culture whose metropolitan centre lay elsewhere. Nowhere in the area covered by this volume is cross-cultural comparison more needed or more difficult to carry out, from either side of the divide. In the present state of play, all that can be said is that few of the periodisations and interpretative schemata which have been applied to western Latin European history in the long tenth century seem to have much relevance to Byzantine or Islamic history in the same period, but that impression may nevertheless represent optical illusion rather than reality.

Some differences must have been real enough, however; the surviving sources and traditions of interpretation no doubt exaggerate the extent to which Byzantium (and its Bulgarian imitator) and Islamic Spain were societies centred on a capital with a fixed court and a ruler who was much more than *primus inter pares*, but no allowance one might make for this could reduce them to the organisational status of the societies shaped by western European itinerant rulership. Cultures which are urbanised and court-centred, whose rulers are normally to be found at a fixed point from which they habitually tax and legislate, are *inherently* different from those of the main area covered in this volume; in particular, the antithesis of core and periphery (or of metropolis and province) is a reality, not simply a metaphor.

The other anomalous historiographical tradition is that of American medievalists (as it happens, hardly represented in the present volume, though this is the result of chance rather than calculation). Their traditions have not always been clearly distinct from European ones; the first generations of American medievalists were largely trained in and inspired by European schools of historical writing, an intellectual dependency sustained in the mid-century era by the influence of a number of important émigrés and refugees, as elsewhere in the American academy. But although the European medieval past is also America's medieval past, it is not its past in the same way. The links with English history, and so, via the Anglo-Norman and Angevin empires, with French medieval history have continued to be important, but they are not the only possible ways of appropriating the past. For Americans whose secondary or primary ethnicity is eastern, central or southern European (there are very few African-American or Asian-American medieval historians), they are not even the most important ones. Moreover, the organisation of studies has favoured a holistic approach to this particular past culture, taking in literary and artistic remains as well as 'straight' history under the umbrella of Medieval Studies, and in consequence exposing medieval historians to the influences of neighbouring disciplines in a way that is only beginning to happen in many parts of Europe. Although American medievalists have taken sides in European medievalists' debates – and they have shown themselves just as liable to Francocentrism as European historians – they have in many cases taken a more detached and also a more innovative approach to the medieval past, and a number of significant recent studies could probably only have been written from the distance provided by the Atlantic.[50]

However fragmented the long tenth century may have been by the accidents of source preservation and divergent historiographical traditions, there are still generalisations which can be made about it, though, as we shall see, few are uncontested. Estimates of changes in the level of economic activity in the long tenth century have on the whole been moving upward in recent decades. Monetisation is perceived positively; the Viking, Saracen and Magyar incursors who caused Marc Bloch to depict the era in such gloomy terms are now thought by many to have given positive impulses by raiding centres of accumulated treasure and releasing it once more into economic circulation.[51] Population is also thought to have risen, though hard evidence is almost impossible to come by. The beginnings of the urban renaissance which characterises the high middle ages have also been sought in this period.[52] To the extent that there is or can be any 'pure' economic history of this period, there is probably more consensus about it at present than about any other aspect of the period.

Yet such developments are more easily described in a broad-brush sense than explained. When we move on to social and political history in search of explanations, consensus recedes. A number of other changes can apparently be identified as characteristic of this period, and historians have been tempted by the idea that many, perhaps even all of them can be linked in some way. There is, first of all, the idea (Marxian in origin, though less so in its exposition or its specific application to the tenth century) that the long tenth century saw a crucial shift away from slavery towards a serfdom which embraced not only slaves but also a good part of what had previously been a free peasantry.[53] Second, we have the view, already mentioned, that settlement patterns, previously fluid and shifting, solidified in this era. Linked with this we have, third, the spread of the 'private', small-scale and residential fortification, by contrast with the refuge fortifications of an earlier era, still being built and planned in the late ninth century.[54] Fourth, such centres of aristocratic

[50] Koziol (1992) and Geary (1994) are two examples; many more could be offered.

[51] Duby (1974), pp. 118–19.

[52] See Johanek, chapter 3 below, and also Hodges and Hobley (1988) and Verhulst (1993, 1994).

[53] Bois (1989); Bonnassie (1991); see also, from rather different perspectives, Wickham (1984) and Müller-Mertens (1985).

[54] Fossier (1982), pp. 182–234; Toubert (1973a, 1973b); Böhme (1991a, 1991b).

domination were significant not only for the exercise of power but also for shifts in family consciousness. Noble families defined themselves less in terms of broad kindreds including relatives on both the male and the female side and more in terms of a male descent lineage; these lineages often took their names from the names of the fortifications which were the basis of their power.[55] Fifth, the lordship exercised from these centres was often of a new kind, based on pragmatic local dominance without much legitimation and certainly with little legitimation through 'public' office-holding. Rather, it came to replace an older 'public' order which had survived in many regions from the Carolingian era. This larger-scale public order was hollowed out to the point of extinction in many parts of Europe during the long tenth century; royal authority suffered earliest and worst, but it was followed into decline by the authority of intermediate powers (dukes, counts, earls, archbishops, bishops).[56] Sixth, what remained was in essence 'ties between man and man': legitimate authority had become privatised and personalised.[57] Linked with all these developments was a seventh: the emergence of a new and enlarged dominant class, a class which still had its own internal divisions but one in which lords and their warrior followers increasingly perceived themselves as members of a single group set apart from (and over) the rest of society; in the course of the eleventh century a separate ideology and initiation rites would be found for this class.[58]

What all this adds up to is the totalising interpretation known as the 'feudal revolution' or 'feudal mutation'. It is a compelling view of the history of post-Carolingian Europe (or at least of the history of Europe's post-Carolingian core); and yet for all its attractions it is a highly problematic one. Even leaving aside those regions of northern and eastern Europe which were clearly following another developmental trajectory altogether (as were Byzantium and Islam, for quite different reasons), and in any case have not preserved the kind of evidence which would enable us to form a judgement, the model does not really seem to work for important parts of Europe: southern Italy, León, England, Germany. As suggested above, this may be in part the product of different historiographical traditions, though at least for England the model has been explicitly rejected as inappropriate.[59] It is in any case a gross oversimplification to call it 'the model': most historians working on this period would acknowledge the existence of at least some of the phenomena enumerated in the previous paragraph and feel tempted by the idea that these phenomena were in some way linked to one another, but, as already suggested, variations in empha-

---

[55] Reuter (1997a) provides a survey of the immense literature on this shift.
[56] The essence of the 'feudal mutation'; see Poly and Bournazel (1991).
[57] The phrase was placed at the centre of interpretation, if not actually invented, by Bloch (1961).
[58] Duby (1978); Flori (1979, 1983).   [59] Campbell (1990).

sis can produce considerable variations in the overarching interpretation which provides the explanation of how these links actually worked.

Moreover, many of the most significant elements of the model are currently under challenge, even for the core regions of west Francia (including Catalonia) and northern Italy, from which the model was derived. The challenges have intensified during the period between conception and publication of the present volume. The extent of slavery in the early middle ages, and the sense in which it was replaced in the long tenth century by serfdom, is highly contentious.[60] So too is what once seemed common ground, the replacement of public authority by personal ties, in other words 'feudalism'. It has been argued that feudalism, in the sense of a homogenous juridification of personal relationships amongst the European governing elites, was an invention of the twelfth century; fiefs and vassals, in this sense, were absent from the long tenth century, and there was in any case no necessary link between vassalage and benefice.[61] It is still not clear whether we should think of a feudal revolution or mutation at all; though Europe in 1100 was clearly very different from the Europe of 800 or 900, not all would see the decades around the millennium as marking a clear period in which most of the transition took place.[62] The consolidation of a small aristocracy and its warrior following into a single, wider class was a process which does seem to have occurred across most of Europe between the Carolingian era and the thirteenth century, but it was hardly a homogenous or simultaneous one.

There are difficulties of perception here: are we dealing with new phenomena, or merely with phenomena which began to be recorded more frequently towards the end of the long tenth century? As local complaints of violence and abuse increase, we are tempted to contrast them with an idealised Carolingian past which may well never have existed, and which would appear quite different to us were we to have as much information about its local look and feel as we do about much of the post-Carolingian core of Europe around the millennium.[63] Equally, the apparent fragmentation of large-scale political authority in many parts of Europe may indicate a new order, but at least at the regional level the polities of this period (notably the French, German and Italian principalities) were in most cases not arbitrary creations but had much older roots as vehicles of being and consciousness, often traceable back through the Carolingian era to the early middle ages. It is even conceivable that the smaller units of lordship which become clearly visible around the millennium had

---

[60] Verhulst (1991); Barthélemy (1993); see also the symposium of responses to Bois (1989) in *Médiévales* 21 (1991). [61] Reynolds (1994); for initial responses see Nortier (1996); Barthélemy (1997).

[62] Bisson (1994), with responses by White (1996), Barthélemy (1996), Reuter (1997b), Wickham (1997) and a reply by Bisson (1997) See also the exchange between Barthélemy (1992a) and Poly and Bournazel (1994). [63] White (1996), pp. 218–23; Reuter (1997b), pp. 178–87.

older roots, now lost to sight. Any attempt to offer a synthesis at this stage
would be futile; as historians from different European traditions become more
aware than they have been of each other's practices and findings, and as interest in the period around the first millennium finds at least a temporary increase
in public and professional awareness from our contemplation of our own position in the decades around the second millennium, debate on these issues,
which are also of central importance to historians of the periods preceding
and following the long tenth century, is likely to intensify and to shift as it does
so.

If we leave the awkward terrain of social and political history and turn to
religious history, then we might at first think that the history of the church in
this period would appear to be a good example of *encellulement*, at least at a
purely institutional level. Ninth-century popes had commanded and occasionally threatened bishops; they had deposed or confirmed some of them in
office; at least a few had been significant figures who could not easily be
bypassed. But papal leadership of Christianity was far more muted in the
period which followed. Ecclesiastics might journey to Rome on pilgrimage, but
they mostly settled their own affairs. Neither the existence of a papal judgement nor the presence of a papal legate was necessarily bankable capital in the
course of a dispute, and the privileges granted by popes were more than once
in this period publicly repudiated. This was not so much a rejection of the pope
qua pope as a reflection of a more general attitude which meant that the
members of the higher ranks of the church hierarchy were largely insignificant
except in their capacity as bishops. Councils were rare, and usually local affairs
when they did meet: bishops were largely sovereign within their own dioceses,
and were the crucial figures of the tenth-century church, as Rosamond
McKitterick's chapter demonstrates.

Ecclesiastical *encellulement* was also visible, in a sense, in the history of monasticism in this period. Historians have been able to free themselves, slowly,
from the notion that monastic reform in this period was spelled Cluny; but it
has been more difficult to dispel ideas of monastic 'orders' projected back
from the twelfth century and later. Yet even Cluny's collection of monasteries
with varying ties of dependence on it was not an order in the later sense: the
ordo Cluniacensis was, as Joachim Wollasch points out, Cluny's 'way of life', not a
legally defined body. Other monastic groupings were still less institutionalised,
depending as they generally did on the attentions of a reforming 'expert'. Yet
the very existence of such 'experts', men like Gerard of Brogne or William of
Volpiano, shows how *encellulement* was not all-determining. Even if such
monastic families had a short-lived and tenuous existence, they could link and
unite, however briefly, monasteries scattered over several dioceses, even kingdoms. The elite owners of monasteries, especially when these were bishops,

were sufficiently knowledgeable to be able to see beyond the rim of their immediate locality.

The localism which is such an evident part of church life in this period was not transcended in the field of monastic life alone. Historians have been inclined to see it as a demonstration of how entangled with the affairs of the world the church became in the post-Carolingian era and certainly there is enough anecdotal evidence of abuse and gross misconduct, at least from some regions of Europe, to support such a view. Yet it is also possible to read the history of tenth-century Christianity as one of remarkable success.[64] It was not only the era in which the Carolingians' attempts to convert the regions beyond the former territory of the Roman empire were continued and largely brought to completion, but also the one in which the Christianisation of Europe's interior finally became reality. It is not so much the evidence from the period which follows that demonstrates this: evidence for an insistence by enlightened laity and clergy alike on the 'Gregorian' themes of a sexually pure clergy and a church untainted by the moral corrosion of payments in cash or in favours. It is also the emergence of a more active lay participation in Christianity, which took many forms: large-scale and long-distance pilgrimages, notably to Rome and Jerusalem; the veneration of relics on a very substantial scale; arguably also the mass participation in the movements known as the 'Peace' and 'Truce of God', though this is stressed much more by some contemporary observers, notably by Adhémar of Chabannes and Radulf Glaber, than by others.[65] Even some of the heresies of the period (and the recording of heresy from about 1000 onwards is itself a novelty) are interpretable in terms of 'leftist deviation', as the products of people who have been reached so effectively by the message as to take it too far; the same is true of the occasional notes of anti-semitism of the period. There is a note of questioning, of self-doubt, in the writings of many ecclesiastics of this period – Rather of Verona, Thietmar of Merseburg, Wulfstan of York – which seems both more strident and more searching than it had been in the Carolingian era. And although it is clear that many of those who lived around the eschatologically significant dates of 1000 and 1033 did not do so in fear (or hope) of the Second Coming, it is, at the end of the second millennium, less clear than it seemed to Ferdinand Lot and his contemporaries that no one at all did. It is more likely that the intensification of religious experience around the millennium, perceptible in a number of ways, was, at least in part, a response to the millennium itself.[66]

Culturally and intellectually the period has often been seen as one of

---

[64] As stressed by Tellenbach (1993).

[65] Head and Landes (1993) stress the links between the peace movement and other aspects of popular religiosity; see also Moore (1980) and Leyser (1994e).

[66] Landes (1988), Fried (1989), Landes (1992, 1993, 1995).

stagnation, even though it was also a period in which some members of the elite invested massively in the arts, whether in buildings, ivorywork, goldsmithery and other metalwork, or illuminated manuscripts, as Henry Mayr-Harting demonstrates. The notion of intellectual stagnation rests on rather superficial judgements: some of the yardsticks which have been used, such as the copying of manuscripts, are inappropriate, and in any case there was, at the level of elite culture, more happening than at first meets the eye, as Claudio Leonardi demonstrates. Nevertheless, there are some signs of decline which are difficult to deny, the most important of which is the reduced importance of schools across Latin-speaking Europe (the trajectories of Byzantine and Islamic intellectual history are not covered here). There were fewer schools, so far as we can judge, than there had been in the ninth century; still more significant, their continuous existence was increasingly precarious and fragile, dependent on the isolated, often highly charismatic figures who had built them up and whom they rarely if ever outlived. This fragmentation and impermanence may perhaps be taken as a cultural and intellectual mirroring of *encellulement*. So also may the decline in the importance of courts as centres of cultural and intellectual production. It is true that modern historians have tended to use the term court as a shorthand for a set of activities in some way connected and interconnected by a ruler and his entourage, thus making courts (like scriptoria) as much a modern social construct as a Carolingian reality. Yet, even making allowance for the gap between present construct and past reality, it remains evident that the royal and princely entourages of the long tenth century had given up much of the functionality of their Carolingian predecessors.

The period has also been seen as one with a sharp decline in pragmatic literacy and a consequent increase in the importance of symbolic and non-verbal forms of communication, though this is a problematic view for two reasons. The decline in pragmatic literacy was in regional terms a very uneven affair.[67] It is not evident that there was much decline, if any, in Italy, or Spain, or Mediterranean France. The paucity of source-material for Anglo-Saxon England is more likely to be the product of post-Conquest neglect of and contempt for the Anglo-Saxon past, which increasingly lacked any legal significance, than of any lack of production at the time. Indeed, it is clear both from contemporary indirect evidence and from later fragments and fossilised practices that tenth-century England must have made extensive use of the written word.[68] Since the newly converted lands on the northern and eastern peripheries had, for all practical purposes, not known literacy previously, the downward curve in the graph of pragmatic literacy really only describes the position in the

---

[67] The contributions to McKitterick (1991) provide the best survey.

[68] Wormald (1977); Kelly (1991); Keynes (1991).

former Frankish kingdoms north of the Alps, and even here it applies mainly to the first half or two-thirds of the century.

As to the use of symbolic and non-verbal forms of communication, these were indeed important in the long tenth century. But, so far as we can judge, they were just as important in those regions which continued to make extensive use of writing. Moreover, they were also important in the periods which preceded and followed them. It is tempting to see the period as one in which politics found expression through liturgy rather than law, or as one dominated by ritual, ceremony and gesture[69] but it would be more accurate to say that historians' eyes for such things have been sharpened in a period superficially poor in other kinds of source, whereas their presence has been more readily overlooked in seemingly more articulate eras like the ninth or twelfth centuries. Whether in the ninth, the tenth or the twelfth centuries, the primary function of social and political ritual was in any case not to act as a substitute for writing as such, but rather to make actions visible and permanent to non-literate lay elites whose members had no other means of defining them and fixing them in memory. Nevertheless, such a cultural approach, rethinking political history through a study of the seemingly inconsequential details of ritualised behaviour, has been of particular significance for the long tenth century for historiographical reasons: however wide the potential applicability of the technique, it happens to have been tested most thoroughly on this period.[70]

How, then, should we 'read' the tenth century? If it is indeed possible to make out at least some trends with a general significance across the period and region, does that mean that we can and should resume the search for general interpretations? The first point is that it *is* possible to read the period. The 'obscure' or 'dark' age is less dark than it seems, in spite of the shortage of large-scale contemporary narratives to provide an initial interpretation (or rather, of rival narratives to provide alternative interpretations). The Braudelian *longue durée* and the medium-term flow are well-enough documented; it is the surface play of the political which is frequently less well recorded. The difficulties lie – to continue the metaphor of reading – not so much in the aporias, in the letters, words, even whole sentences and paragraphs which are missing from the 'text', but rather that we are not always certain what the pieces of 'text' which survive really mean. Literal readings, in other words, are frequently either not possible or merely sterile. Much of what has been preserved from the tenth century simply will not yield to a common-sense understanding, and this is true of the apparently straightforward as well as of the evidently obscure or non-literal.

But reading is difficult, nevertheless, because few of the generalisations

[69] For the first interpretation see Kantorowicz (1957), pp. 87–93; for the second, Leyser (1994d).
[70] Althoff (1990); Koziol (1992); Leyser (1994d); Althoff (1997).

which have been offered, at any level, seem to work for all of Europe, even after we have made allowance for the distorting effects of national historiographical traditions. In that sense, *encellulement* was a reality: we are dealing with regions which did not necessarily transmit their developments to their neighbours, or receive and absorb their neighbours' developments – or not with any speed. And yet, at the level of elite culture at least, the post-Carolingian core of Europe showed a remarkable degree of homogeneity and internationality. There are clear regional flavours to such material remains as writing or building styles, yet they are evidently precisely that: regional flavours, not autonomous practices. It was this post-Carolingian core also which from this period on would provide the model adopted by the emergent societies of northern and eastern Europe;[71] at this time they were still locked in an *encellulement* far deeper than anything found in the west, even if this is now concealed from us by the homogenising effects of ignorance. And it was this post-Carolingian core which came to define itself through opposition to the older, rival Mediterranean cultures of Byzantium and Islam. It would not, as yet, contest their dominance or do more than nibble at their territorial edges, but the sense of difference, so visible from the later eleventh century onwards, was already beginning to form in the period covered in this volume.

Whatever level or form of European history we examine in this period, we appear to be confronted by past behaviour which presents itself at once as having been highly unsystematic and locally specific and as having been widespread: it is this paradoxical relationship between coherence and fragmentation which in the last resort dominates almost all readings of the long tenth century. The reader of the chapters which follow will do well to bear this paradox in mind, and will also do well, in approaching this collective reading of the tenth century, to think of the period not as 'pre' or 'post' anything, but rather as of itself. It is difficult enough, and rewarding enough, even when approached on these terms.

[71] Bartlett (1993).

PART I

GENERAL THEMES

CHAPTER 2

RURAL ECONOMY AND COUNTRY LIFE

Robert Fossier

EVEN THOUGH current historiography still preserves the concepts of ancient and medieval history devised in the nineteenth century, it is becoming steadily more apparent that these divisions – generally drawn up with political history in mind – are unsatisfactory for the historian of the economy or society. In these fields there is a *longue durée* from the decline of slavery in the third century to the first significant use of machine power in the eighteenth century. Nevertheless, undeniable developments in the techniques of production or in the relations between men force us to mark out certain stages in this long period, one in which Europe entered on the stage of world history. At what point was there a transition from the shrunken and undynamic structures still associated with Germanic or Graeco-Roman custom (the two were in this respect very similar) to structures in which the relationships between men and men and a production generating profits announced a more 'modern' economic climate? The question is not otiose; the answer will determine the view one takes on the 'infancy of Europe'. In fact, almost all the observations which one can make, whatever the preoccupations of individual historians, point to the tenth century as the age of growth, of take-off, of rising, or some such phrase. In 898 we find the word *feodum* used in southern France to mean a tenancy by military service; in 910 the foundation of Cluny opened up a new phase in the history of spirituality; in 920 villages began to move on to hilltops in central Italy; in 955 the Magyars were definitively beaten; in 970 the series of commercial contracts surviving from Venice began; in 980 the gold of the Catalan *parias* arrived at Barcelona, and there are other similar examples from all spheres of economic activity.

This transformation of the old world was indeed a 'revolution', if one is prepared to concede that the word does not have the same implications as it does in our own epoch but refers to a slow, indeed a very slow, transformation of the framework of human life. The judgements made by historians on this major turning point in the history of Europe are often marked by scholars' own philosophical convictions. Those persuaded of the fundamental correctness of Marx's analysis will see here the beginnings of a 'feudal' era, which set up, often violently, a kind of tacit contract between a lord who protects and a worker who feeds him; others who remain faithful to 'Romanist' theories will see a generally peaceful transformation from the structures inherited from antiquity to a newer version, determined by conditions equally new; others again will refuse to believe in this transformation and search ardently for proofs of continuity. I find it hard to believe that this latter group can be in the right: it seems to me fairly evident that a new order did indeed establish itself, one which did so with all the slowness familiar to the historical anthropologist but which nevertheless gradually coloured a society nine-tenths of which, it should hardly be necessary to repeat, lived in the countryside. It is necessary to begin by saying a few words about these country-dwellers.

First of all, the two feelings which until then had oppressed everyone in Europe – fear and violence – still dominated. Enthusiasm was not on the agenda; it may be that by the thirteenth century both feelings had come to be held in check, but it is hardly credible to say this about the millennium, even if the well-known 'Terrors' of that fateful year were produced by the dreams of romantic historians. Shortages constantly threatened; one could even say that with the population growing faster than technical progress, their grip tightened; the acts of cannibalism noted for 1033 are a well-known example of this. The fear of want, that fear which prostrated the faithful before an oppressive and vengeful God, did not end, then. Nonetheless, some solutions began to appear in relationships of neighbourhood, profession and family, which we shall return to later. As for the violence of the *armati* (warriors) and the 'terrorism' which they have been described as exercising: the barriers erected against it – justice and the Peace of God – were as yet perhaps not very effective, but unbridled vendetta and constant plunderings were on the decline after 1050 or so. The raiding by warriors, *werra* as it is known in the texts, continued to wreak havoc and misfortune, but it tended towards feud rather than 'warfare'. Gratuitous cruelty and sadism were becoming individual rather than collective failings. The superiority of the stronger expressed itself increasingly in representative and symbolic behaviour: one had to astonish and provoke the admiration of those who could no longer be exploited unrestrictedly. To eat more than necessary, to distribute alms and gifts, not to move about except with a vast entourage, these were the marks of the dominant, the 'noble' man. In such a world of gift-giving, well known to anthropologists, the gesture took on its full value as a symbol: it validated all serious commitment, replaced writing, which was only just beginning to revive, and even speech; the latter, even in the form of oaths, only acquired force from the gestures which accompanied it. A final point, perhaps the most important one here: in southern Europe there was a written law, whether or not we call it Roman, and in the north such law had also been introduced in the writing of law-codes. But who knew how to read these except for a handful of professionals? It follows that the lot of men was largely governed by custom, both spoken and performed. Day-to-day attitudes were shaped by the past, all novelty being in principle both bad and dangerous; this conservatism of spirit was appropriate to a society slow to move. Historians may well attempt to classify individuals into small juridically defined groups, but in fact, in this period, people were what other people thought they were.

The slow expansion of this period, which was only just beginning before the millennium, presents historians, however aware they may be of the issue, with two problems which have still not been fully resolved. First, they are tempted to place the beginnings of these developments around the middle of the tenth century, that hidden turning point of medieval history. Here sources are so thin on the ground, especially north of the Loire and of the Alps, that one has to say in all honesty that we can assume but cannot prove. For this reason there is no shortage of historians to discuss the role played by the Carolingian era. Contrary to what is believed by German historians in particular, the role of the Carolingian dynasty is not a particularly interesting topic: its effects beyond the Channel or the Pyrenees, and even in southern France or Italy, were non-existent or negligible. But it is worth talking about the importance one should give to the period between 700 and 850 as a harbinger of things to come. Anglo-Saxon kings, Frisian merchants, Iberian princes, the Frankish aristocracy, the *litterati* of Italy created a movement which pre-dated Charlemagne, and one might even say that they made him possible. In matters of canon law, in the reinforcement of the nuclear family, in the reform of the church, in the revival of the role of the state, in the taste for antique culture, the period was not negligible. Nevertheless, I do not believe that the changes brought about were universal, and in the two areas to be dealt with here, the economy and rural society, the legacy of the 'Carolingian era' was minimal, and little of it can be traced after about 950 or 1000. A 'mere surface ripple', as Georges Duby has put it.[1]

The other problem is probably still more difficult: that of the 'causes' of the European awakening. This is a classic demonstration of the chicken-and-egg problem: what was cause, and what effect? Technical progress? But how can we determine it? An easing off of the assaults which had afflicted Europe since the third century? But there were still Vikings or Normans in the tenth and eleventh centuries, Magyars until the millennium and Saracens until the end of the eleventh century, quite apart from the internal *werra*, which was hardly a peaceful affair. Demographic expansion is something more certain, and we

---

[1] Duby (1973), p. 121 (= Duby (1974), p. 106).

shall return to it, but where, when and why? Perhaps we can talk of a slight improvement in the climatic conditions in western Europe, favouring an increase in plant life and in human and animal life as well, because this is a datum which is clear, unquestionable and certainly not without effect. The evidence is indisputable: from 850/900 onwards the beech climbs the foothills of the Alps and the Bohemian mountains; the birch yields ground in Scotland and Scandinavia; both the sea and malaria retreat in the coastal marshes. I am not competent to say why these changes took place, but the Christians of this period, if they noticed these phenomena, might perhaps have seen in them the sign of a God finally appeased.

These Christians in their turn, even if they have not left us very numerous sources, did indeed note some of the essential changes which struck them: demographic growth, new family structures and the establishment of fortified residences are referred to in hagiography, biography and historiography, while charters register changes of fortune or status. Iconography remained impoverished and conventionalised, but rural archaeology has compensated for this, and in the last fifty years, especially in northern and north-western Europe, has provided new evidence on human habitat, tools and utensils. The 'dark ages' are lightening a little.

HUMAN GROUPS

Small groups of people, not very numerous, grouped around a *paterfamilias*, a clan chief or a lord, separated by huge areas which were not or scarcely exploited, short of tools and especially of iron ones, scratching a meagre living from the soil with difficulty: that is the countryside of the early middle ages. Here and there, there were larger-scale lordly estates, the descendants of the *villae* of the Romanised regions or of the *curtes* of the barbarian era, worked by slaves. Blinded by classical towns or fascinated by the mosaics which decorated a few exceptionally rich houses, ancient historians have refused to admit, in spite of archaeological evidence, that to the left and to the right of the Rhine, the Germanic and the Graeco-Roman rural economy were in much the same state. In what follows we shall see how these somewhat unpromising characteristics were to soften and reform.

Constraints and relaxations within the family

The basic unit of daily life was the family. Prior both to the state, which it ignored, and to the parish, which was just in the process of formation, it represented the basic unit of production because there was still no exterior element which could replace the labour force of the family group within the rural economy. The history of this group has made substantial progress since 1980: careful study of prosopographical evidence or of the genealogies drawn up in the eleventh and twelfth centuries allows us to identify the various forms of kinship structure which succeeded one another. Even archaeology has made some contribution by dating the settlement forms of the period. The term *familia*, used conventionally by all scribes in this period, is maddeningly vague: the group it denoted might be limited to the nuclear family or extend to very distant clients, and it is probably better not to pursue the matter here.

The historian who examines the family of the first half of the tenth century will find three levels. The 'clan' (German *Sippe*) includes all individuals of the same blood in the sense that they recognised a common ancestor: this might be a group of a thousand or more men and women most of whom had no continuous daily relationships with each other. Sometimes a particular group – we may call it a tribe – imposed its authority on others, as for example when seeking new lands to pass through or cultivate. This pattern was the most archaic, and was found at a very primitive economic level, that of peripatetic hunters and gatherers. Such structures have left traces in the epic literature of the early middle ages; by 900 they were scarcely to be found outside Scotland, Frisia, Scandinavia, and possibly Brittany. Such systems were essentially cognatic, even though women could be excluded from any public role.

The settled clan breaks up into lineages (Latin *gens*, German *Geschlecht*): here a real or mythical but not too distant ancestor defines the group of blood-relatives. Here we are at the heart of the family structure which took shape in the early middle ages in the Christian west. The lineage was sedentary, endogamous and conscious of the purity of its blood, and lived in compact groups of perhaps a hundred members, as the occasional excavation of a great hall of the seventh or eighth century shows. These families were warriors or peasants, hence male-dominated, but because women were evidently the guarantors of purity of lineage their position was better, though they were subject to close surveillance. One can see that this family type remained that of the dominant class, for it was precisely in these kin-groups that they found the elements they needed to maintain their domination over others.

When at the end of the eleventh or in the twelfth century many 'noble' families wanted to establish their genealogy, memory did not take them back beyond a 'wall' in the past – 800–50 for the very noble, 950–80 for the less noble – beyond which it was necessary to invent. This is the result of a second significant shift in family structures, in the late ninth and tenth centuries. The lineage in turn crumbles, breaks up and forgets itself. We are now confronted by the 'house' (*Haus, maison, domus*), with a simple direct line of descent (even when parallel lines also exist). Everything suggests that this simple structure, based on the nuclear family, formed gradually within the lineage, and that if the latter disappeared before the millennium it was as a result of this internal sub-division. The more humble members of the population, to whom we shall return, did not share this preoccupation with the purity of descent. The conjugal system was not simply supported by the teachings of the church; it corresponded to the position of the vast majority, and its triumph would soon come.

It will be recognised that so profound a set of changes did not come about at a stroke in the period with which we are dealing. One of the most visible characteristics of family life around the millennium, and one which would continue to be important long after that, was the powerful constraints exercised by the kindred, not only within noble families, where group interests checked ill-considered personal initiatives, but also among the most humble (at least among those to whom our documents bear witness – a significant restriction). Such constraints could take anodyne forms such as the passing on of the same name from generation to generation, the daily bread of prosopographers in search of lines of descent. Or they could acquire moral or Christian dimensions, which restricted certain freedoms, for example the freedom to bury: one had to lie where one's ancestors were gathered. The earliest examples of genealogical literature – for the counts of Flanders in the mid-tenth century, for the lords of Vendôme at the end of the tenth century – stress this link with one's ancestors. A count of Anjou in the twelfth century was to say: 'Before this I know nothing, for I do not know where my forefathers are buried.'[2] A final superficial point: it is from the end of the tenth century that we begin to find signs in dress and emblems distinguishing one 'house' from another. But it is obvious that it was in the economic sphere that the power of kindred was most important, all the more because the contemporaray shifts in landholding, to which we shall return shortly, threatened to shake the base of its wealth and hence its power. The *laudatio parentum*, by which descendants or collateral relatives gave their consent to property transactions or gifts of land in alms, offers some rough figures, even granted that what we have is only the positive side (should the kin refuse their consent, the transaction would not take place and there would thus be no record of it). In Latium, the proportion of transactions with a collective nature or mentioning the approval of kindred was 35% between 900 and 950 and 46% at the end of the tenth century, and still stood at 41% around 1050. In Catalonia, shortly before the millennium, the figure was a mere 12%, but rose to 30% fifty years later. In Picardy, where fewer documents have survived, it rose from 17% to 36% in the same period. Clearly there are gaps and variations, but the role played by the lineage remained significant, perhaps even grew. Epic literature is replete with examples, from the four inseparable sons of Aymon, to the family of Ganelon, all

---

[2] Fulk le Réchin, in *Chronique des comtes d'Anjou et des seigneurs d'Amboise*, ed. L. Halphen and R. Poupardin, p. 237.

executed along with the traitor, though it is true that this evidence comes from a rather later period.

However, further constraints began to take effect; they were already in place, even though they did not play much of a role before 1080 or 1100. Primogeniture was one, especially for the richer members of society; the lower orders did not here have the motivation driving the dominant classes. The aristocracy could not henceforth with equanimity run the risk of their heirs' joint partition on their death, a source of innumerable difficulties, or of a division of estates. The designation of a preferred heir was not new: Roman testamentary law allowed it. But the combination of an emphasis on male succession and primogeniture was destined to preserve the integrity of family possessions against younger sons and kinsfolk: there are examples from the Loire valley in the 1010s and the practice would spread across north-western Europe in the first instance during the following century. A further path was opened up by the freeing of marriage. By taking wives exogamously, outside one's own kin-group, and by founding the union not on kin interest but on mutual attraction (*dilectio*) and free will (*consensus*), one might hope to escape the intervention of relatives. Such a practice was obviously of interest for the humblest; Roman law, moreover, as well as the Bible, enjoined it. Carolingian church legislation had already laid down exogamy as the norm, and in 1025 Gerard of Cambrai was to back this up with sanctions.[3] It was a key force for the liberation of the individual. But the pressure exerted by the lineage mentioned earlier shows that it would take a long time to triumph.

THE CONTINUING STRENGTH OF FREEDOM

The church asserted it, and both Roman and Germanic law testified to it: the 'normal' man was a free man. He had free disposition of his own body, his goods, his arms; he assisted in the doing of justice, and sustained the prince. Even if he held lands by service, he could leave them and take up another holding. The ideal culminated in the hermit, released from all control and perhaps for that very reason venerated and consulted, as Otto III did St Romuald. Nevertheless, once military skill demanded time for training which work on the fields did not allow, once the complexity of cases and laws coming before tribunals could only be determined by experts, and once the difficulties of subsistence farming meant that workers could not take time off whenever they felt like it – in short, once liberty found its limits – the Roman notion of freedom would become no more than a word. And this was indeed the position for a very large number of people in the tenth century, though not without variations.

---

[3] *Acta synodi Atrebatensi a Gerardo Cameracensi et Atrebatensi episcopo celebrata anno 1025*, pp. 2–5.

Leaving aside for the moment those whose wealth or office placed them beyond all constraints and enabled them to command others, the group of free men, the overwhelming majority of the population, can be divided into at least three groups, which can be distinguished juridically more easily than economically. The highest group was made up of those who were subject only to public authority, either of the count or of the king, who presided at tribunals and gave their opinion as well as enjoying established rights over public land: the allodial landowners (from *al-od*, property held absolutely). They will be known as *Schöffenbarfreien* at the Germanic *mallus*, *sokmen* at the Anglo-Saxon *shiregemot*, *arimanni* in the Lombard plain, *boni homines* in Catalonia, or simply *liberi*, as in Gaul. Since they did not make extensive donations to the church their traces in the documents surviving to us are limited; but the *loci* in northern France which are not part of large estates, the contracts of thirty years' rent followed by outright ownership which formed the *aprisio* of Languedoc, the *pressura* of Catalonia, and the *escalio* of Aragon (this whole region is rich in documentation) from about 820 or 850 onwards, the isolated *casalia* of Tuscany, Sabina and the banks of the Po, as well as the *casae* of the Auvergne and perhaps the Breton *ran*, all show the vitality of the free peasantry. Archaeology has demonstrated, in the proto-villages of the ninth and tenth centuries, the existence of large family enclosures which were certainly not dependent on a lord. In turn, the *libri traditionum* of northern France or the Empire beyond the Rhine multiply examples of the rights held by these *villani* or *pagenses*: access to common lands or to assarts which were to encroach on the commons at the end of the tenth century, in Cerdaña, Normandy and northern Italy. One would like to be able to assess the proportion which this large group represented: as has been said, the sources are often silent, but in Catalonia around 990 (80%) of the charters recording exchanges in favour of the church concern it, and fifty years later in the Mâconnais the figure would be 60%. At the point when seigneurial organisation was being established, this group clearly presented an obstacle, and there are indeed numerous signs of the efforts of the powerful to force the allodial peasantry to submit themselves to their authority, either by personal commendation or by 'receiving' their lands back in dependent tenure. We find these from 975 in Provence, from 1010 in Tuscany and the Thames valley, and from 1040 in Latium and the Loire valley. Public authority, however, had an interest in supporting such free men, and in those regions where comital power remained strong that is what counts did: in the valleys of the Scheldt, Meuse and Rhine, in Bavaria and Saxony, allodial lands (*Eigen*) remained protected.

Nevertheless, the importance of large estates, to which we shall return, is undeniable. Even if he made use of some domestic labour, the master was forced to lease out lands. This was a very ancient 'system', known from the times of antiquity with its peasant *coloni* who paid a rent (*canon* or *tasca*) on the holdings granted to them and who came to owe – but from when? – labour services on their proprietor's own lands. Since we know of the status of these men, for the most part juridically free but all economically dependent, only from the texts of the ninth century, especially the great (so-called 'Carolingian') polyptichs, there have been and still are fierce scholarly debates about them, which can be passed over here, since from 900 or 950 at the latest the silence of the sources is so profound that the debate is irrelevant to us. What we appear to see, around the millennium, is fairly simple. Either in nuclear families or in groups, people held, in return for rent, tenancies thought capable of sustaining them and yielding a surplus with which they could meet their obligations to their lords: the Germanic *hoba*, the Anglo-Saxon *hide*, the *mansus* of Romance-speaking lands or the Italian *colonica*. There is no space here to go into the problems of surface area (ranging from 2 to 24 hectares!), of service obligations, of the nature of renders or the right to commute services. Some of these problems are connected with the origins of the seigneurie, and will be dealt with there. We shall also not spend much time on certain kinds of tenancy, as for example those used by the church (the *censuales* or *sainteurs* of Lotharingia and the lands beyond the Rhine), which the church alone thought were more favourable than other kinds, because in theory their holders were covered by the mantle of ecclesiastical protection, though the price for this was heavy personal taxation. The common characteristic of all these men was straightforward: they were free, served in the army, and were perhaps still able to make themselves heard in public judicial assemblies. But they were weighed down by severe financial exactions which set severe limits on their freedom: they could leave, they could choose wives from elsewhere, but they were then excluded from the group which surrounded them. Their freedom, it has been said, was 'the freedom to choose their lord'.[4]

Some became irrevocably attached to their lords and so came to form a third group: these were men of service (domestics, *Dienstmänner*) charged by their lords with tasks of administration or supervision (*officiales*, *ministeriales*). Generally free (though in Germany they were to become servile), their numbers expanded once the relaxation of the 'system' forced their masters to delegate tasks. One finds them from between 920 and 1000, throughout the zone stretching from Burgundy to Bavaria and from the Alps to the lower Rhine, at the head of outlying estates, as 'mayors' or supervisors; some also had military careers. Normally they lived from a portion of land granted by their lord and from dues, which makes us suppose that they often abused their positions and were detested.

Allodial landowners, tenants, officials: these men were free, but free in the

---

[4] A phrase used by the Marxist historian Bessmertniy (1976).

shadow of the powerful. This is why they were tempted to gather round the powerful and support them. We are still a long way from the rural assemblies of the twelfth century or even from the active confraternities of the eleventh, but the seeds for these developments were sown in the tenth century, in various ways. First, some of these groups were able to obtain tenancy arrangements which were particularly supple and advantageous. This was the case with a number of southern groups: the *libellarii* of northern Italy or Umbria at the end of the tenth century, and the *aprisionarii* of Catalonia and Languedoc fifty years earlier. Once the emphyteutic lease was over, they could become owners of a part of their holdings, and enjoyed guarantees of justice and free access to the *saltus, communia, terra francorum*, even freedom from mercantile tolls. Further north the situation was less favourable, but it is there that we can find convivial meetings providing the basis for conscious solidarity. Groups formed around a patron saint or a drinking-bout are clearly visible from the tenth century onwards at London, Exeter and Cambridge, and scarcely later on the Scandinavian coasts (Birka and Hedeby), then down the Rhine and at St Gallen, and in the early eleventh century in the Low Countries, in the valleys of the Meuse and the Scheldt. True, these *drykkia* or *ghelda* or *potaciones* are generally found in the towns, but their rural echoes are undeniable. Here are the beginnings of those rural solidarities which were to be one of the features of rural life so visible in the twelfth and thirteenth centuries. Perhaps because of a shortage of sources elsewhere, we do not find rural communities outside Spain before about 1020; their early development in Spain was no doubt favoured by the incipient *reconquista*. Was it, at the beginning, merely a question of groups of *fideles* fighting against Islam (*sagreres*), or was it already a matter of agreements amongst peasants (*consejos*)? In any case, the first allusions to *franquezas* can be found from 975–80 onwards in Catalonia, around Cerdaña. There one finds *jurados* (perhaps elected?), who supervise good justice, and *paciarii*, who maintain public order and watch over the observance of custom. These are not yet *fueros*, the *fors* of the period after 1050, but the use of the term *burgenses* around 1020 to designate these peasants – armed, it should be noted – says much about the stages which had already been passed through. When the local church has become a place of refuge and the houses, now regrouped, are surrounded by a palisade (*Etter* in the German-speaking regions), the group of free peasants can emerge from the shades of anonymity: a text from the Mâconnais of 928 calls them the *melior pars*.[5]

---

[5] *Recueil des chartes de l'abbaye de Cluny,* ed. A. Bernard and A. Bruel, II, no. 1240, p. 328.

THE PLACE OF THE DEPENDANT

Responding to a question posed by a count, an officer of the Carolingian court declared that 'there are only two kinds of men, free and slave (*servus*)'.[6] But in 1042 a text from the archives of Cluny could speak of 'two free men, of whom one is a serf (*servus*)'.[7] At the very core of the subject being treated here, there is obscurity and confusion. Historians cannot rescue themselves by talking of certain men as 'half-free': liberty is indivisible, though one may possess it in a different sense from one's neighbour. To make it still more difficult, it is precisely between 900 and 1020 that an essential characteristic of unfreedom emerged. Let us try to see more clearly.

First of all, it should be said that there is no doubt that real personal servitude, that is to say animals with human faces, continued to exist. This wonderful heritage of antiquity, which Byzantium and Islam were to revive cheerfully, remained solid, even if Africans and Goths had given way to Slavs (who from Charlemagne's time gave the institution their name) or Scandinavians. The church condemned the institution, indeed, but very gently: many of its dignitaries, especially in southern Europe, fed and exploited these human cattle. Anyway, she did not admit slaves to her own ranks, and preached acceptance of one's lot in this world in view of the world to come, while at the same time denouncing the Jews guilty of sustaining the trade. It is difficult to estimate the size of this rural labour force: serving-women and concubines, carters, or seamstresses in the women's workshops, were carefully and separately specified, and some polyptichs, moreover, distinguish *mancipia* (a neuter noun) from other subject persons, *servi*. Their presence is visible only in the occasional allusion to the slave trade, at Cambrai, Verdun, Magdeburg or Chur, where in the tenth century the bishop still levied a tax on the sale of any person. Beyond the Channel, those who were shipped at Hull and Bristol around the end of the tenth century, for destinations in Scandinavia and the Islamic world, were probably Welsh and Irish people, boys and girls 'fattened up' before sale. Further south, in Lombardy and the Iberian peninsula around Venice and Barcelona, the embarcation-points for the Islamic world, slaves undoubtedly formed the bulk of the peasants and shepherds working on the great estates. These were real slave-gangs, and rebelled as such, for example in León in 975 and in Lombardy in 980, before they were savagely put down as in all slave wars. True, there were manumissions, either by charter, following the ritual of antiquity (*per cartulam*), or by the more recent ritual of the penny placed on the head (*per denarium*). There are examples of this in Catalonia around 950, in Provence around 960, in León in 985 and in Lombardy around 1000, but it

---

[6] *MGH Cap* I, no. 58, p. 145: *Responsa misso cuidam data*, c. 1.
[7] *Recueil des chartes de l'abbaye de Cluny*, ed. A. Bernard and A. Bruel, IV, no. 3380, pp. 475–7.

should be recognised that it was really the Christianisation of the Slavs and
Hungarians before or around the millennium, coupled with the economic
difficulties of the Byzantine empire after the death of Basil II and of the
Islamic world faced by Seljuk attacks, which were the real causes of the decline
of slavery. Moreover, this was never final: slavery continued in existence.

These beings deprived of all rights were not the only *bondmen*, as they were
known in Anglo-Saxon England. Numerous others are found in the texts,
people whom a long historiographical tradition has agreed to call 'serfs', even
though the word *servus* is not necessarily the commonest term used by contemporary sources, which prefer more complicated but more precise designations such as *homines de corpore, homines de capite, homines proprii* or *homines cotidiani*
(terms all making clear their dependence on a lord), or others stressing their
subordinate role, such as *manuales, bordarii* or *Hausdiener*. Their existence and
status were the subject of excited debates among the historians of the 1950s.
Nowadays we are less concerned with the issue, primarily because they did not
make up a very large part of the population. In Bavaria their share has been
estimated at 18% around 1030, and this would appear to be on the high side;
there were very few in Italy and Spain, or further north in Normandy or
Picardy, though they were more numerous in central France and beyond the
Channel and the Rhine. It seems clear that their appearance, from the end of
the eighth century at the latest, was the product of a number of phenomena,
though these themselves are not easy to study: former domestic slaves housed
(*casati*) on a holding who gradually freed themselves; freemen who had voluntarily entered servitude to secure protection; domestic personnel (*stipendarii,
nutriti*) whose humiliating position had caused them to be regarded as unfree;
tenants who had become incapable of meeting their obligations and so
excluded from freedom. It seems certain that the transformations of lordship
of the tenth and early eleventh centuries accelerated the process. These
people were, first of all, economically affected; they would henceforth be
expected to do days of labour service, and the payments by the next generation for succession to their holdings would allow lords to reclaim the whole or
a part of the wealth they had accumulated. Even their marriages, because of
the consequences for their succession, could be supervised and taxed (*marita-
gium, merchet*), although these constraints do not seem to have been either
established or typical. In the end their lot – their reduced quantity of freedom,
the 'stain', the *pensum servitutis* which would be invoked from around 1000 in
Italy – was undoubtedly characterised by exclusion and mistrust: they did not
bear arms or attend public courts, were pursued with hounds if they fled and
chastised if they committed a crime, were rejected by women of a different
status, were confined to one corner in the church. They were not beasts – they
were baptised, could possess moveable property and have skills – but it is clear

that 'servitude' was a pillar of the authority of lords. To these we must now turn.

THE RICH

It is an established tradition of European historiography to concentrate on the small handful of the very powerful. There are two powerful explanations for this persistent distortion of our view of the past. First, almost the whole of our written documentation, and often a large part of the archaeological evidence, tells us about them. Medieval history has for a long time appeared as a tedious sequence of trivial conflicts between lords and clerics. The second, more significant reason is that this tenth of the population ruled over the others and determined their destiny, especially in the countryside. Their problems have come to flood the history of the period: 'feudal society' or 'feudalism' are the terms used. Let us try to sort out the essentials, beyond what has already been said when we discussed the family.

Wealth at this time undoubtedly meant land; those who owned large chunks of it ruled over others. It is practically impossible to make any assessment of the size of these great estates before about 1050–80; even those of the church evade any estimate. True, the hundreds. of thousands of hectares possessed by the great monasteries of the early middle ages had been partially dispersed, but it has been suggested that ecclesiastical lands amounted to about 25–30% of the total, and that public property and the lands of the warrior aristocracy amounted together to about as much again. The slaves and tenants just discussed lived on these estates, which were generally exploited indirectly: these were to form the basis of the seigneuries still being established. But at this time it was the ties between men which were of greatest significance, and which wove lineage solidarities on the one hand and the great mass of dependants and servants on the other into the *familia*, the word used to refer to the collectivity of those who lived around and were dependent on a lord.

The formation of a loyal but greedy clientele around the rich, who expected aid and counsel from it, goes a long way back and is an inherent characteristic of an inegalitarian society. At the time we are considering, the difficulties of subsistence and the dangers of the environment could only lead to a general spread of such accretions of *amici*, *parentes* and *homines* around anyone owning significant granaries. If besides this he was also invested with some public function, even if this was only theoretical, the pressures making for such an accretion would only be the greater. The presence in or near to the lord's residence of *nutriti* or *prebendarii*, dependants or impoverished relatives whom the lord sustained, *familiares*, *criados*, *gasindi*, *geneats*, to cite a few varied terms, charged with guarding the lord or some other task, created a familial atmosphere which has led to the description of this whole aristocratic ambience as 'smelling of the household loaf'. This complex served as a basis for at least three elements.

The man who fed others and could protect them (the 'giver of bread', the Saxon *hlaford*), whose riches translated into generous presents and favours and an open table, lived *nobiliter*, that is to say without calculating, giving openly, even wastefully. He who did not was thus *ignobilis*, ignoble, as was the case with the pauper or the merchant. The immediate problem is thus the nature of 'nobility', which has so greatly divided historians. Some see in it a supreme group, the only one to enjoy all the elements of liberty, even in the face of public authority where this existed. Others have supposed that in the tenth century it was the blood link with the Carolingians which alone conferred nobility; some have established a link with a real or supposed devolution of public authority. But it is generally agreed that, in this period at least, nobility was an indication of pure blood which was kept in being by a systematic endogamy practised in spite of the efforts of the church to break up its rivals. That did not make every great landowner automatically a 'noble', but he could live like one, could aspire to become one, and nothing stops us assuming that his peasants knew something about this too.

By contrast, the establishing of firm personal ties between lord and dependants did not have to take account of this criterion of 'nobility'. One is surrounded by those commended to one because it is better to keep them on a short rein. We know, moreover, that the Carolingians actively encouraged these practices, which were old established but seemed to them a means of moulding society more closely around them. The rites of vassalage are known from the end of the eighth century, and throughout our period they survived and spread. It should be noted, however, that they were still not clearly fixed, for in 1020 Bishop Fulbert of Chartres was to explain to the duke of Aquitaine the duties – all negative, incidentally – which he could expect from homage.[8] Naturally, it is the material counterpart to this engagement which is of concern to us, because the commended person, having become the man and hence in theory the equal of the more powerful lord, had to perform tasks (these were still called *opera*, 'works', in Saxony in 936[9]) to justify the gift received. At any rate this was a frequent arrangement, though vassalage without a material counterpart is still clearly visible in Germany around 1020, and equally we find grants of land without homage in Italy around the same time. Such grants were also old-established usage, simple temporary loans of land (*laen, Lehn, prestimonio*), then permanent concessions soon to become hereditary. This is not the place to survey the development of 'feudalism' and the distortions which marked it from 1020 onwards, but its role in reinforcing the aristocratic group at a time when, as we

---

[8] Fulbert, *ep.* 51.   [9] Ganshof (1955), p. 71.

have seen, the peasantry were beginning to form their own solidarities made a significant contribution to the hardening of rural society.

This was especially true if the bearing of arms was to become the virtual monopoly of a restricted group. The idea that every free man was a soldier had never vanished. Beyond the Channel, the Anglo-Saxon *fyrd* was still not seriously shaken; but on the continent more and more use was made of heavy cavalry, which excluded the peasant and reduced him to the level of a subsidiary force, patrol, watch or substitute. Henceforth the soldier *par excellence*, the *miles*, would be the man on horseback, the *chevalier* or *Ritter*. But the Germanic languages preserved the domestic origins of such men: *Knecht* (i.e. servant), *knight*. The *familia* of the rich contained enough vigorous boys to make good knights. These were the people armed to defend the lord, though at first it was not necessary to make them into vassals or choose only the noble for the purpose. The *milites*, who appear from about 920–50 in southern Europe and from about 980–1000 in the north, were soldiers in the making, fed, equipped and lodged in their lord's residence. In Germany they were even recruited from among the ranks of the servile. Because of the need for convenient access to the services expected of them and the cost of their arms it was self-evident that they were *casati*, garrisoned, and that they had to do homage. This development, which came to mean that the prestige of the warrior, that of one who had joined an elite *militia* after the magical ceremony of dubbing, was so great that a noble would no longer refuse it and would even strive after it, is already visible, but these elements were not to fuse until around 1100, and in some places even later; around the year 1000 they were still unquestionably distinct.

The study of rural society, which is to say of almost the whole of society, has of necessity taken us to the edge of scholarly fields which need further discussion. A general survey of human society was needed. It will have been noted, finally, that if the inequalities of wealth, rights and power were very strongly marked, the general environment within which all social levels operated had a certain homogeneity. The main reason which can be given for this is that everyone in our period was engaged in what I have called a process of regrouping (*encellulement*), a process which seems to me the most important feature of the break marked in European history by the millennium.

ENCELLULEMENT[10]

There is a solid European historiographical tradition which sees in the countryside of fields and villages which still surrounds us an ancient and even a

---

[10] Translator's note: the French term has been retained here and elsewhere to describe the social, economic and political process of human regrouping accompanied by a restriction of horizons which divided society up into 'cells'.

natural state of affairs. Current upheavals within rural society should, however, make us reflect on whether similar transformations may not have taken place in more distant periods. To put it another way: the 'unchanging serenity of the fields' and 'the eternal village' are figures of the mind. Historians of antiquity, seduced by the disappearance of towns or of some *villae*, have hardly asked themselves about the state of the Roman countryside, and this is even more true of the lands beyond the Rhine–Danube *limes*. Supported by archaeology, it can be said that an organised field system, that is to say one underpinned by a network of paths, and the village itself, are creations of the European middle ages, and that it is precisely in the period before the millennium that we can find the first signs of it.

Since even excavations do not provide an indisputable image of what was going on before the millennium, textual evidence ought to alert the historian to the changes taking place amongst human groupings. The first sign of this is the appearance of new terms to denote equally new forms of exploitation of the soil: *cella* and *curtis* decline, and even *villa* tends to take on more of the meaning of 'village'; *mansus* persists, as does *hide*, but the words lose their association with obligations and come to mean merely 'a holding with a house'. Terms denoting fragments of land – *sors*, *massa*, *quarterium*, *area*, *locus* – follow close behind, and these features are evidently very different from the *mansionale*, *villare* and *casale* of an earlier period. At the same time unambiguous expressions underline the movement of population: *congregatio hominum*, *instauratio tenimentorum*. In short, there are obvious signs of a transition from the former fluidity in the rural habitat to the framework shaping the rural life with which we are familiar today. These are signs of a regrouping and a taking control of men, reassembled into fixed points within the cells of the seigneurie, a process which I have termed *encellulement*.

Besides the general causes for the upheavals which Europe knew at this time, spoken of earlier, various explanations have been offered for these concentrations of population. The decline of tribal wars, for example, and the turning by warriors to more local horizons have been used to explain the quest for authority and profit which required a closer control over the inhabitants of the countryside. So has a decline in rudimentary agricultural methods such as gathering, shifting animal husbandry and long-fallow cultivation, which imply a fixing of the cultivated area and a more determined exploitation of the uncultivated area. It has also been suggested that the evolution of family structure was accompanied by the presence or the persistence of human groupings such as the hundred (*centena*, *hundreda*) or even simply parishes. All these possible explanations – even though the prime mover in the chain of causation would still need to be identified – are not mutually exclusive, and none of them will be privileged here. But it will be necessary to examine the clearest signs of a movement whose beginnings are perhaps found between 920 and 950 on the southern flank of Europe, between 980 and 1010 in the region from the Atlantic coast to the Rhine, and still later beyond the Channel and the Rhine, even if this periodisation is perhaps principally determined by the survival of sources.

If the general tendency towards a disaggregation of the great domains of the early middle ages is borne in mind alongside the effects we have just seen, it seems certain that, by contrast with these elements of disintegration, there was a hard core of demesne lands which resisted all tendencies towards dismemberment, and there were even powerful trends towards the accumulation of lands, especially in the hands of churches and the chief holders of banal powers. Ecclesiastical documents, for example, show the abbey of St Emmeram in Regensburg holding 21% of its lands in demesne between 1000 and 1030; in England, the figures for the abbey of Burton and the bishopric of Winchester are 40% and 22% respectively. Establishments like Farfa or Monte Cassino in Italy, Seo d'Urgel or Liebana in Spain and Saint-Amand or Saint-Bavo in Flanders largely succeeded in reconstructing their patrimonies, often at the expense of allodial peasants who sought protection from these monasteries. As far as we can trace their activities, lay magnates did the same: in Catalonia, Provence and Latium, where documents reveal their activities after 950, there were substantial concentrations of estates (*congregatio fundorum*). Economic motives evidently lie at the root of this, for the appetite of the rich was directed towards soils with good yields or tithes providing a reliable income which was stopped by uncanonical means from reaching its intended recipient. The church, of course, legislated against this (the councils of Trosly and Coblenz, in 909 and 922 respectively) or protested (Ingelheim and Saint-Denis, in 948 and 992 respectively) or threatened (Seligenstadt in 1022); but in vain.

The other side of this process, the disintegration of large estates, can be fairly precisely dated by the development of acts recording sales or exchanges of lands between laymen and the church, which is evidently a more striking sign of a search for profit than the decrease of gifts made in alms; the effect of the latter was no doubt much the same, but the spiritual component can distort our judgement. In almost all the regions where it has been possible to count such things, the peak of change appears to fall between 950 and 1025. This is true of the changes in *alotissements*[11] in Lotharingia, of gifts in Germany, of the dissolving of contracts of *aprisio* in Languedoc. It is difficult, especially given

---

[11] Allocations of small parcels of land.

the details, which get in the way, to follow the broad trend of exploitation in different regions each with its own peculiarities. We may simplify by distinguishing between three large zones with different trends.

England, the Seine basin and its neighbouring regions, the main part of Lotharingia and Germany displayed two related trends. The first is the weakening of the ties, which in these regions had been strong, between dependent tenancies and the remaining lands held in demesne. The *Villikationsverfassung*, to use the German term (the 'manorial system' of English historians), began to break down, especially on its edges, where more distant centres gained their autonomy. One of the human consequences of this relaxation was to cause the lord's hand to fall more heavily on those peasants remaining under his control. From Dijon to Lorsch, from Saint-Bertin to Regensburg, the tenants close at hand were severely exploited, while their counterparts further away largely freed themselves. The other feature is the division of the unit of exploitation into two (*Halbhufe*) or four (*Viertel, quartier vergée*), or even eight, as in England (bovate). The typical holding shrank from 10–12 hectares to 3 or 4, and the new terms which appear, *croada* in Lotharingia (from *corvée?*) or the *boel* imported by the Scandinavians, seem to imply the same size.

Southern France and northern Spain, where the links between the different parts of the estate had always been loose, followed a different route. The initial core, the *mas doumenc*, the *domenicatura*, lost control over outlying holdings. Since the dependent holdings in this zone seem to have had single tenants and not to have been distributed in parcels across the fields as they were further north, each of the *mas* thus liberated was able to form a new little unit. There was often a survival of a render (*tasca, agrière*), which recalled the ancient domanial link, and this can be seen in words like *condamina* which reek of dependency, but these are mere fossils. Besides, the comparatively dispersed nature of settlement and the extent of uncultivated lands in those zones not much favoured by nature allowed the expansion of these isolated *mas*, often by usurpation, up to a size of several dozen hectares.

Italy remained a special case, even if we disregard the contrast between the Lombard plain and the rest of the peninsula. Here the *curtis* held out against disintegration in some areas, but two elements shook this coherence: the leases granted *per libello* to the peasants gave them a lot of elbow-room, largely to their benefit, if their holding (*sors*) was not in the immediate ambit of the *curtes*; and in Latium if not in Lombardy the phenomenon of *encellulement* (here known as *incastellamento*), which here took precocious and powerful forms, broke up the domanial network more completely than in any other region.

These varied developments had important consequences for the general condition of dependants. The loosening of ties with the demesne affected services first of all, especially day-works and plough-works. The time was near when the lord, tired of seeing these performed badly or not at all, would have them commuted for a money payment, liberating the well-off peasant and crushing the poorer one. Then the rents which custom would gradually fix at an unchangeable level became divided into two parts: a render in kind or in silver (once it had begun to circulate again) at a bearable level, or else a portion of the harvest (*tasca, champart*) whose interest for the tenant lay in the possibility of escaping from the consequence of climatic fluctuations, so that he would try to make this a more general practice from about 1020–30, especially on newly cultivated lands. In this context we must also note that the subdivision of peasant tenures reached a new low level, around 3 or 4 hectares (though still with immense variations – in Catalonia around 1050 between 1 and 19 hectares, for example!). This situation can be explained in two ways: either, and this is the optimistic view, technical progress meant that 10 hectares were no longer required to feed a family, or else demographic growth and the evolution of the family proceeded so fast that they forced the break-up and an overloading of tenements.

We can now see why we needed to make this survey of cultivated lands before examining the environment. The allodialists, whether large or small, who continued to direct their exploitation of the land, and the tenants, over-crowded or not, who were freed from 'demesne' constraints, formed a mobile mass, juridically freer and available to be regrouped. True, powerful owners already possessing their 'men' or even their slaves continued to exist. Equally, the disintegration of the 'system' had its negative aspect, for example the wors-ening of the lot of the poorest. But the general effect of *encellulement* was posi-tive.

THE REORGANISATION OF THE ENVIRONMENT.

The floating mass of the peasantry had hitherto lacked centres around which they could crystallise the disparate and disorganised environment inherited from the preceding centuries. It was not enough to scatter their huts haphaz-ardly within a clearing, not even enough to give a name to this agglomeration; there had to be a coherent organisation there, so that a state of mind could take hold. Augustine said that what made a town was 'not walls, but minds'; some-thing similar could be said of the countryside.

It seems to me to start with that it was the dead who fixed the living. The ancient necropolises were laid out along the roads leaving towns, and those of the early medieval countryside on the edges of the lands between settlements, always far from housing, perhaps because of a fear of the dead which the Christian church would slowly uproot, though hardly before 900. Thenceforth, especially as regards magnates, it was, as has been said, psychologically very important to live alongside one's ancestors, to respect them, even to consult them. And since it was hardly easy to move them about, there was a tendency to group settlement around tombs; archaeology has shown, for the whole of northern and north-western Europe at least, that the cemeteries and the protected areas surrounding them which enjoyed peace and functioned as assembly-grounds (*atria*), and are still in use today, date from the tenth century, not before. Indeed, the necropolises of the preceding centuries, set in the open countryside, were abandoned at this time: the cemeteries of Normandy or Württemberg were no longer used after 850 or 900. Unfortunately for historians, the accompanying disappearance of funerary goods and the practice of burying in shrouds of perishable material often mean that dating these new village cemeteries is difficult. Where it has been possible it is by no means uncommon to find that the field of the dead, the 'second village', is earlier than the parish church, as in Lévezou or in lower Saxony. Moreover, the council of Tribur (895) enjoined the separation of church and cemetery, and if that of Toul (971) prescribed the establishing of a cemetery in the middle of each Christian village, it did not require it to be located next to the church.

It is evidently the latter which came to be the heart of the new village, so much so that right across Europe it still symbolises the rural settlement. It is not our purpose here to discuss the slowness with which a parochial system was established, once the Mediterranean shores had been left behind. It is sufficient to recall that around 920 the diocese of Paderborn, which amounted to about 3000 km^2, had no more than twenty-nine parishes, and that there were no more than 3500 in the whole of Germany. As for church buildings themselves, even if there is no shortage of buildings whose foundations are older than the tenth century, nothing shows that they acted as a focal point for settlement in that earlier period. The example of the *fana* of antiquity or of Christian *oracula* in the open countryside are enough to show that this was not necessary. On the other hand, we know that rural Christianisation often took the form – in Gaul or Saxony, for example – of establishing a baptismal font at the centre of a *fundus*, an isolated great estate; the fact that this practice allowed the development of the proprietary church (*Eigenkirche*), with implications evidently counter to the spirit of canon law, is not our problem here. What seems most clearly established is the breaking-up of the giant rural parishes of previous centuries (the *plebes cum oraculis*) into more modest units capable of stabilising a small group of the faithful. This phenomenon has been noted for the *pievi* in Latium between 950 and 1020, in Auvergne and Poitou before 1050, where the word *parrochia* comes to replace the word *villa* as the term for a nucleated settlement, and later on further north. By and large the former kernel preserved a certain primacy over the subsidiary units established within its initial territory, and the present-day parish map often still shows this; but sometimes the churches established in the villages on the uplands led to the remorseless abandoning lower down of the old parochial core church (*Niederkirche*).

If the bell-tower around which the members of the parish came together was a symbol of the village, the castle itself was the symbol of the middle ages. But if for now I merely touch on it, it is because I think it developed later than the other two crystallisation points for the reshaping of settlement, where it developed at all – something which justifies our restricting the concept of *incastellamento* to those regions where its role is clearly established. To set up a fortified location for assemblies protecting and exploiting men is a phenomenon found in all ages. For the centuries immediately preceding those we are here concerned with, archaeology has clearly revealed both the ancient and revived *oppida* which still served as royal palaces in Germany in the tenth century (as at Werla and Tilleda, but also further west), and also the huge earthworks of a more recent age (some seventh- or eighth-, some tenth-century) found in the Auvergne, in Normandy, in England or in the Palatinate (*Ringwallen*, ringworks, etc.). The original feature of the tenth century was the way in which Europe came to bristle with strengthened buildings, towers first of wood and then from the end of the tenth century of stone (*turris, dunio*), set up on a natural or man-made elevated site, surrounded by a moat and possibly a protective enclosure (bailey), and designated by revealing terms – *motte, rocca, podia, colli* – echoed in modern terms like *Wasserburg* and 'moated site'. Their location was rarely chosen at random: they were set up at an ancient assembly-ground (Maine, Oxfordshire), a Roman *mansio* (Piedmont, Burgundy), a *villa* or *casa* (Lombardy, Auvergne, Rhineland), or a cult site (in the Liègeois). Such locations, especially when we note that there was a strategically superior site nearby which could have been chosen instead, show that the aim was much more one of economic surveillance and of social control than of military utilisation.

The material and judicial status of these constructions is fairly well known. Everywhere where public authority retained its force such towers were built only with permission, generally from the count, with or without a genuine devolution of powers in the form of *regalia*. Usurpations by daring allodialists were not unknown, but they rarely survived without either punishment or, more frequently, retrospective legitimisation. Anyway, it could also come about that the rights of control over the men of a neighbouring village (*mandamentum, salvamentum, potestas*) were granted subsequently, either to a landowner who had behaved himself, here functioning as a deputy, or to a military leader whose support was needed (*castlania* in Languedoc and Catalonia). The very force of things meant that possession of a tower, especially where no effective public power could watch over the protection of the villagers, implied the possibility of gaining jurisdiction over them (*districtus*) or exploiting them (*feorum* in England); this was the core of the seigneurial unit. One can thus understand the ties between the powerful man and those without whose aid he could not have built his tower: it has been calculated that forty labourers would have needed fifty days' work to put up a small round motte 10 metres in height and 30 metres across.

The rhythms of growth, which can be revealed only by archaeology (textual evidence being largely absent), are also fairly well known. Once again it was southern Europe which set the pace, perhaps because of the disappearance of higher authority and because of local disturbances and conquests. In Italy the movement began in the peninsula around 920, and around 960–70 in the Lombard plain, with about 120 castles in Sabina by 1050, for example; in Catalonia, with the help of the *reconquista*, the starting point was 950–60, with nearly seventy towers by 1025; in Provence and Languedoc it was between 980 and 1020, often on fiscal lands, with a hundred castles between Lubéron and Costières before 1030; by this last date some 150 castles had also been built in the Massif Central since 970–80. The further north one goes, the later the beginning: in Poitou it was around 980, but with only fifteen castles being built before 1020, as in the Mâconnais. North of the Loire the movement did not get going until after the millennium, in Anjou and Normandy hardly before 1030–40. The wave crossed the channel with the Conqueror from about 1070, and beyond the Seine everything changes around 1060–80. In the Low Countries, Lotharingia and the regions beyond the Rhine it was closer to 1100, well beyond the temporal limits of this chapter.

Of course there was a gap between the building of the castle and development of an accompanying control over men. Sometimes its lord was able to use force to regroup the peasantry around his *rocca* in a *castro* or *castelnau*, a development favoured by geography in Italy, Provence, Gascony or Catalonia. Surrounded by professional horsemen (*caballarii castri*) he was able to control the fortification, carry out police duties and summon before his court at least those cases involving lesser justice. As *castlan* or *castellanus* he was the protector and the lord of custom (*consuetudo castri, ius munitionis*). The relative solidarity of the peasantry in these parts may have forced him to behave more circumspectly: in Auvergne and the Languedoc he will have used persuasion, promising benefits to those peasants who came to populate the *barris* which linked together at the foot of his walls. A better way was to attract artisans whose work would maintain the equipment of the group living in the castle and who soon, headed by the smith (*faber, fèvre. ferrario*), would give a lead to the rustics. Further north violence was less customary, since dukes, counts, kings and emperors were not just vague memories in these regions. Frequently the regrouping of men preceded the appearance of the castle, which would arise a generation later all the richer and more powerful. In Burgundy, villages were formed by the spontaneous grouping of inhabited mansi (here called *meix*), the kernel of a community which would soon gain self-consciousness; in Picardy and Württemberg the palisade (*cingle*, *Etter*) which surrounded the settlement shows that it came first, and here the castle did not engulf the village, but rather looked out over it. In England, the association between dwellings and markets, the distance of the castle and powerful constraints of public or communal obligation (such as armed service in the *fyrd* in Anglo-Saxon England) characterised this slow development. In the end, however, it undermined overall freedom.

BOUNDARIES AND HOUSES

It would have been good to conclude this attempt to classify settlements by saying something on the problems posed by their external appearance. But here we have far more questions than answers. It is much the same with the state of the cultivated area over which the villages, once formed, extended their control and exploitation. To estimate the extent to which they mastered it we would have to be able to say that the full network of roads and paths was in place. Here archaeology is powerless: there have been attempts in England, Alsace or around Limbourg to date either the hedgerows or the fields (*Ackerberg*), but the results are too uncertain for such distant periods. There remain the texts from the Sabina, from Burgundy and from Catalonia in the tenth century which mention boundaries. Alas, three times out of four the scribe mentions the name of neighbours or of a natural feature, and only one in four a road. The conclusion must be that around the millennium the field pattern was not yet established, but still in the course of formation. There is only one exception, of which historians of southern Europe have made a great deal: the traces of Roman centuriation. A number of authors have claimed that field layouts were based on the squares of the centuriation system, and have offered examples from Languedoc and Lombardy. Filled with the desire to emulate this, others have wanted to see centuriation everywhere, even in those places where it would be quite irrational to suppose it. Quite apart from the fact that the architectural remains of antiquity do not coincide with modern cadasters, which are likely to reflect the arrangements of the high middle ages much more closely, I cannot see anything in these possible coincidences other than irritating archaisms which testify merely to a tendency to make some use of what was already at hand.

I cannot any longer avoid a problem often invoked by the partisans of continuity who wish to play down the significance of tenth-century transformations: the antiquity of very many of our village names. It is indeed true that the stock of place-names whose origins are indisputably Celtic, Iberian, Germanic or Roman is impressive and this could suggest that the habitations they designate are just as ancient. But I do not believe it: apart from the possibility that they may merely have designated an isolated element which then served as the centre of a human concentration once all others had disappeared, I would think that such terms often designated human groups (as it certainly did with Roman names ending in -*iacum* or Germanic names ending in -*ing*) and moved around with them, becoming fixed when they did. The baptisms, rebaptisms and displacements of villages which we can still see today in Europe, and still more elsewhere, ought to be enough to convince the advocates of permanence.

There is a third problem, which it is particularly unfortunate that we cannot solve: what did villages and especially houses of the millennium look like? Unfortunately, the conclusion drawn from the foregoing must be that the villages and houses of our period lie underneath those of our own. Although we have many examples of previous habitations, abandoned in the seventh, eighth or ninth centuries, we cannot use them to help us. To describe Chalton (Hampshire), Kootwijk (Guelders), Maizy (Champagne) or Warendorf (Westfalia) and so many others which had been abandoned before 900 would have no interest. Those centres whose displacement has been light enough to allow us to say something – Hohenrode in the Harz or Wharram Percy in Yorkshire for example – are very rare, and what we have been able to discern from them is modest. Houses were still large, 8 metres by 10 or 12, with beamed roofs, perhaps with the addition of a solar in the case of lordly houses. These are traces of a family group which was still large; the houses had exterior doorways and underground foodstores. All the same, change was barely beginning; the task of describing twelfth-century villages can be left to others, but they are evidently the continuation of developments whose origins may be traced in the shadows of the 'dark age'.

THE BIRTH OF THE SEIGNEURIE

We have now arrived at the key result of *encellulement*. From the tenth to the eighteenth century it was the seigneurie in which the men of Europe lived, in forms showing wide chronological and geographical variation. The regions such as Ireland, Scotland, Frisia, the Basque territories and a few valleys in the Alps and the Apennines which did not know it were rare. The fact that one can also show that many towns in western Europe were seigneuries, which is not our concern here, only serves to underline the importance of the problem.

Having said this, it is distinctly difficult to trace the means by which the seigneurie developed. We certainly cannot understand it without taking into consideration all the phenomena we have just discussed, including castles; but a 'political' perspective is also required, even if it has its limitations. We know

that the early middle ages were characterised by a public grouping of men into
territorial units generally known as *pagi*, whose origins have been much discussed. At their head stood an official representing the prince – *comes*, *ealdorman*,
gastald, *Gaugraf*, and so on. Around 920–30 one could have listed about forty of
these units in the British Isles, 160 in western France (two thirds of them north
of the Loire), twenty in Christian Spain, eighty in Lotharingia, and more than
220 in eastern France; in Italy one might estimate them at perhaps 150. At military camps, at the centres of walled towns or at *palatia*, justice was done, fiscal
lands surveyed, free men summoned to arms, and taxation raised if anyone
dared to, or at least imposts for war, service and forage (*Heregeld*, *fodrum*, *alberga*,
hostilicium, etc.). In practice, however, from the ninth century onwards the
count, who in general had none of the characteristics of an administrator,
turned to a deputy to help him out. In England the shire-reeve or sheriff played
an essential role. Nevertheless, this delegation was not enough in those cases
where the size of the *pagus* was too great (was it perhaps a function of the size
of the population?) or where there was need to take rapid decisions, for
example in dealing with Vikings, Hungarians or Saracens, or even, given the
slowness of communications, the need to make on-the-spot assessments of
material needs. or minor problems. For this reason there was a need for more
modest territorial units, grouping at most a few dozen centres of population,
known by terms like *centena*, *vicaria*, *hundred*, *ager* in Germany, western France,
England, Italy, the Alps, etc. Those exercising the rights of a deputy (*vicecomita-*
tus) usually had an official delegation of military, judicial and fiscal duties. But
these could be acquired by people on the spot, and we have found a number of
castle-builders amongst them. After about 940 in Italy, 970 in Catalonia, 990 in
Poitou, 1015 in Normandy and England, to mention only a few, these men held
the law-courts. That 'feudal' or 'vassalic' matters would ultimately also be dealt
with there is a different problem, not relevant here. Serious cases, 'matters of
blood', pertained, in principle, to a higher court, such as that of the count.

Around the millennium the situation appears to have been this. Holders of
the *bannum* (whether lawfully or not), that is to say of the right of pursuit, con-
straint and punishment, came to tolerate, and sometimes to encourage, a
dependent clientele of men who were rich and armed, who were their men or
indeed their relatives, in building towers and holding courts. Such castellans, in
southern Europe at least, were to become more or less independent, or else
simply *seniores* or *domini*, lords. They could not be prevented from dealing with
law-suits affecting land, the most rewarding ones incidentally, before extending
their grasp to others, nor from reclaiming for themselves and their men at arms
the rights of *gistum* and of fiscal assistance. How can we distinguish between
the imposts they exacted from their peasants, allodialists included, which
derived from their 'public' rights (from what the Germans call *Landrecht*) and

those which came to them from their land-holding power? In all cases we find them as lords of 'custom', which ruled the life of all, free to innovate and indeed to expropriate by inventing *malae consuetudines* or *mals usos*, evil customs, which struck so many peasants simply because what is new is inevitably wicked.

In those regions where royal authority, even if enfeebled, still had some force (Anglo-Saxon England, northern France, the western part of the empire), or where comital power remained strong (Catalonia, Normandy, Flanders, Saxony) this development was reined in and bearable. Elsewhere it provoked a lively movement of rejection, which itself deserves to be called revolutionary. The church placed itself at the head of this movement, since it was even more menaced by such developments, both in its judicial rights of immunity and in its enormous landed wealth: the 'peace of God', so often presented as seen through the rose-tinted spectacles of piety. The clerics in fact broke with the class solidarity linking them to the warriors, under the pretext of coming to the aid of the *pauperes*, the *inermes*, deemed to be as dear to God as they themselves. I do not here have to describe the stages of the movement, from the Aquitanian, Burgundian and Languedocian councils of the period 989–1027 with oaths enforcing a truce, moving on to the oaths sworn before bishops and princes between 1023 and 1048. What we need to remember for our purposes here is that the church soon came to terms with the great laymen, especially after the excesses committed by the peasant bands who had rashly been encouraged to settle their accounts, in Normandy, León or Berry for example. Making use of the protection the church enjoyed over its lands – that granted by royal advocacy, for example – it advanced the evolution towards the seigneurial system, whose birth it had so long retarded. Moreover, the network of feudal relations, familial interests and political responsibilities put a long-lasting seal on the *rapprochement* between the first two of the three orders.

Henceforth the seigneurial cells were in working order in villages and around castles. As we are now already beyond the period of this book I can confine myself to these few remarks. It does seem necessary, however, to note a new feature. Whether their authority was of public or private origin, lords soon mingled these two notions, so readily elided in the middle ages. A number of obligations due, strictly speaking, only from those peasants who were tenants of the demesne soon came to be extended to those who had no such ties; these included *corvées*, exacted by right of the ban, but put into effect for the benefit of the landlord. One could even say in this last case that such dues involved a concept of 'banalities' of a particularly 'illegal' kind and hence a source of protests, and this was not a trivial matter: as late as 1000 or 1020 at Milan and Brescia a week's work with oxen was being demanded, as well as two months' labour by hand; several days a week were required in England (*week-*

works), somewhat less on the continent. Doubtless this was less than it had been in the ninth century, but it was now imposed on everyone. So was another banal demand, perhaps more justifiable: the tax in recognition of protection to which the texts give the flattering name of 'request' (*Bede, questa, rogatio*) or the more accurate one of *gistum* (*alberga, gayta*, i.e. (forced) hospitality) or, above all, that termed 'exaction' (*tolta, taille, tonsio*).

The ban affected allodialists and engulfed free tenants; serfs were unaffected because they were the property of an individual and did not, for example, pay the *taille*. This was the fiction. In the villages which made up a seigneurie, all in practice were on the same level *vis-à-vis* the lord. Divisions between them were not lacking; these derived in particular from the economic problems with which all were confronted, and to which I shall now turn.

A STILL FRAGILE ECONOMY

In trying to glean what one can know about the European rural economy of around the millennium, the first line of enquiry should be directed towards men's needs, the only criterion by which we can judge whether their efforts were adequate to satisfy them. This is a difficult subject for the medieval centuries, and especially for those dealt with here. Of course we could assume that the levels of consumption which we can deduce from Carolingian documents continued to be valid one or two hundred years later, but can we be certain? Moreover, there are suspicions of exaggeration and confusions in the numerical data we have, which at Corbie for example envisage that those doing labour services would receive 1.95 kg of bread, a litre of wine, 300 g of legumes, and 100 g of cheese and eggs daily, a somewhat unhealthy and unbalanced diet amounting to about 6000 calories, possibly a ration for a family rather than an individual. Chroniclers, miserly with numbers, are still vaguer. When Helgaud goes into ecstasies over the fact that King Robert allowed beggars to pick up scraps from below the table, or an epic poem tells of a trencherman eating a peacock in three mouthfuls, this tells us nothing. Archaeology in its turn is of little assistance: the finds from the rubbish-pits of Holstein or Hanover in use between 800 and 1000 show proportions of animal bones consumed which suggest a high intensity of animal raising, though the data are random and varied: 15–66% oxen, 10–70% swine, 11–23% sheep. Sparse and late data from Germany have led to an estimate of about 2200 calories daily provided by cereals, though the tenth century has also been described as 'full of beans'. How, too, should we count the roots from the woods, the eggs from the farmyard, the honey from the beehives? In short, none of our data provides any certain indications. What is more or less sure, as has already been said, is that there were acute famines in the early eleventh century. The problem can be summed up in one question, a crucial one: did progress keep pace with the rhythm of needs?

AN ENLARGED CULTURAL HORIZON

In answering yes to this question I am in effect advancing a conclusion which only the succeeding centuries will justify; but such an opening position is indispensable for the observations which follow. Consider in the first place the subject of tools, which some have wished to make one of the most important causes of the rise of Europe. Whereas the middle ages were once credited with inventions, there has more recently been a swing to the opposite extreme of only allowing it a certain talent for popularising others' inventions. This empty dispute hardly takes account of a geographic reality: the Graeco-Roman civilisation of antiquity had brought to a high degree of perfection techniques for dealing with wood, stone and textiles, and ignored water, which in its zone was unreliable, and iron, which was there rare. Central and northern Europe was in a different position; and besides this, the variety of species there permitted progress in the exploitation of animals. To confine myself to what seems uncontroversial, I shall look at three key areas. Historians first claimed that the shoulder-collar for the horse or the breast-yoke for the ox had saved Europe. They then maintained that these techniques had been known to the ancients, just like the hipposandals designed to protect the feet of the horse. In reality, however, the iconography of harness and the archaeology of metal parts have revealed no trace of these practices until the end of the tenth century at the earliest, and in regions distant from the Mediterranean, such as Trier, Savoy or Bohemia. Perhaps the novelty of these things, if it was one, came from the choice of a breed of animal more appropriate to such practices than those of southern Europe.

A second point: iron featured greatly in this equipment, as in mills, from a very early point. Here too we touch on a key sector of medieval technology. Smithies were particularly numerous and relatively easy of access in the Pyrenees, the Rhineland and Saxon regions, Normandy and the north of the British Isles, Burgundy and Champagne. It has also been possible to show that Germanic or Celtic smithery was well in advance of its Mediterranean counterpart: more solid axes, ploughshares, coulters and mouldboards, horseshoes, barrel-hoops and wheel-rims, and of course the armaments used for warfare and hunting. The man who worked them in the midst of the sparks and bellows was indeed the key worker of the village, and its lord was his first and most admiring client. The exploitation of mines and the practice of smelting in low furnaces are found at Canigou from 945, around Fulda and Lorsch about 960, in Poitou and Normandy from 975 or 980, in the Ardennes, in the forest of

Othe in the Champagne and in Yorkshire just after 1000. Before 1030 we can find 'pigs' of worked iron entering into lists of tolls, often heavily taxed as at Pisa or Arras; and increasing numbers of smiths in villages in Catalonia, Sabina and Picardy between 1010 and 1030 are a sign of the growth, from now on unstoppable, of a metallurgy systematically ignored by antiquity. A point should be noted, however, which bears on what was said previously about the reordering of men: furnaces and anvils were first of all used in the woods, near to sources of fuel (there are references to coal in Saxony and near Leicester at the end of the tenth century). In order to make his work more effective, however, the smith moved from the forest to the village, and I would readily claim that the smithy, just as much as the castle, was a crystallising point for the population.

The appearance of a mill for hammering iron in Germany around 987 leads us on to the third area of growth: the harnessing of water power. Little utilised by the ancients, but technologically very relevant to the needs at hand, the water-mill became the first European 'machine'. The regularity of water-flows above a certain latitude, the fortunate nutritional consequences of the fish-ponds that were full of fish (the by-product of mill-sluices), the gain in time and of profit (though this was later) which the rich were able to draw from the use of the mill by the people of the village, all explain the staggering success of these machines. Carolingian texts refer to them, certainly, but one has the feeling that their widespread diffusion did not occur much before 920–35: in Poitou, Catalonia, Berry, the Low Countries. After this period we find them on every water-course. The effects of their installation are known: they were expensive to build, needing beams and mill-stones of high quality as well as lead and iron, but they were estimated in the eleventh century to yield revenues equivalent to those of 20 hectares of land. The rich men who had them built thus knew how to get their investment repaid by those who used them; those who could not afford to use them lost time and energy milling grain at home by hand. Nevertheless, there is no definite evidence of a 'banal' obligation to grind at the lord's mill before about 1030–50. It should be added that, if water was owned and thus had to be paid for, wind was free to all: there is a reference to a mill powered by wind in the region of the Spanish Mediterranean coast at the very end of the tenth century, but it would be a rare phenomenon before about 1150.

It will have been noted that the major effect of this progress in technology was to dispossess the artisans of the demesne of their former omnipotence. Weaving, joinery and smithery had been carried out under the direct control of the lord's agents, or even, in a kind of 'wild artisanry', by those working in the woods as potters or hermits. Henceforth it would be in the village itself, that is to say at the foot of the castle, that the transformation of products and materials would be concentrated. This concentration of technology in the village would allow the peasantry to apply themselves to the key task of mastering uncultivated land, a key to the extension of culture and the food-supply.

The *saltus*, outfield, *bosc*, *foresta* (probably derived from *foris*, 'outside', not from *Föhre*, 'fir') was uncultivated, the zone which might be no more than lightly wooded but which man feared and did not know how to tame. It was the countryside of the Atlantic seaboard of France, the maquis (*mescla*) or *garrigue* of the Mediterranean, the savannah spiked with thorns and isolated trees of north-western Europe, and of course the thick woodland of Lotharingia, Germany and Scandinavia. It rested on poor soils, podsolised and stony, but also on heavy and potentially fertile clays. To clear it was very hard work; it extended over regions where animals stronger than man lived, the wolf for example, or, still worse, those evil spirits who set traps for wanderers. Emperor Henry IV was lost in it for three days, and in Burgundy the least scarcity could cause this wild world to spring up again. The analyses of pollen or charcoal which are today our most reliable indications of the nature and extent of vegetation are very striking: in the Ardennes, Hesse, Schleswig, Kent, Bohemia, Valais, Poitou and Languedoc, for example, we find woodland covering between 50% and 70% (the latter in Germany) of the surface area, while at the end of the eleventh century Domesday Book records some 40,000 km^2 of woodland in England. This huge mass of land was by no means inert or valueless: its role as a zone for hunting and gathering on its borders and for military protection or emergency refuge, quite apart from its role as a source of the principal material from which a wood is made, turned it into a world with a population of gatherers, charcoal-makers, woodcutters and also brigands, as well as, above all, of domestic animals left there to pasture freely, even with the risks which that entailed, because the cleared and cultivated land had to be completely reserved for growing crops for humans.

But if the needs. of the latter grew, because they were now eating more or their numbers had grown or their family groups were breaking up, we should envisage an alternative organisation of the ecosystem. It has even been supposed that in the beginning it was the needs of animal husbandry that prevented the peasantry from eroding away the woodland. In any case, the word 'clearance', in its primary sense of struggle against the bramble rather than against the beech, gives a good idea of this struggle, quite modest at first. There were at least four kinds of attack, no doubt differing in their modalities and their effects. Heavy soils, marles, limestones and sandstones capable of bearing good harvests were tackled at the end of the tenth and the beginning of the eleventh century in the Auvergne, Burgundy and the Rhineland, the Harz, the Weald and Sussex. Rather later, waterlogged lands, marshes and coastal zones – *Schorren*, *moeres*, fens – were taken on; these were more suited to the rearing of sheep. The pebble-strewn floors of the valleys and floodplains of fast Mediterranean rivers (*varennes, ferragina, rivages, bonifachi*) along the coastal plains of the whole of the southern flank of Europe were probably not attacked until 1000 or 1020. Finally, the exhausting conquest of slopes by terracing may have appeared from 975 in Catalonia, but would wait until 1025 or later in Provence or Italy. It goes without saying that where these enterprises were carried through by individuals more or less illicitly on the lands of others they largely escape our observation. We do not find out about them except through the steps taken by the rich in the form of contracts. The classic example, at least that which we find in the documentation which the church provides us with, was the purchase of land by clerics and its putting under cultivation by teams of lay workers: the *quadras* of Catalan pioneers, the *Barschalken* of Bavaria, the *sartores* of Picardy. The lands thus gained might as a result preserve a particular status because the 'guests' (*hospites*) who had come from more or less distant places, and been established there as cultivators with their dwellings, enjoyed seigneurial protection, personal liberty and fairly light obligations as far as renders in kind were concerned, as with the *gualdi publici* of Lombardy, the lathes of the Weald and the *hostalitates* of the Pyrenees.

The trend had hardly begun to show its outlines around the millennium, and it is hopeless to expect to be able to estimate its size at this point. Pollen analysis gives some indications, but no figures. The breaking up of fields into strips might be a proof of its existence, but when does this date from? As for place-names, though their evidence is crucial, they cannot normally offer a precise date. Places ending in *-viller, -hof, -dorf, -sart* or *-bois* are perhaps the products of clearances, but these may go back to the initial timid Carolingian phase. What remain are the micro-toponyms which are certainly linked with the struggle against the *saltus*: *-ley, -den, -hurst* and *-shot* in the British Isles, *-rod, -ried* and *-schlag* in the Germanic regions, *-essart* and *-rupt* in northern France, *-artiga* in the Pyrenees, *-ronco* in Lombardy and many others. But do these date from the tenth, the eleventh or even the twelfth century? And how are we to decide?

THE STIRRINGS OF PRODUCTION

What we today call the medieval ecosystem, which survived in essence until the beginning of the twentieth century, was based on a combination of cereal crops won from the ploughlands, the products of free pasturage in the forest, and meat and dairy produce, complemented by fruits and roots from the uncultivated land and the minor products of the farmyard. Clearly, even if some sort of dietary equilibrium could be attained, this situation constituted, as has been said, a 'vicious circle': to increase the arable at the expense of woodland was to cut off what the latter could supply, but to preserve the woodland was to risk underproduction of cereals. This millenary conflict between the carbohydrates of the plough and the proteins of the forest depended for a favourable outcome either on improvements in technique or on an equilibrium of needs. It is unnecessary to say that those alive around the millennium were not weighed down by the need to find solutions. For many generations they took advantage of *Feldgraswirtschaft*, a system of shifting cultivation on a more or less regular rhythm of years: clearance, followed by years of cultivation until the land started to show signs of exhaustion. Such practices, which the poor could not pursue for lack of sufficient land to do it on, were the preserve of the lords. This is the origin of the quite untenable belief in the general existence of the crop rotation which has been seen in Carolingian documents. In reality we are dealing with an incomplete occupation of the areas covered by the polyptichs and with a shifting between winter or spring grains and a variable fallow period (the famous *tres arationes* of Saint-Amand which have so often been cited). Not until the mid-thirteenth century do we find a conscious and regular rotation; here we are dealing merely with empirical practices.

What was grown? First of all, cereals for bread-making. The best, grains yielding white flour, are known everywhere because of the demands of lords. It has been noted in Catalonia and the Low Countries that after the millennium the hulled wheats of antiquity such as spelt yielded to a naked wheat which did not clog up the mills with which the rich were equipping themselves; barley declined, but beer and oxen saved it; rye resisted because that is its nature, robust and plain, quite apart from the quality of its straw; oats, already in use before 700, source of porridge and soon to be food for horses, begin their career as a 'March' sowing, but are far from equalling the mass of sheaves of wheat in the granaries. Had panic or millet already made their appearance? The economic historian would welcome other details as well. And how was work organised? The wealthy could dispose themselves of the services of their men, and that in abundance, indeed beyond what was useful: at Brescia there were 60,000 man-days to be used, at Saint-Germain-des-Prés 135,000, which is surely absurd. But what was expected of them? How much ploughing, what sowing, what equipment? This last question is crucial, but for the period we are dealing with unanswerable. We know that the plough of antiquity, the *aratrum* with a hardened share, sometimes armed with an iron point, hardly permitted deep or fruitful ploughing, only light and symmetrical furrows. It remained in use in southern Europe, but already in the eighth century the Lombards talk of a *ploum* (evidently a Latinisation of *Pflug* or plough), which no doubt came from central Europe, and indeed asymmetrical shares have been found from the ninth century in Moravia. Unfortunately, the word *carruca*, which ought to imply a more effective instrument, appropriate for the attack on rich and heavy soils, is used by scribes without discrimination. Archaeology has revealed near Utrecht and in the Belgian Campina fossil fields where it seems that the two rival types of plough were in use. What can we say? That the future lay with the wheeled plough drawn by horses on the best soils? That is certain, once we get past 1080–1100, but before that we can only guess.

Progress obviously has to be judged by results: three elements, none of them substantial, seem to me to be signs of a beginning. First of all, what is known about the layout of fields suggests two tendencies: enclosure, even the provisional kind provided by a brush hedge at the time of sowing, appears to give way, except in the special cases of vineyards and olive groves, to an open countryside which can be used for regular pasturage. Besides this, the form of fields is *perhaps* beginning to change: even though the massive, almost square shape (*quaderni* and *aiole* in southern zones) still appears to survive a little longer, it has been noted that in the Low Countries and the Rhineland and Bavaria we can see in outline the beginnings of a system of strip fields, though it is true that before 1025 this seems to be known only in England (with parallel *solskifts* grouped into quarters or furlongs). This kind of layout, which can only coincidentally be seen as associated with a particular kind of plough, appears to represent the abandoning of the very primitive technique of crossed furrows used in antiquity. A second point is that it is possible to estimate from some ecclesiastical examples a growth of the cultivated area: in Catalonia, from 950 to 1000 some estates saw a growth of new cultivated lands amounting to 15% to 35% of the whole; similar figures have been proposed for Provence and central Italy. Finally, we have the fundamental question: what was the volume produced by the cultivated area, whether or not this increased by a third? We know that the estimates made for the Carolingian period are appalling: seed produced twice or at best three times its volume, even if we ignore evidence suggesting a weight for weight return, which would be an absurd negation of agriculture. The few bits of evidence from the mid-tenth century at Brescia or in the Mâconnais suggest a ratio of 3–3.5 to 1, a very modest improvement. But the other side of the millennium at Cluny we have arrived at 4–4.5. The 15 to 1 of Flanders in 1300 is still a long way off, but all progress has to make a start.

The reader will perhaps have been surprised to have heard only about grains. The reason is that about the rest, the *companaticum* (etymologically speaking 'the accompaniment') we know nothing: at the foot of the Italian *rocca* there were 'herbs and vegetables' in the *viridaria* and *orticelli*, as also in Languedoc, perhaps after the millennium. Elsewhere there is silence about gathering berries, rabbit warrens, and the eggs of the farmyard. Essential perhaps, if the weather betrayed the peasant, but outside our reach. What about the vine, the source of the Eucharist, the glory of the peasant, the honour to the table, the tradition of antiquity? Enthusiastic historians have talked of an 'explosion of viticulture'; they have noted the southern European contracts of shared cultivation between vines and olives, the drinking-bouts of castles and peasant communities, and stressed the generous rations allowed wine drinkers. But before about 1100–25 it is not possible to talk about grape varieties, viticulture, wine trade or quality.

Having stressed the importance of the part of the land reserved to animal-rearing, not to mention the role which must be ascribed to hunting and fishing, we find ourselves here still more deprived of reliable information. It has been said that the pig was the animal to which most attention was given because it was the basic source of meat, and this has been deduced from the practice, already found in Carolingian times, of measuring the extent of woodlands by the numbers of swine supported by them or capable of being supported by them, giving an approximate ratio of 0.75 hectares per pig. It is true that we do not know whether the animals were really there, except for the rubbish-tips of northern Germany mentioned earlier, which appear to suggest that cattle were more important. We are reduced to general, supposedly common-sense considerations, which are based on the taxes levied on acorns in the clearings of the Weald (*dens*), or on the passage of transhumant flocks in the Pyrenees and probably the Alps, though the first substantial flocks, in Italy for instance, date from 1050 and later. Quarrels about woodland use, lawsuits over the fisheries on the Saône, references to fisher-villages in the Fens of East Anglia or on the Frisian *terpen*: these are a poor soil where the historian can glean only the first signs of a growth which was still taking shape.

SILVER ARRIVES IN THE COUNTRYSIDE

In an economy of waste, at best of gift and counter-gift, money as a sign of exchange was unable to prevail. Exchanges were of favours, daughters, wine, horses. Towns put up a short-lived pursuit of the coining of money and the sale of luxury goods which can dazzle the Carolingian historian; but there is none of this in the countryside. It was precisely the slow introduction of coins or ingots into the rural world that was a powerful novelty in a growing economy: the pump of exchanges between town and countryside sputtered into life, and it would become an essential motor for the centuries following.

We have some difficulty in following the routes taken by silver from the mines of Germany, Bohemia, or other less rich regions like western France or northern Italy. Was there regular extraction, whether controlled by princes or not, or was it more a case of liquifying thesaurised metal, accumulated especially by the church? Whatever the source, there was abundant striking of coins: Æthelred II had 120,000 pounds of coins circulated; the mint at Pavia emitted 100,000 coins in 1020; In Catalonia, the *parias* imposed on Muslims from 1018–35 onwards allowed coinages, gold in this case, on a very regular basis. The number of mints rose sharply: more than twenty have been counted for Picardy towards 1000, ten in Flanders, fifteen on the Meuse, if we confine ourselves to considering northern France. Hoards recovered from this period show a substantial quantity of *denarii* (pennies) in circulation: the Fécamp hoard, abandoned around 985, contained 130,000 pieces.

Needs increased, in the town in particular, which is not our concern here. But one should also take account of heavy and unavoidable expenses: between 980 and 1010 the Danegeld paid by the English to Scandinavia amounted to 150,000 pounds, and on a more modest scale the erection of a fortified tower cost 2000, that of a mill 500. In order to build a church in the Boulonnais in 1017 the lords of the area had to sell a wood, two granaries and four mills. To cope with these demands the lords were certainly able to count on the income from commuting labour services, the extension of money rents, the expansion of the taille; but in order for these further demands to be met there was a need for peasants to have pieces of silver which could be screwed out of them. Where could these have come from if not from the sale of surplus foodstuffs or craft products, or from a supplementary income? Between 975 and 1000 in Catalonia the documented transactions conducted in silver coin amounted to 32% of those concerning foodstuffs, and 41% of those concerning cattle and horses, though only 15% of those concerning manufactured products. At Farfa in Central Italy in the same period almost all the renders were converted to renders of coin.

Our documents are not distributed sufficiently equally to permit a geography of the penetration of silver into the countryside. We only have a few hints at a chronology: 945–75 on the coastlines of Catalonia and Languedoc, 960–90 in Italy and Aquitaine, not until the millennium and beyond north of the Loire. In northern France and the Rhineland payments by weight or in heads of cattle survived a long time, up to 1030 or 1050. But these were hangovers; by these dates silver had already begun its role of economic and indeed social differentiation within the village; a tripling of the price of livestock has been estimated for Spain and Italy between 975 and 1030, and at this last date a third of all those who made wills in Catalonia had debts.

These were the timid beginnings of a silver-based economy. The foundations of society were still land and freedom, and it was family ties, oaths and rituals which kept them in place. The idea of a society without silver where God had established a division of his creation into 'orders', each with its own responsibilities, still remained the rule. In 1020 Adalbero of Laon was able to express it forcibly, and the poet of *Garin le Lorrain* affirmed that 'that which makes for riches is not ornaments and treasures, but friends, for a man's heart is worth all the gold in the world'.[12] Was this an opinion still held, or merely nostalgia for a world which was disappearing?

We must conclude, and I shall do so in two ways, first by setting out what is known about demography around the millennium, and then by summing up. The question of population has been deliberately avoided up to now; to have inverted the order of exposition by talking first about growth would have suggested that this was undoubtedly a prior cause. I think that it was rather an effect of the transformations which have been surveyed here, or, if one prefers, a coincidental phenomenon, for, as we shall see, the dates where expansion can be noted seem to be rather later than those of the developments we have been discussing, though it must be conceded that research on this is difficult. We have only two approaches: the study of cemeteries, though as has been noted these were in the course of shifting at the time, allows us to say something about the state of health and about the age of those who were buried there; and lists of tenants or those owing labour-services kept by the church, but here numerous and well-spread, in England (Evesham, Bath, Bury St Edmunds), Germany (Fulda, Ghent, Gorze), Italy (Subiaco, Farfa), Spain (Urgel, Braga). Coupled with the signs of increased exploitation of the land revealed by pollen analysis, these data allow some quite precise observations.

The essential common feature is the beginning of demographic growth. It was to last for three centuries. Can we date the beginnings? It was in 930–50 in Sabina and Lombardy, 940–90 in Catalonia, 980–1010 in Languedoc, Provence, Poitou and the Auvergne, 1010–30 in Flanders and Picardy, Bavaria and Franconia, Burgundy and Normandy, 1050–80 in England and the Rhineland, after 1100 in central Germany. Attempts have been made to measure it between its first signs around 950 and the mid-eleventh century, a period which represents the first phase. One author has estimated the global figure for European population rising from 42 to 46 million inhabitants; another confines himself to a rise from 20 to 23 million. These suggestions are interesting, but lack any kind of proof, though one can accept the estimation of a slow annual rise in western Europe, amounting to 11% in the first half of the eleventh century, modest but regular, or the figures for the average number of children born to a fertile marriage, rising from 3.5–4 to 4–5.3 between 980 and 1050. It goes without saying that these figures cannot do more than show a tendency, for too many data escape us. Was it an improvement in nutrition which caused a decline in mortality? Swedish and Polish cemeteries of the millennium still contain 20–30% of children aged less than five. Or was it the 'hidden infanticide' practised against daughters by giving them less care that declined? Or was the social change of earlier marriage accompanied by the physiological

---

[12] *Li romans de Garin le Loherain* ii, verse 268.

change of a growth in wet-nursing, creating a tendency in favour of births? All these problems confront the demographer, whose only certainty is that there were more and more people.

A few remarks will suffice to sum up. The climate may have been better, there were certainly more people, the family was set on a new basis, the framework of the village was stable, the seigneurie with its guarantees and restriction was being put in place: this is the balance-sheet of the decades around the millennium. What about the 'terrors' invoked by the romantics? In 1000, as in 1033, people may have thought about the birth or death of Christ, but they had enough to do to make a living; there was no need to worry about dying. On the contrary, they were participating in a 'birth', that of Europe, and they were conscious of it. How otherwise can we conclude than by citing the words of a Burgundian monk and a German bishop: 'The world, shaking off the dust of its senility, seemed to cover itself everywhere with a white robe of churches',[13] and 'at the thousandth year after the birth of Christ a radiant dawn broke over the world'.[14]

[13] Radulf Glaber, *Historiae* IV, 5.   [14] Thietmar, *Chronicon* VI, 1.

CHAPTER 3

MERCHANTS, MARKETS AND TOWNS

Peter Johanek

THE BEGINNINGS of the European town in the form known to us from the late middle ages lie in the tenth century. Urbanism began its dynamic phase in the late eleventh century, reaching its climax in the thirteenth, but the basic elements were assembled between the decomposition of the Frankish empire at the end of the ninth century and the early decades of the eleventh. In this transitional period the commercial revolution began.

The renewed rise of the town as a social formation is certainly closely connected with the extension and intensification of trade: merchants are therefore an important group in the shaping of the medieval town, in its topography, its institutions and its social networks. Their activities were the most spectacular and impressive, and occasionally overshadow the contribution and activities of the other forces driving developments forward.

The rise in urban development and the changes in the structure and organisation of trade which will be described here presuppose a general expansion of the economy and an increase in prosperity, especially in the agrarian sector. This is the only explanation for the emergence of a broad stratum of consumers able to absorb the goods brought by long-distance trade. From the tenth century onwards this stratum was multi-layered, from clerics and aristocrats acquiring rich oriental cloth to wrap relics in, down to the Frisian manorial officials of the monastery of Werden on the Ruhr, who in the eleventh century had to make renders of pepper and wine to their clerical lords. And indeed the whole of Europe, including the Byzantine empire, shows an evident rise in agrarian production and demographic growth, though obviously there were variations between individual regions.

Those tenth-century Europeans who drew maps of the world did so completely in the tradition inherited from antiquity: they stressed Europe, and in particular the Mediterranean, which was presented as the centre of the continent, from which its other parts and the world outside were viewed. In reality the Mediterranean was a meeting point between the Islamic and the Christian worlds, Christian meaning here both Greeks and Latins.

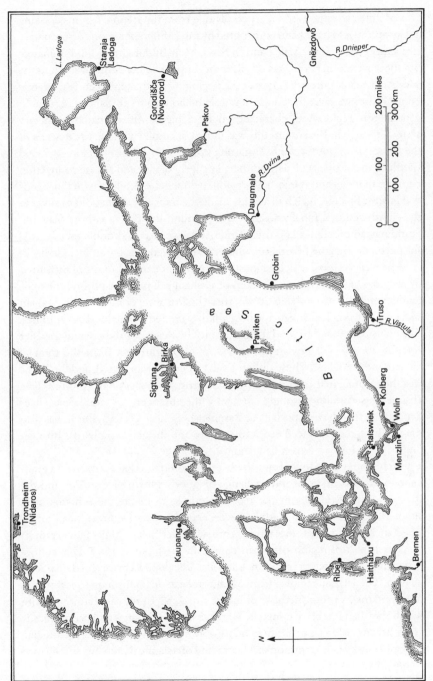

1 Urban settlements and emporia in the Scandinavian and Baltic regions

A Mediterranean observer, especially one from the Islamic regions, looking at Europe, would have been confronted by three different regions of monetary circulation. In Islamic Africa and in Syria, as in Byzantium, gold dominated, but there were other coinages of silver and copper. Whereas in Byzantium the *nomisma* (bezant) entered a crisis at the beginning of the tenth century, Islamic North Africa was able to acquire new gold bullion from sub-Saharan Africa. In general this region was characterised by a highly differentiated monetary system, though in Byzantium this was more concerned with the fiscal needs of the state than with trade. Alongside this south-eastern region we find Carolingian Europe, with a monometallic silver coinage and a close connection between markets and mints. This region included the Anglo-Saxon kingdoms and Islamic Spain, which had already made the transition from gold to silver in the eighth century. Finally, in the north, around the Baltic with its Slav and Scandinavian coastlines and their hinterlands, we also find noble metals used for payment. But the hoards on which our knowledge is based include hack-silver as well as coins, which suggests that it was not coins but metal measured by weight which served as a medium of exchange. Up to and beyond the mid-tenth century, to around 960 or 970, these hoards were dominated by Arabian silver coins from Transoxania, whose mints were fed by the local silver mines. The coins penetrated beyond the Baltic into the Reich, for the oriental traveller Ibrāhīm ibn Yaʿqūb saw in either 961 or 965/6 dirhams from the mint at Samarqand in Mainz.[1] These dirhams subsequently disappeared, and the Baltic was then dominated by pennies from German and Anglo-Saxon mints. This change was certainly brought about by the discovery of additional silver deposits in the Harz (especially at Rammelsberg near Goslar), but it was also the result of the enhanced economic power and the active trade of Ottonian Germany and Anglo-Saxon England.

Our hypothetical Mediterranean observer would thus have perceived a graduation in forms of trade and exchange of goods. North of the Alps and the Pyrenees, and especially in the region around the Baltic, these forms were simpler and less differentiated, but even here the use of coined metal intensified in the course of the tenth century. Nevertheless, the Mediterranean remained the real region of urban culture in the tenth century. This culture rested in part on ancient tradition, but it also developed a powerful dynamic of its own. The Islamic regions, from Mediterranean Spain through to Egypt and Mesopotamia, were noticeably different from the European economy, with which they had intensive contacts. Here we find really large and economically active towns, which can be matched in both eastern and western Christian Europe only by Constantinople. The trading of Islamic merchants was shaped

---

[1] *Arabische Berichte*, p. 31.

by a detailed legislative framework based on writing. Communications between merchants, information about profit and loss, about the availability of goods and means of transport, and about delivery dates were also as a rule carried out in writing.

This urban culture of Islam, which may be seen as a religion of merchants, can be set alongside very varied forms of urbanism in Christian Europe and the pagan north. In Italy there was a great continuity of urban life from Roman times; the *civitates* had remained centres of secular and ecclesiastical administration and nodes of long-distance trade-routes, even if their architectural landscapes had been fundamentally altered by changes in the practice of patronage in the erection of public buildings. North of the Alps, in Gaul and the formerly Roman parts of Germania, most of the *civitates* had shrunk considerably, often being reduced to a core area which functioned as citadel or fortification. In the regions outside the old Roman empire incorporated into the Frankish empire during the Merovingian and Carolingian periods, and especially in the Slav and Scandinavian regions and in the British Isles, we find very varying beginnings for quasi-urban settlements and for mercantile centres. It must be emphasised that at the beginning of the tenth century trade and crafts were not inherently bound up with the social form of the town in these regions, often being organised in connection with lordship outside *civitates*, especially in the lordships of the great monasteries. Writing was used on a large scale in the organisation and regulation of trade only in Byzantium; outside the Mediterranean region law was confined to symbolic forms for concluding contracts. Lay literacy, which survived to some extent in Italy, evidently declined sharply in the course of the tenth century. In the Scandinavian north we find an increase in runic inscriptions, especially around trading centres, but there are no signs of a rune-based mercantile literacy as known from the twelfth century onwards through archaeological finds from Bergen. Only in Haithabu has a runic staff been found, datable to about 900, which may perhaps be interpreted as a merchant's letter.

In spite of this, Europe showed itself an attractive trading partner for the urban culture of Islamic north Africa and the Near East, and indeed it was precisely these trading links which lay behind the flowering of Islamic trading centres on the southern Mediterranean coast in the tenth and eleventh centuries. The cities of the Arab west, especially in the Maghreb and in al-Andalus (Spain), formed the far end of a chain of cities linking the Mediterranean with the Indian Ocean in a unitary trading zone in which goods from Asia, especially spices and luxury goods, flowed to northern Africa and Europe. The Arab west not only expected the same self-evident standard of luxury found in Damascus and Baghdad, it also, through its contacts with west African gold production, disposed of considerable economic strength. In addition, the tenth century saw the height of Islamic power in the western Mediterranean, even if Islamic unity had disintegrated. The Shi'ite Fatimid dynasty established itself in 909 in Kairuan (Ifrīqiyyah) and in 969 it conquered Egypt; the Ummayad amirs of al-Andalus took the title of caliph in 912. This all lent added weight to the region, whose large cities, especially Córdoba and al-Fusṭāṭ Cairo, developed rapidly.

Córdoba, the seat of the Ummayad caliphs, grew sharply in the ninth and especially in the tenth centuries: estimates of its population in the period vary from 90,000 to 500,000, even a million, though the first figure is more realistic. The town was an agglomeration of different settlements, owing their origins to the rulers' initiative. Besides the old city (Medina) with a palace and a central mosque there were other palace cities in the immediate vicinity: al-Ruṣāfa and Madīnat al-Zahrā (Córdoba la Vieja) under ʿAbd al-Raḥmān III (912–61) and al-Madīnat al-Zāhirah under the dictator al-Manṣūr (around 980). The length of the walls around ancient Medina was only 4 km, but at the beginning of the eleventh century there was a moat of some 22 km around the agglomeration, and the palace city al-Zahrā remained outside this. Córdoba was one of the places at which the west encountered Islamic urban culture: Abbot John of Gorze stayed here between 953 and 956 as ambassador of Otto I, guided by merchants from Verdun familiar with the country. Their impression is reflected in the phrase used by Hrotsvitha of Gandersheim to characterise the city: *decus orbis*, the ornament of the globe. Córdoba combined trade, specialised crafts for the production of luxury goods (especially leather), and administrative and military functions, with a strong garrison. It was also a centre of learning with an extensive book production, evidently also organised as an industry. Above all it may be seen as an *exceptionally* large centre of consumption, functioning as the metropolis for an economic region comprising Spain and western north Africa around Fez, and managing its marine trade from Almería, the port founded by ʿAbd al-Raḥmān III in 955.

Comparable with Córdoba in its character as an urban agglomeration created by the ruler was Kairuan, established like Córdoba away from the coast, and the starting point of Fatimid expansion. But the real pendant in north Africa to Córdoba was al-Fusṭāṭ on the Nile, immediately south of the city of Cairo founded by the Fatimids in 969. It grew together with Cairo into a single city, but remained the economically dominant part until well into the twelfth century. Founded in 642 as a garrison by the conquering Arabs, it had developed by the tenth century into a huge agglomeration of separate quarters (about twenty all told, with an average size of 20–40 hectares; al-Qarafa had 300 hectares). Each of these was assigned to a tribe from the conquest era and organised according to its laws. The Arab geographer Ibn Hawqal (d. 988) estimated that al-Fusṭāṭ was about a third of the size of Baghdad, and the population in 969 was probably somewhat under 100,000. From then it grew rapidly and in the eleventh century it lay somewhere between 300,000 and 500,000.

This growth was quite evidently based on the extraordinary economic prosperity about which the encyclopedist Mas'ūdi (d. 956 or 957) reported: 'All the kingdoms located on the two seas which border the country bring to this commercial centre all the most remarkable, the rarest, and best perfumes, spices, drugs, jewels and slaves, as well as staples of food and drink, and cloth of all sorts. The merchandise of the entire universe flows to this market.'[2] The decisive push came around 1000, when the seizure of power by the Karmates in Bahrein made sea transport in the Persian Gulf so dangerous that the great bulk of trade from the Indian Ocean to the west henceforth came over the Red Sea via Aden, 'Adhab on the Sudanese coast and Qusan on the upper Nile to Egypt, thence to al-Fusṭāṭ and Cairo. The cities of Syria and to a lesser extent Byzantium were still the final destinations of the caravans, but al-Fusṭāṭ and its port of Alexandria became the most important emporia of the Mediterranean region.

This is true above all for exchanges between the Islamic world and Christian Europe, which were also stimulated by the military needs of the Fatimid dynasty, whose demand for iron and wood for ship-building could be met only by imports from Italy. There were also traditional imports of goods from the occident, listed already in the ninth century by the geographer Ibn Khordādhbeh: slaves, furs of all kinds, and swords.[3] They can be seen in the presents made by the margravine Bertha of Tuscany in 906 to the caliph al-Muktafī: swords and male and female slaves from the Slav regions. In 949 Liudprand of Cremona also brought weapons and slaves to Byzantium when acting as ambassador for Berengar II.[4] For slaves especially there was an extraordinary demand in the Islamic lands, and indeed in Spain the whole system of government was largely based on slaves from Sclavinia. John of Gorze was accompanied by merchants from Verdun on his mission, and Liudprand of Cremona reports that the Verdunese merchants had become particularly rich by trading in eunuchs with Spain.[5] This flow of trade to the Islamic Mediterranean thus reached deep into Christian Europe, as far as the east Frankish realm, and the rise of Liudolfing Saxony in the late ninth century may be due among other things to the fact that it was the source of these wares.

Islamic merchants did not extend their activity beyond the boundaries of Islamic rule, nor did Islamic rulers encourage activities of this kind. Rather, they allowed foreigners into their own territories to trade with them, though they did not allow transit passages. In Córdoba and in the rest of Islamic Spain

---

[2] Cf. Staffa (1977), p. 46.   [3] *Kitāb al Masālik wa'l-Mamālik*, p. 114.
[4] Cf. Gil (1974), pp. 310–11; Liudprand, *Antapodosis* VI, 6, pp. 155–6.
[5] John of Saint-Arnulf, *Vita Iohannis abbatis Gorziensis*, c. 117, pp. 370–1; Liudprand, *Antapodosis* VI, 6.

these traders came from the Frankish realms, while al-Fusṭāṭ was visited above all by Italian merchants from Amalfi, as we shall see. But the most important group in these exchanges was Jewish merchants. They played a leading role in inner-Islamic long-distance trade, as is shown by the documents from the Geniza of Cairo, which begin towards the end of the tenth century. They were not a substantial part of the population, especially considering the population figures named for the large cities. In eleventh-century Egypt there were probably no more than 15,000 of them, and their most important centre was Alexandria, not al-Fusṭāṭ. But Ibn Khordādhbeh speaks in his report on western trading goods of Radhanites, Jews who were based in the Christian west, probably in southern France, and who carried out a far-flung trade as far as India and China.[6] Jews did indeed play a leading role in the long-distance trade of the Frankish empire from the ninth century onwards, favoured by the privileges granted by Louis the Pious. They were settled here, owning land, vineyards and mills, above all in southern France, for example in Narbonne where they are mentioned in 899 and 919, in Saintes (961) and in Vienne (975–993), but also in Regensburg, where in 981 the Jew Samuel sold a rural estate to the monastery of St Emmeram.[7] Their scattered communities were concentrated along important trading-routes, especially the Rhine. The references in charter sources show that they were seen as long-distance traders *par excellence*. The Raffelstetten trading ordinance (903–906), which regulated the salt trade along the Austrian Danube, calls them 'the merchants, that is the Jews and the other merchants'.[8] Similar phrases are used in privileges for Magdeburg of 965 and 979 and for Treviso of 991, while in Byzantium the *Book of the Eparch*, the main source for the trading history of Constantinople in the tenth century, uses the phrase 'Jews or merchants'.[9]

The activities of these Jewish merchants evidently encompassed the whole of continental Christian Europe, extending into Sclavinia and perhaps into Scandinavia, as is suggested by the fragments which can be deduced of a travel report by Ibrāhīm ibn Yaʿqūb, a Jew from Spain, for he describes Prague as a slave market and Haithabu as a heathen trading-centre with only a few Christians.[10] On the other hand we can see the continuous links to the Islamic regions and their economic centres, even if not all Jews settled in the Carolingian successor-states undertook such long journeys as the Radhanites. Jewish mercantile activity, which reached a marked peak in the tenth and eleventh centuries, linked the Islamic world with Europe and filled the conti-

---

[6] *Kitāb al-Masālik waʾl-Mamālik*, pp. 114–15.

[7] DD Ch S 23 and 102; Lot (1950), pp. 540–1; *Cartulaire de l'abbaye de Saint-André-le-Bas de Vienne*, no. 91, p. 68 (cf. Endemann (1964), pp. 130–1); D O II 247.

[8] *MGH Cap.*, no. 253, II, p. 252.

[9] D O I 300; D O II 198; D O III 69; *Le Livre du Préfet*, p. 33. [10] *Arabische Berichte*, p. 29.

nent with oriental mercantile culture. The comparatively richly transmitted *Responsa* literature of the ninth to the eleventh centuries, in which Jewish merchants posed questions about trading law to legal experts, shows just how far this trading culture was governed by literacy. The statement made by one of these experts in the eleventh century is valid for these traders: 'they used to conduct their affairs by letters which they wrote to one another. And it was their practice that . . . letters were as binding as their words.'[11]

Islamic urban culture thus influenced Christian Europe through Jewish merchants, but these exported goods alone, not the urban forms and institutions of Islamic cities. Here there was no exchange, not even as a result of the experiences of European traders in Islamic lands.

The Islamic cities were centres of dynastic and religious power, controlled by the *'umma*, the Islamic state community. The administration of these cities was – even though Islam was a mercantile civilisation right from the beginning and merchants enjoyed a high social prestige – run by officials of the ruler and his agents. There was no special community of self-administering citizens; only the non-Islamic segments of the population (Jews and Christians above all) enjoyed a certain autonomy. The absence of a community of citizens and the social fragmentation of the Islamic city into ethnic, religious and professional groups also affected its topography. Normally there was no regular network of streets linking all the parts of the city; rather, we find an agglomeration of quarters complete in themselves. The main features of their topography were the palace, the Friday mosque and school as religious centre, and above all the inner-city market, normally situated next to the mosque, which offered the products of urban crafts. Markets for wholesale and long-distance trade, merchants' inns, and also markets for the agrarian produce of the hinterland lay on the periphery. The typical Arab praise of the city stresses besides palaces, mosques, the learning of the schools and the abundance of the markets, the gardens and baths, and above all the number and size of the houses. Ibn Ḥawqāl notes proudly that al-Fusṭāṭ's and Cairo's houses had five, six or even seven storeys and the Persian traveller Nāsir-i-Khusrau had the feeling of having a mountain before him when contemplating Cairo around the year 1000.[12] Admittedly, not all Islamic cities reached the size of Córdoba, Kairuan and al-Fusṭāṭ, but in the Christian lands there was only one city which could be compared with these Islamic metropolises of the Mediterranean region: Constantinople. From this city there also ran in the tenth century an important trading-route for the import of oriental wares into Europe, a trade in which those same Italian cities whose merchants traded with al-Fusṭāṭ participated.

---

[11] Cf. Ben-Sasson (1976), p. 398.   [12] Cf. Wiet (1964), pp. 36, 39–40.

The Byzantine empire, at the height of its medieval power in the tenth century, was a little smaller than the western empire, but it possessed a genuine capital, the largest city in Europe at the time. The walls enclosed an area of 24 km², and estimates of its population extend to a million, though 250,000–300,000 is probably nearer the truth. Constantinople was the heart of an empire with a strongly centralised provincial administration, which came increasingly under the control of the metropolitan elite just at this time. The numerous cities of the Byzantine provinces, in particular those of the Balkan peninsula, came nowhere near the metropolis in size. Even Thessalonika, the most important city after Constantinople, had an area of only 3.5 km², and most of these cities were presumably very small. They were also not pre-eminently centres of craft and trade, least of all long-distance trade, but rather centres of consumption orientated towards their hinterlands, where rich land-lords, following the tradition of Roman antiquity, consumed the surplus wealth of agrarian production. No class of economically active burghers developed here.

To some extent this statement is valid of Constantinople itself. The *Book of the Eparch*, a collection of laws probably published by Leo VI around 911–12, names a great number of crafts and groups of merchants,[13] but these were very strongly aligned with the needs. of metropolitan consumers with a high stan-dard of living. Here too the rich landowners dominated alongside imperial offi-cials. The Byzantine economy, in spite of the increased prosperity of the provinces in the tenth century, tended towards autarky, by contrast with the Islamic world. The *Book of the Eparch* itself shows that there was a considerable import of oriental wares, especially from Persian regions, and also a native pro-duction of luxury goods (silk-production, purple-dyeing), but we can hardly discern long-distance trade and brokerage aiming beyond the borders of the empire. Greek merchants, who had carried out a good deal of early medieval European long-distance trade, from the beginning of the tenth century no longer went abroad: the last reports of Greek merchants in southern France, for example, date from 921.[14]

The Byzantine empire had traditionally organised its trading contacts, both with western merchants and with the Russian and Islamic regions, at fixed points on the border. The admission of foreign merchants to the capital itself, a procedure whose forms become visible in the tenth century, came to be of great importance. But the *Book of the Eparch* imposed a strict regimentation on native crafts and trade, and the same happened to foreign merchants. They had decisive restrictions placed on the length of their stays (as a rule three months); they had fixed living-quarters (*mitata*) in which they could be strictly controlled;

---

[13] *Le Livre du Préfet, passim.*   [14] *Recueil des actes des rois de Provence*, ed. R. Poupardin, no. 39, p. 108.

and for particular wares there were export prohibitions or restrictions on the quantities which could be exported, especially in wares of the highest quality, which were retained for the Byzantines' own needs. Liudprand of Cremona experienced all this when, on his departure from Constantinople in 968, five pieces of purple cloth were confiscated by customs officials; it was in vain that he protested that the merchants of Venice and Amalfi were able to export such textiles from Byzantium and offer them for sale in Italy.[15]

In the course of the tenth century, the contacts of the Italian cities with Byzantium and the Islamic world do seem to have intensified in spite of the restrictions found in normative sources. Amalfi had the greatest successes, but Venice the most lasting ones; Pisa and Genoa appeared on the scene only around the millennium. Both Venice and Amalfi had their roots in Byzantine rule over Italy, and this alone orientated them from the start towards the Levant trade. Amalfi was one of the *castra* erected by the Byzantines against the advancing Lombards towards the end of the sixth century. Almost inaccessible from the land, built on a tiny territory, but endowed with an excellent harbour, it began its rise in the ninth century, especially after it had freed itself from subjection to Naples in 840; like the latter city it pursued, though independently, a policy of occasional cooperation with the Arabs. This led to an early link with north Africa, with the Aghlabids and later the Fatimids in Kairuan and their harbour al-Mahdiyyah, recorded from 870 at the latest. It is therefore not surprising that, following the Fatimid conquest of Egypt, al-Fusṭāṭ/Cairo belonged to their destinations. One hundred and sixty Amalfitans, 'who had come there with their wares', perished in a pogrom in 996.[16] This suggests a real colony, encouraged by the on the whole xenophile policy pursued by the Fatimid rulers. The Amalfitans pursued a triangular business. They brought corn, linen, wood above all and perhaps iron in exchange for gold and spices to Tunisia and Egypt. The gold paid for the imports of textiles, jewels and other luxury items from Byzantium. These activities intensified towards the millennium, and the Amalfitans perhaps received permission to settle in Antioch and Jerusalem around that time; they had been resident in Byzantium from the beginning of the tenth century and backed Constantine VII in the rulership crisis of 944. Because of its Arab connections, Amalfi was probably the most important Christian trading centre in the Mediterranean around the year 1000, ahead of all other south Italian cities but also of its rival Venice.

Ultimately, however, Venice was more successful. This city too, which had its origins in a settlement established by refugees who had retreated before the Lombards around 600 to the islands of the laguna, had been important since the early ninth century. It profited from its special political position, which

---

[15] Liudprand, *Relatio*, c. 55, p. 205. [16] Cahen, 'Un texte peu connu'.

allowed it to appear as a member of the Byzantine empire and so gave its merchants access to Constantinople; from 880 on it was independent of the Frankish empire. Venetians, like Amalfitans, traded with the Arabs, in part in the same militarily significant goods, and this led to friction with Byzantium in 971. But in 992 the Venetians secured a treaty which gave them primacy within Constantinople; in 1082 this culminated in a monopoly, while Amalfi became a backwater following the Norman conquest of 1077. These political facts were important, but Venice also had advantages which Amalfi could not offer: it was in a position to provide the Levant trade with a large-scale and receptive hinterland, northern Italy, which was rich in *civitates* and economically active, and also to open up the transalpine trade. The *caput Adriae* between Istria and the mouth of the Po, along with the Rhône valley, had always been the main entry points for Mediterranean wares into central and northern Europe. Venice was able to bring this region and in addition a part of the eastern Adriatic coast under political control. Its rival Comacchio was eliminated in 933, but it is noteworthy that Venetian activities to secure influence over the harbours of the northern Adriatic intensified around the millennium, when Venice was cooperating more intensively with Byzantium.

The securing of Ottonian rule in Italy placed Venice's access to transalpine regions on a firm political footing and hence facilitated it. In 967 begins the long series of Ottonian *pacta* with the city, based on ancient tradition: these granted the Venetians freedom of movement in northern Italy, especially for the trade with the most important cities between the Adige and the Po.[17] For its trade Venice thus disposed of two privileged zones and enough political influence to be able to restrain all potential rivals in the region at the head of the Adriatic. This made it in the long run the most important interface between the Levant trade and the wares of transalpine regions, which in the tenth century certainly included slaves and furs, perhaps also metals. Venetian trade was evidently closely observed in Germany: already in 860 it was known in Fulda that goods flowed into Venice, and Thietmar of Merseburg noted in his *Chronicon* under 1017 that four Venetian ships with all kinds of different spices had suffered shipwreck.[18]

In the tenth and eleventh centuries German traders were not yet to be found in Venice. Foreigners used the city merely as a starting point for journeys to Byzantium, and Venetian ships as a means of transport, like the 'very rich merchant' Liutfrid from Mainz, whom Liudprand of Cremona met serving as an ambassador of Otto I's in Constantinople in 949.[19] Exchanges between German merchants and Venetians were evidently carried out in Treviso[20] at the

[17] Cf. Rösch (1982), pp. 7–8.   [18] *Annales Fuldenses, s.a.* 860, p. 54; Thietmar, *Chronicon* VII, 76, p. 492.
[19] Liudprand, *Antapodosis* VI, 4, p. 154.
[20] Cessi (ed.), *Documenti relativi alla storia di Venezia*, no. 189, pp. 182–4; cf. Rösch (1982), pp. 80–1.

foot of the Alps, where at the beginning of the eleventh century a German toll-station (*ripaticum teutonicorum*) is recorded, and above all in Pavia.

Pavia had been the capital of the Lombard kingdom, and in Ottonian times also it was one of the preferred *sedes* of the rulers when they were in Italy, alongside Ravenna and Rome. The central administrative apparatus of the *regnum Italiae* with its base in the royal palace at Pavia apparently remained intact. From shortly after the death of Emperor Henry II in 1024 there survives a list of the revenues of the royal chamber, the *Instituta regalia*, also known as the *Honoratiae civitatis Papie*, which shows Pavia at the centre of long-distance trade in northern Italy.[21] It directs attention on the one hand to the ten trading stations in all, the *clusae*, situated at the entry to the Alpine passes from Susa in the west to Cividale in the east, and to the merchants coming from the north (among whom numerous Anglo-Saxons evidently enjoyed a privileged position) and their wares: horses, slaves, wool and linen cloth, tin and swords. On the other hand we find the Venetians and merchants from the south Italian cities, Salerno, Gaeta and Amalfi, who brought in oriental and luxury goods: spices, ivory, mirrors and valuable textiles. At the end of the ninth century Notker of St Gallen had already described the great variety of textiles available from the Venetians to Frankish magnates, and Odo of Cluny in the first half of the tenth century relates how Count Gerald of Aurillac had been offered silk and spices before the gates of the city.[22] Pavia thus appears as a market which was frequented both by rich consumers themselves and by traders, a meeting- and exchange-point between the region north of the Alps and the Mediterranean. The city was a focus for this trade because it was the centre of government in the *regnum Italiae*, not because of any potent stratum of merchants of its own. The role of Pavia, rooted in older relationships, was revived and intensified by the Ottonians' policy in Italy. The increasing frequency of trade on the Alpine route from the Rhine during the second half of the tenth century is also visible in what was evidently the very rapid development of Zurich, which lay in the northern hinterland of the Bündner group of Alpine passes. This concentration of long-distance trade on Pavia and the city's role as a centre of distribution vanished after the royal administration had disintegrated in the course of Henry II's reign and the Pavians destroyed the royal palace.

This action directs our attention to the remaining cities of northern Italy, whose inhabitants also began to develop their independence in the course of the tenth century. This indicates a new stage in urban history. The revival of long-distance trade, in particular the strengthening of communication

---

[21] Cf. *Die 'Honorantie Civitatis Papie'*, ed. Brühl and Violante, *passim*.

[22] Notker the Stammerer, *Gesta Karoli* II, 17, p. 86; Odo of Cluny, *Vita S. Geraldi* I, 27, col. 658.

between two great trading regions, as seen around 1000, gave a powerful shove to economic development and to urbanism. But it coincided with a general intensification of medium- and short-distance trade and a flourishing of handicrafts. All these together favoured the development of urban and quasi-urban forms of life and social organisation in varying degrees. All the post-Carolingian kingdoms were affected by this. Besides the growth of and the emergence of specialisation within the *civitates* we find their penetration of the hinterland with places for the exchange of goods taking the legal form of the market (*mercatum*), which provided those who traded and also the producers of craft and agrarian goods with a stable framework for their activities: peace and protection both at the market itself and while travelling to and from it, legal security and the settlement of disputes arising out of transactions, together with reliable monetary conditions.

This process was stimulated and encouraged by rulers and other lords, who guaranteed the legal setting and derived fiscal benefit from market dues, in particular from tolls. True, market foundations are not an innovation of the Ottonian period, but go far back into the Carolingian era. Yet in the tenth and eleventh centuries they reached a new stage of development, and were used deliberately to intensify lordship in the central regions within which the medieval town developed, that is in Italy, France and Germany.

In Italy the network of *civitates* was finer meshed than in the transalpine regions, an inheritance from antiquity: the distances between episcopal sees ranged between 15 and 50 km. In the transalpine regions they were much greater; even in the German regions west of the Rhine and in Lotharingia they were 50 to 130 km, and further east they could be still larger. For this reason no additional quasi-urban settlements developed alongside the episcopal sees in Italy: urban life is congruent with the episcopal city. The *civitates* in Italy evidently suffered less in the course of the Germanic incursions of late antiquity than the episcopal sees in Gaul, and they did not experience so great a shrinkage. The walled area of the more important towns varied between 20 and 40 hectares, and even the great exception of Rome, with an area of 13.86 km^2, did not achieve the extent of the Byzantine and Islamic metropolises.

Rome played no active economic role. For several centuries it had been a rural town with large farmed areas within the walls. At best it was a centre of consumption. The luxury goods brought by long-distance trade, above all that of the Amalfitans, flowed into the courts of the popes and their clergy, to the numerous churches and their decorations, and to the crowds of pilgrims who visited the tombs of the apostles. Evidently no long-distance trade was plied by Roman merchants. Politically, both city and papacy were in the hands of rival aristocratic families, and even Ottonian rule faced constant revolts: 'Rome and the papacy were at their nadir.'[23] Rome's importance for urban history was not a product of its political or economic role but of the picture of Rome as an urban *caput mundi*, as the city of Christianity itself, shaped by tradition and renewed by Otto III.

The centres of urban innovation in Italy lay in Tuscany and above all in Lombardy. The basis for the *civitates'* economic development was the fertility of the Po basin and its tributary valleys. Liudprand of Cremona formulated this almost epigrammatically when he said that Venetians and Amalfitans brought valuable textiles to northern Italy in order to sustain their existence with the foodstuffs bought in return.[24] But undoubtedly the export of agrarian surpluses was the main driving force behind the early rise of the Lombard cities and the source of their prosperity. The landowning nobility of Italy, unlike that of Gaul, had never left the *civitates*, and so city and hinterland remained closely linked. The *civitas* retained an oligarchic structure even within its walls. Although the bishop, as elsewhere, was the most important figure in the city, and his position was further strengthened by Ottonian privileges, he was still not the real ruler of the city, but had continually to deal with other groups of the urban population and the distribution of power among them. The population was subject to a unitary law, and consisted for the most part of the free. To be able to defend the extensive ring-walls the population bore arms, and took part in the *conventus*, a popular assembly. The nobility naturally played a decisive role in this highly differentiated urban society, and the bishop and the other officials in the city were in effect merely the exponents of the aristocracy and its factions. But their election was the product of inner-urban decision-making. The permanent market within the walls was the economic centre of the city, already equipped with densely built-up market stands often owned by ecclesiastical institutions. It was here that the activities of traders and of the urban craftworkers intermeshed most closely. The differentiation in craftwork and its concentration within the city seems to have been a very important factor in determining the economic power of a city; it was almost as important as trade.

The significance of crafts can be seen in the rise of Milan, which around 1000 was probably already on a par with Pavia. It was not inherently favoured by its position away from the Po, but it was able to concentrate long-distance trade on itself because its archbishop could guarantee the safety of traders along the Alpine route to Chur. This underlines once more the importance of this route for Italian trade with the transalpine region, whereas the western Alpine passes still suffered from the depredations of Saracen bands, who in 891 had set up a base in Fraxinetum, between Marseilles and Nice. From here they made razzias by water and land, and they were not driven out until 973.

---

[23] Krautheimer (1983), p. 145.   [24] Liudprand, *Relatio*, c. 55, p. 205.

That also helps to explain the delay before Pisa and Genoa, with their excellent harbours, were able to take a leading part in long-distance trade. A decisive contribution to Milan's prosperity was made by the development of a productive ironworking industry. This profited from ore deposits on Lakes Maggiore and Como, largely in the hands of the Milanese monastery of S. Ambrogio. At all events it is smiths and ironworkers alongside merchants whom we find among those Milanese citizens who acquired land in the surrounding regions around 1000.

Processes like that just mentioned demonstrate the economic superiority of the *civitas*, as does the fact that around 1000 the price for land in Milan was thirty-six times as high as in the countryside.[25] But the countryside was also subject to increased commercialisation, as seen from royal diplomata granting rights of market, which begin before the middle of the century. Bishops possessed such rural markets, as did individual monasteries and nobles, such as the Vuaremundus who received in 948 from King Lothar the right to collect all the dues pertaining to the king on contracts concluded in his castles and villages or in markets which he might erect in places belonging to him.[26] Trading and the market are here linked with castle-building, *incastellamento*, a practice whereby nobles and ecclesiastics sought to intensify their lordship. These markets and fortifications were only rarely the basis for urban formation. Urban development generally remained linked with the *civitates* and the marketplaces within them. They grew through the accumulation of *burgi*, unfortified settlements outside the walls, which were incorporated into the *civitas* by the walls built in later eras.

It is obvious that the merchants of the Italian *civitates* belonged to the leading groups within the cities, alongside the urban nobility. In the maritime cities, especially in Venice, the nobility itself participated in trade. But it is difficult to get a picture of the social origins of merchants. Some of them were free, such as the Cremonese *milites* active in the Po trade. But links with the bishops appear repeatedly in the sources. Otto III and Conrad II gave the bishop of Asti (at the mouth of the valley of Susa, one of the most important Alpine crossings) in 992 and 1037 respectively a privilege granting freedom from tolls to *his* merchants and to the citizens of *his* city.[27] Regardless of whether they were free citizens or trading agents of the bishop, merchants profited more than all other sections of the population from market, mint and toll privileges and from the episcopal protection guaranteeing their trade-routes. Their room for economic manoeuvre was defined by their link with their *civitas* and its bishop. Archbishop Aribert could therefore justifiably be praised on his death as *mercatorum protector*.[28] Nevertheless, the relationship was not always free from

---

[25] Cf. Renouard (1969), p. 382.   [26] D Lothar 10.   [27] D O III 99; D C II 245.
[28] Landulf Senior, *Historia Mediolanensis* II, 32.

tensions, which show the importance of this group. In Cremona, disputes between the merchants and the bishop are recorded as early as 924, when the merchants sought to move the harbour to a different location to escape episcopal control. Tensions between citizens and bishops increased around 1000: in 983 there is a reference to conflicts between Milanese citizens and Archbishop Landulf, and from 996 there were again disputes over the harbour and the passage of ships in Cremona; these lasted a long time and broke into violent conflict in 1005 and 1030. But the part played by merchants in these disturbances is not clear, and they really belong to the general wave of strivings for autonomy which culminated in the *valvassores'* uprising in 1035. Nevertheless, it is significant that evidence for the right of citizens to participate in the running of the cities refers to economic affairs affecting merchants. Already in 948 King Lothar had granted the bishop of Mantua the mint, with the provision that the *conventus* of the citizens of Mantua, Verona and Brescia was to determine the fineness and weight of the coinage. This strong position of the citizens found around the middle of the century was not seriously affected by the privileges granted by the Ottonians to the bishops, and the economic well-being of the cities was an important precondition for the formation of the communes in the later eleventh century. By the beginning of the eleventh century at all events, Italy ranked as the most advanced urban region of Europe. Her most important cities were Milan and Venice, while the harbour cities of Pisa and Genoa were rapidly gaining ground now that the Saracen danger in the Tyrrhenian sea had been eliminated.

In the transalpine regions of the former Frankish empire, in what were becoming France and Ottonian Germany, the development of towns took a quite different path. The wider mesh of the network of *civitates* (see above) left room for further settlements resembling the episcopal sees in economic and governmental function. But even those *civitates* going back to Roman times operated under different preconditions from those of the episcopal cities of Italy. The Germanic incursions at the end of the third century had led to the fortification of the Gallic cities and so to a drastic reduction in the areas of urban settlement. Only a few episcopal cities retained a substantial area: Lyons (65 ha); Poitiers (47 ha); Rheims (60 ha); Sens (43 ha); Toulouse (90 ha). Remarkably, these included some which lay near the *limes* and set up their defences early: Cologne (96.8 ha); Mainz (98.5 ha); Metz (60 ha); Augsburg (61 ha, though here the fortifications had disappeared by the tenth century and had no influence on the medieval development of the city). Trier, the former imperial residence, had the exceptional area of 285 ha, but only about 15% of this was settled at the beginning of the tenth century. Most of the *civitates* had an area between 6 and 15 ha: Auxerre (6); Limoges (7); Clermont (6); Le Mans (7–8); Paris (15); Rouen (14). The areas in the towns within what later became

Germany were generally larger: Strasbourg (18.5); Worms (23); Regensburg (24.5); Speyer (14). The smaller areas predominating in Gaul evidently provided a model for the bishoprics newly founded in the Carolingian era in the previously townless regions to the east of the Rhine, especially in Saxony: Minden (4.24); Münster (7); Osnabrück (5.25); Paderborn (6.1).

It is clear that these *civitates* essentially had the functions of a mere citadel, and the Old High German glossing of *civitas* and *urbs* with *purc* underlines this fortified character of urbanism. Market, trade, and to a large extent craftwork, largely took place outside these fortifications. The settlements connected with them were adjacent, but legally distinct, creating the characteristic picture of a bi- or multipolarity in the early phase of town formation, which ended only with the creation of a unified town law and wall-building enclosing the separate settlements in the course of the eleventh and twelfth centuries.

The process of town development was roughly similar in France, Lotharingia and Germany, but the pace varied. The trade flows of the period at first favoured Germany and Lotharingia: the links already mentioned across the Alps with Mediterranean trade, which led into the Rhine valley or the region of the Meuse and proceeded along these rivers to the coast; but also the extraordinary growth of the slave trade within Europe. Regensburg was the crucial centre on the Danube route, Erfurt on the Thuringian, Magdeburg on the route across the Elbe. It is no coincidence that it is in Regensburg that we find around 1020 a *civis* and merchant of Slav origin settled there: *Penno filius Liubuste.*[29]

However, the most important impulse for development seems to have been given by the intensification of trade across the Baltic, a flowering of the seeds sown in the Carolingian era. Viking raids functioned here as a motor rather than as a destructive force. The coastal region of northern Europe was bound in this way into the network of long-distance trade; along the Dnieper and the Volga a second trade-route was established with Byzantium and the Islamic east. This Baltic trade also entered via the Rhine, Meuse and Scheldt estuaries to end in Germany and Lotharingia and provided a significant economic thrust. France, by contrast, remained cut off from Mediterranean trade by the hindrance to trade via the mouth of the Rhône due to the Saracen threat; the transit trade of Jewish and Verdunese merchants with Islamic Spain did not compensate. Admittedly, Italian merchants are recorded around 1000 at the Saint-Denis fairs, which go back to the Merovingian era, but the decisive rise of the *Lendit* took place in the second half of the eleventh century.

One also has the impression that the French *civitates* only gradually recovered from the depredations of the Viking raids, to which they had been exposed

---

[29] *Die Traditionen des Hochstifts Regensburg und des Klosters S Emmeram*, no. 327, pp. 246–7.

particularly strongly, even in the interior, during the period of the 'great army' from the 880s through to the foundation of Normandy in 911. In Paris, for example, there is noticeable growth in the settlements outside the walled Ile de la Cité on both sides of the Seine only after the middle of the century; in Rheims the churches of Saint-Denis and Saint-Nicaise still lay in ruins in the mid-eleventh century. In Bordeaux the rebuilding also took place only at the end of the tenth century, and not until the eleventh is a noteworthy flow of trade on the Garonne again recorded.

Nevertheless the London toll regulations of Æthelred the Unready of 984/5 mention long-distance trade with the northern coast of France, especially with Rouen (wine and whale meat), but also with the mouth of the Somme (*Ponteienses*, the men of Ponthieu).[30] Yet in general it seems clear that the final phase of Viking raids retarded French development, whereas overall and on balance they were a favourable impulse to north European trade, and indeed played a decisive part in building up a trade network in the North and Baltic seas.

Tenth-century France also lacked the driving force of powerful kingship. Although the development of towns and markets in France, Lotharingia and Germany was strongly influenced by regional political forces, the Ottonian rulers played a decisive part. Their diplomata suggest that they had a trade policy, one which was to intensify the impulses proceeding from the favourable geo-economic conditions of the period. Their aim was to fill the area with markets, places at which goods could be exchanged in ordered legal circumstances. The need to establish such places in particular regions is explicitly stated. Kings themselves had such markets in their palaces and royal estates, in the *civitates* and elsewhere. From the reign of Otto I the crown increasingly granted the income from such markets in whole or in part, or the markets themselves or at least the right to erect and run such markets, to other lords. Nevertheless, it continued to regard itself as a central regulator, for example in the way in which it issued prohibitions against erecting markets in particular areas, in order to protect the catchment areas of existing markets (as Otto III did for Quedlinburg in 994),[31] but above all in the way in which it sought to guarantee unitary principles of market law and custom. The charters granting rights defined them by reference to those of the nearest economically significant *civitas* (Cologne, Mainz, Magdeburg, Trier, Cambrai, Strasbourg, Speyer, Worms, Constance, Augsburg and Regensburg) or other royal market (Dortmund, Goslar, Zurich). It is clear here that we are dealing with *royal* law, as when for example Otto I in his privilege for Bremen of 965 speaks of the law of merchants in the remaining royal cities (*urbes*) and Henry II grants in 1004 to

---

[30] IV Æthelred 2, 5–6, in *Die Gesetze der Angelsachsen*, ed. Liebermann, I, p. 232. [31] D O III 155.

the market Rincka in Breisgau the peace which is usual 'in the greater places and towns of our empire'.[32] Unified law held together a network of markets owned by different lords, differentiated according to size and distance. The granting of privileges to merchants themselves was a more immediate way of encouraging trade, and this also occurred, though only a few traces of it have survived. The merchants of Tiel, the successor to the Carolingian *emporium* of Dorestadt, claimed at the beginning of the eleventh century to hold royal privileges, and Otto II had already granted the merchants resident in Magdeburg freedom from tolls throughout the kingdom with the exception of those at Mainz, Cologne, Tiel and Bardowiek.[33] This clause, very much in the Carolingian tradition, underlines once more the importance of the great emporia on the Rhine, the entry-points for the North Sea and Baltic trade. It also sketches the radius of action of a group of merchants in Magdeburg, whose members are indeed traceable in Tiel.

What characterises these merchants is their residentiality, their links with a particular place, which is stressed occasionally in the diplomata, reflected in phrases like *Maguntinus institor* or *Verdunenses mercatores* or deducible from their sometimes considerable landed possessions, as when the Regensburg merchant Wilhelm gives land in five different villages to the monastery of St Emmeram in 983.[34] This merchant residentiality also shaped the topography of mercantile settlements and encouraged the formation of social groups with permanent structures.

True, it is clear from the sources that merchants lived both inside and outside the *civitas*, as at Merseburg or Regensburg, but the settlements outside the *civitas*, known as *suburbium*, *burgus*, *vicus* or *portus*, took on a special importance. They were established, sometimes several of them, not only around *civitates* but also at palaces and royal estates, monasteries and aristocratic fortifications. This consolidation of a vocational group will have encouraged the formation of unions of a cooperative nature. The Magdeburg merchants – occasionally named together with the Jews – received their privilege as a corporation.[35] In Tiel, where the *vicus ad portus* of the merchants lay along two lordly settlement-cores – the Walburgis monastery (an aristocratic foundation granted by Otto I to the bishopric of Utrecht) and an important royal estate, which was granted to St Mary in Aachen in 1000 – the outlines of a merchant guild become visible, a 'free association with self-determined law for the pur-

---

[32] D O I 307; D H II 78: 'sicut in maioribus nostri regni locis et civitatibus'.
[33] D O II 112.
[34] Liudprand, *Antapodosis* VI, 4 and 6, pp. 153–4, 155–6; *Liber miraculorum S. Bertini abbatis*, AASS Septembrii II, cols. 595–604: 'Viridunenses negotiatores'; D O II 293, cf. *Traditionen des Hochstifts Regensburg*, no. 212, p. 192: 'urbis Regie negotiator nomine Adalhart'.
[35] D O II 112; D O I 300.

poses of mutual protection and support',[36] which should be seen as a milestone along the road leading to later inner-urban confraternities. Tiel's especially vulnerable position at that time may have encouraged the formation of a guild, but similar associations may be assumed to have existed at other places.

Not all those who traded would have fallen into the categories of *mercatores*, *negotiatores*, *emptores* and *institores*. The Raffelstetten toll ordinance distinguished the *Bavari* (that is Bavarian landowners) trading in salt from the merchants and Jews who to some extent were active in the same markets.[37] The distinction between different groups of traders is difficult, but the inhabitants of *vici* and *suburbia* were probably characterised by their activity in long-distance trade. Their social classification is equally difficult. The rich Regensburg merchant Wilhelm (see above) had been 'granted his freedom' by the king.[38] There were thus free men among the *negotiatores*, but it also means that others were active as agents of the king and in his service, in bonds characteristic of what were later to become *ministeriales*. Similar bonds are to be assumed for merchants in the entourages of other lords, though their activities will have assured them a great deal of flexibility in their legal status and way of life, something which enraged monastic observers like Alpert of Metz, who describes the merchants of Tiel.[39]

The populations of these multiple settlements are frequently described in terms which suggest that they were acting together, especially in conflicts with the bishop of the *civitas*. It was the *Metenses* who blinded the bishop of Metz installed by Henry I in 924.[40] But even when in 958 the citizens of Cambrai sought to drive their bishop from the city, 'united in one and the same will and having made a unanimous oath-taking',[41] we are not yet dealing with an incipient citizens' collective. We must reckon rather with different groups, legally distinct from one another, even within the *civitas*, in which often enough bishop and count were in rivalry. In Cambrai the count held half of the town area and of the dues; in several French *civitates* (e.g. Soissons and Amiens) comital castles are recorded, and the Life of Bishop Burchard of Worms (1000–25) describes impressively how Duke Otto, a son of Conrad the Red, possessed a fortification within the *civitas*, which offered support to those persecuting the episcopal *familia*. Bishop Burchard countered by fortifying the episcopal residence, and so in time brought peace to a city in which within a single year thirty-five members of the episcopal *familia* had been killed. But Burchard's estate law,

---

[36] D O I 124; D O III 347; cf. Oexle (1989), p. 184.

[37] *MGH Cap.*, no. 253, II, pp. 249–52.   [38] D O II 293.

[39] Alpertus Mettensis, *De diversitate temporum* II, 20–1, pp. 78–82.

[40] Adalbert, *Reginonis Continuatio, s.a.* 927, p. 158.

[41] 'cives una eademque voluntate collecti, factaque unanimiter conspiratione': *Gesta episcoporum Cameracensium* I, 81, p. 431.

which set fixed legal norms within the *civitas*, applied only to his own *familia*, not to other groups of persons.

In general the bishops were able to gain the upper hand within the area of the walled *civitas*, not least with the help of the privileges granted them by the Ottonians, and in the palaces, royal estates and aristocratic fortifications which were also adjoined by *vici* and *suburbia* the issue did not present itself. The events just noted do make clear, however, that *civitas* and castle were centres of lordship, though their significance cannot be confined to the merely military. They were also far from serving exclusively as places of refuge for times of war, even if Viking raids and Magyar razzias encouraged the building of fortifications. The *Vita Burchardi* says that after peace had been established the *cives* returned to live there.[42] That is understandable in the case of a *civitas* of the size of Worms (see above), but even in very small settlements, such as that of the castle of the counts of Flanders in Ghent (4 ha) of around 940 or 950, archaeology suggests that craftsmen were working there.

It must be stressed that in multiple settlements around *civitates* and castles, lordship and fortification were closely linked. It was the legal form of the market which proved attractive for the exercise of lordship as well as holding together the individual settlement cores of a *civitas*. Spiritual communities as well as secular magnates set up markets, not least because they saw in them a possibility of selling the agrarian produce of the manorial economy. On occasions this could cover quite a wide area. The monastery of Corvey on the Weser grouped its scattered peripheral possessions by setting up markets (Meppen in 946, and Horhusen (Niedermarsberg) by the beginning of the eleventh century).[43] The most impressive example is that of Lorsch, which intensified lordship in its neighbourhood by establishing a circle of markets about 30 km away (Bensheim 956; Wiesloch 965; Zullestein 995; Weinheim 1000; Oppenheim 1008). These looked in part to the Rhine, in part to the Odenwald, and show us that the region was receptive to commercial exchange. Although the bishopric of Worms, the monastery's great rival in developing the Odenwald, had been able to concentrate large-scale trade on the market in its *civitas*, it had only been able to penetrate the Odenwald itself with a single foundation, Kailbach (1018), and here too only on the periphery. The record of a settlement arranged by Henry II in 1023 shows that there had been a real trade war, escalating at times into violence and even killing.[44]

Secular magnates also made use of this combination of economy and lordship, though records of their activities are much less well preserved. Count Berthold, the ancestor of the Zähringer, set up a market in Villingen in 999, and around the same time Otto III's *fidelis* Aribo established markets in

---

[42] *Vita Burchardi*, c. 6, *MGH SS* IV, p. 835.   [43] DD O I 77, 444.   [44] D H II 501.

Donauwörth, whose later history shows that they were also intended to have functions of lordship.[45] The clearest case is the striving of the counts of Flanders, not only in their building of castles in Bruges and Ghent provided with *portus* and *vicus*, but above all Count Arnulf's seizure in 939 of the fortified *oppidum* Mentreuil at the Pas de Calais. What was at stake in this castle belonging to Count Erluin was not merely its value as a fortification but also the 'great revenues' which 'were to be derived from the landings of ships'.[46]

One may say in summary that the tenth century saw the opening of the countryside for the exchange of goods at markets. This is true of Germany, Lotharingia and France equally, though in the west the process is not visible in such detail, since the west Frankish king did not develop a market sovereignty like that of the German ruler. The establishing of new markets seems to have reached its height in the period around 1000. However, not all the markets set up in the tenth and early eleventh centuries developed into towns. Many disappeared or acquired town law only very late. The market is therefore not the root of the medieval town, but it prepared the ground for the urban economy and can be described as the motor which kept the economic cooperation between the separate settlement kernels going in this decisive phase of transalpine urban development.

Overall we may assume very strong growth for the *civitates* and quasi-urban settlements during the tenth century; occasionally this is visible in topographic development. Thus in Regensburg – perhaps already under Duke Arnulf, certainly before 940 – an area to the west of the Roman legionary camp evidently settled by merchants was taken into its fortifications, effectively doubling the surface area of the *civitas* to about 55 ha. In Worms a wall begun in the second half of the tenth century was completed under Bishop Burchard, and the area of settlement nearly trebled, from 23 ha to 65 ha. In Cologne the land won by filling in the Roman harbour and settled by merchants was fortified around 940 or 950, which increased the *civitas* to 122 ha. Even on the smaller stage of the royal estate at Dortmund, an important trading-centre nevertheless, we find an increase in area from 2.13 to 11.5 ha.

Growth of this kind certainly did not take place evenly everywhere, and we must assume a certain hierarchy within the network of *civitates*, markets and newly founded non-agrarian settlements near castles and palaces. This is occasionally mentioned explicitly, as in a letter of Abbot Othelbert of Saint-Bavo, which describes the *castrum* Ghent as a *caput regionis* which has precedence over other *civitates* (here to be understood as a castle with a *vicus*, not as an episcopal city). To justify his view the abbot pointed to the church buildings and relics

---

[45] DO III 311; DC II 144.
[46] Richer, *Historiae* II, 11, p. 144: 'eo quod ex navium advectationibus inde plures questus proveniant'.

there.[47] Elsewhere also we can observe how both bishops and secular magnates underlined the importance of these places combining military installations, craft and mercantile settlements, and markets by endowing them with a special architecture and sacrality.

The building of walls was necessary for defence and had already been fostered by the Viking threat of the ninth century. In the tenth century it grew and became more effective, drawing in part on labour services from the agrarian surroundings. But the building of new churches, especially new cathedrals within the *civitates*, and their equipping with relics served display purposes and encouraged streams of pilgrims, for whom, as a diploma of Otto III's for the monastery of Selz put it, a market was as necessary as for the monks and the other people living there.[48] We can thus observe a lively building activity in the tenth century, from Otto I, who endowed the cathedral he had built in Magdeburg with a very rich set of relics, through bishops and abbots to nobles, who added monastic or canonical foundations to their castles and also provided these with relics, like for example Manigold, the descendant of the *fidelis* Aribo, who, in order to display more effectively the particle of the Holy Cross which Romanos III had presented to him in Constantinople in 1029, complemented his father's market foundation in Donauwörth with the foundation of a spiritual community.

Large-scale buildings, the monasteries and collegiate churches founded there and their collections of relics increased the attractiveness of these places both for secular vassals and for merchants, who found groups of wealthy consumers to provide for. Besides the general economic conditions and the impulses from lordship, the development of an impressive architecture and the enhanced presence of the saints in their reliquaries belonged to the important factors driving on the emergence of the medieval town in Germany and France.

In the Mediterranean region and in the transalpine sections of the Frankish empire the development of urbanism was shaped by lines of continuity leading back into antiquity, even if these were absent in the easternmost part of the empire. Northern and eastern Europe could not build on such traditions, and even in Britain, where England and Wales had a Roman past, these traditions were not effective to the same extent as on the continent. For the whole of this region, with the exception of England, it must also be acknowledged that our knowledge of urban development owes much more to archaeological research than to written sources. Even in England, the archaeological investigation of towns is further advanced than it is on the continent.

---

[47] *Elenchus fontium historiae urbanae* II, 2, no. 8, p. 295.

[48] D O III 130: 'et mercatus necessaria sunt multitudini populorum undique illuc confluentium, simul etiam monachis et populis ibi commanentibus et habitantibus'.

From the early middle ages onwards England played an important part in North Sea trade, which was of such importance for the economic development of Europe precisely in the tenth century. The Viking raids and Scandinavian settlement brought it, together with the other parts of Britain and Ireland, into still closer contact with Scandinavia, to the point where it became part of a Scandinavian empire under Cnut and his sons.

In England, the monk Ælfric referred to merchants in positive terms, describing and defining their activities in his *Colloquy*, shortly before Alpert of Metz made his harsh judgement on the merchants of Tiel.[49] It is from England also that we have the earliest evidence for medieval European merchants' own thinking, and this in turn shows just how far Scandinavia and the Baltic region lay within the ambit of Anglo-Saxon kings. At the court of King Alfred the Great (871–99) the Norwegian Ohtere described his journeys to the Lapps and to the coasts of Norway and Denmark along as far as Haithabu; the Anglo-Saxon Wulfstan related his knowledge of the Baltic from Haithabu to Truso on the Vistula estuary and beyond into the lands of the Estonians. King Alfred included these reports in the Old English translation of the *World Chronicle* of Orosius.[50]

Alfred's government marked an important turn in the development of Anglo-Saxon urbanism. Until then there had been in essence three kinds of quasi-urban settlement in Anglo-Saxon England. The first consisted of centres of royal power located within the walls of Roman cities – London, York, Canterbury and Winchester – which were also bishoprics. It should be noted, however, that the density of settlement within the Roman fortifications was very low. The next type was that of unfortified trading emporia on the coast, with names frequently ending in -*wic*: Hamwih (Southampton), Fordwich, Sarre, Dover, Sandwich, Ipswich. The ending -*wic* also appears in Eoforwic (later Scandinavian Jorwic = York) and Lundenwic (= London). Archaeology has revealed that west of Roman London there was indeed an emporium of this kind, with an area of at least 24 ha, perhaps 80 ha, lying between what are now Fleet Street and Whitehall, described by Bede as a significant centre of long-distance trade. In York also crafts and trade seem to have been practised mainly outside the area of the Roman legionary camp even before the Scandinavian conquest of 862. It would seem that some of these trading emporia formed a functional unity with nearby royal centres: Hamwih with Winchester; Ipswich with the region around Woodbridge, Rendlesham and Sutton Hoo. A third group was made up of newly established fortified settlements in the interior, such as the Five Boroughs of the Danelaw (Stamford, Nottingham, Derby, Lincoln and Leicester) or else Hereford, about which little

[49] Ælfric, *Colloquy*, pp. 33–4.   [50] *The Old English Orosius*, pp. 13–18.

is known archaeologically. Overall, however, there were probably not more than about fifteen settlements with urban characteristics in Alfred's time.

English scholarship has established a bundle of criteria to determine what marks a town in Anglo-Saxon England: market, mint, fortifications, tenements and open fields (Stenton), special jurisdiction (Lyon).[51] These criteria apply to the majority of a group of settlements which become visible under Alfred and his son Edward the Elder and are linked with a defensive plan directed against the Danes. The *Burghal Hidage*, a list dating from around 914–19, names 30 *burhs* in Wessex and three in Mercia:[52] fortified locations, which were to be kept in repair by the surrounding population and could be manned in times of danger. We are dealing here in part with the use or reuse of Roman or even Iron Age fortifications, but mostly with new settlements. This defensive system, which could also play a part in attack, was the basis for resistance to the Great Army of the Vikings which turned against England from 892 onwards; its development accompanied the recuperation of the Danish north.

To make these settlements capable of surviving and functioning they were mostly equipped with a mint and a market, with the latter appearing in royal legislation as *port*. From the time of Edward the Elder sales were restricted to the *port* and therefore to the *burh*, where they were to be supervised by a royal official, the port reeve, and made before market witnesses. When Alfred occupied London in 886 he evidently caused the *vicus* on the Strand to be incorporated into the walled region; in similar fashion the area of the former Roman town in Winchester was filled with settlement. Economic function and fortification came into line with each other. In the interior both new settlements and ancient urban locations were given a regular street network, so that we can speak, with Biddle, of 'planned towns'.[53]

The kingdom of Wessex thus covered the country with a network of fortified markets, which in their function were comparable with the markets of Ottonian Germany but were all controlled by the king. Their legal and topographical form made them the basis for the medieval English borough, even if – as on the continent – not all the settlements of the tenth century flourished, or are still found as boroughs in Domesday Book. Places like Halwell and Chisbury remained mere hillforts; some, like *Gothaburh*, cannot even be identified with certainty. On the other hand we can already find in the tenth century a fundamental difference between town and rural settlement, as soon as 'greater population numbers, walls, market, mint, income of the population derived partly from trade and craft, market witnesses, royal officials and courts' come together.[54] In the laws, provisions regulating urban conditions become

---

[51] Haslam (1994), p. xv.
[52] Hill (1969).   [53] Biddle and Hill (1971).
[54] *Die Gesetze der Angelsachsen*, ed. Liebermann, II, p. 660, 1 h.

more and more frequent. In Anglo-Saxon England there was also a hierarchy of towns and markets, and for that reason concentrations of commercial activity. The activities of royal mints provide a barometer. Their numbers had risen sharply towards the end of the tenth century, from twenty-seven and later forty under Edgar to seventy-five under Æthelred the Unready, while Domesday Book notes eighty. The laws of King Æthelstan prescribe a mintmaster for every *burh*, but there were exceptions: London 8, Canterbury 7, Winchester 6, Rochester 3, Lewes, Southampton, Wareham, Exeter and Shaftesbury 2. Æthelred tried to reduce the increased numbers, but allowed each *summus portus* (principal town) three.[55] And indeed we find in the various regions places with an above-average mint output (London, Winchester, York, Lincoln, Canterbury, Exeter, Chester and Norwich), accounting together for more than half of total output. It was the south and east which dominated here; in the north only York, with 9% of total production, stood out.

The evidence of written sources, archaeology and numismatics suggests a lively urban life and internal trade, with commercialised forms of goods exchange between town and countryside. Naturally, England was by no means isolated from continental long-distance trade. The London trade regulations of Æthelred reveal the close links with the neighbouring coasts across the channel. Besides the merchants from France and Flanders, mentioned above, we find the 'men of the emperor', German traders.[56] Among these those of Huy, Liège and Nivelles are given particular attention; presumably they traded in bronzeware. Ælfric's merchant, mentioned above, deals in goods which point still further afield: purple and silk, valuable stones and gold, various clothes and spices, wine and oil, ivory and golden bronze (*auricalcum*), iron ore and tin, sulphur, and glass.[57] These names recall the routes over the Alps which brought the Anglo-Saxons to Pavia, where they exchanged their goods for purple dye, silk, spices and other things.

The travellers' accounts of the merchants Ohtere and Wulfstan included by King Alfred in his translation of Orosius point equally definitely to the Baltic and the activities of the Scandinavian peoples, however. They show that the British Isles and the southern North Sea coast of the continent formed a system of trading emporia: Dublin, other Irish sites and York in the west; in the Baltic region Kaupang in the fjord of Oslo, Haithabu in the bay of Schleswig, Birka in the Mälar region of Sweden, Paviken and other locations on Gotland, and the sites of the southern coast of the Baltic – Ralswiek on Rügen, Wolin (Jumne) and Menzlin around the mouth of the Oder, Kolberg (Kołobrzeg) on the Pomeranian coast, Truso in the delta of the Vistula, Grobin in Kurland and

---

[55] *Die Gesetze der Angelsachsen*, ed. Liebermann, I, II Æthelstan, 14, 2, pp. 158–9; IV Æthelred 9, p. 236.
[56] *Die Gesetze der Angelsachsen*, ed. Liebermann, I, IV Æthelred, 2, 8, p. 234.
[57] *Elenchus fontium historiae urbanae*, no. 8, p. 295.

Daugmale on the lower reaches of the Dwina. These sites date back to the eighth and ninth centuries, though they had undergone extensive and very variable change in the course of the tenth century. But all of them had been given new impulses by the Scandinavian expansion from the ninth century onwards, seen most obviously in the razzias and trading missions of the Vikings.

This line of trading sites from west to east pointed towards those sites which organised trade with Islamic central Asia and Byzantium via the Russian rivers. In the tenth century the most important centres at first were Staraja Ladoga on the Volkhov and Gnëzdowo (the precursor of Smolensk) on the Dnieper. The first could be reached by ship across the Gulf of Finland and the Neva, and opened up routes to both Dnieper and Volga. The latter could be reached more directly from the Baltic via the Dwina. Gorodišče on the Volkhov, in the course of the tenth century to be gradually replaced by Novgorod, 2 km further south, and Kiev on the Dnieper, the heart of the Rus' empire, should also be mentioned. Scandinavians were present in all these sites, and indeed played a crucial role. Haithabu, Kaupang and Birka were controlled by Scandinavian kings; Dublin originated in 917 as a Viking foundation, and Scandinavians were of decisive importance in the development of the Russian sites as well, even if details are disputed. The Irish Sea, the North Sea and the Baltic together could count as a Scandinavian sea. The Icelandic sagas reflect this; *Egil's Saga*, for example, calls the journey to Dublin 'the most popular route',[58] and Egil and his companions are shown visiting Norway as well as Wolin and the coast of Kurland. These trading emporia, especially in the Baltic and in Russia, were generally polyethnic formations, rather like the one at Birka described by Adam of Bremen, though in his own time this had long ceased to be important: 'all the ships of the Danes, the Norwegians, the Slavs, the Sembs, and other Baltic Sea tribes are accustomed to assemble there regularly to pursue their necessary affairs'.[59]

Compared with the older Viking era in the ninth century there was considerable growth in these centres in the tenth century, coupled with new foundations and shifts in site: Dublin and Novgorod, as we have seen, and one might also name Sigtuna, which took on Birka's role in the Mälar region from about 980 onwards. Only one of three settlements continued in existence at Haithabu, but this grew in the course of the century to a size of 24 ha. It was precisely the most important sites which displayed such growth: Wolin grew to 20 ha, Staraja Ladoga grew from 4–5 ha to 10 and Gnëzdowo from 4 to 15 ha. Most of the other sites lay between these last two (Birka 13, Dublin 12, Menzlin 10, Ribe 10); some, like the oldest settlement at Danzig (1) or Daugmale (2) were much smaller. Wolin and Haithabu thus headed the league table.

---

[58] *Egils Saga Skallagrímssonar*, c. 32, p. 100 (English trans. p. 82).
[59] Adam of Bremen, *Gesta* I, 60, p. 58.

The growth of these sites points to an intensification of exchange, and the composition of the coin hoards, which in the Baltic regions show a high proportion of Arab silver coins up to about 970, suggests that till then the west had a trade surplus, even if some of the dirhams which came westwards were derived from tribute-payments to the Varangians. Western exports certainly included woollen cloth, mentioned by Adam of Bremen and confirmed by archaeology in Birka and Wolin. Wine evidently also reached at least as far as the Baltic in considerable quantities. The most important role was probably played by the slave trade, however, whereby the product of Viking razzias in western Europe (Ireland in particular) was marketed in Scandinavia and the Muslim east. Haithabu and Brennö at the mouth of the Götaälv, as well as the Volga, are noted as points on this trade-route. The treaties between the princes of Kiev and Byzantium in the tenth century also mention slave-trading; the Russian regions were also a source of slaves. The high proportion of total trade made up by slaves is the most coherent explanation of the import of Arab silver and other wares (silk, for example, has been found in Birka, Wolin and Dublin). In the last quarter of the tenth century the structure of trade relationships changed. From now on western silver flowed towards the Baltic and Russia (see above, p. 66). This means that Russian exports of raw materials must have increased, most likely wax and furs, sought after by the west 'as much as eternal salvation'.[60] By contrast, the export of Christian slaves from the west to the Islamic east will have declined and then stopped; the reasons lay presumably in the monetary difficulties of the central Islamic realms, but also in the gradual Christianisation of the Scandinavian kingdoms from 965 and the increasing prosperity of north-west Europe.

Besides the principal items of trade – slaves, wax, furs and luxury goods – we find a wealth of other raw materials and craft goods, which were traded in large quantities over medium and long distances and marketed in the sites just mentioned: Rhineland glass and pottery, Scandinavian vessels of soapstone and metalware. Trade intensified in the Baltic region as well, and there was a lively exchange with the newly evolving market systems of the central European regions, especially in the Rhineland and in Saxony. That explains the special role played by Haithabu, the link to Scandinavian trade, but also by Wolin, which was of similar importance for its links down the Oder with the emerging lordships of central Sclavinia.

This intensification of trade in luxury consumer goods is certainly also the explanation for the location of craftsmen in the trading-centres of the North Sea and Baltic regions. Metal- and leather-working in particular can be confirmed archaeologically at various sites (Dublin, Haithabu, Wolin, Birka)

---

[60] Adam of Bremen, *Gesta* IV, 18, pp. 244–5.

and grew in importance in the eleventh century. The location of crafts contributed to the growth and the thickening of settlement at north European trading centres. In many cases these were wholly or partially fortified in the course of the tenth century, and there are suggestions that there was a layout of fixed plots. Nevertheless, these quasi-urban settlements were of very varied stability. Kaupang in Norway was abandoned at the beginning of the tenth century; Paviken on Gotland and Menzlin vanished around 1000, and Birka was gradually displaced by the royal centre of Sigtuna from about 970 onwards, while Haithabu was replaced in the eleventh century by Schleswig – the earliest cathedral may already have been built there in the time of Cnut. Dublin, the seat of Irish Viking lordship, the episcopal seat of Ribe, and the Russian princely towns continued in existence.

It is evident that lordship helped to stabilise economic centres as well as drawing economic functions to it. This is most evident in the inland regions of the west Slav peoples, where fortified towns like Gniezno, Cracow and Opole in Poland, Teterow, Brandenburg and Starigard (Oldenburg in Holstein) in the region between Elbe and Oder, or Kouřim, Liubice and above all Prague in Bohemia dominated the picture. These were multiple settlements including a lordly fortification, a *suburbium*, and craft working, for which there is archaeological evidence. They also evidently played a role in trade. Prague in particular, which as a centre of rulership came to surpass all other Bohemian fortifications in the last third of the ninth century, developed in the course of the tenth, with its extended *surburbium*, the Malá straná on the Vltava, to an inland trading-centre, in which, in the words of Ibrāhīm ibn Yaʿqūb, 'the Rus' and the Slavs from the city of Cracow' and 'Muslims and Jews from the lands of the Turks' came together in a polyethnic market similar to those of the maritime trading-centres of the Baltic region.[61] In the Baltic the foundations for the later-medieval trading history of northern Europe, shaped by the Hanse, were laid in the ninth and tenth centuries. The emporia of the northern Baltic on which this development was based had an urban functionality, or at least fulfilled in great part the roles characteristic of towns in later centuries. But in themselves they were mostly not the starting point of the urban development of the high middle ages, tending rather to disappear again. Towns came into being for the most part in places where markets and trade were linked with centres of secular or ecclesiastical power, as in Dublin, Ribe, Sigtuna, Novgorod and Kiev. That is equally true of inland Sclavinia, where although emporia like those on the Baltic were unknown, casual markets are mentioned. But no town emerged from the unlocalisable 'market of the Moravians' mentioned in the Raffelstetten toll-ordinance;[62] it was Prague, a centre of lordship, which was to become a town.

[61] *Arabische Berichte*, p. 12.   [62] *MGH Cap.*, no. 253, ii.249–52.

Thus it was that the north-eastern region of Europe, which contributed so significantly to European economic development, had little effect on the development of the town in the high middle ages. It is also unclear how far tenth-century conditions in this region contributed to the formation of that type of long-distance trader and merchant which was to have such a strong influence on the institutional development of towns in the eleventh and twelfth century. Trade in the Viking era was carried out by merchants who were also often active as raiders or as warlike conquerors demanding tribute. The written sources give the impression that trade was in many cases only a part of their economic activity (as for instance with the landowner Ohtere) or was practised only for a part of their life-cycle. These traders operated in communities, as runic inscriptions occasionally reveal. But we are evidently dealing with short-lived and casual communities with no fixed location, not with long-term unions bound by oaths as with the merchant guilds of the European continent (see above). Such corporations are evidenced in Scandinavia, as in Tiel, only in the runic inscriptions of the eleventh century. By contrast with western and southern Europe we know little about the shaping and maintenance of the market peace, or the self-organisation of the merchants, or the form and extent of the influence exerted by princely power. We must therefore conclude that essential features of the medieval town – both its social and juridic make-up and its topography and visual image – were formed in the core of Carolingian Europe, in the *civitates* of northern Italy, and of the west and east Frankish kingdoms. In these *civitates* and settlements of similar structure the importance of ministerial dependants of lords and of prosperous and increasingly professional long-distance traders, with a tendency to form guilds and settle permanently, grew in the course of the tenth century. Governmental peace ordinances to regulate the market were conceived here. All this was an anticipation of the later distinctions between the legal and social spheres of urban and of rural life, so that already around 1000 Notker the German could contrast *purlich* and *gebûrlich*, 'townly' and 'farmerly'.[63] This distinction took on its final form once institutional structures had been developed for the social formation of the town between the eleventh and the thirteenth century.

But it was above all the growth visible everywhere and its associated building activity which shaped the characteristic picture of the medieval European town. It was the great stone buildings of the church and of rulers which were decisive here, and these were being imitated in the Slavonic east even in our period: Ibrāhīm ibn Yaʿqūb stresses that the city of Prague was built of stone and mortar.[64] The equipping of *civitates* with a ring-wall and a multiplicity of churches, often located according to a preconceived plan, was the manifestation of an urban ideal which lords gave architectural form. It modelled itself

---

[63] Notker the German, *Werke* I, p. 111.   [64] *Arabische Berichte*, p. 12.

on the 'Holy City', as for example when Meinwerk of Paderborn is said to have built his episcopal city 'in the form of a cross'.[65] The rich stores of relics and the frequently attempted or at least invoked imitation of the example of Rome, *the* city of antiquity, are important elements of this tenth-century urban idea. The picture of walls, churches and towers as a city's *ornatus* belongs to the inheritance bequeathed by the tenth century to the cities of the European middle ages, who have preserved it as an abbreviated symbol of urbanity in depictions on their seals.

[65] 'in modum crucis': *Vita Meinverci episcopi Patherbrunnensis*, c. 218, p. 131.

CHAPTER 4

RULERS AND GOVERNMENT

Janet L. Nelson

Tenth-century churchmen emphasised the kingship of Christ, and made kingship Christ-centred. They called on the earthly king to be Christ's special imitator. Like Christ, the king must willingly undergo travails: like Christ's, a king's service, even his humiliation, brought glory to him and well-being to his people. The theologians were also preoccupied with Antichrist. They pondered the end of time, scanning their natural environment for supernatural signs and portents. All of them believed that they lived during the Last of the Four Empires predicted by Daniel in the Old Testament. The Last World Emperor would, according to prophecy, establish a reign of peace, vanquishing the enemies of Christ. Then would follow the Last Days: the brief rule of Antichrist, and the Second Coming of Christ himself. These learned men were ecclesiastics, many of them monks. But they were in close contact with the secular world, and among the leading counsellors of kings and queens. When the learned produced political thought, monarchy dominated their speculations. Kings were frequently their addressees.

Monarchy could take the form of empire. Only in Italy perhaps, among western lands, was there still a sense of Constantinople as the imperial centre of the 'Roman' world. Elsewhere, imperial rule tended to be non-Roman, and defined in terms of rulership over a number of realms. While the Carolingian model inspired the Ottonian Reich, it had become clear by the close of the tenth century that the kings of the west Frankish realm recognised no imperial overlord. In Poland and Hungary, Otto III, strongly influenced by such learned tutors as Gerbert of Rheims, may have seen himself as summoning a new world of kings into existence to redress the balance of the old; but his attempt at a Roman 'renovation' was bound up with ecclesiastical reform and had eschatological dimensions. Kingship too could be viewed in apocalyptic perspective. Adso of Montier-en-Der, writing *c.* 950, believed that the kings of the (west) Franks protected the world from Antichrist: 'as long as their rule endures, the dignity of the Roman realm will not wholly perish'.[1] Tenth-century west Frankish kings could also be credited with a realm that was 'imperial' because it consisted of several entities called *regna* (regions dignified as such whether or not they had once been independent kingdoms).[2] England, another imperial realm in that sense, was actually created in the tenth century. In the 990s, when that new realm was subjected to renewed Scandinavian onslaughts, the theologian Ælfric, who believed himself to be living at the end of time, celebrated Edgar's far-flung overlordship and preached the virtue of obedience to divinely instituted monarchy.[3] His message was spread widely: Ælfric's medium was English, and his audience included the local nobility as well as monks.

Tenth-century historians – Widukind, Liudprand, Flodoard, Richer – produced powerful images of royalty. For these writers, all of them monks or clerics, the deeds of kings continued to be the stuff of history, hence of moral lessons. Classical models, especially Sallust, hovered behind these texts. Yet Widukind seemed also to reflect his contemporaries' confidence in the special qualities of kings: their capacity to bring victory and well-being. Some twentieth-century German commentators have heard echoes here of what they have labelled Germanic notions of *Heil*: Widukind drew, more certainly, on the Old Testament. The lives of royal saints were another lively genre: in Ottonian Saxony Queen Matilda, widow of Henry I, was venerated in a court-linked monastic cult not long after her death, while in England the west Frankish visitor Abbo of Fleury counterposed to the martyred King Edmund of the east Angles (died 871) the martyr's Viking persecutor as archetypical bad ruler.[4] Saint-kings, and -queens, were depicted as holy not *ex officio*, but through special personal qualities. While such ancestors shed charisma on descendants, none of this should be seen as ecclesiastical flirtation with pre-Christian ideas of sacral kingship. Only some fairly heavy interpretation of Flodoard's and Richer's accounts of the deaths of successive tenth-century west Frankish kings has allowed modern scholars to hypothesise popular belief in the last Carolingians' loss of royal thaumaturgic powers.[5] What the *Histories* and the *Lives* alike convey is a profound confidence in Christian rulership, and the capacity of churchmen and -women to construct potent images thereof.

Arbitration and protection were recurrent needs; and, even in regions where kings were weak, or seldom if ever came, it was remembered – in Christian

---

[1] Adso, *Epistula ad Gerbergam reginam*, p. 26.

[2] Richer, *Historiae* IV, 12, p. 162; cf. Hugh, charters 3, 10, (*RHF* 10, pp. 550, 560).

[3] Ælfric, *Lives of the Saints*, pp. 468–70; partial trans. *EHD*, pp. 927–8.

[4] Abbo of Fleury, *Vita Sancti Eadmundi*, cc. 7–10, cols. 511–15.

[5] Flodoard, *Annales*, *s.a.* 954, p. 138, Richer, *Historiae* III, 109, p. 127, as interpreted by Poly and Bournazel (1991), pp. 499–500.

lands, the Bible and the liturgy offered constant reminders – that the provision of justice and peace had been and still were the function of kings. Especially in the western parts of what had been the Carolingian empire, clerical and lay ideals converged on the figure of Charlemagne, dispenser of justice and follower of wise counsel as well as mighty warlord. Several generations before the earliest extant manuscript of the Song of Roland was written, Adhémar of Chabannes wrote of the just rule of Charlemagne and 'knew' that he had extended his realm as far as Córdoba.[6] Social memory, transmitted through vernacular songs, perpetuated for the denizens of secular courts a vision of monarchy capable of bearing apocalyptic expectations. Early in the tenth century, King Louis of Provence, himself (like many leading figures) of Carolingian descent on his mother's side, named his son Charles-Constantine. At the century's close, in the year 1000, Otto III visited Charlemagne's tomb at Aachen.[7]

Though theologians tended to measure by millennia, historians were absorbed by the here-and-now. Flodoard of Rheims, who wrote of his own church's past in the expansive genre of History, used Annals for recent political events, crowding each year with details of royal activity. Yet far beyond the scholar's study, and beyond Rheims, the existence of kings, and the legitimising force of that existence, were known and felt. Monks and clerics in Burgundy, the Limousin, the Midi, used royal reign-years to date the documents of powerful laymen.[8] The cults of saints particularly associated with the monarchy were widespread. A tale recorded in the *Life of Odo of Cluny* shows St Martin concerning himself directly with west Frankish royalty: a hermit somewhere in the south of France saw him one day (it should have been 19 June 936) in a vision – briefly, for the saint explained that it was the day of the king's (Louis IV's) consecration and he had to be there at Rheims.[9] This may not be history, but it resembles the work of the Rheims historians in keeping a whole realm in view. The same is truer still of historiography in the east Frankish realm. Widukind, Hrotsvitha, and the authors of the Quedlinburg Annals, based though they all were in Saxony, narrated the deeds of kings and magnates throughout the kingdom, with the itinerant court providing a strong central focus.

Elsewhere, it was not historiography which promoted any realm-wide vision. This is not surprising in the new and still essentially non-literate kingdoms of the tenth century: Denmark, Norway, Poland, Hungary. In all of these, we shall see (below, pp. 107–12) the deployment of oral, visual and cultic media. Kings found similar ways of fostering the image, and the social reality, of a united realm in England too, and perhaps more surprisingly, an earlier

---

[6] Adhémar, *Chronicon* II, 1, p. 68.   [7] Thietmar, *Chronicon* IV, 47, pp. 184/6; Görich (1998).
[8] Kienast (1969).   [9] John of Salerno, *Vita Sancti Odonis*, c. 27, col. 55.

royal interest in the maintenance and diffusion of a chronicle record was allowed to lapse. In the Italian kingdom, there was, still, a state of sorts, but there had not grown up, since the Frankish conquest, any tradition of royal annals. Literacy, here relatively abundant, remained closely linked with law and government, which turned out to be operable without kings and at local level. Here, in the absence of any court-centred, realm-focused historiographical tradition, laymen wielded power without looking to kings to legitimate it. Where men no longer thought positively about kings, it was difficult to imagine a kingdom. In this respect, Italy in the tenth century was different from other post-Carolingian lands. And even in Italy, but still more clearly elsewhere in Frankish Europe, an ideal-type of Carolingian government was transmitted to the learned through the written residue of capitularies, conciliar decrees and documents. Manuscripts of capitularies continued to be copied in episcopal scriptoria during the tenth century. In the 990s, Abbo of Fleury commended, and cited at length, to Kings Hugh and Robert the conciliar canons with which their predecessors Charlemagne and Louis the Pious had promoted the well-being of both 'state' (*respublica*) and church.[10] Among the books consulted by Bishop Fulbert of Chartres, when *c.* 1020 he wrote to Duke William of Aquitaine on fidelity, was almost certainly a capitulary collection.[11] Sacramentaries and pontificals, in all the realms of the former empire including Italy, continued to include prayers for kings. Law and liturgy, as well as songs and stories, were forms of social memory in which Carolingian traditions survived.

In the course of the tenth century, the patrilinear dynastic link with the Carolingians was broken in both west and east Frankish kingdoms: Carolingian traditions, attached to kingship itself, could be taken up by Capetians as well as Ottonians, and also were readily exported outside the old Frankish lands, most notably to England where Edgar's regime was a passable imitation of Carolingian models. Contemporary writers who imagined, and tried to influence, the workings of kingship did not neglect royal marriages. As the parvenu Henry I sought to extend his power into the Lotharingian heart of the Frankish world and to achieve wide acknowledgement of his legitimacy, he married his daughter to the leading Lotharingian magnate Gislebert and his son Otto married the English princess Edith. Otto looked further afield to find a bride for his son: when Otto II married the Byzantine princess Theophanu, the Frankish world opened out to realms beyond it, prefiguring a wider Europe. Foreign princesses brought the prestige of other royal lineages. Those brides had the advantage of relative detachment from demanding aristocratic families within the realm. Alternatively, kings would marry into just such fami-

---

[10] Abbo of Fleury, *Liber canonum*, PL 139, col 477.   [11] Fulbert, *ep.* 51, pp. 90–2.

lies to gain the countervailing advantage of regional alliance and support: Matilda, second wife of Henry the Fowler and mother of Otto I, was chosen for her powerful Saxon connections; the west Frankish queen Adelaide, wife and mother of the first two Capetians, was herself the daughter of the duke of Aquitaine; while the English king Edgar married successively the daughters of leading nobles in the west and south-east of his realm. The enhanced political role of the queen – as Widukind said of Matilda, 'she would sit while around her the people stood'[12] – was a striking feature of the tenth century. These women were called *dominae*.[13] in translation, the pallid modern English 'ladies' hardly conveys something akin to lordliness in their authority. The Virgin could be imagined as *domina* enthroned, and even crowned.[14]

TENTH-CENTURY KINGDOMS

In 888, the 'old' Carolingian realms had (as Regino put it) created kings out of their own guts.[15] The pattern of the mid-ninth century was resumed: a three-way division, with east and west Frankish kings vying for an increasingly frag-mented Middle Kingdom. The later existence of the separate states of France and Germany has tended to evoke assumptions of historical inevitability on the part of French and German historians. Yet there were forces at work in the successor-kingdoms of Charlemagne's empire which could have led to other outcomes. On the one hand, Frankish unity remained a reality until late in the tenth century. Eastern and western kings continued to vie for Lotharingia; some members of the east and west Frankish elites, and hence the kingdoms they sustained, remained bound together, frontierless. The marriage of Otto I's sister to the west Frankish king Louis IV was at once symptom and agency of a close entente that came close to Ottonian hegemony in mid-century. On the other hand, the regionalisation of the elite had gone a long way, and the leading families of the *regna* most distant from the Lotharingian core – the Billungs in east Saxony, for instance, or the Poitevin dukes of Aquitaine – lacked any perceptible pan-Frankish perspective. Some of the old resources were no longer available to tenth-century Frankish kings in east or west: lack of ancient royal lineage was a drawback for Ottonians and Capetians alike, and there was seldom much to offer in the way of plunder, tribute or territorial expansion. Where earlier Carolingian rulers had sometimes been able to make and, more rarely, break powerful men, by conferring, withholding and redis-tributing comital office, this was manifestly more difficult in the tenth century as countships and the lands that went with them were inherited over several

---

[12] Widukind, *Res gestae Saxonicae* III, 74, p. 125.   [13] Gerbert, *epp.* 62, 66, pp. 61, 64.
[14] von Euw (1991), pp. 122–4; cf. Deshman (1988).   [15] Regino, *Chronicon, s.a.* 888, p. 129.

generations. Aristocrats' own regional power always tended to become entrenched, with house-monasteries and the privatised cults of saints reproducing in their patrimonies the local domination effected by each royal dynasty's religious patronage in its heartlands. In east and to a lesser extent west Francia, the identities of regions still dignified as *regna* within the realm remained clearly etched. In both realms, the period *c.* 920 was especially critical: at that point, it was no foregone conclusion that either would survive as a political unit instead of falling apart into constituent *regna*. By *c.* 1000, however, the survival of both was no longer in doubt.

This change – one of the most striking features of the tenth century – is not easy to explain. It can hardly be attributed solely to the policies and doings of the rulers themselves, given the relative lack of royal resources already noted especially in west Francia. Rather, the focus needs to be widened socially to include the aristocracy, for it was their perceptions of interest and of what constituted legitimate power which allowed the perpetuation, in each case, of a regnal community.[16] Some ideological preconditions have already been sketched: the Carolingian legacy of the preceding century was clearly crucial. As for Italy: its long-term disunity was further crystallised, as the Carolingian *regnum Italiae* became part of the Ottonian empire, though, necessarily, given often distant rulers, a very distinct part with its own forms of devolved and indigenous power, while Byzantines, Lombards and Arabs vied for the south. Thus the three Carolingian successor-states became two; and the tenth century was also the crucial formative period for the long-lasting linkage of Germany and Italy.

The continuity of Burgundy's royal line, acknowledged by other dynasties who intermarried with it, enabled that kingdom to persist throughout the tenth century, though more or less dependent on the Ottonians. This was a sub-Carolingian realm, in which Carolingian traditions and modes of rulership – titles and charter-diplomatic, signs and symbols, the local church's ideological and institutional support – had a continuous history.

A variant explanation is needed when we turn to the lands formerly on the periphery of the old empire. Here, kings newly emerged from the ranks of noble warlords were constructing new realms in León-Castile, Denmark, Poland and Hungary. The timing, and the location, of these changes was not fortuitous: people just beyond the frontiers of powerful states, and hence on the receiving end of their neighbours' aggression, had learned to unite in self-defence, and their leaders to copy something of their adversaries' methods. The brunt of the English kingdom's growing and self-consciously English power was borne by their neighbours. Both Welsh and Scots responded with a

---

[16] 'regnal': Reynolds (1984), p. 254.

growing sense of their own identity, and new manifestations of royal authority, notably in the reigns of Hywel Dda and Constantine II. But, thanks to the vagaries of dynastic alliance, far-flung water-borne contacts and chance, it was also through the English kingdom that Carolingian traditions were to be further diffused to Denmark and Hungary.

Ethnicity played only a limited part in new regnal formations. The world of ninth-century Latin Christendom had been a world dominated by the Franks. Even though the Carolingian rulers had not used an ethnic epithet in their official titles, theirs was a Frankish empire, won by Frankish arms. Yet it was never ruled by Frankish laws: rather what constituted its unity was Latin Christianity maintained by Carolingian power. And it remained polyethnic in legal, and social, reality. The Frankish identity which survived in social memory through story and history, and, extended to western Europeans in general, was acknowledged by outsiders for centuries to come, was more myth than fact. Carolingian traditions were detachable from it, and could help form the base of new identities. A ninth-century Carolingian had entitled himself just *rex dei gratia*. It was in the tenth century, from 911 onwards, that *rex Francorum* became the normal title of west Frankish kings. Though the process was slow, the ruler of the east Frankish kingdom by the end of the tenth century had lost specific close association with Franconia, the properly Frankish area of the eastern realm: the kings of the Franks and Saxons were on the way to becoming German rulers. Other new political formations acquired ethnic labels in the tenth century. *Rex Anglorum* became the usual title of kings who extended their power northwards from Wessex. In Poland, what had been eight distinct groupings were replaced, in the mid-tenth century, by the single Polish *potestas* of Miesco. Invented ethnicities then as now papered over political cracks: in association with kingship itself, they too offered a basis for regnal identity – a basis which could be detached from any particular dynasty, and hence could bridge dynastic change.

Dynastic strategies, dynastic accidents, were in part responsible for the crystallisation of all those tenth-century realms. Kingship remained embedded in family structures and family politics. For most kings, the royal family was the environment in which they were born and grew up. In the kingdoms created out of the ninth-century Carolingian empire, though by 1000 the direct Carolingian line had been extinguished in all of them, the assumption remained that there would *be* a ruling dynasty; and it was around dynasties that new kingdoms were being created, in central Europe, Denmark, England and Wales.

Yet in this same tenth century, kingship became institutionalised in new ways that showed it outgrowing the family. In the evolving identity of realms, kingship came to play an increasingly central role. The distinction between family resources and regnal resources became less blurred. In the east Frankish kingdom, the non-Carolingian Conrad I claimed (even if unsuccessfully) control of regnal lands in Bavaria, far from his own hereditary property. In west Francia, non-Carolingian kings contrived, in the 920s and again after 987, to resume regnal lands from Carolingian claimants: indeed in 987, arguably, it was only thus, by insisting that royal estates *were* regnal, that Capetian power could be established at all. In Italy, the payment of regnal dues (the *fodrum*) was so well established at Pavia that these continued to be collected by royal officers throughout the second half of the tenth century: though the rulers of the *regnum Italiae* were frequent absentees, they stayed there often enough, and for long enough, to maintain plausible claims. Conrad II was depicted by his biographer early in the eleventh century as having a very clear sense of the distinction between a private home and the palace as a public building.[17]

Two aspects of this recognition of the difference between kingship and family deserve special attention. First, the royal succession was more consciously and collectively managed. There were pre-mortem arrangements: in east Francia, Otto I's son and namesake became co-ruler in 961, co-emperor in 972, while in west Francia, Lothar made his son Louis V co-ruler in 979, and Hugh Capet, himself consecrated on 3 July 987, had his own son Robert consecrated as co-ruler on Christmas Day of the same year. The church absorbed surplus royals: the illegitimate younger son of Otto I and the illegitimate oldest son of the west Frankish Lothar. Violence within royal families did not cease, but, when it did occur, was publicly mourned, as in the case of the east Frankish Thankmar whose killing was disavowed by his half-brother Otto I, or the Anglo-Saxon Edward, of whose murder a contemporary asserted: 'no worse deed than this for the English people was committed since first they came to Britain'.[18] The 'people', that is, the aristocracy, were often recorded as electors of kings, not only when there was a change of dynasty, but also on other occasions including the creation of co-rulers. Nobles thus participated actively in the management of the succession, and this was occasionally acknowledged by the draftsmen of royal documents.[19] When noble factions supported rebellion, they aimed at the restoration of king-centred politics and dynastic unity. In 953–4, the supporters of Otto I's rebellious son Liudolf justified their action by alleging that the king's new bride, Adelaide, and his brother Henry had colluded to monopolise counsel.[20] Insisting on their role – at once right and responsibility – as advisers of kings, magnates imposed standards of royal conduct. In the 920s, it was in the name of those standards, because 'Charles [nicknamed *Simplex*, 'the Straightforward'] listened to and

---

[17] Wipo, *Gesta*, c. 7, p. 7.　　[18] Widukind, *Res gestae Saxonicae* II, 11, p. 65; *ASC, s.a.* 978, in *EHD*, p. 230.
[19] D Lo 4; Sawyer, no. 520.　　[20] Hrotsvitha, *Gesta Ottonis*, ed. Winterfeld, lines 735–40, p. 225.

honoured above his leading men (*principes*) his counsellor Hagano whom he had picked from among the lesser nobility (*mediocres*)[21] and, again, 'hearing that Charles planned to summon the Northmen to join him' against his own Franks, that those Franks definitively rejected Charles, chose another king, and kept Charles locked up. (The magnate who, 300 years later, reminded the English king Henry III of Charles' fate was angered, similarly, by royal failure to be counselled aright.[22]) The Frankish chronicler noted parallel events in far-off Italy, where magnates 'disturbed the realm because of their king's insolence'.[23] 'Disturbance' was a legitimate form of resistance. In west Francia, the key point was precisely that Charles was replaced, and another king was chosen. King and magnates needed and sustained each other. By the close of the tenth century, Abbo of Fleury had summarised that mutual dependence in a neat pun: 'since the king on his own is insufficient for all the needs of the realm, having distributed the burden (*onere*) amongst the others whom he believes worthy of honour (*honore*) he too must be honoured (*honorandus est*) with sincere devotion'.[24] Only a few years later, in 1014, the author of the *Anglo-Saxon Chronicle* strongly implied that loss of magnate support rather than Danish invasion drove Æthelred into foreign refuge: he returned when 'sent for' by 'all the councillors', but on condition that 'he would govern his kingdom more justly'.[25]

The magnates' active role as counsellors, hence not just self-appointed but widely acknowledged representatives, of the realm contributed to a second important tenth-century change: the tendency for realms to become indivisible. In transjurane Burgundy a divided succession was rejected when Rudolf I was succeeded by only one of his two sons, Rudolf II, in 912. Three other similar instances occurred elsewhere soon after: in 919, east Frankish and Saxon nobles (though not Bavarians) combined to choose Henry the Fowler as king; in 922, west Frankish nobles acted in similar fashion to replace Charles the Simple by Robert; and in 924–5, the choice of Mercian and west Saxon nobles converged on Æthelstan. With hindsight, these events can be seen as critical for the realms in question: and the near-coincidence was not fortuitous. Though other options were available, in each case a regnal community at most three generations old was recognised, and kept in being. Once an undivided succession had occurred for a further generation or two, division became increasingly improbable, and eventually unthinkable. If Mercia and Wessex parted company again, briefly, in 957, that was symptomatic of the persistence of two regnal communities that long pre-dated the later ninth century. Sundered again briefly under pressure of Danish invasion in 1016, the two

---

[21] Flodoard, *HRE* IV, 15, p. 577.   [22] Bémont (1884), appendix, p. 341.
[23] Flodoard, *Annales*, *s.a.* 922, p. 7.   [24] Abbo of Fleury, *Liber canonum*, *PL* 139, col 478.
[25] *ASC*, version 'E', *s.a.* 1014, p. 246.

were reunited a year later in what proved a permanent union of the crowns. By then, multi-gentile royal titles like 'king of the Saxons, Mercians and Northumbrians' had fallen from use in charters (though this one survived in some *ordines* manuscripts), to be uniformly and definitively replaced by 'king of the English'.

It was not that anyone formulated a principle of indivisibility (*Unteilbarkeit*) or primogeniture. Dynastic accident played a part, allowing unity to persist long enough for custom to congeal. In the east Frankish realm (and also the Italian one) Otto I, then Otto II, died leaving just one legitimate male heir. In west Francia, however, the choice of Hugh Capet in 987 was not imposed by lack of a Carolingian alternative: Charles of Lorraine was deliberately rejected. According to Richer, the archbishop of Rheims recommended Hugh to the magnates as one 'whom you will find a protector of private interests as well as of the public interest'.[26] The dwindling of royal resources had already meant that separate subkingdoms for younger brothers could no longer be funded: hence the dangerous poverty of Charles of Lorraine. In England, the fact that Æthelstan remained unmarried, hence heirless, could suggest a family pact whereby an older man ruled as a kind of stake-holder for younger half-brothers: fraternal succession jostled with filial succession in tenth-century England. Here as elsewhere younger brothers or nephews (and their potential supporters) reconciled themselves, more or less willingly, to exclusion: the several sons of Æthelred II were not endowed with subkingdoms in their father's lifetime (the final, desperate, bid by Edmund Ironside in 1016 was a unique exception). Successions were disputed by would-be rulers of whole realms, with division increasingly infrequent. In the kingdom of León-Castile, as in England, there were several cases of fraternal succession in the tenth century. The nine-year regency (966–75) of Elvira, daughter of Ramiro II and abbess of the royal house-convent of San Salvador in the city of León, for her young nephew Ramiro III (born 961), the first royal minority in Leonese history, indicates a new stability of the realm. Here as elsewhere, the aristocracy's role is better attributed, positively, to support for the dynasty than, negatively, to egoistic hopes of exploiting a royal minority. Where nobles collectively continued to invest in a regnal tradition, that realm tended to survive as a unit; and, where charters are available to document this, nobles' titles and self-presentation suggest that they considered themselves kings' collaborators, subordinates and surrogates. Even if they were normally based far away, they were potentially involved in face-to-face contacts with kings. Their exercise of lordship was in principle legitimated by being part of the realm. There was no alternative ecclesiastical legitimation for nobles: they remained, as Richard Southern observed

---

[26] Richer, *Historiae* IV, 11, p. 162: 'non solum rei publicae sed et privatarum rerum tutorem invenietis'.

of west Frankish counts, 'shockingly unconsecrated and dumb',[27] lacking, that is, theoreticians or apologists: the church called down heavenly blessings upon kings but provided no separate prayers for nobles. The evidence for the development of princely accession-ceremonies of various kinds (though never including anointing) post-dates the tenth century.[28]

In the lands beyond the Carolingian empire, other factors helped determine whether a kingdom materialised and/or persisted. England's formation is partly explicable in terms of the familiar dynamic of acquisition and reward that enabled the west Saxon kings, not without setbacks, to mount a kind of imperial expansion against the Danelaw and at the same time consolidate support in English England. Even the resultant composite realm was relatively small compared with France and Germany; and smallness allowed that greater degree of cohesion which continues to impress modern English historians. Another important factor was linguistic community: despite regional variations, Old English could be understood throughout the realm, the more readily once efforts had been made in the second half of the tenth century to standardise the written vernacular.

How did the Ottonians manage in a realm so very much larger? Because both date and place are recorded in their charters, the Ottonians' itineraries can be reconstructed. There were three core regions: the Harz area of Saxony (where in the 950s, happily for the Ottonians, silver lodes were discovered), lower Lotharingia around Aachen, and the Rhine–Main area (with key bases at Ingelheim and at Frankfurt where Henry's son Otto I stayed often). In holding onto their palaces and estates in the latter two regions, the Ottonians continued Carolingian patterns. In their relentless journeyings, the Ottonians signalled, and exploited, the dual basis of their regime and its legitimacy: they were 'kings of the Saxons and the Franks'. At home in Saxony itself, they preferred the monasteries and convents staffed by their own, and the aristocracy's, kin. Two convents, Quedlinburg and Gandersheim, had special importance, both with Ottonian abbesses who became icons of the royal house in their own right. Between them these places performed the key functions of dynastic centres: guardianship of the tomb of the dynasty's founder, keeping of collective memories of royal deeds, providing of frequent hospitality for the court, hosting of great assemblies, and last but not least praying for the prosperity of king and realm. These indeed provided the ritual centre of the kingdom. The Ottonians were able to draw into it the powerful from the various *regna* of their realm so that the net of intermittent contacts spread wide. Churchmen kept the net in repair. In their minds the realm was a *res publica* – and the distinction between that and private interests remained. Abbot John of Saint-Arnulf, Metz

---

[27] Southern (1953), p. 99.   [28] Hoffmann (1962).

depicted his hero and namesake John of Gorze as ready to leave a rustic 'private life' for the twin challenges of involvement in spiritual reform and in royal service.[29] Thus Carolingian habits of thinking proved resilient: they sustained, at any rate for churchmen, habits of acting that took John of Gorze from country to court and, eventually, far beyond the frontiers of the Reich.

What made the little kingdoms viable, still, was not only their adequate economic base in land and cattle but their rootedness in law and tradition. In Ireland, where geography might seem to have predestined an island-state, the past continued to dominate the present: despite external threats, no High Kingship was established covering the whole island. Regional overkingships emerged fitfully: four eventually survived (Tara, Cashel, Connacht and Leinster), but several others proved shortlived. More important, many little kingdoms, *tuatha* only 16–20 kilometres in radius, survived as well, with kings unsubordinated to any higher-level ruler. In the old Carolingian lands, transjurane Burgundy which became a kingdom late in the ninth century outlasted the tenth, partly because geography protected it, still more because of dynastic continuity. Brittany, on the other hand, failed to survive as a realm into the tenth century. Smallness of scale was not the only, or most, important reason: dynastic disputes at a critical moment inhibited the formation of identity around an indigenous kingship, while Viking attacks crippled the ruler's resources. Still more fundamentally, political traditions, and not least ecclesiastical ones keeping all the Breton sees suffragans of Tours, situated Brittany firmly within the west Frankish realm.

Elsewhere, nascent kingdoms were able to maintain and expand their territorial range, and at the same time to integrate, more or less effectively, their internal spaces. Though scarcely anything can be known of royal itineraries, efforts to establish royal cult-centres can be inferred. In Scotland, under Constantine II, St Andrews became such a centre, representing a substantial eastwards shift in focus and a determined appropriation of the resources of the former Pictish kingdom. Glastonbury, in the ancient heartlands and 'more princely part'[30] of Wessex, especially after Edgar's burial there, bid fair to establish its claims to that role in England. In the 980s, the chain of Harald's fortresses in Denmark linked old and new centres, with a pronounced shift eastwards towards the resources of southern Sweden. Poland and Hungary evinced a similar process of political centring with the choice of sites for the new bishoprics of Gniezno (1000) and Gran (1001). Still-migratory monarchs were nevertheless conscious of where the seat of the realm lay.

---

[29] *Vita Iohannis Gorziensis*, c. 51, p. 351.   [30] Asser, *Life of King Alfred*, c. 12, ed. Stevenson, p. 10.

ROYAL RITUALS

In the tenth century, the king-making rites pioneered by Frankish clergy in Carolingian times became more or less standardised and generalised through much of Latin Christendom, acquiring permanent form as liturgical *ordines*. These rituals were specific to kingship, marking, and demarcating, the uniqueness of monarchy. The role of clergy in elaborating such rituals was crucial, but laity played their part too. Even in the *ordines* themselves, the aristocracy's role is evident, as witnesses and primary audience, even as active participants in the acclamation and enthronement of the new king. While clergy now stage-managed and took leading roles in proceedings inside the church, lay leaders were conspicuous in other rituals performed outside the church. *Principes* acknowledged the new ruler in a form of election preceding the liturgical rite. They served, and joined in consuming, the food and drink at the banquet following the clerical proceedings. They accompanied the new king on the journey through his realm in which he presented himself, symbolically and practically, to his new subjects. The *ordines* thus give only a partial picture. It is the historical writers, and especially Widukind and Byrhtferth, who reveal something of the full and lengthy process whereby kings were made and displayed. Together, the two very different types of source-material, history and liturgy, throw light on one important way in which kingdoms took shape as political communities in this period.

The clericalising of a substantial part of the process did not happen uniformly, or necessarily in linear progression. The Carolingian realms of the eighth and ninth centuries were diverse in substructure, and underwent varying experiences. This diversity in formation helps account for important differences in the tenth century, especially between east and west Francia. In the post-843 east Frankish kingdom, it is possible that no king was consecrated by local clergy before Conrad I in 911 (Charles the Fat apparently had himself consecrated in 880 by the pope). In any event, when Henry the Fowler in 919 decided to forgo anointing by the archbishop of Mainz, he was not breaking with long-established tradition. Modern historians have argued that acceptance of consecration made a king-elect in a sense behoven to his main consecrator, and it is true that Henry mistrusted the archbishop. It is unlikely, though, that Henry was driven by anxieties about clerical control. Complex discussions with lay magnates probably account for the five-month delay between his predecessor's death in December 918 and his 'designation' in May 919 by 'the whole people of the Franks and Saxons'.[31] He may have wanted to display to his key supporters in Saxony his independence of Franconian domination. Perhaps still more important, given the strength of the component *regna* within

---

[31] Widukind, *Res gestae Saxonicae* I, 26, p. 34.

his realm, he needed to reassure the greatest magnates (*duces*) of those other *regna* that he meant to respect what they saw as their customary rights, and would be committed to a consensual style of government: this was what they were to understand by Henry's friendship (*amicitia*). The prestige of Henry's monarchy grew. His successor was not only acclaimed by *duces* and *milites* outside Charlemagne's church at Aachen, but also consecrated inside it.[32] A generation later, an elaborate east Frankish royal *ordo* (formed in part from west Frankish ingredients) was included in the Romano-Germanic Pontifical copied at Mainz and widely diffused.[33] According to this rite, the *designatus princeps* divests himself of cloak and weapons, and prostrates himself in front of the altar steps. Spiritually abased, symbolically annihilated, he rises to assume a new persona. He swears to 'rule and defend his people according to the custom of their forefathers', and clergy and people acclaim him. The anointing signals the transformation of *princeps* into *rex*, making him strong against his enemies and capable of ruling his people justly. There follow his re-arming, and reinvestiture with arm-rings, cloak and sceptre, his coronation, and his enthronement whereby he is raised up in the manner of David and Solomon, 'to be king over God's people'. This *ordo* was used for Otto I's successors. By the end of the tenth century, Ottonian monarchy had reached new heights of exalted representation and display, both in the private form of book-illumination and in the rather public form of table-manners at court, with the ruler dining alone and on high. Otto III was of course an emperor, and imitating Byzantium.[34] By *c.* 1000, though no other ruler in the west would or could match Otto's pretensions, rites of royal consecration were in regular use in Spain, France and England; and even where they were not, as in Scotland or Denmark, Christian glosses were starting to be superimposed on indigenous rulership. Mentions of queen-makings, often linked with marriage, became more frequent in narrative sources, and pontificals began to offer queenly *ordines*: in one widely diffused rite, the prayer accompanying investiture with the ring assigned the queen responsibility for spreading knowledge of the faith among barbarian peoples.[35]

Royal funerals, relatively unremarked earlier, become better documented in the tenth century. In the old Carolingian realms, the explanation is not that these rites had been newly clericalised: rather, increased attention was being focused on them by kings, but also by leading clergy and laymen. In 973, Otto I's funeral became the occasion for a re-enactment of his son's election '*ab integro*, by the whole people', and the *electus* then bore the old emperor's body to

[32] Widukind, *Res gestae Saxonicae* II, 1, p. 55.
[33] *Pontifical Romano-Germanique*, ed. Vogel and Elze, I, 246–59.
[34] Thietmar, *Chronicon* IV, 47, p. 184.
[35] 'Erdmann' *Ordo*, prayer 'Accipe anulum': Schramm (1968), p. 221.

Magdeburg for burial.[36] The west Frankish king Lothar in 986 was given 'a magnificent royal funeral' at Rheims, his corpse, clad in gold and purple, carried on a special royal bed by the leading men (*primates*) of the *regna* (the plural enhances the imperial stature of the kingdom – *regnum* – to which, a few lines further on, his son succeeds), with the regalia and especially the 'gleaming crown' prominently on display in the procession, followed by his retinue.[37] Royal mausolea were numinous places, as Otto III knew when he opened Charlemagne's tomb at Aachen in 1000, and publicised the link between his own 'renewed' empire and his predecessor's. Further north, a no less political message was purveyed when Harald Bluetooth erected a massive runestone at Jelling to commemorate his royal parents and at the same time proclaim his own rulership over all Denmark.

It was in the tenth century that the three Magi of the Gospel story were recast as kings, and began to be depicted with crowns.[38] The crown had now become *the* royal attribute; crown-wearings became great ritual occasions for the Ottonians particularly, and perhaps for other contemporary rulers in west Francia and England too. Sets of regalia, crowns foremost among them, acquired a further significance when power was being passed on not just from one ruler to the next but from one family to another. Widukind describes the dying Conrad sending to Henry I 'these insignia, the holy lance, the golden arm-rings, the cloak, the sword of the kings of old, and the crown'.[39] The lance here is anachronistic: it was only acquired for the Ottonian royal treasury by Henry himself (probably in 926) but thereafter became the kingdom's chief talisman of military success. Later in the century kings of Poland and Hungary would seek to acquire holy lances of their own. The regalia, and especially crowns, contributed to a depersonalising of kingship as, transmitted through generations and across dynasties, they became symbols of state. They were inalienable perquisites of the royal office, and they were (or in the case of the lance, swiftly became) specific to particular kingdoms. Even more homely items of royal attire acquired a unique quality. Those same west Frankish magnates who resented Hagano's hold on Charles the Simple objected particularly to the royal favourite's frequently and in public taking the cap off the king's head and putting it on his own.[40] Otto II's royal banner was publicly displayed before battle.[41] Special rituals of reception and farewell marked the comings and goings of kings. Royal diplomata worked by being multiplied and distributed: the documents themselves, often large and splendidly produced, with seals showing the ruler in majesty, were substantial communicators of regality. Other royal rituals, feasts and fasts, celebrations of peace and friendship and

---

[36] Widukind, *Res gestae Saxonicae* III, 76, p. 127.   [37] Richer, *Historiae* III, 110, p. 142.
[38] *Sacramentarium Fuldense saeculi* x, plate 16.   [39] Widukind, *Res gestae Saxonicae* I, 25, p. 33.
[40] Richer, *Historiae* I, 15, p. 38.   [41] Fichtenau (1984), pp. 71–2 (1991, p. 48).

alliance, displays of largesse and clemency and religious devotion, could be imitated by magnates and by lesser nobles. The availability of an acknowledged ritual repertoire seems to have stimulated inventiveness on the part of laymen as well as clergy: the tenth century was an age not just of ecclesiastically constructed liturgy but of proliferating sign and gesture in a variety of social contexts. These were forms of communication that transcended linguistic barriers and could be received and responded to simultaneously in multiple ways. Rituals of supplication as performed by faithful men (*fideles*) before kings were replicated by faithful men and fighting men (*milites*) before their lords. Ritual thus associated the elite's status and functions with those of the king. Outsiders who learnt the rules could qualify as insiders: Miesco of Poland never remained seated in the presence of Otto I's representative Margrave Hodo,[42] and when he attended Otto's assembly, he presented the young emperor with a camel for his menagerie. Royal zoos were another form of monarchic self-representation, derived in this case from antique and Byzantine models. Most important of all, Miesco had become a Christian and showed himself willing to play by the most fundamental of rules. But ritual was not always about togetherness. It could also assert distance, as when Otto summoned the defeated Count Eberhard of Franconia and his leading followers (*principes militum*) to Magdeburg in 937. Their offence was not only rebellion, but the destruction of a stronghold which had belonged to one of Otto's Saxon trusties, Bruning. The count had to present the king with 100 talents' worth of horses, and his men had to perform the ritual humiliation of carrying dogs. This was political theatre indeed, necessarily performed in public, before Otto's new court (his reign was scarcely a year old) consisting of its essential components: Saxons and Franks.[43] The echo of the Carolingian *harmscar*,[44] a similar ritual punishment, was presumably not lost on such an audience.

Rituals distanced kings from their subjects; rituals closed the gap between them. Kings did not choose between these as alternatives, either cementing loyalty through horizontal bonds of conviviality and *amicitia*, or vertically asserting their own superiority. Friendliness and lordliness were regarded as perfectly compatible; and effective kings operated in both registers simultaneously. Alfred of Wessex, in the 890s, recommended a 'friendship' which bound the receiver of wealth to the lord who gave it: should one's lord call for active service, 'it is better to renounce the gift and follow the giver, who acts as the guardian both of the wealth and of his friendship'.[45] In the Frankish world, such relations of political friendship, though they continued Carolingian prac-

---

[42] Thietmar, *Chronicon* v, 10, p. 232.   [43] Widukind, *Res gestae Saxonicae* II, 6, p. 61.

[44] *MGH Capitularia regum Francorum*, index, *sv.*

[45] Alfred's version of Augustine's *Soliloquies*, trans. Keynes and Lapidge, p. 141.

tice (Charles the Bald had established *amicitia* with Bernard of Septimania in 841, and Charlemagne had surrounded himself with *amici* in baths and bedroom), are more frequently mentioned, and more evidently clothed with ritual, in the tenth century. In the early years of his reign Henry the Fowler was in urgent need of friends to recognise and support his kingship. In 921, he and Charles the Simple swore friendship as between 'eastern' and 'western' kings.[46] Two years later Henry joined Gislebert of Lotharingia to himself in friendship and gave him his daughter in marriage.[47] For contemporaries, context explained, and ritual clarified, the different inflections of the same word: the elaborate arrangements of 921, which culminated in the two kings' meeting on a ship anchored in the middle of the Rhine, expressed equivalence, whereas in 923 friendship between king and non-king, senior and junior, demonstrated Henry's 'liberality' towards Gislebert, and marked distance between them. A ritual reception similarly displayed hierarchy at the same time as it forged bonds. In 924, King Radulf awaited Duke William of Aquitaine on the northern bank of the Loire (as Charles the Bald had awaited Aquitanian magnates in the ninth century): it was William who had to make the river-crossing and, when he met the king, leap down from his horse and approach on foot while Radulf remained mounted. Only then did Radulf offer him a kiss, which signified peace. But peace, as in this case, could restate, rather than elide, distance. The outcome was what Radulf wanted: William 'committed himself to the king'.[48] Kings maintained their prestige and uniqueness in the midst of ritual proliferation. Lay aristocrats could have seals, but the iconography of royal seals remained distinct: only the king was shown seated in majesty. In west Francia, at any rate, he was addressed as Your Majesty. Rituals of friendship found their context in representations of divinely blessed monarchy. The special royal bed on which the dead west Frankish king was laid[49] recalled the uniqueness of the living king. No-one else might lie with impunity in the bed prepared for the king: when a Saxon magnate did this, it was probably meant and understood as a ritual of rebellion.[50] The disposition of kings' daughters made the same point in another way. They were (Henry I's daughter Gerberga was a rare exception) given in marriage to foreign princes, or placed in royally supported convents. Subjects did not share their beds as spouses. Great aristocrats, by contrast, regularly married their daughters into other magnate families to produce the many-stranded patterns of alliance visible in tenth-century genealogies.

The cults of saints linked kings and aristocrats. In east Francia, groups of

---

[46] *Constitutiones et acta publica*, no. 1, p. 1; Altholf (1992).
[47] Widukind, *Res gestae Saxonicae* I, 30, p. 43: '[rex] liberaliter eum coepit habere . . . affinitate pariter cum amicitia iunxit eum sibi . . .'   [48] Flodoard, *Annales*, s.a. 924, pp. 19–20.
[49] Richer, *Historiae* III, 110, p. 142.
[50] Thietmar, *Chronicon* II, 28, as interpreted by Leyser (1994), pp. 198– 201.

royal and noble names entered in the Memorial Books of St Gallen and
Reichenau preserve evidence of particular occasions of collective devotion,
notably in the reign of Henry the Fowler. Kings and nobles alike had their family
saints, their relics, their mausolea. In general, though, even the greatest magnates
could not equal kings in the quantity and quality of their relic-collections and
saint-patrons; and the Ottonians too would set about gaining that edge once
firmly in power. For his son, Henry the Fowler gladly accepted an English bride
of St Oswald's 'holy line'[51] who would help compensate for the Ottonians' own
distinctly un-royal antecedents. More important to Otto I than Oswald was
Maurice, a soldier-saint specialising in victory, but whose relics, unlike Oswald's,
were in Otto's possession. They strengthened his men's morale and so Otto's
own prestige. No tenth-century king was a keener relic-collector than Æthelstan:
'we know you value relics more than earthly treasure', wrote the abbot of Saint-
Samson, Dol, in a covering letter for gifts in point; and Duke Hugh of Francia
sent him St Maurice's standard.[52] Æthelstan may have seen these acquisitions early
in his reign as prerequisites for future military successes. Right relations with the
saints entailed giving as well as receiving. On campaign against the Scots,
Æthelstan paused at Cuthbert's shrine at Chester-le-Street, and offered lavish gifts
to the saint. Such rituals of largesse and devotion at sites of supernatural power,
from Chester-le-Street to Winchester and from Exeter to Canterbury, enhanced
royal authority and underpinned a newly united imperial realm.

ROYAL GOVERNMENT

The west Frankish kingdom has been treated in much recent historiography as
a tenth-century paradigm. 'France', allegedly, was 'without a state', and in its
vast 'kingless territories' such as Aquitaine there was a falling-back on 'order
and social obligations transmitted from the period preceding statehood'.[53]
Generalise from the French model and you have a tenth century for which talk
of royal government would seem redundant. France's typicality can be disputed, however: historians of Denmark, Poland, Spain, Germany and England
represent the tenth century as a period of strenuous royal activity and even
some institutional growth. The notion of 'government' can be variously
defined. It was just a generation after the year 1000 that Duke William of
Aquitaine urgently consulted King Robert II over a portent, the falling of a
rain of blood, that had affected Aquitaine, while Duke Richard II of
Normandy sent a warning to the same king about heretics at Orléans.[54] Both

---

[51] Hrotsvitha, *Gesta Ottonis*, ed. Winterfeld, lines 95–6, p. 207.   [52] *EHD*, no. 228, p. 892.

[53] Fichtenau (1991), p. 423, and cf. p. 391.

[54] The king reported Duke William's request to Abbot Gauzlin of Fleury, Fulbert, *ep.* 2 (appendix B),
pp. 274/6.

dukes still had a sense of the king's uniqueness, and of his responsibility for the religious well-being of the whole kingdom. The king responded with energy to both demands – in the one case demanding learned scrutiny of appropriate books, in the other, arresting and burning the heretics. How had such perceptions survived a century when royal government was allegedly non-existent in west Francia? One answer lies in an exceptionally rich Carolingian legacy, including precociously developed rituals of royalty as well as more long-standing and deep-rooted sub-Roman forms and traditions of monarchy. Are we then to imagine tenth-century west Francia as resembling Clifford Geertz's vision of nineteenth-century Bali where 'power served pomp' – that is, where the state existed merely as a ceremonial display whose sole and solipsistic function was to maintain itself? West Frankish kingship was not as pompous as all that. Moreover, it surely functioned, and not least in its more theatrical moments, for others too. Because it, and the idea of the realm's geographical integrity, were so well entrenched in the minds of its leading subjects, because aristocrats were so habituated to thinking of their own power in terms of delegated royal power, because churchmen were so imbued with ideals of service to the realm, because social memory was so deeply impregnated by written records as well as oral tales and poems in which royal deeds and judgements were central themes, tenth-century monarchy, despite chronic material weakness and in the case of some kings serious loss of prestige, retained legitimising authority. If centralised judicial institutions – a supreme court – are the hallmark of the state, there was no state here. Yet royal authority might generate a kind of power as the imagined guarantor of order and focus of fidelity.

In the 930s, the last heir to the independent kingdom of Provence, the ambitiously named Charles-Constantine, ended his days as a count, the faithful man of the west Frankish king Radulf. Faithfulness to the king still meant something. For the king was no cipher. In Flodoard's *Annals*, just one year (931) in the life of King Radulf shows him incessantly active: he went from Burgundy to Vienne to accept the submission of count Charles-Constantine, then to Saint-Martin, Tours 'for the sake of prayer', then back 'into Francia' to suppress rebellion, besieging two strongholds, and making a truce; he 'sent letters to the clergy and people of Rheims about the archiepiscopal election', moved to Attigny, engaged in further negotiations with the rebels, and headed off the rebels' potential ally, the east Frankish king Henry, by sending hostages; he then captured Rheims after a three-week siege and installed his candidate as archbishop, imprisoned the rebel bishop of Châlons and installed 'his own cleric' in the see; he besieged the rebel leader in Laon and captured it; and so back to Burgundy and the recovery of more castles from rebels.[55] Here then was a king

---

[55] Flodoard, *Annales*, s.a. 931, pp. 46–52.

beset, his control of the heartlands and key churches of Francia threatened, even Rheims and Laon temporarily lost. Yet he rallied, showed diplomatic and military skills, reasserted his control of key churches, recovered the royal seat (*sedes*) of Laon, preserved for his successors something of *dignitas* – royal status. What is missing in all this frenetic activity is the exercise of jurisdiction. Radulf and his successors, unlike their contemporaries in east Francia and England, were unable to impose judgement upon powerful subjects. The west Frankish king simply could not command sufficient resources, could not muster enough troops, to act in the political arena as more than one regional prince (and in military terms a second-rank one) among others. The one trump card he might still play was his kingliness: he could appeal to other kings for help against rebels – as Lous IV did twice to Æthelstan, and many times to Otto I, both of them relatives as well as fellow-kings.

Power in the tenth-century west Frankish kingdom was devolved and regionalised. This was hardly new. A Golden Age of Carolingian justice has been presented in some recent historiography, and the Peace movement portrayed as a response to post-Carolingian 'crisis'. Yet *consuetudines*, in the sense of seigneurial power, had already been mentioned in the edict of Pîtres 864, and so too had castles (*castella*) built 'to oppress the locals' and apparently doing that quite effectively even without mottes.[56] Castles did not *per se* generate change or signify a new phenomenon of seigneurial power. Rather, their effect depended on the diffusion of building technology and on political context; on what other kinds of power existed, in the vicinity, or at a higher level (as when Charles the Bald had asserted his right to authorise fortifications: we have no idea with what success). The same was true of the markets that proliferated in the ninth and tenth centuries: rulers might claim a cut of the profits from commercial exchange, but local aristocrats would stake their claims too. Outcomes would depend on how far the king was able to impose his power in a given region. The notion of a 'degradation' of public to private, and of 'crisis' *c.* 1000, oversimplifies complex processes. If royal power was so weak throughout the tenth century, it becomes hard to explain why the 'crisis' was so long delayed. No one generalisation works for the west Frankish kingdom, less still for the whole of the west. The chronology and the geography of change remain obstinately diverse.

Useful comparisons with west Francia are offered by Denmark, Poland and England: new realms based on military force which borrowed the clothes of Carolingian kingship, where ideological superstructure was attached (in what Marx saw as normal fashion) to material base, pomp serving power. In west Francia, oldest of the old realms, the ruler wore the clothes of majesty; yet thus

---

[56] 'Iniustas consuetudines noviter institutas.'; 'castella et firmitates . . . sine nostro verbo . . . disfactas habeant', *MGH Capitularia regum Francorum* II, 322, no. 272, c. 28; II, 328, additional c. 1.

attired, he could deputise for an absent state. The capital of kingship had dwindled: nevertheless something of its political credit remained. It could not coerce, but it could sometimes impress. This was true, though with a less striking disjuncture between ideal and realities, of other tenth-century realms as well. Kings, in west Francia and elsewhere, worked immensely hard to maintain their credit-worthiness.

Late Anglo-Saxon England is sometimes depicted as such a strong centralised state that it seems more Carolingian than the Carolingians. Before its uniqueness is too enthusiastically accepted (and then celebrated), some discounting has to be done for the centripetal thrust of surviving evidence: while there is an absence here of the kind of thick description supplied elsewhere by chroniclers like Widukind or Richer with their revelations of full-blooded and untidy incident, there is relative abundance of legal material which tends to exaggerate the statelike appearance of the tenth-century realm. Uniquely in this period, Anglo-Saxon England presents a stream of royal legislation. The coinage, meticulously studied, has been proved to be centrally coordinated. Equally well-studied royal charters have revealed the range, and precision, of royal largesse. Scholars working on the laws and the coinage, and also backwards from Domesday Book, have been able to identify agents and agencies of the state. The king might direct ealdormen to publish and implement new legislation, like ninth-century Carolingian counts.[57] Charter witness-lists show that up to half a dozen ealdormen commonly attended the king. Some ealdormen were west Saxons exported to positions of virtual viceroys in the acquired kingdoms of Mercia, east Anglia and Northumbria; others were local magnates who threw in their lot with west Saxon kings. Ealdormen of both types married into the royal family. Kings exercised some control over appointments, and so qualified the tendency towards hereditary office – qualified only up to a point, for men with hereditary claims might well be chosen precisely because they tended to have the local clout that made them effective office-holders. Prescriptive evidence has reeves and port-reeves supervising a range of royal resources in countryside and towns. Income from customs levied on trade at London would, if actually raised, have been far more valuable, and more predictable, than Welsh tribute. Moneyers working to central specifications produced silver coins of standard type, weight and fineness; and the locations of mints and markets were royally authorised. Territorial administration, based on shires, was extended from Wessex northwards. Landowners brought their disputes before shire-courts in the presence of shire-reeves (sheriffs). Fines for crimes were paid to the king. Compared with other contemporary rulers, the kings of England can be shown to have had a large cash income. In the late

[57] iv Edgar, c. 15.1, *EHD*, no. 41, p. 437.

tenth and early eleventh centuries, the king and his advisers were able to organise the payment of large sums of money as tribute to Scandinavian attackers.
Wills and other private documents show royal interests operating through local
judicial institutions on a day-to-day basis: 'shire courts *were* royal courts'.[58]

Nevertheless, these same wills and documents show a fairly rampant and
well-entrenched aristocracy, ecclesiastical as well as lay, sharing in the tasks and
profits of regional goverment. The famous Fonthill case of *c.* 900 is just one of
the best examples of magnate power operating through, and skewing, royal
courts and legal procedures. Armies were recruited from aristocrats and their
followings. Towns, till recently regarded as bastions of royal control, can be
seen as, at the same time, centres of aristocratic power. Urban development,
the coinage and the fiscal system funnelled wealth into the hands of magnates
and town-dwellers as well as (perhaps, cumulatively, more than) kings. Though,
thanks to Edgar's and Ælfthryth's interest in ecclesiastical reform, the king and
queen wielded heavy influence over the church monastic and secular, leading
churchmen were often powerful local aristocrats, who could ease their
kinsmen into lucrative posts as reeves and lease-holders of church land. The
Ely evidence shows Bishop Æthelwold of Winchester doing something similar
to extend his territorial power in east Anglia.[59] Into the picture of a church
integrated particularly closely with the state, involved in organising the performance of military service, systematically praying for the welfare of king and
realm, and offering personnel and resources as agents and instruments of royal
government, there need to be set the provincial prince-bishops of the Tenth-
Century Reform.

Moreover, royal power was very unevenly distributed through the realm.
England, composed of formerly independent kingdoms, remained an agglomeration of provinces. In the midlands and the north, magnates ruled the roost –
one famous example was actually nicknamed 'Half-King'. The reach of intensive royal government was limited effectively to the south – old Wessex, where
the king's lands and residences were concentrated (and even here with some
notable blanks). Further north, and especially northwards of a line drawn from
Chester to the Wash, the evidence of royal action thins dramatically: there were
no mints except for York, no royal monasteries, few royal stays. Here kings
operated through occasional symbolic interventions, often following up military success, rather than day-to-day involvement. When Æthelstan granted a
vast tract of the north-west to the archbishop of York,[60] he was inviting a powerful, but far from reliable, local potentate to make what he could of some
tenuous claims to ecclesiastical jurisdiction in lands that had recently attracted
many Scandinavian immigrants: so, from the king's point of view, a political

---

[58] Wormald (1986), p. 162.   [59] *Liber Eliensis*, ed. Blake, book II, pp. 63–236.
[60] Sawyer, no. 407, *EHD*, no. 104, pp. 548–51.

gesture rather than a sign of prior control. Not long after Eadwig burned Ripon in 948, a west Saxon clerk now attached to St Cuthbert's community at Chester-le-Street took the opportunity to add west Saxon glosses to that prime Cuthbertian relic, the Lindisfarne Gospels, thus appropriating it for Wessex while the book itself remained in its Northumbrian home. Kings based south of the Thames had no option: they relied on ruling at a distance, making extensive use of allies and supporters among the aristocracy of the midlands (Mercia) and the north. Occasionally, these men's attestations of royal charters show them in attendance on the king – often enough, though, to suggest their acceptance of his lordship, and the benefits of attachment thereto.

Thus, if in one sense 'shire courts were royal courts', they were at the same time, and perhaps more routinely (though routine evidence is rare), aristocratic ones. In a famous Herefordshire case, though the shire-reeve was present at the hearing, the proceedings were managed and the outcome was apparently sewn up by the beneficiary, Thorkil, the local strong man who could sway the shire community and also happened to be in favour with the king.[61] In another famous case, that of Wulfbald, what from 'the official point of view'[62] looked like crimes, and were written up as such after the event, one-sidedly, could equally well be seen as aristocratic self-help in pursuit of 'a family dispute about inheritance' and one which, significantly, turned on a woman's claims, for these were the kind that frequently aroused contention and allowed kings to intervene in the name of protecting the weak.[63] Ravaging and murder may well have been usual ways of pursuing such claims in late tenth-century England ('harrying' is mentioned more than once as a royal method for disciplining the recalcitrant[64]). That the king in this case got not one but two large assemblies to support the forfeiture of the property (which the king then gave to his mother) suggests that the king was pushing into a controversial area of property law – indeed pushing his luck. It was the sort of royal action which, pursued in Salian Saxony, would evoke cries of 'calumny' and fierce resistance in the name of custom. The hard cases of Æthelred's reign show politics inseparably entangled in the law. External opposition in the shape of Scandinavian attackers provided a focus for the disgruntled and the dispossessed. Was Æthelred's government strong or weak? The terms on which, after his flight to Normandy, the king was 'sent for' by 'all the councillors' suggest that for those on the receiving end, strength might be hard to distinguish from injustice.[65]

Tenth-century Welshmen no doubt had varied views of English strong government. Welsh kings began to establish a more assertive kind of royal authority of their own, notably in the kingdoms of Gwynedd and Dyfed. A

---

[61] Sawyer, no. 1462, *EHD*, no. 135, pp. 602–3.   [62] Keynes (1991), p. 79.
[63] Sawyer, no. 877.   [64] *ASC, s.a.* 1000, 1014, pp. 237, 247.
[65] *ASC*, version 'E', *s.a.* 1014, p. 246; cf. above, p. 103.

collection of legal tracts is traditionally associated with Hywel Dda (d. 949 or 950) who ruled over both those kingdoms. Coins were issued at Chester in Hywel's name. Son-to-father succession is well attested in tenth-century Wales, and the kingdoms of Gwynedd and Dyfed were transmitted undivided, though not without intra-familial conflict. It seems likely that some if not all these features resulted from contacts with the English: Hywel Dda was not the only Welsh king of this period to spend time at the the the court of an Anglo-Saxon king. But the contacts were very often warlike, as the English raided and plundered and imposed tribute. Poets bemoaned these attacks and invoked heroic resisters of old. Wales' emergence as a slightly more united but distinctly more self-conscious political community was as much a defensive reaction to English aggression as flattering imitation of English ways.

The simultaneously attractive and repellent power of aggressive and ambitious neighbours can be seen in Scandinavia too. In Norway the practice of royal law-making is attested for the first time in the tenth century, on the part of a king who had been brought up at Æthelstan's court. The OE word *hird* for royal retinue was borrowed apparently in the tenth century into Norwegian and also Danish. Englishmen played a series of important roles in the tenth-century Christianisation of Norway, and perhaps (then or slightly later) Denmark and Sweden too. In Denmark, however, the conversion of King Harald in the 960s was the result of the freelance efforts of a German priest. The archbishops of Hamburg-Bremen tried to keep the later Danish bishoprics as their suffragans. Official Ottonian influence is hard to find. Rather, it was Harald who promoted Christianity for his own purposes. He banned pagan rites; and archaeological evidence shows pagan burial practices abandoned by the end of the century. Nevertheless it is not until the twelfth century that ecclesiastical forms of royal inauguration are documented in Denmark. Harald modernised selectively. On the grave-monument he erected at Jelling for his parents he used Christian but also other, indigenous motifs. He chose this medium, in this dynastic cult-site, for the claim to have won 'all Denmark' and Norway as well. The claims were closely linked. Norway emerged as an independent kingdom when the Ottonians temporarily subjected the Danes to tribute-payment. Thus, just as the Danes had reacted to Frankish, then Ottonian power, so Norwegians reacted against Danes. Harald's re-establishment of overlordship of Norway marked a point of conjuncture when both cycles of contact favoured Denmark: Norway was racked by dynastic disputes, while in the later 970s Ottonian resources were concentrated on Italy, then in 983 weakened by Slav rebellion and, again, by the dynastic problem of a minority. Two generations later, the Norwegians reasserted their independence under their own king. Harald's power thus depended on external relations. As for resources within the kingdom, archaeological evidence makes it certain that several impressive timber forts (the largest with an internal diameter of 240 m) were constructed *c.* 980 to a uniform pattern in Jutland and the eastern islands. Harald clearly mobilised very large quantities of manpower and timber and, so the uniform structures suggest, did so directly through his own agents, rather than relying on local aristocrats as middlemen. The forts' location inland rather than on sea-coasts, and their circular form and interior symmetry of design, suggest that, whatever other (military, economic) functions they had, they were aimed at the Danish population as symbolic centres of royal power. According to later medieval sources, Harald's burdensome demands provoked rebellion. His style of rulership may also have been resented. When he was ousted and died in 987, the rebels' choice of successor was his son Sven – who let the forts fall into disrepair and set about amassing silver through foreign raiding, especially in England.

Poland and Hungary also are tenth-century examples of state-formation on the periphery of empire. Both owed their conversion to missionaries from Germany; and direct Ottonian political input continued sporadically important. Boleslav Chrobry in Poland and Vajk-Stephen in Hungary seem to have promoted Christianity under their own steam, exploiting the ideology and organisation which could help them impose and maintain some kind of authority over erstwhile peers, and at the same time resist Ottonian pressure. On the other hand, they were interested in acquiring a veneer of legitimacy through imperial approval: hence their welcome for Otto III in 1000–1. Like Harald in Denmark, Boleslav and Vajk-Stephen were interested in the symbolic representation of their power. They acquired royal titles and attributes, and holy lances of their own. Regular tribute-paying to the Ottonians was discontinued, though the Poles paid again in the eleventh century (as did the Bohemians). Instead they became sometimes uneasy allies. Culturally, they assimilated into Latin Christendom. Though they had never been part of the Carolingian empire, from now on they displayed key forms of the Carolingian inheritance: its diplomatic, its rituals of rulership, its capacity for ethnic invention – and above all its religion. That was the face they turned westwards. On other frontiers, they copied the west's aggression, imposing tribute on and taking slaves from their own northern and eastern neighbours.

The textbook opposition of aristocracy to monarchy would have surprised tenth-century people. Aristocratic power depended on and imitated the power of kings, while kings for their part could conceive of no government that did not involve aristocratic collaboration. Discussions, negotiations through face-to-face encounters, participation in ritual, the use of honour and shame, the deployment of personalised wrath and grace: these had all been fundamentals of Carolingian government. In the old Frankish lands, there is more evidence for all the above in the tenth century. Writtenness, however, takes a lower profile. There are no more capitularies. It is hard to say how far such differences of form entailed differences of governmental substance. If participation in written culture had been very important in the ninth century, in west Francia especially, then the decline of written communication perhaps caused a sense of alienation. But other non-written forms of communication and participation may well have compensated, and had surely anyway always been important. Local courts are poorly documented; but a rare document on political relations in Poitou, the *Conventum* of William of Aquitaine and Hugh of Lusignan, *c.* 1020, refers to such *placita*.[66] It is hard to find any royal input at this level though. The count of Angoulême and his faithful men governed without reference back to the king. They were involved in direct relations with Duke William of Aquitaine, however, and *he* occasionally saw the king: Robert the Pious was his cousin and in 997 actually made a rare trip into Aquitaine to help William besiege a local enemy.[67] Richer's wording suggests, though, that the king acted to help a kinsman rather than to restore order generally.

Continuities can be seen in the role of the church and of churchmen. Kings' rapport with the church became more intimate, in some ways more comfortable. Monks and bishops were more prominent than ever before in the conduct of tenth-century diplomacy. As in the Carolingian empire, the church helped give territorial as well as ideological shape and focus to realms old and new. In west Francia, Rheims played a key role throughout the tenth century in sustaining the monarchy and, in 987, in guiding its transfer from one dynasty to another. In multi-centred east Francia, several churches shared this role, Mainz and Magdeburg prominent among them. Canterbury, Winchester and Worcester in England, Gniezno in Poland, Gran in Hungary, and even St Andrews in Scotland, played analogous roles. But nowhere did monasteries and convents make such a substantial contribution as they did in east Francia to sustaining the monarchy through the provision of hospitality and the exercise of local jurisdiction through advocates.

Alone among the former Carolingian realms, the kingdom of Italy offers a different picture. Here ecclesiastical power, locally strong but divided against itself, provided no cement. In any case, in Lombard, then Carolingian, Italy the institutions of secular government had been peculiarly strong, kings had legislated vigorously, and that legislation continued to be applied in courts. According to some modern historians, the state survived well in Italy through the tenth century. It is true that the palace of Pavia continued to function, and that presupposed organisation of royal economic resources. In 947, Berengar II of Italy collected a poll-tax to pay off the Hungarians (though he allegedly

---

[66] *Conventum inter Guillelmum Aquitanorum comes et Hugonem Chiliarchum*, ed. Martindale, pp. 545, 547.
[67] Richer, *Historiae* IV, 108, p. 330.

kept most of the proceeds).[68] Nevertheless, this is only part of the story. It is from the tenth-century Italian kingdom that the clearest evidence comes for systematic dismantling of structural bonds between centre and localities. The semantic evolution of the word *districtio* is revealing here. In early medieval legal texts, it had meant punishment or legal coercion. In the tenth century it increasingly often had the more general sense of jurisdiction, such as that exercised by bishops or counts; and the word occurs in this sense in Italian charters in which kings granted away such powers. In 940, Kings Hugh and Lothar granted to a count an estate 'with all *districtio* and all public function and capacity to hear legal suits which previously our public *missus* was accustomed to perform'.[69] The unique longevity of the Italian state, then, may have been exaggerated. Here, as elsewhere, what can be seen is devolution protracted to local autonomy. At the same time, the word *districtus*, very rare before the tenth century, and originally meaning 'coercive action', acquired in Italy the sense of 'an area of jurisdiction, especially considered as a source of revenue' – so, a governmental 'district'.

If tenth-century counts can hardly be considered any longer as *ex officio* agents of royal government in Italy, the same is true elsewhere in the old Carolingian kingdoms. The title count, generally hereditary even in the Carolingian heyday, was no less so in the tenth century. Nevertheless, an active Ottonian king gave his formal approval when a count treated his offices 'like an inheritance' and divided them among his sons.[70] Even in west Francia, before such a division occurred on the death of the powerful count Heribert of Vermandois, the count's sons went to the king and were 'benignly received'.[71] In neither east nor west Francia could kings readily remove uncooperative counts, though if a count actually rebelled he might be attacked by a king on grounds of unfaithfulness, his lands ravaged, and eventual capitulation rewarded with nominal reinstatement. Most counts were simply too far away to be involved in regular contact with kings at all. In east Francia there was, however, a higher level of potentate: dukes and margraves. Though these too were hereditary, the king formally appointed them, and may also have had some say in their marriages. In some cases, these men became relatives by marriage of the ruling dynasty. Timely interventions over the marriages of ducal widows and daughters were important means of extending royal influence into duchies, as Otto I showed in Bavaria in 947 when he arranged the marriage of his brother Henry with the daughter of the defunct Duke Arnulf. The facts of demography – the failure of male descent and the frequency of claims through

---

[68] Liudprand, *Antapodosis* v, 33, p. 151.　　[69] D. Hugh 53, pp. 160–1.

[70] Adalbert, *Reginonis Continuatio, s.a.* 949: 'Uto comes obiit, qui permissu regis, quicquid beneficii aut prefecturarum habuit, quasi hereditatem inter filios divisit . . .'

[71] Richer, *Historiae* ii, 37, p. 186.

women – offered the king occasional opportunities to intervene in the transmission of property, and sometimes to claim reversion to the royal estates.

It goes without saying that though the western economy was patchily mon-
etised, no king was in a position to pay salaries. Government was of a type that
could be largely carried on without the activity of full-time specialists.
Chanceries, for instance, consisted of a handful of clerics working as royal
notaries quite intermittently. Government worked in the main through face-to-
face contacts and direct consultations between powerful people. Yet this did
not mean that kings lacked any agents at all. They could deploy the personnel
of their own households, their 'men' (*homines, domestici*) and their 'servants'
(*ministri, ministeriales*). Even in west Francia, at least in a restricted area around
Rheims and Laon, kings could command the services of castellans.[72] In 926, a
tax was raised 'publicly throughout Francia', presumably collected by the king's
own men, to buy off the Northmen: a feat of organisation which, even if we
scale down Flodoard's 'Francia', implies the services of a number of royal
agents.[73] Many senior churchmen too, in however partial and part-time a way,
worked on behalf of kings. When kings granted and confirmed immunities
(and, significantly, such confirmations were often sought) to bishops and
abbots, they had no intention of signing away absolutely the judicial rights and
profits involved. The very closeness of their personal relationships with these
churchmen – over whose appointments they had generally exerted some influence – meant that kings, by and large, could successfully demand from
churches the two things they required: hospitality and the service of warriors
maintained on church lands. In supervising such services, churchmen indeed
worked for the king. And they sometimes worked as a team: in east Francia
especially, the continuing (if intermittent) Carolingian practice of holding
large-scale synods under royal auspices kept in being a sense of a regnal
church. West Frankish bishops preserved something of the same *esprit de corps*;
and some of them manifested it, eventually, in peace councils. In Italy, despite
the pleas of individual bishops like Rather of Verona, such collaborative
efforts were lacking. Rather was a Frank from Lotharingia, overly dependent on
personal ties with the Ottonian court.

There are traces of royal agents in some outer-zone kingdoms as well.
Counts, and local judges called *saiones*, functioned regularly as court-holders in
León-Castile. Sometimes, however, *saiones* are explicitly described as 'of the
count'. The kings' power was based in León. They ruled Galicia and Castile via
personal dealings with the aristocracy of those regions; and the clearest sign of
royal authority there is the presence of regional aristocrats at the king's court.

---

[72] Richer, *Historiae* II, 7, pp. 136/8.
[73] Flodoard, *Annales*, *s.a.* 926, p. 34: 'exactio . . . publice fit per Franciam'.

In Denmark, by the close of the tenth century, adminstrative districts (*syssel*) had apparently been established in Jutland, the core-area of Harald's kingdom: probably an important shift away from the kind of personalised, non-territorial organisation which survived in Iceland into the twelfth and thirteenth centuries. Harald was able to get impressive fortifications built on at least four sites, perhaps by imposing forced labour. Military followers may well have functioned as all-purpose agents. In Wales the prologue to Hywel Dda's legal collection asserts that it was put together by skilled lawyers and clergy acting on the king's orders.[74] But that same legal evidence suggests that the apprehending of criminals was landowners' responsibility. Of special royal agents there is no trace. Kings with their retinues could impose demands, and sanctions, directly in kingdoms barely 95 kilometres across. Interestingly, the only clear evidence for royal law-enforcers and tax-collectors in the Celtic world of this period comes from Scotland, which covered an area seven times larger than the little kingdoms of Wales.

One key activity of government may be identified as the mobilisation and application of force in conflict-management. It was difficult even for English kings to apply force effectively as a sanction against influential uncooperative subjects. Æthelred, as already noted, had to summon two 'great meetings', and took years, before he was able to make Wulfbald, and later his widow, obey the royal command. Wulfbald's story has been taken to show 'the extraordinary feebleness of the government he defied for so long'.[75] It could be argued, instead, that by tenth-century standards, the outcome of this case showed extraordinary royal effectiveness. When Æthelred finally got his way, though, it was not by overwhelming force. True, he was able to use exile successfully against a string of magnates. But in all these instances, he could operate only with substantial aristocratic support. This he relied on when confronting external enemies too, even if local peasants might rally to defend their homes. At Maldon in 991, the army defeated by the Vikings consisted essentially of the followings of Ealdorman Byrhtnoth and his kin and local allies. Contemporary west Frankish kings were generally able to act against faithless castellans in their own neighbourhood, by the standard military tactics of ravaging and besieging. A king, leading a military retinue probably numbered in tens rather than hundreds, was militarily effective therefore within a limited area and with limited objectives: in fact more or less on a par with the *principes* and even castellans who were his routine opponents. West Frankish kings seldom had to confront external enemies, hence did not – could not – invoke 'the defence of the realm'. The Ottonians faced frequent external threats; and organised military

---

[74] *The Law of Hywel Dda*, p. 1: 'six men from every cantred in Wales'.
[75] Whitelock in *EHD*, p. 47; cf. Keynes (1991), pp. 78–9.

resources accordingly. They too relied on their own military followings, which may have consisted of up to a thousand men,[76] but in addition asked their *principes*, ecclesiastical as well as lay, for contingents in particular campaigns: thus, as at the Lech in 955, an east Frankish army might exceptionally have been brought up to a strength of several thousand rather than a few hundred. Miesco of Poland's remarkable success depended not least on his large following – of 3000 men, according to an Arab source[77] (almost certainly exaggerating – Arab historians were as liable as westerners to be fazed by numbers). The Ottonians' military dependence on aristocratic and ecclesiastical contingents was no innovation, for Carolingian armies had arguably been similarly recruited except in cases of local resistance to outside attack. It may be significant though that tenth-century writers labelled these contingents by their leaders as well as (as in the past) by their local origin. The military power of magnates and retinues loomed large in the Ottonians' kingdom as elsewhere. The social power of these men, after all, rested on their status as a warrior elite. Kings' conduct of war thus depended on consent, and the mobilising of faithful ones and friends. Karl Leyser has suggested that warfare might be seen as a normal state, and policy its pursuit by means that were only incipiently violent.[78]

As in the Carolingian period, one thing above all held political systems together, and kept peace of a kind: that was the assembly – to be seen as a regular and sanctioned event, a social conjuncture, a set of interactions, the centre of a field of centripetal force, in short, as an institution. Assemblies were often located at cult-centres. Regnal communities were formed and reinforced through meetings, and by the forging and reforging of personal links, between the king and his great men. These were occasions for multiple forms of collaboration and bonding. The banquet was a cross between working lunch and club dinner, with strong undertones of the public house. For tenth-century rulers it was not just useful, but essential, to combine political discussions with social exchanges: *colloquia*, serious conversations, indeed consisted of both. Forum for personal meetings and the forming of personal relationships through the exchange of gifts and services; marriage market; a job market of sorts; ritual theatre; exercise-ground for companionship in war: the assembly was all these – and all these were more important than what we call bureaucracy in maintaining the community of the realm.

One striking example is the assembly at Senlis in 987, where Hugh Capet's succession to the west Frankish kingdom was settled 'after the opinions of different participants had been collected'. Richer's account telescopes various

---

[76] The estimate of 1000 is that of Werner (1979), chapter III, p. 828.
[77] Ibn Jaqub, cited by Heather (1994), p. 62.   [78] Leyser (1994), ch 3.

arguments into the archbishop's speech:[79] positively, Hugh's physical qualities (nobility of body) and personal qualities (wisdom, credibility, big-heartedness) were required; negatively, Charles of Lorraine excluded himself by his service to an external king (Otto II) and his marriage to a woman of merely knightly status. Absent from the account of the archbishop's speech, but observed shortly afterwards by Richer himself, was the crucial consideration against Charles: his need, as king, to reward and endow his hitherto footloose followers – and this could only be done at the expense of sitting tenants. The 'haves' considered their interests, and voted for Hugh, against the Carolingian candidate.

The linked assemblies of 973 in Bath (attended by 'a great company') and Chester offer another, English, example.[80] These occasions were imposing scenes of royal ritual, but at the same time forums for hard-headed political discussion about coinage reform, law, relations with neighbours and tributaries, contacts with the Ottonian court. Further examples frame the reign of Otto I: in 938, 'a decree went out from the king that an assembly of the whole people' (Widukind's phrasing here echoes St Luke) should meet at Steele near Essen to consider a difference between the customary inheritance laws of Franks and Saxons. The agreed outcome reasserted 'royal power' as well as being in the interests of 'associates'.[81] In 973, Otto held what was to be the last Easter assembly of his reign at Quedlinburg. 'A multitude of diverse peoples' attended to celebrate Otto's return from Italy: at Merseburg for Pentecost, the peoples in attendance included those beyond the eastern frontier, and also 'envoys from Africa'.[82] This last touch evoked Carolingian glories, but it was no fantasy. In contemporary accounts of dealings with peoples beyond the frontiers are hints of Latin Christendom's new self-consciousness.

'OURSELVES AS OTHERS SEE US'?

Cultural contacts often highlight difference. When the north Italian Liudprand visited Constantinople at Eastertime 950 as envoy for King Hugh, he was enormously impressed by the annual distribution of money to the holders of official titles, rank by rank: those of the higher echelons 'needed assistance to drag their money laboriously away'.[83] This was only possible in a regime that taxed on an extensive scale, that is, one that had highly developed mechanisms for creaming off and redistributing wealth. By Liudprand's next visit, on behalf of Otto I in 968, his admiration had gone sour. His famous description of

---

[79] Richer, *Historiae* IV, 11, pp. 158/62.
[80] *ASC*, versions 'D', 'E', pp. 227–8; Ælfric, *Life of Swithin*, trans. *EHD*, pp. 927–8.
[81] Widukind, *Res gestae Saxonicae* II, 10, p. 62.   [82] Leyser (1994), pp. 96–7.
[83] Liudprand, *Antapodosis* VI, 10, pp. 157–8.

Nikephoros Phokas's court ceremonial is not objective reportage: Liudprand parodies the majestic and mystifying self-representation of the *basileus*.[84] Even if you did manage to come into his presence, there was little of the colloquium here. Prostration was not a posture conducive to serious conversations. Basil II was allegedly advised *not* to be approachable.[85] Liudprand's eventual scorn for the style of Byzantine monarchy conveyed more than a change of personal attitude: the subtext was a new western assertiveness, even arrogance, towards 'the Greeks' and their pretensions to romanity.

Like Constantinople, Córdoba in the tenth century was a very big city: both were centres of extensive territories with clearly defined frontiers and crossing-points patrolled by customs-men (as Liudprand learned to his cost in 968). The two regimes commanded standing armies of many thousands, paid for out of tax revenues. In Basil II's reign, the army contained a central component of professional foreign troops known as 'Varangians' (cf. 'Franks'). The military strength of al-Andalus depended on foreign slave-soldiers (many of Slav origin, reflected in the Arabic word for slave), highly trained from youth and highly efficient. Such forces could operate far afield: an army was sent nearly 700 km from Córdoba to sack Compostella in 997; Nikephoros Phokas had dispatched a fleet 900 km from Constantinople to capture Crete in 961. Like the *basileus*, the caliph ran a vast court, geographically distinct from the capital city itself. 'Abd al-Raḥmān III had only recently installed himself in the newly built palace at Madīna al-Zahrā 5 kilometres outside Córdoba, when he sent envoys to Otto I to initiate an exchange. Both caliph and king were concerned to suppress piracy in the western Mediterranean and along the Provençal coast. The result, in 953, was a return embassy led by Abbot John of Gorze in Lotharingia. John's Life was written up some two decades after his death in 974 by the abbot of Saint-Arnulf, Metz, who had known him and used the aged abbot's reminiscences. The Life was dedicated to the archbishop of Trier, and its expected audience consisted of Lotharingian churchmen. Here, in however stylised a form, is purveyed an Ottonian view, or more precisely, a Lotharingian view, of Cordovan power.[86]

John was amazed at the sheer scale of Cordovan officialdom, the amount of paperwork required for every kind of communication, even the size of documents. A thicket of bureaucracy seemed to block access to the caliph himself. John waited for the best part of three years in an official hostel at some distance from the palace before a meeting with the caliph was arranged. The vast scale of the palace complex – impressively confirmed by recent

---

[84] Liudprand, *Relatio.*   [85] Michael Psellos, *Chronographia*, trans. Sewter, p. 43.

[86] John of Saint-Arnulf, *Vita Iohannis abbatis Gorziensis*, cc. 118–36, pp. 371–7; partial English translation Fletcher (1992), pp. 67–8.

excavations – evidently made a profound impression on John. Slave soldiers, infantry and cavalry, guarded access to it, and performed imposing military exercises, making their horses rear up 'to put fear into our people'. John approached through outer courtyards 'covered with the most costly rugs and carpetings', to encounter the caliph 'on a dais, alone, almost like a god access-ible to none or very few, and sitting, not on a throne or seat as other peoples do, but on a cushion'. His offer of the inside of his hand to kiss was a tremen-dous honour 'not customarily granted to any of his own people or to foreign-ers'.

What purports to be a Cordovan view of the Ottonians is also recorded by John's hagiographer. When John asserted that his lord, King Otto, must be the most powerful ruler in the world in terms of men and territory, the caliph riposted:

your [king] does not keep for himself alone the power of his strength [*potestas virtutis suae*] but rather he allows each of his men to wield his own power: he shares out the regions of his realm amongst them, thinking thus to make them more faithful and more subject to him. But the outcome is very far from that! What is nurtured is pride and rebellion . . . and the rebels call the Hungarians into the midst of their *regna* to lay them waste . . .

At this point, unfortunately, the Life, in the single manuscript, breaks off before giving John's rejoinder. Presumably after condemning magnate – and not least Lotharingian – disloyalty (remember for whom the Life was written) through the mouth of the caliph, the hagiographer ended on a high note. By the later 970s, the Hungarian threat was over; and the victory of the Lech, to which Lotharingians contributed, had triumphantly affirmed Ottonian success in 955. The caliph's critique could thus be seen to reflect false generalisation from the revolt of 954, and thence a misunderstanding of Ottonian government. The hagiographer invited his audience *not* to envy caliphal authority, *not* to dis-parage Otto's regime, but instead to relish that extensive devolution of power which was the most striking feature of kingship in tenth-century Latin Christendom. Here was a Lotharingian view refracted. The *Life of John of Gorze* was written, like Montesquieu's *Persian Letters*, not as true ethnography but as commentary on home politics, and for home consumption. Its purpose was to celebrate not only John's holiness, exemplified in his stout refusal to dress up for his audience with the caliph (who allegedly admired his 'unyielding strength of mind' and declared his willingness 'to receive him even if he comes dressed in a sack'), but also the home regime itself. Power-sharing, and a measure of internal conflict, could coexist with a powerful regime – one which could boast the services of a strong-minded saint.

Earlier on in the story, the hagiographer explained why the caliph initially refused to receive John's embassy: the letters sent by Otto contained words that blasphemed the Prophet. This news got out, and the Cordovan populace became angry, reminding the caliph that if he did not punish blasphemy with death, by Muslim law he himself deserved to die. It was a tricky situation. While John was kept waiting, the caliph sent a Spanish-Christian bishop, Reccemund, to Otto to obtain new and inoffensive letters. The author of the Life affects to register John's surprise at the caliph's inability to modify the law, in this case to exempt from a punishment, on his own authority. That was precisely what King Otto not only could do but was expected and invoked to do by his powerful subjects. An essential trait of east Frankish rulership, in other words, was the capacity to judge, and to practise equity – to exercise discretion in applying the law. A ruler with such authority might lack the huge bureaucracy and parading soldiery of Madīna al-Zarhā. In direct contact with his magnates in the relatively intimate atmosphere of his hall, Otto had no need of the mediation of hosts of officials like those who transmitted successive explanations for delay during the three years John was kept waiting in the environs of Córdoba, no need of serried ranks of slave-soldiers. Nevertheless Otto was a mighty ruler: the hagiographer invites readers to admire something very different from caliphal rulership.

Last but not least, the hagiographer implicitly denounces the time-servers who took the orders of the infidel caliph: the Jew Hasday ibn Shaprut, and the Mozarab Christian Reccemund. These men lived under and cooperated with a Muslim regime: 'provided no harm is done to our religion, we obey them in all else and do their commands'. John stood for an alternative. He was defiant, an outspoken witness for Christianity, whom only the threat of causing a bloodbath among Spanish Christians deterred from martyrdom. Like Liudprand of Cremona, the author of John's Life breathed the spirit of a Latin Christendom reformed and militant, and – for good or ill – of a monarchy to match. Gregorianism did not have all the best tunes.

The caliph's response to the tenth-century Ottonian kingdom prefigured that of many modern historians. What kind of a kingship is this which permits so many sharers? How could this be dignified by the name of government? Political anthropologists, familiar with the traditional states of Africa, might take a more percipient, and a less anachronistic, view. For a relevant early medieval comparison and contrast, we might look also at the Icelandic pattern of decentralised power and shared attitudes about lawfulness, including the legitimacy of rebellion and private justice, in a kingless system. This chapter has explored systems which in many ways resembled Iceland, but which functioned with and through kings and kingship. Hence these were states of a distinctive kind, one unappreciated by the hagiographer's imagined caliph. Constantinople and Córdoba alike offer instructive comparisons with the west, but they were fundamentally remote from it. Their writers have left no records of their reactions to the Christian realms, and so we cannot get acquainted with the world of tenth-century kingship and government through foreign eyes. In the end, our most useful go-betweens, for all their limitations, are the contemporary texts – and especially the historians – of the Christian realms themselves. It was, after all, their world.

CHAPTER 5

THE CHURCH

Rosamond McKitterick

THE HISTORY of the church in Europe in the tenth and early eleventh centuries is essentially the history of many local churches, in which the dominant role in secular ecclesiastical and religious life was played by the bishops. Only occasionally can large-scale collective activity be observed; for the most part the very different challenges to religion from within and without the Christian world and the responses to them on the part of various members of the ecclesiastical hierarchy in western Europe mean that it is above all local preoccupations and regional differences that are reflected in the surviving evidence. Nevertheless, the evidence taken as a whole, that is, the synodal legislation and canon law collections, lives of bishops, histories of sees and monasteries, liturgy, music, accounts of saints' cults, books containing patristic and Carolingian theology and biblical exegesis produced for use within ecclesiastical institutions, theological treatises, polemical *pièces d'occasions* and incidental references in the narrative histories of the period, reveals not only lines of continuity with the ninth-century Carolingian church but also many elements of coherence and unity within the remarkable diversity of the tenth-century church. Not all of this coherence can be attributed to the links with monasticism and monks throughout western Europe on the part of the secular clergy, though the zeal for monastic reform undoubtedly was a common bond right across Europe. The evidence itself, moreover, presents particular problems of interpretation, for much of it was designed to present ideals and norms, whether of saints' and bishops' behaviour, of what was expected of the laity in the Christian observance, or of the interaction between the clergy and the laity, which do not necessarily provide a faithful reflection of reality.

Throughout this chapter, therefore, as well as determining the principal activities and achievements of the tenth- and early eleventh-century church, the relationship between the extant sources and the reality they purport to describe will be assessed in relation to the pastoral and political role of individual bishops within their dioceses, the collective activity of the clergy in councils and synods, the function of the law and liturgy of the church, and manifestations of lay piety.

The organisation of the church in the tenth and early eleventh centuries maintained the structures established in the early years of the Christian church and particularly that of the Frankish church in the preceding three centuries, whose principles had originally been based on Roman imperial administrative units. Ecclesiastical provinces, headed by the metropolitan or archbishop, comprised a number of dioceses, whose bishops were under the jurisdiction of their metropolitan. Thus, for example, the province of Trier included the dioceses of Toul, Metz and Verdun. Each bishop in his turn had the charge and care of the clergy and laity of his diocese entrusted to him. Although in principle elected, a bishop was often in practice nominated, either by the existing incumbent, or by lay authorities, the first of which methods was uncanonical and the second, on occasion, ill judged. Kings and other rulers interfered to varying degrees in episcopal elections, and such interference could work to the church's advantage or disadvantage depending on the wisdom of the choice and the degree to which a position could be abused in terms of the self-aggrandisement of the bishop or members of his family. The political complexities such interference could create are discussed below in relation both to the papacy and to particular sees, such as Rheims. Certainly the interest taken in episcopal appointments on the part of local magnates tended to preserve their position within the ranks of the social elite. Robert the Pious, on the other hand, according to Radulf Glaber, 'took great care to fill [any bishopric in his realm which lost its incumbent] preferring a suitable pastor of low birth to a nobleman steeped in the vanities of this world'.[1] It is striking how many members of the episcopate as a whole, even if we discount the hyperbolic attribution of 'noble' origins to many bishops by their biographers, were closely related to the secular rulers of the regions they dominated in ecclesiastical matters. Leadership in secular and spiritual matters in many areas, such as Rheims or Metz, as will be seen below, was a thoroughgoing family concern.

There has been much criticism of this situation, both on the part of contemporaries and by modern historians, for if abused, power and, crucially, property could get into the wrong hands. There are many instances, such as in the dioceses of Metz under Bishop Adalbero II, where church lands had been given out by his predecessors, or of Laon under Bishop Rorico, where episcopal estates were held by the bishop's kindred. The treatise *Dialogus de statu sanctae ecclesiae* of Malcalanus (*c.* 962) refers to the bishop's obligations to look after the interests and immediate necessities of his kinsmen and the poor, and

---

[1] Radulf Glaber, *Historiae* III, 7.

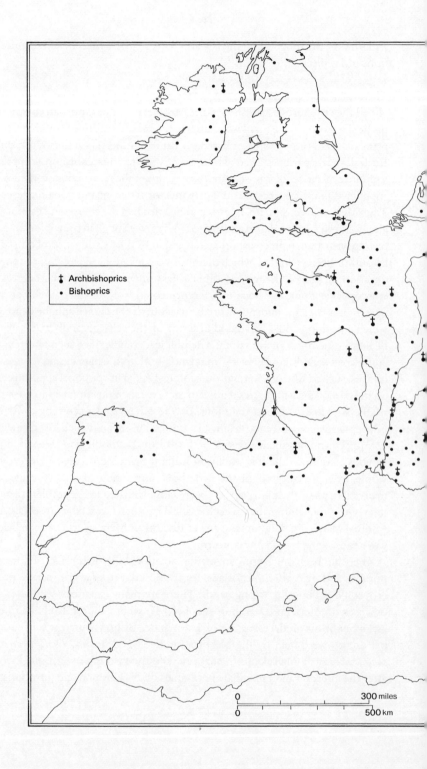

Archbishoprics

Bishoprics

0   300 miles

0   500 km

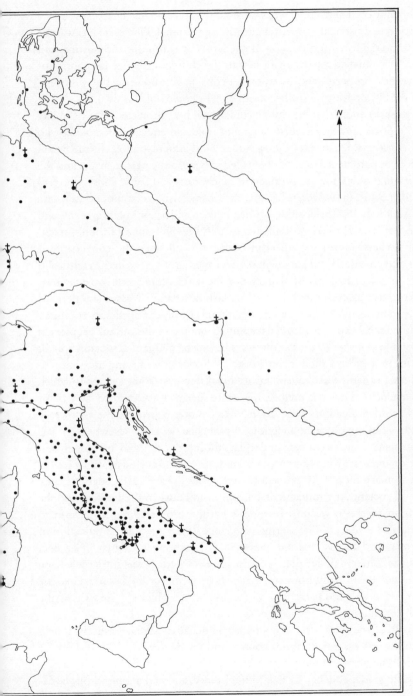

2 Archbishoprics and bishoprics in the early eleventh century

the difficulty of determining what was immoveable and inalienable, especially in relation to episcopal properties already apportioned. Fichtenau has warned against too rigid an interpretation of the terms of such gifts, for they may not always have entailed a permanent loss to the church. Effective lay control of ecclesiastical property gave the lay owner considerable power within a diocese, but if the bishop were of sufficient standing he could hold his own.

There is no doubt that the church could provide both an element of stability within a polity, and an excellent supply of able and educated personnel who could assist in the process of government and administration. In the Saxon kingdom in particular, such work entailed service in the palace chapel and the royal writing office for the production of charters and laws. Those who had worked at court, moreover, subsequently became bishops or abbots elsewhere in the kingdom. But the position of the Frankish and Saxon rulers in relation to the clerical hierarchy had its origin in the careful equilibrium more or less maintained between Germanic rulers in northern Gaul since the conversion of Clovis and enhanced and augmented under the Carolingians in the eighth and ninth centuries. Much of the character of the tenth-century episcopate in relation to secular rulers, notably in the Frankish heartlands, Wessex and perhaps León, can be accounted for, moreover, not only by the extraordinary combination of political expansion and instability recounted in the various chapters in this volume, but also by the various ways in which emergent new states sought to define and express their identity both in their own terms and in relation to the older, primarily Carolingian, institutional framework and norms to which they were heirs. Thus it is unlikely that quite such a clearly defined 'system' or consistent identification of the church as a counter-balance to the aristocracy existed within the Ottonian kingdom in particular, let alone elsewhere, as was once imagined. Such a concept underplays the interlocking and interdependent nature of interest groups and institutions, both lay and ecclesiastical, as well as the customary modes of procedure and social behaviour throughout early medieval society. Any fundamental antagonism between the nobility and the church anywhere in western Europe is hardly to be credited in relation to the available evidence. The German evidence is of a piece in its reflection of the determined use bishops and rulers made of each other and may well reflect a far more coherent policy than is evidenced elsewhere. It was still largely from the ranks of the nobility, however, that bishops were recruited. It remained the continuing wealth and patronage of the nobility on which the survival of the church depended.

Reform of the church in this context, whether advocated by bishops, abbots or princes, was essentially about control and the degree to which bishops or laymen could be permitted to exert the influence and power that each wished. In asserting independence from lay interference, and in defining wholly eccle-

siastical norms for ecclesiastical institutions, the church was arguably, therefore, in danger of cutting off its nose to spite its face in the interest of short-
term imagined advantages. In wishing to assert too heavy-handed an interest,
however, secular rulers were equally in danger of upsetting a delicate equilibrium between secular and spiritual authorities and their representatives, and
this is nowhere clearer than in the history of the popes in the tenth century outlined below. It is, furthermore, not possible to describe the history of the
tenth-century church purely in terms of a loss of such equilibrium, or even
more creditably, a fight to maintain it. There was throughout the kingdoms of
western Europe an ever-changing balance and uneasy shifting of local and
regional interests, like loose ballast in the hold of a ship.

Whatever the source of his patronage and impetus to gaining office may
have been, the bishop's spiritual office was confirmed by the church in that he
was consecrated by his fellow bishops and normally selected by the chapter.
The bishop presided over the cathedral *familia*, whose members had pastoral as
well as liturgical obligations within the episcopal city. The bishop's prerogatives
as well as his sphere of jurisdiction and pastoral obligations were increasingly
emphatically defined in the course of the tenth century. The synod of
Hohenaltheim (916), for example, devoted a number of paragraphs not only to
the definition of a Christian bishop (with reference to both Old and New
Testament statements on the function of a priest) but also to his duties and
expected behaviour and his role in safeguarding the privileges of the church.[2]
In his *Praeloquia*, moreover, the curmudgeonly Rather, bishop of Verona, twice
deposed and restored to his see because of, in his opinion, political opposition
and persecution, is eloquent on the respective prerogatives of the bishop and
secular rulers. A bishop is a powerful and active man. He should serve
emperor, archbishop, clergy and laity and travel throughout his diocese, conferring with the most important clerics and laity about what was to be done in
order to do justice to everyone. Rather invokes a veritable phalanx of Old
Testament priests and prophets to support his ideal of the exemplary bishop,
whose virtues remain vaguely defined even if his possible array of vices is terri-
fyingly detailed.

From the end of the ninth century, it is likely that there were also officials
such as the archdeacons to assist the bishop's work in the city, and deans who
would have particular areas in the countryside under their charge. In addition
there was the parish system, increasingly indicated in such sources as royal and
synodal legislation, episcopal statutes, charters, narrative accounts and references to the collection of tithes (instrumental, for obvious reasons, in the definition of the territorial boundaries of a parish) from the eighth century

---

[2] *MGH Concilia aevi Saxonici et Salici*, no. 1, pp. 19–40.

onwards. Nevertheless, the parish system was by no means fully or coherently organised even in the early eleventh century. Considerable regional variations also existed throughout western Europe. Interpretation is rendered more difficult by the fact that the Latin terms for parish and diocese appear to have been interchangeable. The Aachen capitulary of 818–19,[3] preserved in many late ninth- and tenth-century collections of ecclesiastical legislation as well as in the widely disseminated capitulary collection of Ansegis, was of particular importance in specifying parish provision and stipulating the support for the priest. Some commentary was also provided by Archbishop Hincmar of Rheims (845–82) in his treatise *De ecclesiis et capellis*, who adds the information that a bishop was to be supported in his city work by the archdeacons, and by the deans in the countryside. Similarly the episcopal capitularies, widely disseminated on the continent, and the synodal address *Fratres presbyteri* provided definitions of the expected work of the clergy.

Parish priests, ordained by the bishop, were directly subordinate and answerable to the bishop or his representative on all ecclesiastical matters, whether to do with discipline, administration of the sacraments, pastoral care, income or upkeep of the parish churches. Parish churches are associated not only with smaller units of a city, such as those created by Bishop Burchard in Worms in the early eleventh century, and with areas in the countryside, but also with individual lords' estates, the so-called *Eigenkirchen*. The development of the parish appears to have been piecemeal, but with many similarities in all parts of Europe. In Anglo-Saxon England, for example, pastoral care emanating from the *minsters* (an Old English word used to refer to both monasteries and parish churches) was only gradually supplemented by a parochial system consisting of small rural and urban parishes with a church, a priest, and sufficient endowment to support both. Evidence for its density, particularly in eastern England, is late and indirect, for it is embodied in Domesday Book of 1086, as is information about the number of churches in such towns as Norwich, which had, at the end of the eleventh century, twenty-five churches and forty-three chapels, or York, which appears to have had at least fourteen parish churches.

Some notion of the expected duties of a parish priest can be deduced from such documents as the early tenth-century charters of ordination from Lucca. These specify that the priest is to celebrate Mass and other offices, maintain the lights of the church (that is, keep up the supply of candles and the oil for lamps), obey the bishop and refrain at all times from alienating any church property. Episcopal statutes, such as those of Archbishop Ruotger of Trier (915–31) addressed to all the priests of the churches within his care, and synodal legislation of the tenth century, such as the synods of Koblenz 922 or

[3] *MGH Capitularia regum Francorum* I, 275–80, no. 138.

Trier 927, not only stressed episcopal authority. They also maintained that the priests were to set an example by their conduct, to administer the sacraments punctiliously, not to accept payment for baptism or burial, to teach the people about their faith and to exhort them to proper Christian conduct as defined by the synod.[4]

In all these contemporary discussions and decisions concerning the administration and organisation of the church, little reference is made to the pope and his role *vis-à-vis* the churches, provinces and diocesan sees of Christendom. Archbishops customarily sought the pallium (a band of white wool embroidered with crosses and serving as a badge of office given by the pope to a metropolitan) from the pope. Some are known to have done so in person, such as Dunstan of Canterbury and Oskytel of York who received pallia from Pope John XIII in 960; others were granted it. In the latter case it was presumably received from papal messengers, just as Archbishop Adaldag of Hamburg-Bremen received the pallium sent by Pope Leo VII in about 937. Yet it is only occasionally between about 900 and about 1050 that there is any sign of the pope asserting universal leadership or even being acknowledged to have supreme spiritual authority. A synod of French bishops convened at Saint-Basle, Verzy, had deposed Arnulf of Rheims and put Gerbert of Aurillac, master of the school at Rheims in his place on the instigation of Hugh Capet. At Pope John XV's attempt to intervene, the French maintained their right to independence of action, though John XV did succeed in getting Gerbert suspended at the synod of Mouzon in 995 and his successor Gregory V restored Arnulf to his see. The popes, in short, played a far from consistent role. Their actions and policies depended to an extreme extent on their abilities and on those of the secular rulers with whom they collaborated or on whose protection they depended. They rarely intervened other than when asked to do so.

To some degree it appears to be the case that whatever the character of the incumbent, the standing of the papacy as an institution, as it had been established in the course of the eighth and ninth centuries, survived. One major contributor to this was the papal notariate, which, like the modern British civil service, or, for that matter, the papal bureaucracy during the fifteenth-century Renaissance, provided essential stability and continuity in both its production of documents and its personnel. The notariate was responsible for the issuing of papal letters and charters on a regular basis, often on request from supplicants. The erratic survival of documents emanating from the papal *scrinium* or writing office in the course of the tenth and early eleventh centuries means that conclusions can only tentatively be drawn. Nevertheless, it would appear from

---

[4] *MGH Concilia aevi Saxonici et Salici*, no. 4, pp. 68–74.

the names recorded of the scribes producing letters and charters for each pope that many individual notaries did indeed serve a number of different popes consecutively, patiently coming in to work in the papal writing office regardless of the upheavals connected with the papal throne itself. The papal office was staffed with a number of notaries at any one time, though some predominate in the documents at particular periods. Stephen and Leo for example were the scribes of most of the documents produced between 955 and 973; it is conceivable that it is the same Stephen who then appears as scribe of papal charters right through to 992. Under Gregory V and John XVIII the principal scribe appears to have been Peter, while under John XIV through to Benedict VIII, Benedict the notary is also very active. Other scribes, such as Nicolas, Samuel, Gregory, Sergius, Leo, Melchisadech, Antony, John, Adrian, Theodore and Azzo in the first half of the tenth century and George, Anacletus, Theodore, Bonizo, Gregory, John or Antonius in the early years of the eleventh century, make fleeting appearances. The charters witness to contact being maintained between the papacy and churches in England, France, Spain and Germany as well as in Italy and Rome itself. No doubt as an accident of survival, most of the extant charters, in fact, have to do with matters outside Rome. They witness to the constant stream of requests for papal protection from such monasteries as San Vincenzo al Volturno, Saint-Martin at Poitiers, Cluny, Brogne and Quedlinburg, confirmation of ecclesiastical privileges, especially the designation of metropolitan status and the conferring of a pallium, and confirmations of the position of particular bishops. It is especially notable how many religious houses sought direct privileges from the pope rather than from their local rulers. Occasionally, in addition to the number of charters which relate to political involvement, the pope attempted to take a moral stand. The lay abbot Hugh, *dux* of the Franks and lay abbot of Tours, for example, was abjured not to tolerate the presence of women in the monastery. A quarter of the 630 papal charters surviving from the period 896–1049 are forgeries. Those of near contemporary date, however, attest to the degree of habitual reference to the papacy and its authority on a steadily increasing scale throughout the tenth and first half of the eleventh centuries.

From the perspective of the end of the eleventh century, the tenth-century papacy nevertheless looks a sorry tale of disgrace, political corruption and excess, far worse than mere incompetence. Later historians were to term its period of domination at the beginning of the tenth century by the Theophylact family – Theophylact, his wife Marozia and their sons – as a 'pornocracy'. This is to go too far. The most striking feature of the popes in this period is the degree to which immediate circumstances were responded to, and how much attempts to return to past policies or definitions of papal status, notably *vis-à-vis* the Frankish or German emperors, had the effect, time and time again, of hauling the papacy back onto the rails. Table 1 (p. 692) shows the bewildering succession of popes (striking in its similarities with the succession of fifth-century emperors), with no less than forty-five in 160 years, many of whom served for less than a year. Vicious factionalism accounts for some of the shorter terms of office and the antipopes installed briefly in the Lateran, such as Boniface VII or John XVI. A few popes removed from office, such as Benedict VI, were murdered. Apart from the dominance in Rome itself of the Theophylact and Crescentii families at various stages in the course of the tenth centuries, other strands of political allegiance, to the houses of Wido of Spoleto, Berengar of Friuli, the west Frankish rulers or the German kings, influenced the choice of a pope. Yet this did not always entail corruption and disorder. John X, elected pope in 914, was a vigorous and experienced bishop before his election and managed to form a political coalition of Italian rulers against the Muslims[5] as well as fostering the chant school and the Lateran administration during his fourteen-year reign. It was he who crowned Berengar of Friuli, great grandson of Louis the Pious, as emperor in 915. Under Count Alberic of Rome, moreover, there was a period of relative stability from 932 to 954. Even though the popes in this period, Leo VII, Stephen VII (IX), Marinus II and Agapitus II, were Alberic's nominees and well under his thumb for the most part, much was achieved within the religious sphere, notably in the reform of the monasteries of Rome and in ecclesiastical contacts with Germany. From 1012 to 1044, moreover, there was effective leadership from the papacy provided by the brothers Benedict VIII and John XIX and their nephew Benedict IX. An indication of some popes' aspirations to emulate the early popes and the spiritual status of illustrious bishops of Rome from the 'pure' days of its history lies in their decisions to adopt new names. Silvester II, for example, chose his name in conjunction with the German emperor Otto III in order to recall Constantine and his supposed relationship with Pope Sylvester I. In the frequent choice of the names Leo, Gregory, Damasus and Clement, in particular, earnest good intentions, if nothing more, are mirrored.

The macabre affair of Formosus highlights the very specific objections that could be mounted against a candidate for the papal throne, for it had repercussions for nearly thirty years afterwards. Formosus, before his election to the holy see in 891, had been an active missionary in Bulgaria, a papal legate and, crucially, bishop of Porto, though he had fallen foul of John VIII and suffered a period of excommunication. He proved to be an effective pope in his five years' incumbency, acting with astuteness in relation to England, Germany and Constantinople and crowning Arnulf emperor in 896. But it was against canon

---

[5] Zimmermann, *Papsturkunden*, no. 40, pp. 68–9.

law for a bishop to be translated to another see. Never before had a bishop become a pope and it was held against him, or used as the political excuse for other actions, to an astonishing degree after his death. His successor Stephen VI (VII) convened a synod and had the rotting corpse of Formosus exhumed, dressed up in his pontifical robes, propped againt the papal throne and charged with perjury, breaking canon law by being a bishop before he became pope and coveting the papacy. Unsurprisingly, despite the oral defence offered by a luckless deacon assigned to the task of speaking on behalf of the corpse, Formosus was found guilty and all his acts as pope declared null and void. These of course included all his ordinations and consecrations, and, conveniently, Stephen VI's own disqualifying consecration as bishop of Anagni. The body was then solemnly unfrocked and thrown into the Tiber. Stephen himself did not last long after this gruesome outrage but was imprisoned and killed soon afterwards. Partisans of Formosus subsequently elevated many of their own candidates successively to the papal throne and the validity of Formosus' acts was reconfirmed.

Too much emphasis on some lurid incidents, however, detracts from the proper consideration of consistent elements of papal policy throughout the tenth century and the reiteration of past agreements with the Carolingians concerning their mutual obligations and the conduct of papal elections. At the end of the seventh century it had still been necessary for the Byzantine emperor to be sent a mandate sanctioning the consecration of the new pope once the election had been held. The last pope to seek such sanction was Gregory III (731–41), for the appointment of Zacharias (741–52) was made without imperial ratification: all Zacharias did was to send an envoy to announce his election and consecration. He in his turn was the last pope to send formal notification of any kind to the eastern ruler, for Pope Paul I (757–67) announced his election to Pippin III, king of the Franks and since 754 'protector' of the holy see. It is significant that Paul did so using the same formula that had been used to notify the Byzantine emperors, except that he did not ask for ratification, pledging instead undying loyalty. Similarly Stephen III (IV) (768–77) dispatched an embasssy to the Frankish court to announce his election, as did Leo III, who also sent Charlemagne the keys to the tomb of St Peter and requested a Frankish envoy's presence to receive the oaths of the citizens of Rome. Thus the former ratificatory role of the Byzantine emperor had been replaced by the pope feeling the need to announce his election to the Frankish ruler, who was also the protector of Rome. Yet the balance shifted in 816 when Stephen IV (V) (816–17) anointed Louis the Pious. This was presumably an attempt to make the pope's role in the creation of an emperor a necessary one. In the reign of Paschal I (817–24), who was consecrated the day after his election to pre-empt secular interference, the first major definition of papal and imperial relations was set out in the document known as the *Pactum Ludovicianum* (817). This confirmed the pope in the possession of his papal states and patrimonies, and guaranteed the freedom of papal elections, though it required the new pope to notify the emperor of his election and consecration and to renew their treaty of friendship. Further, in 824, the *Constitutio romana*, ratified at a synod in Rome in 826, granted, among other things, immunity to all under imperial or papal protection and restored the role of the people of Rome in the election of the pope (suspended since 769). The pope was to swear an oath of loyalty to the emperor though papal independence in the spiritual sphere was maintained. It is from this date that we may observe the resumption of local political interest in the papal elections and the re-emergence of factions in Rome whose political ambitions were focused on the papacy.

The *Constitutio romana* and the *Ludovicianum* were reconfirmed or adjusted from time to time in the course of the tenth century. Thus the *Constitutio romana* was revived in 898, to the extent that, while the papal election should be by the bishops and clergy at the request of senate and people, papal consecration should only take place in the presence of imperial emissaries. In 962, on the occasion of Otto I's coronation as emperor, the *Ottonianum* revived the *Ludovicianum*. It confirmed the donations of Pippin and Charlemagne and (possibly after December 963) restored the freedom of papal elections (subject to imperial approval of the man elected and his obligation to swear an oath of loyalty to the emperor).

Individuals also altered the relationship between the Frankish emperors and the pope in practice, either making it even more extreme or asserting papal prerogative. Thus, for example, Gregory IV (827–44) deferred his consecration until the imperial legate had approved his election and he himself had sworn an oath of loyalty to the emperor. Nicholas I was elected in the presence and with the approval of the Emperor Louis II, but Sergius II's consecration was rushed through without waiting for imperial acknowledgement despite Lothar's insistence that a pope should not be consecrated except on his orders and in the presence of his representative. Charles the Bald (emperor 875–7) refrained from claiming a guiding hand in papal elections but Charles the Fat (emperor 881–5) insisted that he ought to be consulted. From time to time in the tenth century it was the pope who made the essential moves for the allocation of the imperial title to a potentially vigorous protector of Rome, but the emperor himself could be called on to nominate a new pope. Thus when Otto III was approached by the Roman nobility, he nominated Brun, son of the duke of Carinthia, who took the name Gregory V and himself crowned Otto as emperor and patrician. Similarly Henry III's appointment as patrician enabled him to take the lead in the appointment of the pope. Even at its lowest ebb the office of pope appears to have been more important than the person. This is particularly the case as far as the coronation of Otto I as emperor in 962 was concerned. The then pope was John XII, consecrated pope when possibly as young as sixteen years old, and the son of the Count Alberic who had per-suaded the Pope Agapitus II to accept John (then called Octavian) not only as successor to Agapitus but also to Alberic, so that he would combine spiritual and temporal rulership of Rome in one person. John however, if we are to believe Liudprand of Cremona's notoriously partial account, was renowned for his dissolute life. Whatever the facts of the matter, John was arraigned at a synod shortly after Otto's coronation and actually deposed. Henry III, on the other hand, appears to have wanted someone reputable to crown him emperor. He deposed no less than three popes at the synod of Sutri in 1046, before installing Suiger, bishop of Bamberg as Pope Clement II. Clement crowned Henry and Agnes his queen on 25 December 1046. It is significant, moreover, that even the emperor's men, such as Gregory V or Sylvester II, championed papal prerogatives once safely consecrated. Their ability to do so was based on that very stability within the papal administration mentioned earlier, as well as the enduring attitude towards papal spiritual authority evident in the contacts with other countries. These are most obvious in the sphere of missionary work, with the establishment of new bishoprics and the determination of their ecclesiastical allegiances and liturgical observance in Denmark, Poland, Hungary, Dalmatia and east of the Elbe. Sylvester II's incumbency, for example, saw the establishment of archbishoprics at Gniezno and Estergom and the sending of a royal crown to King Stephen of Hungary. Occasionally, theological issues as well as those of papal and episcopal jurisdiction in the south of Italy were discussed and sides taken in disputes with the eastern emperor and the patriarch. Papal policy in its various contexts appears, ulti-mately, to have been directed towards enhancing and confirming the authority of the bishops of the Latin church.

Papal relations with the bishops of Latin Christendom are only a small part of the concerns of the bishops themselves, however. Let us look at the careers of some of these bishops and their clergy, therefore, and at the implications of the written records of their activities. Æthelwold of Winchester, for example, the celebrated reformer of the tenth-century English church, scholar, teacher and ascetic, was elevated to the see of Winchester on 29 November 963. According to his biographer, Wulfstan, he was an 'intimate of the distin-guished king Edgar'. He was able to temper the severity of his discipline with coaxing gentleness, but was himself afflicted with frequent pain in his innards and legs.[6] Wulfstan provides a lurid account of the scandalous and wicked

---

[6] Wulfstan of Winchester, *Vita sancti Æthelwoldi*, cc. 25, 28, 30, pp. 42, 44, 46.

behaviour of the canons in possession at Winchester cathedral when Æthelwold arrived. They were married, given to gourmandising and drunkenness, and some even did not celebrate Mass in due order. With permission from King Edgar, Æthelwold expelled the canons, replaced them with reformed monks from his own monastery at Abingdon, and thus became both abbot and bishop. The canons' livings presumably became the corporate possession of the monks. The Life is loquacious on the reforming and monastic practices of Æthelwold. He established Osgar as abbot at Abingdon in his stead, installed nuns at Nunnaminster, and created a monastery at Ely under Abbot Byrhtnoth and monasteries at Peterborough, Thorney and elsewhere. All these were part of the monastic reorganisation throughout Europe described by Wollasch, below, in which the Rule of Benedict was upheld as the ideal. A remarkably successful attempt was made in England to impose the Rule on 'reformed' monastic houses and on new foundations as well as the English variation of imposing it on the cathedral clergy of the episcopal minsters.

The *Vita sancti Æthelwoldi* is conventional in its catalogue of Æthelwold's virtues. He is described as a consoler and helper of widows and orphans, receiver of pilgrims and defender of the church. He refreshed the poor, and set right those who had gone astray. As well as such obligatory pastoral concerns, Æthelwold taught in the school at Winchester. He offered instruction in grammar and translated Latin texts into English for the better understanding of his pupils; many of his pupils became priests, abbots and notable bishops. To complete the picture Wulfstan notes that a number of healing miracles are associated with Æthelwold. Thus Wulfstan's life of Æthelwold at a general level provides a sympathetic account of late Anglo-Saxon religious devotion and expression. Its focus on the career of a saintly bishop, however, is typical of the orientation of sympathy and perception of leadership in the church in Europe in the tenth and first half of the eleventh centuries expressed in the bishops' *vitae* and collective histories of bishops in particular sees. If we compare Wulfstan's account of Æthelwold with those of other contemporary prelates, there are both instructive contrasts and parallels, many of which raise issues of concern to the history of the church as a whole.

Many of the German bishops, for example, accord well with the ideals set out by Æthelwold, yet the career and Life of one in particular, exposes the question of the criteria for sainthood and the recognition of holy status by the ecclesiastical hierarchy. Ulrich of Augsburg was the first saint to be canonised in what later became the normal fashion. It is a measure of his reputation for piety that it was a petition from Augsburg itself in 993, exhorting Pope John XV to acknowledge their former bishop as a saint, which achieved his formal elevation to sainthood. Yet it may also be a measure of the increasing coherence of the ecclesiastical hierarchy and the role of the pope at its head (at least in relation to the bishops of the Saxon empire) that such papal recognition was thought necessary to obtain. This is in striking contrast to the local creation of saints and observance of their cults in earlier centuries. The *Vita sancti Oudalrici*, written in about 982 by Gerhard, a priest ordained by Ulrich and a member of the *familia* at Augsburg, played no small role in Ulrich's recognition. In later years, dossiers on candidates for canonisation were presented to the pope as a matter of course once Innocent III and his successors had assumed control of the cult of saints by defining degrees of holiness and the formal procedure for canonisation.

Gerhard related how the nobly born Ulrich conducted himself in his diocese, with his rounds of episcopal visitation and exercise of pastoral care, observance of the major liturgical feasts, the dedication of new churches, his political service and loyalty to Otto I, especially during the quarrel with Liudolf and his uncle, Henry of Bavaria, his miracles, his journeys to Rome, his attendance at the synod of Ingelheim in 972 and the high example, both in his own conduct and in his attention to the discipline of others,[7] that he provided for the conduct of the religious life. Some of these features are clearly peculiar to the circumstances of Ulrich alone, but others, such as his pastoral care, meticulous ecclesiastical observance, personal piety and miracles, might be generalised as criteria for holiness.

It is the political dimension to Bishop Ulrich's career above all, however, that is a constantly recurring theme in the lives of the bishops of the tenth century. Family politics, larger national tensions and the internal balance of authority and power within the ecclesiastical hierarchy all play a role. Bernward, bishop of Hildesheim (993–1022) is no exception. According to the *Vita sancti Bernwardi* (partly composed by Thangmar, who completed his portions between 1022 and 1024, and partly much later towards the end of the twelfth century), Bernward served in his youth as notary and was with the court in Italy at the court of Otto II, and he and the see of Hildesheim itself were richly rewarded by Otto.[8] Ecclesiastical prerogatives, such as Hildesheim's jurisdiction over the royal convent of Gandersheim, were jealously defended. Bernward left other monuments to his incumbency, not least the magnificent abbey church of St Michael, for the production of whose rich sculptural decorations he was responsible, and the many liturgical manuscripts commissioned by him or presented to him.

The German bishops, moreover, like their colleagues elsewhere in western Europe, had much to do with the maintenance of educational provision in the cathedral schools, actively promoting learning by their patronage of scholars

---

[7] Gerhard, *Vita sancti Oudalrici*, c. 3, pp. 388–90.   [8] Thangmar, *Vita sancti Bernwardi*, c. 19, p. 767.

and book production. Many boys, whether bound for ecclesiastical or for secular careers, were sent for training to these schools – Trier, Augsburg, Cologne, Eichstätt, Liège and Utrecht, under Bishops Ruotbert (931–56), Ulrich, Brun, Ebrachar, Starchand and Balderic respectively, were particularly celebrated.[9] Some visiting scholars, such as Stephen of Novara at Würzburg, provided an added attraction. In the Lotharingian sees of Metz and Toul, in the Bavarian dioceses of Salzburg and Regensburg, and in the newly-founded diocese of Magdeburg, schools flourished. Masters in these schools, such as Ohtrich at Magdeburg, acquired great fame as scholars, and some bishops clearly appointed notable scholars to add lustre to their schools. Under Adaldag of Hamburg-Bremen, for example, the cathedral school was directed by the learned master Thiadhelm. Most of the German bishops themselves, moreover, either had been educated in one of these cathedral schools or came from the schools of the reformed monasteries. Thus Hildiward of Halberstadt and Balderic of Speyer had been educated at St Gallen. Otwin, educated at Reichenau, promoted education as bishop at Hildesheim. They, and others like them, came to their sees ready to apply in their new establishments what they had learnt in their youth.

Many of these bishops were prominent not only in education but also in their patronage of book and artefact production. Some bishops, such as Theoderic of Metz, who in 984 donated a late eighth-century Homiliary embellished with comments and corrections by Rather of Verona,[10] a historical miscellany compiled in the ninth century[11] and a ninth-century collection of texts to do with computus and time[12] to the newly founded monastery of Saint-Vincent at Metz, may have contented themselves with the gifts of older books. Other bishops commissioned new ones for their own or others' use. Archbishop Everger of Cologne (984–99), for example, gave an Epistle Lectionary to the cathedral of Cologne, and had himself depicted therein in abasement before the enthroned saints, Peter and Paul.[13] Gero, archbishop of Cologne (969–76) had himself portrayed offering a Gospel Lectionary to St Peter.[14] Perhaps the most famous German episcopal patron of book production was Egbert, archbishop of Trier (977–93). The scriptorium of Trier during his incumbency produced a number of books both for him and for others (some of which were given to the cathedral at Trier), such as the famous

---

[9] Anselm, *Gesta episcoporum Leodiensium*, c. 25, p. 205.

[10] Berlin, Stiftung Preussischer Kulturbesitz, MS Phillips 1676 (50).

[11] Berlin, Stiftung Preussischer Kulturbesitz, MSS Phillips 1885 and 1896, and St Petersburg Saltykov-Schedrin Library MSS Q.v.IV no. 5 and Q.v. class no. 9.

[12] Berlin, Stiftung Preussischer Kulturbesitz, MS Phillipps 1831 (128).

[13] Cologne, Erzbischöfliche Diözesan- und Dombibliothek, MS Dom 143, fols. 3v–4r.

[14] Darmstadt, Hessische Landes- und Hochschulbibliothek, MS 1948.

Registrum Gregorii with its verses lamenting the death of Otto II,[15] the Egbert Psalter,[16] and the little Greek and Latin Psalter designed to help the Empress Theophanu learn Latin.[17] Yet the German bishops were not unique in their patronage of scriptoria and the commissioning of books. Winchester also produced fine books for its bishops, notably the Benedictional of Æthelwold (963–84)[18] and the Benedictional and Pontifical produced at Winchester c. 980 and subsequently associated with either Robert, archbishop of Rouen (990–1037) or Robert of Jumièges, archbishop of Canterbury (1051–5), of which the former would appear to be the most likely first owner. Arnulf II, archbishop of Milan (998–1018) had a handsome prayer book compiled and decorated in gold, silver and rich colours at Milan for his personal use, of great interest for the personal selection of prayers it contains.[19] The patronage of the arts was not confined to books, however, as is clear from the reliquaries, bronze sculptures, ivory-carvings and buildings also associated with Bishop Bernward of Hildesheim (993–1022), another of the great German bishops subsequently formally canonised.

It cannot be said that the tenth-century archbishops of Rheims, on the other hand, can be described in similar terms to those the German episcopal biographers and hagiographers invoke. Nor is it the case that the Rheims metropolitans upheld the legacy of Hincmar in all respects. In their history there is a tension between the ideal of Rheims' pre-eminence among the provinces of the Frankish kingdoms and the reality of their unfitness for office, their political intrigue with and subservience to members of the Carolingian family, military prowess, immense wealth and the close, often oppressive association between the archbishops and the principal monasteries of the diocese. Heriveus (900–22), for example, led a force of 1,500 warriors to assist the Frankish king against the Magyars; Seulf (922–5) strengthened the city's fortifications. Not till 945 was the monastery of Saint-Rémi finally able to obtain its independence from archiepiscopal control and install a regular abbot.[20] Hugh (925–31; 942–8), son of the Carolingian Count Heribert of Vermandois, was first created archbishop at the age of five and only deposed, with royal intervention, in favour of Artald (931–40), a monk of Saint-Rémi.[21] It is small wonder that Flodoard's account stressed the physical actions and strength of the archbishops, notably in building up the wealth of the archbishopric and retrieving lost estates, at the expense of their spiritual leadership. The stress on property should nevertheless be seen against such provisions as those of the council of Trosly, summoned by Archbishop Heriveus in 909, which mounted a vehement attack on laymen who had taken church land, and on the encroach-

---

[15] Trier, Stadtbibliothek, MS 171a.   [16] Cividale, Museo Archeologico, MS N.CXXXVI.
[17] Trier, Stadtbibliothek, MS 7/9 8°.   [18] BL, MS Additional 49598.
[19] BL, MS Egerton 3763.   [20] Flodoard, *HRE* IV, 32, pp. 583–4.   [21] *Ibid.*, IV, 24, p. 580.

ment on ecclesiastical property, offices and privileges by the king and lay magnates.[22] In the eyes of Flodoard, the retrieval of church land from such predators may indeed have appeared the highest episcopal virtue.

Flodoard had also given himself a much more difficult task than the simple chronicling of one man's life and career. In tackling the history of his see he was attempting to provide not only a collective identity, but also a generalised justification for the pattern of episcopal behaviour over many decades. Ultimately, therefore, the identity and individual careers of the bishops are subservient to the fortunes of the see of Rheims itself, the real hero of his history. He was able to outline a particular conception of the church in Frankish society written in the form of a history and buttressed by copious citation of legal documents which established Rheims' territorial rights. The concentration on property, however much it was at odds with fundamental other-worldly Christian values, has the function of providing continuity and stability within a changing world, beset by human intrigues and attack. Such collective identity and emphasis on territorial possession, together with a firm conception of the bishop's role in relation to the lay world, are arguably the guiding motives in many of the Carolingian, Saxon and Salian histories of bishoprics. The histories of Auxerre, Ravenna, Le Mans, Cambrai, Hamburg-Bremen, Naples, Liège, Trier, Verdun, Metz and Toul were written in the wake of Paul the Deacon's *Gesta episcoporum Mettensium* of the late eighth century and inspired by the example of the collective history of the popes, the *Liber pontificalis*. Their distribution in itself may be significant as far as the existence of possibly different perceptions of the bishops' role in his diocese and in relation to his predecessors and successors are concerned, for no histories in this genre appear to have survived from Spain, England, northern Italy or southern France

Not until the incumbency of Adalbero could Rheims again boast of an archbishop who appears to conform more to the norms established in the episcopal *vitae*. Adalbero was from Lotharingia. His early education at Gorze bore fruit in his own promotion of the school at Rheims, for it was he who installed Gerbert as master of the school at Rheims, re-established a Benedictine community at Mouzon and made over many estates in the wine-producing areas of the Meuse valley and Metz to the monks. A canon's rule, moreover, was reintroduced for the cathedral canons at Rheims and regular monks were restored to the monastery of Saint-Thierry. The scriptoria of Rheims appear to have been active at this stage as well. Adalbero at least, therefore, appears to have resumed his predecessor Hincmar's patronage of the cathedral library as well as devoting himself to the embellishment of existing churches and the erection of a new one in Rheims itself.[23] Nevertheless, even taking the

---

[22] Mansi, *Concilia* 18, cols. 263–308.   [23] Richer, *Historiae* III, 22–3, pp. 28/30.

presentation of Adalbero in Richer's *Historiae* into account, the political involvement of the archbishops of Rheims remained secular in character. Artald's advocacy in the takeover of the west Frankish kingdom by Hugh Capet, for example, is well attested.[24] But then, it was in Rheims' interests to assert to posterity its enabling and crucially supportive role in relation to the crown. Unlike the bishops in England, however, the archbishops of Rheims made little attempt to exert moral authority over their rulers, and the Carolingian tradition of self-seeking ambition and political interference was staunchly maintained by Adalbero's successors.

A similar emphasis on the physical strength of the bishops can be discerned in the meagre account from Sens. Sens under Archbishop Archembald (958–67) had been a disgrace, even if measured against the criteria implied by Flodoard of Rheims. According to the eleventh-century chronicler of Sens, Odorannus (and Clarius, who echoes him), Archembald had actually sold not only the lands and churches of Sens but the actual church buildings themselves. He spent the proceeds on self-indulgence, turning the refectory of St Peter's monastery into a brothel and keeping his hunting dogs in the monastic precincts. Under Anastasius (968–76) and particularly under Seguin (977–99), however, the church of Sens was restored to the position of respect it had attained in the ninth century. Such rapid recovery endorses Fichtenau's less censorious view of the effect of temporary alienations. The chroniclers are most interested in Seguin's devotion to the monastery of St Peter, and give full details of his restoration of the discipline, the fabric and the estates of the monastery and the installation of a new abbot. Seguin also had the cathedral of St Stephen, which had been destroyed by fire in July 967, rebuilt, and he and his fellow bishops of Troyes, Nevers and Auxerre presided over its reconsecration. The needs. of the laity received some attention in the establishment of parish churches in the city and the acquisition of important new relics, including the arm of Pope Leo the Great, to act as a focus of devotion. Both Seguin and Leothericus his successor are reported to have received the pallium from the pope. Although this was the normal recognition received by a new archbishop since at least the eighth century, Odorannus insists that this pallium also conferred the primacy of Gaul upon the archbishop of Sens. Whether this was really the case is doubtful. Rheims too claimed the primacy, yet the precise function of this role, as distinct from its honorific nature, even in the days of Boniface of Mainz and Chrodegang of Metz, is difficult to determine.

Whereas the bishops of Rheims and Sens worked within an ancient ecclesiastical framework in their efforts to cling to their pre-eminence, the archbishops of Hamburg-Bremen, associated as one bishopric from 864, attempted to

---

[24] *Ibid.*, IV, 3–5, pp. 128/32.

exert their ecclesiastical authority in Denmark, Norway and Sweden as well as among the Slavs east of the Elbe. Ever since their first bishop, Anskar, had preached the Gospel in Denmark and Sweden, the bishops, in the way Adam of Bremen tells their story, directed their energies towards establishing the church in Scandinavia. In particular, Unni (bishop 919–36) and a 'very holy man', preached and died in Sweden; Adaldag established the dioceses of Ribe, Schleswig and Aarhus under the metropolitan authority of Hamburg-Bremen and also preached among the Slavs. The bishops worked in such a way as to consolidate the archbishops' own ecclesiastical authority within the northern part of the east Frankish kingdom. Their missionary work in the north, moreover, cannot be divorced from political considerations. A constant, but underplayed, presence in Adam's story of the northern mission is the clashes of interest with England, particularly after the Danish conquest of England and during the rule of Cnut.[25] Similarly, in the overtures to the Slavs, political and ecclesiastical expansion are closely associated, and the lack of Frankish and Saxon success among the northern Slavs is due in part to the peoples of that region's staunch efforts to retain their political autonomy.

Despite the wider horizons of these northern bishops, they exemplify many of the customary episcopal virtues. Thus Adaldag distributed among the parishes of his diocese the relics of the holy martyrs (Quiriacus, and Cesarius, Victor and Corona, Felix, Felician, Cosmas and Damian) and saw to the maintenance of the *xenodochium* of Bremen. Adaldag himself, moreover, was from Hildesheim, 'noble in appearance and behaviour, illustrious in family' and related to Adalward of Verden. He had served Otto I in his chancery. He founded a convent at Hieslingen and a monastery at Reepsholt and maintained a school at Hamburg. Unwan, bishop 1013–29, was similarly of good family, selected from Paderborn, rich and generous. He was the first to impose the rule of canons on the cathedral clergy and did all he could, by loading them with gifts, paid for out of the diocesan treasury of Hamburg, to soften up the kings of Norway towards the ecclesiastical overtures from the German church represented by Hamburg-Bremen.

Adam is more than a biographer of the separate bishops who are his subjects. He provides nothing less than a history of his region in which Hamburg-Bremen is the focus; it is a world where the Saxon kings and the rulers of the Slavs and of the Scandinavian peoples all interact in the political and secular concerns of the archbishops. Although the mission to the heathen is the mainspring of the account, Adam contrives to convey the principles on which political and ecclesiastical expansion can be based. He sets the agenda at the beginning by his unequivocal account of the career of Anskar and its

---

[25] Adam of Bremen, *Gesta* II, 37, p. 98.

significance. He then cuts the careers of the later bishops to the cloth of Anskar. Devotion to Hamburg-Bremen is the highest virtue, and the archbishop who earns the most censure is Hermann (1032–5). Hermann was elected from the chapter of Halberstadt. He rarely visited Hamburg except to come with an army and lay it waste. His one virtue was that he installed Guido as music master in the cathedral at Bremen, who reformed chant and liturgical discipline.

The archbishops of Hamburg-Bremen were not alone in the tenth century as far as expansion of the frontiers of Christendom was concerned. Otto I had extended the frontiers of his kingdom towards the east, and establishment of the church with the assistance of his bishops within that region was a fundamental component of political consolidation. Cnut and the English bishops had, as already noted, mounted an independent missionary enterprise in Scandinavia that clashed with the interests of the archbishops of Hamburg-Bremen. Missionary endeavour elsewhere is signalled on the one hand by the foundation of new bishoprics, such as Bamberg (1007), Magdeburg (968), Gnesen (999), Posen (968) or Prague(973), which were intended to act as missionary outposts and new ecclesiastical centres, and on the other by the celebratory lives of the saints who brought Christianity to the Danes, Slavs, Obodrites, Rus', Poles or Magyars. In their careers, and in the first introduction of Christianity in however superficial a manner, the princes who first accepted Christianity often played a key role, as did Wenceslas, Boleslav I and Boleslav II in Bohemia, Miesco I in Poland, Harald Bluetooth (950–86) in Denmark and Olaf Tryggvason (995–1000) and Olaf Haraldson (1015–1030) in Norway. Recent research, indeed, has tended to emphasise the role of the prince and the leaders in any region rather than that of the foreign missionaries in the decision to adopt Christianity. That the new churches established were essentially state churches certainly supports this view. Conversion to Christianity, therefore, was a decision not merely about religion but also about political association and cultural alignment. Such religious commitment could also lend coherence to different groups of poeple, or enable an individual to consolidate political control, as in the case of Vladimir of Kiev, or Miesco of Poland. In other words, the stabilisation of royal power and Christianisation often went hand in hand. Missions sent out from Salzburg and Aquileia in the eighth and ninth centuries were built upon, and in a number of regions either Italian churches (or even the pope himself) or the Byzantine church played a prominent role initially. Moravia was Christianised, for example, by the Byzantine missionary Methodius (commemorated now in the series of wall-paintings in the lower basilica of S. Clemente in Rome). Rorivoj and his wife Ludmila were baptised together with their son Spytihnev by archbishop Methodius at the court of Sviatopolk. In 895, however, Spytihnev renewed Moravia's allegiance with the

Franks and it has been conjectured that the jurisdiction of the bishop of Regensburg was extended into Bohemia. In the late tenth century a bishopric of Prague was created whose second bishop was Adalbert Vojtech. He had been educated at Magdeburg. He was canonised in 999, and thus gave the Bohemians a national saint, soon to be joined by King Wenceslas. Croatia was reunified under Tomislav (910–29), who was recognised by the pope, for what that was worth, as king of the Croats. For strategic reasons, Venice, Byzantium and Hungary were all interested in the kingdom of the Croats. Thus in this region, political and ecclesiastical interests clashed, for the archbishop of Split aspired to ecclesiastical dominance of the region.

It is difficult to determine the nature and strength of the paganism of these converted peoples; we only hear about them from the Christians who converted them, and who resort to facile judgements and contemptuous references about the religious beliefs and practices of the pagans. Some notion of the strength of the paganism of the eastern Slavs in particular, however, might be surmised from the long resistance of the Elbe Slavs to conversion. Further east, the Lithuanians were not converted to Christianity until the mid-fourteenth century, and then, apparently, more as a political move than from religious conviction. In some cases, moreover, the paganism of some of these eastern regions may have been watered down by long-standing contacts with Christian regions. Resistance to Christianity, moreover, was part and parcel of political resistance. It is significant, for example, that the conversion of Norway was as slow as it was. Although missionaries had been present in the country since the end of the ninth century, ecclesiastical structures did not stabilise for another 200 years. A change in religion transformed the life of the community, though in Iceland, on the other hand, striking adaptations of Christianity to Icelandic society are apparent. The Christian church had to be accommodated physically on the land and socially within the local communities. In the Slav and Scandinavian regions the accommodation to and acceptance of Christianity required the decision not only of the ruler but also of his people. The communal nature of the decision-making is expressed symbolically by the famous Althing of Iceland in 999–1000 when Christianity was declared to be the official religion of Iceland.

It is indicative of the power of the bishops that it was largely through ostensibly Christian means that political ends were achieved. Rather than the careers of founders of monasteries and ascetic monastic saints predominating in the hagiography, as is the case before the tenth century, it is the bishops, sometimes ascetic, sometimes also founders of monasteries and promoters of monasticism and displaying many of the attributes of the saints of the earlier middle ages, as a result in part of earnest efforts on the part of their hagiographers to make them so. In addition, however, they are always practical, involved in politics, energetic, learned, and interested in the material and physical welfare of their flocks. The focus of these bishops' lives, according to the accounts given of them, is, as we have seen from the examples above, essentially local. The fact that we see these bishops primarily through the eyes of their hagiographers might be thought to diminish their credibility as historical evidence, were it not for their indirect display of contemporary expectations of a bishop. Bishop Ulrich, or Bishop Æthelwold, and the others at the hands of their biographers, therefore, each provide a *speculum episcopi*, a model for other bishops to follow and against which laity and lower clergy alike could measure their own bishops. Nevertheless, like much verbal, written image-making, the portraits we have of these bishops are indeed determined in part by their own activities and personalities in reality and in part by the activities of their predecessors, as we saw in the case of the bishops of Hamburg.

More can be learnt of many of these bishops in their own words, in the form of letters exchanged by many of them, sometimes, as in the case of Gerbert of Rheims and Rather of Verona, in copious quantities. From these can be observed the entire gamut of activity on the part of bishops, from political intrigue to pastoral advice. Further, we see these bishops all over Europe participating in the synods of their day, and it is these which establish the degree to which they felt they had a collective identity and acted corporately. A striking feature of much of the ecclesiastical legislation of the tenth and early eleventh centuries, however, is its local and diocesan nature. Very few general or even regional synods appear to have been convened, in marked contrast to the Carolingian period. Rather, the decrees preserved are more often from diocesan, or at best provincial meetings. Nevertheless, they reflect a unity of purpose and similarity of preoccupation among church leaders across the whole of Europe, given local differences. Despite its apparently normative character, moreover, the synodal legislation of the church was usually a response to particular problems and settled local disputes as well as occasionally issuing directives on general religious observance and organisation. A remarkably large quantity of such material survives, albeit it is often difficult to categorise. Some documents, for example, are classified as conciliar proceedings, when they read more like the records of an ecclesiastical court. Others are admonitory or exhortatory in character, or set out to prescribe remedies for a particular set of abuses. Rather of Verona, for example, apparently chose the forum of a synod to address his clergy on their duties, especially celebrating the Mass, the need to teach all parishioners the Lord's Prayer and Creed, the proper days for baptism (Easter Eve, the eve of Pentecost) and what the priest himself should know: the Mass, the Gospels and Epistles, and the rites for the sick, the dying and the dead.[26]

[26] Rather of Verona, *Epistolae*, ed. Weigle, no. 25, pp. 124–37.

Sometimes a synod would be convened as a consequence of a visit from an external ecclesiastical dignitary, such as the synod of Hohenaltheim in 916, prompted by the visit of the papal legate Peter of Orte. Others settled disputes over the appointment of particular bishops, such as the clutch of meetings held at Verdun, Mouzon, Ingelheim, Trier and Rome precipitated by the scandal of the archbishopric of Rheims between 947 and 949, the Cologne provincial synod at Cologne in 920 concerning the quarrel over the bishopric of Liège, or the synods of Duisburg (929), Ravenna (955) and Ingelheim (958). Provincial and diocesan synods in particular discussed general internal ecclesiastical provisions relating to the behaviour of the bishops and clergy, and matters of church discipline or of the religious observance of the laity. The presence of Italian bishops at meetings in Germany from the 950s indicates the extra dimension given ecclesiastical politics by Ottonian involvement in Italy. Many of these synods, particularly those concerning disputes over sees, had an obvious political dimension, though only rarely were synods actually summoned by a king. Those that were, were called on the initiative of such rulers as Henry I or Otto I in such a way as to reflect the king's close interest in the day-to-day running of ecclesiastical affairs and the degree to which this was associated by the king with general good government. One of these, the synod of Erfurt (932), may shed light on the ecclesiastical policy of Henry I, for it is possible that the king had concerned himself intimately with both its agenda and its organisation. Thus, like his Carolingian predecessors, Henry would be, on this reading, implicitly identifying his expectations as ruler with those of his bishops as pastoral and spiritual leaders of their dioceses. His attendance in person endorsed his royal position in relation to the church. The synod of Erfurt in its turn was enhanced by the king's presence and was attended by the archbishops of Mainz and Hamburg-Bremen and the bishops of Verden, Strasbourg, Constance, Paderborn, Augsburg, Halberstadt, Würzburg, Osnabrück, Münster and Minden, as well as a host of abbots and other clergy. In their deliberations, reference was made to the earlier councils of Mainz (852) and Tribur (895), which in their turn reflected earlier Carolingian provisions. The conciliar decisions of the tenth century overall have a clear and acknowledged debt to Carolingian church councils.

This raises the issues of the context in which the records of the proceedings have survived, the development of canon law, the definition and understanding of the authority of the church, and the role of historical precedent. The current understanding of the earlier tenth century, rightly or wrongly, is as one of transition between the concerted activity of the Carolingian synods and the certainties of eleventh-century Gregorian ecclesiology. Although there are not so many supra-regional councils as in the ninth century, there is certainly a respectable number of local and provincial assemblies in the tenth century, especially in the east Frankish kingdom, with records surviving, and many more, of which we have at least notices announcing that they had been convened. As a form of church government and decision-making, the synod was undoubtedly regarded as appropriate. Not only were many Carolingian conciliar decrees incorporated into collections of canon law in the late ninth and the tenth centuries, Carolingian decisions, as has been noted, are also specifically recalled in the deliberations of tenth-century and later ecclesiastical assemblies. If continuities can be so clearly observed, however, it throws doubt on the usefulness of the concept of transition. It suggests, moreover, that the late Carolingian bishops and early Ottonian bishops were, practically speaking, indistinguishable from one another in terms of the traditions and practice they acknowledged.

Certainly from a west Frankish perspective the preoccupations of Carolingian ecclesiastical legislation remained current issues in the context of tenth-century ecclesiastical deliberations. The general concerns of the few surviving decrees of synods between 888 and 987 are, for the most part, indistinguishable from those of their ninth-century precursors, even if particular local and provincial synods can be seen addressing immediate problems. As mentioned above, the synod of Trosly in 909, for example, forsook generalities in its specific attack on laymen who had taken church land and the encroachment of ecclesiastical property, offices and privileges by the king and lay magnates which the tenth-century bishops of Rheims did their utmost to counteract.

Yet the emphasis on discipline and the moral underpinning of the church, on episcopal and priestly accountability, and on the maintenance of the organisation of the church as part of the Christian realm remain the same as in the heyday of the Carolingian councils under Charlemagne and Louis the Pious. In the manuscript traditions of the great councils of the Carolingians in west Frankish sources, moreover, we get exactly the same picture as from the east. It is clear from the context in which many Carolingian conciliar decrees have survived, that individual tenth-century bishops made a direct connection between the preoccupations and concerns of the Carolingian synods and their own. A tenth-century manuscript from Freising, for example, contains the decrees of the Carolingian reform councils in company with the decrees of Hohenaltheim (916), Koblenz (922), Duisburg (929) and Erfurt (932).[27] The compiler, possibly under the auspices of Bishop Abraham of Freising, presumably wished to make a point about the relationship between the two sets of decrees, a century apart in date but not in aspiration. Further, many of these synodal decrees, together with the major conciliar canons of the ninth century, were, in their turn, incorporated into such major eleventh-century collections

---

[27] Clm 27246.

of canon law as that of Burchard of Worms. Older Frankish compilations of canon law such as the *Vetus gallica* were also widely spread throughout western Europe from the early eighth century onwards and were still current in collections of the tenth and eleventh centuries. The *Collectio canonum hibernensium* continued to be popular, as did the *Concordia Cresconii* (in Italy) and the so-called Roman collection, the *Dionysio-Hadriana*, and *Collectio Hispana*. Further compilations drawing on these were consistently compiled in all kinds of contexts. Added to these, of course, was the collection of notorious forgeries known by us as the Pseudo-Isidorean Decretals, though many compilers in the tenth and early eleventh centuries appear to have drawn on both genuine and forged canon law. A notable example is the collection attributed to Remedius of Chur, probably produced in southern Germany *c.* 900 (or 870 according to Reynolds) and found in many German dioceses, and the *Collectio Anselmo dedicata*, dedicated to Bishop Anselm II of Milan (882– 96) which enjoyed fairly wide circulation in Italy in the tenth century.

Obviously, each of the books containing a kaleidoscopic variety of different canons from Carolingian and earlier church councils and canon law collections was compiled for a particular purpose and at a particular time. Some may well have been in relation to the agenda for particular synods or in relation to major disputes. One problem, however, is how the records of a synod were actually made. A few extant tenth-century charters from the diocese of Sens, for instance, indicate that the initial record of a synod was in a form resembling *notitia* from a court case, with decisions made and those present recorded. All such documents imply an agreement by the participants to uphold what had been decided, but there is no intrinsic reason why such decisions should have continued to carry authority once they were translated out of their formal diplomatic context and inserted into a collection of legal material compiled for other purposes. Yet a further consideration is that every synod that met to discuss matters to do with the organisation of the church, belief, discipline or specific and immediate disputes placed itself, whether implicitly or explicitly, in a historical succession. The compiler of a collection of ecclesiastical legislation *c.* 1000 within the province of Mainz, for example, made an explicit link between the early Christian church, Visigothic, Anglo-Saxon and Carolingian decisions and the church of his own day by intermingling synodal decrees from all these regions.[28] The clauses relate to the practical and common concerns of the church, such as the role of the priests, the jurisdiction of bishops, the incidence of superstition, problems of valid marriages and what priests should preach. A west Frankish collection compiled for the use of a bishop includes among other texts the *capitula* of Riculf of Soissons, *ordines* for the convening

---

[28] Wolfenbüttel, Herzog-August Bibliothek, MS Helmst 454.

of synods and much to do with the proper conduct and duties of priests and the relations between a bishop and an abbot.[29] Some collections, such as that of Burchard of Worms or Regino of Prüm, acquired greater authority for reasons that can no longer be established, though their comprehensiveness may have made them particularly attractive to later compilers. One function of these collections, therefore, became that of affirming ecclesiastical and episcopal authority. The individual selections made may also indicate what one person had decided was important from the past legislation at his disposal. A collection compiled for the archbishop of Mainz in the second half of the tenth century, for example, takes as its core Regino of Prüm's *De synodalibus causis et disciplinis ecclesiasticis* and organises round it various decisions concerning the administration of the church, canon law and ecclesiastical organisation, all of which is directly related to the work of the bishop in his own diocese.[30] Similarly, many bishops, such as Ruotger of Trier, continued the ninth-century episcopal practice of issuing *capitula* or sets of directives to the clergy of their dioceses. They mirror diocesan concerns and are especially geared to the day-to-day running of parish affairs, the conduct of the clergy and the faith of the laity.

Faith, coupled with the total reorientation of the life of the laity throughout the Christian year, was expressed in the liturgical rituals of the Christian church, and some of the most creative episcopal activity of the tenth century was in the sphere of liturgy and liturgical chant. The main liturgical books of the early middle ages comprised the sacramentary, containing the texts for the celebrant of the eucharistic prayers and prayers for other rites of the church throughout the liturgical year, and the *ordines*, containing descriptions of and instructions for the rituals of various kinds at which the prayers in the sacramentary were to be recited. Thus we can reconstruct how the liturgy was actually celebrated as well as what was said. Individual bishops (and abbots) were responsible for an intensely local adaptation of the liturgical books and chant repertoire. Thus every surviving liturgical codex provides some slight variation and was designed for use in a particular church or group of churches. In addition, the plethora of commentaries on the Mass produced in the ninth century continued to circulate. Despite efforts to attain liturgical uniformity, indeed, the variety of rite throughout Europe by the end of the ninth century was, if anything, even greater than it had been two centuries earlier, with indigenous traditions heartily preserved. The liturgical evidence from the tenth and early eleventh centuries, moreover, illustrates how this great local diversity was maintained and augmented in an extraordinarily creative period. First, there is the great range of manuscripts extant, from centres as diverse as Regensburg,

---

[29] BN lat. 4280A.   [30] Wolfenbüttel, Herzog August Bibliothek, MS 8321 Aug.2°.

Mainz, Basel, Milan, York, Winchester, St German's in Cornwall, Cracow and Sens. Secondly there was the creation of a new type of composite book, a Missal, which contained mass texts, Epistles, Gospels and Antiphons, though other separate books were created such as Benedictionals, that is, those containing episcopal prayers. Pope Gregory V (996–9) himself requested the monastery of Reichenau to send a Missal for papal use in 998. Further, a new book for bishops, a Pontifical, was devised. It combined prayer texts, rites and *ordines* for a bishop in one volume. The most famous version is the so-called Romano-Germanic Pontifical, put together at Mainz under the archbishops (Frederick, William and Willigis), in the mid-tenth century, incorporating much older Frankish non-eucharistic material, notably from the *Hadrianum* Sacramentary as supplemented by Benedict of Aniane for Charlemagne, with which the *ordines* were combined.[31] Of particular importance for this was a ninth-century compilation from St Gallen.[32] The Romano-Germanic Pontifical rapidly superseded all other collections of *ordines* throughout the huge dioceses of Mainz and Salzburg, though its influence elsewhere in Europe was more limited. It is in the *ordines,* even more than in the texts of the prayers, that the innovations introduced by the Franks may be fully appreciated. They clearly reflect local episcopal initiatives as well as the bishops' ability to have recourse to scriptoria equipped to supply liturgical codices as needed.

Thus in the east Frankish kingdom between 880 and 900 the ritual description of an episcopal Mass (*Ordo* IX) was added to the *ordines* and incorporated into the Mainz Pontifical. Burchard of Worms devised a composite list of Old and New Testament readings for the night office (*Ordo* XIIIC) and a ceremonial description was provided for liturgical functions throughout the Christian year (*Ordo* L). Other *ordines* reflect west Frankish innovations, such as the ceremonial description of the last three days of Holy Week from Saint-Martial of Limoges of the late tenth century (*Ordo* XXXIII).[33] In Rome *c.* 925 was added an *ordo* for the ordination of lectors, acolytes, subdeacons, deacons, priests and bishops (*Ordo* XXXV) and other *ordines* for episcopal consecration were added in about 970 (*Ordo* XXVA and XXXVB). A rite for the coronation of an emperor was used between the death of Charles the Fat and the coronation of Berengar in 915 (*Ordo* XLV).

Liturgical uniformity is thus not in evidence. Even when new collections were formed, as in the tenth century, these were from the older familiar materials with particular liturgical allegiances displayed. An obvious example is the rites of the different regions brought within Christendom in the course of the tenth century – Croatia, Hungary, Bohemia and Poland. The claims of

---

[31] See, for example, BN lat. 13313 and Vienna, Österreichische Nationalbibliothek, MS lat. 701.
[32] St Gallen, Stiftsbibliothek, MSS 614 and 140. [33] BN lat. 1248.

Byzantium and Rome appear to have been equally enticing, but the liturgical orientation, Latin in Bohemia, Slavic in Moravia, Glagolitic in Croatia, Latin in Hungary, reflected a cultural, linguistic, intellectual and political orientation of great significance for the future development of these regions. Choice of which book to adopt in any church clearly rested with the individual bishop. For use in the Aachen palace chapel in the time of the Emperor Lothar, for example, it appears that an earlier stage of Gregorian Sacramentary which had been a Roman priest's Mass Book (as distinct from one for use by a pope like the *Hadrianum*) was used by the scribes of the 'court' scriptorium at Aachen.[34] It was subsequently used at Liège, and migrated to Verona between 900 and 950 where further additions were made to it. Tenth-century examples of the eighth-century Gelasian demonstrate how older Frankish liturgical texts were still in use.[35] In regions but recently brought under Frankish rule there is a predominance of 'non-Roman' rites such as the 'Celtic rite' in use in Ireland, the Ambrosian or Milanese rite which remained current in parts of northern Italy even into the eleventh century, and the 'Mozarabic' and 'Old Spanish' liturgies. The latter is represented, for example, by the reorganisation of the Mozarabic Antiphonary associated with Bishop Akilia of León (917–70).[36] All, nevertheless, played some role in the compilations of the Frankish kingdoms as well, and cannot themselves be said to be completely separate from the Roman-Frankish texts.

Other books were those connected with liturgical chant, such as the Responsaries, Tropars, Sequentiaries and Hymnaries or Hymnals, and those containing texts used during the Mass or in other ceremonies, such as the episcopal benedictionals and martyrologies. It is the lectionaries which demonstrate the greatest local diversity in the arrangements and selection of texts in the early middle ages (apart from the Spanish ones which were relatively stable), though when the Roman Catholic church fixed the readings in 1570, it was an essentially Romano-Frankish system that was chosen.

The most dramatic additions and changes wrought to the chant books, on the other hand, were in relation to their music. In the late Merovingian and Carolingian periods, a hybrid 'Roman' chant repertoire had been created by mixing older material of Roman origin with earlier indigenous Frankish material. This in its turn was combined with what was understood or claimed by the Carolingians to be contemporary Roman music, in order to create a distinctive liturgical chant commonly known as 'Gregorian'. The tenth century continued the remarkable proliferation of musical notations and the expan-

---

[34] Padua, Biblioteca capitolare, MS D47.
[35] Zurich, Zentralbibliothek, MS C43, made 1020–30 and the so-called 'Missal of Monza', Monza, Biblioteca capitolare, Codex F1–1–1 from Bergamo, of the late ninth or early tenth century.
[36] León, Biblioteca capitolare, MS 1.

sion of the chant repertory begun in the ninth century, especially of the new syntheses of melody and prose known as sequences and tropes particularly associated with such centres as Liège, Reichenau, St Gallen, Winchester, and many cathedrals and monasteries in the west Frankish kingdom and in Italy after about 1000. There were also further developments (notably on the part of Hermann of the Reichenau and Guido of Arezzo) in chant theory, the wider use of such musical instruments as the organ, and the emergence of liturgical plays in the late tenth century.

The liturgical year, celebrated in both words and music, included not only the great Christian festivals but also the feasts of local saints. Recent discussions of popular religion and culture in the middle ages have accorded prominence to the evidence of the saints' Lives, and other information concerning the observance of their cults. In the light of such Lives of saints as the *Vita sancti Oudalrici*, however, and the indications of the importance of historical context, it is clear that saints' Lives cannot be regarded as a static genre providing a stable category of historical evidence throughout the early middle ages. The old distinctions between official liturgical cults with written texts and popular oral veneration of saints (thought to be proof of quasi-pagan superstition) are no longer valid. Recent work has stressed how both hagiography and the observance of a cult are far from indifferent to chronology and historical context and that the 'popular' veneration of a saint need not involve non-Christian, magical or pagan practices. In the diocese or Orléans, for instance, the cult of long-dead local fathers of the Orléannais formed the focal point of the cult of saints in the region. Local models of sanctity were provided. Thus, the saints' role in local communities is to be understood within the context of both spiritual and social beliefs; the patronage exerted by a saint was understood in terms of the existing socal system. The 'logic of saintly patronage' has been invoked by Head to explain the way in which laity and clergy interacted. The duties of patronage required the saint to act on behalf of his or her servants; the saint, with his or her miraculous powers, would protect those who chose to become his or her servants, and this relationship in many ways mirrored those of lords and *fideles* in secular society. The submission of a person to the power of a saint and the request that the power be used to protect and intercede for the petitioner governed the full array of relationships between the local 'father' and his servants. God acted through the saint. Saints were live presences who owned property, appeared in visions, cured the sick, meted out punishment and dispensed justice. Miraculous powers were exhibited in their relics. The accounts of their lives provided a means of observing and interpreting the relics. The observance of the Orléannais saints was first recommended by Bishop Walther of Orléans in his statute of 871. In the tenth and eleventh centuries, accounts of these lives were written in order to strengthen and particularise the saints' associations with the Orléannais region. Evutius, Anianus, Benedict, Maximinus, Lifardus and the relic of the Holy Cross treasured at the cathedral of Orléans were firmly associated with a particular religious community and the locality within which it was situated. The relics of other saints – Paul Aurelian and Maurus the martyr – were translated into the diocese in the course of the tenth century. The Orléannais *vitae*, like other early medieval saints' Lives, had both a private and a public function. That is, they were intended for both the *legentes* and the *audientia populi*, and thus were of crucial importance in nourishing the popular devotion of the laity. The cult of saints functioned in many communities all over Europe just as it did in the Orléannais. Despite the fact that hagiography was a well-established literary genre with clear formal conventions and a standard repertoire of stylistic models, the author of each *vita* managed to tailor his material to his own specific requirements, in which immediate and perennial concerns were balanced and images of sanctity modifed to suit the preoccupations of a particular audience. Lay patrons commissioned *vitae* and many laymen and laywomen were celebrated as saints.

The cult of the Virgin Mary in later Anglo-Saxon England, on the other hand, reveals the extraordinarily developed cult of a universal saint, especially in association with the reform movement of the tenth century. Mary is commemorated in a large number of dedications of churches and monasteries, in the composition of private and monastic prayers, the celebration of Marian feasts throughout the liturgical year in ecclesiastical communities, the acquisition, from the tenth and eleventh centuries, of such relics of Mary as fragments of her clothing, hair and sepulchre and some of her milk, her portrayal in art and the writing of texts, especially homilies in Old English describing her life and death.

Relics of the Virgin Mary abound on the continent as well and statues of her as well as of other saints play complementary roles in many public rituals. An example is the council of Rodez convened by Bishop Arnald from his parishes in 1012, an account of which is incorporated into the *Miracula* of St Faith. There the author tells us that it was the customary practice for the bodies of the saints to be brought to synods, and in accordance with this a veritable 'battleline of saints' was drawn up in tents and pavilions, with golden statue reliquaries of Sts Marius, Amantius and Faith (the famous reliquary still to be seen at Conques contains her head), a golden image of the Virgin Mary and a chest reliquary of St Saturninus. There the common people, the *vulgus*, also were gathered together with lay notables and the clergy; they exclaimed in wonder at the miracles performed by St Faith. Such councils and religious gatherings were but one manifestation of the varieties of religious response in Europe in the tenth and early eleventh centuries. The Peace of God movement in France in particular was proclaimed at such councils where, in public gatherings of clergy and laity and in the presence of the saints, the warriors swore an oath of peace within society. The popular participation in the Peace of God movement has been established in recent work, but the episcopal leadership within it and the bishops' attempt to exert social control in their own terms and by means of religious fervour is also of crucial importance.

Devotion to saints and investment in prayer is also reflected in the enormous number of donations to the church, particularly to local monasteries, recorded in the many extant charters of the tenth and eleventh centuries. In this respect there is clear continuity with the eighth and ninth centuries. The monasteries are a most positive and visible reflection of lay piety. Monasteries ministered as effectively to the religious needs of the population as the parish churches; they provided, in many cases, the essential link with the holy and an alternative visible contact with God and his saints to that provided by the secular church. In addition, the charters from such monasteries as Bobbio, Nonantola, St Gallen, Weissenburg, Lorsch, Saint-Bénigne at Dijon or S. Maria at Ripoll reflect how these houses provided one compelling focus of religious devotion and loyalties and service to the cult of a local saint. Grants made to the monastery were insurance against damnation and provided for a donor's immortal soul. Yet they were also a token of the lay Christian's participation in the religious life and a very particular contribution to the promotion of the Christian faith of which every assessment of lay piety needs to take account. Not only did the laity contribute the material base on which a monastery's livelihood depended. They also contributed their sons and daughters to the service of the Christian faith. No doubt in some cases pious motives were not the sole determinant in what prompted the laity to adopt the monastic way of life. The need for refuge, physical unfitness for a secular life, or social and political pressures no doubt played a role as well. Nevertheless, the astonishing varieties of monastic life documented by Wollasch (chapter 6), as much as the successful expansion and consolidation of the secular, episcopal and parochial church described in this chapter, were essentially a consequence of the laity's response to the demands and needs of their religion. The building of churches, the establishment of pilgrimage centres, the devotion accorded relics, the convening of synods, the concentration, in personal and public morality, on Christian norms, and participation in the forsaking of comfort and home in order to go on pilgrimage to the many new sites which were becoming a focus of devotion, such as Compostella, as well as the familiar goals of Rome and Jerusalem, and participation in the liturgical rituals of the church were all possible means of practising Christianity. The developments within the church in Europe in the tenth and early eleventh centuries were extraordinarily rich, varied and creative.

Yet in all the topics treated in this chapter – ecclesiastical organisation, the history of the popes, synodal legislation, missions, canon law, liturgy, music, popular devotion – it has been clear not only how important the eighth- and ninth-century Carolingian foundations were but also how crucial the leadership of the bishops became in the course of the tenth century. To some degree this is what the authors of the many *vitae* of bishops wished us to think. Yet their advocacy, and the fact that there is not the same concentration of episcopal *vitae* in the ninth century, is borne out by the great variety of other kinds of evidence considered in this chapter. In the acceptance, on the part of many modern scholars, of the reform rhetoric of the late eleventh- and twelfth-century bishops and abbots, however, with its stress on the decadence of the clergy as a whole and on the evils attendant on a church in the power of the laity, insufficient acknowledgement has hitherto been accorded the great achievements of their tenth- and early eleventh-century predecessors in the expansion and consolidation of Christianity in western Europe.

CHAPTER 6

MONASTICISM: THE FIRST WAVE OF REFORM

Joachim Wollasch

IN EVERY medieval century in Europe monastic life was renewed, and renewal might indeed be said to have been a characteristic of medieval monasticism. Yet although there is a rich literature on Carolingian monastic reform in the age of Charles the Great and Louis the Pious, for example, it has become customary to describe the monasticism of the tenth and eleventh centuries as 'reform monasticism', just as one talks of the 'reform papacy' and of the 'era of reform'. Is there not here perhaps an inherent contradiction, just as there is in the chapter-title, suggested by the editor of this volume? For if one talks of a 'first wave of reform' in connection with the monasticism of the tenth and eleventh centuries, then this must imply, considering how much we know about Carolingian monastic reform, that tenth-century reform was a much deeper caesura in the history of medieval monasticism, a fundamentally new beginning. Recently Gerd Tellenbach has described the period from the ninth to the eleventh century as 'the great era of monasticism', but he did not talk of reform monasticism and indeed he questioned the notion of monastic decadence in the tenth century.[1] There were indeed many monasteries ruined by warfare, and in west Francia they suffered not only from Norse attacks but also from the long-drawn-out transition from Carolingian to Capetian rule with its concomitant transfer of power from an increasingly weak centre to local and regional lordships, a process which afflicted monasteries in particular. It is probably no accident that it was precisely in Aquitaine, Burgundy and Lotharingia that expectations of the coming end of the world emerged decades before the critical year 1000. Odo of Cluny wrote of the dangerous times and the threatening end of the world: now the time has come, now Antichrist stands before the gate. 'It is precisely this repeated "now" which distinguishes the tenth from the ninth century.'[2]

Tellenbach also quite rightly criticised the view that it was monastic proprietors who should be blamed for all the damage done to coenobitic monasticism

---

[1] Tellenbach (1988/1993), p. 101.　　[2] Fried (1989), p. 413.

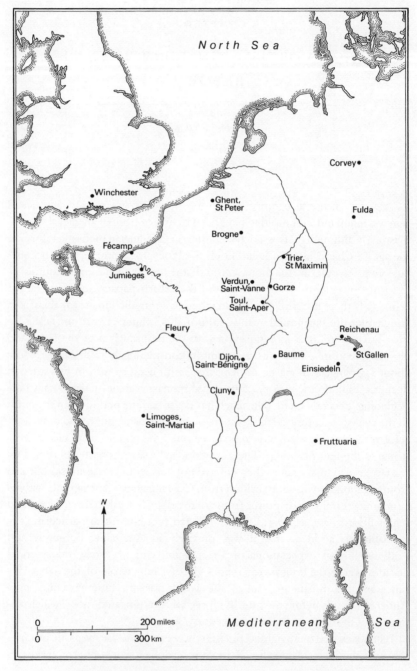

3 Monastic centres in the tenth and early eleventh centuries

during the tenth century. He pointed to those ecclesiastical and lay proprietors of monasteries who supported and endowed their monasteries in such a way as to allow a flourishing of monastic life and so demonstrated their lively interest in their foundations; we shall return to some of the more prominent tenth-century examples later. Moreover, many monasteries, in the German kingdom in particular, did not decline during the Ottonian era from the level they had reached in the Carolingian period. There were many monastic reforms, not just one, and they need to be examined individually. We can indeed note the impressive forces working for a renewal of monastic life in the tenth century; but in order to speak of reform monasticism in the tenth and eleventh centuries and of a movement which experienced a 'first wave' in the tenth century, we would need to find evidence of symptoms common to all the countless monastic renewals, in particular to find signs of an awareness within contemporary monasticism of a need and indeed an imperative to reform monasticism as a whole and not just one's own monastery.

To investigate the customs of coenobitic monasticism in the tenth century no longer entails a wearisome process of gathering together details from the most varied sources – capitularies, accounts of monastic administration, letters, petitions, saints' Lives – as it does for the ninth. By the turn of the millennium the written codifications of coenobitic monastic custom had become a separate genre, though with a great variety of titles, a source whose numbers grew steadily through to the twelfth century. The majority of these *consuetudines* also include – and in this respect they did not draw on the Rule of St Benedict for precedent or inspiration – provisions for the written recording of the commemoration of the dead in the office-book of the chapter (*in libro vitae*, *in libro regulae*, *in martyrologio*, and so on). Such chapter office-books become increasingly numerous in the period before and following the millennium, though many survive only in fragmentary form. Evidently the commemoration of the dead was taking on greater importance for monastic communities and for their sense of themselves, while at the same time the attractiveness of the monasteries for the laity came to lie more and more in the commemoration of the dead, which could be performed by the monastic communities from anniversary to anniversary over generations. In the Tegernsee letter-collection, for example, we find a letter of thanks from Abbot Gozbert addressed to a special benefactor of the monastery, Count Arnold: 'your memory has been preserved up to now in assiduous prayers, but henceforth we have decreed that your name is to be held memorially fast in our monastery in prayers day and night'.[3] Just how much such a commemoration was sought after emerges from a further passage in the letter. For the count's deceased wife the customary commemoration had

[3] '... pro qua extunc usque nunc consuetudinarias complevimus precaminum celebrationes et in semper annuali revolutione temporis vigilias missasque cum oblationibus sciamus facere', no. 22, p. 23.

been practised. Now the community was proposing to celebrate vigils and Mass with offerings every year. The abbot's request to the count shows that this meant yearly commemoration: 'Let the date be written on a sheet of parchment and send it to us by this present bearer of the roll of the dead.'[4] What was now being commemorated in monasteries was no longer the collective memory of the many people whose names had been collected in the books of commemoration since the Carolingian period; rather, it was the commemoration of the individual, carried out on the date of their death and renewed yearly for more and more people.

These codifications of the customs of coenobitic monasticism often implied a claim that they should be adopted by others, to set out customs of a model character. A famous example from the tenth century is the *Regularis concordia* for the monasteries of England. Here, however, one must distinguish carefully, depending on whether the model character of such *consuetudines* was ascribed to the monastery from without – by other monasteries for example, or by kings, bishops or abbots – or whether a community itself intended to disseminate its *consuetudines* among other monasteries. This in turn raises a further point. The spread of two central kinds of text – *consuetudines* and the chapter office-book – up to the turn of the millennium allows us to speak of reform monasticism. But we must distinguish between those cases where the initiative for reform proceeded from an ecclesiastical or lay monastic proprietor and those where a reform-minded chapter cooperated with a ruler: was it a royal order, the expression of episcopal will or the requirements of aristocratic interests which led to reform, or was it the will of the community of abbot and monks itself? Such a distinction is lacking, for example, in Kassius Hallinger's well-known work *Gorze–Kluny*;[5] the title sets the monastery of Gorze, a proprietary monastery owned and reformed by the bishops of Metz, on the same level as the monastery of Cluny, which carried out reforms on its own initiative, and the title equates Cluniac monasticism, whose *caput* Cluny was free of all spiritual and temporal *dominatio*, with that of other 'reform monasticisms' practised in monasteries each of which had its own lord and above these a king. We are thus not dealing with a single reform monasticism including varied observances and opposed tendencies. Any account of monastic reform in the tenth and eleventh centuries must allow for the fact that most monasteries and monastic groupings were locked into structures of lordship and could not move outside narrow limits, regardless of whether they were to be reformed by order from above or whether they wanted to reform themselves and others. The crucial questions are these. How far in such circumstances was independent initiative for monastic reform possible and how did the free monastery of

---

[4] 'Diem kalendarium iubete conscribi membrana nobisque transmitti per presentem pelligerum', *ibid.*
[5] Hallinger (1951a, 1951b).

Cluny conceive of and carry out reform while absorbing other monasteries into an ever-growing monastic group? Where was monasticism renewed, and where did it itself become a force for renewal? Considered in this way, reform monasticism appears not as a static phenomenon with its own inherent norms but rather as a dynamic and multi-faceted movement, which had first to create centres around which it could crystallise.

EREMITIC MONASTICISM

In the face of the well-known monastic foundations of the tenth and eleventh centuries it has often been all too easily forgotten that there were also eremitic tendencies in reform monasticism from the beginning of the tenth century onwards, and that these were more independent of lordly influences. We need not here think only of the male and female *inclusi* who lived in or near monasteries at St Gallen, Verdun and elsewhere. Odo, later abbot of Cluny, was accompanied by a hermit Adhegrinus when he left Saint-Martin of Tours, where he had been a canon, and became a monk in the monastery of Baume. But there were also hermits who participated in monastic renewal. Benno, who was summoned in 927 by King Henry I of Germany from the loneliness of Meinradszelle ('Meinrad's cell'), where he had lived since about 905, to the bishopric of Metz, paid for this by being caught up in the cross-currents of Lotharingian politics, blinded and driven from his episcopal city. He returned to his career as a hermit and, together with the provost of Strasbourg, Eberhard, helped to renew monastic life at Meinradszelle in 934. It is nevertheless characteristic of European monasticism that this eremitical initiative under Eberhard as its first abbot should have led to the foundation of a monastery whose name, Einsiedeln ('Hermitage'), reveals something of its beginnings but which rose under the patronage of the dukes of Suabia to become one of the most highly privileged monasteries of the whole Ottonian kingdom. As such it functioned well into the eleventh century as a source of renewal for other monastic communities. When the bishop of Metz reformed his proprietary monastery of Gorze the archdeacon Einold of Toul became its first abbot under the new dispensation, and he too had begun his monastic career as a hermit.

Petrus Damiani, from 1043 prior of the colony of hermits at Fonte Avellana and later cardinal bishop, has described for us in his *Vita Romualdi* how the Ravennatese aristocrat Romuald 'wished to convert the whole world to eremiticism',[6] and how he sought in vain to win Otto III for a monastic life in the marshes of Pereum near Ravenna. Instead of this the emperor urged

---

[6] 'totum mundum in heremum convertere volens', Petrus Damiani, *Vita Romualdi*, c. 37, p. 78.

Romuald to reform as its abbot the monastery of S. Apollinare in Classe, where Romuald had spent three years as a novice. When Abbot Odilo of Cluny visited Otto III, seeking the *societas* of William of Saint-Bénigne, and stood together with bishops and abbots before emperor and pope in S. Apollinare in Classe itself, the list of participants includes 'Romualdus abbas et eremita'.[7] After Romuald had failed in this task he threw down his staff of office at the feet of emperor and archbishop of Ravenna and left the monastery. There is no doubt that Romuald wanted to be a monk, to win souls for monasticism, and no doubt also that he saw the strictest form of monasticism as eremitism. It is uncertain whether he adapted the Rule of St Benedict for his companions; he had certainly become familiar with it in his period in S. Apollinare, and he also knew Monte Cassino at first hand. As well as Petrus Damiani, another source from the first half of the eleventh century, the Farfese *Liber Tramitis*, tells us that Abbot Hugh of Farfa had undertaken to renew the old institutions of the fathers and especially of Benedict in Farfa, following Romuald's example, and 'shining as an ornament of monasticism' like Romuald 'renewed the norm of ancient justice in both sexes and in both orders [laymen and monks]'.[8] He had many pupils, and lived the coenobitic life with them in different places; indeed he founded monasteries himself before dying at Camaldoli, which in the course of the eleventh century collected a whole group of eremitical colonies around itself. The hermit Nilus, who came from Byzantine southern Italy and so deeply moved Otto III, also acted as abbot and wrote a hymn to Benedict of Nursia.

The careers of Benno and Eberhard of Einsiedeln, Einold of Gorze and Romuald all show that the eremitic monasticism of the tenth and eleventh centuries could not remain independent alongside coenobitic monasticism – it was, after all, not exactly the same as the way of life of the ancient hermits in the Egyptian desert – and also that its representatives found it almost as difficult as did their coenobitic counterparts to escape the influence of their lord's conceptions of monastic renewal and indeed of his demands on their service. As a partial explanation we may note that they were all of high aristocratic origins and that many had held high ecclesiastical office before being summoned to hold bishoprics and abbacies. Although these anchorites of the tenth century, who did not shrink from speaking the blunt truth even to the emperor's face, are impressive figures, their careers show also the tensions between ascetic life in the wastes and the strictly regimented coenobitic life in a monastery which pulled these eremitical fathers this way and that.

It was coenobitical monasticism rather than eremitism which set the route to

[7] DO III 396.

[8] *Liber tramitis aevi Odilonis abbatis*, p. 3: 'decore splendidus monachico Romualdus nomine qui normam priscae iustitiae in sexu renovavit utroque et ordine'.

the climax and turning point of European monasticism in the twelfth century. Examples of this are also provided by monasteries like the Reichenau, St Gallen, Fulda, Hersfeld, Corvey, Lorsch and countless others, all of which were by and large able to maintain the high level of monasticism achieved in the Carolingian period through the Ottonian era and beyond. Nevertheless, this does not mean that they were of continuous importance outside their own immediate surroundings: their wider influence in the Empire and the other European kingdoms depended on several factors, not least on the priorities of kings and emperors, which changed from dynasty to dynasty and from ruler to ruler.

LORDSHIP AND REFORM

If one were to depict the reforms of the tenth century in strict chronological order of the date of foundations of those monasteries which became focuses of reform activity, one would have to begin with the foundation of Cluny in 910. However, the testament in which the first abbot of Cluny, Berno, defined his monastic inheritance dates from 927, when Abbot Odo, under whom Cluny became a centre of reform, took over the monastery. Other prominent centres of monastic reform may thus be considered first, with Brogne in the diocese of Liège coming before Gorze near Metz. These names remind us also that both old and new foundations could become sources of renewal, a further reason for not following the dates of monastic foundations. Any chronology presents us with the thorny problem of evaluating the various reform initiatives. What we find is a simultaneous multiplicity of monastic reforms in the most varied situations both in old-established and in newly founded monasteries. In the old Carolingian core-land of Lotharingia (Flanders, Lorraine, Burgundy, upper Italy), aristocratic and royal monastic proprietors competed with one another in setting up exemplary monastic communities, but there were also impressive reforms in Rome, southern Italy and England, as well as in many parts of the east Frankish/German kingdom. What is common to them all, with the exception of Cluny, is one thing: the proprietors' will to see monasteries functioning to the highest spiritual standards was coupled with the willingness of monastic communities to reform themselves and others. The more we – quite legitimately – look for currents of tradition running from the Carolingian monastic reforms of the era of Benedict of Aniane through to the reform centres of the tenth century, the more we risk losing sight of the elementary connection between lordship and reform, a connection not to be grasped simply in legal or constitutional terms. It was the proprietary lord and founding abbot Gerard who placed his monastery of Brogne under the protection of the bishop of Liège – where it was soon to be granted privileges by the

Ottonians – before offering his services to the margraves of Flanders, for whom he reformed a number of monasteries, not just St Peter in Ghent. In his capacity as lord of Brogne he served not only Margrave Arnulf I of Flanders but also Duke Gislebert of Lotharingia, for whom he reformed Saint-Ghislain. While his Life suggested that he led a sheltered existence (*vitam theoreticam*) within the cloister next to the entrance, the *Miracula sancta Gisleni* note that he directed many monasteries at that time. But this direction had been entrusted to him by the responsible monastic proprietor, occasionally even with reference to the emperor.[9]

In Gorze, the part played by the monks in the reform of the monastery, which belonged to the bishops of Metz, is more clearly visible than in the case of Gerard of Brogne, because we have a whole series of names of men who formed a group of monks leading an eremitical life together with the archdeacon Einold of Toul already mentioned and with John of Vandières, who came from a humble background on the estates of Gorze, of which he was later to be abbot. After John had made a journey to southern Italy, the whole group – Bernacer, a deacon from Metz, Salecho of Saint-Martin near Metz, Randicus of Saint-Symphorian in Metz, and later Frederick of Saint-Hubert in the Ardennes, Odilo from Verdun, Angelram from Metz, Andrew, Isaac and the recluse Humbert – was on the point of quitting the woods around Metz for the south. In 933 Bishop Adalbero I of Metz gave them the monastery of Gorze as a place to live in and renew. Until then Count Adalbert had acted as abbot, having been granted it by Wigeric, formerly bishop of Metz and abbot of Gorze. Adalbert now restored the monastery to Bishop Adalbero. A precondition for reform in Gorze was thus that the episcopal proprietor should commit the task to this group of eremitical monks, and the reform itself had to be begun by Adalbero, who secured the restoration of the alienated lands of Gorze, which had been granted out as benefices to the bishop of Metz's military following. One might thus almost talk of a refoundation of the monastery. The monks mentioned above, who were familiar both with the Rule of St Benedict and with the views of Benedict of Aniane on monasticism, intended simply to lead a monastic life.

Up to the end of the tenth century, according to the evidence of a Gorze necrology which has survived in fragmentary form, fourteen monks of the monastery had been called to be abbot in the monasteries of Senones (twice), Stavelot, Saint-Hubert, Saint-Arnulf in Metz, Saint-Michel-en-Thiérache, Saint-Martin near Metz, Saint-Aper in Toul, Moyenmoutier, Saint-Nabor, Sainte-Marie-aux-Martyrs, Ellwangen, Marmoutier and Saint-Vincent in Metz. A few examples may serve to show who took the initiative in these promotions.

---

[9] *Vita Gerardi abbatis Broniensis*, c. 15, p. 665, and Rainer, *Miracula S. Gisleni*, c. 10, p. 584; cf. Smet (1960), pp. 44, 50.

Before the Gorzian monk Odilo of Verdun became abbot of Stavelot, the monastery had been held by Duke Gislebert of Lotharingia. At Saint-Arnulf in Metz, where Aristeus (and before him Harbert, not mentioned in the necrology) became abbot, Bishop Adalbero I had replaced the canons by monks from Gorze. Frederick, an uncle of Adalbero, had left Saint-Hubert because he could not lead the monastic life there; he became *prepositus* in Gorze and returned to Saint-Hubert as abbot after Bishop Richer of Liège, uncle of Count Adalbert of Metz, had restored coenobitic life there. Senones was also owned by the bishop of Metz.

It cannot be doubted that the participants were conscious of the important role played by the bishopric of Metz within the royal church of the east Frankish/German kingdom. In Saint-Arnulf, Metz and Saint-Aper, Toul, as in Senones, Otto I's consent was sought for the reform of the monastery. Marmoutier in Alsace also belonged to the possessions of the bishop of Metz. In the monasteries which received Gorzian monks as their abbot and Gorzian monasticism, the *ordo Gorziensis*, it was the bishops and counts of Metz and their relatives who dominated. The Gorzian reform in this way brought Lotharingian, and especially Metz monasteries closer together, but it created neither a monastic order as a legally defined organisation nor a network of daughter houses joined by a common observance. Nor did Gorze become a centre of reforming monasticism, even though Einold had a high reputation within the kingdom and John, the second abbot after the reform, had served Otto I on the recommendation of the bishop of Metz as an ambassador to the caliph of Córdoba.

It was the old abbey of St Maximin at Trier which was characteristically used by the Ottonians when they wanted to renew or found a monastery in their kingdom. After Abbot Ogo of St Maximin had reformed his monastery with the help of monks from Gorze and at the suggestion of Duke Gislebert of Lotharingia, Otto I promoted him to the bishopric of Liège. It was with monks from St Maximin that Otto I set up the first community at Saint-Maurice in Magdeburg, and from there that he summoned Adalbert to be the first archbishop of Magdeburg. Otto's brother Brun, archbishop of Cologne, summoned a monk from St Maximin to be the first abbot of his foundation at St Pantaleon; this took place during the pontificate of Ekbert, a relative of the Ottonians, in Trier, showing once again the importance of family connections for reform. Ogo of St Maximin had reformed his monastery, which was not dependent on Gorze, in friendly cooperation with monks from Gorze. When these once again contemplated leaving Gorze in the somewhat constrained period following the renewal there, it was Ogo who offered to take them in at St Maximin. From his time onwards and as a result of Ottonian patronage St Maximin, intellectually and spiritually orientated towards Gorze, became a centre of reform, influencing the imperial monastery of Weissenburg, Ellwangen, Echternach, St Gallen, and Gladbach (a proprietary house of the archbishops of Cologne); Sandrat of St Maximin played an important role here. Even in the later tenth century Otto II still used St Maximin monks to reform Tegernsee, and Bishop Wolfgang of Regensburg was to summon Ramwold from St Maximin to become abbot at St Emmeram in Regensburg. Such examples may serve to show that neither Gorze nor St Maximin was a centre of a self-propelling monastic reform movement establishing daughter houses which followed a similar observance. What cannot be overlooked is the link between the will of imperial bishops in respect of their proprietary monasteries or of the Ottonians in respect of the royal monasteries on the one hand and on the other the readiness of eremitical and ascetically living monks to live a coenobitic life. The most distinguished abbots became transmitters of monastic reform in offering their services to rulers.

When we look at the beginning of the eleventh century and compare those monasteries which under Henry II had replaced the main centres of the Ottonian era, then the connection between lordship and reform becomes evident once more. Gorze itself in the second decade of the eleventh century came to seem so much in need of renewal that Bishop Theoderic II of Metz summoned the abbot of Saint-Bénigne, Dijon, William of Volpiano, to Gorze as abbot. He had already reformed the Metz abbey of Saint-Arnulf on behalf of Theoderic's predecessor. The reform of the English monasteries should also not be forgotten in the context of the interplay of lordship and reform. It is true that recent research by Hanna Vollrath has somewhat modified the previous received view,[10] but there can be no doubt of the cooperation of Edgar and his wife with the abbot-bishops Dunstan and Æthelwold and with other bishops, abbots and abbesses, which aimed at an ordered monastic life within the whole of the *patria*. Dunstan had gone into exile at St Peter's, Ghent, which had been reformed for Margrave Arnulf of Flanders by Gerard of Brogne. After his return, monks from Ghent were summoned to reform English monasteries. But the *Regularis concordia*, on which those assembled at Winchester *c*. 970 agreed as a general and binding statement of coenobitic monastic custom, mentions the *monachi Floriacenses* even before the *monachi Gandauenses*. Contacts had already been made by Fleury with English monasteries before the death of Abbot Odo of Cluny in 942, who had reformed the royal monastery. At the king's orders, so says the *Regularis concordia*, the abbots and abbesses had summoned monks from these two famous monasteries so that they could gather everything which might serve honourable and regular monastic life, just as bees gather pollen from flowers, and bring it together in the book of the

[10] Vollrath (1985), pp 274–85.

Regularis concordia.[11] If one recalls how strongly monks were bound to the observance of their own house when they made their profession, then it will be clear just how much any attempt to impose uniform customs on all monasteries in Edgar's kingdom must have been directed by the royal will. Just as Benedict of Aniane had laid down *una consuetudo* for all monasteries on behalf of Charles the Great and Louis the Pious, so the *Regularis concordia* was a means of unificatory direction of monastic life, a means about which there was no dissent between the abbot-bishops and the king. This is confirmed by the provision that the elections of abbots and abbesses should take place with the king's agreement and following the directions of the Rule of St Benedict – the two conditions are placed in this order by the *Regularis concordia!* The customary singing of psalms for king and benefactors, 'by whose donations we are nourished through Christ's gifts',[12] in the words of the same text, was not to be performed too quickly. The abbots and abbesses of the monasteries should come to perform obedient service for the king and queen as often as was necessary for their houses. The powerful were not to use the monasteries for *convivia*, but were rather bound to the benefit and to the defence of these houses. As early as the *generale concilium* held *c.* 967 Archbishop Dunstan of Canterbury, in accordance with the wishes of Pope John XIII, had threatened clerics that they would lose their churches should they not observe the obligation of celibacy, and indeed the king substituted monks for such clerics throughout his kingdom, especially where they inhabited former monasteries: the secular cathedral clerics in Canterbury, Worcester and Winchester in particular were replaced by monks.

Even allowing that King Edgar, much praised in tradition as the founder of forty monasteries and renewer of many others in England, claimed no more rights than were at that time accorded the king in any case, and even assuming that the abbot-bishops did no more than exercise their inherent powers and allowed the abbots and abbesses to choose whether they would agree to such changes on behalf of their houses, we can still not overlook just how near the prologue to the *Regularis concordia* stands to that text of 966 written in gold letters in the manner of a charter, which catalogues the royal acts in favour of the monasteries, nor ignore the fact that it is precisely the monastic text of the *Regularis concordia* which contains formulations showing just how dominant was the role played by the king in monastic reform. No doubt the abbot-bishops Æthelwold and Dunstan saw royal support as a *conditio sine qua non* for successful reform, and hence they took care to depict reform as a process corresponding to the royal will: for this reason monastic reform under King Edgar reveals a reform monasticism dependent on royal authority: the male houses were,

---

[11] *Regularis concordia Anglicae nationis*, pp. 72–3.   [12] *Ibid.*, p. 74.

according to the third chapter of the *Regularis concordia*, under the protection of the king, while the nunneries were entrusted to that of the queen.

A final prominent example of the ruler's initiative in connection with monastic reforms in the tenth century can be seen in the actions of Alberic II, *princeps atque omnium Romanorum senator*,[13] but because this initiative coincided with another, that of Abbot Odo of Cluny, it will be more convenient to discuss this example in connection with the development of Cluniac reform monasticism.

CLUNY

Cluny differed from all the centres of monastic reform previously mentioned, though there too all the monks wanted to do was to live according to the Rule of St Benedict as amplified by the tradition of Benedict of Aniane. What has always been adduced in discussions of Cluny's unique rise to European significance is the freedom from all ecclesiastical and secular lordship granted at its foundation, and Duke William the Pious of Aquitaine did indeed in 909/10 renounce all proprietorial rights for himself and his heirs and place his newly founded monastery 'under the protection, not the lordship'[14] of the pope. Such a transfer of a monastery to the protection of the Holy See had already been practised on occasion in the Carolingian era, but within the overarching order of the Carolingian empire the act had a different meaning from the *traditio* of Cluny at the beginning of the tenth century; it has been noted frequently enough by scholars that the pope was then in no position to protect the monastery offered to him. The new foundation in the valley of the Grosne lay in the west Frankish kingdom, in a region which from the second half of the ninth century onwards had not been close to the king; the foundation charter was dated later than Charles the Simple's recovery of kingship on the death of King Odo, yet it named King Odo as the feudal lord of the ducal founder and stated that the foundation was also for the remedy of Odo's soul. Cluny was thus, once William had renounced his own claims and those of his heirs, founded outside royal lordship, indeed outside lordship of any kind; unlike other monasteries, it had no lay or ecclesiastical patron. It was thrown back on its own resources, and had to fill the vacuum left in order to secure the freedom it had received. At the time it must have seemed a considerable gamble whether this would succeed. Sixteen or seventeen years after the foundation Abbot Berno in his testament described Cluny as a place which was still incomplete after William's and his own death:[15] poorly endowed and low in number of brethren.

---

[13] Zimmermann, *Papsturkunden*, no. 85, p. 147.

[14] D Ra 12, p. 51: 'apostolicae sedi ad tuendum non ad dominandum'.

[15] Berno, *Testamentum*, cols. 853–8.

If on the other hand one recalls that as late as the early eleventh century Abbot Odilo had to have King Robert II of France confirm that no one might erect fortified towers on the monastery's lands this will give some idea of how long and how hard Cluny was pressed by the nobles of the region.

Although Cluny was so small and defenceless, Abbot Berno – who was also abbot of Gigny, Baume and an unidentified *monasterium Aethicense* with a dependency at Saint-Lothain as well as of Massay and Bourg-Dieu – nevertheless chose it as his place of burial and made gifts to it. Whereas in the first three houses named above he installed his relative Wido as his successor, he appointed Odo to succeed him in Cluny, Massay and Bourg-Dieu; the testament explicitly mentions the consent of the monks to this double designation. Nevertheless, Odo had to ask the pope to mediate in the dispute between Cluny and Gigny after Wido had challenged the validity of Berno's will, and the pope in turn commended Cluny to King Radulf of west Francia. Cluny thus formed a group together with other monasteries from the beginning, thus enabling one member of the group to be supported by the others in crises if necessary. But the abstract notion of a monastic network (*Klosterverband* in German) says little about the nature of the group. When Ebbo of Déols, a vassal of Cluny's founder, himself founded Bourg-Dieu in 917, he gave it the same freedom as Cluny had and forbade his heirs to disturb the freedom of the monastery under the cloak of advocacy and protection. As mentioned above, Berno's testament shows that the new monastery was commended to the abbot of Cluny in personal union, while a relative of William the Pious, Count Bernard in Périgord, transferred his monastery at Sarlat to the power of Abbot Odo. In 929 Countess Adelaide, *abbatissa* in Romainmôtier, placed her house in a state of personal union with Cluny. Sauxillanges was made over permanently to Cluny by its founder, William the Pious' nephew, as were Souvigny, Charlieu, and the monastery of S. Maria on the Aventine in Rome. Monastic proprietors who acted in this way were evidently convinced that it raised their own rank when their foundations collectively practised an exemplary monasticism under the leadership of Abbot Odo of Cluny and were protected from injury through their own heirs by being made over legally to Cluny. In this fashion Cluny grew to be the head of a group of monasteries which participated in its freedom. This was a unique arrangement, and shows how Odo caught Cluny's defencelessness in the safety-net of his own connections. For the whole *raison d'être* of this group of monasteries and of the central position held within it by Cluny lay in the dense and comprehensive work of reform created by Odo with his monks and assistants.

Particularly characteristic here was the way in which Odo made use of confraternity for the purposes of monastic reform, and in this way brought monasteries of quite differing legal status together in a community of the common

monastic life. Fleury had been granted to Count Elisiard by King Radulf;
Elisiard in turn had asked Odo to reform the monastery, and he was in the end
able to overcome the resistance of the monks, who feared for the legal status of
their monastery; he corrected those monks who merely followed the Rule
incorrectly, and at the same time sent four monks *religionis gratia* to Saint-
Martial at Limoges, where they were to ask the abbot to grant them confraternity on Odo's behalf, so that no difference might exist between the monks at
Limoges and Fleury, so that the monks could pass freely between the two
houses, and so that the common way of monastic life might be acknowledged
in all things and the two houses might 'so to speak form one convent'.[16] The
four monks then went on to Solignac, where they succeeded in gaining the
consent of abbot and convent to the same agreement. Following this, the contract of confraternity was written down and read out before the convents
before being copied into the chapter office-book for the notice of coming generations.

To renew coenobitic life Odo needed the consent of monastic proprietors,
and he won over many by his initiative. In the Life by John of Salerno it is said
that 'he was known to kings, familiar to bishops and dear to the hearts of the
great. The monasteries built in their dioceses they transferred to the ownership
of our father [Odo] so that he might order and improve them according to our
custom',[17] an account confirmed by countless examples. Both lay and ecclesiastical proprietors asked Odo to bring the forms of coenobitic life practised
in Cluny (the 'Cluniac way of life', *ordo Cluniacensis*) to their monasteries, for
example in Aurillac, Tulle, Sarlat, Saint-Pons de Thomières, Saint-Marcellin de
Chanteuges, Saint-Benoît de Fleury-sur-Loire, Saint-Julien de Tours, Saint-
Pierre-le-Vif in Sens and various Roman monasteries.

The power of Odo's reforming initiative may be seen in his sermons. At the
Feast of Peter's Chair he said, citing Pope Leo the Great (who in turn drew on
the first letter to Peter), that in the unity of faith and baptism all are of royal
race and participants in the office of priesthood. This was a sentiment evidently well received by the nobles in a land distant from the king. In the first
ever Life written of a holy layman, that of Gerald of Aurillac, Odo offered the
nobility the picture he had formed of the ideal nobleman, who was to use his
power and wealth for the benefit of those entrusted to him by God, so that
lordship meant justice even for the unfree and service to the poor. The interior
life of such a count was that of a secret monk, with a tonsure under his hat: in
this way even the rich and the powerful might become holy. Such examples
draw attention to a further unique characteristic of the Cluniac reform movement. Odo did not confine himself to bringing his own and other monks back

---

[16] *Les documents nécrologiques de l'abbaye Saint Pierre de Solignac*, p. 557.
[17] John of Salerno, *Vita S Odonis abbatis Cluniacensis* II, col. 39E.

to a strict observance of the Rule. He was also convinced of the need to reform the whole of Christendom, imbued as he was with a sense that the Last Days had already begun and the Last Judgement was near. True, the motor for such reform was to be a renewed monasticism; but Odo had held up, as a model which was binding not merely on monks, the primitive pentecostal church recorded in the Acts of the Apostles: 'This is the mean for monks who are bound by the social life.'[18] The foundation charter of Cluny itself says that the foundation was made 'for the state and the integrity of the Catholic faith' and for all Christians, since all are bound together by the one love and the one faith.[19]

We have already cited Odo's sermon on the Feast of Peter's Chair: in his eyes the veneration of Peter was *pietas christianae unitatis*. Since the renewal of coenobitic monasticism from Cluny was to serve as the basis for a comprehensive reform, it was only logical that Odo, when he asked for a papal privilege for Cluny and his monasteries, should not have been content with permission to take in those monks whose abbots could not provide suitable conditions to live according to their monastic profession and who had therefore left their monastery in order to improve their *conversatio*. In the famous privilege of March 931 he also secured the provision that the Cluniacs might with the consent of the owner take a monastery under their lordship to improve it. Odo thus had the pope provide the Cluniacs with a papal command to carry out their work of reform by writing a licence into the privilege. Although Cluny could not reckon with practical protection from the popes, who themselves were hard pressed in Rome, it was nevertheless helpful for the monastery when the pope wrote at Odo's request to the king of France, the archbishop of Lyons, the bishops of Chalon-sur-Saône and Mâcon that they should support Cluny. As a reformer in Fleury Odo also had a privilege issued by the pope which laid down the duty of the archbishops of Lyons, Tours, Bourges, Sens and Rheims and their suffragans to protect himself and the monastery of Fleury. The more lay and ecclesiastical magnates could be made to interest themselves for Cluny and its monasteries – including of course those monastic proprietors who had made their monasteries over to Cluny – the more certainly Cluny avoided the dangers of dependence on a single protector and the more independently it could develop, thanks to a widespread and numerous network of patrons. Cluny as the head of a group of monasteries which all lay and ecclesiastical officeholders in the country were obliged to protect: that was the route taken by the Cluniacs from Odo's time to their goal of filling the protection-vacuum in which the monastery had been placed at its foundation.

---

[18] 'Hic modus est monachis quos ligat vita socialis': Odo of Cluny, *Occupatio* 6, verse 583, p. 136.

[19] 'pro statu etiam ac integritate catholicae religionis', *Recueil des chartes de l'abbaye de Cluny* 1, no. 192, p. 125.

We have contradictory information in the sources of the tenth and eleventh centuries as to who took the initiative in Odo's reform of monasteries of the city of Rome and its surroundings. John of Salerno tells us in his Life of Odo that it was at the urgent request of the pope and that of all the clerical orders of the Roman church that Odo journeyed to Rome to rebuild S. Paolo fuori le mura. The *destructio monasterii Farfensis*, a later source, tells us that *Albericus, Romanorum princeps*, was so determined to return his monasteries to the norm of the Rule that he summoned the holy abbot Odo from *Gallia*, who at that time presided over the monastery of Cluny, and had him made archimandrite of all monasteries around Rome as well as granting Odo his birth-house on the Aventine to build a monastery there. But Odo had commended himself both to Pope Leo VII and to the *princeps*; he had already secured privileges from Leo's predecessor in 927, and among those listed as intervening were Kings Hugh and Lothar of Italy. When Hugh besieged Alberic in Rome it seemed appropriate to ask Odo to mediate with Hugh, Alberic's stepfather, who, following the reconciliation Odo arranged, became his father-in-law as well. We may well ask whether it was mere chance that Odo was asked to reform precisely those monasteries which lay on the great arterial roads leading to Rome: S. Paolo fuori le mura, S. Lorenzo fuori le mura, S. Agnese fuori le mura; certainly a charter of 941 shows that Kings Hugh and Lothar themselves resided in S. Agnese.[20] The pope will not have overlooked the fact that Odo championed the papacy in its period of weakness not only in his support for the veneration of St Peter but also through his links with Rome. Odo did not make his first journey only when Cluny's interests required it; he had already visited the city while he was still canon of Saint-Martin in Tours. His conviction that it was necessary to make a pilgrimage to the prince of the apostles at Rome is reflected in his account of the no fewer than seven pilgrimages made by the count and secret monk, Gerald of Aurillac. The *Romanitas* of Cluny from its earliest phase onwards has thus been rightly stressed, and the way in which it went together with the Cluniac will to reform from Odo's abbatiate onwards can be seen from Odo's reforms in the neighbouring monasteries of S. Elia di Nepi, Farfa, Monte Cassino, S. Andrea in Monte Soracte, Subiaco and Salerno. He installed Baldwin as abbot in S. Paolo fuori le mura, in S. Maria on the Aventine and in Monte Cassino; the remaining monasteries were confided to other pupils. He himself went to S. Pietro in Ciel d'oro in Pavia at the request of Hugh of Italy.

Although the Cluniac reform attempts in the monasteries of Rome and its surroundings scarcely affected these houses permanently – on Odo's death the pope asked for monks from Einold of Gorze, who had Italian experience,

---

[20] D. Hugh 57.

while in Farfa the monks violently expelled their foreign brethren – Cluny's links with Rome and the Cluniac presence in Rome and Pavia remained a fact throughout the tenth century and beyond. After the short intermezzo of the two Gorzian abbots in S. Paolo the monastery was ruled by Ingenaldus, who came from the monastery of Saint-Julien of Tours where Odo was buried. Maiolus followed closely in Odo's footsteps in the journeys he undertook to Rome and Italy during his time as abbot (954–94). Through the Burgundian king's daughter Adelaide, widow of Lothar of Italy and then wife of Otto I, Maiolus received a monastery in Pavia which permanently became Cluny's property. Otto is indeed said to have offered him the overall supervision of all the monasteries subject to him in Italy and Germany, an echo of the continuity in Cluny's links with Rome and presence in Italy and a response to the nature of Cluny itself: unlike so many other monasteries it did not merely radiate reform influences for a short time but continued as a source of reform well into the Cistercian era. Cluny's leadership of a group of monasteries was one reason for this, but hardly the only one. It has rightly been pointed out that from the middle of the tenth to the early twelfth century Cluny had the good fortune to be ruled by only three abbots, all outstanding. This was an essential component of Cluny's steady development. Cluny shared the privilege of free abbatial election with other monasteries, but both its foundation charter and the papal licence for reform laid down, indeed stressed, that the monks of Cluny were to choose their candidate without pressure from outside and indeed 'without consulting any lord',[21] and to make him abbot according to the provisions of the Rule of St Benedict. This provision must have been interpreted very liberally in Cluny, for a custom developed here not foreseen in the Rule. Odo had been designated abbot of Cluny by his predecessor Berno. Since Berno also intended that he should take over the monasteries of Déols and Massay it is conceivable (though not recorded) that the monks in these monasteries had consented to Berno's designation. Since Odo's successor, Aimard of Cluny (*c.* 942–*c.* 954) appears in Cluniac charters during Odo's lifetime it is probable that Odo had designated him successor, especially in view of Odo's frequent absences, though once again we are not told whether the convent consented. What is clearly recorded, however, is that Aimard, ill and blind, made Maiolus his co-adjutor, and then suggested to the whole convent that Maiolus should succeed him, since he alone was qualified to take on the office; Maiolus' consensual election is recorded both in narrative sources and in charters. Maiolus in turn summoned Odilo to be co-adjutor and designated him as successor with the convent's consent. Such a designation of the successor by the ruling abbot is occasionally found elsewhere, and it was known to the author of the

---

[21] 'sine cuiuslibet principis consultu', Pope John XI for Cluny (March 931), Zimmermann, *Papsturkunden*, no. 64, p. 107.

Regula magistri, but in Cluny it was standard practice, though evidently the designation only acquired legal force after the convent had elected the candidate.

Only when abbot and convent were in agreement could the monastery remain a centre of reform and the head of a whole group of monasteries, and only so could it preserve its independence. The cooperation between abbot and convent was an essential precondition for the attraction exercised by Cluny on its environment. Particularly revealing among the increasing numbers of donations made to Cluny by lay and ecclesiastical patrons are those made *ad sepulturam*, in return for the right of the donor and/or his relatives to be buried in the cemetery at Cluny and for their memories to be honoured at Cluny beyond their deaths. The graph of such donations shows a steadily rising curve. Beside the recruitment of the convent of Cluny from ever more families and an ever-widening catchment area it is the gifts *ad sepulturam* – which assured the donors at their death and thereafter the *societas et fraternitas* of the Cluniacs and participation in all the prayers and good works of the monks, ideally the same memorial works as those performed for a monk of Cluny himself – which are the most reliable indicator of the continual growth in the attraction exercised by Cluny on its surroundings.

EUROPEAN REFORM MONASTICISM AROUND THE TURN OF THE MILLENNIUM

We can see how far this evaluation of Cluny as a permanent source of reform corresponds to historical reality if we take a snapshot of reform monasticism in Europe around the millennium and compare this with the conditions visible at the middle of the century. We have already spoken of the uncompromising eremitism of Romuald and Nilus and the deep impression these made on Otto III, and also of the development of Einsiedeln from its eremitical beginnings to one of the most highly privileged abbeys in the Ottonian kingdom. Around the turn of the millennium there was not much trace of the impulses given to reform by Gerard of Brogne in Flanders. Although monks from Gorze and St Maximin had just been summoned to become abbots in royal and episcopal monasteries – Romuald by Wolfgang of Regensburg from St Maximin to Emmeram, Immo of Gorze first to Prüm and then to the Reichenau, where he met with great difficulties – Gorze and Trier themselves then became objects of reform: Gorze at the hands of Bishop Albero II (who had already had Saint-Arnulf of Metz reformed from Dijon in 996/7), St Maximin by Henry II himself. Cluny, by comparison, remained an active provider rather than a passive recipient of reform.

The monastic centres of gravity within Germany shifted with the change to the Bavarian line of the Liudolfings: Bavarian monasteries now became prominent alongside the famous Ottonian monasteries, and monks were summoned from St Emmeram to become abbots in Lorsch, Fulda, Corvey and Bleidenstadt, while Godehard, abbot of Niederaltaich and Tegernsee, went to Hersfeld before becoming bishop of Hildesheim. At the same time the harsh treatment of monasteries which seemed to the emperor in need of reform became clear. The account given by Ekkehard IV – later, but with unusual vividness – of the actions of the Ottonians towards St Gallen makes this evident, as does that of the *Annalista Saxo*, who, writing of the rights and coenobitic customs of the monks of Corvey who opposed the emperor's desire for reform, said that they were 'violently changed by the emperor'.[22] The link established by Empress Adelaide between the Ottonian court and Abbot Maiolus of Cluny remained a strong one under Henry II: Henry II even entered Cluny's confraternity, where he was entered in the chapter office-book as an example of an emperor who was worthy of having his memory preserved.[23]

Not only was Gorze reformed rather than reforming after the turn of the millennium, by contrast with Cluny: William of Volpiano, the man entrusted with the reform by Adalbero II, had himself been a professed Cluniac monk and prior of the Cluniac house at S. Saturnin, whence he had been sent together with twelve particularly distinguished Cluniac monks by Maiolus to reform Saint-Bénigne de Dijon at the request of Bishop Brun of Langres (a relative of William's). William's reforming activity was thus Cluniac through and through, as can be seen in his *consuetudines*. At the same time there can be no doubt that it developed a momentum of its own: its density, geographical extent and subsequent influence made William's reforming work the most significant influence on reform monasticism after the millennium. William was prepared to reform even in those places where Maiolus and Odilo of Cluny had refused a royal request out of concern for Cluny's independence. Brun of Langres confided all the episcopal proprietary monasteries of his diocese except Saint-Seine to William to reform. The bishops of Metz and Toul entrusted Saint-Arnulf of Metz, Gorze and Saint-Aper in Toul to him, as mentioned. The duke of Burgundy and the count of Blois gave him Saint-Vivant-de-Vergy and Saint-Faron in Meaux; the king himself, Robert the Pious, persuaded him to reform Saint-Germain-des-Prés. A further concentration of Wilhemine reform was found in Normandy, after the duke had summoned him there, in Fécamp, Jumièges and Mont-Saint-Michel. William founded Fruttuaria near Turin in 1015/16 together with his own (biological) brothers. Saint-Bénigne's necrological tradition shows not only that William and his

---

[22] 'potestative ab imperatore mutantur': *Annalista Saxo, s.a.* 1015, p. 668.

[23] 'Pro imperatore qui dignus fuerit ita scribatur: Tertio idus iulii depositio domni Heinrici imperatoris augusti nostrae societatis et fraternitatis karissimi' *Liber tramitis aevi Odilonis abbatis*, p. 285.

monks had strong links with Cluny but also that after the time of William and his Cluniac companions in Dijon the community there developed its own self-awareness: the monks of Cluny were no longer recorded among the monks of Saint-Bénigne, but on the facing page of the necrology, reserved for the monks of the houses who had confraternity with Saint-Bénigne. The varying intensity of the contacts between Dijon and these other houses is also confirmed by the necrological evidence. As late as the second half of the eleventh century, contemporaries perceived the houses of Gorze and Fruttuaria – which itself acquired dependencies and whose *transalpini monachi* were requested to reform monasteries as far as the north-west of the empire – together with Cluny as the monasteries of choice for episcopal and lay proprietors who wished to ask for monks to come to reform their houses.

Saint-Vanne in Verdun under its abbot, Richard, was a further monastic centre. He wanted to become a monk in Cluny, but had been persuaded by Odilo that he could do more good as a monk by staying where he had come from. It is worth noting, incidentally, that the most prominent centres of monastic reform now lay on the western border of the German kingdom or beyond it and in upper Italy. We have already noted that Henry II's reign saw a shift of emphasis within the monasticism of the German kingdom compared with that of the Ottonian era; to this it should be added that the emperor himself, following a key experience at Monte Cassino in 1022 when St Benedict cured him of a severe attack of kidney-stones, turned his attention to the reforming monasticism of the west. Alongside his confraternity with Cluny there should be mentioned his close links with Saint-Bénigne, the rich donations he made to Saint-Vanne and his concern for the reform of monasteries in the German kingdom and – together with King Robert II, with whom he had a meeting at Ivois in 1023 – in France. Fruttuaria also accepted Henry II into confraternity. The monasteries to which he now gave most attention developed a greater degree of independence and reform initiative than the monasteries which had been centres of reform in southern Germany earlier in his reign, even if Cluny was here still in a quite different category. Henry sought an abbot from the west who could carry out a general reform of the monasteries in his kingdom. It could not be expected of either Odilo of Cluny or William of Saint-Bénigne or Richard of Saint-Vanne, all of whom the emperor revered, that they would accept a summons to come and assist him. But Poppo of Stavelot, who in the end yielded to Henry II's request after he had been offered the abbey of Stavelot, may count as a pupil of Richard of Saint-Vanne; he became abbot of St Maximin in Trier in 1022, and then, under Conrad II, head of the imperial monasteries of Limburg on the Haardt, Echternach, Saint-Ghislain, Hersfeld, Weissenburg, St Gallen and a whole series of aristocratic and episcopal monasteries.

The opening up of the royal monasteries of Germany to the reform monasticism of the west brought about by Henry II and by some of his bishops (Adalbero II of Metz, Gerard I of Cambrai, Meinwerk of Paderborn) was to take on a new dimension in the era of the Empress Agnes after the middle of the century. But already after the millennium the signs were increasing that Cluny under Abbot Odilo now held the key position within European monasticism. Hundreds. of monasteries already belonged legally to Cluny, and more and more monasteries were from the start founded as Cluniac priories. Under Maiolus and Odilo the second monastic church was built at Cluny; under Hugh the third church, the greatest in the west, was begun, and the infirmary at Cluny, extended under Odilo, became the largest hospital in Europe in Hugh's time. As already mentioned, the number of monks had climbed from around twelve at the beginning to around 100 under Maiolus and Odilo; by Hugh's death in 1109 it had reached 300 to 400. Even in Odilo's time Cluny's catchment area may be seen as Europe-wide, though western and southern Europe dominated. What monks did everywhere – prayer for the dead and feeding of the poor for the preservation of their memory and of their souls – was done in Cluny more intensively and on a broader scale. Odilo and his convent introduced the celebration of All Souls on 2 November to following the celebration of All Saints on 1 November, so as to do more than had been customary for the dead brethren; the feast was subsequently taken up by the Roman church. In Cluny and its monasteries, not only were the eighteen poor who were to be catered for every day fed on this day, not only were masses said and offices prayed for the soul of every dead monk for thirty days following his death, not only was the daily ration which was 'his right'[24] given to a poor person by the almoner; all poor persons 'who chanced to pass by',[25] and whose numbers could therefore not be calculated in advance, were also fed. The Cluniac *consuetudines* show that from the time of Maiolus the word *eleemosynarius* refers to a monastic office-holder responsible for the care of the poor, and the eleventh-century *consuetudines* show very clearly how rapidly the duties of the *eleemosynarius* grew, so that he came to need more and more assistants. The way in which the care of the dead and of the poor were linked in Cluny under Odilo became so famous that a whole series of stories and legends grew up around it: that at the entreaties of the Cluniacs even the pope was granted ease among the purifying fires; that nowhere in Europe were so many souls snatched from the grasp of demons as in Cluny; that Odilo before his death had a monk count up and write down how many masses he had celebrated during his lifetime. The Cluniacs were asked whether it was permissible to sacrifice to God daily for the dead; the answer was that only on Sundays – because of the uniqueness of

---

[24] 'iustitiam vini et panis', *ibid.*, p. 265.   [25] 'omnibus supervenientibus pauperibus', *ibid.*, p. 199.

Christ's resurrection from the dead – was it *not* permissible. The surviving necrologies from Cluniac monasteries show the intensive and extensive nature of the liturgical commemoration of the dead at Cluny. They still include the names of the monks of Cluny in the tenth century – though by no means all – and in their unusual numbers and agreement in their entries impressively confirm what was related in stories and legends.

The community of the living and the dead which thus arose created internally a sense of Cluniac togetherness; externally it enabled the attraction of Cluniac monasticism to penetrate its aristocratic, peasant and clerical surroundings, and touch people at all levels of society. Already in 1006 Robert II could praise Cluny in a charter for Fécamp as 'the most famous monastery', 'whence the source of holy monastic religion has been led in streams to many places far and wide'.[26] At Romuald's suggestion Abbot Hugh 'imposed' on his monastery of Farfa 'the customs of coenobitic life of the monastery of Cluny, which was built in Gaul and flowered above all other monasteries of its time over the whole globe on the path of Regular life'.[27] Even before the question of canonical elections became acute in the course of the so-called Investiture Contest, Cluny's self-determination in this respect became as much of a standard to be matched as was its reputation for exemplary monasticism. In Robert's charter for Fécamp it was laid down in respect of the election, installation and consecration of the abbot that that custom was to be followed which had been preserved in Cluny up until then, in other words the absence of any outside influence. And even before the well-known provisions of the peace councils were issued, Maiolus and Odilo secured from the bishops assembled in Anse in 994 a privilege protecting churches, people and property within the monastery and settlement of Cluny itself, from any act of violence; it also covered certain named centres of Cluniac property and above all it covered all monasteries belonging to Cluny. In this privilege, which was matched in content by a royal charter imprecated by Odilo, general provisions were also formulated on Nicolaitan priests, on the observance of Sunday, on the duty of laymen to fast on Wednesdays and Fridays, and on the care of the poor, all topics familiar from the history of the Peace of God movement. Repentant infringers of these provisions were to be absolved by the abbot and monks of Cluny. Even the negative criticisms of the Cluniacs, as offered for example with satirical exaggeration by Bishop Adalbero of Laon, may serve to show the influence of Cluniac monasticism on public life. In the bishop's eyes the Cluniacs had mixed up the divinely ordained tripartite division of society – clergy (*oratores*), warriors (*bellatores*) and the agricultural population (*laboratores*) – by allowing peasants to become bishops and bishops to become monks, and

---

[26] D Ro II 26.   [27] *Liber tramitis aevi Odilonis abbatis*, p. 4.

in the way in which Abbot Odilo appeared as *rex Oydelo* and the Cluniac monk as *miles*.[28]

The preconditions for Cluny's rise to become the greatest monastery in the west under Abbot Hugh, who at Canossa was able to mediate between Pope Gregory VII and King Henry IV, had thus been created. After the middle of the century a second wave of reform monasticism arose, and Cluny and Fruttuaria were joined as centres by new ones like Vallombrosa, Saint-Victor in Marseilles, Hirsau, Saint-Blasien and Siegburg, to name only these few. Characteristic of this second wave was its powerful impression on the lay world, and the monastic call to follow the apostolic life in poverty and in wandering after the example of the 'primitive church'. It was this second wave of reform monasticism which culminated in the age of monastic orders, beginning with the Cistercians at the end of the eleventh century. This virtually eliminated the risks for the individual monastery within an order, and monastic self-determination was guaranteed by the order's constitution and by the general chapter. The mutual exclusion of the orders, which did not confine itself to self-definition and caused the older representatives of Benedictine monasticism to take on the form of an order, also led in the wake of the ensuing disputes to monasticism's losing a certain degree of credibility, visible not least in the appearance of the first heretical movements of European history in the twelfth and thirteenth centuries. In this period Europe changed from a landscape of monasteries to a landscape of towns; it was these which took over from monasteries as crystallisation points of social life. The forces which concerned themselves critically with the monastic orders and helped to secure the defeat of the first heretical movements no longer built great monasteries in open countryside as previously, but instead took up residence in the towns. It was the exponents of Franciscan poverty and the Dominican community of priests which in turn took on the form of an order as the mendicants.

---

[28] Adalbero, *Carmen ad Robertum regem*, verses 80–169.

CHAPTER 7

INTELLECTUAL LIFE

Claudio Leonardi

INTELLECTUAL life in this period is often given labels which relate to other politico-cultural events and phenomena: the 'post-Carolingian' or 'pre-Gregorian' age. The former view clearly conceives of the tenth century as a continuation of the Carolingian renaissance; by implication, continuation leads to decadence and finally to the Ottonian renaissance. The latter term sees the intellectual and spiritual movement of the monastic tradition (in Gorze and Cluny) and the episcopal tradition (as in Rather of Verona) as precursors of Gregorian church reform and of the Investiture Contest.[1] Such descriptions have long left the tenth century without a name of its own, except perhaps for one of the negative descriptions applied since Baronius' time: the 'iron century', the 'dark century'.[2] Recent reactions against this have led to the period's being described as a great era of cultural renewal and renaissance. Rather than considering the age as particularly obscure or particularly enlightened, it is more useful to look at what was happening in intellectual life at the time. The first thing to consider is schools and book production, which are, at least in part, closely related.

BOOKS, SCHOOL AND INTELLECTUALS

Fewer manuscripts can be dated to the tenth and the early eleventh centuries than to the ninth century and the later eleventh;[3] an oft-repeated fact which tells us nothing about intellectual life during the century. The boom in writing from the last years of the eighth century was a result of the huge cultural developments brought about by Charlemagne. The Carolingian renaissance largely ended Germanic oral tradition and popular culture, and created a need for a written culture based on manuscripts. But given the high cost of books, continued production was unnecessary once demand had been met. This, rather than

---

[1] See in general *Secolo di Ferro* (1991); *Lateinische Kultur* (1991); Jacobsen (1985); Hoffmann (1986).
[2] Baronius, *Annales ecclesiastici*, col 741.   [3] Bozzolo and Ornato (1983), pp. 15–121.

cultural decline, explains the tenth-century fall in manuscript production,[4] though there are some peripheral areas like Benevento and lesser Lombardy where there are more tenth- than ninth-century manuscripts.[5] For the production of written texts to rise, writing must first become a more widespread practice. The numerous surviving charters clearly show that this was true in legal contexts; the tenth century can be accurately described as a period in which the production of documents enjoyed an unusual expansion.[6]

Studies of the surviving manuscripts of classical authors, the best examined field to date, also offer interesting insights into this problem. According to Ludwig Taube's famous remark, the tenth century is an *aetas Horatiana* by contrast with the Carolingian *aetas Vergiliana*;[7] but Horace was not the only or the most important new author of the time. The Carolingians had preferred late classical Christian writers like Sedulius or Arator, as well as Virgil and the *Disticha Catonis*.[8] In the late ninth century Remigius of Auxerre, a typical representative of the period, was also commenting on Juvenal and Persius, and in an early tenth-century Milanese codex (Paris, BN lat. 7900A), Martianus Capella's *De nuptiis Philologiae et Mercurii*, a good representative of the texts studied in the Carolingian schools, appeared alongside new authors such as Terence, Horace, Lucan and even Juvenal.[9] Significantly, the codex is Milanese: Italy had been less influenced by the Carolingian school and was hence more ready to accept the work of authors who did not fit within the rigid scholastic codes of the past.[10]

During the tenth century the entry of other classical authors into the scholastic canon became easier and smoother. But there was also a change in educational theory and thus in the tools used by teachers. The curriculum still mainly consisted of the study of grammar, conceived of as the study of literature through poetry. Teaching followed a manual, the most important being that written in the fourth century by Donatus, whose *Ars minor* had been glossed by Remigius of Auxerre in a successful commentary. During the tenth century Donatus began to be accompanied, though not yet replaced, by the *Institutiones grammaticae* of Priscian as documented in Guadbert's *Epitoma Prisciani*. Other grammars dear to the Irish and Carolingian traditions, such as those of Pompeus, Consentius, Charisius and Diomedes, also began to fall into disuse.[11] Guadbert realised the continuing importance of Donatus and therefore used only the first sixteen books of Priscian (the *Priscianus maior*), and did not adven-

[4] Munk Olsen (1991b), pp. 342–3.
[5] V. Brown in Lowe (1980); Brown (1988); Cavallo (1991), pp. 760–1.
[6] Toubert (1973a), pp. 303–5.   [7] Traube (1911), p. 113.
[8] Munk Olsen (1991b), p. 345; (1991a), pp. 28–32.
[9] Munk Olsen (1991a), pp. 26–7; cf. Leonardi (1960), pp. 435–6.
[10] Ferrari (1991), p. 108. See also more generally Bischoff (1984), pp. 171–94.
[11] Holtz (1991).

ture into the 'revolutionary' territory of books 17 and 18. The importance of
the *Epitoma Prisciani* was clear: pedagogy was placed at a cross-roads, turning
away from the heavy Carolingian overtones of its own French background and
moving towards the Italian teaching tradition which it discusses. Guadbert was
not an isolated figure; comments and glosses on Priscian were also produced
by Israel the Grammarian[12] and Fromund of Tegernsee.[13]

The canon was not simply replaced by a new and equally inflexible system
but altered to fit new needs. The study of grammar lost its Carolingian dominance, being joined by rhetoric (with texts from Cicero and the pseudo-
Ciceronians) and dialectic (using material by Boethius Logicus).[14] At the end of
the century the exceptional but not unique school of Abbo of Fleury
(940–1004)[15] and Gerbert of Aurillac (940/50–1003)[16] slowly added the *quadrivium* to the three subjects of the *trivium* and the study of the sciences was added
to the study of literature. The Bible remained the supreme fount of knowledge
and the focus of study for all the liberal arts, but the classical poets had largely
lost their demonic associations: Jerome's view of the contrast between Christ
and Cicero was now a thing of the past.

The schools were changing internally, but the main innovations took place in
the face they presented to society. During the Carolingian period schools and
intellectual life ran on parallel paths, and schools were equated with culture;
even imperial culture under Charlemagne was conceived of as a school.
Between the beginning of the tenth century and the beginning of the eleventh,
change in this fundamental identity became ever more evident. Schools ceased
to be totally identified with culture and began to take on a preparatory and
introductory role which continued through the eleventh and the beginning of
the twelfth centuries. Culture, in the strict sense of the word, may have originated in the schools but it lost its close relationship with them; and it was no
longer in schools or in school-teaching that culture found its dynamic and creativity.

Typical of this situation were the anti-scholastic debates which seemed to go
beyond the level of topos or habit. Rather of Verona, who had been trained in
Flanders where great schools such as the episcopal school of Liège existed,
had no hesitation in saying of himself, 'he learned little from his teachers, much
more from himself'.[17] This was not an unusual attitude to take; rather, it was
symptomatic of many intellectuals of the time, from Liudprand of Cremona
to Gerbert of Aurillac. The changes taking place also meant that men of
culture began to feel the need for a library of their own, libraries that would

---

[12] Jeudy (1977).   [13] Sporbeck (1991), pp. 369–78.
[14] Van de Vyver (1929), pp. 425–52; Gibson (1991).   [15] Mostert (1987).
[16] Gasc (1986); Riché (1991); Lindgren (1991), pp. 291–303.
[17] 'pauca a magistris, plura per se magis didicit': Rather of Verona, *Phrenesis* II, 70–1, p. 200.

exist alongside those of monasteries and bishoprics and alongside the great court libraries such as that of the new Ottonian emperors from Saxony.[18] Manuscript collecting, characteristic of Italian humanists in the Trecento and Quattrocento, was also typical in this period, although the movement of learning was here the reverse, from the north into Italy.[19] This is true of Rather,[20] and also of Gerbert, who wrote to Raynardus of Bobbio, 'You know with what care I seek copies of books everywhere. You know how many scribes can be found all over Italy in the towns and in the countryside.'[21]

Another important facet of the connection between intellectuals and schools was the writer's relationship to his text. The tradition that the author dictated, or had his work dictated, to a lay or professional scribe came to an end. Henceforth the author no longer merely checked the work of the scribe, which the head of the scriptorium continued to do, but became more directly involved in the text itself, writing or rewriting parts of it, making corrections and additions. In the 870s Anastasius the Librarian (800–79) had edited his own translation from the Greek of the Acts of the Fourth Council at Constantinople, adding extra materials,[22] but this was an exceptional case: since very few knew Greek, the author alone was in a position to revise his translation. Almost a century and a half lies between Anastasius and Radulf Glaber (*c.* 990–1047), during which time the author's attitude to his text changed considerably: the manuscript Paris, BN lat. 10912,[23] shows how Radulf wrote and rewrote his text in different ways. Methods of composition and the intellectual traditions of this period show that, during the tenth century, cultural activity continued to take place in the schools and in courts, bishoprics and monasteries, but also that there was a sense that only individual study, of manuscripts or of various fields of learning, really counted.[24]

Abelard and the other masters of the twelfth century have been seen as the precursors of the modern intellectual in that they were connected with and taught in a school. They were intellectuals whose job was 'thinking and passing on their ideas through teaching', a job which 'allied the development of ideas with the spread of ideas through teaching'.[25] It could be argued, however, that the forerunner of the modern intellectual was the tenth-century author; only during this century did knowledge come to be understood both as being a form of personal achievement and as having a social role. People were aware of the dialectical tension between the scholar's possessive attitude to his subject and

[18] Mütherich (1986); Mayr-Harting (1991a and b); McKitterick (1993).
[19] Ferrari (1991).   [20] E.g. Daniel (1973).
[21] 'Nosti, quanto studio librorum exemplaria undique conquiram Nosti, quot scriptores in urbibus ac in agris Italiae passim habeantur', Gerbert of Aurillac, *ep.* 130, pp. 157–8.
[22] Leonardi (1967).   [23] Garand (1983).   [24] Chiesa and Pinelli (1994); Chiesa (1994).
[25] Le Goff (1957), p. 1.

his intensely critical approach to it on the one hand, and the need to demonstrate publicly (both inside and outside the schools) the knowledge he had acquired on the other: Liudprand of Cremona, trained in Italy and active also in Germany at the Ottonian court, was one example of this new kind of scholar.[26]

THE PERIPHERY OF EUROPE

The dissociation, even alienation, of intellectuals from the schools did not prevent cultural life from being concentrated in particular areas and cities: the historical and geographical context remains fundamental for our understanding of intellectual life in this period.

Spain, largely occupied by the Arabs, enjoyed an extraordinary blossoming of Arab art and culture; the developments in Latin literature were insignificant by comparison. Even taking into account the north of Spain, which had remained outside direct Arab control, Manuel Díaz y Díaz is right in saying that few texts showed any conscious literary content.[27] The Latin tradition continued in Córdoba, the capital of the caliphate during the tenth century. Towards the end of the ninth century Samson maintained the tradition as did Ciprianus and Leovigild later; the Córdoba Penitential was perhaps written here, as was a passion of the St Pelagius martyred in 925 (BHL 6617).

The output of Asturias and León was not much richer. Under Alfonso III (866–912), however, the court of León probably did produce the complex text known as the *Chronicle of Alfonso III*; this includes the *Chronica Visegotorum*, the *Chronicon Albedense* and the *Prophetic Chronicle*.[28] In Navarre under Sancho Garcés I (906–26), the monastery of S. Millán de la Cogolla flourished again; in 924 the monastery of S. Martino was founded at Albeda, in which Vigilianus and Sarracinus composed a set of verses. Little else was written, though towards the end of the century Lupito, who probably lived in Barcelona, produced a number of scientific texts referred to by Gerbert in his work on the astrolabe.[29]

The situation in England, although very different, did have some features in common. As in Spain, intellectual life centred on royal courts and monasteries. King Alfred (871–99) had himself translated several Latin texts he deemed of value into the vernacular: Augustine, Orosius, Boethius, Gregory the Great, Bede's *Ecclesiastical History*. His translations were part of a plan to raise the cultural and social level of the Anglo-Saxon language, and the tenth century did indeed see a substantial rise in the production of vernacular manuscripts. But

---

[26] Vinay (1978a); Sutherland (1988); Staubach (1991).   [27] Díaz y Díaz (1991), p. 95.
[28] *Chroniques Asturiennes*, ed. Bonnaz and ed. Gil Fernandez; cf. Díaz y Díaz (1981); López Pereira (1991).   [29] Gerbert of Aurillac, *Liber de astrolabio*.

this cultural flowering could not have occurred outside the Latin tradition and it also acted as a stimulus to Latin authors.[30]

The first significant work in Latin for fifty years was the biography of King Alfred by Asser (around 893) but nothing important was then produced until the reigns of Æthelstan (924–39) and especially of Edgar (959–75). In Æthelstan's reign there was a considerable growth in scribal activity, thanks mainly to increased document production, the import of manuscripts from the continent,[31] and the arrival of non-Anglo-Saxon teachers such as Israel the Grammarian.[32] In the years that followed, continental influence increased via links with Saint-Bertin, Ghent and especially Fleury. Frithegod worked in Canterbury under Archbishop Odo (941–58) on his *Breuiloquium vitae beati Wilfredi*.[33] Two scholars of outstanding worth, Dunstan, who worked at Glastonbury,[34] and Æthelwold, who lived at court, but retired to Glastonbury on Edgar's death,[35] advanced to high office under Edgar: Dunstan became archbishop of Canterbury, Æthelwold abbot of Winchester (where Wulfstan later worked). Oswald, Odo's nephew, who had studied at Fleury, became bishop of Worcester and later archbishop of York; he also founded Ramsey, where Abbo of Fleury taught for a short time.[36]

The Anglo-Saxon court supported a type of monastic reform which brought with it cultural activity of some distinction. Unlike Spain, which was rather isolated, Anglo-Saxon culture was influenced by the monastic reforms of continental Europe (led by Cluny and Gorze) as well as by the activities of Europe's flourishing centres of manuscript production.[37] Anglo-Saxon text production was mainly of hagiographies, generally though not invariably in verse: lives, translations, miracles (of Swithin, Edmund, Æthelwold and others) and also Æthelweard's *Chronicon*, a Latin translation of a recension of the *Anglo-Saxon Chronicle*.[38] At the end of the century Æthelwold's pupil Ælfric, who became abbot of Eynsham (955–1020), represented the highest pinnacle of Benedictine reform and Anglo-Saxon literature (his works include saints' lives and homilies). Ælfric also wrote in Latin prose and produced a number of important Latin saints' lives.[39]

In Spain and England the tenth century was thus a period not of decadence but rather of renewed interest in study and intellectual activities. Following the Carolingian model, intellectual life revolved around a royal court and was supported by the activities of the Benedictine monasteries, a sign of a certain

[30] Lapidge (1991a).   [31] Keynes (1985).   [32] Lapidge (1992).

[33] Frithegod, *Breuiloquium vitae beati Wilfredi*, ed. Campbell; cf. Lapidge (1988).

[34] Ramsay *et al.* (1992).   [35] Yorke (1988).   [36] Stafford (1989), pp. 187–91.

[37] Knowles (1963), pp. 31–56.   [38] Lapidge (1991b) Cf. also Æthelweard, *Chronicon*, ed. Campbell.

[39] Gatch (1977); Lapidge (1991a).

cultural lag on the periphery. It is impossible, however, to categorise the southern and eastern borders of Europe in this way.

In 881 Monte Cassino was destroyed and the monks who fled to Teano and then Capua were unable to regain the intellectual supremacy they had enjoyed since the end of the eighth century when Paul the Deacon had been one of their number.[40] But by the middle of the tenth century the abbey most closely connected with St Benedict had been completely rebuilt and intellectual life there had begun again. At the end of the ninth century in Capua Erchempert wrote his *Historia Langobardorum Beneventanorum*. In the second half of the tenth century in Salerno, an anonymous author wrote the *Chronicon Salernitanum*,[41] and later Laurence of Cassino, who became archbishop of Amalfi in 1030, wrote sermons and hagiographies.[42]

During this period the Latin-speaking scholarly world – most of southern Italy still spoke Greek, while Sicily was now occupied by Muslims – looked mainly to Naples and the unusual form of literary activity carried out there: translations from Greek into Latin. This work had started in the ninth century and the Neapolitan school continued until well into the second half of the tenth century. Its aim was to produce a Latin hagiographic corpus for southern European Christians incorporating existing religious traditions on the saints; as few of these existed in Latin, works were translated from the Greek. The school was innovatory: its members moved from the traditional theory of word for word towards sense for sense translation. Source texts might in consequence sometimes be partially rewritten to meet contemporary requirements, but the texts produced were generally of a literary quality far superior to that of any literal translation. There were numerous author-translators: John the Deacon, Guarimbotus, Peter the Subdeacon, Bonitus the Subdeacon and Cicinnius, all of whom wrote many saints' lives. John of Amalfi, a monk, translated other hagiographies in the later tenth century; the first Latin translation of a narrative that would later become very popular in the west, the story of Barlaam and Jehosaphat, also apparently comes from the Amalfi area. In Naples at this time Archpriest Leo translated the *Nativitas et victoria Alexandri magni regis* of Pseudo-Callisthenes, the basis of another important western series of narratives.[43]

Although southern Italy was on the edges of the Latin world, it played an important role both by introducing certain aspects of Greek culture into Latin culture and by confirming the vital role played by historiography and hagiogra-

---

[40] Leonardi (1987).

[41] Erchempert, *Historia Langobardorum Beneventanorum*, ed. Waitz; Westerbergh (1957); cf. Taviani-Carozzi (1991). For the *Chronicon Salernitanum* see below at n. 103.

[42] *Laurentius monachus Casinensis archiepiscopus Amalfitanus opera*, ed. Newton.

[43] Chiesa (1991); Kratz (1991).

phy in the artistic self-expression of the time, as well as transmitting the narrative, fantastic themes of Barlaam–Jehosaphat and Alexander into western literature. These are two historical legends of enormous fascination: the story of Alexander the Great and his Asian empire and the legend of Barlaam, the Christianised Buddha. The narratives about ancient Rome and the Trojan War were already popular in the west but were felt to be linked with the roots of western civilisation. The new themes introduced by the writers in Naples and Amalfi represent the arrival of eastern themes in Latin culture.

The eastern borders of Europe were not yet part of the Latin world; these were missionary lands, dominated by the politico-religious interests of the Saxon rulers and the pope. It was not until the eleventh and twelfth centuries that Latin began to be used extensively here. One of the first texts produced was the *Deliberatio supra hymnum trium puerorum* by Gerard, an Italian martyred in 1046 and the first bishop of Csanád in Hungary.[44] The most important texts related to these countries are the two lives of Adalbert, bishop of Prague, martyred in Prussia in 997. The first life was probably written by John Canaparius (who died in 1004) but it has also been attributed to Radim, Adalbert's brother and to Gerbert of Aurillac. John Canaparius was monk and later abbot in the monastery on the Aventine in Rome where Adalbert had spent some time. His work revives several of the themes of ancient martyr literature, such as testimony to the faith in the face of political oppression; but these themes were now integrated into the missionary ones typical of the hagiography of the early and high middle ages.[45]

The second life of Adalbert, written by Brun of Querfurt (974–1009), is of even greater importance. Brun was a chaplain at the court of Otto III but abandoned it to become a monk in the monastery on the Aventine. He later left the monastery for a hermit's life in Romagna as a disciple of Romuald of Ravenna. His desire for monastic perfection became fused with missionary zeal and eventually Brun followed in Adalbert's footsteps. In 1003 he met King Stephen I in Hungary and in 1008 he was in Kiev, under the protection of Grand Duke Vladimir I who had been instrumental in introducing Christianity to the Ukraine from Byzantium. Shortly before his death in 1009 – like Adalbert, he was martyred – Brun wrote Adalbert's biography. This was no mere revision of the first life but a completely new version with new facts and stories inspired by the missionary fervour they both shared. Brun also composed the *Vita quinque fratrum* of his spiritual master Benedict of Benevento, who, along with his companion John and three young Poles, had been killed

---

[44] Gerard of Csanád, *Deliberatio*, ed. Silagi.
[45] *Vita prior S Adalberti Pragensis episcopi*, ed. Karwasinska; cf. Starnawski (1991), but also Kürbis (1991), p. 243.

while preaching in Poland.[46] This text is an even clearer example of a missionary hagiography of saints very recently dead. In this form of hagiography autobiography plays an important, and often clearly stated, part. Of the same *genre* but very different is the *Vita sancti Oudalrici* by Gerard of Augsburg.[47] This recalls the invasions of the Magyars, but the narrative is enriched by a number of different elements including miracles and visions.

TROPES AND HAGIOGRAPHY

The intellectual centre of Europe still lay in France, Burgundy and Lotharingia, where Carolingian culture had developed most fully. But other areas were rapidly growing in importance, including the eastern areas of the old Carolingian territories as far as Saxony, while Bavaria and Italy, especially northern Italy, were becoming increasingly significant.

Many towns continued to maintain schools and be centres of learning; some Carolingian centres of excellence disappeared, to be replaced by new centres. Their rise and the weakened link between schools and culture meant that intellectual life now depended less on schools than previously. Even though tenth-century writings always show a local colouring, it was in this period that many literary genres finally took on a clearly defined individuality; new genres were also introduced. Writings began to be characteristic of their period rather than of their region.

Sequences and tropes are a typical new genre. According to Notker of St Gallen (*c.* 840–912),[48] texts and music not originally included in the canon of the liturgy began to appear at the end of the ninth century; certainly the St Gallen monk's liturgico-literary invention was extremely successful. It consisted of inserting a text into the *vocalise* which prolonged the singing of the Alleluia in the Mass preceding the Gospel lesson: this is the sequence (*sequentia*), also known as the *sequentia cum prosa* or *prosa*. Following a tradition which he claimed to have learned from a monk of Jumièges,[49] Notker regularised the relationship between music and words (one note to a syllable) while maintaining the autonomy of each. From this time on the genre underwent a great development.[50] A trope is also a text produced for the vocalisation within a liturgical text, but unlike the sequence it is not autonomous, since it also includes some of the words of the liturgy; it can thus be inserted in the singing at any point in the Mass. The earliest surviving tropers come from the tenth century; by then the genre had already developed a full range of expression,

---

[46] *Passio sancti Adalberti*, ed. Karwasinska; *Vita quinque fratrum*, ed. Karwasinska; Dunin-Wąsowicz (1972); Sansterre (1989). [47] Gerhard, *Vita sancti Oudalrici episcopi Augustani*, ed. Kallfelz.
[48] von den Steinen (1948). [49] *Ibid.*, pp. 154–5.
[50] von den Steinen (1946, 1947; 1967), pp. 115–50; Huglo (1987); Haug (1987).

reaching its climax in the eleventh century. There are various kinds of trope: the melogenous tropes of the *Alleluia*, which follow the liturgical text, logogenic tropes, which precede it, and meloformic tropes, which are interpolated into a pre-existing text.[51]

While this last kind died out before the end of the tenth century, the other two were further developed and, together with the sequence, undoubtedly greatly changed the liturgy experienced by the faithful in most of the monasteries and cathedrals of Europe. New texts and melodies introduced a previously unknown sense of solemnity to rites in the west. From St Gallen and, according to well-founded hypotheses, from the region between Rhine and Meuse (Mainz and Prüm), perhaps even from Lotharingia (Gorze), the genre spread to England (Winchester) and other areas of France – Autun, Limoges, Aquitaine – and even to Italy. In the tenth century one of the logogenous tropes was the famous trope dialogue between the angel who witnessed the resurrection of Christ and the disciples who ran to the sepulchre: 'Whom seek ye in the tomb, o dwellers in Christ? – The Cross of Jesus Christ, o dwellers in heaven.'[52] This eventually developed into the liturgical drama at the heart of the medieval theatrical revival. Sequences and tropes soon achieved literary and poetic maturity, partly because of the demand for them and partly because of the stimulus of public performance on their authors. This maturity can be appreciated in the dramatic trope written for one of the Masses of Christmas, the *Hodie cantandus* attributed to Tuotilo of St Gallen (d. 913), the only writer of tropes of the period whose name has come down to us.[53]

Less connected with the liturgy were hymns, whose tradition goes back to St Ambrose.[54] There are several large ninth-century hymn collections, probably from St Gallen, Verona and Limoges. The habit of including older hymns in later hymnals continued through the tenth century as the Severinian hymnal, better known as the Umbro-Roman hymnal, shows.[55] Throughout this period the rhythmic line continued to alternate with the quantitative line, which it imitated freely until the year 1000, by which time greater control of the structure of the hymns had become more normal.[56]

While the poetry of sequences, tropes and hymns is often of great depth and high quality, the tenth century offers the first verse masterpieces of medieval Latin literature. Between the middle of the tenth and the beginning of the eleventh centuries there was an outpouring of very significant prose and

[51] See *Corpus Troporum* (1975–90), and also Jacobsson (1986), Silagi (1985), Leonardi and Menestò (1990), Arlt and Björkvall (1993).

[52] 'Quem quaeritis in sepulchro, o Christicolae? – Iesum Christum crucifixum, o coelicolae' See Drumbl (1981); Davril (1986); Iversen (1987).   [53] Jacobsson (1991).   [54] Norberg (1954, 1988).

[55] *Hymnarius Severinianus*, ed. Dreves; cf. Norberg (1977), but also Leonardi (1981).

[56] Stella (1995).

poetry ranging in form from the instructive to the epic. One of the most common forms of writing was hagiographic poetry, often confused with historiographic poetry. When such a confusion occurs there is usually a 'geographic' transfer and the poem ceases to be classed according to where it was produced and is subsequently classed by its genre. As early as the beginning of the Carolingian era Alcuin had written a life of St Willibrord partly in verse and partly in prose, as well as the better-known *Versus de sanctis Euboricensis ecclesiae.*[57] Several typical Anglo-Saxon hagiographies of the tenth centuries written in verse and prose have already been mentioned, and continental European productions were not dissimilar. One of the main differences was that in many hagiographies, especially in those in prose, the hagiographical details accompanied and were often mixed in with historical details, because the stories frequently concerned people who had only recently died, about whom many facts were known that could not be omitted. These are hagiographies in which the transcendental component has become conventional, of less interest than the story of the protagonists and their monastery and/or bishopric. Contemporary hagiography inevitably tends to become historiography.

The famous Life of Count Gerard of Aurillac, who died in 909, written by Odo of Cluny around 925, can be considered the first hagiography of a layman, although the saintly model applied to Gerard is still basically monastic and hardly lay.[58] Hagiographies poured out of Cluny, from John of Salerno's hagiography of Odo in the middle of the century to Sirus of Abbot Maiolus at the end of the century.[59] In these monastic hagiographies it is easy to see an ideological element linked to the monastic reform movement associated with Cluny, based on moral rigour, on distancing oneself from the political world and creating a personal source of power, on prayer and on the celebration of the liturgy.[60] Other centres of monastic reform also produced hagiographies, the most significant being the *Vita Iohannis abbatis Gorziensis* attributed to John of Saint-Arnulf.[61]

There was also a significant reaction against the power of Cluny and its hagiographic writings, for example in Adalbero of Laon's *rhythmus satiricus*, an invective against Count Landri of Nevers. Adalbero, born towards the middle of the century, depicts the count, a member of Hugh Capet's court, as an insidious traitor. The twenty-eight Ambrosian stanzas of the poem throw a shadow over monastic life in Cluny at the time of Abbot Odilo and describe the monks

---

[57] I, Deng-Su (1983); Alcuin, *The Bishops, Kings and Saints of York*, ed. Godman.
[58] Odo of Cluny, *Vita Sancti Geraldi Aurilacensis comitis libri quatuor*; cf. Lotter (1983), Airlie (1992).
[59] Iogna-Prat (1988).　　　[60] Constable (1991).
[61] John of St Arnulf, *Vita Iohannis abbatis Gorziensis*; cf. Barone (1991).

as warriors slaying their foes with the support of the pope. Anti-Roman satire had already begun.[62]

We have already referred to a number of Anglo-Saxon hagiographies and to what might be termed 'missionary' writings from the eastern frontier of Christianity. Other works of equal importance, though perhaps of less importance for the development of the ideal of sanctity, were also being produced at this time: the Lives of two Saxon noblewomen: Queen Matilda, the wife of Henry I, who died in 968 and merited two biographies[63] and the Empress Adelaide, the widow of Otto I, who died in 999 and about whom Odilo of Cluny immediately composed his *Epitaphium*.[64]

The most important characteristic of tenth- and eleventh-century hagiography is its obsession with 'territorial expansion'. Every Christian community seemed to want a written life of the saint that best represented it and with whom it could identify.[65] It was a phenomenon similar to, but different from, the cities' search for patron saints in previous centuries. People sought, perhaps unconsciously, not only for a protector but for a model of saintliness of some kind or other: monastic, episcopal, contemporary or ancient martyrs, a queen or a simple monk. Given the obvious crises of the political institutions of the time, which only towards the end of the century found any degree of order and peaceful government, and then only in a few areas of Europe, and given the crises facing the papacy and the clergy, the problems created by the invasions from beyond the borders, and above all the effects of social and political particularism, the blossoming of hagiography demonstrates the requirements of a number of attitudes which cannot simply be reduced to a need for political and social security. There was also a search for a different code of moral behaviour and greater spiritual awareness, a search which now looked for historical, even 'territorial' points of identification. The hagiographer therefore referred to saints and their real or supposed involvement with the history of a particular town or city to produce a story which was understandable within the context of that particular place or city.

This deep connection between contemporary life, place and model of saintliness can be seen in the antiphrastic utterances of Letald of Micy. Speaking of the miracles of St Maximinus, who lived in Micy during the sixth century, Letald declares, 'I am about to relate not things I have heard but things I have seen',[66] and of the *vita* of the early Christian Julian, bishop of Le Mans, Letald

---

[62] Adalbero of Laon, *Carmen ad Robertum regem*, ed. Carozzi (for the other works see also the edition by Hückel); Brunhölzl (1992) pp. 268–74; cf. Oexle (1978).

[63] *Vita Mathildis reginae antiquior*, ed. Schütte; *Vita Mathildis reginae posterior*, ed. Schütte.

[64] Odilo of Cluny, *Epitaphium Adalheidae imperatricis*, ed. Paulhart; Corbet (1986).

[65] Hofmann (1991); I, Deng-Su (1991).

[66] 'neque...audita sed quae vidi narraturus sum': Letald of Micy, *Liber miraculorum Sancti Maximini Miciacensis*, col. 813D.

writes: 'nothing pleases except what is true'.[67] In the tenth century a fantastic hagiography is consciously trying to become reality.

This is one of the reasons for the appearance of the specialist hagiographer. Some of these were authors of significance: Hucbald of Saint-Amand, whose most important work is the *Vita sancta Rictrudis*;[68] Adso of Montier-en-Der, who wrote a life of Clothilde among others;[69] Theoderic of Fleury (or Amorbach), who also produced a number of lives of Italian saints;[70] Folcuin and Heriger of Lobbes.[71] Other authors, mainly anonymous, were active in many other centres, especially in the Frankish kingdom, Burgundy, and Germany, for example in Trier, where Sigehard added a book of miracles to the Life of Maximinus by Lupus of Ferrières.[72] Ruotpert of Mettlach related the life and miracles of Adalbert of Egmont, but there were also many others.[73] Great scholars like Rather of Verona also produced hagiographies: he rewrote the *Vita sancti Usmari*,[74] while Ekkehard of St Gallen wrote the *Vita sanctae Wiboradae*.[75]

One of the most important of these hagiographies, and a work of great literary merit, is the *Miracula sanctae Fidis* by Bernard of Angers, a student of Fulbert of Chartres.[76] After a pilgrimage to the tomb of the saint in Conques, Bernard decided to write about the miracles he had heard: cures, exorcisms, conversions, but also the resurrection of animals, the freeing of miscellaneous types of prisoner and the punishment and even death of pilgrims who failed to make promised votive offerings to the saint. The tales are told in a free-flowing prose style dominated not so much by linguistic affectation as by a real enjoyment of the narrative process and a dedication to the role of pilgrim extraordinary.

Verse hagiographies are a minor product of the genre, often more stylistically polished but more abstract than the prose versions. Apart from hymns and other short works, there are numerous true hagiographic poems that range from the *Vita sancti Romani* of Gerard of Saint-Médard[77] to the *Vita sancti Richarii* of Angilram of Saint-Riquier[78] and the *Vita et passio sancti Christophori* of Walther of Speyer.[79] The first and longest book of this work demonstrates the flexibility of this literary genre: Walther transforms his hagi-

---

[67] 'nihil placet nisi quod verum est': Letald of Micy, *Vita Sancti Iuliani*, col 782B; cf. Cremascoli (1991).

[68] I, Deng-Su (1990).   [69] Werner (1991).   [70] Poncelet (1908).

[71] Dierkens (1983).

[72] Lupus, *Vitae Maximini episcopi Trevirensis*, ed. B. Krusch, and Sigehard, *Miracula S. Maximini;* cf. Zender (1982).   [73] *Vita Adalberti diaconi Egmundae.*

[74] Rather of Verona, *De Vita sancti Usmari;* cf. Golinelli (1991); but see also Dolbeau (1987).

[75] *Vitae sanctae Wiboradae*, ed. Berschin.   [76] *Liber miracolorum sanctae Fidis*, ed. Robertini.

[77] Gerard of Saint-Médard, *Vita Sancti Romani*, PL 138, cols 171–84.

[78] Angilram of St Riquier, *Vita sancti Richarii abbatis Centulensis;* cf. Manitius (1923), pp. 533–5.

[79] Walther of Speyer, *Libellus scolasticus*, ed. Strecker and ed. Vossen.

ography into an autobiography, speaking of his own training and life and not of those of his hero. This again demonstrates the literary need for hagiography in the tenth century; the hagiographic genre served to identify the writer with his subject.

Hrotsvitha of Gandersheim (*c.* 935–75), a nun, does not fit into the geographic classifications of hagiography. Connected with the Saxon court, she was perhaps the most famous and important of the women writing in the high middle ages, and was above all the first real 'love poet' of medieval Latin culture.[80] Her work can be divided into three groups: eight short hagiographic poems, two historical epics and six celebrated plays.[81] Her hagiographies (all written in Leonine hexameters apart from *Gongolf*, in distichs) are not about local saints but include apocryphal poems (on Mary and the ascension of Christ) unconnected with any particular town or city, She also wrote the life of the Merovingian saint Gongolf and the Cordovan martyr Pelagius (d. 925), the lives of Theophilus and Basil of Cesarea, of Dionysius the Aeropagite and Agnes of Rome. The texts are remarkable in that good always triumphs over evil; even pacts with the Devil (as in the lives of Theophilus and Basil) cannot prevent the saint from achieving communion with God.

Hrotsvitha's hagiography is optimistic. Sin is overcome, the Devil does not conquer, and pacts with him (the Faustian tradition in the west begins with Hrotsvitha) cannot damn the soul of the sinner; she remains immune to all these forces. God Himself would be a rather alien force if her own feminine condition had not revealed His merciful nature to her. The discovery was brought about through her writings on the Virgin Mary (the subject of the first poem taken from the Apocrypha) and Agnes. In both poems the author identifies with her heroine: Mary has made Hrotsvitha's own choice and Agnes has turned her back on romantic love in favour of a different, but no less intense, form of love, that of the Heavenly Spouse, and in fact manages to persuade her partner to share in this new love. Hrotsvitha's saints are often lovers (Agnes, and Proterio's daughter in *Basilius*). Hrotsvitha's hagiography is marked by an enthusiasm for story-telling and a sympathetic attitude to the human condition. She chose her own texts, put them into verse or wrote them herself (as apparently is the case with *Pelagius*) and devised her own narrative scheme based on the conflict between good and evil and the final triumph of good and God's mercy.[82]

---

[80] Vinay (1978b), p. 554.
[81] Hrotsvitha, *Opera*; Vinay (1978b), pp. 483–554; Dronke (1984b).   [82] Schütze-Pflugk (1972).

In her two epic poems, clearly written to commission, the final triumph of good is not so obvious. The *Gesta Ottonis* celebrates the life of Otto I, while the *Primordia coenobii Gandeshemensis* tells the history of her convent. The influence of her sources and of the events which had to be included is large. It is interesting, however, that the unifying force of the *Gesta* is not Otto himself but the government of the world through various people (including Otto, Adelaide, Berengar, Henry I and Liudolf) while in the *Primordia* the unifying force is the monastery. But these forces merely impose an external unity on the historical material and leave Hrotsvitha free to arrange the two poems into a series of tableaux and stories in which she can give her optimism free rein, allowing her once more to merge epic with hagiography.[83]

Critics have identified her literary models as Virgil primarily, but also Prudentius (fourth century) and Sedulius (fifth century), both Christian poets of late antiquity. Her sources have also been identified quite easily as the Bible, hagiography and the liturgy. It has to be said, however, that Hrotsvitha takes a rather free approach to her sources, not in the sense that she ignores them but that she works through them to give her work her own stamp. This is also true of the work of Terence that she explicitly named as the source for her plays: 'for there are others, who stick to sacred writings, and yet although scorning other pagan writers frequently delight in Terence's fictions'.[84]

The plays show even more clearly that her problem (both in life and art) was how to equate human love with the ideal of Christian perfection, how to describe the conflicts this produces and the solutions required. Her drama is not contemporary as it is in the historical poems. *Gallicanus* is set in two periods: that of the Emperors Constantine and Julian (fourth century); *Dulcitius* is set in the Diocletian period and *Calimachus* at the very beginning of the Christian era, in the Ephesus of John the Apostle. With *Abraham* and *Paphnutius* we move to the initial, glorious monastic era of the fourth century, while *Sapientia* is situated in Hadrian's Rome. Hrotsvitha not only sited her 'anti-Terentian' dramas in two different time frames, primitive Christianity and the fourth century, but also used two different historical backgrounds, the persecution and martyrdom of the Christians and the monastic life.

In the plays, even more than in her other works, history does not interest Hrotsvitha; she is entirely wrapped up in her existence as a nun. History has little significance in a nunnery and so is played down in her plays. She is interested in psycho-historical situations that could not have appeared in any drama of her time. In an attempt to resolve the conflict between passion and perfection, Hrotsvitha tried to reduce its immediacy by situating her plays in the

---

[83] Kirsch (1991).

[84] 'Sunt autem alii, sacris inhaerentes paginis, qui licet alia gentilium spernant, Terentii tamen fingmenta frequentius lectitant': *Praefatii*, ed. Homeyer, p. 233, ed. Winterfeld, p. 106 lines 3–6.

distant past. In *Calimachus* and *Abraham* she depicts women in search of love whose deep Christian faith and convictions mean that only God, the Heavenly Spouse, can offer the type of love they seek. As a woman with a true monastic vocation she exalts virginity and chastity and realises that death is often the price that must be paid for the love of this terrible God who demands such self-sacrifice from those who adore Him. Her plays usually end in martyrdom and often deal with terrible carnal temptation (Drusianus in *Calimachus*) or prostitution (Mary in *Abraham* and Thais in *Paphnutius*). This juxtaposition, at times mechanical and superficial, offers, however, a solution to the problem which was already visible in her earlier short hagiographic poems. A merciful God allows men, or rather Christians, who are prepared to accept self-destruction to find a peace and serenity unknown to man: man is kind to woman and the old hermit Abraham is finally able to express all his affection to his niece Mary.

Hrotsvitha's greatest literary achievement coincides with her finest intellectual intuition: monasticism no longer consists in ivory tower contemplation and aristocratic and imperial connections, but is open to mankind and focuses greater attention and love on man. Hrotsvitha perceives man as love, even though she is unable to show the love between man and woman openly. In some plays there is only a female protagonist because woman is the one true ally of God in the conversion of men, but in *Abraham* both man and woman with their delicate tenderness and affectionate outpourings are protagonists and the keyword of the drama is *pietas*, 'divine piety, which is greater than all created things'.[85] In this sense *Abraham* is Hrotsvitha's masterpiece.[86]

The greatest of the epic poems written in the tenth century is *Waltharius*. But it was not the only epic poem produced. In the first half of the century an anonymous author in northern Italy wrote a panegyric on Berengar, which is principally a description of the struggles between Berengar and Wido of Spoleto. The *Gesta Berengarii*, composed in 1,090 rather elegant hexameters, has numerous hellenisms and many references to Virgil, Statius, Prudentius and Sedulius. Unusually, the author supplied his own glosses.[87] While the anonymous *Gesta* in its celebration of contemporary power is close in spirit to Hrotsvitha's *Gesta Ottonis*, her *Primordia* was perhaps the model for other poems celebrating monastic and episcopal life such as the *Gesta Witigowonis* of Burchard of the Reichenau.[88]

Two epic poems of a different type each represented the beginnings of a real literary tradition. The *Gesta Apollonii*, possibly written in Tegernsee, tells the life and adventures of Apollonius of Tyre and is a reworking in hexameters of a

---

[85] 'superna pietas maior est omni creatura': *Abraham* VII, 10, ed. Homeyer, p. 316, ed. Winterfeld, p. 158, line 4. [86] Vinay (1978b), pp. 532–53. [87] *Gesta Berengarii imperatoris*, ed. Winterfeld.
[88] Purchard, *Gesta Witigowonis*, ed. Strecker; cf. Autenrieth (1985), pp. 101–6.

Latin prose story of the fifth century, in its turn a Christianisation of an old Greek text.[89] Even more successful were epics about the animal world, such as the *Ecbasis cuiusdam captivi per tropologiam*, the first epic of its kind in the middle ages. In classical times satirical writers from Aesop to Phaedrus had made animals the main characters in their fables. This tradition was taken up again – for example by Sedulius Scottus – in the Carolingian period and reached a high point in the eleventh century with the work of Adhémar of Chabannes (988–1034).[90] But until the *Ecbasis* no-one had produced a whole story about animals in a single narrative that was neither instructive nor satirical but epic; it is this epic structure, even though fragile and subtle, that holds the poem together. Consisting of 1229 Leonine hexameters, composed perhaps in Lotharingia towards the end of the tenth century, it is really two stories, one within the other. Although the meaning of the poem is enigmatic, its literary worth is undeniable. The anonymous writer of the only successful comedy written in the early middle ages gives us a series of well-described scenes portraying animals and characterising them figuratively and psychologically (with references to Horace).[91]

Waltharius (a poem of 1,453 hexameters) is poetry of a rather higher calibre.[92] Its dating is still disputed, but opinion now tends towards the middle of the tenth century rather than the earlier dating to the first half of the ninth century. The revised dating also means that Ekkehard I of St Gallen (910–73), known to have been author of a *Vita Waltharii manufortis*, has now been put forward as its author.[93] Although Dieter Schaller has recently claimed that Ekkehard's authorship has not been proved beyond doubt,[94] the likelihood of the poem's having been written in St Gallen and therefore being attributable to Ekkehard has been strengthened by Schaller's own conclusions: there is no evidence for the existence of a *Waltharius* poem in the Carolingian period, while there are strong links between early eleventh-century Mainz and Ekkehard IV of St Gallen, who undoubtedly knew and reworked a *Vita Waltharii* written by Ekkehard I.[95]

The theme of *Waltharius* is neither Christian nor classical – this is a story in the Germanic tradition. By the high middle ages the cultural heritage of the Germanic peoples had already become the subject of Latin literature, with masterpieces such as Bede's *Historia ecclesiastica* and Paul the Deacon's *Historia Langobardorum* telling the great tales. These were works of history and not epic

---

[89]   *Gesta Apollonii*, ed. Dümmler and ed. Ermini.
[90]   Adhémar of Chabannes, *Fabulae*, ed. Gatti and Bertini.
[91]   *Ecbasis cuiusdam captivi per tropologiam*, ed. Strecker; cf. Gompf (1973).
[92]   *Waltharius*, ed. Strecker; cf. Langosch (1973); Önnerfors (1988).
[93]   Brunhölzl (1992), p. 63.   [94]   Schaller (1991), p. 437.
[95]   *Ibid.*, p. 436. Cf. also Werner (1990), pp. 101–23.

poems. In the Carolingian period the Germanic tradition had found a voice in *Karolus Magnus et Leo papa*; but *Waltharius* was something new and different: it was no longer a single poem but an entire story, that of Walther's flight and return to his homelands.

There was probably an oral Germanic version of the story in existence before the appearance of the Latin text but the theory that the Latin is a later version of a German text can now be excluded. What is clear, however, is that the Germanic tradition itself is the subject of the poem although the references to Virgil in the flight theme, in the description of the battles and in the sense of adventure which runs through the work are obviously important, as are the references to Prudentius. Hrotsvitha's optimism is also present in the poem, with a vein of Christianity tempering the Germanic tale. The main influence is Carolingian poetry with its occasionally rather laboured metric structure and somewhat creaky imagination. But from this structure Ekkehard (or the anonymous author from St Gallen) has created a broad poetic narrative that allows the Germanic epic to make a welcome entry into the Latin-Christian tradition. Walther is not on a great mission: this is the story of man who has reached maturity and full possession of all his powers returning home after many adventures to the woman he loves (Hildegund is a shadowy figure whose only real function is to represent a haven of security for the hero). It is the story of a man who is strong and heroic, but who shares the anxieties, the uncertainties of travel, the fear of the night, of the unknown and of the enemy with his friends/enemies, that is with other men. Walther seems almost overcome by the trials of life and the final battle and its uncertain outcome (because Walther knows that he may be the loser) are at the heart of the poem. Walther's best quality is not his strength but his desire for peace and light which – like Hrotsvitha's merciful *pietas* – runs through the work:

> Behold, however things may turn out, here I shall lie
> Until the revolving sphere brings back the longed-for light,
> Lest the land should say 'That king, the proud king,
> Has stolen a thief's flight through the shadows, as is his wont.'[96]

Waltharius marks the beginning of the great Germanic epic tradition.[97]

The tenth century produced another surprise. Far from St Gallen, in Micy in the Loire Valley, a monk named Letald (*c.* 945–96) wrote a short farcical epic

---

[96] En quocumque modo res pergant, hic recubabo,
Donec circuiens lumen spera reddat amatum,
Ne patriae fines dicat rex ille rex superbus
Evasisse fuga furis de more per umbras.
Waltharius, ed. Strecker, p. 71, lines 1151–4

[97] Von den Steinen (1952); Vinay (1978c); Dronke (1984a).

poem: a tragedy with a happy ending, but in this case the ending is a comic parody. In *Within piscator, Versus de quodam piscatore, quem ballena absorbit*, Letald tells how the Englishman Within (he who is within) one day goes fishing and ends up inside the belly of a whale. He tries desperately to escape but in vain, until he remembers that he has a knife and with this he keeps slashing at the whale's stomach, wounding it ever more gravely until finally, after several days imprisonment he reaches the heart and kills the fish, which beaches on the coast he set off from. The reference to Jonah in the Bible is obvious. The ending, however, bears no relation to the biblical story. The inhabitants of the village run down to the beach to see the whale and open it up and share out the meat. Within cries for help and is taken for the Devil. The villagers then organise a propitiatory procession and an exorcist, but in the end they recognise the fisherman and all ends happily.[98] In *Within* Letald gives us a pleasant, fantastical story that is almost a joke and which parodies both the high-minded ideological example of the biblical Jonah and the committed epic poetry about kings, queens and knights.

HISTORIOGRAPHY AND LITERATURE

Intellectual production during the whole century was notably historiographic. With its hagiography and its epic-historical and biographical poetry, the period is best characterised by its interest in contemporary and past events and its varied historiographic output. It is as if the enormous quantity of historiographical writing by often anonymous authors answered a need. This was no longer the need to rediscover a cultural past as the Carolingian era had rediscovered Latin and the works of the *auctores* and Christian writers, rather the need to rediscover the history of a people and to regain a lost sense of cultural awareness and responsibility. No other literary genre of the tenth century produced so many works as historical writing, from *annales* to *chronica*, from *gesta* to biographies and autobiographies, a form which made its first medieval appearance in this period.

The *annales* formula, ennobled during the Carolingian period by its pre-eminence in court literature, once more became the accepted form of memoirs, especially in the monasteries. Talented writers such as Flodoard of Rheims had no hesitation in calling their historiographies *annales*. At least thirty annalistic works date from the tenth and beginning of the eleventh centuries: many come from eastern Europe, including Bavaria and Saxony, but several others were written in northern France, in the valleys of the Loire and the Rhine, and a few were produced in other places like Spain and Italy.[99]

---

[98] Letald of Micy, *Within piscator*, ed. Bertini; cf. Bertini (1991). [99] Hofmann (1991).

Flodoard's *Annales* follow the tradition of chronicling events year by year.[100] But he also innovates, and his chronicles are rich in details which show a design tending more towards the narrative than towards the documentary and an alternation of local news with news of more general interest. In Flodoard's writings, the annalistic genre, which continued to enjoy great popularity for a number of centuries, acquired several structural features which extended its meaning but also brought it to the brink of extinction.[101]

Apart from his work in continuing a great cultural tradition, Flodoard is also remembered for two other, equally innovative works: the *De triumphis Christi* and the *Historia Remensis ecclesiae*. The first is an apparently incomplete hagiographic epic poem, which recounts the exploits of the saints of Palestine, Antioch and Italy. The work sets out to be a legendary of the universal church and is innovative in its hagiographic scope because of its historico-geographic structure, which extends out from Palestine to the whole Christian world. Flodoard can be considered the historian and hagiographer *par excellence* of the period. Like many other writers of the time, he considers historiography and hagiography as the two components of historical conscience: history as a series of events and personages and history as sublimated in the *viri Dei*: human history and divine history that together lead to an understanding of the times.[102] Flodoard's *Historia* also starts another tradition, or at least reinforces an existing one. He uses public and archival documents such as epigraphs, private charters and letters as a further basis for his historical narratives, following the model of Agnellus of Ravenna's *Liber pontificalis* and John Hymmonides' *Vita Gregorii* from the first and second half of the ninth century respectively.[103]

The *chronica* genre also continued to be employed both in bishoprics and in monasteries, but its heyday came later in the eleventh century. Nevertheless, the tenth century also produced several great *chronica*: Widukind of Corvey's *Res gestae Saxonicae*, the story of the house of Saxony; Benedict of St Andrew by Monte Soracte's *Chronicon*, about Rome; and an anonymous south Italian writer's *Chronicon Salernitanum*. The last of these is a local chronicle of facts and extraordinary happenings.[104] Benedict describes Rome and its surroundings from a monastic point of view, which imposes a distance on events, as if seen from another form of reality.[105] Widukind, by contrast, is aware that he is telling a story about power; he has no illusions about the world he is describing and no time for the unreal.[106] All three chronicles share one feature, however:

[100] Flodoard, *Annales*, ed. Lauer.   [101] Sot (1993).

[102] Flodoard, *De triumphis Christi*; Jacobsen (1978).

[103] Flodoard, *Historia Remensis ecclesiae*, ed. Stratmann.

[104] *Chronicon Salernitanum*, ed. Westerbergh; Oldoni (1969).

[105] Benedict of Soracte, *Chronicon*, ed. Zuchetti; Oldoni (1991).

[106] Widukind, *Res gestae Saxonicae*, ed. Hirsch and Lohmann; Beumann (1950).

the historian identifies entirely with the place he is writing about (monastery, city or kingdom). In consequence universal chronicles, such as Regino of Prüm's *Chronica seu libellus de temporibus dominicae incarnationis* completed in 908,[107] are of little interest to him.

Two historians stand out: Richer of Rheims and Liudprand of Cremona. Richer, who had studied with Gerbert, was still alive at the end of the century. The heir to a great historiographic tradition, his conception of the art was completely different from Flodoard's. Richer's writings follow no chronological or any other apparent order, and seem determined only by his own opinion of the history of his time. In selecting the contemporary events to record in his *Historiae*, Richer makes no use of existing sources or judgements and shows his skill in using literature as a basis for his historiographical texts.[108]

Richer was following in the footsteps of Liudprand (*c.* 920–72), one of the greatest strictly literary geniuses of the century, whose achievements dwarfed Richer's. Liudprand had studied and was perhaps born in Pavia, but he did not dedicate himself to a life of study. Instead, he made an early entry to Berengar II's court and later, controversially, left for the Saxon court of Otto I, who created him bishop of Cremona. He continued in the emperor's service, however, and in 967 went to Constantinople to request the hand of Theophanu for Otto II (having already been to Constantinople previously on a mission for Berengar).[109]

Liudprand's historiographic works all have contemporary settings and often drift into autobiography: the *Antapodosis* or *Liber retributionis regum atque principum Europae*; the *Liber de rebus gestis Ottonis magni imperatoris*, and the *Relatio de legatione Constantinopolitana*.[110] In the last two books the titles point to his role as Otto's counsellor and ambassador but he is also present in the first (and most famous) of the works. Liudprand's historiography abandons all pretence of objectivity, even the apparent objectivity of the various types of annal, chronicle and history which try to present a list of facts in an attempt to conceal the historiographic and ideological selections made. Liudprand conceals nothing and describes his facts with a crudity and immediacy unknown in Carolingian historiography. His stories do not only or even principally describe greatness and nobility of intent and action; they are more concerned with their brutality, unmasking foul intentions, dirty affairs and the vulgarity and obscenity of relations, including sexual relations, between men. If a Christian God exists in his writings, His actions are mechanical, so that Liudprand, of Lombard descent, seems to be reintroducing a primitive Germanic spirit into the literature of the period.

[107] Regino, *Chronicon*; Schleidgen (1977).   [108] Richer, *Historiae*; Kortüm (1985).
[109] Lintzel (1933); Sutherland (1988).   [110] Liudprand, *Opera*; Chiesa (1994).

The unrivalled greatness of his historiographic writings stems from his despair at finding himself impotent in the face of events, and from his obstinate, furious reaction to events he has understood or believes he has understood. From the literary point of view, this gives an aggressive edge to his narrative, which increases the more as he manages to convey anger in his narrative-fictional interpretations of events which he has heard at third-hand and which may be either truth or fiction. Liudprand produced a number of unforgettable realistic portraits and tableaux. His view of history was anti-epic and he regularly de-epicised every event: epic in reverse. His portraits such as those of Nikephoros Phokas or of Marozia and Theodora, the libidinous debauchers of Rome, or of Berengar and Willa are justly famous. His portraits and tableaux are generated by an autobiographical style of writing, which contemplates the meaninglessness of history with its irrationality and earthly brutality and uses descriptions to expose this.[111]

Other notable authors besides Liudprand were working in Italy in the Po valley in the tenth century. They included Atto of Vercelli, the author of a commentary on the *Epistles* of St Paul and especially of a *Polypticum quod appellatur perpendiculum*, an extremely obscure political treatise which is also a political satire and compendium of wisdom.[112] The Ottonians also imported teachers and codices from Italy (not only north Italy), often via Milan. Gunzo and Stephen of Novara were at Otto I's court at the same time as Liudprand,[113] while the manuscripts from Otto III's library, still in Bamberg, include works by contemporary Italian authors such as Eugenius Vulgarius.[114] Mainly from southern but also from northern Italy, the texts on Roman history were clearly used by the Ottonians to appropriate imperial ideology. Both John Philagathos, the bishop of Piacenza (later abbot of Nonantola) and John, the German bishop of Vercelli, played important roles in this ideological transfer.[115]

The cultural relations between Italy and Germany, two countries relatively little touched by Carolingian culture, cannot explain the quality of Liudprand's prose (which made use of *prosimetrum* in the *Antapodosis* and inserted poetry into the *Relatio*)[116] or the prose of the other genius of the period, Rather of Verona (*c.* 890–974). Rather came from Flanders and was educated at Lobbes. Like Liudprand, he was an autodidact, although he had received an excellent scholastic education. He too was a bishop, of Verona, and was twice expelled from his see by clergy and politicians who disagreed with his policies, only to be later reinstated.[117]

Like Liudprand's, Rather's personality was bizarre and eccentric, and so

---

[111] Vinay (1978a), pp. 391–432.   [112] Atto of Vercelli, *Polipticum*, ed. Goetz; Wemple (1979).
[113] Ferrari (1991), pp. 110–14.   [114] Pittaluga (1991).   [115] Ferrari (1991), pp. 110–14.
[116] Jacobsen (1985); Scherbantin (1951).   [117] Jacobsen (1989).

was his prose: it is like Liudprand's in being rich and full of rare words and apparently irregular constructions, but it is also very different and not strictly comparable. Liudprand narrates a story which happens to include his first-hand experience; Rather narrates himself, though he hides this behind moral or legal debates about the nature of hostility towards him. Liudprand recounts a story and its action; Rather is defeated by a problem he never explicitly admits, the difficulty of reaching truth and of making it reflect reality. As a result Rather is a lonely character and the consciousness of unbearable solitude is the thread running through all his works from *Praeloquia* to the *Qualitatis coniectura cuiusdam*, to *Phrenesis* and the letters.[118]

Recently the influence of the *Consolatio* of Boethius has been pointed out in the works of the older Rather and his junior Liudprand (especially the *Praeloquia* and *Antapodosis*) as the *Phrenesis* is written in a prosimetric structure like the *Consolatio* and the *De nuptiis* of Martianus Capella. It has been claimed that Rather, and later Liudprand, took Boethius' concept of seeking consolation within oneself for the antagonism of the powerful and used it as the model for radical satirical criticism of the moral and political condition of the time.[119] This may define the literary genre to which they belonged but it can only offer a limited explanation of their literature and of the spiritual meaning they both gave to their lives and works.

In describing Rather's *Praeloquia* as a book in which 'whoever reads it will find many things while reading which can provide as much pleasure as profit to the minds of those reading',[120] Liudprand is speaking less of Rather than of himself; his own view of history finds a way to salvation in writing and narration, the means of achieving inner calm and taking pleasure in life. Rather, by contrast, cannot do this; in his work there is the consciousness of an absolute solitude which can be described but not resolved through writing, for the resolution of his predicament would have to come through an absolute truth he knows he can never express. As a result, Rather' despair gives rise to the first true form of 'autobiographical representation in the high middle ages'[121] but it also leads to an absolute desire for existence beyond history, which history cannot satisfy. He expresses this desire through his hope and fear that history will end in the millennium, allowing him to escape from the cruelty and despair of history into true metahistory.

The period between the ninth and eleventh centuries was rich in many other forms of intellectual activity and saw the rise of many other literary forms, both old and new. But above all, the period was characterised by its sense of

---

[118] Vinay (1989a, 1989b).   [119] Staubach (1991).

[120] 'Quem si qui legerit, nonnullas ibi hac sub occasione res expolitas inveniet, quae legentium intellectibus non minus placere poterunt quam prodesse': Liudprand, *Antapodosis* III, 52, p. 101.

[121] Vinay (1989a), p. 135.

historical awareness. Hagiography, biography and true historiography, in all their various forms, sprang from this basic realisation of the need to match oneself against history.

One of the greatest writers of the age, Gerbert of Aurillac (940/50–1003) was also one of the most aware of the period's historical context. While other writers contented themselves with descriptions of the past and/or the present, or invented the legends of men, such as saints, who were historical representations of perfection in God, and while Rather and Liudprand measured themselves against history and came away defeated after having merely touched it through their writings, Gerbert dominated and took control of history, determining its course. Gerbert too had known defeat, but not like Rather in Verona or Liudprand at the hands of Berengar. Gerbert was a victor and in him we have an extraordinary phenomenon: the intellectual who holds the reins of power, literature as power. While other great writers carried historiography to its greatest literary peaks, Gerbert plunged it into the world of politics.

Gerbert was born in the Auvergne and became a monk in Aurillac. He studied in Catalonia, where he came into contact with Arab learning, and Pope John XIII called him to Rome where he met Otto I. He left Rome for Rheims to become director of its school. In 981 he was back in Rome and in Pavia Otto II created him abbot of Nonantola. He won a famous disputation with Otric of Magdeburg before the emperor in Ravenna, but Otto II died in 983 and Gerbert returned to Rheims. On the death of Archbishop Adalbero in 989 he succeeded to the see, but his title was not confirmed by the pope. He therefore left Rheims for the court of the Saxon emperors and became tutor, but mainly counsellor, to Otto III, who was still a minor. Otto had him enthroned as archbishop of Ravenna and in 999 as pope. Gerbert, the first French pope, assumed the name of Sylvester II and enjoyed a relationship with Otto III similar to Sylvester I's with Constantine: that of the greatest ecclesiastical and temporal powers in the western world working together in close harmony.[122]

Gerbert was no historiographer, but both a political intellectual and a great writer. His work shows how far Carolingian culture had now been left behind. He was a master of the arts of the *trivium* and his travels to Italy were partly made in order to find the works and stimuli needed to complete his training in logic, as he was not satisfied with the few Ciceronian references in Carolingian rhetoric and dialectic. His extraordinary scientific, technical and practical work reinjected arts of the *quadrivium* from Spain into the general culture of the time. France had been the centre of Carolingian culture but Gerbert makes it clear that innovation now comes from outside France, from the Arabs and from the traditions still maintained in Italy.

[122] Gerbert of Aurillac, *Opera; Opera mathematica*, ed. Bubnov; *Epistolae*, ed. Weigle; *Gerberto* (1985).

In his letters Gerbert's successful prose style is consciously modelled on that of the ancient *auctores* and is careful and controlled but effortless, far from the linguistic contortions of Rather and Liudprand, for all their literary effectiveness. He is immersed in writing and culture, 'in study and politics we teach what we know and learn what we do not know';[123] though in politics as well, as the sentence just quoted makes clear. Not surprisingly, Gerbert was believed to have made a pact with the Devil: his successful and glorious career could only have been achieved with Lucifer's aid.[124] Nor is it surprising that his vision of God has much in common with Boethius, perhaps his most influential model. For Gerbert, God is total intelligence and perfect understanding of the world because the world can be controlled by the intellect.[125] In this respect Gerbert's views are diametrically opposed to those of Rather. Both are ill-at-ease with the theory of the perfect unity of truth and history, but while Rather considers it impossible, Gerbert believes the intellect could grasp the concept and use it.

THE MILLENNIUM

The most striking feature of the era is the eschatology provoked by the imminent arrival of the millennium: history must be told and should be understood and directed but it can also come to an end. The great intellectual and spiritual inheritance of the time is the understanding that history may have no future but, in so far as it exists, is a function of the future. Beatus of Liébana, Ambrosius Autpert and Aimo of Auxerre between the eighth and the end of the ninth centuries had all interpreted the Apocalypse of John the Apostle as a message to the individual, free of any historical context. In the tenth century a different interpretation of the book produced a fear of the millennium and the possible end to history that might accompany it.

It was one of Gerbert's friends, Adso of Montier-en-Der (910/15–992) who reintroduced the eschatological reading of the Apocalypse. In his widely read *Epistola de ortu et tempore Antichristi* dedicated to Gerberga, Otto I's sister, Adso describes the Antichrist as a person, the son of Satan, who at the end of the millennium is freed from his chains and brings history to an end. Adso voiced a common tension: the fear of, but also the longing for, an end to history.[126]

Through Augustine, and in particular his *De civitate Dei*, the west perceived history as a single process produced by the war between God and the Devil, and understood the one thousand of the Apocalypse to mean the historical millennium. The end of the world was perceived as a historical event following

---

[123] 'in otio, in negotio, et docemus, quod scimus, et addiscimus, quod nescimus': Gerbert, *ep.* 4, p. 73.
[124] Oldoni (1977, 1980, 1983).   [125] Riché (1991), p. 421.
[126] Adso of Montier-en-Der, *Epistula ad Gerbergam reginam de ortu et tempore Antichristi*, ed. Verhelst; Konrad (1964).

a last battle in Jerusalem between the Christ and the Antichrist. This possibly is why Adso, already very advanced in age, took ship for the east in 992, dying at sea after five days. The desire to see the end of history was also a desire to see the final outcome of the last battle and the ultimate victory of Christ for all men.

The great legacy of the time is its view of the future. This formed the basis for thinking in the west for many centuries to come: not only the expectation of the end but also the knowledge that Christian perfection is to be found within history. In this sense the works of Gerbert and Adso are both parallel and convergent.

CHAPTER 8

ARTISTS AND PATRONS

Henry Mayr-Harting

ARCHITECTURE

The architectural world of the tenth and eleventh centuries is not easy to recover either from what is now to be seen or from the literary sources. First, although we have the literary and archaeological evidence for Ottonian royal palace complexes such as those in Magdeburg or Ravenna, our evidence is predominantly that of churches. And second, as to churches, we see some remarkable experimentation in what has survived, but the literary texts, our only evidence for so much that has been destroyed or rebuilt, tend to present building by abbots and bishops in its traditionalist aspects. Often we have to work from analogies. The church of Romainmôtier in modern Switzerland is probably our best chance of seeing what the second church of Cluny looked like, and Nivelles, where around 1000 a cousin of Otto III called Adelaide was abbess, and where the church has a transept at each end of the nave, is likely to reflect the appearance of Bishop Notker's (972–1008) cathedral at Liège.

One church of novel character which can still be seen is that of St Martin de Canigou, dating from the earliest years of the eleventh century, and built under the patronage of Count Wifred of Cerdaña. The Pyrenees, as Puig y Cadafalch long ago showed, was an important region for the early development of Romanesque styles. It would be a great mistake to regard this region as out of the way, despite the impression of remoteness the monastery of Canigou now gives, standing on a magnificent spur of the mountain of that name, and commanding staggering views upwards from its cloister. For it was close to the great route which linked Spain and the Mediterranean to the heart of rich and productive Lotharingia via the rivers Meuse, Saône and Rhône. Canigou is a traditional, 'first Romanesque' church in its use of small, unsmoothed stones and its triple-apse plan, but its remarkably slender pillars support a daring barrel vault over the nave.

However, the chief object of this discussion is not to engage in an analysis of stylistic development, but rather to ask how the ecclesiastical architecture of the period is related to what went on inside the churches. Carolingian monasticism, with its interest in Roman and eastern chants, was already more liturgised than the Rule of St Benedict had envisaged, and tenth-century monasticism, whether we consider the so-called Gorze Reform, Cluny and Fleury, or the English Benedictine revival, heightened this tendency. We know one of the *raisons d'être* of the various tribunes, the west work and the separated areas of Agilbert's church of Charles the Great's time at Saint-Ricquier, for it is clear from his Ritual Order. It was to enable choirs of monks and boys, separated from each other, to answer each other antiphonally across the church with impressive echoes, rather as the various tribunes of the dome of St Mark's, Venice, were intended to echo with the trumpets of Gabrieli's music. One cannot understand Carolingian churches, for all the importance of saints' shrines and relics in their lay-out which has been rightly stressed, without recreating for oneself the sounds which they were intended to contain. It is quite as much so with the churches of the succeeding age. The musical stave was only invented in the eleventh century, and it is clear that choirs of monks, nuns and canons were still in the ninth and tenth centuries expected to know their musical notes by heart, and the neums which positively sprouted in the chant books of this age are considered to represent the movements of a conductor's hand, as well as reminding the choir of melody, and indicating rhythm and ornamentation. An inspired precentor must have been able to elicit dramatic effects from his schola cantorum. We know that Liège was famous for its chants under Bishop Stephen (903–20), that it was an experience to hear the chants on Christmas night in Trier Cathedral or in the open air at Augsburg on Palm Sunday, that hymnals spread far and wide from the abbey of St Gallen (the Solesmes of the day), and that a spate of Marian anthems began to be composed at Reichenau at the latest in the early eleventh century which apparently gave us among others the *Salve Regina*. The tenth-century English show a near craze for building organs, whose main function must have been to accompany the chants; the evidence is mostly English, but one may doubt whether the phenomenon itself was so confined.

One notable musical composer was Odo of Cluny. While he was abbot of Cluny (926–44) he was approached by the monks of his former monastery of Tours to write some longer antiphons for Saint-Martin than those they had, whose length might relieve them 'of the monotony of repeating these very short ones'. He praised the brevity of their antiphons and expressed disgust at the prolixity they demanded; they warned him that he would displease Saint-Martin if he refused and that his excuse signified a hidden pride. Odo gave way and composed antiphons 'in which the meaning and sound agreed so well, that it seemed that nothing could be added or taken away from the sense, nothing found more sweet in the modulations of the melody'. His biographer adds that they were retained to that day in Benevento, not an uninteresting observation, since it shows the power of music to unite a politically fragmented world, as between Liège and St Gallen, Tours or Cluny and Benevento.[1] There is much evidence for the interest in musical theory at this time, derived above all from the writings of Boethius, and Odo is part of it, but this story shows that he was no mere musicologist.

We have unfortunately little hard evidence of how the various parts of a tenth-century church were exploited musically, though that does not invalidate hypotheses drawn from the nature of the architecture itself, but there is a suggestive story from amongst the tenth-century miracle narratives of St Faith at Conques about the cure of a blind man called Gerbert. In the night of the vigil of the feast of St Michael, St Faith appeared to this man in a dream and told him to join the procession of monks to the altar of St Michael the following day after Vespers where God would restore his sight. And so it was done. Gerbert accompanied the monks' procession to the oratory of St Michael, where, while they sang the antiphon in honour of the coming festival, the heavenly artifex or creator enabled him to see.[2] From the account it is clear that we are dealing with a kind of Westwork, whether of the tenth century or the ninth we cannot tell, of which the oratory of St Michael constituted the third level, above a solarium which was itself supported by a vaulted structure on the ground floor. It is not clear, therefore, if the oratory gave onto the church as a second level must have done, but it is quite likely, since we also learn from the account that above the oratory was yet a fourth level with bell-tower (all this of course disappeared in the great rebuilding of the eleventh and twelfth centuries). The important point for our purposes, however, is the use of the high galleries for music.

A church of striking originality for its galleries along the length of the nave at triforium level is Gernrode in the heartlands of tenth-century Saxon rule. Close to the royal nunnery of Quedlinburg with its staggering views across to the Harz Mountains, Gernrode was founded as a nunnery in 961 by Margrave Gero, one of the great military commanders of Otto I on his eastern frontier with the Slavs. Having lost his son Siegfried in the Slav wars, Gero founded here a house of canonesses with his widowed daughter-in-law, Hathui, as their abbess. Hans Jantzen, in his brilliant analyses of the aesthetic of Ottonian churches, wrote of the strong rhythmical counterpoint between the arches of this triforium and the great openings of the nave arcade underneath it, and he developed the pleasant conceit that the austere and noncommital exterior of the building, in contrast to its lively and solemn interior, was just like the taci-

---

[1] John of Salerno, *Vita S Odonis abbatis Cluniacensis*, c. 10, col. 48C.
[2] *Liber miraculorum sanctæ Fidis* II, 1, pp. 91–2; see Lehmann-Brockhaus (1955), pp. 27–8.

turnity of its founder himself as described by Widukind.[3] Be that as it may, one cannot look at these remarkable galleries without supposing that the nuns, whose understanding of their liturgy was so little staid and conventional that soon after the foundation of Gernrode they gave us our first known commentary on the psalms in the Old Saxon vernacular, would not sometimes have tested their musical possibilities. Anyone who has tested the acoustics of the west work in Archbishop Brun of Cologne's (953–65) great church of St Pantaleon will know that the cool well of space contained within the solemn rythms of its arcaded galleries must provide a veritable echo chamber for a choir of monks or boys. Here is another church whose building was initiated by a patron close to Otto I, in this case his brother. The building at St Pantaleon was continued in a later campaign apparently stimulated by the Empress Theophanu, wife of Otto II, around 984, from which period some exceptional fine stone sculptures have been discovered, including a head of Christ and angel reliefs, which probably adorned the west facade.[4] The nave of Bishop Bernward of Hildesheim's (993–1022) great early eleventh-century church for the monastery of St Michael, Hildesheim, has no galleries in the nave, but the galleries at two levels in the transepts, together with the majestic vistas of the interior and arrangement of external towers, must have contributed to the designation of this church by contemporaries as a *templum angelicum*.

This was a very angel conscious society, as one sees from the often domineering postures of angels when they appear in art and literature. Whether the monks and nuns of whom we have been writing always wanted to live like angels may be doubted, but when one looks at their architecture there is a stronger case for thinking that they sometimes wanted to sound like angels.

The liturgical efflorescence of the tenth century partly found expression in small dramas, which were now for the first time fitted into the structure of the monastic liturgy, and of which the best known was that of the Three Women at the Tomb, performed on Easter morning. A monk clad in white was to represent the angel at the tomb, and three monks, vested in copes and holding thuribles, were to approach it 'step by step as if looking for something'. At the appropriate moment the angel was to begin singing softly and sweetly the words 'quem quaeritis' (whom do you seek). The stage instructions for this drama are contained in the English *Regularis concordia* of *c.* 970, while the musical score is in the Winchester Troper (Bodleian Library, Oxford).[5] The music perhaps came immediately from Corbie, whence Bishop Æthelwold derived his singing-master for Winchester. It has been plausibly argued that replicas of Christ's Tomb, as shown to pilgrims in Jerusalem, may well have

---

[3] Jantzen (1947), pp. 11–14; Widukind, *Res gestae Saxonicae* II, 20 and III, 54, pp. 84, 133.

[4] Brandt and Eggebrecht (1993b), pp. 221–4.

[5] *Regularis concordia*, c. 51; Oxford, Bodleian Library, MS 775, fol. 17r.

been connected to these dramas. Bishop Conrad of Constance, for instance, who died in 975 and who had three times visited Jerusalem, had 'a sepulchre of the Lord similar to that at Jerusalem' made for the church of Saint-Maurice in his city and adorned with fine goldwork.[6]

A feature of early medieval churches which was of great importance but which is difficult to recover from the surviving evidence was wall-painting. Wall-paintings depicting the main scenes of Christ's life must have been common in Carolingian churches, where they were used to instruct the illiterate, and some remarkable schemes of wall-painting survive from more educated contexts in the Carolingian period, such as Auxerre, Müstair, Mals and Brescia, while we know of others, notably at the royal palace of Ingelheim and the monastery of St Gallen, from written sources. We know extraordinarily little about how wall-paintings were related to pictures in manuscripts, or for that matter to each other, at this period. One might be tempted to wonder whether wall-painting would not have been a vast store of iconography now lost to us, and whether it is not as likely that wall-paintings were primary models for book-illuminations rather than the other way round. Final pronouncements seem impossible on these issues, but it has been shown that in the case of tenth/eleventh-century wall-paintings at Saint-Julien of Tours the models were ninth-century Turonian book-illustrations, while very few of the scenes in the large St Gallen Christ cycle of the ninth century are not also found in Ottonian books, presumably use being made in each case of similar late antique sources which, practically speaking, could only have been available in book form. Gauzlin, abbot of Fleury, of whom more will be said later, obtained a painter from Tours called Odelric to paint the walls of his church with scenes from the life of St Peter and the Apocalypse.[7] It is hard to see how their model would not have been books, for there was a rich iconography of the Apocalypse in Carolingian books, and the St Peter scenes could have been taken from an illustrated Arator or some such book of illustrated lives of the Apostles as Bede had earlier seen. Indeed from the ninth century onwards there was a brisk business in hagiographic illustration both on walls and in books, with many of the scenes easily adaptable from one saint to another. That scenes could have been taken from books and put on walls does not prove that they were, but it is not easy to cede the primacy to wall-paintings in these circumstances.

One especially interesting patron of wall-paintings in the tenth century was Bishop Gebhard of Constance (980–96), in his *Eigenkirche*, the monastery of Petershausen. This bishop had the walls of the church covered with pictures, on the left hand side with Old Testament subjects, on the right with New

---

[6] Oudalschalk, *Vita Chounradi episcopi Constantiensis*, cc. 7, 11.

[7] Andrew of Fleury, *Vita Gauzlini abbatis Floriacensis monasterii*, cc. 62–4.

Testament. The idea of such sacred parallels was of course an old one, being found in late antique manuscripts of the New Testament, in the painted wooden boards which Benedict Biscop acquired for his monastery of Wearmouth/Jarrow, later in the bronze doors of Bishop Bernward of Hildesheim, and in revived form in Byzantium after the Iconoclastic Controversy with their Sacra Parallela. So far, then, the bishop in his murals was being no more than a professional teacher of his flock. More notable was the fact that whenever the image of Christ appeared His image was gilded. The liberal use of gold was an important adjunct of episcopal majesty in this period; almost all reproductions fail to bring out the way the Benedictional of Æthelwold of Winchester shimmers with gold. But most remarkable of all was Gebhard's abundant use of 'the Greek colour', lapis lazuli, for the colouring of his walls.[8] This was acquired from the Venetians. It has a double significance. It showed to his people the far-reaching access of their bishop to luxury goods, probably at a time when the Ottonians had trade agreements with the Venetians before the initiative in Venice passed to the Byzantines with Basil II in 992; and, as a brilliant blue, the colour which in scriptural exegesis always sig-nified heaven itself, it was an alternative way to tribunes and galleries of con-veying the idea that a church was a piece of heavenly space.

PRECIOUS OBJECTS

There was a time when all the arts such as those in gold and silver, enamel, ivory or embroidery, were known in English parlance as 'the minor arts', by comparison with art in manuscripts, or with painting generally; but happily that time has passed, and Peter Lasko's volume of 1971 in the Penguin History of Art, covering the period 800–1200 and dealing (admirably) with these arts, was entitled *Ars Sacra*, i.e. sacred art. There is a sad reflection even in that title of the loss of a whole non-ecclesiastical artistic world. For instance we think of ivories as covers for liturgical books, or perhaps as pyxes or holy water buckets, because that is how they have mainly survived. So the following gloss on 'ivory' in a late tenth- or early eleventh-century manuscript of Prudentius' *Psychomachia* at Cologne may take us aback: 'ivory', it reads, 'is elephant bone with which the handle of a sword is ornamented'.[9] Such glosses sometimes reflect only the old books from which they derive, but the comments in this book are in general far removed from the mere mindless repetition of antique flotsam and jetsam. We are familiar with the art of the goldsmith in various ecclesiastical forms, but it is refreshing to read that when Otto I wanted to reward the warrior grandfather of the bishop and chronicler Thietmar of

---

[8] Cames (1966), p. 17.   [9] Cologne, Dombibliothek, MS 81, fol 73r.

Merseburg for making peace between himself and the archbishop of
Magdeburg, he gave him a golden collar which he wore with pride, to the joy of
his friends and the sadness of his enemies.[10] Would that we could hire a time
machine for a group of art historians to go and study this collar while Count
Henry of Stade was wearing it at a feast! Perhaps they would find that it had
repoussé, foliated scrolls, inhabited by birds and beasts, like the rare but purely
ceremonial Ottonian sword sheath at Essen.

Certain as it is that many finely ornamented books of our period have disappeared, the losses in the ecclesiastical world of the *ars sacra*, not to speak of the
secular equivalent, must have been far greater. C. R. Dodwell has brilliantly
evoked this lost world, and the idea of it as such, in his book on *Anglo-Saxon
Art*. What he has done for England with the help of literary sources – and one
could use the same method for the continent – can in a way be achieved
through a short cut by using Bernhard Bischoff's edition of early medieval trea-
sure-lists for the empire.[11] Here a breath-taking world of bygone book covers,
reliquaries, chalices, crosses, candlesticks, thuribles, altar frontals, fine linens
and embroidered vestments meets our gaze, and speaks eloquently of the marriage of art and ceremony, of the marriage between the monastic or canonic
life and high liturgical culture, in our period. These lists were drawn up to commemorate the munificence of a benefactor to a church or to record the valuables in its treasury or sacristy at the moment when a new custodian or provost
took office.

Did they fantasise, imagining treasures sometimes on a Beowulfian scale
which never in fact existed? Occasionally some part of a treasury survives, as at
Hildesheim with the wonderful artefacts of Bishop Bernward (993–1022),
including two famous silver candlesticks inscribed with his name, or at
Conques in the Massif Centrale of France, where spectacular reliquaries and
other objects have been jealously guarded by the local community down the
ages. Such survivals, and the resplendent book covers which have come down
to us, show that we need not think of these lists as fantasies. But what I wish
particularly to consider is the Ottonian treasure at Essen. Essen was a royal
nunnery and from the time of its Abbess Matilda (971–1011), grand-daughter
of Otto I, there survive in the first place three splendid golden processional
crosses set with all manner of precious gems and first-rate enamels. They are
likely to be Cologne work. The gold figure of Christ crucified in the most
famous of these has something of the feeling of the limewood Gero crucifix
(probably 969–76) in Cologne cathedral, and the best cut stones, two amethysts
of different shades and a garnet, are reserved for the cross in his nimbus. At its
base is an exquisite enamel, depicting Abbess Matilda and her brother Otto,

---

[10] Thietmar, *Chronicon* II, 29, p. 78.   [11] Bischoff (1967b).

duke of Suabia, ceremonially presenting the cross itself to the abbey. Another similar cross has at its foot a small enamel of Matilda, dressed now in pure white and kneeling at the feet of a hierarchically seated Virgin Mary and Child. Among the precious stones in this cross are a sardonyx engraved with a fisherman, an antique cameo with female bust, and an amber carving of a lion at rest immediately under the feet of Christ. The third processional cross, from the same period, has particularly profuse filigree work and enamels of the crucifixion scene and the evangelical symbols.

What are these crosses actually about? First of all they are about religious ritual and symbolism; manuscript illustrations of the time showing ecclesiastical ceremonies are full of processional crosses. A nice example of symbolism is the amber lion, for the *Physiologus* saw the lion, which supposedly slept with its eyes open, as typifying Christ crucified, asleep so to speak in his humanity but wakeful in his divinity.[12] The crosses are, however, just as much about the authority of the abbess. Matilda was a Liudolfing, but we may be sure that under her were many other high-born nuns, and we know from the documented experiences of St Radegund and St Leoba how searchingly the authority of an abbess (as of an abbot) could be put to the test in the early middle ages. Unexpectedly small as the enamels of Matilda are, once the eye has caught them, they both make an impact at a distance of as much as twenty feet. The Matilda/Otto cross must fall more or less within the first decade of Matilda's forty-year period of office, since Duke Otto died in 982, in other words during her least secure time, before she could draw on that natural respect accorded in the tenth century to long life (one need only consider the analogy of Otto I's reign and the chronology of rebellions against him). We know that tenth-century nuns could be hard-bitten people, and whether a few small enamels by themselves could cause many of them to quake at the knees when they beheld their abbess may be doubted. The important consideration, however, is what effect this kind of art could have had on the self-confidence of the actual persons who ruled, on their sense of the canonisation of their own authority. Moreover, countless medieval hagiographies and histories of religious houses show us the importance of architectural beautification and material enrichment for sustaining the authority of an ecclesiastic, and Matilda herself embarked also on a new campaign of building at Essen which produced another interesting west work of which a partial impression can still be obtained. In that west work stands now a remarkable and huge bronze candelabrum of seven branches with great ornamental knops, while the famous freestanding gilded Madonna and Child can be seen in another part of the church, both of them from Matilda's time.

[12] See Wessel (1966), p. 27.

There are other fine objects in the Essen treasury from the later period of
Abbess Theophanu (1039–58), grand-daughter of the empress of that name.
One other work from Matilda's time, however, should not pass without
comment, namely the dazzling gold and jewelled crown, edged with continuous rows of pearls, which may reasonably though not certainly be associated
with her young cousin, Otto III. Here a large red stone is engraved with a
crowned head, while below the fleur-de-lys-type cross which one supposes
represented the front of the crown, in a raised golden setting, is a huge sapphire. In the famous representation of Otto III in the Aachen Gospels, the veil
or scroll held by the evangelist symbols not only 'clothes the heart' of the
emperor with the Gospels, but also in some way distinguishes a heavenly
sphere of God-given rule from an earthly; in another way this symbol of the
heavenly sphere (as a sapphire was always taken to be), placed so prominently
on this crown, seems to make the same point.[13]

The greatest of all goldsmiths' workshops in our period were those of
Archbishop Egbert of Trier (977–93), which carried out commissions for
other churches, such as the golden book cover (still surviving in Nuremberg)
which the Empress Theophanu ordered for the monastery of Echternach, or
the enamelling with which they adorned a golden cross from Rheims (as is evidenced by a letter of Gerbert of Aurillac).[14] We know from the work of
Hiltrud Westermann-Angerhausen that Egbert did not bring these workshops
into being, for they were in Trier before him,[15] but he did use them richly and
imaginatively to propagate an image of the majesty of his church as well as a
sense of Christian mission.[16] Amongst the inflated claims to antiquity which
the great Ottonian churches made in their rivalries with each other, Trier
claimed to have been founded by none other than St Peter, and to validate its
claim it preserved the relic of St Peter's staff, which Egbert had encased in a
gold and bejewelled container (still surviving in the Limburg cathedral treasure), with enamelled representations of the earliest bishops of Trier, the first
three, Eucharius, Valerius and Maternus, reputed followers of Peter himself.
As if that were not apostolic support enough, Egbert also had St Andrew's
foot, a great relic of his church, placed in a priceless container, a chest with the
finest enamels set into it, topped by a golden foot (to be seen in the Trier cathedral treasury). Egbert was also a great patron of illustrated books, in two of
which, a book of Gospel readings known as the Codex Egberti (at Trier) and a
psalter (at Cividale del Friuli), he was himself depicted on the frontispiece in
hieratic posture, staring straight ahead as if seated in a world divorced from the
earthly one. In these and other books which were written under Egbert,

---

[13] Aachen, Dom, Schatzkammer.   [14] Gerbert of Aurillac, *ep.* 106.
[15] Westermann-Angerhausen (1987); (1990), esp. p. 20 .
[16] Westermann-Angerhausen (1983); (1973), pp. 66–72.

Westermann-Angerhausen has shown that there are depicted capitals with masques and other ornaments, which would have derived from the capitals of Bishop Nicetus' sixth-century cathedral, covered over by Egbert's own building works on the cathedral. Egbert had twice visited Italy in the entourage of Otto I and Otto II, but Trier itself had an imperial and historic past, if not quite so historic as its church claimed at this time. It had Roman buildings and other remains (a gold coin of Constantine is set into the St Andrew reliquary), and it had Carolingian books, derived from Tours, which were demonstrably the source of many of the ornamental motifs used in the goldsmiths' workshops.[17]

As patrons of art Archbishop Egbert and Abbess Matilda may have had at least one point in common, desire to bolster a vulnerable authority. It is easy to think of Egbert's art as expressing the pinnacle of might reached by one of the dominant churches of the tenth century; but it was probably otherwise, for in the ecclesiastical power game of that time, Trier under Egbert appears to have been losing rather than gaining influence. Averil Cameron has shown that similarly in ninth- and tenth-century Byzantium new rituals (and new art) are as much a response to political pressure as an articulation of effortless superiority, that the divine and earthly harmony of imperial art and ceremony could gloss over a much tenser reality.[18] Authority is again at issue in a most remarkable phenomenon of the goldsmith's art in southern France during our period, the statue-reliquary, of which the extraordinary example of St Faith at Conques survives, a statue of gold (over wood) studded with jewels, and representing the saint seated in a hieratic posture like an oriental potentate. Public authority in that region had given way to castellans like the counts of Rouergue exercising power from local castles, and the monastery of Conques was anxious to stress, in this image, that its authority over its lands and men was embodied in a patron saint well capable of giving predators nightmares and worse. All the same, the northern French rationalist Bernard of Angers, a pupil of the great master Bishop Fulbert of Chartres, disapproved of such things. They were common in the Auvergne, he observed, but were a form of idolatry of which he doubted that Jupiter and Mars would think themselves unworthy.[19]

A great collector of *objets d'art*, as well as patron of artists, was Gauzlin, abbot of Fleury (1004–30) and half-brother of Robert the Pious; doubtless this relationship to the king of France put him in a useful position to accumulate goodwill offerings, and his monastic biographer, Andrew, was nothing loath to detail them. Bishop Bernard of Cahors, an alumnus of the Fleury school, gave him a golden altar frontal and some finely embroidered altar cloths; and Arnold, count of Gascony, sent him thirteen silver vasa and two pounds of 'Arabic metal' as well as some oriental silks. The abbot himself had a

[17] Westermann-Angerhausen (1987).   [18] Cameron (1987).
[19] *Liber miraculorum sanctae Fidis* i, 13.

lectern of 'Spanish metal' made, as well as using Spanish copper plaques to enclose the choir at Fleury, while the precentor Helgaud, biographer of King Robert as well as craftsman, made a precentor's baton with a handle of crystal, sparkling with precious stones.[20] We are seeing in all this, amongst other things, the build up of a luxury traffic between Spain and the region of the Meuse, connected by the rivers Rhône and Saône and spinning off into other parts of France. The general importance of this great river trade route was long ago established by Maurice Lombard, and in 1950 J. M. Lacarra published a remarkable customs document issued by King Sancho of Navarre in the 1060s, detailing commodities which passed through Jaca at the foot of the Somport Pass in the Pyrenees.[21] Here we can see dyed Flemish cloths and various forms of weaponry coming down from the north, while Constantinopolitan textiles, Castilian horses and Spanish gold are coming up from the south. Awareness of Spanish wealth helped to draw French knights into an involvement with the *reconquista* in the eleventh century, and the Cordovan as well as Greek textiles and silks witnessed in King Sancho's document contained, we can be sure, those zoomorphic stylisations and geometric designs which held such profound inspiration for the Romanesque sculptors who would translate them into stone capitals.

One cannot ignore the function of fine objects for a political world whose relationships were still sustained as much by gift exchange as by legal contract. The Emperor Otto III, who sought to run his relationship with Doge Peter II Orseolo of Venice (991–1009) along the Byzantine lines of expressing his superiority through the godfatherly status, was offered rich gifts by the Doge when he visited Venice in 1000. He did not accept them all, for fear of looking as if he had visited Venice not purely out of love for his godson (who would have thought of any other motive?), and finally left with only an ivory chair, a silver goblet and a jug with rare ornament.[22] Probably it was important for him, as the greater ruler, to accept gifts only of lesser value than he would give, and he subsequently sent the Doge fine works of gold from Pavia and Ravenna. Again, the courtiers of the Emperor Henry II loved to visit Magdeburg because they were always rewarded with splendid gifts from the archbishop, who could tap into an important trade of oriental luxury goods passing down the River Elbe.

BOOK-ILLUMINATION

Whatever the relatively low importance of book-illumination amongst the arts to contemporaries of our period, it speaks to us across the centuries, partly

---

[20] Andrew of Fleury, *Vita Gauzlini abbatis Floriacensis monasterii*, cc. 38, 39, 65, 47.
[21] Lacarra (1950), text pp. 19–20.   [22] Uhlirz (1964).

because of its high rate of survival compared with artefacts in other forms of art, and partly because it is certainly no less effective a medium to express the ideas, attitudes and aesthetic of the age. The principal problem in making an even study of the whole west European world of book art is that the books of the German, or Ottonian, empire bestride that world like a colossus. However much we may give parity to French/west Frankish or Italian metalwork or ivories, when it comes to book-illumination, the Ottonian art runs away with the prize.

One may say this while acknowledging that there were undoubted master-pieces of book art in other regions. In England the Benedictional of St Æthelwold, the *chef d'œuvre* of the Winchester School (*c.* 970–80), reigns supreme, with its early openness to Byzantine influence, and its majestic Christ scenes and saints' images framed with ebullient foliage ornament derived from Carolingian manuscripts of Rheims. There is also a wealth of other English manuscripts, such as the Bury St Edmunds Psalter (*c.* 1020) with its brilliant drawings in the margins, while the debt to Anglo-Saxon art of the great art patron and artist Abbot Otbert of Saint-Bertin (probably 989–1007) in Flanders, particularly in his Gospel Book and Psalter now at Boulogne, is gen-erally acknowledged. English book art was very different from Ottonian. Expressed briefly, one might say that whereas Ottonian illumination derives its character from work in gold and enamel, English art is more linear (to take up a theme expounded by Nikolaus Pevsner in his *The Englishness of English Art*),[23] more draughtsmanly, more closely related to the world of its great calligra-phers, though great calligraphers worked on Ottonian books too. The impulses of patronage, however, from kingly rule and the episcopal *Tremendum* which was so important a means of sustaining that rule, were similar in both societies; Æthelwold, bishop of Winchester (964–84), is comparable to Egbert, arch-bishop of Trier (977–93), in his closeness to a royal court and in the projection of his own mighty image through art. The vital difference – and it is a point which always has to be borne in mind when considering art patronage in this period – is that while Æthelwold's art reflects a waxing of Winchester within the English church, Egbert's would appear more as a response to the waning of Trier within the imperial church.[24] Æthelwold rides on the crest of a wave; Egbert faces the pressure of a stormy sea.

The finest French book art of the tenth and early eleventh centuries drew its inspiration first and foremost from Carolingian and pre-Carolingian traditions of that region. The so-called First Bible of St Martial, Limoges (*c.* 1000, BN lat. 5), has a wonderful series of ornamented initial letters with very lively zoo-morphic and plant decoration, which takes one back to the great bibles of

[23] Pevsner (1956), ch 5.   [24] Mayr-Harting (1991b), pp. 82–8.

ninth-century Tours, and, in their animal forms, to works such as the eighth-century Gellone Sacramentary. We are dealing here with first-rate artists, but ones who appear indifferent to the figural art of the Ottonian books, or indeed of the Turonian bibles. The concern of these artists was not with projecting the image of an all but non-existent west Frankish royal power or of an episcopate which had little existence independent of the aristocratic power structure; it was with embellishing the studies and liturgy of an important monastery far from the islet of effective Capetian rule.

Neither Spain nor Italy is lacking in notable works of book art in our period. In Spain we have above all the series of illustrations to Beatus' Commentary on the Apocalypse. If one wishes to see in something of their purity the late antique traditions of Apocalypse illustration, which were transformed in style by the Mozarabic modifications, one should consider (as Florentine Mütherich has pointed out) the Beatus commissioned by Abbot Gregory of Saint-Sever (1028–73), for which the artist used a Spanish model.[25] In south Italy there is the rich series of Exultet Rolls, and, in the eleventh century, the rise of narrative illustration connected to the life of St Benedict, at Monte Cassino; in the north there were interesting provincial schools like that of Bishop Warmund of Ivrea (c. 969–1011), another bishop who liked to have himself depicted in books, but who in real politics was (as a supporter of the Ottonians) under great pressure from Arduin of Ivrea. The illuminated books of Warmund, principally his Sacramentary and Psalter, both at Ivrea to this day (Codd. 85 and 86), show a variety of iconographic influences from Carolingian and Ottonian art, and no doubt from earlier Italian books which also influenced these. The Psalter shows the liking for monumental standing figures evidenced also in the Prayer Book of Archbishop Arnulf of Milan (c.1000, BL, MS Egerton 3763), and in early Italian wall-paintings, as Hans Belting has shown.[26] The Warmund style, however, is a world away from anything Carolingian or Ottonian, showing how little political influence carries with it the assumption of accompanying artistic influence. The draughtsmanship is clumsy, but for all that, its potentiality for great liveliness is realised in a series of feverish illustrations to the *ordo in agendis mortuorum* in the Sacramentary, showing the death and burial of a man while his grieving wife or mother becomes more and more distraught, until she has to be restrained at the graveside. As to the principal colour tones of blue, green, pink and yellow in the Sacramentary, they have little to do with the work of goldsmiths and enamel workers, but rather more, perhaps, with that of muralists who were so important in north Italian art at this time. One may confirm this from the nearby contemporary wall-paintings in the cathedral baptistery at Novara.

[25] Mütherich (1973), pp. 195–6.   [26] Belting (1967).

Because of the supremacy of Ottonian book-illumination in our period, however, we shall make our points about patrons and artists largely through it. First, we have to ask how Ottonian book-illumination began, after the long hiatus (for the most part) from the late ninth century to the 960s, generally presumed to be caused by external threats and unsteady politics. My answer would be that Otto I and his court played no small part as a stimulus, but this must remain in the nature of an argument or a hypothesis, for it cannot be proved. The Ottonians never had any court school of illumination as the Carolingians had, where production of de luxe manuscripts, especially of the Gospels, was directly under their control. Under Otto III and Henry II, and also under Henry III, certain monasteries, such as Reichenau, St Emmeram of Regensburg, and Echternach, worked for the ruler, but in the cases of Otto I and Otto II we cannot even name any surviving manuscript which was certainly produced for either of them. The case for Otto I's stimulus, therefore, is based on a number of convergent indicators. His general interest in books is explicitly testified, not in the early part of his long reign when he gave a very exiguously ornamented Gospel Book to his brother-in-law, Æthelstan of Wessex, but in the later part. Widukind says, 'after the death of Queen Edith [946], whereas previously he knew nothing of letters, he learned them to such an extent that he could read and understand books fully'.[27] Culturally Otto I's horizons broadened manifestly in the latter half of his reign. In 968 he finally established the archbishopric of Magdeburg as a lynchpin of his ecclesiastical organisation to the Slav east, together with several suffragan sees and dependent monasteries. In his foundation document he stressed his own initiative, and indeed this had been a central project of his since 955. Suddenly a huge new need arose for fine liturgical books as well as library books; Otto I realised this, for Thietmar of Merseburg says that he endowed Magdeburg generously 'in estates, books, and other royal splendour' (suggesting ornamented books).[28]

There seems little doubt now that perhaps the two greatest works in the initial Ottonian revival of book-illumination, the Gero Codex (Darmstadt, MS 1948) and the Codex Wittekindeus (Berlin, Staatsbibliothek, MS theol. lat. fol. 1), were made respectively at the monasteries of Reichenau and Fulda. Both these monasteries had particularly close connections with Otto I and his court; the emperor is known to have visited Reichenau in 965 and again in 972, the very period when the Gero Codex would have been in the making. Moreover the Gero Codex, which is a book of Gospel pericopes, has a liturgical calendar in which the only non-New Testament based feasts are those of St Laurence and the Maccabees. These two feasts were amongst the normal celebrations of the Roman calendar in the tenth century, but singled out in this way they

---

[27] Widukind, *Res gestae Saxonicae* II, 36, p. 96.   [28] Thietmar, *Chronicon* II, 30, p. 76.

represent a virtual hall-mark of Otto I because both bear significantly on his victory over the Hungarians at the Lechfeld in 955. He spent the tenth anniversary of this victory, the feast of St Laurence 965, at Merseburg, where he had vowed on the battlefield to establish a church in honour of that saint whose feast it was. The liturgy of books and the liturgy of public life were not two separate issues in his time. The Maccabees' resistance to the Seleucids was seen as a veritable biblical type of the Ottonians' resistance to the invading Hungarians. The Gero who commissioned the book and is shown receiving it cannot be identified with certainty, but there are several good reasons for regarding that Gero who was archbishop of Cologne from 969 to 976 as the likeliest candidate, and he had been a court chaplain of Otto I before his elevation. As to the Codex Wittekindeus, a book of the four Gospels, its earliest known provenance was the monastery of Enger, which was granted by Otto I to the archbishopric of Magdeburg in 968.

The greatest book painter of the early period of Ottonian artistic efflorescence was the Gregory Master; he was an expert calligrapher and furthermore no other artist shows such mastery of how to handle his late antique prototypes, their modelling and perspectives. We cannot name him; indeed it is a sad fact that we cannot name a single Ottonian book painter in relation to any particular book; but we can trace him through his work in a period of activity which spanned the last three decades of the tenth century. Art historians have given him his title from a double page of miniatures depicting Pope Gregory the Great dictating his *Dialogues* (Trier, MS 171/1626) and the Emperor Otto II seated in majesty surrounded by personifications of imperial provinces (Chantilly, MS 146). He appears to have been based at Trier in Archbishop Egbert's time (977–93), but he also worked with and for the churches of Lorsch, Reichenau and probably Fulda. He was very peripatetic, which might suggest that he was a layman but was by no means incompatible with his being a monk in those times of so many connected monasteries with their confraternity arrangements. Now if Hartmut Hoffmann is right that he was the artist of the Marriage Roll of the Empress Theophanu (972), a magnificent document written in gold letters on purple grounds with vivid drawings of lions and griffins, and the case is a persuasive one,[29] then this becomes his first known work, and it was produced under the patronage of the Ottonian court in the reign of Otto I. Hoffmann has also established that the script of this document was Fulda, and so it was produced in conjunction with Fulda, around the period of the Codex Wittekindeus. And by 972 Egbert, who would become the Gregory Master's principal patron, was a court chaplain. Hoffmann himself prefers to regard this Marriage Document as a feature of the new culture of

---

[29] Hoffmann (1986), pp. 103–16.

Otto II, co-ruler with his father from 961, rather than of the *aurea mediocritas* of Otto I. It makes little difference to the main argument – the likely court stimulus of early Ottonian book art, even though there was no court school.

The high point of Ottonian book-illumination comes with a series of books made at Reichenau or Regensburg for Otto III (983–1002) and Henry II (1002–24), such as the Aachen Gospels (Aachen Minster), the Gospel Book of Otto III at Munich (Clm 4453), the Bamberg Apocalypse (Bamberg, Bibl. 140), the Pericopes Book of Henry II (Clm 4452) (all Reichenau) and the Regensburg Sacramentary of Henry II (Clm 4456). These are amongst the summits of western civilisation. They contain images of the rulers which give the royal/imperial ideology a very high pitch, not to speak of their superlative series of New Testament scenes. Of the ruler image in the Aachen Gospels, for instance, Hagen Keller has observed that, whereas Carolingian kings are depicted as in this life and as interacting presidents of their courts, Otto III is removed from his sub-kings and courtiers and sits in a 'super-earthly sphere', stiff and frontal in posture like a Christ in Majesty.[30] That is typical for the Ottonians.

Given that Reichenau and Regensburg were not court schools but rather monasteries which undertook work for the court, it is reasonable to pose the question whether these ruler images stem from the court ideology, whether they are painted on the instructions of the court patrons so to speak, or whether the monasteries themselves actually formulated this ideology through art in order to win court favour for themselves. These are, however, stark alternatives; they suggest too low an idea of the cultural integration of the great imperial monasteries with the court itself. We have to remember that Ottonian kingship was itinerant, a fact which would have brought the kings to such monasteries more often that we can now tell from the surviving evidence. Moreover their abbots were often close friends, or *familiares*, of the rulers; in an itinerant kingship the circle of *familiares* is not confined to those 'at court'. Abbot Alawich II of Reichenau (997–1000) was on friendly enough terms with Otto III to join him at Rome in 998 and to be made bishop of Strasbourg by him two years later. Henry II knew personally not only Abbot Berno of Reichenau (1008–48) but also others of the monks in the monastery, while he had himself been educated at St Emmeram of Regensburg, as had his earliest principal adviser, Tagino, archbishop of Magdeburg (1004–12).

We do not have any evidence to know how court patrons actually dealt with monastic artists in the case of Ottonian books, but in so far as we can make deductions, these have to allow for a positive court input to explain the ruler imagery and other ruler-related imagery in them. For instance, the Otto III

[30] Keller (1985), pp. 302–5.

image of the Aachen Gospels, which most commentators would now date to after his imperial coronation of 996, appears to draw on the inspiration of tenth-century Byzantine ivories of the Ascension, depicting Christ not standing in the usual western fashion, but seated on an orb as he ascends to heaven. Reichenau had been an eager recipient of Byzantine culture throughout the tenth century; however, this is not something which sets it over against Otto III's court, but something which the two institutions share. More particularly, it is hardly likely that Reichenau was responsible for fixing Ascension Day, with all its connotations of Christ ideology and apotheosis, as the feast on which Otto III's imperial coronation was set in 996. Equally the Rome emphasis in the ruler imagery of the Munich Gospel Book could not possibly be explained without reference to the influence of the court chaplain, Leo of Vercelli, on Otto III in this respect. The rare splendour for this period of the depiction of St John the Baptist's Nativity in the Pericopes Book of Henry II, and its hieratic character, may have been the idea of the Reichenau artist, but if so, it cannot have been conceived without a good knowledge of ideas already existing in Henry II's head. For he had celebrated the feast of the Baptist's Nativity at Reichenau itself in 1002 during his *Umritt*, that is, when he travelled around his kingdom to gain acceptance for his kingship by public ritual acclamation after an intense struggle earlier in the year. It was certainly not Reichenau which was responsible for the subsequent emphasis on the *Umritt* as a validation of Henry's kingship. One could say much more about the correspondence between court thinking and ruler imagery if space permitted.

The question whether it was patron who specified the ruler images or artist who suggested them is therefore to some extent an unreal one. When Rubens painted his great cycle of pictures glorifying the Regency of Marie de Medici, the latter's conception of her political *persona* and aims are not the less dominant in Rubens' scenes because many of their subjects derived from his own suggestions. Rubens was a learned man and so were many Ottonian artists. We may not be able to name any artist in connection with a particular work, but we know something about artists generically. The scheme of illustration for the Uta Codex of Regensburg, highly theological in content, was devised by a monk called Hartwic, who had studied under the learned Fulbert of Chartres.[31] A Trier artist called Benna, painting at Wilton in the 980s, was not only renowned for his art but also respected for his learning. At Fulda, whose main business in book-illumination appears to have been the production of mass-books, not least for export, we know, from the monastery's records of deaths, of a person called Ruotbraht, subdeacon, monk and painter (*pictor* could mean a wall painter, or book painter, or most likely both), who died in 977. A subdea-

---

[31] Bischoff (1967a).

con, if only in his twenties, must have had a certain degree of learning as well as clearly defined liturgical responsibilities within the Mass. Whichever way we look at it, therefore, the most satisfactory idea to have in mind is neither that of the rigid orders of a patron nor that of the surprise packet of a clever artist, but of an interaction between the requirements of patron and their creative realisation by artist, through intelligent dialogue.

This area of relations between patron and artist is where an important point established by Hartmut Hoffmann may fit in. In several Ottonian manuscripts we find a picture of a cleric proferring the book to its ultimate earthly recipient (I am not speaking here of the *traditio* to a saint), such as Liuthar to Otto III in the Aachen Gospels, or Ruodpreht to Archbishop Egbert in the Egbert Psalter at Cividale (MS 136), or the two Reichenau monks Kerald and Heribert in the Codex Egberti (Trier, MS 24). Hoffmann has shown that such a figure would perhaps never have been the artist, and that only in rare cases can he be said to be the scribe, as with Eburnant in the Hornbach Sacramentary of Reichenau. *Stifter*, or donors, is the term he uses for these clerics.[32] That does not necessarily mean that they paid for the materials and work of the manuscript; though it could mean that, even if such a one were a monk, for monks often had rich families. Liuthar, Hoffmann says, could have been the scribe, or he could have been the current leader of the Reichenau scriptorium, but what matters is that he acts here as a respected representative of his community. Ruodpreht, of the Egbert Psalter, is an even more interesting case. If he was a scribe, why should he be singled out amongst the several Reichenau scribes whom Hoffmann shows to have participated in the manuscript? Indeed, he need have had nothing to do with Reichenau, and was probably a monk or abbot of Egbert's circle, the *Stifter*. Now when one studies the Codex Egberti and the Egbert Psalter as a whole (as I have done elsewhere), it is clear that they are deeply shot through with Archbishop Egbert's own concerns and preoccupations. Their mode and matter can in no way have been left to the unaided discretion of Reichenau. Egbert himself had probably visited Reichenau at least once during his archiepiscopate, on his way back from Italy in 983. But Egbert's protégé, the Gregory Master, himself painted the first illustrations in the Codex Egberti, and should he not be seen, together perhaps with the Reichenau monks Kerald and Heribert, as the ideal mediator between patron and scriptorium? Likewise, perhaps, Ruodpreht in the case of the Egbert Psalter?

CONCLUSION

As we contemplate Ottonian art we are drawn back ever and anon to liturgy, to art as a means of ritualising religious experience and political power relations.

---

[32] Hoffmann (1986), pp. 42–7.

Rulers, especially Henry II, appear constantly as if they were the central actors in church services, and several sacramentaries, or mass-books, of Henry II's time carry in their calendars the day of his kingly consecration, his *dies ordinationis*. It is vital, however, not to treat Ottonian art as if it were all ideology, even religious ideology, that is, as if its sole function was to be an instrument in the Ottonian power game. In any power game religious art would be a worthless instrument unless it could appeal to a body of believers whose own religious experience was at least in some degree independent of political motivations. That is why it is important to study the religious culture of the great centres of Ottonian artistic production without seeing politics round every corner, and the religious culture of their patrons. For example, let us by all means remember that in the Munich Gospel Book of Otto III the Christ scenes project an image of a Christ-Emperor, who thereby in some sort canonises the authority of the earthly emperor; but let us not overlook, when we contemplate, say, the poignant scene of the Repentant Mary Magdalene in that same book, that Otto III owned a prayer book, one of whose prayers, headed 'whoever prays this prayer shall not feel the torments of hell in eternity', says, 'be mild to me as you were to Mary the whore, and fill my eyes with tears as you filled hers when she washed your feet and wiped them with her hair'.[33]

[33] Pommersfelden, Schloss, MS 347, fols 31r–34v.

Plate 1 Canigou, church of St Martin du Canigou, early eleventh century

Plate 2 Gernrode, church of St Cyriacus, late tenth century

Plate 3 Cologne, church of St Pantaleon, interior of Westwork, late tenth century

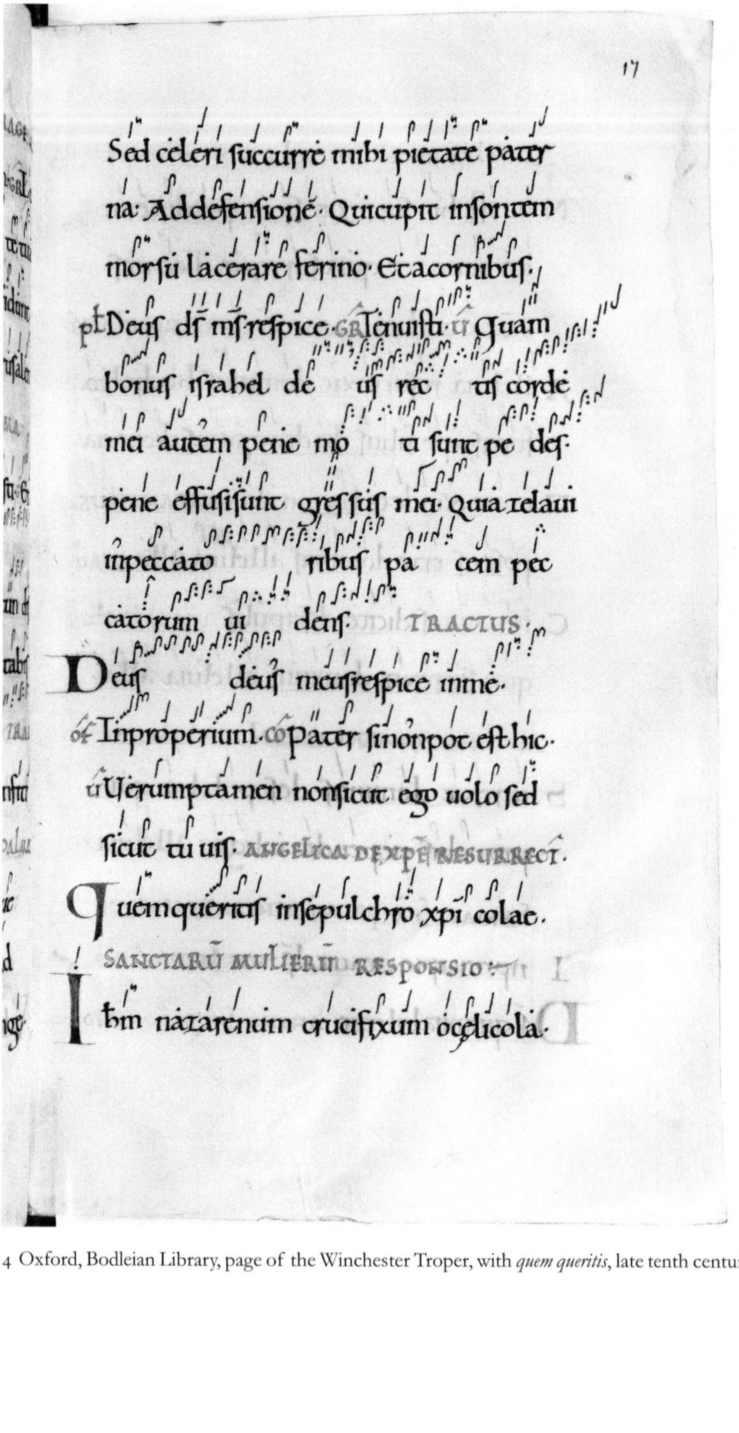

Sed celeri succurre mihi pietate pater

na· Addefensione· Quicupit insontem

morsu lacerare ferino· Etacornibus·

pt Deus ds mr respice catenuisti· u quam

bonus israhel de· us rec us corde

mei autem pene mo ti sunt pe des·

pene effusi sunt gressus mei· Quia zelaui

inpeccato ribus pa cem pec

catorum ui dens· TRACTUS·

Deus deus meus respice imme·

of Inproperium· co pater sinonpot est hic·

u Verumptamen nonsicut ego uolo sed

sicut tu uis· ANGELICA DE XPI RESURRECT

Quem queritis insepulchro xpi colae·

SANCTARU MULIERU RESPONSIO·

Ihm nazarenum crucifixum occelicola·

Plate 4 Oxford, Bodleian Library, page of the Winchester Troper, with *quem queritis*, late tenth century

Plate 5 Essen Minster, sheath of a ceremonial sword, late tenth century

Plate 6 Cologne cathedral, Gero crucifix, *c.* 970

Plate 7 Essen minster, processional cross of the Abbess Matilda of Essen, 971-82

Plate 8 Essen minster, interior of Westwork, late tenth century

Plate 9 Essen minster, crown of ?the boy Otto III, late tenth century

Plate 10 Trier cathedral, reliquary of St Andrew's foot, 977-93

Plate 12 Essen minster, statue of the 'golden Madonna', tenth century

Plate 11 Conques, statue of St Faith, tenth century

Plate 13 Paris, Bibliothèque Nationale, Ms. lat. 5 (2), fo. 173, first Bible of St Martial, Limoges, showing initial letter to the Acts of the Apostles, c. 1000

taculo tuo. Quod
operatus es dñe·
Sctuarium dñe qð
firmauert manus
tuae· Dñs regna
uit in eternum &
ultra·
Ingressus est enī
pharao cucurrib·
&equitab: in ma
re· Et reduxit
super eos dñs aqs
maris·
Filiaur isrt am
bulauerunt
per siccum in
medio eius·

ABBACVC PRO PHETANS·

CATC

ABBACC

Plate 14 Ivrea, Biblioteca Capitolare, Ms. 86, psalter of bishop Warmund of Ivrea, showing the
standing figure of Habakkuk, *c.* 1000

Plate 15 Ivrea, Biblioteca Capitolare, Ms. 85, sacramentary of Bishop Warmund of Ivrea, showing a grieving woman at the graveside, *c.* 1000

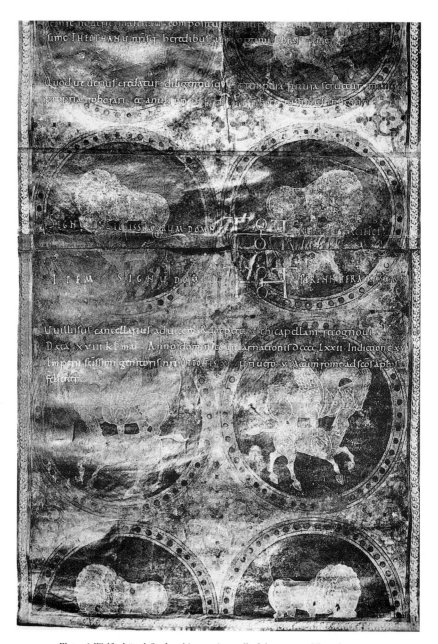

Plate 16 Wolfenbüttel, Stadtarchiv, marriage roll of the empress Theophanu, 972

Plate 17 Aachen minster, Aachen Gospels, showing the emperor Otto III seated in majesty, *c.* 996

Plate 18 Florence, Museo Bargello, Byzantine ivory of seated Christ ascending to heaven, tenth century

Plate 19 Cividale del Friuli, Museo Nazionale Ms. 136, fo. 17, psalter of Archbishop Egbert of Trier, showing Ruodpreht presenting the book to the archbishop, 977–93

Plate 20 Bamberg, Staatsbibliothek, Ms. Lit. 53, fo. 2v, pontifical made at Seeon, showing the solemn entry into church of the emperor Henry II flanked by two bishops, 1014-24

PART II

POST-CAROLINGIAN EUROPE

CHAPTER 9

THE OTTONIANS AS KINGS
AND EMPERORS

Eckhard Müller-Mertens

THE POST-900 POLITICAL CRISIS: THE DISSOLUTION OF THE
FRANKISH KINGDOM RULED BY ARNULF AND THE DEVELOPMENT
OF REGIONAL AND ETHNIC PRINCIPALITIES

The Emperor Arnulf died in Regensburg on 8 December 899. The illegitimate son of King Carloman of Bavaria and Italy had brought about the fall of Charles the Fat in November 887, which had led to his own election by the east Frankish magnates and to the election of non-Carolingian rulers in other parts of the Carolingian empire. Charles the Fat had been able to reunite the Carolingian kingdoms and, apart from Provence, had exercised direct rule over all of them. Unlike Charles, who had accepted the west Frankish crown offered him in 885, Arnulf of Carinthia rejected a corresponding offer from the west Frankish magnates. This incident, whose significance, especially for the development of a German kingdom, has been much discussed, did not mean that Arnulf of Carinthia wished to confine his rule to east Francia, *Francia orientalis*. He established a relationship of feudal overlordship, or at any rate allowed one to be established. The other rulers elected in 888, Odo of west Francia, Rudolf of upper Burgundy, and Berengar of Italy, as well as, later, Louis of Provence, acknowledged his overlordship. He sent Odo a crown, with which Odo had himself crowned a second time in Rheims. After Charles the Simple had been set up as king in west Francia in 894 he too submitted to Arnulf, who acted as mediator in the dispute between Odo and Charles over the west Frankish throne. Arnulf disputed the claim by Rudolf of upper Burgundy to rule over the whole of the former kingdom of Lothar II; and when Wido of Spoleto challenged his overlordship by having himself made emperor, Arnulf intervened in Italy and acted directly as Italian king.

Arnulf, as king over other kings, exercised an imperial kingship. It was in keeping with this when in 895 he transferred the kingdom of Lotharingia to his son Zwentibald. The latter's newly independent position, within the ambit of imperial kingship, was intended to act as a check on the aspirations of Rudolf I.

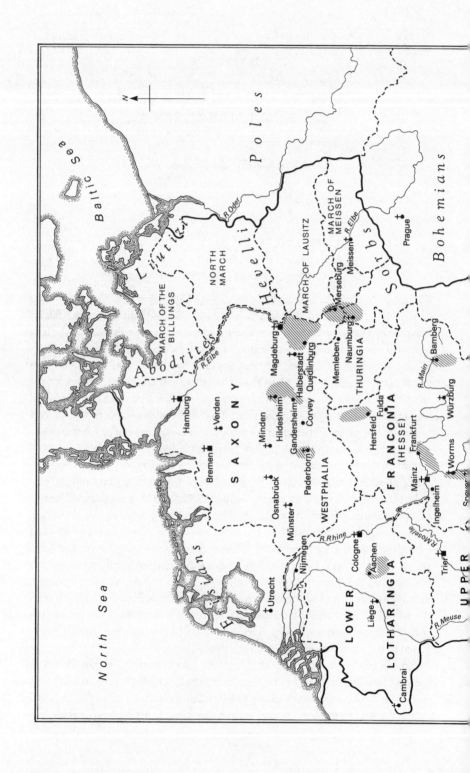

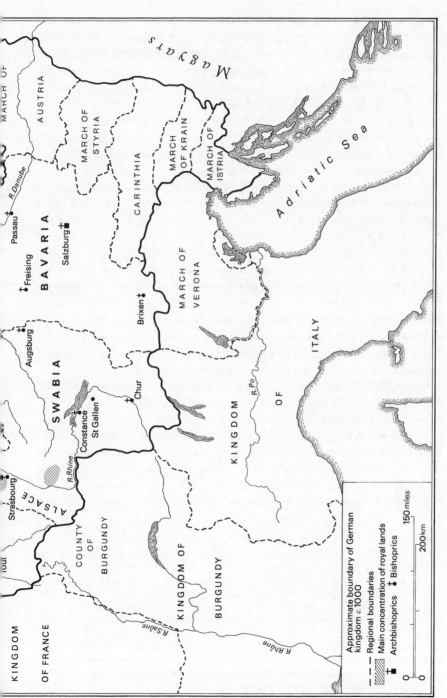

KINGDOM
OF FRANCE

KINGDOM

Strasbourg

ALSACE

Toul

R.Rhine

COUNTY
OF
BURGUNDY

KINGDOM OF
BURGUNDY

BURGUNDY

R.Saône

R.Rhône

Augsburg

SWABIA

Constance
St Gallen

Chur

KINGDOM

OF

ITALY

R.Po

Adriatic Sea

Passau

R.Danube

BAVARIA

Freising

Salzburg

MARCH OF
AUSTRIA

MARCH OF
STYRIA

CARINTHIA

Brixen

MARCH OF
VERONA

MARCH
OF KRAIN

MARCH
OF
ISTRIA

Magyars

MARCH OF

Approximate boundary of German
kingdom c. 1000
Regional boundaries
Main concentration of royal lands
Archbishoprics † • Bishoprics

150 miles

0

0   200km

4 Germany

This policy was a successful one until the point at which Arnulf was attacked by an illness, shortly after his imperial coronation in February 896, which in the end made him incapable of ruling. He exercised his kingship itinerantly: its core regions were Bavaria, with its centre Regensburg, and the lands around the confluence of the Rhine and the Main, with their centres Frankfurt, Tribur and Worms as the principal locations for meetings with the magnates.[1] For journeys between these core regions he preferred the Main valley area of Franconia, with the royal palace of Forchheim as the place of choice for assemblies. Arnulf visited Suabia and Lotharingia only occasionally, and Saxony only once, in the course of a campaign against the Abodrites. Yet he was nevertheless able to exercise influence in these provinces: indeed, Suabian, Lotharingian and Saxon churches and magnates received significantly more royal diplomata than did their counterparts in Bavaria and the Rhine–Main area. Arnulf drew his counsellors from the high nobility of all regions of his kingdom, including members of families which were later to produce dukes: Conradines, Luitpoldings and Liudolfings. The bishops Hatto of Mainz, Solomon III of Constance, Waldo of Freising and Adalbero of Augsburg played a significant role at the court as well as acting as a link between Suabia and the king. There were certain differences between Arnulf's treatments of the two core regions: the lands around Rhine and Main, and Bavaria. The Rhine–Main area was of greater importance for assemblies dealing with regnal affairs, for synods and for meetings with the magnates from other parts of the kingdom. Bavaria was less significant as a centre of integration for the kingdom: it had more the role of a base domain for Arnulf's kingship, with significant direct seigneurial exploitation and intensive contacts between Arnulf and the Bavarian magnates. These can be seen in the large number of individual Bavarian recipients of diplomata, both ecclesiastical and secular, who did not receive their diplomata at assemblies, unlike the practice in the Rhine–Main area. The latter was easily the most important central region for the politics of the kingdom. Bavaria came a poor second here, playing rather the role of a

[1] *Translator's note:* In the discussion here and at intervals in what follows it may be helpful to have the terminology of German medievalists, as developed by Müller-Mertens, Moraw and others, explained. In this the spatial divisions of the kingdom are conceived of as having different aspects. As *Zonen* (zones, which may be 'distant', 'open' or 'close'), one thinks of these regions primarily in terms of the way in which the elites in politically or geographically determined areas saw themselves in relation to the ruler and the consequent political opportunities for the ruler there. As *Landschaften* (translated here as domains), one thinks of concentration or absence of royal resources in terms of palaces, fiscal lands and rights within an area (so that a 'base' or 'core' domain is one with a particularly high concentration of such resources). Finally, as *Räume* (translated here as regions), one thinks of the absence or presence of the itinerant ruler himself and of the magnates in attendance on him: there are 'central' regions where the ruler stayed for long periods, 'transit' regions which he visited not infrequently but usually on the move between 'central' regions, and other regions where the ruler was rarely found. See now Bernhardt (1993), especially pp. 45–70.

basis for Arnulf's own power; he had made his bid for the kingship as margrave of Carinthia with the backing of an army of Bavarians and Slavs. All this demonstrates the east Frankish and Carolingian structure of Arnulf's kingdom, though his chancery no longer used the term *Francia orientalis* for the kingdom: when either it or the historians of the period used a name at all, it was plain *Francia*.

Arnulf of Carinthia left a single legitimate son, who was still a minor. The magnates of the kingdom were soon agreed on the succession, and had no qualms about setting up the six-year-old child as king. This was done on 4 February 900 in Forchheim. Louis IV, the Child, received the allegiance of Zwentibald's followers, who had defected from him on Arnulf's death, shortly after this in Thionville. Arnulf's realm thus continued to lack a ruler capable of acting, for the emperor had already lost control of events as a result of his illness in the final years of his reign. This was to call in question the characteristic elements of Arnulf's earlier rule: the position of imperial kingship and the predominance of direct royal rule within east Francia. A loosely organised, legally undefined regency, which included the Bavarian margrave, Leopold, and Bishop Adalbero of Augsburg, carried out the government on Louis' behalf. The numerous diplomata include an unusually high number of Frankish, Suabian and Bavarian intervenors. The principal points on the itinerary were, as they had been under Arnulf, Regensburg and the palaces of Rhenish Franconia. After 907, however, the regency council withdrew from Bavaria, which ceased to be a base domain for Louis' kingship. The council was dominated by magnates whose power-base lay in the Rhine–Main area: Archbishop Hatto of Mainz and his church, and the Conradines (Conrad the Elder and later his son Conrad the Younger, and Gebhard). Hatto concerned himself with the question of the unity of the empire, and may even have contemplated an emperorship for Louis, but the practical politics pursued by these men were rooted in regional issues of rank, property and power in Franconia, Lotharingia and Thuringia. The Conradines were able to establish themselves in Lotharingia, where Gebhard received ducal office on behalf of the king. This produced rivalries with the Matfridings; after their defeat, the Reginarids took over their position and worked against the Conradines and for the defection of Lotharingia. In Franconia the Conradines pursued a struggle for supremacy with the Babenberger; Conrad the Elder was killed in the course of this, but with the assistance of Hatto of Mainz the Conradines won, and after the Babenberger Adalbert had been executed the lord and duke of Franconia was Conrad the Younger, the future King Conrad I.

In the politics of the kingdom it was now the *regna*, the large-scale political areas, which dominated the stage. Franconia and Lotharingia were former royal provinces, whose political organisation stemmed from the Carolingians;

Suabia, Bavaria and Saxony were ethnically defined regions. It was here that rival noble kindreds struggled for supremacy and leadership; it was here that the defence against the Magyars was organised and led; and it was here that the transformation of ducal power into viceregal or quasi-regal positions took place. In Suabia the Hunfriding Burchard of Raetia sought supremacy; he was opposed by Solomon III of Constance and by the Alaholfings Erchanger and Berthold until his murder in 911. In Bavaria and Saxony the development of ethnically based dukedoms by the Luitpoldings and the Liudolfings respectively took place without such rivalries. Margrave Luitpold fell in 907 in battle against the Magyars, and this marked the loss of the Carolingian marches on the south-eastern frontier. Luitpold's son Arnulf was able to defeat the Magyars on several occasions. In Saxony the Liudolfing Otto the Magnificent was able to extend his hegemony in Saxony to cover Thuringia following Margrave Burchard of Thuringia's death fighting the Magyars in 908. Having achieved his majority, Louis himself led an army against the Magyars in 910. He was defeated near Augsburg; the numerous dead included the Lotharingian duke Gebhard, the uncle of the future king Conrad I.

With the premature death of Louis the Child on 24 September 911 the east Frankish line of the Carolinigans came to an end. Only a few weeks later, at all events before 10 November 911, east Frankish magnates set up Conrad the Younger from the Conradine house as king. He was the first east Frankish king to be anointed, and was acknowledged without difficulty. The Lotharingians had already defected to the west Frankish ruler Charles the Simple during Louis' reign, but the decision to do so was not based on principles of hereditary succession. The main force behind it was the powerful count and *missus* Reginar Longneck, who tried in this way to secure his own claims within Lotharingia and to exclude his Conradine rivals. It is doubtful if those east Frankish magnates who mattered seriously considered the question of whether to stick with Carolingian hereditary right and offer Charles the Simple the succession. Such a decision would have represented more of a break with tradition than did the election of Conrad, who should be seen as providing continuity with the east Frankish Carolingians, to whom he was related on his mother's side. He dominated the lands around Rhine and Main, the central region of the east Frankish kingdom, both as duke of Franconia and as the head of the Conradine family. He had played a significant role in the regency council and could point to successes in the struggles for supremacy within Franconia and Lotharingia. His first efforts were devoted to winning back Lotharingia: these failed, and were abandoned in 913. In the same year the margrave Arnulf of Bavaria and the Suabian count palatine Erchanger with his brother Berthold fought a victorious campaign against the Magyars; Conrad was unable to organise the defence against the invaders. It may be that the new ethnically based powers already prevented him from doing so; they took up the task themselves and consolidated their position in Conrad I's reign. In Bavaria it was Arnulf, and in Suabia it was first of all Erchanger and then the Hunfriding Burchard II, who became duke of the people. Conrad was determined to reduce their power. In Suabia he was able to avoid an immediate conflict with Erchanger by marrying Erchanger's sister Kunigunde, the widow of Luitpold and the mother of Arnulf of Bavaria; once the breach had come in spite of this, he was able to drive Arnulf out of Bavaria. At the synod of Hohenaltheim in 916 the pope, in the person of the legate Peter of Orte, intervened decisively in support of Conrad. Whoever rose up against the Lord's anointed, so it was decreed, should suffer severe punishments: penances, excommunication, even execution. Conrad did indeed have the Suabian brothers Erchanger and Berthold executed in 917. Yet the successes trickled away, the king was defeated, the new duchies established themselves.

Following attacks by both sides a rather different and more promising arrangement was reached with the Saxon duke, a settlement accompanied by truce. In 915 Conrad probably acknowledged the standing of the Liudolfing duke and future king Henry as regards his ducal rank, his conquests and what in effect was his viceregal position. This Franco-Saxon agreement, which even then may have included a friendship alliance, probably contributed to Conrad's proposal that Henry should be his successor, an acknowledgement that a continuation of Conradine kingship had no future. Conrad, whose power no longer extended beyond Franconia, died on 23 December 918.

In May 919 Frankish and Saxon magnates elected the Saxon duke Henry in Fritzlar as their king. Either before or after this, Bavarian and other Frankish magnates chose the Bavarian duke Arnulf as their king. Duke Burchard of Suabia and the Suabian magnates did not take part in these elections. These events offer as it were a snapshot of the east Frankish subkingdoms in action, as these had been established by the marriage alliances and succession arrangements made by Louis the German in 872 and continued as independent kingdoms after his death in 876. Evidently a king based only on Franconia as a base domain and on the Rhine–Main area as the central region of the kingdom was no longer able to sustain a direct and dominant royal lordship extending over several large provinces. In the eastern *regna* of the former Carolingian empire, as well as in the west, regional aristocratic forces had established themselves in positions of leadership with a regal, quasi-regal or viceregal status. At the end of the Carolingian era it may well have seemed possible that successor states could be established on this basis; we can appreciate this more clearly if we compare the size of, say, Franconia and Saxony taken together or of Bavaria alone with the size of the two Burgundian kingdoms or the *regnum Italiae*.

THE *TRANSLATIO REGNI FRANCORUM AD SAXONES*: FOUNDATION AND
CONSOLIDATION OF OTTONIAN *FRANCIA ET SAXONIA*

The Bavarians set up Duke Arnulf as king 'in the kingdom of the Teutons':[2] it
is a matter of dispute whether this view of what happened was already present
in the original Salzburg annals composed around 950 or whether it was introduced at a later time. The now lost original of the annals is preserved only in a
copy produced as an exercise by novice scribes in the middle of the twelfth
century. By then the notion of a 'kingdom of the Germans' or a 'German
kingdom' had become a commonplace; but when Arnulf and Henry became
kings that was by no means the case. It is probable that the word *Teutonicorum* is
the result of a latter correction or addition, but even if it did occur in the original manuscript it still poses the question of what was understood by *Teutonici* in
Salzburg in the middle of the tenth century: hardly a German people comprising Franks, Suabians, Bavarians, Thuringians and Saxons. There is no evidence
that Arnulf's kingship extended beyond Bavaria, and it is probably most easily
understood as a resurrection of the Bavarian kingship practised by Carloman
from 876 to 879. Arnulf was later also to follow in Carloman's footsteps when
in 934 he intervened in Italy and sought to win the Italian crown for his son
Eberhard.

The Frankish and Saxon electors of the duke of Saxony, Henry, came from
the subkingdom allocated to Louis the Younger in 876. Henry I went beyond
this from the start. Immediately after his election in Fritzlar he took the field
against Burchard of Suabia, who submitted. Henry concluded a friendship-
pact with him, as he had already done with Eberhard of Franconia. The new
Saxon king received Burchard's submission and at the same time confirmed
the viceregal position of the Suabian duke. Before enforcing acknowledgement in Bavaria Henry turned to Lotharingia, with which he had links through
his sister Oda, the widow of King Zwentibald and the wife of Zwentibald's
rival, the Matfriding Gerhard. Henry's accession had coincided with a revolt
against the rule of Charles the Simple in Lotharingia, led by Gislebert, son of
Reginar Longneck, who had died in 915. Henry gave Gislebert his support and
intervened in 920 or 921 against Charles the Simple in Lotharingia. The campaigning was ended by an armistice in the summer of 921. Later that year
Henry forced Arnulf of Bavaria to submit. Once more the king made use of a
friendship-pact to define the future nature of the relationship. Arnulf
renounced his royal title and became Henry's man, but Henry confirmed his
viceregal position. When in 925 Henry finally succeeded in bringing
Lotharingia under his rule he made a similar pact with Gislebert and strength-

---

[2] 'in regno Teutonicorum': *Annales ex annalibus Iuvavensibus antiquis excerpti, s.a.* 919, p. 742.

ened the relationship by giving Gislebert his daughter Gerberga in marriage in 928.

These friendship-pacts with the dukes were an expression of Henry I's new policy, of his intention to redefine kingship. He was more than forty years old when he became king, and had had extensive experience in establishing his supremacy and defending his possessions; he was evidently able to recognise realities and take account of them in pursuing his claims and purposes. The Liudolfings had established themselves as dukes without meeting any significant rivalries, which suggests a degree of consensus with other noble lords, itself perhaps the product of the somewhat archaic character of the socio-economic and socio-political organisation of Saxony. Henry had also experienced the failure of Conrad's kingship in the struggle with the duchies. Elected by Frankish and Saxon magnates as king, the Saxon duke established his lordship by recognising the intermediate powers in the other provinces and duchies. He allowed the dukes a viceregal position and bound them to him with pacts of friendship; at the same time he used vassalitic bonds to subordinate them to the king. Henry also entered into pacts of friendship with leading noble families from Saxony and lower Lotharingia and with the Conradines. The new king established a relationship of *primus inter pares* with the magnates, or simply continued such a relationship from his time as duke. This is probably one of the reasons why Henry refused to accept the unction which would have set him above the magnates. But here other factors were at work: Henry intended to stress a break in continuity with the kingship practised by Conrad I and the east Frankish Carolingians and to emphasise a new, specifically Liudolfing style of rulership based on Saxony. The break in continuity was also visible in the fact that Henry did not take over Conrad's royal chapel and chancery personnel; only slowly did he build up a new royal chapel of his own, which from the start displayed its own, specifically Liudolfing characteristics.

The main feature of Henry's rule was the recuperation of Lotharingia and his relations with the rulers of west Francia and Burgundy. He did not seek a military solution, nor did he allow himself to become involved in factional infighting, choosing rather to pursue a policy of compromise and reconciliation while retaining the threat of military intervention as a last resort. In November 921 he concluded the treaty of Bonn, a pact of friendship with Charles the Simple, in which the latter appeared as *rex Francorum occidentalium* and Henry I as *rex Francorum orientalium*. Neither before nor after this did Henry use the east Frankish royal title; his aspirations went further. He was quite prepared to break the pact with Charles and to enter into another one with the west Frankish anti-king Robert of Francia at the beginning of 923. By 925 Lotharingia was already incorporated into Henry's kingdom, just as it had belonged to the kingdom of Louis the Younger, whose wife Liudgard was an aunt of Henry's. At an assembly in Worms in 926 Henry concluded a friendship-pact with Rudolf II of Burgundy. The Burgundian ruler acknowledged Henry's overlordship, commended himself with the Holy Lance and, in handing this over to Henry, also handed over his claims to rule in the kingdom of Italy. The meeting of the three kings – Henry I, Radulf of west Francia and Rudolf of Burgundy – at Ivois in 935 demonstrated the predominance which Henry had reached among the kings of the Carolingian successor-states; the imperial kinship of the Liudolfing-Ottonian house was now established.

The other main feature of Henry's rule was the defence against the Magyar invaders and the efforts made to bring the Elbe Slavs under his rule. Already in the period before his kingship Henry had campaigned against the Daleminzi on the middle Elbe, who in their turn had called on the Magyars for assistance. It was via the territory of the Daleminzi that the Magyars made their first attack on Saxony, in 906, and thus defence against the Magyars and control of the neighbouring areas inhabited by the Elbe Slavs went hand in hand. By paying a substantial tribute the king was able to purchase a nine years' truce from the Magyars; in 927 Duke Arnulf also renewed a truce first concluded in 918. As a result there was an end to Magyar raids from 926 in Saxony and Franconia, and from 927 in Bavaria, Suabia and Lotharingia. At an assembly held by Henry with his magnates at Worms in 926, defensive measures were decided on. These consisted of enlarging existing and setting up new fortifications, and were to apply throughout the kingdom. In Saxony, whose military obligations still reflected those of an archaic period, free peasant warriors (*agrarii milites*) were entrusted both with the building of the fortifications and with their subsequent garrisoning. Henry also took steps to increase the number of mailed horsemen available, in other words to modernise the Saxon army. The new troops were tried out in the campaigns of 928–34 against the Elbe Slavs, where they played a significant role. The territories of the Slav peoples as far as the Oder were largely subjected to a still impermanent over-lordship and to tributary dependence. In 929, furthermore, Henry compelled Duke Wenceslas of Bohemia to submit. In the territory of the Daleminzi he established a centre for his lordship in the fortification at Meissen. As commanders we find Count Siegfried in Merseburg and the margraves Bernard and Thietmar on the lower Elbe: in 929 these defeated a Slav army which had advanced across the Elbe at Lenzen, a battle in which mailed horsemen played a crucial role. By 932 Henry felt strong enough to risk open conflict with the Magyars; he cancelled the tribute payments. When in 933 the Magyars appeared in Saxony in response to this affront, they were defeated by an army whose main component was heavily armed cavalry and which consisted of levies drawn from all the *gentes* of east Francia. In the following year Henry defeated a Danish petty king on the northern frontier. The victories over both invaders, the Magyars and the Norsemen, brought the first Saxon king a reputation which extended well beyond the borders of his kingdom.

Henry's practice of kingship reflected both his own aspirations and the changes which had taken place in the structure of the kingdom. The Saxon king did not set foot in Bavaria and Suabia after the submission of their dukes;[3] these remained distant zones in relation to his kingship. The investiture of the Conradine Hermann as duke of Suabia in 926 made no difference to this. The central political region of the former east Frankish kingdom, the area around Rhine and Main, was now joined by east Saxony and Thuringia as a new base domain. In addition the area between the lower Rhine and Meuse centred on Aachen took on a new role as a region for the exercise of kingship. This area, a core domain in the Carolingian empire, had never been of central importance for the Carolingian east Frankish kingdom. When we consider its structure in this way, Henry I's kingdom appears not so much a continuation of *Francia orientalis* (the east Frankish kingdom with its core regions around the Rhine–Main confluence and in Bavaria linked by a transit region consisting of Suabia and east Franconia) as a renewal of the political constellation established by Charles the Great, in which the core regions had been those around lower Rhine and Meuse, around Rhine and Main, and in Saxony, linked by transit regions in Westfalia and in Hesse and east Franconia. It was Henry I's practice and the political reorganisation during his reign which established the Ottonian kingdom of *Francia et Saxonia*, acknowledged in diplomata issued by Otto I in 936 and 938 as the provinces represented by his kingship.[4]

The first Saxon king saw himself as a *rex Francorum*, but he did not follow the dynastic practice of the Franks by dividing the kingdom between his heirs. The kingship which the Liudolfings had won was to remain indivisible. At the assemblies of 929 in Quedlinburg and 936 in Erfurt Henry's first son by his Immeding wife Matilda was chosen as his successor. The older son by his first marriage, Thankmar, and the younger son by Matilda, Henry, who had been born after Henry had already become king, were given no part of the kingship. Henry here followed a general trend becoming visible both in the practice and in the new conceptions of the state which were developed in the Carolingian successor-states and in the aristocratic principalities. For the kingdoms as feudal states, as the form of political organisation taken on by an aristocratic society, it came to be established that their basis was the community of aristocratic and ecclesiastical magnates. The kingdom was conceived of as existing

---

[3] The visits to these provinces posited by Schmid (1964), pp. 113–22 for 929/30 have no direct basis in the sources; the Liudolfing entries in the Suabian *libri memoriales* do not require us to assume that Henry I was present in person See Althoff (1992), p. 111.   [4] DD O I 1 and 20.

apart from the ruling family, and the royal office was contrasted with the person of the king. To preserve the unity of the kingdoms evidently corresponded to the interests and intentions of the new non-Carolingian dynasties as well as of the princes and the major churches. On 2 July 936 King Henry died in the palace at Memleben. Later generations saw him, according to Widukind, as the greatest of the kings of Europe, who left his son a great and broad kingdom which he had not inherited from his fathers but acquired by his own efforts and by God's grace.[5]

Only five weeks later, on 7 August 936, Otto I was raised to kingship in Aachen by all the dukes and other magnates, and was crowned and anointed by the archbishops of Mainz and Cologne. Otto appeared in Frankish clothing and was enthroned both on the throne in the arcaded court in front of the Aachen palace chapel and on the throne in the chapel's upper storey. Henry's successor had thus taken possession of Charles the Great's throne in a manner so visible as to leave no doubt. It was a politically motivated and programmatic act, one which should be seen in a line of the continuity with Henry I's kingship. Liudolfing (henceforth Ottonian) kingship did not merely stand in succession to the east Frankish kingdom of Louis the German. It had now established itself in succession to Charles the Great in Aachen, in a core domain of great importance for the self-definition of Charles the Great's empire, the area around the lower Rhine and Meuse which had been associated with the imperial title in the division of 843.

The new king proceeded without delay from the Carolingian centre of Aachen to the Ottonian centre at Quedlinburg, Henry I's principal palace and his burial place. The nunnery founded there by Queen Matilda, Otto's mother, received a rich endowment. Otto moved against the rebellious Elbe Slavs as early as September 936. New margravates were established on the lower Elbe and on the middle Elbe and Saale, a sign of a policy of more intensive domination and of an intention to claim and establish hegemonial kingship over the west Slav areas up to the Oder. The foundation of the monastery dedicated to St Maurice at Magdeburg in September 937 was a further sign of this. The new royal foundations in Quedlinburg and Magdeburg were significant for Otto's programmatic conception of kingship in another respect as well. Quedlinburg was dedicated not only to Peter and Mary but also to the Maastricht saint, Servatius, and to the west Frankish royal saint, Denis. The new monastery at Magdeburg was staffed by monks from St Maximin's in Trier and had St Maurice and his companions as patrons. Relics of one of the companions, St Innocentius, had been donated by the king of Burgundy, Rudolf II, who had just died and whose minor son and successor Conrad had been taken under

---

[5] Widukind, *Res gestae Saxonicae* I, 41.

Otto's control. These actions with their associated relics and dedications established links with Lotharingia, Burgundy and west Francia; they implied an imperial kingship. Otto himself described his kingship in the diploma for Quedlinburg (D O I 1) as being based on the royal throne *in Francia ac Saxonia*, a throne which he saw as something separate from his own dynasty and at the disposal of the electors.

The appointment of Hermann Billung as margrave on the lower Elbe and of Gero on the middle Elbe and Saale infringed the claims of Hermann's brother Wichmann I and of Otto's half-brother Thankmar. Otto was equally unprepared to accept Eberhard of Franconia's behaviour towards a Saxon vassal, and later on he rejected an agreement which Archbishop Frederick of Mainz had made on his behalf. He thus injured duke and archbishop in their dignity and reputation. On the death of Duke Arnulf of Bavaria he reduced the extent of the ducal rights enjoyed by his sons. These incidents produced waves of disapproval, of outrage; they affected the balance of power between and the ranking of the aristocratic kindreds, connections and communities, and those offended were prepared to defend their claims with feud. An early failure by the young king against the sons of the Bavarian duke in 938 triggered off a series of uprisings in Saxony, Franconia and Lotharingia which lasted until 941. The heads of the rebellions and conspiracies were members of the royal family: Thankmar, who was killed in 938, and then Otto's younger brother Henry. Duke Gislebert of Lotharingia sought his own advantage in supporting Henry. Henry wanted to dethrone Otto and become sole ruler himself. The Suabian duke Hermann and other members of the Conradine family supported Otto. The issue was decided in favour of the king at Andernach on the Rhine in September 939. The resistance and revolt offered by substantial parts of the church and the lay aristocracy were rooted in the claim by the new ruler to an enhanced kingship. However, it should not be overlooked that at that time every change of ruler produced tensions, and disruptions of the pecking order and of the possessions and influence of the lay and ecclesiastical magnates. Even if the succession question had been decided otherwise, even if the relationship with Eberhard of Franconia had taken a different course in 936 and 937, the new ruler of an undivided kingdom would still have been faced with conflicts and trials of strength. Without a predominant central power, which in turn required a sacral basis and legitimation, a transethnic, hegemonial and imperial kingship of the kind established by Henry I and passed on undivided to his son could neither be maintained nor made permanent. Otto broke with his father's practice of presenting himself as first among equals. He was not prepared to enter into *amicitiae*, into agreements with other magnates which placed obligations on both sides. He insisted on submission and made decisions arbitrarily after the fashion of Carolingian kingship. He demanded the precedence due to him as the Lord's anointed; he was convinced of the nature of his kingship as kingship by the grace of God.

Otto did not appoint a new duke in Franconia after Duke Eberhard had been killed at Andernach together with Gislebert of Lotharingia. Like the Saxon ethnic dukedom, the dukedom of the royal province of Franconia was taken under direct Ottonian rule. Otherwise Otto pursued his father's policy of recognising the dukedoms established over ethnic areas and royal provinces as established parts of the kingdom's organisation. As a counterpart to this he continued with the practice, already found under Arnulf of Carinthia and reactivated by Henry I, of entering into relationships of feudal overlordship with non-Carolingian rulers in the Carolingian successor-states. Otto introduced a new element into this policy. He sought to link the royal dynasty with those of the dukes by marriage alliances and to secure the dukedoms for members of the royal family. In Bavaria Duke Berthold, Arnulf's brother, was intended to be married to Otto's sister Gerberga or her daughter. The marriage did not take place, but Otto's brother Henry succeeded Berthold, and he had been married to Arnulf's daughter Judith since 936 or 937. In Suabia Otto set up his son and heir-presumptive Liudolf as duke; he had been married to Ida, the daughter of Duke Hermann, who had no sons, in 947. In the same year Otto's daughter Liudgard was married to Duke Conrad the Red of Lotharingia. Following Conrad's deposition in 953 Otto made his brother Brun, who at the same time became archbishop of Cologne, duke of Lotharingia.

From the beginning of his rule Otto was locked in to west Frankish, Burgundian and Italian politics as a consequence of existing relationships. This involved disputes over kingship, transregnal aristocratic connections and conflicts between kings and aristocratic factions. Otto, who disposed of superior forces and armaments, soon found himself in a hegemonial position. In west Francia he encouraged a balance between King Louis IV and Duke Hugh of Francia, both of whom were married (from 939 and 937 respectively) to sisters of Otto: Gerberga, Gislebert's widow, and Hadwig. Otto met Louis no fewer than seven times between 942 and 950, for example at the general synod of Ingelheim in 948, which settled the schism in the archbishopric of Rheims and allowed Otto to display himself in the full glory of his hegemonial kingship in alliance with the papacy. After the deaths of Louis and Hugh their widows, Otto's sisters, managed Carolingian and Robertine power in west Francia, and their brother Brun, archbishop of Cologne, was *de facto* regent. Conrad of Burgundy had grown up at Otto's court. In 942 he reached the age of majority, and with Otto's backing was able to achieve a kingship extending over Provence as well as Burgundy. As to Italian affairs, Otto provided from 941 onwards a refuge for Margrave Berengar of Ivrea, the rival for the throne to the kings, Hugh and Lothar. Berengar returned to Italy in 945 with Otto's agreement, drove out Hugh, who died in 948, and was a serious threat to the kingship of Hugh's son Lothar. Lothar's death in 950 established a new political situation. Berengar had himself crowned king of Italy, imprisoned Lothar's widow, Adelaide of Burgundy, and so provoked independent interventions in Italy by Otto's brother Henry of Bavaria and his son Liudolf of Suabia. The disturbances this created in the balance of power in Italy, Burgundy and southern Germany compelled Otto to intervene in Italy himself.

During his first Italian expedition, between the autumn of 951 and February 952, Otto received kingship over Italy and married Adelaide, the dowager queen. But he was able neither to drive out Berengar II nor to organise an expedition to Rome to receive imperial coronation. The collisions of interest and decisions in and around Italy provoked new disputes within Otto's own family, which developed into a new general uprising against Otto's kingship. Conrad the Red, who had remained in Italy, made an agreement with Berengar that the latter should retain the kingship over Italy under Otto's overlordship. Otto was furious, and wanted to institute proceedings for high treason; but the agreement held. But before Berengar was finally able to receive investiture with the kingship in return for homage at the assembly in Augsburg in 952, Otto had ostentatiously demonstrated his displeasure with Conrad and Berengar at the Easter celebrations that year. For Conrad this was a reason to join Liudolf's conspiracy; Archbishop Frederick of Mainz had already done so.

Liudolf, who had himself had hopes of the crown of the Lombard kingdom, found not only that he was excluded in Italy while his uncle Henry was favoured, but also that his own succession was threatened. He set himself up in opposition to the excessive influence of Henry and the new queen at court. These conflicts revived the latent tensions between Otto's claims to kingly rule and the claims of lay and ecclesiastical magnates to participate in government. When in 953 Otto rejected an agreement which had been negotiated at Mainz between himself, Liudolf and Conrad by Frederick of Mainz on the grounds that it had been extorted, Liudolf's rebellion broke out openly; it lasted until 955. Liudolf, Conrad and Frederick could rely on existing aristocratic friendship agreements which implied obligations of mutual assistance. Liudolf was backed by Suabia; the old conflicts with the church of Mainz and with the Saxon nobility broke out afresh; opposition within Bavaria to Henry's rule became visible. Otto was not able to suppress the rebellion by military force. The Magyars renewed their attacks on the Reich in 954, and the Abodrites east of the Elbe rebelled. The revolt collapsed in the face of the threat from the invading Magyars, especially after Conrad and Liudolf had seemed to ally themselves with the invaders. The rebels submitted; Conrad and Liudolf lost their duchies, and the last centre of resistance, Regensburg, surrendered in April 955.

When in 955 the Magyars again raided into Bavaria and Suabia, Otto met them with an army of Franks, Suabians, Bavarians and Bohemians. The Lotharingians were absent because of the long distance, and the Saxons were pinned down by conflicts with the Elbe Slavs, who had been joined in the course of Liudolf's uprising by the Billungs, Wichmann the Younger and Ekbert. Otto, who led his army into combat carrying the Holy Lance, forced battle on the Hungarians while they were besieging Augsburg. They were crushingly defeated on 10 August 955 at the Lechfeld and on the two following days while fleeing. Immediately after his triumphal victory against the Hungarians Otto moved against the Abodrites, who were defeated at the Recknitz in eastern Mecklenburg on 16 October 955.

Before the battle the king received an offer of terms from the Abodrites: they were willing to pay tribute, but they wanted to retain freedom and lordship over their own land.[6] Otto's conception was one of direct rule over the neighbouring Polabian and Sorbian settlement areas. He aimed at immediate lordship over land and men, accompanied by renders and services from the rural population and ultimately the formation of manorially organised estates. To this end a military and political organisation was set up, in the first instance in the form of the wide-ranging marches controlled by Hermann Billung and Gero. On Gero's death in 965 the march on the middle Elbe and on the Saale was divided into six smaller marches. Besides the marches there were smaller-scale organisational units in the lands of the Sorbs and Hevelli; in the Latin diplomata of the time these are denoted by their Saxon name of *burgward*. A *burgward* comprised some five to twenty villages grouped around a fortification which was a centre of administration and lordship. The fortifications were to be erected and maintained by the Slav population. Alongside these organisational units of secular lordship went a new church organisation. The bishoprics of Brandenburg and Havelberg were set up in 948, and were joined from 967 onwards by bishoprics at Meissen, Merseburg and Zeitz and at Oldenburg in east Holstein. Otto planned from an early date to transform the monastery of St Maurice at Magdeburg into a new archbishopric which should be the centre of church organisation and missionary activity for the conquered Slavic territories. He sought the pope's agreement to the foundation of bishoprics at Magdeburg and elsewhere immediately after the battle on the Lechfeld, but this idea was wrecked by the opposition which came from the church of Mainz under its new archbishop, William, a son of Otto's by a Slav concubine of royal descent.

The structures established by Henry I were consolidated by Otto I and continued under his successors. Compared with the east Frankish Carolingian

---

[6] Widukind, *Res gestae Saxonicae*, III, 53.

kingdom, the Ottonian Reich had a new central region and base domain in the lands around the Harz in eastern Saxony and northern Thuringia. A second central region lay in the lands around the confluence of Rhine and Main; this had been established in the time of Charles the Great and had been the principal central region of the east Frankish kingdom. Henry I and Otto I reactivated a third central region, that established by Charles the Great in the lands around lower Rhine and Meuse with its centre at Aachen, as a core domain of the Ottonian Reich. In all three central regions Otto exercised direct royal rule at periodic intervals, and this was accompanied by regular transit passages and assemblies in Angria/Westfalia and in Hessen/Thuringia/east Franconia. It was in the central regions above all that the assemblies took place and the principal acts of rulership, the religious representation of the ruler on the high feasts of the church, implying a ritualisation of the ruler by the grace of God which displayed his sacrality and his God-given nature. The remaining political regions – Bavaria, Suabia, Alsace, upper Lotharingia, Frisia – were visited only occasionally by Otto, either in the course of rebellions or in transit to Italy or west Francia. The dukes, counts, bishops, abbots and other magnates of these distant zones met the king either in one of the central regions or in the east Franconian transit region. As a result each region developed its own catchment area for the lay and ecclesiastical magnates of the kingdom, and this led to the creation of supra-ethnic and supra-regional sets of connections based on the central regions, each with its own infrastructure of roads and supplies. The main east–west lines of supply and communication were those established by Charles the Great, either the Hellweg from the lower Rhine to Saxony or those roads running from the middle Rhine to Saxony via Main, Hesse and east Franconia. To this the Ottonians added a north–south axis which linked east Saxony/north Thuringia via east Franconia with southern Germany. The existence of such structures does not permit us to call the Ottonian Reich a continuation of the *regnum Francorum*, even though contemporaries like Widukind of Corvey used this term for it and conceived of it in this way. The Ottonian Reich displayed new Saxon characteristics in its political structure over and above the ones which it had inherited.

The phrase *Francia et Saxonia*, used by Otto I in 936 and 938 and later by Widukind of Corvey and Adalbert of Magdeburg, corresponds better to the actual structure of the Reich. The reality of Ottonian kingship in the period before Otto's imperial coronation was reflected in the works of writers of the 960s, who talked of the *populus Francorum et Saxonum* and developed the idea of a 'translation' of the Frankish empire to the Saxons. But there was also a specifically Saxon conception of the Reich, which could be seen as a *regnum Saxonum*.

OTTO THE GREAT AS EMPEROR AND THE APOGEE OF THE OTTONIAN
REICH

It is only following the imperial coronation of Otto I in 962 that an Ottonian historiography can be said to begin; from the preceding period we have only Liudprand of Cremona's *Antapodosis*. There had been no serious historiographical activity since around 900, but now as well as Liudprand we have Widukind of Corvey, Hrotsvitha of Gandersheim, Adalbert of Weissenberg, Ruotger and the author of the older *Vita Mathildis* as well as Rather of Verona and a number of significant hagiographers. Most of these authors saw Otto I's imperial coronation as marking the beginning of an epoch and the papal coronation as constitutive for the imperial quality and dignity. The imperial aspect of his kingship was stressed for the period before the coronation, something which had already been done by the royal chancery during Otto's kingship. Some of the historians even projected the imperial title back into the royal era. Apart from Liudprand and Rather, only Saxon authors of this period gave the Ottonian emperorship a Roman name. This took place before Otto II actually assumed the Roman imperial title in 982, and suggests a stress on the Roman element of emperorship which was not merely literary or historiographical. Widukind by contrast stressed a non-Roman imperial idea: he derived Otto's imperial rank from an acclamation as *imperator* by his army following the victory on the Lechfeld in 955. The idea of a non-Roman emperorship is also implicit in an *ordo* for the coronation of an emperor composed *c.* 960 in Mainz, probably in the entourage of Archbishop William. Like Widukind, William was an opponent of Otto's project to establish an archbishopric at Magdeburg with the help of the pope and of his imperial title.

From the beginning Otto had practised a hegemonial and imperial kingship. It expressed itself in supremacy and hegemony over the other Carolingian successor-states and in a policy of political and military expansion against the Slavonic lands to the east; here and in the north it was also linked with mission and the development of church organisation. Otto had already negotiated about an imperial coronation in 951. The Roman *patricius* Alberic, who had Rome and the *patrimonium Petri* firmly under control, opposed the request. Following Alberic's death in 954 the political constellation in Rome shifted. In 955 Agapetus II consented to the foundation of an archbishopric at Magdeburg, but the plan failed against the opposition by William of Mainz. On this occasion too Otto may have put out feelers about an imperial coronation. It was only very reluctantly in 952 that he had recognised Berengar II as Italian king under his overlordship. When he was once again master of the situation after the suppression of Liudolf's revolt, he sent Liudolf into Italy to drive out Berengar II and his son Adalbert, who had become effectively independent;

Liudolf had the prospect of himself becoming subking in Italy. Following Liudolf's death in the autumn of 957 the two recovered and extended their power. They came to threaten the pope, who was also menaced by the princes of Benevento and Capua and by opposition within Rome itself. John XII invited King Otto to free the Roman church and the pope from the tyranny of Berengar and Adalbert. The new disturbance of the balance of power within Italy and the inner-Italian threat to the papacy gave Otto the opportunity to acquire the emperorship. Just as his Carolingian predecessors Pippin and Charles had responded to the calls for help by the popes, Stephen II, Hadrian I and Leo III, so Otto responded to John XII's appeal. He made arrangements for the period of his absence, ordered the succession and had his son Otto II elected and crowned as co-king. On 2 February 962 Otto received the imperial crown from Pope John XII, and Adelaide was crowned and anointed with him. After John XII had agreed to the setting up of an archbishopric in Magdeburg and given Otto a free hand to organise the church in the Slavonic east, the new Ottonian emperor confirmed Pippin's donation of 754 and the other privileges granted by the Carolingians to the pope and to the Roman church, and secured for himself the imperial right to a promise of fidelity from the pope after he had been elected by the nobility and clergy of Rome and before he was consecrated. Otto assumed neither Charlemagne's imperial title with its reference to the Roman empire nor an imperial title which referred to the Romans; he was content with the simple title *imperator augustus* customary from the time of Louis the Pious onwards. In the chancery the designation *magnus* for Otto became customary after 962; he has gone down in history with this honorific title, 'the Great'.

Following the imperial coronation Otto began warfare against the kings, Berengar and Adalbert, and continued this with interruptions and pauses. Berengar surrendered at the end of 963 and was sent into exile at Bamberg. Adalbert fled, returned after the emperor's departure from Italy, and was defeated by an army sent by Otto I in 965 under Duke Burchard of Suabia; only after this did he cease to be a factor in Italian politics. Otto did not appoint a new subking, and ruled directly in the Italian kingdom from the autumn of 961. Otto and his successors employed a policy of exploiting aristocratic conflicts of interest, of preserving the balance of power between margraves, counts and bishops, of encouraging the development of new smaller margravates and granting privileges to the bishoprics. In this way they were able to stabilise their rule in the *regnum Italiae*. The main problem following the imperial coronation was to settle the relationship between emperor, pope and Rome. The Roman aristocracy and their aristocratic pope had no interest in a serious practical application of imperial power over Rome and within Italy. In the period after the coronation there was a series of uprisings and judicial hearings with rapid changes of control over Rome. Typically for his style of rulership, Otto demanded submission to his will in an intensified and previously unknown claim to rulership. After John XII's rapid defection Otto had him deposed by a Roman synod and an antipope, Leo VIII, elected, here infringing the legal principle that a pope is not subject to any earthly tribunal. The Romans also had to take an oath to Otto that they would never elect and consecrate a pope without permission from Otto and his son. John won Rome back, and a new Roman synod condemned Leo's election. Following John's death in May 964 the Romans asked Otto for his consent to the election of a new pope, as they did not recognise Leo VIII. The emperor insisted on having his pope. He besieged Rome in June 964 until the Romans had handed over their pope, Benedict V, who was kept prisoner in Hamburg until his death. Otto had thus compelled papacy and Romans to acknowledge a genuine exercise of imperial power. At the beginning of 965 he returned to the German lands of his empire.

It was not until 967/8, during the third Italian expedition, that the emperor managed to have an archbishopric set up at Magdeburg. The new province of Magdeburg included the existing bishoprics of Brandenburg and Havelberg as well as the newly erected sees at Merseburg, Zeitz and Meissen. The new foundation at Oldenburg, like the bishoprics of Schleswig, Ribe and Aarhus established in the course of the Danish mission which Otto had patronised, came under the archbishopric of Hamburg-Bremen. The resistance to the establishing of an archbishopric at Magdeburg, led by William of Mainz and Bernard of Halberstadt, shows the practical limitation of royal power by institutions like the churches of Mainz and Halberstadt and also reveals communities of interest between these and groups of magnates. Only after the death of Bernard in February and of William in March 968 was Otto finally able to complete the foundation of Magdeburg in cooperation with Pope John XIII at a synod at Ravenna in October 968. It is still disputed whether the bishopric of Posen, also founded around this time, belonged to Magdeburg's province or not. Its existence hints at the rise of a new concentration of power to the east in the form of the nascent Polish state and its church organisation. Margrave Gero had concluded a pact of *amicitia* on Otto's behalf with the increasingly powerful Polish prince Miesco in 963, which included the obligation to pay tribute for the western part of the Polish realm as far as the Wartha. In 966 Miesco received baptism, and the bishopric of Posen was founded shortly afterwards in the heart of his realm: a new Christian power was establishing itself firmly.

Otto's brother Brun, who had simultaneously been archbishop of Cologne and duke of Lotharingia, died in 965. He is held to have been a prototype of the Ottonian imperial bishop, the inaugurator of an Ottonian imperial church system. The imperial church itself was a Carolingian inheritance. By contrast with the situation in the west Frankish kingdom the east Frankish rulers had retained lordship over all the bishoprics and over many monasteries, so that there was here a much greater element of continuity between the Carolingian and the Ottonian eras. This imparted a special flavour to the church in the Ottonian Reich and in the end led to the development of a specifically Ottonian and Salian imperial church; Brun's activities lie at the beginnings of this. He combined and conflated episcopal and ducal office in the service of the Reich and had clerics drawn from the high nobility for the service of church and Reich trained at the cathedral school of Cologne, whom he then had appointed to Lotharingian bishoprics. Otto took over this conception, or rather it fitted in with his existing style of rulership. He extended the royal chapel, and staffed it above all with cathedral canons drawn from the high nobility; he increased the proportion of chaplains promoted to bishoprics. This began before Brun's death, and indeed the beginnings of the practice can be traced to the reign of Henry I, who had established a new royal chapel and appointed cathedral canons as *capellani*. Brun himself had been educated at the Utrecht cathedral school, and served from 941 to 953 as chaplain and chancellor before he became archbishop. What was to become the characteristic feature of the imperial church in the Ottonian and Salian eras – the interconnections between royal court and royal chapel and the cathedral chapters, and bishoprics held by former chaplains – set in before 967 and was not linked with specific events like Liudolf's uprising or the death of Brun. A second characteristic was the religious legitimation of the widespread and traditional practice that the bishops performed secular services for the king. These stood in contradiction to the episcopal ideal established in the course of the ninth century, which was orientated towards Benedictine monasticism and a monastic-ascetic way of life. In his *vita* of Brun, Ruotger justified the involvement of bishops 'with political affairs and dangerous wars'.[7] He worked out a new episcopal ideal, which Brun incorporated. Service for the king, who for contemporaries was the image of God and Christ's representative as well as the defender of the church, hence a priest-king, was here depicted as a duty which conformed with the divinely willed order of things. Service for the Reich – a part of the divine order of things, entrusted to the ruler by God – was the service of God.

A new Roman uprising against Pope John XIII recalled Otto to Italy, this time for what was to be a stay lasting six years, from 966 to 972. Otto, drawn by his Roman policy into the relations between the papacy and the Lombard principalities, came into conflict with Byzantium about the disputed overlordship over the latter. Finally war broke out, with a number of unproductive expeditions by Otto into Byzantine southern Italy. The result was a compromise:

---

[7] 'rem populi et pericula belli': Ruotger, *Vita sancti Brunonis archiepiscopi Coloniensis*, c. 23.

Otto retained feudal overlordship over Benevento and Capua, and his western emperorship was recognised by the east Roman empire. He also secured a Byzantine princess – Theophanu, the niece of the new, peaceably inclined emperor John Tzimisces – for his son, who had been crowned co-emperor in 967. The brilliant marriage of Otto II and Theophanu in St Peter's in Rome in 972 displayed Otto I at the height, though also at the limits of his power; there were rumbles of discontent in Saxony at this time over the ruler's long absence. The emperor returned; he died on 7 May 973, like his father in the palace at Memleben.

OTTO II AND OTTO III: MILITARY DEFEATS AND THE COLLAPSE OF THE POLICY OF *RENOVATIO IMPERII ROMANORUM*

Otto II had already been chosen king and emperor during his father's lifetime. He succeeded Otto I, aged not quite eighteen years, without a new election as king or a new imperial coronation in Rome. The questions of pecking-order and claims to power of the magnates associated with the succession soon led to conflicts and trials of strength in the south German duchies and in Lotharingia. In the west these centred around the claims of those magnates who had been driven into exile in 958 and now returned. Otto II restored Reginar IV and Lambert, the sons of Reginar III, to their allodial lands and in 977 appointed the Carolingian Charles, who was at loggerheads with his brother, the west Frankish king Lothar, as duke in lower Lotharingia. The consequence was war with Lothar, which was ended in 980 by an agreement to restore the status quo. In Bavaria Henry the Quarrelsome, the nephew of Otto I and cousin of Otto II, together with the Luitpoldings, revealed their ambitions; Otto responded by favouring his other nephew Otto, the son of Liudolf, and granting him Suabia in 973 and Bavaria in 976. Henry II of Bavaria tried to depose his cousin, and organised several uprisings in alliance with Miesco of Poland and Boleslav II of Bohemia. In the course of the struggle Carinthia was separated off from Bavaria and made into a duchy in 976, the Main-Frankish family of the Babenberger were given the Bavarian northern march, set up after 955, and finally in 978 Henry II lost his duchy. In these years the most influential advisers at the royal court were the empress Theophanu, Willigis, the last chancellor of Otto the Great and from 975 archbishop of Mainz, and Hildibald, the chancellor and bishop of Worms.

Royal or imperial rule remained undisturbed in Italy after Otto I's death, but not in Rome. Roman aristocratic factions, among whom the Crescentii were the most powerful during the second half of the tenth century, and popes established either by the emperor or by the Crescentii continued fluctuating struggles for power. At the end of 980 Otto II left for Italy. Theophanu, hostile to the new regime in Byzantium following the change of dynasty in 976, together with Gerbert of Aurillac and Adso of Montier-en-Der, introduced the young emperor to the Roman imperial conception and the idea of bringing the whole Italian peninsula under Roman imperial lordship. In Rome he decided to drive back the Saracen offensive in the south Italian mainland and in this way to conquer the Byzantine areas of southern Italy. In order to strengthen his army Otto ordered 2100 additional mailed horsemen from Germany, of which around 1500 were to be provided by the imperial churches. In the course of the siege of Tarento in March 982 the emperor adopted the Roman imperial title and thus proclaimed his claim to rule over a *Roman* empire against that of Byzantium. The campaign in southern Italy ended in a disaster: at Cotrone on the Calabrian coast the imperial army was crushingly defeated by the Saracens in July 982.

Saxon magnates demanded a meeting with the emperor, who summoned an assembly to Verona in May 983. Since Duke Otto of Suabia and Bavaria had died in Italy, the south German duchies were vacant. The vacancies were filled by members of the old ducal families: Bavaria reverted to the Luitpoldings in the person of Henry the Younger (who had been deposed as duke of Carinthia in 978), while Suabia was granted to the Conradines in the person of Conrad, a nephew of Duke Hermann. A further crucial matter dealt with at the assembly was the settling of the succession. The emperor's three-year-old son, Otto III, was elected as king with the participation of the Italian magnates present. The young Otto was sent to Germany to be crowned at Aachen by the archbishops Willigis of Mainz and John of Ravenna and to be brought up by Warin, archbishop of Cologne. Otto's election in Verona by German and Italian princes, and his coronation by the archbishops of Ravenna and Mainz, show the wish of the court and the participating magnates to treat the German territories and the *regnum Italiae* as one kingdom, to stress the one imperial kingship which integrated the various *regna*. Otto II had made intermittent use of the Roman imperial title in the course of the struggle with Byzantium. Following the Veronese assembly he renewed his attempt on southern Italy; in the course of this he died at Rome, on 7 December 983.

The news of the great uprising by the Elbe Slavs probably reached Otto before his death. The Liutizic confederation formed in the preceding years, an alliance of the Elbe Slav tribes with the Redarii at its core, had risen in the summer of 983 together with the Abodrites against Ottonian lordship. The Saxon march and church organisation was swept away. The Abodrites burned Hamburg. The attack was checked only west of the Elbe at the Tanger, where a Saxon army defeated the insurgents. The defeat at Cotrone and the Elbe Slav uprising brought the Ottonians and the Reich they had founded their first serious defeats. The extension of Ottonian power into southern Italy, already checked under Otto I, was halted once again, and Saxon expansion into the areas of Polabic tribal organisation and settlement was reduced to its starting-point at the Elbe.

The dispute about the guardianship over the royal child Otto III (claims were made by Henry the Quarrelsome and the west Frankish king Lothar) or indeed about the succession (Henry the Quarrelsome had himself elected king at Easter 984) ended in favour of Empress Theophanu. She was supported above all by Archbishop Willigis of Mainz, who, together with Hildibald of Worms, continued to exercise decisive influence at court. This did not change when the regency was taken over by Empress Adelaide following Theophanu's death on 15 June 991 at Nijmegen. The basis of royal rule remained intact during the years of regency under the two empresses, both in the German lands and in the kingdom of Italy; Adelaide exercised royal authority in Italy for years. Henry the Quarrelsome was restored to Bavaria in 985, and later to Carinthia. The structures and style of rulership, as visible in the itineraries of the empresses and the grants of privileges, corresponded to those practised in the time of Otto the Great. Promotions of royal chaplains to bishoprics continued, and in 985 Theophanu made the first grant of a whole county to a bishopric, Liège.

In 989 and 990 Theophanu made a journey to Italy. She exercised imperial power in Rome and Ravenna, and issued diplomata as *Theophanu imperatrix augusta*, even as *Theophanius imperator augustus*, but avoided getting involved in the Roman factional disputes. In spite of her involvement in west Frankish affairs and in the rivalry between Capetians and Carolingians for the throne, which culminated in the election of Hugh Capet in 987, her activities did not go beyond securing Lotharingia with diplomatic means. The renewed claim of the west Frankish Carolingians to this were rejected, and Hugh Capet, supported by Theophanu in his bid for the throne, as newly-elected king of France renounced Lotharingia. A comparison of the Rheims electoral dispute of 989–97 with that of 940–8 clearly shows how France and the Ottonian Reich had developed away from each other. In the latter dispute the influence both of the papacy and of the Ottonian court were less visible; it was Hugh Capet who dominated. The old imperial position of the Ottonians no longer had a basis in France.

In almost every year of her regency Theophanu organised campaigns in the Elbe Slav territories and often participated herself. These were conducted in alliance with Duke Miesco of Poland, who did homage to Otto III in 986, and provided Polish armies for the campaigns. Saxon and Polish forces also cooperated against Bohemia. The Bohemian duke, Boleslav II in turn concluded an alliance with the Liutizic confederation. Here the conflicts between the Polish Piasts and the Bohemian Przemyslids became visible; from about 990 the two families fought for lordship over Silesia and Cracovia, and in the last resort for hegemony over the whole area of west Slav settlement. A third family was also concerned in these rivalries, the Bohemian Slavnikids, who were of some importance for Ottonian eastern policy and provided the bishop of Prague in the person of the subsequently canonised Adalbert. The leadership in the wars for the reconquest of the areas of Polabian settlement and the securing of the marches of Meissen and Lausitz was taken by the archbishop of Magdeburg, Giselher, who had worked for the absorption of the bishopric of Magdeburg by Magdeburg in 981, together with Margrave Ekkehard I of Meissen, who had been appointed by Theophanu. All these efforts were in vain; the Liutizi and Abodrites retained their independence and freedom.

This was not altered by the campaigns undertaken by Otto III after he reached his majority: in the autumn of 995 together with the new Polish duke Boleslav Chrobry; in the summer of 997, when the Liutizi threatened the Arneburg on the Elbe and for a time even conquered it. After this Otto turned away from this aspect of Saxon and Ottonian policy and towards Rome. His policy of renewal of the Roman empire changed the angle of vision of Ottonian policy, though it should be noted on the one hand that Rome and the imperial position in Rome had played an important part in Ottonian policy since 962 and on the other that the political and ecclesiastical developments in the east did not lose their importance for Ottonian policy: the expansion of the Polish realm of the Piasts; the menacing of the Czech realm of the Przemyslids in Bohemia by Poland; the persecution of the Slavnikids in Bohemia by the Przemyslids; the formation of a Hungarian kingdom under the Arpáds. Otto III had a particular link with missionary activities in these areas through the bishop of Prague, Adalbert, who after being driven from his bishopric sought a life as monk and missionary and was martyred by the Prussians in 997.

In September 994 Otto III, now fifteen years old, received the arms which marked his entry into manhood and hence his ability to rule in person. The new king had received an education in Latin and Greek. He was imbued with a belief in his divinely sanctioned and unrestricted imperial rule and with an enthusiastic religiosity directed towards asceticism and mission; through his mother he inherited a particularly strong orientation towards Byzantium. This was combined with an admiration for the example of Charles the Great and for Carolingian tradition. These conceptions found expression in a programme of renewal of the Roman empire, which Otto developed following his imperial coronation in 996 under the influence of the chancellor Heribert, Leo of Vercelli and Gerbert of Aurillac in particular. Gerbert, whom Otto made pope in 999, addressed Otto as the new Constantine and as pope took the appropriate name of Sylvester II. As emperor Otto combined the vision of a *renovatio* with that of his apostolic status, which gave him the duty to see through an apostolic renewal of the church. On his first Italian expedition in 996, while still king, he behaved as if the papacy were an imperial bishopric in appointing his relative and chaplain Brun as pope, who as Gregory V became the first German to hold the see of St Peter. Following the imperial coronation on 21 May 996, Otto refused either to renew the *Ottonianum*, the confirmation of the Roman see's privileges by Otto the Great, or to acknowledge the Donation of Constantine; he persisted in this attitude and indeed later rejected the latter document as a forgery. He also claimed leadership within the church. He was determined to exercise imperial rule over Rome and within the *patrimonium Petri*; the result was tensions with the Roman nobility and the curia. Although Otto in effect conceded their wishes in the end, the concession of the eight disputed counties in the Pentapolis in January 1001 took the form not of a recognition of papal privileges but of an imperial donation.

The Christian renewal of the Roman empire was practised by Otto III and his court after Otto had, in the course of his second Italian expedition, which lasted from the end of 997 to the beginning of 1000, renewed control of Rome in February 998. At the beginning of this process stood the cruel tribunal over the antipope John Philagathos who had been set up by the Crescentii, the execution of Crescentius II and the exiling of his supporters. The emperor had an imperial palace built on the Palatine hill. Court titles derived from ancient Rome and a court ceremonial on Byzantine lines were introduced. Like those of the Byzantine emperors and the popes, the diplomata were validated by metal bulls with the device *renovatio imperii Romanorum* ('renewal of the empire of the Romans'). The chancery had already adopted the title of Emperor of the Romans from the time of the imperial coronation. To this Otto added the apostolic devotion formula *servus Jesu Christi* ('servant of Jesus Christ') on his journey to Poland, and from January 1001 the formula *servus apostolorum* ('servant of the apostles').

The most important actions with practical political consequences in the course of the four years of the *Renovatio* were the diplomata and other acts of Otto III and Sylvester II which reorganised imperial and papal connections with Poland and Hungary. In Rome negotiations were conducted with representatives of the Polish prince which led to the decision to found a Polish archbishopric. This was carried out in the course of a pilgrimage which Otto III undertook in February and March 1000 to Gnesen, where Boleslav Chrobry had had the body of the martyred Adalbert buried. The emperor concluded a pact of friendship with Boleslav. As a sign of his new status he set the imperial diadem on his head, presented him with a copy of the Holy Lance, and turned him, as Thietmar of Merseburg grumbled, 'from a tribute-payer into a lord'.[8] It

---

[8] 'tributarium faciens dominum': Thietmar, *Chronicon* v, 10, p. 232.

is even conceivable that Otto made Boleslav king in a secular ceremony, though if this did occur it was not followed by the ecclesiastical consecration necessary for the full legitimation of kingship. On the journey through the German territories which followed, Otto had the crypt of Charles the Great in Aachen opened and removed from it the emperor's golden breast-cross. By the summer of 1000 Otto was once again in Rome. The discontent within the Roman nobility and at the curia against imperial rule grew; in the end a Roman uprising forced emperor and pope to leave Rome in February 1001. Otto and Sylvester took themselves off to Ravenna, where at Easter they gave their sanction in a synod to the reorganisation of the Hungarian church planned by Stephen I and based on an archbishopric at Gran. Stephen, who like Miesco presented his kingdom to St Peter and sought royal status, was sent a royal crown by Otto III, the crown of St Stephen, with which he was crowned by the new Hungarian metropolitan. An aristocratic conspiracy in Germany at this time, about which we learn from Thietmar of Merseburg, may have had as its driving force the injured rights and claims of the churches of Magdeburg, Salzburg and Passau. News of its outbreak probably did not reach the emperor before his death: he died on 24 January 1002, not yet twenty-two years of age, near Rome, which he had not yet been able to reconquer. In the wake of the cortège bringing his body to Aachen the opponents of Ottonian rule in Italy rose.

In the era of Otto III the Ottonian imperial structure and style of rulership were developed, extended and intensified. There was an increase in the interaction between royal court and the imperial churches and the use of the latter for royal service. The absolute numbers of the royal chaplains, as well as of those chaplains who were at the same time holders of canonries at cathedrals or other foundations, increased substantially. Chaplains are found as royal messengers, participating in or presiding over the royal court, and also intervening in royal diplomata. The most important political advisers of Otto III were court chaplains and they remained permanent advisers of the king even after they had become bishops or popes. After a pause between 984 and 989 the promotion of chaplains to bishoprics became more and more frequent. The imperial churches had their rights of immunity extended both in nature and in extent. It was in the second half of the tenth century that most churches had their first grant of immunity coupled with bannus, the right to command and to hold courts; there was a concentration of such grants in the 980s. These also saw the first grants of whole counties to bishoprics. From the 970s a fresh wave of privileges granting annual markets, mint, toll and roads began, reaching its high-water mark around the year 1000. Around 1000 Otto III also issued the earliest privileges permitting weekly and daily markets. The counterpart to these changes in the organisation of the kingdom was a new form of

legitimation of rulership: it was in these years that the ruler portraits so characteristic of the late Ottonian and early Salian period first appear. The ruler,
though still alive, is here depicted as translated from his earthly surroundings
into the celestial sphere, projected on to the same level as Christ and the saints.
The new type of portrait corresponded to developments within the Ottonian
theology of rulership. The king or emperor received his legitimation and his
promised position as Christ's representative on earth through the service he
performed for God. The policy towards Rome was also marked by both continuity and intensification. The Ottonians had concentrated to a remarkable
extent on Rome and Italy since Otto's departure for his imperial coronation.
Of the forty years and five months between August 961 and January 1002,
sixteen years and ten months had been spent on Italian expeditions. The
numerous Italian expeditions, which followed on one another in rapid succession, the lengthy courts held in Italy, the journeys across the Alps which these
entailed for German princes and their followings – mailed horsemen and other
fighting men as well as servants – and the journeys in the reverse direction for
Italian magnates all led to a lengthening and strengthening of the north–south
axis of integration of the Ottonian Reich, which now extended from the lands
around the Harz, through east Franconia into southern Germany and across
the Alps into Italy. For the first time in the Ottonian period Otto III's reign saw
assemblies, meetings with magnates and the issuing of diplomata in Bavaria
and Suabia as the court moved to and from Italy. It was such practical matters
which helped to integrate *Francia et Saxonia* with the south German duchies, the
remaining German territories and the *regnum Italicum*. Emperorship, emperor
and the whole empire came to be orientated towards Rome.

RENOVATIO REGNI FRANCORUM UNDER HENRY II: THE EMERGENCE OF
THE *REGNUM TEUTONICUM* AND THE DEVELOPMENT OF EMPERORSHIP

Otto III left no son, nor was there a surviving brother or brother of his father
who could succeed by hereditary right to the throne. There was only one surviving member of the royal house in the male line: Henry IV of Bavaria, a
great-grandchild of King Henry I and the representative of the Bavarian line
of the Liudolfings. He at once made a bid for the crown. In addition there were
candidates in the persons of Duke Hermann II of Suabia, a Conradine, and
Margrave Ekkehard I of Meissen. Henry was supported by Archbishop
Willigis of Mainz, who had lost his previously dominant influence at court
under Otto III. On 6 or 7 June 1002 the Bavarian Liudolfing was elected as king
by his Bavarian, Frankish and upper Lotharingian supporters in Mainz and
anointed and crowned king by Willigis. By this time Ekkehard had already been
killed in a feud unconnected with the dispute over the succession. After an

indecisive campaign against Hermann of Suabia, Henry in the course of a perambulation of the kingdom successively won the recognition of the Thuringians, Saxons and lower Lotharingians either by homage or by a renewed election. Finally Hermann submitted in Bruchsal on 1 October 1002. The new king did not retain Bavaria in his own hands, but he also did not grant it, to the margrave of the Bavarian northern March, the Babenberger Henry of Schweinfurt, as he had at first promised, but to one of the four brothers of his wife Kunigunde, a member of the Luxemburg line of the clan of the Ardennes counts. Henry of Schweinfurt, backed by Boleslav Chrobry, rose against this decision and was crushed by Henry.

In Italy an anti-Ottonian group had set up Margrave Arduin of Ivrea as king on 15 February 1002. As soon as Henry had established his kingship in Germany he sent Duke Otto of Carinthia against Arduin around the turn of 1002/3. As early as the spring of 1004 he himself came to Italy, where on 14 May 1004 he was elected *rex Langobardorum* and crowned; between May 1004 and May 1005 he issued several diplomata under the title of *rex Francorum et Langobardorum*, thus acknowledging a certain independence of Italy from the Frankish kingdom, his realm north of the Alps. Henry insisted on Burgundy's feudal dependence. He had himself acknowledged as heir by the childless King Rudolf III in 1006 and had his overlordship confirmed on several occasions. On 14 February 1014 Henry received imperial coronation in Rome. Benedict VIII sought him out in 1020 in Bamberg to ask for armed assistance against Byzantium. It was here that Henry II confirmed the Ottonianum of 962; he responded to the pope's appeal and led a powerful army against Byzantium in southern Italy on his third expedition in 1021–2. The three Italian expeditions were short, lasting seven, three and nine months respectively, and the two stays in Rome were measured in days. The emperor refrained from any interference in Roman affairs, and within the Italian kingdom reverted to the policy of preserving the balance of power as practised by Otto the Great.

The Bavarian Liudolfing thus broke with the orientation towards Rome, and with the intention of exercising practical and decisive imperial authority over and in Rome, both of which had been determinant features of Ottonian policy in the previous forty years. Instead of the device *renovatio imperii Romanorum* used by Otto III Henry adopted the formula *renovatio regni Francorum* ('renewal of the kingdom of the Franks'), which had already been used on the imperial bulls of Louis the Pious, Charles III, Arnulf and Wido of Spoleto. Possibly it had already been formulated under Charles the Great, and at all events it expressed continuity with him. Henry was the first ruler to use the device as king – between the beginning of 1003 and 1007 – and evidently he announced in this way his conception of imperial kingship with a concentration on the *regnum* north of the Alps.

Henry made another U-turn in his eastern policy. From the end of the 970s onwards the Ottonians had supported Polish expansion against the Przemyslid principality, in the Baltic areas and against Kiev Rus', and received in return armed help of the Polish dukes in their attempts to reconquer the lands of the Liutizi and Abodrites. Then Otto III had made Boleslav Chrobry a member of the *imperium Romanum* at Gnesen in 1000. Boleslav was henceforth able to claim to be 'brother and cooperator of the empire, friend and ally of the Roman people'.[9] In the course of the succession dispute of 1002 he occupied the lower Lausitz and the Milzener land around Bautzen following Ekkehard I of Meissen's violent death, presumably in agreement with the Ekkehardings. Henry gave him these marches as benefices when Boleslav took part in the renewed election by the Saxon princes in July 1002 at Merseburg and with these acknowledged the new king. At the beginning of 1003 the Polish duke seized Bohemia. Henry demanded that he should do homage for the Bohemian dukedom, which Boleslav refused. It was then that Henry broke with previous Ottonian policy: he renounced further attempts to reconquer the territories of the Elbe Slavs lost in 983; at Easter 1003 he concluded an alliance with the Liutizi and together with them took up arms against Boleslav Chrobry with the intention of driving him out of Poland and out of the Saxon eastern marches which had remained under German rule after 983. Like Otto III's Roman and Polish policy, Henry II's alliance with the pagan Liutizi against the Christian prince of Poland aroused violent criticism within Saxony. It can be found in the chronicle of Thietmar, from 1009 bishop of the see of Merseburg restored by Henry II in 1004, and in an admonitory letter written by the missionary archbishop Brun of Querfurt in 1008. The Saxon nobility conducted the Polish wars reluctantly and without enthusiasm. The Liutizi, who were themselves interested in preserving a balance between the two opponents, did not contribute to a decisive victory by Henry. Henry and Boleslav conducted three campaigns, in 1003–5, 1007–13 and 1015–18. The emperor was not able to deprive the Piast prince of the lower Lausitz and the Milzener land: by the peace of Bautzen of 1018 he confirmed the possession of these territories as benefices. On the other hand he did prevent the incorporation of Bohemia into the Piast empire and did preserve Ottonian overlordship over Bohemia.

Henry II remained within the paths and conceptions of Ottonian sacral kingship. Having succeeded to the throne after his grandfather Henry had been excluded from kingship in 936, he regarded himself as specially chosen by God. His, the Henrician line of the Liudolfings, had been exalted by God after a long period of trial and humiliation. This idea can be found in the younger *Vita Mathildis* written between 1002 and 1012. With his sense of ruling as God's

---

[9] Gallus Anonymus, *Chronicae et gesta ducum sive principum Polonorum*, c. 6: 'fratrem et cooperatorem imperii constituit, et populi Romani amicum et socium appellavit'.

viceregent, Henry perceived all secular and ecclesiastical lordship as hierarchically subordinated to his kingship, and it was part of God's order that it should obey his power of command unconditionally and respect his authority in matters of law and peace. Just as the Liuthar evangeliary of Aachen shows Otto III as living ruler in earthly surroundings but directly in contact with Christ and the divine sphere, so there is a portrait of Henry II in a Regensburg sacramentary which does the same. Here the figure of Henry extends into the nimbus around the figure of Christ, who with His left hand sets the crown on the head of the praying king. Henry sought to shape the constitutional reality according to such conceptions. He opposed private concentrations of lordship and power and was concerned to stress the nature of aristocratic lordship as office. In spite of this intensified Christian and sacral idea of kingship the king remained, like all Ottonians, in fundamental consensus with the aristocratic ducal and comital families. He completely respected their hereditary rights and their expectation that the bishoprics and abbacies of royal monasteries would be bestowed on members of the high nobility.

In the real world of rulership the king acted as umpire, judge and peacemaker in the struggles for position which were produced by the formation of regional lordships, in particular between the houses of the dynastic nobility and between counts and dukes and the episcopal churches. Conflicts in Lotharingia forced the king to undertake repeated campaigns between 1005 and 1012. Between the Meuse and the Scheldt the struggles turned around the formation of what were later to become the territories Brabant, Hennegau, Holland and Flanders, in particular between the Reginarids and the Ardennes counts. In upper Lotharingia it was the Luxemburg branch of the Ardennes comital house, related to Henry II by marriage, whose attempt to extend their power by seizing the archbishopric of Trier in 1008 (the relationship had already brought them the bishopric of Metz in 1005) set off a conflict which lasted years. In Saxony too lay nobles sought to extend their power at the expense of archbishops and bishops; as the king valued and favoured the latter, tensions arose between him and the lay nobility which culminated in 1019–20 in a full-scale uprising by the Saxon duke and Saxon counts. Such struggles were normally concluded by a compromise.

Henry II continued the policy of the Ottonians in integrating the imperial churches – bishoprics, cathedral chapters and other canonries, and large monasteries – into royal lordship and orienting them towards the court through personal connections. The number of cathedral chapters linked with the royal chapel rose, as did the number of royal chaplains promoted to bishoprics. Between 1002 and 1021, twenty-two of the thirty-six episcopal vacancies were filled by royal chaplains; twenty of the forty-seven bishops who died during Henry's reign were former chaplains. Henry was persistent and determined in having his candidates appointed. Occasionally he even invested these against the will of or contrary to the proposal made by the cathedral chapter; in his confirmations of privileges for bishoprics he occasionally deleted the right of freedom of election granted in earlier privileges. At the end of his reign his ability to get his own way may have been somewhat reduced; almost all the bishops appointed in 1022 and 1023 were not members of the royal chapel. The king-emperor encouraged the incipient territories being built up by the imperial churches. He granted immunities with ban and entire counties to bishoprics and royal monasteries. In all this Henry's church policy shows no real innovation, only development of existing tendencies, but the quantitative extension and intensification of the links between court and imperial churches during his reign was so great as to give the whole institution a new quality; Henry brought to fruition the specifically Ottonian characteristics of the imperial church. Henry's own contribution to this is to be seen in the support he gave as king to the movement of monastic reform, which established something like an 'imperial monasticism'; already in his period as duke he had supported monastic reform movements of differing observances. He imposed Gorzian reform on the most important imperial monasteries and reorganised both monastic life and the administration of monastic property, in some monasteries provoking by this resistance and even secessions by the monks. Possessions which exceeded the needs implied by the Rule of St Benedict were taken over for the use of the kingdom.

Henry II's practice of government shows that as king he took over the Ottonian positions in the lands around the Harz and based his lordship on them. The political central regions in east Saxony/north Thuringia, in the lands around Rhine and Main, and in the lower Rhine/Meuse area continued to exist. But the continuity was coupled with change. Henry extended the areas where the court stayed for longer periods to include Alsace and the south German duchies. At the same time he increased the speed of his itineracy and shortened the length of his stays in the various parts of the Reich: these were visited for shorter intervals more frequently. Bavaria, Suabia and Alsace, previously distant zones in relation to royal lordship, now became close zones. Correspondingly the duchies of Bavaria and Suabia lost their special status. They had continued to exist in the Ottonian Reich after 918 as duchies with an ethnic basis, and so differed fundamentally from the duchies in upper and lower Lotharingia and in Carinthia as well as from the Billung dukedom in north-east Saxony. Henry II curbed the quasi-regal ducal lordship in Bavaria and Suabia which he himself had exercised as duke, following the death of Hermann II of Suabia in 1003 and with his own renunciation of Bavaria in 1004. By founding the bishopric at Bamberg in 1007 Henry created a new political centre within the Reich which lay on the north–south axis connecting the Harz region via east Franconia with south Germany and northern Italy. This reorganisation of government was carried out from Saxony, where Merseburg played a special role as a place particularly favoured by Henry both to stay and to hold assemblies at. The new bishopric at Bamberg received a substantial landed endowment in order to fulfil its role as a centre of royal lordship, which extended over the whole of the southern half of the kingdom and down along important Alpine crossings.

Henry's practice of rulership – adoption of the Ottonian central regions in order to extend the practice of periodic royal presence over most of the German territories, creation of a new centre of lordship in east Franconia in the bishopric of Bamberg, curtailing of the viceregal dukedoms and other prominent noble lordships, intensification of the use made of the imperial churches for royal service and of their orientation towards the ruler's court – led to a new phase of integration of the kingdom, which now included Franks, Lotharingians, Saxons, Bavarians and Suabians. The Roman and Italian policy of the period from 961 to 1002 had given a new quality to the organisational structures employed by rulership within the *imperium* in Germany and Italy. At the end of the Ottonian era both *imperium* and *regnum* were more integrated than they had been.

The emperorship of the Ottonians had already been linked with the Romans by Otto II and Otto III. Contemporaries soon linked Henry II's kingship with the Germans. Around the turn of the millennium we find in Venice and southern Italy the first references to a *regnum Teutonicum* and a *rex Teutonicorum* (German kingdom, king of the Germans) applied to Henry II; his kingdom north of the Alps, like that of Otto III, was a *regnum Teutonicum*. That contemporaries saw Henry II as a king of the Germans in his own lifetime is shown by the diploma issued in 1020 for the Bavarian bishopric of Brixen near the border with the Italian kingdom, which was drawn up by the recipient. The bishop of Brixen's scribe gave Henry the title *rex Teutonicorum, imperator augustus Romanorum*.[10] This title remained an isolated instance during the eleventh century, but it nevertheless clearly shows the processes of integration and conceptions of reform of the Reich during the first decades of the new millennium: the German and imperial components of the Ottonian Reich; the king elected by the German princes with a claim to an emperorship of the Romans and responsibility for the Roman empire, conceived of as simultaneously king of the Germans and emperor of the Romans.

Emperor Henry II died childless on 13 July 1024 and was buried in the cathedral at Bamberg. A cult soon grew up around Bamberg and the grave in the

---

[10] 'king of the Teutons, august emperor of the Romans': D H II 424.

cathedral, culminating in the canonisation of Henry in 1146 and of Kunigunde in 1200. Henry II was thus the first ruler in the succession to the Frankish rulers to be perceived by contemporaries as king of the Germans, and the only saint among the German kings and emperors.

CHAPTER 10

SAXONY AND THE ELBE SLAVS IN THE TENTH CENTURY

Gerd Althoff

SAXON POLITICS IN THE SHADOW OF OTTONIAN KINGSHIP

Saxony after Carolingian incorporation

The conquest and incorporation of Saxony into the Carolingian empire, which Charles the Great achieved after long and bitter struggles, had far-reaching consequences for the political and institutional organisation of the Saxons. The three Saxon 'armies' of the Ostfalians, Westfalians and Engrians, and the 'national' assembly of all castes – nobles, free men and freed men – ceased to contribute to the coherence of Saxon political life. From 785 all assemblies in Saxony were forbidden except for those summoned by a count or royal *missus*. It was the so-called comital organisation which henceforth determined the structure of lordship in Saxony; but no more fundamental Frankicisation of the ruling strata in Saxony took place. The Saxon nobility allied itself with the Franks, presumably by ties of marriage, and the Carolingian rulers did not replace it with Frankish magnates. A second characteristic of the Carolingian conquest was to have long-term consequences: Saxon territory did not become a core region of the Carolingian kings, even after the divisions of the empire among Louis the Pious' sons. Carolingian visits to Saxony remained exceptional events. Already by the mid-ninth century we can observe nobles in eastern and western Saxony termed *dux*. Between Rhine and Weser in the west it is Ekbert, with his *ducatus Westfalorum*; in the east it is the *dux* Liudolf, ancestor of the Ottonians and founder of the nunnery of Gandersheim. In Saxony, therefore, as in other parts of east Francia, we find that phenomenon known as the 'younger tribal duchy': an aristocratic lordship claiming exclusive pre-eminence within a *gens* (a source of lengthy feuds in Franconia and Suabia), and consequently bound to clash with the king. In Saxony such conflicts are not recorded at first, and it is in any case doubtful whether the *dux* Liudolf already claimed a leadership within the whole Saxon territory. He seems rather to have confined himself to his own lordship in eastern Saxony, in the Harz mountains.

Liudolf's position was inherited by his son Brun, who fell against the Northmen in 880 while leading a Saxon army including the bishops of Hildesheim and Minden among others. Liudolfing predominance was apparently not affected by this, for Brun's brother Otto 'the Magnificent' simply took over his position. The influence exercised by the Liudolfings is seen not least in the way their women married east Frankish Carolingians: Liutgard married Louis the Younger and Oda Zwentibald. Multiple alliances with the royal family were accompanied by marriage links with powerful noble families *outside* Saxony, for example with the Babenberger of eastern Franconia, but not apparently by marriages among the Saxon nobility itself. Several of Liudolf's daughters remained unmarried as abbesses of Gandersheim, a very clear indication of the Liudolfings' prominent position.

Henry, son of Otto and later to become king, was the first to break with these marriage practices. He first married a widow from the Merseburg regions for her rich inheritance, and then fell in love 'because of her beauty and her wealth',[1] with the young Matilda, a descendant of the Saxon duke Widukind, whose lands lay mainly in western Saxony. Ecclesiastical protests against the first marriage made possible its dissolution and Henry's remarriage; linked with it was a thrust into western Saxony, which soon brought Henry into conflict with the Conradines. The Liudolfings' position was consolidated by Henry's successful conduct of his dispute with King Conrad I, who had at first tried to restrict his succession to his father after the latter's death in 912. Henry's rise is all the more remarkable when we consider that no other Saxon aristocratic group succeeded in continuously extending its position in this way: neither the descendants of the *dux* Ekbert nor those of the Saxon leaders Widukind and Hessi achieved such a continuity, though the reasons are not clear.

However, one very forcible reservation must be made when considering Saxony in the late ninth and early tenth century: any judgements are made very difficult by the fact that many evaluations come from the later 'Ottonian' historiography, which bathes early Liudolfing history in a flood of transfiguring light. This is true not only of the works written in Gandersheim but also of Widukind of Corvey's *Saxon History*. It is thus ultimately unclear how the Franks and the Saxons came to elect the Saxon duke Henry as king in 919 following King Conrad's death.

The Saxon dukedom in the tenth century

Henry I's elevation to kingship at Fritzlar in 919 had a less-noticed consequence for the Saxon people: its duke was now king. Henry I is not known to

---

[1] Thietmar, *Chronicon*, I, 9.

have taken any steps to install a substitute as duke in Saxony, and nor do the Saxons themselves appear to have been active in this direction. This was the start of a development which had great significance for the tenth century. The king, frequently absent, was able to shape Saxon politics less continuously than would have been possible for a duke. He nevertheless refrained from establishing an 'office-like' dukedom there, by contrast with the position in the south German duchies. This had three characteristic consequences for Saxon history in this period: noble families forced their way into the resulting power vacuum; it became more difficult to reach an expression of political will at royal and popular assemblies, for a number of different forces had or claimed positions of rough equality; cooperative forms of association (*coniurationes*) were widespread, which is probably also a result of the organisation of lordship within Saxony.

The Ottonian rulers naturally could not avoid giving offices and tasks to Saxon nobles from which a pre-eminence within the people might have been derived. The best-known such example was the appointment of Hermann Billung as *princeps militiae* by Otto I in 936.[2] This had particularly important consequences because with time Hermann's position gradually broadened into that of a duke, a position which became heritable within his family. But Otto's decision is also of great interest because it lit the fuse for a whole series of conflicts. These show that even in the early tenth century Saxon nobles thought of themselves as having claims to particular offices and were not prepared to accept royal decisions they perceived as arbitrary. Otto I's choice was a – probably deliberate – breach of the internal ranking of the Billung family and of the Saxon nobility as a whole, intended to demonstrate his right to make such decisions. Resistance articulated itself immediately: Hermann's older brother Wichmann left the royal army and allied himself with Otto's enemies, while an Ekkehard, 'son of Liudolf', tried by an act of hare-brained courage to show that he was a more appropriate choice for military leadership than Hermann. With eighteen companions he risked an attack on the enemy against royal orders, and perished with all his comrades.[3] In the following period we can see how Otto I repeatedly entrusted his *princeps militiae* with representing him (*procuratio*) in Saxony when he went to Italy. These *procurationes* came to be quite lengthy ones, for the emperor spent almost all his time in Italy after 961. It is therefore significant that the royal chancery refers to Hermann only as *comes* or *marchio*, while Widukind of Corvey terms him *dux*, though he also uses this term for other Saxon nobles of the period, such as Margraves Gero and Dietrich. In spite of this it is clear that Hermann's exalted position was also reflected in his titles.

[2] Widukind, *Res gestae Saxonicae* II, 4.   [3] *Ibid.* II, 4.

The independence with which he acted can be seen from two events from his second *procuratio*. Otto wrote to the *duces* Hermann and Dietrich, ordering them not to make peace with the Redarii; although the letter was read out at a popular assembly in Werla, the peace, already concluded, was kept, since the Saxons feared to divide their forces while threatened by a war with the Danes.[4] Even more striking than this overriding of orders from a distant emperor determined by the military position was a reception which Hermann arranged for himself in Magdeburg in 972. Here he usurped the reception ceremony reserved for the king, sat in his place and slept in his bed. He had, of course, assistance in this, notably from the archbishop of Magdeburg, Adalbert, whom Otto condemned to a hefty fine for his presumption.[5]

It is not until the time of Bernard I, however, who had inherited all his father's rights in 973, that we learn that the position of the Billungs within Saxony had come to approach that of a duke. In the crisis period after the death of Otto II, who had left only his three-year-old son Otto III, just crowned as co-ruler in Aachen, to succeed him, decisions by the Saxon people were particularly necessary because Otto's nearest male relative and guardian, Henry the Quarrelsome, himself aspired to kingship and sought a decision in Saxony. He summoned a Saxon assembly for Palm Sunday 984, and suggested to it that he should be elected king. Some of those present expressed reservations, claiming to be unable to act without the permission (*licentia*) of Otto III. We can tell that Duke Bernard was among them, even though this is not recorded explicitly, from the fact that he headed the participants at an assembly held at the Asselburg immediately afterwards, intended to rally those who wanted to resist Henry's usurpation.[6] Although several Saxon counts besides Bernard took part in this meeting, they were evidently not strong enough to prevent Henry from being proclaimed king by his supporters at the Easter celebrations of 984 in Quedlinburg. These supporters included the dukes Boleslav of Bohemia and Miesco of Poland and the Abodrite prince Mistui. So we cannot deduce an established ducal position for Bernard from these events, even though he is named among Henry the Quarrelsome's principal opponents.

The Saxon opposition to Henry, in alliance with forces outside Saxony, notably Archbishop Willigis of Mainz, ultimately forced Henry to abandon his plans for kingship and affirmed Otto III's succession under the regency of his mother Theophanu, while Henry was restored to the duchy of Bavaria. The reconciliation and compromise were celebrated and publicly demonstrated at the Easter celebrations at Quedlinburg in 986, certainly not by coincidence. Four dukes served at table, as if participating in the coronation banquet of a

---

[4] *Ibid.* III, 70.   [5] Thietmar, *Chronicon* II, 28.   [6] *Ibid.* IV, 2.

newly crowned king: Henry of Bavaria as steward, Conrad of Suabia as chamberlain, Henry the Younger of Carinthia as butler, and Bernard I as marshal.[7] When four dukes had participated in the coronation feast of Otto I in 936 there had been no Saxon duke present, and Widukind, to whom we owe the description of the scene, talks of Siegfried in this connection as the 'best of the Saxons and second after the king', not as *dux*.[8] This may serve to underline the Billung's growing into a new role.

The royal succession following Otto III's death also proved difficult; it is our next opportunity to observe whether Bernard exercised ducal functions. First he favoured his relative Ekkehard of Meissen, which made him a member of a group ultimately unable to prevail even within Saxony. It was this partisanship which perhaps explains why Bernard played no specially prominent role in the formation of a Saxon view, for another Saxon, Margrave Liuthar from the Walbeck family, was able to raise his profile as an opponent of Ekkehard of Meissen. The Bavarian claimant to the throne, the later Henry II, even turned in letters to his cousins, the Ottonian abbesses Adelaide and Sophie, in order to win them and the Saxon magnates for his cause, with decisive effect. Details like this show what varied forces could operate within Saxony alongside and also against the duke.

Bernard's partisanship for Ekkehard evidently did not damage him. At Henry II's so-called 'subsidiary election' (*Nachwahl*) in Merseburg, which brought Saxon recognition of the new king, the duke appeared as a representative of the people before Henry II, who had appeared in full regalia, set out the Saxons' view of the matter and their own position, and demanded binding promises. After Henry had given these, 'Duke Bernard took up the Holy Lance and entrusted him with the care of the Reich in the name of all'.[9] The scene has become a *locus classicus* for the scholarly investigation of the Saxon dukedom: the Saxon duke can here be seen transformed from a 'king's representative among the Saxon people' to a 'representative of the Saxon people before the king'.[10] However, this is the *only* occasion when we can point to a Saxon duke's taking an important position at the head of the people. It should also be noted that the later Ottonian rulers no longer entrusted the Billung dukes with representing them in Saxony during their absences in Italy, preferring instead to make use of people who stood closer to them. Otto III chose his aunt Matilda, abbess of Quedlinburg, famous for the care with which she presided over the Saxon assemblies, and Henry II used the archbishop of Magdeburg and his wife Kunigunde for the purpose. Such details should make us think hard when asked to determine the essential nature of the Billung dukedom. Signs of a

---

[7] *Ibid.* iv, 9. [8] Widukind, *Res gestae Saxonicae* ii, 2.

[9] 'Bernhardus igitur dux, accepta in manibus sacra lancea, ex parte omnium regni curam illi fideliter committit': Thietmar, *Chronicon* v, 16– 17. [10] Jordan (1958), p. 8.

steady evolution of the Billungs into dukes are matched by others which cast doubt on whether kings, Billungs and other forces within the Saxon nobility shared a consensus about the rights and duties of the Saxon duke. There is thus every reason for modern scholarship to rethink the characteristics of ducal lordship in the east Frankish/German kingdom.[11]

Observations on the Saxon nobility in the tenth century

It may be dynastic coincidence or not, but apart from the Liudolfings we know of no Saxon noble family whose genealogical connections can be traced with certainty from the ninth through to the tenth century. This is linked with another observation. In ninth-century Saxony we can make out five noble groups: the Liudolfings, the Ekbertines, the descendants of Widukind, the Hessi-clan and the so-called older Billungs. In the tenth century, by contrast, we can make out more than twenty-five possessing some sort of firm genealogy and visible history. Such a comparison suggests fairly certainly that the Saxon nobility's lordship profited to a considerable extent from the Liudolfings' rise to kingship and from the Ottonian dynasty. The connection becomes still clearer if we ask whereabouts in Saxony the families visible only from the tenth century onwards resided: for the most part they came from the Liudolfing and Ottonian core region around the Harz mountains. This was the home of the families associated with Margraves Siegfried and Gero, of the Ekkehardines, Walbecks, Haldenslebens, of the counts of Weimar, Northeim and Katlenburg as well as others, and if one notes that it was also here that the well-known Ottonian palaces and house monasteries like Quedlinburg, Gandersheim and Nordhausen lay and that Otto had by founding Magdeburg and its suffragans of Merseburg, Zeitz and Meissen installed further ecclesiastical centres in the region, then one gets a picture of a concentration of lordship unparalleled in the rest of the Ottonian Reich. Here we should note that the borders between Saxony and Thuringia seem to have been permeable. There are clear signs of a specific consciousness among both Thuringians and Saxons, culminating in the election of Ekkehard of Meissen as duke of Thuringia, reported by Thietmar of Merseburg,[12] and the demonstrative visit by Henry II to Thuringia in the course of his itinerary round the Reich following the royal election in Mainz. But on the other hand Thuringian magnates like the Ekkehardines or the counts of Weimar appeared at Saxon popular and royal assemblies and cannot be distinguished from the Saxon magnates there. It is more plausible to speak of a Thuringian special consciousness within Saxony.

---

[11] See now Becher (1996).   [12] Thietmar, *Chronicon* v, 7.

Similar concentrations of lordship are not found in the other regions of Saxony outside this east Saxon/Thuringian core region. In the tenth-century north two noble groupings, the Billungs and the counts of Stade, achieved prominence and shared the military command on the Slav border. Even this cannot be paralleled in western Saxony, in the bishoprics of Minden, Osnabrück, Paderborn and Münster, apart from some evidence for lordships held by the wider Billung family in these regions. It thus seems reasonable to suppose that the concentration of noble families in the east Saxon/Thuringian region, the Ottonian heartland, is connected with the patronage of these families by the royal dynasty. It has also been noted that in the tenth century royal gifts of land to the nobility lay in the area where the recipient held office, in sharp contrast to Carolingian practice. In other words, the gifts favoured the development of a centre of lordship, and so in the long term the emergence of 'territorial lordships' held by nobles and prelates. Indirect evidence for such concentrations around a centre of lordship is also provided by the numerous monastic foundations of the tenth-century nobility. These were mausolea, centres preserving the *memoria* of the family's relatives, and so providing points of crystallisation around which noble family consciousness could be preserved and cultivated. The cultivation of *memoria* also allows us to see the very close ties between individual noble families. In the course of the tenth century the Saxon nobility had become quite exceptionally interrelated, even if dynastic marriage for political reasons is hardly a Saxon invention. It is noteworthy how closely the most eminent Saxon families were related to each other: the Billungs to the counts of Stade, the family of Margrave Gero and the Ekkehardines; the counts of Stade in turn to the counts of Walbeck; the Ekkehardines also to the counts of Walbeck. This list, owing much to the genealogical information provided by Thietmar of Merseburg, could easily be extended, but it can hardly be doubted that the most influential sections of the Saxon nobility in the Ottonian era were all related to one another. This did anything but prevent conflicts – one might offer examples from the history of the Billungs and of others – but it also certainly offered chances for the members of this stratum to act together and to exchange information, very necessary at royal and popular assemblies but also for the successful conclusion of *coniurationes*.

Problems of political consensus-formation in Saxony: popular assemblies and
coniurationes

Saxony in the Ottonian era was rich in centres from which royal lordship was exercised. For this reason it is clear that the politics of the *gens* were to a large extent decided at such places, for example at the Easter palace at Quedlinburg or the *urbs regia* Magdeburg. Alongside such centres, however, Werla grew in importance as a location for Saxon popular assemblies. It must be stressed that the popular assemblies there of the Ottonian period all took place without kings: the generally held view that tenth-century kings often appeared at these assemblies has no foundation. Werla was certainly an *urbs regia*, and the Ottonians frequently stayed there, but their stops were spread across the year and do not suggest regular participation at a regional popular assembly in springtime. It is, however, very questionable whether there was a *yearly* popular assembly at all. Three of the four pieces of relevant evidence come from periods when there were problems with royal succession following the deaths of Otto II, Otto III and Henry II in 984, 1002 and 1024 respectively. The fourth piece of evidence comes from 968, when the Saxons met in Otto I's absence in Italy under the leadership of their *duces* Hermann Billung and Dietrich.

These instances also show that it was not the duke who summoned these assemblies; rather, the cooperative forms of organisation among the Saxon magnates brought about the meetings at Werla. In 984 Henry the Quarrelsome hurried to Werla in order to prevent or pacify a *coniuratio* which was taking place there. In 1002 Saxon magnates pledged themselves at a *secretum colloquium* in Frohse that they would elect no one as king before a meeting to take place at Werla. Thietmar of Merseburg gives us a very precise account of the course of this *colloquium*, showing the form such an assembly took. The claimant Henry sent a messenger to the assembly, in particular to the Ottonian abbesses Sophie of Gandersheim and Adelaide of Quedlinburg, as well as to the Saxon magnates, showing the important role played by Ottonian princesses in such meetings. At the meeting the messenger revealed his master's offer to reward generously all who would help him to kingship. Thietmar shows that by no means all politically relevant forces participated, for Margrave Ekkehard of Meissen and his following were absent, and it is pretty certain that this included Duke Bernard and the bishops Arnulf of Halberstadt and Bernward of Hildesheim. Ekkehard, together with Bernard and Arnulf, provoked the Ottonian ladies and their guests by usurping a festive banquet and eating up the meal probably intended in favour of those who had decided for Henry as king.[13]

The active role played by female members of the Ottonian family in Saxon politics is also evident in the succession of Conrad II in 1024–5. The Saxons again organised an assembly in Werla to discuss the royal election and other outstanding problems, including a reconciliation between Bishop Meinwerk of Paderborn and the Billung count Thietmar. But the main effect of the assembly

---

[13] *Ibid.* v, 4.

was that the Saxons took no part in the election of Conrad II at Kamba; yet there was, in contrast to 1002, no longer talk of a native Saxon candidate. When Conrad then proceeded to Saxony via Lotharingia the Ottonian abbesses Adelaide and Sophie behaved differently from the other Saxon magnates, who did homage to the king in Dortmund and Minden. The 'imperial daughters and sisters', as they are termed in the Quedlinburg annals, received the new king, their distant relative, with demonstrative affection as the *ius consanguineum* prescribes, in Vreden in western Saxony.[14] It is evident that in so doing they largely predetermined the outcome of the Saxons' decision.

All these details show that in Saxony there were traditional forms of reaching political decisions, held for preference in Werla but also in other places like Frohse, Seesen or the Asselburg. Equally clear is the fact that the Saxon duke had no pre-eminent role in the summoning and conduct of these assemblies; it is rather the variety of political forces operating in Saxony which is noteworthy, including the female members of the Ottonian house in a prominent position. It was not only Sophie and Adelaide who were to be found in the first row at such assemblies; Matilda of Quedlinburg – as already mentioned – is also praised for her careful presidency over them during Otto III's absence, 'sitting amongst the bishops and dukes'.[15] But it was not only members of the royal family who might take a higher profile than the dukes at these assemblies. Margrave Liuthar clearly dominated an assembly at Frohse in 1002; he summoned the 'better part' of the assembly from a consultation to a *secretum colloquium*, after the larger assembly had failed to reach consensus. The confidential meeting allowed the controversy to be worked through; it had arisen over the aspirations of Ekkehard of Meissen to kingship and culminated in the well-known piece of dialogue: 'What have you got against me, Count Liuthar?' 'Can't you see that your wagon is missing a fourth wheel?'[16] These details also reveal the cooperative forms and structures of such meetings, which do not fit with a model of a popular assembly directed by the duke. It would seem that the lack of continuity in the duke's position on the one hand and the sense of dignity held by margraves, archbishops, bishops and royal abbesses on the other hand both helped to shape political structures within the Saxon people. Since ducal lordship was inadequately established, the politically active forces made use of forms of communication and interaction customary among cooperatively structured groups. This helps to explain why oath-takings played such an important role at these assemblies. Thietmar of Merseburg calls the arrangements made by Henry the Quarrelsome's opponents at a meeting in Werla in 984 a *coniuratio*. Henry took it so seriously that he sent a bishop to negotiate with it, who fixed a date for a meeting. This *coniuratio* had already been

---

[14] 'imperiales filiae ac sorores': *Annales Quedlinburgenses, s.a.* 1002, p. 78.
[15] *Annales Quedlinburgenses, s.a.* 999, p. 75.   [16] Thietmar, *Chronicon* IV, 52.

prepared at a meeting at the Asselburg; Thietmar names those who took part, calls them *consocii* and their actions *conspirare*.[17] It was also an oath which bound the participants at the meeting in Frohse to act in common at Werla in choosing a king; they too were a sworn confederation.

These forms of cooperative *coniuratio* associated with the royal elections of the late tenth century remind us that in early tenth-century Saxony magnate *coniurationes* stood at the beginnings of actions against the king. For the conclusion of such sworn confederations there was a traditional location, Saalfeld in Thuringia. The *coniuratio* into which Henry, Otto I's brother, entered with Saxon magnates in 939 and Liudolf, Otto's son, in 951, was marked by a *convivium*, a festive banquet intended to create and strengthen community and generally characteristic of such cooperative associations. Members of the royal house initiated sworn confederacies, in other words; they joined Saxon nobles in taking oaths. Contemporary historians claimed that observers regarded the very existence of such meetings as sinister, for their purpose was evidently unambiguous: people met to enter into a *coniuratio* at a specific place, confirmed it with a banquet and then hastened to turn their oath into reality. In both of the cases just mentioned this meant beginning a feud against Otto the Great. The possibility of summoning *socii* and *coniuratores* to assistance in seeking revenge for any injustice suffered strengthened, as will easily be seen, the position of all members of such *coniurationes*. Even though such associations need have had no institutionalised continuity, we should not underestimate the permanence of the links they created. The circle of participants in tenth-century conspiracies against the king leaves an impression of remarkable constancy. After all, Tacitus had already pointed out that among the Germans both *amicitiae* and *inimicitiae* were inherited from father to son. This was undoubtedly strengthened by the fact that cooperative ties were joined by familial ones. It is, of course, not a Saxon peculiarity, but we should once again stress how closely related all politically relevant forces in Saxony were; it can be said without exaggeration that all were locked into this network of cooperative and familial ties. Admittedly, this did not prevent conflicts, but it did create or facilitate the possibility of regulating them, because comrades and relatives were familiar with the idea of 'compensation through satisfaction'. How this worked can be seen from the example of the members of the Billung family Wichmann and Ekbert, the 'classic' rebels of the Ottonian era. Following their feuds and actions against king or duke, they repeatedly found mediators and advocates, who secured their re-entry into the king's grace or provided them with an opportunity to flee. This 'system' of conflict resolution was so familiar in tenth-century Saxony that in 984 Henry the Quarrelsome's cause was severely

---

[17] *Ibid.* IV, 2.

damaged by his behaviour towards two Saxon counts, Dietrich and Siegbert: he spurned them as they begged forgiveness, barefooted, for earlier offences. They responded appropriately by persuading their friends and relatives to quit Henry's following.

Overall, ties of family and sworn association made a substantial contribution in tenth-century Saxony to the stabilisation of political relationships. This is certainly due to the fact that the structures of lordship within the *gens* were underdeveloped, there being no clearly defined ducal position. The Ottonian kings from Saxony provided the people with an enhanced sense of being an 'imperial people', but such a consciousness had little effect on Saxony's internal political structures. This situation naturally became highly problematic as soon as Saxony ceased to provide the ruler, as happened in 1024 and already in effect in 1002, when Henry II, a Bavarian Liudolfing, ascended the throne. His relationship with the political forces in Saxony was fraught with problems. Substantial parts of the Saxon nobility and episcopate were united in rejecting Henry's policy towards the Elbe Slavs and Poland, and this led to more or less open conflicts throughout his reign. Henry's measures towards 'centralisation of governmental power in the Reich' thus inevitably met with severe constraints in Saxony.[18] It is symptomatic of this that in 1020 Duke Bernard II 'moved all Saxony with him in rebellion against the king'.[19] Bernard's rebellion had no consequences for him, for Archbishop Unwan of Hamburg-Bremen and Henry's wife Kunigunde were able to mediate a peace without any diminution of the Billungs' possessions and rights. Once more we find the characteristics of Ottonian ruling practice, which owed more to mediation and royal clemency than the assertion of claims to power. But this already prefigures the severe conflicts between the Saxons and the Salian rulers, in which the claims of the Salians to lordship and the quite different customs of the Saxons clashed openly. This clash between hierarchical and cooperative principles and structures of lordship culminated in the 'civil war' under Henry IV and Henry V, but these kings remained unable to destroy the established organisational forms of the Saxons. In the Saxon wars under the Salians we again hear of the *conventicula* and *colloquia* of secular and ecclesiastical magnates, which led to *coniurationes*, in other words of cooperative forms of organisation, without the duke's playing a decisive role. Henry the Lion was ultimately to fail in the face of this inheritance.

---

[18] See the title of the article by Weinfurter (1986).
[19] 'totam secum ad rebellandum cesari movit Saxoniam': Adam of Bremen, *Gesta* II, 48.

SAXON RELATIONS WITH THE ELBE SLAVS

Conquest and incorporation?

For a long time German historiography depicted the politics practised by the Ottonians and Saxons towards their Slav neighbours as a particularly dynamic aspect of the 'German eastward movement', while the historians of the Slav states took the same subject as the basis for a diagnosis of an aggressive 'German drive to the east'. For the Ottonian period it was established that the kings had had a plan of expansion which aimed at extending the Reich at least as far as the Oder, in other words to incorporate the countless small Slav peoples between Elbe and Oder or Neisse. Scholars assumed that these expansionary plans were accompanied by a plan of missionary activity, as developed and realised by Otto the Great in particular, with his foundation of an archbishopric at Magdeburg and of suffragan bishoprics at Meissen, Zeitz, Merseburg, Brandenburg and Havelberg. Just as Charles the Great simultaneously Christianised the Saxons and incorporated them into his empire, so the Ottonians and their helpers are supposed to have intended to act similarly towards the Elbe Slavs, perhaps even towards the already Christianised Poland and Bohemia. By contrast with Charles the Great, however, the plans of the tenth century met with little success.

As early as the nineteenth century German historiography had sought and found an explanation for this in the rulers' Italian policies, which had absorbed essential energies of both the German Reich and its rulers and distracted them from the national tasks awaiting them in the east. It is certainly true that the results of both expansion and mission were only modest. The well-known Slav uprising of 983 largely destroyed what had been established before that date; the episcopal sees of Brandenburg and Havelberg remained orphaned until the twelfth century. Only in the south did Ottonian lordship in the Slav regions have some permanence. Astonishingly, succeeding kings did not make any serious effort to wipe out this disgrace. In spite of a few military actions it may be doubted whether the last Ottonian rulers even had such a recuperation as their primary goal. Otto III enhanced the position of both the Polish and the Hungarian rulers through some spectacular actions, and was prepared to concede them an independent church organisation by helping with the foundation of their own archbishoprics. Henry II by contrast concluded an alliance with the pagan Liutizi in 1003 against the Polish ruler, probably entailing a renunciation of missionary activity.[20] The last two Ottonian rulers thus did not orientate themselves according to the plans which scholars have assumed to

---

[20] Brun of Querfurt, *Epistola ad Heinricum regem*, ed. Karwasińka, pp. 101ff.

have motivated their predecessors, and in consequence contributed not a little to the poor balance-sheet – seen from a nationalistic perspective – of the Ottonians' eastern policy.

This in sum is the dominant view of Ottonian eastern policy. Since the 1960s there have been strenuous efforts to write about the situation along the German–Slav borders as a history of relations, to shift attention away from confrontation towards varied exchange and a neighbourly living together. This reorientation was important and justified, but it concentrated largely on other themes of German–Slav history; the older view of Ottonian eastward expansion was not explicitly replaced by a new assessment. One may well ask, however, whether it really corresponds to the political conceptions of the tenth century to see expansion, extending of borders and incorporation of the Elbe Slavs, perhaps even the Poles, as a major goal of Ottonian and Saxon policy. If that had really been so, we should have to ask why the military might of the European hegemonial power was unable to conquer and incorporate the small Slav tribes along the eastern border. One answer is readily available: it was not brought to bear. Although this may seem at first sight surprising, the Ottonian rulers did indeed refrain from applying their Reich's military power and potential to eastward expansion. 'Imperial expeditions' eastward, by analogy with Italian expeditions in which forces from the whole Reich partici-pated, did not exist in the Ottonian period, apart from Henry II's wars against the Poles. Military conflict with the Elbe Slavs was essentially a matter for the Saxons, and as far as we can see primarily for the Saxons living along the borders. Ottonian rulers from Henry I to Otto III certainly participated in campaigns against the Slavs, but leading Saxon contingents. Even when the Slav uprising of 983 brought the 'bold arch of Ottonian eastern policy', in Brüske's phrase, so to speak to the point of collapse, it was an exclusively Saxon contingent under the leadership of the margraves and of the archbishop of Magdeburg which met the insurgents.[21] In the following decades there is little to be seen of military attempts to reconquer the areas lost in 983.

If the ineffectiveness of the alleged expansion already suggests doubts about its putative dynamism, these are strengthened once one asks how con-quest and incorporation are to be envisaged in concrete terms. There is no echo of the Carolingian model of an exchange of elites based on a newly intro-duced comital system. By contrast with the behaviour of Carolingian armies in Saxony, Saxon contingents never remained for long stretches in the lands of the Elbe Slavs; they returned home successful or unsuccessful, a pattern which hardly suggests an intention to expand permanently.

What expansionary plans can in any case be ascribed to an Ottonian kingship which within the Reich largely did without an administration of its own, and in many respects contented itself with an acknowledgement in principle of its overlordship or primacy, without drawing concrete advantage from such an acknowledgement? Certainly, Ottonian and Saxon eastern policy aimed at recognition of its overlordship by the Slav peoples, which was to find expression in regular tribute-payments. Certainly, Otto the Great undertook considerable efforts to create the preconditions for successful evangelisation of the Elbe Slavs, through founding and endowing bishoprics. Had these peoples become substantially Christianised, their relations with the Ottonian Reich would undoubtedly have had to be rethought, as the examples of Bohemia and Poland show. But conquest and incorporation are notions which characterise the aims and goals of warfare in the early modern or modern period. Their transfer to the political and military conflicts of the medieval period, especially of the tenth century, is distinctly problematic: expanding and conquering rulers like Charles the Great were the exception rather than the rule. Whether Otto I of all people had set himself the task of building up a 'centrally directed and firmly organised and effective administration' in the lands of the Elbe Slavs is something which has to be proved in detail and not merely assumed,[22] not least because such an assumption is difficult to sustain, given the other limiting conditions affecting Ottonian lordship.

If we repeatedly hear about campaigns, surrenders, payments of tribute, submissions and recognition of overlordship, followed by renewed conflicts and submissions, without our being able to detect any steps towards more permanent incorporation, then we must ask whether the basic aim of Ottonian rulers was not precisely to secure this recognition of overlordship, though there was certainly also a missionary aim, pursued with varying degrees of intensity. The dubious role played by the medieval eastern policy of Germany in the political arguments and practice of the twentieth century, from the Weimar Republic through the Third Reich to the period after the Second World War, makes it essential to ask whether the situation along the eastern border in the tenth century has not been fundamentally misinterpreted. In what follows, the sources – not in any case numerous – will be interrogated again to see what they actually have to report about relations between Saxons and Elbe Slavs. The aim is to show that contemporary reports describe the conflicts using categories which leave little room for concepts like expansion and incorporation.

---

[22] Ludat (1968/1982), p. 46.

Border warfare: submission, tribute, reprisals, peace

The situation along the border between Saxons and Elbe Slavs, which had always been characterised by plundering expeditions on both sides, changed after Henry I became king for a specific reason: the Slavs east of the Elbe served as a testing ground for the troops, in particular mounted soldiers, whom Henry was training for a defence against the Hungarians following his nine years' truce with them in 926. The years 928 and 929 saw a campaign by Henry against the Hevelli with the conquest of the Brandenburg, another against the Daleminzi followed by the erection of the fortification at Meissen, a counter-attack by the Redarii leading to the destruction of the fortification at Walsleben, the destruction of a Slav army in the battle of Lenzen under the leadership of the 'legate' Bernard and his 'colleague' Thietmar, and finally a campaign by Henry against the Bohemians. According to Widukind,[23] Henry I did not repudiate the truce with the Hungarians until he had sufficient warriors trained in mounted combat.

That such conflicts followed different principles from those customary in the feuds of an aristocratic society can be seen from two examples. After the conquest of the fortification Jahna, the Saxons killed all the adults, and took off the young boys and girls into captivity, meaning slavery. In Merseburg Henry installed a legion formed of thieves and robbers. He remitted their punishment and gave them the instruction to undertake as many plundering expeditions against the Slavs as possible.

We can see a similar difference under Otto the Great. In October 955, immediately after the victory at the Lechfeld, Otto moved with Saxon contingents against the Wends under their *princeps* Stoinef, who by this time was harbouring the Billung brothers Wichmann and Ekbert, members of the Saxon high nobility and relatives of the royal house. We know the details of this campaign from the extensive account given by Widukind of Corvey.[24] After the victory, in which Stoinef was killed, the Slav leader's head was hacked off and stuck on a pole on the battlefield; seven hundred prisoners were beheaded. Stoinef's adviser's eyes were gouged out, his tongue was torn from his mouth, and he was left helpless among the dead. The cruel treatment may be explained in part by the massacre carried out by a previous Slav raiding-party, which had preceded Otto the Great's reprisal expedition. Duke Hermann had ordered the garrison of a fortification to surrender to its Slav besiegers under Wichmann's leadership on condition that the free and their families should have safe-conduct, and only the slaves should be left to the Slavs. However, during the departure there were clashes, and the Slavs promptly killed all the males and

---

[23] Widukind, *Res gestae Saxonicae* I, 38. [24] *Ibid.* III, 52–5.

took off the women and children into captivity. But this explains the cruelties only in part. One must also bear in mind that the normal restraint shown in dealings with relatives, fellow-members of a caste or people, and Christians, did not apply to dealings with the Slavs.

Widukind's account of the negotiations between Otto and Stoinef is given much space, and it shows that the campaign aimed not at incorporation but rather at satisfaction or revenge. The first step was that a Slav embassy appeared before Otto, and offered that the Slavs would pay tribute as usual, but would exercise lordship in their lands themselves; otherwise they would fight. Otto answered that he was denying them peace only because they were not prepared to render satisfaction for their misdeed. Then he laid waste his opponents' territory, but not without in turn sending an embassy to Stoinef, led by no less a person than Margrave Gero. Otto's offer was this: if Stoinef would submit, Otto would be his friend and not treat him as an enemy. It should be stressed that here a pact of friendship was being offered to a heathen Slav *princeps*. The friendship was not to eliminate all traces of lordship: a surrender, a *deditio* was to precede the grant of friendship. Yet such behaviour does not suggest a plan of conquest.[25]

That rituals of friendship and treacherous cruelty were found side by side in the conflicts between Saxons and Elbe Slavs can also be demonstrated from Gero's 'friendship banquet', in which he had thirty Slav princes killed while drunk. Widukind excuses this act with the argument that Gero was here merely anticipating a trick intended by the Slavs themselves, who planned Gero's death.[26] Quite apart from the question of whether these accusations are justified, it is noteworthy that the rituals of peace and friendship also had a place alongside bitter conflicts. The boundary conditions of these conflicts included situations in which Gero could invite thirty Slav princes to a *convivium* or Otto I become the *amicus* of the Christian duke of the Poles, Miesco I, and make a similar offer to the pagan Stoinef.

Nevertheless, contacts between the leading strata of the Slavs and the Saxons were, taken as a whole, very limited. Only for a few Slav magnates were Christianity and the Saxon alliance attractive enough for them to surrender their traditional beliefs and their local ties. One rare example is the Hevellic prince Tugumir, held in prison by the Saxons since the time of Henry I. He finally allowed himself to be bribed to betray his own lordship to the Saxons; the entry of his death in the necrology of Möllenbeck shows that he must have become a Christian.[27] Pretending to have fled from prison, he returned home, had his nephew and rival for lordship treacherously killed, and then submitted himself and his people to Otto's lordship. According to Widukind, his example

---

[25] *Ibid.* III, 53–5.   [26] *Ibid.* II, 20.
[27] *Das Nekrolog von Möllenbeck*, ed. Schrader, p. 355 (17 May).

was followed by all the Slav tribes up to the Oder, who 'were ready to pay tribute'.[28] Here again we must stress the distinction between payments of tribute and the associations evoked by the word incorporation. Widukind's account makes very clear that the Slav tribes were generally prepared to pay tribute, but the question was whether they would have accepted more wide-ranging restrictions on their freedom.

Apart from Tugumir, we hear of only a small number of cases of collaboration with the Saxons. The normal function of marriages in strengthening peaceful ties was here ruled out by the impossibility of marriages between pagans and Christians. We know nothing about the background to Otto's liaison with a noble Slav woman, the mother of the later archbishop of Mainz, which could take us further here. Only once do we hear of such a marriage plan in Adam of Bremen's account, which he explicitly describes as based on oral tradition.[29] A Slav duke is said to have sought the Saxon duke Bernard I's niece for his son in marriage, and this was agreed to. The Wend in return provided a thousand mounted soldiers for Duke Bernard's contingent on the Italian expedition, where they almost all fell. Nevertheless, Margrave Dietrich frustrated the planned marriage with the remark that the duke's kinswoman was not to be given to a dog. This, according to Adam (and to Helmold of Bosau, who follows him), was the reason behind the great Slav uprising of 983. It was certainly not the only reason, but the anecdote demonstrates the Saxon attitude very clearly; at all events the peace-bringing function of marriage was little seen in relations between Saxons and Slavs. The unnamed Slav duke may well have been the Abodrite Mistui, who according to Thietmar had a *capellanus* Avico in his entourage,[30] and so presumably was not wholly opposed to Christianity, which would certainly have favoured the marriage proposals. If our fragments of information do not deceive us, then participation in the uprising of 983 and a receptive attitude to Christianity were not mutually exclusive; certainly Mistui appeared only a year later at an assembly held by Henry the Quarrelsome in Quedlinburg.

In assessing the nature of these conflicts we may further adduce those Saxon magnates who fought on the side of the Slavs. These included not only the Billung brothers Wichmann and Ekbert, already mentioned, but also a Saxon noble named Kizo who went over to the Liutizi out of annoyance with Margrave Dietrich. It has been argued that the *inclitus miles* Kizo (Christian), who came from the Merseburg region, was a member of Margrave Gero's kindred. This would show a remarkable similarity of behaviour among members of the two leading margraval families, Billungs and Geronids: in each case relatives of the margrave go over to the Slavs as a result of internal

---

[28] 'tributis regalibus se subiugarunt': Widukind, *Res gestae Saxonicae* II, 21.

[29] Adam of Bremen, *Gesta* II, 42.   [30] Thietmar, *Chronicon* IV, 2.

Saxon conflicts, because they feel that they are not able to get justice in Saxony.

Still more significant is the fact that these magnates were entrusted by the Slavs with important command positions. Wichmann led Slav attacks against Saxony and against Miesco I of Poland; Kizo was in charge of the garrison in the Brandenburg, whence he also led attacks against Saxony. Even more interesting than the trust and esteem shown by the Slavs towards these 'traitors' is the fact that they were not condemned by other Saxon magnates for their behaviour. Wichmann and Ekbert were able to flee to Hugh of Francia after the massacre of Stoinef's army in 955, until no less a person than Archbishop Brun of Cologne secured Ekbert's pardon from Otto the Great. We can observe this member of the Billung family enjoying unrestricted rights of political action in Saxony in the period which followed. Wichmann, by contrast, who like his brother had previously been declared a 'public enemy',[31] was reconciled with Otto by Margrave Gero. Even after he once again broke the reconciliation oath he had taken, Gero allowed him to go off once more to the Slavs, because he saw that Wichmann was in fact guilty. In other words, Gero had deliberately prevented Wichmann's condemnation. Kizo offers a similar story. After he had again changed sides in 993 and submitted himself and the Brandenburg to Otto III's lordship, he was allowed to retain his position and given support in his defence against the Liutizi. It was one of his vassals, with the Slav name Boliliut, who made himself master of the fortification during Kizo's absence; Kizo was killed trying to reconquer his position. Thietmar of Merseburg, who describes the episode at length, makes no criticism of Kizo's behaviour; he explicitly allows him the right to change sides 'to come to his right'.[32]

All details of the border wars as revealed by Widukind and Thietmar point in the same direction: the wars were an exclusively Saxon affair, concerned with submission – recognition of overlordship and payment of tribute – but equally often with revenge, for every attack demanded reprisals. Opponents were treated savagely and cruelly, often treacherously; but alongside this we also find negotiations, offers and conclusions of peace agreements, rituals of solidarity and so forth, which show that *all* the forms of conflict familiar from the early middle ages were practised here. The only thing we do not hear of explicitly in the narrative sources is any plan to incorporate the Elbe Slavs into the Ottonian Reich, or of measures taken by the kings to do so.

---

[31] Widukind, *Res gestae Saxonicae* III, 60.   [32] Thietmar, *Chronicon* IV, 22.

Organisation: *legates, margraves,* burgwards, *bishoprics*

As was said at the opening of this section, it has been customary even in recent scholarship to talk of the 'introduction of a strict military, administrative and ecclesiastical organisation' intended by Otto the Great to produce a 'definitive subjugation and incorporation into the Reich' of the districts east of the Elbe.[33] The sources offer no specific account of when these organisational innovations were introduced; the conventional view has been derived from various indications offered by the sources, which require a critical examination.

The first margraves we meet in the tenth century are Hermann Billung and Gero, both appointed by Otto the Great in 936 and 937, though here not yet called margrave. The Saxon reaction to these appointments shows that the offices were not new ones; indeed, relatives of the appointees, the Billung Wichmann the Elder and Otto's own half-brother Thankmar, displayed irritation at having been passed over for positions to which they felt they had greater claims. The two new office-holders succeeded the Saxon magnates Bernard and Siegfried, whose position is described in the sources as a *legatio*. This is probably to be understood as a military command in a border region, as exercised for example by Bernard at the battle of Lenzen in 929. Besides *legatio* (*legatus*) Widukind of Corvey[34] also used the term *princeps militiae* to describe Hermann Billung's position. Until the death of these two 'margraves' Hermann and Gero, in 973 and 965 respectively, both narrative and charter sources use a whole range of titles for them, among others *comes, marchio, dux, dux et marchio*, but there is no reason to suppose that royal reorganisation had changed in any way the tasks assigned to these magnates. In other words, the sources do not suggest that Otto introduced a 'margraval organisation'. We have absolutely no information about any powers the two may have possessed over and beyond their military commands – whether, for example, they also exercised jurisdiction or command over other counts in the border regions. The two 'officials' gained their high profile exclusively through military activities, which they evidently carried out with a high degree of independence.

There is also considerable uncertainty about what happened to Gero's sphere of office after his death. We find no fewer than six counts from the area under Gero's command with the title of *marchio* in the period following his death, a fact very difficult to interpret. The sources give no indication of why a single successor to Gero was not appointed; but to deduce that the situation was now so secure that a single leader was no longer needed is hardly plausible in view of the uprising of 983. We do not even know whether the various margraves were appointed by the king or not. Even after the deaths of the various

---

[33] Ludat (1968/82), p. 46.   [34] Widukind, *Res gestae Saxonicae* II, 4.

marchiones we cannot observe the appointment of successors. Rather, we find from the beginning of the eleventh century that three large margravates had evolved out of the area formerly under Gero's lordship: the North march, the East march and the march of Meissen. The transition phase following Gero's death does not therefore suggest that precise regions of office had been laid down in a royal plan which would have allowed a smooth succession following the death of an office-holder.

The military independence of the margraves also argues against a carefully worked out royal plan of expansion. Even substantial campaigns were not necessarily cleared with the king in advance, as we can see in 972, when Margrave Hodo attacked the Polish duke Miesco, even though the latter was *amicus imperatoris* and a tribute-payer. Otto the Great used messengers to threaten both participants in the conflict with the withdrawal of his grace, if they should not keep the peace until his return from Italy. Around the same time the margraves Hermann and Dietrich made peace with the Redarii and kept it even when Otto sent written orders from Italy to the contrary.[35] These incidents hardly speak for royal organisation and planning of activities east of the Elbe; they tend rather to support the view arrived at in the previous section of local forces taking *ad hoc* and repressive measures.

Interestingly enough, one of the most 'well known' of these independent actions probably derives from a misunderstanding by Thietmar of Merseburg. He describes how Margrave Gero subjugated the Polish duke Miesco and his followers to imperial *ditio*.[36] This statement, which scholars have discussed at length and controversially, is in all probability a result of Thietmar's misreading of Widukind.[37] Thietmar simply summarises Widukind's cc. 66–8 in two sentences: Gero subjugated the Lausitz and Miesco; Hermann Billung Selibur and Mistui. But Widukind writes in c. 66 that Gero returned Wichmann to the Slavs to save him from being condemned, and Wichmann twice defeated Miesco; his formulation makes it easy to confuse Gero and Wichmann. There is no reason to suppose that Thietmar is here drawing on his own knowledge of a campaign by Gero against Miesco, and this may be struck from the record.

The origins, powers and tasks of the margravates are thus noticeably more complex than the picture offered by previous scholarship. This is even more true of the assumption that Otto the Great introduced a *burgward* organisation after the marches had been set up. Certainly, the word *burgwardium* or *burgwardum* is found in the sources from the middle of the tenth century onwards. Certainly, fortifications had a central function for the population living in their vicinity; in times of need the population could take refuge there and they were also obliged to perform services and make renders. Naturally, such an organ-

---

[35] *Ibid.* III, 70.   [36] Thietmar, *Chronicon* II, 14.   [37] Widukind, *Res gestae Saxonicae* III, 66.

isation was particularly important in the marcher regions, so that the map drawn by Walter Schlesinger of the *burgwards* shows a concentration which is impressive but hardly surprising. The question is rather how we are to visualise the organisational measures taken by Otto the Great to install the *burgward* system as a miniature version of the entire Ottonian state structure.[38] From which groups were the garrisons recruited? Where did the commandants come from? Who determined the estates and services for the maintenance of the warriors? Such a bundle of organisational measures would have required considerable activity and the participation of significant numbers of people, most prominently the members of the Saxon nobility, in their planning and execution. But such plans have left absolutely no traces in the sources. Moreover, the fact that Otto donated several of these *burgwards* to the newly founded bishoprics does not suggest that there was any kind of strict organisation for the purpose of expansion; it would have been hollowed out as soon as it was introduced had that been the case.

By contrast we do find organisation and planning in another aspect of eastern politics, which must be set against the facts sketched so far: ecclesiastical organisation. Scholarship has tended to see Otto's missionary and church policy as a part of his expansion policy. Ottonian missionary activity cannot be treated as a whole in a chapter devoted to Saxony; but there is no doubt that it is the history of the episcopal foundations which provides the most detailed knowledge of property-holding and lordship in the regions east of the Elbe. The foundation charters for Havelberg and Brandenburg show that Otto the Great was able to transfer *civitates* and tithes in regions of Slav settlement to the new churches. Later gifts to Magdeburg confirm the impression that the ruler disposed of a whole range of possessions and rights east of the Elbe; that, in other words, the idea of state boundaries in our modern sense is quite anachronistic for this period. But equally anachronistic would be any impression gained from such information that these rights and possessions were an index of the success of Ottonian expansion. To deduce from the ability to found and endow bishoprics in the regions of the Elbe Slavs that there must have been an intention to expand will not work; at precisely the same time (948) three Danish missionary bishoprics were founded as suffragans of Hamburg-Bremen, but no one has deduced similar expansionary intentions towards the Danish kingdom from these foundations. Because Charles the Great had an interlinked strategy of mission and conquest in his Saxon wars, we do not have to assume that this must also have been so in the Ottonian period.

There are a number of indications in the sources that ecclesiastical and military activities were not coordinated with each other, rather that the forces

[38] Cf. Schlesinger (1937/61).

involved frequently blocked and disturbed each other's activities. Here we may mention the energetic resistance by the bishop of Halberstadt and the archbishop of Mainz to the plan to erect an archbishopric in Magdeburg. We may also mention Otto's stern warning from Italy to the Margraves Wigger, Wigbert and Gunther that they should obey the instructions of the new archbishop and furthermore should endow the new bishops of Zeitz, Merseburg and Meissen adequately, so that these should not be taken to be poor peasants. The fact that this warning was evidently much needed gives a deep insight into the contemporary situation, and it fits in well with later ecclesiastical complaints that it was the cruelty and greed of the Saxon margraves which prevented missionary successes and in the last resort was responsible for the great Slav uprising of 983. The foundation of the archbishopric of Magdeburg was certainly part of an organisational conception due in essence to Otto I and realised by him in Italy. What are lacking are convincing demonstrations that this conception was only a part of a greater plan of expansion.

SAXON HISTORIOGRAPHY IN THE TENTH CENTURY

The works of so-called 'Ottonian' historiography, to which we owe most of our knowledge of the problems discussed so far, were almost all written in Saxony, the core region of the Ottonian Reich. To characterise them as 'Ottonian' implies that the works were written from the perspective of the king. But this assessment conceals essential characteristics of these works. More recently there has been a strong tendency to ask how far they witness to others' opinions and positions, not identical with positions of the ruling house. The idea of an Ottonian ruling house in any case plays down the divergent forces operating within this 'house'. The new view of 'Ottonian' historiography proceeds from the observation that almost all works of Ottonian historiography were written within ecclesiastical communities – Corvey, Quedlinburg, Gandersheim, Nordhausen, Merseburg – and often at crucial phases in the development of these communities. We are thus confronted with a basic question about the function of such historical writing, which is probably much more linked with and aimed at influencing its own present than one normally assumes of historical writing. In Ottonian Saxony, historiography allowed forces to articulate themselves whose opinions and interests were very different from those held by the Ottonian rulers.

The anonymous Lives of the Ottonian Queen Matilda, written in her foundation of Nordhausen, provide a very specific view of the history of the Ottonian dynasty. The older work, written around 974, is aimed at Otto II; the younger was intended for Henry II, which led to the rewriting of important passages. Henry II's direct ancestors were transformed in the younger Life into central figures in Matilda's life. Her whole love and care was devoted to them, as were her mourning and her memory. There is thus a remarkable adjusting of historical writing to accommodate its addressee. But both Lives have a central theme in common: Matilda devoted all her energy to ensuring that the future of her foundation of Nordhausen should be secured by all kinds of legal protection. She did this, allegedly, with the understanding and close cooperation of her son Otto the Great. For – and this is also a central message of the works – he had learned that the preservation and well-being of his rule depended in decisive measure on whether he supported his mother's attempts to found and endow ecclesiastical communities using her dower lands. Not until his rule met with failures and crises and he had been warned by his wife Edith did the king change his behaviour towards his mother.

This remarkable pointing up of Ottonian family history, accentuating the discord between mother and son with all its consequences, becomes comprehensible only when one realises that the two Lives were written at a point when new queens were about to receive their dower. In the case of Otto II and his wife Theophanu, the dower charter has survived in the form of the famous purple dowry charter.[39] In this we read that Theophanu's *dos* includes Nordhausen, and it is stated explicitly that this means everything which Queen Matilda possessed there. This threatened the monastic community in Nordhausen, should the new queen decide to disturb Matilda's work. To prevent this the Nordhausen community composed the Life of Matilda and dedicated it to Otto II. After the warning implicit in the Life had been successful, the procedure was repeated when Queen Kunigunde, wife of Henry II, came to the throne. In other words, a spiritual community used spiritual means in a position of existential threat by depicting its founder's life as an *exemplum* for the new queen, and it reinforced this admonition with the clear warning that action contrary to Matilda's intentions would bring down God's anger and punishment.

The depiction of the early history of Gandersheim by the nun-poet Hrotsvitha starts with a redirected Annunciation. It was prophesied by no less a person than John the Baptist to Aeda, the mother of the foundress Oda, that her seed should found a monastery, Gandersheim. This would ensure the peace of the Reich, 'as long as its vows are protected by the kings' care'. As a reward for its foundation the family would receive so high a dignity 'that no other of the kings on earth would dare to place himself alongside it in rank and powerful majesty'.[40] This is of course a retrospective prophecy; but we must ask why Hrotsvitha linked the well-being of the Ottonian house so explicitly with the furthering of Gandersheim. Moreover, this theme shapes the

---

[39] D O II 21.   [40] Hrotsvitha, *Primordia coenobii Gandersheimensis*, ed. Homeyer, p. 452.

subsequent account in the *Primordia*. The members of the Liudolfing house are
implored to do everything necessary to secure the safety, the protection and the
material endowment of the monastery. The account lays particular stress on
the appropriate actions of Duke Liudolf and his wife Oda and those of Duke
Otto, all of whom, according to Hrotsvitha, knew very well just how much the
success of their house depended on the merits and prayers of the
Gandersheim nuns. Just as in Nordhausen, so in Gandersheim a clear warning
was issued to the ruler in the form of a historiographical work which tried to
oblige him to follow the example of his ancestors. Hrotsvitha's second work,
the *Gesta Ottonis*, should also be seen in the context of this warning. It was
written at the request of Abbess Gerberga and interestingly enough was to be
laid before Archbishop William of Mainz, Otto's chief opponent in the
Magdeburg question, for his approval. Unfortunately, the fragmentary nature
of the work makes the author's intentions ultimately unclear, but one thing is
certain: the *Gesta* stress the internal crises of Otto's rule and his relatives' uprisings against him. They also depict his opponents very positively, and they stress
repeatedly that it was God's grace alone which rescued Otto from great peril
and preserved his rule. If Otto is again and again compared with David in this
context it must be asked whether the comparisons are intended to be praising
or warning.

The most famous work of 'Ottonian' historiography, Widukind's *Saxon
History*, was dedicated in 967 or 968 to Matilda, abbess of Quedlinburg and
daughter of Otto I. Although each of the three books of the *Saxon History*
begins with a prologue dedicated to Matilda, scholarship has largely ignored
the question of why such a work should have been dedicated to an imperial
daughter, and why this should have happened in the years 967–8. The historical
context of the dedication offers a number of clues. The young Matilda (she was
eleven years old) had been made abbess of Quedlinburg at Otto's request by all
the archbishops and bishops of the kingdom at a great festival in April 966 at
Quedlinburg, before the emperor set out for his third Italian expedition. In the
autumn of 967 his son and co-ruler Otto followed him south. The only
members of the royal house remaining north of the Alps were William of
Mainz and Queen Matilda, with William acting as regent. The old queen fell
seriously ill at the beginning of 968. William hurried to her sick bed, and must
have realised that her death was imminent, but surprisingly he himself died
before the queen at the beginning of March; she followed him on March 14.
The young Abbess Matilda was thus the only member of the royal house left
north of the Alps, and this remained the case for four years. She now had the
task of representing Ottonian rule in Saxony in a very difficult situation. Otto
the Great ordained the foundation of the archbishopric of Magdeburg and its
suffragans of Merseburg, Zeitz and Meissen from Italy; up to the last minute

there had been serious opposition to these plans in Saxony. It was precisely in this situation that Widukind dedicated his *Saxon History* to the abbess; it contained just what she needed in her current position, the knowledge of the past required to be able to rule in Saxony. This was the precise function of the *Saxon History*. It allowed Matilda to act as the highest-ranking person in Saxony, as the *domina imperialis*, because she had been informed about the history of the Saxon people, about her father's and grandfather's achievements, and not least because she knew about the difficulties which her father's decisions, in Saxony in particular, had brought about. For this purpose Widukind included a number of pieces of information really belonging to the *secreta regis*, to that area which a historiographer would normally have discreetly passed over. One must read Widukind's work in the light of the situation in which it was composed in order to understand why it is precisely those things referred to over and over and not others which are dealt with; it was *these* which Matilda had to know about in order to act independently and as a member of the imperial house in Saxony from 968 onwards.

The Quedlinburg annals are equally shaped by their situation. They were written in Henry II's reign, at a time when Quedlinburg lost its former dominant role as a royal centre. Among other things, Henry broke with the Ottonian tradition of celebrating Easter there and hardly visited the place at all, which evidently wounded Quedlinburg sensibilities deeply. These were expressed by the annals in their account of the year 936: Queen Matilda intended to make Quedlinburg a 'kingdom for the gentiles' and had therefore collected only well-born persons, for these seldom go astray.[41] The term *regnum gentibus* is evidently an echo of the title *rex gentium*, 'king of the peoples', used by Widukind for Otto I at the end of his Saxon history.[42] How did this community react to its downgrading by Henry II? None of his actions finds a good word. The annals from 1003 are a drastic demonstration of how openly criticism of a ruler might be practised in a royal monastery. A few examples: 'The king, very downhearted because he had won no good peace, returned with a miserable army and brought the bodies of the dead with him' (1005);[43] 'As the king learned of this he was troubled in his heart and enjoined his men not to leave the matter unavenged. But – I know not for what reason – up to the present so great an anger has not been turned into deeds' (1007).[44] When Henry II chose a different candidate for the archbishopric of Hamburg-Bremen not the one elected by the chapter, the annalist commented on the events as follows: 'But the king's crude ways/ and his thirst for gain, thrust the petitioner back,/ turn from the weeping his gaze.'[45] Henry's Roman expedition of 1014 is summed up thus:

---

[41] *Annales Quedlinburgenses, s.a.* 936, p. 54.   [42] Widukind, *Res gestae Saxonicae* III, 76.

[43] *Annales Quedlinburgenses, s.a.* 1005, p. 78.   [44] *Annales Quedlinburgenses, s.a.* 1007, p. 79.

[45] *Annales Quedlinburgenses, s.a.* 1013, p. 81.

'After he had . . . ordained official matters well, as he thought, and collected huge sums of gold from everywhere, he accelerated his return homewards, though not without inflicting damage on many people'.[46] Such unrestrained criticism of the ruler corresponded completely to the contempt which Henry had showed towards Quedlinburg by staying in Saxony frequently enough but never visiting the place, and by making it no gifts until 1021. It is hardly possible for a community to lose the king's grace and presence more quickly than Quedlinburg did. Seen in the context of other changes which Henry's reign brought with it, such an observation also shows how far he broke with the tradition of his Ottonian ancestors, indeed distanced himself from them. The loss of royal favour did not last for the whole of Henry's reign, however. In 1014 he granted Abbess Adelaide of Quedlinburg the headship of the nunneries of Gernrode and Vreden. In 1021, at last, he attended the consecration of the newly built monastic church at Quedlinburg and made a rich gift to the convent. It can thus hardly be coincidence that the negative comments on Henry II cease from 1014 onwards and that from 1021 the author is once again capable of panegyric descriptions of Henry II's deeds of a kind familiar to us from the early years of Ottonian rule. Historical writing thus reacted directly to changes in the political climate.

To ask about the cause and historical context for the origins of 'Ottonian' historiography is to sharpen one's perception for the specific functions of each of these works; none was written exclusively from the king's perspective, and some were written directly contrary to it. Forces within Saxony with interests not unconditionally identical with those of the rulers could articulate themselves in this way: ecclesiastical communities like Nordhausen, Gandersheim and Quedlinburg, and then a little later Thietmar of Merseburg, who wrote the history of his precarious and threatened bishopric in such a way that it can also be written as a history of the Reich and the Saxon people. Widukind of Corvey wrote not so much as a representative of the oldest monastery in Saxony as of those forces within Saxony who wished to avoid conflicts, and so he took care to instruct the young imperial daughter about positions and patterns of behaviour of which her father would certainly not have approved. Saxon historiography of the tenth century can thus hardly be characterised adequately as 'Ottonian' historiography, still less as 'Ottonian house tradition'. It should rather be seen as formulating the perspectives of forces within Saxony which were certainly not fundamentally opposed to Ottonian kingship but were equally not prepared to identify themselves unreservedly with all the positions and decisions taken by these kings.

---

[46] *Annales Quedlinburgenses, s.a.* 1014, p. 82.

CHAPTER 11

BAVARIA IN THE TENTH AND EARLY ELEVENTH CENTURIES

Herwig Wolfram

THE CAROLINGIAN INHERITANCE

The restoration and expansion of the Frankish empire in the eighth century were possible not least because the ruling Carolingians accepted the existence of the regnal structure of the Franco-Lombard core region of Europe and indeed took this on board as a permanent aspect of Carolingian tradition. The sources distinguish between three kinds of *regna*. In its first sense, *regnum* means the whole Carolingian empire; in its second sense it refers to a Frankish (or the Lombard-Italian) subkingdom; and in the third it denotes a political and regional entity with a name drawn from that of a people living there under a common law. The first two kinds of *regna* were invariably ruled by kings, whereas a *regnum* of the third type might be ruled by kings' sons (with or without a royal title) or by princes without kingly rank. The Carolingian empire was thus a flexible polity built up of prefabricated parts, an organisational form which allowed an imperial extensiveness together with a governmental intensiveness in smaller regions.

The Carolingians had in general to associate their leading men with the government of the empire; the 'imperial aristocracy', to use Gerd Tellenbach's term, were still more entitled to political participation in the *regna* of the third type. Representatives of the most successful aristocratic groupings emerged from the competition for closeness to the king, power and influence as the 'second after the king'. Diplomata and other sources written in the royal entourage never call such magnates anything except *comites* or, in the late Carolingian era, *marchiones*. A *secundus a rege* of this kind might nevertheless acquire a princely position, even in the Carolingian period. Occasionally such a comital or margraval office-holder might even have to take on royal duties, if royal authority had failed or been withdrawn from an area for one reason or another. Thus Odo of Paris and other non-Carolingian 'princes of the Franks' were elected as kings in 888 because on Charles III's death his *regna* 'were deprived of their natural lord'.[1]

---

[1] Regino, *Chronicon, s.a.* 888.

One of the most prominent *regna* of the third type was Bavaria, which had had the status of a *regnum* even in pre-Carolingian times and had consolidated this position in the course of the ninth century. In the summer of 814 Louis the Pious had organised the Frankish subkingdoms, among which Bavaria was named for the first time. Three years later he issued the *ordinatio imperii*. Louis' namesake, known to historians under a title whose inaccuracy is sanctioned by tradition as 'Louis the German', received as his kingdom 'Bavaria, the Carinthians, the Bohemians and the Avars, as well as the Slavs who live in the east of Bavaria'.[2] In other words, Louis became king of two regionally defined *regna*: the Bavaria which had been ruled over by the Agilolfing duke Tassilo III and the peoples of the Bavarian Eastland, which included semi-autonomous Slav peoples and the dependent Avar khaganate on the middle Danube. Between 830 and 833 Louis the German even used the title *rex Baioariorum* in the charters he issued in his own name, so that Bavaria received the highest form of political recognition for the first time.

In 833 the three adult sons of Louis the Pious rebelled against their father, and Louis the German took on the *regnum in orientali Francia*.[3] This 'kingdom in eastern Francia' lay largely east of the Rhine, and corresponded roughly to the term *Germania* as used in classical literature. The struggles over Louis the Pious' inheritance led Louis the German to set up a Bavarian viceroyship, a *secundus a rege* ('second after the king'); he and his immediate successors, however, remained strong enough to keep the holders of this office in their places. Kings' sons and princes established themselves in one of the two parts of the Bavarian double *regnum* in accordance with, not against the will of, the east Frankish king. After Louis the German's death in 876 Bavaria was briefly reunited under his oldest son Carloman. However, the new king conferred the Bavarian Eastland on his illegitimate son Arnulf 'of Carinthia', in much the same way as he himself had held it during his father's lifetime. It was from here that Arnulf set out with a powerful army of Bavarians and Slavs in 887 via Regensburg to Frankfurt, where in November of that year he was set up as king. The *regnum* in the Bavarian Eastland had grown noticeably in strength. The person who held it was not just able to take over first parts and then the whole of old Bavaria, as in Carloman's time; its possessor could now also become the heir to the whole of Louis the German's kingdom, provided that he moved quickly to take control of the region around the confluence of Rhine and Main, and so dispose of the most important transport routes of the east Frankish kingdom and of the royal fisc in Rhenish Franconia.

On 8 December 899 Arnulf, who had been crowned emperor in Rome nearly four years earlier, died at Regensburg; he was succeeded by Louis 'the

---

[2] For the terminology see Eggert (1973).
[3] The title used in DD L G 13 and following diplomata.

Child', who was at the time not quite seven years old. In Bavaria a certain Luitpold seized the initiative and prevented a power vacuum from arising, thus showing both fidelity to the Carolingian house to which he was related and an eye to the main chance. Luitpold, whose family is known to historians as the 'Luitpoldings', had to share power with other magnates, but stood at their head. Already in the year which followed Arnulf's death Luitpold began campaigning against the Hungarians on his own initiative and erecting fortifications against them. In the summer of 907 he took the offensive against these enemies, who had already conquered a great part of the Bavarian east; on 4 July 907 he lost the battle, a Bavarian army and his life near Bratislava on the Danube. Bavarian influence on the king and the rest of the east Frankish kingdom declined sharply after the battle; Louis the Child shifted his principal residence from Regensburg to Frankfurt. The Carolingian period had already come to an end in Bavaria before the east Frankish royal house died out on the death of Louis the Child on 24 September 911.

Like other similar magnates in the other *regna* of the east Frankish kingdom, Luitpold had achieved the status of a prince in Bavaria. In spite of his catastrophic failure as leader of the Bavarian army, Luitpold's position was so strong that his son Arnulf was able not only to succeed him but to rise to the rank of a quasi-royal prince of the Bavarians, a *dux Bavvariorum*, a basis from which he too could undertake a 'new start on the basis of Carolingian tradition'.[4] This tradition included a rich variety of possibilities, contradictions and challenges. It corresponded to Carolingian tradition that the rulers of Bavaria were to intervene in Italian affairs even before those of Alemannia did so, and even to seek the imperial crown, just as Carloman, the oldest son of Louis the German, had tried to do and as his son Arnulf was to succeed in doing. But Louis the German had also given his second son Louis a kingdom which in 876 had already united Franconia and Saxony and provided a basis for possession of Lotharingia, a decision which anticipated the political situation under Conrad I and Henry I. A further aspect of Carolingian tradition was that of the unanointed king in east Francia, whereas the other kings in the *regna* of the second type had generally been anointed. So also were the settlements between these *regna* on the basis of treaties of friendship, which the kings made with each other for the preservation of peace; in addition to these, the Carolingian feudal system came to establish 'interregnal' ties. Avar, Slav, Lombard and Breton princes became the men of Carolingian kings. The end of the ninth century also saw vassalitic treaties within the Frankish core lands which enabled a Carolingian ruler to establish himself as high king, as *primus inter pares* among his own kin or non-Carolingian competitors alike. Rule over the church

---

[4] Cf. the title of Althoff and Keller (1985).

was a self-evident part of Carolingian kingship. The episcopate preferred on the whole to be a part of a supra-regional regnal church rather than of a church confined to a regional *regnum* of the third type. The four older archbishoprics in the east Frankish kingdom were here concerned not least with their own rank in the court chapel and the royal chancery. Mainz stood for Franco-Saxon unity, while from the time of Carloman's rule onwards Salzburg could be certain of pre-eminence within Bavaria or any east Frankish kingdom dominated by Bavaria. Trier and Cologne disputed pre-eminence within Lotharingia.

Tensions between norm and reality continued in existence in Bavaria. To take only two key examples: it was the king, according to Bavarian law, who nominated the duke, and yet as late as 1002 King Henry II could refer to the Bavarians' right of election, which forbade him an independent decision.[5] Already in the Agilolfing period the dukes had governed the church, and yet the Bavarian law contained a provision that the king installed the bishop and that the people elected him.[6] Counts and counties, feudalism and royal vassals, military and court service were equally part of the Carolingian tradition in the various *regna*, and were to be particularly significant in regions like Bavaria, where such institutions had merged with or overlaid native traditions. 'Comital organisation proved to be one of the most essential instruments of royal government of the kingdom, the fundamental organisational unit of the kingdom in matters of administration, justice, and the raising of armies'.[7] The beginnings of Carolingian feudalism are to be found in Bavaria in the late Agilolfing era. There were Bavarian vassals of the Frankish rulers both within and beyond the *regnum*. By the second half of the ninth century at the latest the relations between the east Frankish king and the Slav princes were also organised on feudo-vassalitic lines.

A further tradition of Carolingian Bavaria was its polyethnic structures based on Roman, German and Slav traditions, and its openness to the south and west. Bavaria was the only east Frankish *regnum* which had frontiers on to both the Slavic world and the areas of Romance speech. It was Bavarians who were the first to be termed *Nemci* by their Slav neighbours, and they were to be termed 'Germans' (*Theotisci*) by the Lombards of northern Italy long before this name came to denote all 'Germans'.[8]

Among the Slav neighbours of Carolingian Bavaria the Moravians had formed the most powerful polity both in political and in ecclesiastical terms. It had not been possible to conquer the Moravian kingdom; all attempts to treat the successors to the Avars north of the Danube in the same way as the Bohemian, Pannonian or Dalmatian Slavs had failed. Louis the German's counts were left to

---

[5] Thietmar, *Chronicon* v, 14.   [6] *Lex Baiwariorum* i, 10.   [7] Schulze (1973), p. 347.
[8] Wolfram (1991).

master the situation using their own resources; yet all those who tried to establish peace on the middle Danube with the help of negotiations and treaties sooner or later came to seem like rebels in the eyes of the east Frankish rulers. Numerous counts lost their positions, but the king's son Carloman and the comital generation which succeeded the 'unfaithful' ones did not do any better. Bloody and bitter campaigns alternated with peace agreements until the Hungarians destroyed the Moravian kingdom, by 906 at the latest.

The 'Avars, who are now called Hungarians',[9] had thus come to replace their predecessors, which meant for the Bavarians that they were to be combatted with all the means available, but also that one sat down at the same table with them, and that not just in order to murder them treacherously but also to negotiate honestly and conclude treaties with them. In this way it was possible for Duke Arnulf, who had defeated the Hungarians three times in 909, 910 and 913, to go into exile among them in 914 and then again in 916, which presupposes the existence of a peace agreement at the very least. The same holds true for 937, when the Hungarians 'peacefully' marched through Bavaria on their way west. The phrase 'the raging sword of the heathen' was used on the Danube as well as elsewhere,[10] but it was only in the distant hinterland that the Hungarian was seen as a 'Scythian', as a member of a people whose name called forth apocalyptic associations which, significantly, were being noted for the first time west of the Rhine in this period.

The Bavarian view of the treaty which Charles III had made with the Northmen at Asselt in 882 reveals a similarly nuanced view of 'heathens and barbarians'. The Mainz version of the *Annals of Fulda* saw in it the shameful capitulation of a weak non-ruler advised by a traitor, Liutward of Vercelli; the Regensburg continuation stressed the friendship between the two sides, who spent two days in joyous conviviality and underlined the peace treaty with mutual gifts.[11] Not to defame the enemy from the east as the product of hell, or to do so only half-heartedly, an attitude already adopted by Tassilo III and his wife Luitpirc, and to treat him as an object of international law, to use modern terminology, made him into an enemy like any other; 'any other' in this context might mean a Frankish king like Charles the Great, Conrad I or Henry I. In other words, not much distinction was drawn between Avars and Hungarians on the one hand or an opponent who came from the equally foreign parts of Franconia and Saxony. As late as 937 the view was taken in Regensburg that 'the Saxon Henry had invaded the land of the Bavarians as an enemy', and that before him King Conrad I had entered the country 'not as a king but as an enemy'.[12] This means that it was not a question of treachery or high treason

---

[9] *Annales Fuldenses, s.a.* 894, 896, 900, pp. 125, 129, 134.

[10] *Fragmentum de Arnolfo duce Bavvariae*, ed. Reindel.   [11] *Annales Fuldenses, s.a.* 882, pp. 98–9, 108–9.

[12] 'Non regaliter sed hostiliter': *Fragmentum de Arnulfo duce Bavvariae*, ed. Reindel.

when Berthold of Reisenburg, the grandson of Duke Arnulf, is said to have warned the Hungarians of the approach of Otto I and his army before the battle of the Lechfeld on 10 August 955; it was merely part of an unsuccessful alternative to the policies successfully pursued by the Saxon Otto which so impressed both his contemporaries and later observers. It is not surprising that these later observers should have attributed a rapid and terrible end to Berthold, but in reality he was still alive in 976 and was treated respectfully by Otto II, the son of the 'betrayed' king of 955, even though he had evidently supported Duke Henry II (the Quarrelsome) and thus once again resisted royal authority. The Bavarians of the tenth century neither belonged to a kingdom of Germany, which did not yet exist, nor were capable of betraying an equally non-existent German national consciousness.

ARNULF OF BAVARIA, 907–37

It was not an accident that Arnulf, 'who came from the stock of emperors and kings',[13] bore the name of the last Carolingian emperor, whatever his relationship to Arnulf of Carinthia may have been in reality. The exact chronology of his rise to a quasi-regal duke of Bavaria is not congruent with either a precise terminology or a strict view of constitutional history. Arnulf was evidently still a young man when he began to restore and consolidate the Bavarian *regnum* after his father's death in 907. It is worth noting that though he presumably needed the Bavarian magnates to do this he did not need the king, nor was he hindered by his father's closest rival, Arbo, and his family. Margrave Arbo, whose county had originally stretched from the Traungau in today's Upper Austria to the River Raab in western Hungary, had held a powerful position on the Danube for more than thirty years. The Hungarians penetrated upstream only gradually, until in the aftermath of the battle at Bratislava, in which Arbo and his followers had probably not taken part, they reached the Enns and thus confined the old die-hard to the small patch west of the river. In February 909 Arbo received a royal grant in the Traungau; Arnulf played no part in this, which is probably to be interpreted as an attempt by Louis the Child, or rather his entourage, to foster a representative of a powerful Bavarian aristocratic family against the lord of Bavaria. This interpretation is also supported by the fact that the formula of intervention in the royal charter names at the head of the lay magnates 'our relative, Count Conrad', that is, the later king.[14]

It was on their return from Suabia that the Hungarians had probably taken the episcopal see of Freising and burned down its cathedral 'at noon on Friday' 4 August 909.[15] But only seven days later the invaders encountered 'black

---

[13] *Fragmentum de Arnolfo duce Bavvariae*, ed. Reindel. [14] D L C 67, 19 February 909.
[15] *MGH Nec. Germ.* III, p. 82; Schneider (1991), 100.

Friday', when on 11 August 909 Arnulf, and no other Bavarian magnate, defeated them at the River Rott in lower Bavaria. When the Hungarians invaded southern Germany in the following year it was near Augsburg that they secured a victory over the royal army of Franks and Alemans, while on their way home they were caught by Arnulf's army at Neuching, which deprived them of their booty and inflicted a decisive defeat on them. The Bavarian duke had thus succeeded in doing something which neither the king nor another prince of the Frankish kingdom was able to do at the time, namely to protect the country and to defeat the Hungarians. His ability to do this is generally explained by the assumption that he took appropriate administrative and organisational measures in order to restore the fighting strength of the Bavarian forces. It is supposed to have been as a result of these comprehensive secularisations, for which later generations in the monasteries affected made Arnulf alone responsible, that the Bavarian duke had been able to realise enough liquid assets to compensate to some extent the powerful aristocratic families and bishops in Bavaria for the lands lost in the Bavarian east after 907. This would have been a continuation of a policy already visible in the Carolingian era, for example in the so-called lay abbacies or in Carloman's distribution of monasteries. The confiscations, which were certainly not intended to support supposed plans by Arnulf to become king himself, are held to have put the Bavarian quickly in a position to conduct a successful defence against the invaders.

Such explanations cannot, because of the shortage of sources, be simply refuted, but they nevertheless pose more questions than they answer. One would like to know first of all how it is that the accusations were raised only many generations later, if Arnulf and his men had really conducted secularisations on a grand scale. It was not until the end of the tenth century that Arnulf was to be explicitly accused of having destroyed the monasteries and deprived them of their holdings, which he gave to his vassals. A royal diploma of 979 which restored the lands of the monastery of Tegernsee complained in general terms about its destruction but did not mention any prince or ruler held responsible by name. The diploma was issued by Otto II on the intervention of his nephew Otto, duke of Suabia and Bavaria, so that there was not the slightest reason to have spared the Luitpolding Arnulf had he really been responsible.[16] Genealogical studies based upon two lists of alienations written in the monastery of Tegernsee around 1030 and 1060 respectively suggest that almost 50% of the alienated property was held by families descended from Arnulf, and the rest was held by three other families.[17] The alleged secularisations cannot have been very successful if their intention was to provide for a substantial number of *milites*.

[16] D O II 192.   [17] Tyroller (1953/4), pp. 302–9.

One would further like to know why it was that Arnulf's measures in restoring and consolidating the Bavarian *regnum* should have enabled him to conduct a successful defence against the Hungarians while on the other hand leaving him the weaker every time in the conflicts with Conrad I and Henry I. Arnulf's military potential was enough to deal with the Hungarians; he was able to meet them on equal terms and defeat them several times. Was the 'death toll of the Bavarian nobility on the field at Bratislava' by contrast too great, so that he had no chance against his kings?[18] Or did he run into difficulties with his great men and with the bishops when the kings came to Bavaria? Since all his early victories were won against Hungarians returning home laden with booty it may well have been that it was the prospect of rich pickings which allowed him to gather large numbers of Bavarians to fight against these external enemies; the danger for the Hungarians would then have been one which all marauding warriors from the Goths to the Avars had had to face. The prospects of success were by contrast much less rosy when east Frankish rulers attacked with their Frankish and Saxon armies. Apart from a possible internal opposition to Arnulf there was one certain further reason for his failure against the east Frankish kings; these held the Rhine–Frankish royal lands and the regions around Rhine and Main, and were thus both economically and demographically in a much stronger position.

At all events the Hungarians were defeated for a third time by the Bavarians under Arnulf and Alemannic troops led by his mother's brothers Berthold and Erchanger in 913 at the Inn. Once again, the Hungarians were returning from a raiding tour through Alemannia. Sometime after 13 September 908 and before 924/6 Arnulf issued a charter which, though it has only survived as a copy, nevertheless reveals royal form in almost everything except the ducal title. Opening formula, *arenga* and *narratio* seem royal, as do the reference to a seal and the absence of witnesses: 'In the name of the holy and undivided trinity. Arnulf, by the ordination of divine providence duke of the Bavarians and even of the surrounding regions to all bishops, counts, and princes of this *regnum*.'[19] The document confirmed an exchange of lands between Bishop Dracolf of Freising and his *chorepiscopus* Kuno, who was evidently Arnulf's *capellanus*. There is no dating-clause, however, so that the piece cannot be precisely dated. *Intitulatio*, addressees and in general the language of the diploma suggest that it could only have been issued after Arnulf had been formally set up as *dux* by the Bavarian nobility. The most likely time for this to have happened was after Arnulf's victory at the Inn in 913, especially as his companion and uncle Erchanger was raised as *dux* after winning a battle against the Hungarians in

---

[18] Störmer (1988), p. 281.

[19] 'Arnulfus divina ordinante providentia dux Baioariorum et etiam adiacentium regionum omnibus episcopis comitibus et regni huius principibus': Reindel (ed.) *Die bayerischen Luitpoldinger*, p. 78, no. 48.

915. An independent election as *dux* within a *regnum* of the east Frankish kingdom was a provocation to Conrad I, who had been king since November 911. It is thus probably no coincidence that the first conflict between king and *dux* should have occurred in 914, even though Conrad had married Arnulf's mother the year before.

Arnulf had no chance against the king. Conrad had the stronger battalions and his position as king. Although it was probably only after agreement had been reached between Henry I and Arnulf that a Bavarian synodal sermon invited its audience to pray *pro rege et duce nostro et eius uxore ac filiis*, but whether or not Conrad had been anointed, he was seen as 'the Lord's anointed', *christus domini*, as was decreed unambiguously by the synod of Hohenaltheim on 20 November 916 held with papal support and the participation of Bavarian bishops.[20] The episcopate of the east Frankish kingdom, though by no means fully assembled there, thus approved and blessed the king's military and political steps against the ducal 'rebels', among whom both Arnulf and his uncle Berthold are named. In spite of this Arnulf was able to recapture Bavaria in 917 and ward off the attacks by both Conrad and his brother. It was in the course of these conflicts that the king received a severe wound, of which he was to die on 23 December 918.

ARNULF'S QUASI-REGAL RULE IN THE *REGNUM* OF BAVARIA

Since Ernst Klebel first discovered an eleventh-century manuscript in the library of the monastery of Admont in 1921 which contains excerpts from the Greater Salzburg Annals covering the period from 725 to 956, scholarship has repeatedly concerned itself with the entry found only here under the year 920 (*rectius* either 919 or 916/17): 'the Bavarians submitted again freely to Duke Arnulf and caused him to reign in the kingdom of the Teutons'.[21] This has been linked with a passage in the *Antapodosis* of Liudprand of Cremona, which says that Arnulf after his return from exile in Hungary was received by the Bavarians and eastern Franks with honour, 'and not only with honour, but he was also urged by them to become king', a sentence which is followed by the information that King Henry attacked Arnulf as his only enemy with a powerful army in Bavaria.[22]

The events recorded here have generally been seen by scholars as a Bavarian reaction to Henry I's election as king in Fritzlar in northern Hesse in May 919 by Franks and Saxons, though some have suggested, probably correctly, that the passage in the Salzburg Annals should be dated to 916/17. Whatever one's

---

[20] *Concilia aevi Saxonici*, no. 1, p. 28, c. 21.
[21] 'et regnare eum fecerunt in regno Teutonicorum', *Annales ex annalibus Iuvavensibus antiquis excerpti*, p. 742.　　[22] Liudprand, *Antapodosis* II, 21.

views may be about the possible existence of a *regnum Teutonicorum* in the first half of the tenth century – whether this is seen as a variant of a *regnum Bavvariorum* or as an anachronism dating from the eleventh or twelfth centuries – one cannot describe the polity over which Arnulf was intended to rule as a 'kingdom of Germany'. Above all, it is nowhere recorded that Arnulf was really made king, quite apart from the question of who might have made him king and over what they might have made him king. Liudprand talks of the intention of the Bavarians and a few east Franconians to make Arnulf king; the Salzburg Annals make him rule in a *regnum* of the old Frankish kingdom, just as other *duces* before and after Arnulf had done and were to do. When Henry I took up arms against Arnulf the question was not whether the latter was to renounce the throne but on what terms he would acknowledge Henry's kingship.

After two campaigns in 920 and 921 an agreement was reached before the gates of the old royal city of Regensburg, which Arnulf had been able to hold against Henry even in the second campaign, an agreement which was then ratified by the Bavarian magnates. The king and the duke of Bavaria concluded a treaty of friendship, an *amicitia*; Henry thus extended the Carolingian tradition, which had been to make such treaties with external rulers only, by making one with a magnate from his own kingdom. This by implication also settled the question of the status of the two participants and their recognition of each other's rank and status. Arnulf acknowledged the integrity of the east Frankish kingdom and in return was able to retain his quasi-regal rule over Bavaria; indeed, it was probably Henry's recognition which first enabled him to establish it firmly.

The duke continued to exercise control over justice, call out armies, maintain peace and govern the church, which was happy to pray for both the king and the duke as well as for the latter's family;[23] he disposed *de facto* over crown lands and the counts and royal vassals in Bavaria as well as over the coinage, and he was able to practice an independent 'foreign policy' *vis-à-vis* Bohemia, Hungary and north Italy. A further consequence of this sworn friendship was probably the adoption of the royal name Henry in the Luitpolding family. Arnulf's youngest son, who was probably born about this time, was called Henry, as also were one of his grandsons and the only son of his brother Berthold.

From the treaty of 921 until the death of Henry I in 936 each side kept its part of the bargain. The Bavarian duke fought against the Bohemians both at

---

[23] See Schneider (1991), pp. 98–9 and 115, who adduces a Freising synodal sermon of uncertain date. The prayers in the Regensburg Sacramentary (Brussels, Bibliothèque Royale, MS 1814–16, fols. 241v–242r) also refer to 'Arnolfum ducem nostrum', but are still less precisely datable. As there is evidence for Bavarian synods in Regensburg and Dingolfing in 932 it is possible that the Freising and Regensburg texts should be dated to around this point.

the side of the king and on his own account; after some successes of his own against the Hungarians, he followed in 927 the example of the truce made between them and Henry the previous year; in 933–4 he tried to secure the Lombard *regnum*, or at least Verona, for his son Eberhard. Royal diplomata were issued for Bavarian recipients only at Arnulf's request; in 932 there is evidence for two Bavarian synods held at Regensburg and Dingolfing 'under the rule (in Bavaria) of Arnulf the (venerable) duke'.[24] After the failure of the Italian venture Arnulf designated his oldest son Eberhard as his successor in the *regnum* of the Bavarians and had him publicly acknowledged, probably in Salzburg.

After Henry, as whose friend Duke Arnulf is named, had died on 2 July 936, the ecclesiastical and lay magnates of the east Frankish kingdom met on 7 August in Aachen and set up Otto, the oldest son of the dead king, as king. Arnulf, like the other princely dukes, exercised a court office and 'served' as marshal. But the new king broke with what in modern terms might be called the federalistic policy of his father and wanted to return to being a king in the Carolingian tradition, anointed and crowned in Aachen, even though (or perhaps precisely because) his father's predecessor Conrad I had failed in the attempt. It was once again a question of the renewal of Carolingian tradition, something which was seen as a duty; if this is not comprehended, the history of the following two generations seems to be simply a meaningless sequence of rebellions and reconciliations, renewed rebellions and constantly changing alliances.

RESISTANCE AND CHANGE OF DYNASTY, ACHIEVEMENTS AND SETBACKS

It was probably while Arnulf was still alive that the new king Otto succeeded in making the best match available in the east Frankish kingdom for his younger brother Henry, who was ambitious and dangerous because 'born in the purple' after his father had already become king: the younger Liudolfing married the Luitpolding Judith, Arnulf's daughter. Arnulf himself died on 14 July 937; already by the following year there was an open breach between Otto I and the new Bavarian duke Eberhard supported by his brothers. The king prevailed and conferred the duchy of Bavaria on Arnulf's brother Berthold, who ruled from 938 to 947, evidently after having renounced rule over the church and the right to appoint bishops.

Berthold had already had the title of *dux* during Arnulf's lifetime, for the lands south of the Alps: in effect the Carinthian *regnum* together with what

---

[24] 'regnante Arnolfo (venerabili) duce (in Bavvaria)': prologues to the synods of Regensburg and Dingolfing, *Concilia aevi Saxonici*, nos. 7 and 9, pp. 95, 120.

today is south Tirol. Just as Berthold had earlier served his older brother, so now he was to be a faithful representative of his royal lord. No fewer than six royal charters for Bavarian recipients show either Berthold intervening or Otto confirming his decisions. In 937 the Hungarians had passed peacefully through Bavaria on their way west; this took place either at the end of Arnulf's reign or at the beginning of Eberhard's. In Arnulf's early years they had been attacked only when laden with booty on their journey home. Under Berthold, by contrast, they suffered their most severe defeat yet at the hands of an east Frankish army while still in the offensive phase of their campaign; Berthold's troops caught the aggressors near Wels on the Traun in upper Austria on 12 August 943.

Arnulf's sons, above all the count palatine Arnulf, stood aside and waited for their moment. This took some time to arrive, for after the death of Berthold in the autumn of 947 King Otto installed his brother Henry, Arnulf's son-in-law, as duke of Bavaria. This quasi-regal prince achieved what his predecessors had sought in vain: the power and influence of the Bavarian duke extended from the Moldava to the Po, and from the Lech to beyond the Enns – Bavarian troops are even said to have crossed the Thissa. After successes in the Nordgau against Hungarian invaders, the first large-scale counter-attack followed in 950, penetrating deep into Hungary. In the same year Bohemia was placed under ducal rule in a revival of traditional Carolingian policies, and in 951 the duke of Bavaria, if not Bavaria itself, was granted the Italian marches of Verona and Friuli, much as Arnulf had once sought them for his son Eberhard.

The first consequences of the change of dynasty in 947 were admittedly precisely the opposite of what the king had intended: instead of a pacification and incorporation of Bavaria into the royal sphere of influence, resistance and internal fragmentation were extended by a new element, that of jealousies and conflicts between the members of the ruling family. Thus Otto's son Liudolf, who had felt passed over and rebelled openly in 953, found full support from the Luitpoldings, who continued in their resistance even after Otto's reconciliation with Liudolf had led to catastrophe for most of them. This was in the early months of 955; the battle against the Hungarians in the summer of that year saw Luitpoldings still active against the foreign king. It was not only the majority of the Luitpoldings, especially Arnulf's direct descendants, who remained irreconcilable; the Bavarian Liudolfings themselves were soon to fight not only against the members of the native ducal family but also with the king's enemies against the king. Henry I of Bavaria remained loyal to his brother, but he died in the autumn of 955, leaving a namesake of four years, 'the Quarrelsome', who probably did not begin ruling in person until 967.

Otto's great victory against the Hungarians, his rise to emperorship in 962, the severe losses suffered by the Luitpoldings and the minority of the Bavarian duke Henry II, all meant a breathing-space of some two decades. But in 974, in the first year of Otto II's reign, the game began afresh: Henry the Quarrelsome allied himself with Bohemia and Poland, found support from the last Luitpoldings, and began a conflict for which the sources give no reasons, so that one can only guess. Once again it was probably a question of 'honour', which took on a value quite the opposite of that given to it by Falstaff: 'A word. ... Air. A trim reckoning.' In this period 'to pass over the claims by magnates to honor could easily be seen as a slight or insult, *offensio*. If they did not react then their position was affected in two ways. Their followers lost confidence in them, which meant a loss of real power; and their rivals and opponents lost respect for them, which threatened their position still further.'[25] In such a situation the magnates had to defend their own rights by arms, in order to restore their reputation and their power, in other words their honour, by force.

The struggle lasted for more than ten years, from 974 to the beginning of 985, and hence even beyond the death of Otto II; in the course of them the Bavarian duke lost some influence, though only temporarily, and the land itself was freshly divided into its former component *regna*. Henry's attempts to draw on Bohemian support were countered by Otto II, which led to the setting up of a bishopric at Prague in 976. Since this new bishopric was subordinated to the metropolitan see of Mainz, the Bavarian church lost its traditional jurisdiction over its old missionary districts, and there was a consequent decline of Bavarian influence in Bohemia. In the same year, 976, the Carinthian and Lombard regions of Bavaria were divided off as a separate duchy of Carinthia and given to the Luitpolding Henry, the son of Duke Berthold. The new duke took up where his father had left off in reviving a modified Carolingian tradition. The installation of the Babenberger in the Bavarian march on the Danube, the core of what was to become Austria, was of particular significance for the future. The origins of the family, which begins with a Margrave Luitpold I, are disputed; Bavarian historians have generally insisted on a Frankish origin, while their Austrian colleagues have pointed to the leading name Luitpold and seen them as a collateral line of the Luitpoldings.

The erection of a duchy of Carinthia was intended more as an acknowledgement of the princely position of a magnate close to the king than the creation of a strong institution which might shape the polyethnic south-east Alpine region. The march east of the Enns remained attached to Bavaria, though the margraves who held office there acquired the hitherto unimagined chances which went with a border and colonial land in the 'wild East'. They seized their opportunity, established a dynasty and created a territory whose economic potential and real power began, in spite of its small size, to compete with its

[25] Althoff and Keller (1985), p. 124.

more substantial Bavarian and Carinthian neighbours. The old royal city of Regensburg gradually lost its role as capital, while the much younger Vienna was by the mid-twelfth century to become the residence of the Danube margraves, who by now were dukes of Austria.

This development was naturally neither inevitable nor the result of a conscious plan drawn up in the tenth century. But the policy followed by Henry, the last Bavarian duke to have been elected by the nobility, once he had become king, shows that the era of extensive ethnically based principalities was coming to an end. After the compromise of 985 Henry the Quarrelsome was able to rule powerfully in Bavaria for another decade. He was lord of the Bavarian church, the royal demesne in Bavaria, and in effect the vice-king 'in respect of the advocates and counts of his province', as the decrees of the provincial assembly at Ranshofen issued around 990 so impressively demonstrate.[26] In 995 Henry's son and namesake, who had already participated in government during his father's lifetime, succeeded with the consent and by the election of the nobility. Henry the Quarrelsome's presence was felt not only in Bavaria but also in much of Carinthia, whose independent development was thus hardly fostered. He also renewed the conflict with the Hungarians between 985 and his death in 995. He must already have disturbed the peace which his uncle wished for at an early stage in his reign, for an embassy from Géza of Hungary appeared at the assembly in Quedlinburg in 973, obviously with the intention of restoring peace. There is clearly a connection between Henry's active Hungarian policy and the fact that in the former Bavarian Eastland a number of marches from the Danube across the middle Mur and Drava as far as the Sann and Save are named in the 970s. He evidently renewed his attacks on the Hungarians after his restoration, no doubt partly in retaliation for Hungarian raids during the confusion of the early 980s in the Reich. In 991 'Duke Henry triumphed over the Hungarians'.[27] The Hungarian border defences were still set as outposts some distance in front of the region of Hungarian settlement proper; it was not until the peace settlement of 1043, following the first definition of the River Fischa as the border in 1030, that these were lost. At that time the tributaries of the middle Danube, the March and the Leitha, were established as the eastern boundaries of Bavaria and hence of the emerging German kingdom.[28]

Following the defeat of 991 the Hungarian ruling house, the Árpáds, had to come to terms with its western neighbours. Stephen, the later saint, married Gisela, the daughter of Henry the Quarrelsome and sister of the young Henry IV, who had just become duke in 995. The match was obviously made with the agreement of the Ottonian court, and by making Stephen the brother-in-law

---

[26] *Constitutiones Heinrici ducis Ranshofenses.*   [27] *Annales s. Rudberti Salisburgensis,* p. 772.
[28] *Annales Altahenses maiores,* p. 33; Hermann of the Reichenau, *Chronicon,* p. 124.

of the future Emperor Henry II established a permanent basis for relations between Hungary and the Reich. With Gisela came not only Christian missionaries but also a substantial following. The influence of these 'guests' (*hospites*) ranged from military affairs through the use of charters to legislation. Stephen, who had previously been called Vajc, took his name from that of the Passau patron saint, a sign that the easterly bishopric on the Danube had shaken off its rivals in the conversion of the Hungarians. However, the great hopes which had been raised in Passau about a permanent subjection of Hungary to Passau's diocesan administration, even the promotion of Passau to the status of an archbishopric for the lands of the Danube basin, were disappointed. Pope, emperor and duke of the Bavarians agreed on the recognition of Hungary as a Christian kingdom and the more or less simultaneous erection of a new church province in Hungary, once Stephen I had been crowned and anointed the first Christian king of the Hungarians in 1001.[29]

After the death of his cousin Otto III, the Bavarian Liudolfing prevailed against powerful opposition and was elected and anointed king as Henry II in June 1002 in Mainz. 'Bavaria now triumphs', as an Italian observer put it,[30] but it was not the Bavarian duchy as a whole which profited from the policy of the new king but individual lay and ecclesiastical magnates of Bavaria, who began to take on important offices and positions within the kingdom. It was a logical response to the demands of the time that Henry II should have wanted to preserve the resources of the Bavarian duchy for the crown, even after he had reluctantly agreed to give the land its own duke. This was what lay behind the origins of the bishopric of Bamberg in 1007, following the defeat of the rebellion by the Babenberger Henry of Schweinfurt, margrave in the Nordgau. Henry II had at first promised this most prominent member of a powerful rising family the duchy of Bavaria as a reward for his support in the struggle for the kingship, and then reneged on his promise. Now the bishopric of Bamberg was to take the place of the Babenberger margraves. Besides this, Bamberg received rich endowments of royal lands throughout Bavaria and in what is today Austria down to Italy, as well as scattered lands on the Rhine, in Suabia and in Thuringia. The new bishopric was immediately subject to the king and hence received no privilege of immunity; to a large extent it enjoyed the means of power previously enjoyed by the Bavarian duke. As the duchy was in the hands of the king or his family for a total of fifty-three years between 995 and 1096, the last chance to create a 'genuine dynastic connection between the people and the intermediate power of the duke' was missed.[31] One can talk of Bavaria as a crown land by the time of Conrad II, Henry II's successor, at the latest. Although these policies threatened Bavaria's integrity, there was in the

---

[29] Thietmar, *Chronicon* IV, 59 See most recently Fried (1989a), pp. 66–7 and 132–3.
[30] Leo of Vercelli, *Versus de Ottone et Henrico*, p. 482.   [31] Prinz (1981), 390.

end to be no fragmentation of the region as there was in other *regna* of the east Frankish kingdom. Rather, the greater part of Bavaria remained undivided and in the twelfth century was to provide the basis for the emergence of a medieval territorial state, once royal influence had been radically reduced. It is not inconceivable that it was the Bavarian magnates themselves, with their insistence on 'custom and law' and on participation, who preserved the unity of the duchy, considered to be the noblest dignity in the empire.

SPIRITUAL AND INTELLECTUAL LIFE

Almost one monastery in two of those which had existed in the ninth century disappeared in the course of the tenth; in the 'antimonastic' diocese of Freising only three monasteries out of fourteen survived. Those which did survive did so for a long time only in a radically reduced form, mostly as episcopal *Eigenklöster*. Apart from the monasteries we have only the Bavarian bishoprics: Passau, Regensburg, Freising, Brixen, and the metropolitan see of Salzburg. The books of traditions kept under the Archbishops Odalbert (923–35), Frederick (958–91) and Hartwig (991–1023) contain a systematic collection of copies of the charters issued during the pontificates of the archbishops concerned. These pieces have the simpler form of a *notitia* and, compared with the Carolingian period, have a much more straightforward language. The period of generous and unconditional donations was long over; what we have here are often exchanges of property, many using the instrument of the *complacitatio*, whereby the donor's property was increased during his lifetime, but fell completely to the bishopric on his death.

In spite of both decline and retrenchment it was still possible for this 'age of iron' to throw up a man like Bishop Pilgrim of Passau (971–91). Whether or not he as patron actually stimulated a Latin version of the *Nibelungenlied*, he was at least so firmly rooted in the aristocratic tradition of the material that the anonymous poet who composed the surviving Middle High German poem around 1200 made him Kriemhild's uncle. Pilgrim was also a student of Roman history, as can be seen from his forgeries. By present-day standards these elaborations may seem very dubious products, but they reveal a comprehensive knowledge of the history of the region from antiquity to the Carolingian period and beyond, and a high level of intellectual activity which allowed such knowledge to be placed in the service of a struggle for an independent church province. 'Pilgrim's backward-looking utopia of an archbishopric of Passau in the Danube basin may have been a product of its time, but it would be unfair to see it as merely a product of its time; great ideas always have a certain timeless component.'[32]

---

[32] Fichtenau (1971), 133.

The most distinguished figure among the Bavarian bishops of the later tenth century was without doubt Wolfgang of Regensburg (972–94), who brought Lotharingian monastic reform into the land and began his pontificate by separating the Regensburg monastery of St Emmeram from the bishopric. He was followed in this by his archbishop, Frederick, who summoned the monk Tito from St Emmeram to Salzburg in 987 and there made him the first independent abbot of St Peter with a separate monastic endowment. The bishop of Freising, Abraham (957–93), who had looked after the affairs of government during the minority of Henry the Quarrelsome together with the dowager duchess Judith, had extensive intellectual contacts with the west of the kingdom, from where he was demonstrably able to procure texts of the Latin fathers and Latin school literature. The scriptorium of Freising reached a high artistic level in his pontificate. Equally famous is the collection of Slavonic material in Munich, Clm 6245, a kind of handbook for pastoral practice in the Slav regions of Bavaria and Carinthia. It includes both the oldest continuous text and the oldest records of a Slav language written in a Latin alphabet.

In the second half of the tenth century there was a noticeable increase both in intellectual activity and in the use of writing in the Bavarian bishoprics. The intellectual equipment for a renewed mission in the Bavarian east was there, but the Bavarian episcopate was not able to exploit the roll-back of the Hungarians in the years following the victory of 955 to the extent the Carolingian tradition might have suggested. As we have seen, the foundation of bishoprics in Bohemia and Hungary cut Regensburg, Salzburg and Passau off from their traditional missionary territories, and gave them clear diocesan boundaries to the east.

The modest level of literary activity produced no distinguished historiography: the *Great Salzburg Annals* of the mid-tenth century owe their title not to their importance but to their place in the family tree of the south-east German annals worked out by modern scholarship. The panegyric on Duke Arnulf does indeed speak a clear language of Bavarian consciousness, but it has survived, significantly, only as a mere fragment. It is not until the achievement of an Otloh of St Emmeram (d. *c.* 1070) that what has otherwise survived here and there from this period in Latin and the vernacular can be seen to have been a tentative new beginning. There was still not enough leisure, *otium*, for such activities; men were still too preoccupied by daily affairs, *negotia* (etymologised by a play on words as *nec-otia*, 'no free time'). It is thus not surprising to find no Bavarians among the chorus of millenarians at the end of the tenth century; those who had to deal simultaneously with Hungarians, Bohemians, Saxons and Franks had enough problems in this world without having to speculate about the end of time and the ruin of the world.

CHAPTER 12

LOTHARINGIA

Michel Parisse

FROM 900 TO 939

The kingdom held by Zwentibald, who died on 13 August 900, became a duchy with the same boundaries, known from the start by the convenient designation of Lotharingia. The borders were delineated by Frisia and the North Sea in the north and by Burgundy in the south, along the line where the diocese of Toul met the dioceses of Besançon and Langres. As far as the borders with the kingdom of west Francia and the neighbouring Germanic duchies are concerned, matters are less clear. One must concede that the ancient principle of boundaries defined by major rivers, as followed in the partition of Verdun in 843, still remained essentially valid: thus the Meuse and the Scheldt in the west and the Rhine in the east were in theory the borders of Lotharingia in this period. The reality was rather more complex. In the absence of other administrative units with precise borders it was the dioceses which counted, and their bishops were dependent on the ruler of east Francia. If in the west one traces the western bounds of the dioceses of Toul and Verdun, one finds that these extended some way to the west, beyond the left bank of the Meuse, and it must be asked whether the *pagi* on the left bank within these dioceses were subject to the authority of the king of west Francia or not, a question which applies in particular to the Ornois and the Barrois, thus for the Lingonian part of the Bassigny. Traditionally, the three eastern *pagi* of the diocese of Rheims – Astenois, Dormois and Castrice – were held to be 'imperial'. Given such uncertainty, and given also the slow evolution characteristic of the tenth century, it should probably be said that the rulers regarded the Meuse as a boundary, but that the authority of the east Frankish kingdom extended some way to the west of this river. Along the Rhine, the dioceses of the Lotharingian bishoprics extended beyond the river to the east, but the boundaries ascribed to the duchies normally followed the great river itself. This was no longer true, however, of the Alsatian section, since from 911 onwards the duchy of Alemannia/Suabia had won back lost ground and reincorporated Alsace, thus extending its western frontier as far as the Vosges.

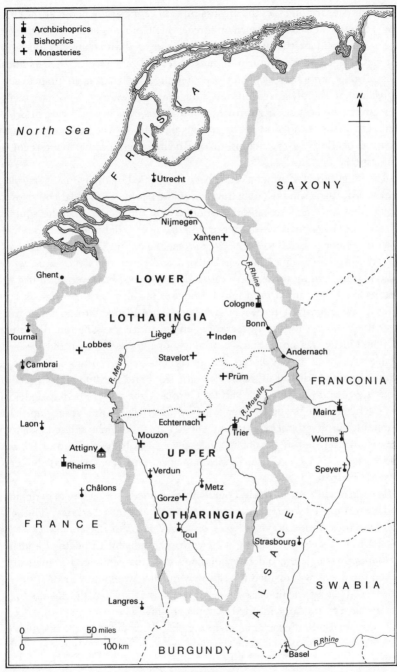

5 Lotharingia

Within these boundaries the most significant centres were naturally the episcopal cities, which can be placed on three levels. Cologne, Trier and Metz were the most important, the largest and the best endowed with churches and monasteries; Liège and Verdun can be ranked second by virtue of their political role; Toul, Cambrai (which had been reunited with Arras in France) and Utrecht were slightly less significant. One must be aware of Cambrai's membership of the ecclesiastical province of Rheims, which posed certain problems, especially at the moment of episcopal elections, when the king of west Francia, 'overlord' of the archbishop of Rheims, might be able to intervene in this imperial 'city'.

The kingdom of Zwentibald had been designated by the name of its ruler. After his death he was no longer mentioned and people confined themselves to noting that the kingdom had once belonged to Lothar. The narrative sources of this epoch – annals, chronicles and saints' lives – did not agree on which ruler this name referred to. Some, when speaking of the 'kingdom of Lothar', intended to refer to the Emperor Lothar I and hence to *Francia media,* while others were alluding to his son Lothar II. Historians, however, have had no doubts about this, and if occasionally one uses the term 'Lotharingian axis' to refer to a long strip of territories stretching from Flanders to northern Italy, Lotharingia always means the territory defined above, the kingdom of Lothar II. This duchy was not ethnically homogenous, including as it did Frisians, Franks, Alemans and Walloons. Its inhabitants spoke various languages: a Latino-Romance dialect in the dioceses of Toul and Verdun and in parts of Trier, Liège and Cambrai, and various Germanic dialects in the remainder of the duchy. The linguistic frontier followed the crest of the Vosges up from Burgundy, turning to the right from Dabo to Audun-le-Tiche and so passing to the east of Metz before turning up once again towards the north in such a way as to pass round Liège, which was Romance, and then proceed due east towards Tournai.

The inhabitants of the duchy could only be named by referring to their king, and the terms used were thus *Lotharii, Lotharienses* and then *Lotharingi.* The geographical region was known as *regnum quondam Lotharii* or *Lotharii regnum.* From the end of the tenth century a new word gradually came to dominate, *Lotharingia,* though the older terminology was not eliminated immediately. When the duchy was divided the two new duchies were known as *Lotharingia superior* and *inferior,* the first also being known as the duchy of the *Mosellani;* historians have by and large referred to upper and lower Lotharingia.

In 900 the Lotharingian aristocrats were hardly troubled by the question of which ruler they owed allegiance to, and the court of the young son of the emperor Arnulf, Louis the Child, had little trouble in keeping control of Lotharingia. To the west King Charles (the Straightforward) exercised a still more limited power, and he had only been sole ruler since 898. It was the lay aristocracy of Lotharingia who had brought down Zwentibald, and it claimed to have a say in the government of the country. The resistance was led by a number of counts. The most important of these were the two brothers Gerhard and Matfrid, whose ancestors, from the kindred of Matfrid and Adalhard, had held important positions under Carolingian emperors. Their power was centred on Metz; Gerhard extended his influence by taking to wife the widow of the fallen Zwentibald, Oda, a daughter of the *dux* of Saxony. Another family was that of Reginar Longneck, whose mother was a daughter of Lothar I who had been carried off and married by Count Gislebert of the Meuse. His power was firmly based on the great monasteries like Echternach and St Servatius in Maastricht, and on his allodial lands between the Meuse and the Scheldt; he felt himself to be Carolingian, and had ambitions which extended over Hainault and Brabant. Other counts played a lesser role: Stephen, for example, a member of a somewhat obscure kindred which was well endowed in the Saar region and included two bishops of the same name, those of Cambrai (*c*. 911–34) and of Liège (901–20); or Wigeric, count of the palace, who married the Carolingian Kunigunde. All these princes disposed of wealth based on hereditary lands, monasteries held in benefice and *pagi* which they administered.

None of them was invited to take over the duchy; Louis the Child's entourage entrusted it to the *dux* Gebhard, who with his brother Conrad was the head of an important Franconian family, the Conradines. Gebhard, the first man to rule over Lotharingia without bearing a royal title, stood up to local resistance successfully, but fell in 910 in battle against the Hungarians, at the same time, incidentally, as his Metz adversary Gerhard. In the following year the death of Louis the Child renewed the question of Lotharingia's allegiance; this time there was a switch to the king of west Francia, Charles. It is difficult to know with certainty whether this change took place before or following the death of the young German ruler, but the person responsible was probably Count Reginar, whom a chronicler calls *dux*.

Charles the Simple

The posthumous son of Louis the Stammerer had been able to impose his rule on his own kingdom only with difficulty; at first he had been passed over in favour of Odo, count of Paris, but he had been raised to the kingship during Odo's own lifetime before becoming sole ruler in 898. His ambition was to recover control of the lands of his ancestor, of that *Francia media* which had now become Lotharingia. He had lands there and had visited them on a number of occasions even before he came to rule there. He had to wait until

911 before gaining full control of them; then he moved immediately to take possession, obtaining the allegiance of its counts and bishops with little difficulty. It was the policies he pursued and the excessive favour shown to his favourite Hagano which led to his downfall. Although he thought he had made a wise move in marrying a Lotharingian woman, Frederuna, by whom he had numerous children, he made the mistake of endowing Hagano with monasteries already held in benefice by local counts, or at least this was the explanation offered for the tensions which arose. Wigeric seems to have remained loyal, but Gislebert, the successor and heir of Reginar Longneck, who died in 915, did not. He had ambitions to recover the leading role played by his father, who had still borne the titles of *marchio* and *missus dominicus*. He could not tolerate being the victim of the favours shown to Hagano and led the opposition to Charles; from 919 onwards he supported the new king of Germany, Henry I. If one believes Flodoard, Gislebert himself was elected *princeps* by his equals, but it is not clear what we are to understand by this title – perhaps the kingship itself?[1] He failed in his subsequent attempt to establish his candidate Hilduin as the new bishop of Liège against the royal candidate Richer, abbot of Prüm and brother of the Matfriding counts, in 921. Somewhat later, at a meeting organised on the banks of the Rhine at Bonn in November 921, the two kings made an alliance. Charles was subsequently able to appoint his notary Gauzlin to the see of Toul in 922, but if everything was still running fairly smoothly for him in Lotharingia things were very different in west Francia. There the aristocratic opposition had become strong enough to elect an anti-king in the person of Robert the Strong, brother of King Odo, in 922. Shortly afterwards Henry I made contact with this opponent of Charles, which enabled him to set foot in Lotharingia. He had calculated well, for in 923 war broke out in the west and at the battle of Soissons in June 923 Charles was defeated and Robert killed. The west Frankish nobility was not dispirited and set up the brother-in-law of the slain leader, Rudolf of (ducal) Burgundy, as a new anti-king. Charles, weakened and disarmed, hoped to find support from Heribert of Vermandois, who lured him into a meeting at which he was imprisoned; he remained in captivity until his death in 929. The Lotharingians never seem to have intended going over *en bloc* to Rudolf, who possessed neither Charles' Carolingian descent nor his Lotharingian connections. The reaction to the assassination of Count Ricuin of Verdun in 923 by the brother of the new king of France, the intriguer Boso, demonstrated that Rudolf enjoyed scarcely any support in the country. Henry I was thus free to undertake the reconquest of the kingdom of Lothar and Zwentibald.

He began this in 923 and had largely completed it by 925 when he broke the

---

[1] Flodoard, *Annales, s.a.* 920.

resistance of Saverne, defended by Bishop Wigeric of Metz. Henry immediately took steps to establish his power. In 927 he appointed a devout Strasbourgeois cleric, Benno, to the see of Metz, conferred important economic rights on the bishop of Toul, and gave support to Barno, the new bishop of Toul. In the following year he went still further by giving his daughter Gerberga in marriage to Count Gislebert, who was also entrusted with ducal powers. However, none of this was straightforward, and the local aristocracy was still very active; in 929 the inhabitants of Metz did not hesitate to depose and martyr Benno, following which they appointed a bishop from among their local lords: Adalbero, the eldest son of Count Wigeric, a cleric who was also said to have been responsible for the murder of Count Ricuin. The king was unable to put up any resistance to this coup.

There was thus still some transient opposition, and one may also observe the attention paid by the king of west Francia to the desires of the Lotharingian aristocracy, but in the end things stayed as they were up to the death of Henry I in 936. In that year there were two significant changes: the accession of Otto I in the east and the almost simultaneous accession of Louis IV 'd'Outremer' in the west. After the short reign of the Burgundian Radulf, a Carolingian, the son of Charles the Straightforward, was once more on the throne of France, and he had retained ancient Carolingian ambitions intact. Initially there was peace, but then the new king of east Francia found himself faced with opposition at both ends of his kingdom. Otto I could see that power was drifting away from him in Lotharingia, where his own brother-in-law Gislebert was gathering bishops and counts behind him, but he first had to settle problems in Bavaria and in Saxony before coming across the Rhine. Two of Otto's supporters were victorious at the battle of Andernach in 939 at the end of which Gislebert drowned in the Rhine. This success was enough to secure Otto's position. The bishop of Metz rallied to the king and had him confirm the reform undertaken at the monastery of Saint-Arnulf. The king of France, by contrast, now took a more active role: in effect he scooped up Gerberga, Gislebert's widow, and married her on the spot, thus simultaneously becoming a member of the extended Ottonian family and marking his intention of continuing to show interest in Lotharingia.

FROM 939 TO 965

Otto I had to find a replacement for Gislebert, and at first thought that he had acted well by generously conferring Gislebert's position on his young brother Henry. But Henry remained disloyal, and the king soon replaced him by a local noble of high standing, Otto, count of Verdun, the son of Ricuin. About Otto we know very little in respect either of the powers which he really exercised or of his own landed wealth, though in Verdun he held a fortification which played an important role on the frontier with west Francia. He scarcely had a chance to show his mettle, for he died in 944, to be replaced by a Conradine, Conrad, a descendant of Duke Gebhard, later known as the Red. His career reveals him to have been an able and energetic man and a good appointment. Pursuing his familial policy, Otto I gave Conrad his own daughter Liutgard in marriage and thus bound him more closely to the king's own dynastic interests, in 947 or 948. Unfortunately this family *entente* remained purely superficial. Otto I would later discover this with his natural son William, archbishop of Mainz, and he was soon to suffer under the opposition of his son Liudolf and of his son-in-law Conrad. These two princes, dukes of Suabia and Lotharingia respectively, had either been angered by some royal actions or else themselves aspired to a still more brilliant career; at all events they combined forces in a coalition which by 953 had become dangerous. Otto I reacted firmly, and deprived the two culprits of office. He replaced Conrad by an ecclesiastic, his youngest brother Brun, who had already been promoted from the archchancellorship to the archbishopric of Cologne. Promotion to the archbishopric and to the duchy occurred within a very short space of time. Conrad, furious, took revenge by summoning the Hungarians into the duchy in 954, after himself having attacked Metz. Subsequently he submitted, and was to find a splendid death on the battlefield at the Lech; with Archbishop Brun at its head Lotharingia was to enjoy a few years of relative peace.

One might say that from the accession of Otto I to that of Otto III, even up to the accession of Hugh Capet, Lotharingia had the character of a *Francia media*, disputed between its two neighbours much as the kingdom of Lothar II had been earlier. The Carolingians of the west – Louis IV and Lothar – were just as much concerned to get and keep possession of this intermediary duchy as were the Ottonians; the history of these struggles is all the more interesting in that it consists of alternating periods of familial rapprochement and hostility.

We have already seen that Louis IV married Otto's sister Gerberga in 939. A year earlier the *dux Francorum*, Hugh the Great, who was Louis' main adversary, had taken another sister of Otto as his third wife, Hadwig. The king of Germany was thus able to exploit the permanent state of potential hostility between his two brothers-in-law by supporting first one and then the other. It was the king of France whose position was weakest and who turned most frequently to his relative beyond the Rhine. They met frequently, as political circumstances or family preoccupations directed: at Visé (942), Cambrai (946), Aachen (947, 949), Mouzon (947), Ingelheim (948), and somewhere in Lotharingia in 950. The list of names is itself not without interest, for it reveals the role of frontier played, as already noted, by the Meuse and the Rhine. Otto enjoyed acting as patron and was able to put on a dazzling show in the midst of his own court at Aachen, where he had been crowned, as he twice did at Easter. Louis took a more defensive position, and had more and more to appear as the suppliant to preserve his throne. Men like Hugh of France and Heribert of Vermandois represented a permanent danger: in 940 they had even done homage to Otto. Louis always sought to preserve his territory, as in 951 when he protested against the attempt by the Lotharingian count Frederick to establish a castle at Fains on the borders of the two kingdoms.

This family arrangement was shortly to take a turn for the worse. The king of France died the year after Brun's promotion, leaving a minor as his heir; two years later Hugh of France also died and left a minor to succeed, the future Hugh Capet. The two widows, Queen Gerberga and Duchess Hadwig, naturally turned to their brothers, Otto and Brun, archbishop of Cologne, whose ducal title has been disputed by some historians. Brun in particular carried great weight under the circumstances. He was the youngest of the sons of Henry I and Matilda, born in 925 and entrusted to Bishop Balderic of Utrecht from 929 for an education which could only be a clerical one. When Otto became king, he summoned his young brother to him to become a member of the chancery; Brun had been chancellor from 940 and thus intimately familiar with his brother's difficulties. In 951 he was made archchaplain, a rank giving him control over the court personnel, and in 953, as we have seen, received in rapid succession the Lotharingian archbishopric of Cologne with the attached title of archchancellor, and the ducal function, granted here for the first time to an ecclesiastical prince. A historiographical tradition has led historians, inspired by Ruotger's *Vita Brunonis*, to see in this prelate the symbol itself of the union between secular and sacerdotal power, the developer of that imperial church which was to underpin the power of German rulers for a century.

Brun's task was a double one: on the one hand to secure the submission of a Lotharingian aristocracy which had lost none of its reputation for turbulence, and on the other to act as a mediator in the delicate diplomatic relations between the two kingdoms. Within the duchy he found a relatively healthy position. Most of the great families had been effectively decapitated. Boso, the Burgundian trouble-maker, had disappeared from the scene in 935 and the head of the house of Verdun in 944, as had the head of the comital lineage of Metz, Adalbert, assassinated that same year. The powerful Hugh of Chaumontois, who claimed Carolingian descent, was confined to the south of the province and was in any case loyal, while Gislebert's relatives, Reginar and Lambert of Hainault, always dangerous and long exiled in France, had still not been able to restore the family's position in its full pride. Conrad the Red had achieved good results by energetic action; Brun continued this by exercising supervision over castle-building. There were other families besides those mentioned, but they were less powerful: the lineage of the Folmars in the Saar region, for example, or the descendants of Wigeric, count of the palace.

It was a heavy burden, and Brun wore himself out in travelling back and forth between Germany and France and in exercising his ducal and archiepiscopal functions. His northern adversaries, Reginar of Hainault and Immo of Chèvremont, did not lay down their arms, and Brun had to intervene militarily on several occasions. He thought he had found the solution by dividing up the over-large duchy between two subordinates: the northern part was granted to Godfrey, a son of the count palatine and descendant of Count Gerhard of Metz, in 959, and the southern part, corresponding roughly to the province of Trier, to a Count Frederick. The latter merits our attention as closely linked with the Ottonian dynasty: in 951 this count – who should not too readily be termed count of Bar, and still less readily count of Metz – had been betrothed to Beatrice, the daughter of Hugh of France and Hadwig, hence the niece of Brun. The fortune of this Lotharingian aristocrat was in practice due to the position enjoyed by his elder brother, Bishop Adalbero I of Metz. Another of his brothers, Gauzlin, held Verdun and was to pass it on to one of his sons, one of those Godfreys whose name was to dominate Lotharingian history up to the time of Godfrey of Bouillon; a third was to found the lineage of the counts of Luxemburg. As we shall see, family alliances constituted an intricate network throughout this period, and their influence outlasted the death of Brun, who died prematurely, on a journey back from Rheims in October 965. In that same year, Otto I had returned from Italy and celebrated Whitsun in his city of Cologne in the full splendour of his imperial crown, having gathered around him his German family and his French relatives. This included a couple who were a product of that same family policy: Lothar, king of France, had married Emma, the daughter of the empress Adelaide by her first husband, the Italian king Lothar.

The powers of *sacerdotium* and *regnum* were united in the hands of the archbishop. The first term was still more important for Lotharingia than the second. Brun had received an excellent education from which his lively intelligence had drawn great benefit, and he had been able to complete it at his brother's court before putting it to powerful use at the head of his duchy. He had made contact with the royal chapel and soon became its head; he thus surveyed the whole field of good candidates for bishoprics here and among the great monasteries. He supported monastic reform without hesitation, familiar as he was with its effects through the contacts which he had with the centres at Gorze and Metz and at Trier. He had intervened personally with Duke Conrad in order to have Gorze's properties confirmed in 945. But his main interest was devoted to episcopal elections. In the course of a few years he intervened in almost all the Lotharingian dioceses: in 953 he conferred Liège on the learned monk of Lobbes and bishop of Verona, Rather; in 956 he placed his relative Henry on the archiepiscopal throne at Trier; and in 959 he appointed the Bavarian Wigfrid to Verdun. At Liège again, where Reginar of Hainault had succeeded in appointing his own relative Balderic, Brun imposed a distinguished candidate in 959, Eraclius; in early 963 he summoned the canons of Toul, still prostrated by the death of Gauzlin, and gave them as bishop a cleric from his own entourage, Gerard, who returned with them to Toul and led an exemplary life there for thirty years. Brun then waited two years until his brother had returned before establishing his cousin Dietrich as bishop of Metz and another Dietrich as archbishop of Trier. In 962 he extended his influence into France, appointing Odelric, a canon of Metz from the comital family of Chaumontois, as archbishop of Rheims. In this way we can observe him setting up an episcopate of very high quality, characterised by its piety, by its intellectual curiosity and by its loyalty to the empire. His followers were keen to continue his work in the field of intellectual life, and his influence thus made itself felt long after his own death.

FROM 965 TO 1033

The division of 959 took effect on Brun's death, but Godfrey, to whom lower Lotharingia had been entrusted, had already died in Italy in 964, and was not replaced immediately. It was not until 977 that Otto II conferred the duchy on Charles, the brother of King Lothar of France: the nomination had a political character which was in effect an act of defiance, and it established or confirmed the latent or genuine hostility between the two brothers. The personality of Charles 'of Lorraine' has engaged historians' attention, but not sufficiently for a biography of him to have been written. He was a complex personality, who undoubtedly suffered in the course of his repeated failures to become king or at least duke of all Lotharingia. In the course of Otto II's expedition into France, to be discussed shortly, he had himself proclaimed king at Laon, but the nobility of the kingdom regarded him with suspicion, no doubt because of his dependence on the empire and because of his marriage, which was seen (wrongly?) as unworthy of the son of a king. His final adventure was in 987 against Hugh Capet, when Archbishop Adalbero of Rheims declared him once again unworthy of the crown. The duke once again captured Laon, the last Carolingian bastion, in 987, then Rheims in 989; in 990 he fell into the hands of the new king and died in captivity in the following year. The vacant duchy was granted to his son Otto, about whom little can be said. On Otto's death it was bestowed on Godfrey, of the family of the counts of Verdun, who held it from around 1012 until his death in 1023. During this period the country experienced many changes, including the division of the over-large *pagi* and the beginnings of economic and urban growth. Thus the beginnings of the future town of Brussels are normally dated to the reign of Charles. During the same era the two episcopal cities of Cambrai and Liège flourished, thanks to the personality and activities of the two bishops Notker of Liège and Gerard I of Cambrai.

Upper Lotharingia became more and more the main stage of political activity. Duke Frederick, appointed in 959, had no trouble in governing a country which was slowly fragmenting as a result of the combined effects of the formation of episcopal principalities and of new comital seigneuries. Things became different on his death in May 978. The king of France, angered no doubt by the enfeoffment of his hostile brother with lower Lotharingia, took advantage of the vacancy in the other duchy, which was now held by the child Dietrich I, to launch an attack aimed at capturing both Aachen and its occupant, Otto II. The latter barely escaped the surprise attack, but then took up the pursuit of the French troops. Lothar had vainly attempted to capture Metz on the way; he had to flee before the German assault as far as Paris and experience the proclamation of his brother as anti-king. The French aristocracy did not leave him in the lurch, and the emperor had to withdraw his army, not without losses. In this tense atmosphere peace was made at a meeting in May 980 on the banks of the Chiers, near Mouzon, but it was in practice no more than a postponement of conflict, which bubbled up again as soon as the news of Otto II's premature death had become known. While the deposed duke of Bavaria, Henry, seized the young Otto III and attempted to usurp the throne, Lothar launched himself into the conquest of Lotharingia, beginning with Verdun, the imperial town closest to the kingdom, at the end of 984. By that time the political situation within the empire had largely been clarified. Faced by the alliance between the two widowed empresses and their relative Duchess Beatrice of upper Lotharingia, Henry of Bavaria had submitted and handed over the child king. As a reward Adalbero, the son of the duchess, was granted the see of Verdun, only to pass in October to the see of Metz, which had become vacant on the death of Dietrich I, whose last days had been overshadowed by his alliance with the usurper. Lothar had moved on Lotharingia at a time when the empire did not have a ruler in a position to organise resistance; this came from the Lotharingians themselves, given moral support by princesses and prelates. The young duke Dietrich was not yet of an age to act effectively, and his allies the counts of Verdun and Luxemburg had little more success. Verdun was taken at the beginning of 985 and a number of Lotharingian nobles made prisoner. The situation remained precarious for the whole of 985; Beatrice negotiated for assistance with her brother Hugh Capet. The matter was resolved by two events: first by the death of Lothar in March 986, and then a year later by that of his son Louis V in June 987. Order was restored. The election of Hugh Capet as king of France was to mark for a long period the end of French claims to Lotharingia.

The duchies enjoyed a moment of respite. With the accession of Henry II in 1002 opposition once again broke out. Baldwin, count of Flanders extended his control over Cambrai and Valenciennes, with the assistance of Lambert of Louvain; the king had to come in person to subdue his opponents, and he took the opportunity to confirm and extend the immunity of the bishopric of Cambrai in 1007. In 1012, on the death of Duke Otto, the king turned to Godfrey of Verdun to replace him, thus confirming the rise of this family, as we shall see. Lambert of Louvain remained insatiable, claiming the duchy by virtue of his marriage with a sister of the dead duke and attacking the bishop of Liège from his castles at Brussels and Louvain. He was killed at the battle of Florennes in 1015, and his son Henry took up the struggle. The count of Holland was also restive.

By contrast, the duchy of upper Lotharingia entered into a kind of lethargy. Its history was not a little troubled by the quarrels between Dietrich I and his mother Beatrice, who was reluctant to relinquish power. The period between 970 and 1050 was dominated by the various activities of the different branches of the great kindred of the counts of the Ardennes. The ducal branch was not the most dynamic, and it receives little mention right up to its extinction in the male line in 1033. A second branch, that of the counts who were established at Luxemburg from 986 and whose power was based on the advocacies of the monasteries of Echternach and St Maximin of Trier, was to have a brilliant future. Count Siegfried was succeeded by Henry, who later became duke of Bavaria; his daughter Kunigunde married the man who in 1002 became emperor as Henry II; a son, Dietrich, had a long career as bishop of Metz from 1006 to 1047; another, Adalbero, vainly attempted to set himself up as archbishop of Trier between 1008 and 1015 against the candidates supported by his brother-in-law. This branch caused the ruler a good deal of trouble, and in order to break its opposition he twice had to lay siege to Metz, where the allied brothers had taken up residence, in 1009 and 1012. The third branch, that of the counts of Verdun, was no less active than the second and destined to rise even higher. Its founder was without doubt Godfrey, known to historians as 'the Old' or 'the Captive' and distinguished for his longevity (he died sometime after 1000). During his own lifetime he saw his brother Adalbero become archbishop of Rheims in 969 and dominate politics on the borders of the two kingdoms until his death in 989, and his nephew (also called Adalbero, or Ascelin) play the trouble-maker for successive kings of France during his tenure of the see of Laon between 977 and 1031.

A chronological coincidence which is not wholly surprising given the composition of the contemporary aristocracy meant that four related Adalberos were simultaneously bishops of Metz, Verdun, Rheims and Laon in the years from 984 to 988. The mention of these two last towns reminds us that part of Champagne was closely linked with Lotharingia at the end of the tenth century, as we can see from the letters of Gerbert, himself no stranger to Lotharingian affairs. The lay descendants of the count of Verdun also had impressive careers. Godfrey, as we have seen, was granted the duchy of lower Lotharingia, and his brother Gozelo I succeeded him in 1023, before becoming duke in both duchies from 1033 until his death in 1044. Two other sons occupied important positions at Verdun and in the Argonne. All in all, the whole of Lotharingia appeared to be dominated by members of this dynamic family around the year 1000. A map of its allodial lands, of the counties it ruled, the bishoprics it held and the monasteries whose advocacies it enjoyed would cover the whole of Romance-speaking Lotharingia, extending also into Champagne and nibbling at the edges of Germanic Lotharingia. The region around Trier escaped its grip, however, in spite of the advocacy of the monastery of St Maximin enjoyed by the family.

The territorial development of the two duchies has been mentioned on a number of occasions, and it is now time to discuss it at greater length, for this period saw a considerable remodelling of secular and ecclesiastical units of government. The first thing to be noted is the secular power of the episcopate, whose constant consolidation led to the birth of the great episcopal principalities of the region. Otto I took up the principles of Carolingian government in relying on the episcopate in order to govern. He did not abandon the practice of immunities, whose origins go back to Merovingian times and whose possession exempted their holder from public burdens and the direct intervention of royal agents. The immunists' territories, often held by bishops and abbots, spread out with or without royal assent. Advocates represented the immunists before courts. In the ninth, and still more in the tenth century, many lay lords, dukes and counts held the abbacy of one or more monastic houses and relied on these as a source of power and income, used to raise mercenary soldiers. The Ottonians and their successors showed themselves doubly generous towards the bishops and the abbots or abbesses, and granted huge territories, counties, royal hunting-grounds and fiscal lands, as well as rights, particularly of an economic nature (the most frequently encountered formula referred to rights of market, toll and mint). Thanks to these grants, the bishops, though in varying degrees, established powerful lordships in which they alone were lords over men and over taxation, and exercised banal rights in all their domains. There were few diplomata marking these grants. In the case of Cambrai we know that the prelate was granted comital rights over the city in two stages, which made him the sole lord there; by 1007 he had complete control. In the case of Metz usurpation is suspected, and in that of Verdun Otto III's grant is known only from local tradition. Everywhere mints were set up which struck coins with the name of the prelate, at first alongside that of the sovereign, later without it. One could not enumerate all the grants of abbeys, counties and forests made to Lotharingian bishops from the mid-tenth to the mid-eleventh centuries: the result was the formation of principalities which, though scattered, were often on a very large scale. Cologne, Liège and Metz benefited from this process, as to a lesser extent did Cambrai and Verdun.

Since these cannot all be examined here, we may take Liège, which has been well studied, as an illustration. The most impressive gains took place during the episcopate of Notker (972–1008). In 980 Otto II confirmed all older donations and granted him a general immunity to cover all his lands; in 985 Otto III granted the powers and endowments of the county of Huy; in 987 he granted 'the county of Brugeron, the mint and toll at Maastricht, the abbeys of Lobbes and Fosses to which was added the new monastery of Gembloux'.[2] In 1006 Henry II confirmed all this, and then, as he did for Metz around the same time, offered a huge forest, a gigantic royal reserve set aside for hunting and fishing. In this way a territorial state was born, as similarly at Cologne, Verdun or Metz. The bishop of Metz recovered free control of the salt-works at Saulnois; his neighbour at Toul recovered the monasteries of the Vosges and extended his power into the neighbouring valleys around the city; the bishop of Verdun's acquisition of the county of Verdun made the ecclesiastical and the secular territory almost coterminous. For the later history of Lotharingia all these facts are of extreme importance: it was at this time that the 'Three Bishoprics' (Metz, Verdun and Toul) and the principalities of Liège and Cologne were born; Trier followed later.

The territorial fragmentation of the former *pagi*, which meant that counts could no longer operate within the lands of immunists, led to a progressive redistribution. There were soon more counts than *pagi* to be ruled over. Instead of designating these 'counties' by the names of the places which had long been their centres of operations, men now referred to them by the names of castles, the centres of residence, defence and control of a new class, first of counts, and then of mere lords, all of whom exercised banal powers. Even before this the *pagi* and *Gaue* had hardly maintained a fixed form. The largest, like Condroz or Brabant, had been divided into two or four; there are also isolated references to seemingly ephemeral *pagi*. The comital lists are full of gaps, not least owing to irregularities in nominations or successions and the progressive dismantling of the counties. Thus Siegfried was established in the castle at Luxemburg at the head of a territory which incorporated fiscal lands like those at Thionville, allodial lands and the advocacies of two large abbeys. In certain places the new

[2] Kupper (1981), p. 425.

counties were a continuation of the old ones, as in the Astenois (Dampierre) or in the Dormois (Grandpré). The huge county of the Chaumontois was eroded by the numerous monasteries within it; Hesbaye, Limbourg and Nahegau followed the same path. This period was thus particularly important for the way in which the transformations of Carolingian government into that of the feudal regime can be localised in time and space. Feudal institutions were still in an incipient form, but were gathering power. Oaths of fidelity were met with grants of benefices; lords surrounded themselves with bodyguards of professional mounted warriors; dukes and bishops were still able to slow down the tendency towards the building of fortifications, but not for very long. Lotharingia here followed general trends. It was perhaps in the effectiveness and the survival of the advocacy, the high advocacy which the counts had substituted for their earlier lay abbacies, that imperial influence was still felt most forcibly in the country.

A DYNAMIC TRANSIT REGION

Lotharingia has always been a transit zone. Long before *Francia media* had been established, the valleys of the Moselle and the Meuse, and the highways parallel to them, had been followed by travellers, pilgrims, merchants and armies moving from the region of the North Sea, Flanders and the Low Countries to Burgundy and northern Italy. These valleys were linked to the Alpine passes, notably that of the Little St Bernard, reached via the upper Rhône valley, and of the Mont-Cenis, reached via Lyons and Savoy. Commercial products came from Genoa, Venice and the orient to Paris or the great Lotharingian cities. The merchants of Verdun were familiar with the route which came down from the Rhineland and passed over to Spain via the valleys of the Saône and Rhône. The valley of the Meuse enjoyed a variety of fortunes. Verdun and Liège were successful towns; the upper valley was for the time being somewhat somnolent, while the lower section from the Ardennes to the river-mouth was by contrast a centre of an active commerce, which gave employment to the metal-workers of Namur, Huy and the Liègois. There was heavy traffic on the Meuse by the standards of the time. Here we are at the heart of the 'Pays Mosan' dear to the heart of Félix Rousseau. The Moselle valley was lined by abbeys, cities and castles destined to become towns: Remiremont, Epinal, Toul, Dieulouard, Metz, Thionville, Trier, Coblenz. To the north there was a junction with the densely populated valley of the Rhine up to Cologne, and to the south an ascent of the valley and the pass of Bussang led to Basel and the Suabian Jura.

This region was not as yet, any more than others, affected by the economic and urban growth which characterised the millennium, and which was not really to take off before the end of the first third of the century. Nevertheless, the first stirrings are visible: in the attention given to fairs and markets in the vicinity of the great monasteries and outside cities; in the striking of coins; in the artistic activity which enriched ecclesiastical treasuries; and in the mentions of travellers found in *miracula* and *vitae*. A number of towns in the process of foundation come to mind, such as Epinal, established by the bishop of Metz between 970 and 1005 with the double foundation of a castle and a religious community, followed by a market, at Lunéville, Dieulouard and Huy. Fifty or a hundred years later such examples will become more numerous.

Should we not be tempted to ascribe this growth in economic activity not only to the linguistic frontier and the contact between the two cultures but also to the reform dynamic which crossed *Francia media* from Brogne to Fruttuaria via Trier, Verdun, Metz, Toul, Dijon and Cluny? From around 934 we can find in Lotharingian monastic centres a radiating out of new forms of monasticism as a reaction to the monastic decline which was ascribed to a lay overlordship which devoured revenues and handed out benefices to soldiers and followers. We find ardent leaders, themselves often drawn from the secular clergy, filled with an ascetic vocation and attracting crowds of disciples before entering monasteries given or commended to them by leading abbots, and rigorous customs governing the application of the Rule of St Benedict. The movement began simultaneously in Gorze, in Saint-Evre in Toul, in St Maximin in Trier and in Brogne, and reached Flanders, Champagne and Saxony after swarming out into Lotharingia and Alsace. This growth contributed to the revival of cities, where new monasteries and chapters of canons were founded: Metz, around 1000, had eight Benedictine monasteries; Liège accumulated monasteries and chapters; so did Trier; in the course of fifty years Verdun moved from one to four religious houses. These phenomena are important because they help us to understand the intellectual activity of the period.

There is no question of the primacy of Liège as a centre of study in the tenth and eleventh centuries. At the beginning of the tenth century, Stephen had been at once a man of letters, a liturgist and a musician. For the following period historians have rescued from the shadows masters who attracted disciples from far afield and then became bishops. The name of Rather (of Lobbes, or Verona, or Liège) is on everyone's lips but it is not the only one. The real take-off came under the episcopates of Eraclius and Notker, the second building on the creations of the first. Was there perhaps an intention of turning Liège into 'a training centre for the imperial episcopate'?[3] At all events the teaching there was brilliant and varied, open in particular to science and mathematics under the influence of the Rheims *scholasticus*, Gerbert. Chartres,

---

[3] *Ibid.*, p. 119.

Rheims and Liège were in contact with each other; Adelman, who taught at Liège, had resided at Chartres. The main centre at Liège was the cathedral chapter of Saint-Lambert, but the abbey of Lobbes, distinguished by its master Heriger, was not far behind. The basis of teaching was of course the *trivium* and the *quadrivium*, but mathematics enjoyed a more important position than elsewhere; Rodulf of Liège discussed mathematics with Raimbold of Cologne. However, one should not underestimate the importance of divine sciences and of reflection on the exercise of power, and there were remarkable historians also: Folcuin of Lobbes, whose chronicle is filled with archival material, may serve as an example.

The other cities followed with greater or lesser success, led without doubt by Trier and Metz. Literary production reached a new height in this era, with chronicles, annals, saints' lives and collections of miracles succeeding one another. Authors were inspired to retrace the history of the most significant founders and benefactors, either by bringing ancient hagiography into line with contemporary taste and embellishing and thus transforming it, as with the Lives of the ancient fathers of Remiremont (Amatus, Romaricus and Adelphus) and of the older bishops, or by inventing miracles for those saints of whom there was no longer any knowledge, or by composing lives for the more recent. The *scholasticus* Adso was a master in this field; he came from Luxeuil to Toul, where he immediately wrote the *Lives* of St Mansuy, of St Evre and of Berchair of Montier in a fairly academic style, and took charge of the episcopal *Gesta*. From there he moved to Montier-en-Der, where he became abbot and composed a work on the Antichrist dedicated to Queen Gerberga; a list of his small personal library has survived. A whole literature grew up at Metz around St Clement, while Gorze and Saint-Arnulf produced *miracula* for St Gorgon and St Glosindis as well as giving us the admirable life of the reformer John of Gorze. The movement spread to monasteries outside cities, as one can see from the production of chronicles at Moyenmoutier and Saint-Mihiel. A similar enthusiasm can be found at Cambrai, Liège or Trier.

Besides literary and artisanal production, one should mention the flourishing of art. Lotharingia had a tradition in the production of fine illuminated manuscripts going back to the ninth century, though not such an important one as in the major German or French centres, and Rheims still had a strong influence on the productions of Liège. Metz comes readily to mind, though the scriptoria of this centre had not yet reached their height in the production of illuminations, but few other examples do. This should not be interpreted as meaning lack of activity, for the workshops of the monasteries, cathedrals and chapters copied and produced plenty of books. Their production, however, was plain: books meant to be studied, read and meditated upon. The library catalogues which are preserved for Liège, Gorze and Saint-Evre in Toul show ample and varied libraries, with a place for the sciences and philology as well as for the ancient and more recent patristic literature. The reputation of the scriptoria was so high that the bishops of Freising summoned scribes from Metz and Toul or sent their own scribes there to copy works; calligraphy was a Lotharingian speciality.

In the fine arts proper the Walloon lands had already achieved an honourable level, soon to be surpassed. Leaving sculpture aside, where the most important works date from the end of the eleventh century and beyond, one may mention goldsmithery, enamelwork and ivory-carving. There was an ancient tradition of metal-working in the Meuse valley, which showed itself especially in the production of liturgical utensils, crosses and reliquaries; here bronzework supported gold- and silverwork. Ivory workshops appear to have had a continuous existence at Metz during the ninth and tenth centuries. One or two book-covers provide a firm basis for dating, and it would appear that there were two distinct phases of production, the second around the year 1000 and linked with a panel bearing the name of Adalbero II of Metz. Besides such panels, which decorated the finest manuscripts and generally included scenes from the life of Christ, especially the Crucifixion and the Resurrection, combs and small boxes were also produced. But Metz certainly had no monopoly, and one is tempted to suppose that Liège and Cologne also had a part in this production. The Crucifixion of Tongres corresponds to that of Adalbero of Metz. The experts are by no means unanimous on all these matters, and the resultant uncertainty probably helps to maintain Metz's claim to primacy; the famous cathedra of St Peter, firmly dated to the tenth century and definitely attributable to Metz, provides some further support for this.

CHAPTER 13

BURGUNDY AND PROVENCE,

879–1032

Constance Brittain Bouchard

THE REGION known as Burgundy has had some of the most elastic borders of any region of France, and some of the various regions called 'Burgundy' at different times barely overlap at all. The name comes from the tribe of the Burgundians, who in the fifth century established a kingdom centred in the region between Geneva and Lyons, which kingdom stretched south towards Arles. After this kingdom was conquered by the sons of Clovis in the 530s, 'Burgundy' became one of the three principal Frankish kingdoms (with Neustria and Austrasia) and covered essentially all the Loire and Saône–Rhône river basins, stretching from its capital at Orléans to the Mediterranean.

A somewhat diminished version of this Merovingian kingdom of Burgundy was divided between the sons of Louis the Pious in 843. Charles the Bald of France received the western part, essentially the region between the Saône and the Loire, reaching from Sens and Troyes south to Autun and Mâcon. This is the region which later (and without Sens and Troyes) became the French duchy of Burgundy. French Burgundy, and indeed the entire French *regnum*, was divided from imperial territory by the Rhône–Saône river basin. At various times and in various places both French Burgundy and imperial Burgundy reached across to the other side of the river, and south of Mâcon imperial Burgundy was often considered to include at least a narrow strip of the river system's west bank, but for the most part these rivers can be considered the dividing line between the two Burgundies, French and imperial, which were permanently separated after 843.

At the same time as Charles the Bald received the French portion of the old Frankish kingdom of Burgundy, the emperor Lothar I took both that part of Burgundy east of the Saône and that south of Mâcon. Imperial Burgundy included both the region around Besançon and Geneva, the heart of the Burgundian kingdom of four centuries earlier, and the region from Lyons and Vienne south to Arles and the Mediterranean. This latter, more southerly part of imperial Burgundy was sometimes called lower or cisjurane Burgundy (to

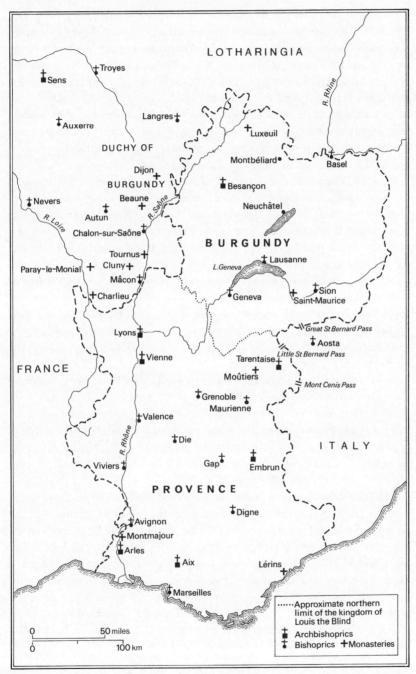

LOTHARINGIA

Troyes

Sens

Auxerre

Langres

Luxeuil

DUCHY OF

Montbéliard

Basel

Dijon

BURGUNDY

Besançon

Nevers

Beaune

Neuchâtel

Autun

R. Loire

Chalon-sur-Saône

R. Saône

BURGUNDY

Tournus

L.Geneva

Lausanne

Paray-le-Monial

Cluny

Mâcon

Geneva

Sion

Charlieu

Saint-Maurice

Great St Bernard Pass

Lyons

Aosta

Little St Bernard Pass

FRANCE

Vienne

Tarentaise

Moûtiers

Mont Cenis Pass

Grenoble

Maurienne

Valence

R. Rhône

Die

ITALY

Viviers

Gap

Embrun

PROVENCE

Digne

Avignon

Montmajour

Arles

Aix

Lérins

Marseilles

R. Rhine

......Approximate northern
limit of the kingdom of
Louis the Blind

■ Archbishoprics

† Bishoprics + Monasteries

0   50 miles

0   100 km

6 Burgundy and Provence

distinguish it from upper or trans-Saône Burgundy) and sometimes called Provence. The Carolingians divided imperial Burgundy into these two parts in 855, when Provence, the Lyons–Vienne–Arles region, was made into a separate kingdom for Charles, son of the emperor Lothar I.

This chapter will focus on the history of both halves of imperial Burgundy (i.e., upper Burgundy and Provence) as well as that of the region which later became the French duchy of Burgundy, between the late ninth century and the early eleventh century. For imperial Burgundy, I shall primarily follow the activities of the kings. For French Burgundy, however, an area in which royal power was weak, I shall concentrate on the dukes and counts.

Imperial Burgundy became the first area for over a century in the heartland of Carolingian hegemony to have a non-Carolingian king when, on 15 October 879, King Boso of Burgundy and Provence was elected at Mantaille, near Vienne. Boso was one of a group of relatives known to modern scholars as the Bosonids (see Table 7, p. 698). They constituted at least three separate though related lineages, but all seem descended from people who had held power along the Rhône since the eighth century. Boso took full advantage of what has been termed *Königsnähe*, closeness to the king, to move from responsibilities within the royal court to semi-autonomous authority within the royal domains, from marriage with a woman of the royal family to a claim to the royal throne itself. Indeed, Boso is the classic case of such a process in the ninth century.

Boso and his brother Richard (known as Richard le Justicier since the eleventh century) became extremely powerful members of the court of Charles the Bald. Boso quickly acquired property and *honores*, both in French Burgundy, where he was count of Mâcon and became count of Autun, and in imperial Burgundy, of which Charles the Bald acquired part in 869, after the death first of Charles of Provence and then of his brother Lothar II, and the rest in 875, when he became emperor.

Like his paternal uncle, who had earlier served Louis the Pious, Boso began by serving as royal *ostiarius*, but was soon given the title of archminister of the palace and named royal chamberlain for Aquitaine. In 869 Boso received the abbey of Saint-Maurice of Agaune from Charles, an abbey which had once been held by Boso's maternal uncle Hubert (d. 864). This abbey, located in upper Burgundy, had, like nearby Luxeuil, been an important monastic model in Merovingian times, although it was much less influential under its ninth-century lay abbots. In 871, Charles the Bald named Boso count of Vienne, which city Boso made his capital. He accompanied the king on his Italian campaigns and was given the title of duke of Pavia in 876. According to Regino of Prüm, although Regino's accuracy has been challenged on this point, Charles even made Boso his viceroy for the region of Provence (lower Burgundy) in

877, shortly before his own death.[1] At any rate, Boso acted as if he were viceroy there during the two-year reign of Charles' son, Louis the Stammerer.

In the meantime, Boso also forged links of marriage between his family and the Carolingians. In 869, he offered his sister Richildis to Charles the Bald as the king's concubine, and Charles married her a few months later. In 876, with Charles' approval, Boso himself married the king's great-niece Ermengard, daughter of the late German emperor Louis II and his wife Angilberga. The widowed empress Angilberga seems to have wanted to be reconciled with the new duke of Pavia, a formidable competitor, and recognised that her daughter, who had no living brothers and thus had enormous potential as an heiress, would remain a target until she was married.

With these marital alliances and a considerable accumulation of secular power, Boso was in an excellent position to claim the crown for himself. After the death of Charles the Bald in 877 and, in 879, of Charles' son Louis the Stammerer, who left only two under-age sons born to a repudiated concubine (Charles the Simple, his third son, was born posthumously), Boso moved quickly to have himself elected king by a major portion of the bishops of Burgundy (both imperial and French Burgundy); he was crowned by the archbishop of Lyons.

He had been assisted in his rise to the throne by his formidable wife, Ermengard. She had as a girl been engaged to the Byzantine emperor Basil, and was quoted by the *Annales Bertiniani* as saying in 879 that she, daughter of the Roman emperor and formerly affianced to the Greek emperor, would not want to live if she could not make her own husband king.[2] Boso may have intended originally to succeed Louis the Stammerer as king of the Franks, but he ended up as king only of Burgundy and Provence. Indeed, Regino of Prüm, writing half a century later, distinguished between Boso's rule in Provence (*Provintia*), his by gift of Charles the Bald, and his rather abrupt entry into upper Burgundy (*Burgundia*).[3]

At the time, however, the consensus of Boso's enemies was that Boso had no right to any sort of royal title. His eight-year reign (879–87) was almost entirely filled by the unsuccessful wars he waged against the sons of Louis the Stammerer and their allies. Among those allied against him was Pope John VIII, even though the pope had referred to Boso as his 'adopted son' only a year earlier.[4] Hugh the Abbot, of the powerful Welf family (discussed further below), also joined the alliance against Boso. The duke of Aquitaine, for which territory Boso had once been royal chamberlain, was rewarded in 880

---

[1] Regino, *Chronicon, s.a.* 877; Bautier (1973), pp. 46–7.   [2] *Annales Bertiniani, s.a.* 869, 879.

[3] Regino, *Chronicon, s.a.* 879.

[4] '... Bosonem gloriosum principem per adoptionis gratiam filium meum effeci': John VIII, *Epistolae,* no. 110.

with Boso's county of Mâcon, for his role in driving the beleaguered king out of it.

One of Boso's bitterest opponents was his own younger brother, Richard le Justicier. Once Boso was elected king, Richard moved quickly to create his own centre of power in French Burgundy. It is easy to appreciate why Boso had tried to create kindred ties with the Carolingians, since at this time one's closest male relatives were potentially one's fiercest rivals. Richard made his capital at Autun, which Boso had acquired in 879, shortly before being elected king. In 880, Richard asked Carloman, son of Louis the Stammerer, to recognise him as count of Autun. Here Carloman was rewarding Richard for supporting the Carolingians against his own brother. It is interesting to note that wielding effective rule in a region was not enough; one needed to have royal confirmation of one's comital office as well. Two years later, in 882, Richard captured Vienne, Boso's capital, and took Boso's wife and daughter back to Autun as his prisoners.

Although Boso remained uncaptured, the last five years of his life, from 882 to 887, were marked by a complete lack of military and political success. When Boso died, on 11 January 887, it was as a discredited usurper. Interestingly, however, he was still respected by the Burgundian churches. He was buried at the cathedral of Vienne, his old capital, and the obituary there recorded the gifts he had given the church. The monastery of Charlieu, located in the southern part of the county of Mâcon, considered Boso its founder. While others forgot him after his death, the monks there preserved his memory and featured him prominently in the church's twelfth-century sculptural programme.[5] Only one year after Boso's death, in 888, several more non-Carolingians were elected kings within the area of former Carolingian hegemony. Interestingly, however, none of these claimed Provence. These 'kinglets' (*reguli*), as the *Annales* of Fulda disparagingly called them,[6] included Odo of France (son of Robert the Strong, ancestor of the Capetians), Berengar of Italy (grandson of Louis the Pious through his mother), Arnulf of Germany (a Carolingian through his father though born to a concubine), and Rudolf I of upper or trans-Saône Burgundy.

In the meantime, the widowed yet determined Queen Ermengard of Burgundy and Provence had been released from Richard's captivity and set about trying to establish the fortunes of her two children by Boso. She seems to have quickly come to terms with Richard le Justicier, from now on the undisputed head of French Burgundy. Ermengard's children were named Angilberga and Louis, for her own imperial parents. Angilberga was married to William I, duke of Aquitaine, who seemed eager to make peace with the

[5] Bouchard (1988), p. 428.   [6] *Annales Fuldenses, s.a.* 888.

Bosonids – and use a marriage connection to further his own position – once King Boso was dead.

One of the most significant results of the marriage between Angilberga and William of Aquitaine was the foundation of the monastery of Cluny in 909. The duke's own centre of power was in the Auvergne, fairly far from the county of Mâcon where the monastery was founded, and he himself had been accused of wasting the resources of Saint-Julien of Brioude (in the Auvergne), which monastery he ruled as secular abbot. He might thus seem like a somewhat odd person to found a monastery which later became a symbol of religious reform and freedom. But this foundation makes excellent sense as the work of the duchess Angilberga.[7]

William was willing to take the lead from his wife, as is indicated by the fact that they named their son neither William nor Bernard (his father's name) but Boso, her father's name (young Boso predeceased his father). The county of Mâcon had been Angilberga's father's until William's father had won it from him in battle, and the regular monks established at Cluny were of the same sort her own family had patronised for two generations. Interestingly, after William's death, when the county of Mâcon broke away from the duchy of Aquitaine (the latter now ruled by the counts of Poitou), the dukes paid no more attention to Cluny for a century. Yet throughout this period the monks continued to receive gifts from Angilberga's Bosonid relatives.

Cluny's foundation in 909 was the culmination of a fifty-year period in which a number of monasteries had been founded or refounded within French Burgundy. These included the monasteries of Vézelay and Pouthières, both founded by Count Gerard of Roussillon and his wife in 858/9; the monastery of Saint-Bénigne of Dijon, the oldest house in the region, which was reformed and rebuilt by the bishop of Langres in 869/70; the monastery of Charlieu, founded by the bishop of Valence in 872 and given much of its early possessions by King Boso, as noted above; and the monastery of Saint-Philibert of Tournus, founded in 875 in the old house of Saint-Valérien with the support of Charles the Bald, by monks fleeing the Vikings.

While marrying her daughter to the duke of Aquitaine, Boso's widow also tried to get her son Louis elected king. According to the *Annales* of Fulda (though the accuracy of this has been questioned), in 887, once Boso was dead, Ermengard persuaded her cousin Charles the Fat to adopt Louis as his son – he had no sons of his own.[8] It may be this potential legitimacy of a claim to Provence in 887 that kept any of the new kings of 888 from taking that kingdom.

---

[7] *Cartulaire de Brioude*, nos. 26, 66, pp. 48–50, 87–8. Bouchard (1988), pp. 425–6.

[8] *Annales Fuldenses, s.a.* 887: '. . . quasi adoptivum filium eum iniunxit'.

At any rate, Charles the Fat was deposed later in 887 and died early in 888, and no one else immediately took up the imperial title. This left the broad strip of Burgundy and Provence which had been attached to the empire since 843 without a ruler, making possible both Rudolf's accession to upper Burgundy in 888, as already noted, and Louis' election to lower Burgundy (Provence) in 890. He was elected in an assembly at Valence without any apparent opposition.

Louis' kingdom was smaller than his father's, as it did not include upper Burgundy, taken by Rudolf, nor any of French Burgundy, taken by his uncle Richard le Justicier. Louis' kingdom of Provence stretched from Vienne, his capital as it had once been his father's, down to Arles and the Mediterranean. He was supported by the bishops of the region; by Dukes Richard and William, his uncle and brother-in-law, who had opposed Boso but now came to the aid of Boso's son; and by the secular lords of Provence, who were feeling the increasingly frequent attacks by the Saracens along their coast.

Louis ruled successfully in Provence for ten years, then determined to extend his rule into Italy. Louis' initial Italian campaigns against King Berengar I were highly successful. In 900 he was crowned king of Italy, and in 901 Pope Benedict IV crowned him emperor. He capped his success by marrying Anna, daughter of the Byzantine emperor Leo VI and mother of Louis' heir, Charles-Constantine. But his success was short-lived. King Berengar, who continued to call himself king of Italy even while Louis also held that title, soon renewed the war. After several years of campaigning, Berengar captured Louis in 905. Rather than executing him, he blinded him and sent him home to Burgundy. Blinding was a relatively common punishment in Italy (and Byzantium) at this period; it incapacitated one's enemy, yet, because it left him alive, did not create a power vacuum into which a potentially more dangerous rival might move.

While Berengar consolidated his hold on Italy, and shortly had *himself* crowned emperor, Louis the Blind returned to Vienne. Louis lived for over twenty more years, probably until 928, and continued to style himself emperor, but no one outside of lower Burgundy seems to have paid him the slightest bit of attention. His last known activity with any political ramifications was his second marriage, to a woman named Adelaide, most likely the daughter of Rudolf I of upper Burgundy.[9] After Louis' death, lower Burgundy (Provence) was never again a separate kingdom with an independent king.

Louis' oldest son, Charles-Constantine, with a name that represented his Roman and Greek imperial parentage, never became king. He had to be content with the title of count of Vienne, his father's and grandfather's capital. His cousin King Radulf of France finally gave him this county in 931, three years after his father died; between 928 and 931 it had been held by Heribert of Vermandois.[10] Charles-Constantine kept control of Vienne after the

---

[9] Poupardin (1901), p. 208.   [10] Flodoard, *Annales, s.a.* 928, 931.

Carolingians regained the French throne; he received the Carolingian king Louis IV there in 941 and 951. But the county of Vienne was but a small part of what his father had held, much less his grandfather; even the county of Arles within the old kingdom of Provence was lost to Charles-Constantine. He and his wife Tetburgis had two sons, named Richard and Hubert, but nothing certain is known of them beyond their names. They did not even succeed to their father's county of Vienne. After Charles-Constantine died around 962, King Lothar of France (son of Louis IV) granted Vienne to King Conrad of Burgundy in 966, as part of the dowry of his sister Matilda.

Although scholars have been tempted to make one or the other of Charles-Constantine's sons (or perhaps his younger brother Rudolf, doubtless born to Adelaide, Louis' second wife) the ancestor of the counts of Arles, or of Savoy, or of Vienne of half a century or a century later, all that can be said with assurance is that the descendants of the emperor Louis the Blind disappear into both documentary and political obscurity. During Louis' twenty years of seclusion, other men had taken over the kingdoms and even the imperial title he had called his, and it was much too late for his descendants to reacquire them.

Radulf, the king of France who confirmed Charles-Constantine as count of Vienne after the death of Louis the Blind, was also a Bosonid, son of Duke Richard le Justicier of French Burgundy. Richard, King Boso's younger brother, had been instrumental in leading Burgundian forces against the Vikings towards the end of the ninth century. Interestingly, he never took the route of his brother Boso of Burgundy and Provence, of his brother-in-law Rudolf I of trans-Saône Burgundy, of his nephew Louis the Blind of Provence, or even (later) of his own son, in trying to become king himself. Rather, he served the Carolingians faithfully during his long life. It may well be significant that only after Richard's death in 921 did Duke Robert I of Francia, Richard's ally and friend, rebel against Charles the Simple, which rebellion ended with Robert's own coronation as king of France in 922 (see Table 13).

But when Robert was killed in battle less than a year later, French Burgundy produced its first king, Radulf, son of Richard le Justicier and son-in-law of Robert I (Robert's own sons were too young to inherit in 923). Radulf kept Charles the Simple imprisoned while he was king, but Charles' son, the future Louis IV, was alive and well in England, with his mother's family. And when Radulf died without an heir in 936, the Carolingians regained the French crown for another fifty years. The tenth-century dukes of French Burgundy did not again produce a king of France, although the Capetian kings of France did produce later dukes of Burgundy.

Radulf had continued to play a major role in French Burgundy at the same time as he was king of the Franks. After his death, French Burgundy was dominated in the tenth century by several lines of counts related to Richard le Justicier (see Table 10). Initially, while Radulf was still alive, according to the eleventh-century *Chronicle* of Saint-Bénigne of Dijon, the duchy was divided between his two younger brothers, Boso and Hugh the Black. Neither of these brothers had an heir of his own, and Boso died even before Radulf. According to the *Annales* of Flodoard, the duchy was then divided in 936 between Hugh the Black, the son of Richard le Justicier, and Hugh the Great, son of Robert I. Hugh the Great was confirmed in the duchy of Burgundy by the Carolingian Louis IV in 943. Hugh the Great spent little time in French Burgundy, concentrating instead on Francia, the other duchy Louis confirmed to him in 943, but two of his sons did become dukes in Burgundy later in the century, as indicated below.

In the meantime, two other lines of counts, both connected to Richard le Justicier, also played a key role in French Burgundian politics in the tenth century (see Table 10). These were the counts of Atuyer and Dijon, descended from one Gibuin who seems to have been an illegitimate son of Richard's,[11] and the descendants of Count Manasses, who was probably Richard's nephew.[12] Both of these lineages also produced powerful bishops as well as counts. The first of these lineages, the descendants of Gibuin, never had more than a narrow area of power, being restricted to the region immediately around Dijon. Gibuin's son, Count Hugh I of Dijon (d. 954), was the father of Count Richard of Dijon, Count Hugh II of Atuyer, and Gibuin, bishop of Châlons for most of the second half of the tenth century. During the eleventh century, when the dukes of Burgundy made Dijon their capital, the descendants of Hugh II became lords of Beaumont. Count Manasses, often called Manasses 'l'Ancien' by modern scholars, the brother of Bishop Walo of Autun (893–919), was the father of Bishop Hervé of Autun (919–35) and of Count Gislebert. After the death of Hugh the Black in 952, this Count Gislebert briefly became the most important figure in French Burgundy, but in 956 both he and Hugh the Great died.

The title of duke of Burgundy was then taken by Otto, son of Hugh the Great and brother of Hugh Capet, the future king of France (see Table 9). Otto married Letgardis, Gislebert's daughter (his other daughter, Adelaide-Werra, married Count Robert of Troyes and Meaux). Then, after Otto's death in 965, the title of duke of Burgundy was taken by his brother Henry (or Henry-Odo) (d. 1002). Henry had originally been intended to be a cleric, but he emerged from the church to become one of the most important secular lords of the late tenth century.

---

[11] Bouchard (1987), pp. 319–23.

[12] Based on Duchesne's reading of a now illegible section of the *Series* of the abbots of Flavigny (BN, Coll Baluze 57, fol. 210). His printed text of 1625 (Duchesne, *Histoire généalogique*, preuves, p. 17) diverges from this, probably erroneously. See also Hlawitschka (1968), p. 242 n. 4.

Several other major lines of counts were established in French Burgundy during the tenth century and influenced local politics into the eleventh century and later. These included the counts of Mâcon, descendants of the viscounts of Mâcon, who took the comital title early in the century, after the death of William I of Aquitaine; the counts of Chalon, established around 970 in a county which had earlier been held by Hugh the Great; and the line of the counts of Nevers, which became established around the same time Henry became duke of French Burgundy.

Although during much of the tenth century the various counts and dukes within French Burgundy took advantage of the absence of strong royal authority to become extremely powerful in their own right, by the end of the century some of their own power was weakening, as indicated by such evidence as the virtual disappearance of public counts' courts and the lessening of their authority over the local bishops. Especially in the southern part of French Burgundy, the rise of independent castellans, exercising banal rights and extracting dues from all people living in their castellanies, challenged former comital monopolies during the eleventh century. In the northern part of French Burgundy, however, especially in the region around Dijon where, beginning with Duke Henry, the Capetian dukes had their greatest power, these dukes were the chief threat to comital independence. Close ties of marriage or alliance were established between Duke Henry and all of these counts.

In the 970s he married the daughter of the first hereditary count of Chalon and adopted her son William (or Otto-William), fathered by her first husband, Adalbert, last king of Italy. Otto-William, as he is usually known to modern scholars, seems to have taken the 'Otto' at the time of his adoption. He became the most important figure in French Burgundy at the turn of the century, as well as continuing to control considerable domains in northern Italy, inherited from his father.[13] Not long after his mother married Duke Henry, he himself married the widowed countess of Mâcon, taking over that county, probably in 981. Countess Ermentrude of Mâcon was a very well placed woman in her own right, being sister of Bishop Brun of Langres and niece of the Carolingian King Lothar of France. Otto-William cemented an alliance with Landric, who became first hereditary count of Nevers, by engaging his daughter to him and giving him the county of Nevers at the same time. It should be noted that, although the Nivernais was separated from the French duchy of Burgundy in the late middle ages under the Valois dukes, in the tenth and eleventh centuries it was very much part of the duchy.

When Duke Henry died in 1002, without legitimate sons of his own, the duchy of French Burgundy was disputed between Otto-William, the duke's

---

[13] Poupardin (1907), pp. 420–9.

adopted son, and King Robert II, the duke's nephew. In the protracted wars which ensued, almost all the Burgundian lords rebelled against the king; only Hugh, count of Chalon and bishop of Auxerre (999–1039), remained loyal to the king, even though he was Otto-William's uncle. The king's principal ally in the fighting was the duke of Normandy. These wars were finally settled around 1015, with the king's victory over Otto-William and over Landric, count of Nevers, who had been the king's bitter enemy – to the point that some contemporary chroniclers virtually ignored Otto-William's own role in the wars.

This final generation of the tenth century and early years of the eleventh century was also the period in which Cluny began to be an important influence on monasticism within French Burgundy. During the first fifty or sixty years after its 909 foundation, Cluny had reformed more houses in the Auvergne and in Italy than in the various regions of Burgundy, although Cluny's abbot became abbot of Boso's house of Charlieu in 932, when King Hugh of Italy gave it to Cluny.

But in the late tenth century Cluny helped many ruined or dissolute Burgundian monasteries recover their regularity. In many instances the monks went on to elect abbots of their own, rather than becoming Cluniac priories; one cannot speak of Cluny as being the head of an institutionalised 'order' until the twelfth century. Cluny's abbot helped, around 970, establish the monastery of Paray-le-monial, a foundation of the counts of Chalon, but Paray only became a Cluniac priory in 999, when the count of Chalon gave it to Cluny. Around 990, that count's mother had given the old, ruined monastery of Saint-Marcel-lès-Chalon to Cluny, also as a priory. In other cases Cluny's reform led to no permanent affiliation. The abbot of Cluny reformed the monasteries of both Saint-Germain of Auxerre and Saint-Bénigne of Dijon, at the request of Duke Henry of Burgundy, in 986 and 990 respectively, by sending monks from Cluny to be abbots there, without establishing any permanent tie to Cluny. The old abbey of Moûtier-Saint-Jean, the second oldest in the duchy after Saint-Bénigne, had become a Cluny priory in 984, but in 986 the abbot of Cluny gave it instead to Saint-Germain. Both Saint-Germain and Saint-Bénigne became important centres of monastic reform in their own right in the first half of the eleventh century.

After King Robert and his Norman allies finally made peace with the French Burgundians around 1015, the son of Landric of Nevers married a Capetian girl, and Otto-William had his heir marry a daughter of the duke of Normandy. Otto-William contented himself after this with the county of Mâcon and with the title of count – rather than duke – of Burgundy. Although Otto-William's descendants later acquired a 'county of Burgundy' east of the Saône, in imperial Burgundy, as noted below, the title pre-dated the county itself. Indeed, the title *comes Burgundie* seems originally to have been attached to the county of

Mâcon, which Otto-William had acquired through marriage; his predecessor Count Leotold of Mâcon appeared with this title in 951 and 955.[14] Even while King Rudolf III of upper Burgundy was still alive, before Otto-William's descendants carved out a county around Besançon for themselves, Otto-William had begun exercising power there; Thietmar of Merseburg said that he was the king's dependant or knight (*miles*) there in name but lord in fact.[15] The French duchy of Burgundy was meanwhile intended for Henry, King Robert II's second son; young Henry began appearing there with his father around 1016. Then, when the king's oldest son died in 1025 and Prince Henry became the royal heir, the duchy of Burgundy was designated for the king's next son, Robert. After the end of the fighting between the brothers and their mother which followed King Robert's death in 1031, Duke Robert settled down as duke of French Burgundy, and all subsequent dukes until the fourteenth century were descended from him.

Count Otto-William of Burgundy and Mâcon died in 1026 and was succeeded as count of Burgundy by his son Rainald. Rainald gradually pushed his way eastward, especially after the death of King Rudolf III in 1032. Although the counts of Mâcon lost a good deal of authority to the castellans of the Mâconnais in the eleventh century, members of the family were able eventually to outcompete the castellans of upper Burgundy and exercise virtual royal authority in the region. When Rudolf had died, the royal Burgundian title went to the German king, but after the first few years the kings of Germany paid no attention to imperial Burgundy for over a century. Instead, it became part of the territory ruled by the counts of Burgundy and Mâcon, the 'county of Burgundy' itself, although, interestingly, after Rainald's son William succeeded, it was called the county of Count William as often as it was called the county of Burgundy.[16]

This kingdom of upper Burgundy – or the Jura and cisalpine Gaul as Flodoard called it – was the northern part of imperial Burgundy, east of the Saône from French Burgundy. It had itself had an eventful history between Rudolf I's accession in 888 and Rudolf III's death in 1032. The Rudolfian kings of Burgundy were not related to the Bosonids originally. Their family, known as the Welfs to modern scholars (see Table 8), had established power throughout much of the Carolingian empire during the ninth century, in part again by tying themselves closely by marriage to the Carolingians. They were descended from an early ninth-century powerful lord named Welf, who married his daughter Judith to Louis the Pious, as the emperor's second wife, and married another daughter, Emma, to Louis the German, Louis the Pious' son by his first wife.

---

[14] Flodoard, *Annales, s.a.* 951; D Lo 7.

[15] Thietmar, *Chronicon* VII, 30: 'miles est regis in nomine et dominus in re'.

[16] Bouchard (1987), p. 272.

Welf's successors had made the family very powerful in the next three generations. His son Conrad ruled in Bavaria, and his grandson, also named Conrad, became count of Auxerre. The first Conrad married Adelaide, sister of Lothar I's wife Ermengard. The second Conrad's brother Hugh (d. 886), often known as Hugh the Abbot because he held the abbeys of Saint-Martin of Tours and Saint-Germain of Auxerre, succeeded to the *honores* of Robert the Strong when that count, the ancestor of the Capetians, died in 866, leaving only under-age sons. Thus the Welfs were well established even before the second Conrad's son Rudolf, who had already been a count in imperial Burgundy, took the royal crown of upper Burgundy at Saint-Maurice d'Agaune in 888.

Almost immediately upon becoming king, Rudolf I created the same sort of marriage tie to the royal family that had immediately preceded him in imperial Burgundy as both Rudolf's ancestors and King Boso had created with the Carolingians. Shortly after Rudolf's coronation, he had his sister Adelaide marry Richard le Justicier, who as brother of King Boso and duke of French Burgundy in his own right was someone whose allegiance Rudolf needed, and yet as one of the leaders in the wars against Boso perhaps represented the forces of legitimacy. In 929, Adelaide gave the monastery of Romainmôtier, located in upper Burgundy, to Cluny, the house her husband's niece had helped found.

Rudolf I seems originally to have hoped for a much larger kingdom, including much of what had once been ruled by Lothar II. But after negotiations with Arnulf, the new German king in 888, Rudolf was forced to limit himself to the Jura and the diocese of Besançon, allowing Alsace and Lorraine to be attached to the German crown. Indeed, Arnulf attempted unsuccessfully to appropriate the kingdom of upper Burgundy for his own son in 895. Rudolf I died in 912 and was succeeded by his son, Rudolf II.

Rudolf II was king during a period in which the region was ravaged by repeated Magyar incursions. But his principal battles were not against the Magyars but rather part of an expansionist policy. He continued his father's attempts to increase the size of the kingdom of upper Burgundy, but in a new direction. When Lotharingia had been broken off from the German kingdom in 911 it was taken not by the king of Burgundy but by Charles the Simple of France. But Rudolf II pursued the kingdom of Italy with greater success – at least initially. In 922, in the midst of strife, Rudolf marched into Lombardy, where he was accepted as king by the counts and bishops. In 923, Rudolf defeated Berengar I, but he was immediately faced by another claimant to Italy, Count Hugh of Arles.

Hugh was a Bosonid, grandson of Hubert, lay abbot of Saint-Maurice, and second cousin of Louis the Blind (see Table 7). He had served Louis faithfully for years, acting as count of Provence while Louis was in Italy, even helping restore the churches of Vienne that had been sacked by the Saracens. He made no attempt to challenge Louis for the throne of Provence after that king's humiliation, even though he, rather than Louis's son Charles-Constantine, took the county of Arles once Louis was dead. Rather than trying to be king of Provence, Hugh always seems to have had his eye on the kingdoms of upper Burgundy and of Italy.

In 912, after Rudolf I died, Hugh promptly married his widow, Willa, and unsuccessfully challenged Rudolf II for the Burgundian throne. By 920 at the latest, Hugh turned his attention to Italy, wracked by wars involving Berengar I, the pope and a number of counts. After Rudolf II had defeated Berengar and, in 924, Berengar had died, Hugh gained quick and decisive victories. In 926, he had himself crowned king of Italy. Immediately upon taking the throne he began distributing political and ecclesiastical offices to the large group of Burgundian and Provençal allies and relatives he had brought with him. Hugh would rule Italy without major setbacks, in spite of constant wars, for the next twenty years (926–47), before finally being driven back to Provence in the last year of his life.

In consolidating his hold over Italy, Hugh was willing to reduce drastically his role in Provence. He appeared in Vienne with the title *rex* in 928, probably shortly after the death of Louis the Blind, but since he had been king of Italy for two years at this point one probably should not read too much into his use of the title there. At any rate, his visit to Vienne was brief. According to Liudprand of Cremona, around 933 he offered Rudolf II a bargain, that Hugh would not challenge Rudolf in his Gallic territories if Rudolf stayed out of Italy.[17] Essentially Hugh seems to have been willing to concede Provence to Rudolf in return for Italy. Hugh spent little more time in Provence after this, even though he did lead a major battle against the Saracens there in 942. Although Rudolf II did not in fact move into Provence, the area's last chance of being an independent kingdom was gone.

But if Hugh was willing to give up to Rudolf II any claim to be king of Provence, he continued to eye the kingdom of upper Burgundy. When Rudolf II died in 937, leaving only a young son, Hugh immediately married his widow, Bertha of Suabia, as he had earlier married Rudolf's mother, and affianced his son Lothar to Adelaide, Rudolf II's daughter. But in spite of Hugh's new claim to upper Burgundy, Rudolf II's young son Conrad succeeded (937–93).

Conrad, known to historians as 'the Pacific', faced more potentially serious challenges from the German king than from the king of Italy. Otto I, who had just succeeded in 936, marched into Burgundy in 938 and took Conrad under his protection. He arranged for Conrad's coronation in 940. By 942, when

---

[17] Liudprand, *Antapodosis* III, 48.

Otto began allowing the young king of upper Burgundy more independence, it was on the clear understanding that Conrad owed allegiance to Otto. Otto considered the king of Burgundy useful primarily in advancing his own ambitions. As already noted, Conrad's sister Adelaide had married Lothar, son of King Hugh and heir to Italy, and they had a daughter, Emma, who eventually married King Lothar of France. But after the death of Lothar of Italy in 950, leaving no sons, his widow Adelaide married Otto I of Germany, giving, in her position of queen of Italy, greater legitimacy to Otto's claim to be king of Italy.

Initially, the young Conrad was in no position to make any claim to Provence, in spite of his father's agreement with King Hugh of Italy. Boso, younger brother of King Hugh, ruled as count of Arles in his brother's place. But during the 940s, especially after the death of King Hugh in 947, Conrad expanded Burgundian rule into the old kingdom of Provence. Although Charles-Constantine continued to be count of Vienne until his own death around 962, owing allegiance to the Carolingian king of France rather than to the king of upper Burgundy, his county was attached to the kingdom of Burgundy in 966. Conrad's expansion meant that Provence, like upper Burgundy, increasingly fell under the authority of Otto I of Germany, for Otto continued to keep Conrad firmly in his train. It was Otto, not Conrad, who attempted to drive the Saracens out of the southern Alps in 968.

Conrad ruled as king of Burgundy until 993, when he was succeeded by his son Rudolf III. Conrad had married Matilda, daughter of the Carolingian Louis IV. As well as Rudolf, Conrad fathered Bertha, who married Count Odo I of Blois and, after his death, King Robert II of France – although the couple were forced to separate after a great deal of debate and scandal. His other two daughters, Gisela and Gerberga, created connections between the Burgundian royal house and the emperors of the early eleventh century. Gisela, who married Duke Henry of Bavaria, was the mother of the emperor Henry II; and Gerberga, who married Duke Hermann of Suabia, was the mother of Gisela (sometimes known as Matilda), wife of Emperor Conrad II.

Conrad's son Rudolf III (993–1032), often called 'le Fainéant' by modern scholars, has been accused of indolence since the eleventh century. Thietmar of Merseburg, who called him 'soft and effeminate', complained that no other king was so careless of his kingdom, not even defending his bishops.[18] During Rudolf's reign, the counts and castellans of the kingdom of upper Burgundy acted increasingly independently. The first revolt of his *fideles* took place shortly after his coronation. The elderly empress Adelaide, his aunt, had to intervene in Burgundy in 999 to restore peace. The emperors who succeeded

---

[18] Thietmar, *Chronicon* VII, 30: 'mollis et effeminatus'.

the Ottonians after 1002, first Henry II and then Conrad II, renewed the authority over the kingdom to their west which Otto I had first attempted to establish seventy years earlier.

Rudolf III and his wife Ermengard had no sons. It was agreed that after he died his kingdom would become attached to the imperial crown. The process by which this happened has been debated, but the overall lines are clear. In 1016, Rudolf asked for help from the emperor (his nephew), Henry II, promising in return to leave Henry his kingdom when he died. Their agreement at Strasbourg seems to have been in reaction to Count Otto-William's intervention in the episcopal election of Besançon, in which the count drove out Rudolf's candidate in favour of his own. Although the emperor was no more successful than Rudolf had been against Otto-William, he did remember Rudolf's promise to leave him the kingdom of Burgundy, and forced the king to renew the Strasbourg agreement in 1018.

In the event, Henry died before Rudolf, but in spite of Rudolf's attempts to reassert his independence, the new emperor, Conrad II (Rudolf's nephew by marriage), made Rudolf submit and renew the earlier agreements. When Rudolf died, on 5 or 6 September 1032, he sent the emperor his insignia of authority. Conrad returned quickly from his wars in the eastern part of his empire to claim Burgundy. He was crowned king of imperial Burgundy on 2 February 1033.

His haste was due to the threat of another candidate for the Burgundian throne, Rudolf's nephew Odo II of Blois. Odo claimed Burgundy through his mother Bertha, Rudolf's sister. But Odo was preoccupied with French affairs in the early 1030s and was killed in battle in 1037, and Conrad was able to consolidate his position. However, once the emperors had secured the Burgundian throne, they paid little more attention to it. Conrad II had his son Henry, the future Henry III, named as king of imperial Burgundy in 1038, but after Henry succeeded to the German throne he virtually ignored Burgundy. After having been the first kingdom within the area of Carolingian hegemony to have a non-Carolingian king in the late ninth century, and after having been the centre of lively politics in the tenth century, the imperial kingdom of Burgundy and Provence disappeared in the eleventh century. Not just the line of its kings but its very existence as an independent kingdom came to an end. From this time until the middle of the twelfth century, imperial Burgundy – or the kingdom of Arles, as the emperors called it – was essentially governed by its counts without reference to a king.

By the late tenth century, Provence too had become a county rather than a kingdom, ruled by a line of counts who took their names from the Bosonids and from the dukes of Septimania. It seems most likely that these counts were originally from Provence and that, since they served under the Bosonids, they took the names of their lords in imitation of them, rather than because they were related to them.

In the middle of the tenth century, the brothers William and Boso of this line, sons of one Robold, held the county of Provence under King Conrad of Burgundy. This Boso had made a brilliant marriage with Bertha, niece of King Hugh of Italy, and probably owed the county of Arles to this marriage, because her father (also named Boso), King Hugh's brother, had also been count of Arles. The younger Count Boso did however leave her around the time of the death of King Hugh to marry another woman, named Constance.[19] The brothers William and Boso initially had to share the rule of Provence with a Bosonid, King Hugh's nephew Manasses, archbishop of Arles (914–62/3), who had gone to Italy with his uncle, had become archbishop of Milan, then had come back to Provence in 945, and dominated politics there until his own death close to twenty years later.

By the final decades of the tenth century, Count Boso's son, Count William I, held the county of Arles without any effective opposition. King Conrad of upper Burgundy gave William the title of marquis of Provence. William and his brother Robold led the Christian armies which finally drove the last of the Saracens out of Provence in 972, after Saracens had captured Abbot Maiolus of Cluny. William married Adelaide-Blanche, formerly the wife of the Carolingian Louis V. As well as his heir, William II, he had Constance (named for her grandmother), wife of King Robert II of France.

In the meantime, monasticism in Provence had suffered serious setbacks during the Saracen invasions. Most Provençal monasteries and even several of the bishoprics have lacunae in their history in the late ninth century and the first half of the tenth. Monasticism in Provence was restored during the second half of the tenth century, at the same time as the new line of counts of Provence was being established, beginning even before the last of the Saracens were expelled. The number of churchmen in the county remained very small, however, until the eleventh century. The beginning of monastic renewal in Provence can be dated to the foundation of Montmajour, just outside Arles, in 954. Fifty years later, this house began receiving small churches of the region; Cluny had already been given several small Provençal churches during the preceding generation. Other monastic houses, however, which had long been under the control of the local bishop (most notably the bishop of Arles), tended at the end of the tenth century and beginning of the eleventh to come under the control of the counts.

---

[19] Liudprand, *Antapodosis* v, 31 For the identification of Bertha's husband Boso as the son of Robold, rather than the son of Richard le Justicier, as is often assumed, see Poly (1976), pp. 32–3.

As the foregoing should make evident, the history of the various Burgundian regions was far from simple during the 150 years in which the French duchy of Burgundy was continually redefined, and the imperial kingdoms of upper Burgundy and Provence were created and disappeared again amidst great political turmoil. The continually shifting kaleidoscope of persons, lineages and territorial designations can be daunting, even bewildering. If one focuses on the building of the nation-state in the tenth century, then Burgundy must be considered a failure. But the very complexity of the history of these regions, and of the families that constituted their principal lineages, indicates that there was no real distinction in the minds of the chief actors between personal, familial, ecclesiastical and political alliances or conflicts, and their activities continually involved an amalgam of all of these.

CHAPTER 14

THE KINGDOM OF ITALY

Giuseppe Sergi

THE CAROLINGIAN INHERITANCE AND THE STRUGGLE FOR POWER

At Charles the Great's deposition, the *regnum Italiae*, whose capital was Pavia, included north Italy from Piedmont to Friuli, Emilia as far as Modena, Tuscany, the Marches and the Abruzzi. From Romagna as far as central Italy the lands of the kingdom were interlinked with those of the *patrimonium Petri*, the temporal possessions ruled by the Roman church with varying degrees of success. From 888 to 923 Berengar, margrave of Friuli, was a major, though not the only dominant figure of the kingdom of Italy. Berengar's coronation as king preceded that of his rival Wido, duke of Spoleto by a year. Wido had made unsuccessful attempts on the kingship in France and Burgundy, returning to Italy at the end of 888. Although his first battle with Berengar at Brescia was indecisive, he defeated him later at the River Trebbia and was crowned at Pavia in February 889.

The tumultuous immediate post-Carolingian period was dominated by the rivalry between Berengar and Wido, who were both typical products of a political transformation which had its roots in the hierarchical social order of the Frankish empire. Berengar's family came from the lower Rhine and Wido's from the Moselle region. Both were related to the Carolingians, and above all both governed large Carolingian territories by well-established dynastic right. Their ambitions were therefore the result of the status they had achieved within the previous administration and it was also natural that they should apply the dynastic-seigneurial power schemes which had already proven their worth in the marcher commands each held. Apart from Friuli and Spoleto-Camerino, there were two other large marches important enough to affect the balance of power in the kingdom: Tuscany and Ivrea (which included all of Piedmont and Liguria). The margrave of Tuscany, Adalbert, remained neutral during the first few years of the conflict between Berengar and Wido. The margrave of Ivrea, Anscar, had come to Italy from Burgundy in Wido's train and so his family was initially instinctively pro-Wido. But Wido's greatest immediate

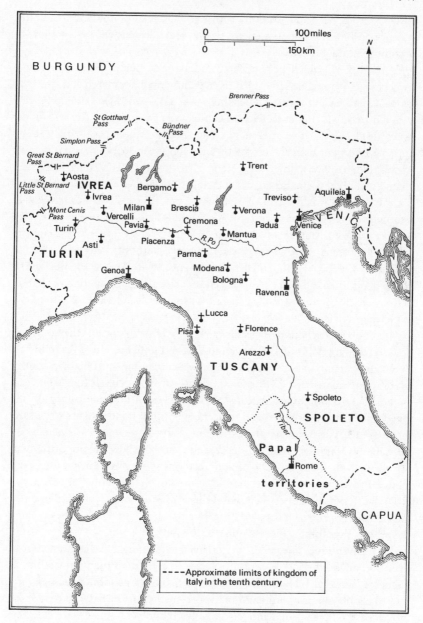

7 The kingdom of Italy, *c.* 1000

advantage was his good relations with the church of Rome and it was this which won him the imperial crown in 891 and allowed his son Lambert to become joint ruler in 892.

From Verona, which became his headquarters, Berengar exercised such royal powers as remained in his hands over his hereditary march and also over Padua, Cremona and Brescia. Thus there were now two *de facto* kingdoms: one in north-east Italy (under Berengar I) and another comprising the rest of the *regnum* (under Wido), the latter being designated the empire, as the right to the imperial title went with the crown of Italy. The year 894 was a decisive one. Arnulf, king of Germany, and his son Zwentibald entered Italy, were welcomed and offered obedience, but they failed to achieve a convincing victory over Wido. Towards the end of the same year, after his two new rivals had returned to their home beyond the Alps, Wido died, but Berengar was in no position to take advantage of the situation since extensive areas of the country (especially Emilia) now recognised Lambert's authority and also because several of Berengar's influential followers looked to Arnulf for the future; hopes that turned out to be badly placed because, after his imperial coronation in Rome at the beginning of 896, Arnulf fell gravely ill and was forced to return to Germany.

There followed a period of deadlock. The River Adda became the boundary between the kingdoms of Berengar and Lambert until the latter's death in 898. Berengar's patience was rewarded when for a certain time he obtained control over the entire kingdom. Unfortunately these were particularly turbulent years as the Magyars' intensive, repeated attacks revealed the inefficiency of the kingdom's military defences and won them an important field victory at the River Brenta. The permanently discontented anti-Berengarian aristocracy, led this time by Margrave Adalbert of Tuscany, did not allow the opportunity to slip through their fingers. Diplomatic relations were established with Louis, king of Provence, and between the end of 900 and the beginning of 901 he was given the Italian and imperial crowns. Louis was active in Italy but suffered two military defeats between 902 and 905. Berengar had him blinded for breaking their treaty, thus forcing him to return to Provence.

From now until 915 began the period in which Berengar had greatest control over the kingdom of Italy, and in 915 we find the first mention of him as Emperor Berengar I. He was probably crowned by Pope John X, perhaps as a reward for his role as coordinator in the destruction of the Saracen base at the mouth of the River Garigliano (also involved in the enterprise were Adalbert of Tuscany, Alberic of Spoleto, Landulf of Capua and the Byzantines in Calabria and Apulia). This base was less important than the Provençal base at Fraxinetum, but it posed an endemically insidious threat to the whole of central and southern Italy.

The kingdom did not rest, however, on a solid foundation of aristocratic consensus, and it was the strength of anti-Berengarian feeling which established an efficient network of alliances. Bertha, the widow of Adalbert of Tuscany, married her daughter Ermengard to Adalbert, margrave of Ivrea, allied her party with Uldarich, the count palatine, and with Lambert, archbishop of Milan, and also managed to work together with Margrave Alberic of Spoleto, who wielded enormous influence with Rome and the papacy. Berengar was once more driven back to his secure domains in the Veneto–Friuli regions and was forced to hire Magyar mercenaries to break out of his siege position, a move which won him a short-lived victory and the hatred of his contemporaries.

Rudolf II of Burgundy was invited to Italy by the anti-Magyar and anti-Berengarian factions and defeated Berengar at Fiorenzuola d'Arda in 923, one of the bloodiest battles in the history of the kingdom. The huge number of deaths on both sides decimated Italy's aristocracy. The nobility which survived looked to Ermengard for leadership, as she represented the interests of the marches both of Tuscany and of Ivrea. Berengar was put to death in Verona in 924 (while the Magyars, who were still overrunning the country, entered and devastated Pavia) and after Rudolf II returned to Burgundy a disappointed man, in 926 the country turned to Hugh of Provence as guarantor.

But guarantor of what? Not of 'order', as traditional historiography has claimed, but rather of a status quo which favoured the magnates of the time. At the end of the Berengarian period the Italian aristocracy wanted a government that would take into account the large degree of autonomy enjoyed by the various regions. This autonomy had been long desired and temporarily achieved thanks to the check the rival kingdoms had exercised over each other and also to the long periods of weak rule during Berengar's reign. When Berengar I attempted to rule more effectively – and more widely – or when Rudolf II threatened to put his services at the disposal of the crown, services which ignored local power structures, the reaction of the powerful members of the nobility was inevitable.

The forty-odd years between 888 and 926 saw enormous changes in the kingdom. Despite the great disorders and the huge bloodbaths there was no revolution, and Carolingian institutions were merely adapted to suit the new needs of dynastic continuity and territorial stability desired by the Frankish aristocracy resident in Italy. Pavia's chancery still existed and until 898 continued to issue capitularies, the final legislative output of Wido and Lambert. After this date chancery activities were limited to the issuing of diplomata containing specific royal decisions in favour of various recipients. The activities carried out in Pavia reflect the transitional character of the reign. The other legislative activities remained along Carolingian lines: the recalling of smallholders (the *exercitales* or *arimanni*) to their military obligations, and the defence of these men's rights against abuse by public officials (who, together with the bishops, were still expected to look after the peace in the various districts of the kingdom); the restoration and upkeep of public buildings; the guardianship of women's rights and of their goods; the regulation of the registration by notaries of the sale of property; the passing of laws to prevent the usurping of parishes and ecclesiastical tithes. Later, the system of diplomata, which had become the only normal form of royal intervention, proved to be the perfect way of setting up and maintaining a heterogeneous network of relations, and by the beginning of the tenth century the management of this network had become the sole form of government in the kingdom.

In the meantime the whole social context of the country was changing. The uncertainties of the agricultural situation led many smallholders to seek help from large landowners and to hand over their lands to them in exchange for a guaranteed right to live on and work them and the promise of protection by the private armies and fortifications of the owners of the great *curtes*, the largest of the agricultural holdings. As a result, the *curtes* increased in size and in the number of their dependent tenant-farmers and the number of small independent landowners dropped, though it is important to note that they remained quite numerous.

These social changes, and the reduction in the number of smallholders, accelerated what was already an on-going process: the king and his officials lost the habit of mobilising all free citizens of the kingdom for the army and found it more convenient to call on vassals and the large landowners who could guarantee to provide a certain number of men. The king and his officials ended by considering direct politico-military relations with smallholders in the countryside as exceptional, where once they had been the norm. In some cases, when these relations survived, they were no longer considered the remains of a once common practice but seen rather as privileges of groups which had once enjoyed a special personal relationship with previous rulers. This explains why medievalists have only recently realised that the *arimanni* documented in the kingdom of Italy from the tenth century on are simply descendants of the *liberi homines* or *exercitales* of the Carolingian period, and are not necessarily ethnic descendants of the Lombards or holders of a legal status originally different from that of ordinary free men.

The disappearance of legislative activity in the form of capitularies did not, however, mean that there was a clean break with Carolingian models. Not only did the capital Pavia and its chancery continue to operate, but the territory of the kingdom was subdivided into marches, counties and minor districts (*iudiciarie, fines, gastaldi*-ships) which were either traditional Carolingian administrative districts or else survivals of Lombard territorial divisions. The intermittent activities of the king, the military mobilisations, the administration of justice, and the dynastic ambitions of the counts and margraves were all played out in the framework of the Carolingian system, which used the province as its basic administrative unit.

The diplomata, particularly those issued by Berengar I, offer interesting proof of how the system was maintained by minor adjustments within this framework. The bishops of Modena, Reggio Emilia, Padua and Bergamo were allowed to fortify their towns and were given a free hand to improve the military defences of their territories. The abbesses of the convents of Pavia and Brescia obtained similar fortification rights (in the case of St Julia of Brescia the abbess was one of Berengar's daughters). It is important to note that both the bishops and the nunneries obtained these rights in the form of immunity (either *de facto* or formally recognised), preventing access to their lands by royal officials. The concept of immunity was a development of the institution imported and well tried by the Carolingians. By the tenth century it had evolved from being a mere exemption from certain duties to becoming the positive exercise of all forms of *districtus* (the right to judge, punish or levy troops). But by this time immune lands no longer formed part of any coherent plan to govern Italy through a network of allied ecclesiastical bodies. Berengar accepted that parts of his kingdom would provide their own defences, simply because he had no other choice. Initially, immunities were granted to more or less important public authorities, but by now this had given way to true political fragmentation, and Berengar made concessions even to minor ecclesiastical authorities. Thus a parish priest in Voghera was recognised as having *districtus* and was granted the various forms of public income that went with the title, and concessions were even made to a group of lay subjects: twenty-nine inhabitants of the Novara region were allowed to build a castle on their private lands.

During the troubled years of Berengar's rule the state of emergency meant that the government of the kingdom was based on the reinterpretation of the Carolingian models. What resulted was not original, but it provided fertile ground for the development of local magnates, who became more important as the century progressed.

THE MIDDLE OF THE TENTH CENTURY: THE TENSION BETWEEN PARTICULARISM AND ROYAL POWER

In a society characterised by an extremely fragmented politico-military situation, the few existing areas of territorial stability began to assume particular importance. The marches of Tuscany, Ivrea and Friuli and the duchy of Spoleto, the largest and most solid of these territories, offered a sense of continuity and became powers which could not be ignored by aspirants to the

throne. At this point in the tenth century, Ermengard, now the widow of
Adalbert, margrave of Ivrea, represented this continuity, and with her enduring influence she restored the family of the margraves of Tuscany to their previous position, while also convincing the Italian aristocracy to turn to her
brother Hugh, one of the powerful counts in the kingdom of Provence. In
appealing to Hugh the Italian nobility moved in unaccustomed unison: its
united presence at his landing at Pisa in June 926 and at the later meetings at
Pavia and Mantua shows the strength of Hugh's relations with the magnates of
the kingdom and with Pope John X.

Hugh's plan to re-establish the authority of the monarchy and to introduce
sweeping alterations to the power structure must have been helped by these
powerful relations. Hugh introduced two principal changes, both of which
may have seemed spontaneous at the time: first, he favoured the holders of the
largest territorial units; second, he recruited a new class of leaders from among
his relations and followers. The latter move only became possible after sweeping changes had been made in the ranks of the aristocracy. The gaps in the
ranks of the nobility following the battle of Fiorenzuola made it possible to
establish a new elite, but even so it was Hugh's inflexibility, later to become a
characteristic of his reign, which pushed through the changes.

Samson, one of Hugh's military commanders, quashed a revolt in Pavia with
great cruelty and was immediately created count palatine as a reward. When
Wido of Tuscany died in around 929, Hugh was given the opportunity to interfere extensively in local affairs and to go against the rule of dynastic succession.
He had the new margrave of Tuscany, his step-brother Lambert, imprisoned
and blinded, and replaced him with his brother Boso; a relative, Tedald,
became margrave of Spoleto-Camerino, and since he considered the diocese
of Verona to be of vital importance he gave it first to another relation, Ilduin,
and then to Rather, one of Ilduin's trusted followers, when the latter was promoted to the more prestigious see of Milan. Hugh's marriage to Marozia, the
widow of Wido of Tuscany, was perhaps not as successful as he had hoped,
however. Marozia was a member of the Theophylact family, the most influential of the aristocratic Roman families, and the marriage should have given
Hugh considerable influence with Rome, but instead Marozia's son, Alberic,
became the leader of a revolt in Rome against the new king.

As was only to be expected, these first moves met with great opposition, not
only in Rome, and Hugh reacted with energy. In 931 he created his son Lothar
joint king of Italy and came to an agreement with Rudolf II of Burgundy:
Hugh renounced all rights to the throne of Provence, in exchange for eliminating the risk that Rudolf might intervene at any moment to gain the Italian
crown. Then, after the failure of Arnulf of Bavaria's abortive expedition into
Italy in 935, Hugh began the second violent stage of his political changes.

Arnulf had been invited to Italy by Milo and Rather, respectively count and bishop of Verona. Hugh took advantage of the situation not only to remove the traitors but also to reinforce his position in the north-east of Italy. He set up a new, strong, mixed (ecclesiastic and lay) district authority that included the patriarchate of Friuli, the dioceses of Verona, Mantua and Trent, and the Tridentine march and placed it in the hands of his kinsman, Manasses, archbishop of Arles.

In 935 and 936 several more opportunities for a general reordering arose. On the death of Tedald, margrave of Spoleto, Hugh intervened in the marches of Spoleto and Ivrea. He promoted Anscar to Spoleto, thus separating him from an environment in which he could count on both landed wealth and vassals, and gave Ivrea to Berengar, who was Anscar's brother but was more under Hugh's control (Hugh had in fact married him to Willa, the daughter of his brother Boso). Boso himself, meanwhile, was removed from his position as margrave of Tuscany, on suspicion of treachery, and was replaced by Hugh's illegitimate son Humbert. Humbert was now Hugh's most trusted follower and was created first count palatine and later duke of Spoleto and Camerino after a military force had been sent to the dukedom to depose Anscar in 940.

In the meantime, Hugh married Bertha, the widow of King Rudolf II of Burgundy in 937 and betrothed Adelaide, the daughter of Rudolf II and Bertha, to his son Lothar. Hugh's ambitions in Provence may have been rekindled; he was certainly seeking to protect the western borders of the kingdom and to make an entrance onto the European stage as one of its leading players. In a new diplomatic move he established links with the German king Henry, and with the Byzantine court, in the latter instance to merge forces against the Saracens on the coasts of Provence; and in fact Hugh did send some ships against the Saracens.

Between 940 and 943 Hugh was at the height of his power. His decisions clearly demonstrate that his governing policy was an original combination that made use of both a reinforced central authority and a loyal network of relatives and supporters. He was intolerant of any independent development of local power (so that during his reign the transfer of power to local families slowed in pace), but at the same time he placed little emphasis on the restoration of royal power as a 'public authority' and restricted positions of trust to relations (such as his now extremely powerful son Humbert) and to the vassals he could be sure of (such as his faithful follower Sarlio, who was sent against Anscar at Spoleto and who later obtained the monastery of Farfa and other royal monasteries in central Italy). The king granted the bishop of Reggio a *districtus* of 3 miles around the city, making his bishopric the temporal equal, from a territorial point of view, of those of Modena, Bergamo and Cremona.

This was a hybrid method of government, suited to the times except in one respect: the new officials were insufficiently familiar with the social reality of the regions they governed. When he had been contacted by the *Italienses* to bring order into the kingdom and act as arbiter in their disputes, Hugh had been too optimistic in his interpretation of the initial consensus he had achieved; in a sense he had exceeded his mandate. His radical, energetic measures had burst upon an unprepared nobility and had made him enormously powerful. But as soon as the aristocracy had recovered from this onslaught and society was able to reorganise, it was Hugh's anachronistic moves back to a centralised form of government – perhaps more than the cruelty which both the chronicler Liudprand and traditional historiography stress – which led to a general reorganisation of the opposition.

Hugh's aim of installing trusted followers in the main marches of the kingdom led him to make a bad decision in the case of Ivrea. Here he did not destroy the ruling family but placed power in the hands of Berengar, one of its younger members, in the belief that marriage to one of his own nieces would be enough to ensure his loyalty to the crown. For a time it did, but later it was to Ivrea that the malcontents began to look for leadership. Berengar's flight to Germany in 941 or 942 was probably because he had been found in some way disloyal, but in retrospect the period of exile proved to be extremely profitable because his protector, Duke Hermann of Suabia, helped him establish relations with Otto I, a move which over the following two years made him look increasingly attractive to Italians wishing to get rid of Hugh. Berengar's exile, however, also meant the end of the great march of Ivrea, which for half a century had included the westernmost lands of the kingdom of Italy. New counts and their families were on the ascendant in Piedmont and Liguria, and Hugh agreed to further their ambitions for two reasons: first, to break up the huge political formation in the north-west of Italy which wielded too much power within the kingdom; and second, to assist the rise of new, more controllable families in the different, uncoordinated counties within the march of Ivrea.

The results of the operation were contradictory. Berengar eventually managed to return to Italy and to use his prestige as margrave of Ivrea to aim at the throne, and to this extent it can be said that Hugh failed. But the old march was never fully re-established. It was unable to subject the powerful new counts whose first allegiance was to Hugh. Berengar himself realised this while he was fighting for the throne and so retained for himself and his family a reduced territory around Ivrea while accepting the creation of new hegemonies (smaller, rather ill-defined marches) under the new margraves – Arduin in Turin and Aleram and Otbert in south-west Piedmont and Liguria.

But when did Berengar return to Italy and why had Hugh's power declined? The margrave of Ivrea returned in 945 when it was clear that Wido of Modena, the most powerful bishop in northern Italy and one of the king's critics, had become the focus of a group of new opponents of Hugh, such as Bishop Manasses and Milo, count of Verona. Berengar set up his headquarters in Milan and initially did not aspire to the throne, but remained faithful to what might be called the mission assigned him by those who had recalled him to Italy; this was to safeguard the rights of the magnates that Hugh had oppressed. An unusual compromise was reached: the powerful nobles would recognise Lothar as king if he nominated Berengar his chief counsellor. Although Hugh could also have had recourse to this compromise, he preferred to flee to Provence. This is one of the most overlooked passages in Liudprand's chronicles; it describes Hugh fleeing 'with all his wealth' and may mean that he decided to abandon the struggle and to content himself with securing the throne for his son.[1] Hugh died in 947 in Arles.

Between 947 and 950, with the formal approval of Lothar, under the growing influence of his wife Adelaide, Rudolf's daughter, and with the margrave of Ivrea acting as guarantor and coordinator, the Italian nobility overhauled the political system to ensure the *de facto* heritability of ecclesiastic and public offices and power. Hugh's son Humbert was allowed to remain margrave of Tuscany (presumably to avoid violating the rule that such offices were heritable) but he lost the dukedom of Spoleto to Boniface, whose family had supported Wido of Spoleto at the end of the previous century, and he also lost the office of count palatine. Bishops more likely to maintain the new status quo were nominated to Brescia (Anthony), Como (Waldo) and Reggio (Adalhard). Bishop Boso of Piacenza was able to hold on to his diocese but not to his position as arch-chancellor, which was given to Bruningus, bishop of Asti.

In the middle of the tenth century the politico-military situation in Italy had led to a complex transition period, with a general changeover in the major offices of the *regnum Italiae*. This was accompanied by a revision of territorial boundaries and meant that the new political geography of the land – now composed of a great number of generally independent local power-bases – was largely irreversible. When Lothar died in November 950, his successor to the throne of this fragmented kingdom was the ex-magnate Berengar II, who immediately named his son Adalbert joint king. Berengar was well liked by the Italian aristocracy, who had put him to the test for a few years as guarantor of the settlement with Hugh and Lothar, and he was probably supported by Otto I, who, according to the chronicler Widukind, considered him his vassal.[2]

During the course of 951 Berengar II's rule was made more turbulent by two factors. The first, more structural, factor was the discovery that his acknowledged *de facto* power was more respected than his new formalised power. The

---

[1] Liudprand, *Antapodosis* v, 31. [2] Widukind, *Res gestae Saxonicae* i, 31.

second, less important but more explosive, factor was his behaviour towards Adelaide, Lothar's widow, whom he persecuted in an effort to force her into submission. Part of the Italian aristocracy was opposed to this treatment and a new, powerful entrant on the scene, Adalbert Azzo of Canossa, helped the dowager queen escape from a siege. Meanwhile, Bishop Manasses, who was still extremely powerful, abandoned the Berengarian camp, to which Bishops Bruningus of Asti, Azzo of Vercelli and Wido of Modena still remained faithful, and backed Otto I's plan to become more involved in Italy, giving his aid to the military force.

Between 951 and 952 Otto I gained widespread support in Italy and issued diplomata which described him as *rex Langobardorum* or *Italicorum*, even if there was no official election.[3] He married the widowed Adelaide, who had become a symbol of opposition to Berengar II in Italy and was a member of the Burgundian royal family. Adelaide was the ideal wife for Otto, who planned to extend his rule to include the three Alpine kingdoms of Germany, Burgundy and Italy. If Otto had not faced so much opposition within Germany at this time and if the marauding incursions of the Magyars had not already begun, Berengar's reign would probably have ended here. However, Otto I was forced to return to Germany, and in August 952 an agreement was concluded at Augsburg. Berengar II kept his crown, but had to acknowledge himself the vassal of Otto I, and he lost Verona, Trent and Friuli to Germany.

Although reluctant to issue diplomata, Berengar behaved like a king for a number of years. It is true that he had to accept that Ivrea, his hereditary march, was much reduced territorially; but he was not threatened or opposed by the neighbouring margraves. His revenge on Manasses was immediate – he was deprived of the archbishopric of Milan – and the king also made his displeasure with several of his allies felt. This is probably the reason why Bruningus was replaced as arch-chancellor by Bishop Wido of Modena, the real new force on the scene. In the meantime, Otto's difficulties in Germany were being resolved. His victory over the Magyars at the Lechfeld in 955 not only led to peace but also greatly increased the political prestige of the king – who now put his plans for rule in Italy into full operation.

The situation in Italy, on the other hand, remained so fluid that the land was almost ungovernable. One example of this is the alliance between Berengar and Humbert of Tuscany, which was counterbalanced by the anti-Berengarian alliance of Pope John XII (son of the powerful Roman aristocrat Alberic) and margrave Theobald of Spoleto whose family had originally been pro-Berengarian. The years had seen alliances overturned and power redistributed, but all new systems of authority were eventually unsettled by the Italian aris-

---

[3] DD O I 138, 139, 140.

tocracy's unceasing fascination with any foreign leader who appeared to offer authority without really effective control. In this case the foreign leader was Otto I. The Ottonian party, which for many years had included Bishops Waldo of Como and Walpert of Milan, rose in numbers on the arrival of margrave Otbert. With Germany now pacified (the king had now created his son joint king) and Italy in a state of unrest, Otto I entered Pavia almost unopposed. At some time between August 961 and February 962, he received general acknowledgement based on his assumption of power in 951, and he was crowned emperor in Rome in February 962.

The sporadic resistance by Berengar's camp was unsuccessful. In June 962 Otto I successfully concluded the siege of the island of S. Giulio d'Orta in the Novara region, where Willa, Berengar II's wife, had fled with part of the army. In May 963 Berengar himself was dislodged from his eyrie at S. Leo in the Montefeltro region and together with his wife was exiled to Bavaria. Under the command of Berengar's son Adalbert, troops faithful to Berengar continued to harass the kingdom after Otto's return to Germany. Adalbert obtained some temporary diplomatic success, persuading Pope John XII to join his side (the imperial party had already installed Leo VIII as a counterbalance) and inducing Wido of Modena to rethink his position (he had already agreed to remain arch-chancellor under Otto I); but he was eventually defeated by one of Otto's commanders, Burchard of Suabia, in June 965. This marked the end of the long and profitable Italian adventure of the Anscari family from Burgundy. One of Berengar II's sons, Wido, died in battle, while Adalbert fled to Burgundy, never to return. Otto I re-entered Italy in 966, generally recognised as ruler of the kingdom.

The ruling class now grouped around Otto I was largely composed of new men. This was a result partly of the political changes made by its predecessors and partly of the outcomes of the power struggles at local level. The increase in the episcopate's temporal powers, energetically initiated by Berengar I, had become an unstoppable process, even though it had received only intermittent support from Hugh and Berengar II. It was probably these men's lack of enthusiasm in promoting their interests that led the bishops to give such enormous support to Otto I. What Hugh and Berengar II had both done, on the other hand, was to upgrade the status of the counts. They did this, however, for diametrically opposed reasons. Hugh's centralising policy, aimed at overturning local power-bases, meant that he had to improve the official position of the followers he was moving into local positions of power, by making them the representatives of royal authority. Berengar II's experience as guarantor of aristocratic interests and as chief counsellor of the kingdom during Lothar's reign led him to seek support from among the aristocrats who were in the process of establishing their territorial interests. As a result, he tended to offer them formal recognition of their new military and landed power by creating them counts or margraves.

By the middle of the tenth century, the administration of the country was based on a contradiction which had to some extent been evident even in the Carolingian period. The government of Italy was supposed to be based on a system of relatively homogeneous provinces, but at the same time it also had to acknowledge the importance of local magnates and their power. In the middle decades of the century public recognition of magnate power had two distinct aspects: first, episcopal immunity was extended to include *districtio* in areas beyond town boundaries; second, the aristocracy's hereditary rights to power were acknowledged. Each successive king of Italy tried to gather support and to survive by recognising *de facto* situations and giving them formal recognition. This meant that they became directly and permanently enmeshed in the realities of life in the country. By recognising the temporal powers of the bishops, by granting public offices as hereditary rights, or by acknowledging the jurisdiction of castles, they were becoming part of the power-base of the new magnates. Following coronation at Pavia, each king of Italy and his itinerant administration acted as a spasmodic centre of coordination which, while trying to establish the dynastic rights of the royal house, in fact established a rather provisional and general dominance, working *ad hoc* both with and against the local magnates, on a case by case and area by area basis.

The relationship between the king and local magnates did not depend on any formally recognised system of hereditary or feudal rights. Kings like Berengar II who sought the support of established families presented the unthreatening face of a royal power which had coordinated rather than restructured the social framework. By contrast, kings like Hugh who were notable for their interventionist policies had to promote new families to positions of authority to achieve their aims. In order to avoid having to endow his protégés too richly Hugh chose men from those families who, although distinguished militarily and large landowners, had held no public office in the immediate post-Carolingian period. This excluded the Frankish or German aristocrats, who had all been involved in the public affairs of the previous reigns to a greater or lesser extent, but it did include the Lombards. Thus from Hugh's reign on it was mainly the Lombards who became the new men in Italy, supporters of a crown which had promoted their families to the ruling class. Typical of the new class was Adalbert Azzo of Canossa, who received King Hugh's help in transferring his family from Tuscany to the Parma area in around 940, a move that laid the foundations for its very rapid rise in power, in recognition of which he was later granted the title of count. Another example was Otbert, probably one of Hugh's new men but created margrave by Berengar II and founder of an extremely secure dynasty.

The leading characters on the political scene in the middle of the tenth century included well-established bishops, and bishops like those of Reggio and Genoa who had recently seen their positions strengthened by the concession of new areas of jurisdiction; they included hereditary counts and margraves, and newly appointed men. The sovereigns of Italy made no distinction between the old guard and the newcomers; all were treated as Grand Electors, who needed to be either persuaded into voting for the king or appointed for the purpose. But in 951 something happened to change all this. Like all the others, Otto I had been invited to come to Italy by a group of the most influential nobles in the kingdom, but unlike them he did not seek formal approval and election by the Italian aristocracy when he reached Pavia. Instead, the similarity of his reactions to those of Charlemagne in the period following the victory over the Lombards foreshadowed the many similarities his reign would have to that of Charlemagne, and gave his rule a more public flavour.

OTTONIAN ITALY

Otto I's concept of kingship, a truly imperialist ideology, was at odds with the turbulent period in which he lived. He was crowned king in 951 and emperor in 962, but his sovereignty was only fully accepted after 966. In fact, he only succeeded in consolidating his rule by paying more attention to the power of the local magnates. It is in this light that we should consider the exile but also the subsequent pardon of Bishops Sigulf of Piacenza and Wido of Modena – although the latter was replaced by Bishop Humbert of Parma as arch-chancellor – and also the way in which families which had traditionally held public office (such as the Supponidis, who had been counts of various areas) since the ninth century, and newer families who had recently been appointed such as those of Arduin and Aleram, received exactly the same treatment at the hands of the king. Otto also accelerated the progress of several careers, for example that of Canossa, although in this case a determining factor in Adalbert Azzo's advancement must have been Adelaide's gratitude to him for saving her from Berengar II shortly after the death of her husband, King Lothar.

Otto had already unified the dukedoms and bishoprics of Germany and he now applied the same successful techniques to Italy. The status of the officials in closest contact with the administration was enhanced: for example, on 13 February 962 he decreed that a pope could not be elected in the absence of imperial envoys. The support of the bishops possessing temporal powers was obtained: between 962 and 965 he issued diplomata to the bishops of Parma, Reggio, Modena and Asti. Equal attention was paid to ensuring that there was an efficient county structure: Otto created new counts whose families in their turn eventually began to show an interest in episcopal careers. In general, Otto recruited new members of the nobility from among the local families and, unlike Wido and Hugh, who had imported their followers from Burgundy and Provence, he did not completely transform the composition of the ruling class.

Otto's reign immediately distinguished itself by the interest shown in Rome and in central and south Italy. He did not limit his sphere of actions to the area bounded by the Po valley and the Apennines, as previous kings had done. He opposed Popes John XII and Benedict V and arranged the election of Leo VIII, but peace was reached after Leo's death with the election in 965, against the wishes of the people of Rome, of the bishop of Narni, who assumed the title of John XIII. The prince of Capua, Pandulf, who had offered hospitality to the fugitive Leo VIII, one of Otto's supporters, was rewarded with the march of Spoleto and Camerino, and as a result was accepted into the highest levels of government in the Italian kingdom.

In 967 Otto I raised his son to the position of co-emperor and began negotiations to obtain the hand of the Byzantine princess Theophanu for him. Despite the dealings between the two courts, there remained a certain amount of tension between them because of the renewed royal and imperial interest shown by Otto I in south Italy. Otto I and his representative Pandulf were kept busy with expeditions to Capua, Benevento and Apulia. Although the chronicler and bishop of Cremona, Liudprand, made his celebrated mission to the court of Constantinople during an interlude of peace in 968, this came to nothing. The marriage of Otto II to Theophanu was therefore not celebrated until 972, when peace had been established with the eastern empire under its new emperor John Tzimiskes. In 972 Otto I left Italy for Germany, where he died in the monastery of Memleben in May 973. Throughout his reign, he had maintained a constant flow of diplomata to churches and followers and had held innumerable meetings of his *proceres* (counts and bishops), who carried out the new legal and administrative business of the land, so that on his departure Italy was enjoying a period of relative stability.

It was because of this stability that in the seven years following Otto's departure Italy found itself in the unusual situation of being kingless but having no new pretender to the crown. It was therefore the imperial legates who dealt with serious disturbances in Rome fomented by Theodora's nephew Crescentius, and with the pardoning of old opponents of the regime such as the Lombard Count Bernard. The system, whose overhaul and efficiency had caused Otto I such trouble, had proved it could work.

Otto II became personally involved in Italian affairs again at the end of 980, after he had quashed a certain amount of opposition in Germany and had regained the support of his mother; Adelaide's quarrels with her son were serious enough to make her flee to the court of her brother Conrad, king of Burgundy. On reaching Italy, he discovered that his representatives had already solved many of his problems. He was particularly pleased to discover that Pope Benedict VII was one of his supporters. Otto II himself dealt with the Milanese disorders which were precursors of the social upheaval that characterised Lombardy between the tenth and eleventh centuries. Later, in the tranquil atmosphere of Ravenna and Rome he discussed the Italian situation with his counsellor Gerbert of Aurillac, recently appointed abbot of Bobbio. It was decided that the interest in south Italy shown in the previous reign should be continued. Agreements were easily concluded with the Lombard nobility in the principalities of Benevento and Naples and there were few obstacles to the extension of the kingdom into Apulia and Calabria between 981 and 982. In July 982, however, despite the arrival of substantial military reinforcements from Germany, Otto's army was largely wiped out by the Muslims in a battle south of Cotrone in Calabria.

Otto II and Theophanu retreated with their few remaining troops to Salerno, Capua and then Rome. Given his military defeat and the existing political situation, the emperor returned his attention to the northern heartlands of his Italian kingdom. He issued a number of important diplomata which will be examined as part of the overall achievements of the dynasty; but more especially, in May 983, during an assembly of his most powerful nobles in Verona, he arranged for his three-year-old son to be elected king as Otto III. During the same assembly he dealt with the matters troubling a nearby city, Venice. As the tenth century neared its close, the authority and independence of the doge of Venice had increased, accompanied by a rise in the number of violent clashes between the Candiano and the Morosini families jockeying for hereditary control of this position. Otto managed to negotiate a lasting peace between them, thus asserting his royal authority over the region. After this final act, he died suddenly in Rome at the end of 983.

Otto's administration differed from that of the kings of Italy in the first half of the century in that it was not totally dependent on the sovereign and was also able to function in transitional periods. It may be that the fact that it ruled over two complex kingdoms which were too large to allow the king to be present at all times had made the administration used to doing without his permanent attendance, so that many mechanisms functioned automatically. In 984, therefore, even in a context where the king was only three years old, the efforts made by Duke Henry of Bavaria to oppose Theophanu's regency for the three-year-old Otto were timid and soon withdrawn. Theophanu in fact remained in Germany, and the real regent of Italy was Adelaide, now an old woman but able to count on the support of a few absolutely loyal magnates such as Margrave Hugh of Tuscany. South Italy, beyond the confines of the kingdom, was now ungovernable, however, and Rome had to be abandoned to the anti-imperial Crescentii.

When Theophanu died in 991, Otto III was eleven. His remaining guardians were Adelaide and the archbishop of Magdeburg. Adelaide exercised the regency for Otto until he came of age in 994; in 996 Otto began to turn his attention to Italy. He sent his troops to quash a revolt in Verona and in Pavia; he filled the vacant pontifical seat with one of his cousins who assumed the title of Gregory V. He then entered Rome, where he was crowned emperor in May. The situation in Rome exploded again that autumn. Pope Gregory V was put to flight and John XVI was set up in his place by Crescentius, who was excommunicated in Pavia in 997. The repression of the Roman rebels between February and April 998 was carried out with a cruelty that churchmen, such as the monk Nilus and the reformer Gerbert, supporters of the new emperor at that time, found difficult to understand. John XVI (John Philagathus, one of Otto's tutors) was mutilated and exiled. Crescentius was killed after a siege, even though he had been promised immunity.

The concerted and complementary action of Otto III and Gregory V introduced a form of government based on the universalistic view which both powers held of themselves. This was clear from the two councils held at Pavia and Rome between the end of 998 and the beginning of 999. The new system was clearly intended to continue beyond the death of Gregory V and the election to the papacy of Gerbert of Aurillac in April 999 as Sylvester II. In Germany and especially in Italy Otto III was extremely dexterous in counterbalancing the intensive military activity needed to suppress the risings in the Po Valley and Rome (some of which had distinctive social connotations) with equally intensive administrative activities. He made frequent trips to the cities of his kingdom, maintained large numbers of contacts, and issued numerous diplomata to the bishoprics. Otto III died in Paterno in January 1002 while awaiting the arrival of troops from Germany with which he, like his father and grandfather before him, planned to eliminate the dangers and rival powers in south Italy. Adelaide had died at the end of 999 and Pope Sylvester II followed in May 1003. All the great names who had played a role in the creation of the kingdom of Italy as it stood at the end of the tenth century were now gone.

During Otto's reign there was an increase in seigneurial powers whose territorial basis did not correspond to boundaries defined by the limits of public jurisdiction but necessarily straddled them. These included monastic immunities (often scattered among several regions but no less independent for all that) and the immunities of the lay nobility established around castles originally constructed to offer military protection to the lands of the *curtes*. It was now no longer only the bishops but also the leading aristocratic families who tended to associate their hereditary strength with a region and to prefer this stable form of influence to the more precarious positions of courtier or court official who might be transferred to wherever the king required.

The regional power structure in Italy just before the millennium shows the balance achieved between stability and innovation. In some areas the larger holdings were on the way to becoming territorial principalities while in others the figure of the count still played an important role. In these latter regions there were areas where the counts often changed, either because the family had no roots in the region or because of frequent intervention by the royal authorities, and others where one family had ruled for at least a few generations. Within Piedmont, Liguria and Lombardy, the incipient territorial principalities included the marches of the Arduin family (based in Turin), the Aleram family (basically rural, with no urban bases) and the Otbertians (which extended irregularly from western Liguria to south-east Piedmont and in some years also included the Milan area). There was also the march of Ivrea which, after the final disappearance of the Anscari and despite the absence of a ruling family, had managed to maintain some of its territorial identity, although this was much reduced as compared with the beginning of the century. Ivrea was now being taken over with some vigour by an ambitious count named Arduin, who had no connection with the Torinese family. The powers of the bishops were attaining formal recognition to an increasing extent throughout Piedmont, while Lombardy was divided between the juridically unofficial but *de facto* authority of the archbishop of Milan, the intermittent presence of a family with waning powers, that of the counts of Lomello closely connected with the royal capital of Pavia, and the rising Otbert family of margraves. A good number of local counts and their families (among whom the Bernardingi family and the counts of Lecco should be mentioned) created a growing network of administrative functionaries, which expanded while repeatedly clashing with powerful ecclesiastics such as the bishops of Como, Mantua and Cremona. In the north-east of Italy the patriarchate of Aquileia had established a strong ecclesiastical principality which included all of Friuli and acted as a genuine march patrolling the areas from which the Magyar threat had come, up until the middle of the century. At the same time the most western of the Venetian possessions, centred on Verona, found themselves in an ambiguous position: although Italian by geography and social structure, they were formally linked to Trent, having been theoretically ceded to the German duchy of Carinthia. This area had been the object of such ardent royal attention during the Ottonian period that territories had changed hands continually; thus even the most important of the counts of Verona had been unable to set up any stable form of dynasty.

The biggest changes of this period took place on the plains of the Po valley and in Emilia. Canossa's influence grew first throughout the countryside and later managed to become established in several cities, although it did not completely destroy the temporal power of all of the bishoprics, several of which easily lasted through his assault and survived to ease the transition to the first urban communities. Romagna was under the firm control of the archbishop of Ravenna, by position a mediator between the regions with Byzantine traditions and the kingdom of Italy.

Tuscany, like the Veneto-Trentino area, was always so central to the interests of the kingdom that it was unable to act very independently. However, the authorities in the region were powerful and formed stable dynasties. During the lifetime of Margrave Hugh, Tuscany enjoyed a period of great peace under a ruler who was a trusted follower of the king and co-existed peacefully with the various minor counts in the area. The duchy-march of Spoleto-Camerino (in time it came to be called a march), with its important appendage Fermo, deserves special mention. During the course of the tenth century this area became peripheral to the kingdom of Italy. For some time it had ceased to put forward candidates for the crown and for quite a long period it had been clear that it was now the southernmost border of a kingdom whose real centre lay in the Po valley. Nevertheless, Spoleto-Camerino continued to play a vital role in the political history of the period between the tenth and eleventh centuries because it had become closely linked with the papacy. The story of the march of Spoleto-Camerino, at one time tied to that of Tuscany, on another occasion given to the duke of Benevento as a reward, still later disputed between the Crescentii and the counts of Tusculum, is often a vital part of the tortuous history of Rome and the *patrimonium Petri*, and although it is essentially extraneous to the history of the kingdom of Italy, at times it did influence the train of events significantly.

At the end of the tenth century it is impossible to speak of Italian national characteristics, but certain regional characteristics were developing: on the threshold of the millennium, the marches of Spoleto and Ivrea were more distant from each other than they had been a century before.

FROM THE STRUGGLES WITH ARDUIN OF IVREA TO CONRAD II

During this period, the nobility's habit of making public offices hereditary appurtenances coexisted with a royal capacity to intervene in individual public jurisdictions. By the last decades of the tenth century the Anscari margraves of Ivrea, who had produced candidates to the Italian throne and dangerous opponents of the king's authority for much of the period, were in irreversible decline. The power gap was filled by a Count Arduin, who descended from an aristocratic family based either in Lombardy or in the county of Pombia, an internal jurisdiction of the march of Ivrea. Arduin had therefore become margrave of Ivrea not by hereditary right but presumably because his enterprise and military ability had brought him to the attention of the royal court (heavily influenced by Adelaide during the minority of Otto III).

For some time the march of Ivrea had in Arduin a lord who was unusually attentive to its domestic affairs and this was because, unlike the members of the family who had ruled before him, he was not yet involved in the great political rivalries of the kingdom. But within the territories of the march lived some of the most powerful bishops in Italy, so that the margrave's new interest in domestic affairs inevitably led to hostility. The most violent clash was with Peter, bishop of Vercelli. An influential man, he had been a trusted follower of Otto II and, thanks to immunities granted in the past and to the accumulation of new landed wealth, he now occupied a dominant position within his diocese. However, Peter had also gone about systematically rescinding the episcopal grants made too liberally by his predecessor Ingo. This alienated local families, who had partly usurped the possessions and partly obtained them as benefits from Ingo, using them to lay the foundations of their own wealth and social advancement.

Backed by the lay malcontents and by those ecclesiastics who did not share the tough views of the new bishop, Arduin had no difficulty in launching his policy to re-establish the authority of the march. On closer inspection, this proves not to have been revolutionary but rather a rejigging of the power structure within a large public jurisdiction. But Arduin's policy was met with armed resistance and by 997 the situation had degenerated to the point that Arduin's army marched on Vercelli and set fire to the cathedral, killing Bishop Peter. Arduin had this murder thrown in his face for years and in 999 in Rome he made partial reparation for it to Pope Sylvester II, although still blaming the excesses which led to the death of the bishop on his followers rather than on himself.

Two acquiescent bishops, Reginfredus and Adalbert, followed Peter; but then Leo, an extremely faithful German follower of Otto III, was created bishop of Vercelli, and he proved instantly hostile to the margrave. Warmund, bishop of Ivrea, also turned against Arduin, complaining about the arrogance with which he was treated. Warmund's letter provides an interesting insight into the bases of Arduin's support, for the bishop lamented that 'all the citizens living in the city of Ivrea' were tempted to back the margrave at the expense of the traditional support shown to their pastor.[4]

As we have already seen, before 999 it was impossible for bishops to seek redress from the pope against Arduin. These were the years in which Pope Gregory V, Otto III's cousin, lived in exile, having been hounded from Rome by Crescentius and his followers. The pope managed to return only some time between 998 and 999, shortly before his death. Arduin was tried as soon as Gerbert of Aurillac was elected pope, or in other words as soon as the situation

---

[4] 'omnes cives in Eporeia civitate habitantes': Provana, *Studi critici sovra la storia d'Italia*, p. 339, doc. 12.

in Rome was quiet enough for the authorities to begin to busy themselves also
with what was happening in the distant regions of north Italy. During this
period Otto III and Sylvester II were prodigal in their granting of concessions
to the churches in Piedmont, in this way trying to compensate them for the
wrongs they were suffering. The result of their efforts, however, was to alienate
all those damaged by the granting of the concessions and thus to enlarge the
social basis of Arduin's support.

Within the boundaries of his march Arduin had therefore applied methods
of government which made him very attractive to a large proportion of the
nobility. He was particularly attractive to those vassals whose wealth was based
on church fiefs and who lived in constant fear of their loss. This class was not
sympathetic to the rising power of the bishops, who demanded total subservience as the price for the retention of their land grants. Arduin was thus the
natural leader not of some minor nobility composed of *vavassores* (vassals of
vassals) as has been claimed in the past, but of two large aristocratic classes: the
vassals who depended on the ecclesiastic *seniores* and whose allodial lands were
not extensive enough to complete and support the income from their feudal
lands; and the great families who had long enjoyed public office and who, notwithstanding their plans to found a dynasty, also wished to maintain the
authority of the counts. The first group backed Arduin because he was a strong
opponent of interventionist bishops and a more or less conscious champion
of the hereditary principle when it came to ecclesiastic fiefs. The great families
admired the margrave of Ivrea for his opposition to the over-enthusiastic royal
granting of ecclesiastic immunities. Among those who fell into this second category were the Aleram and Otbertian marcher dynasties, who were supporters
of the new king, unlike Tedald of Canossa who was hostile, and unlike
Uldarich Manfredi, the neutral margrave of Turin whose family shared a name
with the rulers of Ivrea but had no other connection with them.

At Otto III's death, Arduin was crowned king of Italy by the bishop of Pavia
on 15 February 1002. His election did not express any Italian national or anti-
German feeling and it would be anachronistic to think it did; equally, it would
be anachronistic to make him out to be the champion of the secular. On the
contrary, he enjoyed good relations with the abbot of Bobbio and with the
bishops who did not oppose him such as Peter of Asti and Peter of Como.
Peter of Como had retained his position as arch-chancellor of the kingdom
and had been rewarded for his fidelity to Arduin with the *districtus* of the county
of Chiavenna, a concession similar to those he accused his predecessors of
accumulating. The new king's diplomata show his gratitude to certain clerics in
Vercelli and Ivrea who appear to have gone against the wishes of their bishop
and supported Arduin. The diplomata also demonstrate the favour shown the
monasteries of Lucca and Pavia and the new cathedral at Lodi.

The new king of Germany, Henry II, did not passively accept the separation of the kingdoms of Germany and Italy. A conference of Italian magnates was convened by Archbishop Arnulf of Milan at Roncaglia and, following the messages he received from this body, Henry sent an expeditionary force into Italy under Otto, duke of Carinthia and count of Verona. There was a vigorous counter-offensive by Arduin at Campo di Fabbrica near Verona somewhere between 1002 and 1003 and Henry's force was routed. Henry II then himself entered Italy in April 1004, becoming the focus of anti-Arduin discontent, and without the need for great field battles he dispersed the Italian king's followers. Following a triumphal entry into Verona and Milan, Henry went to Pavia to receive the royal crown of Italy on 12 May 1004, but his reception there was unenthusiastic and the citizens of Pavia later turned to full-blooded rebellion, which was firmly crushed. The differences between the Italian nobility did not make any real opposition to Henry possible, and as a result between 1004 and 1005 Arduin retired to the lands which were most faithful to him, his old march; for a time he was virtually under siege in his castle at Sparone near Ivrea.

Henry returned to Germany in 1005 and for some time was fully involved with the war on his Polish front; for a number of years his Italian chancery in Pavia ceased to exist. Arduin once again became *de facto* king, but for a little-documented decade between 1005 and 1014 there were in fact two powers in the kingdom. Arduin roamed through the land wreaking revenge on his opponents and exercising an authority which was temporally and territorially patchy. In Germany, Henry II received the Italian bishops faithful to him and offered them concessions through his Italian chancery under the bishop of the new see of Bamberg. Huge areas of Italy were now beyond the control of any central power. In Tuscany, with Henry II's backing, Boniface had become margrave, but during this same period the cities of Tuscany had shown enterprise and autonomy, organising an expedition against the Saracens independently of the margrave. They were also restless and quick to fight among themselves, Pisa against Lucca and Florence against Fiesole. For the first decade of the eleventh century, during the papacies of John XVII, John XVIII and Sergius IV, Arduin was indirectly advantaged by the dominance in Rome of the anti-German Crescentian party. However, in 1012 the situation changed and Pope Benedict VIII was elected. Benedict was a member of the family of the counts of Tusculum, and after a brief period of uncertainty he established stable relations with the king of Germany, Henry II. Arduin still had important allies, such as his relations the Otbertians and the monks in the Abbey of Fruttuaria (indicative of the support he continued to enjoy in the march of Ivrea), but they were not enough to enable him to oppose Henry II's return in the autumn of 1013.

Henry plunged into north Italian politics with a series of astute moves. When he lost the endorsement of Archbishop Arnulf of Milan he did not hesitate to take steps to attract the backing of the vassals of that diocese, thus undermining one of the bases of Arduin's support. It is significant in this context that Henry nominated two of his *missi* from Milanese families. Even for the years preceding this it is difficult to distinguish a purely pro-episcopal policy for Henry and a purely anti-episcopal one for Arduin, and such an interpretation is even more inadequate for this later period. Henry limited the powers of the bishop of Mantua, and exempted numbers of free men in the diocese from the bishop's temporal jurisdiction. He listened to the arguments of the bishop of Savona, but only to grant the *cives* of his town important exemptions from their obligations to the margraves. This decision was probably a measure against the Otbertians and was similar in spirit to the decision to create the diocese of Bobbio and to place it in the hands of a friendly bishop.

Henry II went to Rome in February 1014, where he was crowned emperor by Benedict VIII. He presided over a synod on simony in Ravenna and it was probably his decision to repress a revolt in Rome before returning to Germany. Immediately after this, Arduin marched on Vercelli, putting his bitterest enemy, Bishop Leo, to flight, and then on Novara and Como. When the bishop of Vicenza changed sides to join him, Arduin may have thought that Henry's support was waning. But this illusion was short lived. Boniface, margrave of Tuscany, gathered an opposition force against Arduin of such strength and unity – it included the nobility, bishops and citizens – that he was forced to retreat to his march and seek refuge in the monastery at Fruttuaria. It is uncertain whether Arduin retreated to Fruttuaria because of his isolation or because of ill-health, but in any case he survived there only slightly more than a year and died on 14 December 1015.

The years immediately following Arduin's defeat and death were ones of far-reaching political change. The huge confiscated possessions of Arduin's followers were now redistributed, showering lands and new rights on the bishoprics of Pavia, Como, Novara, Vercelli and the monastery of S. Abbondio of Como. The resistance to the new order from Arduin's descendants and followers was mainly successful in the areas of Vercelli and Ivrea and was occasionally aided by Uldarich Manfredi, the margrave of Turin, but it did not make much real impact and was not considered important enough to warrant any great reprisals from Henry. In fact when Henry II was able to return to Italy his was a pacifying presence, in line with decisions taken at Strasbourg and Bamberg in 1019 and 1020 during meetings with his most influential Italian supporters and Pope Benedict VIII. Many opponents exiled to Germany were pardoned and allowed to return to Italy. Henry now had allies in several key positions in the country: the archbishop of Ravenna was first his brother-in-law Arnulf and later his relative Heribert; the Bavarian Poppo became patriarch of Friuli and Aquileia; Aribert became archbishop of Milan, and Boniface of Canossa held everything between Tuscany and Emilia.

Even then, however, Henry's position in Italy was not secure. He came to Italy between 1021 and 1022 with an army large enough to carry out a campaign in the south of the country and although his success was limited it did strengthen his relations with Pope Benedict VIII. At the end of the campaign Henry and the pope held a council in Pavia, attended by the bishops of Pavia, Milan, Como, Tortona, Turin and Vercelli, at which the new social and religious problems of the kingdom were discussed (the flight of serfs from church lands, the marriage of serfs to free women and the marriage of clerics). An attempt was made to solve these problems but there was no real effort to rationalise and reform the situation. Henry died in July 1024 in Germany leaving no children, the last of the Saxon kings who had left such a mark on the history of Italy over the preceding sixty years. Conrad II, his successor as king of Germany, was much less interested in Italy than his predecessors.

In Italy, some of the nobles tried to offer the crown first to Robert the Pious, king of France, and then to Duke William of Aquitaine but no-one was interested in venturing into Italy at a time when Henry II's supporters had not disbanded and, flanked by the papacy, still represented a well-established, pro-German majority. Representing the Italian nobles, Aribert of Milan and Leo of Vercelli went to Magdeburg to invite Conrad II to accept the Italian throne. The simultaneous assault on the royal *palatium* in Pavia by the *cives* of the capital, the embassy by the citizens of Pavia to Magdeburg to beg for royal forgiveness and the difficulties Conrad encountered in trying to enter Pavia for his coronation all foreshadow the contradictions and problems of a period in history in which the sheer number of heterogeneous local influences made royal coordination of government increasingly difficult.

The Saxon period which lasted from the middle of the tenth century until 1024 presents some of the main institutional problems in the history of the kingdom of Italy. Research carried out over the last twenty years has undermined the previously held notion that the Ottonians' policy in Italy was to increase the independence of the bishops and as a result nominate them as royal representatives and officials (to the detriment, it was believed, of the counts whose consolidated dynastic ambitions had begun to pose too great a threat to the central authorities). More comprehensive recent research has shown that the Ottonian monarchs in reality operated on an *ad hoc* basis, intervening in each case to restore the status quo. They took into account the existing situation and backed the local families when these did not get in the way of their plans, forming alliances with them if the situation was fluid and removing them only when they went into opposition. This probably explains the favour enjoyed by the bishops of Piedmont, who had been influential before the Ottonian period but increased in power during it; it also explains the decline of the bishops of western Emilia, where Otto I was so unfavourably impressed by the authority and independent decision-making powers of Wido of Modena that he created a number of new counts to counterbalance the power of the bishops of Emilia. It should be noted, finally, that it was only with Otto III and Henry II that there was any significant import of German bishops into Italy; until the end of the tenth century, in other words, the acceptance of the increase in episcopal powers was such that the king was prepared to admit local men to the rank of bishop and only later were such positions assigned to trusted courtiers.

It is not surprising that the Ottonian policy of 'corrective acceptance' of the status quo should have been applied to a kingdom which, in the second half of the tenth century, was influenced by many important and powerful bishoprics. The first king to make use of the charisma and military power of the bishops was Berengar I. Berengar also laid the foundations of the rise in the temporal power of many bishops. The rise of the bishops was aided by what might be termed 'moral legitimacy', a phenomenon based on the priestly rank of the holders of power and on the prestige of their urban strongholds and the importance these had for the surrounding regions. All these factors aided the consolidation of the episcopal lordships during the tenth century, so that their importance during the Ottonian period is due more to natural historical development than to any new royal policy.

Where bishoprics were endowed with royal diplomata the temporal sphere of action of their holders increased considerably, but the latter did not formally become royal officials or 'count-bishops', and it was not until the middle of the eleventh century that any bishop began to use the title of count. The bishops of the cathedrals with diplomata were endowed with greater temporal responsibilities within the government of the kingdom at the level of secular lordship or mixed secular-ecclesiastical lordship, but only when royal supremacy extended over all magnates in the entire region. The bishop was endowed with jurisdiction over the city and parts of the county surrounding the city, but he performed no function as official mediator between subjects and the government of the realm. It is no accident that in areas where the authority and power of the bishop were self-evident, as in the case of Milan, the bishops did not feel the need to ask for diplomata granting them *districtus*, as the seigneurial powers they already held, along with the immunities granted in individual castellated towns in the county, were enough.

The Carolingian division of the kingdom of Italy into counties continued to exist both in areas with more stable power structures and in those where major restructuring was occurring. This is true both of Tuscany (where the counties retained their character and governments under the higher authority of the margraves) and the large marches of Liguria and Piedmont (where the absence of any counts did not lead to the abolition of their territories, now supervised by the margraves either directly or with the aid of *vicecomites*). It is true also of the Po areas ruled by the Canossa family, quickly recognised by the king, who rationalised the lands and divided them into *comitatus* and *marcae*, and true of many territories where bishops' powers increased, also classed as *comitatus*. This was not merely an exercise in terminology. The most ambitious men and families, while rising socially and moving around the country in a way new to the geography of the kingdom, continued to use amended versions of the basic Carolingian system of territorial offices as the springboard for their ambitions, and as a way of legitimising the territorial basis of their power.

The rights and powers of regional authorities (comital dynasties and bishops), but also those of smaller but territorially more coherent signorial domains, were particularly shifting between the tenth and eleventh centuries; the transfer of these rights and powers were referred to in the language of private law. After its beginnings in the Carolingian period, the allodial concept of power had grown in scope under the protection of the reigns which followed. The king granted jurisdiction and public office *in alodium* or *in proprium*, thus associating the rights of jurisdiction with landed property, making the jurisdiction transferable with the land itself. The coexistence of a spontaneous seigneurial power structure with a continuing system of public government had become particularly evident during the reign of Henry II and in the kingdom he left to Conrad II. The last king of the Saxon dynasty had diverged from the models of government left by Otto III and his plans for an imperial restoration based in Italy. The ever more frequent absences of the king from Italy in the early eleventh century made clear the function royal power was now aiming at: one of coordinating the dominant factions via spasmodic royal intervention as a way of regulating and correcting new developments in the status quo. The sovereign no longer acted systematically as a stable, centralising source of power.

CHAPTER 15

WEST FRANCIA: THE KINGDOM

Jean Dunbabin

THE TENTH century was crucial in the evolution of the west Frankish kingdom.[1] Whereas in 898 its future was uncertain, with either reabsorption into a larger empire or disintegration into smaller units clearly possible, by 1031 it was firmly on the map, albeit with ill-defined frontiers and a debatable political character. From the northernmost tip of Flanders to the Pyrenees, from the Atlantic to the eastern frontier of the duchy of Burgundy, only one king, Robert II, was recognised. And time had weakened the potential alternative configurations. With hindsight, therefore, we can detect in the course of the tenth century the increasing cohesion of a unit that was later to emerge on the European stage as one of the great national monarchies.

But to contemporaries this shadowy entity was a largely irrelevant abstraction, evident chiefly in the use of regnal years for dating charters. In the real world they conceived of kings as personal rulers, their authority co-extensive with their presence, while *regnum*, the term which in other contexts is translated 'kingdom', they applied to the act of ruling, and thus to a wide variety of political and semi-political authorities. They had no vocabulary for describing the area in which Robert II was recognised as king; nor would they have thought of it as a unit – 'west Francia' is a historian's abstraction. Worse, they had no word for the lands over which the last Carolingians and the early Capetians exercised political authority: *Francia* in tenth- or early eleventh-century sources was defined by the past, not the present. It meant either the area north of the Loire in which Franks were thought to have settled in the early middle ages, or the area between the Seine and the Lotharingian border that had once been part of the Austrasian kingdom.[2] It did not describe a political hegemony.

Yet despite contemporaries' inability to pinpoint a west Frankish kingdom, to modern eyes the chronicles and charters of the period prove that there was such an entity. In the narrow sense it consisted of an initially shadowy but

[1] I am grateful to Dr Patrick Wormald for constructive criticism of an early draft of this chapter.
[2] Schneidmüller (1987), pp. 17–19.

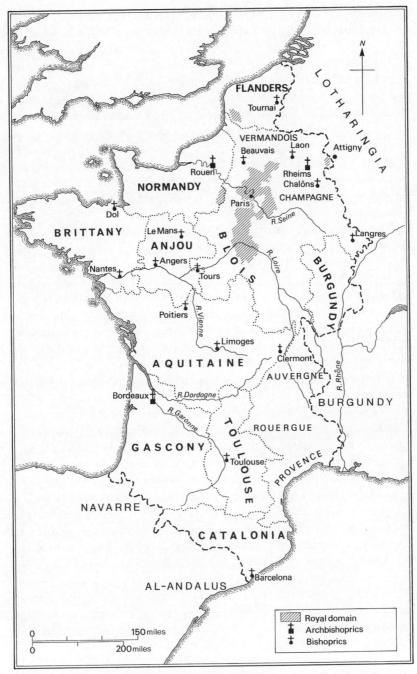

8 The kingdom of France, *c.* 1000

increasingly well-defined royal principality, under the Carolingians centred on Laon and Rheims, under the Capetians on Orléans and Paris, over which the kings enjoyed a measure of real control. And more broadly, it referred to west Francia north of the Loire, excluding Normandy, Brittany and Flanders but sometimes including Lotharingia, the region where royal policies clashed with those of other great lords but frequently prevailed and always deeply influenced events. Within this ill-defined area, the west Frankish king was powerful in some localities, he engaged in conflict elsewhere, he was impotent in yet other places; and the pattern changed with time. Generalisation about the quality of his rule is as difficult as definition of the geographical boundaries within which it operated. But the rule itself remained a reality that could not be ignored. Beyond these frontiers he did not rule, although he might on occasions substantially influence events.

The difficulty of describing the kingdom arises from the uneven quality of the sources at our disposal. The period 898–919 is very inadequately chronicled. But from then until 966 the historian can draw on Flodoard's *Annales*[3] and his history of the Rheims church,[4] which together offer a reliable skeleton account of events as seen through monastic spectacles. Flodoard's accurate and unemotional recording excites confidence; he uses titles with care, he draws on documents where possible. More surprisingly, he seems remarkably detached – he offers no overt judgement on the deposition of Charles the Simple, or on the elections of Robert and Radulf. But nor does he attempt to explain motive, a restraint that makes some of the tergiversations he describes very puzzling.

From 966 until 995 we have to rely on the chronicle of Richer, a monk of Saint-Rémi of Rheims who, though he drew on Flodoard in the early part of his work, was temperamentally very different from his predecessor.[5] For him, the point of relaying the past was to produce a didactic tale, in which the good characters were portrayed as he thought they ought to have been, and virtue was conceived in the ancient Roman mould. Those for whom he had less affection were presented as intriguers, sometimes with unclear ambitions. The chronicle was suffused with an ancient republican spirit that sits uneasily with tenth-century concerns. Yet Richer had good sources of information; and occasionally he drew on his personal knowledge of people and events. His *History* is a challenging source to exploit.

In putting flesh on Flodoard's dry bones and in resisting the allure of Richer's idiosyncratic didacticism, the historian can only call on one other tenth-century chronicler, Folcuin,[6] who concentrated almost exclusively on

---

[3] Floadoard, *Annales*.   [4] Floadoard, *HRE*.   [5] Richer, *Historiae*.
[6] *Cartulaire de l'abbaye de Saint-Bertin*, pp. 4–168.

Flemish affairs. In addition there are scraps of information to be found in various annals such as those of Saint-Vaast, St Peter's, Ghent, and Saint-Amand.[7] Of the eleventh-century chronicles, only that of Sens is principally concerned with the kings.[8] The writings of Adhémar of Chabannes,[9] Dudo of Saint-Quentin,[10] Radulf Glaber,[11] and the anonymous authors of the chronicles of Nantes and Saint-Maixent[12] all offer the odd corroboration or even correction of Flodoard and Richer at various points, but mainly deal with other parts of west Francia. Helgaud's *Life of Robert the Pious*,[13] which promises well, in fact yields more information about the monastic ideal of kingship than on Robert himself.

The inadequacy of chronicle stories, even when fortified by the occasional saint's life or miracle story like those found in the *Miracles of St Benedict*,[14] is somewhat redressed by a body of royal charters which have received careful study,[15] and by a quantity of other charters, including those issued by great princes. Unfortunately only a small percentage of these survive in the original; consequently there are problems of authenticity. And because the compilers of the monastic cartularies to whom we are indebted for most of what we know were largely unconcerned by the affairs of the laity, their material is very unbalanced. Yet charters have been made to yield a rich harvest of information on princely titles, on the areas within which royal authority was exercised, and on the ways in which lordship enhanced wealth and power.[16] The declining number of royal charters – there were on average five a year for the reign of Charles the Simple, three for Louis IV, and less than two for Lothar – has been used as an index of the decline of royal power.[17] The rising number of charters produced not in the royal chancery but by the recipients has been similarly interpreted. And, more controversially, changes in diplomatic form have been linked with a failure to preserve intact the royal ideological inheritance.[18]

Given the patchiness of the sources, interpretation and hypothesis inevitably dominate royal history. Furthermore, the subject can be approached in two very different ways. On the one hand, recent study of the various French principalities and of Lotharingia has recast our historical perspective, forcing us to

---

[7] *Annales Vedastini* ed. von Simson (1909); ed. Grierson (1937).

[8] *Historia Francorum Senonensis.*   [9] Adhémar, *Chronicon.*

[10] Dudo of Saint-Quentin, *De moribus et actis primorum Normanniae.*

[11] Radulf Glaber, *Historiae.*   [12] *Chronique de Nantes; Chronicon Malleacense.*

[13] Helgaud of Fleury, *Vie de Robert le Pieux.*

[14] Books 2 and 3 of the *Miracula sancti Benedicti*, for example, cast light on the Viking raids in the Loire area.

[15] See in general Tessier (1962); for the charters of particular kings, see the editions of Charles the Simple's *Acta* by Lauer (1940–9), Robert's and Radulf's by Dufour (1978), Louis IV's by Lauer (1914), Lothar's and Louis V's by Halphen and Lot (1908), Robert II's by Newman (1937).

[16] Lemarignier (1970), pp. 155–6.   [17] Lemarignier (1965), p. 30.

[18] *Ibid.*, pp. 42–3; for criticism, see Brühl (1989a), pp. 589–95.

rethink the role of the kings, now that they are no longer seen as isolated figures representing legitimate authority on a stage otherwise occupied by bold, bad men intent on self-aggrandisement. The princes were entitled to act as partners in ruling. Therefore, not withstanding the innate conservatism of the royal chancery, the titles 'duke' and 'marquis', long claimed in their own principalities by men such as Richard le Justicier, William the Pious, Robert the Strong and Baldwin II, could not reasonably be withheld. On this line of argument, the emergence of the duchies and marquisates of west Francia implied not weakness but pragmatism on the part of the kings. The century thus saw an interesting constitutional experiment in decentralised government, during which political control intensified as it became more localised. On the other hand, the emergence of the principalities clearly excluded kings from regularly exercising their powers within them, and threatened the valuable royal protection over the church. Therefore any historian looking at tenth-century history from the ruler's point of view is bound to be drawn to the more traditional line of argument, comparing unfavourably the kings' authority against that wielded by their predecessors and successors, and also by their contemporary kings in east Francia or England. If the decline of the monarchy is no longer the only theme, it remains a central one.

In 898 the wind seemed set fair for Charles the Simple. With the support of Robert, Odo's brother, enthusiastically championed by Fulk, archbishop of Rheims, and attracting the loyalty a Carolingian could usually command from the magnates of the south, he was apparently in a strong position. Even his name promised well for the future. Naturally he could not attempt to turn back the clock; he would have to cooperate with Richard le Justicier in Burgundy, William the Pious in the Auvergne, Baldwin II in Flanders, Rannulf II in Poitou and Odo in Toulouse. But he might aspire to rally them to his court, to take a directive role in their policy-making, to underline their duties as his *fideles*. They, after all, needed him to legitimise their position at least as much as he needed them to hold his realm together. It was in this spirit that Charles permitted the royal chancery to address Richard le Justicier as marquis in 900,[19] to favour Robert the Strong similarly in 905,[20] and to call William of Aquitaine 'our great marquis' in 919.[21] He was simply developing a policy that went back at least to the days of Charles the Bald.

But in relation to Neustria, Charles the Simple faced a radically new situation. Here, by the terms of the agreement he had made with King Odo in 897, a new principality was in the process of formation. Not only had Robert received all Odo's honours and possessions, which made him virtual lord of west Francia from the Seine to the Loire; he was also permitted to claim the

---

[19] DD Ch S 32, 33.   [20] DD Ch S 9, 65, and all subsequent charters relating to him.
[21] D Ch S 102.

fidelity of royal servants, including the important count of Le Mans, and to enjoy the lay abbacies of Saint-Germain-des-Près, Saint-Martin of Tours, Saint-Denis, Saint-Amand, Saint-Aignan of Orléans and Marmoutier.[22] Charles' reliance on Robert for support, particularly in the period after 911 when he was himself engaged in Lotharingia, gave permanency to these acquisitions. The 'Robertine wall' (the phrase is Werner's[23]) was now excluding the king from an area that had recently been under royal control. Consequently Charles was obliged to cling tightly to the fiscal land he still retained between the Seine and the Lotharingian border.

Yet even here he faced a challenge, this time from a quarter hitherto well disposed towards him. Baldwin II of Flanders, who had long striven to gain control of the monastery of Saint-Vaast and the fertile land surrounding it, saw King Odo's death in 898 as the opportunity to try again. On the advice of Archbishop Fulk of Rheims, Charles resisted Baldwin's aggression as vigorously as he could. But Baldwin, bitterly resentful of the archbishop's influence, had Fulk murdered in 900. Ominously, Charles was able to punish only the perpetrator, not the instigator, of the murder. And although he managed to postpone for about twenty years the Flemish annexation of the Artois, he had to concede to Baldwin Boulogne and the Ternois.[24]

Within the territory still remaining to him, the king moved from royal palace to palace, stayed occasionally at Rheims and Laon, and accepted hospitality from the abbeys under his protection.[25] Though he seldom travelled outside the limits of his fiscal lands, he kept alive the tradition of special masses for the king's feast day in churches across the realm; he granted charters in places as far apart as southern Flanders and Catalonia; he recorded judgements made in the royal court;[26] he issued copious coinage (of poorer workmanship and lower silver content than previously);[27] and he gathered at least his more northern *fideles* around him. For the first decade and more of his reign he was a figure of authority.

At this time west Francia was continually threatened by Viking and Hungarian attacks. Although the appalling destruction of the 880s along the north-west coast was not repeated (Flemish defences preventing it), further south there were almost annual raids, violent and widespread, which disrupted harvests and spread panic among the peasants. Worse, small groups of Vikings established themselves for the winter in camps along the Loire and on the Norman coast, creating apprehension. And in the second decade of the tenth century there were occasional but devastating raids across the Lotharingian border by Magyar horsemen.

---

[22] DD Ch S 45–7, 54, 77; Dufour, Introduction to Robert I, *Acta*, p xci. [23] Werner (1984), p. 438.
[24] Ganshof (1949), p. 19. [25] Brühl (1968), pp. 49–50, 232 and n. 47.
[26] Lemarignier (1965), pp. 30–3 and map 1. [27] Belaubre (1986), pp. 50, 51.

Had Charles been confident of his military skills, he would have united the forces of the realm behind him to expel the invaders. But lacking talent and finding his own lands reasonably secure, he left the task to others. Richard le Justicier of Burgundy took on the role of chief defender of the kingdom, ably backed by Robert of Neustria. They, along with the count of Poitou, were responsible for the famous rout of the Vikings at Chartres (911?) which threatened the enemy settlements on the Loire and put to flight the notorious Viking commander Rollo.[28] Thus the princes amply demonstrated that they could work together without royal leadership.

But if it was their victory, Charles was the peace-maker. According to Dudo of Saint-Quentin, the Franks suggested that Rollo be given the land from the river Andelle to the sea, to settle in return for assistance against any future Viking incursion.[29] The treaty of Saint-Clair-sur-Epte in 911 created the nucleus of what was to become the future Norman principality, carved out of the possessions of Robert and Charles. Despite his losses, Charles benefited from the arrangement in that his authority to make peace had been recognised; and later he was to gain from the Norman prince's readiness to challenge the dominance of the Robertines in Neustria.

If the victory at Chartres did not put an end to invasions on west Frankish soil, it did create a substantial breathing space. Immediately Charles determined to exploit this by attempting to reverse the 880 restoration (at the peace of Ribemont) of Lotharingia to the east Frankish crown. This was a step for which he had long been preparing, particularly since his marriage in 908 to Frideruna, a Lotharingian lady of wealth and power. In 911, with the death of the last Carolingian ruler of east Francia, the moment was ripe: the Lotharingians under the command of Reginar, count of Hainault, offered their realm to him. Towards the end of 911 in Metz Charles was acclaimed as their king, and he in turn nominated Reginar as his representative in the newly acquired lands.

Lotharingia brought Charles fiscal land, wealth, troops and prestige, which compensated him for what he had lost in Neustria. And in the short term its acquisition suited both Robert and Richard. In 914 Robert obtained for his son Hugh the right of succession to all his land and honours, and in 918 Richard assumed the title of duke, which concessions might well have been refused had the king not been absorbed in the affairs of his eastern possessions. Yet the princes became apprehensive of interference by Lotharingians in west Frankish affairs, and in particular of the dominant influence in Charles' counsels from 918 of Hagano, a relation of the king's now deceased wife. So alienated were they on his account that in 919 they refused to assist Charles in

---

[28] *Cartulaire de l'abbaye de Saint-Père de Chartres*, pp. 46–7.
[29] Dudo of Saint-Quentin, *De moribus et actis primorum Normanniae ducum* II, 23, p. 162

repelling a Hungarian invasion. Thus after twenty-one years of reasonably har-
monious rule, the king faced serious opposition. In 921 Robert made a treaty
with the Normans without royal confirmation.[30] When in 922 Charles took the
rich abbey of Chelles from Rothilde, Charles the Bald's daughter (related by
marriage to the Robertine house), and gave it to Hagano, the crisis boiled over.
His opponents apparently regarded this instance of royal patronage as subvert-
ing justice and thus undermining Charles' right to rule. But it is most unfortunate that our sources on this crucial incident are so unforthcoming.

Under the combined leadership of Robert and his nephew Radulf, son of
the recently deceased Richard le Justicier, the west Frankish aristocrats threw
off their allegiance to Charles and had Robert crowned king at Rheims in 922.
Before the year's end Robert had been recognised by the pope and by King
Henry I of east Francia. Of Charles' potential allies, Arnulf of Flanders preferred his ambitions in the Artois to loyalty to his royal relation, and Heribert
II, count of Vermandois, who took pride in his descent from Charlemagne,
had recently married Robert's daughter, which neutralised his support. When
neither Rheims nor Laon held out for him, Charles had no option but to flee.
Though he returned in 923 with Norman help, it did him no good. At the battle
of Soissons on 15 June, his forces were defeated so seriously that even Robert's
death in the course of the fighting could not alter the outcome. Charles was
imprisoned by Heribert, who guarded him until his death in 929. And immediately after the battle, the west Frankish lords elected Radulf as their king. The
coronations of 922 and 923 thus constitute proof of the princes' determination to have the kind of ruler they wanted.

Radulf's accession was naturally welcomed in Burgundy. Led by his brother
Hugh the Black, the Burgundian lords hastened to display their loyalty to the
new king. The great monastery of Cluny followed suit, describing him in charters in terms once reserved for the Roman emperors.[31] Radulf kept the
Autunois, Senonais, Auxerrois and Dijonnais for himself, thereby bolstering
the dwindling resources of the crown; and he gave the rest of his lands and
offices to Hugh, with whom he preserved continuously good relations. It was
not surprising that the king should spend much time, especially in the early
years of his reign, within the frontiers of the duchy his father had created. This
has been interpreted as evidence of his weakness,[32] but the judgement is surely
anachronistic. Had Radulf's son Louis (by his wife Emma, daughter of Robert
I) not predeceased his father, west Francia might have become a realm centred
on Dijon rather than Rheims, Laon, Orléans or Paris. In the early years of the
tenth century the kingdom was still sufficiently malleable to accommodate
such a change.

---

[30] Flodoard, *Annales*, p. 6; Sassier (1987), p. 82.   [31] D Ra 12.   [32] Werner (1984), p. 457.

Initially at least Radulf also enjoyed the support of Hugh the Great, Robert's son. According to Radulf Glaber, it was Emma, Hugh's sister and Radulf's wife, who brought this about.[33] But in 924 the king was careful to compensate his brother-in-law for his assistance in the Aquitanian campaign by recognising his de facto suzerainty over Le Mans. He also bought the temporary goodwill of Heribert of Vermandois by a grant of Péronne, and Arnulf of Flanders, threatened by the Vikings, came into line. Alone of the northern princes, Rollo of Normandy refused allegiance, gladly capitalising on Charles' misfortunes as justification for onslaughts on his neighbours. He was finally induced to pay homage to Radulf in 933.

The southern princes at first regarded Radulf with no more enthusiasm than they had felt for Odo in 888. To overcome their apathy, in 924 Radulf, supported by Hugh and Heribert, invaded the lands of William II of Auvergne, defeated him, and persuaded him to submit, in return for the restoration of Bourges, taken from him some years previously. The count of Poitou did not accept Radulf's accession before 927, Raymond III Pons of Toulouse and the count of the Rouergue postponed their homages until 932 (well after the death of Charles the Simple), and the count of Barcelona omitted that ceremony entirely. Nevertheless, before his death in 936 Radulf had won over the great majority of the southern aristocrats. And if their adherence came very slowly, once committed they were loyal.

Outside west Francia Radulf was less successful. Although Flodoard insisted that many Lotharingians wanted him as their king,[34] by 925 he had lost control there to a local aristocrat, Gislebert, who enjoyed the backing of Henry I of east Francia. Recognising that a non-Carolingian without allies had no ground for complaint, Radulf accepted the fait accompli. His decision was probably popular among the bulk of the west Frankish lords, who had learned to distrust the Rhinelanders as rivals in the competition to counsel the king and receive royal patronage.

Meanwhile there was plenty to occupy Radulf at home. The Vikings took advantage of the crisis of 922–3 to re-establish themselves and cause serious havoc around the Loire. It was a measure of the confidence felt by the people in the son of Richard le Justicier that in both 924 and 926 they paid Danegeld for the defence of the realm – the last occasions on which this tax was collected. In 925 Radulf proclaimed the ban across Francia north of the Loire, thus uniting behind him the whole fighting force of the north. His resolution was crowned by major if costly victories, at Eu in 925 and at Faucembergues in 926. After this, although the worst of the danger was over, occasional campaigns against marauders burnished Radulf's reputation as a warrior in the last decade of his life.

[33] Radulf Glaber, Historiae I, 6–7, pp. 14–16.   [34] Annales, p. 17.

In one respect the resounding victory at Faucembergues brought trouble in its trail: Arnulf I of Flanders now felt free to attack the Artois again, and Radulf could neither prevent his depredations nor deny him control there because he needed his assistance to counter a new and more dangerous enemy. In 925 Heribert II of Vermandois decided to throw off the mask of friendship, revealing himself as the would-be creator of a principality north of the Seine, centred on Rheims and Laon, the traditional Carolingian heartland. As the great-grandson of Pippin, king of Italy, Heribert had impeccable Carolingian ancestry. If Charles the Simple's possessions were regarded as belonging to his family rather than to the crown, Heribert's claim to them was certainly better than Radulf's, if not as good as the absent prince Louis'. But his scheme posed a serious threat to Radulf, for whom the retention of Laon and Rheims constituted proof that he was Charles' legitimate successor.

By assisting Seulf, archbishop of Rheims, both against rebellious vassals and against the Vikings, Heribert had for some time been building up his influence in Rheims. Consequently when Seulf died in 925, Heribert was able to persuade the people to elect his five-year-old son Hugh to the archbishopric, despite the clear violation of ecclesiastical law involved. During the child's minority the spiritualities of the see were to be commended to the bishop of Soissons, while Heribert himself held the temporalities. King Radulf, though obviously concerned, could not withhold his consent while the Viking attacks continued, especially since Heribert, as Charles the Simple's gaoler, was in a position to threaten his own tenure of the throne. However, the events of the following year shocked Radulf. Heribert began by seizing the town of Amiens from its count, and then disputed the succession to Laon, whose Count Roger died in 926. Despite Radulf's clear prohibition, Heribert captured Laon by force, held it until 931, and then contrived to retain until 938 a citadel he had built in the town. His presence there threatened to undermine Radulf's hitherto undisputed right of appointing counts across north-eastern Francia. War was therefore inevitable.

It was unfortunate for the king that Heribert's wife was Hugh of Neustria's sister; during the first four years of the war, family loyalties assured Heribert of Hugh's somewhat episodic support. But in 931, as a result of a family quarrel, Hugh threw his weight on Radulf's side, and almost at once the tide turned decisively in favour of the king. The royal army captured Laon (though not Heribert's citadel) and Rheims; Radulf deposed Heribert's son from the archiepiscopal see and substituted his own candidate Artald, thereby creating an ecclesiastical dispute that dragged on till the 960s (a major theme in Flodoard's *History of the church of Rheims*); and the army went on to besiege some of Heribert's castles. At this point Heribert, apparently vanquished, turned for help to King Henry I of east Francia, who successfully interceded on his behalf. The mercy Radulf now accorded to the count of Vermandois demonstrated the king's fear of endangering the aristocratic consensus on which his authority rested.

In 935, after four relatively peaceful years, Radulf fell ill; and at the beginning of 936 he died. His reign had proved a turning point in that, apart from the famous Hungarian raid of 937, west Francia had now been freed from invaders. Although his defensive measures were not the only factor responsible for this change, he had ensured that the country was no longer easy prey. In calling the *ban* and in exacting Danegeld, he had also kept alive essential elements of the Carolingian inheritance (though the appearance in *c.* 925 of the first coin issued in the name of a territorial prince – William II of Auvergne – has rather unfairly been interpreted as a serious infringement of royal rights);[35] and he had been compensated for the loss of Lotharingian fiscal land by drawing on his Burgundian revenues. Significantly for the future, he had proved that a non-Carolingian ruler could impose himself, if rather slowly, on all the princes of west Francia except the Catalans. Indeed, his had become a popular rule.

Radulf's lengthy illness had given the west Frankish lords plenty of time to contemplate the succession problem. Perhaps the childless king had designated Louis d'Outremer, Charles the Simple's son, as his heir: certainly Louis' uncle, Æthelstan of Wessex, was pressing his nephew's cause. Nevertheless Hugh of Neustria's solicitude for Louis has excited surprise. Hugh, after all, was the son of a king; his second wife, Eadhild, was Æthelstan's sister; and he was a mature and experienced politician. His concession of the crown to Louis has been taken as indicating that the Robertines still regarded the Carolingians as having a better claim to the throne.

Alternatively, it has been suggested that Hugh's motive in promoting Louis was to secure his own possessions.[36] If he thought himself obliged to imitate his uncle Odo, who had surrendered all his counties to his brother Robert when he became king in 888, then a coronation would have placed him in an unfortunate predicament, since he had at this point no near relation on whom to bestow his extensive possessions. By 936 he held the counties of Paris, Etampes, Tours and Orléans; the *pagi* of Blois, Chartres and Châteaudun; and a fistful of important abbeys. Effectively his power stretched from the Seine to the Loire, with rather few intervening territories. To surrender what Flodoard called *terra Hugonis* to lesser men would have been unbearable.[37]

But whether Hugh was indeed bound by Odo's precedent is questionable. Robert I had reigned so briefly that his disposition of his lands and honours is unknown. But Radulf certainly had not surrendered all of his Burgundian inheritance on assuming the throne; nor was Hugh's son, Hugh Capet, to divest

[35] Dumas-Dubourg (1971), pp. 49–50.   [36] Werner (1984), pp. 456, 457, 463.
[37] Flodoard, *HRE* IV, 33, p. 425.

himself of much in 987. Some compromise would surely have been open to Hugh. His apparent altruism may therefore have been prompted by the realisation that this was not yet the moment for self-promotion. On the one hand, he needed heirs to bolster his family claims; and on the other, he was concerned about a threat to his authority in Neustria, since in 929 the viscount of Angers had assumed the title count of Anjou and begun to exercise comital functions around the city.[38] So Hugh may have decided to postpone his challenge, and concentrate in the meantime on extending his power and building up his dynasty.

During the two years in which he acted as the young king's guardian, Hugh's gains were considerable. Immediately after the coronation at Laon, he swept Louis off to campaign against Hugh the Black of Burgundy, in an effort to claim for the Robertines at least some of Radulf's lands, probably in the name of his now deceased sister Emma, Radulf's wife.[39] As soon as he had acquired Sens and Auxerre, along with some future rights in the duchy itself, he recalled the troops and returned home, leaving Louis (whose only gain was the city of Langres) sensing that he had been manipulated. But the young king could not yet afford a breach with Hugh. Indeed in 937 he bestowed on him the title 'duke of the Franks' and glossed this by calling him 'second to the king throughout the realm'.[40] In 938, after the death of his west Saxon wife, Hugh enhanced his prestige yet further by marrying Otto I's sister Hadwig, who not only gave him an entrée to the Ottonian court but also bore him three sons of impeccable royal descent. He now held the trumps he had lacked in 936.

Meanwhile the other west Frankish princes, with one exception, welcomed the return of the Carolingian dynasty. After the initial friction, Hugh of Burgundy proved a loyal friend to Louis; Count William of Poitou was among his firmest allies; and the count of Barcelona was swift to acknowledge his rule. Though Raymond III Pons of Toulouse only paid homage in 944, his tardiness was not symptomatic of coolness. Only Heribert of Vermandois determined to renew his earlier claims, even against a relation. Since Louis had begun his reign in possession of less fiscal land that any other king since 751,[41] he could not tolerate this. In alliance with Hugh the Black, he stormed Heribert's castles and in 938 succeeded in capturing the citadel in Laon that had been the lynchpin of his opponent's designs. Unfortunately for Louis, this sign of competence so alarmed Hugh (by now called 'the Great') that he threw his weight on Heribert's side.

At this point west Frankish affairs become embroiled in Lotharingian politics. In 939 Duke Gislebert of Lotharingia joined the rebellion against Otto I engineered by Henry of Bavaria and, to strengthen the anti-Ottonian party,

[38] Guillot (1972a), pp. 131–8.   [39] Sassier (1980), p. 17.   [40] DD L IV 1, 4.
[41] Brühl (1968), p. 231.

offered to restore his duchy to the west Frankish kingdom. After hesitation born of fear, Louis accepted, in hopes of enriching himself. Immediately Hugh the Great rallied to his east Frankish brother-in-law, supported by Heribert, by Arnulf of Flanders, and by William Longsword of Normandy. The west Frankish realm was once again riven by Carolingian pretensions in Lotharingia. Then in 939 Otto defeated his opponents, and Duke Gislebert was drowned while crossing a river. Louis' only consolation was his swift marriage with Gislebert's widow Gerberga, Otto's sister, who overcame Otto's wrath and bore her new husband male heirs of royal stock on both sides. By 942 Louis had renounced Lotharingia in the interests of peace with his brother-in-law.

However Hugh's and Heribert's opposition to the king was not so easily overcome. In 940 they attacked Rheims, captured it, put Archbishop Artald to flight, and restored Heribert's son Hugh to the see. Louis' attempt to reverse this step led to his total defeat. His plight was now so miserable that Pope Stephen VIII wrote to the west Frankish lords ordering them to support their king. Appalled by the scale of the disaster, Hugh the Black, William of Poitou, William Longsword, Arnulf of Flanders, and the counts of Rennes and Nantes rallied to Louis. In the resulting stalemate, both sides agreed to accept the arbitration of Otto I, who in 942 imposed an uneasy truce that lasted until the death of Heribert of Vermandois in the following year.

This event took the pressure off Louis. To safeguard royal interests in Laon, he decided to appoint no successor to Count Roger II who had died in 942. Instead, he had his illegitimate brother Rorico promoted to the vacant bishopric of the city and expected him to govern Laon. Similarly, he had conferred the county of Rheims on Archbishop Artald in 940. These instances of the suppression of important lay offices to the benefit of bishops illustrated a new policy – probably inspired by Ottonian example – that was to commend itself to west Frankish kings for the rest of the tenth century. Extensions of the long-familiar grants of immunity, these measures on the whole paid off; independent bishops usually supported the king against third parties, and provided much-needed military assistance from the episcopal militias. However, the disadvantage of boosting episcopal power lay in the enhancing of bishops' already substantial hold on the royal coinage; the policy thus contributed to the dramatic decline of royal monies and mints in the second half of the tenth century.

Louis' more immediate problem in west Francia was solved by invoking the principle of hereditary right: Heribert's sons divided their father's lands and offices among themselves. They still caused occasional trouble; Louis was particularly angry when the eldest of them, Heribert the Old, count of Omois, abducted the queen mother Eadgifu and married her in 951. But the threat their father had posed to Carolingian dominance north of the Seine receded into the distance. Then Albert of Vermandois' marriage to Louis' stepdaughter Gerberga helped to calm past animosities.[42] The worst was apparently over.

However, another and equally serious crisis blew up in Normandy, where the murder of William Longsword in 942 at the instigation of Arnulf of Flanders left the succession insecure and led to dissension among the Norman lords. Louis, perhaps hoping to claim the duchy for his younger son Charles, intervened and, to gain support, offered the town of Bayeux to Hugh the Great, who brought his army to join the king's. Certain Norman lords, anxious to safeguard the rights of William's heir, the young Richard, then turned to the Danish prince Harald for military assistance. At a crucial moment in the campaign Louis revoked his promise of Bayeux to Hugh, who promptly withdrew. In 945 Louis was captured by Harald and his Danes, which put paid to his ambitions in Normandy; under duress he recognised Richard's right to succeed his father. This renunciation did not, however, secure his release. Instead, Harald handed Louis over to the still-smarting Hugh. The king's imprisonment by one of his *fideles* caused widespread outrage, with both Otto I and Edmund of Wessex demanding his immediate release – a demonstration of kingly solidarity against aristocratic pretensions. At the behest of an assembly of west Frankish magnates, Hugh did indeed release Louis, though not until the town of Laon had been surrendered to him in compensation. The king was therefore restored to his throne, but on the sufferance of his lords. A repetition of the events of 922 had only just been averted.

Seeking revenge for this humiliation, in 946 Louis attacked Laon, where he acquired a fortress, and then Rheims, which he captured from Archbishop Hugh (which again led to Hugh's expulsion and Artald's restoration). In 948, at a synod at Ingelheim, in the presence of Otto I and the papal legate, Louis obtained the excommunication of both Hughs. But bringing Hugh the Great to heel proved impossible (partly because Otto wished to hold a balance between his two brothers-in-law). Finally in 953 the adversaries agreed a compromise at Soissons, by which Hugh unreservedly recognised Louis both as his king and his lord, but kept Laon (apart from the king's fortress), acquired suzerainty over Normandy (a substantial blow to Louis' hopes), and probably also obtained royal endorsement for his plan to take Aquitaine from Louis' ally Count William of Poitou. The Robertine family interests thus were strengthened and broadened by Hugh's rebellion.

Yet Louis emerged from Soissons with some positive gains. He had recovered Rheims; he had maintained his fortress in Laon; he had probably secured his son's succession to the throne; and he had prevented the formation of an

---

[42] Bur (1977), p. 103.

alliance between Hugh and Heribert of Vermandois' sons. Heribert the Old, Robert of Troyes and Albert of Vermandois were all men of ambition; but they no longer looked to the Robertine house to get what they wanted. From the king's point of view, their neutrality in the years 945–53 was a real achievement. On the other hand, Louis had had to sacrifice royal interests in Amiens, Ponthieu and the Artois to the wily count of Flanders, whose support against Hugh had been essential.[43] And the loss of Normandy had been a bitter blow. When he died as a result of a hunting accident in 954, contemporaries probably counted as his principal successes his mere survival as king and his possession of a male heir with both Carolingian and Ottonian blood in his veins.

Lothar's accession to the throne marked an interesting divergence from past Carolingian practice: his younger brother Charles was denied any part in the inheritance, because Louis could not afford to divide his small possessions. Too young in 954 to register his protest, Charles' ambition was later to cloud Lothar's reign. In the meantime, because the young king was only thirteen, his mother assumed the guardianship of the kingdom, assisted by her brothers Otto I and Archbishop Brun of Cologne (who had been put in charge of Lotharingia in 953). Gerberga's policies were predictable: no west Frankish intervention in Lotharingia, cooperation with the bishops, an Ottonian bride for Lothar (in 966 he married Otto's step-daughter Emma), and peace with Hugh the Great and his heirs. From this last, Hugh at once benefited. Although his attempt to claim the duchy of Aquitaine in 955 was foiled by Duke William III, he did acquire the duchy of Burgundy in 956 on the death of Hugh the Black's heir Gilbert.[44] This he bestowed on his second son Otto. Whether it was actually in the long-term interests of the Carolingian house to allow such a build-up of Robertine power may be doubted. But Lothar was spared from any immediate adverse repercussions by the death of Hugh in 956.

The king at once determined to prolong the minorities of Hugh's heirs, thereby encouraging the fragmentation of ducal authority across Neustria and Burgundy. Between 956 and 960, the year in which the young Hugh Capet was recognised as duke of the Franks, the duke of Normandy threw off Robertine overlordship, the count of Blois annexed Chartres and Châteaudun to his principality, and the count of Anjou extended his influence into the Massif Central.[45] The consequence was that Hugh's domains shrank to the Paris basin (where the counts of Senlis, Corbet, Melun, Dreux and Vendôme proved consistently loyal), and a corridor stretching south to Orléans, of which he retained the county. To assert himself beyond these bounds was to prove difficult. Yet his task was rather easier than that which faced his brother Otto in Burgundy.

Lothar used the breathing space thus created to consolidate his links with his

---

[43] Ganshof (1949), p. 22.   [44] Sassier (1980), pp. 15–18.   [45] Werner (1980).

bishops. On Brun of Cologne's advice, he approved the election of Olderic, canon of Metz, to the archiepiscopal see of Rheims in 961. This set an important precedent. In 969 Olderic was succeeded by Adalbero, son of the count of Verdun; and in 976 a relative, also called Adalbero, received the see of Laon. These three Lotharingian prelates loyally upheld the rights of the Carolingian king in west Francia, so long as he remained committed to the Ottonian alliance. But in the last resort, as was to become clear in 987, they preferred the Ottonians to the Carolingians. Their elections therefore created, in the Carolingian heartland, pressure points for the continuance of pro-Ottonian policies.

With royal protection of Rheims re-established and that of Sens removed from the hands of Otto of Burgundy, Lothar was then able to exploit his influence over Langres, which had been returned to Louis IV in the course of Hugh the Great's Burgundian campaign of 937. Under the royal eye, the bishop ruled the county of Langres and a large part of the diocese as a territorial principality.[46] From him, Lothar obtained financial, political and military support. When in 980 he secured the election of his kinsman Brun of Roucy to the bishopric, the benefits to the crown expanded, as did the boundaries of the bishop's power.

In dealing with his secular magnates, Lothar had one stroke of luck: in Flanders he exploited the succession crisis of 965 to acquire temporarily the rich lands of the Artois that had long been a bone of contention between the kings and the counts of Flanders, in return for recognising the rights of the young child Arnulf II.[47] Furthermore he skilfully obtained the alliance of Heribert the Old, who by 968 enjoyed the titles *comes Francorum* and count palatine, to signal their friendship.[48] Lothar thus overcame the isolation that had so often plagued Louis IV.

Nevertheless Hugh Capet, once out of his minority, demonstrated abilities that could not be overlooked. He won back Richard of Normandy's goodwill and built up a firm alliance with Geoffrey Grisegonelle of Anjou. He acquired the county of Ponthieu (probably from Lothar in 965), which gave him a convenient foothold between Norman and Flemish territory. Finally, in 967 or 968 he married Adelaide, daughter of Count William III of Poitou, thereby formally renouncing his father's claims on the duchy and acquiring both an ally and a wife who bore him a sizeable family. Though he could never dominate west Francia as Hugh the Great had done, he was becoming a substantial force in its political life.

Consequently, Lothar was moved to attempt the extension of his power

[46] Bautier (1990a), p. 175. [47] Flodoard, *Annales, s.a.* 962, pp. 152–3; Dunbabin (1989).
[48] Bur (1977), pp. 113–14.

elsewhere in west Francia. Hemmed in as he was by his princes, the only chance he saw was in the Massif Central, where the marriage of Geoffrey Grisegonelle's sister Adelaide with the viscount of the Gévaudan had opened up a new prospect. Since Adelaide was now a widow, Lothar sought her hand for his son Louis, hoping that the Gévaudan might become the kernel of a revived subkingdom of Aquitaine. The wedding took place in 982. But within two years, dissatisfied both with his wife and with the poverty of his prospects there, Louis demanded a divorce.

The alternative strategy for expansion, the revival of Carolingian claims on Lotharingia, seemed less dangerous after the death of Archbishop Brun in 965, especially since the emperors' preoccupation with Italian affairs distracted their attention from the region. But Lothar would probably have refrained from intervention had it not been for his brother Charles' ambitions and Otto II's willingness to pander to these. In 974 Charles joined the rebellion of Reginar and Lambert, sons of the erstwhile count of Hainault whom Brun had expelled in 957/8 and who sought restoration to their father's rights. Otto II, plagued by problems elsewhere, surrendered Hainault to Reginar and Lambert and, more surprisingly, conferred the duchy of lower Lotharingia on Charles.[49] Instead of calming the storm, this generosity infuriated Lothar, who saw his own claims to Lotharingia violated by his brother's promotion, and regarded it as insulting that he had not been consulted over the affair. At the same time, Hugh Capet was disturbed by the news, because his sister, widow of Frederick, duke of upper Lotharingia, feared the effects of Charles' aggression on her son's inheritance.[50]

Therefore in August 978, assisted by Hugh Capet and his brother Henry, now duke of Burgundy, Lothar set out to demonstrate his anger. His target was Aachen, Charlemagne's capital, which the army found undefended after the emperor's flight. They pillaged the palace and then retreated, hoping to return soon. At once Otto reciprocated. Accompanied by Charles, whom he now proclaimed king in his brother's stead, he swept towards Paris, intent on humiliating Lothar. There he met and was defeated by the royal army, reinforced by Capetian, Angevin and Burgundian troops, in an encounter that was to be remembered in legend.[51] Abandoning his ambitious plans, Otto sued for peace, asking only that Lothar renounce his claims in Lotharingia. At Margut in 980 the terms were agreed. But the exclusion of Hugh Capet from the treaty (perhaps his concern for his sister would have made it impossible for him to

---

[49] *Editor's note:* in English and French literature Charles is normally called 'Charles of Lorraine', but as lower Lotharingia is quite different from present-day Lorraine, he will be referred to in this volume as 'Charles of Lotharingia'.

[50] For the origin of the Robertine interest here see Parisse (1989), p. 343.

[51] *Gesta consulum Andegavorum*, p. 38; *Chronique de Nantes,* pp. 97–101.

recognise Charles as duke of lower Lotharingia) led to a rift between Hugh and Lothar that lasted for the rest of the reign. The tensions of the years 945–53 thus returned to plague west Frankish politics.

The 978 adventure had sharpened Lothar's appetite. Otto II's death in 983 provided the ideal opportunity to revive his claims to Lotharingia. Admittedly a campaign there would antagonise both the pro-Ottonian bishops and Hugh Capet, who was still concerned to defend his nephew's rights. But the lure was too great to be resisted. In 985 Lothar sent Odo, count of Blois, and Heribert the Young, count of Troyes, to besiege Verdun, where Count Godfrey, brother of Adalbero of Rheims, was flying the Ottonian banner. The capture of the town, its defender, and the young duke of upper Lotharingia who was sheltering there, brought about an alliance between Adalbero and Hugh Capet that was potentially dangerous. Nevertheless the fighting was all going Lothar's way when, on 2 March 986, he died after a short but very unpleasant illness.

Louis V, who had been crowned as his father's associate in 979 (in opposition to Otto II's proclamation of Charles of Lotharingia),[52] succeeded without difficulty to the throne. Although there are indications that he wished to continue the Lotharingian campaign,[53] he was prevailed upon by his mother and the west Frankish princes to desist. Peace negotiations with the east Frankish regency government were therefore begun, only to be disrupted by Louis' death in May 987 without an heir.

Thereupon a council of the west Frankish aristocrats, guided by Adalbero of Rheims, rejected the claims of Charles of Lotharingia to the throne, and elected Hugh Capet. The precedents of 922 and 923 were carefully followed. Hugh, grandson of a king and son of an Ottonian princess, was brother to the duke of Burgundy, brother-in-law to the duke of Aquitaine, and suzerain of the duke of Normandy. His election was acceptable to all the west Frankish princes except the house of Vermandois and its allies; and it was welcomed by the Ottonian interest because it would mean peace in Lotharingia. Charles, on the other hand, was only a collateral claimant, who had limited west Frankish connections and was personally unpopular; furthermore the union of west Francia with Lotharingia that he intended to achieve revived bitter memories of Hagano's dominance. Therefore the accession of the Capetian dynasty to the west Frankish throne, later seen as a momentous event, was achieved quite smoothly. And on 3 July 987 Hugh Capet was crowned at Noyon.

The circumstances of his election made Hugh determined to establish his dynasty securely. By Christmas 987 he had overcome magnate opposition to the coronation of his eldest son Robert as joint king. This ceremony, drawing on the precedent of Lothar's emergency measure of 979, set a pattern for

---

[52] On the general significance of this see Lewis (1978).   [53] Sassier (1987), pp. 186–94.

Capetian kings until the time of Philip Augustus. Then Robert needed a royal bride to enhance his claims against those of Charles of Lotharingia. After an abortive attempt to obtain a Byzantine princess,[54] Hugh settled on Rozala, daughter of Berengar, king of Italy, a lady whose distinguished ancestry was outweighed in the eyes of her young bridegroom by her relatively advanced years.

The coronation and subsequent royal marriage forced Charles of Lotharingia's hand. Helped by the counts of Vermandois, Troyes, Roucy, Soissons and Rethel, in May 988 he invaded the lands that had been held by his brother. Laon fell easily to him; but only by the treachery of its new archbishop, Arnulf, was he able to capture Rheims in August 989. Since Hugh continued to enjoy the backing of most French magnates and bishops, stalemate ensued. In the early spring of 991, through the cunning and deceit of Adalbero, bishop of Laon, Charles was captured and imprisoned in Orléans, where he died, probably within a year. From now on the Capetian dynasty had no rival in west Francia. Hugh could therefore allow his headstrong son Robert to divorce Rozala, who had served her purpose.

Hugh's recapture of Laon and Rheims put an end to the division of west Francia that had endured since Odo's treaty with Charles the Simple in 897. By uniting Carolingian and Robertine lands, and by steadfastly refusing to perpetuate the title 'duke of the Franks' (of whose emotive power he, as its long-time bearer, was fully aware), Hugh performed a decisive service for the west Frankish monarchy. Although he and his successors found themselves surrounded by powerful princes, they never had to face a rival for the throne of the standing of Hugh the Great. Nor were they forced to look beyond the west Frankish realm for the means of stabilising their authority; Lotharingia and the Ottonian connection ceased to play more than a shadowy role in royal politics. And in the moral support they received from their cadet branch in the duchy of Burgundy, the early Capetian kings were fortunate. The change of dynasty in 987 therefore largely resolved the tensions of the past century.

Yet relief from external pressure and internal rivalry created its own problems. While the crown had been contested, the princes had automatically considered their own interests within the context of royal politics. Now they no longer had to do so. Though acknowledging Hugh's sacrality, in matters of everyday dispute they could afford to treat him as one of themselves without endangering the realm or shocking the pope or the emperor. Indeed one of their number, Count Borrell of Barcelona, disappointed by Hugh's failure to assist him against al-Manzur in 987, ceased to request royal charters at all.[55] If the loss of this tenuous connection was hardly noticed at the Capetian court,

[54] For an explanation of the rapid abandonment of this scheme, see Poppe (1976), pp. 232–5.
[55] Lemarignier (1965), pp. 31, 38; Bonnassie (1975), pp. 138, 337.

its long-term implication – the ultimate alienation of Catalonia from the west Frankish realm – was important. Elsewhere in the south Hugh – *faute de mieux* – was accepted as king; but neither he nor Robert made much impact there. Hugh's marriage to Adelaide of Poitou and Robert's third marriage to Constance of Arles, along with Robert's famous pilgrimage to S. Jean d'Angély in 1004, aroused only limited interest.

North of the Loire, after 991 Hugh had little to fear. No longer plagued by Vermandois enmity, he was supported by Richard II of Normandy, and the young Baldwin IV of Flanders depended upon his goodwill. Though his authority in the Carolingian heartland was less than strong, he could call upon most of the bishops to display their traditional loyalty. Within Robertine lands he retained the county of Orléans, his chief centre of power, and he kept Ponthieu, and also the lordship over many viscounties and castellanies; he was ably assisted by the count of Paris, his old friend Bouchard of Vendôme; and with the exception of Marmoutier, he preserved his authority over the great religious houses that had contributed so much to his father's standing.[56]

The one fly in the ointment was the growing independence of the counts of Blois and Anjou who, in their ambitious extension of their principalities, were engaged in conflict on Breton soil. Of the two, Odo I of Blois was the greater immediate danger to Hugh, on the grounds that, as count of Tours, he threatened Hugh's authority in Saint-Martin and took Marmoutier from him, as issuer of a remarkable comital coinage he blatantly contravened a royal right, and as cousin of the Vermandois he had claims north of the Seine.[57] When in 993 Odo was tempted into rebellion by Bishop Adalbero of Laon, Hugh took the easy way out, encouraging Fulk Nerra of Anjou to attack his rival in Brittany and in the Touraine. Although this served Hugh's immediate purpose, it facilitated the emergence of a powerful Angevin state with Poitevin connections that later threatened Capetian interests.

In 996 Hugh died, leaving the kingdom to Robert II. Despite the sobriquet 'the pious' bestowed on Robert by his biographer Helgaud of Fleury, the new king was ambitious and designing. In his determination to assert himself in west Francia he was assisted by Otto III's absorption in Italy, by a change in the direction of Flemish expansionist designs from Picardy and Ponthieu to the imperial march of Valenciennes, and by the death of Odo I of Blois in 996. This last provided an opportunity not to be wasted. Robert at once married Odo's noble widow, Bertha of Burgundy, a marriage which embroiled him in much trouble with the church and which was ultimately (in 1003) dissolved on grounds of consanguinity. But in the short term it smoothed relations between the king and the house of Blois, allowing Robert to contain Fulk Nerra's

---

[56] Sassier (1987), p. 148.
[57] Bur (1977), p. 158. On the Blois-Chartres coinage see Dumas-Dubourg (1971), p. 53.

designs in the Touraine. This, however, proved to be Robert's sole achievement in that quarter. In 1008 Fulk Nerra arranged for the murder of the king's favourite Hugh of Beauvais, count palatine, an event greeted only by royal complaint.[58] And in 1016, when Fulk unexpectedly won a great victory at Pontelevoy against the army of Odo II, thereby extinguishing the Breton ambitions of the house of Blois, Robert could again only wring his hands.

The major success of the reign was in Burgundy. In 1002 duke Henry, the king's uncle, died, having designated as his heir to the duchy his step-son Otto William, count of Burgundy and Mâcon. Supported by Hugh, bishop of Auxerre and count of Chalon, Robert challenged Otto William, and by 1006 had won Burgundy, which he ruled directly until his second son Henry was old enough to become duke. Thus he imitated the aims and family policies of his grandfather Hugh the Great. Then he permanently detached Auxerre from the duchy of Burgundy, retaining it himself for the rest of his life; in face of considerable resistance he imposed royal protection on the archbishopric of Sens; and he taught the bishops of Chalon, Autun and Auxerre to turn again to the crown in times of trouble.[59] The royal demesne thus benefited substantially from the restoration of Robertine rule over the duchy.

In 1022 a quarrel broke out between the king and his erstwhile protégé Odo II of Blois, Bertha's son. The cause was the count's growing ambition following his (contested) inheritance of the counties of Meaux and Troyes in 1021. Although Robert initially gave his consent to Odo's succeeding his second cousin Stephen, son of Heribert the Young, he never liked the consequence: Odo's control of lands both to the south-west and to the north-east of the royal demesne. The count's attempt to extend his sway over Rheims may have been the spark that ignited the tinder box.[60] In the five-year war that followed, Robert tried in vain to deprive Odo of Meaux and Troyes; in 1027 he finally agreed to recognise Odo's rights again. The count subsequently devoted his time to campaigning in imperial Burgundy; like Baldwin IV of Flanders, he now preferred to turn his aggression eastward.

Robert's failure to disinherit Odo should be ascribed not only to the traditional fear of alienating other lords but also to the problems he faced on the royal demesne. The bundle of lands and rights he had acquired from his father was proving increasingly difficult to control. The death of Bouchard II in 1007 had deprived him of a faithful servant, and paved the way for Vendôme's annexation by Anjou. Robert's recovery of the county of Paris and, temporarily, of Melun and Corbeil, was a welcome consequence of Bouchard's heir being an ecclesiastic – he was Reinald, bishop of Paris – but it increased royal responsibilities. Then, throughout the demesne, castellans and other officials

[58] Fulbert, *ep.* 13, p. 26.   [59] Sassier (1980), pp. 31–41.
[60] Bur (1977), pp. 158–65; but see also Sassier (1980), p. 12 and n. 12.

took advantage of the king's absences in Burgundy to put their own interests before his. During the war with Odo II, that count built up a network of allies on the royal demesne, including the counts of Meulan and Dammartin.[61] It was a situation demanding from the king a degree of concentrated attention that he could not give. Consequently he left to his heir Henry I a legacy of trouble and discord there.

Robert had done his best to ensure a smooth succession; in 1027, when his eldest son Hugh died, he had arranged at once for the coronation of Henry in his place. But he could not prevent his third wife, Constance of Arles, from trying to upset his arrangements. The trouble that broke out in the early years of Henry's reign is symbolic of the achievements and failures of the first two Capetian kings. In the absence of external pressure, they had secured their dynasty against other west Frankish pretenders; they had brought a degree of peace to the realm, had incorporated Carolingian lands, bishoprics and abbeys within the extensive Capetian demesne,[62] and had prevented the duchy of Burgundy from slipping out of Capetian control. But they had not imposed their will firmly on dissidents, whether within the royal family or among the princes, and they had devised no new means of controlling their lesser *fideles*. Therefore they remained vulnerable to pressure. Though the west Frankish kingdom was firmly on the map by 1031, their own future was still questionable. A succession crisis might still prove dangerous.

Any history of the west Frankish kingdom from 898 to 1031 inevitably highlights the king's relations with his princes. And yet during this period the king was less likely to encounter his great men than either his predecessors had been or his successors would be. Odo was the last king to call the *ban* across the whole kingdom; Radulf's 925 *ban* was the last north of the Loire. After this 'the nation in arms' became an obsolete concept. Large assemblies of magnates for peaceful purposes, like the one convoked by Lothar in 961, were rare events. The emergency gatherings at which Robert, Radulf and Hugh Capet were elected to the throne, sizeable though they were, were very incomplete; each king had subsequently to gather allegiances from absentees. Coronations tended to attract only neighbouring lords. And as the royal demesne took shape and kings travelled less beyond its frontiers, their opportunities for meeting distant nobles declined. The rulers of Gascony and Toulouse, and after 987 Catalonia, effectively withdrew from the kingdom; the duke of Aquitaine only episodically participated.

Even north of the Loire, contacts between king and princes were becoming occasional. This trend was partially obscured in the second half of the reign of Radulf and that of Louis IV, when Heribert of Vermandois' ambitions

---

[61] Lemarignier (1965), pp. 61–2.   [62] Brühl (1968), p. 235.

embroiled the northern princes in royal politics; as it was again in the last years of Lothar, when the Lotharingian campaigns polarised opinion. But in 'normal' times, the princes were too much engaged within their own lands to come often to court. It was therefore natural that the kings should rely increasingly in day-to-day matters on the advice of those bishops who remained in their sphere of influence, and of their lesser *fideles*: in the case of Louis IV and Lothar, the lords of the Laon–Rheims area; for Hugh Capet and Robert, the castellans of the Orléannais and the Île de France. This development inevitably blurred the distinction between kingdom and principality.

Lemarignier, who counted the declining number of royal charters in the tenth century, the shrinking area from which came requests for such charters, and the royal chancery's increasingly frequent departure from Carolingian diplomatic form, concluded that the kings, by their growing isolation from many of the princes, were becoming irrelevant in much of west Francia; and that, even within the confines of their contracting rule, their power to command (as opposed to confirming the initiatives of others) was disappearing. Not until the last two decades of the eleventh century was this trend slowly to be reversed.[63]

Dumas, who brought together the scattered numismatic evidence, produced a similar though steeper graph of decline. In the reign of Charles the Simple, all coinage was issued in the king's name; it was relatively abundant, and was produced in mints in the south as well as in his centres of power. By the time of Hugh Capet, it was scarce and had become just one of many coinages circulating in the realm; even in the royal demesne it enjoyed no monopoly.[64]

Earlier, Dhondt had painted a somewhat similar picture by charting the losses from the royal fisc throughout the century, and drawing out their implications for royal revenue. Though his conclusions were too gloomy, recent work has confirmed the validity of his approach.[65] When Arnulf I finally seized the Artois, he deprived his king of income from well-cultivated and productive estates which could ill be spared. By the middle of the tenth century, Louis IV was finding it difficult to hold on to fiscal land in any of the principalities; it was above all financial pressure that caused him to risk the campaign in Normandy in 945, and led his son Lothar to attack Lotharingia, although he knew how much opposition he would arouse. Similarly the much richer Robert II had to fight rather than allow the whole Burgundian duchy to escape from his family's hands.

But it was not just revenue that was at stake. When Louis IV granted away the last piece of fiscal land in the Mâconnais, royal authority collapsed in that

---

[63] Lemarignier (1965), p. 139; (1970), pp. 153–8.   [64] Dumas (1992).
[65] Dhondt (1948), pp. 267–75; Martindale (1984), pp. 171–2.

area for two centuries.[66] Appreciating this, Brühl investigated the impact of fiscal grants on royal itineraries and hence, kingship being largely personal, on royal power.[67] As Louis IV and Lothar lost control of palaces, abbeys and bishoprics, their authority was increasingly restricted to the area around Laon and Rheims; and even there Louis at least faced strong competition. However, the situation did ease after 987, with the very substantial addition of the Robertine lands to the royal demesne; and Robert II's intrusions into northern Burgundy broadened further the scope of royal journeyings. By 1031 he had been seen in places long unvisited by the last Carolingians.

There are clear differences of opinion among modern historians as to when the nadir of the west Frankish monarchy was reached. But there is general agreement that the tenth century saw the balance of power tilting strongly towards the princes. The elections of 922, 923 and 987 offered real choices to the electors, as did the events of 936. After each of these occasions the king was restricted by the terms of his elevation.[68] Furthermore, there were moments, as in 945, when it seemed that the west Frankish king was nothing more than the pawn of his magnates. And even the revival of royal fortunes under the early Capetians was primarily owed to their exploitation of essentially princely talents – only by becoming like a prince could the king bolster his authority. West Francia was thus apparently on the brink of becoming a loose confederation.

Yet looked at from another perspective, the kings retained and even enhanced some of their specifically royal advantages during the century. As a consequence they contrived to bequeath to their successors an inheritance of alliances and political ideas that was to prove crucial to the later development of the French monarchy.

In the first place, tenth-century kings remoulded and applied to new ends the traditional bonds with the church. Appreciative of the military significance of episcopal troops, Louis IV permitted a marriage between his step-daughter Aubrée and the leader of the Rheims archiepiscopal *militia*, Reinald of Roucy, which stood his family in good stead until 991.[69] Lothar's campaign of 985–6 in Lotharingia owed much of its *élan* to troops supplied by abbeys and bishoprics of the royal demesne. Though these forces proved inadequate to protect the king against a united aristocratic front, and they could not be called upon to act against the wishes of churchmen, they did permit a significant degree of royal initiative (which was why the kings took pains to prevent them from falling into the clutches of princes). The union of those abbeys and churches the Carolingians had protected with the extensive Robertine ecclesiastical

---

[66] Duby (1953), p. 91.   [67] Brühl (1968), pp. 220–39 and Itinerarkarten III and IV.
[68] For a different opinion, see Lewis (1981), p. 5.   [69] Bur (1977), pp. 134–5.

demesne in 987 radically improved the royal position. The archbishopric of
Tours, the bishoprics of Paris and Orléans and the abbeys of Saint-Martin of
Tours, Fleury and Saint-Denis were merely the most significant additions to
the crown. Bolstered by Amiens, which Baldwin IV of Flanders surrendered,
and the gains Robert made in Burgundy, by 1031 the Capetian dynasty felt reasonably secure against most rebellions (except those led by members of the
family, who could divide its assets).

To consolidate their positions, Hugh and Robert followed the Carolingian
precedent of granting bishops comital rights, sometimes over the city alone,
sometimes over the whole county. By 1031 Le Puy, Rheims, Châlons, Noyon,
Langres, Laon, Beauvais, Paris and Auxerre had all become small episcopal
states. The suppression of lay countships could not totally extinguish secular
power within them; the bishops needed advocates and commanders of their
armed forces, some of whom, like the Roucys in Rheims, grew to be very significant figures. But it did exclude the princes from absorbing the towns into
their principalities. And in the long term this ring of episcopal states around
the royal demesne was to reinforce royal authority in areas where it was otherwise weak.

The alliance between church and crown brought other advantages.
Ecclesiastics continued to address kings in terms framed for the heirs of
Charlemagne. Abbo of Fleury, writing for Hugh and Robert, exploited classical and Carolingian sources to exalt what he took to be an unchanged and
unchanging monarchy.[70] The coronation ceremony rubbed in the same point
of view. Nor were churchmen afraid to embellish their inheritance in the interests of helping their king. Aimo of Fleury in his *De gestis regum Francorum* took
Hincmar's original story of the dove who had brought from heaven an
ampoule of oil for the coronation of Clovis, and added to it the important
claim that the ampoule was miraculously refilled for all subsequent coronations;[71] thus all west Frankish kings became the special beneficiaries of God's
grace. Similarly Helgaud of Fleury described Robert II as a holy man, compared him with King David, and attributed to him healing powers.[72]

However, tenth-century kings were not simply passive recipients of propaganda; they manufactured it for themselves. By imitating Ottonian diplomatic
forms in some of his charters of the 960s, Lothar surrounded himself with an
aura of majesty, while Hugh Capet twice referred to his *imperium* in his charters.[73] Both late Carolingian and early Capetian seals consciously imitated
Ottonian forms.[74] The equation of kingship with empire proved popular
among west Frankish churchmen; Abbo of Fleury defended it enthusiasti-

---

[70] Mostert (1987), pp. 137–8.   [71] Aimo of Fleury, *De gestis regum Francorum*, p. 40.
[72] Helgaud of Fleury, *Vie de Robert le Pieux*, pp. 59, 139, 129.
[73] Schneidmüller (1979), pp. 100, 175.   [74] Rezak (1986), pp. 94–6.

cally,[75] and Adalbero of Laon flattered Robert II with references to his imperial ancestry.[76]

More concretely, tenth-century kings innovated to preserve. Here they have sometimes had less than their due from historians, whose obsessive concern with Carolingian precedent has led them to interpret all modifications of tradition as proofs of weakness. But Louis IV's abandonment of his family custom in choosing Lothar as his sole heir was a sound move in the circumstances; the precedent he set was to be followed by and become a source of pride for the early Capetians, as was Lothar's coronation of Louis as his co-ruler. In the same way, Robert II's suppression of Carolingian counties, 'the disintegration of the *pagus*', once interpreted as the clearest symptom of royal decline, is now appreciated as a successful endeavour to uphold royal at the expense of comital authority.[77] Furthermore the creation of the large royal principality was an achievement of equal magnitude with the emergence of the duchies of Burgundy and Normandy. Imitating princes did not derogate noticeably from royal power in the short term; and over time it proved vital to the restoration of the monarchy on a new footing.

Therefore, beneath the fragmentation of royal authority and the localised wars of the tenth century, other forces can be descried. The assumptions of the Carolingian era, many of them deriving from imperial Rome, no longer fitted circumstances. New solutions to governmental difficulties had to be found. It is easier to admire the response of the princes to this challenge, because their principalities were largely new creations. Set against them, tenth-century kings appear rather inert. Yet not all the changes that occurred were forced upon them by their more vigorous neighbours; they were capable of constructive innovation. And their twelfth-century successors were to reap the benefits of some of their more far-sighted policies.

[75] Mostert (1987), p. 131.   [76] Adalbero of Laon, *Carmen ad Robertum regem*, p. 2.

[77] Sassier (1980), pp. 39–40. Lemarignier accepted this interpretation in his introduction to Sassier (1980), p. viii.

CHAPTER 16

WEST FRANCIA: THE NORTHERN PRINCIPALITIES

David Bates

THE AREA over which the 'west Frankish' kings exercised meaningful authority contracted during the tenth century and new units of power emerged.[1] These have customarily been termed 'territorial principalities' since the publication of Jan Dhondt's important book.[2] By the early eleventh century the monarchy was effectively confined to what can justifiably be called a royal principality, situated around Paris and Orléans, and even within this area its control was patchy. The rest of the region was dominated by five major principalities: Flanders, Normandy, Brittany, Anjou and Blois-Chartres, the last of which was from *c.* 1021 combined with Champagne.[3] Between the great principalities were zones containing several smaller lordships, over which no prince exercised real authority, and in which counts who dominated a single county, or a small group of counties, had power in some respects analogous to that of the greater princes. This was particularly the case in the lands surrounded by Normandy, Anjou, Blois-Chartres and the royal principality, and in the area between Flanders, Champagne, the royal principality and Normandy. The principalities were themselves far from being monolithic entities; Normandy and Flanders were close to being territorially compact units, but Anjou, Blois-Chartres, Brittany and the royal principality all contained enclaves under the control of lords who were vassals of other princes. In broad terms, the period as a whole was one of dramatic and profound change which shaped the history of the region for centuries to come. Commentators such as Werner and Fossier have firmly emphasised that the 'age of the principalities', that is, the period roughly speaking from 900 to 1200, is a crucial phase in the creation of the

---

[1] I am grateful for advice and assistance which I have received in the preparation of this chapter from Jean Dunbabin, Véronique Gazeau, Michael Jones, Katharine Keats-Rohan, Janet Nelson, Cassandra Potts and Timothy Reuter.   [2] Dhondt (1948).

[3] Unlike the others, this principality has never received a convenient name. It was constructed by a family whose members were originally counts of Blois and at different times included different counties. See below, pp. 407–8. For convenience, its rulers are henceforth called counts of Blois.

French state.[4] However, the precise character and extent of change across the whole period have been, and remain, matters for discussion, with the question of the extent of continuity from the Carolingian patterns of the ninth century a particularly vexing one.

The process whereby the principalities were formed and consolidated began in the middle of the ninth century when the Neustrian march was created for Robert the Strong by King Charles the Bald. It continued with the start of the conflict for the kingship between the Carolingians and the Robertines, with the evolution of what became Flanders and Normandy in the late ninth and early tenth centuries and of Brittany, Anjou and Blois in the mid-tenth century. As it developed, the process involved both the division of the west Frankish kingdom and the disintegration of its supposed constituent part, the Neustrian march. Three structural factors shaped the region's destiny during the period under discussion. First, there was the prolonged rivalry of the Carolingians and the Robertines/Capetians which continued until a descendant of Robert the Strong, the duke of the Franks, Hugh Capet, was chosen as king in 987. Second, there were the disruptive effects of Breton incursions into the western parts of the west Frankish kingdom in the ninth century, and of Viking raids in the second half of the ninth century and the first half of the tenth, which affected most parts of the region more or less severely. Third, there was the shift towards the inheritance of a principality by a single member of the family which became general in the early tenth century. The first, which is analysed by Jean Dunbabin (chapter 15), obliged the two families to concentrate their activities in the area between the Seine and the Somme where their lands met, thereby allowing others to develop their power in the western and northern parts of the region. The second meant that once the two families had by the late ninth century abandoned any attempt to control what later became Normandy and Brittany, they had to install 'marcher' lords to contain the threat of further Breton and, especially, Norman expansion. By the time that Brittany and what became Normandy were beginning to stabilise in the second half of the tenth century, the new units of power established to confine them had become so entrenched as to be unmovable and were themselves taking shape as principalities or lordships. The third ensured that, although individual principalities might be disrupted by succession conflicts, they were not divided up, after the pattern of ninth-century *regna*. This was a crucial factor in their consolidation.

The ethnic continuities from pre-Carolingian times, which arguably explain the evolution of the southern principalities of Burgundy and Aquitaine, do not, except in the case of Brittany, exist north of the Loire. The antecedents

[4] Werner (1978), pp. 275–6; Fossier (1979), p. 10.

which can be used to argue for continuity from Carolingian times are of a different kind. Dhondt, while referring to the developments of the period as 'une profonde révolution', emphasised that both the Neustrian march and Flanders can be traced back to territorial creations which Carolingian kings set up to buttress their rule against the assaults of the Bretons and the Danes. Karl Ferdinand Werner, by far the most important modern commentator, has taken this approach much further by suggesting that the first principalities were not 'illegitimate', that is, creations founded exclusively in the violence and acquisitiveness of their founders, but rather the successors of territorial units which originated in a grant by a king.[5] This argument is even possible in the case of the one principality which is manifestly an intrusion, Normandy, since its territory was formed from a combination of grants made by Carolingian and Robertine kings. Werner would, however, admit that the creation of Anjou and Blois, his so-called 'second wave' which followed the partial disintegration of the Neustrian *regnum* of the Robertines, was less controlled: 'this last type would correspond to the conventional scholarly picture of "amasser of counties"'.[6] But even here, he has argued for what is called 'biological continuity', by showing that the families responsible for the creation of the 'second wave' principalities can almost invariably be traced back to already powerful families, which existed in the time of Charles the Bald at the latest, and which built upon lands and offices which they can be shown to have held in the middle of the ninth century.

A more subtle version of the 'continuity' thesis dwells on the continuity of the language and structure of power. Werner has argued, and a number of the regional studies which will be discussed in this chapter have demonstrated, that tenth-century princes generally ruled through methods which were observably Carolingian and used titles which were equally respectful of Carolingian usage. The principalities can therefore be seen as a kind of post-Carolingian phase, a twilight of the Carolingian world before the social changes of the later tenth and early eleventh centuries associated with the emergence of seigneuries, which are seen as ushering in a new feudal age. The inspiration for much of this approach lies in the conclusions of Georges Duby's influential study of the Mâconnais, published in 1953, and his subsequent writings.[7] A parallel line of argument, associated above all with Jean-François Lemarignier, saw such features as the spread of multiple ties of allegiance and the devaluation of the language of authority through the proliferation of terms such as *consuetudines* in the late tenth and early eleventh centuries as indicative of a society teetering on the edge of anarchy.[8] At the extreme it is even possible to see the principalities as a continuity representing

[5] Werner (1978), pp. 247–52. [6] *Ibid.*, p. 250. [7] Duby (1953, 1978).
[8] Lemarignier (1965), pp. 59–65; (1968), pp. 106–11.

the final stage in the decline of the Carolingian world, before the process of renewal through the seigneurie commenced.

Modern French historiography nevertheless remains undecided on the extent of continuity from the Carolingian period.[9] The notion of the northern principalities as 'un prolongement carolingien' is deeply embedded in modern discussions.[10] It is an approach which has accomplished a great deal. It means that we are able to think in terms of a credible evolution, rather than the violent break which was proposed by Marc Bloch,[11] and that when we examine the essentials of government and power, such as *fidelitas*, coinage and charters, we are able to construct a conceptual framework for their operation, even when we choose to reject or modify ideas of continuity. A less than enthusiastic acceptance of 'continuity', set out in the 1970s by Robert Fossier and developed, seemingly independently, by American and British scholars such as Bernard Bachrach, Constance Bouchard and Jean Dunbabin, has queried the way in which 'continuity' and 'biological continuity' have been defined. Fossier, for example, emphasised that it was neither devolution, usurpation nor inheritance that created a principality, but rather the ability of one family to secure acceptance of its superiority by those around it.[12] Bachrach has pointed out that inherited rights and powers 'only delineated the broad limits of available opportunity, but could not ensure that opportunity would be grasped',[13] while Jean Dunbabin has employed a musical metaphor to draw attention to the creative genius of the territorial princes, stating that 'a *regnum* was a series of brilliant improvisations, not the carefully balanced slow movement in a symphony of Carolingian decline'.[14] With regard to 'biological continuity',[15] Constance Bouchard has argued that it cannot be taken as signifying either direct or smooth descent of office, land and power, since many of the families, such as the counts of Anjou, Blois and Champagne, advanced by combining advantageous marriages and clever dynastic manoeuvres with violence; the result, it is suggested, could be tantamount to a 'social revolution'.[16] As far as the special case of Normandy is concerned, old debates about the relative role of Frankish and Scandinavian influences have recently been revived by Eleanor Searle,[17] even rejecting notions of the two-sided character of Norman society and 'dented continuity'.[18]

---

[9] Autrand, *et al.* (1991), pp. 103–4.

[10] Thus, 'L'époque carolingienne se poursuit en France du nord, comme le veut l'histoire de la dynastie, jusqu'au terme du Xe siècle': Fossier (1968b), p. 445. More recently, 'Le système carolingien n'est donc pas mort avec le changement dynastique', Sassier (1987), p. 282; and '980–1030, c'est une phase décisive de la "dislocation" du royaume carolingien, déjà amorcée depuis 877 au profit des principautés', Barthélemy (1990), p. 9.   [11] Bloch (1962), pp. 195, 422–6.

[12] Fossier (1979), p. 12.   [13] Bachrach (1984), p. 816.   [14] Dunbabin (1985), p. 92.

[15] The phrase 'biological continuity' was coined by Génicot (1962), p. 3. See also Martindale (1977), p. 10, n. 22.   [16] Bouchard (1981), p. 527.   [17] Searle (1988), pp. 1–11.

[18] Musset (1979), pp. 50–4; Bates (1982), pp. 15–24.

All these generalisations will be examined in more depth in the discussions
of individual principalities which follow. It is important at this stage to emphasise very strongly that all the above-mentioned scholars, with the exception of
Eleanor Searle, are working within the framework first articulated by Dhondt,
and developed much further by Werner, even if all would undoubtedly wish in
one way or another to modify it. This said, it is necessary to recognise that a
vital component in an analysis of the notions of 'continuity' and 'biological
continuity' – and indeed in deciding whether to accept them at all – is a clear
idea about where we start, how we travel and where we end. If we begin from
the recent observation that '[ninth-century] *regna* were artificial things.
Carolingian rulers didn't just receive them as given: rather they created, recreated, shaped them for themselves',[19] we can see that the Carolingian structure
from which we have to start was more flexible than has often been recognised,
and that the territorial consolidation achieved by the tenth-century princes represents something more creative than a mere *prolongement* and, ultimately, something more permanent. Genuine state-building is typical of the tenth-century
aristocracy/princes in a way which appears not to be typical of their ninth-
century predecessors.

It is also important to recognise that the often-observed continuity of titles
and political language can equally well represent devices designed to mask ille-
gality and change as a continuation of an existing structure – Werner himself has
pointed out that the way in which the Norman rulers used the increasingly elevated titles of *marchio* and *dux* was not universally accepted.[20] What appear to be
grants may well represent concessions made under duress; it is hard to believe,
for instance, that the creation of the Neustrian march and the duchy of the
Franks by 'grants' from Charles the Simple and Louis IV did not have something
to do with the potential power of the Robertines, or that the grants to the
Normans were not made against a background of threats of further violence.
Similarly, it can hardly be a coincidence that the power of the counts of Anjou
and Blois was consolidated during the minority of Hugh Capet from 956 to 960.

At the latter end of the period under discussion, an assessment of long-term
continuity and change needs to recognise that the new social structures associated with the rise of the seigneuries emerged against a background of principalities most of which were able to survive the disruptions, and most of which
sought to use the seigneuries to consolidate their internal structure. The result,
as will be seen later, is that while the significance of continuities from
Carolingian times often has to be played down, there were at the same time
principalities where Carolingian tradition continued not only beyond the early
eleventh century but even into the twelfth. For these reasons, the majority of

---

[19] Nelson (1992), pp. 2–3.   [20] Werner (1976), pp. 707–8.

those who have written on the northern regions of west Francia in this period
have in part or whole rejected the applicability of Duby's model of social
change built around the emergence of the seigneurie. In the context of the
history of the northern French principality, the scale of change in the first half
of the tenth century may deserve greater emphasis and the scale of change in
the first half of the eleventh century, less.

The principality of Flanders certainly evolved directly out of arrangements
made during the reign of Charles the Bald, but its final shape was the result of
the military achievements of its rulers. Count Baldwin I, a relative of a family
who already held comital status, abducted Charles' daughter Judith in 862,
reached a settlement with the king in the same year, and in 864 appears as count
of Ghent and Waas. By the time of his death in 879 he had made further acquisitions, which were greatly expanded by his son, Count Baldwin II 'Iron Arm'
(879–918), who beat off Viking attacks in the 880s, was established in Artois in
883 by King Carloman, and then proceeded to take over lands which stretched
as far south as Vermandois. His successor Arnulf I (918–65) pushed even
further south and west.[21] Along with violence – these early counts of Flanders
were involved in the murders of Archbishop Fulk of Rheims in 900, Count
Heribert I of Vermandois in 900×907, and Count William Longsword of
Rouen in 942 – the basis of power looks to have been landed wealth, much of it
taken by Baldwin II from the church and from the royal estates he was supposed to be protecting. The counts thereby acquired enormous possessions,
especially in the north of the county.[22] Yet, despite their massive achievements,
the power of the Flemish counts became somewhat insecure in the last years of
the long life of Count Arnulf I, and especially so after Arnulf's son Baldwin III
predeceased him in 962, leaving Baldwin's infant son, the future Count Arnulf
II, as heir. Arnulf I's solution was to swear fealty to King Lothar in 962, place
the county under royal protection, and permit the transfer of the counties of
Boulogne and the Ternois to a collateral line. Arnulf II's reign is now regarded
as a period of consolidation, after which territorial expansion was resumed,
but this time towards the east, under Count Baldwin IV (989–1035).[23]

The political shape of the rest of the north-eastern part of the region
remained fluid for much of the tenth century. At one stage it appeared that a
principality was being forged by the exploits of Count Heribert II of
Vermandois, who died in 943. Heribert had all the credentials of a proto-terri-
torial prince. He was of Carolingian descent. He had inherited the counties of
Vermandois and Soissons, which had been brought together in the later ninth
century to form a march on the River Oise against Viking incursions, and he
used them as a base from which to absorb neighbouring *pagi*. He played a

---

[21] Ganshof (1949), pp. 15–27.   [22] Warlop (1975), pp. 29–30.   [23] Dunbabin (1989), pp. 53–6.

central part in the struggle between the Carolingians and the Robertines, as well as against the Vikings, siding with the Robertines and acting as King Charles the Simple's jailer at the time of his death in 929 and campaigning against Vikings in Brittany in 924×925 and 927.[24] However, his 'principality' was too close to the heartlands of Carolingian and Robertine power for these two powers to allow it to continue, as well as being in a region whose stability was regularly disturbed by the incursions of the Normans and the counts of Flanders. After 943 Heribert's lands were split up among his sons, none of whom was able to control much more than a single *pagus*. When the power of the counts of Flanders retreated in the second half of the tenth century, Heribert's descendants came to share control of the area between Flanders, Normandy and the Capetian lands around Paris with the collateral branch of the Flemish comital family which had been established after 962 in the Boulonnais and the Ternois, the counts of Ponthieu who were set up there by the Robertines/Capetians, and another family of impeccable Carolingian descent, the counts of Amiens-Valois-Vexin.[25] During this period, the most important of Heribert II's descendants, Count Heribert the Old, established the principality of Champagne on the base of the *pagi* of Troyes and Meaux. His death without direct heirs in 984 led eventually to Champagne being acquired in 1021 by Count Odo II of Blois, on the basis of his descent from one of Heribert the Old's sisters.

Normandy evolved from a sequence of grants of territory to Viking war-bands, who were the successors of raiders who had been active in the Seine valley since 841. Evidence for the initial gift, the so-called 'treaty of Saint-Clair-sur-Epte', is either late or indirect. A grant was certainly made – probably in the year 911 – by the Carolingian King Charles the Simple to the Viking chieftain Rollo after the latter had suffered a military defeat near Chartres. Flodoard's chronicle indicates that further grants were made in 924 and 933, the total of which produced a territory approximating to that which became Normandy.[26] What must initially be emphasised is that these grants to the Vikings were a regular feature of late Carolingian politics, a world in which kings and nobles sought to manipulate Viking war-bands to assist their own complex rivalries and to appease and perhaps assimilate a highly volatile threat to the region's stability. There were similar, earlier grants to Bretons and Vikings, and contemporary grants to Vikings based on the River Loire. To an extent, therefore, ideas of the 'legitimacy' of Normandy's creation are justified. However, as Eleanor Searle has rightly emphasised, neither the survival of such territories nor their rulers' acceptance of the restrictions which the 'grants' theoretically imposed on them can be taken for granted. Most similar Viking settlements did

---

[24] The best modern account of Heribert and his sons is Bur (1977), pp. 87–114.
[25] Feuchère (1954), pp. 1–37.   [26] Musset (1970), pp. 96–9; Bates (1982), ch. 1.

not endure. Rollo, his successor William Longsword (*c.* 927–42) and other war-leaders campaigned extensively in northern Francia, with the undoubted purpose of acquiring even more territory. The new settlement was almost overthrown when the Franks made a determined attempt at reconquest in the 940s. As in the case of Flanders, the dual themes of princely violence and creativity are once more evident. A more controversial aspect of recent discussion of Normandy's origins is Eleanor Searle's suggestion that 'Normandy' was not controlled by Rollo and those who followed him as counts of Rouen, but by a number of independent war-bands which the rulers established at Rouen were not able fully to control until well on into the eleventh century.[27] Lucien Musset's restatement of the argument that Normandy's exceptionally well-defined frontiers must have been created *ab initio* suggests the relative political coherence of early Normandy, however.[28] So does the considerable evidence for William Longsword's activities in Brittany,[29] and so does the extent of the lands held by the counts of Rouen/dukes of Normandy in the west of Normandy in the early eleventh century.[30] These general points are only slightly modified by the demonstration that the location of the Norman rulers' lands in the Hiésmois fell some way short of the later frontier.[31]

The nature and the extent of Scandinavian influence within what later became the duchy of Normandy remains a subject of lively controversy. The contributions of Professors Musset and Yver, both broadly in favour of institutional continuity from the Carolingian era, are of fundamental significance to the whole subject. The institutional emphasis of Yver's work can give a misleading impression that there was not extensive disruption and violence, but it is without doubt the basis on which all discussion of Normandy's early history must now be based.[32] That Normandy evolved in many respects towards a typically post-Carolingian territorial principality seems beyond denial; the rulers' titles were Carolingian, churches were re-established on Carolingian sites, the settlers' language was undoubtedly French by the early eleventh century and their culture largely Christian. From William Longsword's reign there are numerous indications of developments in the minting of coin, of the construction of princely palaces, and of written documents, which are recognisably influenced by Carolingian models.[33] On the other hand, the frequency of

---

[27] Searle (1988), chs 3 and 10.   [28] Musset (1989), pp. 309–16.

[29] Guillotel (1979), pp. 64–5, 70–3.

[30] I shall return to the subject of ducal lands in lower Normandy in the second edition of Bates (1982).

[31] Louise (1992), pp. 137–50.

[32] Fundamental is Yver (1969). For continuity at the level of rural society, Musset (1946). For law and government, Musset (1976b) and (1979). Note also Musset (1970). By way of contrast see de Bouard (1955).

[33] Musset (1946), pp. 42–52; Bates (1982), pp. 24–38; Tabuteau (1988), pp. 4–6, 294, 307–8; Renoux (1991), pp. 343–447; Potts (1990a), pp. 23–6, 43–5.

fresh Scandinavian incursions into the settlement and its enduring connections with Scandinavian colonies elsewhere until well into the eleventh century, along with features such as the lengthy persistence of Scandinavian folk-memories, indicate a settlement both integrated into and distinct from its Frankish environment.[34] There have also been recent advances in the study of Norman place-names which emphasise settlement on a relatively sizeable scale, notably in the two regions where Scandinavian place-names proliferate, the Cotentin and the Pays de Caux, and a good survey of the archaeological, linguistic and place-name evidence.[35] In the case of Normandy, as with all the principalities, we should think of the Scandinavians as in essence new and distinctly exotic masters who built on old foundations. The activities of the settlers and their sea-borne visitors remained an unpredictable threat to the region's stability until beyond the middle of the tenth century, but by the time of Duke Richard II (996–1026) Normandy had become a very powerful principality. It had also ceased to be the threat it had once been to the region's stability. Although Richard fought a war against Count Odo II of Blois, his people's long-standing loyalty to the kings was thought worthy of comment by an early eleventh-century writer who was not a Norman.[36] 'Normandy' became 'respectable' in the sense that its rulers and aristocracy came by the early eleventh century to share the same ambitions and aspirations as their counterparts elsewhere in the region.

The two principalities of Anjou and – as it had become by the 1020s – Blois-Champagne-Chartres-Châteaudun-Tours emerged from within the Neustrian march, in both cases through the social ascent of families appointed to office by the Robertines. Fulk the Red first appears as *vicomte* of Angers in 898. In 929 he uses the title 'count of Anjou', a dignity at first denied to him by Hugh the Great, but subsequently accepted in 942 at the latest.[37] He also appears as *vicomte* of Anjou and count of Nantes in 907, 908 and 919 and lay-abbot of the abbey of Saint-Aubin of Angers in 924. How Fulk acquired these positions has been much discussed. The family genealogies compiled in the late eleventh and the twelfth century name three generations of ancestors, one of whom, Ingelgar, is a historical figure recorded in other sources; the others, the earliest of whom appears in the genealogies as a rustic who was made a royal forester by Charles the Bald, have been regarded by some commentators as legendary and by some as historical figures.[38] Werner suggested that it was through his marriage to a woman named Roscilla that Fulk the Red obtained his various dignities, which can be shown to have been held by a family from which she

---

[34] Musset (1979); Bates (1982), pp. 15–24; Searle (1988), pp. 44–58, 79–90; van Houts (1984).
[35] Fellows Jensen (1988), pp. 133–4; Renaud (1989), pp. 109–203.
[36] Radulf Glaber, *Historiae* I, 21, p. 36.   [37] Werner (1958), pp. 264–71; Guillot (1972a), pp. 131–8.
[38] The most recent discussion is Bachrach (1989a).

was presumably descended back in the mid-ninth century. For him this established a biological continuity with the Carolingian nobility which he believed to be the basis of the power of the counts of Anjou. More recently the accent has been placed firmly on a rapid rise, either through successful marriage alliances or through a larger paternal inheritance than Werner believed.[39] 'Continuity' – if indeed the word can be used in this situation – is evident in the manner in which the Angevin family took over an existing unit of responsibility. Yet we are left with a clear impression of a family who rose dramatically out of the ranks of the *vassi dominici* to achieve a regional superiority which was unprecedented. The power of the tenth-century counts of Anjou was to all intents and purposes that of 'new men'.

The beginnings of the principality of Blois-Chartres-Tours are similar. In 905, Fulk the Red occurs as *vicomte* of Anjou and Tours, but in 908, there is a first reference to a *vicomte* named Theobald. This same Theobald was probably *vicomte* at Blois shortly afterwards, and is almost certainly the father of the first count of Blois, Theobald 'le Tricheur', who began to call himself count in *c.* 940. As with the counts of Anjou, later accounts of the family's origins have a legendary feel about them; Richer of Rheims records the gift of Blois to a certain Ingon, another forester, for his heroic deeds at the battle of Montpensier (892) by the Robertine King Odo. In all probability we are again dealing with a family which may well have been related to the established aristocracy, but one whose rapid social ascent seemed perplexing to later medieval commentators and, as far as we are concerned, must be regarded as dramatic.[40]

The power of the two comital families of Anjou and Blois should not be seen as at the beginning developing in opposition to that of the Robertines within the Neustrian march. Both were promoted in order to foster and protect Robertine power against encroachment from south of the Loire and against Viking incursions from the north and west. Both were the beneficiaries of the Robertines' patronage; Hugh the Great, who became duke of the Franks in 936, may well have positively sanctioned the transformation of the erstwhile *vicomtes* into counts, as a reflection of his own elevated status.[41] It was only later that the Robertines/Capetians lost control over affairs on the Loire, because of their preoccupations elsewhere, and because of the skill with which the two families expanded their power and territory. Theobald 'le Tricheur' and his family acquired control over Tours in the early tenth century, Chartres in *c.* 950, Châteaudun in *c.* 960 and, much later, in *c.* 1021, in the time of Count Odo II, Champagne. The counts of Anjou pushed southwards into Aquitaine, Poitou and the Saintonge in the time of Geoffrey Grisegonelle (960–87) and,

---

[39] Bouchard (1981), pp. 514–16; Bachrach (1989a), pp. 10–15.   [40] Boussard (1979).
[41] Sassier (1987), pp. 131–2.

massively so, during the long reign of Fulk Nerra (987–1040). They also
acquired lordship to the north and east over formerly independent families of
the Neustrian march such as the counts of Maine and Vendôme and influence
over the former Robertine protégés, the lords of Bellême.[42] As a result of this
expansion, the two counts had lands and vassals within each other's sphere of
influence; the counts of Blois built up control over land on both banks of the
Loire to the west of Tours almost up to Angers itself, while Amboise on the
river to the east of Tours became subject to the counts of Anjou, as were
Loches and Buzançais to the south. After 977 the two principalities embarked
on a bitter struggle for supremacy which ended only in 1044 with the battle of
Nouy and the Angevin capture of Tours. Their rivalry and, in particular, the
ambitions of Counts Fulk Nerra and Odo II, were the chief cause of instability in the region in the late tenth and early eleventh centuries. Neither principality was ever as compact or territorially consolidated as Flanders and
Normandy, and, in the case of Blois, its over-extended and loosely unified territories are reasonably seen as the fundamental cause of the decline which
began in the eleventh century.[43]

   In the case of Brittany, we are dealing with a principality with origins much
more ancient than those of the others. Brittany had never been incorporated
into the Carolingian empire; its rulers had called themselves kings in the second
half of the ninth century, and had sometimes, if not altogether willingly, been
recognised as such by the Carolingians. The policy adopted by Charles the Bald
had allowed the Breton kings to extend their authority to the western regions
of what later became Anjou and Normandy.[44] This enlarged 'state' collapsed
under the impact of Viking attacks after the death of Alan the Great in 907. By
921, an embryonic Scandinavian principality had been created around Nantes
and the mouth of the Loire, and the Normans settled around Rouen had
invaded the westerly regions of Cornouaille. Religious institutions had been
destroyed, and the count of Cornouaille, Mathuédoi, along with his son Alan,
fled into exile in England at a date between 913 and 931.[45] Viking domination
eventually proved to be unsustainable, however, and in 936 Alan was allowed to
return, probably as the result of an agreement reached between the dominant
Franks, Hugh the Great and Count Heribert II of Vermandois, and the
Norman count of Rouen, William Longsword. By 939 the Vikings had been
completely defeated. But, the new Breton principality was no more than a pale
reflection of the old. Although Alan established himself as count of Nantes,

---

[42] Boussard (1968a), pp. 27–8; Bachrach (1976), pp. 111–22; (1985), pp. 17–28; (1993), pp. 147–226.

[43] Boussard (1979), pp. 109–11.

[44] For a useful account see Guillotel in Chédeville and Guillotel (1984), pp. 249–374.

[45] The chief modern accounts of this period are Guillotel (1979), pp. 63–76; Chédeville and Tonnerre
    (1987), pp. 23–30; Price (1989), pp. 23–54; Galliou and Jones (1991), pp. 148–74.

his heirs were unable to prevail against the rival counts of Rennes after his death in 952. The contest for power between these two families was a long one, not even partially resolved until *c.* 1030, when Budic, count of Nantes, witnessed a charter of Alan III, count of Rennes, and still likely to re-emerge after that. Former Breton territory was removed by the Normans when the Cotentin and the Avranchin were granted to them in 933, and, further south, during the course of the tenth century, by the counts of Anjou and Maine. The tenth-century Breton counts, while sustaining their territorial independence, became something of a pawn in the rivalry of the counts of Anjou and Blois, with the counts of Nantes usually allied with Anjou and the counts of Rennes with Blois. When Blois began to decline in the eleventh century, the counts of Rennes gravitated into the orbit of the Norman dukes.

Although there are numerous occasions in the tenth and early eleventh centuries when all or some of the princes acted in unison with the kings, the undoubted reality is that conflict and rivalry for power and territory underlay many events in the tenth century in the northern part of western Francia. A dramatic instance of cooperation is the support which Hugh Capet brought to assist King Lothar in 978 when the emperor Otto II's army advanced through the ancestral lands of the Carolingian kings to the gates of Paris. There are many other demonstrations during the tenth century of the new territorial rulers' basic respect for kingship. Alongside Count Arnulf I of Flanders' oath of fealty to King Lothar in 962 we can place a series of charters from Lothar's reign in which the king confirmed grants within the principalities.[46] Charters involving Count Geoffrey Grisegonelle of Anjou demonstrate an apparently irreproachable respect for the acknowledged structures of authority, since royal confirmations were obtained through the agency of his lords, Duke Hugh Capet and Duke William of Aquitaine, and he acknowledged that he held the county of Anjou from Duke Hugh.[47] However, the way in which Geoffrey manipulated Lothar into agreeing to an unsuccessful marriage for his son Louis V, which assisted the count's ambitions in Aquitaine, shows that such primarily legal evidence cannot be taken at face value, and how far self-interest influenced the princes' policies and actions.[48] Similarly, the apparent moment of unity of 978 in fact reveals the deep divisions among the rulers of north-west Francia; Richer tells us that Lothar's separate peace with Otto was seen by Hugh Capet as the start of an alliance against him, and a period of tension between Lothar and Hugh followed.[49] This quarrel replicates earlier ones; for example, the break-down of the alliance of Louis IV and Hugh the Great during their invasion of the Normans' lands in the 940s and Lothar's resent-

---

[46] DD Lo 1, 5, 7, 15, 16, 18, 19, 21, 22, 24, 25, 26, 36, 41, 44, 48, 52, 53, 54, 62 (on which see further Guillot (1972a), p. 6 n. 28), 68.   [47] Guillot (1972b), pp. 2–7.   [48] Richer, *Historiae* III, 92–4.
[49] *Ibid.* III, 81–5; Sassier (1987), pp. 160–70.

ment that Hugh Capet did not assist him, Count Theobald le Tricheur and Count Geoffrey Grisegonelle in a war against the Normans in the 960s. All these events raise questions about the nature of the *fidelitas* which supposedly bound the princes to the kings and the precise character of the policies the princes were following.

At the summit of society were the latent or overt rivalry between the Carolingians and the Robertines/Capetians and the wars between Anjou and Blois which commenced in earnest after 977. And throughout the region there was a mass of lesser rivalries, of which the tenth-century conflict between the counts of Maine and the bishops of Le Mans drawn from the family of Bellême[50] and the rivalry of the Norman dukes and the counts of Rennes over Mont-Saint-Michel can serve as examples.[51] The failings of kingship probably lie at the root of the disorder, causing all who claimed power and status to have to fight to hold on to it; there was no one dominant power capable of sustaining extensive authority or keeping the peace. Whatever the explanation, all the rivalries fuelled the violent politics which are typical of the region's history. It should not, however, be thought that this signified that the major principalities lacked solid foundations. A series of important developments show that this was very much the case.

The most powerful princes developed what can legitimately be termed 'foreign' policies. All astutely combined warfare, diplomatic and marital alliances, and the manipulation of *fideles* to expand and consolidate territory. A succession of Angevin counts from Fulk the Good through to Geoffrey Martel (1040–60) used exactly this mixture of methods to push southwards into north-east Aquitaine, Poitou and the Saintonge.[52] The Normans, with their long coastline, had relations with the British Isles and Scandinavia, and from the 990s onwards they became involved in the convoluted politics of the English succession.[53] Duke Richard II (996–1026) was an ecclesiastical patron on a European scale and provided warriors to assist the papacy in Italy, a development which was at the beginning of the Norman settlements in southern Italy.[54] There were several marriages involving princely families and the royal families of Europe. Count Baldwin IV of Flanders and Count Odo II of Blois both became involved in the politics of the empire. Odo was especially energetic in pursuing the dynastic possibilities created by his family's and his own marriages, at one time or another claiming the county of Champagne, the kingdom of Italy and the kingdom of Burgundy. It was in pursuit of this last ambition that he was killed in battle in 1037 against the German King Conrad II. What deserves emphasis is the relatively early date from which princes were

---

[50] *Actus Pontificum Cenomannis in urbe degentium*, pp. 353–9; Louise (1992), pp. 222–45; Keats-Rohan (1994, 1997).   [51] Bates (1982), pp. 70–1; Potts (1990b).   [52] Bachrach (1976, 1983, 1985, 1993).
[53] Musset (1954); Keynes (1991).   [54] France (1992).

developing relations with powers outside the region; Count Baldwin II 'Iron Arm' of Flanders married a daughter of Alfred the Great, while Count William Longsword of Rouen was involved in negotiating the return from England of King Louis IV in 936 and the Breton Count Alan in *c.* 937. Arguably, the princes envisaged themselves as participants in a political world which extended beyond modern-day conceptions of west Francia. Family networks exercised a considerable influence on policy.

By the end of the tenth century – and probably earlier – all the princes commanded formidable military machines, adept at siege warfare and, if necessary, at fighting full-scale battles. The methods of the Angevin counts have been particularly thoroughly analysed; Count Fulk Nerra, the great castle-builder, has been seen by Bernard Bachrach as following a well-worked policy of constructing fortifications with both attack and defence in mind, and shown to have been able to call on at least 4000 effective fighting troops for war.[55] Richer provides the first two known instances of the employment of paid troops by the counts of Anjou and Blois in the 990s, and Professor Boussard suggested that the armies which fought the princes' wars increased considerably in size at that time.[56] Duke Richard II of Normandy also has a great reputation as a recruiter of warriors from distant lands; it is a measure of the power of the other princes that he and his fellow Normans had to call on help from Scandinavian war-bands in order to assist in their northern French wars.[57] Although the evidence is sparse, it is clear by the end of the tenth century that princes were advancing men of relatively humble aristocratic origins in order to further their military and political purposes, and also that they were benefiting from a movement of social mobility which was fuelled by fortune-hunters among whom Bretons were prominent.[58]

The veneer of royal authority throughout the region in many significant respects peeled away in the last years of the tenth century to reveal the power which the princes had long been developing. Whereas, for example, Geoffrey Grisegonelle in 966 acknowledged that he held the county of Anjou from Hugh Capet, no such acknowledgement was forthcoming from his son Fulk Nerra (987–1040) after Hugh became king.[59] Similarly, no royal charter exists relating to Normandy after 1006 and none to Brittany after 986.[60] The practice whereby principalities were styled *regna*, although an infrequent usage, is an almost universal one, and, by the mid-tenth century, Flanders' territorial identity, and, by the early eleventh century, Normandy's, were sufficiently secure for

[55] Bachrach (1983, 1989b).   [56] Richer, *Historiae* IV, 82, 90; Boussard (1968b), pp. 148–68.

[57] Bates (1982), p. 99; Radulf Glaber, *Historiae* II, 3, p. 56.

[58] Chédeville (1974), pp. 315–21; for 'new men' in the entourage of Count Fulk Nerra see Bachrach (1984), pp. 808–10.   [59] Guillot (1972a), p. 2 n. 5.

[60] Lemarignier (1937), p. 34 n. 30; Jones (1990), p. 5.

them to be called on occasion *Flandria* and *Normannia*.[61] The dukes of Brittany practised an inauguration ritual from the time of Conon I which is apparently unique.[62] The Normans were especially precocious in the development of a princely ideology, perhaps because their origins made it more necessary that they do so. The *Historia Normannorum* of Dudo of Saint-Quentin, commissioned in the late tenth century for the Norman counts Richard I and II, is the first instance of 'history' written to present a version of a principality's history. Its precise purpose is currently controversial; Eleanor Searle's argument in favour of a history written for a predominantly Scandinavian court seems less persuasive than Leah Shopkow's emphasis on a Carolingian inspiration and an underlying intention to identify a formerly pagan people with their Frankish environment, while at the same time pushing the case for Normandy's independence within the west Frankish kingdom.[63] A further demonstration of the growing individuality of particular principalities is the emergence of regionalised custom, expressed in the middle years of the eleventh century by phrases such as *mos patrie, mos Normannie* and *consuetudines Andecavinas*.[64]

Nonetheless, there were distinct and significant limitations to princely autonomy and independence. Although most of the princes articulated their evolving authority from the mid-tenth century onwards through the Carolingian language of power, this was apparently done within a set of universally understood ideas. Thus, the Normans and the Bretons called themselves on occasion *marchio* and *dux* and the counts of Flanders used *marchio*, in every case implying a ruler with authority over counts. That they usually did so with royal authorisation does not prove that the kings truly approved; agreement could be extorted by force. What is, however, exceptionally interesting is the conservatism with which the new titles were used. *Dux*, rather than *comes*, is once, and only once, employed to describe a count of Anjou in the tenth century, and then abandoned as if inappropriate;[65] while a thorough analysis of the titles used by the 'dukes' of Normandy shows the frequency with which the titles *dux* and *comes* were combined together, rather than used separately, as if betraying a lack of confidence in the much more assertive *dux*, and how *comes*, with its implication of a dignity conferred by a higher authority, remained the more common even as late as the reign of William the Conqueror.[66] In the same vein, it is noteworthy how the great princes are called *comites Francie* in a charter of 1017 and that, with one exception, they never used their territorial

[61] Werner (1978), pp. 248–54; Bates (1982), pp. 56–7; Ganshof (1957), p. 346.

[62] Radulf Glaber, *Historiae* II, 4, p. 58.   [63] Searle (1984); Shopkow (1989).

[64] *Recueil des actes des ducs de Normandie*, nos. 85, 132; *Cartulaire de l'abbaye de Saint-Aubin d'Angers*, ed. de Broussillon, no. 5 (Guillot (1972b), p. 109, no. C147); Tabuteau (1988), pp. 93, 223–9.

[65] 'fortissimus dux ac nominatus in universo mundo comes',*Cartulaire de l'abbaye de Saint-Aubin d'Angers*, ed. de Broussillon, no. 131, cited by Bachrach (1985), p. 38.   [66] Bates (1982), pp. 148–50.

titles in royal charters.[67] It should also be noted that the principalities on the Loire were somewhat less forward in adopting the full trappings of a princely ideology; Olivier Guillot suggested that one appeared in Anjou only in the time of Count Geoffrey Martel, and Michel Bur noted no evidence of one in the lands of the counts of Blois.[68] Although this conclusion has been somewhat modified for Anjou,[69] in both cases the apparent reticence may reflect their later origins, or a continued recognition that they had evolved out of the Robertine Neustrian march at a lower social level than the others, or that Blois in particular was less compact than the other principalities. It is notable too that some recently discovered charters have shown that Capetian authority was exercised much more frequently in Anjou in the 1030s and 1040s than had up until that point been thought.[70]

The nature of princely *fidelitas* points to a similar conservatism. The most recent treatment of the famous early twentieth-century controversy about whether or not the princes continued to be royal *fideles* has advocated a middle course, emphasising the continuity of princely fidelity, while at the same time stressing the fragility of the relationship.[71] What is interesting about this debate is the princes' consistent wish to remain within the structure of fidelity. Documents relating to the career of the buccaneering Count Odo II of Blois sum up the contradictions which were involved. Odo coveted and used the ancient Carolingian title of *comes palatinus* at the court of King Robert the Pious, yet after 1019 he was at war with that king.[72] A letter written on Odo's behalf to King Robert in 1023–4 calls Robert Odo's lord (*dominus*) and acknowledges that the king may set up a court to try him. It denies that Odo holds any *beneficium* granted from Robert's lands, but opines rather that his lands come by hereditary right from his ancestors with Robert's consent.[73] The whole argument is a recognition of lordship and authority; indeed it may be as much an appeal that the king behave as a good lord should, as an exercise in obfuscating any implications that fidelity may have been involved: 'For how can I honourably forgo defending my benefice? I call on God and my soul to witness that I would prefer to die with honour while defending it than to live dishonoured by its loss.' Radulf Glaber actually tells us that the Normans were consistently faithful to the kings after the initial phase of settlement, and the counts of Flanders were also generally loyal.[74] It was recognised that royal authority could confer legitimacy, as when, for example, Duke Robert I of Normandy had his designation of his young son William as his heir confirmed by King Henry I, and, on occasion, it

---

[67] *Recueil des actes des ducs de Normandie*, no. 22; Lemarignier (1965), pp. 128–9.
[68] Guillot (1972a), pp. 353–66; Bur (1977), pp. 461–99.   [69] Bachrach (1993), pp. 46–7.
[70] Fanning (1985).   [71] Lemarignier (1955).   [72] Lemarignier (1965), p. 129 n. 263.
[73] 'per tuam gratiam ex maioribus meis hereditario iure contingunt': Fulbert, *ep.* 86. On this subject, see also Hallam (1980), pp. 153–4.   [74] Radulf Glaber, *Historiae* I, 21, p. 36.

could become a reality, as when in 1047 Henry's intervention as overlord guaranteed William's survival. Despite the principalities' increasing independence from any kind of royal authority, kingship remained the theoretical lynchpin of the political society of north-west Francia. Neither the notion of Francia as a unit nor that of meaningful personal fidelity disappeared in northern Francia during the tenth and early eleventh centuries. A statement such as Dhondt's that there were no fidelities but merely interests in the eleventh century does not fully do justice to the subtleties of the situation.[75] What happened is that powerful, new identities evolved within the existing structure and that the specific obligations consequential on fidelity – about which we have only generalised accounts – reduced as princely independence grew.

A development which was crucial to the evolution of princely power was the practice whereby princely titles and lands were passed almost without exception either entirely or substantially undivided to a single son. With the exception of the succession in the Vermandois family after the death of Count Heribert II in 943, this practice took root in the early tenth century. It should not be regarded as an adjustment accepted by all, since in both the tenth and the eleventh centuries, several of the principalities were disrupted by feuds within the ruling kindred. Nonetheless, it went a long way to guaranteeing the integrity and survival of the principalities, and, from the middle of the tenth century, it was increasingly reinforced by the practice of designating the heir.[76] Later partitions, such as the grant of the Boulonnais and the Ternois to a branch of the Flemish comital family in the last years of Count Arnulf I's reign are the result of special circumstances; in this case, the need to resolve a family feud. The division of the holdings of Count Odo II of Blois after 1037 may reflect either royal interference against the development of a principality which threatened to encircle the royal lands, or the family's decision that the maintenance of geographically separate territories would be best served by division; whatever the case, the division respected the territorial integrity of the constituent units of Odo's lands.[77] A refinement, which both unified a kindred and sought to provide for its ambitious members, was that provision within a principality was often made for cadet branches; the Norman *comites* of the late tenth and early eleventh centuries are a well-known case in point. The overall result was that *regna* had ceased to be the flexible entities that they had been in the ninth century, to the extent that, by the eleventh century, it was possible for contemporaries to talk about the frontiers of principalities.[78]

[75] Dhondt (1967), p. 148.

[76] Lewis (1978), pp. 911–15; Searle (1988), pp. 91–7; Martindale (1989); Garnett (1994).

[77] Dunbabin (1989), pp. 54–5; Bur (1977), pp. 195–6.

[78] Musset (1989); Bates (1982), p. 56; Bachrach (1983), p. 549 n. 53; Chédeville and Tonnerre (1987), pp. 52–7.

Princes' charters only start to appear in any numbers from the late tenth century onwards. A good modern edition of them currently exists only for Normandy,[79] although there are calendars and selected *pièces justificatives* for Anjou and for the reign of Count Odo II of Blois.[80] Although sparse, the evidence suggests that the tenth-century princes increasingly exercised on their own behalf powers which had once been the monopoly of the ninth-century kings. The best and earliest evidence of how a responsibility to supervise the operation of a delegated royal power was transformed into a princely prerogative is provided by coinage. The Normans were notably precocious, since coins were minted on behalf of both William Longsword and Richard I; under Richard, it should be noted, in a style which broke away from the rules set out in Charles the Bald's edict of Pîtres. Coins were being minted in several former Carolingian mints on behalf of Theobald le Tricheur of Blois by the 960s. The Norman coins notwithstanding, there is a general tendency in northern regions of western Francia for coinage not to depart too radically from Carolingian models – the mints within the lands of Hugh Capet actually reverted to issuing Carolingian royal coins in the years immediately before he became king – which indicates yet again the conservatism with which princes developed their authority.[81] Archaeological evidence has also shown that the majority of them built palaces in a style which was typically Carolingian, although by the second half of the tenth century the most powerful were adorning their residences with high towers.[82] Charters, treated as cultural artefacts, can also show how Carolingian models were followed by scribes producing documents for the assertive princes.[83] The great increase in the numbers of princely charters from around the year 1000 is another indication of the much more open displays of princely independence which became normal from that date.

Other frequently mentioned 'continuities' from Carolingian times are control of fortifications and the minting of coin, both of which were at the heart of ducal authority in Normandy; also, taxes such as the *bernagium* and the *gravarium* which have discernible Carolingian antecedents, and the chief officials of Norman local government, the *vicomtes*, controlled territories whose boundaries were usually those of the Carolingian *pagi*.[84] The counts of Anjou relied heavily on the *fodrum* to provision their armies, had a monopoly control

---

[79] *Recueil des actes des ducs de Normandie.*

[80] For Anjou, Guillot (1972b), based on the earlier catalogue in Halphen (1906), pp. 237–342, and with some omissions noted in Bachrach (1984), p. 802 n. 27 and Fanning (1985). For Odo II, Lex (1892), pp. 283–358. An edition by Hubert Guillotel of the *acta* of the counts of Brittany is announced. There is a catalogue of the acts of the counts of Maine in Latouche (1910), pp. 139–59.

[81] Dumas-Dubourg (1971).   [82] Renoux (1991), pp. 302–7.

[83] Potts (1992), pp. 30–4; Guyotjeannin (1989), pp. 44–5.

[84] Musset (1979), pp. 51–4; Bates (1982), ch. 4.

over coinage, and had extensive forest rights.[85] As has recently been stressed by several scholars, such 'continuity' was not mechanistically achieved. Rights and obligations had to be enforced in order to be sustained; it is no accident that many among the most successful princes have reputations for ruthlessness and brutality. The evidence of coinage, which is in many ways the most precise available, shows that 'continuity' is not a simple concept. The prerogative was once royal, but decisions to mint in a style which broke from Carolingian traditions, like those taken by the Normans and by Count Odo II of Blois, were made by the princes; arguably, one might think, this is not continuity at all. Instances of manifest innovation from the early eleventh century, such as the castellanries of Flanders,[86] the incipient chanceries in Normandy and Brittany,[87] the ubiquitous *prepositi*,[88] and the Norman *camera* with its capacity to perform financial operations of some sophistication, illustrate the long-standing dynamic of princely rule.[89]

The formulae of charters show that princely power was exercised *Dei gratia*. Although the notion that this implies divine favour has been questioned on the grounds that it may simply be a reference to providence,[90] the point remains that the princes are shown as considering themselves to have a place within the divine scheme. All took responsibility for the church within their lands and some, such as Duke Richard II of Normandy, have a reputation for personal piety. The princes invariably played a dominant role in the choice of bishops within their lands. A recent study has shown that the counts of Anjou were choosing the incumbent of the bishopric of Angers from the middle of the tenth century at the latest and that the counts of Blois influenced the choice at Tours and Chartres, even if the nominations were theoretically still royal. In Flanders and Normandy, the counts chose the bishops, but in Brittany, hereditary family possession of dioceses circumscribed the dukes' control and local comital families often provided the bishop. It is interesting also to note how families with power in the spaces between the great principalities came to influence appointments; the family of Bellême, for instance, in the bishoprics of Le Mans and Sées and the counts of Amiens-Valois at Amiens.[91] Most of the princes were patrons of monasticism and heavily involved in the spread of monastic reform. The counts of Flanders had a great reputation in this respect: Duke Richard II of Normandy patronised the influential monastic reformer William of Volpiano, and the counts of Anjou reformed and patronised abbeys such as Saint-Aubin of Angers, Loches and La Trinité of Vendôme.

---

[85] Guillot (1972a), pp. 379–96.   [86] Ganshof (1957), pp. 399–402; Warlop (1975), pp. 105–36.
[87] *Recueil des actes des ducs de Normandie*, pp. 42–3; Chédeville and Tonnerre (1987), p. 48.
[88] Werner (1978), pp. 256–61.   [89] Bates (1982), p. 154.
[90] Guillot (1972a), pp. 354–5.
[91] Boussard (1970); Louise (1992), pp. 150–61, 224–45; Lemarignier (1965), pp. 53–5.

The last major aspect of government is the appearance everywhere of castles – normally, it seems, wooden structures – and the emergence around them of seigneurial lordships or castellanries. As already noted, following on from Georges Duby's work on the Mâconnais, this has been regarded as a decisive and disruptive episode, a secondary phase of disintegration when authority shifted downwards to a new and lower social level. Throughout most of the northern parts of western Francia the period when the castellanries began to emerge can usually be placed in the late tenth or early eleventh century – Normandy is somewhat exceptional – but the broad conclusion to be drawn from the recent monographs devoted to the region is that, in the strongest principalities, most castellanries were not only not disruptive, but were actually princely creations. Much depends on the part of the region under discussion. It is clear, for example, that independent castellanries were much more likely to emerge around the royal principality and some of the lands of the counts of Blois, where war and rivalries encouraged the development of multiple ties of allegiance, than in the stronger principalities.[92] The 'independence' of a castellan family was also very much a mixed blessing, since the family concerned was often obliged to defend itself against more powerful neighbours, a point very well made by recent studies of the lords of Bellême.[93] Within the major principalities, the emergence of castellanries was for the most part a controlled process which represents a modification of the obligations of *fideles* rather than a reconstruction of society from below. The families involved were usually long-established ones; as will be seen from the studies cited in the next paragraph, the thesis of 'biological continuity' can largely be seen to apply at this social level as well.

Within Flanders, the first castellanries appeared in the late tenth and early eleventh centuries. They were established as the basic unit of comital government and their holders can clearly be shown to have been drawn from already established families. It was only in the lands to the south of the county, in the region from which Flemish power retreated after the death in 965 of Count Arnulf I, that local families established more independent lordships, although, even in these cases, their holders continued to accept that they were vassals of the count.[94] Princely control over the emergence of the castellanries within the lands of the Vermandois family and of the counts of Blois has also been argued for Champagne and the county of Chartres, with, again, the holders of the castellanries being drawn from the existing aristocracy.[95] For Anjou, where the subject has been analysed in considerable depth, Counts Fulk Nerra and Geoffrey Martel have been shown to have created castellanries and to have

---

[92] Lemarignier (1965), pp. 69–70; (1968), pp. 106–10; Bur (1977), pp. 174–92; Guyotjeannin (1987), pp. 19–31.   [93] Thompson (1985, 1991); Louise (1992, 1993).

[94] Warlop (1975), pp. 105–36.   [95] Bur (1977), pp. 127–47, 393–402; Chédeville (1973), pp. 254–93.

maintained firm control over them.[96] Even a more pessimistic analysis of the situation in Anjou, heavily influenced by Duby's approach, sees the period of major weakening in comital authority to have taken place after 1060.[97] In Normandy, in the time of Counts Richard I and II, the castellans bore the title of *comes* and were drawn from the rulers' close family circle; acts of disobedience by members of this group were ruthlessly punished. A second phase, this time of independent aristocratic castle-building, occurred during the civil wars of the Conqueror's minority, but no one would deny William's ultimate success in controlling its consequences. Again, although the thesis that the origins of the Norman aristocracy should be seen as based on 'biological continuity' from the tenth-century Scandinavian settlers has not proved universally acceptable, there are strong arguments for seeing the dominant castellans as descended from long-established families.[98] In Brittany, the dukes' control is less secure, but once more the developments often involved established families participating in a scheme to defend the principality's frontier.[99]

By 1025 the region had by and large acquired the territorial shape which endured until the great expansion of Capetian power which brought about the re-establishment of a dominant royal authority in the early thirteenth century. For that reason 1025 is a good date at which to end. It is, however, far from a perfect one, since princely rivalries and princely government continued to evolve. It is also important, in conclusion, to re-emphasise the sheer violence of the period from 900 to 1025; it was this which fascinated an earlier generation of scholars, whose attentions were focused on the literary sources, and who saw the age as one of minimal achievement. Recent research has convincingly and definitively provided a much more positive picture, yet it should still be borne in mind that the destiny of the region was effectively reshaped by the ruthlessness and violence of a small number of dominant families who exploited the crumbling of authority at the top of west Frankish society, a process which began in the last years of the ninth century. Their achievement was much more than 'un prolongement carolingien'. It is true that Carolingian forms survived into the late tenth century and beyond, and that Richer could write as if old-style Carolingian kingship still existed,[100] but the royal confirmation charters which continue up until the end of Lothar's reign and the advice and military support which the princes gave to the kings show beyond any doubt the creativity of the great princely families. The enterprise shown by individual princes, the territorial consolidation which they achieved and the

[96] Bachrach (1983), pp. 536–7.   [97] Guillot (1972a), pp. 299–317.

[98] Bates (1982), pp. 111–37; Musset (1976a), pp. 72–7; Tabuteau (1984), pp. 612–14; Hollister (1987), pp. 230–40.   [99] Jones (1981), pp. 160–7; Chédeville and Tonnerre (1987), pp. 111–75.

[100] Richer, for example, calls the war between Count Odo I of Blois and Count Fulk Nerra of Anjou 'bella civilia': *Historiae* IV, 79, 81, 90.

evidence for change within the principalities from a date early in the tenth century, all pin-point a powerful evolutionary process which began long before the last years of that century. On the one hand, the resilience and, on the other hand, the conservatism of princely power both require a final emphasis. Although new developments, such as the spread of castles, were taking place by the early eleventh century, there was no crisis of fidelity throughout most of the region, and princely power, which had developed in the tenth century, endured on into the eleventh and twelfth centuries. The princes' collective achievement was one of effectiveness; new units were created with great political skill on the basis of the traditional language of power. Yet, for all the princes, kingship remained the fundamental source of legitimacy and authority. Although, therefore, the tenth-century princes laid the foundations for at least another two centuries of achievement by their successors, the survival of an earlier political language supplied a basis of ideas from which the authority of kings was subsequently to be recreated.

CHAPTER 17

WESTERN FRANCIA: THE SOUTHERN PRINCIPALITIES

Michel Zimmermann

THE SOUTHERN half of the west Frankish kingdom created at Verdun led a troubled existence. Charles the Bald placated Aquitanian separatism by re-establishing a kingdom of Aquitaine for his son in 855, but royal control remained insecure. Rulers crushed an Aquitanian revolt and disposed of Aquitanian honours for the last time in the 870s; thereafter royal inadequacy left the south in comfortable isolation, though southerners continued to profess loyalty to the monarchy. In 888 the nobles of Neustria elected the non-Carolingian Odo as king, and the various peoples gave themselves 'kings born of their own entrails', as Regino put it.[1] In Aquitaine, Ramnulf II, count of Poitiers, proclaimed himself king, or at least behaved like one. Odo did not attempt to subdue Ramnulf by force; instead, he went to Aquitaine with only a small escort. Early in 889 Ramnulf submitted, and in return Odo granted him the title of *dux maximae partis Aquitaniae*, giving him control over Aquitaine under royal authority.

For the western kingdom, Odo's reign (888–98) initiated the era of princi-palities: hegemonies over cultural or ethnic entities which revived the former territorial units making up the *regnum Francorum*. South of the Loire, this phenomenon was especially significant. Throughout the tenth century, rival claimants to the kingdom came from the north; southerners were largely uninterested in the struggle, being more concerned to consolidate their own positions. William the Pious' adoption of the title of duke in 898 marked the beginning of a period in which the king was effectively absent from the south. The change of dynasty in 987 only made absence complete. The lengthy visit by Robert the Pious in 1019–20, the last royal intervention south of the Loire for over a century, was a mere pilgrimage. The only sign that the southern principalities belonged to the kingdom was the use of regnal years in the dating-clauses of charters.

---

[1] 'de suis visceribus': Regino, *Chronicon, s.a.* 888.

This royal absence was earlier and more complete in some regions than in others. The south was not homogeneous, and the nobility was divided; the king's remoteness encouraged a redistribution of power. Historical loyalties, ethnic traditions and more recent political alliances gradually created a division into four zones: Aquitaine proper, stretching broadly into the Auvergne; a Gascon zone beginning south of the Garonne; a Gothic zone covering Septimania, the mid-Garonne region, the Toulousain, the Rouergue and Albigeois; and the kernel of the later Catalonia, also Gothic but originally part of *Hispania*. These zones were not rigidly defined, and the powers controlling them were themselves unstable, as seen from the varying titles they assumed. But from 900 onwards they constituted the political framework of that France-without-a-king now occupying the former kingdom of Aquitaine.

The early tenth-century equilibrium remained stable for over a century. Around 1020–30 the principalities came under threat from within. Links of personal dependence, forged through private wars and nourished by an early intensification of economic activity, spread throughout the whole of society. From 1020, feudalism created a new social and political order. Some principalities disintegrated, others reformed or consolidated themselves. But the feudal order, itself shifting, was to come to birth only after decades of social and institutional chaos.

SOURCES FOR THE HISTORY OF SOUTHERN FRANCE: GAPS AND INEQUALITIES

How do we know about the history of the southern principalities? There were no local historians to carry on where the palace historians left off. If we want to know the history of southern France we have to look beyond narrative sources; our knowledge of events is consequently patchy; even our knowledge of institutional structures is fragmentary and speculative. Sources from north of the Loire largely ignore what was happening in the south: the *Annales* of Flodoard (919–66) contain only a few scattered references to southern events, mainly during Radulf's reign. Richer's *Historiae*, which offer occasional glimpses of the south in books III and IV, have long been judged very severely, but he expresses views current in northern Gaul, and reveals the (sometimes uncertain) terminology used there for political realities south of the Loire. He has less to tell us about the situation itself than about royal reactions, the kings' attempts to keep a presence, or regain a foothold, either directly or via the rulers of Anjou, in the furthest reaches of their realm.

Diplomatic sources, on the other hand, supply essential information, not only about 'institutions, titles and dates', as Leonce Auzias remarked,[2] but also

---

[2] Auzias (1937), introduction and pp. 216–32.

about the development and effectiveness of royal policy. The distribution and frequency of royal diplomata confirm the 'royal absence' from certain areas; the standing of the recipients emphasises that political attitudes varied, while that of the subscribers conveys the retrenchment of royal influence. This did not depend merely on proximity to the court: in Catalonia, the only part of the kingdom south of the Pyrenees, the number of royal letters did not decline until the mid-tenth century, and then only slowly. J.-F. Lemarignier has calculated that Gothia and the Spanish marches attracted one-sixth of the diplomata issued by the Carolingians in the tenth century;[3] even the counts were eager to nourish a 'royal memory' which still lay at the root of legal and political order. Hugh Capet's reign ended this kind of documentation abruptly: from 987 to 1025, no royal diplomata were issued for recipients south of a line drawn from S. Jean d'Angély through Bourges to Thiers.

Whereas narrative sources record only notable events, diplomatic sources show us day-to-day interactions. The southern princes ceased to frequent the court at the end of the tenth century: from 987 to 1108, the duke of Gascony, the count of Toulouse, the duke of Gothia and the Catalan counts never attended, and the duke of Aquitaine did so only in exceptional circumstances. The subscriptions show that from the Bay of Biscay to the Mediterranean there was a wide band of territory in which the king had no influence.

Most of our information comes from local sources. Even there we must still distinguish different types. There is no genealogical or dynastic literature from this region before the twelfth century; except for one chronicler, there is no southern French historiography. Numerous monastic annals and a few episcopal lists supply a trickle of information, mostly local. The only really historical work is the chronicle (*Chronicon*, *Historia*) of Adhémar of Chabannes, reaching to 1028. After 829, the author's work is original, and his horizon narrows; he draws heavily on local sources and oral tradition. From 980, the history of the Franks becomes a chronicle of the Aquitanian nobility. Other areas are even less well provided. There is no narrative history for Languedoc, either the Toulousain or Septimania; and only three very brief 'pseudo-chronicles' deal with the history of the Auvergne.[4] No narrative source survives for Gascony, only numerous documents turned into histories at a later date, and needing to be treated with great caution. Catalonia has no original historiography before the eleventh century; the 'writing of history' there was entirely dependent on the Frankish tradition. The events of 985–87 caused an abrupt change in historiographical perspective. The chronicles cease to make any mention of Frankish history and concentrate exclusively on local events. But this narrowing of perspective was not sufficient to sustain a regional history.

---

[3] Lemarignier (1965), p. 22.   [4] The expression is that of Lauranson-Rosaz (1992), p. 14.

By contrast, hagiography – saints' lives, miracles – is an essential, but uneven souce for southern French society. There is no hagiography from Catalonia from the tenth century, and little from the eleventh. It is much richer north of the Pyrenees: and some works, such as the *Life of Gerald of Aurillac*, or the *liber miraculorum* of St Fides of Conques, are of great importance. Yet however rich the hagiographical sources, they are no basis for historical writing. It is archival sources which supply the bulk of our knowledge of tenth-century history.

Southern societies characteristically produced an abundance of archival documents, though their conservation has been very uneven. Catalonia's documentation is the most abundant. Pierre Bonnassie estimates that there are at least 5,000 documents from the tenth century and over 10,000 from the eleventh in Catalan collections.[5] They allow us to trace the development of prices and inheritances, the growth in trade and the diffusion of gold coinage; we can also discern different cultural spheres, gauge how long a formulary remained in use, note the appearance of a vernacular expression.

The other areas are less well favoured. Documentation concerning the Bas Languedoc consists mainly of cartularies and is solely ecclesiastical; it provides incidental information about lay society, but it takes no account of relationships among members of that society. The absence of 'public' documents conceals the mechanisms of government, and the relationship between the church and the nobility. The disappearance of originals is a serious handicap: the cartularies contain only a small selection of older documents, depending mainly on earlier copies full of misreadings.

Documents relating to the Toulouse region are even scantier. No original survives; for the most part we have selected copies in monastic cartularies, and even these documents are few. Around the turn of the millennium the documents become more numerous, but the absence, or at least imprecision, of dates (after 980, over half omit to mention even the name of the reigning sovereign) means that they must be used with caution. Here again, we can only deplore the absence of any 'public' documents concerning the comital house of Toulouse; we know nothing about the relationship between the count and the viscounts who governed the various counties.

The Auvergne is slightly better supplied, but the documents are spread very unevenly, with some peripheral regions entirely unilluminated. The cartularies are all monastic; they are complemented by some fragmentary collections of charters and some administrative documents, catalogues and inventories. As for Aquitaine itself, the cartularies of Poitou (Saint-Hilaire and Saint-Cyprien), and also those of Brioude and Cluny, supply valuable information on the

[5] Bonnassie (1975), pp. 22ff.

'institutions' of the duchy and the use of titles, but several of these documents are of uncertain date and doubtful authenticity.

No original documents for our period survive from Gascony. Some items were transcribed from the end of the eleventh century in cartularies, but these themselves have rarely survived in their original form. Evidently there is a problem with the transmission of texts: scribes often simplified or omitted the formal protocols; they committed many errors, which sometimes make the text incomprehensible; above all, they introduced alterations and interpolations intended to strengthen the rights and claims of their abbeys. Usually, the content of charters is inserted into historical narratives – notices or *historiae* – and has presumably been edited in the process, while many have no dating system. It is easy to see why historians of Gascony disagree about the reliability of the available documentation and tend to be either hypercritical or undercritical.

The importance of diplomatic sources, and also the occasional abuse of them, can be explained by the state of contemporary society. This is a region of written law, with a positive cult of the written word. 'It is stipulated in the law that writing should be used in all cases' ('Decretum est in lege ut in omnibus causis scripturae intercurrant'), as the preambles of Catalan charters constantly repeat. This respect for formalism, the scrupulous pursuit of *reparatio scripturae*, the familiarity with wills and written oaths, and the attention given to reconstituting lost titles to property, all bear witness to the importance of the written word in southern French societies.

The documentary abundance allows us to trace the spread of vocabulary and the special forms taken by the development of feudalism in the southern regions. It does not contribute much to our knowledge of political history. Nonetheless, the documents can be read indirectly, with more attention to form than to content: methods of dating, forms of address, geographical and political vocabulary, the spread of technological terms and the appearance of vernacular terms are all indicators which take us beyond domestic history. The continuity of political development is not always perceptible, and some 'reigns' are poorly represented, but stages and interruptions of development can be grasped inductively – though excessive systematisation in reconstituting developments may lead to disputes and contradictions.

BENCHMARKS: THE SOUTH OF THE KINGDOM *C.* 900

The heading chosen raises immediate questions. What was the 'south' of *Francia occidentalis*? Why 900? What was the origin of these unexpected principalities?

Identifying the south

The 'south' is primarily a geographical fact: the part of the kingdom south of the Loire and west of the Rhône extending across the Pyrenees to the bounds of Frankish domination: in early medieval terms Aquitaine with a fringe in Hispania. It had remained distinct from the Frankish lands; in the tenth century a traveller still did not enter *Francia* until he had crossed the Loire. Seen from the Frankish palace, Aquitaine was a peripheral region with an undeniable cultural individuality. But during the Carolingian era the region changed greatly: Aquitaine shrank and the Midi grew, so that the two were no longer coterminous.

Charles Martel and Pippin III brutally 'liberated' Septimania in the mid-eighth century. It was integrated into the kingdom of Aquitaine, but for local scribes and the notaries of the Frankish chancery it remained *Gothia*. Further Frankish expansion, cautious after the disaster at Roncevaux, went no further than Barcelona. South of the Pyrenees, 'liberation' also met resistance from locals proud of their Hispanic inheritance and 'more favourable to the Moors than to the Franks'.[6] The future Catalans, wrested from *Hispania*, loudly proclaimed their Gothicness. The Carolingian monarchs took account of this, calling themselves *rex Gothorum* in several diplomata sent south of the Pyrenees. The future Catalonia was still threatened by renewed Islamic aggression; it was organised for defence, and determined to enlarge itself at infidel expense, hence its boundaries extended into a no-man's land peopled with adventurers and other *mali homines*. Henceforth separate from Spain, it delineated a shifting *marca Hispanica*, a term wrongly understood by modern historians as meaning all the counties south of the Pyrenees.

The fourth southern unit was Gascony, between the Garonne and the Pyrenees. It soon separated from Carolingian Aquitaine, and even became a threat to it. Its history remains obscure; its ethnic composition is itself enigmatic. A massive Gascon immigration was imposed on a Celtic population, but the sources do not distinguish these intolerably insubordinate *Vascones* from the Basque hillmen who inhabited most of the Pyrenean chain, and some modern historians have also favoured the identification. Frankish power was felt late here, and the region escaped the Merovingian divisions. After 840, Frankish power ended at Bordeaux: the Gascons under 'national'

[6] Urbs erat interea Francorum inhospita turmis,
   Maurorum votis adsociata magis,.
   Quam Barcinonam prisci dixere Latini,.
   Romanoque fuit more polita nimis
                 Ermoldus Nigellus, *Carmen in
                 honorem Hludowici Pii*, lines 102–5.

dukes evaded control, and the kings of Aquitaine could only turn Bordeaux into a bridgehead. The history of Gascony begins with the government of Sancho Mitarra around 850; he organised the defence against Vikings and Muslims, and behaved like an uncrowned king. His nephew Arnold was ejected from Bordeaux before 887 by García Sánchez (almost certainly a grandson of Sancho Mitarra), who assumed the title 'duke of the Gascons'. Gascony soon became a 'national' principality, in which a culturally and linguistically homogeneous population was subject only to the authority of native chieftains. It was an anomaly in the constellation of southern territorial units. Viking invasions created a permanent insecurity, accelerating the loss of royal influence.

Cultures of the south

The Frankish presence in the south was based on conquest. The south remained peripheral to the Frankish state, with distinct traditions. Frankish presence was limited, strengthening a separatism quick to emerge at the first signs of a weakened central authority. Aquitanians and Gascons had lived under their own sovereigns before the Carolingians, and the collapse of Carolingian power restored their own history to these regions.

The south was culturally heterogenous, but awareness of its Roman past gave it cohesion. The principle of personality of law perpetuated ancient ethnic and legal distinctions. Documents attest the knowledge and practice of Roman law as late as 1000. Several libraries had a copy of the *Breviarium*, or even of the *Code* of Theodosius, and charter-protocols appealed to the authority of *lex Romana*. Some 20–30% of Aquitanian nobles still bore Roman names in the tenth century. Names emphasised ethnic contrasts, though they also followed fashion: Count Raymond of Toulouse adopted Pons as a second name, initiating the common practice of double names. Early genealogies all attempted to establish a link with the era of the senators, saints and martyrs. Southerners lived in a landscape stamped with the memory of Rome. Ancient cities were still inhabited, surviving monuments a reminder of past splendour; enthusiasm for antiquity explains the reuse of materials and models. Many rural settlements were the successors of ancient *villae*. In the middle of a Catalan *villa*, still with its mosaic pavement, a tower and a place of worship might appear; the mosaic of a Gascon *villa* may show the post-holes of a more recent dwelling. There is no doubt that slavery persisted, and the retention of the old public titles made it possible to locate individuals clearly within the social hierarchy.

The south also bore the mark of later upheavals. Septimania and Catalonia were Gothic; in Catalonia, pride in Gothicness was coupled with a nostalgia for the lost *Hispania*. Its inhabitants called themselves *Gothi*; males bore names constructed on the root *Gothus* or recalling early sovereigns of Toledo. The locals always appealed to Gothic law (*lex Gothorum*), a national heritage (*lex patrum*) and a territorial law (*noster lex*); abbey libraries and even those of rural parishes kept copies of the *Forum Iudicum*. Public institutions themselves incorporated Gothic survivals, and the first monasteries restored after the expulsion of the Saracens were governed by the old system of the 'pact' derived from the rule of St Fructuosus.

Gascony seems largely to have escaped the Roman inheritance, or at least this was heavily overlaid by the sixth-century migrations. There was a strong feeling of national identity which nourished aggressiveness towards both Franks and Aquitanians. Gascony apart, the southern regions felt more solidarity with one another than with the north of the kingdom; the king took note of this by addressing diplomata to all Catalan and Septimanian counts. They shared a rich cultural tradition which embraced a large part of the lay population; the cult of writing, the survival of notaries, the large number of autograph signatures, the elaborate preambles and the renewal of Latin writing conferred a real supremacy upon the south.

THE RISE OF THE PRINCIPALITIES (900–80)

The title of 'duke' implied not so much an office within a hierarchy as leadership of a people. But the claims remained intermittent and competing; the kings sometimes granted the title themselves. *Dux* was less a title than a form of address: dignitaries could be 'designated' dukes. The tenth century saw a stabilisation. The *ducatus* became a territorial reality with autonomous existence, and the title of duke became hereditary. The underlying structure of the Frankish kingdom was exposed: a collection of *regna*, gatherings of peoples under a 'national' leader, a prince, hence the name 'principalities' given to these new subdivisions. French historians stress the geographical and institutional aspects, and speak of 'territorial principalities', whereas their German colleagues see them as '"tribal" duchies'.

The tenth century was the age of the principalities: still in formation in 900, they were in decline before 1000. This development affected the whole kingdom but royal influence made a difference. North of the Loire, the king remained a partner: the princes decided the fate of the monarchy. In the south, the principalities formed without reference to the king, occasionally in opposition to him. Kings strove to keep links with the southern princes, but these were broken every time the throne was seized by a non-Carolingian 'usurper'. For several centuries 'royal absence' was the backdrop to southern French history. The area combined a deep attachment to Carolingian legitimacy with a precocious institutional development towards control by dynastic, territorial comital powers: both favoured the formation of principalities.

The stages of royal withdrawal

In the course of the tenth century the southern half of the kingdom slowly drifted away. There was no sudden break: the southern princes upheld Carolingian legitimacy, while the rulers missed no opportunity to assert their authority. But increasingly they lacked the means to exercise it *within* the principalities; the quasi-royal status they had conceded the princes shut them off from the counties, churches and revenues of the new *regnum*. Non-Carolingian kings faced particular problems, and in effect had to attempt a 'reconquest' of the southern principalities.

The reign of Odo (888–98) began the dissociation between a royal office denied by nobody and the king's ability to exercise it. The beginning of the tenth century saw the end of the Carolingian order south of the Loire; the king was no longer able to grant comital honours, which had become hereditary; the first usurpations of regalian rights occurred; abbeys, later bishoprics, came under aristocratic control, with the king now confined to confirming nominations, only occasionally imposing his own candidate (as at Saint-Hilaire, Poitiers and Saint-Julien, Brioude). To gain the nobles' grudging allegiance, Odo abandoned the last remnants of the royal revenues. The royal vassals themselves transferred their allegiance *en masse* to the 'duke of the Aquitanians'; only Gerald of Aurillac remained faithful to his king, and Odo of Cluny duly records this as evidence of his sanctity.[7] Royal diplomata for recipients south of the Loire continued, but only as confirmations of privileges or grants of immunity.

Odo tried to compensate for his growing weakness by interventionism. As guest and overlord of William the Pious, he appeared in Brioude, Périgueux, Limoges and Poitiers; he presided over assemblies attended by Catalan prelates and counts, often on the Loire. They continued to attend the court; they renewed their homage and accompanied their sovereign hunting, as Bishop Gilbert and Count Raymond of Nîmes did in 889. This contrast between an enfeebled royal authority and frantic efforts to exercise it persisted throughout the tenth century: kingship in the absence of a kingdom.

The nobles of Aquitaine were by no means anxious to see the Robertine dynasty firmly established, and supported Charles the Simple as Odo's successor. Charles immediately tried to restore royal authority in Aquitaine. He confirmed possessions and rights abandoned by Odo, and granted new ones (such

---

[7] Odo of Cluny, *Vita Sancti Geraldi Aurilacensis comitis libri quatuor*, I, 32, col 658.

as the mint at Vic granted to Wifred Borrell); generally recognised, he resumed interventions in episcopal elections. In exchange for renewed fidelity the king granted the princes unlimited autonomy. He acted only at their request, confirmed rather than determined, and never ventured across the Loire. The southerners refused to accept his elimination in 923: they ignored or rejected Radulf, 'traitor to the Franks', 'elected to the kingship after the faithless Franks had deprived King Charles of his honour', and they continued to date documents by the years of the Carolingian Charles' reign.[8]

The Catalans never acknowledged the usurper; in Aquitaine, Radulf was acknowledged only tardily and incompletely. To gain the homage of William the Younger he surrendered Berry in 924; but from 926 William protested against Charles' imprisonment and Radulf's usurpation. William died a rebel, and his successor Acfred governed his duchy independently. Ebles of Poitou, by contrast, who had dated documents by Charles' reign *in custodia*, dropped his opposition in 928 so as to secure Acfred's inheritance. Radulf subsequently visited Aquitaine twice: in 932 he received the homage of Raymond III Pons of Toulouse and Gothia and of the Gascon Lupus Aznar. He regained a foothold south of the Loire; but his reign marked a further stage towards princely autonomy, and for the first time princes struck coins in their own names (William the Younger at Brioude, for example).

The Carolingian restoration of 936 was the decision of Hugh the Great, 'in all our kingdoms the second after us' as Louis IV declared.[9] The southern princes took no part in it, but in the struggle between Louis IV and his burdensome protector, Louis sought the support of all still faithful to the dynasty. William Towhead, count of Poitou and Auvergne, directly threatened by Robertine expansion, did homage in 942; in the following years, the king made several appearances in Aquitaine. In 944, it was the turn of Raymond Pons to come to Nevers and declare his fidelity; the king thanked him by granting him the title 'prince of the Aquitanians'.[10] Realising that the south was a focus of resistance to him, Hugh the Great claimed lordship over Aquitaine immediately after Lothar's accession. In the spring of 955 he took the young king on a tour of Poitou. It was wasted effort: William Towhead avoided him and himself assumed the title of duke of the Aquitanians. The south resisted Robertine hegemony.

It was probably this which impelled Lothar to revive the kingdom of Aquitaine. Having made his son Louis joint king in 979, he married him to Adelaide, widow of the count Stephen of Gévaudun. Immediately after the ceremony Louis was crowned king of Aquitaine; but the marriage proved a

---

[8] The formulae are found in the genealogies or catalogues of the Frankish kings; cf. Zimmermann (1981) for details.   [9] D L IV 4.

[10] Richer, *Historiae* II, 39–40; for the formula 'princeps Aquitanorum' cf. D L IV 17.

failure, and in 984, Lothar recalled his son. After this Frankish rulers ignored the south, while the southern princes no longer took part in a kingdom whose centre of gravity had shifted towards Lotharingia. Hugh Capet's election merely revealed changes which had already come about. Richer claims that Hugh was elected unanimously by the assembled peoples of the *regnum*,[11] but the south saw it as an exterior event: a northern prince had usurped the legitimate dynasty's rights to exercise an ephemeral power. The count of Barcelona – perhaps after repeating his appeal for help against the Muslims – rejected the new power, declaring the kingship vacant and referring ironically to a king who was no more than an ex-duke; some Catalan documents are even dated by the reign of the king of Navarre, or of Charles of Lorraine *qui est in vinculis*. The same thing happened in Gascony, only more often. However, Jean Dufour has shown that apart for some abbeys which remained obstinately legitimist throughout the tenth century, the southern princes soon recognised Hugh Capet.[12] As far as they were concerned, the accession merely confirmed a royal insufficiency they had long lamented. There could be no better evidence of Capetian weakness in the south than the insolent reply given by the count of Périgord to Hugh's imprudent question, 'Who made you count?': 'Who made *you* king?'[13] He did not here so much reject the ruler as complain about a political deal from which southern princes had been excluded.

Whether it provoked indifference or resistance, the advent of the first Capetian made royal absence complete: the king was generally acknowledged, but he sank below the political horizon. Abbo of Fleury, venturing into the duchy of Gascony in 1000 to visit the priory of La Reole, remarked bitterly, 'I am more important in these parts than the king of France, for here nobody fears his domination.'[14] The king existed, maybe even reigned, but he no longer ruled.

The principality: a new way of organising the kingdom

The principality has been defined as 'a territory in which the king no longer intervened except through the prince',[15] an area closed to royal activity, though the prince's sovereignty was a question never posed. It did not fit traditional categories, being a sovereignty within the Frankish kingdom, a *regnum* within the *regnum*. Catalonia drifted into independence rather than seeking it. The phenomenon was undeniably earlier in the south. The emergence of the southern

---

[11] Richer, *Historiae* IV, 12.   [12] Dufour (1991).

[13] Adhémar of Chabannes, *Chronicon*, appendix, p. 205.

[14] 'Potentior, inquiens, nunc sum domino nostro rege Francorum intra hos fines, ubi nullus ejus veretur dominium, talem possidens domum': Aimo of Fleury, *Vita S Abbonis abbatis Floriacensis*, c. 20, col. 410A.   [15] Dhondt (1948a), p. 19.

principalities raises three questions. Who were the princes, and what territories did they control? Was this redistribution of authority produced by emancipation, delegation or a consensus on how to adapt to circumstances? What was the exact nature and extent of the princes' power?

Historians have long viewed the principalities as the products of essentially ethnic regional identities. Carolingian weakness allowed peoples never completely subdued or assimilated to claim freedom under a 'national' leader. The concept of a 'tribal' duchy would on this view be just as legitimate for Gaul as it is for Germany. The form of the princely title – *dux* followed by the name of some ethnic group – seems to fit this view, and Dhondt has offered a skilful defence of the argument.[16] The principalities arose during Odo's reign: imitating the Franks who had chosen a king 'from their own entrails', the other peoples of the kingdom claimed their freedom. A principality was not a mere collection of counties: it reflected a striving for internal cohesion. When, as in Aquitaine, the land was divided among several princes, their rivalry for the title of *dux Aquitanorum* reveals the same desire for unity.

But only Gascony fits this purely ethnic definition fully. It never had a comital structure, and all attempts to put it under an assimilated or 'Frankicised' Gascon ended with the restoration of some descendant of the Lupus who submitted to Charlemagne in 769. The other principalities had no such 'national' coherence. Under William the Pious, Aquitaine included the county of Mâcon. The duchy may have reflected some early tradition, but it was territorially unstable, for the title of duke was borne successively by the counts of Clermont, Toulouse and Poitiers. As for Catalonia, throughout the tenth century its Gothic inheritance could not sustain leadership over the entire principality. Gascony apart, the southern principalities were new phenomena, empirical and fragile, born of division as much as reassembly. Even where the families were of local origin, as were the counts of Barcelona, the princes were still descendants of Carolingian officials drawn from the high aristocracy, though from political expediency they might encourage the local particularism in which their power was rooted.

The principalities of the first half of the tenth century were royal creations, not the products of princely ambition; their rulers were marcher lords before they were princes. The awful damage inflicted on Aquitaine by Hungarian invasions in the early tenth century could only reinforce its cohesion and show the 'need' for it. The princes did not usurp a power granted by the king: they merely exercised it autonomously. Kings would later officially recognise an authority no longer exercised according to their ideas, one which inaugurated a new order more appropriate to reality. By accepting the legal transfer of some royal

[16] *Ibid.*

prerogatives to princes in a part of the kingdom, they effectively reorganised it. The movement began in the southern marches, whose separate identity had long been acknowledged by the term *regnum*. The title conferred on the first princes was thus that of marquess. The first to receive it was Bernard Plantevelue. In a diploma from Charles the Simple, William the Pious and his son, William II, were given the title of 'great marquess'.[17] The same sovereign entrusted to Bernard Pons, count of Toulouse and marquess of *Gothia*, the care of 'our realm of Septimania'.[18] Both in the minds of contemporaries and in the language of the chancery, the marquesses were indeed entrusted with a *regnum*, a halfway stage between the counties and the *regnum Francorum*. The acknowledged lords of *regna*, endowed with sovereign powers, were naturally called *principes* by their followers; they themselves gradually assumed the title of *dux*. This redistribution of powers meant a weakening of royal authority, but it ensured the survival of royal office, and the last Carolingians successfully traded on this in their dealings with the dukes. For instance, Richer tells us how Louis IV met Raymond Pons and the nobles of Aquitaine at Nevers in 942: 'The king discussed with them the government of their State, and as he wished all their possessions to be subject to him, he demanded homage from them for their province, but readily granted them the administration of it; he delegated it to them and commanded them to govern it in his name.'[19]

The princes were thus the acknowledged masters of their provinces, though subjects and 'delegates' of the king. But what powers did they really have? How did they deploy them, and express them in their titles? Though the princes governed *regna*, they never thought of calling themselves kings: that title was reserved for the *rex Francorum*, and everyone remembered that Bernard of Gothia had fallen in 877 because he had 'truly behaved like a king'.[20] However, like their German counterparts, they did not hesitate to take the title 'duke'. The southern princes were ahead in this: Richard of Burgundy did not become a duke until 918/20; Hugh the Great did not bear the title *dux Francorum* until 936. The prince (or duke) ruled over a people rather than a territory: while *princeps* was used alone, *dux* always had a complement, normally the name of a people (*Aquitani*, *Vascones*). It should be noted, however, that while the expression *dux Aquitaniae* is rare, *dux Vasconiae* and *dux Gothiae* occur, as if both notions had a clear geographical referent, unlike the uncertain and disputed area of Aquitaine.

Historians attribute the creation of the principalities to dukes of strong

---

[17] Dhondt (1948b); Kienast (1968), p 167; D Ch S 102.

[18] Devic and Vaissette (eds.), *Histoire générale de Languedoc* V, preuves no. 36.

[19] 'Apud quos de provinciarum cura pertractans, ut illorum omnia sui juris viderentur, ab eis provincias recepit; nec distulit earum administrationem eis credere. Commisit itaque ac suo dono illos principari constituit...': Richer, *Historiae* II, 39.   [20] *Annales Bertiniani, s.a.* 877.

character whose nicknames are a memorial to their glory and whose exploits fill contemporary chronicles, but the extent and cohesion of the principalities varied with political circumstances: William the Pious' Aquitaine, for example, did not survive its ruler. The southern principalities had no legally recognised existence or institutional continuity. If some, like Aquitaine, fed on lasting images, others, like Catalonia, remained implicit, and one might conclude that principalities had no existence beyond that of their prince. His principality was a collection of counties, and his power derived from his office as count. The extent of his power thus depended on the number of counties he held directly and could appoint viscounts to administer, and on the control he exercised over other counts.

The princes' attitude to the king varied from formal acknowledgement (before 923, the southern princes regularly went to court to do homage) to indifference. But they all 'acknowledged' the ruler, who remained the keystone of Christian society, provided that he did not interfere in the principality unless asked to do so. Even to confirm an immunity or grant some fiscal advantage, the king needed the prince's permission. In 890 Odo granted the town of Manresa 'all royal powers concerning the city of Manresa, so far as the count himself agrees'.[21] Royal authority was mediatised; if princes dated their documents by the years of the *rex Francorum*, they immediately referred to their own reign. Only the Robertine 'usurpers' attempted to cross the Loire, seeking a recognition never accorded except for a price. Whether or not they paid allegiance to the sovereign, the princes exercised all the royal prerogatives within their own duchies; the idea of a transfer of power was clearly formulated in 1019 by the count of Empuries, who declared that he had within his own county the *potestas* formerly held by the king.[22]

The traditional organisation of public authority now worked to the exclusive benefit of the princes. They inhabited royal palaces, usually in towns; they held courts and established administrations, some more substantial than others (viscounts, advocacies); they incorporated fiscal lands into their own territory (after Odo's reign no royal demesne remained in Aquitaine); and the *vassi dominici* transferred their fidelity and homage to them. They dispensed justice according to custom, presided over judicial assemblies amongst *boni homines*, enforced judgements and received the fines which formerly went to the royal treasury. Gradually they monopolised the coinage, either by controlling a prelate with a royal grant of mint (such as Adalhard of Le Puy in 924), or by striking their own coins. William the Younger first presumed to put his name in place of the king's, around 920; he had few imitators before 950. In spite of royal resistance the princes finally got hold of the churches: first of the abbeys,

---

[21] 'omnes regias dignitates de Manresa civitate, quantum ipse comes consentivit': *Catalunya carolingia* 2, 1 B, p. 298.   [22] Pierre de Marca, *Marca Hispanica sive limes Hispanica* ed. E. Baluze, appendix 181.

where they made themselves lay abbots or established burial-places (William the Pious at Saint-Julien de Brioude, the counts of Poitiers at Saint-Hilaire, the counts of Toulouse at Saint-Gilles), and which they later distributed amongst relatives and friends; then of the bishoprics, where they controlled elections. From the first half of the tenth century onwards, all the southern bishoprics except Le Puy fell into princely hands. Ecclesiastical possessions became an essential part of their wealth, which put the church in danger if their authority weakened: when Duke Acfred died in 927, the viscount Dalmas seized the abbacy of Saint-Julien de Brioude and made inroads into its possessions; Saint-Chaffre and Sauxillanges met the same fate. Quarrels among great families destroyed monasteries, and left some bishoprics temporarily without an incumbent.

By appropriating regalian powers, the princes replaced the king in the working of Carolingian 'public' institutions. They held on to their role as arbitrators: until 980 in both Aquitaine and Catalonia the prince ensured that judicial assemblies were held regularly and that sentences were carried out, even those unfavourable to themselves. The same concern for public order appears in the Peace of God movement, which began in Aquitaine at the end of the tenth century. By associating himself with the church's attempts to curb the nobility and re-establish *justitia* and peace, the prince showed himself the successor of ninth-century kings.

The Frankish kings, having retreated north of the Loire, saw the principalities as preserving the kingdom and their own authority; having recognised the emergent principalities, they claimed the right to confer the title of duke and create further 'royal' duchies. By granting the duchy of Aquitaine to Hugh the Great when the Poitevin dynasty was just beginning its rise to prominence, Louis IV showed his gratitude to the man to whom he owed his crown, but he also intended to exclude him from the recently opened competition for that crown.

Coexistence and competition among the princes

As the tenth century progressed, four princely groupings emerged. Their creation was neither simultaneous nor similar. Gascony existed by the end of the ninth century, but no durable centralised authority had been established, and the outermost counties enjoyed a growing autonomy which suggests a condominium. Aquitaine took final shape towards 930 with the advent of the Poitevin dynasty, but competition from the Toulousain dynasty continued until this withdrew to its own principality, itself very heterogenous. As for Catalonia, even in the late tenth century it was still no more than a collection of counties linked by the need to defend the borders and by the common origin of the ruling families. The history of these principalities is hard to write; it amounts to discontinuous sequences of events corresponding to variations in princely power.

Aquitaine was the least cohesive of the principalities. After Bernard Plantevelue's death in 886, his son William the Pious remained master of central and eastern Aquitaine, to which he added the regions of Lyons and Mâcon. In the west the leading character was Ramnulf II until his death in 890. Ramnulf's heir was his young bastard son Ebles Manzer, but in 891 Odo ceded the county of Poitiers to Adhémar, count of Perigueux, the son of a former Poitevin count. This caused a revolt by the Aquitanian nobility, instigated by William the Pious. Odo had to intervene to install Adhémar, and in 893 he made an agreement with William, restoring his honours and acknowledging his hegemony over Aquitaine, a hegemony William continued to consolidate until his death in 918. From 898 he called himself *comes, marchio et dux*; in 909 he assumed the title *dux Aquitanorum*. Charles the Simple, to whom he did homage as *rex Franciae et Aquitaniae*, recognised his title of *marchio* and even, in 914, *marchio maximus*.[23] His prestige further increased by his marriage with Engilberga, sister of Louis of Provence, he intervened in western Aquitaine: in 902 he expelled Adhémar from the county of Poitiers, which was immediately reoccupied by Ebles Manzer.

William died leaving only two nephews. The elder, William the Younger, inherited the title of duke and all William's honours except Berry, which passed to the Robertines. His brother Acfred succeeded him in 926 and declared himself independent of Radulf. He died without issue on 11 October 927, and with him the Auvergne dynasty of Aquitanian dukes ended. His nearest relative was Ebles Manzer, who claimed William's inheritance and assumed the title of duke, while remaining faithful to Charles *qui est in custodia*: thus it was not until 928 that he was reconciled with Radulf and took possession of Aquitaine.

On his death in 934 his son William Towhead inherited his titles and honours without dispute, but he soon had to face up to Neustrian expansion. After seizing Burgundy, Hugh the Great turned to Aquitaine in 936, and, probably with Louis IV's connivance, seized the county of Poitiers, retaining it for two years. At the same time, Raymond III Pons, count of Toulouse since 924, assumed the title *dux Aquitanorum* in a charter of 28 August 936 and continued to bear it until 941; in 940 he even used the expression *primarchio et dux Aquitanorum*.[24] Hugh the Great may have encouraged this claim; Louis IV supported it as long as he remained in alliance with Hugh, but in 939 he was reconciled with the Aquitanians against the coalition of northern princes, and in 941 the Auvergnac nobles renewed their allegiance. In 942 Louis was in Poitiers,

[23] Dhondt (1948b); D Ch S 102.   [24] Kienast (1968), pp 185–6.

where he granted William the abbey of Saint-Hilaire. In the course of this reversal of alliances he probably put an end to Toulousain ambitions; henceforth, only William bore the title of duke, while Raymond Pons had to content himself with *comes Tolosanus, princeps Gothorum, dux Gothiae* until his death in 951.[25] Hugh did not renounce his ambitions in Aquitaine. In 954, he induced Lothar to grant him the *ducatus Aquitaniae* and went off to conquer it. Meeting resistance from William, the invaders were forced to raise the siege of Poitiers; Hugh died shortly afterwards. Hugh Capet inherited his father's claims, but could not put them into practice without the king's consent. In 960, Lothar restored to him his father's duchy, and added Poitou to it, but in 962 he returned it to William.

William Towhead's reign was a turning point in the formation of the principality. Drawing strength from his own county of Poitou and from Aquitanian separatism, he behaved like a king. His marriage with Adela, sister of William Longsword, gave him the entrée into the circle of princes who decided the kingdom's fate when the king died. On his death in 963 his son William Fierabras took over his titles and inheritance. A double marriage sealed the reconciliation with Hugh Capet: in about 968 William married Emma, daughter of Theobald count of Chartres; in 970, Hugh married Adelaide, sister of the duke of Aquitaine. After the failed attempt to revive a Carolingian subkingdom of Aquitaine in the early 980s, nothing prevented William from claiming a fully sovereign authority: the title *dux totius monarchiae Aquitanorum* which he took in 984 pre-emptively rejected any attempt at external interference in his duchy. When he died in 993, the Poitevin dynasty could safely expect to control the destiny of an independent Aquitaine for many years to come.

However, at this date being a duke did not automatically mean exercising real power or institutional authority: the title was used only internally, and never in isolation before the twelfth century. Its recognition by the royal chancery in 989, and the papal in 1033, celebrated its holder's greatness without confirming it legally. It was as count of Poitiers, Limoges or Auvergne that dukes summoned judicial assemblies, appointed viscounts and exercised regalian rights. William Towhead called himself *comes* on *denarii* struck in his name after 950 at Brioude and Clermont. No doubt he tried to get the counts and viscounts in the principality to acknowledge his lordship, but it remained purely theoretical outside Poitou. Some of the remoter counties led a largely independent existence, most strikingly the episcopal lordship of Clermont.

The principality or *regnum* of Toulouse was an assemblage of fourteen counties stretching from Quercy to the Rhône valley. The counties belonging to the house of Toulouse (Toulouse itself, Albi, Cahors, Rodez) must be distin-

---

[25] *Ibid.*

guished from those belonging to the marquisate of Gothia, the former Septimania (Uzès, Nîmes, Lodève, Substantion, Béziers, Narbonne, Conflent and Roussillon); the two counties of Carcassonne and Razès formed a 'hinge' held by their own dynasty. The principality's origins go back to the death of Bernard Plantevelue in 886. Odo, brother of Bernard of Toulouse, who had died in 872, received the Toulousain, the Rouergue and Gothia. The county of Toulouse and Gothia thereafter went together, and the latter was again called a march or marquisate.

Odo died in 919, leaving two sons. Raymond II succeeded him as count of Toulouse; Ermengaud, the younger, received the Rouergue; they administered Gothia jointly. In 924, Raymond III Pons succeeded his father. Jointly with his uncle Ermengaud, he was called *princeps Gothiae*, and his reign (924–50) marks the real beginning of the southern principality. On his uncle's death in 937, he took the title *marchio Gothiae* and ruled alone over all the lands of Languedoc, as well as briefly claiming hegemony over the whole of Aquitaine (see above). After 950, the counts of Toulouse dropped all contact with Aquitaine and the rest of the kingdom; they confined their activities to Languedoc, and made much of a Gothicness which enhanced the links with neighbouring Catalonia: initially these were familial, then religious, until they acquired a distinctly political dimension in the mid-eleventh century.

For a century the history of the principalities of Toulouse, Rouergue and Gothia remains confused. The almost complete absence of documents makes it hard to examine how territories alternated between the two branches of the Raymondine dynasty, and the comital succession is itself very problematical. Elsewhere, the fog is still thicker. In the Albigeois, the Pons traditionally held to have been count of Albi (985–1000) seems never to have existed, since the only document said to be from him is a forgery. A Count Raymond appears at Cahors between 972 and 983. Was he count of Toulouse? Or of Rouergue? Or was he count only of that particular *pagus*? Only in the Rouergue does the institution of count seem to have had some stability: the counts, a cadet branch of the house of Toulouse, succeeded one another from father to son from 919 onwards.

In Gothia the Toulouse and Rouergue branches ruled alternately, though some counties, like Carcassonne and Nîmes, continued under a co-suzerainty. Septimania led its own private and institutionally precarious existence: a 'province without counts'.[26] In the tenth century the viscounts usurped regalian rights and exercised the count's delegated authority for their own profit. The office became hereditary in Nîmes and Narbonne at the beginning of the century, and soon elsewhere: viscounts steadily supplanted counts. While the

---

[26] Magnou-Nortier (1974), p. 232.

viscounts of Narbonne shared the lordship of the town with the archbishops, the Trencavels gathered into their own hands the viscounties of Nîmes, Béziers, Agde and Albi. In this dismembered principality, the power of the distant count of Toulouse was perceived rather as was the king's power elsewhere in the south, which is perhaps why the principality of Toulouse, the most artificial and heterogeneous of them all, was also the one in which the least attention was paid to the Frankish king, even in the dating of documents. Only the county of Carcassonne-Razès retained real coherence. The rise of the viscounts, who gained control over episcopal elections from 980 onwards (the bishops of Nîmes, Agde, Béziers, Carcassonne and even Narbonne were often the sons of viscounts), prevented the rise of real ecclesiastical lordships, despite the wealth and power of the churches. In about 990 William Taillefer's marriage to Emma of Provence added Tarascon and the lands of Argence to the Raymondine possessions. We cannot really speak of a principality of Toulouse, however: it was more a conglomeration of counties controlled by two branches of the same family, rather like the situation in Catalonia.

Gascony had genuine territorial and political cohesion, being ruled from 836 to 1063 by the same family which had seized it amidst the Viking invasions. Furthermore, the Gascons had a real national consciousness and were seen from the outside as a separate ethnic unit. However, at the end of the ninth century the principality seemed to be disintegrating. It was shorn of the county of Bordeaux, which was repeatedly attacked by the Vikings. Bigorre, under its own dynasty, controlled the roads into Spain. With the disappearance of the metropolitan see of Bazas, the ecclesiastical framework collapsed. The demands of defence against Saracens and Vikings isolated the region.

García Sánchez (886–920) gathered up most of the counties between the Garonne and Navarre and added Agen as his wife's dowry, after which he called himself *marchio* or *marchio in limitibus Oceani* (904).[27] He reorganised the church, ruined by the invasions, on the basis of the abbeys. Around 900 he founded Saint-Pierre de Condom, to which he granted more than twenty parishes; and he took up residence nearby. By marrying his three daughters to the counts of Bordeaux, Toulouse and Aragon, he opened up his principality and strengthened his links with Navarre. He divided his counties among his three sons, leaving Greater Gascony to the eldest, Sancho Garcés, while the younger sons received the minor counties of Fezensac and Astarac. All three brothers bore the title of count, but Sancho Garcés kept that of count of Gascony; he was the only one to be called *marchio et princeps*, and his two brothers acknowledged his *dominatio*. This confraternity did not outlive the brothers, and the three Gascon counties pursued an autonomous existence. Sancho García

---

[27] Mussot-Goulard (1982).

bequeathed Greater Gascony undivided to his three sons, but only the eldest, Sancho Sánchez, inherited the title of count. Fezensac, which contained the new metropolis of Auch, was an enclave and hampered by the fact; the count of Astarac, by marrying his daughter to the lord of Aure, secured access to the Pyrenean passes.

Sancho Sánchez died in 960, leaving Greater Gascony to his brother William Sánchez (960–99), who completed the pacification and reorganisation of the country. Married to the sister of the king of Navarre, he fought at his brother-in-law's side against al-Manṣūr. In 977, he succeeded his cousin William the Good as count of Bordeaux, whereupon he took the title *totius Gasconiae dux*. Having subdued the allodial lordships, he strengthened his control over the country by creating viscounties: first Lomagne; then, in about 991, Oloron, Dax and Bearn; and finally, in about 996, Marsan. He imposed his authority on the holders of minor counties, weakened by successive subdivisions, by the growing autonomy of the viscounties in Astarac and Bigorre, and by the zones of power emerging around the first castles.

The government of William Sánchez was the apogee of the Gascon principality: its prince exercised all regalian rights, struck coins in his own name, reorganised the church, built fortresses and *castella*; he called himself *dux* and spoke of his *regnum*; his contemporaries saw him as *dominus totius Vasconiae*.[28] Though he acknowledged that the duchy belonged to the *regnum Francorum* and recognised Hugh Capet in dating-clauses, he refused to pay any formal allegiance to the distant sovereign.

One of William's most important initiatives was to create a bishopric of the Gascons in 977 for his brother Gombaud, including the territories of the dioceses ruined by the Vikings. This allowed him to evade control by the archbishop of Auch; it involved a sharing of authority between the brothers, since in 978 Gombaud's title was that of *episcopus Vasconiae et totius regionis dux*, and he exercised comital powers in the Bazas, Agen and Lomagne areas. This bishopric survived until 1059 independently of the two metropolitans of Auch and Bordeaux. During this period monastic life flourished. The ruined bishoprics were replaced by monasteries at Aire and Lescar, and several new monasteries were also founded: La Réole in 977; Sorde and, most important, Saint-Sever, between 988 and 989. These abbeys, dedicated to local saints and not yet influenced by Cluny, contributed decisively to parochial organisation, and were also focuses of agricultural and urban development.

William Sánchez was succeeded by his two sons, Bernard William (999–1009) and Sancho William (1009–32). The tendency to fragmentation intensified: in 1028, Astarac was in turn divided into three counties (Astarac,

---

[28] See on this Mussot-Goulard (1982, 1991).

Aure and Pardiac). The dukes did their best to contain the southern viscounts, especially the Centulles of Bearn: confined at first to the environs of the ancient city of Beneharnum, they spread northwards, established a vicecomital residence at Morlaas, then absorbed the viscounty of Oloron. All the lords, however, acknowledged that they belonged to the duchy, and ducal authority was never clearer. Sancho William called himself *totius Gasconiae princeps*, spoke of his *regnum* or *monarchia*, and claimed an authority of divine origin (*gratia Dei dux*). A notice in the cartulary of Saint-Seurin mentions a rite of ducal investiture in use in about 1009.[29] Sancho William, who had spent part of his childhood at Pamplona, strengthened his links with Navarre and took part in its affairs alongside Sancho the Great, with whom he had regular meetings; the duchy looked more and more to Spain.

On the other hand, links with the Capetians were non-existent. Though some Gascon charters do mention the regnal year, others do not; no source refers to any relationship between Gascony and the king after 932. In 1010, it was as sovereign that Sancho William met Robert the Pious, Sancho of Navarre and William of Aquitaine at Saint-Jean d'Angély; he did not dream of doing homage to a king who was his equal and to whom he owed nothing.

THE GENESIS AND EMANCIPATION OF CATALONIA

In about 900 the future Catalonia was a loose assemblage of ten counties, successive fruits of Frankish 'liberation'. Some counties were recent formations, like Vic, restored in 885, while others, like Ripoll, were short-lived, and others came and went, like Berga and Conflent. By 897 the three central counties of Barcelona, Gerona and Vic constituted an undivided bloc belonging to the descendants of Wifred the Hairy. The western counties of Pallars and Ribagorza were a special case; Ribagorza became an independent political unit, in 957 acquiring a bishopric at Roda, which was steadily attracted into the ambit of Aragon. Under its own dynasty, but with no ecclesiastical organisation, Pallars became dependent on the county of Urgell, whose count governed what was now merely *terra Palliarensis*.

There was no institutional unity among the eastern counties. Historians long supposed, incorrectly, that the term *marca Hispanica* referred to a military territory composed of all the frontier counties under the authority of a single count of the marches. Recent research has shown that the expression means the same as *limes Hispanicus*: the frontier of the empire with Muslim *Hispania*, wherever that might be. The title 'marquess' was borne in competition by various frontier counts and even, in 917, by a viscount, Ermenard.

---

[29] Mussot-Goulard (1982, 1991) and Zimmermann (1992), pp. 260–2 and 295–300.

This was the only region in the kingdom on a frontier: Christians and Saracens were separated south of Barcelona by a wide no-man's-land around the ghost town of Tarragona. The Carolingians chose native counts (acknowledging Gothic separatism) alternately with Frankish counts drawn from their court officials. From 821 to 878 the two groups more or less changed places: after 820–5 the Gothic counts, who held the interior counties, showed an exemplary loyalty, whereas the Frankish counts several times fomented Aquitanian separatism. It was when the rebel Bernard of Gothia was stripped of his honours that the fortune of the house of Barcelona was established. In 878 Louis the Stammerer granted the counties of Barcelona and Gerona to Wifred, who was already count of Urgell and Cerdaña, and the county of Roussillon to his brother Miro. Almost all Old Catalonia thus fell to a single family, a local family which for at least two generations had supplied the Frankish kings with loyal administrators. Wifred and Miro, the last counts to be appointed by royal authority, inaugurated a dynasty which was to reign until 1410.

In the history of Catalan identity, the events of 878 have been passionately debated. It has been tempting to interpret the ninth century as a confrontation between the Gothic people and the Frankish state, an interpretation suggested by the *Gesta comitum Barcinonensium*, written between 1162 and 1174, which clearly associates the origins of the dynasty with the clash between two peoples.[30] But this 'nationalist' argument must be rejected, since it presupposes a Catalan nation struggling for liberty. Gothic separatism found expression *within* the *regnum*, and the formation of a Catalan principality can be explained only in terms of a weakened monarchy incapable of preventing comital honours from becoming heritable, and of a tendency to redistribute power by linking strategic necessity with ancient cultural community.

Wifred's government was preoccupied with practical considerations. He aimed to repopulate central Catalonia, and focused the spontaneous colonisation by founding abbeys (Ripoll, 880; Sant Joan, 885). In 885 he established the new county of Ausona and restored its bishopric, transferred to the town of Vic. His main aim was safeguarding his counties against the permanent threat of a Muslim counter-offensive: he died in battle in 897.

Between 897 and 987, the contours of the incipient 'principality' emerged. Catalonia's incompleteness has two main causes: the temporariness of the territorial groupings, and the absence of any title expressing an acquired supremacy. For strategic and emotional reasons the links with the Carolingian monarchy remained very strong. The Frankish sovereign might no longer intervene, but he still existed, and his documents maintained law and order.

---

[30] *Gesta comitum Barcinonensium*, pp. 3–4.

The break was to come from the sovereigns themselves, since the Capetians' accession forced the counts to assume a sovereignty they did not actually want.

Regroupings

Cerdaña absorbed Conflent, Berga and Ripoll in the tenth century; Besalú swallowed Vallespir. Zones of dominance emerged, with one noble ruling several counties which came apart or together according to the vagaries of succession: thus double counties came into being, such as Cerdaña-Besalú and Empuries-Roussillon.

From 897, the three counties of Barcelona, Gerona and Vic formed an indivisible bloc which the counts bequeathed to the eldest son and which exercised a real pull on the neighbouring counties. The county of Urgell joined this core by escheat; when Borrell died in 992 it broke away again, but the holders of the various counties – brothers, and later cousins – kept up a relationship which was closer than mere politeness. After 878 all the Catalan counties, with the exception of Pallars and Ribagorza, remained in the hands of the same family. Catalonia was ruled by a lineage rather than a prince; more than once the heirs preferred a joint exercise of the comital function to a division of the inheritance. Whereas north of the Pyrenees a pre-existing county aroused rival ambitions, the fraternal condominium in Catalonia denoted an area of power which had no existence apart from it. It was in this way that Catalonia expanded across the Pyrenees, incorporating Roussillon to the north of ancient *Hispania*. Before 985, no Catalan count had tried to gather a large number of counties which would justify his using a title expressing his supremacy.

The fading of royal influence

During the tenth century Catalonia became part of the area of 'royal absence', a development endured rather than accepted: the Catalan counts were not content to be abandoned. They long tried to mitigate its effects, and always showed unreserved loyalty to the dynasty which had liberated them.

From the first third of the tenth century, royal commands became infrequent; new grants became the exception, and diplomata were usually confirmations at the request of their recipients. Local lay and ecclesiastical dignitaries, like the lowlier scribes, tried to keep the withering relationship alive and preserve the 'royal memory': notaries still dated documents exclusively by regnal years; libraries and scriptoria kept up with royal genealogies; comital documents repeated that royal precepts (*praeceptum regis, praecepta regalia*) were the fount of law and order. The hereditary counts continued to distinguish lands held from the king and 'fiscal lands' from those acquired by purchase or clearance; even here, land clearance (*aprisio*) implied the existence of wastelands (*ermes*), fiscal lands which could not be possessed without a formal grant. The counts legitimised their power and wealth with reference to their royal origin, and responded readily to any manifestation of royal authority. Until late in the century (at Laon in 944, Rheims in 952), Catalan counts went to the king to have the privileges of their churches confirmed, though they hesitated to express their loyalty by doing homage.

Nothing shows the loyalty of the Catalan counts more clearly than their refusal to accept the Robertine usurpations. They would not recognise Odo (888–98) until he had promised the Carolingian claimant the succession; during the reign of Radulf (923–36) the counts were in a state of insurrection. The monarchy's inadequacies, its inability to ensure the protection due in exchange for fealty, loosened the bond. The Catalan counts gave up journeying to 'France': Wifred of Besalú (d. 957) was the last to do homage to a descendant of Charles the Great. The abbeys clung longer to what was by then an illusory protection: eight of the nine diplomata from after 952 are for abbeys; the last dates from January 986, and was requested by the abbot of Saint-Cugat.

Imitatio regis

The retreat of the monarchy, even if accepted unwillingly, forced the Catalan counts to claim new powers. This changed their image, and their titles adapted to this increase in power. The changes found practical acceptance before being given precise legal expression. The vocabulary of power remained shifting, approximate and contradictory throughout the tenth century. Its most notable aspect was the proliferation alongside ordinary titles of honorific and often hyperbolic terms like *illustrissimus* or *praeclarissimus*. All tenth-century Catalan counts assumed some such title at some time, though never officially.

Other titles were regularly used and acquired institutional standing. 'Marquess' appears at the beginning of the tenth century, when it was no more than a title for the frontier counts never granted or acknowledged by the king. Its status was prestigious enough to provoke emulation. The counts of Barcelona, who controlled most of the frontier, were the first to bear the title 'marquess' and would have liked to monopolise it. It was not until 981 that the count of Cerdaña took it up; in 992 the count of Urgell followed suit. In the middle of the tenth century the phrase *gratia Dei* came in and immediately became part of the counts' titles. Borrell of Barcelona seems to have 'invented' the formula, following the major crisis in relations between Catalonia and the monarchy during the reign of Radulf. He saw it as a way to defend the legitimacy of his own dynasty against the kingdom's political uncertainties. Between

960 and the turn of the eleventh century the other comital families also adopted the formula.

Besides the affirmation of power common to all the counts, titles could show a desire to differentiate between various different people in authority. This is true of the title *dux*, which was fought over in Aquitaine. It was very rare in Catalonia; it was attributed several times to Borrell in the last twenty years of his reign, though it was totally unknown previously. Two documents from 972 call him *dux Gothiae*; in 988 he gave himself the title *gratia Dei Hibereo duci atque marchiso*; and in 991 a court summons still calls him *comes atque dux*. The 'duchy' of Barcelona had no precise localisation and appeared irregularly. It also had competition: in 981, King Lothar himself granted the title of duke to count Gausfred of Roussillon-Empuries, while Hunifred, count of Pallars, added it to his titles on his own account. Bernat Tallaferro, count of Besalú, revived the title in 1015. Ramon Borrell and Berenguer Ramon occasionally (e.g. in 1006 and 1017) used the title to distinguish themselves from the surrounding counts. None of this should lead us to posit any awareness of a 'Catalan duchy'. Borrell's use of *dux Gothiae* or *dux Gothorum* means only that he wanted to participate in the reorganisation of powers in the kingdom on the basis of 'ethnic' units.

Princeps is a word which, by general agreement among historians, implies a claim to independent sovereign power. Pierre Bonnassie emphasises that in Catalonia the word 'keeps its pure Isidorean meaning of a holder of sovereign authority'.[31] Its ambiguity permitted a claim to supremacy which did not pronounce on the question of royal sovereignty. From 906 it was attached to the memory of Wifred the Hairy, and was used several times to describe Wifred II and Sunyer, before becoming habitual under Borrell; gradually it was stripped of adjectives and became the normal term for a sovereign count. Its popularity grew at the end of the tenth century. Borrell seems to have wanted to reserve it for the counts of Barcelona, but Bernat of Besalú assumed it in 1005; and it was as *princeps et pater patriae* that his memory was perpetuated by his brother Oliba.[32]

The supremacy of Barcelona: a principality without a prince

Catalonia in the second half of the tenth century does, however, answer to the definition of a territorial principality. The counts exercised all the powers which had formerly devolved on the king. Awareness of a common history and the demands of defence created a feeling of solidarity which transcended the bounds of the counties. The counts of Barcelona enjoyed a supremacy which,

---

[31] Bonnassie (1975), p. 165.   [32] *Diplomatari i escrits literaris de l'abat i bisbe Oliba*, p. 318.

though never legally formulated, was acknowledged by the other comital dynasties. In the course of the tenth century, they acquired a pre-eminence in areas of power and wealth which was close to real sovereignty. For three-quarters of a century they accumulated land tirelessly; after 950 clearances gave way to systematic purchase. This policy gave them a clear superiority. The possession of several counties and the importance of the marches, suitable areas for colonisation, explain the wealth of the Barcelona dynasty and the consequent amassing of land. The comital domains ceased to increase after 960, because towards 980 the tendency was effectively reversed. The counts started selling, though mostly lands recently or fortuitously acquired. They thus created an intricate network of feudal allegiances.

Here again, the counts of Barcelona were exceptionally successful; in particular, they had large quantities of a currency which they spent freely from 960 onwards: castles. Between 963 and 992, they sold several dozen *castra*; most of them were 'in the marches', of a private origin quickly legitimised by the count. The sale did not mean that the lands attached to the *castrum* were considered as allods. The operation did not surrender power, it exercised it: the castle, as a fortress against peril from outside, was not to be a centre for the exercise of private power.

Another element in the counts' power base was their control of ecclesiastical affairs. Control of the church was primarily a means of government, but also gave the counts extra-political powers: participation in the life of the church lent their authority an eschatological overtone often expressed in the preambles of documents. The bishop of Barcelona addressed Ramon Borrell as *Dei cultor*, and the notary Bonushomo, writing about the razzia on Córdoba in 1010, describes it as a holy war. The counts effortlessly assumed a quasi-royal dignity. Ermengol of Urgell 'reigned' equally with King Robert; Bernat of Besalú referred to his *regnum*. In 1019, Hugh of Empuries roundly declared that 'the power which the kings once had there this count Hugh had'.[33]

There was no name for the Catalan region as a whole, but the behaviour of the nobility reveals that their interests extended across the future Catalonia. Wills show private individuals holding lands in several counties: when Gerosolima made an inventory of the lands she had passed to her son in 993, she went through the whole catalogue of the Catalan counties.[34] The wills of the counts were ordered according to an immutable cartography which ignored county boundaries: Ripoll always comes first, emphasising its importance as a place where Catalan unity, which it symbolised from an early stage, was collectively affirmed.

[33] 'potestatem quam reges ibi pridem habuerunt iste Hugo comes ibi habebat': Pierre de Marca, *Marca Hispanica*, ed. E. Baluze, app. 181.
[34] Udina Martorell, *El archivo condal de Barcelona en los siglos IX–X*, doc. 242.

Counts and bishops met to plan action outside their own counties or dioceses. Several counts would band together to dispense justice or endow an abbey. The reform of the cathedral chapters was the occasion for what could truly be called Catalan councils, when several counts came together with the bishops of the province. The vague sense of a common destiny also encouraged the repeated attempts to create a Catalan metropolis; these finally succeeded in 970 when the bishopric of Tarragona was transferred to Vic.

Several sovereign counts claimed to rule a homogeneous Catalonia, but the count of Barcelona enjoyed a genuine pre-eminence by the end of the tenth century. The representative of the senior branch of Wifred's lineage and master of several counties, resident in prestigious Barcelona, he combined all the attributes of *imitatio regis*. Increasingly he monopolised the title *princeps* and ruled with the assistance of a small team of *proceres regni*. He controlled the revenues, struck coins bearing his name and effigy, granted privileges and extended his foreign policy into Spain; in his disputes with other counts he always invoked the authority of Gothic Law. The other counts acknowledged his supremacy by asking him to settle their disputes, or to dispense justice or attend the consecration of churches in their own counties. This supremacy had no permanent juridical basis: the count of Barcelona was a sovereign prince, but only in his own counties. And since there was no *princeps*, the principality of Catalonia remained nameless and incomplete.

From 'openness to the world' to forced 'independence'

Royal inadequacy favoured the first stirrings of collective consciousness, but the Catalan counties were also permanently threatened by a revival of militant Islam from Córdoba. Unable to ensure their own defence, they sought protection in exchange for concessions. Catalonia's 'openness to the word' first began around 950.[35] They sought papal protection to replace that which the king could no longer give: papal privileges replaced royal diplomata. By 1000 the great Catalan abbeys were under the direct authority of Rome. The lay nobility soon followed. As early as 951, Count Sunifred of Cerdaña went to Rome with the bishop of Urgell, and thereafter such joint voyages became commonplace. The pope's exalted protection complemented that of the kings: a document of 956 alludes to 'the pope of Rome and the king of the Franks, princes of our region'.[36] Rome was constantly asked to intervene in the affairs of the Catalan church, and it was there that the Catalan counts 'discovered' the new Ottonian emperors; in 970 Borrell met Otto I, and in 998 and 1001 Ermengol of Urgell met Otto III.

[35] The phrase is that of d'Abadal i de Vinyals (1960).
[36] Pasqual, *Sacra Cathaloniae antiquitatis monumenta* III, pp. 76–8.

The dynasty's origins, an intense awareness of the Gothic inheritance, and a common language created a reassuring feeling of solidarity between the nobles of Catalonia and Septimania. Borrell increased it through marriage alliances (he married Ledgarde of Rouergue, and then Aimerud of Auvergne). The counts and great nobles also made numerous grants to Aquitanian churches (Conques, Le Puy, Saint-Martial and especially Lagrasse).

However, an understanding with the powerful caliphate of Córdoba was the safest way out of isolation for the Catalan counts. In 940, when the caliph's fleet blockaded Barcelona, Sunyer was forced to conclude a peace which extended Córdoba's influence over the Catalan counties. In 950, Borrell's embassy renewed the agreement; three further embassies, in 966, 971 and 974, finally made Catalonia dependent on the caliphate. This gained the counts their powerful neighbour's neutrality, if not his benevolence; gratefully, he overwhelmed the counts with protestations of friendship. This alliance gave Catalonia a window on the Islamic world and the position of a privileged intermediary between Christendom and Islam. For several decades, the counties south of the Pyrenees owed far more to Córdoba than to the Frankish kingdom: the former supplied them with manpower, cloth and priceless manuscripts, and, above all, with gold.

Yet Borrell's submission did not give the Catalans the lasting security they had expected. In 985, al-Manṣūr, who had proclaimed holy war against the Christian kingdoms of Iberia in 981, launched an expedition against Catalonia. He laid siege to Barcelona on 1 July; on Monday, 6 July, the city was stormed and burned, the inhabitants put to the sword or taken captive. The tragedy was a cruel refutation of Borrell's policy; in later Catalan historiography it was dignified with the status of the first event in a 'national' history. In his despair, the count of Barcelona turned to the Frankish king. An embassy was sent to Compiègne in the first days of 986 to ask Lothar's help. But his death and the brevity of Louis V's reign made it impossible to send any expedition. Borrell renewed his appeal just after the accession of Hugh Capet – or at least, that is what is suggested by the letter written by Gerbert in the king's name at the end of summer 987. In it, Hugh promises help on condition that Borrell undertakes to meet him in Aquitaine to do homage.[37]

This offer by the new king received no reply. By early 988 al-Manṣūr's troops had left Barcelona, and Hugh, bogged down by the rebellion of Charles of Lorraine, would have been unable to keep his promise. Moreover, the Catalans refused to acknowledge him: when dating documents they reverted to the habit of alluding to royal absence, or maliciously stated that he who reigned *in Francia* was no more than an ex-duke (*qui dux fuit pridem*).[38] Catalonia, betrayed by the

---

[37] Gerbert, *ep.* 112. [38] Zimmermann (1981, 1991).

caliphate and abandoned by its natural protector, was compelled to exercise full sovereignty. The episode tacitly ended all relations with the Frankish kingdom; the Capetian kings sent no more diplomata south of the Pyrenees, and all allusions to royal decrees disappear from local documents. Notaries still dated documents by Frankish regnal years, but all memory of the king disappeared. It is easy to see why the Generalitat wanted to celebrate the millennium of the country's 'political independence' in 1988. The peoples of Catalonia had to reorganise their view of things, delineate their own space between the kingdom and the caliphate, invent a history which assigned to them the task of liberation hitherto attributed to Louis the Pious and his successors, and dispute with other Christian kingdoms in Spain the honour of preserving the Gothic inheritance.

Catalonia was a frontier zone, a march; and while the title 'marquess' was slow to adhere to the Catalan counts themselves, it reappeared with increasing frequency in the last third of the tenth century to refer to the shifting area in which sovereignty was disputed between Saracens and Christians, where fortresses were guarded, colonists laboured to clear the land, and brigands and renegades lurked. It was a dangerous and frightening place, but also a place for the enterprising and adventurous. New sovereignties were made there; liberty was reborn there. A frontier society arose, with its own identity. Throughout the tenth century, the Catalan frontier did not advance more than a few dozen miles south of Llobregat. Territorial expansion was neither a political aim nor a religious imperative: it was the result of individual initiatives or fortunate chance. The march was a buffer zone, but also a zone of interchange: it encouraged cultural and commercial exchanges, making Catalonia highly favourable to encounters between the Christian and Arabic worlds.

It was the ecclesiastical framework which gave shape to the 'principalities' and a basis for the hegemonic pretensions of princes, whether 'dukes' or not. The province of Bordeaux, split between the principalities of Aquitaine and Gascony (the dukes jointly designated the metropolitan bishop), lost importance to Bourges, which was geographically equated with Aquitaine; the creation of a bishop of the Gascons answered to the duke's desire to possess 'his' province and give his power a religious basis. In Catalonia, the desire for religious emancipation led in 971 to the restoration of a native metropolis at Vic; for a few months after the assassination of the new archbishop, Ato, on 22 August, the Catalan province was detatched from the metropolitan of Narbonne.

Shortly after their liberation, Septimania and Catalonia were described as wastelands, fiscal reserves open to colonisation, and they remained largely in this state in the tenth century. The exploitation of the country was never the result of Frankish immigration; on the contrary, the documents show a regular influx of Christian *Hispani*, Gothic settlers who set their stamp on local place-names. But most of the settlement was by mountain peoples moving towards the plains below. Successive waves of invaders had chased so many people into the safety of the mountains that the area had become saturated and could supply manpower to colonise the lower valleys, depopulated by conquest and reconquest. The settlement, attested in Septimania as early as Charles the Great's reign, started in Catalonia in the last decades of the ninth century. It was inaugurated by peasants on their own initiative, but public authorities and abbeys soon took it over and extended it. The most striking example is the exploitation of the plains of Vic and Bages. By 897, several thousand colonists had settled there, mostly from Cerdaña, but a few from the Llerida region still under Muslim control.

The settlement of fiscal lands took place through *aprisio*: settlers acquired full ownership after thirty years' uninterrupted farming. Colonisation produced liberty: new villages were allodial communities, which had sometimes moved *en bloc* from the mountains under the guidance of a priest. Outside the zones of settlement, the peasant allod was less prominent: it was the result of more intensive farming, and led a precarious but perpetual renewed existence on the fringes of power, in disputed zones, or carved out of the wasteland.

The shadow of the castellans fell on these free lands. As colonisation progressed, a network of castles was constructed to protect and delimit the 'micro-societies' of the frontier, with an analogous development in less recently colonised areas. The castellans, who held office from the counts, were remunerated by a grant of fiscal land called a fief. Small peasant holdings rubbed shoulders with great aristocratic domains, which had been fortified since 950 in Languedoc. In spite of the rapid decline of slavery, the latter was still exploited by direct labour dues, and the *corvée* remained unknown. The towns, surrounded by peasant populations, retained a power and prestige inherited from Roman times. The counts resided there, and the towns remained centres for the distribution and display of power.

The southern princes, anxious to make their fragile principalities as cohesive as possible, heirs to a Carolingian tradition of collaboration between the secular power and church leaders, were aware of the profound changes within that institution, and in reformed monasticism they saw the agent for a regeneration of society as a whole. After the foundation of Cluny by William the Pious, the southern princes contributed to the success of reform. The influence of Cluny was immediate and direct in Aquitaine, late and indirect in Catalonia and Septimania. The centre from which its influence spread was the abbey of Lezat: in 965 its abbot, Gari, was asked to reform Saint-Michel de Cuza. In 993 this union developed into a congregation of five abbeys headed by Gari, from which the reform spread through all of Languedoc and into Catalonia.

THE DECADES OF CHANGE AND THE OVERTURNING OF THE OLD
ORDER, *C.* 985–*C.* 1025

The decades around the millennium were a turning point in the history of the
southern principalities. The Capetian accession removed the last barrier to full
princely sovereignty, and the principalities reached their apogee in the first
third of the eleventh century. Simultaneously, economic progress sharpened
appetites and encouraged violence and the fragmentation and privatisation of
power. The crisis did not erupt until after 1030, but from 1000 the stakes were
set and the partners decided.

The advent of Hugh Capet in 987 was fiercely resisted in places before
Charles of Lorraine formally recognised him, but the new king was generally
accepted within two years; only in the Limousin, Quercy, Poitou and the
Catalan county of Pallars did Carolingian legitimism sustain rejection of the
usurper. The Velay, Gothia and most of Catalonia treated the first years of
the Capetian monarchy as an interregnum during which real power was exercised by Christ; subsequently the Catalans acknowledged Hugh but treated him
with sarcasm. The southern princes thus forcibly declared an independence
hitherto restrained by their loyalty to the Carolingian order. William IV of
Aquitaine wanted acknowledgement as a partner and equal by the king, his
brother-in-law. In Gascony, the charters of William Sanchéz make no mention
of the king, whereas the clerks of Saint-Sever use the names of both king and
duke in their documents. Catalan documents hesitate to use the name of the
local rulers, but make it clear that the monarchy was in a distant and foreign
land (*rex in Francia, rex francigenus*). After 1020, the king had almost no contact
with the churches in the south and none with the nobles and counts, who now
dealt only with the prince.

His image was never more prestigious than at the beginning of the eleventh
century. Gascony, the Toulousain and the future Catalonia were at their height.
Gascony loudly proclaimed its independence; its dukes forgot the king of
Francia and strengthened their links with the king of Navarre. The counts of
Toulouse had to share the marquisate of Gothia with their Rouergue cousins.
Doubtless they regretted having lost the title 'dukes of Aquitaine', but after the
death of William III Taillefer in 1024, they exercised 'an undisputed and virtually sovereign authority, alluding to their "kingdoms" . . . exercised full public
authority and controlled three-quarters of the fortresses in the counties under
their sway'.[39] The princely title was arrogated by the counts of Barcelona,
Borrell (948–92) and Ramon Borrell (992–1018), who claimed rights of senior-
ity and at times used the title *dux*, making them the equals of the Capetian

---

[39] Magnou-Nortier (1974), p. 255.

usurper; and they referred to their *potestas regalis*. The most extravagantly praised of all the princes was the Aquitanian William V the Great (993–1030), *totius tunc temporis Aquitaniae monarchus*, on whom Adhémar of Chabannes wrote an enthusiastic panegyric.[40] Not only did he possess all the kingly virtues, he also dealt on equal terms with contemporary sovereigns, with whom he exchanged gifts: Alfonso of Castile, Sancho of Navarre, Cnut and even the emperor Henry II. In 1024, the nobles of Italy contemplated offering him the crown; the king of France treated the duke on a footing of absolute equality. Not only did William subjugate the whole of Aquitaine as far as Anjou; his marriage with Brisca, sister of Sancho William, initiated the reunification of the two southern duchies. His pilgrimages to Rome and Compostella show an international reputation which he dreamed of enhancing by accepting the crown of Italy. 'He gave the impression of a king rather than a duke' is Adhémar's conclusion.[41]

Chroniclers considered Aquitaine a *monarchia*, the count of Toulouse spoke of his *regnum*, and the compiler of the *Miracles of St Benedict* saw the future Catalonia as a *regnum Barcilonense* shared between four *duces*; yet none of the southern princes attained kingship. Did they retain vague memories of their origins as Carolingian officials? Were they still attached to the idea of a *regnum Francorum* which they equated with western Christendom? Were they overawed by the image of sacred kingship? Or were they aware that their idealised authority did not accord with contemporary political reality? William V would have found it exceedingly difficult to 'ignore' a king to whom he was bound by family ties. Hugh Capet was his uncle by marriage, and Robert the Pious, already related by his first marriage, became his brother-in-law when he married Constance of Provence. It was to S. Jean d'Angély that Robert came on the last journey south of the Loire made by any Capetian for many years; and William was present at the coronations of Hugh in 1017 and Henry I in 1026.

At the end of the tenth century the principalities allowed the effective exercise of public authority. But the king's absence did not automatically transfer all regalian prerogatives to the prince. Princely power had limits; the title of prince did not guarantee the rigorous control of a territory. William was to all intents and purposes a king, but without a capital: he had to move ceaselessly about to convey his orders and hold judicial assemblies at which he merely arbitrated. The prince's authority was limited to his inherited status as a former royal official. He always appended to his princely title the name of the county which was the root of his power (*dux Aquitanorum et comes Pictavensis*). The count of Barcelona did not even develop a new series of titles: his power had a territorial definition (*comes Barcilonensis*, not *comes Barcilonensium*).

---

[40] Adhémar of Chabannes, *Chronicon* III, 41.   [41] Adhémar of Chabannes, *Chronicon* III, 10.

The principality was simply a collection of *pagi*, begun on the king's initiative, and the power of the prince was measured by the cohesion of the area under his direct control. Every principality had an inner zone, made up of the *pagi* held directly by the prince where he acted as count and was represented by viscounts but where he mainly held fiscal rights and lands, and an outer zone, the *pagi* held by vassal counts. This had been progressively added to the principality, and might fall away again if princely authority showed any signs of weakening, since it depended on a consensus worked out at princely assemblies. The largest principalities, like Aquitaine, with a huge outer zone, were the least stable.

Until about 1000 the princely system worked well in the whole area. This is shown by the princes' common attachment to Romano-Visigothic law: incarnate in the *lex Gothorum* used everywhere, it exalted public sovereignty (*potestas*) and private property. The princes retained an influence sustained by lands and revenues which had often been granted to them quite properly by the king. Their delegated power was quite legal, and their representatives – viscounts or provosts were public officials. Until 1020, the word *fevum* meant 'a tenure granted over public land by public authority to an agent of that authority',[42] and these agents demanded services from the nobles by comital order. Though slavery had become much less common, cultivation still partly depended on the labour of serfs, though it was commoner for landowners to rent their land to free peasants for payment in kind. Finally, the vigorous colonial advances created and sustained important communities of peasants working their own allods.

From 980 the first symptoms appeared of a crisis which was to erupt and spread after 1030, a new stage in the collapse of Carolingian institutions and the establishing of feudalism. Recent research has shown that this transformation was the result of economic changes affecting the rate of production and the extent of cultivated land, as well as the increase and acceleration of trade. Land clearance to cope with an increased population; new villages; new technology (mills) in the countryside; new crops (vines): all these encouraged local trade and an increased number of markets, and also the revival of long-distance trade when in the 990s Muslim gold began to flow into Catalonia and then north of the Pyrenees. This sudden increase in wealth provoked conflicts disturbing to public order. The counts lost control over viscounts and castellans – the 'collapse of the *pagus*' analysed by Lemarignier.[43] Public documents constituting proof in themselves were succeeded by mere notices, agreements, and oaths, whose effectiveness depended on the power of the beneficiary.

The administration of justice was the first to be affected by the crisis. The

---

[42] Magnou-Nortier (1964).   [43] Lemarignier (1951).

courts lost confidence; disputes were submitted to arbitrators less interested in applying the law than in drawing up an acceptable compromise. The elements of society supposedly protected by public law – the church, the 'poor' – were denied legal redress and left to the arbitrary power of the nobility. The collapse of the judicial system made violence endemic. Public officials – viscounts or castellans – in charge of public fortresses were the first to band together and make private war: their castles became operational bases and public lands were used to reward their followers. Until 1020 the castellans drew their strength from a privatisation of what some of them still called their *functio*. The nobles of the marches, tired of the peace along the frontier, started remunerative expeditions on their own account.

The count retained power only over those areas he controlled directly. His authority, already fragile in the outer zone, was now threatened in the inner zone as well. Some resisted better than others, creating a whole typology of princely power in the eleventh century. In the early eleventh century we have only disturbing forebodings of a coming crisis. The 'rise of the castellans' is still a matter of comital officers under the count's authority: of the eighty-eight castles known to have existed in the Charente region, only twelve are earlier than the year 1000, and most of those earlier than 1020 were built on the count's initiative, or with his approval.

In a sort of chain reaction, the emancipation of the castellans promoted a diversification of power right across the hierarchy, leaving the prince with an authority which was largely theoretical. Former viscounts, some of whom usurped the title of count (as in the Auvergne) while others (as in Bearn) retained their former title, made themselves virtually independent, extending their own territory at the expense of the prince or of ecclesiastical immunities: they inaugurated a second generation of principalities. The counts in the outer zones of the principalities regained independence within a system previously dominated by princely prestige.

On the southern fringes of Aquitaine, princely power was eliminated: the Massif Central entered a new period without either king or prince and with an extreme dispersal of power. On the fringes of the inner zone of his duchy, the count of Poitiers had to come to terms with secondary counts, attempting to foment strife among them. William V allied with William Taillefer, count of Angoulême, against the counts of La Marche, Périgord and Limoges; in his first year he seized Charroux, the capital of La Marche. In the heart of Poitou he was challenged by the lords of Lusignan, Déols and Châtellerault, whom he succeeded in buying off with important concessions. In Gascony the rise of the viscounts and castellans, together with dynastic problems, speeded the collapse of a principality soon to become part of Greater Aquitaine.

In the county of Toulouse the old political order began to fade from as early as 980. 'The ruin of royal power was echoed by the loss of authority by the counts. They could neither impose judgements which they had made nor hold regular judicial assemblies. The county of Toulouse had no territorial basis, and in every little enclave, local dynasties appeared descended from the viscounts or provosts of the preceding era'.[44] The counts rarely appear in documents; they may still have presided over judicial assemblies, but they were no longer the only ones to do so. In Septimania, the counts had long ceased trying to intervene; from Narbonne to Nîmes, the vicecomital families were struggling with the bishops to control cities which were still centres of political organisation. Narbonne, together with Nîmes, Maguelonne, Agde, Lodève, Béziers and Carcassonne, were centres of both lay and episcopal power.

The church was the first victim of a noble violence no authority was able to restrain. It was also the first to react. The Peace of God was born in the southern principalities, where the disorder was most serious and the weakness of the dukes was most obvious. The first peace councils met at Charroux in 989 and at Le Puy in 990 and 994. Conciliar legislation, backed only by ecclesiastical sanctions, aimed to compensate for the failings of a public authority no longer able to protect the church and the 'poor'. By requiring troublemakers to acknowledge conciliar decisions the bishops attempted to create a new public order. Though a spiritual impulse lay behind this notion of peace, the first assemblies were clearly directed against the castellans. The Truce of God was intended to contain violence within ever narrower limits. It first appeared in the diocese of Elne (at the synod of Toulouges in 1027), and reached Vic in 1031 and then the whole of Languedoc. But the prince could use the new legislation to prop up his authority: in 998, William V presided over a peace council. Where the power of the princes had completely vanished it was the abbey of Cluny which attempted to limit violence, as in the Auvergne under Abbot Odilo (994–1049).

The princes' attitude to the church remained contradictory. They interfered in episcopal elections and disposed of ecclesiastical offices and lands, but they also encouraged the reform movement. It was at their initiative that Cluny spread its influence over the monasteries of the south. William V illustrates this perfectly. He seized the lay abbacy of Saint-Hilaire, twice appointed bishops of Limoges (in 1014 and 1022), and in 1027 even appointed the archbishop of Bordeaux. But he also corresponded with Fulbert of Chartres and tried to retain him by appointing him treasurer of Saint-Hilaire; he entrusted to Cluny the reform of Saint-Jean d'Angély and Saint-Cyprien; in 1028, at Charroux, he summoned a council to 'exterminate the Manichaean heresy which was spreading among the people'.[45] In 1030 he retired to die at the abbey of Maillezais built by his father. Aquitaine also saw the development of

---

[44] Ourliac (1988), p. 117.   [45] Bonnassie and Landes (1992), p. 440.

a new kind of sanctity, illustrated by Odo of Cluny in his *vita* of Gerald of Aurillac.

Around 1000 the façade of princely power was preserved, but behind it, power was dispersed and there was an improvised quest for palliatives to the unending violence. During this time, the Catalan territories achieved a precocious unity leading to a new national consciousness. The traumatic fall of Barcelona in 985 and the accession of Hugh Capet were soon to be elevated by local chroniclers into the founding episode of Catalan history.

A new cultural and spiritual identity emerged, and Catalonia itself acquired a political structure. The two oldest oaths of allegiance which have survived, sworn by Ermengol, bishop of Urgell to Count Wifred of Cerdaña and by the same Wifred to Ermessent, countess of Barcelona, date from the 1020s, and were exchanged by holders of public power. The vassal–lord relationship, the basis for a radical transformation of society, was already making it possible to clarify the political situation: a family condominium was becoming a feudal principality. Catalonia emerged as other principalities were collapsing. The expedition to Córdoba in 1010, which was attended by almost all the Catalan counts and bishops under Ramon Borrell of Barcelona, can be seen as the first collective manifestation of a national identity, though this found no political expression until after a long crisis which began around 1020; nothing in the 1020s suggested that the coming disturbances would later give the count of Barcelona the opportunity to rebuild his power on fresh foundations.

Despite its shifting and imprecise political divisions, the south of the Frankish kingdom had a real coherence, extending, as recent research has shown, into Provence and Italy, Aragon and Galicia. Yet it was a heterogeneous region. The dispersal of power did not occur everywhere to the same degree, and the titles of the princes were as confusing as they were numerous. Doubtless the south 'forgot' the king while continuing to see him as the keystone of a moral and political order of which it was part. But that is not the most important aspect. Behind the persistence, even the reinforcement, of cultural and political units a new system of relationships and social institutions was emerging which in the north would take on a fixed juridical form. The south did not develop a bastard imitation of northern feudalism: it was there that feudalism developed. The importance of oaths and contracts, the role of women, the prestige of towns, the fascination with the enemy across the frontier – all these are characteristics of a different society. The north, which borrowed so much from the south, would later have to 'reconquer' it.

CHAPTER 18

ENGLAND, 900–1016

Simon Keynes

THE MORE that is known of any period in the history of Anglo-Saxon England, the more we can appreciate the limitations of our knowledge. A framework for the momentous events of the tenth century is provided by the *Anglo-Saxon Chronicle*; charters, law-codes and coins supply detailed information on various aspects of royal government, and much else besides; and the surviving works of Anglo-Latin and vernacular literature, not to mention the numerous manuscripts written in the tenth century, testify in their different ways to the vitality of ecclesiastical culture. Yet it does not follow that the tenth century is better understood than more sparsely documented periods: the evidence may allow great scope for the kind of detailed analysis on which generalisations must depend, but at the same time it generates supplementary questions which expose how much remains beyond our reach.

It is easy enough to identify the themes which seem in retrospect to give shape to the period under review, though it must be emphasised that the themes are interwoven to such an extent that it is unwise to treat any one of them in isolation from the others. During the course of the tenth century the West Saxon kings extended their power first over Mercia, then into the southern Danelaw, and finally over Northumbria, thereby imposing a semblance of political unity on peoples who remained conscious nonetheless of their respective customs and their separate pasts. From time to time, the kings also received the submission of certain Welsh and Scottish rulers. The prestige and the pretensions of the monarchy increased, the institutions of royal government were strengthened, and kings and their agents sought in various ways to establish social order. England was brought into closer contact with the mainstreams of the European world; religious learning and the decorative arts were stimulated by the importation of manuscripts from the continent, and in certain quarters there was new zeal for organised monastic life. A land-owning and office-holding aristocracy of ealdormen and thegns spread across the country, nurtured by the kings who needed its support; but while its members

Bishoprics
Towns
Battles

Bamburgh

N O R T H U M B R I A

Durham

York

GWYNEDD

Lincoln

Derby Nottingham

M E R C I A

Tamworth Leicester Stamford

Tettenhall

Worcester

DYFED

E A S T
A N G L I A

Oxford Maldon

London Ashingdon

W E S S E X Canterbury

Winchester Dover

Exeter

CORNWALL

0   100 miles
0   150 km

9 England in the tenth century

accumulated great wealth and power, their loyalty to anything other than a calculation of self-interest could hardly be taken for granted. Religious houses prospered to varying degrees under the patronage of those who identified with their interests, acquiring and consolidating substantial endowments of land by purchase, gift and exchange; at the same time, the heads of these houses gained influence in high circles, and found themselves in control of the services of increasingly large numbers of men. Rural estates continued to be managed in accordance with local customs; markets thrived where surplus produce could be sold, or exchanged for more useful commodities; and towns flourished on domestic and foreign trade. Large quantities of gold and silver were in circulation, and the economy could support a well-regulated coinage. Meanwhile, life for the great majority of people followed its natural course: some may have prospered, and may have come to enjoy the prospect of larger horizons, but many must have felt their world closing in ever more tightly around their manorial lord.

The challenge which confronts the historian of tenth-century England is first to assess the variety of sources on their own terms, and then to correlate the different kinds of evidence in an attempt to produce a composite whole; if the process is likened to solving a jigsaw puzzle, the problem is not merely that so many pieces are missing, but that the pieces themselves come from several different puzzles. It is important to stress, moreover, that few things in the tenth century are likely to have been quite what they now seem to be. For example, we might be tempted to represent the 'unification of England' as a remorseless progression towards a preconceived end; in other words, as the fulfilment of a deliberate policy which could be traced back to the visions of the 'unity' of the English people current in one form or another in the eighth and ninth centuries. One could not doubt that grandiose notions of such a kind were entertained by some; but in the event the unification of England proved to be a far more complex process, involving as much accident as design. Again, we always have to bear in mind that of their very nature the available sources encourage the supposition that all things proceeded from a royal initiative, and that matters can be understood in terms of the personal characteristics of particular kings. Of course this is true, up to a point; but to think exclusively in terms of the policies of successive kings is to subscribe to a rationale which could be at once misleading and artificial. Similarly, it is the case that for our understanding of ecclesiastical affairs in the tenth century we are largely dependent on sources which emanate from the circle of the monastic reformers, and which thus invite us to take a fundamentally 'Benedictine' view of the condition of the church. Yet there is no obvious reason why the modern historian should be expected to share the prejudices of one party as opposed to another: to do so would be to deny the viable varieties of religious life, and also to miss the more complex dimensions of the reformers' own activities. Finally, it must be emphasised that the available 'narrative' sources, such as the *Anglo-Saxon Chronicle*, can hardly be expected to tell the whole truth. Analysis of charters has much to reveal about a king's dealings with the great and the good of his kingdom, about the composition of the royal household, and about attendance at meetings of the king's council. Sometimes it is possible to detect patterns which seem to be significant, and which help to complement the narrative record; but often one is merely left with the impression that there was something going on at court, without any basis for knowing what to make of it. In the same way, analysis of coinage can suggest much about the gradual extension of royal authority into different parts of the country, about the complexities of local administration, and about changing patterns of economic activity. The question is whether this evidence should then be interpreted in the light of what we already know about such matters, or whether it should be given the opportunity to tell its own story.

A review of the major political developments in England during the course of the tenth and early eleventh centuries must begin during the reign of King Alfred the Great (871–99). Æthelred, ruler of the Mercians, had submitted to King Alfred in the early 880s, and it was at about the same time that Alfred's authority was recognised in the formerly Mercian city of London; in 886 Alfred took measures to secure the city's defence, 'and all the English people that were not under subjection to the Danes submitted to him', whereupon the king 'entrusted the borough to the control of Ealdorman Æthelred';[1] then or soon afterwards, Æthelred married Alfred's daughter Æthelflæd (sister of Edward the Elder), later known as 'the lady of the Mercians'. There is reason to believe that the events of the 880s, and perhaps of 886 in particular, established a new polity in southern England: Alfred came to be recognised by those around him as 'king of the Anglo-Saxons', a formulation which seems in this context to have been intended to express an amalgamation of the 'Anglian' and 'Saxon' peoples, and in this way to symbolise the aspirations which cast Alfred as the leader of the English people against the common enemy.[2] Of course, not all parties would have subscribed to such a grandiose view of King Alfred's position: some may have continued to regard him, quite accurately, as 'king of the West Saxons', and there may well have been others who were reluctant to acknowledge that his authority extended over themselves. Nonetheless, it seems clear enough that Alfred's status at the end of his reign was significantly different from his status at its beginning: in the words of a chronicler reporting his death, on 26 October 899, 'he was king over the whole English people except for that part which was under Danish rule'.[3]

---

[1] *ASC,* p. 199.   [2] *Alfred the Great,* pp. 38–41 and 227–8.   [3] *ASC,* p. 207.

Against this background, it is important to consider the precise nature of the relationship which existed in the first quarter of the tenth century between the established powers in Wessex and Mercia. The matter is naturally judged in the first instance by a reading of the various sets of annals incorporated in the extant manuscripts of the *Anglo-Saxon Chronicle*, which show that the events of these years could be presented in very different ways, depending on the chronicler's point of view. A series of 'West Saxon' annals (covering the years 897–914, with a continuation from 915 to 920) happens to provide the core of the narrative, and a series of 'Mercian' annals (covering the years 902–24) seems merely to supplement it; so it is all too easy for the modern historian subconsciously to adopt what is fundamentally a 'West Saxon' point of view. This means, of course, that he may give more than a due share of credit to Edward the Elder, at the expense of the Mercian contribution to the English conquest of the southern Danelaw; but it also means that he may receive a distortedly 'West Saxon' impression of the nature of Edward's position. These sets of annals are usefully supplemented by Ealdorman Æthelweard's *Chronicon*, written (in Latin) towards the end of the tenth century and dedicated to Æthelweard's kinswoman, Abbess Matilda of Essen; for Æthelweard's account of Edward's reign appears to be largely independent of the material in the extant manuscripts of the *Chronicle*, and thus represents yet another point of view. It is always the case, however, that overtly 'narrative' sources can create a very misleading impression of the course of events; and for the reign of Edward the Elder, as for any other period in Anglo-Saxon history, it is necessary to pay close attention to the evidence of charters, law-codes and coins.

In the inscrutable words of the West Saxon chronicler who reported King Alfred's death in 899, 'his son Edward succeeded to the kingdom'. All this need have meant in practice was that leading members of the secular and ecclesiastical hierarchies chose Edward as their lord and formally recognised him as their king; it need not follow that Edward would have been able from the outset of his reign to command the loyalty of all those who had made submission to his father, or that he would have been able to take immediate and effective control of a fully functioning state. The natural assumption is that Edward succeeded his father as king 'of the West Saxons', and that English Mercia was left in the hands of its own ruler, Ealdorman Æthelred; certainly, the chronicler could not be expected to dwell on the political consequences of Alfred's death from anything other than a West Saxon point of view, and it is conceivable, therefore, that Ealdorman Æthelred and the Mercians immediately recovered their independence.[4] Even in Wessex itself Edward's own position was far from secure. Soon after his accession, Edward's cousin, the ætheling Æthelwold,

---

[4] See, e.g., Stenton (1971), pp. 317–21; John, in Campbell (1982), p. 161; Stafford (1989), pp. 25–6.

'rode and seized the residence at Wimborne and at *Twinham*, against the will of the king and his councillors'. As the son of Alfred's elder brother, King Æthelred (865–71), Æthelwold would have had good reason to resent Edward's assumption of royal power; and his seizure of Wimborne (in Dorset), where his father had been buried, and of *Twinham* (Christchurch, Hants), one of King Alfred's network of fortifications, suggests that he was determined to make a bid for power in his own right. In other words, the incident arose from residual dissension within the West Saxon royal family, and soon developed into a serious threat. Edward responded by bringing his army to Badbury, near Wimborne, whereupon Æthelwold slipped away 'to the Danish army in Northumbria, and they accepted him as king and gave allegiance to him'; a series of Northumbrian coins struck in the name of 'Alvvaldus' appears to confirm Æthelwold's success in gaining some form of recognition in the northern Danelaw.[5] Edward's position would have been significantly strengthened by his coronation, on 8 June 900;[6] but in late 901 or 902 the ætheling Æthelwold returned to the south with a naval force, 'and submission was made to him in Essex'. Æthelwold induced 'the army in East Anglia' to break the peace, crossing the frontier into English territory and penetrating as far as Cricklade on the Thames, before returning 'homeward'. In retaliation, Edward took his own army into East Anglia, and 'harried all their land between the Dykes and the Ouse, all as far north as the fens'. After a while, Edward gave orders for his army to withdraw; but the Kentish contingent in his force lingered behind, and in the ensuing battle 'of the Holme',[7] 'a great slaughter was made on both sides'. The Kentish casualties included two ealdormen, and several others of whom the chronicler names the most distinguished; the casualties on the 'Danish' side included King Eohric, Æthelwold himself, and a certain Brihtsige, who was apparently a disaffected Mercian prince. The inclusion in the Mercian annals of a reference to 'the battle of the Holme between the people of Kent and the Danes' suggests that the battle was widely understood to have been a significant event; and it is interesting that the West Saxon chronicler who provides the fullest account of the battle seems to have been at pains to explain why Edward and the rest of the English had apparently left the Kentish forces to their fate, as if they had been criticised for their absence from a battle which had put an end to a most dangerous threat.

At once, therefore, we get a sense of the difficulties which confronted Edward in the opening years of his reign. Indeed, it may be that we should see him at this stage as one who operated in a relatively restricted West Saxon context, with his centre of power at Winchester and not yet in full control of

---

[5] Blunt (1985); Blunt *et al.* (1989), pp. 4 and 102–3.   [6] Æthelweard, *Chronicon* IV, 4.
[7] Perhaps Holme, in Huntingdonshire; see Hart (1992), pp. 511–15.

other parts of his extended kingdom. There is certainly a strong 'Winchester' flavour to Edward's regime in the first decade of the tenth century. Within a year or two of his accession, Edward founded the 'New Minster', with the apparent intention that it should serve the particular interests of the royal family; his charters suggest the existence of close links between the clergy of the royal household and the communities of both the Old and the New Minsters; and it is interesting that the earliest of the coins struck in Edward's name appear to have been minted at Winchester, though other mints came into operation at a later stage.[8] For their part, Æthelred and Æthelflæd were in firm control of the West Midlands, and (one must suppose) of the south-eastern portion of the former kingdom of Mercia which lay between the Thames and the frontier with the Danes; the main seat of their power appears to have been at Gloucester, where they too had founded a 'new minster' to serve their own interests.[9] A charter issued at Shrewsbury in 901, in which they are described as 'holding by the assisting grace of God the monarchy of the Mercians and governing and defending them in an honourable manner', demonstrates the reality of their power over lands which had formerly belonged to the Mercian kings, and illustrates their good intentions towards one of the ancient Mercian minsters (the community of St Mildburg at Much Wenlock, in Shropshire).[10] Another charter, dated 904, shows that the bishop and community of Worcester were eager to establish mutually beneficial relations with their rulers: the bishop and community leased land within and outside the town walls of Worcester to Æthelred and Æthelflæd, described as 'lords of the Mercians', for the duration of their lives and for that of their daughter Ælfwyn.[11] The impression that Æthelred and Æthelflæd were autonomous rulers of the Mercians is further strengthened by the report in the West Saxon annals that in 911, following the death of Ealdorman Æthelred, 'King Edward succeeded to London and Oxford and to all the lands which belonged to them', and by the report in the same source that in 918, following the death of Æthelflæd, Edward occupied Tamworth, 'and all the nation in the land of the Mercians which had been subject to Æthelflæd submitted to him' – as if Edward had seized each opportunity to impose his control over areas or peoples which had not been his before. Moreover, the Mercian annals refer quite pointedly to Æthelflæd's death as occurring 'in the eighth year in which with lawful authority she was holding dominion over the Mercians', adding that Ælfwyn 'was deprived of all authority in Mercia and taken into Wessex'. One might well suppose that Edward, as king of the West Saxons, had effected a two-stage *coup d'état*, and that the Mercians had been forced to submit to his sway.

It is possible, however, to read the evidence in a rather different way. Edward

---

[8] For the coinage, see Blunt *et al.* (1989), pp. 21, 29–30 and 264–5.

[9] See Heighway (1984), pp. 40–6.   [10] Sawyer, no. 221.   [11] Sawyer, no. 1280.

may have succeeded his father in 899 not as king 'of the West Saxons', but as king 'of the Anglo-Saxons', representing the distinctively Alfredian polity which had been established in the 880s, and which would have given Edward notional authority over English Mercia from the beginning of his reign. Examination of the religious service used for the coronation of kings in the tenth century suggests that in its earliest form it had applied not to the kingship of the West Saxons, as such, but rather to the kingship of the 'Angles' as well as the 'Saxons'.[12] In this respect the service appears to reflect the Alfredian polity of the 880s, and it is by no means unlikely that it was used for the first time on the occasion of Edward's coronation in 900. It is significant, furthermore, that the royal styles accorded to Edward in the small corpus of his surviving charters (all of which were issued in the first decade of his reign) indicate quite emphatically that he was regarded, like his father before him, as 'king of the Anglo-Saxons'. One charter, dated 901, alludes to a judgement given during Alfred's reign 'by all of the councillors of the Gewisse [i.e. the West Saxons] and of the Mercians', as if the two peoples had been acting together;[13] and if this is what the Alfredian polity had entailed, a polity of a very similar kind seems to have obtained from the beginning of Edward's reign. It emerges, for example, that in 903 a Mercian ealdorman called Æthelfrith 'petitioned King Edward, and also Æthelred and Æthelflæd, who then held rulership and power over the race of the Mercians under the aforesaid king, as well also as all the leading men of the Mercians', that they should allow him to have replacements made for certain charters which had been lost in a fire. Three of the charters produced in these circumstances have survived: one concerns an estate in Somerset, and the two others concern estates at Risborough (Buckinghamshire) and at Islington (Middlesex), in the heart of territory known to have been in Æthelred's charge.[14] Another 'Mercian' charter, issued in 904 in respect of an estate in Oxfordshire, was drawn up on behalf of a certain Wigfrith who in the same way had petitioned King Edward, and Ealdorman Æthelred and Æthelflæd and all their *senatores*, for a new charter to replace one damaged by water.[15] One might add that Mercian bishops regularly attest Edward's 'West Saxon' charters; and although Æthelred and Æthelflæd were clearly empowered to issue charters in their own right, without explicit reference to Edward,[16] it is no less significant that coins seemingly produced in Mercia during the first and second decades of the tenth century were struck not in their names but in the name of King Edward himself.[17]

The conclusion seems inescapable that the Alfredian polity of the kingship 'of the Anglo-Saxons' persisted during the first quarter of the tenth century,

[12] See Nelson (1986), pp. 365–7.   [13] Sawyer, no. 362 (*EHD*, no. 100, pp. 541–3).
[14] Sawyer, nos. 367, 371, and 371 MS 2.   [15] Sawyer, no. 361.   [16] Sawyer, nos. 221, 224 and 225.
[17] See Blunt *et al.* (1989), pp. 21, 42–3 and 264–6.

and that the Mercians were thus under Edward's rule from the beginning of his reign. It is arguable, therefore, that our dependence on sets of annals which cover the events of this period from either a West Saxon or a Mercian point of view has served to polarise matters in what could be a misleading way, perpetuating the appearance of antagonism between the peoples and concealing a more complex truth. The one-sided views of the chroniclers were the natural product of their partisan interests, and it is only by accepting that the annals are complementary accounts that we can begin to restore the balance. The truth, of course, was that the campaign to bring the areas of Danish settlement in eastern England back under English control entailed sustained cooperation between Edward, Æthelred and Æthelflæd, so much so, indeed, that it is difficult to imagine that it was not orchestrated by one party, in overall command. The strategy appears initially to have been directed against the threat of any renewed hostility from the Danish forces based in East Anglia and Northumbria. In 906 Edward is said to have made peace with the East Angles and the Northumbrians, at Tiddingford (Buckinghamshire, in Ealdorman Æthelred's territory), in circumstances which may not have been quite as much to his advantage as the West Saxon chronicler would like us to believe.[18] Edward himself seems to have broken the peace in 909, sending an army 'both from the West Saxons and from the Mercians' to ravage 'the territory of the northern army'; but in the following year it was the northern army which took the offensive, striking south into English Mercia as far as the (?Upper) Avon and thence crossing the Severn into the 'western districts', before returning homewards via Bridgnorth (in Shropshire).[19] An army sent by Edward 'both from the West Saxons and Mercians' overtook the invaders at Tettenhall (in Staffordshire), and won a decisive victory; several of the Scandinavian leaders were killed, perhaps disrupting the political stability of the north for some years thereafter. Another dimension of the English strategy in its earliest stages is revealed only by the evidence of charters. It seems that men were being encouraged, already in the first decade of the tenth century, to purchase estates from the 'pagans', thereby to reassert some degree of English influence in territory which had fallen under Danish control; and since the recorded instances concern land in Bedfordshire and Derbyshire, the fact that the purchases are said to have been made 'by the order of King Edward and also of Ealdorman Æthelred along with the other ealdormen and thegns' supports the view that Edward's authority was considered to extend deep into 'Mercian' territory.[20] Following Æthelred's death in 911, King Edward assumed direct responsibility for the south-eastern part of English Mercia, and it was at this

---

[18] Compare the chronicler's account (*ASC*, p. 209) with the northern annals preserved by Simeon of Durham (*EHD*, no. 3, p. 278). [19] *ASC*, pp. 210–11; cf. Æthelweard, *Chronicon* IV, 4.

[20] Sawyer, nos. 396 (*EHD*, no. 103) and 397.

point that Edward and Æthelflæd took the offensive. The details of the campaign, which involved the establishment of fortified sites (or burhs) at strategic locations in a broad band of territory stretching diagonally across central England from the Wirral to the Thames estuary, are best followed in the *Anglo-Saxon Chronicle*; suffice it to say that the strategy proved remarkably effective, precipitating the submission of one region after another until the process was complete.

It is unfortunate that we know so little about those aspects of Edward's reign about which we should like to know much more: for example, the operation of royal government, the condition of the church, and the king's relations with the local nobility in the various parts of his extended realm. The coinage reflects in its own way the extension of Edward's control into the southern Danelaw, though it is interesting that East Anglia appears to have been less well integrated than the east midlands, and that Lincoln appears to have retained links with York.[21] A reference in one of Edward's law-codes to the 'oath and pledge' given by 'the whole people' may allude to an oath of loyalty sworn by the people to the king; and since the code goes on to address the treatment of offences committed 'here', as distinct from their treatment 'in the east' or 'in the north',[22] it seems that the conception of Edward's kingdom had come by this stage to embrace an area exclusive only of East Anglia and Northumbria. The law-codes reveal much more about the maintenance of social order; but it is the shortage of charters issued in Edward's name which prevents us from reaching a better understanding of other internal and domestic aspects of his reign. A small number of charters survive from the first decade of the tenth century, but charters are lacking for the fifteen years from 910 to 924, when the campaign to reduce the Danes to submission was at its most intense. Unless we are to posit a dramatic upheaval in land-holding following Edward's death, attended by the loss or destruction of Edwardian title-deeds, the inference must be that relatively few charters were produced during his reign, and that latterly their production was curtailed to such an extent that they have left no trace at all. It is unlikely that the explanation was very simple. Edward may have felt constrained by the particular terms of his father's will from disposing freely of any 'royal' estates which in other circumstances should have been his to give away.[23] He would, on the other hand, have received many estates from his subjects, by bequest or by due process of law; and while he may have disposed of some of these estates by transferring existing title-deeds. into new hands, he may have kept much of the land in his own possession, granting it to others only on lease. Yet the issuing of charters was always an effective way of raising

---

[21] See Blunt *et al.* (1989), pp. 20–55 and 264–6; Smyth (1979), pp. 6–9.

[22] II Edward, c. 5, in *Gesetze der Angelsachsen* I, p. 144, trans. Attenborough, p. 121.

[23] For Alfred's will, see Sawyer, no. 1507 (*EHD*, no. 96).

substantial sums of money for a short-term advantage (at the expense of smaller but steady returns over many years), or a way of rewarding particular factions for their support (sometimes at the expense of other parties), or a way of earning the prayers of churchmen who could intercede with God; and since Edward must have needed all the money, support and prayers he could get, it would certainly appear that he was exercising considerable restraint in creating so few estates of bookland (land held by a 'book', or charter, with privileges including exemption from certain forms of taxation). Perhaps Edward felt that the creation of privileged tenures on any 'normal' scale would have an adverse effect on the preparations for the campaign against the Danes, and would threaten to compromise its execution; perhaps he had resolved to place restrictions on the creation of bookland simply as a matter of principle; or in view of the evidence indicating that Edward had ordered some men to purchase land in areas of Danish settlement, it may be that he then extended this policy by rewarding his supporters with grants of land in the territories newly conquered from the Danes, and that any charters issued in respect of such grants have not chanced to survive.[24] The scarcity of Edwardian charters is thus a matter of considerable interest in its own right; but these speculations are poor compensation for our ignorance of so much else.

Edward the Elder was succeeded by his son Æthelstan (924–39), who has long been regarded, with good reason, as a towering figure in the landscape of the tenth century. He may once have been renowned principally for his victory over a coalition of his enemies at the battle of *Brunanburh* in 937, celebrated by a famous poem in the *Anglo-Saxon Chronicle*; but he has also been hailed as the first king of England, as a statesman of international standing, and as the one Anglo-Saxon ruler who will bear comparison with King Alfred the Great. The basis for our knowledge of Æthelstan's reign is provided by a remarkable series of royal charters, complemented by a coinage of intriguing complexity and by a corpus of legal texts of unusual richness and variety. These sources, interpreted separately and in relation to each other, enable the historian to form a particularly good impression of the operation of Æthelstan's government; and one senses that it is only the lack of a contemporary biography, to do for Æthelstan what Asser had done for Alfred, that prevents us from appreciating the extent to which the king's own personality suffused the age. Further details emerge from the account of Æthelstan provided by the Anglo-Norman historian William of Malmesbury;[25] and although the precise quality of this information is open to doubt,[26] it retains its interest as a considered statement based in part on earlier written sources which do not survive and in

---

[24] See Dumville (1992), pp. 151–3.
[25] William of Malmesbury, *Gesta Regum*, II, 131–40).   [26] Lapidge (1993), pp. 50–9.

part on traditions current in the early twelfth century at the place of the king's burial.

The circumstances of King Æthelstan's accession to the throne expose the tensions which still existed within the West Saxon royal family, and help to explain what may have been distinctive about his rule. On Edward's death, the kingdom 'of the Anglo-Saxons' appears to have fractured into two of its component parts: Æthelstan 'was chosen by the Mercians as king',[27] and his half-brother Ælfweard appears to have gained recognition as king in Wessex. It is far from clear what lay behind this interesting state of affairs. Edward may or may not have intended that his kingdom should be divided after his death, and whatever his intentions had been those who survived him may or may not have been inclined to carry them out; if both Æthelstan and Ælfweard gained recognition in the immediate aftermath of their father's death, it remains uncertain whether different parties had taken it upon themselves to 'choose' a king 'of the Anglo-Saxons', or whether one party chose a king of the Mercians and the other a king of the West Saxons; and since Ælfweard lived for barely two weeks after Edward's death, it is also possible that the Mercians were simply acknowledging a second successor to Edward, who had already been 'chosen' in Wessex. The lack of charter-evidence for the years from 910 to 924 means that it is now impossible to form any impression of the composition of the king's court (or of that of the Mercian court) in the period leading up to Edward's death, and it is accordingly difficult to put the events of 924 in what might have been their appropriate political context. One can, however, gain a sense in other ways of at least some of the issues which may have been involved. Æthelstan is said to have been the offspring of an irregular liaison between Edward and a woman considered to be of low birth;[28] and there is reason to believe that he was brought up at the Mercian court of Æthelred and Æthelflæd.[29] Ælfweard, on the other hand, was the legitimate son of Edward by his wife Ælfflæd, and had presumably passed his youth in Wessex itself. It is by no means unlikely that power-brokers in Mercia would have favoured Æthelstan (who may well have taken charge of his father's Mercian interests after the death of Æthelflæd in 918), and that power-brokers in Wessex would have favoured Ælfweard; but Ælfweard soon died (and was buried in the New Minster at Winchester), whereupon Æthelstan and his supporters would have to have taken whatever steps were necessary to gain his recognition in Wessex. In a charter dated 925, which appears to have been issued at a time in that year when Æthelstan's authority was not yet recognised outside Mercia, the king is described as 'supervisor of the Christian household of the whole region

---

[27] *ASC*, Mercian Register, p. 218.

[28] Hrotsvitha of Gandersheim, *Gesta Ottonis*, trans. Hill (1972), p. 122; William of Malmesbury, *Gesta Regum*, ii, 131 and 139.   [29] William of Malmesbury, *Gesta Regum*, ii, 133.

well-nigh in the whirlpools of cataclysms',[30] perhaps an oblique reference to current political difficulties. There is some evidence that Æthelstan had encountered political resistance at Winchester in particular,[31] and it may be significant in this connection that the bishop of Winchester does not appear to have attended the king's coronation in 925 and was again conspicuously absent from the witness-lists of charters issued in 926; moreover, Æthelstan's reign was pointedly ignored in a late-tenth-century account of the history of the New Minster.[32] There may have been some residual dissension in high circles, if only to judge from the fate of the ætheling Eadwine (Ælfweard's brother) in 933,[33] and from the fact that Eadgifu (Edward's surviving queen) does not attest her step-son's charters. One should also note that when Æthelstan died (at Gloucester, in 939) he was buried not in the Edwardian mausoleum at the New Minster, but in Malmesbury abbey. Of course it is quite impossible, on the basis of such a miscellaneous set of observations, to comprehend the political manoeuvring of the mid-920s. It is conceivable, however, that Æthelstan's claim to the throne had been pressed in the first instance by his Mercian supporters, in opposition to the favoured 'West Saxon' candidate; that even after Ælfweard's death the matter had taken some time to resolve; and that even after Æthelstan's coronation some elements of dissension lingered on. Æthelstan was a member of the West Saxon dynasty; but he stands apart from what may have been the West Saxon establishment at Winchester, and should perhaps be seen as one whose political background was distinctively 'Mercian'.

To judge from the evidence of his charters, Æthelstan was regarded initially as 'king of the Anglo-Saxons',[34] in continuation of the polity established by his grandfather Alfred the Great, and perpetuated by his father Edward the Elder. It was not long, however, before this polity was overtaken by events, and replaced by a yet more grandiose perception of the king's position. In 926 Æthelstan had given his sister in marriage to Sihtric, king of the Northumbrians; and when Sihtric died, in 927, 'King Æthelstan succeeded to the kingdom of the Northumbrians'.[35] It is not clear whether Æthelstan was quick to exploit the political vacuum left by Sihtric's death, by mounting a military campaign to bring the north under subjection to his rule, or whether he 'succeeded' to the kingdom by virtue of a prior agreement;[36] but whatever the case, he was able to go from strength to strength. The chronicler who reported Æthelstan's succession to the kingdom of the Northumbrians continued, as if

---

[30] Sawyer, no. 395.   [31] William of Malmesbury, *Gesta Regum* II, 137; see also Sawyer, no. 436.

[32] *Liber Vitae*, p. 6; Keynes (1996), pp. 00–0.

[33] *ASC*, version 'E', p. 219; see also *EHD*, no. 26.   [34] Sawyer, nos. 396–7; see also no. 394.

[35] *ASC*, version 'D', p. 218.

[36] Cf. William of Malmesbury, *Gesta Regum*, II, 131 and 134.

in the same breath: 'and he brought under his rule all the kings who were in this island: first Hywel, king of the west Welsh, and Constantine, king of the Scots, and Owain, king of the people of Gwent, and Aldred, son of Eadwulf from Bamborough. And they established peace with pledge and oaths in the place which is called Eamont, on 12 July, and renounced all idolatry and afterwards departed in peace.'[37] Æthelstan thus established a polity of his own, which was to endure until the end of his reign. His charters indicate that he was regarded henceforth as *rex Anglorum* ('king of the English'), and by extension as *rex totius Britanniae* ('king of the whole of Britain'); a poem apparently composed in direct celebration of the great events of 927 alludes to *ista perfecta Saxonia* ('this England now made whole');[38] and the king was proclaimed as *rex totius Britanniae* on his coins.[39] One suspects nonetheless that many of those who fell under Æthelstan's sway would have preferred to reserve their judgement. In *Armes Prydein Vawr* ('The Great Prophecy of Britain'), a Welsh poet foretold the day when the British would rise up against their oppressors and drive them back to the sea: the Saxon 'foxes' would flee 'through ramparts of the fortress'; the stewards of the 'great king' at Cirencester would collect afflictions, not taxes; the English 'will flee straightway to Winchester'; and 'when the men of Wessex will come together in council, in a single party, of one mind with the Mercian incendiaries, hoping to bring shame on our splendid hosts', they would meet with a crushing defeat.[40] So much, in the hearts of the Welsh, for Æthelstan's 'kingdom of Britain'; but what of his 'kingdom of England'? In 937 Norsemen from the Viking kingdom of Dublin, under the leadership of Olaf Guthfrithsson, combined forces with Constantine, king of the Scots, in what was evidently a bid to re-establish the Viking kingdom of York and thereby to destroy Æthelstan's supremacy in the north. Æthelstan and his half-brother Edmund, at the head of an army which included both West Saxon and Mercian contingents, defeated the invaders at *Brunanburh*, prompting a chronicler to wax lyrical on what he perceived as the greatest victory since the distant days when the 'Angles and Saxons' had won their country.[41] There is no mistaking the reality of Æthelstan's control of southern England, or his ability to rise to a challenge; but his position in the north was far more tenuous, and there remained many conflicting interests within his kingdom which had yet to be resolved.

The profusion of evidence testifying to the operation of Æthelstan's government throughout the period from 925 to 939 stands in stark contrast to the 'Edwardian gap', creating an impression that these were the formative years of the late Anglo-Saxon state. Indeed, it is as if the monarchy had emerged

[37] *ASC*, version 'D', p. 218.   [38] See Lapidge (1993), pp. 71–81.

[39] See Blunt *et al.* (1989), pp. 55–6.

[40] *Armes Prydein: The Prophecy of Britain*, ed. Williams (1972) and Dumville (1983).

[41] *ASC*, s.a. 937, pp. 219–20.

from the vicissitudes of war, eager to reassert its peacetime role and to consolidate its power over a greatly extended realm. Our attention focuses initially on
a remarkable series of charters produced in Æthelstan's name between 928 and
935, by a scribe known to modern scholarship simply as 'Æthelstan A'.[42] There
may be relatively little to be gained from the information provided by any one
of these charters on its own (for example, that in 931 the king gave an estate of
9 hides at Ham, in Wiltshire, to his thegn Wulfgar); but their significance is
transformed when they are taken as a group. In the first place, they reveal that a
single person had responsibility for the production of all of the king's charters
during the period in question; and since it would appear that charters had been
produced hitherto in a variety of different circumstances (in some cases by
royal priests, and in other cases by members of religious houses operating in
the king's name on behalf of the beneficiaries), it seems that King Æthelstan
had taken an unprecedented degree of control over what had become a most
important aspect of royal activity. Secondly, the charters conform to a pattern
which is of considerable literary interest in its own right: they are composed in
a highly elaborate style, reflecting well on the intellectual attainments of the
scribe himself and throwing light on the cultural milieu of the king's court; and
they follow a regular development in terms of their structure and formulation,
of a kind which suggests that the scribe took considerable care and even pride
in their production. Thirdly, they incorporate distinctively precise information
on the date and place of the meetings at which the charters were issued,
making it possible to trace the movements of the king and his councillors
around the kingdom. And fourthly, they are furnished with lists of witnesses
remarkable not only for their length but also for their unusual scope (including
'subkings' from Wales and elsewhere, bishops of sees unknown, abbots, and
earls from the 'Scandinavian' parts of England). It can be no coincidence that
the charters of 'Æthelstan A' make their appearance in the first years of
Æthelstan's rule as 'king of the English' and as 'king of the whole of Britain'.
They must be seen, first and foremost, as the work of an individual scribe; but
they are symbolic of a monarchy invigorated by success, developing the pretensions commensurate with its actual achievements and clothing itself in the
trappings of a new political order. One would like to know more of 'Æthelstan
A' himself, because he clearly deserves recognition as a figure of singular
importance at King Æthelstan's court. He seems to have retired from his duties
during the course of 935; and while his successors in the royal writing-office
soon established standards of their own in the form of royal charters, they
were less flamboyant than their predecessor, and seem to have been more
inclined to take King Æthelstan's achievement for granted.

---

[42] For an example of one of these charters, see *EHD*, no. 104, pp. 548–51.

Without any doubt the most impressive aspect of King Æthelstan's government is the vitality of his law-making.[43] Kings had long been bound, by ideology and custom as well as by the specific terms of their coronation oath, to
exercise their power in the interests of peace, prosperity and the common
good; and it is by a king's laws, above all else, that we are able to judge his success
in the fulfilment of his appointed role. The law-code promulgated by King
Alfred the Great remained in force throughout the tenth century, suggesting
that Alfred's successors were conscious of its cardinal importance in the establishment of social order; yet while the surviving acts of legislation which run in
the names of tenth-century kings developed from the Alfredian foundation,
they were also complementary to a body of unwritten and customary law. It is
always difficult, therefore, to ascertain when a particular provision was first
introduced, because it is possible that the subject had been covered in a code
which has not chanced to survive, or that its first attested appearance represented the explicit statement of a practice or procedure which had previously
been taken for granted; equally, it is dangerous to assume that a provision when
first introduced was necessarily observed thereafter, or that it would prove any
more effective by constant repetition. Under these circumstances, it would be
hazardous to fasten on any particular aspect of King Æthelstan's legislation as
indicative of the special quality of his rule. The significance of his law-making
lies more in the demonstration which it affords of the principle that a king
should be *seen* to govern. Æthelstan's legislation shows among other things how
the king drove his officials to do their respective duties, and how uncompromising he could be in his insistence on respect for the law; it also reveals the persistent difficulties which confronted the king and his councillors in bringing a
troublesome people under some form of control. One might add that King
Æthelstan's coinage conveys the same impression of the invigorated application of established practices: his concern was to regulate rather than to reform,
and the significance of the coinage lies in its capacity (under expert analysis) to
expose the local variations which nonetheless endured.[44]

Æthelstan was evidently perceived by his contemporaries to have established himself in a position which none of his predecessors had enjoyed, and
for that reason alone his claim to be 'king of the English' must command our
respect; but it is important to bear in mind that the process which we recognise
in retrospect as the making of England still had some way to go. Indeed, it
may be said that the crucial developments took place in the twenty years which
followed King Æthelstan's death in 939, and that it was only when the dust had

---

[43] Æthelstan's laws are in *Die Gesetze der Angelsachsen*, ed. Liebermann I, pp. 146–83, and ed. and trans.
Attenborough, *The Laws of the Earliest English Kings*, pp. 122–69; see also *EHD*, nos. 35–7, pp. 417–27,
and Keynes (1990), pp. 235–41.

[44] See Blunt (1974), and Blunt *et al.* (1989), pp. 108–13 and 266–8.

settled from the political ructions of this period that the unified kingdom of England began to assume its familiar shape. The major political problem for Edmund (939–46) and Eadred (946–55) remained the difficulty of subjugating the north. The Hiberno-Norse rulers of Dublin still coveted their interests in the Viking kingdom of York; terms had to be made with the Scots, who had the capacity not merely to interfere in Northumbrian affairs but also to block a line of communication between Dublin and York; and the inhabitants of northern Northumbria were doubtless a law unto themselves. It must be emphasised, however, that the matter depended largely on the changing attitude of those with power and influence in York itself. It was for them to make and break their political allegiances, in accordance with their own estimation of where their best interests lay. Anglo-Danish York had become a thriving centre of trade, and commercial considerations must have loomed large in the determination of the city's future. Wulfstan, archbishop of York from 931 to 956, must also have played a crucial, if largely unknown, role in the politics of the north; for to judge from the several references to him in the 'northern recension' of the *Anglo-Saxon Chronicle*, and to judge from the curious pattern of his attestations in the charters of Æthelstan, Edmund and Eadred, he pursued a line which left him sometimes in and sometimes out of favour with the royal court.

Events unfolded with a bewildering speed, though many people in the north were probably untouched by the shifting of loyalties which took place above their heads. The men of York took the opportunity presented by Æthelstan's death to choose Olaf Guthfrithsson as their king; whereupon Olaf seized his own opportunity to strike south into the east midlands, leading to the establishment of a frontier at Watling Street.[45] When Olaf died (in 941), it was Edmund's turn to take the initiative, and he soon managed to redeem the 'Five Boroughs' (Lincoln, Leicester, Nottingham, Stamford and Derby) from Norse control. In 943 Edmund stood sponsor to Olaf Sihtricsson at baptism and to Ragnald Guthfrithsson at confirmation, seeking in this way initially to extend his influence over those who now held power in York; but in 944 these kings were driven out, and Edmund 'reduced all Northumbria under his rule'.[46] In 945 Edmund sought to protect his position by granting all Cumberland to Malcolm, king of the Scots, 'on condition that he should be his ally both on sea and on land'.[47] When Edmund died (in May 946), his brother Eadred immediately went north and 'reduced all Northumbria under his rule';[48] but in 947 the

---

[45] See the northern annals in *EHD*, no. 3, p. 279.

[46] According to the *ASC*, p. 222, the kings were expelled by Edmund; but according to Æthelweard, *Chronicon* IV, 6, they were expelled by 'Bishop Wulfstan and the ealdorman of the Mercians' (?Æthelstan Half-King).   [47] *ASC*, p. 222.

[48] Sawyer, no. 520 (*EHD*, no. 105, pp. 551–2) reveals that this was accomplished before the king's coronation.

Northumbrians took Eirik Bloodaxe (the exiled son of Harald Fairhair, king of Norway) as their king, prompting Eadred to ravage Northumbria in 948 (and at the same time to make a new agreement with the Scots). Even so, the Northumbrians soon re-established their independence, initially under Olaf Sihtricsson (950–2) and latterly under Eirik Bloodaxe (952–4); but finally they drove out Eirik, and submitted to Eadred again, apparently of their own volition. It is as if the men of York had been playing the field, and eventually decided in the interests of their own peace and prosperity to throw in their lot with the English king.

It is hardly surprising, under these circumstances, that the draftsmen of charters and the designers of coins seem to have exercised a certain degree of restraint when choosing how to describe Edmund and Eadred, at least in comparison to the practices which had prevailed during the reign of King Æthelstan. Gone, for the time being, were the heady days of the 'king of the whole of Britain', though both kings were styled 'king of the English' even at times when their rule did not extend over Northumbria, as if they had never been prepared to relinquish their claim to the north. More instructive, however, are the royal styles employed by the draftsman of the distinctive series of 'alliterative' charters produced in the 940s and 950s.[49] Edmund was 'king of the Anglo-Saxons' (in 940 and 942); and Eadred was 'king of the Anglo-Saxons, Northumbrians, pagans, and Britons' (at various points throughout his reign). It would be dangerous, of course, to press such evidence too far; but it is interesting nonetheless to be reminded that in the eyes of at least one observer the whole was no greater than the sum of its component parts.

The question remains whether the political base in southern England was itself both stable and secure. Examination of the charters issued by King Æthelstan in the 930s, and by Edmund and Eadred in the 940s, suggests that there was a considerable degree of continuity at various levels of royal government, reflecting a smooth transition from one reign to another. It is unfortunate, however, that it is so difficult on the basis of the available evidence to get much impression of the currents which lie beneath the surface of recorded events. The unfolding pattern of attestations in the charters of the 930s and 940s shows who among the bishops, ealdormen and thegns may have been the more significant figures in the domestic affairs of the day, and we can guess that they played their respective roles in a complex story; but since it is impossible to identify the competing interests and to separate the different factions, the plot itself lies beyond our reach. We can imagine what may have been involved: bishops pressing for the resources necessary to improve the fortunes of their

[49] For these charters, see Hart (1992), pp. 431–44.

respective churches, and seeking support from the secular powers;[50] members of the secular nobility sating their appetite for land and office, forming personal alliances with and against each other;[51] the king doubtless concerned to bring a violent and unruly society to order,[52] though fully immersed himself in all the rivalries and jealousies at court.[53] The plot would have thickened as new factors and personalities came into play: Abbot Dunstan, for example, was established at Glastonbury by King Edmund, and enjoyed special favour from King Eadred;[54] and Æthelstan 'Half-King', who had been appointed an ealdorman by King Æthelstan in 932, assumed an increasingly dominant position in the secular hierarchy.[55] It might be supposed from a reading of the *Anglo-Saxon Chronicle* that Edmund and Eadred were preoccupied throughout the 940s with the subjugation of the north; but although we cannot articulate the course of domestic affairs during the same period, there could be little doubt that they would prove to have been of no less significance.

Matters appear to have come to a head in the 950s. It is known that King Eadred suffered from a serious illness throughout his reign,[56] and it is possible that he was incapacitated by it for some years before his death in November 955. It may or may not be significant in this connection that no law-codes issued in Eadred's name have survived; but there is certainly good reason to believe that royal government was affected in some way by peculiar conditions obtaining in the last four or five years of Eadred's reign. The production of charters by scribes of the royal secretariat, which had lent an impression of such great cohesion to the period from the late 920s to the late 940s, was all but suspended; and although charters were produced in the king's name in the early 950s, they are fewer in number and strikingly different in appearance. Some belong to the distinctive group of 'alliterative' charters, examples of which had been produced from time to time since the early 940s, by an agency perhaps to be associated with the bishop of Worcester;[57] others belong to a no less distinctive group apparently associated with Glastonbury and characterised by (among other features) the absence of the king from the list of witnesses.[58] Eadred is well known to have preferred Abbot Dunstan above all his men, and to have entrusted him with 'all the best of his goods, namely many title-deeds and also the ancient treasures of preceding kings, as well as various precious

---

[50] Cf. I Edmund, ch. 5. See also Dumville (1992), pp. 173–84.

[51] For instructive sudies of tenth-century ealdormen and their families, see Hart (1992), pp. 569–604, and Williams (1982); see also Fleming (1991), pp. 22–39.

[52] Cf. II Edmund, and III Edmund, ch. 1.

[53] Cf. *Vita S. Dunstani*, c. 13 (ed. Stubbs, pp. 21–3; trans. *EHD*, no. 234, pp. 898–9).

[54] For a survey of Dunstan's career, see Brooks (1992).

[55] For Æthelstan 'Half-King', see Hart (1992), pp. 574–85.

[56] *Vita S. Dunstani*, c. 20 (ed. Stubbs, p. 31).

[57] Hart (1992), pp. 431–44.   [58] Keynes (1994).

things he had acquired himself, to be faithfully kept in the security of his monastery';[59] and it is difficult, therefore, to resist the supposition that the king had also entrusted Dunstan with powers which extended to the production of charters in his absence. King Eadred made provisions in his will which reflect in a no less interesting way on his priorities towards the end of his life.[60] He bequeathed 'to the place where he wishes his body to rest two gold crosses and two gold-hilted swords, and 400 pounds'; three estates were to pass to the Old Minster at Winchester, three to the New Minster, and three to the Nuns' Minster; and 30 pounds were to be given to each of the nunneries most closely associated with the royal family (the Nuns' Minster, Wilton, and Shaftesbury). Eadred then made elaborate arrangements for the distribution of a further 1600 pounds, to be used on behalf of his people so that 'they may redeem themselves from famine and from a heathen army if they need'; in addition, an amount of gold was to be taken sufficient for minting into 2000 mancuses (the equivalent of about 250 pounds), to be distributed throughout the bishoprics. Eadred's mother, Eadgifu, was to receive three specified estates in Wiltshire, Berkshire and Hampshire, 'and all the booklands which I have in Sussex and Surrey and Kent, and all those which she held before'; and relatively small sums of money were to be disbursed to the archbishop, bishops and ealdormen, and to the various officials of the royal household. Finally, the king stipulated that twelve almsmen from each of the estates were to be supported for ever thereafter; 'and if anyone will not do this, the land is then to go to the place where my body shall rest'. Of course it is difficult to judge the significance of Eadred's will in our ignorance of whatever provisions may have been made in the wills of other tenth-century kings. The land to be given to the three minsters at Winchester seems in itself to have amounted to a substantial bequest; but it is more remarkable, perhaps, that Eadred should have made such generous provision for his mother, in the sense that it would place in the hands of another party a quantity of estates which a successor might wish to keep at his own disposal. It is also worth noting that the penalty clause at the end of the will distinguishes implicitly between the intended recipients of land and the place where he wished to be buried, suggesting that Eadred expected to lie at a place other than Winchester; if so, either Glastonbury itself (where his brother Edmund was buried) or Abingdon (where he had taken special interest in the building works)[61] would be the obvious choice, and thus the prospective recipient of the opening gift. And while the arrangements for setting aside large sums of money for good purposes must have proceeded from the best of intentions on Eadred's part, one does wonder whether the gesture might have

---

[59] *Vita S. Dunstani*, c. 19 (ed. Stubbs, p. 29; trans. *EHD*, no. 234, p. 900).
[60] See Sawyer, no. 1515 (*EHD*, no. 107, pp. 555–6).
[61] Wulfstan of Winchester, *Vita S. Æthelwoldi*, c. 12.

been regarded by others as a rather extravagent indulgence. In short, Eadred's will could be interpreted as a highly charged document, reflecting in a most interesting way on his own preferences but perhaps not likely to meet with the complete approval of those left in power on his death.

When Eadred died, on 23 November 955, the throne passed from the last of the sons of Edward the Elder to the first of a new generation. Eadwig (955–9) was the elder son of King Edmund. According to the chronicler Æthelweard (his kinsman), Eadwig 'for his great beauty got the nick-name "All-Fair" from the common people. He held the kingdom continuously for four years, and deserved to be loved.'[62] Be that as it may, Eadwig has gained a reputation as one unfitted to the responsibilities of his high office, who lost control of the affairs of his kingdom and forfeited the support of many of his people, receiving his come-uppance in 957 when the Mercians rebelled against his authority and set up his younger brother Edgar in opposition to him, and whose timely death in 959 enabled Edgar to succeed to a reunited kingdom of all England. The reputation proceeds from the portrait of Eadwig presented in the late tenth-century Life of St Dunstan,[63] and is given substance by the quite exceptionally large number of charters issued by Eadwig in 956; but while the legend may have some basis in truth, the closer we look the clearer it becomes that the events of Eadwig's reign had more complex dimensions. Ealdorman Æthelstan 'Half-King' remained the dominant secular figure at the royal court, and must have had a significant part to play from the outset of the new reign; and since there is reason to believe that he had been made responsible for the upbringing of the young Edgar, it may have been Edgar's interests that he was most concerned to protect. Initially, King Eadwig himself seems to have been determined to assert his own independence, breaking free from the influence of those who were closest to his late uncle. The fact that Eadred was buried at the Old Minster, Winchester, may itself be symbolic of a reaction in certain quarters against the late king's wishes, if he had actually expected to be buried elsewhere.[64] Indeed, it is conceivable that Eadred's will was largely ignored, for not even the minsters at Winchester appear to have been able to gain full possession of the lands he had bequeathed to them,[65] and Eadred's mother Eadgifu is known to have been deprived of her property soon after Eadwig's accession.[66] But the main target of Eadwig's reaction against his uncle's regime was probably Dunstan himself. There must be some truth behind the lurid

---

[62] Æthelweard, Chronicon IV, 8.

[63] For the Vita S. Dunstani (ed. Stubbs, pp. 3–52; extracts trans. EHD, no. 234, pp. 897–903), see Lapidge (1993), pp. 279–91.

[64] Eadred was later remembered as 'a particular friend and champion of the Old Minster at Winchester': see Wulfstan of Winchester, Vita S. Æthelwoldi, c. 10.   [65] See Sawyer (1983), p. 280.

[66] See Sawyer, no. 1211; see also Vita S. Dunstani, c. 24 (ed. Stubbs, p. 36; trans. EHD, no. 234, p. 902).

story in the Life of St Dunstan, to the effect that the abbot incurred Eadwig's wrath when he interfered with the king's pleasures on the occasion of his coronation; and although we may suspect that the whole truth was more complex, the event led directly to the confiscation of Dunstan's goods and to his enforced exile.[67] Further understanding of Eadwig's activities emerges from analysis of his numerous charters. It might be assumed that he was appropriating land from churches on an unprecedented scale, or that he was dissipating the resources of the monarchy in an irresponsible manner; but in fact it would appear that much of the land which changed hands in Eadwig's reign had been confiscated (by fair means or foul) from men who had prospered during the reigns of his predecessors, and that the king was redistributing this land among men who had managed to remain in favour, or among new favourites of his own.[68] Of course there must have been other factors behind the extraordinary events of 956. It may be, for example, that the king was simply too young to control the competing factions among his aristocracy, and found himself unable to resist pressure to favour one party at the expense of another; whatever the case, the evidence amounts to a social and political upheaval in the heartland of Eadwig's kingdom, which can hardly reflect well on the quality of his rule.

In 957 'the ætheling Edgar succeeded to the kingdom of the Mercians'.[69] This momentous event, recorded in such bland terms by the *Anglo-Saxon Chronicle*, was represented by the author of the Life of St Dunstan as the outcome of a rebellion against King Eadwig 'by the northern people', involving a division of the kingdom along the line of the river Thames;[70] and as the story was retold, it was cast increasingly in terms appropriate to civil war.[71] The reality of the division of the kingdom is not in doubt: it is mentioned incidentally in other sources;[72] charters of Eadwig issued in 957 can be shown on the basis of their witness-lists to have been produced before or after the division; and both Eadwig and Edgar issued charters for estates in their respective kingdoms in 958–9. Perhaps one should not be surprised to find that bishops whose dioceses lay to the south of the Thames stayed with Eadwig, and that bishops whose dioceses lay to the north transferred to Edgar's court; nor is it

---

[67] *Vita S. Dunstani*, cc. 21–3 (ed. Stubbs, pp. 32–5; c. 23 trans. *EHD*, no. 234, pp. 900–1); see also Brooks (1992), pp. 14–18.　　[68] Cf. *Vita S. Dunstani*, c. 24 (ed. Stubbs, p. 36; trans. *EHD*, no. 234, pp. 901–2).

[69] *ASC*, versions 'B' and 'C', p. 225. For discussion of the division of the kingdom, see Stenton (1971), pp. 366–7; Yorke (1988), pp. 75–9; Stafford (1989), pp. 47–50; Hart (1992), pp. 582–5; Brooks (1992), pp. 18–20.

[70] *Vita S. Dunstani*, c. 24 (ed. Stubbs, pp. 35–6; trans. *EHD*, no. 234, p. 901).

[71] See, e.g., *Memorials of Saint Dunstan*, pp. 102 (Osbern), 194 (Eadmer) and 291 (William of Malmesbury).

[72] Sawyer, no. 1447 (ed. and trans. *Anglo-Saxon Charters*, no. 44, pp. 90–3); and Bishop Æthelwold's account of the establishment of monasteries (*EHD*, no. 238, p. 920).

necessarily remarkable that ealdormen remained with Eadwig if they held office in the south, and went over to Edgar if their responsibilities lay in the north. Yet it is precisely because the division of the kingdom is reflected so neatly in the witness-lists that one is led to suspect that it was the outcome not of a rebellion against King Eadwig but of a political settlement amicably agreed by all the parties concerned. The two courts separated on a purely territorial basis in 957, and were combined again when the kingdoms were reunited in 959, as if questions of conflicting loyalties had not been involved. But under what circumstances and under what conditions was the division of the kingdom arranged? One need not imagine that the unity of England would have been regarded in the 950s as something necessarily desirable for its own sake, not least because it was of such recent creation. It is possible that a division had been contemplated in Eadred's reign, to be implemented after his death, and that it had been put aside in 955 perhaps because Edgar was considered too young to assume his share of the responsibilities; it is also possible that Edgar had been brought up in the expectation of succeeding his elder brother, but that circumstances soon recommended or demanded an element of power-sharing. One important factor may have been the position of Ealdorman Æthelstan 'Half-King', for it seems significant that he gave up his office (and retired to Glastonbury) at the same time as the division was arranged:[73] he may have stepped down when Edgar was ready to take over, or perhaps Edgar took over when he wished to step down. The several charters issued in Edgar's name as king of the Mercians suggest that he enjoyed complete freedom of action within his own domains. One, dated 958 and still extant in its original form, is attested by Edgar as 'king of the Mercians and of the Northumbrians and of the Britons',[74] suggesting that he had succeeded, in effect, to a major part of the composite whole. Three other charters, also issued in 958, belong to the group which appears to have been associated in some way with Dunstan at Glastonbury;[75] all three are attested by Dunstan, as bishop, and lack the attestation of the king himself, raising interesting questions about the possible circumstances of their production. Yet it is important to note that Edgar did not issue a separate coinage in 957–9, and that during these years moneyers serving 'Mercian' mints continued to strike coins in Eadwig's name;[76] for this may indicate that Edgar, like Ealdorman Æthelred and Æthelflæd before him, was prevented under the terms of the agreement from issuing and profiting from a coinage of his own. One should add that while the draftsman of Eadwig's charters exercised a certain degree of restraint, after the

---

[73] This statement depends on detailed analysis of the charters of 956–7; cf. Hart (1992), p. 584.

[74] Sawyer, no. 677 (*EHD*, no. 109, pp. 557–9).

[75] Sawyer, no. 676 and 678; for the third, see Keynes (1994), p. 166.

[76] See Blunt *et al.* (1989), pp. 146–56, 272–3 and 278–80.

division of the kingdom, in their choice of royal styles, they persisted in calling him 'king of the English'. It is conceivable, in other words, that Eadwig remained king of a notionally unified kingdom throughout his reign, and that Edgar was assigned his apparently subordinate role when the opportunity arose. Political arrangements in the mid-tenth century could still be adapted to suit the changing circumstances.

Eadwig 'the All-Fair' died on 1 October 959, whereupon Edgar 'succeeded to the kingdom both in Wessex and in Mercia and in Northumbria, and he was then 16 years old'.[77] In any appraisal of the reign of King Edgar (959–75) there is a temptation at once to dwell on the impetus he gave to the cause of monastic reform. Initially, the king's patronage of the monastic party found expression in the favour he showed towards Abingdon abbey in particular, under the rule of his mentor, Abbot Æthelwold;[78] it was extended thereafter by his backing of the expulsion of priests from the minsters at Winchester and elsewhere in 964;[79] and it is symbolised by the sumptuous charter of privileges granted to the New Minster in 966.[80] The effects of the policy are reflected in the steady increase, from the mid-960s, in the number of abbots who attest the king's charters;[81] and latterly the king reaped his reward, in the honour accorded to him in the *Regularis concordia* as one who had always given his encouragement and active support to the monks and who had been instrumental in summoning the synodal council at Winchester to coordinate their efforts.[82] It comes as no surprise that Edgar won extravagent praise from those who were among the direct or indirect beneficiaries of his policy, including Æthelwold himself,[83] Lantfred of Winchester,[84] Wulfstan of Winchester,[85] Ælfric,[86] and Byrhtferth of Ramsey.[87] One wishes nonetheless that it were possible to set the views of the monastic party beside the views of those who were no less directly affected by Edgar's activities as king, though in different ways.

---

[77] *ASC,* version 'B', 'C', p. 225.

[78] See Æthelwold's account of King Edgar's establishment of monasteries (*EHD*, no. 238, p. 921), and Sawyer, no. 937 (*EHD*, no. 123, p. 583); see also Thacker (1988), pp. 52–4. For Æthelwold as Edgar's mentor, see Wulfstan of Winchester, *Vita S. Æthelwoldi*, c. 25, and Byrhtferth of Ramsey, *Vita S. Oswaldi*, p. 427); see also *Regularis concordia*, c. 1.

[79] *ASC,* version 'A', p. 226; and Wulfstan of Winchester, *Vita S. Æthelwoldi*, cc. 18 and 20.

[80] Sawyer, no. 745.

[81] Byrhtferth of Ramsey (*Vita S. Oswaldi*, pp. 425–7) describes the holding of an Easter council at which King Edgar ordered the foundation of more than forty monasteries; but this was perhaps a rationalisation, in retrospect, of the king's promotion of the monastic cause.

[82] *Regularis concordia*, esp cc. 1–12 and 69.

[83] Æthelwold's account of King Edgar's establishment of monasteries (*EHD*, no. 238, pp. 920–3).

[84] *Translatio et miracula S Swithuno*, Preface (ed. and trans. Lapidge (forthcoming)).

[85] *Vita S. Æthelwoldi*, c. 13; and Wulfstan Cantor, *Narratio metrica de S. Swithuno* 11, lines 440–65 (ed. Campbell, pp. 154–5; trans. Whitelock (1981), p. 84).

[86] *EHD*, no. 239 (g) and (i), pp. 927–8. [87] *Vita S. Oswaldi*, p. 425.

Edgar is said, for example, to have 'loved evil foreign customs and brought too firmly heathen manners within this land, and attracted hither foreigners and enticed harmful people to this country';[88] though it is far from clear what lies behind this complaint. More particularly, Edgar appears to have succeeded where to some extent his predecessors had failed in the suppression of wrong-doing and in the maintenance of social order. His reign, indeed, was renowned for its 'peace'; but by what means was this peace achieved?

A general impression of Edgar's government can be gained from the evidence of his charters and law-codes. When Edgar became king of all England in 959 he retained the services of at least one of the scribes who appear to have worked for him as king of the Mercians; the scribe in question, known to modern scholarship as 'Edgar A', was entrusted with responsibility for the production of the majority of the king's charters in the early 960s, establishing practices which set the pattern for the rest of Edgar's reign. The charters of the 960s and early 970s are thus remarkably uniform in their structure and content, and do not in themselves convey much sense of political development or change. It is worth noting, however, that from the late 960s the northern provinces came to be represented on a regular basis among the attestations of the ealdormen, most notably in the person of Oslac; and that in the early 970s the secular hierarchy as a whole came to be dominated by four great men, namely Ælfhere of Mercia, Æthelwine of East Anglia, Oslac of Northumbria and Byrhtnoth of Essex. One would like to know more about the standing of these men in relation to the king, and about their role in the government of the constituent parts of the kingdom; but one would also like to know more about the role of thegns and reeves in relation to local administration throughout the country, and about the particular arrangements which obtained in the heartland of Wessex itself. King Edgar's legislation is instructive in a different way. As we have seen, the extant tenth-century codes, whilst never approaching Alfred's in grandeur or scope, afford a good indication of the particular aspects of the law which were of current concern to a king and his councillors, and which needed restatement, modification or reform. In the case of King Edgar, the emphasis appears to have been more on the administration than on the substance of the law, as if his primary concern was to ensure the efficient operation of procedures which may not have been new in themselves, but which had not perhaps been properly observed in the past. For example, every man was to provide himself with a surety, who would hold him to every legal duty; hundred courts, borough courts and shire courts were to be convened on a regular basis; all transactions were to take place in the presence of appointed

---

[88] *ASC*, version 'D', *s.a.* 959 (*EHD*, no. 1, p. 225), written in the style of Wulfstan, archbishop of York 1002–23.

witnesses; and delinquents were to be relentlessly pursued.[89] Yet when Edgar insists on the enforcement of those provisions 'which I and my councillors have added to the decrees of my ancestors, for the benefit of all the nation',[90] one begins to suspect that there was rather more to his law-making than meets the eye in the extant codes. Lantfred of Winchester (writing in the 970s) credited King Edgar with the introduction of 'a law of great severity', whereby convicted felons were to be blinded, mutilated and scalped, and their bodies thrown out to wild beasts and birds.[91] It was perhaps for good reason that Edgar was hailed as 'the strongest of all kings over the English nation',[92] who suppressed evil-doers everywhere, and subdued tyrants;[93] but should we be disposed to admire the great 'peace' which Edgar brought to his people, perhaps we should bear in mind at the same time that it depended in some measure on the enforcement of laws of such a kind.

By the early 970s, after a decade of Edgar's 'peace', it must have seemed that the kingdom of England was indeed made whole, and that its unity was something to be respected and secured. In his formal address to the gathering at Winchester which led to the production of the *Regularis concordia*, the king urged his bishops, abbots and abbesses 'to be of one mind as regards monastic usage . . . lest differing ways of observing the customs of one Rule and one country should bring their holy conversation into disrepute'.[94] A similar desire to advance from diversity by the imposition of uniformity appears to underlie King Edgar's great reform of the coinage, *c.* 973; certainly, there could be no better illustration of the capacity of Edgar's government to achieve its purpose, for as a result of the reform the coinage was standardised in such a way that coins of one and the same type were produced by mints throughout the country. It is as if the kingdom was being remade in a new mould; and the same could be said of the king himself. He had presumably been anointed and crowned soon after his accession in 959; but on 11 May (Whitsunday) 973, in a service conducted in the Roman city of Bath, Edgar was consecrated for what would appear to have been a second time, and immediately afterwards took his naval force to Chester, where he received the submission of a number of Welsh and Scottish rulers.[95] The events represented the reaffirmation, in religious ceremony, of Edgar's divinely appointed role as a Christian king, and the celebration, in public display, of his supre-

[89] For Edgar's legislation, see *EHD*, nos. 40–1, pp. 431–7; see also no. 39, pp. 429–30.
[90] IV Edgar ch 2.1a (*EHD*, no. 41, p. 435).
[91] *Translatio et miracula S. Swithuni*, ch. 26 (ed. and trans. Lapidge (forthcoming)); see also Wulfstan Cantor, *Narratio metrica de S. Swithuno* II, lines 440–65 (ed. Campbell, pp. 154–5; trans. Whitelock, 'Wulfstan Cantor and Anglo-Saxon Law', p. 84).   [92] Ælfric, in *EHD*, no. 239 (i), p. 928.
[93] See *Vita S. Dunstani*, c. 25, pp. 36–7; trans. *EHD*, no. 234, p. 902; see also *Vita S. Oswaldi*, p. 425.
[94] *Regularis concordia* c. 4.
[95] *ASC*, pp. 227–8; Ælfric, in *EHD*, no. 239 (g), p. 927. See also Nelson (1986), pp. 296–303.

macy throughout Britain. Edgar was only twenty-nine years old, and at the zenith of his power.

It is a sign of Edgar's 'strength' as a ruler that when he died, on 8 July 975, the 'peace' of his kingdom was immediately disturbed. The succession was disputed between his surviving sons Edward and Æthelred (born of different mothers), and in the event it was the supporters of Edward who prevailed; but while it is significant that there appears no longer to have been any thought of dividing the kingdom, the dispute itself undermined the stability of government, exposing tensions which had previously been kept under control. We know most about the disorders during the reign of Edward the Martyr (975–8) in so far as they affected the interests of the reformed monasteries, and for that reason they are often characterised as an 'anti-monastic reaction'. It must be emphasised, however, that the disorders proceeded from a variety of local circumstances, and found expression in a number of different ways. Earl Oslac of Northumbria, described by one chronicler as 'a grey-haired man, wise and skilled in speech', was driven into exile,[96] perhaps the victim of a reaction against the part he had played in Edgar's regime. In Mercia, Ealdorman Ælfhere began to oppress some of the monasteries which had been founded during Edgar's reign, if only because he had the power and could not now resist the opportunity to seize their estates for himself and his friends; but when the disturbances threatened to spread eastwards, a certain Ælfwold, his brother Ealdorman Æthelwine and Ealdorman Byrhtnoth are said to have taken a firm stand in defence of the monks.[97] At Abingdon, estates which properly belonged to kings' sons and which had been given to the abbey by King Edgar were forcibly withdrawn by the councillors, and reallocated to the ætheling Æthelred;[98] while at Rochester, a certain widow and her kinsman applied after Edgar's death to 'Ealdorman Eadwine and the section of the public (folc) which was the adversary of God', and compelled the bishop to give up the title-deeds to a disputed estate.[99] The evidence from Ely abbey in Cambridgeshire is of special interest, because it reveals in unusual detail how Bishop Æthelwold and Abbot Byrhtnoth had set about the task of accumulating land for the abbey from the local nobility in the early 970s, and how people had then taken advantage of the disorder precipitated by King Edgar's death to renege in one way or another on previous agreements, in an attempt to recover their money or their land.[100] The case of Ely illustrates, in other words, the conflict of interests generated within a local society by the establishment of a major monastery in its midst, and exemplifies what could happen when the

---

[96] ASC, p. 229.

[97] ASC, p. 229, and Byrhtferth, Vita S. Oswaldi, pp. 443–6, trans. EHD, no. 236, pp. 912–14. See also Williams (1982), pp. 159–70.   [98] Sawyer, no. 937 (EHD, no. 123, p. 583).

[99] Sawyer, no. 1457 (Anglo-Saxon Charters, no. 59, pp. 122–5).   [100] See Liber Eliensis, pp. 72–117.

pressure was released. Yet the case is only unique in so far as the evidence from Ely is good enough to bring the local society to life: Glastonbury and Abingdon may have experienced something similar in the mid-950s, and many houses must have shared Ely's experience in the mid-970s. In general terms, the disturbances of Edward's reign should be regarded as a manifestation of the kind of social and political disorder which might be expected to attend the unexpected removal of one who was seen as the personification of an overbearing regime. Of Edward himself nothing of any substance is known. He was murdered at the gap of Corfe in Dorset on 18 March 978, by some 'zealous thegns' of his younger brother;[101] his body, initially abandoned in a secret place, was miraculously 'discovered' in February 979, whereupon it was taken to Wareham and then borne with great honour to Shaftesbury.

The reign of King Æthelred the Unready (978–1016) witnessed the resumption of Viking raids on England, putting the country and its leadership under strains as severe as they were long sustained. The raids began on a relatively small scale in the 980s, became far more serious in the 990s, and brought the people to their knees in 1009–12, when a large part of the country was devastated by the army of Thorkell the Tall. It remained for Swein Forkbeard, king of Denmark, to conquer the kingdom of England in 1013–14, and (after Æthelred's restoration) for his son Cnut to achieve the same in 1015–16. The sorry tale of these years incorporated in the *Anglo-Saxon Chronicle* must be read in its own right,[102] and set beside other material which reflects in one way or another on the conduct of government and warfare during Æthelred's reign.[103] It is this evidence which provides the basis for the indictment of the king as one who lacked the strength, judgement and resolve to give adequate leadership to his people in a time of grave national crisis; who soon found out that he could rely on little but the treachery of his military commanders; and who throughout his reign tasted nothing but the ignominy of defeat. Any attempt to escape from the pervasive influence of the received tradition is bound to be perceived as an exercise in special pleading. One could argue, for example, that the account of Æthelred's reign in the *Anglo-Saxon Chronicle* represents the view of a man writing in the immediate aftermath of the Danish conquest, whose purpose was to trace the events which led ultimately to defeat; and it might be supposed, therefore, that his account is not necessarily representative of the whole truth. Yet the more excuses which have to be made, the less convincing the exercise becomes. Perhaps the reign of Æthelred was, after all, a simple

---

[101] See *ASC*, pp. 230–1, and *Vita S. Oswaldi*, pp. 448–51, trans. *EHD*, no. 236, pp. 914–16. See also Ridyard (1988), pp. 154–75.   [102] *ASC*, pp. 230–51.

[103] See, e.g., *EHD*, no. 10 (the poem on the battle of Maldon), nos. 42–6 (law-codes), nos. 117–29 (charters, etc.), nos. 230–1 (letters), and no. 240 (Archbishop Wulfstan's *Sermo ad Anglos*). See also Hill (1978), Scragg (1991) and Cooper (1993).

story of a king unequal to the challenges which confronted him, and is best left at that. If we learn anything, however, from the history of England in the tenth century it is that events unfolded in ways which can scarcely be reduced to such simplistic terms. We may be impressed by the fact that King Alfred the Great and his successors had created a unified kingdom of all England, and had at the same time developed the means to govern their realm and to impose order on their people. We may also be impressed by the piety and good intentions of certain kings, and by their will to create conditions in which religious houses would prosper and learning would flourish. But when we reach the reign of King Æthelred, our attention is diverted from such uplifting matters to the Viking raids, and we are brought back with a bump to the grim realities of life in Anglo-Saxon England. It is obvious enough that the raids exposed tensions and weaknesses which went deep into the fabric of the late Anglo-Saxon state; and it is apparent that events proceeded against a background more complex than the chronicler himself was concerned to reveal. It seems, for example, that the death of Bishop Æthelwold in 984 had precipitated further reaction against certain ecclesiastical interests; that by 993 the king had come to regret the error of his ways, leading to a period when in some respects the internal affairs of the kingdom appear to have prospered; that in 1006 there were significant developments at court which brought another party of councillors to the fore; that during the disturbances caused by the activities of Thorkell's army, in 1009–12, Eadric Streona, ealdorman of Mercia, managed to establish himself in a dominant position in the secular hierarchy; and that it was Eadric's pivotal role in the last years of Æthelred's reign which undermined whatever capacity the English still had to resist.[104] If we seek to judge King Æthelred in terms of his ability to defend his country against its enemies, the verdict is clear; and even if we seek to understand what happened, nothing can conceal the fact that his reign ended in shambles and disaster. We should bear in mind, however, that the king and his people had endured all manner of trials and tribulations in the earlier part of the reign, and indeed had risen to many challenges before their powers of resistance finally crumbled; and that if it is tempting to regard the Danes as no more than an instrument by which the English inflicted hurt upon themselves, it would be as well to give them credit, on their own terms, for bringing a campaign of relentless aggression to an effective conclusion.

[104] Keynes (1980); Keynes (1986), pp. 213–17.

PART III

NON-CAROLINGIAN EUROPE

CHAPTER 19

EUROPEAN RUSSIA, *C.* 500–*C.* 1050

Thomas S. Noonan

INTRODUCTION

Histories of European Russia during the early medieval era normally focus upon the origins and development of the Rus' state centred at Kiev. This approach is, however, much too parochial. Politically, it ignores the Byzantine Crimea, the Khazar khaganate, and the Volga Bulgar amirate, the non-Rus' states which existed in European Russia after 500 A D. Socially, it omits the vast majority of the population who did not belong to the ruling elites of these states. In order to reflect these new historical perspectives, this chapter will focus on two major themes: the peoples who inhabited European Russia and the states which sought to govern these peoples.

First, however, a few comments about terminology are necessary. There are no universally accepted terms in English for what is referred to here as European Russia. Most Soviet scholars used the phrase eastern Europe (*Vostochnaia Evropa*), which is fine except that many in the west consider Poland, the Czech Republic, Hungary and the Balkans as eastern Europe. On the other hand, Ukrainians and other non-Russians object to being classified as part of Russia, even if only for geographical purposes. With apologies to the non-Russians, European Russia has been adopted because it best describes in English the region being examined here. Great controversy also surrounds the use of the word Russian to describe the eastern Slavs and their state in the pre-Mongol era. Ukrainian scholars in particular have insisted that Rus' is a far better term, especially since it was the word most used by the medieval east Slavic sources to denote themselves and their state. Since this argument has much merit, the term Rus' will be employed here.

The peoples of European Russia did not provide many written sources for their history prior to *c.* 1050. The only substantive Khazar source is the tenth-century *Correspondence* between the Khagan Joseph and several Jews in Spain;[1]

---

[1] *Evreisko-khazarskaia perepiska v X veke*, ed. P. K. Kokovtsov.

487

the authenticity of this *Correspondence* has been challenged, and there is considerable controversy over the interpretation of its passages. The Volga Bulgars left no written sources and the peoples of Cherson apparently kept no local chronicles. The Rus' *Primary Chronicle*, whose coverage starts *c.* 850, was only compiled after the mid-eleventh century and there is a lively debate about the veracity of its information for the period before *c.* 1050. Byzantine, Islamic and Scandinavian sources provide much valuable information but also present serious problems. Only one Islamic author, Ibn Faḍlān, ever visited European Russia and thus wrote from personal experience.[2] The Scandinavian sagas were composed primarily in Iceland, starting in the thirteenth century, and are thus debatable sources for European Russia in the ninth to eleventh centuries. Byzantine sources, as might be expected, treat European Russia from a strictly Byzantine perspective. The paucity of written primary sources means that we are very dependent upon the information derived from archaeology, linguistics and numismatics. Although these disciplines illuminate many aspects of medieval life, they do not provide satisfactory evidence for many key historical questions. They do not, for example, help us resolve the question of whether feudalism existed in the early Rus' state. The scarcity of sources is a major obstacle to a reconstruction of the early history of European Russia.

THE PEOPLES OF EUROPEAN RUSSIA

The peoples of European Russia inhabited five different geographic-economic zones during the early middle ages. In each zone, the inhabitants had developed a distinct survival strategy over the course of time, that is, had adopted distinct ways of living to conform with specific climatic and environmental conditions. These five zones were:

1   the Black Sea littoral, where a Byzantinised population perpetuated the urban life originally transplanted from the Mediterranean;
2   the steppe or prairie, where various Turkic and some Iranian groups practised a pastoral nomadism which arose here even before the coming of the Scythians *c.* 700 BC;
3   the forest steppe and forest zones, where east Slavic agriculturalists supplemented the erratic yields of their crops with the products of the forest;
4   the forest zones of central and north-central Russia, where Baltic and Finno-Ugrian tribes combined hunting, stock raising and agriculture;
5   the tundra and northern taiga of the far north, where the Lapps/Saami and Samoyed Nentsy survived by fishing and hunting.

---

[2]   Ibn Faḍlān, *Risalah*.

10 European Russia in the ninth and tenth centuries

The above divisions are not rigid. Both nomads and agriculturalists, for example, inhabited the forest steppe while agriculturalists and hunters-trappers came together in the forest zones of central Russia. Similarly, agriculturalists did engage in some foraging and both nomads and hunters practised some agriculture. Few medieval peoples would have survived if they had confined themselves exclusively to just one means of survival.

The Black Sea littoral

Around 700 BC, Greek colonists began to settle along the coasts of the northern Black Sea. By the early centuries AD, Rome had replaced Greece as the major Mediterranean power in the northern Black Sea. The Greeks and Romans brought to their northern Black Sea colonies much of their civilisation, and in the course of time a number of indigenous peoples were assimilated into the societies of the northern Black Sea cities. The Hunnic invasion of southern Russia c. 375, which touched off the 'great migration of peoples', threatened the very existence of these cities. When conditions stabilised during the sixth and seventh centuries, Byzantine influence in the northern Black Sea was confined to a few towns along the Crimean coast, most notably Cherson on the southwestern shore and Bosporos along the western side of the Kerch strait. Bosporos soon came under the Khazars, leaving Cherson as the principal bastion of Mediterranean society on the northern Black Sea coast.

Cherson is located on a narrow strip of coastal land separated from the Crimean steppe by mountains. For most of the early medieval era, it was the only major town in all European Russia. The city's dwellings were situated along streets laid out in a rectangular pattern inherited from classical time. Protected by massive walls, which were periodically rebuilt, and possessing a fine natural harbour, Cherson was able to pursue its commercial interests in relative peace. Beyond the mountains to its north lay the Crimean steppe. From its steppe neighbours, the city obtained sheep and horses, while those living in the forest steppe and further north sent furs, honey, wax, slaves and perhaps grain. Cherson itself was the centre of a major fishing industry. All these products were then shipped to the markets of Asia Minor and Constantinople. In return, Cherson obtained luxury goods such as silks, fine glassware and glazed pottery, as well as wine and olive oil. These products were then exchanged for the goods of the north. Some of the wine and oil sent north was shipped in amphorae and other pottery vessels specially made in the city whose workshops also produced tiles for the northern trade. Cherson survived and prospered owing to its role as an intermediary in this commerce.

The archaeological evidence suggests several long-term cycles in Cherson's economy. The fifth, sixth and seventh centuries were a time of prosperity which resulted in widespread building activity (rebuilt walls, new churches, new areas of habitation). Fishing and fish processing flourished, as did pottery production. The eighth and first half of the ninth century are considered a period of decline, meaning that there is little archaeological evidence of building or workshop production at this time. The second half of the ninth and the tenth century witnessed an economic revival. The city's walls were repaired, many churches were constructed or rebuilt, the population became denser in many parts of the city, new areas were inhabited, and local coinage resumed. Pottery and tile production increased, as did imports of Byzantine glazed ware. Prosperity abruptly ended *c.* 989 when the Rus' Grand Prince Vladimir sacked the city and ushered in a new 'dark age' which lasted till the late eleventh or twelfth century.

In perspective, Cherson was a provincial version of Constantinople, located on the periphery of a vast 'barbarian' world to the north. It actively traded with this world but, aside from a secondary role in the conversion of Rus', it had no lasting impact on its neighbours to the north. This explains why Cherson and the Byzantine Crimea are usually ignored in the medieval history of European Russia. Cherson's lack of influence upon European Russia followed a long tradition. The Greeks and Romans never attempted to conquer European Russia or convert it into a large tributary domain. As a result, there was no Graeco-Roman legacy in European Russia, no experience of a highly organised and bureaucratic state, no military presence to facilitate Romanisation, no Christian church or episcopal structure to bind the peoples together, no Roman road system or Roman technology to produce and transport goods by land, and no law or philosophy to help order people's lives. In short, Greece and Rome did not provide Russia with a usable past.

The nomads of the steppe

Before the appearance of the Scythians in southern Russia *c.* 700 BC, some people had already begun to abandon agriculture, hunting and gathering as their primary means of survival and had turned instead to nomadic pastoralism. These nomads found that the herds of animals (primarily sheep and horses) raised in the lush prairie lands stretching across southern Russia and Ukraine provided a more reliable subsistence than the alternatives. The Pontic steppe, however, is just one part of a larger steppe belt which extends from Mongolia to modern Hungary. Nomads from the east periodically moved into southern Russia, attracted by its rich steppe lands. Some of these migrants had been defeated in military conflicts and were forced to seek new pasture lands. Others headed westward because of natural catastrophes such as diseases which decimated their herds or droughts which parched their grazing lands.

Whatever the causes, periodic westward migrations by new nomads into the Pontic steppe were a consistent feature of Russian history from *c.* 1000 BC to *c.* 1300 AD. Until *c.* 370 AD, the nomads of south Russian were almost entirely Iranian speaking. The Hunnic invasion initiated a long period of dominance by Turkic-speaking nomads. During the early medieval era, the main nomadic groups in the south Russian steppes were the Turkic Khazars and Pechenegs. The Ugrian Magyars inhabited the steppe for some time before being forced to migrate to the Hungarian plain shortly before 900. Remnants of the Iranian Alans and the Turkic Bulgars were also found in the Don and north Caucasian steppe.

Nomadic pastoralism was not a self-sufficient way of life. While some agriculture and handicraft production existed among the nomads, they were dependent upon sedentary peoples for food and various goods. These products were obtained either by trading or by raiding. The steppe nomads thus became famous for the commerce which ran through their lands and for their attacks upon neighbouring sedentary states. Since the nomads were not literate in the early medieval era, the historical sources describing them were composed by the sedentary 'victims' of their raids. These sources paint a picture of barbarous nomads who raped, killed or enslaved the innocent inhabitants of 'civilised' lands and wantonly destroyed their villages and towns. In truth, Rus' princes subjected other Rus' princes and their peoples to every atrocity for which the Pechenegs and other nomads were so strongly condemned by the Rus' chroniclers. Furthermore, as early as *c.* 1015, Rus' princes recruited Pechenegs and other nomads as auxiliaries in Rus' civil wars. Much of the damage done by nomads in the Rus' lands was perpetrated on behalf of the Rus' princes.

The Rus' and other neighbours of the steppe nomads came from primarily agrarian states. They found it difficult if not impossible to fathom the nomadic way of life. From their perspective, nomads seemed to roam aimlessly. The reality was quite different. Successful pastoral nomadism required a very regulated system. The steppe lands occupied by a nomadic horde were divided among various tribes and clans to prevent conflict. During the mid-tenth century, for example, the Pecheneg horde was divided into eight tribes, four of which were located on each side of the Dnieper. These eight tribes were in turn divided into forty clans. The peoples in each nomadic tribe also followed a strict annual cycle. Each year in the spring, after the snow melted, the tribes moved north so that their herds had good pasture lands during the summer. In the autumn, the herds were brought south to land where the winter snow depth would not impede grazing. Every person within a nomadic group also had specific responsibilities. Women and children put up and took down the felt *yurts* or tents and performed other domestic chores, while men watched the flocks, hunted, traded and waged war. In short, nomadic life was far from aimless roaming; rather, it was a fairly regimented way of life designed to ensure the survival of the group.

The Rus' capital of Kiev was located along the northern frontier of the forest steppe, a region utilised by both cultivators and nomads. As east Slavic peasants settled in this region they converted some of the best summer pasturage into black earth fields. Obviously, the Pechenegs and other nomads opposed this threat to their survival. Their resistance was viewed as unprovoked aggression by the Rus' chroniclers, who did not understand that nomads also needed these lands. Rus' 'retaliation' against the 'hostile' nomads was considered legitimate, while nomadic incursions against the Rus' were condemned as outrages.

Trade with sedentary peoples was crucial for nomads. The Khazar khaganate, for example, was famous as the centre of an international commerce which took place in its capital of Itil' located somewhere in the delta of the Volga. The khagan received a tithe from each foreign merchant who visited Itil'. In return, the Khazars provided a safe market where traders from the Near East, Central Asia, the Caucasus and European Russian could conduct their business. While Khazaria had a fixed centre where merchants from many lands would bring their merchandise, nomads like the Pechenegs with less of a political structure entered into direct trade with their neighbours. The Rus', for instance, purchased cattle, horses and sheep directly from the Pechenegs, while the Pechenegs also had an active commerce with Cherson. The nomads of the Pontic steppe created safe markets where merchants could meet, allowed merchants to pass through their lands safely to other countries, and exchanged their products with neighbouring peoples directly.

The society of the medieval steppe nomads was far more organised and complex than was realised by sedentary authors. The nomads had adopted a survival strategy based on the herding of sheep, horses and other animals which, for the most part, proved very successful. But, because the steppe nomads were often cast as brutal villains, their way of life has been little understood or appreciated.

The agriculturalists of the forest steppe and forest

Since classical authors provided no precise information on the origin of the Slavs, almost all the evidence is archaeological. Archaeology, however, cannot demonstrate a continuity of Slavic settlement dating back to the early Iron Age in either Poland or Ukraine, the two leading contenders for the hypothetical Slavic 'homeland'. Thus it is best to start the history of the early medieval Slavs around 500 AD, when they can be located along the lower Danube and immediately to the north. Under pressure from the Avars, groups of Slavs began to migrate in increasing numbers towards the south, west and north-east. Those Slavs who moved north-east were the original ancestors of today's three east Slavic groups: the Ukrainians, Byelorussians and Great Russians. Some of the Slavs who had migrated to what is today Poland later moved east-ward and were assimilated by the early east Slavs. Over the course of a millennium, the east Slavs kept moving northward and eastward. In the process, they conquered and assimilated, exterminated or expelled the indigenous Finnic and Baltic peoples who had occupied much of the forest steppe and forest zones. Thus, while the east Slavs were the last major people to migrate into European Russia, they slowly became the dominant group.

In the early middle ages, the east Slavs lived primarily in small hamlets along the tributaries of major rivers. Some of these hamlets were hillforts while others were open villages located near hillforts. The hillforts were normally sited on the top of high river banks and often had deep ravines on both sides. This provided good natural protection and minimised the need for earthen ramparts and ditches to keep out intruders. The siting of these settlements also took into account sources of fresh water and access to rich alluvial fields along river banks. The simple houses in the hamlets were scattered about in no particular order, and there is little evidence of specialised handicrafts. Most families were self-sufficient and lived at subsistence level, with no sign of surplus or sophistication: almost all pottery was handmade. The society of the early medieval east Slavs was much less advanced than that of the pre-Hunnic peoples of the Cherniakhovo culture which occupied much of southern Russia from *c.* 200 to 370 AD.

The early east Slavs are considered to have been cultivators and many scholars claim that they lived in extended, communal families. Only in the fifteenth and sixteenth centuries, however, do we begin to find sufficient written sources to justify generalisations about the east Slavic peasantry. By combining the limited evidence of early medieval times with the insights obtained from studies of late medieval agriculture, it is possible to construct a picture of east Slavic peasant life before *c.* 1050 that is probably closer to reality than hypotheses based on modern political ideologies. The vast majority of the early medieval peasantry lived as independent, nuclear families, not as extended families in communes. The life of the peasant family revolved around a very difficult struggle for survival. The peasants planted low yield seeds, using primitive implements. The resulting harvest gave barely enough to feed the family until a new crop came in and to provide a small surplus for tribute and a few necessary purchases. Draught animals like oxen and horses could not be left outside to graze during the winter like the sheep of the nomads. Such animals had to be stalled and fed. Since most peasants could not transfer much crop land to the raising of hay, they could not keep draught animals. This meant that they had no dung with which to fertilise their lands and thus increase their yields The absence of natural fertiliser required the east Slavic peasant constantly to clear new land for planting. With the use of axe and fire only, new plots were continually cleared in the virgin forests, planted with crops for a few years, and then abandoned as the mobile cultivators brought new plots into service. The peasant was thus trapped into a way of life that afforded subsistence but little more in a normal year.

Normal years were rare. Too much rain or too little, too much sun or too little, all reduced peasants' yields. As the peasants could not live by agriculture alone, their margin of survival came from the forest: the animals of the forest provided food and furs, while the fish in forest streams were probably the major source of protein in the peasant diet. Both the log cabins of peasants and the fire in their hearths came from the trees of the forest. Mushrooms and berries were additional sources of food. In short, the east Slavic agriculturalists of the middle ages were cultivators and foragers. If they had depended on agriculture alone, they would have perished.

Limited yields also restricted the size of the peasant family. Models of peasant farming project a maximum yield per person given the constraints under which agriculture operated. This maximum is achieved with a nuclear family consisting of a husband, wife, and several children. When children grew up and married, the new family had to move on and find virgin land upon which to begin farming. It was probably this process of new families bringing new lands under cultivation which precipitated the movement of the east Slavic peasantry across the forest steppe and forest zones of European Russia.[3]

The creation of the Kievan state led the Rus' princes to advance certain claims which affected peasant life. The most important of these claims was the right to collect tribute in kind, one pelt per hearth, from the peasants. Marxist historians often interpret this tribute as the payments owed by serfs to their feudal lords. There is little evidence to support this view, and most scholars believe that the enserfment of the east Slavic peasantry began in the fifteenth and sixteenth centuries. In addition, the Rus' princes began to establish private estates, primarily for raising livestock and horses, as well as promoting agriculture and hunting. On these estates, most, if not all, of the workers and overseers were slaves or debtors. It is not certain, however, when this process began. Judging from the *Pravda Russkaia*, the earliest Rus' law code, private landholding can be confirmed only from the second half of the eleventh century. Thus, apart from the collection of tribute, the princely economy had relatively little impact on the peasantry before about 1050.

[3] This analysis draws very heavily on the many insights found in Smith (1977).

Hunters, stock breeders and peasants in the forest zones

At the start of the middle ages, a number of Finno-Ugrian and Baltic peoples
inhabited the forest zones of European Russian all the way from the middle
Volga to the Baltic. They did not leave written sources like the east Slavs and
Vikings, form states like the Khazars, Volga Bulgars and Rus', or invade the
lands of their sedentary, literate neighbours like the Pechenegs and other
steppe nomads. As a result, the Balts and especially the Finno-Ugrians have
been the neglected peoples of early medieval European Russia. Since the
Finno-Ugrians were more numerous and occupied a far greater territory, this
section will focus upon them.

The Finno-Ugrians had traditionally been hunter-gatherers. Given the
abundance of animals, fish and raw foods in the forests of central and northern Russia, this was a rational adaption to their environment. After 500 AD,
however, the roles of agriculture, stock breeding and metallurgy all increased
significantly. Since the new ways did not take root uniformly, socio-economic
differences amongst the Finno-Ugrian peoples increased. The Mordvins, for
example, had extensive plough farming while the chief occupation of the
Udmurts and Komi-Permians was slash-and-burn agriculture. The
Mari/Cheremis had probably adopted slash-and-burn agriculture by the
eleventh century. The economy of the Merians and Muromians was based on
animal husbandry while the Komi-Zyrians remained primarily hunter-gatherers. Despite these differences, all the Finno-Ugrian tribes had mixed economies. The hunting of elk, bear and deer, fishing, and the trapping of sable,
marten, beaver and other fur-bearing animals were pursued everywhere. Stock
breeding, especially horses, cattle, swine and sheep, had spread throughout the
forest zone. The cultivation of grains by various methods had increased dramatically. Furthermore, the growing need for tools and weapons combined
with the existence of local sources of iron ore had fostered the widespread
development of ferrous metallurgy. In fact, prior to the tenth century, there
was even an era when women dominated casting among the Merians; it was a
domestic craft. Finno-Ugrian metallurgy in the early medieval forest zone
reached its artistic zenith among the Komi-Zyrians and their ancestors (the
people of the Lomovatovo and Rodanovo cultures). Their artists-artisans used
a variety of techniques to produce a series of metal plaques, pendants and idols
in the so-called Permian animal style. Combining realistic and fantastic elements, they depicted birds, animals and humans in a variety of scenes. During
the early middle ages, the Finno-Ugrian peoples of the forest zone made the
transition from predominantly hunting-gathering societies to mixed economies where agriculture, stock raising and craft production were also important.

The numerous fur-bearing animals of the central and northern regions of

European Russia had always attracted the attention of outsiders. In the early middle ages, Vikings from Norway, east Slavs from Novgorod and Bulgars from the middle Volga all sought to obtain furs from this area through trade and tribute. The history of these regions centred, in large part, around the competition amongst outsiders to exploit their rich natural resources. Whatever isolation existed prior to the ninth century came to an abrupt end as the Finno-Ugrians were made part of history by those seeking their furs and their lands.

The Finno-Ugrian tribes of northern Russia could not avoid an active trade with their neighbours. Trade was not only necessary to acquire certain goods, but was also forced upon them and was indeed preferable to the compulsory payment of tribute to colonial officials and armed expeditions. In any event, the persistent intrusion of outsiders altered the life of the Finno-Ugrian peoples. To avoid Rus' and/or Bulgar rule, many Finnic peoples migrated further north and east. Some of those who remained were exterminated or assimilated. As a result, several Finnic tribes like the Muromians and Merians, who are mentioned in written sources, disappeared during the middle ages. At the same time, historians of the Great Russians acknowledge their strong Finnic substratum just as historians of the Byelorussians recognise their prominent Baltic substratum. The assimilated Finns and Balts slowly became Rus', agriculturalists and Orthodox. Those tributaries who resisted assimilation and still survive, the Mari/Cheremis for example, have been subjected to considerable Slavicisation. For better or worse, the Finno-Ugrian world of European Russia has evolved significantly, starting in the early middle ages.

Northern hunter-gatherers: the Lapps/Saami and Nentsy of the tundra

Since early modern times, the dominant native peoples of the tundra and northern taiga zones in European Russia have been the Lapps or Saami of the Kola peninsula and Samoyed Nentsy of what is now the Nenets Autonomous Okrug. There is considerable disagreement about the time when the Saami and Nentsy first occupied these regions as well as the period when they adopted specialised reindeer nomadism as the basis of their existence. In his report of *c.* 885 to King Alfred, the Norwegian sailor Ottar (Ohthere) noted that the coasts from northern Norway to the White Sea were inhabited by Saami who hunted during the winter and fished in the summer.[4] However, some domesticated reindeer were also kept. It thus appears that the Saami, and by extension the Nentsy, maintained a hunting-fishing culture in the early medieval era and only became specialised reindeer herdsmen at some later period.

---

[4] Pritsak, O. (ed.), *The Origin of Rus'*, pp. 692–5.

Despite the harsh climate, the tundra and northern taiga possess great natural wealth. The Saami and Nentsy trapped valuable fur-bearing animals like marten and otter, hunted reindeer and bear, gathered numerous bird feathers, made ship ropes from whale, seal and walrus skins, and collected the ivory of walrus teeth. The early medieval era witnessed the start of the long campaign by peoples to the south to exploit this wealth. The Norwegians appear to have been first, since the purpose of Ottar's northern voyages was to collect a tribute of furs, feathers, whalebone and ship ropes from the Saami. Later Norse sources such as *Egil's Saga*, confirm that by the late ninth century Norse bands travelled to the Saami areas by land and sea to collect tribute and conduct trade.[5] The Volga Bulgars, who were next in exploiting the riches of the north, developed a different strategy. They relied on trade rather than tribute and used intermediaries like the Ves' of the Beloozero region who traded with the Saami and Nentsy as well as the Bulgars. The initial Rus' expansion to the north came primarily from Novgorod and focused almost entirely on forcibly imposing tribute upon Finno-Ugrian, Saami and Samoyed peoples of the taiga and tundra. In short, by 1050, a twofold battle was under way in the Russian north. One aspect was the subjugation and exploitation of the Saami, Nentsy and Finno-Ugrians by their southern neighbours. The second aspect was the growing competition amongst the Norwegians, Rus' and Bulgars, each of whom sought to gain control over the natural wealth of the north at the expense of the others.

THE STATES OF EUROPEAN RUSSIA

In the year 500 AD no organised states existed in European Russia outside the northern Black Sea littoral. By the year 1000, a Christian east Slavic Rus' state had appeared along the middle Dnieper with its capital at Kiev, while an Islamic and Turkic Bulgar state ruled the middle Volga region. In addition, the Khazar khaganate, a nomadic and Turkic state whose ruling elite had converted to Judaism, had dominated the Volga–Don steppe, eastern Crimea and northern Caucasus for approximately three centuries (*c.* 650–*c.* 965). The appearance of these three states, combined with the spread of several major religions of the book, marks the transition of European Russia from prehistory to history.

The Crimea: Byzantium's outpost in European Russia

The early medieval era brought major political changes to European Russia. The appearance of the Khazar and Rus' states along with the migrations of the

---

[5] *Egil's Saga*, cc. 9–17.

nomadic Pechenegs and Magyars into the steppe created a host of problems for Byzantium. Byzantine possessions along the eastern Black Sea coast and in the Crimea were threatened, while there was a constant danger that one or more of the newcomers might invade the Balkans or launch a naval campaign against Byzantine cities. As Bosporos and the eastern Crimea passed into the Khazar sphere of influence, Cherson emerged as the crucial Byzantine outpost on the northern Black Sea. The city's primary political function was to monitor movements in the steppe and to keep Constantinople informed of any development which might threaten Byzantine interests.

Using Cherson as an intermediary, the Byzantine government formed alliances with various peoples in southern Russia directed against those who might endanger Byzantium. In the early seventh century, when Sasanian Persia invaded Asia Minor, Byzantium persuaded the west Turks/Khazars to attack the Sasanian lands in the southern Caucasus. In the 630s, the Bulgars of the Don–Azov steppe were the chief Byzantine partner in the steppe. Between 650 and 750, Byzantium aligned with the Khazars on several occasions against a common enemy, the Umayyad caliphate. During the first half of the ninth century, the migrations of the Pechenegs and Magyars into the steppe weakened the Khazar position there. The initial Byzantine response, c. 837, was to construct the fortress of Sarkel on the lower Don river for the Khazars in order to impede hostile movements in the steppe. A new military province or theme was also created in the Crimea c. 839. By c. 900, Byzantium decided that the Khazar alliance no longer served its interests. Consequently, Byzantium made the Pechenegs its chief proxy in the north. Each year imperial ambassadors journeyed north from Cherson into the steppe to meet with the leaders of the Pecheneg tribes. These leaders and their retinues were given numerous gifts so that they would keep Byzantium informed of developments in the steppe, and, when requested, attack those who threatened Byzantine interests. This Pecheneg threat deterred the Magyars, Rus' and Khazars from attacking Byzantine territories. In emergencies, Byzantine envoys were even taken by ship to some mutually convenient location along the northern Black Sea coast to meet with Pecheneg chieftains. However, most of Byzantium's contacts with the Pechenegs were conducted via Cherson.

In theory, the Byzantine policy of hiring proxies to fight imperial enemies in the northern Black Sea appeared simple and effective. In reality, this policy was often difficult to implement. The Pechenegs, for example, constantly demanded more 'gifts' and even when appropriately bribed could not be relied upon to fulfil their side of a bargain. Often the Pechenegs were more interested in attacking lands promising rich booty than peoples who threatened Byzantium. Thus Byzantium found that it was not always easy to get the Pechenegs to fight its battles.

Besides the Pechenegs, Byzantium also used the Alans of the north-central Caucasus and the Rus' of Kiev as its proxies during the late ninth and tenth centuries. The Alans were engaged to keep the Khazars in line, while in the mid-960s Byzantine envoys from Cherson bribed Grand Prince Sviatoslav to attack the Danubian Bulgars. The example of Sviatoslav shows how crucial Cherson was to Byzantium's entire northern defence policy. It also demonstrates the basic flaw in this policy: having defeated the Bulgarians, Sviatoslav claimed their lands for the Rus' and had to be driven out of the Balkans by Byzantine forces.

THE KHAZAR KHAGANATE: EUROPEAN RUSSIA'S FIRST MEDIEVAL STATE

While pastoral nomads had occupied the Pontic steppe since prehistoric times, the Khazars were the first to create a lasting state. The Khazar khagans traced their ancestry back to the royal clan of the west Turk khaganate (552–c. 630) in Mongolia, the Ashina. Following west Turkic traditions, the Khazars also had a dual kingship. The khagan was the 'charismatic', ceremonial ruler, whose ancestry gave legitimacy to the khaganate. The day-to-day ruler who ran the government and implemented decisions was known as the *Shad* or *Bäk/Beg*. The Khazar state was held together, in part, because its rulers claimed descent from a clan with strong claims to rule the Turks.

The Khazar khaganate also endured because it rested on a solid economy which provided the revenues for a powerful military. In addition to the tithe collected from merchants, the Khazars collected tribute from all their subject peoples. Much of the tribute from European Russia, for example, was paid in fur. The substantial revenues from tribute and trade enabled the Khazars to supplement their own nomadic forces with large groups of auxiliaries, especially from Khwārizm and other parts of the Islamic world. The large Khazar army kept the numerous clans and tribes of the khaganate in line and helped the Khazars create and maintain a vast tributary state. Because of its political and military strengths, the khaganate dominated southern Russia for over three centuries, longer than even the Mongol Golden Horde.

During the second half of the sixth century, west Turkic elements had extended their control into the Pontic steppe. There had also been relations between Byzantium and Sogdian merchants from Central Asia since the mid-sixth century. Given these connections, it is not surprising that when the Byzantine Emperor Heraclius needed help against Sassanian Persia in the Caucasus, c. 625, he turned to the west Turks. These Turkic allies of the emperor were also called Khazars. While the Turkic/Khazar campaign against the Persians was successful, the Turks disappeared soon after the defeat of

Khusraw II in 628. Their disappearance was due to the death of their leader and to the civil war which broke out in the west Turkic khaganate *c.* 630.

By 650 or so, the Khazars reappeared in the north Caucasian–Pontic steppe, this time as an independent entity. Very quickly they came into conflict with the Bulgars who dominated the Don–Kuban steppe. By 680, the Bulgars had been defeated and, from this time until the 830s, the Khazars were the uncontested masters of the steppe. The Khazars were also confronted by a major challenge in the south. During the 640s, the Arabs began their successful conquest of the southern Caucasus, a process which inevitably led to Arab expansion into the northern Caucasus. The Khazars had hoped to reassert their short-lived position in Georgia and Caucasian Albania which they had lost *c.* 628–30. They also considered Daghestan in the north-eastern Caucasus as a key part of the khaganate; some scholars even see Daghestan as the real centre of the early khaganate. In any event, the period *c.* 650–*c.* 750 was marked by a series of Arab–Khazar wars. Arab incursions into the northern Caucasus were followed by Khazar raids into the southern Caucasus. In the end, neither the Arabs nor the Khazars could defeat the other decisively, though each enjoyed major if ephemeral victories. After the collapse of the Umayyads and the establishment of the ʿAbbāsid caliphate in Baghdad, the Caliph al-Manṣūr (754–75) decided to make peace with the Khazars in order to focus on more serious problems elsewhere. It required almost half a century and several further clashes before a *modus vivendi* could be reached. But, in the end, the Arabs abandoned their pretensions to the northern Caucasus while the Khazars abandoned their designs on the southern Caucasus. As many authors have noted, it was the Khazars who blocked the large-scale expansion of Islam into European Russia.

While engaged in their hundred years' war with the Umayyads, the Khazars also extended their influence into the Crimea and areas of the western Caucasus. By *c.* 700, Khazar governors were established in Phanagoria/Tamatarkha and Bosporos, on both sides of the Kerch strait, while Khazar officials (*Tuduns*) were apparently found elsewhere in the Crimea including Cherson. While the Khazars were not able to retain their position within Cherson, their protectorate over most of the Crimea was still intact during the 780s, when they suppressed a revolt by the Crimean Goths. For some time the Khazars also tried, without success, to subordinate the Alans of the north-central Caucasus. The latter, however, retained their Byzantine orientation. The Khazars did have more success in western Georgia (Abkhazia and Egrisi) where in 786 the local ruler switched his allegiance from Byzantium to Khazaria. Despite frequent allusions by historians to the 'traditional Byzantine–Khazar alliance', an alliance based on cooperation against the Persians and Arabs, it is clear that the Khazars and Byzantines were also competitors in both the Crimea and the northern Caucasus. Given Byzantium's many problems with the Arabs and Danubian Bulgars, it chose not to pursue this competition too vigorously in the eighth century. After all, it was the Khazars who kept new nomadic intruders out of the Pontic steppe and thus provided safety for Cherson and the Balkans. As long as the Pax Khazarica was maintained in the steppe, Byzantium could accept some loss of influence in the Crimea and northern Caucasus.

The Khazars are also famous for the conversion of their ruling elite to Judaism, an event which probably took place in the early ninth century. Little is known about Khazar shamanism, although it is thought by analogy with that of the north Caucasian Huns to have included a holy forest cult, the worship of lightning and thunder, horse sacrifices, and the sky god Tängri. There has been a long discussion of when the conversion to Judaism took place and what form of Judaism was involved. The most salient fact, however, is that the Khazar rulers accepted one religion of the book to deflect pressures from the Arabs and Byzantines to convert to Islam or Orthodoxy. In 737, the future caliph Marwān successfully penetrated Khazar defences in the Caucasus mountains and pursued the khagan north to the lower Volga. To gain peace, the khagan agreed to accept Islam, a promise which was quickly forgotten when Marwān returned home. This campaign also led the Khazars to move their capital to Itil' in the lower Volga. The Byzantines apparently attempted to establish eight Christian bishoprics in Khazaria around the mid-eighth century. While this effort did not bear fruit, it was clearly intended to bring various peoples in the khaganate within the Byzantine orbit. Faced with these pressures, the Khazar elite decided to abandon their native shamanism and accept Judaism. Judaism was apparently chosen because it was a religion of the book without being the faith of a neighbouring state which had designs on Khazar lands.

The position of Khazaria in the Pontic steppe began to deteriorate during the first half of the ninth century. Around 837, in response to the khagan's request, the Byzantines constructed the fortress of Sarkel along the lower Don to help the Khazars defend this region against an anonymous enemy. Scholars have identified this unnamed enemy with a number of peoples, including the Rus' and the Magyars. Most probably it was the Pechenegs who threatened the Khazars. During the early ninth century, the Turkic Pechenegs, under pressure from the Oghuz Turks to the east, forced their way westward through the khaganate into the Don–Dnieper steppe. The migration of the Pechenegs helped to destroy the Pax Khazarica in the steppes. At the same time, the Rus' princes established themselves in Kiev and other centres, putting an end to Khazar domination over the east Slavs of the middle Dnieper and their rich tribute in furs. The Khazars were unable to drive the Pechenegs from the steppe or resist Rus' expansion in the forest zone. Internally, the Khazars had to suppress a rebellion by the Kabars sometime before *c.* 900. By the early tenth century, Byzantium had switched its support to the Pechenegs and now actively encouraged the Alans and others to attack Khazaria so that it could reassert its former position in the Crimea and western Caucasus. The Rūs/Rus' exploited Khazaria's weakness to launch a series of raids in the Caspian Sea between *c.* 880 and *c.* 945. The tenth century thus saw the Khazars engaged in a series of conflicts against Alans, Rus', Pechenegs and Byzantium. During the first half of the tenth century, Khazaria held its own in these struggles, though it had lost control over the Volga Bulgars by 950. In 965, the Rus' Grand Prince Sviatoslav defeated the Khazar army and took Sarkel and possibly Itil'. With Sviatoslav's victory, the khaganate collapsed. The Khazars mentioned after 965 were clearly remnants of the former khaganate who had survived its demise. The end of Khazaria can be attributed to both military and economic factors. The appearance of the Rus' and Pechenegs in the ninth century slowly eroded the Khazars' vast tributary empire and thus weakened its economic viability. Unable to defeat its enemies, Khazaria was destroyed by them.

The disappearance of the khaganate did not mean that the Khazars disappeared or moved. Rather, in typical nomadic fashion, it is probable that they were subsumed, in a subordinate status, into a successor horde. The horde ruling the steppes at any given time was known by the name of its dominant tribe. This horde usually contained a number of diverse tribes who, through coercion or choice, acknowledged the leadership of the dominant tribe. Thus, Alans and Bulgars did not disappear form the Pontic steppe after *c.* 650; they were simply incorporated into the Khazar khaganate as secondary tribes.

THE VOLGA BULGAR AMIRATE: TURKIC EXPANSION NORTH OF THE STEPPE

In the aftermath of the Hunnic invasion, various Turkic peoples known as Bulgars entered the south Russian steppe from Kazakhstan. Aside from a few isolated references, little is known about them until *c.* 635 when a leader named Kubrat overthrew Avar domination of the Bulgars with the help of Byzantium and became head of Great Bulgaria, a Bulgar-led horde in the Don–Kuban steppe. When Kubrat died sometime after 640, he left Great Bulgaria to his five sons. The Khazars soon challenged the Bulgars and replaced them as masters of this region. Some of the Bulgars remained in the Don–Kuban steppe as Khazar subjects; in the tenth century, they became known as Black Bulgars. A second group, led by one of Kubrat's sons named Asparukh, migrated westward and by 679 had crossed the lower Danube and started to settle in the Balkans. Another group moved northward and settled in the region of the Volga–Kama confluence. Here, they conquered the native Finnic peoples and,

by the early tenth century, created a state of some size. Historians refer to this
last group as the Volga Bulgars.

The Volga Bulgar amirate suddenly emerged from obscurity in the early
tenth century. Almost nothing is known about the earlier development of this
state. The period around 922 is particularly well documented because Ibn
Faḍlān wrote an account of his embassy to the Bulgar amir in that year. The
ruler at that time was Almish ibn Shilkī who had the Turkic title of Yiltawār. As
the result of Ibn Faḍlān's visit, Almish decided to call himself Jaʿfar ibn ʿAbd
Allāh and assume the title of amir. Externally, the Volga Bulgars were tributaries of the Khazars, paying the latter one sable pelt annually per household. The
amir's son was also held hostage by the Khazars. In fact, one of the main aims
of Ibn Faḍlān's mission was to help the amir build a fortress to protect him
from the Khazars. Internally, the amir's power was restricted by tribal or clan
leaders who could defy his order. Besides the amir and the tribal leaders, the
ruling elite also included 500 prominent families. This ruling elite dominated a
large state. While precise boundaries are unclear, Volga Bulgaria included substantial Finnic and Ugrian areas north of the Volga, a large part of modern
Bashkiria to the east, much of the Volga region south of the Bulgar territory
itself, and the lands of the Finns and east Slavs to the west perhaps as far as the
Oka River. Volga Bulgaria was a multi-ethnic state, with large numbers of
Turkic Bulgars and Bashkirs, a variety of Finnic and Ugrian peoples, and many
east Slavs.

The emergence of the Volga Bulgar state was closely linked with its key role
in international trade. It was no accident that Islamic sources suddenly became
aware of the Bulgars shortly after 900. At the beginning of the tenth century,
the Sāmānid amirate of Central Asia became the leading exporter of dirhams
to European Russia. Much of the commerce which formerly went north
across the Caspian and Caucasus from Iran and Iraq now ran from
Transoxiana and Khwārizm to Khazaria and Volga Bulgaria. The Bulgar
market along the Volga, so vividly described by Ibn Faḍlān, became a real competitor with the chief Khazar market of Itil'. Rus' merchants with their furs
and slaves regularly visited the Bulgar market to meet their Islamic counterparts while Bulgar merchants obtained sable and fox pelts from the Wīsū/Ves'
to the north. Caravans went back and forth between the Sāmānid lands and
Volga Bulgaria, completely circumventing the Khazars. Al-Muqaddasī even
mentioned the various furs, wax, amber, swords, slaves and other products
which reached Khwārizm and Central Asia via Volga Bulgaria. The Khazars
made the Bulgars their tributaries primarily to keep control over this trade and
tap the wealth of Bulgaria. The Bulgars sought independence in order to
control their trade themselves and sell their own pelts. The Volga Bulgar conversion to Islam, which was already well under way during Ibn Faḍlān's visit,

was, in part, defiance of the Khazars whose ruling elite was Jewish and, in part, a means to obtain support from co-religionists against Khazar domination.

By 950, at the latest, the Bulgars had become independent of the Khazars. For some time before then, the Bulgars had been striking unofficial coins which imitated Sāmānid dirhams. In 949/50, the Bulgar amir, Ṭālib ibn Aḥmad, began to issue official Volga Bulgar dirhams bearing the mint name Suwār. The official coinage continued until 986/7 and bore the names of several amirs and the mint names Bulghār and Suwār. The fact that the official coinage made no reference to a Khazar overlord reflects Bulgar emancipation from the Khazars. The loss of control over the Volga Bulgars by 950 was one of the factors which facilitated the collapse of the khaganate during the 960s.

With the demise of Khazaria, relations with the Rus' became of primary importance for the Bulgars. Conflict was inevitable as the Rus' princes established their domination over the upper Volga and pushed eastward into the Bulgar sphere of influence. This probably explains the 985 Rus' campaign against the Volga Bulgars. In addition, the Rus' and Bulgars were competitors in the struggle to extract a fur tribute from the Finnic peoples of northern Russia. The Rus', for instance, claimed tribute from the Ves'/Wīsū, who were also a major source of fur for the Bulgars. Relations between the Bulgars and the Rus' were thus marked by a struggle for territory and tribute. At the same time, both sides had an interest in maintaining an active trade along the Volga. In 1006, for example, the Rus' and Bulgars concluded a trade agreement which allowed Rus' merchants to trade freely in Bulgar cities along the Volga and Oka. The value of this treaty became evident in 1024 when a famine in the upper Volga lands forced the Rus' to buy grain from the Bulgars. The Bulgars clearly profited from good commercial relations with the Rus'.

The Volga Bulgar amirate demonstrated that Turkic and Muslim peoples could create a viable state in the forest zones of European Russia and compete successfully with the Rus'. This fact is too often forgotten by those who see the history of medieval European Russia solely as a history of the Rus' and their state.

KIEVAN RUS': EUROPEAN RUSSIA'S FIRST EAST SLAVIC STATE

The origins and development of the Kievan state constitute the most contentious topic in medieval Rus' history. Ever since the eighteenth century, one group of historians, called Normanists, has argued that the Kievan state was founded by Normans or Vikings: the Rus'. In response, another group, known as anti-Normanists, has claimed that the east Slavs (= Rus') created their own state. I tend to agree with those who see the Rus' as essentially a multi-ethnic group of merchants and mercenaries; within this group, however, the

Scandinavian element was clearly dominant. In any event, the long Normanist controversy has both distorted and retarded the study of the early Rus' state. For too long, the written and archaeological sources have been viewed solely in terms of how they related to this debate.

The authors of the *Primary Chronicle* tell us very little about the political structure in the east Slavic lands prior to the emergence of the Kievan state. In part, this omission may be due to ignorance. At the same time, the authors most probably deliberately suppressed information about those who ruled the Rus' lands before their patrons, the Rus' princes. The chroniclers refer to a number of east Slavic tribes. Unfortunately, it is not known when or how these tribes arose or what role they played in east Slavic society. The chroniclers also mention a Prince Mal of the Derevlianian tribe as well as the 'best men' who ruled the Derevlianian land. Elders from the Derevlianian capital of Iskorosten' are also noted in passing. One can only speculate on the functions of these princes, best men and city elders. In short, very little can be said about the political organisation of the east Slavic peasants who gradually migrated into the forest steppe and forest zones and settled there.

Much more is known about the Vikings who came to European Russia and created the Kievan state. During the sixth to eighth centuries, Scandinavians periodically raided along the coasts of the south-eastern Baltic and even established one or more settlements there, for example Grobin/Seaborg on the Latvian coast. From 750 on, some of these Scandinavians began to visit an emporium at Old (*Staraja*) Ladoga which is located on the west bank of the Volkhov river near its confluence with Lake Ladoga. It is not clear why this emporium arose, since the Finnic graves in the hinterland surrounding Old Ladoga are very poor. Soon the Scandinavians established a permanent settlement at Old Ladoga and began to explore the interior of European Russia. By the 780s, hoards of Islamic silver coins or dirhams began to appear in the Ladoga region. By 800, the Scandinavians, now called Vikings, had discovered how to reach the Near East via the Black and Caspian Seas. In other words, the primary aim of Viking penetration into European Russia was apparently to obtain silver in the form of Islamic dirhams. By the mid-ninth century, Islamic sources describe how Rus' merchants from the north brought furs and swords to the Black Sea and lower Volga where they paid a tithe to the Byzantine emperor and Khazar khagan. These merchants were then able to cross the Caspian Sea to Jurjān, on the south-eastern coast, from whence they joined the main land route leading to Baghdad.

By the tenth century, Rus' trade with Islam via European Russia had changed dramatically. The Rus' no longer travelled to Baghdad. Instead, Rus' and Islamic merchants met in the Khazar capital of Itil' and at a special market along the Volga in the Bulgar lands. In other words, the Khazars and Volga

Bulgars had become key intermediaries in this commerce whose centre had now shifted from the Near East to European Russia. Furthermore, most of the dirhams used by Islamic merchants to obtain the furs, swords, slaves, amber and other products brought by the Vikings were now struck in the Sāmānid mints of Central Asia, for example al-Shāsh/Tashkent, Samarqand, and Bukhārā. Rus'–Islamic trade had now become quite complex. The Rus' brought swords from the Rhineland and Baltic amber to Old Ladoga, where raw glass was turned into glass beads. These beads were then traded with the indigenous Finnic peoples of north-central Russia for furs. The Rus' also captured slaves in this region and, no doubt, forced the natives to pay them tribute in furs. These goods were then taken to the Bulgar market along the Volga described by Ibn Faḍlān.[6] Here, Rus' merchants prayed to their pagan idols that a rich Islamic merchant with many gold and silver coins would buy all their furs and slaves without haggling. These prayers were apparently answered, for Ibn Faḍlān noted that the wife of a Rus' merchant wore a neck band for each 10,000 dirhams her husband possessed; some of these wives wore numerous neck bands. The Rus'–Islamic trade resulted in the export of millions of dirhams to European Russia and the Baltic while huge numbers of slaves and furs were sent to the Islamic lands in return.

The development of a lucrative Rus' trade with Islam had political repercussions. Originally, the Rus' seem to have operated from select commercial-handicraft centres along the main routes. Inevitably, the Rus' who spent much time in European Russia sought control over various areas there in order to guarantee regular supplies of furs, easy access to captive slaves, and secure river routes. In short, some Rus' became political rulers as well as merchants. Local Rus' states had already begun to appear by the second half of the ninth century. In the north-west, Novgorod, located at the headwater of the Volkhov River, replaced Old Ladoga as the major Rus' centre in the north. Old Ladoga was simply too exposed to Viking raids while the rapids along the middle Volkhov protected Novgorod. Another centre was Kiev, on the high, right bank of the middle Dnieper. The Rus' first became acquainted with Kiev on their way to the lower Volga via the Black Sea. However, they quickly found that Kiev was a perfect centre for travelling to Constantinople. Already in 839, Scandinavians called Rhos reached Constantinople, although it is not certain they came from Kiev. In 860, Rus' from Kiev launched a major attack on Constantinople and a second raid, *c.* 907, led to the conclusion of the first recorded Rus'–Byzantine treaty *c.* 911. In addition to Novgorod and Kiev, other Viking centres were located at Beloozero (White Lake), Polotsk, Gnëzdovo/Smolensk, Timerovo, Chernigov, and elsewhere.

---

[6] Ibn Faḍlān, *Risalah*, pp. 127–35.

The *Primary Chronicle* relates how one group of Rus', descended from the semi-legendary Rurik, came to rule over all the Rus' principalities, thus creating the Kievan state. Perhaps because their patrons traced their ancestry to Rurik, the chroniclers generally ignored the other Rus' groups and instead recorded that Rurik had been 'invited' by the native Finns and Slavs of northern Russia to come and rule over them. The descendants of Rurik, the Rurikovichi, were thus cast as the only legitimate rulers of the Rus' lands. Nevertheless, other Rus' principalities existed until at least the late 970s when the future Grand Prince Vladimir killed Rogvolod of Polotsk and seized his lands.

While Novgorod remained an important centre, because of the Baltic trade, the Rurikovichi moved their headquarters to Kiev *c.* 880, when Oleg succeeded the deceased Rurik as leader of this group. Since Kiev was already controlled by other Rus' led by Askold and Dir, Oleg had to kill them first before claiming the city for the Rurikovichi. Oleg then began to conquer the various east Slavic tribes of the middle Dnieper and to impose a tribute in fur upon them. These actions created conflicts with the Khazars but laid the basis for an active trade with Constantinople. The relationship of Askold and Dir to the Khazars is uncertain. However, various Khazar officials resided in Kiev and collected tribute from the east Slavic tribes on the left bank of the Dnieper. The Rus' chroniclers would have us believe that the Khazars put up no resistance to Oleg's seizure of Kiev and the subsequent conquest of their tributaries. In any event, the appearance of Oleg and the Rurikovichi marked the beginning of the end of Khazar rule over the middle Dnieper and the real start of the Rus' state centred in Kiev.

The Rus' princes of Kiev needed over a century to conquer the east Slavic tribes and impose their control over the Finns and Balts who also inhabited north-central European Russia. The Rus' conquistadors encountered strong and persistent opposition from the natives, who were compelled to pay tribute as a sign of their subordination. The east Slavic Derevlianians, in particular, resisted Rus' domination. They revolted when Igor succeeded Oleg as head of the Rurikovichi *c.* 913. Igor restored Rus' control and imposed a larger tribute. Some years later, *c.* 945, Igor tried to collect even more tribute from the Derevlianians. Outraged by his avarice, the Derevlianians killed him. Igor's wife, Olga, then wrought triple revenge upon them, culminating in the destruction of their capital and the massacre or enslavement of its inhabitants. These events apparently led Olga to reform the way in which tribute was collected. Prior to this time, it was customary for the Rus' prince and his retinue to make the rounds of the subject peoples during winter, collecting the tribute. This practice was now seemingly replaced with the payment of tribute to local governors at a trading post or other regional site. With the tribes of the middle and upper Dnieper as well as the Novgorod lands subdued, Olga's son, Grand

Prince Sviatoslav, began the conquest of the east Slavic tribes of the upper Volga in the 960s. His son, Vladimir, had to reconquer them and suppress another revolt in the 980s before they paid tribute to the Rus' princes of Kiev on a regular basis. By *c.* 1000, almost all the lands which formed part of Kievan Rus' had been conquered, even though resident Rus' princes had not yet been installed everywhere.

The expansion of the Rurikovichi tributary state brought in huge quantities of tribute, primarily in furs. Each spring, a large convoy of ships left Kiev carrying these furs along with wax, honey and slaves to Constantinople. Thanks to Oleg's treaty of *c.* 911, Rus' merchants had gained entry into the Byzantine capital to sell their goods. The tribute collected from the peoples of European Russia was thus converted into great wealth for the Rurikovichi and their retinues. Despite this mutually profitable trade, conflicts between Rus' and Byzantium periodically erupted. In 941, for example, Igor raided the Byzantine cities along the Asia Minor coast of the Black Sea. The Byzantine navy, however, destroyed the Rus' fleet using Greek fire. In the aftermath of this raid, a new Rus'–Byzantine treaty was concluded in 945 which specified in considerable detail how the Rus' merchants were to conduct their trade in Constantinople. While many Rus' made their fortunes in the trade with Islam, the Rurikovichi of Kiev grew rich from their Byzantine commerce.

The territorial expansion and increasing wealth of the Rurikovichi tributary state led to the rapid growth of its capital city of Kiev. Prior to *c.* 880, Kiev consisted of perhaps 100–200 inhabitants occupying a few small villages with an area of 2–3 hectares. By the early tenth century, Kiev had become a large town of about 50 hectares and several thousand inhabitants. At that time, the centre of the town was Vladimir's City on the *Starokievskaia Gora* or old Kiev Hill on the high, right bank, along with the adjoining commercial centre or *Podol* located along the shore of the Dnieper. In Vladimir's City, ramparts over 6 m high and a deep moat encircled an area of some 10 hectares which contained the dwellings of the political-religious elite, the stone Church of the Blessed Virgin or Tithe Church and the stone palaces of the princes. A variety of workshops to service the elite as well as others were found throughout the city.

Because of the close ties with Byzantium, a number of Rus' began to travel to Constantinople to enter Byzantine military service, while the emperors began to turn to the Rus' for military assistance. Byzantine agents visited Kiev in 967 and gave Sviatoslav a huge bribe to attack the Danubian Bulgars. After defeating the Bulgars, Sviatoslav decided to move his capital from Kiev to the town of Pereiaslavets on the lower Danube. The Byzantines were thus forced to drive Sviatoslav out of the northern Balkans. Two decades later, the emperor Basil II requested military assistance from Grand Prince Vladimir to help suppress a revolt in Asia Minor. Vladimir complied, but this time the provision of military support by the Rus' was linked with the complex series of events leading to conversion of the Rus'.

For over a century, Christianity had been spreading slowly in European Russia, mainly because of the efforts of Vikings converted to Catholicism in Scandinavia and Rus' converted to Orthodoxy as the result of contacts with Byzantium. The new religion had a growing number of supporters in the Rus' elite. In 945, part of the Rus' who ratified the new treaty with Byzantium swore a Christian oath at the Church of St Elias in Kiev. The most famous convert was Princess Olga, heroine of the Derevlianian massacres, who accepted Christianity c. 955–8. Sviatoslav, however, was a staunch pagan, as was Vladimir for the first decade of his reign (c. 980–8/9). Vladimir even inspired a pagan revival after he ascended the throne. In 988/9, Vladimir converted to Orthodoxy, married the emperor's sister, and launched the Christianisation of his subjects. The accounts of Vladimir's conversion found in the sources mix and perhaps confuse several different themes. The most convincing account for me has been advanced by A. Poppe, who argues that in May–June of 987 the emperor Basil II sent envoys to Vladimir requesting military assistance to suppress a serious rebellion within Byzantium. An agreement was reached under which Vladimir was to convert to Orthodoxy and marry Basil's sister Anna while 6000 Rus' troops were dispatched to assist the emperor. By the summer of 989, the Rus' had helped to defeat Basil's enemies while Vladimir put down a revolt in Cherson against Basil, accepted Orthodoxy and married Anna.

Why did Vladimir convert to Orthodoxy in 988/9? When Vladimir ascended the throne (c. 980) after a bitter civil war, he ruled a highly hetero-geneous state. His subjects belonged to a number of diverse ethnic groups and religions and were at very different levels of socio-economic development. The major peoples – the east Slavs, Balts, Finns and Vikings – had no tradition of a unified state. Rather, they were each divided into numerous clans, tribes and groups. Vladimir very much needed a cohesive force which would unite all his subjects while providing legitimation for his position as grand prince. The pagan revival of Vladimir's early reign was an effort to find cohesion in a syn-cretic paganism. Unfortunately, there were varieties of paganism (east Slavic, Finnic, Baltic, Scandinavian), a growing Christian population among the ruling class, neighbouring states that were Islamic (Volga Bulgaria) and Catholic (Poland), and a recognition that a pagan Rus' state would be culturally and politically isolated. Thus, Vladimir turned to Orthodoxy to provide the cement which paganism lacked. Orthodoxy was already familiar to an elite whose pros-perity arose from the trade with Constantinople. The emperor and patriarch in distant Constantinople would find it difficult to interfere successfully in Rus' affairs. Finally, Orthodoxy legitimised Vladimir's role as grand prince. In the new system, all subjects, regardless of language and background, were now united as Christians who were governed by the god-given princes of Kiev.

The conversion of Vladimir brought more than Byzantine religion and monasticism to Rus'. Greek artisans were invited to build brick and stone churches and to decorate them with mosaics, frescoes and icons. The new religion came into conflict with indigenous traditions and practices, resulting in the need for a written law-code. Schools for the elite and chronicle writing soon developed. In addition to art, masonry architecture, law and literacy, imported technology helped Kiev to develop into a major European centre for the production of glassware, glazed ware, jewellery, etc. during the pre-Mongol era. The high culture and handicraft production of Kievan Rus' were profoundly influenced by Byzantine practices.

The unity provided by a common religious identity quickly proved essential. On the deaths of both Sviatoslav and Vladimir, bitter and protracted civil wars had erupted. The Rus' system of succession did not specify which son would succeed the deceased grand prince. All sons were eligible and most pressed their claims by force. It took Vladimir around eight years and the assistance of Viking mercenaries to defeat his half-brother Iaropolk and take Kiev *c.* 980. When Vladimir died in 1015, the Rus' state was almost permanently split into two parts. Iaroslav, aided by Viking auxiliaries, drove his brother Sviatopolk from Kiev in 1019 only to face a new challenge from another brother, Mstislav. At the battle of Listven' in 1024, Mstislav prevailed. Two years later, the brothers divided the Kievan state along the Dnieper. Mstislav ruled the eastern half from Chernigov until 1036 when he died without heirs. Iaroslav, who had ruled the western half from Novgorod, realised that only luck had prevented the fragmentation of Kievan Rus'. Consequently, just before his death in 1054, he divided the Rus' lands among his sons, with the oldest ruling in Kiev, and he admonished his sons to respect each other's inheritance. Regrettably, Iaroslav's 'last testament' was soon forgotten and the Kievan state was consumed by endless strife amongst the Rurikovichi princes.

The unresolved problem of succession became more serious as various steppe nomads threatened the southern regions of the Rus' state. Already during the early years of Igor's reign (*c.* 915), the Pechenegs had invaded the Rus' land. Soon the Pechenegs besieged Kiev itself (968, 1036) and they conducted regular raids against the Rus' settlements in the forest steppe. To defend Rus', Vladimir constructed a series of forts along his southern frontiers and staffed them with soldiers from all over the Rus' lands. The Pechenegs also endangered Rus' commerce with Byzantium, especially at the Dnieper rapids, where they waited to attack as the Rus' merchants had to transport their goods and slaves around each rapid. At the same time, the Pecheneg threat should not be exaggerated. As long as the Rus' state was united, the Pechenegs could be contained. In 1036, the Pechenegs, already under pressure in the steppe from the Torks/Oghuz, attacked Kiev but were defeated by Iaroslav. This ended the Pecheneg danger and ushered in almost a quarter-century of peace along the steppe frontier.

Iaroslav the Wise, whose reign is often considered the high point of the entire pre-Mongol era, was a very fortunate man. Defeated at the battle of Listven', he was able to share rule over Rus' till his brother Mstislav died in 1036 without heirs. Then between 1036 and his death in 1054, Iaroslav was able to use the peace created by the collapse of the Pechenegs to strengthen his state internally and to embellish its capital at Kiev. The origins of the first written law-code, the *Pravda Russkaia*, are usually connected with Iaroslav's reign. The city of Kiev grew markedly. A new fortification 3.5 kilometres long surrounded an area of 72 hectares adjacent to Vladimir's City which became known as Iaroslav's City. Four gates led into Iaroslav's City, the most famous of which are the monumental Golden Gates (26.8 m deep, 10.5 m wide, 12.5 m high) modelled on those of Constantinople. Inside 'his' City, Iaroslav had Byzantine masters construct the great Cathedral of St Sophia. With its five naves and apses, two galleries, thirteen domes, and interior frescoes it was a fitting centre for the Rus' metropolitanate. In addition to St Sophia, Iaroslav's City also included several other masonry churches, palaces for the princes and metropolitans, and numerous residential buildings for the lesser members of the elite. Under Iaroslav, Kiev was clearly one of the largest cities in medieval Europe.

Iaroslav's foreign policy was dominated by problems with Byzantium. In 1043, his eldest son led a disastrous campaign against Constantinople. Forced to make peace, Iaroslav later appointed the Rus' monk Hilarion as metropolitan in 1051. Since the patriarch in Constantinople was supposed to appoint the metropolitan of Rus', Iaroslav's action is considered a direct challenge to Byzantium. The fate of Hilarion is not known but most historians believe he had to be replaced when Iaroslav again made peace with Byzantium. Iaroslav also presided over a very cosmopolitan court. His wife, Ingigerd, was the daughter of King Olaf of Sweden, while his daughters were married to King Andrew I of Hungary, King Harald III of Norway and King Henry I of France. His sons married into royal families in Byzantium, Poland and Germany. No Rus' ruler had so many foreign connections as Iaroslav.

There are many genuine accomplishments to explain why Iaroslav has been so highly regarded by posterity. Indeed, he is the only east Slavic ruler ever to become known as Wise. At the same time, Iaroslav was very popular with the chroniclers who created our image of him. He built many new churches, founded monasteries, had church books translated from Greek into Slavic, and was highly praised for his devotion to priests and monks. Obviously, those clerics who composed the entries on Iaroslav's reign had reason to recognise his wisdom.

The death of Grand Prince Iaroslav marks, in retrospect, the end of an era. Despite many difficulties and some setbacks, the Rurikovichi princes had created from scratch one of the largest and most advanced states in all Europe. In 1054, the future looked propitious for Rus'.

CHAPTER 20

BOHEMIA AND POLAND: TWO EXAMPLES OF SUCCESSFUL WESTERN SLAVONIC STATE-FORMATION

Jerzy Strzelczyk

THE WESTERN SLAVS

From the end of the fifth century or the early sixth century the presence of Slavs in the central European area is indisputable. They settled in the eastern parts of central Europe first and spread westward, that is, to the eastern parts of modern Germany, in the second half of the sixth century. The south Slavs in the Balkans soon lost contact with the remaining Slav groups, but the mutual contacts between the two constituent parts of 'northern Slavdom' (the western and eastern Slavs, of whom the latter were incorporated into the Rus' state in the ninth and tenth centuries) were lively and intensive in the early middle ages and remained so as late as the first half of the thirteenth century.

The western Slavs included the ancestors of the peoples known later as Poles, Pomerani, Czechs, Slovaks and Polabi. From the linguistic point of view they were and still are divided into two fundamental groups. The northern, so-called Lechitic group includes, along with Polish, the dead Polabian and Pomeranian languages; the southern language group embraces Czech and Slovak. The languages of the southern part of the Polabian area, preserved as relics today in Upper and Lower Lusatia, occupy a place between the Lechitic and Czecho-Slovak groups. The western extremities of the region settled by the western Slavs embraced the tribes of Polabia: the Sorbo-Lusatic and Polabian-Baltic peoples called *Elb-* and *Ostseeslawen* in German. We know a good deal about the social and political formation of this area and about what in the last analysis was the lack of success of the tribes there in establishing a native socio-political organisation. By contrast with the Polabian Slavs, the Polish and Czech tribes succeeded in creating their own polities, which became important and lasting political agents in this part of Europe almost as soon as they emerged.

For the prehistories of Poland and Bohemia we must underline the supra-regional role played in the ninth century by the (Great) Moravian state. Under the rule of Sviatopolk (870–94) Great Moravia became a significant power and

11 Poland, Bohemia and Hungary

managed effectively to defend her independence from the eastern Frankish empire. She expanded her frontiers and her sphere of influence into Little Poland and Silesia, the areas between the Danube and the Tisza, and the part of Pannonia to the west of the Danube, as well as into Bohemia and at least a part of southern Polabia. Despite numerous conflicts with the Germans, Great Moravia acquired an impressive degree of internal consolidation and prosperity, and also mediated between the Byzantine empire and the western Slavs and Latin Christendom. The collapse of Great Moravia at the beginning of the tenth century under Hungarian pressure enabled or even accelerated the processes of consolidation in Bohemia, and also affected what was happening north of the Carpathians in what was later Poland.

The tenth century proved decisive for the future history of central, eastern and northern Europe. As in Rus' and Scandinavia, the western Slavs (and Hungarians), except the Polabi, embarked on the road to creating their own strong state organisations. This was achieved by various means, sometimes with the help of foreign powers (particularly in Rus' and Bulgaria), and it exhibits similar common basic features. However, the stabilisation of settlement, inevitable inter-tribal contacts and the progressive decline in the social significance of clan organisation led to variations in Slav societies and the creation of diverse forms of power. Previously ineffective attempts to propagate the Christian faith among the Slavs now became attractive to rulers, as the new religion began to be taken up as an ideology promoting the unity of its own social group and assuring the sacral nature of the ruling power. Christianity was strongly supported as a unifying factor for, and stabiliser of, the new political creations which had been wrought with such great effort. The western Slavs, at first positioned 'between Rome and Byzantium', came under the Roman sphere of influence and soon afterwards formed an integral part of Latin Christendom, thanks mainly to their close proximity to the Germans.

BOHEMIA

Tribal geography

The Bohemian Plain is blessed by its convenient position in the centre of Europe and by natural conditions which favour human settlement. It lies in the basin of the River Vltava, which flows into the Elbe. It is surrounded on almost all sides by belts of mountains and was inhabited from the fourth century BC by the Celtic *Boii*, who gave the land the name by which it is known in many languages: *Boiohaemum, Bohemia, Böhmen*. We learn of the names of the Slav tribes which colonised it after the Germanic tribes had abandoned it during the great migrations only significantly later, often through intermediate accounts.

The central part of the country in the lower reaches of the Vltava was occupied by the Czechs in the narrow sense of the word, who extended northward to the rivers Elbe and Oder. Their main towns were: Prague (and the associated town of Vyšehrad), Tětín, Kazin, Libušín, Levý Hradec and Dřevic. The Czechs had the greatest influence on the fate of the whole country, giving it their name and enjoying dominant status within it during historical times. In the east the Czechs shared a border with the Zličani, whose settlements lay between the rivers Sázava and Elbe. Their main towns were Stara Kouřim and Libice. To the north of these, eastern and western Croatian settlements stretched through the upper basin of the Elbe as far as the Izera basin. Between the western Croats and the Czechs dwelt the small tribe of Psovi (main town Pšov, later called Melnik). According to the sources there were three smaller tribes north of the Czechs: Litomeri, Dečani and Lemuzi. They inhabited both banks of the Elbe, which in that region flows through the Sudeten mountains. Their main towns were Litoměřice, Děčin and Bilina. To the Czechs' west on both banks of the River Ohre lived a Lucanic people known from their main town, Zatec, as Satcenses. Further west still lived the Sedličane of Sedlce. The geography of the southern Bohemian tribes is very unclear. This should probably be understood in the light of the early domination of this part of the country by the Czechs. It seems that the Dulebi played the main part among the tribes which first inhabited that region.

The unification of these regions was achieved between the eighth and tenth centuries. To the reign of Boleslav I (929/35–72) we should date the subordination of the whole of the Bohemian plain by the Czechs, who until that time had controlled only central Bohemia directly. Boleslav II's elimination of Slavnikid power in Libice in 995 can be taken as the completion of the process. We should add that the scope and political position of the Slavnikids' power are subject to academic dispute. While some are inclined to think their territory covered the whole of eastern Bohemia and was completely separate, other scholars regard the area as much smaller (at any rate they probably occupied the lands close to the Zličani) and treat the power of the Slavnik clan as a usurpation of the higher prince's rights. From that time the political unity of Bohemia was never actually put to the test – the country did not follow the path of disintegration through dynastic partition – and at the beginning of the eleventh century the long-lasting union between Moravia and Bohemia was established.

Between Moravia and the empire: the unity of Bohemia under the Přemyslids

Bohemian unification was speeded up by pressure from the east Frankish kingdom in the west and from Great Moravia in the east. Our oldest sources for Bohemia pre-date the rise of Moravia: references in Frankish sources in 791, 805, 817 and 822 suggest a loose Frankish hegemony over Bohemia. However, this domination was weakened by the Frankish crisis of the 830s, and there are references to campaigns against the Bohemians in the late 840s and the 850s, and occasional references during the next forty years imply that the Bohemians were as much under Moravian as under Frankish control. Only in 895 did 'all' the Bohemian princes appear before King Arnulf; two of them were *primores* and victorious princes: Spytihnev and Vitislav. This indicates the continuing process of consolidation in Bohemia and the formation of supra-tribal organisations.

The first indisputably 'historical' Bohemian ruler from the house of Přemysl (the legendary ancestor of the Czechs) was Bořivoj. Later sources claim that he was baptised by St Methodius, although the date given (894) is incompatible with this. He is taken to be the founder of the church of the Blessed Virgin Mary recently excavated in the Prague citadel, and died around 890. According to the *Legend of Christian*, Bořivoj's opponent was Strojmir, who returned from exile in Germany and forced Bořivoj to flee to Moravia. He was about to usurp the king's place when Bořivoj returned with Moravian reinforcements. The details of the story are questionable, but it may reflect rivalries between two parties in Bohemia at the end of the ninth century. Bořivoj's group favoured the Moravians, while Strojmir's wanted closer links with east Francia.

Bořivoj was succeeded by his sons Spytihnev (-905?) and Vratislav I (*d.* 921). Bořivoj's wife Ludmila, the daughter of the ruler of Pšov, was an ardent Christian. The collapse of Moravia at the beginning of the tenth century freed Bohemia from Moravian domination but it also deprived her of the Moravian counterbalance in her dealings with east Francia. It may have been around then or a little later under Boleslav I in the 940s that the Bohemians expanded through the girdle of mountains into Silesia and Little Poland. Vratislav I allied himself with the Polabian Slavs, marrying Drahomira the Stodoranian princess. Pressure from Germany became difficult to resist, especially after the rise of the Liudolfings. To counterbalance the pressure from Henry I, Vratislav's son and heir Wenceslas I (921–9) fostered close relations with the Bavarians. In the campaign of 928/9 Henry I defeated Wenceslas and compelled him to pay tribute. This failure provoked Wenceslas's younger brother, Boleslav I (929/35–972) to mount a coup, kill his brother and seize power. As early as the tenth century the Bohemian church recognised Wenceslas as a saint and he was to become the national patron saint. Boleslav first had to overcome some unnamed rival (*subregulus*) aided by the Saxons and Thuringians. For a long time he kept his distance from the Germans, maintaining contacts with the Polabian Slavs, and allowing Hungarians to pass through his lands to Thuringia. Thus he constructed defence outposts, later to be the kernels of urban organisation in

Bohemia. However in 950 he had to submit to Otto I, and in 955 he fought with the Germans against the Hungarians. This relationship of dependence on Germany forced on the Bohemians would turn out to be long-lasting.

The marriage of Boleslav I's sister Dobrava to the Polanian duke, Miesco I, in 965 signalled a weakening of Bohemian relations with the Polabian tribes whose strength was waxing, and the temporary stabilisation of Bohemian rule in southern Poland. Good relations with the neighbouring Polanian state did not last long, given the rivalry of Prague and Gniezno for supremacy among the western Slavs. Boleslav's son and heir, Boleslav II (967/72–999) continued his father's policy. He succeeded in obtaining his own bishopric in Prague, dependent on the archbishop of Mainz; previously Bohemia had been under the jurisdiction of the bishop of Regensburg.

Bohemian eastward expansion established relations with Kievan Rus'; Boleslav II's son Boleslav married a daughter of the Grand Duke Vladimir. Relations with Poland were soon set on a proper footing and the leaders of both polities willingly cooperated with the German regency in 983 in an attack on the Polabian Slavs. This collaboration with the Saxon dynasty, which dates back to 978, was preceded by cooperation between the Bohemian ruler (along with the Polanian duke Miesco) and Henry of Bavaria. Boleslav II's wife Emma was of Bavarian descent and his brother Strachwas became a monk in Regensburg. By 995 Boleslav had concluded the political unification of the Bohemian plain, a process already significantly advanced by Boleslav I. This he achieved through the violent elimination of the Slavnikid dukes based in Libice in eastern Bohemia. Slavnikid rule, supported by Saxony and Poland, did not accord with the aspirations of the government in Prague. A few survivors of the Slavnikid clan took refuge in Poland or Germany, including the then bishop of Prague, Adalbert-Vojtech.

The crisis of the Přemyslid state at the turn of the tenth and eleventh centuries: the Polish interlude and Břetislav I's reconstruction

Under Boleslav III (999–1003) the Bohemian state reached a crisis point. Coupled with an internal dynastic quarrel and the conflict between the ruler and the bishop of Prague were social disquiet, opposition from a section of the nobility and disputes with neighbouring lands. Boleslav's brothers Jaromir and Oldřich took refuge along with their mother Emma at the court of the duke of Bavaria (later Emperor Henry II). St Adalbert's successor, Bishop Thiedag, fled to Margrave Ekkehard of Meissen. The noble party which opposed Boleslav deposed him and summoned his cousin Vladivoj from Poland to rule; he acknowledged Henry II's overlordship but did not manage to bring order to the realm during his brief reign (1003). After his death, the nobles invited first

Jaromir and then Oldřich from their Bavarian exile to assume power. However at this moment, the duke of Poland, Boleslav Chrobry (a grandson of Boleslav I of Bohemia), intervened. Making use of Boleslav III, who had been handed over to him, the Polish duke first launched an armed intervention in Bohemia to return the exile to power. The subsequent bloody settlement of scores by Boleslav III with his influential enemies, the Vršovci clan, turned Bohemian opinion against him. The Polish duke exploited this by intervening; he imprisoned and blinded Boleslav III and assumed personal rule in Prague. Henry II was prepared to acknowledge Boleslav Chrobry as duke provided that he acknowledged imperial rights, but Boleslav refused to do homage to Henry for Bohemia. This led to open conflict in the course of which the Germans brought Jaromir and Oldřich to Prague and the Polish garrison was obliged to leave Bohemia. However, Moravia and Slovakia remained under Polish control.

Jaromir (1004–12) became a faithful vassal of the emperor and on several occasions fought alongside him against Poland. In 1012 he was deposed by his brother Oldřich, who maintained a pro-German policy during the reign of Conrad II. Around 1030 Oldřich's son Břetislav drove the Poles from Moravia and ruled there himself. However, relations with the Empire soon deteriorated and a punitive expedition was sent by the new king, Henry III. Oldřich was deposed. Power was taken by Jaromir who returned from exile and later (from 1034) both brothers shared rule in Bohemia with imperial blessing. However Oldřich had his brother blinded and expelled his own son Břetislav from Moravia. Oldřich's death obviated the need for a new imperial intervention. Břetislav I (d. 1055) became prince in 1034, receiving Bohemia and (for the first time in this manner) Moravia as imperial fiefs in Bamberg. Under Břetislav the creation of the Bohemian monarchy was completed. An attempt to take advantage of Polish weakness following the death of Miesco II met with imperial opposition. An armed expedition of Bohemian forces was directed against Poland in 1038, in the course of which, *inter alia*, Cracow, Wrocław, Gniezno and Poznań were captured and large areas of the country laid waste; the relics of St Adalbert were taken from Gniezno along with those of his brother Radzim-Gaudentius and the five martyred brethren (hermits who had been murdered *c.* 1000). Emperor Henry III feared excessive increase in Bohemian power. A Bohemian–German war in 1040–1 ended with the capitulation of Břetislav in the Prague citadel. After his surrender the Bohemians swore homage in Regensburg and handed over his Polish captives, though Silesia was not returned to Poland until 1050, and ratification of Polish control in Silesia came about only in 1054 through Henry III's arbitration.

By remaining a generally faithful vassal of the emperor after the homage of Regensburg, which brought considerable consequences for his foreign policy (i.e., respecting imperial arbitration in his disputes with Poland and taking part in military expeditions against the Hungarians), Břetislav maintained his power uncurtailed within his own country. He used his power to consolidate the state and his own dynasty's position. Břetislav resettled citizens of Giecz (in Great Poland) near present-day Hedčany, east of Kralovice and also (but this is less clear) some of the citizens of Kruszwica. He is credited with consolidating (or rather codifying) the principle of succession by the seniorate, a development linked with the principle of the indivisibility of the state and the royal patrimony. Břetislav's younger sons received lands in Moravia to be held as fiefs from the eldest brother. Attempts to obtain an ecclesiastical province from the Roman curia ended in failure, but Břetislav patronised and even spread new church institutions throughout his lands. He patronised the monastery at Sázava which had been founded during his brother Oldřich's reign, and the first Latin monastery in Moravia was built at Rajhrad, *c.* 1050. He also established a collegiate chapter in Stara Boleslav. Around 1050 he introduced monetary reform, establishing the Prague *grivna* as the basis of the currency, which lasted for many centuries. At an unknown earlier point, traditionally associated with the Polish campaign in Gniezno in 1038, he promulgated a collection of eight decrees settling various legal questions within his realm. His close collaboration with Bishop Šebir of Prague (1031–67) ended during the war with Germany, when the bishop and a group of nobles deserted to his opponents.

POLAND

Tribal geography

The beginnings of Slavonic settlement north of the Carpathian and Sudeten Mountains are more difficult to determine than those in Bohemia and Moravia, among other reasons because significantly less is known of the decline of earlier ethnic and settlement structures in that region. Matters are complicated further by the support that is continually found for the autochthonists' view that part or even the whole of Polish territory formed the 'ancient homeland' of the Slavs. When the ethnic situation in Polish territories becomes a little more decipherable in the ninth century – from three independent sources, the Bavarian Geographer, King Alfred's description of Germany and the anonymous Old Church Slavonic *Life of Methodius* – it appears that there were several large tribes whose settlement pattern corresponded, roughly speaking, to the later divisions of the Polish state under the first Piasts. Ninth-century sources confirm only that the Vistulani (*Wiślanie*), Goplani (*Goplanie*) and, less clearly, the Lendizi (*Lędzianie*) belonged to this group. To this list of large tribes (tribal confederations?) we must certainly add the Polani (*Polanie*) in Great Poland, the

Slezi in Lower Silesia, who are named by the Bavarian Geographer but placed among the 'lesser' tribes, the Mazovi and the Pomerani. The tribal structure of Silesia is best known. Alongside the aforementioned Slezi the Bavarian Geographer names the Dziadoszani (around Głogów), Opolani (around Opole), Golęszyce (near Raciborz) and the enigmatic Lupiglaa (Glupczani?). From later sources we learn of the Bobrzani (on the river Bóbr?) and the Trzebowi (?). By contrast with Silesia, where the Bavarian Geographer lists the usual 'lesser' tribes, in Little Poland the sources name only the Vistulani on the Upper Vistula (around Cracow and Sandomir). To the east of these, on the Rus' border, were certain Lendizian settlements which Constantine Porphyrogenitus mentions twice (*Lendzanenoi*) and from whose name the eastern neighbours derive their name for the Polish tribes (*Liakh* in Rus' sources, *Lenkas* to the Balts and *Lengyel* among the Hungarians).

The absence of the Polani from the work of the Bavarian Geographer and other sources needs some discussion, given that this tribe, later powerful in northern Poland, lent its name to both Poland and the Polish. The name Polani in the general sense (all the first subjects of the Polish dukes) appears in sources only at the turn of the tenth and eleventh centuries, when the state formed by Polanian leaders appears on the historical stage. It appears that in the mid-ninth century the Polani were a less significant tribe which was inferior to its eastern neighbours, the inhabitants of Kujawy. It is surely the latter which are hidden in the Bavarian Geographer under the name of *Glopeani* – Goplani (named from Lake Gopło) who were centred on Kruszwica. Traces of the competition between the Goplani and Polani were probably preserved in Polish historical tradition in the form of a tale of the violent overthrow of the (Goplanian?) Popiel dynasty; the Popiels were succeeded in their control of Gniezno by the Polanian Piasts. Polanian settlements were in what later became Greater Poland. They were centred on the middle stretches of the Warta and their main towns were Gniezno, Poznań, Ostrów Lednicki and Giecz. No source mentions the Mazovi and Pomerani (among the latter we may distinguish the Wolini on the island of Wolin and Pyrzyczani in the Pyrzyce region) before the eleventh century. Some scholars consider that they were not actually tribes, but groups which formed distinct entities later within the context of the Piast state.

Without counting the Pomerani, who were fully (but not continuously) connected with Poland only at the beginning of the twelfth century (although they formed part of the realms ruled by Miesco I and Boleslav Chrobry), Poland under the first Piasts was divided into two clearly distinct geographical regions: northern Poland, encompassing the lowlands of Great Poland, Kujawy and Mazovia, and southern Poland, encompassing the highlands and great mountains and including Silesia and Little Poland (the Cracow and Sandomir regions). We know the names of Miesco's predecessors, Siemowit, Lestek and Siemomysl, from the tradition recorded at the beginning of the twelfth century by the first Polish chronicler, Gallus Anonymus.[1] Their achievement was to unite northern Poland, at a time and in a manner unknown to us. In the time of Miesco I, Polanian expansion spread over Pomerania, Lubusz and, in its final stage, over southern Poland so that finally under Boleslav Chrobry the Polani came to control Bohemia, Moravia and Slovakia (along the Danube), part of southern Polabia and the so-called Czerwień towns (Grody Czerwieńskie) on the borders with the Rus'.

Two state-creating groups: the Vistulani and the Polani

The silence of the sources on the Polani and their impact on the Vistulani in the ninth century is not coincidental. The lands of southern Poland had long been significantly more advanced, and their natural resources favoured human settlement more than did the wooded and swampy terrain of northern Poland. Moreover the influence of external polities – Rus', Byzantium, Moravia and Germany – was significantly stronger in the south than in the Polanian lands, long subject to physical and political isolation. Admittedly, around 875–80 Little Poland and Silesia found themselves under strong political influence from the Great Moravian state, and in the tenth century from Bohemia. They were subject for a longer time to the influences of the south, for example in the matter of conversion to Christianity. All this, despite occasional swings in scholarly opinion, cannot be overstated. The 'conquest' of Little Poland by Sviatopolk of Moravia merely proves that the Vistulani had seemingly lost the chance to gather around themselves other eastern-Lechitic (Polish) lands and assume hegemony over lands north of the Carpathians.

At that time, unthreatened by outside powers, the Gniezno state of the first Piasts emerges from the shadows of the sources. After gaining control of Polanian and Goplanian territories, the Polani seized their chance to annex Mazovia, Pomerania and the lands of the Lendizi. The conquest of Pomerania was achieved by the first 'historical' Polanian leader, Miesco I (*c.* 960–92), who managed towards the end of his life to gain the Silesian territories disputed with Bohemia (990?) and Little Poland together with Cracow,[2] thus completing the lengthy process of uniting the Polish lands.

Although under Miesco I the terms 'Poland' and 'Polish' (*Polonia, Poloni*) are not yet in the sources, authors used various circumlocutions for Miesco and his

---

[1] Gallus Anonymus, *Chronicae et gesta ducum sive principum polonorum* i, 3.

[2] I respond to the view expressed by Labuda (1988), chapter 8, that the date of the Polish capture of Cracow must be corrected. Cosmas of Prague, *Chronica Boemorum* i, 34, dates it to just after the death of Boleslav II (999).

realm, such as 'prince of the Slavs', 'the realm of Miesco', *Licikaviki*[3] and 'prince of the Vandals'. Above all, Miesco I engaged the attention of the west, where his main aim was to conquer Pomerania and Lubusz and neutralise the threat posed to him by the Veleto-Bohemian alliance. The first we hear of him is his battles with the Veleti between 963 and 967. He also aimed to establish links with the German empire and its eastern clients. His marriage with the Bohemian princess Dobrava in 965 was symptomatic of the Polono-Bohemian *rapprochement*. The baptism of prince and people in 966 and the establishment of a missionary bishopric at Poznań in 968 were important decisions affecting Poland's place in Europe.

Miesco was on good terms with Otto I; Widukind refers to the Polish ruler as *amicus imperatoris*.[4] The tribute paid *usque ad Vurta fluvium* presumably refers to lands newly annexed to Poland (Pomerania, Lubusz) nominally subject to German overlordship.[5] The arbitrary attack by Margrave Hodo of the Ostmark on Miesco's realm was unable to destroy him and it ended in German defeat at Cedynia (Zeden) in 972. After Otto I's death the princes of Poland and Bohemia followed separate policies in their relations with Germany, making use of internal conflicts within the empire, especially the rebellions by the Bavarian duke, Henry the Wrangler, from 974 and again from 984. The defeat and death of Otto II in Italy, the great revolt of the Polabian Slavs which erupted in 983 and the troubles of the regency governing in the name of the minor, Otto III, all facilitated the realisation of Miesco I's plans. From 985 Miesco supported the young emperor's party, and around 986 he repudiated the alliance with the Bohemians. He developed closer relations with Hungary and around 990, as a result of his war with Bohemia, Miesco annexed to Poland both Silesia and Little Poland.

After the death of Dobrava, Miesco married for a second time around 980. His new wife was Oda, the daughter of Margrave Dietrich of the northern March. In 991 Miesco placed his lands (*civitas Schinesghe*: the realm of Gniezno) under the direct protection of the Holy See.[6] Despite his desire to secure his realm for the future against an overpowerful German influence, Miesco was certainly driven by the wish to ensure that, after his death, Poland would be governed by Oda and her young sons, which went against the interests of Miesco's first-born son from the Dobrava marriage, Boleslav Chrobry.

---

[3] Widukind, *Res gestae Saxonicae* III, 66: 'Misacam regem, cuius potestatis erant Sclavi, qui dicuntur Licicaviki' The etymology and actual meaning of this name are still a matter for scholarly debate.

[4] *Ibid.* III, 69.   [5] Thietmar, *Chronicon* II, 29.

[6] We know of this from a description of the letter given a century later in a papal register. The text begins with the curious words: 'Dagome iudex et Ote senatrix', hence the usual scholarly name for it. The form *Dagome* may be a conjunction of the alleged Christian name of the Polish duke (Dagobert) and his family name: Dago[*bertus*] Me[*sco*].

However, after the death of Miesco I on 25 May 992, Boleslav paid no attention to his father's wishes. He exiled his step-mother and her sons, and crushed the not particularly strong resistance to his succession. By these means Boleslav came to enjoy complete control throughout the land.

The Polish state seeks hegemony among the western Slavs

Early in his reign Boleslav the Brave was careful to maintain his alliance with Germany where Otto III came into his majority in 994. Boleslav assisted the Germans in their campaigns in Polabia. At the same time he supported the anti-Přemyslid opposition in Bohemia. After Boleslav II of Bohemia had crushed the Slavnikids of Libice in 995, Boleslav Chrobry welcomed the exiled Slavnikid bishop of Prague, St Adalbert. Adalbert was martyred on 23 April 997 while on a mission to the Prussi undertaken at the behest of Boleslav Chrobry. By recovering the martyr's relics and preserving them in the capital Gniezno, Boleslav's Poland gained its own sacral centre and increased respect in the eyes of Christendom. The Polish ruler knew how to exploit this situation. In March 1000 Emperor Otto III came on pilgrimage to the tomb of his friend Adalbert, who had been canonised in Rome the year before. At the synod of Gniezno, called because of the imperial visit, the Polish capital was raised to the rank of the seat of an archbishopric with control over three (newly created?) sees in Cracow, Wrocław and Kołobrzeg and – later – an earlier missionary see, now restricted to western Great Poland, based in Poznań. The political decisions taken at the imperial assembly in Gniezno are less clearly defined. According to later Polish tradition, the emperor raised the Polish ruler to royal status and accomplished at least the first, secular part of the coronation. However, the prevalent view is that by placing a crown on Boleslav's head and addressing him as *frater et cooperator imperii*,[7] Otto granted him imperial rights over the government of the Polish church (primarily in the investiture of bishops). This was in accordance with the general political conception of Otto III, who intended to revive the Roman empire with Poland (*Sclavinia*) as an equal member of the empire alongside Rome, France and Germany, a conception given visual formulation in the Reichenau Gospels.

The change in imperial policy after the death of Otto III and the accession of Henry II (1002) soon produced Polono-German conflict. At first, relying on strong support in Germany – from Ekkehard and Gunzelin of Meissen and from the Bavarian margrave of the northern March, Henry of Schweinfurt and others – Boleslav seized Lusatia, Milzen and Meissen. He sought to hold the first two as fiefs at an assembly in Merseburg. Open conflict followed his

---

[7] Gallus Anonymus, *Chronicae et gesta ducum sive principum polonorum* 1, 6, p. 20.

seizure of Bohemia and Moravia in 1003 and his refusal to do homage for them. German intervention forced Boleslav to leave Bohemia in 1004, but he maintained control over Moravia and Slovakia. In 1005, with the help of the Bohemians and the Liutizi (the alliance of Henry II with the archpagan Liutizi scandalised public opinion), a great German expedition was launched against Poland. This campaign ended unfavourably for Poland with the peace of Poznań, by which Boleslav was compelled to surrender his earlier gains in Lusatia, Milzen and Bohemia. Next, the newly formed bishopric of Kołobrzeg collapsed. This should be interpreted as the decline of Polish influence in Pomerania, probably because of pagan reaction from across the Oder (the Liutizi alliance). The next phase of the Polish–German war began in 1007 when the Polish ruler attacked Lusatia, and continued for several years until the peace of Merseburg in 1013. By this Boleslav kept Lusatia and Milzen as fiefs of the empire. Boleslav's son Miesco II married Richeza, the daughter of Ezzo, count palatine of the Rhine. Both parties could expect the use of a force of 300 fighting-men when need arose, but the Polish side did not fulfil this part of the agreement. The last stage in the Polono-German wars lasted from 1015 to 1018 and was provoked by the Germans. It ended with the peace of Bautzen (1018) which, considering the length of the whole war and the degree of commitment to the fight by the Germans, worked out to Poland's advantage. Boleslav kept Lusatia and Milzen, and the silence of the German sources suggests that he held them without paying homage to the empire.

In 1018 there was a Polish expedition to Rus', following an unsuccessful campaign four years earlier, which received help from German, Hungarian and even Pecheneg auxiliaries. Having defeated the enemy on the Bug, Boleslav captured Kiev without a fight and set Sviatopolk on the grand ducal throne. In the spring of 1019 the Polish armies returned home without encountering further resistance from the Rus'. They took with them booty and prisoners and held the Czerwień towns (headed by Czerwień and Przemyśl) for Poland. These towns and part at least of the Lendizi territory had been seized from Bohemia in 981 by Grand Duke Vladimir of Kiev.

As Thietmar of Merseburg's chronicle falls silent the shadows close round the last years of Boleslav Chrobry's reign. The deaths of Henry II and Pope Benedict VIII in 1024 perhaps facilitated the coronation of the Polish ruler in Gniezno in 1025, undoubtedly at Easter. This did not long precede the death of Boleslav Chrobry on 17 June 1025. He continued the policies of Miesco I, established more fully the short-lived splendour of the young Polish state and assured its dominance among the western Slavs. However he overestimated his own powers and exposed his people to exhausting military endeavours and his state to the antagonism of almost all her neighbours. Soon after his death, Poland lost all her extra-Polish possessions and fell victim to great internal crises.

Miesco II and the collapse of the first Piast state after 1034: the beginnings of the restoration

Miesco II (1025–34), crowned immediately on his accession to the throne, was not perhaps the equal of his father in skill or energy, but he also had to pay the price of Boleslav's excessively expansionist policies. The Polish monarchy, inaugurated essentially by Boleslav Chrobry in 992, and formally sanctioned by the coronation of 1025, was a new phenomenon and led to conflict within the dynasty. Miesco's elder brother from his father's Hungarian marriage, Bezprym, had been disinherited by Boleslav and sent to a monastery, probably like his second son Otto. Both pretenders soon found themselves outside Poland, Bezprym in Rus', Otto in Germany; both sought aid against Miesco II. In 1028 the Polish king invaded and so provoked retaliation from Conrad II in 1029. Matters came to a head in 1030, when concerted German and Rus' attacks on Poland began, supported by simultaneous onslaughts from Bohemia. The Bohemians seized Moravia, thenceforth inseparable from Bohemia. Iaroslav the Wise of Kiev attacked the Czerwień towns. In 1031 German forces captured Lusatia and Milzen, which were thenceforth lost to Poland for good. With the armed support of the Rus' and undoubtedly of a section of Polish society disaffected with the king, Bezprym seized power in Poland, driving Miesco into exile in Bohemia. Queen Richeza and her son Casimir fled to Germany, taking the royal insignia with them. Bezprym's regime met with resistance from a large sector of Polish society and he was murdered after a few months, in March or April 1032. Despite having been maimed by the Bohemians, Miesco II returned to Poland and assumed the throne once more, but he was not in a position to resist a new German attack. He submitted to Conrad II in Merseburg in 1032 and renounced his royal title. In accordance with the emperor's wishes, Miesco had to agree to a role as subject prince and his other brothers, Otto and Dietrich, received, or were supposed to receive, their own portions. Shortly before his death in 1034, Miesco II succeeded in regaining control of a reunited kingdom. At the moment of his death, the only living head of the dynasty was his son Casimir, who was in Germany with his mother.

After Miesco died, the Polish state embarked on a period of violent disintegration. There were separatist movements in the provinces, especially in Mazovia and Pomerania, the latter having fallen away completely from Polish control. Pagan opposition raised its head with a call to return to an earlier tribal freedom, a reaction supported by a part of the rural population and by the warriors. The pagan revolution swept through Great Poland in particular, and in central Poland it destroyed a significant part of the ecclesiastical infrastructure. However it had no, or at least only a very minor, effect on Little Poland and Mazovia, which remained under the effective control of Duke Miecław. These

misfortunes were increased by the destructive invasion of Břetislav of
Bohemia in 1038 (see above, p. 520). Silesia was filled with Bohemian garrisons
and was lost to Polish control for more than ten years.

Faced by the evident dangers posed by a political vacuum in Poland and by a
pagan revival, as well as by what from a German point of view was an excessive
growth in Bohemian power, the German court supported the only claimant to
the Polish throne, Casimir I the Restorer (1034/9–1058). With the help of a
small German party, he returned to Poland, probably in the autumn of 1039,
and won support from influential Polish circles exhausted by the conflict. After
considerable exertions Casimir annexed Mazovia (1047), restored supremacy
over Pomerania (1048) and re-established control of Silesia (1050). This Polish
state, smaller in territorial extent and international significance than the empire
created by Boleslav Chrobry, was well knit, with lasting ethnic bonds, and
strengthened by the consolidated influence of its governing apparatus. With
the exception of Pomerania, this realm would be the basis of the Polish
kingdom in the future – Silesia broke away only in the fourteenth century. The
heart of this restored 'second' Piast state clearly shifted, not only as a result of
the Bohemian depredations, from Gniezno in Greater Poland (though this
continued to be the metropolitan see) to Cracow in Little Poland.

'A STATE WITH PRINCELY LAW': BOHEMIA AND POLAND, SOCIAL AND POLITICAL STRUCTURES, THE CHURCH AND CHRISTIANITY

'In those days there were four kings among them: the King of the Bulgars,
Bojeslav, king of Faraga, Bojema and Karako and Meshko, king of the north
and, on the western borders, Nakon.'[8] Among the four west Slavonic leaders
mentioned by Ibrāhīm ibn Yaʿqūb (who travelled across Europe from the caliphate of Córdoba around 965/6), we find the Bohemian duke (the king of
Prague, Bohemia and Cracow) Boleslav I, and the king of the north, Miesco I,
duke of the Polani. Ibrāhīm could have learned about the western Slavs in
Magdeburg or Prague.

Despite features peculiar to each of them, the history of both western
Slavonic states exhibits a range of common characteristics. As most of these
are also found in the Hungarian state we may speak of a central European
model of early medieval state formation. Ignoring the short-lived extra-Polish
acquisitions of Boleslav Chrobry, the history of early medieval Poland was
played out in a much broader context than the history of Bohemia, even
including Moravia. By contrast with the geographic unity of Bohemia within
clear boundaries, Poland lacked such natural borders to the west and the east,

---

[8] *Relatio Ibrahim ibn Ja'kub*, p. 145.

but it benefited from a consciousness of common ethnic identity among the Polish tribes, as against their neighbours, the eastern Slavs, Balts (Prussi, Sudavi and Lithuani) and Germans. Poland formed under different conditions from those prevalent in Bohemia, whose neighbours were the southern Polabi, Poles, Germans and Hungarians. Moreover the Germans were much closer to the Bohemians than to the Poles, who until the 960s were completely cut off from the Germans and were later to some degree protected from them by a 'buffer zone' in Polabia.

The medieval Polish and Bohemian states are characterised by an almost ideal ethnic homogeneity, each drawing her related tribes around her into one entity and uniting all the tribes of a given group, be it Polish or Czech, though this is not to deny the existence of intermediate regions such as Upper Silesia or the development of local separatist tendencies in Moravia, Mazovia and Pomerania. The latter (with the exception of the Pomerani, only weakly integrated into the first Piast state) did not play an important role in the creation of the state, or they became significant only at a later period. It should be added that the linguistic differences among the western Slavs were not as great around AD 1000 as they are today.

The details of the formation of the first Bohemian and Polish states are not very clear, especially as there is an almost complete absence of local contemporary sources; the historical tradition known to us for the first time in the early twelfth century, almost simultaneously from the works of Cosmas of Prague and Gallus Anonymus, grew up in an exiguous and selective way, filtered through the chroniclers' erudition and distorted by later fantasy and social requirements.

In Bohemia there was one significant political centre in the middle of the country, reflecting the position of Prague in the Bohemian state. In Moravia two centres competed for prominence – Olomouc and Brno. However, in Poland at the end of our period the main political centre was transferred from Gniezno in Great Poland (Poznań, although not without importance, was secondary to Gniezno) to Cracow in southern Poland.

The influence of neighbouring polities on Poland and Bohemia was different. The Moravian state exercised substantially more political and cultural influence on Bohemia than on Poland, even southern Poland, for a time probably a part of Moravia's possessions. Moravo-Bohemian relations, often exaggerated by scholars, were limited, although they led to Moravian domination in the ninth century, when Bohemia appears as a province on the very periphery of the Moravian empire. Real contacts were hindered until the thirteenth century by the almost impenetrable band of forest and mountain separating Moravia from Bohemia. At first the Bohemians appropriated Moravian traditions cautiously; the theory of *translatio regni*, by which Bohemia was the heir to

Moravian power, appeared only in the later middle ages. In the eleventh
century the earlier relationship between Moravia and Bohemia was reversed.
Thenceforth Moravia was under Bohemian dominion and, although she
retained a certain distinctness within Bohemia (from 1182 Moravia was a separate imperial fief), her unequal union with Bohemia was never seriously questioned.

The clan as the fundamental unit of social organisation existed in both societies long before the tenth century. This gave way to units based on territorial
bonds, such as village communes: the *opole* in northern Poland and the *osada* in
Bohemia and southern Poland. The clan (except the royal clan) did not play
much part in the creation of the state. The prevalent view is that the aristocratic
families in later Bohemia and Poland were not descended from the clans of the
tribal period. Gradually, but inevitably, the tribes also lost their political pre-
eminence in the creation of the new states. They declined in Moravia by the
ninth century and in Bohemia and Poland they functioned as shadows of their
former selves under the levelling policies of the dukes. This contrasts with the
Polabian Slavs where, especially among the Liutizi, the tribes maintained their
pre-eminence even after other groups developed and effectively paralysed any
attempt at state consolidation.

Despite the traditional view which assigns democratic (communal government) structures to the ancient Slavs, and social differentiation and the creation
of an aristocracy to the Germans, we cannot doubt the existence of an upper
class among the Slavs in the early period, though it had no clear legal definition.
In the tenth century this class was still not on an equal footing with the rulers,
but depended on them, deriving status and wealth above all from state service.
In the course of time (fully only in a later period) they came to draw power
from control of land and people, becoming great landholders. The significance
and relative (but increasing) autonomy of the aristocracy is shown by the fact
that, in the event of political collapse (royal disfavour or foreign invasion), part
of the nobility always remained powerful and retained its rank. However it is
probable that the Přemyslids (and surely the Piasts too, although in this case the
sources are less clear) physically eliminated almost the whole 'old aristocracy'.
At the same time there arose differences between the aristocracy and the
common people, warriors and peasants alike. The 'new' nobility, purposely
created by the rulers and corresponding to the German *ministeriales*, although
the legal status of freemen was not questioned, came to ever greater prominence.

The majority of the population was divided into two basic classes. The warriors owed military service to the state and received land in return as allods
('warriors' law'). This land they maintained at their own expense with the help
of their family, retainers, prisoners of war and, occasionally, slaves. The village

people were directly dependent on the ruler (and state officials) and owed military service only in defence of the realm (*pospolite ruszenie*: levy in mass). They also owed various other services to the state such as tribute and labour services. The unfree population was mostly on the ruler's estates and was not very numerous, gradually merging with the mass of commoners.

The fulcrum of the newly created states was the ruler (duke or king) with his court and local administrative centres. From the ninth century the sources, which until then had usually called Slav rulers king (*rex*) without distinction, begin to differentiate between normal (tribal) dukes and 'kings', the latter term being reserved for those leaders with control over other dukes. The lack of an actual coronation in the Christian sense (since only the pope or the emperor may dispense crowns) had no effect at first on internal relations, although in Poland this lack of inauguration rites tended to favour centrifugal tendencies within the ruling dynasty. There is no doubt that the dukes of Bohemia enjoyed a status equal to that of a king, as did the first two Polish leaders before the coronation of Boleslav Chrobry.

The question of kingship is connected with the problems of Bohemian and Polish relations with the empire. From the mid-tenth century Bohemia had permanent links with the German empire, whose constitutional significance is controversial. From 1041 Bohemian dependence on the empire was not questioned until the Hussite movement of the later middle ages, and in the course of time Bohemia (and Moravia) came to be regarded as a constituent part of the German empire, although the Bohemian rulers maintained full control of internal affairs, and enjoyed a special position among the imperial princes. Poland, like Hungary, remained outside the empire, being connected only temporarily with the empire on a tributary basis for a part of its territory, though it was sometimes subject to the political influence of the German rulers.

The dynasties, whose names, the Přemyslids and Piasts, were devised in modern times, were respected as 'natural lords'. They alone enjoyed the right to govern. Until the end (the Přemyslids became extinct in 1306 and the main Piast line died out in 1370), no-one questioned their right to rule. Tradition has preserved the first traces of magic elements in the dynasty's rule – both Přemysl and Piast were supposed to have been ploughmen. At first, all male leaders of the dynasties theoretically had a right to rule, but who actually did so depended on support from factions within society. Dynastic territorial partitions were thus the norm. In Bohemia they were opposed by the seniorate which was strengthened by Břetislav I (it was introduced into Poland in 1138). In Poland, royal coronations led to the unity of the state and excluded collateral lines from succession to the throne.

Given the lack, or primitive nature, of original state institutions, the ruler's power was at once both strong and shallow, being limited by customary law, the need for popular acceptance and the realities of enforcing royal will. The absence of taxation compelled the state to embark on an active policy of plunder and conquest. A political system based on such methods could not last long and, as a rule, ended in collapse, as in Bohemia at the end of the tenth century, and in Poland after 1034.

The basis of the ruler's power was a monopoly on land (in as much as it was not parcelled out among the nobles and warriors as allods or had not been conferred on them) and supreme power over the people. Both were in this early period practically unchallenged, diminishing rapidly only in the twelfth and thirteenth centuries as a result of privileges and immunities for ecclesiastical and secular magnates. The actual base of the ruler's power was tribute and services rendered by the prince's servitors alongside a strongly established system of service-settlement peculiar to Poland, Bohemia and Hungary. This provided the ruler with almost complete control over the economy, while his court and state organisation gained essential commodities and special services. The ruler's most important armed force, apart from the general warriors' service and the levy in mass which was occasionally summoned, was the *druzhina* (following). This assumed various forms, centralised and local, and sizes. It consisted mainly of young men, who had special contacts with the ruler, and it is reminiscent of vassal bands in western Europe, as can be seen in the classic description of the princely *druzhina* by Ibrāhīm ibn Ya'qūb in his account of Miesco I's realm.[9] Initially, the members of the *druzhina* were maintained by their lord with gifts and the opportunity to participate in military raids. Gradually, beginning perhaps as early as the tenth century in Bohemia, they were settled on estates. This relieved pressure on the princely treasury and created a lasting bond between the retainer and the prince. Once the retainer held land in fief, and hence inevitably came to be rooted in local society, there was a potential conflict of interests between him and his lord; but the formation of private landholdings in Bohemia, still more so in Poland, probably did not get beyond the preliminary stages in the tenth and eleventh centuries.

Local government, in Poland as in Bohemia, relied, given the paucity of cities in the western European sense, on a close network of towns based around tribal centres – what Frankish sources call *civitates*. As the state developed these were reorganised. They were centres of power combining military and administrative functions. Amongst them a small group of central towns evolved such as Prague, Levý Hradec and Libice in Bohemia; Cracow, Sandomir and Wrocław in southern Poland and Gniezno, Poznań and Ostrów Lednicki in Great Poland. Kalisz, Głogów and Santok formed along the border of the Piast lands. In Bohemia the closest and earliest network of towns was

[9] *Ibid.*, p. 147.

created in the eastern and central, 'Přemyslid', part of the country. The reform of the town system in Bohemia is clear from archaeological evidence from the time of Boleslav I. In Poland at the end of the tenth century we see the fall of many 'tribal' towns and the creation of new ruling centres; the link between this and the unifying policies of the rulers is evident. Similarly, in central Bohemia some of the old towns lost their importance as the government became centralised, and they fell into decline.

In Poland there was perhaps a higher tier of administration above the town organisation which formed the basis of the administrative system: the provinces, which corresponded roughly to the ancient tribal territories. In the oldest period these territories were subject to members of the same dynasty, as Little Poland had been to Boleslav Chrobry and (less certainly) to Miesco II before they assumed power.

The church played a common role in the early phases of the development of societies and states in central Europe. After a Moravian phase, whose extent is disputed, there followed in the tenth century a period of German influences first from Bavaria and later from Saxony. Bohemia, until the erection of her own bishopric in Prague in 973, fell under the pastoral care of the bishop of Regensburg; Moravia was dependent on Passau, and thus both came under the archbishop of Salzburg. The newly created see of Prague was excluded from the province of Salzburg and came under the control of the metropolitan of Mainz where it remained until the creation of the province of Prague in 1344. The bishopric of Prague covered the whole of Bohemia. The early history of the Moravian church remains clouded. The see of Moravia, Olomouc, appears in the sources in 976; we do not know whether it was created along with the bishopric of Prague or whether it is a hangover from the Great Moravian state.

Bohemia, as we saw above, did not obtain its own ecclesiastical province until the later middle ages. Each bishop of Prague sought investiture from the emperor and consecration at the hands of the archbishop of Mainz. Nevertheless, the ruler of Bohemia had the deciding voice in appointing to the bishopric of Prague, as later with the see of Olomouc. He also supervised the activities of the bishops. By contrast, the church in Poland and Hungary soon broke away from the German church. The beginnings of Christianity in Poland – leaving aside the puzzling and disputed origins of Christianity in southern Poland in the Moravian period – are connected with Bohemian and Bavarian influences. By 968 there was a missionary see in Poland (with Bishop Jordan, of origins unknown) and this was directly dependent on the Holy See. It controlled the whole of the Piast state, the *civitas Schinesghe* of the *Dagome iudex* text. At that time Little Poland and Silesia were under Bohemian control and thus subject to Regensburg or Passau. In 1000 a Polish province was created with its centre at Gniezno. The first archbishop was St Adalbert's brother, Radzim-Gaudentius. Gniezno controlled the three sees which were created at the same time to cover the whole of Polish territory: in Cracow for Little Poland, Wrocław for Silesia and Kołobrzeg for Pomerania. The latter fell into disuse when the Polish state disintegrated after Boleslav Chrobry died. The missionary bishop, Unger (992?–1012), Jordan's successor, had to be satisfied with the see of Poznań which governed the church in western Great Poland. At the beginning of the eleventh century the see of Poznań was temporarily transferred to Magdeburg but Magdeburg's pretensions to supremacy over the church in Poland were without foundation and could not be realised. The lists of the oldest Polish bishops are incomplete and disputed, but it is clear that the early bishops were mainly foreigners. The same is true of the earliest bishops of Prague. After St Adalbert-Vojtech (982–997) came Strachwas-Chrystian, a member of the Přemyslid clan (994–6) and a monk in Regensburg. The other bishops of this time were German: Thietmar (973–82) and Thiedag (998–1017) were both former monks of Corvey; Ekkehard (1017–23) had been the abbot of Nienburg. The origins of Hizzo (1023–30) are unknown. Only Šebir (1030–67) was probably a Bohemian.

Further development of church structures in the shape of archdeaconries and parishes came later. Benedictine monasteries were few and, naturally, the first were established by the ruler. Around 970, that is, before the creation of the diocese of Prague, the monastery of St George was founded in Prague. In 993 Bishop Adalbert, not the duke, founded the monastery at Břevnov outside Prague. Ostróv, south of Prague, was the next royal foundation (c. 1000). C. 1032 we find the semi-private monastery founded in Sázava (St Procopius and Prince Oldřich) to the south-east of the capital. Here the liturgy was celebrated in Slavonic until the end of the eleventh century. The oldest Benedictine house in Moravia, Rajhrad near Brno, was built, perhaps on Břetislav I's orders, around 1050. In Poland the oldest are the Benedictine hermitage at Międzyrzecz (1001–2) and the monastery at Łęczyca (c. 1000?). The greatest wave of Benedictine foundations accompanied the Cluniac reform after the catastrophe of 1038–9. This included Tyniec, near Cracow, Wrocław (?), Lubin and Mogilno.

The Polish and Bohemian churches of the early middle ages were in the fullest sense 'national' churches, despite the strong links of the latter with Germany: bishops, monastic communities and the clergy were completely dependent on the ruler. Only the bishops of Prague could to some extent counterbalance this by their links with the German emperor and the archbishop of Mainz. Any attack on royal power thus had to be directed against the church too, as is shown by the pagan reactions in Bohemia in the early tenth century and especially by the revolts in Poland and Hungary in the eleventh century. The same can be said of Rus'. As everywhere, the cult of the saints had an important role to play, especially those which were open to use for maintaining socio-political order. In Bohemia St Wenceslas, as St Stephen in Hungary a little later, was taken from the start to be the patron of the state and the ruling dynasty. In Poland (as in Germany) there was a shortage of 'dynastic' saints, and St Adalbert could only partially function as national patron, especially after his relics had been plundered; the role was in the end filled by St Stanislas of Cracow, martyred in 1079.

It is in our period that we must date the formation of a sense of common bonds among the Bohemian and Polish peoples, as seen for example in the way in which the dynasty and the state weakened regional ties, though of course without eliminating them completely. The most obvious sign of this is the growth of a fundamental awareness of the foreignness of neighbouring peoples and enmity towards them. A further symptom is the disappearance from the sources of the terms for 'general Slavonic' phenomena such as *Sclavi*. Tribal terminology disappears in a similar way, in Poland earlier than in Bohemia. In both states there gradually developed terms which formulated an essentially hostile attitude to the Germans, *Niemcy* meaning 'dumb, alien'. Following the conversion of southern Polabia, Poland and Hungary, the Bohemians had no pagan neighbours, unlike Poland, who had heathens on her western and northern borders. A characteristic and quite lasting trait of relations between Bohemians and Poles, in spite of their shared roots, is mutual dislike. This is expressed in sources as early as the eleventh century and can be interpreted as the result of the conflicts of interest in southern Poland and southern Polabia, and probably also of the ruling classes' competition for supremacy among the western Slavs. Contrary to the traditional view, we can find no evidence for sentiments of alliance or general west Slavonic mission in the policies of either Boleslav Chrobry or Břetislav I.

The political unity of Bohemia was practically never questioned. In the first half of the twelfth century, Poland was divided amongst the various branches of the ruling house for almost two hundred years. The achievements of the first Přemyslids and Piasts were solid, and laid the foundations for the whole of the later history of these two important European peoples. The examples of Moravia, in whose lands there were nation-building tendencies in the ninth century halted by the fall of the state, or of the Abodrites, who despite all efforts were unable to form their own lasting state and as a consequence never became a nation, show eloquently that in medieval Europe only the existence of a strong endogenous state could ensure the independent growth of an ethnic group and facilitate its development as a distinct nation: the only exception in central Europe is the Slovaks, who did not have their own state until the twentieth century, though they constituted a separate people in the nineteenth century.

CHAPTER 21

HUNGARY

Kornél Bakay

IT WAS in 862 that the Hungarians first indisputably appeared on the European scene: an attack by *Ungri* on the kingdom of Louis the German is recorded for that year, and further attacks are recorded for 881 and 884,[1] though it is very probable that Hungarians are already referred to in Byzantine sources in 837 or 838. The missionaries Cyril-Constantine and Methodius met Hungarians personally. Cyril encountered them around 860 in the Crimean Peninsula, while Methodius found them around 884 at the lower reaches of the Danube; he met the *rex Ungarorum*, perhaps Prince Árpád himself.[2] Regino of Prüm's *Chronicon* for 889 says: 'the hitherto unknown and incredibly fierce Hungarian *gens* has come from Scythia', from where the Pechenegs had driven it,[3] yet it is clear from the earlier encounters mentioned that the *gens* cannot have been completely unknown. Nevertheless, it is unproven, despite certain hypotheses and theories, that the Carpathian Basin was inhabited by Hungarian-speaking people earlier than the end of the ninth century. We have not as yet managed to excavate a complete Hungarian settlement from the tenth and eleventh centuries; the pits and huts dug into the ground which we have found could not have served as permanent dwellings. Apart from log cabins and tents it may be assumed that there were stone and brick buildings built in this period.[4]

We are dependent on Frankish and Byzantine sources for our information, and these do not refer to the Hungarians by the name they used for themselves:

---

[1] *Annales Alamannici, s.a.* 863, *MGH SS* I, p. 50 (Gombos, *Catalogus fontium historiae Hungaricae* I, p. 91); *Annales Bertiniani, s.a.* 862, p. 93 (Gombos I, p. 111); *Annales ex Annalibus Iuvavensibus antiquis excerpti, MGH SS* xxx, p. 742.

In the notes to this chapter, references to primary sources are given both to the current edition and to the convenient collection of early Hungarian sources by Gombos (I–III).

[2] *Vita ss Cyrilli et Methodii, Legenda Pannonica II:* Gombos (III), p. 2331.

[3] 'gens Hungarium [sic] ferocissima et omni belua crudelior, retro ante seculis ideo inaudita quia nec nominata': Regino, *Chronicon, s.a.* 889, p. 131; Gombos (III), p. 2038.

[4] Kiss (1985) provides a convenient recent guide to the state of archaeological research.

Mogyeri or *Magyaeri* ('Man of the Earth';[5] cf. *gyermek*, meaning 'little man', hence 'child'). This brings us up against a fundamental problem of early Hungarian history, paralleled by the early histories of the Slavic and Germanic peoples. Contemporary written sources were compiled by 'outsiders' – Franks and Byzantines above all – who were not familiar with the Hungarians, and used older names and models drawn from more familiar peoples to describe them and their institutions. Written sources from within Hungary are of a much later date, and the information they yield must be treated with caution, while the archaeological evidence can rarely be linked precisely with the information found in contemporary written sources.

Ninth- and tenth-century written sources used a number of names for Hungarians, many of them taken from the names of older peoples known to have inhabited the same area, like the Huns and the Avars: *Hunni, Avari, Avares, Ungari, Hungri, Agareni, Pannonici, Vandali. Tourkoi*, the name used for them in Byzantine sources, has the same origin as the names used in Latin sources. The *gens* which appeared in western view at the end of the ninth century was clearly one still in the process of formation, and will have included confederates with other ethnic identities as well as the Magyars themselves. Magyar is known to be a Finno-Ugric language, but it includes many Bulgarian loan-words, and the language alone is no clue to ethnic origins.[6]

According to Constantine Porphyrogenitus, the Hungarians consisted of seven tribes apart from the Kabar tribe (*gens Cabarorum*) whose names are Nyék (*Nece*), Megyer (*Megere*), Kürtügyarmatu (*Curtugermati*), Tarján (*Tariani*), Jeneh (*Genah*), Keri (*Carem*) and Keszi (*Casem*).[7] But whereas in the case of the Pechenegs he listed their chieftains by name, in the case of the Hungarians he did not do so.[8] The Hungarian chronicles, by contrast, do not mention tribal names but they do enumerate chieftains and captains. Despite the high proportion of toponyms rooted in tribal names, all attempts to form an authentic picture of the tenth-century tribal system have so far failed, and so have attempts to clarify it by grouping archaeological data.

In the ninth century the Bulgarians can be shown to have ruled the lower reaches of the River Tisza, the Temes region and the Maros valley, especially the Transylvanian salt mines. The Bulgarians had in the course of the ninth century become a major power. They had occupied the territories formerly held by the Avars and invaded Frankish territory as well, but the Bulgarian khan

---

[5] Anonymus, *Gesta Hungarorum*, preface: 'populus de terra Scithica egressus per ydioma alienigenerum Hungarii et in sua lingua propria Mogeri vocantur', ed. Silagi (1988), p. 28; Gombos 1, p. 230.

[6] For the external terminology see Moravcsik (1958), Móor (1959), Antonopoulos (1993); for Magyar ethnogenesis see Lipták (1983), Györffy (1988b), Róna-Tas (1988), and especially Golden (1990), pp. 243–9.   [7] *DAI*, c. 40, lines 3–7 (Gombos 1, p. 743).

[8] *DAI*, c. 37, lines 15–25 (Gombos 1, p. 741).

had been an ally of Louis the German and Arnulf in their struggles against the Moravians. The Hungarian warriors who appeared in the Carpathian basin in the last third of the ninth century encountered only Slavic peoples on the banks of the Tisza (*Tisia, Tibiscos, Parisos, Pathisus, Parthissus*), the Danube (*Danuvius, Istros*), the Körös (*Cresia*), the Maros (*Marisos*), the Drava and the Mura (*Dravos et Murius*), the Szamos (*Samus*), the Garam (*Granios, Granua*), the Zala (*Sala*) or near Lake Balaton (*Peiso-Pelso*). All these river-names are Slavic; we know almost nothing of Avar toponyms. The *Conversio Bagoariorum et Carantanorum*, written around 871, says that Slavic peoples were settled near the Danube beyond the Avars (whom it refers to as Huns),[9] and this is well supported by the frequency of Slavic toponyms in Pannonia, the Tisza region and Transylvania and also by the significant number of Slavic loan-words in Hungarian. The subsequent ethnic and linguistic dominance of the Hungarians, whose numbers are estimated at a few hundred thousand, suggests that vast regions of the Carpathian basin must indeed have been depopulated or even uninhabited by the end of the ninth century, as suggested by Latin sources, which say that 'the region was ideal and empty of peoples' or 'they [the Hungarians] laid the whole land waste'.[10]

The eastern province of the Carolingian empire was divided into two parts; what was later to be called Transdanubia and the territories north and south of the River Drava were called *Pannonia superior* and *Pannonia inferior* respectively.[11] Ecclesiastically it came under the bishopric of Passau and the archbishoprics of Salzburg and Aquileia. At the end of the ninth century Carloman's son Arnulf ruled Pannonia, from 888 on as king; he was the first western ruler to enlist Hungarian help, against Sviatopolk of Moravia in 892.[12] In the *Annals of Fulda* for 894 it is said that Hungarians (*Avari, Ungri*) had killed off the population of Pannonia. In the same year Prince Sviatopolk of Moravia, against whom Arnulf had also been supported by the Bulgarians, died, and in 895 Arnulf entrusted *Mosapurc* and Pannonia to the Slav prince Braslav, who had taken part in Arnulf's campaign against the Moravians of 892.[13]

The counterpart to the Bulgarian–Frankish alliance of 894 against the Moravians was the Byzantino–Hungarian military pact against the Bulgarians

---

[9] *Conversio Bagoariorum et Carantanorum*, 6, ed. Koš (1936), p. 132, ed. Wolfram (1979), p. 44, ed. Lošek, p. 110.

[10] 'regnum erat optissimum et gentibus vacuatum', Simon de Kéza, *Gesta Hungarorum*, c. 95, p. 123 (Gombos III, p. 2156); 'Ungaris . . . omnem illam regionem incendio devastandam versabatur', *Annales Fuldenses*, ed. Kurze, *s.a.* 892, p. 121 (Gombos I, p. 132).

[11] *Conversio Bagoariorum et Carantanorum*, c. 7, ed. Koš (1936), p. 132, ed. Wolfram (1979), p. 46, ed. Lošek (1996), p. 112.   [12] *Annales Fuldenses*, *s.a.* 892, p. 121.

[13] *Mosapurc* was probably located in Carinthia, not, as often stated, near Lake Balaton. The recently much debated question of the location of Moravia and the nature of east Frankish Moravian policy will not be discussed here; for a judicious survey of the problem see Innes (1997).

in 895.[14] The campaign in Pannonia in 894 and that against the Bulgars in 895 have usually been seen as the beginning of the Hungarian conquest of the habitable regions of the Carpathian basin. It is difficult either to prove or to disprove conclusively the hypotheses which have been offered on this subject, but it does seem highly probable that between 895 and 900 the regions around the Garam and east of the Danube, including the river valleys of what had been Dacia, came to be ruled by Hungarians, though the archaeological finds from this period are rarely suitable for accurate dating.

Arnulf's Bavarian army intervened in the fratricidal conflict within the Moravian princely family following Sviatopolk's death, and did severe damage to Moravia in 898. Arnulf also encouraged Hungarian campaigns against both the Moravians and Berengar in Italy. On 24 September 899 the Hungarian forces fought a victorious battle against Berengar at the River Brenta, whence they proceeded as far as Bologna and even Venice. In the summer of 900 Hungarian troops returning from this campaign in Italy united on the Tisza with forces from the east. As the earlier pact had lapsed on the death of Arnulf in 899, they attacked first the Moravians and then the Bavarians, conquering the whole of the eastern province up to the River Enns. In the new situation the Moravians quickly made peace with the Bavarians and started to prepare for war against the Hungarians, but it was too late; by the early years of the new century Moravia had ceased to exist.

THE TERRITORY OF HUNGARY IN THE TENTH AND ELEVENTH CENTURIES

There were vast forest regions not only in the Carpathians but also between the Rivers Drava and Sava and near Lake Fertő, as well as large moors in the vicinity of Moson, Sopron and Győr and in the territories of the later counties of Fehér, Baranya, Békés and Csanád. The military defence of the territories occupied by the Magyars and their confederates was facilitated by leaving uninhabited regions (*gyepü*) at the edges, as well as by building abattises and similar kinds of artificial defence works.[15] There were *kapuk* (*portae*, gates) in the *gyepü*, which were guarded by *őrök* (*speculatores*, guards). The approximate borderline marked by these defences in the tenth and eleventh centuries can thus be drawn using ancient toponyms containing the words *gyepü*, *kapu* and *őr*. This evidence suggests the following boundary. In the south-west, between the confluence of the Rivers Mura and Drava and the River Raba it ran along the line Őrtilos–Zalalövő–Őriszentpéter–Gyepüfalva. The western frontier changed frequently between the end of the ninth and the eleventh century. From the

---

[14] See chapter 23, below, pp. 567–70.   [15] Göckenjan (1972).

River Enns the Hungarians first withdrew to the River Traisen, and then to the Rivers Pinka and Leitha (also called Lajta or Sár). The Annalista Saxo and Wipo note that the forces sent against the Hungarians under Conrad II in 1030 had to make a 'hard and laborious journey' into the 'country fortified by rivers and forests'.[16] The western frontier, running from Felsőőr via Alsóőr to Őrsziget (now in Austria), was probably established no earlier than the middle of the eleventh century. At the River Répcze there was a second *gyepü*, as can be seen from the name *Kapuvár-Lövő*. The so-called royal ditch (*fossata regis*) must also have been part of the defences. In the north-west the borderline was marked by the Hanság and Lake Fertő (*Vertowe*) and north-east of them by Oroszvár (Rušovce) The villeins of the abbey of Borsmonostor were not freed from the burden of preparing *gyepü* until the beginning of the thirteenth century.

North of the River Nitra the country was almost unpopulated even in the early thirteenth century, as was the valley of the River Árva (Orava). The *gyepü* here may have been at the junction of the Rivers Vág and Dudvág, as is suggested by the presence of the village Őr Sztraža (*villa speculatoris*). North-east of Nagytapolcsány we find Kőkapu and Kolos (from *clusa*, meaning closure or fortification). The Garam valley and the district of Zólyom were once a royal estate (*praedium*) and hunting ground; this too suggests an originally defensive function. What later became Szepesség and the northern Sajó valley also used to be a *gyepü*, as is suggested by the name of the Poprád valley's Gömörőr (*Stražky, Gumureur*).[17] Until the thirteenth century what was later to be the county of Torna was uninhabited, while the lower Hernád valley was guarded by the frontier guards (*speculatores*) of Bárcza near Kassa. The Zemplén hills, the district of the River Laborcz and Ung, were *gyepü-elv*, meaning 'across the border', as can be seen from the place-names Gyepüelve and Or near Ungvár. The regions along the Rivers Latorcza and Borsova were sparsely populated, and as late as the thirteenth century they belonged to the forest county (*silva regalis*) of Bereg. The region around Máramaros and Nagybánya was an uninhabited forest; the ruler's authority probably extended to the valleys of the Tisza and Szamos, as can be seen from Őr near Vaja and Őrpátroha in Szabolcs.

There were *gyepü* at Meszes and Szamos as late as 1068 and after, although the eastern border defences were built at Kolozsvár (the name is derived from *clusa*; cf. Cluj). The 'Messes gate'[18] is the gate to Transylvania. The name of this region is derived from *Erdő-elü*, *Erdő-elve*, meaning 'beyond the forest' (compare the Latin 'ultra' or 'trans silvam'); the name 'beyond the forest' indi-

16 'difficili et laborioso itinere': *Annalista Saxo, MGH SS* VI, p. 677 (Gombos I, p. 221); 'munitum regnum fluviis et silvis': Wipo, *Gesta Chuonradi*, c. 26, p. 44 (Gombos III, p. 2666).
17 Anonymus, *Gesta Hungarorum*, cc. 22, 34, pp. 72 and 86 (Gombos I, pp. 241, 244).
18 'porta Mezesina': Anonymus, *Gesta Hungarorum*, c. 22, p. 72 (Gombos I, p. 241).

cates that it was populated from Hungary. In order to defend the borders of the country, Erdély was settled with frontier guards (*székler*).[19] The archaeological evidence shows that apart from the valleys of the Rivers Olt and Zsil the territory was settled by Hungarians. The Danube served as a border in the south as far as Szerémség, which was completed by the Roman *kőárok* (= stone fosse) at Szávaszentdemeter (formerly Sirmium, now Mitrovica) and the River Szava. In the county which was later to become Baranya county (called Pozsega county from the twelfth century onwards) there lived *székler* (bowmen) as well.

According to written sources Hungarians were divided into tribes (*generationes*) in the same way as the Pechenegs and Cumans, and their settlement was organised accordingly. Although several attempts have been made to substantiate this using archaeological and toponymic evidence, these have not so far produced convincing results. Attempts to prove that the chieftains or heads of clans led a life of seasonal nomadism have been equally unsuccessful. An alternation of winter and summer dwellings, as implied for the Khazars in a letter of Khagan Joseph (957–61),[20] must have been unusual within the Carpathian basin; toponyms implying such practices are not enough to prove the practice, just as tribal names are inadequate to define the territories settled by the tribes.

MAGYAR CAMPAIGNS IN WESTERN AND SOUTHERN EUROPE IN THE FIRST HALF OF THE TENTH CENTURY

Both archaeological and written sources leave no doubt that Hungarians in the ninth and tenth centuries must be classifed socially with the nomadic peoples of the east, with a way of life characterised not only by the dominance of livestock breeding but also by a highly developed military organisation, by authoritarian rule under chieftains (princes and heads of clans), and by constant warfare. They shot their arrows with frightening accuracy from their strong reflex bows, their hardy and undemanding horses enabled them to cover enormous distances, and their disciplined tactics enabled them to perplex their enemies completely. From the point of view of those who lived and thought as Christians, Hungarians, like the earlier Avars, Huns and Scythians, were pagan hordes of barbarian murderers who looted western and southern Europe. However, the fact that from the time of their settlement at the end of the ninth century they built a circular system of defence works around their land suggests that they themselves held a rather different attitude, and many of their campaigns in the early tenth century should be seen as being preventative and defensive rather than mere razzias. The purposefulness of their conquest of

[19] 'in confinium regni Hungariae, scilicet in Erdelw': Anonymus, *Gesta Hungarorum*, c. 11, ed. Silagi, p. 52, cf. also c. 24, p. 74 (Gombos 1, pp. 235, 241).
[20] *Evreisko-khazarskaia perepiska v X veke* For a contrary view see Györffy (1975).

the Carpathian basin is shown very clearly by the campaign against the Bulgarians, by the pact made with Byzantium and by their military ventures as allies of the emperor Arnulf. As a parallel, we may note that in 1240–1 the Mongols invaded the territory of Hungary with a similarly well-elaborated military plan. It should also be noted, however, that successful warfare was indispensable for sustaining and maintaining the ruling dynasty among nomadic peoples.

After their triumph over King Berengar on 24 September 899, Hungarian troops spent the winter in Italy, a serious venture for a cavalry force whose numbers have variously been estimated at two, five or eight thousand; this too may perhaps be interpreted as part of the Hungarians' deliberate preparations for the conquest of Pannonia. In 901 Hungarians fought against the Carinthians, in 902 they turned against the Moravians, in 903 they attacked the Bavarians and in 904 they looted Italy, where they spent the winter of 904–5 as well. King Berengar entered into an *amicitia* with the Hungarians, that is, they became his allies. In 906 the Slavs (Dalaminci) hired Hungarian mercenary troops against Henry, *dux* of Saxony. That the Hungarians were here acting in a defensive and preventive manner is suggested by the Bavarian offensive against the Hungarians in July 907. The army led by Margrave Luitpold of Bavaria was, however, annihilated near Bratislava. In this 'terrible battle' the Bavarian duke Luitpold was killed together with Theotmar archbishop of Salzburg; nineteen counts, two further bishops and three abbots also fell.[21] The Hungarians' campaign in 908 was directed against Saxony and Thuringia, in 909 against Suabia, and in 910 against Bavaria. The contemporary annals imply a Bavarian victory at Nauching, after earlier defeats of Suabian and Franco-Lotharingian contingents. In 911 Suabia was again looted by Hungarians, who then crossed the Rhine for the first time and invaded eastern France and the Aargau in Switzerland. In 912 they continued looting the Frankish empire, and following the death of Louis the Child they now demanded tribute from his successor, King Conrad. In 913 they crossed the Rhine again, but the Bavarian *dux* Arnulf inflicted a serious defeat on them at the River Inn; in 914 Arnulf in turn, together with all his family, sought refuge among those he had defeated when he turned against King Conrad! They made peace with Arnulf, and the pact was respected for many years, not only in 915 when they reached Fulda via Suabia but also in 916 and 917 when they campaigned in the regions around Regensburg and Basel but left the Bavarian heartland. Moreover, they supported Arnulf in 918 in his return to Bavaria. There may be a connection between the fact that Henry, rather than Arnulf, was made king in east Francia

---

[21] *Annales ex Annalibus Iuvavensibus antiquis excerpti, MGH SS* xxx, p. 742; for other contemporary accounts see Reindel (ed.) *Die bayerischen Luitpoldinger*, pp. 62–70.

in 919 following Conrad's death and the Hungarian raids of that year against Saxony, Lotharingia and west Francia.

Another argument against the assumption that the Hungarians simply carried out aimless and uncontrolled lootings is the fact that from 905, when the Hungarians and Berengar had formed an *amicitia*, as noted above, fifteen years passed without Hungarian troops entering Italy. In 920, perhaps at the request of King Berengar, they fought against Rudolf, king of Burgundy, and his supporters in Lombardy. In 921 the Hungarian friends of Berengar, the kings *Dursac et Bugat* (Tarhos and Bogát?) arrived in Verona and defeated Berengar's enemies; in 922 they reached Apulia. In 924 Berengar made a new alliance with the Hungarians, who following his death sacked and burned Pavia and crossed via the St Bernard pass into southern France, where they penetrated as far as the Pyrenees. In 925 they appeared at Nîmes. After 924 they ceased to loot Saxony, as Henry I had made a pact with them for nine years and bought peace by high tribute payments. In 926 they ravaged Suabia and Alsace across the Rhine, but they also campaigned through the territory of present-day Luxemburg and reached as far as the Atlantic. In 927 Peter, brother of Pope John X, 'sent his ambassador to the Hungarians, calling them to rule Italy'.[22] The Hungarians marched into Rome, and enforced large tribute payments on Tuscany and Tarento. It is probably only because of gaps in the sources that there are no data for similar campaigns between 927 and 933. In 933 the pact with the Saxons expired and a substantial Hungarian army appeared in Saxony, where they were defeated by Henry I at Riade (near Merseburg). This put an end to the significant taxes levied for the peace. It is worth noting that the archaeological finds from Hungary contain no western jewellery or art treasures, only coins.

Apart from the Bulgarian campaign in the Balkans at the end of the ninth century no sources mention any military ventures directed southward before 934. In this year, while reaching Metz in the west, they made an alliance with the Pechenegs and fought their way through Thrace to Constantinople, killing off the inhabitants, inflicting severe damage on the countryside and forcing both Byzantium and Bulgaria to pay them tribute. The looting of the west continued with attacks against upper Burgundy in 935, and against Saxony in 936 after Henry I's son Otto I had become king of Germany. On their return journey from this raid they also crossed the Rhine and turned against Rheims, Sens, Orléans and Bourges. In 937 a troop of Hungarians marched from Burgundy to Italy via the Rhône valley in the service of King Hugh, who sent them against Capua, Monte Cassino and Naples. In 938 Hungarians repeatedly attacked Saxony. In 940 they ravaged the region of Rome and in 942 they

[22] Benedict of Soracte, *Chronicon*, c. 29, pp. 159–60; cf. Liudprand, *Antapodosis* III, 43, pp. 95–6.

crossed into Spain over southern France from Italy to besiege the town of Lerida in Andalucia, thus against the caliphate of Córdoba. According to Ibn Haijan, the Hungarians had a vanguard and seven military contingents with seven leaders.[23] In 943 smaller Hungarian forces appeared at the River Enns and near Wels, while significant forces were fighting in the Byzantine province of Hellas. There are then gaps in the sources until 947, when we find Hungarian troops fighting in Italy under Prince Taksony (*Toxus dux*) for three months. First they levied a tribute of ten bushels of silver in Lombardy; then they ravaged through Apulia, reaching as far as Otranto. In 948 Bulcsú harka and Prince Tormás went to Byzantium, this time not to fight but to confirm an alliance. Around 949 and 950 they fought with the Bavarians at Laa and in 951 they reappeared in Italy and in Aquitaine. At the request of Otto I's son Liudolf and of Conrad the Red, who had revolted against Otto, a large Hungarian army appeared at Augsburg and Worms in 954, which proceeded to Cambrai in upper Lotharingia before returning home via Burgundy and Italy. In 955 the Hungarians also marched against Otto under their leaders Bulcsü, Sür and Lél. The decisive battle took place near Augsburg at the River Lech, where the Hungarians were defeated and Duke Henry of Bavaria had the leaders hanged. This marked the end of large-scale Magyar raiding abroad, though there were some skirmishes with Byzantium and Bavaria until late in the century.

PRINCES, MILITARY LEADERS AND CHIEFTAINS

There are no substantial records of the Khazar, Hun or Avar languages, though Khazaric and Avaric are thought to have been Turkish. None of the names for rank which have survived from the Khazars and Avars – *kagan, katun, bej-beg, tegin, jabgu, iugur, capcan, tudun, šad, čoban, čur-caus (csősz,* 'guards') – can be found among the Hungarians. The Hungarian rulers are called *kende* and *djila* by Ibn Rusta,[24] *voivoda* and *archon* by Constantine Porphyrogenitus,[25] and *kral* ('king') by Methodius.[26] Western sources use the same term *dux* for the princes of Hungary as the later Hungarian chronicles; Liudprand of Cremona uses both *rex* and *dux* for their military leaders.[27] Other sources sometimes denote Hungarian leaders – chieftains and heads of clans – as kings (*Iulus rex, Chussol rex*) and at other times simply as military leaders (*milites Lelu et Bulsuu*).[28] Arabic sources make it certain that the first in rank was called *djila* who was fol-

---

[23] Chalmeta (1976), p. 343.

[24] Ibn Rusteh, *Les Autours précieux / Kitāb al-A'lāq an-Nafîsa,* trans Wiet, p. 160.

[25] *DAI,* c. 38, lines 5, 7, p. 171.   [26] Gombos III, pp. 2330–1.

[27] Liudprand, *Antapodosis* II, 61, pp. 64–5 (Gombos II, p. 1473).

[28] *Annales Alamannici, s.a.* 904, *MGH SS* I, p. 54; *Annales Heremi, MGH SS* III, p. 140; *Annales Sangallenses, s.a.* 902, *MGH SS* I, p. 77 (Gombos I, pp. 91, 140, 199).

lowed by a *kharkhas* (*horca*). The meaning of the rank *kende* mentioned by Ibn Rusta is uncertain. Constantine Porphyrogenitus calls Árpád the 'great prince of Tourkia',[29] but Árpád's name cannot be found in western sources.

The supposition that in fact it was Kurszán (*Chussol, Kusid*), killed together with his retinue in 904 at a banquet in Bavaria, who was the grand prince of the Hungarians (*kende, kundu*), and that Árpád was merely a *djila*, seems very questionable. A more plausible conjecture is that Kurszán was the military leader (*djila*) in charge of the campaigns, much like the Taksony (*Taxis-dux, dux Tocsun*) who led Hungarian armies in 927, 942 and 947 and is also referred to as a prince in the ten years following the Italian campaign of 947. In 948 Bulcsú harka, who was third in rank after the *gyula* (*gyla*) and the grand prince (*megas archon, magnus princeps*) visited Byzantium.[30] During the military campaigns to the west and the south princely power had diminished. This is apparent in the fact that the role of military leaders (*Bulcsú, Lél*) grew more significant and in 948 and 953 Bulcsú harka and Gyula (*gyla*) were baptised in Byzantium.

Taksony was the grandson of Árpád; succession to power in the Árpád period was a dynastic matter. It remains uncertain whether legitimate succession within the dynasty was defined by the principle of the seniorate, as Constantine Porphyrogenitus informs us was the case among the Pechenegs.[31] The principle means that ranks and titles are inherited by the oldest surviving male member of the dynasty rather than by sons or younger brothers. This is what John Cinnamus says in the twelfth century about the Hungarians when he writes that the law is that live brothers inherit the crown and the title 'Urum';[32] the title seems to refer to the position of heir-apparent to the throne. Although succession by right of being the closest male relative can be found among the Árpádians, the primary principle applied in practice was apparently that of primogeniture. Almos was certainly followed by his son Árpád. It is uncertain whether Árpád was succeeded by Falicsi or Zulta. Zulta was followed by his son, Taksony (c. 956–72); Taksony was succeeded by his son Géza (972–97); Géza in turn was followed by his first-born son Vajk, christened as Stephen (997–1038). If we consider all the Árpád princes and kings between the late ninth century and the end of the dynasty in 1301, then we find that on twelve occasions the ruler was succeeded by his first-born son, while on a further twelve occasions he had no son to succeed him. In only three cases that we know of was he not succeeded by a surviving first-born son (Béla I, Salamon, László I). Since the right of the eldest male relative seems to have been

---

[29] 'ho megas Tourkias archōn', *DAI*, c. 40, line 53. [30] *DAI*, c. 40, lines 63–5.

[31] *De cerimoniis* II, 48, *PG* 112, cols 1277–8: 'archontes Patzinacorum'.

[32] *Epitome historiarum*, I, 9 and V, 1: Migne, *PG* 133, cols 318, 551 and *Fontes Byzantini*, ed. Moravcsik, pp. 195, 215. The interpretation of the title is much debated; see Ostrogorsky (1951) and Makk (1989), p. 87.

acknowledged in certain cases, however, as for example with King Kálmán and Álmos, it seems highly probable that collateral succession existed in the period before the existence of written law, at least as a rival principle.

PRINCES TAKSONY AND GÉZA

Although the military power of the Hungarian principality was not destroyed by the defeat at the Lechfeld in 955, it did bring about certain changes which are clearly visible even from the sparse data. The time of Prince Árpád's death is unknown (Hungarian chronicles mention the year 907)[33] and it is uncertain who was his successor (there may have been several), but it is obvious that after 955 Taksony became prince. His father, Zulta, had married a Cumanian-Pecheneg woman. Taksony established a new type of relationship with the high nobility and reigned in power and peace over his country. In the 950s a monk called Hierotheus had been consecrated as the bishop of Tourkia in the southern parts of Hungary by the patriarch of Constantinopole, Theophylact, a sign of the role played by Byzantium in the spread of Christianity amongst the Magyars, and presumably a consequence of the baptisms of Bulcsú and Gyula mentioned earlier. Among the finds from tenth- and eleventh-century Hungarian graves there are objects implying the use of Christian rites. Liudprand mentions that a bishop was sent to convert the Hungarians by Pope John XII in 963, but the delegation, led by Salec, was captured by Otto I's men.[34]

Prince Taksony, according to the chronicles, died in the same year (971) that the Hungarian troops sent out to loot the Balkans in alliance with Sviatoslav of Kiev were defeated. The new prince, Taksony's son Géza, was soon baptised, according to Adhémar of Chabannes, and took the name Stephen.[35] This must have happened in 972, when Wolfgang, later bishop of Regensburg, was sent to Hungary by Pilgrim of Passau. Taksony's other son, Calvus Zyrind, was also christened and given the name Michael. Géza sent twelve of his noblemen to Quedlinburg at Easter 973, to the court of that very Emperor Otto I whom Pope John XII had called 'rex carissimus et christianissimus' precisely because of his 'triumph over the barbarian Hungarians',[36] a people who had up to then answered the Christian 'Kyrie eleison' with the 'diabolic and vicious cry huj-huj'.[37] The conversion of the Hungarians involved violence as well, since Géza

---

[33] Anonymus, *Gesta Hungarorum*, c. 52, p. 120 (Gombos I, p. 253).

[34] Liudprand, *Historia*, c. 6, p. 163 (Gombos II, pp. 1474–5).

[35] 'Gouz . . . nomine in baptismo Stephanum vocavit': Adhémar, *Chronicon* III, 31, p. 153 (Gombos I, p. 16).

[36] 'devictis barbaris gentibus, Auaribus scilicent ceterisque quam pluribus': Zimmermann, *Papsturkunden*, no. 154, pp. 282–3.   [37] Liudprand, *Antapodosis* II, 30, p. 51 (Gombos II, p. 1472).

did not merely invite priests (Brun and Adalbert) to spread the Christian faith but ruled as a tyrant over his people. According to Thietmar of Merseburg he killed large numbers of people,[38] though he met considerable difficulties in oppressing rebels and rooting out pagan rites. It is not quite clear whether Géza had one or more wives. According to Thietmar his wife was Beleknegini (Sarolt in later legend), the daughter of Gyula of Transylvania, who was not only beautiful but also good at drinking and riding; it was also rumoured that she had killed a man in her fury. Polish sources on the other hand say that Géza married the sister of Miesco I, Adelaide.[39]

Géza organised a strong army, whose existence is suggested by archaeological evidence.[40] Since in Géza's reign we know of only one campaign outside Hungary, when Henry the Quarrelsome, duke of Bavaria, attacked the western borders in 991 – the legend of St Stephen refers to this peaceful policy when saying that he 'began to keep peace with the neighbouring provinces faithfully'[41] – the army must have served the purpose of consolidating central power. Géza also established new dynastic relationships by marriage. Besides his own marriages with Transylvanian and possibly Polish princesses, he married one of his daughters to Miesco's son Boleslav Chrobry and the other to the ruler of Bulgaria, Samuel. It is highly probable that Géza's brother Michael also married a Bulgarian woman, who gave birth to two sons, Wazul and Szár László (Calvus Laizlaus); the latter may be identified with the Koppány of whom we shall hear more under Géza's son Stephen.

The capital of Géza's principality was Esztergom, where the ruins of the royal chapel (*rotunda*) have been found. There are suggestions that the son of Géza, Vajk, who was born sometime between 969 and 975, was baptised by Adalbert of Prague himself, but this remains unproven. Géza asked for the hand of Gisela, daughter of the Bavarian Duke Henry II, for his son. Henry died in 995 but Vajk, by now baptised as Stephen, did marry Gisela and thus became the brother-in-law of Duke Henry IV of Bavaria, who was later to rule as Emperor Henry II (1002–24). Prince Vajk-Stephen was very well educated. After the death of Géza, *senior magnus*, in 997, Stephen became ruler, though he was still a child, and he had to carry on the struggle against rival magnates who burnt and ravaged the country and against pagans who did not refrain from insulting the king. His most powerful enemy was his close relative, Koppány, the son of Tar Szörénd, who had inherited the title of duke of Somogy. If we

---

[38] Thietmar, *Chronicon* VIII, 4, p. 496 (Gombos III, p. 2203); see also *Legenda S. Stephani regis maior*, c. 2 (*MGH SS* XI, p. 230; *Scriptores rerum Hungariuim* II, pp. 378–9).

[39] Thietmar, *Chronicon* VIII, 4, p. 498 (Gombos III, p. 2203); *Annales Kamenzenses, s.a.* 965, *MGH SS* XIX, p. 581 (Gombos I, p. 145).   [40] Bakay (1967).

[41] 'cum omnibus ... provinciarum vicinis de pace ... cepit attente tractare': *Legenda S. Stephani regis maior*, c. 2 (*MGH SS* XI, p. 230; *Scriptores rerum Hungaricum* II, p. 379).

are correct in assuming that Koppány is to be identified with Prince Géza's nephew, Calvus Laizlaus, we can see why it is that he is said in later sources to have wanted to marry Stephen's mother incestuously and hence establish his claim to be the rightfully succeeding prince.[42] Stephen defeated him with the help of a force of German warriors, and had him executed and his body quartered. The sites of the battles against Koppány are uncertain, though the ruins of Somogy Castle have been found.

HUNGARY UNDER ST STEPHEN

From Thietmar's account it is certain that after his triumph over Koppány Prince Stephen, son-in-law to Henry, Duke of Bavaria, received a crown and blessing from the pope with the approval of Emperor Otto III.[43] King Stephen sent Bishop Astrik to Pope Sylvester II to ask for a royal crown. The date of the coronation has not been definitively established. Although the fourth year after the death of Prince Géza (i.e. 1001) seems more probable, there is evidence to support the year 1000 as well. The crown of King Stephen is, according to the latest Hungarian research, identical with the present Holy Crown of Hungary. It does not, in other words, consist of a *corona graeca* and *corona latina* united only at some later date. The Holy Crown of Hungary is a completely unified piece, most probably commissioned by the pope himself. Its complicated symbolism, material, size, jewels and enamel icons, as well as its mystic power, make it a truly remarkable piece of regalia.[44]

Otto III died in 1002, soon after the coronation of Stephen, and was succeeded by Henry II, Stephen's brother-in-law. It was Henry who promoted the organisation of the chancery of Hungary. The basic principles of King Stephen's royal administration were summarised in the 'Exhortations' written for his son (*Libellus de institutione morum*).[45] Stephen compiled two law-codes. The first must have been drawn up not long after his coronation and twelve of its clauses define the position of the church and the practice of religion; it emphasises that whoever dares to damage or attack the house of God will be excommunicated at the command of the lord king. Counts and judges should support the bishops. Sundays, fasts and Christian faith should be strictly kept. On Sundays each and every person should go to church, except for those who tend the fire. The estates and riches of the king should be respected by all, and

---

[42] Gombos I, p. 615.

[43] Thietmar, *Chronicon* IV, 59, p. 198 (Gombos III, p. 2203); *Diplomata Hungariae antiquissima*, no. 1, pp. 17–18.

[44] Bakay (1994) The origin and nature of the crown of St Stephen as we have it today have been the subject of much debate; for other views see Déer (1966); Studien (1983).

[45] Ed Balogh (Gombos III, pp. 2167–71).

none should loot or defraud them. Everyone should have the power to divide his own properties among his heirs. Every lord should have warriors (*milites*), but neither the counts nor their warriors should dare to force any free persons into servitude from the time of the making of the law henceforward. Murderers are to pay 110 golden coins. Whoever kills his wife should be punished with a fine of fifty cows if he is a count, of ten cows if he is a warrior and of five cows if he is a commoner (*vulgaris*). If anyone kills somebody by the sword he should be killed with the same sword. If anyone attacks another's house with his warriors, the owner of the house may kill the attacker; if the latter had merely sent his warriors he should pay a fine of 100 cows. If a warrior attacks another's estate or house ten cows should be paid. Whoever breaks his vow should have his hand cut off. Any commoner who does not respect the Holy Mass should be flogged and have his head shaved.[46]

Servants and handmaids may be liberated by their lords but no servant may testify against his lord. Whoever fornicates with another person's handmaid should be punished with servitude, and similarly whoever marries a handmaid should be punished with eternal servitude. Stephen made strict laws against theft. If a free man's wife should steal, after the third theft she is to be sold as a slave. If a servant should steal, he is to be punished on the first occasion by the loss of his nose, on the second by the loss of his ears and on the third by the loss of his life. The same goes for a free man who steals. There were laws to protect forsaken wives, widows and orphans and unmarried girls from rape. He tried to protect the people weak in faith against pagan practices. He made laws against witches (*strigae*), poison brewers (*venefici*) and those who worked with evil spells (*malefici*), who were punished by flogging or in the case of recidivists by being branded in the shape of a cross on the breast, forehead and between the shoulder blades, using to do so the red-hot key of the church.

In order to keep these strict laws Stephen needed a strong army which he used – much as his father had done – against potential rivals and magnates indifferent to his authority (for example Ajtony-Achtum) rather than abroad. He did not even intervene in the Polish–German war of 1003–18 until Boleslav Chrobry had occupied certain territories of the Hungarian kingdom in 1018. Instead he concentrated on converting the people, waging war in 1003 against Black Hungary (*Ungaria Nigra*), where his uncle *Iulus rex* ruled. The king defeated him and captured him together with his wife and sons.[47] Missionary activity also increased in the lands controlled by Gyula of Transylvania after this; Byzantine priests played a significant part.

---

[46] The two law-codes are conveniently accessible in Gombos III, pp. 2172–9; see also Stephen, King of Hungary, *Szent István törvényeinek*, and *Laws of the Medieval Kingdom of Hungary*, pp. 1–11.

[47] Thietmar, *Chronicon* VIII, 4, p. 496 (Gombos III, p. 2203); cf. also Adhémar, *Chronicon* III, 33, p. 155 (Gombos I, p. 16).

THE ORGANISATION OF THE CHURCH

Stephen used his power and the riches gained by his triumph over rich people, in Transylvania amongst others, to build churches and monasteries like the richly endowed basilica of Fehérvár. As can be read in his 'Exhortations', 'after faith, the second place of honour in the royal palace should be given to the Church'.[48] He ordained that every tenth village was to build a church and to present this church with two units of land held in villeinage, two servants, a horse, a foal, six oxen, two cows and thirty pieces of 'small livestock', that is, sheep or pigs. It can also hardly be doubted that Henry II played a significant part in the conversion of the Hungarians to Christianity: links between the Hungarian and German churches can be seen in the fact that the 'archbishop of the Hungarians' subscribed the protocol of the council of Frankfurt in 1007, at which the bishopric of Bamberg was founded,[49] and that Archbishop Astrik consecrated an altar in Bamberg in 1012, while Brun, bishop of Augsburg, the brother of Emperor Henry II and Queen Gisela of Hungary, also visited the royal court. In missionary work the leading role was played by western priests. They came from Rome, Bohemia (Vojtech-Adalbert, Anastasius/Gaudentius and Radla/Radim), Italy (St Romuald and his fifteen fellow-priests around 1015, and St Gerard of Csanád), France, and Saxony, whence Brun of Querfurt came in 1004 and 1007 to convert the people of Black Hungary.

The legends relate that Stephen divided his country into ten bishoprics; as defender of the faith, as vicar of Christ, and as king and priest he appointed bishops and abbots for the monasteries himself. The hierarchy was headed by the church of Esztergom, dedicated to St Adalbert, whose archbishop was Astrik. The bishopric of Veszprém and the archbishopric of Esztergom must have been founded at the same time. The bishopric of Veszprém was dedicated to St Michael; the third bishopric, at Győr, was dedicated to the Assumption of the Blessed Virgin Mary and the bishopric of Pécs, founded in 1009, to St Peter. The foundation charter of the bishopric of Pécs implies that the archbishopric of Kalocsa, dedicated to St Paul, already existed by then, though the text is interpolated.[50] Eger and its bishopric was dedicated to St John Cooked In Oil. Since the dedications of the bishoprics of Vác, Transylvania and Bihar – the Blessed Virgin Mary, St Michael and St Peter – duplicate those already mentioned it may be assumed that these were founded later, since bishoprics at that time were named after the dedication, not the see. The tenth bishopric, in Csanád, dedicated to St George, can have been founded only after the defeat of

---

[48] 'In regali quidem palatio post fidem ecclesia secundum tenet statum': *Libellus morum*, c. 2, p. 621 (Gombos III, p. 2168).   [49] *MGH Const* I, no. 29, p. 60.
[50] *Diplomata Hungariae antiquissima*, no. 9, p. 58 (cf. pp. 56–7).

the lord of the Maros region, Ajtony, in 1030.[51] It is probably in this southern region of the Hungarian lands that the orthodox 'bishop of *Tourkia*' was most authoritative, and it is worth noting that there were also Greek monasteries dotted along the Danube basin.

King Stephen had founded the Benedictine convent on the Hill of St Martin before his coronation and had endowed it with similar rights to those of the bishoprics. The legend compiled by Bishop Hartwig describes how tithes not only from conquered people but even of every tenth child were given to the monastery.[52] The numbers of the monks here may soon have increased, since in 1030 four of them were sent to Csanád. There were also prominent monasteries functioning in Pécsvárad, in Bakonybél, in Zobor near Nyitra, and in Zalavár, the last founded in 1019. The house of St Ipoly in Zobor was the mother house of the monasteries of St Andrew and St Benedict Killed By Thieves. The nuns' convent in Veszprémvölgy is probably also very early since its foundation charter, written in Greek, has come down to us in a transcript dating from 1109.[53] Although the bishopric of Csanád was founded in 1030, the monastery of St John continued to play an important role in Marosvár.

After Basil II had defeated the Bulgarians, Stephen opened the pilgrimage route to the Holy Land and transferred his royal see from Esztergom to Székesfehérvár (Alba Regia). Relationships with western Europe became more intensive. Odilo, abbot of Cluny, and Fulbert, bishop of Chartres, sent greetings to the king of Hungary; Abbot Richard of Verdun, Abbot Eberwin and Bishop Poppo of Trier travelled through Hungary as pilgrims to the Holy Land. William, count of Angoulême, also visited Stephen's court.

ROYAL SUCCESSION IN THE ELEVENTH CENTURY

As suggested above, the previous sequence of Hungarian princes makes it likely that Stephen I would also have been succeeded by his son Henry, had the latter not predeceased him, dying suddenly on 2 September 1031. Henry, who had been born around 1007, had received a royal education and been well treated by his father; though the *Legend of St Henry* suggests otherwise,[54] he spent much of his time hunting, and the notice of his death in the *Annals of Hildesheim* says that he was gored by a boar.[55] Other explanations are conceivable, since he is referred to there as *dux Ruizorum*. If Aventine's conjecture that Ruisi is to be identified with Rugiland is correct,[56] this would imply that Henry

[51] *Legenda S. Gerhardi episcopi*, c. 8 (10), pp. 489–92 (Gombos III, pp. 2424–6).
[52] *Legenda S Stephani regis ab Hartvico episcopo conscripta*, c. 6, pp. 409–10 (Gombos III, p. 2584).
[53] *Diplomata Hungariae antiquissima*, no. 13, p. 85.   [54] *Legenda S. Emerici ducis*, c. 4, pp. 453–4.
[55] *Annales Hildesheimenses, s.a.* 1031, p. 36 (Gombos I, p. 141).
[56] Györffy (1988a), p. 199, suggests a derivation from *orosz* ('body guard, housecarl').

had succeeded to the Ostmark following the death of Henry II in 1024. However this may be, we certainly know that Conrad II campaigned first against Poland in 1029 and then against Stephen I in the following year; there may be a link with the marriage planned for Henry, of which we otherwise know nothing, and it is possible that Henry was assassinated. Following Henry's death, Stephen nominated Peter Orseolo, the son of his sister, thus passing over Vászoly, the second son of his uncle Michael. The crushing of an attempted revolt by Vászoly and his noble following and the blinding and mutilation of Vászoly which followed is testimony to the effectiveness of Stephen's rule. He died on 15 August 1038, and was buried in the church at Székesfehérvár.

Any account of early Magyar history risks oversimplification. What we have by the end of Stephen's reign is an established and Christianised kingdom with a defined territory and some sense of ethnic identity, a polity not dissimilar to (though certainly not identical with) those of Poland and Bohemia, discussed in the previous chapter. It is very difficult not to read early Magyar history as in some way leading up to this; but the reader should be aware that the processes of ethnogenesis (the emergence of the Magyars as the dominant ethnic component) and state-formation (the emergence of a Christian kingdom looking to the Latin west more than to the Byzantine east) were protracted, and that there was nothing inevitable about the path they were finally to take.

CHAPTER 22

BYZANTIUM IN EQUILIBRIUM, 886–944

Jonathan Shepard

IN THE late ninth century the Byzantine emperor's dominions were straggling and vulnerable. The survival of the state was not in question but the government of Leo VI (886–912) faced harassment and humiliating reverses on several fronts, while fears of rebellions were all too lurid for a royal family which owed everything to a bloody palace coup barely a generation earlier.

It is against this background that one should view the various manuals of governance and law-collections dating from Leo's reign. They evince his enthusiasm for order, godliness and good learning. Besides commissioning, compiling or interpolating these works he wrote numerous sermons. He aspired to be acknowledged as the fount of wisdom and pious enlightenment, judging by the description of his bath-house near the palace complex.[1] Leo's sobriquet, 'the Wise', implied in the bath-house imagery, acclaimed by contemporary courtiers and derided by Symeon of Bulgaria, was not wholly undeserved. Like his father Basil I, he wished his rule to be associated with illustrious figures of the Christian empire's acknowledged heyday, notably Constantine and Justinian. At the same time he propagated the idea of renewal in, for example, his highly euphemistic version of Basil's accession: the former state of affairs had been removed together with Basil's senior co-emperor, Michael III, 'for the purpose of fresh and well-ordered change'.[2]

The concept of 'cleansing' government and society of the corrupt and the obsolete is threaded through the *Novels* of Leo VI, an assemblage of 113 ordinances, mostly dating from the earlier years of his reign. They are largely concerned with morality and church discipline, and envisage a well-tempered society whose laws apply to all men save the emperor: he has been granted 'discretionary powers' (*oikonomia*) over earthly affairs by God. The laws, it is repeatedly asserted, are to help men, bringing benefits to their souls as well as to their

---

[1] Magdalino (1988), pp. 103–10, 116–18.
[2] 'pros kainēn kai eutakton metabolēn', Vogt and Hausherr (eds.), 'Oraison funèbre de Basile I', p. 56.

bodies.[3] How far Leo's *Novels* were practicable administrative instruments and how far they were enforced is, however, uncertain.

The *Book of the Eparch* was issued in 911 or 912 in the name of Leo VI. Its preface invokes by way of analogy the Tables of the Law which were disclosed by God's 'own finger',[4] but its scope is confined to Constantinople, whose administration was supervised by the Eparch. It regulates the conduct of nineteen guilds, and lays down harsh penalties for those who breach the regulations. General professions of concern for the welfare of the emperor's subjects are here juxtaposed with detailed administrative procedures. The *Book of the Eparch* reveals something of the government's assumptions and priorities. It is particularly concerned with top-quality products such as silks, purple dyes, silver- or goldwork and spices. Five guilds connected with the silk industry receive detailed attention, whereas tanners and leather-softeners get cursory treatment and numerous other known guilds are not mentioned at all. The monopolisation and rationing out of luxury goods was the stock-in-trade of imperial statecraft, at home and abroad. Great efforts were made to ensure that the various stages of production and retail of silk remained in the hands of different professions, and dealers in less valuable goods such as 'groceries', meat and soap were also not to merge their enterprises. Small-scale units could safely be allowed to monitor their own operations and their own tax-assessments and -collections to a large extent; fewer officials were thus required for them. The *Book of the Eparch* essentially envisaged self-regulation by craftsmen and traders in conjunction with the City authorities.

A still more urgent priority for the government was provisioning at affordable prices. The heads of the fishmongers' guild were to report to the Eparch at dawn on the night's catch, whereupon he set a price. The prices of meat and bread were likewise set by him; rigorous inspection of all weights and measures was enjoined. The drafters or revisers of the *Book of the Eparch* assumed that residence in Constantinople was a privilege, and 'exile' was a harsh penalty in itself. No clear distinction was drawn between provincials and foreigners: for example, anyone 'from outside' bringing any kind of merchandise 'into the God-protected City' was to be closely supervised by the Eparch's deputy; a list of their purchases was to be made at the end of their stay, 'so that nothing forbidden should leave the reigning City'.[5] The sale of pigs and sheep was regulated in detail; the express aim was cheaper food for the populace, and the interests of provincial producers were secondary.

All this probably had a positive effect on the citizens' well-being, but it also

---

[3] Leo VI, *Novels*, pp. 131, 197, 329–31, 345, 361.

[4] 'daktylō . . . idiō', *Eparch, prooimion*, p. 72.

[5] 'hōs an mēden kōlyomenon tēs basileuousēs exerchētai', *Eparch*, xx, 1, p. 132; see also xiii, 2, p. 120; xv, 1, p. 122, xvii, 4, p. 128, xviii, 1 and xviii, 4, pp. 128, 130.

publicised the emperor's solicitousness. An emperor enjoying the citizens' goodwill was screened against would-be usurpers. Leo broadcast his piety and accentuated the mystique of emperors born in the Purple Chamber (himself and his son Constantine). He maintained the festival celebrating the consecration of the 'New Church' built by Basil I. A dirge composed soon after Leo's death linked Constantinople and the reigning family thus:

> O City, sing, intone the praise
> of Basil's noble offspring,
> For they impart a deeper hue
> To thy imperial purple.[6]

Bread and butter issues were at least as important as pomp in winning the sympathies of the populace. Leo seems to have realized this.

Concentration on the capital rather than the provinces is not particularly surprising. More striking is Leo's assumption, in compiling his *Tactica* in (for the most part) the 890s, that the provinces are vulnerable to enemy attack and that this will continue indefinitely. He states that the work is for fighting the Saracens, who harass his subjects 'day by day'.[7] Warfare is essentially defensive, and commanders must ensure that all necessities are removed from areas under attack to safe places, livestock dispersed and the population evacuated. The Arab raiders should be attacked only when returning, weary and preoccupied with booty. Here, at least, the emperor was attuned to life as it was lived in the eastern provinces. The same tactics are advocated in *Skirmishing*, which drew on first-hand experience and was composed in the milieu of the Phokas family; it presupposes that humans as well as livestock will be amongst the raiders' encumbrances, and the *stratēgos* (military governor of a theme) is to assume that his troops will be numerically inferior to the raiders.[8]

The subterranean settlements of Cappadocia provide material evidence for the insecurity of the south-eastern provinces. Some pre-date the Arab invasions, but others, such as Salanda, 80 kilometres west of Caesarea, were created then. Several of the mill-stones which closed its numerous entrances are still extant, though such ingenuity did not prevent this redoubt from being captured in 898 and again in 906/7. *Skirmishing* sets notably less store by man-made fortifications than by familiarity with mountain heights and natural defences

---

[6] Hymnēson polis, hymnēson, tous Basileiou paidas,
　　Houtoi gar porphyrizousi mallon sou tēn porphyran
　　　Ševčenko (ed.), 'Poems on the Deaths of Leo VI and Constantine VII',
　　　　　ed. pp. 202 (Greek text), 205 (translation); cf. pp. 225, 227.

[7] 'to kath' hekastēn', Leo VI, *Tactica* XVIII, 142, col. 981.

[8] Leo VI, *Tactica* XVII, 76–80, cols. 932–3; XVIII, 126–7, col. 976; XVIII, 134, col. 977; Dennis (ed.), *Three Byzantine Military Treatises*, pp. 146, 156–8, 214.

from which observers can gauge enemy numbers and movements.[9] Rapid movement was here at a premium, thus limiting what the mounted raiders could take back. Their numbers seldom exceeded 10,000, and were often far smaller. The brunt of the seasonal land-raiding was borne in the south-east borderlands. Nonetheless, *Skirmishing*'s preoccupation with finding out the raiders' targets betrays the difficulty of keeping track of them, let alone in mustering soldiers from widely scattered agricultural holdings. Its detailed provisions for coping with major invasions, replete with siege-equipment, bespeak a state of alert and uncertainty as to where the next blow would fall.

No less uncertainty overhung the southern and western coastal districts of Asia minor. The amir of Tarsus despatched or led naval razzias, and these, like the piratical fleets operating from north Syrian ports, enjoyed a safe haven in Crete, if needed. It was there that Leo of Tripoli withdrew after sacking Thessalonika, the empire's second city, in 904, and there 22,000 prisoners were counted before being auctioned to the Cretans. For a while Leo's fleet was expected to attack Constantinople; it was probably this, rather than just the humiliation at Thessalonika, that spurred Leo VI into large-scale countermeasures. But a combined operation soon collapsed. The commander of land forces, Andronikos Doukas, had recently led a successful incursion into Cilicia. He now fell under suspicion of rebellion and fled to Baghdad after holding out for six months in 905 in the fortress of Kavala.

A later task-force under the command of a trusted civil servant and relative-by-marriage of Leo VI, Himerios, was directed against Crete, from which the Byzantines had vainly tried to dislodge the Arabs in the ninth century. Himerios was no more successful in 911–12, even though he seems to have followed the precepts of Leo's *Tactica*, and Leo of Tripoli remained at large in the Aegean for ten more years. Arab raids are quite commonplace in tenth-century hagiography: the tales may be fabulous, but their setting has substance. The sermons of Peter, bishop of Argos (*c.* 852–*c.* 922), and his *Life* concur in suggesting that the locals looked to the saints and Peter himself rather than to the emperor for protection.[10] Peter regularly ransomed captives from pirates who put in at Nauplia; and, reportedly through the miraculous production of flour, he acted to relieve a famine. Peter's ransomings were not far removed from tribute, and it seems that a form of tribute was exacted from the inhabitants of southern Aegean isles such as Naxos.

At one level these facts of provincial life make a mockery of the *bien pensant* Leo's public pronouncements. Yet the raiding fleets were normally modest,

---

[9] Dennis (ed.), *Three Byzantine Military Treatises*, pp. 150, 152, 154, 164, 184, 186; Howard-Johnston (1983), p. 259.

[10] Cf. *Hagiou Petrou episkopou Argous Bios kai Logoi*, pp. 34, 48, 174 (sermons); 242, 244, 246, 250 (Life); cf. Morris (1995), pp. 113–14.

and the boats in everyday piratical use needed to be small and light, to facilitate swift concealment in Aegean coves. So their carrying capacity was restricted. In any case, not even Byzantine or Muslim authorities could achieve high standards of seaworthiness: naval technology did not allow either side to dominate the seas, and vessels of any bulk tended to ply a limited – and predictable – range of routes. The Muslim fleets seldom seem to have liaised with one another, being intent on plunder, not conquest. The account of one of Leo of Tripoli's captives of 904 suggests there was more or less covert trafficking between the Muslim and Christian zones, involving redeemable prisoners and other commodities.[11] The smattering of Cretan amirs' copper coins found on the Greek mainland may hint at exchange. In the border regions, local self-reliance and deals with the men of violence were unavoidable.

Some of the areas most exposed to enemy raids indeed showed signs of increasing economic activity and wealth. In Sparta and Corinth the coin-sequences which had begun in the mid-ninth century continue uninterrupted through the first half of the tenth. Still more suggestive is the proliferation of painted chapels and churches in the rocks of Cappadocia. Some formed part of monasteries, but most were lay foundations, serving as shrines, marks of piety, and oratories. Similar monuments may well have been raised above ground in other provinces, particularly those in north-west Asia Minor, long secure from Arab raids. On the fertile southern shore of the Sea of Marmara lay several large wealthy monasteries, and ports such as Kyzikos, Pylai and Trigleia offered outlets to convey produce and livestock to the megalopolis. Under intensive police and customs scrutiny, the Sea of Marmara was the prosperous inner sanctum of the empire. There are signs of economic dynamism at Constantinople itself in the early tenth century. The size of the population remains uncertain, but the number of buildings was apparently increasing. Leo's *Novels* regulate building land and the spaces to be preserved between buildings, in ways not found in the Justinianic planning legislation, and this hints at greater building density.[12]

Yet even in the megalopolis the scale of economic activity and growth was modest. The citizens' needs could apparently be met by twenty-four notaries. Five of the nine owners of the shops listed in a mid-tenth-century rental note were officials or title-holders, only one identifiable by his trade. The richest pickings came from supplying the state or holding office, and the government was by far the largest employer in Constantinople. The palace complex will have required many hundreds of servants; eunuchs, pages and foreign body-guards were reportedly numbered in their thousands. Most of those who attended banquets or other ceremonies were holders of offices, heads of guilds

---

[11] John Kaminiates, *De expugnatione Thessalonicae*, pp. 59, 63.   [12] Leo VI, *Novels*, pp. 257, 373–5.

or other such City worthies, but persons who held titles yet lacked a state function could attend. A text deriving from Leo's reign specifies the sums payable
for certain court titles and offices, and indicates the *roga* (stipend) payable annually by the treasury to title-holders according to their rank. Provided that the
purchaser lived on for several years, he could make a profit, but the advantage
lay mainly in the conspicuous connection with the imperial court, significant
given the multifarious dealings which any man of property would have with
tax-inspectors and other officials.[13]

The purpose of the unremitting palace ceremonial was set out by
Constantine VII in the preface to the handbook on ceremonies he commissioned: 'may it be an image of the harmony of movement which the creator
gives to all creation, and be regarded by our subjects as more worthy of reverence and therefore more agreeable and marvellous'.[14] The establishment over
which the emperor presided was as just and as immutable as God's, and to
attempt to overturn it was tantamount to challenging God's order of things,
and no less wicked or futile. The ceremonies also dramatised the emperor's
role as the sole source of legitimate authority, and of serious wealth. Leo VI
recommends the appointment as general of a 'good, well-born and rich [man]'
even while piously urging a more meritocratic approach.[15] Leo probably
appreciated how much the running of his army in the provinces depended on
officers' local connections and resources. The rank-and-file did not receive
substantial regular cash wages, and Leo's *Tactica* discusses how to ensure a high
turn-out of well-drilled soldiery after a call to arms. His solution is a combination of fiscal privileges for the soldiers with the arousal of religious fervour
throughout provincial society, so that non-combatants would be predisposed
to contribute unstintingly to the war-effort.[16] The reforms would have to be
carried through by one of the army's few full-time components, officers above
the rank of *droungarios*. These were appointed directly by the emperor and
drew their salaries from him, but their effectiveness would not be the less for
their being gentlemen of private means. The *stratēgos* who commanded them
had to cope with enemy incursions. He had to take major decisions, and possessed sweeping powers to requisition and to evacuate civilians. He was left
largely to his own devices, but the term of office was short and he was forbidden from owning land in the theme he governed, a provision evidently
designed to prevent close ties growing up between the governor and local
society. It could not always be enforced, especially in the distant south-eastern

---

[13] *DC*, pp. 692–4; Lemerle (1967), pp. 80–3, 99–100.
[14] 'eikonizoi men tou demiourgou tēn peri tode to pan harmonian kai kinēsin, kathorōto de kai tois
hypo cheira semnoprepesteron, kai dia touto hēdyteron te kai thaumastoteron', *DC*, ed. Vogt, vol. I,
I, p. 2.   [15] 'agathos, eugenēs, plousios', Leo VI, *Tactica* II, 25, col. 688.
[16] Leo VI, *Tactica* XVIII, 128–33, cols. 976–7; Dagron (1983), pp. 221–3, 230, 233–9.

borderlands. Yet on the whole a balance was struck between affiliations, imperial and local.

Imperial propaganda did not merely proclaim an ideal of good order from the palace. The palace rites nearly all involved prayer or the veneration of the sainted. Many involved liturgical celebrations in St Sophia or churches outside the palace complex. The emperor constantly led his entourage in prayers for the welfare of his subjects, acting together with the patriarch and fortified by the concentration in his palace of Christendom's finest relics. The rhythmical intercession possibly gained in significance from the disorder which many provincials endured, constituting both an oasis and a clarion call for supernatural aid. Such a combination of imprecation and material splendour amidst turbulence could be found in Cluny, and the spell which Cluny's sumptuous liturgies cast on the propertied classes of Francia was perhaps akin to that of the *basileus'* festive prayers in Byzantium. His ritual displays of intimacy with God and *philanthrōpia* for his subjects were the visible accompaniment of works of legislation and tabulations of good administrative practice.

Those who did not view their interests or spiritual salvation as best served by the imperial establishment were too poor, localised and ill-equipped to take concerted action: the nearest they came was to respond tardily, if at all, to the general call-to-arms which the authorities periodically issued. Widespread if unchronicled apathy meant that *stratēgoi* had little hope of turning their forces against the government successfully. Their regular soldiers were too few and often too dispersed, and their principal mode of warfare was ill suited for an assault on Constantinople's formidable walls, ringed by water.

These underlying stabilisers of 'the great laden ship of the world'[17] are virtually unnoticed in the chronicles composed in Constantinople, which focus on the colourful factional rivalries between leading courtiers and generals. Thus the eunuch Samonas tried unsuccessfully to flee to the caliphate *c.* 904, but was soon restored to favour in the palace, rising to the position of *parakoimōmenos* ('chamberlain') in 906. But ultimately he depended on the emperor's favour, and once this was withdrawn, in June 908, Samonas became a political nullity confined to a monastery. The patriarch could sometimes, if determined enough, exert moral pressure on the emperor about matters with some religious or ethical content. In 906/7 Patriarch Nikolaos Mystikos made an issue of the marriage of Leo to his mistress, who had recently borne him a longed-for male heir, Constantine. This, Leo's fourth marriage, flagrantly violated canon law and a recent edict issued by Leo and his father Basil. Nikolaos caused the emperor great political embarrassment, and his involuntary abdication in 907 was galling to many churchmen. But deposed he was. One of the charges laid

---

[17] 'pēn kosmikēn holkada', *DAI*, 1/7–8.

against him was that he had written a letter to the Domestic of the Schools, Andronikos Doukas, urging him to continue with his stand at Kavala (see above, p. 556) and promising that 'the City by our exhortations will soon ask for you'.[18]

Whether authentic or not, the letter touched on the rawest of political nerves. Andronikos belonged to one of the families which had risen to prominence in the army in the later ninth century through martial talents and imperial favour. Andronikos' son, Constantine, who had fled with him to Baghdad, later returned, to be pardoned and even promoted. He became Domestic of the Schools in the last years of Leo's reign or during that of Leo's brother, Alexander. However, the latter's death and the infancy and debatable legitimacy of Constantine VII presented Doukas with an opportunity, and he is alleged to have been 'ever longing for the crown'.[19] His attempt to seize control of the palace met with stiff resistance from the reigning emperor's bodyguards, in the course of which he was killed. After this foiled coup attempt in June 913, the Doukases ceased to hold senior army commands.

The family which became the military mainstay of the Macedonian dynasty was neither illustrious nor particularly wealthy by origin. Its first outstanding member, Nikephoros Phokas, rose thanks to the favour of Basil I. He must have acted largely on his own initiative while Domestic of the Schools on the eastern frontier, yet his exploits are approvingly mentioned by Leo VI, who repeatedly calls him 'our general'.[20] Nikephoros was, during Leo's childhood, the *prōtostratōr* ('chief groom'), a post entailing close contact with the emperor. He most probably won Leo's trust then. The emperor on the Bosphorus, culling ancient writers on strategy for his generals' benefit, was demonstrating that he was still supreme commander, making his unique contribution to the war effort. The artificial convention of imperial omniscience was one to which the Phokases were normally willing to subscribe. *Skirmishing* cited Leo's work as the source for an exploit of Nikephoros, *even though* the account given is much fuller than that in Leo's *Tactica*.[21] The two families had risen together and their interests were furthered by mutual praise and aid. The build-up of lands, wealth and local connections of the Phokas family in Cappadocia was set in motion by imperial patronage and office.

Nikephoros' elder son, Leo, was seemingly made *stratēgos* of the single most important theme, the Anatolikoi, in the early tenth century. The post was held

---

[18] 'hē polis tacheōs dia tōn hēmōn paraineseōn epizētēsei se', Nikolaos I Mystikos, *Miscellaneous Writings*, p. 16.

[19] 'tou stephous aei ephiemenos', Theophanes Continuatus, *Chronographia*, p. 382.

[20] 'ho hēmeteros stratēgos', Leo VI, *Tactica* XI, 25, XV, 38, XVII, 83, cols 800, 896, 933.

[21] Leo VI, *Tactica* XI, 25, XVII, 83, cols 800, 933; *Three Byzantine Military Treatises*, ed. Dennis, pp. 218, 223 n. 1; Nikephoros Phokas, *De velitatione*, pp. 167–8.

subsequently by Leo's younger brother, Bardas. The Doukases were then in the limelight and Andronikos Doukas was clearly regarded by some courtiers as a budding usurper. Perhaps for that very reason ties were kept up with the Phokases. Constantine Doukas' *coup* attempt appeared to confirm the courtiers' suspicions. It could well be a sign of contemporary Byzantine preoccupation with *coups* that Symeon of Bulgaria's march on Constantinople later that summer was assumed to be aimed at the throne. Nikolaos Mystikos, the chief regent, had no special reason to cherish the boy emperor: his refusal to sanction Leo VI's marriage to Constantine's mother, Zoe, had cost him his patriarchal throne. He regained it only after Leo's death, and upon becoming chief regent in June 913 he expelled Zoe from the palace. Nikolaos is not implausibly alleged to have incited Constantine Doukas' attempted coup. In a letter to Symeon of July 913 Nicholas seems to hint that if only Symeon will stop short of outright usurpation, a role as guardian of the boy emperor may yet be found for him. Nikolaos' position was insecure within the palace, understandably enough given his attitude to Constantine VII, and early in 914 the boy's yearning for his mother was cited as grounds for ousting Nikolaos from the regency council. Zoe returned to the palace, and took charge.

The following six years are commonly regarded as a break in the generally orderly political history of tenth-century Byzantium. However, the period of overt jockeying for power was relatively brief. Moreover, Zoe seems to have maintained a stable regime for some three years, renewing the imperial axis with the Phokases. Leo Phokas was appointed Domestic of the Schools, probably at the same time as or soon after the eunuch Constantine was restored as *parakoimōmenos*, early in 914. Leo is said by the main chronicle to have been endowed with 'courage, rather than a commander's judgement'.[22] A court orator was even less flattering, dubbing him 'the deer-hearted brother-in-law'[23] of the *parakoimōmenos*. But the expeditions sent to Armenia and central Italy were successful, and the government felt confident enough to attempt to 'annihilate' Symeon of Bulgaria with a surprise attack.[24] Bitter recriminations followed the disastrous defeat on the Acheloos on 20 August 917. An attempt was made to lay heaviest blame on the admiral of the fleet, Romanos Lekapenos, for failing to ferry the Pechenegs across the Danube to attack Symeon from the north, and also for not picking up survivors. These allegations probably represent an official attempt to exonerate the land army's commander, Leo Phokas. He stationed himself at Constantinople with his surviving soldiers, as did Lekapenos with the imperial fleet.

The naval commander Romanos Lekapenos was a provincial without court

---

[22] 'andria mallon ē epistatikē phronēsis', Theophanes Continuatus, *Chronographia*, p. 388.

[23] 'elaphō tō gambrō', Dujčev (1978), p. 276.

[24] 'aphanisai', Theophanes Continuatus, *Chronographia*, p. 388.

connections, but he exploited the fact that Constantine was now too old to be ignored. Romanos struck early in 919, benefiting from surprise, sympathisers in the palace and the apparent paralysis of Zoe and Phokas, once the intelligent *parakoimōmenos* had been seized and stowed aboard one of Lekapenos' ships. Lekapenos claimed to be acting in response to a handwritten appeal from the boy emperor. On the morrow the thirteen-year-old announced that he would assume imperial power in conjunction with Patriarch Nikolaos and a veteran courtier, Stephen *magistros*. Zoe was to be expelled from the palace – although her tearful pleas at once made him relent – and Phokas was to be replaced as Domestic of the Schools. Remarkably, Phokas' reaction was merely to insist, before leaving the palace, that a brother and nephew of the *parakoimōmenos* be appointed to key commands. Still more remarkably, when these were also immediately expelled from the palace, Phokas turned to Lekapenos for consolation and support. Oaths of mutual assistance were sworn between them. Phokas' prominence at court had not been in reward for political skills. Romanos Lekapenos, in contrast, was a politician to his finger-tips, who even capitalised on his status as an outsider to the palace and posed as the disinterested arbiter. He made the modest request of access to the palace, the better to guard the Porphyrogenitus. Although in late March he resorted to a display of force, arraying the entire fleet in the main harbour of the palace, he relied heavily on a small number of active sympathisers in the palace and acceptance by courtiers loyal to the Porphyrogenitus. He entered the massively fortified precincts with only a few followers 'to perform obeisance' to the emperor,[25] exchange oaths and be appointed commander of the imperial bodyguard. Once installed in the palace, he acted promptly yet circumspectly. Letters in Constantine's name were sent to Leo Phokas, who had withdrawn to Cappadocia, warning him not to contemplate rebellion. Equally promptly, Romanos betrothed his daughter to Constantine. The marriage was celebrated on 9 May 919 and Romanos assumed the title *basileiopatōr* ('father of the palace'). His rapid rise now alarmed well-wishers of the Porphyrogenitus; but he controlled the fleet and the palace, as well as Constantine's person and so his validating authority. It was the last of these cards that he played against the large army which Phokas led from Cappadocia to Chrysopolis, across the straits from Constantinople. A letter from the emperor was read out to the rebels, singing Romanos' praises as his most trustworthy guard and denouncing Phokas as a traitor who had 'always' coveted the throne.[26]

Upon hearing this, the soldiers apparently deserted *en masse* and Phokas, who tried to flee, was caught and blinded. These events suggest the focal role of the emperor, in whose cause all parties professed to be acting, even though

---

[25] 'proskynēsōn', Theophanes Continuatus, *Chronographia*, p. 394.
[26] Theophanes Continuatus, *Chronographia*, p. 396.

Constantine's forbears had only worn the purple for half a century and even though he had been born out of wedlock. It was Romanos' talent to harness this sentiment to his own interests. More than eighteen months elapsed before Romanos induced his son-in-law and Patriarch Nikolaos to crown him co-emperor, on 17 December 920. By mediating between Nikolaos and his enemies Romanos had given Nikolaos a stake in the perpetuation of his rule. Romanos was now about fifty years old and so he needed to move fast, yet any outright deposition of Constantine would outrage the very sensibilities which he had harnessed to seize power. On 17 or 20 May 921 he induced the Porphyrogenitus to crown his eldest son, Christopher, co-emperor. The 'unusual profusion of patterns and ceremonial issues'[27] of coins in the 920s reflects Romanos' aspirations, but also his hesitation about promoting Christopher to the exclusion of Constantine VII. On certain classes of *solidus* Constantine appears smaller than Christopher and (unlike him) beardless, while on the commonest class of the 920s only Romanos and Christopher are depicted. Nonetheless, Constantine retained his formal position as second after Romanos in the palace ceremonies. In the early 920s Romanos constructed, in effect, an alternative palace with adjoining monastery on the site of his private residence, over 1 kilometre to the west of the Great Palace. The new complex, though small by comparison, was clearly intended to be the shrine of the Lekapenos dynasty, and Romanos' wife was buried there in 922. The Myrelaion might lack a Purple Chamber, birthplace of emperors, but the monastery implied that in piety, at least, the new imperials were unimpeachable. Romanos also sought to demonstrate his philanthropy to the citizens of Constantinople through charitable foundations.

Even so, Romanos could be branded a 'stranger and intruder' by Symeon of Bulgaria,[28] and charged with imposing himself upon Constantine. The furiousness of Romanos' denial was real; the acute Bulgarian had put his finger on the speciousness of the pretext for Romanos' rise to power.[29] However, if Symeon hoped to destabilise Romanos' regime, he was to be disappointed, and his armies' repeated attacks on the City may well have rallied support behind the seasoned naval commander. In autumn 924 Symeon led his host in person, and at a preliminary meeting with Patriarch Nikolaos he requested an encounter with Romanos. Romanos is credited with delivering a miniature homily, exhorting Symeon to desist from slaughtering fellow Christians and demonstrate his Christianity by making peace. Symeon is depicted as being shamed by these words and agreeing to make peace, though in reality nothing firmer than an accord was negotiated: the account probably

---

[27] Grierson (1973b), p. 529.

[28] 'xenos kai allotrios', Theodore Daphnopates, *Correspondance*, p. 73.

[29] Theodore Daphnopates, *Correspondance*, pp. 71–3.

echoes contemporary imperial propaganda. Romanos also turned the Bulgarian problem to political advantage in 927, when emissaries from Symeon's heir, Peter, arrived, proposing peace. A treaty was soon ratified and on 8 October the young tsar was wedded to Maria, daughter of Romanos' eldest son, Christopher.

Romanos had his reasons for publicising the wedding. Losses in the Bulgarian war had been substantial, and peace must have been welcome to the citizens and to the provincials who had lived through Bulgarian occupation. Romanos probably also sought to advance his own son's status through the marriage: the Bulgarians were 'barbarians', and Peter's father had styled himself emperor only since, probably, 913, but Peter's family had long been royal. It was most probably at Romanos' prompting that the Bulgarians insisted that Christopher's name be acclaimed before that of Constantine at the wedding, and Romanos bowed to their protests. The predilections, and imperial style, of the Bulgarians could thus be yoked to Lekapenan aspirations. In so far as the interests of these two families converged, the court rhetoric about 'union' and fellowship had an unsuspectedly solid foundation. Christopher's imperial credentials were enhanced and he could be described as revitalising his father's old age through 'flourishing in his turn in majesty, and he nourished [it] with hopes of [his] succession to the throne'.[30]

Romanos Lekapenos is said to have been devastated by Christopher's death in August 931. He does not seem to have had the heart to set about advancing his younger sons Stephen and Constantine ahead of the Porphyrogenitus; they were still only boys. Constantine was restored to the gold coins, even occupying a position senior to Romanos', which reflects the uncertain political outlook. Constantine was neither assured of the succession nor involved in decision-making. His bitter disdain for his father-in-law is patent in his *De administrando imperio*, most explicitly in his dismissal of the Bulgarian marriage arranged by the 'common and illiterate fellow'.[31]

This uneasy *ménage* was upset publicly by Romanos' show of favour towards Constantine VII: he proposed that Constantine's son should marry the daughter of his Domestic of the Schools. Stephen and Constantine Lekapenos protested vehemently and the plan was dropped. It is striking that the Domestic, John Kourkouas, was brought into play by Romanos to counteract the tensions of court factions, inevitably aggravated by his advanced age. Romanos' alertness to the post's significance is suggested by the brevity of Domestics' tenure

[30] ... en skēptrois epakmazōn.
    kai tais elpisin etrephe diadochēs tou kratous
        Sternbach (1899), p. 17, lines 5–6.

[31] 'idiōtēs kai agrammatos anthrōpos', *DAI*, c. 13/149–50.

early in his reign, in contrast with Kourkouas' twenty-two-year stint. Kourkouas was under thirty when appointed in 922, and he had no record of associations with the Macedonian house, probably a prime recommendation in Romanos' eyes; his experience of pitched battles on the eastern borderlands was then minimal. But Kourkouas proved to have military talents. From the later 920s onwards, he was repeatedly sent eastwards and won praise from Byzantine chronicles for all the towns, forts and castles, allegedly numbering over 1000, that he captured from the Saracens. The troublesome Muslim raiding bases of Melitene and Theodosiopolis were repeatedly attacked. Melitene was finally annexed in 934, and Theodosiopolis was eventually captured in 949. Muslim forts along the upper Euphrates and its tributaries were turned into Byzantine strongpoints. One of them was renamed Romanoupolis, in the emperor's honour. The Domestic, who was aptly compared with Belisarius, gained for his sedentary master an aura of expansion. He is credited with having doubly benefited *Romania*, stemming the Muslim raids deep into Asia Minor and extending Roman borders as far as the Euphrates and even the Tigris.[32] More impressive is the fact that Kourkouas' offensives could be sustained for almost twenty years without much overt foreboding of *coups d'état*.

Romanos chose the theatres of operations no less shrewdly. They lay for the most part in Armenia and Mesopotamia. He did not mount ambitious combined operations of the sort that had come to grief in Leo's reign, nor was there much concentrated effort in the south-eastern borderlands. Instead, the pressure was applied further north, on Armenia. Theodosiopolis and Melitene lay in fertile countryside and were important trading centres. They could yield ample revenues and Melitene was declared an imperial *kouratoreia*, an estate whose proceeds went straight to the emperor's coffers. The rocky slopes of the Taurus and the Anti-Taurus, by contrast, were neither fertile nor well populated, while the Cilician plain was studded with Muslim forts. One further advantage of Romanos' eastern strategy was that it did not rely on Byzantine military resources alone. John Kourkouas and his brother Theophilus were able to gain the collaboration or formal submission of certain Armenian princes, while Romanos himself sought to forge bonds with individual princes, offering titles or a residence and estates in Byzantium. He thereby complemented and, at the same time, kept track of Kourkouas' activities. The princes' ties were with Romanos himself.

The most spectacular of Kourkouas' *tours de force* induced the citizens of Edessa to surrender their famed *mandylion*, the cloth with the miraculous imprint of Christ's features. In return, Romanos issued a chrysobull, pledging

---

[32] Theophanes Continuatus, *Chronographia*, p. 427.

that Byzantium would never again molest the region of Edessa.[33] Edessa lay little more than 100 kilometres south from Melitene, but was clearly not regarded as a desirable candidate for annexation. The gaining of the relic showed up the impotence of the caliph and it was conveyed through the provinces to Constantinople. But the high-pitched celebration of its arrival had much to do with Romanos' domestic problems. Some time earlier he had had to yield to his son's protests at his scheme to marry Constantine VII's son to Kourkouas' daughter. Now he was too ill for the lengthy processions and ceremonies, and the advent of the image may unintentionally have bolstered the standing of his two unfavoured younger sons: they played a leading role in the celebrations whereas Kourkouas is not recorded as having been present. By the autumn of 944, Kourkouas had been dismissed. That same autumn Romanos made another gesture in favour of Constantine, issuing a testament declaring him 'the first emperor' and threatening his own sons' imperial status should they attempt anything against Constantine.[34] Acting, presumably, in light of this, the young Lekapenoi struck against their father, on 20 December 944. He was secretly abducted to one of the islands in the Sea of Marmara. It is uncertain whether Constantine VII connived with the plotters: what is (and was) clear is his status as the sole adult emperor to have been born in the Purple Chamber. When a rumour spread that he had been murdered by the two Lekapenoi, the populace gathered outside the palace, calling for Constantine. It was placated only by his appearance, poking his bare head out through a lattice.

The citizens apparently associated the Macedonian house with their own well-being, just as Leo VI had intended. But the Porphyrogenitus did not rely on aura alone. He is said to have immediately appointed Bardas Phokas as Domestic of the Schools, the brother of the man against whose alleged ambition for the throne Lekapenos had launched his own political career.[35] Bardas' first loyalty was patently to Constantine VII, and the appointment was a first step towards the undoing of the Lekapenoi. They themselves were apparently hatching a plot when they were seized in the palace on 27 January 945. They were, without any reported popular outcry, abducted to the Princes' Islands and a new life as involuntary clerics. Had their father backed them whole-heartedly they might perhaps have supplanted the Porphyrogenitus. But Romanos had not repeated his efforts to advance Christopher. At home, as abroad, his hard-headed ambition did little more than maintain the status quo.

[33] Theophanes Continuatus, *Chronographia*, p. 432; Dobschütz (1899), p. 75**. The environs of Edessa were traversed by Byzantine forces on several occasions, and as early as 949 Samosata, a city named in the chrysobull, was attacked and, nine years later, devastated. However, these were essentially countermeasures against Saif al-Dawla, who was the first to breach the terms of the chrysobull: Canard (1953), p. 751; Segal (1970), p. 216.

[34] 'tō prōtō basilei', Theophanes Continuatus, *Chronographia*, p. 435.

[35] Theophanes Continuatus, *Chronographia*, p. 435.

CHAPTER 23

BULGARIA: THE OTHER
BALKAN 'EMPIRE'

Jonathan Shepard

THE HISTORY of Byzantium in this period cannot be divorced from that of Bulgaria, with which it shared borders for over 1,000 kilometres. The accord of 870 between Khan Boris and Emperor Basil I conceded Bulgaria an archbishopric of its own, 'autocephalous' but under the moral lead of the patriarchate of Constantinople; the archbishop was high in the order of precedence of imperial court banquets. The Byzantine ruling elite enshrined the notion of Bulgaria's religious indebtedness in the fiction that the Bulgarians were the 'spiritual children' of the Byzantines, while each successive Bulgarian ruler was the 'spiritual child' of the emperor and the patriarch.[1]

After major expansion westwards in the mid-ninth century and the subsequent establishment of metropolitanates and bishoprics, Bulgaria constituted a large, populous and well-ordered power. Its newly Christian rulers were committed to abhor warfare against fellow-Christians and especially against their 'spiritual father', but their polity aroused apprehension on the Bosphorus. The various clashes between Symeon (893–927) and Byzantium might seem to vindicate such unease. But the colourful career of Symeon has deflected attention away from the problems inherent in Byzantino-Bulgarian relations, and tensions are also discernible during the reign of his eirenic son, Peter; the personalities of individual rulers were by no means the sole determinant of relations.

The events of Symeon's reign are narrated relatively fully by Byzantine sources, and these have swayed modern historians' appraisals of his aspirations. Already before 913 'not a few persons were . . . whispering' that he intended to seize the Byzantine throne, according to a letter of Patriarch Nikolaos Mystikos ostensibly urging him against such a course.[2] Yet Symeon could be described by Theophylact of Ochrid, a much later Byzantine churchman writing in Bulgaria, as one who 'showed most fervent trust in those manifesting purity of morals and a most Christian way of life'; he had 'extended the

---

[1] 'pneumatika/on tekna/on', *DC*, p. 690; Dölger (1939), pp. 188–90, 191–3.

[2] 'ouk oligōn kai prin . . . phēmizontōn', Nikolaos I, Patriarch of Constantinople, *Letters*, pp. 28–30.

holy preaching of the Gospel and through his foundation of churches everywhere established orthodoxy as unassailable'.[3] A contemporary encomiast in Bulgaria had compared Symeon with the founder of the library in Alexandria, Ptolemy.[4] Clearly, this Bulgarian image of Symeon the bibliophile jars with the barbarous warmonger presented in the Byzantines' writings of the tenth century.

Amidst the uncertainties enshrouding Symeon's aims and actions, three features of the earlier years of his reign stand out. First, his accession was fortuitous. He had withdrawn to a monastery, probably without expectations of accession. His elder brother Vladimir is said as khan to have tried 'with all his might' to turn his subjects back to paganism.[5] He was stopped not by Symeon but by their father, Boris, who emerged from monastic retirement, seized and blinded Vladimir and designated Symeon in his stead, 'threatening in front of everyone that he would suffer likewise if he deviated one jot from the correct Christian way'.[6] Symeon was therefore committed to maintaining orthodoxy, a policy publicised on his lead seals: their iconography is very similar to that on Boris', and their Greek legends invoke the help of the Virgin and of Christ for 'Symeon, prince of Bulgaria', just as his father's did.[7]

Second, the opening years of Symeon's reign saw an outburst of clerical literary activity, especially by former pupils or associates of Cyril and Methodius. This meant primarily translating Greek prayers, hymns, sermons and other works of doctrinal exegesis into Slavonic, but also copying manuscripts. In 893–4 a scholar residing in Preslav, Constantine, compiled the so-called 'Didactic Gospel-Book'. Its central section comprises a collection of sermons expounding in plain words the Gospel readings for each Sunday through the year. Constantine states that he had been pressed into this task by Naum, another of Methodius' pupils, who had arrived in Bulgaria as a refugee after his master's death.[8] Within a few months of his accession, Symeon transferred Clement, yet another pupil, from the extreme south-west to become the bishop of 'Dragvista or Velitza', most probably an extensive region arching from the south-west of Thessalonika to the Rhodope range north of the city.[9]

---

[3] 'malista de pros tous semnotēta tropōn epangellomenous kai biou christianikōtatēn emphaneian, pistin thermēn epedeiknyto'; 'epauxēsas to theion kērygma kai tais hapantachou domētheisais ekklēsiais egkatastēsas tēn orthodoxian asaleuton': *Gr'tskite zhitiia na Kliment Okhridski*, p. 128.

[4] Kuev (1986), pp. 11, 13; Thomson (1993), p. 52.

[5] 'omni conamine', Regino, *Chronicon*, p. 96.

[6] 'Interminatus coram omnibus similia passurum, si in aliquo a recta christianitate deviaret', Regino, *Chronicon*, p. 96.

[7] 'Symeōn archonta Boulgarias', Jurukova (1985), pp. 17–18; cf. Jordanov (1984), pp. 91–3 and fig. 2 on p. 92; Jurukova and Penchev (1990), pp. 28–9.   [8] See Georgiev (1962), p. 158; Kuev (1986).

[9] Both names of the diocese derived from those of Slav tribes living in the region: *Gr'tskite zhitiia na Kliment Okhridski*, p. 128; Soustal (1991), pp. 88, 197–8.

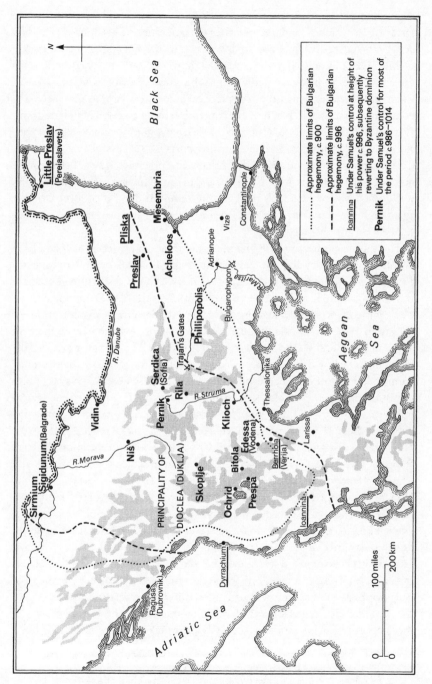

12 Bulgaria in the tenth century

Legend:

.... Approximate limits of Bulgarian hegemony, c.900

‒ ‒ ‒ Approximate limits of Bulgarian hegemony, c.996

Ioannina Under Samuel's control at height of his power c.996, subsequently reverting to Byzantine dominion

Pernik Under Samuel's control for most of the period c.986–1014

According to Clement's *Vita*, Symeon had been impressed by reports of 'the virtue of the teacher', and it emphasises the ignorance of his flock.[10] Symeon's choice to succeed Clement as roving pastor in the huge area encompassing Ochrid, Diabolis and Glavenitsa was Naum, whose earliest *Vita* describes his mission there as being 'for education', the same priority as in the *Vita* of Clement.[11] Neither Symeon nor his clerical associates seem to have seen any contradiction in the despatch of bookmen to remote places. They shared with Cyril and Methodius the assumption that learning, godly living and lucid exposition of the Scriptures were interlocking parts of successful evangelisation. Constantine of Preslav translated St Athanasius' polemics against the Arians in 906/7, on the instructions of Symeon, and in the following year the translation was copied out by Symeon's nephew, the monk Todor (Theodore) Doksov, again on his instructions: Symeon's zeal for learning and its transmission continued long after his accession.[12]

The third clear feature of Symeon's earlier years in power is his formidable talents for diplomacy and war. Nothing in his life as monk or student can have provided much outlet for them, and the shock of their disclosure goes some way to explaining his ill repute in Byzantium. According to Byzantine chronicles, Symeon was provoked into war by the arbitrary manipulation of Bulgarian trade in Constantinople (business being switched from there to Thessalonika), and by the raising of customs dues. The emperor's reportedly blithe dismissal of Symeon's protests was a slap in the face to a ruler recently enthroned in somewhat demeaning circumstances. Symeon led his army into the Byzantine theme of Macedonia and defeated the large force sent against him with heavy losses. But he withdrew to Bulgarian territory without pressing his advantage. It was Byzantium which made the next move, inciting the Hungarians to attack Bulgaria from their vantage-point in the south Russian steppes. The imperial fleet ferried the Hungarians across the Danube and Symeon's forces were overwhelmed. Symeon himself barely escaped and the Hungarians ranged as far south as Preslav. Symeon negotiated for peace, playing for time while bringing the Pechenegs into action as his own proxies. These nomads of the steppes to the north-east of the Black Sea were incited to drive westwards into the Hungarians' grazing grounds. The worsted Hungarian clans migrated westwards across the Carpathians. Byzantium determined upon a direct attack, but the great army was defeated by Symeon at Bulgarophygon in 896 before it had entered Bulgarian territory. Symeon used the allegedly 120,000 prisoners as bargaining-counters in his negotiations with the emperor and his emissary, Leo Choerosphaktes. Symeon had within a

---

[10] 'tēs aretēs tou didaskalou', *Gr'tskite zhitiia na Kliment Okhridski*, p. 128; cf. pp. 130, 132.

[11] 'na ouchitel'stvo', Ivanov (1930), pp. 306–7, 308; Kusseff (1950), p. 143.

[12] Georgiev (1962), pp. 192, 330–1; Athanasius, *Contra Arianos*, p. 7 (introduction).

couple of years deprived Byzantium of its main fighting force. But the feared Bulgarian assault on Constantinople never materialised, and the peace-treaty concluded in (probably) 897 apparently made no sweeping concessions to Symeon.

The empire continued to enjoy significant strategic advantages over Symeon. It kept its bases at Mesembria and Develtos, while Thessalonika and Dyrrachium represented tight clamps on Symeon's flanks. It is no accident that the two known occasions of apparently serious strain in Symeon's early relations with Byzantium concerned these two formidable military bases. Our principal source is a self-serving letter of Leo Choerosphaktes in which he claims credit for dissuading Symeon from grabbing 'the thirty forts of Dyrrachium' and for preventing the Bulgarians from occupying Thessalonika after its sack by Leo of Tripoli in 904.[13] Epigraphical evidence suggests that Symeon sought demarcation of the borders near Thessalonika then, staking his claim to a strategic pass north of the city. But the inscription extant on one of at least two marble columns erected there implies no departure from peaceful coexistence with Byzantium. The 'Romans' are named first, following Byzantine diplomatic convention, and Symeon is called *archōn*, 'prince', as on his earliest seal-type, leaving the *basileus'* monopoly of imperial status intact.[14]

Symeon's first two decades as ruler thus offer contrasts but not contradictions. His late-blossoming talents as diplomat and general did not exclude a persistently ascetic private life. In 920 Patriarch Nikolaos Mystikos saluted, albeit ironically, Symeon's monk-like regimen.[15] Symeon was strong willed, inheriting from his father both high moral seriousness and ruthlessness. Already in the mid-890s he derided (if enviously) Byzantine claims to superior wisdom, inviting Leo Choerosphaktes to give his master's prediction of whether Symeon would release his prisoners-of-war. Two years earlier Leo VI had correctly forecast a solar eclipse. Now Symeon seized upon the hapless envoy's response to his invitation: 'Your emperor, for all his knowledge of the heavens, knows nothing at all about the future.'[16] By keeping Choerosphaktes in suspense about the release of prisoners he was turning the tables on a government which had not consulted him about trading policy or heeded his protests. After his first victory he cut off the noses of the captured Khazars and sent them back to Constantinople 'to the humiliation of the Romans'.[17]

Such gestures were spectacular: the Khazars had been part of the emperor's bodyguard, symbolising his wide-ranging power. But Symeon's insults may well

---

[13] 'ta tou Dyrrachiou triakonta phrouria', Kolias (1939), p. 113.

[14] Ivanov (1970), pp. 16–20; Beševliev (1979), pp. 170–2.

[15] Nikolaos I, Patriarch of Constantinople, *Letters*, p. 94.

[16] 'Oide de kai ho sos basileus kai meteōrologos oudamōs to mellon loipon', Kolias (1939), p. 79.

[17] 'eis aischynēn tōn Rōmaiōn', Theophanes Continuatus, *Chronographia*, p. 358.

have been intended to warn Leo VI of the need to take Bulgarian interests into account and to lay the foundations for more stable relations. Symeon undoubtedly aspired to emulate Byzantium, but not, during the first two decades of his reign, to conquer it. He aimed rather at a viable Christian polity, distinct from Byzantium yet impeccably orthodox in religion. His concern with evangelisation among ordinary people is manifest not only in his 'foundation of churches everywhere' but also in his efforts to bring social norms into line with Christian teaching.[18] Symeon may well have been responsible for disseminating copies of the *Zakon Sudnii Liudem* ('Law for Judgement of the People'), a Slavonic translation of a brief collection of extracts from Leo III's law-code, the *Ekloga*.[19] He enjoyed from early on a reputation for 'justice and philanthropy'.[20] His apparent sense of a duty to provide his subjects with cults, churches and justice realised the ideals of Christian rulership as expounded by Patriarch Photius in a lengthy letter to Boris, which may have been heeded rather more carefully than modern scholarship has allowed.[21] His education and intellect enabled him to develop his role as teacher, sage and moral guide to an unprecedented extent, and he was probably not joking when he compared himself to Moses.[22] His personal interest in theology is apparent in his independent selection from the sermons of St John Chrysostom: he drew extensively from the vast range of Chrysostom's works, marking the passages to be translated by his scholar protégés.[23] Symeon's anonymous encomiast was one recipient of his instructions. He praised the use to which Symeon put the variegated book-learning which he had collected 'like a labour-loving bee': 'he pours [it] like sweet honey from his lips, before his boyars'.[24]

Symeon was devising a hierarchy of knowledge and piety. His superior endowment in these qualities entitled him to direct everyone else, including his 'boyars' (nobles). Their nature, numbers and origins are unknown, but the halls and courtyards excavated in and around Symeon's palace complex at Preslav were their residences. Eight monasteries have now been discovered there and most date from the reigns of Symeon or Peter. Symeon's reasons for making his principal residence there rather than at Pliska have not been convincingly explained: Pliska's pagan associations had already been obscured by Boris'

---

[18] *Gr'tskite zhitiia na Kliment Okhridski*, p. 128.

[19] The questions of where and when the translation – part loose, part literal – was made remain debatable. See *Zakon sudnyj ljudem (Court Law for the People)*, ed. H. W. Dewey, p. viii; *Oxford Dictionary of Byzantium*, ed. A. P. Kazhdan, 3 vols., Oxford (1991), III, p. 2219.

[20] 'to dikaion meta tou philanthrōpou', Kolias (1939), pp. 81, 83.

[21] Photius, *Epistulae et Amphilochia* I, pp. 1–39; Simeonova (1988), pp. 96–101.

[22] Nikolaos I, Patriarch of Constantinople, *Letters*, p. 176.

[23] Thomson (1982), pp. 22, 45–7.

[24] 'aky p'chela liubodel'na'; 'prolivaiet aky str'd slad'k iz oust svoikh pred boliary', Kuev (1986), p. 11; Thomson (1993), p. 52.

foundation of a monastery and building (or rebuilding) of churches there. Strategic considerations probably weighed heavily. The middle-sized fort at Preslav had not fallen to the Hungarians and had perhaps discouraged them from pressing further south. Around the turn of the ninth and tenth centuries, Symeon enlarged the fort and incorporated a palace complex and a grid of squares and streets paved with limestone slabs and lined by stone residences. Particular care was taken to ensure abundant clean water and a limestone aqueduct carried water to the citadel from the 'outer town'. The outer town was itself fortified with crenellated ramparts of regularly laid blocks of stone; this entire fortified area comprised approximately 3.5 km^2, abutting to the east on the River Ticha.

The painstaking provision of drinking water, the massive gate-houses which could act as mini-forts and the innovatory techniques of the walls' foundations (designed to withstand blows from catapults or battering rams) all bespeak a preoccupation with defence. The ensemble was at the same time designed to proclaim the prince's majesty and it is noteworthy that John the Exarch in his celebrated evocation of Symeon's court treats the prince and his nobles as the centrepiece: the tall palaces and churches would astonish the stranger, especially if he beheld the prince sitting in his pearl-studded robe, 'and on both sides his boyars sitting with gold necklaces, belts and rings'.[25] Symeon's decorators used ceramic tiles extensively, decorated to resemble more precious materials such as marble or mosaic.

This long-term building-project unmistakably emulated Constantinople, but it suggests a determination to hold on to Preslav against all comers rather than the preliminaries to an attempt on Byzantium. Symeon apparently sought to hold Byzantine power at arm's length, while still drawing on its funds of religious knowledge and technical know-how. Symeon could not, even with his well-stocked library, aspire to full cultural self-sufficiency. Byzantium remained the fount of religious knowledge, and Greek was the language of Symeon's seals, court acclamations and inscriptions. It was taught in monastic schools, and the sung parts of the liturgy continued to be in Greek, as they had been from long before Boris' conversion. Several bilingual inscriptions have been found, as well as beginners' alphabets.

Upon Leo's death in 912 Symeon is said by our chief Byzantine chronicle to have sent envoys to his successor, Alexander, expressing enthusiasm for peaceful relations 'just as in the reign of Emperor Leo'.[26] Symeon is depicted as having been provoked into war by Alexander's insulting and threatening dismissal of his envoys – plausibly enough, as Leo VI had been almost as high-

---

[25] 'i obapoly ego bolery sediashchia v zlatakh griv'nakh i poiasekh i obruch'kh', John, Exarch of Bulgaria, *Hexaemeron* VI, 3–5.

[26] 'hōsper dē kai epi tou basileōs Leontos', Theophanes Continuatus, *Chronographia*, p. 380.

handed with Symeon. Symeon is said to have determined on war, but there is no firm evidence for hostilities before the death of Alexander on 6 June 913; and while Symeon most probably proclaimed himself *basileus* around that time, and in the late summer of 913 led a huge army to the walls of Constantinople, no deliberate bloodshed occurred even then, judging by the silence of the Byzantine sources. The Byzantine chronicles' statement that Symeon withdrew without having made any peace-treaty is contradicted by an almost contemporary letter of Patriarch Nikolaos Mystikos, regent for the seven-year-old Constantine VII.[27] Even the most summary outline of events must therefore be tentative. There can be little doubt that Symeon and Nikolaos met publicly in the Hebdomon palace complex outside Constantinople in 913, or that a rite involving a crown was carried out by Nikolaos. Its exact nature and significance is controversial, but there is general agreement that a marriage was arranged between a daughter of Symeon and Constantine and that Symeon probably believed that the ceremony implied recognition of his imperial title by Byzantium. It was probably now that he began to strike seals whose legends included the terms *Symeōn basileus* and, on the reverse, *eirēnopoios basileus*, 'peacemaking emperor', a phrase chanted in Byzantine court acclamations which is probably also an allusion to the peace which Symeon believed he had established in 913.[28]

While some recent scholars have questioned whether Symeon coveted the Byzantine throne from the outset, they tend to accept that Alexander's provocations and the opportunity presented by Constantine VII's minority raised his sights to the 'Roman' throne.[29] His deal with Nikolaos on this view manoeuvred him into court circles as future father-in-law of the boy Constantine, with every prospect of supreme power thereafter. There is some support for this interpretation: soon after his encounter with Symeon Nikolaos was ousted from the regency by Zoe, the boy emperor's mother, and while the chronicles mention neither the agreement of 913 nor any formal abrogation of it, they do describe Symeon as ravaging Thrace; in September 914 Adrianople was briefly in his hands. At about the same time a letter of Nikolaos Mystikos accused Symeon of not being content with the 'honour' or 'title' he had received and persistently trying 'to appear and to be someone of different standing'.[30] This phase could be regarded as ending with the Byzantine invasion of Bulgaria 'to

---

[27] Theophanes Continuatus, *Chronographia*, p. 385; Leo Grammaticus, *Chronographia*, p. 292; Nikolaos I, Patriarch of Constantinople, *Letters*, pp. 50–2.

[28] Gerasimov (1960), pp. 67–9; Dujčev (1961), p. 249; Beševliev (1962), p. 18; (1963), p. 332; Dujčev (1971), p. 188; Jurukova and Penchev (1990), pp. 29–30. Gerasimov (1976), pp. 126, 128, later changed his reading of the reverse from *(eirēnop)oios basileus* to *hyios basileōs* ('son of the emperor'), but it seems unlikely that Symeon's pride could have stomached, let alone sported, such an epithet; cf. Božilov (1986a), p. 81, n. 47.   [29] Božilov (1983), pp. 111–12; Fine (1983), p. 144.

[30] 'kainoteros tis einai kai dokein', Nikolaos I, Patriarch of Constantinople, *Letters*, p. 50.

overcome and annihilate Symeon'.[31] The strategy resembled that of twenty years before, with the Pechenegs playing the part formerly taken by the Hungarians while a Byzantine army advanced up the coast. However, the Pechenegs failed to cross the Danube, and the main Byzantine army was cut to pieces beside the River Acheloos, on 20 August 917.

The historicity of the disaster on the Acheloos is unquestionable, but various letters of Nikolaos Mystikos to Symeon give serious grounds for doubting whether there really was 'a continuing war' from 914 onwards.[32] In a letter of late summer 917 Nikolaos is unable to cite a single aggressive action of Symeon to justify the Byzantine invasion; he merely repeats others' allegations about Symeon's war plans and Bulgarian encroachments on Byzantine possessions near Dyrrachium and Thessalonika. Nikolaos leaves Symeon to judge the force of these, and urges Symeon not 'to renew the war against the people of your spiritual father', Constantine.[33] The chronicles' allegations of Bulgarian depredations in Thrace may have been equally government-inspired.[34] Nikolaos' complaint about a *timē* ('honour, title') may also represent a Byzantine initiative: Nikolaos may in 914 have been implicitly retracting such recognition as he had accorded to Symeon's imperial title in the Hebdomon; the title implied in Nikolaos' letter, *archōn ek theou* ('prince from God'), had been borne by khans since the early ninth century, and was perhaps an oblique affirmation that this was Symeon's rightful title, not *basileus*.[35]

There were undeniably strains in Byzantino-Bulgarian relations after Symeon's massive show of force in 913. But the title of *basileus* (Slavonic *tsar*) probably carried for Symeon connotations of legitimacy and Christian 'sovereignty', while a marriage-tie held out the hope of equilibrium in Byzantino-Bulgarian relations for at least a generation. It did not necessarily guarantee Symeon access to his daughter; her role would be almost that of a hostage guaranteeing his own behaviour towards the empire. Symeon may indeed have reckoned himself worthy of an imperial title, after twenty years of nation-building in strict accordance with Orthodox precepts. But those same precepts bore on his foreign policy. His scruples were such that, according to Nikolaos Mystikos, he was still, in 913, doing penance for his warfare against fellow-Christians in the 890s.[36] His zeal for evangelisation and learning remained strong. He was still urging the aged Clement to continue his diocesan pastoral

---

[31] 'pros to katapolemēsai kai aphanisai ton Symeōn', Theophanes Continuatus, *Chronographia*, p. 388.

[32] Cf. Fine (1983), p. 148.

[33] 'polemon analabesthai kata tou laou tou sou pneumatikou patros', Nikolaos I, Patriarch of Constantinople, *Letters*, p. 64; cf. p. 62, and chapter 22, p. 561.

[34] Theophanes Continuatus, *Chronographia*, pp. 386, 388; George Monachus Continuatus, pp. 879–80; Leo Grammaticus, *Chronographia*, pp. 293, 294; Shepard (1989 [1991]), pp. 24–5.

[35] Beševliev (1979), pp. 71–2.   [36] Nikolaos I, Patriarch of Constantinople, *Letters*, pp. 34–6.

work on the eve of Clement's death in 916.[37] This in itself suggests that Symeon was not then envisaging aggressive warfare even on a limited scale near the borders: Clement's diocese most probably stretched to the north of Thessalonika, one of the trouble spots cited by the Regency Council to Nikolaos. At about the same time Symeon commissioned the translation of a Greek collection of extracts from church fathers and snippets of religious and literary knowledge, including a brief chronicle listing emperors from Augustus 'even up to Constantine and Zoe, the Greek imperials';[38] the translation was probably made between 6 June 913 and August 920. The legitimacy of 'the Greek imperials' is not impugned, although Symeon himself is 'great among emperors', according to the encomium added to the translated materials;[39] this emphasises Symeon's love of books, and makes no mention of war.

The Byzantine attack of 917 may thus have been intended to take Symeon by surprise, after a period of formal peace. Nikolaos Mystikos repeatedly acknowledged that the attack had been unjustified, and besought Symeon not to be embittered by it. That Symeon neither forgave nor forgot is suggested by the fact that seven years later he rode his old war-horse to his second encounter with Nikolaos and pointed out the scar from the sword-thrust it had suffered on the Acheloos; this, he said, had been the result of Nikolaos' prayer![40] Symeon was probably not just scoring a debating point but highlighting what seemed to him the hypocrisy of his 'spiritual father' Nikolaos, and the entire Byzantine 'establishment'.

Symeon's meeting with the aged and failing patriarch took place at Constantinople in September 924. If his conduct over the previous seven years sometimes appears erratic, this reflects the impasse in which the Byzantines' perfidy had placed him. He could hardly trust any future agreement, yet presumably he still abhorred shedding Christian blood. He sent troops to ravage Constantinople's suburbs soon after Acheloos, but seemingly did not possess the siege engines needed for an assault on the City. In any case, his chief concern after the battle was with Prince Peter of Serbia, who had allegedly received a Byzantine proposal to join the Hungarians in attacking Bulgaria. Symeon is said to have 'raved' at this news,[41] and sent an army which managed, by deception, to abduct Peter and install as prince another member of the Serbian ruling clan, Paul. He sent armies into Byzantine territory in 918 and 919 and units ranged as far south as the Gulf of Corinth, but no assault was mounted on Constantinople.

Symeon may still have nursed hopes of a marriage-tie; the raiding could have

[37] Gr'tskite zhitiia na Kliment Okhridski, pp. 138–40; Obolensky (1988), p. 33.
[38] 'dazhe i do Konstantina i Zoia, ts'r' gr'ch'skykh', Ianeva (1987), pp. 100–1, 104; Bibikov (1991), pp. 98–9, 101–2.   [39] 'velikyi v tsarikh', Kuev (1986), p. 11; Thomson (1993), p. 51.
[40] Nikolaos I, Patriarch of Constantinople, Letters, p. 208.   [41] emmanēs, DAI, c. 32/91–101.

been a means towards attaining it. But his apparent indecisiveness after Acheloos was perhaps governed by simpler considerations: internal political discord left Byzantium in no position to launch an offensive against him. It was the emergence of Romanos Lekapenos as the new strong man at Byzantium that precipitated demands from Symeon for Romanos' abdication and a move towards full-scale war. Symeon sent or led armies to the walls of Constantinople nearly every year from 920 to 924; they pillaged the suburbs but made no major assault. At the same time, Bulgarian forces occupied much of Byzantine Thrace. The *vita* of St Mary the Younger indicates that they garrisoned Vize and other towns there for some years.[42] They also infested parts of northern Greece for several years and were most probably responsible for prolonged rampages of bands of that region's Slavs into the Peloponnese. Symeon also tried at least twice to acquire a fleet, making approaches *c.* 922 to the Fatimid caliph in north Africa and to the amir of Tarsus. Their fleets would have allowed him to blockade Constantinople from a vantage-point such as the Dardanelles or make an outright assault, if Romanos' usurpation could be supposed to have forfeited divine protection for the City.

Symeon's escalation of hostilities might seem to confirm that he had long been stalking the Byzantine throne and was now acting from pique at having been pre-empted by another non-Greek aspirant, Lekapenos. But as we have seen, it is not certain that Symeon wanted the throne in 913, and the Byzantines' reading of his subsequent actions may have been no better inspired. Fear of a further attempt to annihilate him can only have sharpened his interest in affairs at court; government in the hands of the inexperienced Constantine would have held few threats. But this is not the same as bidding for the throne itself, and his propaganda in the early 920s contrasted Constantine's legitimacy with Lekapenos' usurpation. Symeon for a while even declined to address correspondence to Romanos, writing to the senate instead.[43] This might be the petulance of a loser, but could also be an attempt to fan intrigue inside the City and to foster Romanos' suspicion of senior palace officials.

Whatever Symeon's aims, his attacks failed to bring down Romanos. The vainglorious facets of his conduct in the mid-920s may well register his frustration that war had proved no more effective than diplomacy or Christian forbearance in resolving his problems with Byzantium. He cannot, given his evident distrust of the government, vilification of Romanos and long-standing ridicule of 'the old fool' Nikolaos, have set much store by his meetings with them in September 924.[44] Indeed, it is perhaps more remarkable that they

---

[42] *Vita S. Mariae iunioris, AASS Novembris* IV, p. 701.
[43] Nikolaos I, Patriarch of Constantinople, *Letters*, pp. 194–6.
[44] 'mōrantheis'; 'mōros', Nikolaos I, Patriarch of Constantinople, *Letters*, pp. 68–72.

occurred at all and that an accord of some kind was negotiated than that it proved more or less fruitless. Bulgarian forces may have withdrawn from some portions of Byzantine territory, but they remained in control of former naval bases such as Mesembria, towns such as Vize and parts of northern Greece.

Not long after his meeting with Romanos, Symeon proclaimed himself 'emperor of the Bulgarians and Romans'.[45] His seals now termed him 'emperor in Christ of the Romans' and depicted him for the first time in full imperial vestments.[46] He may well also have sought to raise the status of his senior churchman to that of patriarch; for if the senior churchman was accorded titular patriarchal status by Romanos in 927, as is most likely, this probably represented a compromise based on the *status quo* rather than a sweeping concession *de novo*. Symeon's new title would have looked all the more empty without the company of a patriarch.

Symeon's 'Roman' title may represent a quest for legitimacy as well as compensation for his failure to impose a settlement by force of arms. Through the earlier 920s he suffered from the quicksilver loyalties of the princes of Serbia, as one protégé after another turned from him to the Byzantine *basileus*. After a number of setbacks, Symeon sent a second invasion force together with yet another princely pretender, Časlav, who was used as a decoy to assemble the Serb chieftains and then deport them to Bulgaria. A substantial part of the population was likewise deported: Serbia was to be erased as a political entity. In 926 Symeon tried to extend his Balkan hegemony with an attack on Tomislav of Croatia. Tomislav, however, inflicted a heavy defeat on the Bulgarians and, in a sense, vindicated Symeon's decision to attend to his western flanks. Shortly beforehand, Tomislav had invited the papacy to involve itself in Dalmatian and Croatian affairs. A synod had convened in Split in 925 to determine the status and jurisdiction of its archbishop. John X, who addressed Tomislav as *rex Crovatorum*, became keenly interested in restoring papal supervision of the Dalmatian clergy.[47] He also tried to end hostilities between Tomislav and Symeon, and papal legates destined for a second synod of Split paid a visit to Bulgaria in late 926 or early 927. They are credited in the acts of the second synod with having made peace between the Bulgarians and the Croats.[48] If this really was the case, Symeon's hands were, by the spring of 927, rather freer for other ventures than is commonly supposed. All earthly ambitions were, however, terminated with his demise on 27 May 927, aged about sixty-three.

---

[45] 'basileus Boulgarōn kai Rōmaiōn', Theodore Daphnopates, *Correspondance*, p. 59.

[46] 'en Christō basileus Rōmaiōn', Gerasimov (1934), pp. 350–6; Beševliev (1963), pp. 330–1; Jurukova and Penchev (1990), p. 30.　　[47] *Historia Salonitana Maior*, p. 96; Klaić (1971), pp. 290–1.

[48] 'peracto negotio pacis', *Historia Salonitana Maior*, p. 103; Klaić (1971), p. 283; Fine (1983), pp. 267–8, 271–2.

Bulgaria still had a substantial military capability: a major incursion was launched into the theme of Macedonia; then the Thracian towns under Bulgarian occupation were evacuated and razed to the ground. But there were in Bulgarian ruling circles persons who hoped for a *modus vivendi* with Byzantium. Their first overtures were made 'secretly' (*kryphiōs*), probably to evade detection by 'Symeon's magnates',[49] who tried to supplant the new Tsar Peter with his brother John not long afterwards. The Byzantines themselves had supposed that hostilities would drag on and the peace was hailed as 'the unhoped-for transformation' by a court orator in the autumn of 927.[50] No source records the terms of the treaty, but Byzantine recognition of a Bulgarian titular patriarchate is very probable and it is equally likely that Peter was recognised as '*basileus* of Bulgaria'; mid-tenth century protocols for addressing letters to him indicate that this title was formally in use then.[51] The Byzantines also probably agreed to pay tribute, presumably annually. This supplemented a more solemn bond, the marriage of Maria, a grand-daughter of Romanos, to Peter. The elaborate wedding at Constantinople had a clear message: the union of Maria to 'an emperor . . . husband' constituted standing recognition of the legitimacy of his realm and Maria's name was changed to Eirene ('peace') as a symbol of the hopes vested in the marriage.[52]

These expectations were not empty, and peace lasted for approximately forty years. The *modus vivendi* owed something to the recognition that military stalemate had been reached and something to the character of the new tsar. Byzantine sources depicted Peter as peace-loving and averse to bloodshed. His piety is suggested by his frequent letters to the Byzantine monk Paul of Latros,[53] and also by his unflagging veneration of John, a hermit lodged on a remote crag south of Sofia. Peter tried to visit John and after John's death in 946 he had his body translated to a church which he built to accommodate it in Sofia. Peter's lead seals affirmed his piety. The most commonly found type bears the legend 'Peter the pious emperor'.[54] Peter faces the beholder, grasping with one hand a patriarchal cross, while Maria, wearing an empress' crown, clasps the cross from the other side. Maria is not known to have played any active role in Bulgarian political life, but the seal design gave a general intimation of her parity of status with Peter and of Bulgaro-Byzantine rapport.

Yet *détente* was not unqualified. It is clear from the *De administrando imperio* that even during Maria's lifetime amicable relations could not be taken for

---

[49] 'megistanōn tou Symeōn', Theophanes Continuatus, *Chronographia*, pp. 412, 419.

[50] 'tēn par' elpida metabolēn', Dujčev (1978), p. 266.   [51] *DC*, p. 690.

[52] 'basilei . . . andri', Theophanes Continuatus, *Chronographia*, p. 415; Liudprand, *Antapodosis* III, 38. See previous chapter, p. 564.   [53] *Laudatio S. Pauli iunioris*, ed. Delehaye, pp. 122, 143.

[54] 'Petros basileus eusebēs', Jurukova (1980), pp. 4–6; Gerasimov (1938), pp. 360–3; Jurukova and Penchev (1990), p. 34; Shepard (1995), p. 143.

granted. Constantine advises that the Pechenegs can be incited to attack the Bulgarians, who are bracketed with the Hungarians and the Rus', actual adversaries of the empire in the 940s, as being highly vulnerable to the nomads.[55] Constantine does not devote a complete chapter to the Bulgarians, but at several points he notes details of Bulgaria's relations with its neighbours, and he is particularly concerned to establish that the princes of the Serbs and the Croats had been subjects of the 'Roman' emperor since Heraclius' reign. It is stated in identical terms in the two chapters on the Croats and the Serbs that their princes were 'never made subject to the prince of Bulgaria'.[56] There is no evidence that Peter was actively asserting hegemony over them, but his very piety and Bulgaria's rich and still expanding repertory of Slavonic religious writings are likely to have had some impact on neighbouring Slavs of the Orthodox rite. Manuscripts of the Slavic translations carried out in Ochrid and elsewhere in Bulgaria may have appealed to all the Slav-speakers in the western borderlands where Clement and Naum had toiled, and been in demand among the Serbs. Constantine thus faced a potential rival Orthodox commonwealth. Moreover, Peter's piety rested on a political structure not bereft of material resources.

The evidence for the structure is mostly indirect, but not undetectable. A quest for political leverage against a basically stable power is suggested by Lekapenos' support for Prince Časlav of Serbia after his flight from Peter's court back to Serbia, probably in the early 930s. There was an active administration of some complexity functioning throughout Peter's reign. Some twenty-one seals of Peter are known, considerably more than the combined totals for his father and grandfather.[57] The fact that more than half of them were found in the citadel and the outer town of Preslav suggests their use for internal administration, not merely for correspondence with foreign rulers. A silver seal of Peter has been excavated at the site of the key fortress of Pernik. No earlier Bulgarian ruler can be unimpeachably credited with a silver seal, and the intricate construction of Peter's seal is not characteristic of tenth-century Byzantine seals, which are of gold or lead. Peter lacked the resources to strike coins, but his seals imply a writing office at Preslav. The regularity and scale of Peter's central administration evoked comment from a well-informed Jewish traveller, Ibrāhīm ibn Yaʿqūb, who mentions the secretaries and heads of other departments.[58]

In so far as material remains can be an index of political health, those at Preslav suggest not merely continuity from Symeon's reign but expansion. There was extension work inside the palace complex; the original north wall of

---

[55] *DAI*, c. 5/3–9; c. 8/20–1.

[56] 'oudepote tō archonti Boulgarias kathypetagē', *DAI*, c. 31/59–60; c. 32/147–8.

[57] Jurukova (1984), p. 230; Totev (1989), p. 40.   [58] Ibrāhīm ibn Yaʿqūb, *Relatio*, p. 148.

the citadel was demolished late in Peter's reign, presumably to create more space; new churches were built. Each of the quarters of the outer town expanded. There was also development beyond its walls in the new conditions of relative security: not only rebuilding in unfortified monasteries such as those at Tuzlal'ka and Patleina but also massive new structures which seem to have belonged to wealthy notables. Highly refined and sumptuous artefacts were manufactured, mostly in complexes belonging to the tsar or his senior officials, and in the great monasteries. Glazed wall- and floor-tiles were produced in the Tuzlal'ka and Patleina monasteries; some of their ceramic icons are of exquisite quality. Another hint of the capital's wealth is a hoard of jewelry, probably deposited during the Rus' occupation *c.* 970.

Government exactions were the mainspring of economic activity, but the shops and stores adjoining the citadel's outer wall illustrate how the ruler's resources could generate further economic transactions: glass vessels and amphorae, probably of Byzantine manufacture, were excavated in them, while Byzantine white-clay ceramic vessels have been found in Preslav's more substantial secular and monastic properties. The export of Bulgarian linen and honey to Constantinople mentioned in the *Book of the Eparch* probably continued up to about 970.[59] It is difficult to gauge the situation in the countryside, upon whose produce the pomp of Preslav depended. The numerous stone fortifications and strongpoints which made up a series of 'defence systems' in northern and southern Bulgaria probably date largely from Symeon's reign or earlier, but there is no indication that they were abandoned wholesale during Peter's. In fact it has been suggested that Peter's interest in John of Rila was not exclusively religious; his attention to the districts of Rila and Sofia may have been keened by their strategic significance.[60] There is archaeological evidence for rebuilding during the tenth century at forts between the River Maritsa and the Rhodope range. Their garrisons probably relied, like Preslav's denizens, on mandatory exactions from the surrounding population, but a mid-tenth-century critic of society, Cosmas the Priest, associated 'towns' with markets, and denounced monks who frequented 'towns'.[61]

Cosmas' *Treatise against the Bogomils*, composed most probably during the 960s, is often taken to depict a society bereft of true religion: rich persons neglect the poor, and the less well-off frequent the houses of the rich, feeding there 'like crows on carrion'.[62] Monks and clergy are devoted to worldly pleasures and neglect the laity, in stark contrast with the proselytising zeal of the

---

[59] *Eparch* IX, 6, p. 108.   [60] Jurukova (1980), pp. 8–9.

[61] Cosmas the Priest, *Treatise against the Bogomils*, ed. Popruzhenko, pp. 56–7; ed. Puech and Vaillant, pp. 104–5.

[62] 'aky vranove na mertvechine', Cosmas the Priest, *Treatise against the Bogomils*, ed. Popruzhenko, p. 68; ed. Puech and Vaillant, p. 116.

Dualist heretics. These 'Bogomils' were named after one Bogomil the Priest, who preached total renunciation of material things, which were the creation of the devil; he adduced passages from the New Testament to show that the good God was pure spirit. Cosmas likens their show of asceticism and interpretation of the Gospels to a fish-hook's bait, drawing people to perdition.[63] Cosmas' explanation for the Bogomils' success is consistent, but there was no necessary contradiction between ecclesiastical discipline and material splendour during the reign of Peter any more than in his 'monk-like' father's reign. In fact the *Treatise* suggests that the church's problems sprang as much from obsession with personal salvation as from moral laxity. Cosmas upbraids those who, from fear of pollution by the world, abandon everything to become monks: many are ill suited to monastic discipline and 'if you condemn married life on the grounds that one cannot be saved with such a way of life, you are no different in thought from the heretics'.[64] Priests and bishops should attend more to instructing their charges than to fasting: cows and horses, too, abstain from meat and wine! Independent evidence exists for numerous new monastic foundations in southern Bulgaria during Peter's reign: John of Rila was only the most prominently patronised holy man. The land apparently teemed with individuals setting lofty spiritual goals, emulating the desert fathers rather than sinking into torpor and vice. Cosmas' *Treatise* is itself an example of concern for high standards. He is exercised by the inadequacies of episcopal supervision of local clergy and implicitly endorses the heretics' condemnation of clerical drunkenness and lechery. But he also assumes that copies of the Bible are available to all wealthy persons, lay and clerical, and urges them not only to read the Scriptures but also to make their books available to those 'desiring to read and to copy [them]'.[65] This, too, breathes an atmosphere of spiritual endeavour.

Cosmas was not alone in his stand. John of Rila in his testament enjoined his acolytes to shun heresy, greed and vainglory, and a certain Peter the Monk wrote several tracts and sermons on such subjects as *Fasting and Prayer* and *Salvation of the Soul*. Addressing laymen, he urges penitence and church-attendance and he raises most of the points upon which the Bogomils diverged from the Orthodox church.[66] Such works may lack the polish or intellectual depth of Symeon's era; but the very fact that they are written simply, apparently by rank-and-file clergy and monks, suggests that Christian values and monastic

[63] Cosmas the Priest, *Treatise against the Bogomils*, ed. Popruzhenko, pp. 24–5; ed. Puech and Vaillant, p. 76.

[64] 'ashche li . . . zhitie s zhenoiu otkhouliaeshi nemoshchno tvoria spasti sia sitse zhivoushchemou, to nichim krome esi mysli eretichesky', Cosmas the Priest, *Treatise against the Bogomils*, ed. Popruzhenko, p. 58; ed. Puech and Vaillant, p. 106.

[65] 'khotiashchikh pochitati i pisati', Cosmas the Priest, *Treatise against the Bogomils*, ed. Popruzhenko, p. 72; ed. Puech and Vaillant, p. 121.   [66] Dimitrov (1987), p. 34; Pavlova (1991), pp. 81–4.

ideals were sought after outside the gilded political culture of Preslav. Moreover, the established church was not totally inert. Cosmas indicates that Bogomils were being imprisoned and persecuted, and already in the 940s or early 950s Tsar Peter wrote to Patriarch Theophylact describing the doctrines of certain heretics active in his land and requesting background information and advice about punishment.[67] Peter's request probably came less than twenty years after Bogomil began spreading his message. And if, as is quite possible, the Bogomils' preachers and their followers constituted only a small minority of the population, Tsar Peter's letter, Cosmas' tract and the works of Peter the Monk suggest vigilance on the part of at least some of the Orthodox.

Cosmas' *Treatise* is thus not unequivocal testimony to the enfeeblement of church and state. Ibrāhīm ibn Yaʿqūb was aware of translation work done in Bulgaria and regarded its administrative apparatus as befitting a great ruler.[68] That the Bulgarian realm was taken seriously by Byzantium is suggested by the care which was taken to divest Boris II of his regalia ceremonially in 971; the detailed, if somewhat divergent, accounts suggest that these symbols were treated as inherently valid. A different testimony to Bulgaria's properties comes from the *Russian Primary Chronicle*. Prince Sviatoslav is represented as deciding to take up residence at Pereiaslavets ('Little Preslav') in the Danube delta, since 'all good things converge there'.[69]

The sequence of events which brought Sviatoslav to the Balkans is controversial, because our main sources show discrepancies. But that tensions between the two empires should have unleashed conflict is not so extraordinary, given the clear evidence for continuing Byzantine apprehensions about Bulgaria. After Maria's death, Peter sent his two sons as hostages to Constantinople, presumably to allay Byzantine unease. Relations were put under further strain by intensifying Hungarian raids from the late 950s, probably the consequence of their defeat at the Lechfeld. Two small bands ravaged Macedonia and the environs of Thessalonika in early spring 968; similar incursions probably precipitated Nikephoros' armed excursion into Thrace in June 967 and also the repairs to fortifications attested in inscriptions. But these may well also have been designed to counter the Bulgarians' southern fortification system, and Nikephoros, while putting on his show of force in Thrace, complained to Peter that he was letting the Hungarians cross his lands and ravage Byzantium. Peter apparently replied that his earlier requests to Byzantium for aid had been disregarded and that he was not prepared to set aside the 'treaty' he had had to make with the Hungarians.[70] Peter's diplomacy had, in fact,

---

[67] Theophylact's reply is extant: Petrovskii (1913), pp. 361–8; Grumel (1936), no. 789, pp. 223–4.

[68] Ibrāhīm ibn Yaʿqūb, *Relatio*, p. 148.

[69] 'tu vsia blagaia skhodiatsia', *Povest' Vremennykh Let*, p. 48; trans. Cross, p. 86.

[70] 'spondas', John Zonaras, *Epitome Historiarum* III, p. 513.

reached beyond the Hungarians: in 961 or 965/6 Ibrāhīm ibn Ya'qūb observed Bulgarian envoys bound for Otto I's court, possibly looking for aid against the Hungarians' latest round of depredations.[71]

Nikephoros' response to Peter's defiance was to try and deal an indirect but devastating blow to his power-base. His choice of the Rus' as agents is suggestive. He may have hoped to embroil them in Balkan warfare, distracting them from attacking Byzantine lands during his own campaigns in Syria and Mesopotamia. But he probably also reckoned that only a militarily formidable power such as the Rus' could overwhelm Bulgarian defences. Sviatoslav led an attack on Bulgaria in, probably, the late summer of 968. The Rus' sacked 'many towns' and took much plunder,[72] but they did not reduce Preslav, where Peter remained as tsar until his death some months later. Meanwhile the Pechenegs raided as far north as Kiev itself, a move which Byzantine statesmen had probably envisaged. What Nikephoros did not foresee was that Sviatoslav would return northwards, make a pact with the nomadic raiders and then journey back to the Danube; he enlisted not only the Pechenegs but also a Hungarian host as his allies there. Sviatoslav did not depose Peter's son and heir, Boris, who stayed on in Preslav. He assigned garrisons to the forts and settlements along the river-way, and Pereiaslavets was to be 'the centre of my land'.[73]

Sviatoslav's venture was destroyed by John Tzimiskes in a brief but hardfought campaign in 971. Boris and his family were taken prisoner in their capital. Although Tzimiskes announced that he had come to avenge the Bulgarians, many Bulgarians fought on out of antipathy towards the Byzantines. Tzimiskes' overriding concern, however, was that the Rus' might return: forts were refurbished and naval installations built along the Danube's south bank. Preslav became the Byzantine centre of government, and was renamed Ioannoupolis after its new ruler. The various permutations of the names of command-units on seals of the 970s and earlier 980s attest the intensity of Byzantine administration in north-east Bulgaria and the Danubian basin. The rival empire had in effect been decapitated. Significantly, the insurrection which flared up in Bulgaria after Tzimiskes' sudden death in 976 was not fanned into full blaze by former officials of the Bulgarian state: the leaders were the four sons of an Armenian officer in the Byzantine army. Their lengthy wars with Basil II are recounted below.[74] Samuel, the ablest of the four Kometopouloi, had to construct a new, impregnable, culturo-administrative centre in a formerly outlying area. But he showed political acumen in his respect for the beliefs and totems of its heterogeneous inhabitants. Among

---

[71] Ibrāhīm ibn Ya'qūb, *Relatio*, p. 148.   [72] 'pollas poleis' Skylitzes, *Synopsis* p. 277.
[73] 'sereda zemli moei', *Povest' Vremennykh Let*, p. 48; trans. Cross, p. 86.
[74] See below, ch 24, pp. 596–600.

these was Romanos, the eunuch brother of Boris, who had managed to flee back from Constantinople. Like Sviatoslav, Samuel appreciated the Bulgarians' sentiment for their old royal house and, conveniently for Samuel, Romanos lacked the means of begetting a rival dynasty. Samuel emphasised his Orthodox piety through church-building and patronage of the patriarch. Basil II himself recognised, in the church's organisation, a means of gaining acceptance from his new subjects after 1018. The political culture of Boris and Symeon had been laid on very firm foundations, which circumstances tempted Rus', Armenian and Byzantine adventurers to exploit.

CHAPTER 24

BYZANTIUM EXPANDING, 944–1025

Jonathan Shepard

THE REIGN of Constantine VII Porphyrogenitus as senior and dominant emperor (945–59) has long been viewed as the apogee of Byzantium as a great power resplendent in culture and learning. Constantine, like his father Leo, saw himself as a writer and instructor, and he was interested in many branches of written knowledge. This was partly a matter of theoretical knowledge or erudition about the past, but Constantine regarded the practical experience relayed by writings as indispensable to an emperor, as he stated in his preface to the *De administrando imperio*, a secret handbook devoted principally to foreign peoples and compiled for the instruction of his young son so that foreign nations 'shall quake before thee as one mighty in wisdom'.[1]

Constantine's public stress on learning reflected his own views and there is no reason to doubt the characterisation by the author of a *Synaxarium*, a history of the saints celebrated through the church year, commissioned by the emperor. Constantine, rising before the birds, was zealous to study 'every book' and read through 'the ancient . . . histories' from which one could become 'experienced . . . in all kinds of matters'.[2] This, like the standard preface to the fifty-three instalments of extracts from classical and early Byzantine historical works commissioned by Constantine, asserts the special access of the emperor to wisdom through the books amassed in his palace. An emperor who exploited these reserves of past experience and piety was uniquely wise and reverend. But Constantine was simultaneously offering the 'benefit' of his digests 'to the public', in the words of the preface.[3] This exaltation of book-learning was in the tradition of Constantine's father, Leo 'the Wise'; both were palace-dwellers, and both asserted that the books and learning accumulated behind its closed doors were, through their mediation, relevant and advantageous to their subjects.

---

[1] 'ptoēthēsontai gar se hōs megalophyē', *DAI*, *prooimion*/28.

[2] 'pasan biblon'; 'tas palaias . . . historias'; 'empeiron . . . pantoiōn . . . pragmatōn', *AASS Novembris, Propylaeum*, col. xiv; Ševčenko (1992), p. 188, n. 52.

[3] 'ōpheleian'; 'koinē': e.g. *Excerpta de legationibus*, p. 2.

Constantine may have known of the example of another early tenth-century emperor, who had also filled his palace with books and whose reputation for learning was known to the Byzantines: Symeon of Bulgaria. Constantine and Symeon both accepted the ruler's duty to educate his people. This notion had been propounded by ninth-century scholar-ecclesiastics like Photius, and became engrained in the propaganda and self-image of the Macedonian dynasty, although Constantine's education had in fact been very limited. His piety was sometimes patently dynastic. Thus he appropriated the acquisition of the *mandylion* from Edessa; the sermon composed in the opening years of his reign represents the arrival of Christ's image as prefiguring and even precipitating Constantine's advance to sole rule.[4] By January 947 Constantine had brought 'home' to the capital the relics of St Gregory Nazianzen; the casket was borne to the palace on purple cloth, restoring the 'sanctity and reverence' of which it 'had previously been deprived'.[5]

Constantine emphasised most prominently his least controvertible qualities, invaluable assets even in his infancy: birth in the Purple (declared on his silver coins from 945 onwards); and the supposed link between his well-being and that of the citizens of Constantinople, asserted in the acclamations chanted before large crowds in the Hippodrome. Constantine, by commissioning the *Book of Ceremonies*, in large part an almanac of the emperor's participation in church festivals and celebration of imperial power, showed his regard for both book-learning and the rhythm of the ritual; he claimed to be both restoring old practices and introducing new ones.[6] The rites he described and prescribed amounted to one long round of intercession, and the relics which Constantine amassed underlined the traditional designation of the palace as 'sacred'. They also enhanced his ability to gain supernatural protection for favoured subjects, such as soldiers out on campaign; the saints seconded, as it were, the prayers of the emperor. The power of imperial prayer is stressed in the *Vita* of Basil I, yet another of the works issued under Constantine's auspices, and it is a theme also implicit in three works of art probably emanating from court circles which show Constantine venerating a relic or in prayer.[7]

Yet prayer and book-learning were not enough. The balance between piety and practicality ascribed to Basil I in the *Vita* probably represents Constantine's own aspirations. One symbol of his concern for those beyond the City walls was the promulgation of laws valid throughout the empire. Eight are extant, at least one more known. One strengthens the sanctions and impediments on the

---

[4] Dobschütz (1899), pp. 79**, 85**.
[5] 'sanctitatem reverentiamque'; 'qua pridem privatae fuerant', *AASS Maii*, II, p. 452.
[6] See his preface: *DC*, ed. Vogt, I.1, pp. 1–2; Jolivet-Levy (1987), pp. 452–4; Moffatt (1995), pp. 379–84.
[7] Theophanes Continuatus, *Chronographia*, pp. 299, 315–16; Weitzmann (1971), pp. 242–6; (1972), pp. 59–60; Jolivet-Levy (1987), pp. 452–4, 458 n. 68.

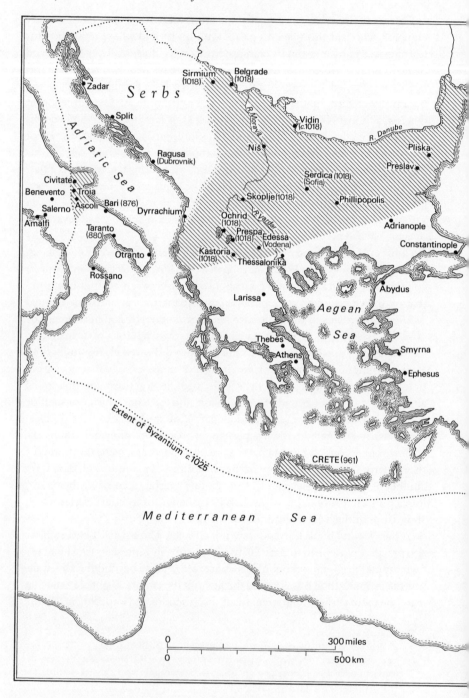

13 Byzantium in 1025

N

Cherson

Black   Sea

Extent of Byzantium, c.1025

Sinope

Trebizond

TAO(TAYK)
(1000–22)   Ani

Ancyra

Theodosiopolis (949)
(Erzerum)   Manzikert

Tephrike   TARON
(967)

Amorium

Kizil Irmak

Caesarea   Melitene   Bitlis
(934)   VASPURAKAN

Hadath

Germaniceia   Samosata (958)
(Ma'rash)   Edessa

Mosul

Adana (964) Mopsuestia
Tarsus   (965)
(965)

Antioch   Aleppo
(969)

R. Tigris

CYPRUS (965)

R. Euphrates

Beirut

Damascus

Jerusalem

	Territorial gains, 900–1025
Kastoria (1018)	Dates in brackets are those of acquisition by the empire

purchase of land from 'the poor' by 'the powerful' laid down by Romanos in a novel of 934. Another attempts to protect the land-holdings of those enrolled to supply military service in the themes.[8]

There seems little doubt that small peasant proprietors were increasingly alienating their lands to 'the powerful'. But it is unclear how far they were acting involuntarily and how far they were trying to profit from a more active property market. The two explanations are not mutually incompatible and, taken together, they could imply a gradual increase of population and quickening of commercial transactions (albeit mostly in agricultural produce). It appears that 'the powerful' causing keenest concern to the emperors were those trying to take over lands in the fertile coastal region of western Asia Minor; in some of its towns there is evidence of construction work and economic revival during the tenth century.

The legislation of Constantine implies governmental concern about the material underpinning of the theme army at a time when Kourkouas was engaged in operations in the east. Constantine's novel on 'military lands' was issued about the time of the expedition of 949 to reconquer Crete, a cherished project. Extravagant rhetoric celebrated the emperor's supposed victories and his extension of the frontiers. In a poem in honour of Romanos II, Constantine is described as growing weary from writing down the roll of subjugated cities.[9] Tarsus and Crete tremble, every people and city races to submit to the emperor, though most of these towns were sacked rather than occupied, and the Cretan expedition ended ignominiously. It was part of the continuity Constantine sought to maintain, especially with his father's reign; then, too, a Cretan expedition had been launched and land-campaigning concentrated on the south-eastern borderlands. Equally, Constantine looked to the Phokas family to provide military leaders, and the poem likens Bardas Phokas, Domestic of the Schools since 945, to 'a glittering broadsword or a flame of fire, kindled by thy father's [Constantine's] prayers'.[10] These lines evoke the 'special relationship' between the Phokases and the Macedonian house which Romanos Lekapenos had so dexterously disconnected in 919. Constantine seems nevertheless to have balked at entrusting major command to any military man of repute. The commander of the Cretan expedition, Constantine Gongylios, had been in charge of the imperial fleet since 945, but was

---

[8] *Ius graecoromanum* i, pp. 214–17, 222–6; Lemerle (1979), pp. 87, 94–8, 117–25.

[9] Odorico (1987), p. 91.

[10]   'romphaian hōs stilbousan ē pyros phloga
                 tou sou proseuchais patros ekpyroumenēn'
                                  Odorico (1987), p. 91

The 'Phokas' of the poem seems more likely to be the head of the family, Bardas, than one of his sons.

described as 'without experience of war'.[11] Our sole detailed account of the expedition blames him for its failure and alleges that he failed to take the elementary precaution of establishing a secure camp on the island.[12]

Constantine's early years as senior emperor remained within the framework of essentially static, palace-based rule implied by the preface to the *De administrando imperio*. This work, compiled at his command between *c.* 948 and *c.* 952, bears his fingerprints more markedly than any of the other works associated with him. Diplomacy was an activity which a sedentary emperor could conduct highly effectively on his own account, and its ceremonial workings were focused on his mystique alone. But even as the compilation got under way, a military crisis developed in the east which was eventually to force Constantine to depart from the strategy of previous generations. The catalyst was Sayf al-Dawlah, a scion of the Hamdanid dynasty of Mosul. By the end of 947 he was in firm control of Aleppo and its commercial wealth. He embarked on a series of devastating, if strategically insignificant, raids into Asia Minor. The Byzantines responded to this energetic war-lord on their borders with major reprisals, taking captives and razing the walls of foreposts such as Hadath and Maʿrash. Hadath, a fortress on a key pass leading towards Byzantine-occupied Melitene, was the scene of several battles involving sizable Byzantine armies intent on demolishing the walls and Muslim units no less determined to defend or rebuild them. Bitter as the fighting was, it formed part of a broader strategy. At the same time as attempting to deny Sayf secure bases, Byzantium sent embassies proposing truces and prisoner-exchanges. However, Sayf took these as signs of imminent Byzantine collapse. He rejected an exchange of prisoners, and the poets in his entourage proclaimed his courage and the prospect of victory.

His militancy and obduracy seem to have persuaded the reluctant Constantine that he would have to be worsted or removed, if his own authority was not to be diminished. In, probably, 955 Nikephoros Phokas was appointed Domestic of the Schools. He is said to have raised his soldiers' morale and trained them to attack in good order and to occupy enemy territory confidently 'as if in their own land'.[13] The reason for the more aggressive strategy is given by Abū Firās, a member of Sayf's entourage: after incessant incursions and after Sayf had refused a truce except on extraordinary terms, Constantine made treaties with neighbouring rulers, sought military aid from them and sent out a large and expensive expedition to break Sayf's power.[14] In the summer of 958 Samosata, on the Euphrates, was captured and demolished and Sayf was heavily defeated trying to relieve Raʿban, in October or November. Next

---

[11] *apeiropolemon*, Skylitzes, *Synopsis*, p. 245; cf. Theophanes Continuatus, *Chronographia*, p. 436.

[12] John Skylitzes, *Synopsis historiarum*, pp. 245–6.

[13] 'hōs en idiō chōrō', Theophanes Continuatus, *Chronographia*, p. 459.　　[14] Vasiliev (1950), p. 368.

spring the Byzantine force reached Qurus, only about 40 kilometres from Aleppo, and took many prisoners. Muslim sources suggest that Byzantium was fielding much larger forces than before.

Whether Constantine would have refrained from launching a large-scale *reconquista* must remain uncertain: death, on 9 November 959, relieved him of the problems posed by departure from his own model of static, 'Solomonic' kingship. Constantine's right-hand man, Basil Lekapenos the *parakoimōmenos*, was arguing for another assault on Crete during Constantine's last months. Even in court circles, the temptation to put to new uses the military machine assembled to break Sayf al-Dawla was growing all but irresistible.

Basil Lekapenos was dismissed by Constantine's heir, Romanos II, but the new *parakoimōmenos*, Joseph Bringas, also urged an attack on Crete, and Romanos himself seems to have been enthusiastic for a success at the outset of his reign. The greater part of the empire's armed forces embarked for the island in a huge flotilla, in June 960. The ensuing hard-fought campaign lasted until March 961. Contemporaries were well aware of the significance of this feat. The author of a poem composed just after Crete's fall looks forward to the invasion of other Muslim lands: the vultures of Egypt will devour the victims of the emperor's sword. As the preface acknowledges, the real hero of the poem is Nikephoros Phokas, for all the dutiful praise awarded to Romanos.[15] Nikephoros was now allowed to strike at Aleppo, from which Sayf had continued to harass the empire. Sayf's army proved no match for the Byzantine heavy cavalry and he fled ignominiously. Byzantine soldiers entered the town on 23 December 962.

Double question-marks now hung over Byzantium: would the offensive against the Muslims be sustained, now that Sayf had been humbled? And how would relations fare between Nikephoros and the young emperor, depicted in chronicles as a dissolute youth much given to pig-sticking?[16] The second question was resolved by Romanos' sudden death on 15 March 963, from poison according to some sources, and before the slighting of Aleppo had been celebrated. Phokas was summoned to the capital by Joseph Bringas, was hailed as 'the conqueror',[17] a pun on his first name ('victory-bearer'), and then withdrew to the east, but the temptation or pressure to claim the throne was strong. Nikephoros had, unlike his uncle Leo in 919, a large victorious army at his disposal and the officers seem to have felt prime loyalty to him. If we may believe a source biased heavily in his favour, they proclaimed Nikephoros emperor willy-nilly, maintaining that he, rather than an 'ignoble eunuch with sucklings [the infant Porphyrogeniti] should be giving out orders to men of

---

[15] Theodosius the Deacon, *De Creta capta*, pp. 1, 36.

[16] Theophanes Continuatus, *Chronographia*, p. 472; John Skylitzes, *Synopsis historiarum*, p. 248.

[17] 'o conqueror!' = *nikēta*: *DC*, p. 438.

blood'.[18] Nikephoros also enjoyed active support among the Constantinopolitan populace, and whereas Leo Phokas had been opposed by the fleet under Romanos Lekapenos, Basil the ex-*parakoimōmenos* managed to seize the docks and their warships armed with Greek Fire. Basil's web of patronage was extensive, while in the palace the mother of the Porphyrogeniti, Theophanu, seems to have been in sympathy with Nikephoros. Basil sent ships, including the imperial yacht, inviting him into the City and on 16 August 963 Nikephoros made a triumphal entry, receiving such acclamations as 'Nikephoros for emperor the public interest demands'.[19] He was crowned in St Sophia. In little more than half a dozen years, the army had become not only a battering-ram against distant Muslim foes but also a sought-after presence in the political life of the capital.

Constantine VII had claimed the inheritance of Constantine the Great through his veneration of the True Cross; Nikephoros bid for the succession by acts of conquest. An inscription on an ivory reliquary from his reign reads: 'Formerly, Christ gave the Cross to the mighty master Constantine for his salvation. But now the lord by the grace of God Nikephoros, possessing this, routs the barbarian peoples.'[20] It fits with the notion that the empire's military fortunes hinged upon Nikephoros' personal survival, expressed in a book of prophecy, the *Visions of Daniel*, shown to Liudprand of Cremona at Constantinople in 968.[21]

Nikephoros, acclaimed as 'conqueror' at his coronation as well as at his triumphs, kept his forces engaged; in some years there were two or three expeditions in progress on different fronts. The disastrous outcome of the 964 Sicilian expedition did not prevent Nikephoros from reducing the numerous Muslim fortifications beyond the Taurus and Anti-Taurus ranges, in Cilicia and northern Syria. He is plausibly credited with the capture of 'more than a hundred towns and forts'.[22] This was a very fertile, well-populated region which had not suffered ruination from Byzantine campaigning earlier in the century, being a 'hard' target. The forts, most notoriously Tarsus, had served as

---

[18] 'andras haimatōn agennēs ektomias meta nēpiōn tithēnoumenōn kathypotassoi, hē an autō dedogmenon eiē', Leo the Deacon, *Historiae*, p. 40. According to Leo, this was the argument put by Phokas' second-in-command, John Tzimiskes, to other senior officers.

[19] 'Nikēphoron basilea to pragma to dēmosion aitei', *DC*, p. 439.

[20]
> Kai prin krataiō despotē Kōnstantinō
> Christos dedōke stauron eis sōtērian.
> Kai nyn de touton en Theō Nikēphoros
> Anax tropoutai phyla barbarōn echōn.
>
> Frolow (1961), p. 240; (1965), p. 101.

[21] Liudprand, *Legatio*, c. 39; Morris (1988), pp. 94–5.

[22] 'pleon tōn hekaton poleis kai phrouria', John Skylitzes, *Synopsis historiarum*, p. 271.

bases for raids, and in 965 Tarsus surrendered. That same year, a Byzantine force occupied Cyprus. Nikephoros commanded an expedition as far as the outskirts of Aleppo in 966 and briefly laid siege to Antioch. Pressure was resumed in the autumn of 968: he initiated another siege of Antioch and then left a blockade under subordinates; almost a year later, on 28 October 969, Antioch surrendered.

The fall of Antioch had considerable *éclat*, for this was an ancient Christian city. The Muslims' execution of its patriarch on a charge of treachery in 967 gave edge to claims that Nikephoros was 'armed with the holy spirit'.[23] Yet the fundamentally defensive cast of his strategy is indicated by the truce which Peter Phokas concluded with the amir of Aleppo in January 970: a blueprint for coexistence, biased in Byzantium's favour but leaving the amirate as a semi-autonomous power. The amir was to inform the emperor of the military movements of his fellow-Muslims, and 'if any Muslim troops arrive to invade the Rum . . . [he is] to hinder them, saying "Pass through other regions and do not come into the land of the truce!"'[24] The terms were probably not very different from those initially offered to the amir of Melitene some forty years earlier, and they presupposed that Byzantium would rest content with its gains in Cilicia and along the Euphrates valley.

The terms had almost certainly been approved by Nikephoros, but by the time the truce was made he was dead, murdered during the night of 11 December 969. His fall was a quintessential palace coup: his wife, Theophanu, had been attracted to his former right-hand man, John Tzimiskes, who personally participated in the killing of Nikephoros and had the severed head displayed to the guards who came, too late, to the rescue. Tzimiskes' first measure, after consultation with Basil the *parakoimōmenos*, was to decree that looting or violence would be punished with death, a stern pronouncement against the lawlessness that had been dogging the City in the later part of Nikephoros' reign. This endeared him to the propertied classes, as did his remission of the hearth-tax, and he increased the stipends payable to senior officials and title-holders. He was also more attentive to the material needs of ordinary citizens than Nikephoros had been. Reportedly, he had to be restrained by the *parakoimōmenos* from emptying the treasury through distributions to the poor.[25] He took steps to alleviate famine in the countryside, but the pacification of the City was probably his priority. When celebrating a triumph through the streets, he had them bedecked with laurel branches and cloths of gold 'like a bridechamber',[26] thus invoking the emperor's role as bridegroom of the City. The procession was staged to mark his victory over the Rus' on the Danube,

---

[23] 'theiō pneumati kathōplismenos': Petit (ed.), 'Office inédit en l'honneur de Nicéphore Phocas', p. 401. This comes from an office venerating Nikephoros, written soon after his death.

[24] Canard (1953), pp. 833–4; Farag (1977), pp. 2–3.   [25] Leo the Deacon, *Historiae*, p. 97.

[26] 'dikēn thalamou', Leo the Deacon, *Historiae*, p. 158.

but it gave him the opportunity to demonstrate to the citizens 'ignorant of military matters'[27] the utility for their own security of large, well-equipped armed forces, and the indispensability of military leadership.

The need to rekindle personal loyalties among the former soldiers of Nikephoros Phokas was one of the reasons for the spectacular campaigns against the Muslims which Tzimiskes launched from the autumn of 972 onwards. Byzantine propaganda even claimed that in 974 he led an all-conquering army to Baghdad itself; he certainly levied tribute from the amir of Mosul. In 975 Tzimiskes penetrated as far south as Damascus, levying tribute from its governor and taking Beirut by storm. Relics were sent back to Constantinople, as they had been by Nikephoros II after several of his campaigns. In a letter to Ashot III, king of kings of Armenia, Tzimiskes claimed to have received tribute from Ramla, Jerusalem and other towns, and that the liberation of Jerusalem was his ultimate goal.[28] Such propaganda was partly for domestic consumption, but it also provided moral, and eventually political, authority over the Armenian princes.

Tzimiskes' designs on Armenia had, however, no time for fruition. On 11 January 976 he died of typhoid or poison. The elder son of Romanos II, Basil, was seventeen. No formal regency was required, although his great-grandfather's bastard son, Basil the *parakoimōmenos* dominated the administration for a further ten years. Basil II's speech was staccato, 'more that of a peasant than a gentleman',[29] a description which would surely have pained his bookish grandfather. In fact Basil, with his single-minded devotion to his army and preoccupation with drill and military formations, had far more in common with Nikephoros Phokas, another celibate ascetic. The role of war-leader, which he assumed in early adulthood, became habitual and congenial. He is depicted in military uniform on the frontispiece of a celebrated psalter, opposite verses explaining such images as the archangel Michael handing Basil a spear.[30] The epithet 'Bulgar-slayer' seems to have been engraved on his tomb, together with verses:

> No one saw my spear lie still . . .
> but I was wakeful through all the time of my life
> and guarded the children of the New Rome . . .[31]

---

[27] 'polemikōn ergōn agnōtes tygchanontes', Leo the Deacon, *Historiae*, p. 63. The 'Bamberg silk', commonly associated with Basil II, may well commemorate this triumph: Prinzing (1993), pp. 218–31.

[28] Matthew of Edessa, *Chronicle*, pp. 30–1; Walker (1977), pp. 319–27.

[29] 'kai agroikikōs mallon ē eleutheriōs', Michael Psellos, *Chronographia* I, p. 23, trans. Sewter, p. 45.

[30] Venice, Bibl. Marciana, Codex gr. 17; Cutler (1984), p. 115 and fig. 412, p. 253.

[31]
> ou gar tis eiden ēremoun emon dory . . .
> all' agrypnōn hapanta ton zoēs chronon
> Rōmēs ta tekna tēs neas eryomēn.
> Mercati (1970), p. 230

Basil's watchfulness in reality was directed as much at his subjects and officers as at foreign foes. The resentment of the Bulgarians at the dissolution of their state was exploited by four sons of an Armenian officer in the Byzantine occupation army. Soon after Tzimiskes' death, if not before, the Kometopouloi ('sons of the *komēs*') deserted, and were soon leading Bulgarian rebels. More immediately menacing was the revolt of the eastern army within months of Tzimiskes' death. The new claimant was Bardas Skleros, the general upon whom the government had relied to combat the Rus' and also to quash the rebellion of Bardas Phokas (nephew of Nikephoros) in 970. Skleros forced the Taurus mountain passes, and after further battles he gradually closed on Constantinople. Basil the *parakoimōmenos* turned to none other than Bardas Phokas, but the troops which Phokas mustered in his family heartland around Caesarea were no match for the host which Skleros could field, and Phokas was defeated twice in the summer and autumn of 978. The Macedonians' plight was undoubtedly dire, even though Skleros hesitated to march straight for Constantinople. The day was saved by the arrival of a 12,000–strong force of cavalry despatched by David Curopalates, the ruler of the region of western Georgia adjoining Theodosiopolis, Tao (Tayk). The Georgians joined up with the remnants of Phokas' army and surprised and defeated the rebels to the west of Caesarea, in the theme of Charsianon, on 24 March 979. Bardas Skleros fled to Muslim territory and lengthy negotiations ensued between Byzantium and Baghdad.

Skleros eventually returned, but as a claimant to the throne, not a deportee. In 985 Basil dismissed the *éminence grise* of tenth-century politics, Basil the *parakoimōmenos*, and subsequently exiled him from the City, upon suspicion of plotting with various generals of the eastern army. Basil II resolved to take charge of the army himself and to undertake an operation independently of the great families of the south-eastern borders. Bulgaria offered an opportunity and a real threat. In 985 and early 986 Samuel, who was emerging as the dominant Kometopoulos, was systematically reducing important forts and towns in Thrace and northern Greece. He transplanted the inhabitants of Larissa to Bulgaria and enrolled the males for military service. Basil led a large army to Serdica (Sofia), a key strategic centre, but he failed to reduce the town and his army was ambushed withdrawing through the pass at Trajan's Gates; Basil himself barely escaped. His first steps in soldiering thus ended in ignominy and Bardas Skleros seized the opportunity to negotiate his release with the authorities in Baghdad and make his second bid for the throne early in 987. Then, on 15 August 987, Bardas Phokas, to whom Basil had turned for assistance against Skleros, was himself proclaimed emperor. With the help of Maleinos and other Cappadocian notables he raised local troops, supplementing the *tagmata* already under his command. A pact was negotiated between the rebel generals, whereby Skleros would become master of Antioch and other recently gained or still unconquered territories to the south and east of that city.

By the end of 987 Phokas had gained control of most of Asia minor and was able to send a detachment to Chrysopolis, in the footsteps of Leo Phokas in 919. He himself laid siege to Abydos, at the other end of Byzantium's 'inner sea'. Once again, the mystique of imperial authority seems to have dispersed a Phokas-led army, but this time the mystique worked on a foreign ruler, and not on rank-and-file Byzantine soldiers. A marriage was negotiated between Basil II's sister, Anna Porphyrogenita, and the ruler of the Rus', Vladimir Sviatoslavich. In return for Anna's hand, Vladimir would send warriors to the emperor's aid, and according to an almost contemporary Armenian writer 6,000 arrived at Byzantium. They surprised and routed the rebel force encamped at Chrysopolis.[32] However, they were infantrymen, and probably could not have prevailed over the heavy cavalry of the eastern army. It was greatly to Basil's good fortune that on 13 April 989 his enemy died suddenly of a stroke and the rebel army dispersed. Bardas Skleros emerged to make common cause with the dead man's sons. In June, Skleros wrote to the Turkish general in charge of Baghdad, requesting his aid. No prompt aid was forthcoming, and this may well have been one reason why Skleros entered into negotiations with the Byzantine government. Basil granted him an amnesty in the autumn of 989. Only then did the citizens of Antioch drive Leo Phokas (Bardas' son) out of their city and acknowledge Basil II's regime.

Basil, the ruler of an enlarged empire, became his own general, thereby dispensing with the military 'establishment' upon which he had relied earlier in his reign. His intimate knowledge of the characters of individual soldiers and his supervision of promotions reduced the risk of plots and coups. He maintained the strictest military discipline. This martinet-like stance probably sprang from a mixture of personal inclination and political calculation. He had, in any case, little choice but to take up the challenge which Samuel of Bulgaria was posing. On 14 June 987 or 988 Samuel had his own brother Aaron and most of his family put to death, becoming in effect sole ruler. He was determined to found a new dynasty based in the Macedonian highlands, forswearing Symeon's Preslav. The gain of Dyrrachium – apparently without violence – relieved him of danger from the west. Samuel married Agatha, daughter of John Chryselios, 'the leading man',[33] who presumably swung the town behind him. He also aspired to control Thessalonika, the counterpart of Dyrrachium. Both stood where the Egnatian Way reached the sea. There were

---

[32] Stephen of Taron, *Histoire universelle*, p. 164; Michael Psellos, *Chronographia* I, p. 9, trans. Sewter, pp. 34–5; John Skylitzes, *Synopsis historiarum*, p. 336.

[33] 'tou . . . prōteuontos', John Skylitzes, *Synopsis historiarum*, p. 349.

already, in the *massif* traversed by the Egnatian Way, a number of towns, comprising bishoprics and monastic centres, which stood to benefit from the grain grown in the plains of northern Greece, which Samuel was set to dominate. Byzantine and Armenian captives were settled in areas adjoining the Egnatian Way and so, probably, were the deportees from Larissa. Samuel made an island on Lake Prespa his principal residence, building an immense cathedral, some 44 m long, and also a palace. He installed in the church the relics of St Achilleus, removed from Larissa in 985 or 986. He was thus acquiring for his seat not merely supernatural protection but also legitimacy, for the erstwhile patron and guardian of Larissa would not have allowed an impious usurper to abduct his remains. Samuel could hope to gain through such measures acceptance and even allegiance from his diverse subjects: Bulgarians, Vlachs, Albanians, Armenians and Greeks.

Samuel's dispositions give no hint of designs upon the Byzantine throne. Nonetheless, an upstart astride the Balkans menacing the emperor's revenues from the Thessalian plain would have been unpalatable to rulers less martially minded than Basil, and by about 990 the lower Danube was under Samuel's sway. Basil turned to the Bulgarian problem once he considered the eastern provinces to be quiescent, in early spring 991. Four years of campaigning brought the recapture of Berrhoia (Veroia), some 60 kilometres south-west of Thessalonika. Basil had it and several other recaptured fortresses demolished, evidently assuming that they could not be held indefinitely against Samuel. In 995, while Basil was on the eastern front, Samuel counter-attacked, sending patrols up to the walls of Thessalonika itself. In one clash the duke of Thessalonika himself was killed, and Samuel's raids ranged further south. His incursions were interrupted in the autumn of 997 or the spring of 998, when his army was surprised during withdrawal from a raid on the Peloponnese. Many Bulgarians were butchered in their sleep and Samuel and his son Gabriel-Radomir were seriously wounded.

The general responsible for the victory on the Spercheios, Nikephoros Ouranos, could now undertake bolder forays into enemy territory. Basil himself moved east, taking advantage of the death of David of Tao. David had lent troops to the rebels in 987–9 and had subsequently been overawed into bequeathing his principality to the empire. The cavalrymen whom Basil transplanted from Tao were probably of assistance to him on his subsequent campaigns. Byzantine authority was reimposed on north-east Bulgaria, and around 1002 Basil exploited his new-found control of the lower Danube to advance upstream. He besieged Vidin and the defenders gave in after eight months. Basil strengthened the fortifications, clearly intending to establish an outpost to Samuel's north-west. He was most probably allied with a local Hungarian magnate, Duke Ahtum-Ajtony, who is said to have 'received power from the

Greeks' and to have been baptised.[34] Basil then drove far to the south and received the surrender of Skoplje.

Basil's spectacular circumscription of Bulgaria may well explain why Dyrrachium's leading family transferred its loyalties back to the emperor in, probably, 1004 or 1005. John Chryselios' two sons each received the title of *patrikios* and an imperial official was admitted to the city. Recovery of Dyrrachium tipped the strategic balance in Byzantium's favour, but neither side could deliver a death-blow. In fact, the gains made by Basil's long march were fleeting. Skoplje was back in Bulgarian hands at their final surrender in 1018. Even Dyrrachium, Basil's most significant acquisition, seems in effect to have been neutralised, though probably not wholly lost. The ruler of Dioclea (Duklja), the Slav principality north of the city, was endowed by Samuel with 'all the land of the people of Dyrrachium'.[35] The prince, John Vladimir, had been forced to submit to Samuel; but after a spell in detention at Prespa, he had been married to the daughter of a relative of Samuel, one Theodorites. Samuel seems to have felt sufficiently in control of Dyrrachium's hinterland to entrust it to a local prince linked to his own family.

Basil's annual razzias in the period following his long march were carefully organised. His insistence on tight formations, 'making his army into a kind of tower',[36] assured it invincibility in open countryside and enabled it to brave mountain passes. But the absence of any known victories between about 1005 and 1014 throws into doubt their effectiveness. Basil's adversary did not merely rely on natural defences. He was 'most expert in strategy',[37] and was ultimately responsible for the fortifications which guarded the passes. The large earthwork at Kleidion (Kliuch) comprised three lines of ramparts and two ditches aligned with the terrain, and protected the population very effectively from Basil's incursions. Until the end of his reign Samuel was able to deploy large armies, 'the numberless Bulgarian phalanx'.[38] There is no sign that the war-effort overstrained either the Bulgarians' manpower reserves or loyalty to their new tsar. Samuel presided over various ecclesiastical building works. At Ochrid a large basilica was apparently built or refurbished, and the head of the Bulgarian church installed there. Samuel's relocation of the patriarchal see from Prespa to a place famed for its associations with Clement and Naum reflected his rising confidence that Ochrid was reasonably secure, even though it lay on the Egnatian Way. He made Ochrid his own principal residence and the location of his treasury. Reportedly, 'much money' and 10,000 lb of

---

[34] 'Accepit autem potestatem a Grecis', *Legenda S. Gerhardi*, p. 490.
[35] 'totamque terram Duracenorum', *Letopis popa Dukljanina*, p. 335.
[36] 'hoion katapyrgōsas to strateuma', Michael Psellos, *Chronographia* I, p. 21, trans. Sewter, p. 47.
[37] 'strategikōtatos', Kekaumenos, *Strategikon*, p. 152.
[38] 'tēs Boulgarikēs anarithmētou phalangos', Sullivan (ed. and trans.), *The Life of Saint Nikon*, p. 148.

'stamped gold',[39] as well as imperial crowns, were kept in the heavily fortified and extensive citadel. He gained an aura of legitimacy, being called *rex* by a contemporary Italian chronicle,[40] and his descendants enjoyed imperial status in eleventh-century Byzantium.

Samuel's treasury may well have been filled with revenues from his southern towns, as well as spoils of war. However, the reconstituted political structure was inevitably shaken by his death on 6 October 1014. Byzantine writers maintain that he was overcome by the spectacle of 14,000 or 15,000 men returning, most of them blinded, from Byzantine captivity.[41] Undoubtedly, he had suffered a humiliating defeat: an army guarding the Kleidion pass had been surprised and routed by a Byzantine unit, and Samuel himself only just escaped. But it was his demise, not the débâcle, that tipped the scales in Byzantium's favour. Samuel's son, Gabriel-Radomir, was bellicose and forceful, but lacked his political skills. Gabriel's first cousin, John Vladislav, begrudged his succession, and on 15 September 1015 he had him assassinated. John became the new tsar. Basil II tried to exploit the rivalries of the ruling family, seizing the town of Edessa (Vodena). He sacked several Bulgarian royal residences and the town – though not the citadel – of Ochrid. However, John Vladislav was able to renovate and strengthen the fortifications of an alternative base, Bitola, commemorating the work with an inscription. Moreover, Basil's eighty-eight-day siege of Pernik ended in failure and heavy losses, while his siege of Kastoria, in late spring or summer 1017, was also unsuccessful. He seems still to have been unsure of Edessa's loyalty, seeing that he had to 'set everything in order there' on his way back to Constantinople.[42]

The ambivalence of the Edessans was prudent. John Vladislav was still capable of attacking the hardest targets. After Basil's withdrawal, he resumed personal command at Dyrrachium. In February 1018 a pitched battle was fought before the city walls. John Vladislav was, 'like another Goliath', 'invincible', engaged in single combat when two footsoldiers managed to deal fatal blows to his stomach.[43] This changed everything, as Basil realised. He 'immediately' set forth for Adrianople,[44] but no forcible entry into Bulgaria was necessary. John had not designated an heir and there were tensions between his widow and Samuel's descendants. So the prospects of an agreed succession looked faint. Krakras, the magnate who had defended Pernik for eighty-eight days, now surrendered not only Pernik but also the thirty-five other forts

---

[39] 'chrēmata polla', 'chrysou episēmou', John Skylitzes, *Synopsis historiarum*, pp. 358–9.

[40] Lupus Protospatharius, *Annales*, p. 57.

[41] John Skylitzes, *Synopsis historiarum*, p. 349; Kekaumenos, *Strategikon*, p. 152.

[42] 'panta ta ekeise katastēsamenos', John Skylitzes, *Synopsis historiarum*, p. 356.

[43] 'hoia dē Goliath', 'amachon', Michael Psellos, *Scripta minora* I, p. 160; Grégoire (1937), pp. 287–90.

[44] 'parautika', John Skylitzes, *Synopsis historiarum*, p. 357.

forming an elaborate system round it. Other war-lords and community leaders saw that the game was up, and as Basil advanced along the Egnatian Way, their envoys brought offers of surrender. Basil responded with honours, titles and other blandishments, making Krakras, for example, a *patrikios*. Contemporary historians in Armenia and the west show awareness that Basil's triumph owed little to pitched battles.

Basil's settlement of Bulgaria should be viewed against this background. Ochrid and the other residences of Samuel and John were divested of their royal trappings. John's widow, Maria, and her children were drawn into Basil's court circle, receiving titles. Several of the males rose to high office in the imperial administration. Basil is credited with the desire 'not to innovate at all',[45] letting revenues be raised in grain and wine rather than coin. It is probable that these and other administrative duties were, in the remoter regions, left to local notables bedecked with titles and offices. Basil had never recognised the patriarchal rank of Bulgaria's head churchman, but he now reaffirmed the special status of the Bulgarian church. His appointee as archbishop was a Bulgarian monk named John, a concession to his new subjects' sensibilities, and his concern for the church's well-being is expressed in three charters confirming its rights. That of 1020 sternly forbids other metropolitans (subject to the Constantinopolitan patriarch) from encroaching into the Bulgarian province. Archbishop John is to have authority over the same number of sees as his precursors in the time of 'Peter the emperor and Samuel'.[46] Officials, including tax-collectors, were forbidden to interfere in the churches' or monasteries' affairs on pain of the 'great and pitiless . . . wrath of our majesty'.[47]

To the north-west, Basil consolidated his possession of Vidin, and pushed further north-westwards. The recalcitrant potentate who controlled Sirmium was assassinated and the town became the headquarters of a new Byzantine theme. Even the Croats, a people hitherto only spasmodically connected with Byzantium, now came within its orbit. The ruling brothers, Gojslav and Krešimir III, formally submitted to Basil and received titles, thus acknowledging his commanding position in the Balkans and beyond. King Stephen of Hungary was now his ally, and he may well have taken part in the last stages of the campaign against John Vladislav and the final occupation of Ochrid in 1018. That same year, Doge Otto Orseolo of Venice drove the Croats back from the region of Zara, and imposed tribute on some of the cities on islands off the Dalmatian coast. The Croats were hemmed in by Byzantium's possessions, allies and vassals.

---

[45] 'mēde metakinēsai ta pragmata', Skylitzes, *Synopsis*, p. 412.

[46] 'Petrou tou basileōs kai tou Samouēl', Gelzer (1893), p. 44; *FHGB*, vol. 6, p. 44.

[47] 'megalēn kai asympathē . . . apo tēs basileias hēmōn aganaktēsin', Gelzer (1893), p. 46; *FGHB*, vol. 6, p. 47.

Basil showed no signs of being prepared to let his 'spear lie still' after his subjugation of the Balkans. Although in his early sixties, he embarked on a massive expedition to Caucasia in 1021 and 1022. He superintended the take-over of the administration of Vaspurakan, whose King Sennacherim had been induced to cede his realm to Basil. He fought a series of engagements against King George I of Georgia, in order to retrieve all the forts and lands claimed as the inheritance of David of Tao. After George had renounced all title to Tao, Basil returned to Constantinople. His energies now swung towards the west and still more aggressive campaigning. He was about to embark with reinforcements for an invasion of Sicily when he fell ill and died, on 13 or 15 December 1025.

Basil's dominions were half as large again as those of Constantine VII. Constantine seems to have had little appetite for expansion, preferring like his father to emphasise his role as the wise guarantor of order and justice. Basil, by contrast, appears to have presented conquest as his prime aim, without any palpable regard for the question of who would succeed after the deaths of himself and his younger brother, Constantine. But he had managed to maintain the army's loyalty by becoming its general and personally directing its affairs, a stance which had much in common with that of Nikephoros II Phokas. He was consciously contending with the prestige which great military families or individuals still enjoyed. They were bracketed with other, less politically involved, families whose wealth and influence seemed to occlude imperial authority locally. Some versions of a novel concerning the purchase of property by 'the powerful' from 'the poor' cite as examples of malefactors members of the Maleinos family and the Phokases in general, convenient political targets.[48] The most active admirers of the tenth-century heroes were themselves in or connected to the army, and it was from their ranks that a coup was attempted during Basil's last Caucasian campaign. We are told that 'many of those who were in the camp had walked with their feet behind the emperor, but in thought and words they were behind the rebels'.[49] According to Psellos, he treated his subjects as if he had subjugated them.[50] His ability to maintain a large standing army probably owed much to the vulnerability of the well-to-do to his arbitrary seizure of property and commandeering of resources. Only the patriarch of Constantinople and other senior churchmen and monks seem to have presumed to object to a new measure to make large landowners responsible for the tax liabilities of missing petty landholders. Basil promised Patriarch Sergios that he would lift the obligation if he were to prevail over the Bulgarians.[51] At the same time, Basil seems to have hoped for the gratitude of

[48] *Ius graecoromanum* I, p. 264, n. 24.   [49] Aristakes of Lastivert, *Récit*, p. 20.
[50] Michael Psellos, *Chronographia* I, p.18, trans. Sewter, p. 44.
[51] 'ei': John Skylitzes, *Synopsis historiarum*, p. 365.

his non-Greek and non-Chalcedonian subjects in return for his consideration for their rites and customs. They might provide soldiers no less effective, and perhaps more loyal, than his Greek troops. In this way, he could turn the 'diversity' of the empire to his advantage, binding 'the elements of power in imperial harmony'.[52] One feature of this policy is the generous scale of the lands and forts granted to eminent Armenian expatriates.

The expansion was not ruinous in itself. Bulgarians served on the eastern front, while Armenians fought in Basil's Bulgarian wars. And, if Bulgaria's economy was largely agrarian, Armenia's towns and smaller settlements offered important new sources of revenue. The prosperity of towns in the western Armenian borderlands had already attracted the notice of Constantine VII, and they seem to have expanded in the eleventh century. In Cappadocia, a former Byzantine border zone, building work and decorative programmes continued in the rock-chapels and -monasteries. The numerous churches and monasteries erected by Syriac Jacobite immigrants in the Euphrates valley south from Melitene and in parts of Cilicia attest their wealth as well as their piety in Basil's time. And Antioch, a *kouratoreia* of the emperor, seems to have prospered. Many Armenians, initially soldiers but probably subsequently craftsmen and traders too, were settled in its vicinity. The increase in population and in economic transactions involving coin should have worked to the government's advantage. However, a major problem was posed by the instrument of the empire's enlargement, the army. Materials upon which even the roughest estimate of its size and cost to the state might be based are lacking, but the armed forces were certainly very substantially larger than they had been during the first half of the tenth century, and much more dependent on money for their maintenance and remuneration. More men needed to be employed full-time for Basil's ceaseless campaigning, while key points such as Dyrrachium or Sirmium needed substantial garrisoning. The administrative apparatus responsible for their upkeep was not radically different from the one which had operated the smaller theme armies of the tenth century, and many of the military units were still based on long-established themes in Asia Minor. At the same time, the increasing security of many parts of Asia Minor and mounting prosperity called for larger numbers of non-military officials. By the early eleventh century, towns in Greece and Asia Minor's western coastal plain were witnessing building development and more use of coin for commercial transactions. The towns' purchasing power signalled the emergence of local elites, while local landholders gained opportunities for enrichment through supplying produce to the town-dwellers.

---

[52] 'poikilian', 'ta tēs archēs eis harmonian basilikēn', Michael Psellos, *Chronographia* I, pp. 13–14, trans. Sewter, pp. 39–40.

The interests of these provincial groupings were not directly opposed to those of central government, and many of their members looked to Constantinople for status if not office, while the 'professional', expensively equipped soldiers relied more on state pay and other subventions than their early tenth-century precursors had done. But there were conflicts of jurisdiction and fiscal rights between the military and the civilian administrative apparatuses: labyrinthine and rival nexuses of tax-collectors and imposers of charges and services to the state sprawled across the empire. Those who were not shielded by office, court titles or connections with local dignitaries had reason to seek the patronage of those better-placed, in order to minimise exposure to what were – in their eyes at least – arbitrary or extortionate demands.

These tendencies were not necessarily lethal to effective central government. The very care which major landowners took to gain charters exempting them from state charges suggests as much, and the state took steps to increase the number of peasants labouring on its own domain. The overall increase in the population of the empire also potentially benefited the state's tax rolls. However, this combination of administrative problems with the need to finance and maintain recruitment to a large standing army was primed by the political threat which the generals seemed to pose. Basil II masked the problem by marrying his army. Booty from foreign campaigning and ruthless seizure of properties brought in enough for him to keep it operational and, according to Psellos, to hoard 200,000 gold pieces in his palace treasury.[53] But strong-arm methods were no substitute for the administrative reform needed to cope with success. Expansionism would unleash disarray.

---

[53] Michael Psellos, *Chronographia* 1, p. 19, trans. Sewter, p. 45.

CHAPTER 25

BYZANTIUM AND THE WEST

Jonathan Shepard

BYZANTINE LINKS WITH THE WESTERN CHRISTIANS, 900–950

Byzantium's relations with the Latin west in this period have a 'Cheshire cat' character in comparison with ninth-century exchanges. Very little attention is paid to the Christian west by Byzantine writers even when Saxon potentates begin to intervene in Italy and bedeck themselves with imperial trimmings. A memorandum of diplomatic procedures, compiled partly from older materials in the mid-tenth century, lists the standard form of address for letters to various *reges*, of 'Gaul' as well as Bavaria and Saxony: each is to be addressed as 'spiritual brother', unlike the numerous other addressees. But the protocols for receptions of ambassadors make no special provision for western ones: formulaic greetings for envoys from the Bulgarians and eastern Muslims are rehearsed, presumably because their visits were more important or frequent.[1]

A somewhat later compilation would probably have paid western ambassadors little more attention than the *Book of Ceremonies* did on the eve of the imperial coronation of Otto I. For Basil II, as for his predecessors, the existence of a rival Bulgarian *basileus* was far more important. But if events beyond the Adriatic were generally of secondary importance to Byzantium's rulers, the very powers which troubled them in the Balkans or hindered communications with the west obliged them to maintain outlying bases from which to disrupt their activities. Byzantine claims in Italy were based on quite recent military actions and not merely on the inheritance of the old Roman empire. The *De administrando imperio* recognises the territorial losses to the Lombards, but stresses the help which Basil I had provided against the Arabs, and claims authority over Capua and Benevento on the basis of 'this great benefit rendered to them' then.[2]

Great expectations continued to be vested in Sicily. Byzantine bases there provided platforms for speedy *démarches* towards any figure of note in Italy or

---

[1] *DC*, pp. 689, 681–6.
[2] 'tēn eis autous genomenēn megalēn tautēn euergesian', *DAI*, c. 29/215–16.

even southern Francia, and a ready means of monitoring and hindering the passage of Arab vessels, a capability not open to Christian magnates without fleets. The *De thematibus*, a work commissioned by Constantine VII, claims that Sicily is 'now' under Byzantine rule 'since the emperor of Constantinople rules the sea as far as the Pillars of Hercules'.[3] This should be inverted: a presence in Sicily gave Byzantium disproportionate influence and status in the western Mediterranean world, and to abandon claims to it would have been demeaning. Thus *stratēgoi* residing in Calabria were officially designated governors of 'Sicily' through the first half of the tenth century. Sicily was, together with Calabria and Illyricum, under the patriarch of Constantinople, and some contacts with orthodox churchmen on the island persisted. Partly because of this, the Byzantine military position was not utterly hopeless: Taormina fell to the Arabs in 902, but was regained by 912/13; it was only fully taken over by the Arabs in 962.

If imperial ambitions showed great resilience, loss of control of the straits of Messina had in reality eroded Byzantium's capacity for intervention in Rome or further north. Expeditionary forces or major diplomatic *démarches* could no longer be funded from the island, and Calabria was too poor and too harassed by Sicilian Arab razzias to provide much before the end of the tenth century. Byzantium thus had greater need of allies in the west and there were indeed occasional contacts between Constantinople and some western courts. The temerity of Muslim raiders and the existence of stray Arab colonies further north could affront the Christian sensibilities and prestige of enough parties for joint action to be attempted, but actual operations were rare. Those best placed to provide effective land forces were those Lombard princes whose patrimonies had been most impaired by the Byzantine recovery in southern Italy. Only after skilful negotiation and manoeuvring by Nicholas Picingli, the *stratēgos* of *Longibardia*, and by Pope John X, could the lords of Gaeta and Naples be induced to cooperate with Capua-Benevento, Roman nobles and Picingli's fleet and army to expel the Arabs from the Garigliano valley. The coalition captured the Saracens' base in August 915, but did not long survive its victory. Soon Landulf of Capua-Benevento and other Lombard princes were in 'rebellion', raiding Byzantine possessions in southern Italy and regaining control of much of them.

Otherwise, few important rulers had interests which clashed or converged with Byzantium's strongly enough for intensive relations to be maintained with them. The main fixed points on the Byzantine political map were cities. Venice's interests were aligned quite closely with the empire's and its ruling families were willing to designate themselves as *servi* (*douloi* in Greek), a vague

---

[3] 'nyn'; 'dia to ton autokratora Kōnstantinoupoleōs thalassokratein mechri tōn Hērakleiōn stēlōn', Constantine Porphyrogenitus, *De thematibus*, p. 94.

term ranging in meaning from 'slave' to 'subordinate' of the emperor. The *basileus* felt no need to show particular favour towards the managers of Venice, being well aware of the Venetians' need of the sea for protection, sustenance and income. Reliance on the import of bulk goods made them vulnerable to famine or financial ruin since merchantmen were small, unwieldy and even in summer unseaworthy. Byzantium was the obvious and most lucrative of the limited outlets available to the Venetians for their re-export of weaponry, wood and slaves, while Byzantine luxury goods were much in demand among the elites of north Italian towns. The deficiencies of navigation and the revitalised Byzantine presence along the island-studded Dalmation coastline thus made Venetian maritime communications highly sensitive to the actions of the imperial authorities.

Fortunately for the Venetians, it was in Byzantium's interests to foster a self-financing and largely self-reliant naval capability on the outermost fringe of its Adriatic possessions, since this relieved it from maintaining a significant fleet of its own there. Each party stood to gain from the status quo, in which direct contacts between Constantinople and the northern Adriatic were monopolised by the Venetians, while taxed and supervised by the Byzantine government. The Venetians' returns were substantial, and guaranteed access to secure markets in Constantinople helped to offset the delays and losses of the sea voyage. They also tended to profit from their ability, very rare among westerners, to monitor events in Constantinople and, most probably, to speak Greek. Even Venice, however, ranked low in Byzantine priorities and its rulers' compliance was assumed. Of far greater weight was the city of Rome, with its indelible imperial connotations and especially its role as the residence of the pope.

The importance attached to the papacy is demonstrated by the protocols for the reception of envoys: those for 'ambassadors' from the pope feature first, and are detailed and full.[4] Long-standing tradition played its part here, but there was also a more dynamic reason. The pope was the sole western figure who could intervene substantively in the empire's affairs and within its sphere of influence. Apulia's subjection to papal jurisdiction was not formally disputed, and as the population was mostly Lombards under Latin priests and bishops it was imperative for the Byzantine government to keep in touch with its spiritual leader. In the Byzantine 'mainland' the papacy's reputation had been enhanced by its stand against iconoclasm. A few monks and holy men continued to make their way to venerate Rome's churches and the tombs of Sts Peter and Paul; eastern churchmen were in contact with the Greek monasteries – still prominent, although not numerous in Rome – and also with the *curia*.

---

[4] *presbeis, DC,* pp. 680–1.

Papal verdicts on religious questions mattered; hence emperors, too, looked to the papacy in their efforts to manage their own patriarchate. Romanos I seems to have regarded papal support as pivotal to his plan to impose his son, Theophylact, as the patriarch of Constantinople, and papal legates carried out the act of enthronement on 2 February 933. There was another equally cogent reason for the intensity of imperial relations with Rome. The papacy had been slow to abandon hopes of Bulgaria. In papal eyes, Bulgaria fell within Illyricum, a province rightfully under its jurisdiction. Symeon's imperial pretensions and his later hostility towards Romanos may have made him seem amenable to papal overtures, as Patriarch Nicholas apparently suspected when, in the early 920s, he detained two papal emissaries whose declared aim was to persuade Symeon to make peace with Byzantium. Symeon's proclamation of himself as 'emperor of the Romans' may well have been known to the papacy. The papal legates who mediated between Symeon and Tomislav of Croatia in 926/7 may have investigated a possible accommodation between pope and self-declared emperor.[5] The papacy had originally been responding to an approach from Tomislav, Symeon's enemy, and papal interest in south Slav affairs need not have been wholly repugnant to the imperial government at that time. Nonetheless, the papacy's title to Illyricum could have made for some sort of concordat between Rome and a Bulgarian ruler seeking recognition. All this underlay the golden bulls for, and ritual attention to, 'the spiritual father of our holy emperor'.[6] Formal exchanges were probably accompanied by unofficial contacts with other churchmen and notables in Rome. The pope might thus be deflected from undesirable initiatives and his undeniable authority put to the emperor's uses: papal approval of Theophylact's appointment is said to have been bought by Romanos.

The benefits to the emperor of papal cooperation made others' intervention in Rome a matter of some concern, since these might yoke the papacy to their own ambitions, seeking the irritatingly grandiose title of emperor; yet they might also provide leverage over a recalcitrant pope. A masterful occupant of the Italian kingdom's throne like Berengar of Friuli was uncongenial, but even Berengar's imperial coronation in Rome in December 915 seems to have been received with equanimity on the Bosphorus. If Byzantium showed a penchant for closer ties with more distant potentates in southern Francia, this probably sprang from an abiding concern about Sicily as well as from fears that a Lombardy-based 'emperor' might intervene more effectively in Roman affairs. For the *basileus* nurtured a dream of his own: with the cooperation of a southern Frankish ruler, the chances of driving Arab predators from their bases and

---

[5] See chapter 23, above, p. 578.
[6] 'ho pneumatikos patēr tou basileōs hēmōn tou hagiou', *DC*, p. 680. The Logothete of the Drome termed the pope thus in his greetings for envoys from Rome.

eventually isolating and subduing the occupiers of Sicily became slightly less remote. There is suggestive evidence from the mid-tenth-century diplomatic memorandum that the emperor maintained contacts with the *archōn* ('prince') of Sardinia.[7] Greek inscriptions there suggest that court titles were still being sported by members of the ruling elite towards the end of the century.[8] It may be no coincidence that the marriage of Leo VI's infant daughter Anna to Louis III of Provence was negotiated and contracted in 899/900, shortly before the fall of Taormina to the Arabs. This commitment of the emperor's only daughter to a western spouse, the first such match to be actually contracted by a member of a Byzantine ruling house, yielded no tangible aid, and Romanos I seems to have responded tepidly to an embassy from Hugh of Arles, who, upon being crowned king of Italy in Pavia, 'took care to make his name known even to the Greeks placed far from us'.[9]

Emperor Romanos showed keen interest in the marriage of one of his other sons into the leading Roman family which included Pope John XI himself, his half-brother and enemy Alberic, and Marozia. An imperial letter of early February 933 offers more warships to ferry her to Constantinople and shows willingness to entertain John's request for help.[10] But the letter was already out-of-date by the time of writing: Marozia had married Hugh of Arles and he had come to Rome, only to be expelled by Alberic and the citizens under his command. Alberic himself sought a marriage-tie, but Romanos was now looking for an ally against the Muslim corsairs and the Lombard princes. A mission was despatched with money, dress tunics and *objets d'art* for Hugh, *rhex Italias*, and his magnates; they were to attack the Lombard 'rebels'.[11] The subsequent operations were successful and Hugh's relations with Romanos became close. But the commander of the mission had received contingency instructions in case Hugh sent an army without leading it in person; he was also supplied with a reserve of costumes, presumably for others whom he might find serviceable. Such flexibility was of the essence. In late 944 or early 945 Byzantine warships attacked Fraxinetum and destroyed many Muslim boats with Greek Fire, acting in response to a request from Hugh. Romanos had made his assistance conditional upon a marriage-tie: Hugh was to give one of his daughters in marriage to Constantine VII's infant son, also called Romanos. Liudprand of Cremona regarded the threat to the Byzantine south from the Lombard princes as underlying Romanos' request.[12] Hugh, lacking a legitimate daughter, sent Bertha, his child by a concubine. She was brought to Constantinople in the late summer of 944 and married to Romanos.

---

[7] *DC*, p. 690.   [8] von Falkenhausen (1978), p. 44 and n. 135; Boscolo (1978), pp. 111–15.

[9] 'studuit et Achivis nomen suum longe a nobis positis notum facere', Liudprand, *Antapodosis* III, 22.

[10] Theodore Daphnopates, *Correspondance*, pp. 14, 39–41.

[11] 'apostatēsantas', *DC*, pp. 661–2.   [12] Liudprand, *Relatio*, c. 7.

There is a tone of family feeling and pride in the sketch of Bertha's lineage provided in the *De administrando imperio*, a work commissioned and partly written by her father-in-law, Constantine.[13] In 948, after the death of Hugh, Constantine wrote to Berengar of Ivrea, urging him to act as faithful guardian of the late king's son, Lothar. But at the same time he wrote another letter, urging Berengar to send an ambassador who would return with proof of Constantine's love for Berengar.[14] Constantine was discreetly shifting towards the more important figure in Italy: Berengar was already sidelining Lothar. Even the injunctions to protect Lothar – who might, at around twenty years of age, have been expected to fend for himself – were somewhat double-edged. The emperor had to preserve decorum but also to do business with whoever prevailed in northern Italy or Rome, so long as they did not persistently offend against his interests. His main concern at that time was the reconquest of Crete; elsewhere in the Mediterranean he sought tranquillity. Liudprand, who had travelled with an envoy of Otto I, reached Constantinople during or just after the expedition, and the diplomatic activity he records turned essentially on Crete. Constantine's sense of kinship with Hugh's family could not outweigh the requirements of Crete. Any possible tensions between sentiment and strategy were relieved by the deaths of Bertha-Eudocia in 949 and Lothar in 950.

BYZANTIUM AND OTTO I

Byzantium had also maintained some contacts with potentates based north of the Alps and the Mediterranean littoral. The Greek embassies who visited Otto I in 945 and 949 may well be the tip of an otherwise unrecorded iceberg of diplomacy. The *pallia graeca* presented by King Edmund to St Cuthbert in 944 could have been brought by emissaries of the *basileus*, a title west Saxon kings from Æthelstan onwards sometimes bore in their charters. But the emperor's most active concerns lay in the Balkan and Mediterranean worlds. Increased Byzantine attention to Otto during the late 940s may have been induced by recent Bavarian victories over the Magyars: Constantine, too, was interested in the Magyars, devoting three chapters of the *De administrando* almost exclusively to their history, and seeing to the baptism and investiture with the title of *patrikios* of at least two of their chieftains.[15]

In September 951 Otto led an army across the Alps. Probably in the same year Constantine requested the hand of Hadwig, daughter of Duke Henry of Bavaria, for his widowed son Romanos. He may have believed that Hadwig's uncle might one day reign as *imperator*, or at least exercise lordship over the kingdom of Italy: Greek envoys were present when Berengar of Ivrea swore

---

[13] *DAI*, c. 26/1–5, 44–5, 66–72.   [14] Liudprand, *Antapodosis* VI, 2.
[15] *DAI*, cc. 38–40; Skylitzes, *Synopsis*, p. 239.

fides to Otto at Augsburg in 952. But he may also have envisaged Henry as a prospective in-law because of his occupation of Aquileia, which bridged Byzantine interests in Venice and the Dalmatian coast. Around this time Henry went on the offensive against the Hungarians and captured 'much booty',[16] which cannot have escaped Byzantine notice. Allegedly, however, Hadwig herself refused the match and Byzantine bids lapsed. Instead, Constantine intervened directly in the central Mediterranean. In 956 he sent a large expeditionary force to overawe rebels in Calabria and Apulia, reduce Naples to submission and attack the Saracen raiders in their Sicilian base. All this was accomplished, but the underlying purpose was apparently the defensive one of relieving southern Italy of Muslim pressure.

Substantive change in the tempo and tenor of east–west relations was, however, imminent. Other westerners were trying to correspond with Byzantium, judging by a decree issued by Doge Peter IV Candiano in June 960. This implies that the Venetians' carriage of letters from northern Italians, Bavarians, Saxons and others to the emperor was increasing and bans the delivery of letters other than those customarily passing 'from our palace'.[17] Byzantium soon began to deploy its newly enlarged armed forces elsewhere, notably in Sicily. Taormina fell to the Muslims for a second time in 962. A huge Byzantine force including heavy cavalry landed on Sicily in the autumn of 964, but it was soon crushed at Rametta; the fleet was destroyed in a subsequent action. An attempt to assemble another, more modest, task-force in Calabria in 965 was abortive. Byzantium was nevertheless better placed and disposed to flex muscles in the west than it had been since the seventh century, and the later 960s saw some administrative reorganisation: the newly instituted *katepano Italias* ('katepano of Italy') was of high rank and may have had some supervisory duties over all Byzantium's possessions on the peninsula. It was coincidence rather than cause and effect that the two leading Christian powers simultaneously turned their attention towards parts of Italy. Already in the late 950s Byzantines envisaged the reconquest of Crete as the prelude to victory in Sicily, while Otto I's intervention in Italy came in response to appeals from nearly every prominent figure, including John XII. While it is difficult to assess Otto's understanding of his title of *imperator*, his crowning by the pope or the relevance to this rite of the city of Rome, they undoubtedly gave him reason to care about the pope's future allegiance. John XII soon tried to make contact with Constantinople and so did Berengar's son, Adalbert. Otto was aware of John's appeals for Byzantine assistance, judging by the allegations which Liudprand puts into his mouth.[18]

[16] 'praeda magna', Widukind, *Res gestae Saxonicae* II, 36, p. 95.
[17] 'de nostro palatio', Tafel and Thomas, *Urkunden* I, p. 21.
[18] Liudprand, *Historia* c. 6, p. 163; Hiestand (1964), p. 219 and n. 129.

Several other issues troubled relations between the new *imperator* and his eastern counterpart. These were probably not all clearly understood at the time and this and the delays caused by distance made the course of events still more tortuous. First, there was the question of the interrelationship between two empires, each of which had some call on the imperial Roman past. One of the foundation-stones of Byzantine imperialism was that Constantine the Great had by God's will moved legitimate leadership from 'old Rome' to 'the reigning city' on the Bosphorus. Much self-congratulatory ceremonial affirmed that inheritance, as did the emperor's title, 'emperor of the Romans', on his seals and coins. The *De thematibus* – not a work of propaganda – stated flatly that the city of Rome had 'put aside' imperial power and was mainly controlled by the pope.[19] A mid-tenth-century Arabic historian, Ma'sudi, noted that the city's ruler wore no diadem and did not call himself emperor.[20] The Byzantine government must have been aware that Louis III and Berengar of Friuli had called themselves *imperator* following a papal coronation, and Berengar's realm is even termed a *basileia* ('empire') by Constantine.[21] But if Byzantium did not actively oppose the western war-lords' pretensions, neither did it actively encourage them. Hugh of Arles adapted various Byzantinising modes of depicting his majesty, such as gold bulls and documents written in gold on purple parchment, and his daughter married a porphyrogenitus. This rendered Hugh's status comparable to that of the *basileus*, and Bertha's large dowry was probably meant to indicate parity. It was perhaps in deference to Byzantine sensitivities that he abstained from the imperial title. That these could be awakened is shown by Leo Phokas' denunciation of Liudprand's master in 968: he was not an *imperator*, but a *rex*.[22] Nikephoros, like most tenth-century *basileis*, had personal grounds to be vigilant about unauthorised use of the imperial title: he was an intruder in the palace, while even Constantine VII deemed it necessary to flaunt his purple birth. The Saxon *arriviste* was a different class of *imperator* from his tenth-century predecessors. He showed himself both more blind to the Greeks' concerns and less pressed to gain their recognition of his title than Charlemagne had been in 800.

A second potential source of tension was the Christianisation of eastern Europe. In 961, on the point of departure for Italy, Otto I sent a religious mission to Princess Olga of Kiev. The enterprise folded almost immediately and does not feature in Byzantine sources, but it displayed a certain readiness to intervene in the Byzantines' patch. Not that Byzantium was wholly inert: a Bishop Hierotheos had been sent to *Tourkia* (= Hungary) with the chieftain Gyula *c.* 948 and ecclesiastical ties were subsequently put on a permanent footing. A metropolitan of *Tourkia* was in office in 1028 and the see probably

---

[19] *apothesthai*, Constantine Porphyrogenitus, *De thematibus*, p. 94.
[20] Vasiliev (1950), p. 404.   [21] *DAI*, c. 26/37.   [22] Liudprand, *Relatio*, c. 2.

remained in existence through the eleventh century. The papacy was also interested in Hungary, and in 965 John XII was accused of trying to send two emissaries there among the envoys destined for Byzantium. More alarmingly for Byzantium, the appearance of Bulgarian envoys at Otto's court in 961 or 965/6 and in 973 suggested that the Hungarians were ceasing to act as a barrier between the east Franks and the Balkans.

Otto's actions in Italy touched some of these sore points. In December 967 he came to terms with Venice, largely renewing earlier *pacta* between rulers of the Italian realm and Venice. Doge Peter IV was married to a niece of the emperor. Otto had already gained the fealty of Pandulf Ironhead of Capua-Benevento, the leading power in south-central Italy. At the same time, the Greeks' very ability to make trouble in Rome confronted Otto with their continuing presence in the peninsula. There were more positive reasons for an accommodation with the *basileus*. A Greek marriage alliance would not merely demonstrate that Otto's predominance in the west was acknowledged by the other outstanding Christian ruler; it would also transfuse purple-born blood into his own descendants' line, enhancing their imperial status. Moreover, the connection would open up the *basileus'* store of portraits, emblems of authority and valuables. After Otto's imperial coronation in 962, his seals began to show him frontally, wearing a cross-topped crown and holding an orb and a sceptre, echoing though not copying contemporary Byzantine coins and imperial seals.

There were thus strong reasons for Otto to regularise his relations with the eastern emperor. The build-up of Byzantine armed forces in the central Mediterranean need not preclude an accommodation. Judging by one interpretation of a prophecy then current in Constantinople, some Byzantines viewed Otto as a future junior partner in a coming fight-to-the-death with the Saracen 'wild ass'.[23] Yet the negotiations reached an impasse with the visit of Liudprand to Constantinople in 968. It seems clear that Otto I, after Otto II's coronation as co-emperor, was impatient for a number of objectives: a fittingly purple-born bride for Otto II; the destruction of the Muslims' notorious lair in Fraxinetum as a demonstration of his God-given invincibility; and his own return to his northern power-base. Most of these aims are enumerated, and the impatience evinced, in a letter dated 18 January, 968. Time spent away from Saxony probably seemed time wasted, and this, rather than any positive desire to conquer the Byzantine south, probably made for Otto's bluff, fitfully minatory, tone towards the eastern empire. In the letter, Otto asserts that the Greeks 'will give up Calabria and Apulia ... unless we consent';[24] he had already given a

---

[23] *onagrum*, Liudprand, *Relatio*, c. 40.
[24] 'Apuliam et Calabriam provincias ... nisi conveniamus dabunt', Widukind, *Res gestae Saxonicae* III, 70, pp. 146–7.

hostage to fortune by publicising his bid for 'the step-daughter of Nikephoros himself, namely the daughter of Emperor Romanos'.[25] Otto's close counsellor Adalbert penned these words in, most probably, early 968, when Otto still publicly aspired to a top-ranking bride for his son. Otto II's coronation on 25 December 967 may well have originally been planned as a preliminary to the wedding. Otto's exasperation is understandable if, as is likely, his envoy Dominicus had returned with the news that Nikephoros was favourably disposed; for the Byzantine embassy which arrived on Dominicus' heels brought words of peace, but no porphyrogenita. Otto miscalculated badly in supposing that he could jolt the Greeks into compliance by an assault on Bari. Soon afterwards, Liudprand was despatched to finalise a marriage agreement and, seemingly, to fetch the bride. Otto probably planned to use Bari as a bargaining chip, while affirming to regional magnates such as Pandulf Ironhead, whom he had recently invested with the duchy of Spoleto, his ability to better the *basileus*.

Liudprand's mission was no more effective than Otto's assault on Bari had been. The venomous *apologia* which he wrote soon afterwards, the *Legatio*, registers a certain pattern of development. Dominicus had sworn that Otto would never invade imperial territory and according to Nikephoros he had given a written oath that Otto would never cause any 'scandal' to the eastern empire.[26] This sweeping undertaking had been flagrantly violated by Otto's simultaneous attack and styling of himself as emperor. Then Nikephoros proceeded to demand that Otto relinquish his bonds of fealty with the princes of Capua-Benevento, Pandulf and his brother Landulf. Nikephoros reiterated that they were rightfully his *douloi* and demanded that Otto 'hand them over',[27] but he may essentially merely have been seeking a disclaimer to these borderlands. That these were Nikephoros' top priority is shown by a subsequent proposal: even if a 'perpetual friendship' was no longer in play,[28] Liudprand could at least ensure that Otto would not aid the princes, whom Nikephoros said he was planning to attack. At the eleventh hour the prospect of a 'marriage treaty' to confirm 'friendship' was dangled before Liudprand;[29] the price would presumably have been an undertaking on Otto's behalf about the Lombard princes. Thus Liudprand's fulminations do not quite conceal the Byzantines' continued willingness to negotiate, and indeed he returned with official letters for emperor and pope. Otto's was sealed with a gold bull whereas the pope was only accorded silver, against custom. It may be that one, perhaps the principal, purpose of the *Legatio* was to counteract such emollient effects as the letter might have on Otto.

---

[25] 'privigna ipsius Nichofori, filia scilicet Romani imperatoris', Adalbert, *Reginonis Continuatio*, p. 178.
[26] *scandalizare*, Liudprand, *Relatio*, c. 25; cf. c. 31.   [27] 'eos tradat', Liudprand, *Relatio*, c. 27.
[28] 'perpetuam . . . amicitiam', Liudprand, *Relatio*, c. 36.
[29] 'firmare amicitiam foedere nuptiarum', Liudprand, *Relatio*, c. 53.

In the short term Liudprand's militancy was in key with Otto's. Otto invaded southern Italy again and in an Italian charter of 2 November 968 was represented as seeking the reconquest of all Apulia.[30] Otto's advance was, however, hindered by the numerous *kastra* whose construction Nikephoros and earlier emperors had encouraged. In 969 Byzantine forces went on the offensive. Pandulf Ironhead was captured while besieging Bovino and was shipped to Constantinople. In 970 Otto sent another mission to the new *basileus*, John Tzimiskes; one of the envoys may have been none other than Liudprand. The eventual outcome was a marriage agreement. Princess Theophanu was sent to Italy, and married to Otto II on 14 April 972. Soon afterwards, Otto and his father returned to Germany. Otto I had stayed on in the south four years longer than his letter of January 968 intimated. If the main reason for the delay was his quest for an imperial bride for his son, it is at first sight surprising that Theophanu was not in fact a porphyrogenita but 'the most splendid niece' of Tzimiskes, as Otto II's dowry charter terms her.[31] More than forty years later a chronicler could comment openly that she was *non virginem desideratam*; all the Italian and German magnates mocked at the match, while some urged that she be sent home.[32] There was at least one porphyrogenita available, but Tzimiskes apparently did not feel sufficiently threatened or tempted by Otto to offer her. Otto, for his part, could see that the Greeks' presence in the south was ineradicable. Moreover, his former adjutant, Pandulf, now urged peace, and although he continued to be Otto's vassal, he could no longer be counted on in future hostilities. Otto probably concluded that some sort of royal 'from the palace of the Augustus' was better than none.[33] The other issues do not seem to have carried the same weight with him. His very insistence on retaining Pandulf as his vassal suggests this: he was essentially trying to provide for his own inevitably prolonged absences from Rome, by forging close bonds with the leading potentate to the south. These alarmed the *basileus*, but really they signalled the marginal role which the city of Rome and central Italy played among Otto's concerns. Once Pandulf had been neutralised, Otto let other Mediterranean matters rest and returned to his Saxon grassroots.

OTTO III, ROME AND BYZANTIUM

The nature and extent of the impact of Theophanu on Ottonian court culture is controversial and ambivalent.[34] The Byzantine late tenth- or early eleventh-

---

[30] D O I 368, p. 504. [31] 'neptim clarissimam', D O II 21, p. 29.

[32] Thietmar, *Chronicon* II, 15, p. 56.

[33] 'regalis'; 'augusti de palatio', *Vita Mathildis reginae antiquior*, c. 15, p. 141. See also Leyser (1995), p. 19.

[34] See Wentzel (1971), pp. 11–84; Leyser (1995), pp. 19–27; Westermann-Angerhausen (1995), pp. 244–64.

century *objets d'art* still extant in German cathedral treasuries and museums probably arrived by a variety of routes, not merely from Theophanu's sumptuous dowry. The emperor, however, remained the principal distributor. Some of the works had important symbolic functions beyond conspicuous display. Otto II is shown on an ivory – probably Italian-carved and now in the Musée de Cluny – wearing an imperial *loros* (a richly embroidered pendant sash) and other ornamented vestments. Theophanu also wears Byzantine imperial vestments and the couple are being crowned with *stemmata* (crowns) by Christ. Such depictions were current in contemporary Byzantium; in Germany they counterbalanced the fact that Theophanu had needed to be crowned by the pope before her wedding to Otto. The Byzantine origins of this visual statement – diffused through crude lead medallions[35] – may have been lost on most of Otto's subjects. But one should not underestimate the comprehension of the political elite; in 984 Gerbert of Rheims could assume that Archbishop Egbert of Trier would be familiar with the Greeks' custom of associating 'a new man' on the throne as 'co-emperor'.[36] It was probably in such matters that Byzantium had most to offer the Liudolfings. Its arsenal of symbols could help each ruler pass on the imperial crown – itself partly of Byzantine inspiration – to his chosen son. For a family with pretensions to being the *beata stirps* ('blessed family'), the emblems of long-established authority were of inestimable value.

Otto II, for his part, seems to have been more positively interested than his father in the imperial Roman past and its Italian foundation stones: the use by his Italian chancery of the title of *imperator Romanorum augustus* from March 982 signalled a keener commitment to Italian affairs. He tried to subjugate Venice, attacked Byzantine Taranto and aspired to the extra moral authority and power which expulsion of the Saracens from southern Italy would bring. In the 980s and 990s their depredations surpassed those of Fraxinetum's Muslims, whom a Byzantine naval blockade possibly helped local lords to destroy *c.* 972. A victorious Otto could have complemented his Roman title with the reclamation of Apulia and Calabria, eclipsing the *basileus* as *pallida mors Sarracenorum*.[37] However, Otto's army was virtually destroyed by the Saracens at Capo delle Colonne and he himself escaped only by swimming out to a Byzantine warship anchored offshore. He died fifteen months later, on 7 December 983, and was laid in an antique sarcophagus beneath a porphyry lid in St Peter's, Rome; here too, Byzantine imperial symbolism was echoed.

Considering Otto II's misadventures, his son might be expected to have emerged from his long minority with the limited goal of tightening control over his Teutonic subjects and rebellious Slavs. In fact Otto III showed

---

[35] Schramm and Mütherich (1962), p. 144 and plate 74.

[36] *novum, conregnantem,* Gerbert, *ep. 26.* Theophanu's uncle, Tzimiskes, was one such 'new man'.

[37] Liudprand, *Relatio,* c. 10; Ohnsorge (1983), pp. 199–200, 203–4.

unprecedentedly fervent attachment to both the city and the imperial mystique of Rome. He also came to envisage his hegemony as extending spiritually and ecclesiastically as far east as Poland and Hungary. Yet these tendencies did not manifest themselves all at once, and they were neither wholly consistent nor the product of Otto's whims alone. It was most probably his advisers who were responsible for the decision to seek a marriage-tie with Byzantium, only four or five years after Theophanu's death in 991. Her presence was evidently remembered as benign; it had presumably inspired Hugh Capet to seek a Byzantine princess for his son and heir, Robert, in 988. Gerbert, who had a hand in this *démarche*, was esteemed by Otto both as counsellor and as polymath: Otto expressed the desire that Gerbert would bring out his 'Greek exactitude' while banishing 'Saxon rusticity'.[38] But this serious-minded, highly strung adolescent was also strongly drawn to holy men whose vision was focused on God's kingdom or on spreading the Gospel on earth. First among these was Adalbert of Prague, who became Otto's spiritual father in 996. He seems to have aroused in Otto a longing for spiritual regeneration which intensified after Adalbert's martyrdom by the Prussians in the following year. Otto's yearning for personal salvation fused with a sense of mission to save others, itself a facet of his desire to resurrect the empire. Thus he joined with Boleslav of Poland in venerating Adalbert, personally laying the relics on the altar of Gniezno's cathedral in 1000. Otto came under the influence of other fathers, such as the group of hermits around Romuald whom he met in Rome in 1000; and St Nilus, the Calabrian Greek holy man who had moved from Rossano to a monastery near Gaeta, was urged by Otto to come and take charge of any monastery he might wish in Rome. Nilus was later visited by Otto, who is said to have wept and placed his crown in the old man's hands upon departing.[39]

Otto seems to have been able to converse freely with Nilus, and he had a reading knowledge of Greek. Thus one of the most formidable barriers to intercourse between Greek and western courts was, temporarily, lowered. But Theophanu's 'splendid retinue'[40] from Constantinople included no-one who emerged as a dominant figure in the Ottonian court or as a special adviser to the young Otto. The one Greek high in Theophanu's favour came not from Constantinople but from southern Italy. John Philagathos instructed Otto, his godson, in Greek for several years. In 989 or 990 he was put in charge of the administration at Pavia, overriding entrenched customs and interests there. Subsequently John was sent to Constantinople to negotiate the marriage alliance. He returned in late 996 with a Greek envoy, Leo of Synada. Soon he had been acclaimed pope in lieu of Otto III's appointee Gregory V; but before long John's chief patron, Crescentius, had been beheaded and he himself blinded, deposed and paraded around Rome,

---

[38] 'Greciscam . . . subtilitatem'; 'Saxonicam rusticitatem', Gerbert, *ep.* 186.

[39] *Vita S Nili iunioris,* col. 153.   [40] 'comitatuque egregio', Thietmar, *Chronicon* II, 15, p. 56.

seated back to front on a donkey, in the spring of 998. Leo of Synada claimed to have had a hand in John's elevation,[41] but this cannot have formed part of his original brief and the key axis was that between John Philagathos and the Crescentii. Nonetheless, Byzantine support for John was probably suspected by contemporaries, as it was by later writers, and the episode can scarcely have encouraged Otto to employ other Byzantine Italians.

In 1000, after his visit to Adalbert's shrine, Otto had Charlemagne's remains at Aachen exhumed and the body laid on Byzantine silks, evidently acting here as heir. He contemplated making Aachen his most favoured residence, but then chose another city, like Aachen on the periphery of his lands but still more deeply imbued with historical legitimacy. Otto determined in effect to abandon the essentially absentee lordship of Rome practised by his father and grandfather. He would make Rome a 'royal city' as a conscious riposte to the papacy's self-proclaimed 'apostolic' status and to self-willed local nobles.[42] The phrase was probably also a conscious evocation of the Byzantines' term for their own 'reigning city'. His choice of site is highly significant: the Palatine Hill, where the Caesars' palaces had stood from the reign of Augustus onwards. The outpourings of Otto's clerical staff reflect his residence there: some sixty-five diplomata were issued in or near Rome between May 996 and February 1001, two of them expressly stating that they were issued *in palatio monasterio*, probably an allusion to the adjoining monastery of S. Cesario on the Palatine.[43] Otto's installation of his court there for quite lengthy stretches from 998 onwards blatantly flouted the idea that the area within the city walls had been made over to the papacy by the Donation of Constantine.[44] There was no recent precedent for a large-scale secular court in Rome, but the citizens were acquainted with the luxury products and authority symbols of the Byzantine emperor. Otto's predecessors had used Byzantine-style media, such as the flamboyantly de luxe copy of Otto II's dowry charter for Theophanu. If Otto III borrowed more extensively, this was because he was trying to root his court in a city where such things clearly appealed to some of the leading families and where at the same time elaborate ceremonial trappings and liturgies daily glorified St Peter and his heir. The Byzantine extravaganza of palace ceremonies and street parades could bring to life the idea that the emperor conferred preeminence on the City by residing there and ensured divine favour for it through prayer. The new establishment on the Palatine was intended to be the node of a fresh network of bonds with laymen and clerics.

[41] Leo, Metropolitan of Synada, *Correspondence*, ed. and trans. Vinson, pp. 8, 16, 20.

[42] Schramm (1957), pp. 30, 168; Brühl (1968), p. 503. The fact that 'urbs regia' occurs in only one *arenga* of Otto's documents is emphasised by Görich (1993), p. 196.   [43] DD O III 383–4.

[44] Tellenbach (1982), pp. 243–4, 250; Brühl (1989a), pp. 4–6, 19 with n. 82, 24–9. For a different approach, see now Görich (1993), pp. 263–7.

A farrago of terms for officials emerges from Otto's diplomata. Two are of unmistakably Byzantine stripe, *logothetēs* and *prōtospatharios*. Otto began in 998 to call his chancellor for Italy, Heribert, *cancellarius et logotheta* (or *archilogotheta*). The title *prōtospatharios* is consistently borne by only one individual but he too is associated with the palace, as *comes palatii* in Italy. Most of the other terms come from the contemporary civilian administration of Rome or, as in the case of *imperialis palatii magister*, were Otto's own coinings. They feature principally in documents issued in or after 998, and exemplify Otto's efforts to represent himself as legitimate, palace-based master of the city.[45] From 1000 Otto also experimented with his own title, varying it in accordance with his location north or south of the Alps. Very little is known about the ceremonial envisaged for the palace. The descriptions in the *Libellus de caerimoniis aulae imperatoris* are mainly due to Peter the Deacon's mid-twelfth century fascination with classical Rome, though three protocols seem to date from Otto's time.[46] One conspicuous feature of court life was that Otto would sometimes sit at a separate table, elevated above his fellow diners. To dine apart, or with a few guests at a separate, raised, table was also the practice of the *basileus* at certain banquets, and this was probably the chosen model of Otto's dining ritual.

Otto also tried to earn the appreciation of Rome's citizens through his promotion of the cult of the Virgin as protectress of Rome. He even commissioned a hymn in her honour: 'Holy mother of God, look after the Roman people!'[47] The Virgin, rather than Sts Peter and Paul, is associated with the City, and Otto is acclaimed by name, a combination also to be found in contemporary Constantinople. The hymn was chanted through Rome's streets by the 'Greek School' on the Vigil of the Assumption in 1000. The impact of such rites was all the greater at a time when there was still a significant number of Greek-speakers in Rome; there seem to have been fresh arrivals of monks from the south then. Rome was both central to Otto's designs and the haunt of influential persons conversant with Byzantine ways, including Byzantine forms of punishment and degradation for rebels, such as those inflicted on Philagathos.

North of the Alps Otto's experiment with a new political culture could expect fewer sympathisers. The fairly plentiful finds in northern Germany of *objets d'art* showing distinctively Byzantine traits or workmanship do nevertheless show that some members of the north German elite had an appetite for

---

[45] See Schramm (1969a), pp. 288–97, who emphasises the un-Byzantine uses to which the terms *logotheta* and *protospatharius* were put. But that Byzantium's court culture was being consciously invoked to add solemnity and mystique to Otto's entourage is in itself significant. See also Leyser (1995), p. 27.

[46] Bloch (1984), pp. 87–9, 90–105, 119–27, 141–2; (1988), pp. 799–800, 823–6.

[47] 'sancta Dei genetrix, Romanam respice plebem!', *MGH Poet.* v, p. 468, line 59; Berschin (1980), p. 224.

such luxuries, and there is evidence that they adapted motifs like the symmetrical double portrait and *proskynesis* to their own family needs. Authority symbols such as the *loros* were assimilated by the reigning family. *Stemmata* of Byzantine design retained a place among the insignia of Henry II, while other items, such as the orb, seem to have belonged to an easily comprehensible vocabulary of God-given power common to eastern and western courts. Otto III's newly mounted political culture travelled in 1000 to the Slav north-east, to Gniezno. Otto is said to have removed a crown from his own head and placed it on Boleslav's, rendering him 'brother and partner of the empire'. Otto declared him 'friend and ally of the Roman people'.[48] A comparable crown-transfer is attested only once in Byzantine chronicles, but the emperor was accustomed to crown junior emperors and Caesars personally. Otto seems to have been consciously drawing on Byzantine rites and terminology to convey his own notion of his relationship with Boleslav as a kind of *primus inter pares*. He presented him with a gilded lance; for the Liudolfings a 'Holy Lance' – perhaps inspired by Byzantium and its cult of Constantine the Great – had long been a symbol of imperial authority. Nonetheless, Otto's new political order required frequent displays of military *virtus* and ample bounty, as well as ceremonial, and time would have been needed to instil it. Thietmar of Merseburg voices the incomprehension and dissatisfaction of some northerners in describing Otto's aim as being to revive 'the ancient customs of the Romans, now largely destroyed'.[49]

The reaction of the Byzantine government to Otto's experiment was as mixed as that of the Saxon nobility. Otto's initial attempts to tighten his hold on Rome are unlikely to have been welcome, but Leo of Synada's embassy implies at least willingness to sound out the young ruler; negotiations were still in progress, and Leo still in the west, in September 998. His observations of the turmoil in Rome could have persuaded the government that Otto was too weak to warrant a porphyrogenita. Yet a few years later, in response to another request or proposal from Otto, Byzantium acceded and a daughter of Constantine VIII landed at Bari, probably in February or March 1002, too late to find Otto alive. Why was the eastern empire now so much more forthcoming, subjecting Zoe to a sea-voyage in winter? Otto's pretensions and claims had grown in the meantime, and Gerbert's assumption of the name 'Sylvester' upon becoming pope in 999 signalled that Otto himself was a new Constantine. The signal was aimed mainly at Otto's heterogeneous subjects and the newly Christianised peoples in eastern Europe. But a poem composed

---

[48] 'fratrem et cooperatorem imperii'; 'populi Romani amicum et socium', Gallus Anonymus, *Chronicae*, pp. 19–20.

[49] 'antiquam Romanorum consuetudinem iam ex parte magna deletam', Thietmar, *Chronicon* IV, 46, p. 184.

soon after Gregory V's return to Rome in 998 claims that 'golden Greece' and the Muslims fear Otto and 'serve [him] with necks bowed'.[50] The poem, probably chanted at a festival in Rome, challenged Byzantine claims to be sole continuators of the *imperium Romanum* and thus the crucible of legitimate earthly authority. Yet these various manifestations of Otto's God-given majesty did not win round all the leading families or the mob in Rome and his experiment with an *urbs regia* could therefore have been dismissed by the Byzantines as tawdry and ill-starred: Otto had to abandon his residence there in 1001. Such things probably did not go unnoticed by easterners passing through Rome. Otto's one foray into southern Italy, in 999, took him only to Benevento and Capua, and was not notably effective, nor is there evidence that he claimed southern Italy.

Otto did show a pronounced interest in Venice, and visited Doge Peter II Orseolo in April 1001. Already the godfather of a son of Peter named after him, he now became godfather to the Doge's daughter. Otto's visit may have been viewed with unease from Byzantium; the empire's position in the Adriatic was hard pressed after the loss of Dyrrachium to Samuel of Bulgaria. Samuel lacked a fleet to reduce Byzantium's subject cities on the Dalmatian coast; his incursions probably ranged no further north than Ragusa. But they may well have occasioned Doge Peter's show of force down the coast in 999, when he received oaths of *fidelitas* from the notables of Zara, Split and most of the other Dalmatian towns.

Whether this operation was undertaken with prior Byzantine approval is uncertain, but Venice's fleet had proved its efficacy in an area where Byzantine possessions were beleaguered. This alone could account for Byzantium's close attention to Venice and any other power exercising leverage over it. Another, related reason may lie behind Byzantium's readiness to oblige Otto III. Basil II was about to lead his army up the Danube against Samuel. As Samuel was probably linked to Stephen of Hungary through two marriage alliances, Basil was liable to be attacked by Stephen, and he most probably joined forces with a Hungarian potentate in the region of Vidin, Ahtum-Ajtony. Otto may have appeared a useful potential restraint on Stephen, for Stephen was married to the sister of Duke Henry of Bavaria and through 'the grace and urging' of Otto he received a crown and, most probably, a gilded lance in late 1000;[51] such links gave Otto a certain moral leadership. If word of Otto's *démarches* towards Hungary reached Byzantium in 1001, while preparations for the daring venture up the Danube were afoot, this could have tipped the balance in favour of Otto's repeated requests for a marriage-tie.

---

[50] 'aurata Grecia'; 'collis flexis serviunt', *MGH Poet.* v, p. 479 and apparatus criticus. See also Gerbert, *Lettres*, ed. Havet, p. 237.

[51] 'gratia et hortatu', Thietmar, *Chronicon* IV, 59, p. 198.

This explanation, though hypothetical, fits the pattern of east–west relations throughout the tenth century. The Balkans, especially Bulgaria, loomed large among the concerns of the Byzantine government; matters further afield were mostly of secondary importance. A well-disposed Otto might do little more than discourage Stephen of Hungary from attacking Basil's Danubian expedition, but Otto will have seemed likely to be a force in east-central Europe for many years to come, and for his good offices a porphyrogenita probably seemed a price worth paying.

Otto III's death and his successor's preoccupation with affairs north of the Alps loosened Byzantino-German relations for almost two decades. Basil II for his part was embroiled in the Bulgarian war. It was the Venetians who came to the relief of Bari when it was in danger of falling to the Saracens in 1003, and the Sicilians and North Africans continued to pillage the south Italian coastline through the opening decades of the eleventh century. Imperial authority suffered another blow when an Apulian notable, Melo, instigated a revolt *c.* 1009. This was far from being the first local insurrection, but it was serious, involving Ascoli as well as Bari. The imperial authorities took several years to suppress it and Melo then fled to the courts of Lombard princes. Subsequently, in 1017, he mounted another challenge to imperial power, relying heavily on a band of Normans, at first exiguous but later reinforced. This is the first occasion when the Normans' armed presence in the south is indubitable. Melo now ventured to fight pitched battles and several important towns such as Trani renounced imperial authority. However, in October 1018 Melo and his Normans were defeated at Cannae by Basil Boioannes, the *katepano* of *Italia*.

Boioannes was assisted by the fact that Bulgaria was being pacified. The forces which he led onto the battlefield were like 'bees issuing forth from a full hive'.[52] But he showed great organisational talent, building numerous strongholds in northern Apulia. Several towns were founded in a system on the Byzantine side of the River Fortore, including Civitate and Fiorentino. Others were founded in Calabria. Boioannes expressly claimed to be restoring at Troia a town long abandoned; the name and site of Civitate likewise evoked classical antiquity. Troia lay only 215 kilometres from Rome.

Boioannes' prime objective was to consolidate Apulia's northern defences and overawe the borderland princelings. But the effect was to provoke the German emperor and aggravate the hostility which Pope Benedict had already shown in granting a fortress on the Garigliano to Melo's brother-in-law, Datto. In 1017 Benedict had probably put the band of Norman fortune-seekers in contact with Melo and the Lombard princes of Capua and Naples. Benedict

---

[52] 'comme li ape quant il issent de lor lieu quant il est plein', Amatus of Monte Cassino, *Storia de'Normanni*, p. 29.

also looked to the German emperor as a patron of church reform and counter-weight to the Crescentii, and it was to Henry II's court that Melo fled after Cannae. In 1020 Benedict himself accepted Henry's invitation and crossed the Alps to Bamberg, where he exchanged the kiss of peace with Henry and cele-brated the liturgy using the *filioque* clause in the creed, a heretical interpolation in Byzantine eyes. Henry seems to have made explicit his claim to overlordship in the south by conferring on Melo the title of *dux Apuliae*. However, on 23 April 1020 Melo died. The following spring Boioannes suddenly attacked Melo's brother-in-law on the Garigliano. The fortress was handed over to Pandulf IV of Capua, now a Byzantine vassal; Datto himself was paraded through Bari's streets on a donkey, then thrown in the sea. Henry II marshalled a large army and reached Ravenna at the end of December, 1021. A detach-ment was sent to deal with Pandulf and his cousin Atenulf, abbot of Monte Cassino. Henry led the main force towards the base which had assisted Boioannes to operate so effectively on the Garigliano, an area where Picingli had required allies a hundred years earlier. Henry besieged Troia for about three months, until his army succumbed to dysentery, the *basileus'* abiding ally against intruders from the north. Henry eventually managed to extract token submission from Troia, but soon after his withdrawal the inhabitants opened the gates to Boioannes. So long as Henry stayed in the south, he could overawe the Lombard princes. Pandulf IV, besieged in Capua, sued for terms and was stripped of his principality; the prince of Salerno, Guaimar, surrendered; and a new abbot was installed at Monte Cassino in lieu of Atenulf. But Boioannes' barrier fortress stood undemolished: Henry's southern foray had made no more impact on Byzantine Apulia than Otto I's or Otto II's had done.

In 1025 the eastern empire appeared on course towards reconquering Sicily and dominating traffic in the central Mediterranean when Basil II died and his expedition lapsed. But Byzantine Italy was becoming more prosperous and populous than it had been for centuries. Many of its inhabitants seem to have preferred the distant, undemanding *basileus* as the safeguard of their interests, while Byzantine emperors contemplated yet another Sicilian expedition. Byzantium's build-up of power in southern Italy antagonised the papacy and the western emperor, but it was small groups of predators whose energies, greed and organisational skills wore down the Byzantine authorities in the mid-eleventh century. The spoils of the burgeoning towns and, eventually, power over them would go to these self-reliant freebooters, hailing from the shores of a northern sea.

CHAPTER 26

SOUTHERN ITALY IN THE TENTH CENTURY

G. A. Loud

THE SEVENTY years before 900 were an era of disorder and continued crisis in southern Italy. The government of the principality of Benevento, which ruled over most of the south of the peninsula, was riven by succession disputes which led to the formal partition of the principality in 849. But, far from ending the contention, this division gave only a brief pause in the internecine strife. Muslim attacks from Sicily and North Africa threatened to swamp a feeble and divided Christian defence, and the local rulers were far more intent on their internal power struggles than on making any coherent and effective stand against the invader. However, the years round about 900 marked a very significant change, with regard both to the internal stability of southern Italy and also to its relative freedom from external threat (or at least from the threat of conquest rather than sporadic raiding). For much of the tenth century the land was to be, if not exactly peaceful, at least freed from the dreary litany of civil war and the establishment of territorial footholds for further Muslim advance that had made the previous period a time of trouble and strife, the impact of which was reflected in the prevailing pessimism of contemporary chroniclers such as Erchempert, and in the number of contemporary charters mentioning relatives captured by the Saracens.

This change was marked by three factors. First, there was the revival of Byzantine power in the late ninth century. Under the governorship of Nikephoros Phokas in the 880s the Byzantines had recovered much of northern Calabria and consolidated their hold in southern Apulia. The creation of the new *thema* (province) of *Langobardia* at this period was part of the process of consolidation, as was the creation of new dioceses in Calabria after 886. Visits by local rulers to Constantinople (those of Guaimar I of Salerno in 887 and Landulf I of Benevento in 910), as well as the use once again of the regnal years of the Byzantine emperor in the dating clauses of documents from both the cities of the west coast and the Lombard principalities, demonstrate the

14 Southern Italy

restored prestige of the empire.[1] Secondly, there was much greater internal stability in those parts of southern Italy not ruled by Byzantium. In 900 a bloodless coup had installed Atenulf I of Capua as ruler of Benevento as well, and a few months later another coup displaced Guaimar I of Salerno, who was despatched to end his days as a monk. But while these events might seem to have been merely a continuation of the chaos in the Lombard principalities of the ninth century, in fact they marked an end to it. The union of the two principalities of Capua and Benevento was to last for eighty-one years, and Guaimar I was merely replaced by his son, who remained as prince, apparently unchallenged, until his death in old age in 946. Thirdly, there was the threat from Islam. The conquest of Taormina, the last major Byzantine bastion in Sicily, early in 902, was indeed the prelude to a renewed invasion of the mainland, into Calabria in the late summer of that year. But the death of its leader, Ibrāhīm ʿAbd-Allāh, at Cosenza in October marked not just the end of that invasion, but also the end of serious threat for many years, as internal instability proved as much of a problem in Islamic Sicily in the tenth century as it had in Lombard south Italy in the ninth.

Thus from *c.* 900 onwards the political structures of southern Italy remained, at least outwardly, more or less in equilibrium. Apulia and Calabria were ruled by the Byzantine empire, each with its own provincial government, based respectively at Bari and (probably) at Reggio. The southern Campania and the Cilento region formed the Lombard principality of Salerno, which had been created by the division of 849. The central mountain region and the bulk of the Terra di Lavoro, the two principalities of Capua and Benevento,[2] were ruled by the descendants of Atenulf I of Capua, to judge by their surviving diplomata largely from Capua. Three coastal duchies, from north to south Gaeta, Naples and Amalfi, retained their independence from the Lombard principalities, as they had always jealously done, but each of them was really only one city with a very small dependent territory. Given how limited their hinterlands were, their economies were largely dependent on overseas trade.

The effective cessation of Muslim attempts at conquest after 902 still left one very serious problem for the security of the principalities of the west coast unresolved, namely the Saracen colony at the mouth of the River Garigliano, established *c.* 881. From here the north of the principality of Capua and the Abruzzi region lay at the invaders' mercy. Indeed in 881-3 raiders from the

---

[1] Imperial regnal years were used in Gaeta up to 934 and in Naples throughout this period In Capua and Benevento usage was more sporadic, but the princes referred to their title of *patrikios* up to 920: von Falkenhausen (1967), pp. 32, 37.

[2] Cilento (1966), pp. 149–50 argues that the use of terms like 'the principality of Capua' is anachronistic since the early tenth-century rulers described themselves as prince without any territorial designation, but cf. the *Chronicon Salernitanum*, c. 159, p. 167: 'Atenulfus Beneventanus princeps' and c. 172, p. 175, 'Beneventi fines'.

Garigliano had destroyed the famous and prosperous inland monasteries of Monte Cassino and S. Vincenzo al Volturno, whose surviving monks had had to take refuge for a generation or more in Capua. A first attack on the Garigliano base, launched by Atenulf I of Capua in 903, failed, not least because of support lent to the Saracens by the forces of the duke of Gaeta.[3] Under papal auspices a second, and this time successful, attack was made in 915. A prolonged diplomatic campaign, conducted by both the papacy and the Byzantine government, deprived the Muslims of their Christian allies (the coastal cities of Amalfi and Gaeta whose trading interests had led them to seek accommodation with the Arabs), and secured the reinforcement of the local armies of Capua and the duchy of Naples by troops from central Italy and from Byzantine Apulia, under the personal command of the *stratēgos* of *Langobardia*.[4] The destruction of the Garigliano colony ensured that southern Italy was in future to be free from serious Muslim threat, even though raids on Calabria continued intermittently for much of the century, often bought off by the payment of tribute. Occasionally such attacks also menaced the southern part of Apulia. Oria was, for example, sacked in 925, and Taranto in 928. But these were essentially plundering expeditions, not attempts to establish bridge-heads for further conquest, and as such they were of only very limited significance.

Indeed, after 915 the problem for the Byzantine government was rather disaffection among the inhabitants of their provinces, combined with the ambitions of the princes of Capua to extend their rule towards the Adriatic coast. The *stratēgos* of Calabria, John Muzalon, was assassinated in an uprising near Reggio in 921, and soon afterwards the *stratēgos* of *Langobardia*, Ursoleon, was killed at Ascoli fighting against the forces of Capua-Benevento, which went on to occupy much of northern Apulia, apparently with the support of the local inhabitants. The fiscal pressure of Byzantine rule was undoubtedly one factor creating disaffection, and it was, as the Calabrian revolt shows, by no means confined to the Latin areas under Byzantine rule.[5] But the desire of the princes of Capua to recover those parts of Apulia which had been under the rule of their predecessors at Benevento up to the middle of the ninth century, and to secure control of coastal towns like Siponto and Bari which benefited from trade in the Adriatic, should not be underestimated. That this was a very real ambition is clear from the attempt of Landulf I after his victory at Ascoli to persuade the Byzantine government to appoint him as *stratēgos* of *Langobardia*, something which not surprisingly the authorities at Constantinople were reluc-

---

[3] *Chronica Monasterii Casinensis* I, 50. [4] Vehse (1927) remains the best discussion.

[5] Gay (1904), pp. 202–4 shows that the two revolts were separate, despite some confusion in the sources. For a later revolt in Greek Calabria, protesting against exactions for military service, see the *Vita S. Nili iunioris*, cc. 60–2.

tant to do.[6] It seems, although details are obscure, that the Byzantine position in Apulia was restored for a time after 921, but a second Beneventan invasion in 926, this time with the support of the prince of Salerno (apparently not involved in 921) proved more serious. For some seven years substantial parts of Apulia were in the hands of the princes of Capua-Benevento, and parts of Lucania and northern Calabria under the rule of the prince of Salerno, and the status quo was only restored when the Byzantine government secured an alliance with King Hugh of Italy which, combined with substantial military reinforcement from Constantinople, achieved the withdrawal of the Lombard princes.[7] But from *c.* 934 onwards, for more than thirty years, the frontier between the principality of Benevento and the Byzantine province of *Langobardia* remained relatively secure, if not entirely uncontested, especially in the late 940s.

Despite problems on the province's northern border, Byzantine rule in Calabria was largely unaffected by the tense relations with the Lombard principalities, and indeed for some considerable period Calabria was also free from Arab raids from Sicily. Tribute money paid from the province to Sicily apparently ceased after 934, and in the latter part of this decade the Muslims on the island were in the grip of civil war. It was only after internal peace was restored in Sicily in 947 that Calabria was once again threatened. Reggio was captured in 950, and a further attack took place in 952, but once again the payment of protection money secured a period of truce.

The Byzantines were therefore able to maintain, albeit with some difficulty, their dominions in Italy more or less as they had been secured by the reconquests of the 880s. What they were not able to do, more than very sporadically, was to enforce any recognition of their rule in the petty duchies of the west coast, or still less in the Lombard principalities. Only in Naples did documents continue to be dated by the regnal years of the Byzantine emperors, and such links were of far more cultural than political significance. Indeed in 956, when the government in Constantinople was able to release sufficient troops for a major expedition to Italy, the first target of that offensive was apparently Naples (although that may quite possibly have been to secure Neapolitan naval assistance against renewed Arab attacks on Calabria). Furthermore, it would seem that at this period, once again, there was disaffection in those areas under direct Byzantine rule.[8] Byzantium was a 'super-power', unlike the independent south Italian states. But for its government southern Italy was of far less

---

[6] Nikolaos Mystikos, *Letters*, no. 85, pp. 338–42.

[7] The period of seven years is given by Liudprand, *Relatio*, c. 7. From 935 the regnal years of the emperors appeared occasionally in Beneventan charters: Mor (1952), p. 263. Details of the troops sent to Italy are given by Constantinus Porphyrogenitos, *DC* II, 44.

[8] Theophanes Continuatus, *Chronographia*, pp. 453–4.

moment than either the frontier with the Muslim world in Asia Minor or the defence of its European provinces against the Bulgarians, and it was not surprising that for the most part the defence of its Italian dominions was left to local efforts, and that only very occasionally could imperial troops or ships be spared in any numbers. Even in 956 the policy was essentially defensive, to secure a commitment by the Lombard princes not to attack Byzantine territory, to enforce effective government in that territory, and to prevent further raids on Calabria. The one exception to this limited policy came with the launching of a large-scale expedition to Sicily by the Emperor Nikephoros Phokas in 964, but the disastrous defeat which resulted cannot have encouraged further such ambitious enterprises, and renewed military operations in other theatres anyway prevented a fresh attempt.

Moreover, in 966 the balance of power in southern Italy was to be, for a time, seriously affected by a new player on the stage, the German ruler Otto I, who in reviving Charlemagne's western Roman empire also revived Carolingian imperial claims to overlordship over southern Italy. The means through which Otto sought to vindicate his claims were both direct military action and an alliance with the strongest of the local rulers in the south, the prince of Capua and Benevento, Pandulf I Ironhead (961–81). What this meant in practice was that the Capuan pressure on the Byzantine frontier in northern Apulia of the 920s and 930s was once again revived, but with the formidable military assistance of the German emperor.

The alliance with Pandulf Ironhead served a further purpose for the German emperor too. By conceding, as he did, the margravate of Camerino and the duchy of Spoleto to the prince of Capua, he not only secured a vital ally and recognition of his overlordship in the south, but also created a viceregal power in central Italy through which he could the more effectively control the Roman nobility, understandably restive at the prospect of a series of Ottonian clients being placed on the papal throne. For Pandulf it ensured not merely the chance to revive his ancestors' ambitions to encroach on Byzantine territory in Apulia, but also the protection of his own dominions from incursions from the north, as had apparently occurred in the early 960s.[9] Otto himself made a brief visit to Benevento in February 967, and in the spring of 968 a full-scale attack was made on Byzantine Apulia which reached as far as Bari before the allies withdrew. A further attack took place in the winter of that year which took the imperial army as far south as the Calabrian border. But in the end very little was accomplished. After Otto I had returned to northern Italy the prince of Capua was captured while besieging Bovino on the Apulian frontier and sent as a prisoner to Constantinople. It was in good measure due to his intercession, after a

---

[9] *Chronicon Salernitanum*, c. 166, p. 170.

further year's inconclusive warfare, that a peace between the two empires was eventually patched up, sealed by the marriage of the young Otto II to a Byzantine princess, Theophanu.

The overwhelming impression given by this period of conflict, as indeed by the sporadic border warfare of the earlier part of the century, was of its essential sterility. Each side was capable of deep penetrations into the other's territory – Byzantine troops briefly got as far as Capua in the summer of 969 – but neither was strong enough to make any permanent impression. While the Byzantines held on to key border fortresses like Ascoli and Bovino the province of *Langobardia* was essentially safe. Furthermore the enhancement of the prince of Capua's authority was hardly in the interests of the other local rulers, who, while they had no wish to be Byzantine clients, were equally unwilling to be those of the prince of Capua and the German emperor. The duke of Naples supported the Byzantine invasion of Capuan territory in 969, and while the prince of Salerno did not, and in fact sent a relieving force to Capua, he seems to have otherwise tried to keep on good terms with the Greeks. Significantly the late tenth-century Salerno chronicle took a favourable view of the Emperor Nikephoros, very different from the famous (and libellous) portrait of the emperor by Otto's envoy to his court, Liudprand of Cremona.[10] And around 966 the duke of Amalfi was once again, after a long interval, using a Byzantine title, sign of renewed contact with the government at Constantinople.[11]

The conflict between the two empires in the 960s had a further aspect, however, and one which was of very considerable significance for southern Italy. In 966, while he was taking refuge with Prince Pandulf from the hostile nobility of Rome, Otto's client Pope John XIII raised the see of Capua to be a metropolitan archbishopric. Two years later, at the height of the military conflict in Apulia, he did the same for that of Benevento. While the creation of the archbishopric of Capua should almost certainly be seen as a recognition of Capua's status as Pandulf's *de facto* capital and as an attempt to boost princely authority over the rest of the principality (the first archbishop was his younger brother John), the creation of the new ecclesiastical province of Benevento was overtly anti-Byzantine. The authority granted to the archbishop stretched deep into Byzantine territory, and among the new suffragan sees to be subject to it were Ascoli and Bovino, the two key border fortresses under siege from Otto's and Pandulf's forces. Since the bulk of the population of Byzantine Apulia were Latins, the loyalties of their churchmen were clearly of crucial importance to the Byzantine government, and the creation of the new archbishopric of Benevento, which was intended to destabilise northern Apulia,

[10] 'Vir bonus et iustus', *ibid.*, c. 173, p. 176.
[11] Schwarz (1978), pp. 37, 243, for the dating, contra Gay (1904), p. 321.

was to have wide-ranging repercussions. The Byzantines moved in turn to reorganise the church in Apulia, to create new archiepiscopal sees to rival Benevento, and to ensure that the Apulian church remained loyal to Constantinople. In the 980s, when Otto II tried once again to invade Byzantine territory, the creation of the archbishopric of Salerno by Benedict VII was a further anti-Byzantine ecclesiastical measure, including as it did the subordination to Salerno of the sees of Cosenza and Bisignano in Calabria, previously suffragans of the Greek archbishop of Reggio and in areas clearly under Byzantine jurisdiction, but which, unlike most of Calabria, almost certainly contained a substantial Latin population.[12] Here too the Byzantine authorities reacted with ecclesiastical changes of their own, including the creation of an archbishopric at Cosenza in defiance of papal authority.

The ecclesiastical changes after 970 were part of a more general overhaul of the administrative structure of Byzantine Italy. In part this was a reaction to the renewed threat to its borders, but it also reflected changes in the distribution of its population. Quite how extensive these were has been a matter of some debate among historians.[13] But it seems clear that Arab raids on Calabria, which while not by any means continuous were undoubtedly alarming and destructive, encouraged the population both to retreat from coastal settlements to more defensible hill sites inland and, in some cases, to move northwards towards the borderlands with the principality of Salerno. Some Greeks living in Sicily under Arab rule may also have crossed the Straits of Messina and moved northwards, although the evidence for this is almost entirely derived from contemporary saints' Lives, and we cannot be certain that the movement of these holy men was accompanied by any substantial numbers of laymen. Christian monks may well have been more obviously at risk in periods of disorder in Sicily, as in the 940s, than the laity who were less of a provocation to the Muslim devout.[14] But, whatever the case here, nearly all the saints' Lives from tenth-century Calabria show their protagonists settling around the northern frontiers of the province, in the regions of Mercourion and (further north still) Latinianon, the second of which had in the ninth century been a gastaldate of the principality of Salerno. The saints' Lives certainly imply that their subjects were not the only Greeks present in these regions. St Luke of Armento, for example, spent some seven years in the Val di Sinni in Latinianon before he fled

---

[12] The earliest evidence for Salerno as an archbishopric comes in a papal bull of 989, which is clearly retrospective; Gay (1904), p. 358 argued convincingly that the promotion should be dated to the summer of 983, and this has been generally accepted, e.g. by von Falkenhausen (1967), p. 148, Taviani-Carozzi (1991b), p. 673.

[13] Notably between Ménager (1958) and Guillou (1970), especially essay no. IX.

[14] For example St Elias the Speleote (*c.* 865–*c.* 960) left Sicily after his companion at his hermitage was killed by the Arabs, *AASS Septembrii* III (11 September), col. 851; Ménager (1958), p. 763.

to escape a crowd of would-be disciples.[15] Some Greeks, both monks and laymen, crossed into Lombard territory. The most famous example was St Nilus of Rossano, who towards the end of the century spent some fifteen years at Valleluce, near Monte Cassino. But his was not the only case. In the eleventh century there were at least four Greek monasteries in the vicinity of Salerno, and one as far away as Pontecorvo, near the northern border of the principality of Capua.[16]

The expansion of the Greek population of Calabria into the heel of Italy led to administrative changes both lay and ecclesiastical. From the 880s onwards there had been two separate and apparently independent provinces of Byzantine Italy, *Langobardia* (that is Apulia) and Calabria up to the 940s still officially and anachronistically known as the theme of Sicily, although the Byzantines only retained a few isolated strongholds in the north-east of the island). In the time of Nikephoros Phokas there came a change. The theme of *Langobardia*, strategically the more significant of the two since through its ports the mouth of the Adriatic was in Byzantine hands and easy access was possible to the European mainland of the empire, was placed under an official known as the Catepan, of more senior rank and status than previous governors. It is probable that he was placed in overall authority over Byzantine Italy, and it is also likely that at the same time, although the dating is far from certain, a new province was created, that of Lucania, which embodied those areas to the north of Calabria into which there had recently been an influx of Greeks, namely the Latinianon, Lagonegro and Mercurion regions. A new diocese, Tursi, was set up as the bishopric for Lucania.[17] Tursi was made part of a new metropolitan province, subject to the previously autocephalous archbishopric of Otranto. Both these sees had Greek clergy, but in addition four Latin sees in southern Apulia, Tricarico, Acerenza, Matera and Gravina were also subjected to the archbishop of Otranto. In the next few years two further Apulian sees were raised to the status of archbishoprics, Taranto in 978, and Trani in 987. The process was continued in the early eleventh century when archbishoprics were erected at Lucera, Brindisi and Siponto. The intention here was to bind the Latin clergy of these sees firmly to the Byzantine government, and to combat the claims of the archbishop of Benevento. The policy was not anti-Latin. Given that the majority of the population in all but the extreme south of Apulia was Latin it could not be, and the claim by Liudprand of Cremona that

---

[15] *AASS Octobrii* vi (October 13), col. 339; Ménager (1958), pp. 767–8.

[16] Borsari (1950); (1963), pp. 58–60, 71–5; Loud (1994a), pp. 38–41. For examples of Greek laymen in the principality of Salerno see *Codex diplomaticus Cavensis* II, pp. 235–6, no. 384 (986) and III, pp. 88, no. 521 (999).

[17] von Falkenhausen (1967), pp. 46–7, 65–8, 104 would argue that the theme of Lucania was created in the eleventh century and had only an ephemeral existence, and that Calabria was not subject to the Catepan's authority. Guillou (1965) makes a very convincing case to the contrary.

Nikephoros Phokas and the Patriarch Polyeucht wanted to forbid the Latin rite in southern Italy is clearly ludicrous.[18] Sees with Latin bishops and clergy remained Latin, even in towns like Taranto where most of the population were Greek. But these ecclesiastical changes were clearly political, to exclude the influence of the papacy, which was under the control of the Ottonians, and of the archbishopric of Benevento, which was an agent of the ambitions of Pandulf Ironhead and (perhaps, in so far as they had any power) his successors. The policy seems to have worked. In 983 the then catepan conceded a privilege to the Bishop of Trani in reward for his support during the recent siege of the town.[19] But no chances were taken. Latin churches in Apulia remained under very tight supervision. Sees were often combined together, and then split up once again. Officials of the government acted as the advocates (i.e. legal representatives) of churches. Occasional exemptions from taxation given to Latin clergy were very specific and very limited,[20] although this was part of a more general desire by the Byzantine authorities to preserve the fiscal base of the state.

Despite the continued hazard of Muslim raids on Calabria, a problem which, after a period of intermission, became serious once more from the mid-970s, the Byzantine provinces retained their cohesion, and even, in at least a modest way, flourished. Not only did Greek influence increase and push the border northwards in Lucania – and the creation of the theme was a recognition of this – but in the last years of the century, after Ottonian policy in southern Italy had collapsed and Pandulf Ironhead's dominions split, the Apulian frontier shifted northwards as well, from the River Ofanto to the River Fortore. The area of northern Apulia thus incorporated in the theme of *Langobardia* became known, significantly, as the Capitanata. At the end of the century the Byzantine administration can be seen in full operation as far inland as Tricarico on the Apulia–Lucania border, redefining boundaries and setting up new *khoria* (taxable units).[21] Monasteries were often the focus for the clearance of land and new settlement, particularly in the hitherto under-exploited Lucanian region, and the villages which developed around them were then officially incorporated as *khoria*. The population, it would seem, was expanding, although in Lucania (as described above) migration can explain new settlement. In a few cases population transfers may have been deliberate, although the evidence for this relates mainly to the reign of Leo VI (886–912), who is known to have sent settlers from the Peloponnese to southern Italy. By the end of the tenth century agriculture was apparently flourishing in at least parts of

---

[18] Liudprand, *Relatio*, c. 62. For the ecclesiastical changes generally see von Falkenhausen (1967), pp. 147–57; Martin (1993), pp. 563–72.

[19] *Le Carte che si conservano nell'archivio del capitolo metropolitano della città di Trani*, pp. 32–5, no. 7.

[20] E.g. *ibid.*, pp. 37–8, no. 8 to the archbishop of Trani (999), discussed by Borsari (1959), pp. 128–34.

[21] Holtzmann and Guillou (1961).

Calabria, with extensive vineyards and the beginnings of silk production which by the middle of the next century was on a considerable scale. Evidence for the external trade of the Byzantine provinces is so slim as to be virtually non-existent, but it would appear that in the tenth century Otranto and Brindisi were probably the most important ports, with Bari becoming more important in the eleventh.

While Calabria and Lucania, with a largely, if not exclusively, Greek population, might seem very much like other Byzantine provinces, Apulia was undoubtedly very different. The presence of a substantially Latin populace meant that the Byzantine government had to concede a degree of local autonomy, or at least variation, which was inconceivable in entirely Greek parts of the empire. While the provincial governors and some of their more senior officials were Greeks sent out from Constantinople, and in the case of the *stratēgoi* and catepans generally holding office for fairly brief periods (about three years on average), many of the more junior officials were Latins. At Bari in the late tenth and early eleventh centuries eight out of eleven recorded turmarchs (probably by this date town judges or governors rather than the immediate deputies of the provincial governor) were Latins, and only three Greeks. (In Taranto, by contrast, all but one known turmarchs were Greeks.) Such use of locally born Latin officers was probably even more prevalent in inland Apulia, where on occasion they might use titles such as gastald derived from the Lombard principalities, and in one case at least, from Lucera at the end of the century, model their documents on Beneventan princely charters.[22] Most significant was the widespread sanction given to the use of Lombard law. The growth of a fairly prosperous class of small-scale landed proprietors in Apulia, judged by their own law and with their own Latin churches, approved of but closely supervised by the provincial government, was probably the best guarantee for the stability of Byzantine government in Apulia. But it was by no means infallible. Revolts in the coastal towns occurred a number of times in the tenth century,[23] and intensified after 1000, although the role of contributory factors such as the abnormally harsh winter of 1007/8 should not be underestimated. Nor should the burden of taxation, which in Italy as in the rest of the Byzantine empire probably increased with the ambitious military policy of the late tenth-century emperors. While the Latin chroniclers tend to ascribe instances of disaffection in the Byzantine provinces to the demands or the cruelty of particular governors, one might well conclude that it was rather the reaction of the populace to a governmental system which was far more efficient, and thus by definition more oppressive, than that in the Lombard principalities.

---

[22] Von Falkenhausen (1973).

[23] E.g. at Conversano in 947, Trani in 982/3 and Bari in 986: Lupus Protospatharius, *Annales*, pp. 54–6; *Carte...di Trani*, no. 7.

These latter states, if one can use such a term about markedly inchoate organisations, presented a great contrast to Byzantine Italy. They were undoubtedly much more stable in the first three-quarters of the tenth century than they had been before 900, and whereas in that period the princely office had at times seemed little more than a football to be kicked back and forth among local gastalds and other members of the office-holding aristocracy, in the tenth century hereditary succession was the norm. This was made more certain by the nomination of sons as co-rulers in their father's lifetime, which was also the practice in the duchies of Naples and Amalfi. In the principality of Capua-Benevento family stability was ensured by joint rule between brothers, as well as father and son. On one occasion, very briefly in 939–40, this meant that there were no less than four persons using the princely title: Landulf I, two of his sons and his younger brother, Atenulf II. But generally there were no more than two princes holding office at any one time, and a younger brother associated with his elder could not expect to pass the title down to his children. There were never more than two brothers holding the princely title at the same time. Pandulf Ironhead associated only his eldest son with him as co-prince, although he had several younger ones as well, and he did that only after his younger brother's death in the winter of 968/9. It may sometimes have been the case that one prince (probably the senior) held Capua, while the other was associated with Benevento, as may at first sight be implied by the *Chronicon Salernitanum*'s account of Pandulf Ironhead hastily abandoning Otto I's army while it was on the Calabrian border on the news of his brother Landulf's death, and going to Benevento to secure his son's enthronement as prince. However, the same chronicle also shows the two brothers acting together at Capua a few months earlier, conducting the prince of Salerno to meet their overlord the Emperor Otto, and the significance of the incident may simply be that the palace church of St Sophia at Benevento remained the traditional place for a new prince to be enthroned, as it had been back in the eighth century.[24] Charters generally show princes acting together, as in fact Pandulf I and Landulf III invariably did in the 960s. In 943 Atenulf III, acting by himself, issued a group of charters for Monte Cassino, from Benevento. Although he did this in the name of his absent father and younger brother as well as on his own behalf, his action was almost certainly a symptom of a political crisis, for soon afterwards he was expelled from Benevento, according to the Salerno Chronicle for his 'sins and cruelty', and took refuge with his son-in-law, Guaimar II of Salerno.[25] It looks as though the attempt to associate several members of the princely family together as co-rulers in the late 930s had not

---

[24] *Chronicon Salernitanum*, cc. 169–70. It is, however, noteworthy that the Beneventans installed Landulf's son as their chosen prince in 982.

[25] Poupardin (1907), pp. 97–8, nos. 89–91; *Chronicon Salernitanum*, c. 159, p. 167.

been a success, or perhaps he was simply displaced by his younger brother, to whose sons the princely title was eventually to pass. But the episode suggests that a division of Capua or Benevento between individual princes was neither normal nor wise.

The association of a son with his father was clearly important in ensuring a smooth succession. Gisulf I of Salerno was made co-prince when only three years old.[26] From the few chronicle accounts we have it would seem, however, that whatever the importance of such designation and of the appearance of the co-prince in diplomata, in practice the senior ruler was the effective one who was considered to dictate policy. Only in exceptional circumstances would matters be different, and the most obvious would be when the inheriting prince was still a minor. This was the case with Prince Landenulf of Capua, who succeeded in 982 and was for some years under the tutelage of his mother, Aloara. Similar examples occurred in the duchy of Amalfi in the 950s and at Gaeta in the early eleventh century. But minorities were of course potentially very dangerous: the minor duke of Amalfi in the 950s, Mastalus II, was murdered in 958, and his family replaced by a new dynasty.

Yet for the most part princely rule, and that of the dukes in the coastal cities, seems to have been stable, at least up to the 970s in Salerno and the 980s in Capua and Benevento, and when compared with the chaos of the preceding century. But it is paradoxical that while this was the case the foundations of princely authority were being eroded. In contrast to the ninth century, when the embattled princes of Benevento were careful not to alienate parts of their fisc and regalian rights, preferring to give out property which had reverted to them essentially by accident (for example from men lacking heirs) or judicially, their successors in the tenth century were less cautious, particularly after 950. It was under Pandulf Ironhead, when the prince was at least nominally at his most powerful, that the most extensive concessions were made. For example, in 964 Pandulf and his brother conceded the county of Isernia to their cousin Landulf with an extensive immunity which essentially withdrew the county from their jurisdiction. A similar abdication of public power can be seen in Pandulf II of Benevento's concession of Greci and regalian rights over its inhabitants to a certain Count Poto in 988, and of Trivento on very similar terms to Count Randisius in 992.[27] It may be that Pandulf Ironhead's ambitious policy made him more reckless than his predecessors in securing support from his nobles (many of whom were relatives) and from churchmen. Certainly more of his diplomata survive, nearly all embodying grants, from the twenty years of his rule as senior prince than for

---

[26] *Chronicon Salernitanum*, c. 159, p. 166.

[27] Poupardin (1907), pp. 105–6, 117–18, nos. 112, 140–1; Wickham (1981), p. 162 has a useful discussion of the first of these grants.

the preceding sixty years, since the union of Capua and Benevento. But it may also be that his policy was pragmatic, and that such grants as that to the count of Isernia were not really giving much away, but recognising alienations that had already happened. There could also have been sound reasons for such concessions as that to Count Poto in 988. Greci was on the frontier with Apulia, and the grant of the right of fortification was an obvious security measure, while the generous judicial and financial concessions may have been necessary to persuade an aristocrat to settle an apparently deserted and quite possibly dangerous site.

But there was in fact a longer-term process at work in this privatisation of authority. Gastaldates were probably effectively hereditary by *c.* 900, and already in the ninth century the authority of the prince was very obviously ineffectual in the more remote areas of his principality. Furthermore, to judge by the *Chronicon Salernitanum*, by far the lengthiest and most circumstantial historical work of the time, concepts of princely authority were still very personal, rooted in a traditional framework of fraternity, mutual obligation and gift-exchange, and a condominium of prince and aristocracy. Vassalic links were not merely weak, as for example in tenth-century Francia, they had never existed. *Fidelitas* in Lombard south Italy implied a contractual relationship, not one of dependence.[28] In Benevento the role of the princely palace as an effective institution of government had probably already begun to diminish *c.* 850, after which date its officials ceased to appear in princely *diplomata*. By making grants to nobles the princes were at least making also a statement that authority still ultimately came from them, however remotely, and creating some sort of short-term link and mutual goodwill, particularly when most of those receiving such concessions were kinsmen, who doubtless came to expect these marks of favour; even if in the long-term such hereditary grants (and there is very little evidence for temporary and revocable concessions) led to a haemorrhage of central authority outside the immediate vicinity of the princely residences.

The symptom, and also one of the causes, of this privatisation of authority was *incastellamento*. The development of private fortifications (in southern Italy rather fortified villages than castles pure and simple) had several functions. It was partly defensive, and even after the cessation of the Saracen threat there was still external danger. Hungarian raiders penetrated deep into the principality of Capua in 937, and as far as Apulia in 922 and again in 947. The *castello* was too a means of protection against greedy neighbours, especially when central authority was weak or distant. But it was also a means for effective exploitation by patrimonial landowners, attracting new settlers, imposing common rents

---

[28] Delogu (1977), ch 2, and especially Taviani-Carozzi (1980), (1991b), pp. 686–702.

and services, and providing a centre for collection of such rents and for local judicial authority. The creation of *castelli* and the attraction of immigrants could also repopulate areas abandoned or under-exploited, although we should be cautious about taking at face-value the claims in monastic chronicles as to the extent of such desertion before the age of *incastellamento*. Concessions by the princes of the regalian right of fortification, largely from the second half of the tenth century, were a symptom of central authority in decline. They were not necessarily the mark of a society in decline. Indeed, the tenth century was an age of growing population and increasing agricultural prosperity, though in southern Italy more than in most areas of Europe there might be quite striking regional variations. What might hold good for such fertile areas as the Capuan plain or the broad and flat Liri valley in the north of the principality of Capua was not necessarily the case for more mountainous areas like Molise.

There were also contrasts between the different principalities. In Salerno the capital city and the princely court continued to act as a magnet for the nobility in a way that no longer applied in the more decentralised principalities of Capua and Benevento. This was probably a function of the greater size of the city of Salerno, and its correspondingly greater influence, both social and economic, within the principality. A mark of the city's development is that in the period 980–1000 twenty-nine notaries, all of them laymen, can be found operating there.[29] Furthermore the other main centres of habitation within the principality lay relatively close to the city. The prince's relatives continued, for the most part, to reside at Salerno, whereas in the other two principalities they lived in their *castelli* and established their territorially based dynasties.

The comital title, which had begun as a personal distinction signifying relationship to the princely family, evolved, in Capua and Benevento, into a territorial designation. The counts replaced the gastalds as the chief local princely officials. (The gastalds in the ninth century had fulfilled a role which was analogous to that of the counts in the *regnum Italiae*.) But the emergence of the territorial counts in southern Italy signified not merely a change in title, but also one of function, a step along the way to the privatisation of authority. There were far more counts in the principality of Capua in the later tenth century than there had been gastalds in the ninth, as local authority not only became more entrenched but also more fragmented, and the process spread eastwards into Molise and the principality of Benevento, although with less density in these more mountainous and sparsely settled regions.[30] The role of princely cadets in this process is clear. Two of Landulf III's sons became counts at S. Agata and

---

[29] Taviani-Carozzi (1991b), pp. 541–2.

[30] Martin (1980), pp. 573ff. provides a most valuable discussion, on which I have drawn heavily. For Salerno, Taviani-Carozzi (1991b), especially pp. 449–51, 573–4, 725–7, 769–70.

Larino. Two of Pandulf Ironhead's younger sons in turn became count of Teano, replacing an existing line of counts descended from Atenulf I. The descendants of one of them were in the eleventh century counts at Venafro and Presenzano. This fragmentation of local authority was encouraged by the partible inheritance of Lombard law. The change in usage seems to have occurred particularly in the 950s and 960s, in the years when Pandulf Ironhead was co-ruler with his father and in the early years of his own rule, and in one case, that of the creation of the county of Isernia in 964, he can be seen expressly sanctioning this development. But it is also interesting that the gastalds of Aquino, who were not descended from the Capuan princely dynasty, did not use the title of count until some twenty years later.

In the principality of Salerno the process was much slower and less complete, for reasons which have already been outlined above. It has been suggested that a count had been established by 947 in a territorial lordship at Nocera on the border with the principality of Capua, at a period when relations between the two princes were hostile. But the evidence for such a supposition is at best inconclusive, and it is more probable that the count was simply a princely relative who held property at Nocera. A son of either Atenulf II or the exiled Atenulf III of Benevento was established in a lordship at Conza on the southern border of the principality, facing Byzantine territory, but he appears not to have had a comital title, and his relationship with Prince Gisulf later deteriorated to such an extent that he was driven into exile once again, at Naples.[31] Hence comital titles in Salerno remained a mark of personal status, not institutional function. Furthermore, the princes retained their control over the church and their monopoly over public justice until well into the eleventh century. Legal cases first heard under local officials in outlying parts of the principality were often concluded at Salerno itself.

In the principality of Capua-Benevento the princes sought to bolster their authority in the north of their principality by allying with and favouring the two great monasteries of the region, Monte Cassino and S. Vincenzo al Volturno. Both of these were not just major landowners, but also possessed coherent blocks of territory, and could be used as counter-weights to the local nobility in localities some distance away and geographically separate from the centres of princely authority. Both monasteries had been destroyed by the Arabs, Volturno in 881 and Monte Cassino in 883, and in the early years of the century both communities were still in exile. The monks of Volturno returned to their

---

[31] *Chronicon Salernitanum*, cc. 161, 175, pp. 168, 178; *Codex diplomaticus Cavensis* II, pp. 62–3, no. 260 (969). Mor (1953), pp. 139–40. The chronicle is infuriatingly vague as to which Atenulf he was son of, and the genealogical charts in Mor (1952), pp. 294–5, Cilento (1971), table 2, and Taviani-Carozzi (1991b), p. 397, do not agree either. For Nocera, see Taviani-Carozzi (1991b), pp. 492–6; *Codex diplomaticus Cavensis* I, pp. 224–5, no. 174.

mother house in 914, but those of Monte Cassino remained in exile, first at Teano and later at Capua until 949. This long residence at Capua was, to judge both from a contemporary papal letter and from later Casinese tradition, the result of direct pressure from Landulf I in his greed to exploit the monastery's property.[32] If so, this policy was short sighted, for the chief profiteers were not the princes but the nobles of the Liri valley, who alienated much of the abbey's land. But under Landulf II and Pandulf I the policy changed. The monks returned to Monte Cassino, and the princes actively supported them, forcing the local nobles to disgorge their stolen property and respect the abbey's lands in future. The gastalds of Aquino were brought to heel by direct military action, and a series of land pleas in the early 960s consolidated this process. Landulf II similarly took action to protect Volturno's territory from the incursions of the counts of Venafro.[33] In the 960s Pandulf Ironhead conceded both fiscal immunities and, in 967, the right to erect fortifications to the monasteries.[34] Admittedly one must not over-estimate the extent of the *incastellamento* on the lands of either monastery. Pandulf's charter to Monte Cassino mentioned only two *castelli* by name, and a tower at a third site, and the development of fortified sites on the abbey's lands was gradual. By *c.* 1000 there were no more than half a dozen *castelli* there. On the *Terra Sancti Vincenti* the fortification of settlement was largely confined to the central portion of the monastery's lands in the immediate neighbourhood of the mother house, and to some eastern parts about which the abbey of S. Vincenzo was in dispute with the counts of Isernia.[35] The beginnings of *incastellamento* on the lands of these abbeys were more part of the reorganisation of their system of land exploitation than intended for directly military purposes (although those *castelli* founded in the lands of S. Vincenzo claimed by the counts of Isernia were set up above all to symbolise the abbey's claims to this property). The abbeys could, however, rely on princely support, and indeed that of the emperors Otto I and II, in case of difficulty. The princes could use their relationship with these abbeys to validate their rule in the north of their dominions, and to limit the building of local power-bases by nobles whose activities they might otherwise find difficult to check. After the two principalities of Capua and Benevento separated in 981 the relationship between the prince of Capua and Monte Cassino became that much closer when Prince Pandenulf appointed a kinsman, Manso, as abbot of

---

[32] Agapetus II (JL 3664), Zimmermann, *Papsturkunden*, no. 109, pp. 191–3; *Chronica monesterii Casinense* I, 59, p. 147, which clearly used this letter.

[33] *Chronica monasterii Casinense* II, 1–3; *I placiti cassinesi del secolo X col periodi in volgare*; *Chronicon Vulternese del monaco Giovanni* II, 64–8.

[34] The latter are edited in Tosti (ed.), *Storia della badia di Montecassino* I, 1226–8, and *Chronicon Vulturnense* II, pp. 162–4.

[35] Wickham (1985), especially pp. 250–1; Loud (1994b), pp. 54–6. Cf. also Del Treppo (1955), pp. 74–100, for the social and economic consequences of *incastellamento*, and also Toubert (1976).

Monte Cassino, and in 1011, while the two principalities were briefly reunited, Pandulf II installed one of his sons as abbot. But by that stage S. Vincenzo al Volturno was no longer playing any part in this policy. After 981 there were no further princely diplomata for the monastery, and by the eleventh-century Molise had slipped entirely from princely control.

The coastal duchies of Amalfi, Naples and Gaeta were very different from the Lombard principalities. For one thing, the small size of their territories meant that they did not face the problems of distance and control which undermined effective government in the principalities. In Naples and Gaeta hereditary dynasties were already established by 900, and in Amalfi a ruling family was in the process of consolidating itself by that date when the city's governor, Manso, associated his son with him in its rule. By 907 the Byzantine government had recognised his position by granting him the rank of *spatharo-candidatus*, although the comparatively low status of the *parvenu* Amalfitan dynasty is suggested by the fact that at the time of the Garigliano expedition the rulers of Naples and Gaeta were granted the much higher rank of *patri-kios*.[36] Manso's family was displaced by a coup in 958, but otherwise the ruling dynasties in the coastal duchies were stable enough to endure unchallenged throughout this period, and indeed well into the eleventh century. The new Amalfitan ruling family lasted until the time of Robert Guiscard in the late eleventh century, and that of Naples until the death of the last duke in 1139.

The economy of all three duchies was based on trade, but not to the same extent. Amalfi, with the smallest territory (and that very mountainous), was the most active in such trade; Naples, with the largest hinterland, the least. According to Ibn Ḥawqāl, an Arab traveller writing *c*. 975, Amalfi was 'the richest city of southern Italy, the most noble and most illustrious by its condi-tion, the most affluent and the most opulent'.[37] By the 940s Amalfitan mer-chants were present in some numbers at Constantinople, and by the end of the century in Egypt. But the primary trading destinations were North Africa and Sicily, to which timber, grain, linen and other agricultural products from south-ern Italy were transported. Naples was a centre for linen production, which was praised for its quality by Ibn Ḥawqāl. Such trade required good relations with Islam, which explains the reluctance of Amalfi and Gaeta to participate in military operations against the Arabs in the ninth and early tenth centuries, and indeed the provision at times of actual assistance to the invaders. That the duchy of Naples played a more active role in combatting the Arabs of the Garigliano suggests that the city's trade was less significant to its well-being than to the other two duchies. But the fact that grain was certainly imported from the interior of southern Italy to Amalfi, and probably to Gaeta as well,

---

[36] Schwartz (1978), pp. 31–2.   [37] *Medieval Trade in the Mediterranean World*, p. 54.

shows that the economy of the Campanian ports required links with the
Lombard principalities as well. Furthermore the role of Salerno in such trade
cannot be entirely excluded. It was Islamic gold which was used to mint imitation quarter-dinar coins called tari, which were the principal money of southern Italy outside the Byzantine provinces, and from *c.* 1000 these were minted
at Salerno as well as Amalfi.

Profits from such trade helped particular families to establish their rule at
Gaeta in the mid-ninth century and at Amalfi in the 890s, and to consolidate
their regimes thereafter. The surviving wills of two rulers of Gaeta, Docibilis I
in 906 and Docibilis II in 954, show the very considerable movable wealth that
these men had at their disposal, for which trading profits are the most obvious
source.[38] The possession of mills was also an important facet of their power.
The duke of Gaeta had a monopoly over mills, which he granted out to others
only in exceptional circumstances. In Amalfi the number of mills attested in
surviving documents was far more than the relatively small population of the
duchy can have needed for its domestic supply, and yet their value was high.
While not possessing a monopoly as in Gaeta, the Amalfitan rulers held quite a
number of mills and could thus benefit from the income that they generated.
In these, as in other ways, rule in the coastal duchies was very different from
that in the Lombard principalities. Unlike the Lombard princes, the dukes did
not assert the ultimately divinely sanctioned nature of their rule (except in
Amalfi from the 950s when the *dei gratia/providentia* style may well have been an
attempt to legitimise the new and usurping dynasty), nor could they look to a
tradition of rule hallowed by time. Their position rested rather on their wealth,
both from the remains of the public fisc and on their private family property,
on their role as lawgivers and military leaders, and on their control of the local
church, in which their relatives were frequently given high office. In the early
part of the century the rulers of Amalfi were often content to refer to themselves as 'judges', while the adoption in the early eleventh century of the title
magister militum by the rulers of Naples reflects their military role as defenders
of their people. Byzantine titles were an important element of legitimisation
for the newer dynasties of Gaeta and Amalfi, although their use of such titles
might vary depending on how far they felt that they might need Byzantine
support and alliance. With the coming of the Ottonians in the 960s and their
support of Pandulf Ironhead of Capua, the dukes of Naples and Amalfi gravitated once more towards friendship with the eastern empire, and their documents once again made reference to their Byzantine ranks, while the duke of
Naples actively supported the Byzantine invasion of the Campania in 969.

In the 970s the growing power of the prince of Capua-Benevento was

---

[38] *Codex diplomaticus Caietanus* I, pp. 30, 87, nos. 19, 52. For Gaeta, Skinner (1995), especially ch. 3.

threatening to take over those parts of southern Italy not under Byzantine rule. In 973 there was an abortive coup in Salerno in which the childless Prince Gisulf was packed off to Amalfi as a prisoner. The ringleader of this coup was the former lord of Conza (the son of either Atenulf II or Atenulf III of Benevento) whom Gisulf had expelled many years earlier, but then allowed to return. Swift and decisive action by Pandulf Ironhead restored Gisulf to his throne. However the price of his restoration was that Pandulf's son be associated with him as co-ruler, and when Gisulf died in 977 that son, also called Pandulf, was his successor. Thus in theory at least the unity of the old principality of Benevento, as it had existed in the Carolingian period before the division of 849, was restored. But such unity proved illusory, for the death of Pandulf Ironhead in 981 was the precursor to the break-up of his empire. Despite the presence of an imperial army under Otto II both Salerno and Benevento revolted. The Beneventans installed as their prince Pandulf's nephew, the son of his brother and co-ruler Atenulf (d. 968/9). The Salernitans turned first to Duke Manso of Amalfi, and then in December 983 to a palace official, John of Spoleto, who succeeded in holding on to the principality and founding a new ruling dynasty.[39] Thus from 982 onwards Lombard southern Italy was once again divided into three separate principalities.

The year 982 also saw the catastrophic eclipse of Ottonian influence in the south. Otto II had decided to abandon the peace of 969 and to launch a fresh invasion of the Byzantine provinces. His army marched first into southern Apulia where it besieged, but failed to take, Matera and Taranto. Then he marched south into Calabria, which was once again menaced by Arab incursions from Sicily. Quite what his intentions were is unclear. The German chronicler Thietmar of Merseburg implied that his primary objective was to free Calabria from the Arab menace, but though circumstantial this account is too tendentious and unreliable to be taken entirely seriously, and the emperor's main intention may rather have been the annexation of Byzantine territory. Near Cape Colonna, half way down Calabria, his army was comprehensively defeated in a pitched battle with the Arab invaders and it was only with great difficulty that the emperor himself escaped.[40] Landulf IV of Capua and his brother Pandulf, the deposed prince of Salerno, were both killed.

The defeat in Calabria, followed by Otto II's death little more than a year later and the minority in the empire which followed, meant that there was no further German intervention in southern Italy for some sixteen years. It also ensured that there would remain three separate Lombard principalities and that no ruler would dominate the non-Byzantine south with imperial assistance, as Pandulf Ironhead had done. His rule over Spoleto and Camerino was

---

[39] For the dating, Schwartz (1978), pp. 39–41. The number of Amalfitans living within Salerno undoubtedly facilitated Manso's takeover. [40] Thietmar, *Chronicon* II, 20–2.

granted to others. The principality of Capua was left in the hands of a minor, under the tutelage of his mother. And in both Capua and Benevento the forces of decentralisation, of which *incastellamento* was a symptom, reduced princely authority little by little. In the principality of Benevento the development of *castelli* accelerated *c.* 1000, and the rule of the prince became limited to little more than the immediate vicinity of Benevento itself. The growing weakness of central authority was certainly not helped by a fragmentation of interests within the ruling families. For a time in 985 Duke Manso of Amalfi was displaced by his brother Adelferius. More seriously, in 993 Prince Landenulf of Capua was murdered in an uprising in Capua, and there are some indications that this was with the connivance of his brother Laidulf, who succeeded him as prince.[41] Soon afterwards Archbishop Aion of Capua was also murdered, and in 996, after a period of virtually open warfare in the north of the principality between the abbey of Monte Cassino and the neighbouring counts of Aquino, Abbot Manso of Cassino, who was, it will be remembered, a princely kinsman, was captured while on a visit to Capua and blinded. Authority within the principality of Capua was seemingly near collapse in the 990s.[42] The intervention of the Emperor Otto III in 999 did nothing to cure this. He deposed Laidulf and installed his own nominee as prince. But as soon as his army withdrew his protégé was expelled, and replaced by a brother of the prince of Benevento (whose capital the emperor had besieged but failed to capture).

While we have no such spectacular manifestations for other areas as we have for Capua, the decentralisation of authority would appear to have been a fairly general phenomenon. Even in the minuscule duchy of Gaeta the same fissiparous tendencies as in the Lombard principalities manifested themselves, with cadet branches of the ducal house setting up their own, almost independent, counties in outlying parts of the duchy, at Fondi, Traetto and Suio. In the Byzantine dominions with their strong central administration there was not, of course, the same problem. But the recurrence of Arab attacks in the 980s and 990s was a serious phenomenon, not least because imperial attention was devoted almost exclusively to more pressing matters elsewhere, notably revolt in Asia Minor and then war with Bulgaria. These Muslim raids penetrated not merely into Calabria, but also deep into Apulia. The outskirts of Bari were ravaged in 988, Taranto attacked in 991, Matera captured after a long siege in 994, and Bari itself besieged for nearly five months in 1003 and rescued only by

---

[41] Otto III justified his deposition of Laidulf in 999 because of his alleged involvement, *Chronicon monasterii Casinense* II, 24. A more contemporary Capuan chronicle does not go this far, but describes Laidulf 'coming joyfully' to Capua after his brother's murder: Cilento (1971), pp. 308–9. Most damning is the *Vita S. Nili*, c. 79.

[42] Cf. Prince Laidulf's unprecedented oath to respect the possessions of Monte Cassino, *c.* 993: *Accessiones ad historiam abbatiae Casinensis*, p. 90.

a Venetian fleet. In northern Calabria, Cosenza was sacked in 1009. If a note of pessimism creeps into contemporary documents this is hardly surprising; an inhabitant of Conversano (in central Apulia) lamented in 992 that, while he had made suitable provision for his elder sons in a time of peace, now in 'a time of barbarism' he could not do the same for his younger son.[43]

Nor indeed was the west coast exempt from attack. The duchy of Amalfi, whose trading links had hitherto protected it, was raided in 991. And in 999 the outskirts of Salerno were the victim of a further piratical raid. According to the chronicle of Amatus of Monte Cassino (admittedly written some eighty years later) there was general panic before a group of forty pilgrims from Normandy, returning from a visit to Jerusalem, volunteered to combat the invaders, caught them unawares and routed them. Impressed with their prowess, the prince (Guaimar III) invited them or their relatives to enter his service as mercenaries. So at least ran the legend, and perhaps even the sober fact, of the arrival of the Normans in southern Italy.[44] For some years to come they were to be only a minor factor in the region's history. But, as the eleventh century wore on, the Normans were to change its course for ever.

---

[43] *Codice diplomatico Pugliese*, no. 20; *Le Pergamene di Conversano*, pp. 56–8, no. 26.
[44] Amatus of Monte Cassino, *Storia de'Normanni* I, 17–19, pp. 21–4. For the date, cf. Hoffmann (1969).

CHAPTER 27

SICILY AND AL-ANDALUS
UNDER MUSLIM RULE

Hugh Kennedy

BY THE beginning of the tenth century Muslim expansion had come to an end in most areas of the Mediterranean world. On the south-eastern frontiers of the Byzantine empire the border was firmly established in the Anti-Taurus mountains, leaving the Muslims in control of the plains, the Byzantines of the uplands. The weakened ʿAbbāsid caliphate was no longer in a position to mount major expeditions using the resources of the entire Islamic near east as it had a century before. Malatya, the Cilician plain and Antioch still remained in Muslim hands but they would be lost to Islam in the next century.

The eastern Mediterranean saw the gradual resurgence of Byzantine sea-power. Until 905 the Tulunid rulers of Egypt had controlled most of the eastern coast and had maintained a fleet in Tarsus, but the ʿAbbāsid reconquest of Egypt in that year seems to have put an end to this. In 969 the Fatimids moved east from Tunisia to Egypt and attempted to regain the initiative at sea, but by this time Tarsus and the other northern ports had been lost and the Fatimids were forced to make do with Tripoli and Acre, much further to the south. The loss of Crete to the Byzantines in 961 marked another important step in this process.

In the western Mediterranean, Sicily, the Balearic Islands and much of the Iberian peninsula remained firmly in Muslim hands. It was in these areas that the Muslims were able to set up strong and effective states and the tenth century was in many ways the golden age of al-Andalus. Even in these areas, however, expansion had virtually ceased. Raids were still made on Christian communities in Italy and Spain, but the age of conquest was over, and the age of bureaucracy had arrived.

MUSLIM SPAIN, 912–1031

In October 912 ʿAbd Allāh b. Muḥammad, the aged and depressive Umayyad amir of Córdoba, died, nominating his grandson, ʿAbd al-Raḥmān as his successor. The inheritance he left was not an impressive one. In the time of his grandfather, 'Abd al-Raḥmān II (822–52) the power of the amirs had been extended from the heartlands of the amirate around Córdoba, to include all the main centres of power in the more distant provinces, including Merida, Toledo, Zaragoza and Valencia. The half-century which followed his death saw this power gradually being dissipated under the rule of Muḥammad (852–86), al-Mundhir (886–8) and finally 'Abd Allāh himself. The causes of this collapse went beyond the personal failings of the rulers. One underlying reason was the strong separatist tendencies found among the Muslim elites in the provinces, tendencies which had been barely controlled by 'Abd al-Raḥmān II even at the height of his power. To these were now added tensions at the centre caused by the very success of Islam itself. As the number of native converts (*muwallad*s) to the new religion increased, they began to demand equality of political and fiscal status with old-established elite groups of Arab and Berber descent. These disputes not only undermined the effectiveness of the Cordovan government but also poisoned relations with provincial magnates, many of whom came from *muwallad* backgrounds.

The power that 'Abd al-Raḥmān inherited barely extended beyond Córdoba and the fertile Campiña around it. The army was a small and unimpressive force which subsisted mainly on pillaging the nearby areas, while the bureaucracy had shrunk with the diminishing resources of the state. In the provinces, local magnates enjoyed undisputed control: Badajoz and much of the western part of al-Andalus was ruled by the descendants of a *muwallad* chief, Ibn Marwān al-Jillīqī (*d. c.* 889), whose family had been important in the area for a century while Merida and the pastoral plains to the north and east were dominated by a Berber chief, Mas'ūd b. Tajīt. Toledo had a long tradition of autonomy under *muwallad* leadership which had been only temporarily interrupted in the time of 'Abd al-Raḥman II. Zaragoza was ruled by the Tujībī family, a dynasty claiming Arab descent which also had branches in Calatayud and Daroca and had by this time almost completely supplanted the *muwallad* Banū Qāsī in the Ebro valley. The highlands to the east and south-east of Toledo were largely populated by Berber tribes. From the late ninth century the leading family among them had been the Banū Zannūn (Arabised to Banū'l-Dhū'l-Nūn), whose influence extended as far as the plains around Valencia where many of the transhumant Berbers wintered.

Local autonomy in the centre and north of al-Andalus had long been a feature of the political life of Muslim Spain. More immediately challenging to the power of Córdoba was dissidence in the south, traditionally the centre of the power of the amirs. Seville itself, probably the second city of *al-Andalus*, had been taken over by a local Arab family, the Banū'l-Ḥajjāj and most of the smaller centres of the south-west had their own local lords. Even more serious was widespread revolt led by a *muwallad* landowner, 'Umar b. Ḥafṣūn. This had begun in the reign of the amir Muḥammad and had gathered recruits from *muwallad*s and *mozarab*s (native Christians under Muslim rule) throughout the southern mountains from Almeria in the east to Medina Sidonia in the west, though it was concentrated around 'Umar's mountain stronghold of Bobastro in the Serrania de Ronda. Ibn Ḥafṣūn's movement was violently opposed by local Arab leaders, especially in the area of Elvira (a now deserted site to the north of Granada) but the attempts of the Amir 'Abd Allāh to pacify the region were spasmodic and ineffective.

From the first year of his reign, the young 'Abd al-Raḥmān began a systematic extension of his power by using both his limited army and his diplomatic skills. He enjoyed the rock solid support of leading families among the Umayyad *mawālī* (the descendants of freedmen of the early Umayyads who formed an elite group in Córdoba), notably the Banū Abī 'Abda who had played an important military role under 'Abd Allāh, the Banū Shuhayd and others. In the beginning he could also count on the support of experienced members of his own family, notably his paternal uncles, Abān and al-'Āṣī b. 'Abd Allāh. In relying on these groups, 'Abd al-Raḥmān was following the example of his predecessors but he also began to look for military support from outside *al-Andalus* altogether. He greatly increased the practice of buying white slaves, mostly Slavs originally captured in wars on the eastern frontiers of the Ottonian Reich and brought south by slave-traders. These men (known as *ghulām* or *fatā*, both words meaning page) were then used to form the core of his new model army, becoming, in the process, increasingly influential in the military hierarchy and eventually in the Umayyad state in general. In this way he created an effective military machine responsible directly to him and independent of pressures from native Arabs and *muwallad*s alike. Along with this went a vast expansion of the bureaucracy, new titles and positions being created partly to service the new professional army but partly, no doubt, to provide lucrative positions for the elite of Cordovan political society.

None of this would have been possible on the very restricted resource base 'Abd al-Raḥmān took over in 912. Campaigns were launched in the first winter of his reign (912–13) showing the urgency with which he regarded his task and the next summer he was leading his troops on an extensive royal progress around the edge of the Sierra Nevada. His technique was always to offer terms to local war-lords, who were encouraged to hand over their castles peacefully. He was aided in this by the fact that his major rival in the south, Ibn Ḥafṣūn, had by this time reverted to his ancestral religion of Christianity and most Muslims preferred to accept the overlordship of a Muslim amir to an apostate rebel, even if it meant paying more taxes. A further stroke of luck occurred in 913 when the cunning old ruler of Seville, Ibn al-Ḥajjāj, died;

while his family disputed his inheritance, ʿAbd al-Raḥmān's troops took over the city.

By 914 ʿAbd al-Raḥmān had regained control over the richest and most populous areas of *al-Andalus*, but the final reduction of Ibn Ḥafṣun's rebellion in its mountain strongholds proved a more lengthy task. The rebel leader himself died in his bed in 917, but the struggle was continued by his sons until the last one surrendered on terms in 928, bringing to an end half a century of dogged resistance to Cordovan authority in the southern mountains.

Well before this, however, the amir had begun to extend his influence outside the confines of *al-Andalus*. His vehicle for doing this was the *ṣāʿifah*, the summer raid against the Christian north which was an important symbol of the amir's role as leader of the Muslim community. ʿAbd Allāh had allowed this duty to lapse; ʿAbd al-Raḥmān revived it as one of the most effective instruments of his policy: for example in 924 he led his army up the east coast (probably the first time a reigning amir had ever visited the area) and then to the Ebro valley whence he led the Muslims in the sack of Pamplona. Such a campaign not only affirmed his status as leader of the whole Muslim community of *al-Andalus*, it also brought him into direct contact with such local magnates as the Tujībīs of Zaragoza and the Dhū'l-Nūnids, who were duty bound to serve in his armies.

In 929 he felt confident enough to arrange that he should be proclaimed as caliph and to take the official title of al-Nāṣir ('the Victorious') on the model of ʿAbbāsid caliphs. There were a number of reasons for this move. The Umayyads of *al-Andalus* were of course the descendants of caliphs, indeed they were sometimes referred to as 'Sons of caliphs' before they took the title for themselves: no one could call them upstarts and no one else in *al-Andalus* could claim the same status. But there were also more immediate reasons; the Islamic ideal of one caliph for the whole community was already in ruins. During the early tenth century the ʿAbbāsid caliphate of Baghdad slipped into chaos, paralysed by political and economic problems which left the caliph himself as an impotent figurehead. At the same time the Fatimids had set up a rival caliphate in Tunisia in 909. The Fatimids claimed descent from the Prophet's daughter, Fāṭima (hence the name) and his son-in-law ʿAlī and they proclaimed their intention of assuming the leadership of the entire Muslim world. Not only did this mean that there were already two rival caliphs but their pretensions posed a particular danger to the Umayyads of *al-Andalus* since they claimed authority over the Maghreb and Spain. The dangers that this could pose were made clear when Ibn Ḥafṣūn at one stage accepted them as his overlords.

All these factors meant that the assumption of the title of caliph, with its claims to religious as well as secular leadership, was a logical step. Along with it went the decision to mint a gold coinage, as the Fatimids had done. In part this reflected the increased prosperity noticeable in the country at the time, but it certainly had a symbolic importance as well.

Armed with these new claims to authority, al-Nāṣir immediately set about extending his authority in the centre and north of *al-Andalus*. In the summer of 929 he reduced the Lower March including Badajoz and the Algarve to obedience. The local leaders were leniently treated but they were obliged to settle in Córdoba while Umayyad garrisons were installed in their erstwhile strongholds. In 930 it was the turn of Toledo. This proved a more difficult problem and it took a two-year siege to reduce the city to obedience. His next objective was to assert control over the lands of the Dhū'l-Nūnids and Zaragoza and the Ebro valley, held by the Tujībīs and other powerful local lords. Al-Nāṣir struggled to subdue this area for much of the 930s but it proved beyond his resources. Recalcitrant lords could be forced to make terms but they seldom kept to them and al-Nāṣir could find no substitute for Dhū'l-Nūnid or Tujībī power. Even serving in the *ṣā'ifah* was something they did reluctantly since it meant serving under his orders in lands they considered their own and, perhaps worse, serving with and under upstart slave soldiers. It was these tensions which finally led to disaster. In 939 al-Nāṣir led an expedition to the middle Duero region where, caught in broken and difficult terrain, he was decisively defeated at an unidentified site the Arabs called al-Khandaq (the Trench) by the Leonese army, at least in part because of the desertion of Fortūn b. Muḥammad, lord of Huesca, at the height of the battle. The caliph left the battle-field in ignominious flight.

The defeat marked a major turning point in al-Nāṣir's fortunes and seems to have destroyed both his ambition and his self-confidence. He never ventured on campaign again and seldom left Córdoba. Activity on the frontier was confined to small-scale expeditions mounted by local leaders. The lords of the upper march and the Berber chiefs of the eastern highlands (where the old established Banū Dhū'l-Nūn were joined by the up and coming Banū Razīn of Albarracin) continued to exercise power undisturbed.

Al-Nāṣir's reign also saw Córdoba taking a more active role in North Africa. The area of modern Morocco, known to the inhabitants of *al-Andalus* as al-'Udwa (literally 'the other side'), was very much less developed than Muslim Spain. Apart from Fes, there were few towns and little Arab settlement and it remained essentially a land of Berber tribes. The Idrisids, a dynasty which like the Fatimids claimed descent from the Prophet himself, exercised a feeble and intermittent leadership but real power lay with tribal chiefs and local dynasts. The Umayyads of Córdoba had shown little interest in this poor and intractable land beyond establishing friendly relations with some of the nearest dynasts, like the Banū Ṣāliḥ of Nakūr on the Mediterranean coast. The coming of the Fatimids, however, meant that this hands-off policy was no longer adequate and al-Nāṣir became concerned, not to rule the area directly, but to prevent the Fatimids from taking it over and using it as a base for attacks on *al-Andalus*. This he achieved by finding allies among the local Berbers. The Fatimids sent major expeditions in 922, when Fes and the southern trading outpost of Sijilmassā were taken, and in 935 and 953 but each time they found that they were unable to control the areas they had taken and local tribal leaders, sustained by Umayyad support, were able to reclaim their independence. The threat reached the coast of Spain itself and in 955 a Fatimid fleet burned Almeria. In order to monitor events in North Africa more closely, al-Nāṣir took over the ports of Melilla (927), Ceuta (931) and Tangier (951) and established a permanent but limited presence on the African littoral. One result of this was the increasing recruitment of Berbers, originally known as *ṭanjiyyūn* (men of Tangier), for the Umayyad armies, a trend which was to have a major impact on the Umayyad state.

In the years after 939, the caliph seems to have remained near Córdoba, consoling himself perhaps with the construction of a new palace city at Madīnat al-Zahrā outside the town, where the wealth and sophistication of the court was employed to dazzle a whole range of local people and foreign ambassadors, including John of Gorze from Otto I some time between 953 and 956 and the monk Nicholas from Byzantium in 951. It was in this increasingly large and ornate palace complex that he died in 961.

There was no problem about the succession. His chosen successor al-Ḥakam al-Mustanṣir, born in 915, was already experienced in administration and warfare. His reign is marked by a broad continuity with his father's and he seems to have continued the largely stationary court life of al-Nāṣir's later years. Madīnat al-Zahrā became a sort of Andalusi Versailles where potentially disruptive local magnates like the Tujībīs of Zaragoza or Berber chiefs from Morocco were encouraged to settle in luxurious idleness. Increasingly government functioned by people coming to the ruler rather than by the ruler travelling to lead armies or solve problems. Al-Ḥakam was a man of great culture, both as patron of writers and bibliophile, but his style of government certainly contributed to later problems.

His relaxed style of government meant that great influence was acquired by a small number of powerful individuals connected with the palace. Foremost among these was Ghālib b. ʿAbd al-Raḥmān. He was a slave soldier who had been elevated by al-Nāṣir to the highest military commands. He had also established a territorial base at Medinaceli at a crucial point on the Christian–Muslim frontier and the main road from Córdoba to the Ebro valley, where he and his Slav followers were established. He also seems to have enjoyed authority over the other lords of the middle march. He served al-Ḥakam well on the frontier and in North Africa and further honours were showered on him.

His opposite number in the civil administration came from an equally obscure background. Jaʿfar b. ʿUthmān al-Mushafī seems to have been the son of a teacher of Berber origin from the Valencia area who had been appointed as tutor to the young al-Ḥakam. Jaʿfar and the young prince became friends, and on the latter's accession, Jaʿfar became his secretary. He was skilled not only at preparing formal legal documents but also at arranging the elaborate ceremonies which were such an important part of life at Madīnat al-Zahrā. Although Jaʿfar had no personal power-base his nephew Hishām b. Muḥammad was an important figure in the military, being in command of the family's home base of Valencia. Relations between Ghālib and al-Mushafī were close and cordial.

The main outside preoccupation of al-Ḥakam's administration seems to have been with North African affairs. In 969 there was a radical change in the balance of forces when the Fatimids conquered Egypt. Soon after, they abandoned Tunisia as their seat of government, leaving a Berber chief, Zīrī b. Manād as their agent. This removed the threat of an invasion of *al-Andalus* and al-Ḥakam seems to have attempted to conquer the area. He was opposed by many, including an Idrisid prince, al-Ḥasan b. Qannūn. Al-Ḥakam sent a major expeditionary force under the command of Ghālib but progress was slow and very expensive and it was not until 973 that he was finally defeated. Even then, Córdoba found it was too demanding to rule the country directly and appointed an adventurer known as Ibn al-Andalusī to organise the country in their interest. The results of this long and costly campaigning could only confirm the wisdom of al-Nāṣir's policy of minimum intervention. However, the efforts to find reliable allies in Morocco did lead to intensive diplomatic and personal contacts between officials at Córdoba and Berber leaders.

In this rather closed, even claustrophobic, political society where access to the ruler was tightly controlled, it was easy for a few individuals to wield enormous power quite unrelated to their origins or their wider political support. The most successful of these political operators in the later years of al-Ḥakam's reign was Muḥammad b. Abī ʿĀmir. He claimed Arab origin and, indeed, that one of his ancestors had participated in the original conquest of *al-Andalus* in 711, meaning, amongst other things, that his family could claim to have been in *al-Andalus* longer than the Umayyads themselves. They settled in Algeciras where they maintained a modest and undistinguished prosperity, ignored by the chroniclers, until the time of the young Muḥammad, born in 938. According to the Arab sources, he determined early on to make himself the most powerful figure in *al-Andalus*, and since opportunities for Arabs in the military were very limited he went to Córdoba and acquired a firm grounding in religious law.[1] In

---

[1] Lévi-Provençal (1951), pp. 201–2.

circumstances which are not entirely clear, he established close relations with members of al-Ḥakam's harem, notably Ṣubḥ, a Basque who was mother of the heir apparent Hishām; he became manager of her considerable wealth and that of the young prince. This patronage led to further promotion and in 973 he was appointed as *qāḍī* (judge) of the areas of Morocco which the Umayyads held, in effect to act as a political officer alongside the military commander Ghālib and his successors. Ibn Abī ʿĀmir became the main link between the Berber chiefs of the area and Córdoba.

He returned from this posting just before the death of al-Ḥakam in October, 976. Hishām, the heir apparent, was still a boy and some senior officers in the Slav military tried to push the claims of one of al-Ḥakam's brothers, but they were outmanoeuvred by Ibn Abī ʿĀmir and al-Muṣhafī, working in close cooperation, and a group of Berber troops, newly arrived from North Africa. The new caliph was duly proclaimed and given the title of al-Muʿayyad but real power lay with his guardians Ibn Abī ʿĀmir and al-Muṣhafī. From this moment, Ibn Abī ʿĀmir worked with cold and systematic cunning to remove his partners. His first move was to dismiss all those leaders of the Slav military who had opposed him. In 978, with the support of the veteran warrior Ghālib, still based at Medinaceli on the frontier, he had al-Muṣhafī put in prison where he later died. By 981 Ibn Abī ʿĀmir felt himself strong enough for a showdown with Ghālib, now an old man. He marched north to meet him on his home ground. Against Ghālib's frontier troops and his Castilian allies, Ibn Abī ʿĀmir could rely on the support of the Berber troops led by Ibn al-Andalusī and the troops of the upper march led, as usual, by the Tujībī family with whom he had established good relations in his North African days. In July 981 a major engagement was fought near Atienza, during which Ghālib was accidentally killed and his forces dispersed.

This victory meant that Ibn Abī ʿĀmir's power was now unrivalled and, to celebrate this, he took a regnal title, that of al-Manṣūr ('the Victorious'), a title which had been held by one of the greatest of the ʿAbbāsid caliphs. For the next twenty years he was to be undisputed ruler of *al-Andalus*, a period which in some ways saw the apogee of Muslim Spain in terms of territorial security and internal peace and prosperity. He was careful to maintain the fiction that he was only acting as a regent for the young Umayyad Hishām, and when the prince reached his majority it was given out that he wished to devote himself to religion and had entrusted al-Manṣūr with running the state. He was rigorously confined to the Alcazar at Córdoba, whose fortifications were strengthened to prevent anyone entering or leaving without express permission. Al-Manṣūr himself founded a new centre of government, which he called Madīnat al-Zāhirah, just to the east of Córdoba and transferred thither all the offices of the state.

This effective usurpation did not go entirely unchallenged. In 989 there was an abortive conspiracy led by a descendant of al-Ḥakam I called ʿAbd Allāh b. ʿAbd al-ʿAzīz, known as al-Ḥajar ('the stone', because of his avarice) and one of al-Manṣūr's sons ʿAbd Allāh with the support of García Fernandez, count of Castile, but it failed, and al-Manṣūr ordered his son's execution. In 996 Hishām's mother Ṣubḥ attempted to secure his liberation but her attempts were immediately uncovered by al-Manṣūr's agents. Apart from this, there was little internal dissidence and the Umayyad family were obliged to accept their effective exclusion from power. Elsewhere some local magnates managed to retain their influence. As usual, this was particularly marked in the upper march, where the Tujībīs managed to maintain their power even though individuals sometimes fell foul of al-Manṣūr. We hear less about such Berber chiefs as the Banū'l-Dhū'l-Nūn and the Banū Razīn, but their influence continued undiminished into the eleventh century.

The new regime undoubtedly enjoyed some popular support, partly because of the prosperity and stability it brought but also because of a strong commitment to rigorist Islam. Al-Manṣūr himself made his personal devotion clear, copying the Qurʾān by hand and building a massive final extension to the mosque in Córdoba, an austere contrast to the luxuriant decoration of al-Ḥakam II's work in the same building. He also took strong measures against any sign of heterodoxy, purging al-Ḥakam's great library of any works which might upset orthodox opinion and publicly crucifying a scholar accused of Muʿtazilite thought.

The most important part of this populist commitment to Islam, however, was his systematic pursuit of the *jihād* (Holy War) against the Christians. Previous rulers, notably ʿAbd al-Raḥmān II and al-Nāṣir in the first part of his reign, had used leadership of the Holy War to legitimise their rule and keep them in touch with outlying areas of *al-Andalus* but no one had developed this as a policy to the same extent as al-Manṣūr. The Arabic sources mention more than fifty raids, from small-scale expeditions to major campaigns like the 985 sack of Barcelona and the 997 sack of Santiago de Compostella.[2] Despite the fact that he seems to have had no military background or training, his expeditions were usually successful, suggesting that he was a competent organiser and had a good relationship with the military. Very striking is the way in which al-Manṣūr made certain that news of his triumphs, real, exaggerated or imagined, was spread in Córdoba. The most notable example of this came after the fall of Santiago when the bells of the cathedral were carried south to Córdoba by prisoners of war.

The propaganda effect of these triumphs was immense, both inside *al-*

---

[2] See Lévi-Provençal (1951), pp. 233–59, for details.

Andalus and among the Christians of the north where the constant raids and continuous destruction caused real fear. In the end, however, they achieved little in military terms. Christian resistance was strong and remained so right up to the end of al-Manṣūr's life when in the summer of 1000 Sancho García, count of Castile inflicted major losses on the Muslims and nearly clinched a remarkable victory. Cities were sacked but, apart from a brief and abortive attempt to establish a Muslim garrison at Zamora in 999, no effort seems to have been made to advance the frontiers of Muslim settlement. Paradoxically, this policy of aggression went along with the development of kinship ties across the frontier. As has already been noted, Ṣubḥ, mother of the titular caliph Hishām, was a Basque, and al-Manṣūr continued the connection by marrying ʿAbda, daughter of King Sancho Abarca of Navarre, who was the mother of his son ʿAbd al-Raḥmān, known as Sanchuelo, born around 983. In 993 he is said to have taken a daughter of King Vermudo II of León as a concubine whom he subsequently liberated and married.

Al-Manṣūr also pursued an active policy in North Africa. As before, Cordovan policy was concerned with finding local tribal leaders who would be strong enough to defend Cordovan interests and yet be prepared to accept its overall authority. There was no longer any third power, like the Fatimids in the time of al-Nāṣir, seeking to exploit the situation; but this did not make it easier to find reliable allies. From 988 the head of the Maghrāwa tribal confederation, Zīrī b. ʿAṭīya, seemed the best agent Córdoba could find and he founded a new centre at Wajda to base himself in. He was invited to the capital and established in a luxurious palace but the Berber chiefs always seem to have found this sumptuous environment constraining and he was soon back on his native territory. In 997 he rejected the authority of al-Manṣūr who then decided on a more active policy. Up to this point, Cordovan forces had only occupied Ceuta but in 998 al-Manṣūr sent his leading Slav commander, Wāḍiḥ, who had taken over Ghālib's role and position at Medinaceli, with a large force. Fes was occupied and an Andalusi administration installed which survived until al-Manṣūr's death.

The expense was considerable and the conquests ephemeral but the most important legacy in *al-Andalus* was the large number of new Berber troops. These new troops were usually recruited not as individuals but in tribal groups under their own chiefs who continued to command and lead them. This meant that they retained much of their tribal group spirit (the *ʿaṣabiyyah* of the Arabic sources). Combined with the fact that few of them spoke Arabic and that they were wholly unused to an urban environment such as the great city of Córdoba, it meant that they remained a very alien presence, uncomprehending and uncomprehended at the heart of Andalusi society. The most important group came not from Morocco but from Zirid Tunisia. The authority of the

Zirid ruler Bādīs was challenged by two of his great uncles, Maksān and Zāwī, and when their attempt to overthrow him failed, they and their followers were invited to Córdoba by al-Manṣūr where they were established as a new section of his growing army.

Al-Manṣūr's reign was in many ways a culmination of trends which had been evident in *al-Andalus* throughout the tenth century, especially the growing professionalisation of military and civil hierarchies and the concentration of military power in the hands of non-native groups. At the same time there were a number of new factors, not all of them beneficial. Al-Manṣūr had significantly undermined the prestige of the Umayyad dynasty which had been the focus of unity in Muslim Spain for so long. Not only was the caliph a feeble recluse but other members of the family were completely excluded from power and influence. He had systematically destroyed the authority of anyone who could command a following in the state, and his subordinates were often people of little independent standing. While he remained in charge the system worked, despite the cruelty it exhibited at the highest level: under less competent management, its future was less assured.

Al-Manṣūr was succeeded by his adult son, ʿAbd al-Malik al-Muẓaffar, who had extensive experience of frontier warfare and of managing the military, and he stepped into his father's shoes to become effective ruler of *al-Andalus* from 1002 to 1008. For Ibn Ḥayyān, writing in Córdoba after the collapse of the caliphate, and the writers who depended on him, the reign was a sort of Edwardian summer, when al-Andalus was peaceful, strong and prosperous, in marked contrast to the chaos of the years which followed. Reading between the lines, it is clear that things were not quite so settled and discontent surfaced repeatedly. Part of the problem was the personality of the ruler himself. ʿAbd al-Malik was a competent soldier but he had little time or enthusiasm for day-to-day administration, a problem which was aggravated by the fact that he drank wine, heavily and often. This in turn meant that ambitious and unscrupulous men could take advantage of the situation to assume absolute power in the administration. In addition, the government was generally unpopular among the people of Córdoba, who resented high taxation and the pretensions of the ʿAmirids and their followers.

The new generation of leaders who had risen in al-Manṣūr's years had now reached political maturity and had acquired followings and ambitions of their own. This was particularly apparent among the Slavs. They had been left largely leaderless by al-Manṣūr's purges but now a new cohort of leaders had emerged, Ṭarafa, Mujāhid and above all Wāḍiḥ, who had taken over Ghālib's position at Medinaceli. These new men now formed a powerful bloc opposed to the Berber tribal chiefs.

Two senior officials attempted to use their position to take control of the government into their own hands. The first of these was the Slav Ṭarafa, who in 1003 was denounced, arrested and executed after having been entrusted with the most important offices. In 1006 it was the turn of the chief *wazīr*, ʿĪsā b. Saʿīd al-Yaḥṣubī. Although himself of modest origins, al-Muẓaffar's negligence in ordinary administrative affairs had allowed ʿĪsā to assume almost absolute authority and he had developed close links with old established families in the civil administration. He planned a coup to restore the Umayyads to real power, under his tutelage of course, but the plan was denounced and both ʿĪsā and his candidate for the throne, a grandson of al-Nāṣir, were put to death. It is said that after this al-Muẓaffar determined to take a serious interest in administration but he died before this could bear any fruit. Both incidents showed serious instability among the ruling elite.

Al-Muẓaffar's way of dealing with, and perhaps escaping from, these problems, was to devote himself to the Holy War and he launched annual raids against the Christians. Here again the Arab chroniclers portray this as a stream of victories but in truth the results were pretty meagre and amounted to the sack of a few frontier forts. Unusually, al-Muẓaffar did try to encourage settlement of a castle near Lleida by offering fiscal inducements to anyone who would live there, but it is not clear that this came to anything. Disturbingly for the future, Christian resistance was fierce and Count Sancho García of Castile, especially, showed himself to be an opponent who could take on the Muslims on equal terms. The most noticeable feature of these campaigns was the care with which al-Muẓaffar, like his father, publicised his achievements in Córdoba, writing letters which were to be read out in the mosque at Friday prayers (letters which may form the basis of our chronicle accounts), and organising victory parades. But even then, people complained that he did not send as many new slaves as his father had done. Only against the background of subsequent disaster did al-Muẓaffar's reign acquire a golden glow. In reality, the instability of the ʿAmirid state was increasingly apparent.

On the death of al-Muẓaffar, his brother ʿAbd al-Raḥmān, known as Sanchuelo ('little Sancho', after his maternal grandfather, Sancho Abarca of Navarre), succeeded to his position. ʿAbd al-Raḥmān had been his brother's right-hand man but his extensive experience did not bring political wisdom. He immediately decided to break with the policies of his father and his brother in two distinct ways. In November 1008 he obliged the Caliph Hishām to appoint him heir apparent: both the two previous ʿAmirids had been careful to maintain a screen of constitutional legality but this was now swept away. Despite the circulation of prophecies and alleged traditions of the Prophet, nothing could disguise the fact that the ʿAmirids were not members of the Prophet's tribe of Quraysh, a qualification which almost all Muslims agreed was necessary to become caliph. In making this arrangement, ʿAbd al-Raḥmān completely alienated the numerous members of the Umayyad family, who realised that their remaining status would be destroyed.

His second move was to demonstrate openly his reliance on the Berbers, most obviously by ordering his court to appear on 13 January 1009 dressed in turbans, a typically Berber headgear. Al-Manṣūr's system had depended on balancing different elements within the military, notably the Slavs and the Berbers, but also the Arabs from the upper march led by the Tujībīs. By relying on one group, ʿAbd al-Raḥmān inevitably alienated the others.

He attempted to surmount the obvious opposition in the traditional ʿAmirid way and, even though it was midwinter, he immediately set out on an expedition against the Christians, hoping to win a victory and justify his title. The opposition realised that his absence gave them their opportunity and as soon as they knew he had entered Christian territory, they struck. The leadership seems to have come from the Umayyad family, headed by Muḥammad b. Hishām b. ʿAbd al-Jabbār b. ʿAbd al-Raḥmān al-Nāṣir. His father had been executed by al-Manṣūr for conspiring with ʿĪsā b. Saʿīd in 1006 and he himself had led a fugitive existence since. At the same time, he had attracted a considerable following among the people of Córdoba.

The news of Sanchuelo's entering Christian lands arrived on 15 February and the conspirators struck that night, attacking first the Alcazar, where they obliged the Caliph Hishām to abdicate in favour of Muḥammad, and then Madīnat al-Zāhirah, the ʿAmirid stronghold, which was thoroughly pillaged. The new caliph took the title of al-Mahdī to announce his role as a restorer of legitimate Muslim government. His first appointments showed that he intended the Umayyad family to play a major role and he appointed his cousins as both ḥājib (chief minister) and the ṣāḥib al-shurṭa (commander of the security police). He also began to recruit a militia from the people of Córdoba. It was a deliberate attempt to break the stranglehold of Berbers and Slavs over the military and to arm the people of the city. The chroniclers tend to be very disapproving of this, criticising him for employing tradesmen and the riff-raff of the market place in his army,[3] but in fact it was a bold move to develop a new power-base.

The new regime may have been popular in the streets of the capital, but it faced formidable problems. The least of these was Sanchuelo who, despite all advice, determined to return immediately. His troops melted away and he was arrested and executed at a monastery near Córdoba where he had stopped for the night, his only companion the Christian count, García Gomez of Carrion. He was the last of the ʿAmirids and no attempt was subsequently made to revive their fortunes.

---

[3] Ibn Idhārī al-Marrakushi, *Kitāb al-Bayan al-Mughrib*, III, ed. Lévi-Provençal, pp. 49–51.

More serious was the fact that the established military groups rightly saw al-Mahdī and his new army as a threat to their position. The Slav leader Wāḍiḥ at Medinaceli threw in his lot with the new regime, which he no doubt preferred to a Berber-dominated government, but many of the Slavs left Córdoba and established themselves in the Levante, so depriving al-Mahdī of a military force to balance the Berbers. The Berbers themselves were not so accommodating. Hostility between them and the citizens of Córdoba was a continuous problem which ran through all the chaotic events of the period. The Berbers were dependent on having a friendly government in Córdoba without which they could not survive, but al-Mahdī had his own constituency to satisfy and they demanded the humiliation of these alien soldiers. He introduced a series of measures like forbidding them to carry arms in the city, which left them vulnerable to any attack. Zāwī b. Zīrī, the most prominent leader, was refused access to the palace, and the quarter where most of them had their homes was pillaged. This humiliation culminated in their expulsion from the city after an abortive coup attempt.

In order to press their claims, the Berbers adopted a member of the Umayyad family, Sulaymān b. al-Ḥakam, as their candidate for the throne. They moved north, where their advances were rejected by the Slav commander Wāḍiḥ at Medinaceli but where they negotiated the support of Sancho García of Castile. Then the joint Berber-Castilian army attacked the capital. The hostile accounts we have of the Cordovan army show clearly that this was a town militia of tradesmen with little equipment and less experience in warfare. Not surprisingly, they were severely defeated by their professional opponents. In November 1009, Sulaymān entered the city and was proclaimed caliph with the title of al-Mustaʿīn. Amid a sullen populace he was acclaimed by the Berbers and gave his ally Sancho García a formal reception.

Inevitably there was a reaction. Al-Mahdī escaped to Toledo and Wāḍiḥ obtained Christian support from the counts of Barcelona and Urgell. This time the Berbers were defeated in May 1010, and once more al-Mahdī was accepted as caliph in Córdoba. Now, however, his regime was based on the support of the Slav soldiers led by Wāḍiḥ rather than the populace and they tired of him rapidly. In July 1010 he was murdered and replaced by the useless Hishām II once again. These events took place against the background of a siege by the Berbers which lasted from 1010 to 1013 and resulted in terrible hardship among the inhabitants. Within the city Wāḍiḥ attempted to assume the role of his erstwhile master al-Manṣūr, but this aroused the apprehensions of the Cordovans and, in October 1011, he too was murdered. By May 1013 the citizens had had enough and they asked for terms. Although a safe conduct was granted, the Berber troops were unrestrained in their pillage and destruction of the city. In many ways, the sack of Córdoba in 1013 marks the end of its role as a capital; from this time on it was an important city but it had lost the dominance which it had enjoyed in the tenth century. From 1013 other centres of power in *al-Andalus* were possible.

Attempts to restore central authority continued to be made. The most sustained of these was made not by the Umayyads but by the Ḥammūdī brothers, Berbers who claimed Arab descent. The Ḥammūdīs were late arrivals on the Andalusi scene. It was not until the second reign of Sulaymān from 1013 that ʿAlī was given the governorate of Ceuta, and his brother al-Qāsim received Algeciras and Tangier. The family did have one advantage over other Berber leaders, their ancestry. Much of the original success of the Umayyads in establishing themselves in *al-Andalus* had been due to their descent from the caliphs of Damascus and their consequent prestige and ability to stand apart from and above local feuds and jealousies and so attract loyalty from a wide cross-section of society. The Ḥammūdīs were Idrisids and so ultimately descended from the fourth caliph, ʿAlī b. Abī Ṭālib, and belonged to the house of the Prophet himself. They were of Quraysh descent and they had more chance of attracting widespread support than even the most powerful Berber chiefs.

In 1016 ʿAlī b. Ḥammūd took advantage of growing Berber disenchantment with their Caliph Sulaymān and, claiming to be the legitimate heir and avenger of Hishām II, he marched on Córdoba. For a while he made a serious attempt to build up a broad-based coalition of Cordovan people and Berbers, but their mutual hostility meant that he had more and more to depend on Berber military force and in 1018 he was assassinated by some domestic slaves.

His disconcerted supporters then sent for his brother al-Qāsim who was, for a time, more successful. He conciliated the Cordovans and had good relations with the Slav leaders, confirming Khayrān in Almeria and Zuhayr in Jaen. In an attempt to free himself from total dependence on the Berbers, he began to build up a bodyguard of Negro troops. As always, the Berbers felt their position threatened and joined ʿAlī's son Yaḥyā in rebellion in 1021 in Malaga; the resulting civil war destroyed the Ḥammūdid attempt. Its fate serves to illustrate the almost insuperable problems faced by anyone who tried to restore a state which would be acceptable to all Andalusis, rather than be dominated by Berbers, Slavs or any other group.

Other Umayyads were chosen by the Cordovans to occupy the Alcazar of their ancestors but none of them was able to sustain his power, having neither reliable troops nor a regular income to call upon. For most of *al-Andalus*, the caliphate was now an irrelevance. In 1031 a leading local notable, Abūʾl-Ḥazm b. Jahwar, persuaded the Cordovans that it was more trouble than it was worth, and the Umayyad caliphate of *al-Andalus* was definitively and finally abolished. So bitter had the experience of the last quarter of a century been that no serious effort was made to revive it.

The abolition of the caliphate in 1031 had little impact beyond Córdoba itself. The real change had come much earlier, during the long siege of the capital between 1010 and 1013 when central government had been paralysed. This period saw a clear change of attitude among some of the Berber chiefs. The Zirid leaders of the Ṣanhāja Berbers established themselves in the Granada area, apparently on the invitation of the local inhabitants who wanted protectors in these uncertain times. By 1013, the Zirids already had effective power there and their priorities had shifted: they no longer wished to control the central government in the interests of the Berbers but rather sought to keep it weak so that their rule in their own area would not be challenged.

A similar process occurred in other areas of *al-Andalus*. Sometimes it was other groups of Berber soldiers who established local power-bases, like the Banū Birzāl in Carmona. As noted, the Slav leaders tended to gravitate towards the Levante and the east coast, and from Tortosa in the north to Almeria in the south the cities were ruled either by Slav leaders or, like Valencia after 1021, by scions of the ʿAmirid dynasty, in this case a son of Sanchuelo. The preference of the Slavs and ʿAmirids for this area probably reflects the fact that the Levante had no well-established Islamic elite to challenge them. Until the tenth century, the area seems to have been very sparsely populated and much of it was used as winter pasture by transhumant Berbers from the eastern Meseta. In the tenth and eleventh centuries, however, the area was won over for settled agriculture and became one of the richest parts of Muslim Spain.

Elsewhere, power was seized by people of local origin. In Seville the Banū'l-Ḥajjāj who were ruling in 912 disappeared during the course of the tenth century, but they were replaced by another long-established elite family of Arab origin, the Banū ʿAbbād. On the collapse of Cordovan government, Muḥammad b. Ismāʿīl b. ʿAbbād used his position as *qāḍī* to become effective ruler of the city. The centres of the lower and middle marches (Badajoz and Toledo) were in a slightly different position. The conquests of al-Nāṣir in 929–30 had largely destroyed the power of the local elites, and in the period of the crisis at Córdoba we find Badajoz taken over by a Slav commander and Toledo, like Seville, by the local *qāḍī*. Neither was able to sustain himself for long. Badajoz and the lower march were seized by a Berber dynasty called the Banū'l-Aftas. This had long been a Berber-dominated area and it seems that the Aftasids were old-established pastoral Berbers, not newly arrived mercenaries. Toledo, too, was soon taken over by a Berber dynasty based in the surrounding countryside, the Banū'l-Dhū'l-Nūn.

In contrast to the lower and middle marches, the upper march, together with the mountainous areas of the eastern Meseta, had not been effectively brought under control by al-Nāṣir and traditional local power structures survived here almost unaltered. The Dhū'l-Nūnids effectively dominated the Huete and

Ucles areas from the ninth century and they made their peace with al-Nāṣir. We do not hear of them in the period of al-Manṣūr and al-Muẓaffar, but the fact that they reappear as local magnates with the collapse of the caliphate strongly suggests continuity. The Banū Razīn at Albarracin too had survived unscathed and there was one curious survival from the very earliest days of *al-Andalus*: the little town of Alpuente was ruled by a member of the Fihrī family, who had challenged the Umayyads for power in *al-Andalus* in the eighth century and who had long had contacts among the local Berbers.

Zaragoza and the upper march continued to be ruled by the Tujībīs as they had been for well over a century. Al-Manṣūr had favoured Maʿn b. ʿAbd al-ʿAzīz al-Tujībī, described as *fāris al-ʿarab* ('the knight of the Arabs'), as the leading Arab commander in his army. When ʿAbd al-Raḥmān b. al-Mutarrif al-Tujībī, increasingly apprehensive about his position and feeling himself the one important figure in the state not liquidated by al-Manṣūr, joined the abortive rebellion of al-Manṣūr's son and was executed, he was replaced in Zaragoza by his nephew: al-Manṣūr could execute individual members of the family but he was not powerful enough to remove the whole dynasty from its seat of power.

In some cases, like the settlement of the Berbers in the south, new elements in Andalusi society consciously broke with the centralised regime which had nurtured them because they felt more secure in charge of their own sources of income. In many other areas, the passing of the caliphate allowed well-established local powers to become independent rulers in their own right. The break up of the caliphate into Taifa kingdoms cannot really be understood without remembering that *al-Andalus* had usually been a land of *taifas*; it was central control from Córdoba that was the exception.

By 1025, *al-Andalus* had broken up beyond repair and already the Christians were taking advantage, as when Sancho García paraded his men in triumph through the streets of Córdoba in 1010. However, at this stage they were content with payment, loot and the new-found domestic security they enjoyed; it was not until the second half of the eleventh century that the Christian powers began to make territorial gains at Muslim expense.

SICILY

In the tenth and early eleventh centuries, Sicily was an integral part of the Islamic world and was becoming increasingly populous and prosperous as time went on. The court of the amirs in Palermo was a cultural centre of some importance and both jurists and poets found patronage there. It is all the more frustrating, therefore, that the Muslims of the time did not leave more extensive records. Apart from the brief and uninspired chronicle, known, rather bizarrely, as the *Cronica di Cambridge*, they left no surviving histories.[4] Other contemporary Muslim sources are not much more helpful and the only first-hand account we have is the geographer Ibn Ḥawqāl's record of his visit in the mid-tenth century, full of incidental detail and acerbic comment but too short to give a full picture.[5] Nor is the archaeological evidence much more substantial, and there are no surviving buildings on the island which can be reliably attributed to this period. Instead we are obliged to depend on late compilers, Ibn al-Athīr (*d.* 1234), Ibn Idhārī (*fl.* 1300), al-Nuwayrī (*d.* 1332) and Ibn Khaldūn (*d.* 1406). All were conscientious and careful historians but their material is naturally abbreviated and lacking in depth.

An interesting problem is posed by the evidence from the Norman period, some of it in Arabic. This tells us a good deal about the administration but it is by no means clear that it can be projected back into the tenth and early eleventh centuries; Arabic administrative practice may well have been further developed under Norman rule. An example is posed by the well-known division of the island into Val di Mazara, Val di Noto and Val Demone. While the word Val represents the Arabic *wilāyah*, meaning a district, the usage is first attested in Norman times; does the division represent the administrative arrangements of the Muslim period or a terminology devised by Arabic clerks working for the Norman kings? It is impossible to tell.

The result of this paucity of sources is that the history of Muslim Sicily 900–1025 amounts to little more than a thin chronicle of the comings and goings of rulers and raids on the Byzantine mainland. It is difficult to give a rounded picture of what must have been one of the more complex and advanced societies in the tenth-century Mediterranean world.

At the beginning of the tenth century, Sicily was ruled by governors who were more or less under the control of the Aghlabid rulers of Ifrīqiyyah (the Arab province corresponding approximately to modern Tunisia). Sicily was close to the centre of Aghlabid power but it was by no means a docile province. The history of the island since the Muslim conquest in the previous century had been troubled by repeated tensions, as governors, often with the support of the Muslim population of Sicily, attempted to establish their independence from the Aghlabids. Muslim Sicily remained very much a conquest state. The last Christian outpost on the island itself, at Taormina, fell in 902, but it is clear from tenth-century history that many Christian areas, especially in the western half of the island, continued to enjoy considerable autonomy in practice. Raids on the Italian mainland were still an important feature of military activity and probably an important source of revenue as well, and they had reached a new

---

[4] For the *Cambridge Chronicle*, which exists in both Arabic and Greek versions, see Vasiliev (1935), pp. 342–6 and (1950), pp. 99–106.   [5] Ibn Ḥawqāl, *Ṣūrat al-arḍ*, pp. 118–31.

intensity at the turn of the century under the leadership of the Aghlabid amir Ibrāhīm who was killed in 902 besieging Cosenza.

Perhaps because of this concentration on the *jihād*, Muslim Sicily remained a brigand polity and does not seem to have developed very much in the way of government institutions. Political activity seems to have been confined to Palermo, where the *jund* (military of North African origin) dominated the scene. There is little mention in the brief annals of this period of provincial governors, fiscal administration or native Sicilian converts.

The immediate reaction of the Sicilian Muslims to the Fatimid takeover of Qayrawān, capital of Ifrīqiyyah, in 909, was to expel the Aghlabid governor and install a man of their own choice, Ibn Abī'l-Fawāris to represent the new dynasty. This display of local autonomy tinged with submission did not, however, please the new masters of Ifrīqiyyah, and when the governor went to receive his investiture in the capital he was detained and a prominent supporter of the Fatimids, al-Ḥasan b. Aḥmad, known strangely as Ibn Abī Khanzīr ('son of the father of the pig') was appointed. On his arrival, he appointed his brother as governor (*ʿāmil*) of Agrigento, which emerges at this time as the second city of Muslim Sicily. He also appointed an official called the *ṣaḥib al-khums*, who effectively functioned as deputy governor. The *khums* was the name given to the fifth part of the booty captured in wars against the infidels which was reserved for the ruler. This may suggest that booty was still an important source of state revenue but may also mean that the management of these revenues was becoming more formalised. Interestingly, the office has no parallel elsewhere in Islamic administrative practice and seems to be distinctively Sicilian.

This high-handed treatment of local feelings provoked a major uprising in the late summer of 913. Not only did the Sicilian Muslims revolt and appoint a scion of the dispossessed Aghlabid family as their governor, but the Christians in the Taormina area refused to pay the *jizyah* (poll-tax), thus rejecting Muslim rule. A further element was soon added to the chaos when the largely Berber Muslim population of Agrigento rejected the Aghlabid governor, who was captured and sent to Ifrīqiyyah, where he was executed.

These disturbances were suppressed by a full-scale invasion by Fatimid troops in 916. These were led by Abū Saʿīd Mūsā b. Aḥmad al-Ḍayf and were largely composed of Kutāmah Berbers, a tribe whose members formed the backbone of the Fatimid army both in North Africa and later in Egypt. They crushed the resistance of the Sicilian Muslims, destroying the walls of Palermo and disarming its inhabitants. When Abū Saʿīd returned to Ifrīqiyyah in 917 he left a large garrison of Kutāmah and a Kutāmī governor, Sālim b. Rashīd behind him.

The invasion of 916–17 saw the effective imposition of Fatimid rule in the island. This was characterised by a reliance on a garrison of outside troops (the Kutāmah in this case), the disarming of the local Muslim populace and the imposition of more regular taxes to pay for this new military presence. As was so often the case in the Islamic world, this led to the development of a new and separate official quarter in Palermo, where the governor and his military forces could live a separate life from the rest of the population and defend themselves if necessary; in 937 Sālim's successor, Khalīl b. Isḥāq began the development of the Khāliṣah quarter (whose position and name are commemorated in the Piazza della Kalza in Palermo). These changes have many parallels in the medieval Muslim world, but perhaps most strikingly in Muslim Spain in the reign of ʿAbd al-Raḥmān III (912–61). Like his Spanish contemporary, Sālim made a point of distinguishing himself in the *jihād* in Calabria, winning both booty and prestige.

The changes drastically reduced the privileged position of the existing Muslim inhabitants and led to open rebellion in Agrigento in 937. The immediate cause of the uprising is said to have been that the inhabitants were obliged to cut wood for the fleet, but there was more general resentment about taxation and loss of status. There may have also been religious factors at work: the overwhelming majority of the Muslims of Sicily were Sunnis and regarded the claims of the Shiʾite Fatimid caliphs to divinely inspired leadership of the whole Muslim world with incredulity or contempt. This would have been especially true of the Kharijites, who opposed all of the established caliphates. In 909 the Fatimids had destroyed the Kharijite community at Tahart and some of its members seem to have come to Sicily, settling in mountainous Enna and other areas of the island. The revolt rapidly spread to Palermo and soon the whole island was involved, leaving the governor powerless.

The Fatimid caliph al-Qāʾim responded by sending a large army led by Khalīl b. Isḥāq b. Ward, who set about putting down the rebellion with great brutality, ravaging the country and leaving famine in his wake. Despite help from the Byzantines, to whom the insurgents appealed, resistance was finally crushed in 939, when Agrigento was forced to surrender. Khalīl left the island in 941 since his services were required to combat the revolt in North Africa of Abū Yazīd, 'the man on the donkey', which threatened the very existence of the Fatimid caliphate. He left behind him a ruined country, but one in which the bulk of the Muslim population was subjected. It was on these foundations that his successors were able to create the prosperous, stable and comparatively peaceful Muslim Sicily of the late tenth and early eleventh centuries.

The departure of Khalīl was followed by a period of anarchy while the Fatimids were preoccupied with the North African revolt. The notables of Palermo attempted to regain their lost status. It was not until 948 that the caliph was able once more to spare any resources to re-establish order. In this year the

Caliph al-Manṣūr appointed al-Ḥasan b. ʿAlī al-Kalbī as governor, whose family were to rule the island for the next century. Al-Ḥasan claimed descent from the Arab tribe of Kalb, powerful in the Syrian desert at the time of the first Muslim conquests, but his most loyal supporters were not Arabs but the Kuāmah Berbers. He himself had become important as a leader of the Fatimid forces in the struggle against the rebellion of Abū Yazīd and he was therefore a natural choice to send to troublesome Sicily.

Having first overcome the opposition of the established Palermo elite, al-Ḥasan played an important part in wider Mediterranean rivalries as the Fatimids struggled with the Byzantines and the Umayyads of Córdoba for mastery. Fatimid–Umayyad rivalries were mostly played out in the western Maghreb (Morocco and western Algeria), where each side attempted to control the area through its clients among the Berber tribes, but there was also a maritime dimension to the conflict. In 953 the Fatimids made a treaty with the traditional enemy, the Byzantines of Calabria, and in 954 open warfare with *al-Andalus* broke out when a Sicilian merchant ship was captured. Al-Ḥasan led the Sicilian fleet to burn Almeria and in 955 ʿAbd al-Raḥmān III responded by making an alliance with the Byzantines. This resulted in sporadic and inconclusive naval warfare off the coasts of Calabria and Sicily as well as raids by the Muslims into Calabria. The events are interesting as an example of long-distance diplomacy and strategic thinking in the tenth century but had few lasting results.

In 960 the Caliph al-Muʿizz recalled al-Ḥasan. The caliph's eyes were now firmly turned on Egypt and he wanted the Kalbīs to lead his fleet. He also needed peace in Sicily so that he would not be distracted by events on the island, so he was prepared to allow al-Ḥasan's son Aḥmad to succeed to his father's office. There was certainly no intention at this stage to make the Kalbīs hereditary rulers of Sicily but this was in effect what happened. When Aḥmad in turn was recalled in 969 to lead the Fatimid navy to Egypt there was an immediate uprising against the Fatimids and their Kutāmah military. The caliph was obliged to send Aḥmad's brother Abū'l-Qāsim (970–82) to restore order, thus effectively confirming the family's position. After the conquest of Egypt in 969, Fatimid priorities changed completely: Egypt, Syria, Byzantium and even Iraq were the objects of their concern and North Africa and Sicily were relegated to the backburner. They were happy to allow the Zirids in Ifrīqiyyah and the Kalbīs in Sicily to enjoy hereditary governorships, as long as they accepted the nominal overlordship of Cairo, looked to the caliphs for formal investiture and had the caliph's name inscribed on their coins and pronounced in the *khuṭba* (the sermon in the mosque at Friday prayers).

The period of Fatimid rule saw a greatly increased rate of conversion to Islam. The sources do not give us clear evidence about this but it is likely that at the beginning of the tenth century only a small fraction of the population of the island were Muslims and that most of these were concentrated in Palermo and the Val di Mazara in the south and west of the island. It is probable that the percentage increased significantly in the course of the next hundred years, and by the early eleventh century it is possible that around half the total population of the island was Muslim. Although churches and a few monasteries still survived, it seems that the ecclesiastical hierarchy was no longer functioning. Conversion, however, was very unevenly distributed and areas in the Val Demona and the western half of the island were still largely Christian, though under Muslim political control.

This process was partly the result of government action. The Fatimids claimed to be the rightful leaders of the Muslim community and it was natural that they should encourage the spread of the religion to enhance their claims. In 962 al-Muʿizz sent vast amounts of money and fine robes as presents for 14,000 Sicilian boys who were circumcised at the same time. He also wrote to the governor ordering him to build a mosque and a *minbar* (pulpit) in each of the fourteen administrative districts (*iqlīm*) into which the island was divided, which shows the caliph's concern for the spread of Islam but also that there were areas, which had previously had no mosque to speak of. The Kalbīs also put an end to the semi-independent Christian communities which survived in the Taormina and Rametta areas, and in 963, despite Byzantine military help, Rametta fell to Muslims. The continuing *jihād* in Calabria must have sharpened religious differences on the island and made the Christian population suspect among many Muslims.

The pace of conversion in Sicily was increased by further waves of immigration from North Africa, especially after the famines of 1004 and 1015, while some Christians continued to emigrate to Calabria. As in all early Muslim states, conversion to Islam was encouraged by the imposition of the *jizyah* on non-Muslims, which meant that there were fiscal advantages in becoming a Muslim. This naturally decreased state revenues and it may have been as a result of this that the Amir Jaʿfar b. Yūsuf al-Kalbī (998–1019) and his *wazīr*, al-Ḥasan b. Muḥammad al-Baghāyī imposed the tithe (*ʿushr*) as a compulsory levy on agricultural produce. Even though this was standard practice in other Muslim countries, it caused great resentment among the Sicilian Muslims and a revolution which cost the *wazīr* his life.

Along with the Islamisation of Sicily went the continuing *jihād* in southern Italy. This enthusiasm stemmed partly from the desire to legitimise Kalbid rule and partly, no doubt, from the desire for booty. No effort seems to have been made to expand Muslim rule into southern Italy on a permanent basis but the raids were far reaching. The most aggressive of the Kalbī amirs was Abūʾl-Qāsim (970–82). In 976 he drove out a Byzantine force which had occupied

Messina and went on to attack Cosenza, Taranto and Otranto, all of which paid tribute. He raided southern Italy again in 978 and 981. He faced his biggest challenge when the Emperor Otto II invaded Calabria in 982. In July Abū'l-Qāsim confronted him at Capo Cotrone. At first the German forces had the upper hand but the Muslims counter-attacked and defeated them. It was a fitting end to his career that Abū'l-Qāsim himself was killed in this battle, a martyr for Islam. Raids did not cease with his death and Muslim expeditions continued to invade Calabria and places further afield: in 994 Matera was taken, and Bari, the capital of Byzantine Italy, was threatened in 988, 1003 and 1023. The early eleventh century saw a diminution in this aggressive activity and the shape of things to come was clearly demonstrated when a Pisan fleet appeared in the straits of Messina in 1005–6 and defeated the Sicilian navy. At the beginning of the eleventh century, too, the Kalbid state, as far as we can judge, had ceased to be a conquest polity, dependent on booty and raiding; the amirs now lived a sedentary life in luxurious palaces in Palermo, and they and their military elite were maintained by a tax-collecting bureaucracy.

The second half of the tenth and the early eleventh century seem to have been a period of growing prosperity and increasing population. Palermo itself became a very large city with a population of perhaps 100,000 and new settlements seem to have spread in rural areas. This prosperity was partly based on the introduction of new crops, citrus fruit, sugar cane and cotton among them. It also seems that the great grain producing latifundia of late Roman times were broken up into smaller, more intensively cultivated areas, where irrigation was practised. Crops like cotton and mulberries fed a thriving textile industry. International trade developed and Sicily benefited from being a centre of exchange between Amalfi and other Italian cities and the Fatimids. Trade with Ifrīqiyyah was especially important, with the Sicilians sending agricultural products in exchange for slaves and gold. Throughout the Fatimid period, the rulers of Muslim Sicily minted the *ruba'ī*, the distinctive gold quarter-dinar which the Italians imitated and called the *tari*.

After the move of the Fatimids to Egypt in 969 the political history of the island was fairly uneventful. The martyred Abū'l-Qāsim was succeeded by three short-lived amirs from his family and then from 990 to 998 by Yūsuf b. 'Abd Allāh, who was given the title of Thiqat al-Dawla by the Fatimids and whose reign saw the high point of Kalbid power and prosperity, the court becoming a centre for poetry and intellectual activity. The Kalbids continued to rule as vassals of the Fatimids and the family was closely involved with politics in Cairo. When the Caliph al-Ḥākim was proclaimed in 996, the Kutāmah troops in Cairo insisted that al-Ḥasan b. 'Ammār al-Kalbī should be appointed *wāṣitah* (essentially, prime minister) to support their interests against those of their Turkish rivals.

Yūsuf's successor, Jaʿfar b. Yūsuf (998–1019), continued in his father's ways but towards the end of his reign the internal peace of the island was shattered by a series of upheavals whose causes are not entirely clear. In 1015 the Kutāmah and black slaves of the army, led by the amir's brother ʿAlī, revolted. They were defeated, and after their rout Jaʿfar ordered that all the Kutāmah, who had been the mainstay of family power for so long, should leave the island. Three years later, in 1019, there was the further uprising in protest against taxation mentioned above. Jaʿfar went into exile in Cairo and was succeeded by his son Aḥmad (1019–36), known as al-Akḥal (the man who blackens his eye with *koḥl* or antimony), whose reign saw increasing internal disorder, especially when the amir's son was perceived to be favouring new immigrants from Ifrīqiyyah over native Sicilian Muslims. In 1035 al-Akḥal made a treaty with the Byzantines and received the Byzantine honorific of *magister*, which again sharply divided Muslim opinion in the island. The amir's opponents invited in al-Muʿizz b. Bādīs, the Zirid ruler of Ifrīqiyyah, who defeated and killed al-Akḥal in 1036. Though another member of the family, Ṣamṣām b. Yūsuf (1040–1053), was able to claim the title, internal division and renewed Byzantine invasions in the 1040s prevented a real revival of Kalbid power, and Muslim Sicily was laid fatally exposed to outside invasion.

CHAPTER 28

THE SPANISH KINGDOMS

Roger Collins

THE KINGDOM OF LEÓN (910–1037)

The Arab conquest of most of the Iberian peninsula in 711 destroyed the centralising governmental structures of the Visigothic monarchy and of the Spanish church. One of the first beneficiaries of this was the small kingdom that developed from *c.* 718 onwards in the northern mountains. This Asturian realm aggrandised itself primarily at the expense of its Galician and Basque neighbours until it was able to extend itself southwards on to the plateau of the Meseta. This southwards shift of the frontier which occurred during the second half of the ninth century led to a comparable displacement of the political centre of gravity, symbolised by the transfer of the main royal residence and administrative centre from Oviedo in the Asturias to the former Roman legionary settlement of León.

The deposition of Alfonso III of the Asturias by his son García (910–913/14) in 910 marks the formal divide between the Asturian and Leonese monarchies, but there was no break in dynastic continuity. Even the transfer of the principal seat of royal government from Oviedo to León may not have taken place before the reign of the second of Alfonso's sons, Ordoño II (913/14–924). This move was a sign of a greater sense of security, in that the new site was more vulnerable to attack from the Arab-ruled south. However, the dissolution of the central power of the Umayyad amirate of Córdoba during a period extending from the 880s to the 920s must have made such a danger seem increasingly remote. At the same time, the political and economic importance of the rapidly expanding southern frontier districts of the former kingdom of the Asturias made the removal of the centre of royal authority to a site closer to and better placed to supervise those regions increasingly desirable.

Although the monarchy had since its inception remained in the hands of a single dynasty, it was not inherently strong. Its governmental apparatus was minimal. There may have been no permanent royal writing office, and the

670

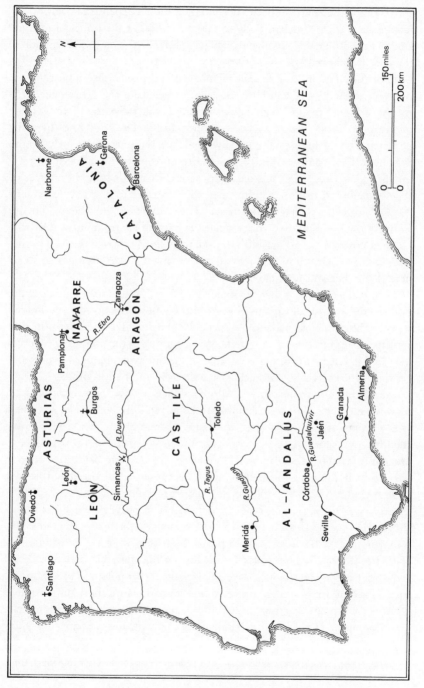

15   The Spanish peninsula, c. 1000

extension of the kings' authority beyond their capital depended largely on the maintenance of a sufficient body of support amongst the principal regional landowners. While it is possible that some at least of the kings were anointed, this usually followed a process of selection on the part of the principal lay magnates of the kingdom, and all male members of the royal house appear to have been considered as eligible. It is possible to delineate the genealogies of a number of the principal regional aristocratic families. Several of the leading members of these held the office of count. Comital duties cannot be easily designated on the basis of the available evidence, but they clearly included the holding of local courts of justice as well as responsibility for raising and directing the military resources of their districts. It is clear, although the sources of the obligation are not, that all free men were required to take part in royal or comitally directed military expeditions.[1] These, together with the building up of their own landholdings on a generally expanding frontier, enabled the regional aristocracies to establish considerable local power-bases *vis-à-vis* the Leonese monarchs. From the 930s onwards comital offices, although formally in royal gift, became inheritable.

The greatest problem that has to be faced in trying to understand both the politics and the social organisation of the Leonese kingdom is the limited nature of the available evidence. In particular, the dearth of narrative historical records makes this period considerably more arid than the preceding Asturian kingdom in terms of our knowledge, let alone our assessment, of events and personalities. Only one chronicle was written in the period of the Leonese kingdom, probably in the reign of Alfonso V (999–1027). This was the work of a certain Sampiro, almost certainly a royal clerk and probably to be identified with a bishop of Astorga of the same name. Regrettably, the work, which took the form of a series of brief accounts of the reigns of the individual Leonese kings and was thus modelled on Isidore of Seville's *Historia Gothorum*, does not survive in its original form. It is, however, preserved incorporated in two twelfth-century histories. In one of these, the *Liber chronicorum* of Bishop Pelayo of Oviedo (1097–1130), Sampiro's text is heavily interpolated, and greater reliance is normally placed on the version of the text preserved in the anonymous *Historia Silense*, a work probably written in León.[2] In addition to these problems of its transmission, the text of the chronicle itself is exceedingly brief and tantalisingly allusive and lacking in chronological precision. As in the case of the Asturian kingdom, the limitations of the Latin narrative sources can in part be compensated for in the occasional references in Arab historiography. However, the fragmentary state of the principal text, the

---

[1] Sánchez-Albornoz (1965, 1970).

[2] *Sampiro, su crónica y la monarquía leonesa en el siglo X*, ed. Pérez de Urbel; *Historia Silense*, ed. Pérez de Urbel and González Ruiz-Zorilla.

Muqtabis of Ibn Ḥayyān (d. 1076), which contains extracts from an otherwise lost late tenth-century Arab work, means that only certain years are thus illuminated.

Where in evidential terms the Leonese kingdom considerably excels its Asturian predecessor is in the survival of charters. Most of those that are known have been preserved in a small number of twelfth- or thirteenth-century monastic cartularies, not all of which have yet been edited. Forgery and interpolation are relatively rare in these collections, though the *Liber testamentorum* of the cathedral of Oviedo is a notorious exception.[3] However, while they can provide excellent evidence for the accumulation of ecclesiastical and to a lesser extent lay landed estates, relatively few of the charters are of royal origin. It is thus difficult to build up pictures of the personnel and activities of the royal court in the tenth century in the way that it has been possible to do for its equivalent in the Castilian–Leonese kingdom of the late eleventh and early twelfth centuries.[4] One consequence of this has been that modern scholarly interest in the Leonese kingdom has tended to confine itself to the editing of charters and the study of monastic estates, while avoiding broader interpretations of its history.

Such materials survive from virtually all of the component sections of the Leonese kingdom. As its history in the tenth and early eleventh centuries shows, a fundamental flaw in the structure of this state was its inability to turn itself into something that was more than the sum of its parts. Territorially it expanded very little in the course of this period. The boundaries of the kingdom remained more or less those created in the preceding Asturian period. What did take place from the later ninth century onwards, however, was its intensive repopulation and resettlement, especially of the southern frontier districts. This involved the movement of population from the northern mountainous heartlands of the Asturias, Galicia and Cantabria, and the immigration into the kingdom of new elements both from the adjoining Basque regions to the east and from the Christian communities under Arab rule in the south. These latter, now known as Mozarabs, brought with them distinctive elements of the material and intellectual culture of al-Andalus.[5]

The frontiers of the kingdom were delineated roughly by a series of natural features. The central valley of the Duero, with a more tenuous southern extension towards the Sierra de Guadarrama, marked the borderlands across the south. To the west an earlier frontier represented by the lower Duero had been surpassed in the Asturian period and new fortified settlements had been established in the centre of what would later become Portugal in the mid-ninth

---

[3] Fernández Conde (1971).   [4] Rodríguez (1972, 1982, 1987) shows what can be done.
[5] See Hitchcock (1978) on nomenclature.

century. Coimbra, on the Río Mondego, was the principal southern bastion in this region. To the south-east the upper Duero was the frequently contested divide between the county of Castile that had come into existence around Burgos in the later ninth century and the middle march of al-Andalus, while the eastern boundary of Castile and therefore of the Leonese kingdom, which here fronted that of Pamplona, was normally to be found around the Sierra de Orbasa and the Río Glera. In both the eastern and western sections of the kingdom, just as the region of León had developed as a southwards extension of the Asturias, the frontier regions of Castile and Portugal had grown out of Alava and Galicia. In both cases the comital families, which had established themselves as hereditary dynasties by the mid-tenth century, came to outstrip in military power and political influence other noble lineages established in the earlier areas of settlement, now far removed from the frontiers.

The preceding Asturian kingdom had been able to extend itself territorially, and then to move its centre of government southwards to León, largely thanks to a period of political disintegration and military weakness in the Umayyad amirate of Córdoba. This had commenced in the final years of the reign of the Amir Muḥammad I (852–86), and lasted into the 920s.[6] A continuing consequence of this was the ability of the earliest of the Leonese kings to launch large-scale raids on their southern neighbours with relative impunity. García (910–913/14) sent at least one such expedition prior to his premature death at Zamora, and in 913, while he was still ruling, his brother Ordoño led another one from Galicia as far south as Evora. The town was captured and sacked and its Arab governor killed.

It is possible to suspect, on the basis of a comment in the work of the Arab historian Ibn Ḥayyān, that Ordoño had established an independent regime for himself in Galicia and was in conflict with his brother García at the time of the latter's death.[7] However, he was accepted as heir to the whole kingdom, and may have then carried out the transfer of its capital from Zamora to León. During his ten-year reign (913/14–924) he was able to continue raiding the Arab-ruled territories to the south and east. In 915 he led an expedition south towards Mérida, and in 918 he cooperated with Sancho Garcés I (905–25) of Pamplona in a large-scale raid in the upper Ebro valley, threatening the towns of Nájera, Tudela and Valtierra. Although none of these settlements were taken, the primary purpose of both of these campaigns appears to have been the looting of the countryside and the taking of captives. This was identical to the kind of warfare the Arab armies had waged against the Christian kingdoms in the ninth century. By the end of the decade, however, political conditions in the south had greatly improved, with the virtual elimination of the leading

---

[6] Lévi-Provençal (1950a), pp. 300–96.
[7] Ibn Ḥayyān, *Al-Muqtabis*, ed. Chalmeta and Corriente, p. 82.

rebels against Umayyad authority. Thus when the amir (and from 929 caliph) ʿAbd al-Raḥmān III (912–61) learnt in the autumn of 919 that Ordoño was planning a raid on the middle march in the following year, he felt able to launch a pre-emptive strike northwards in June 920. Under the amir's personal direction the Arab army invaded the Leonese territory in the upper Duero valley, taking Osma, before defeating the hastily gathered forces of Ordoño II and his ally Sancho Garcés on 25 July. Two Leonese bishops were captured in the rout. The Arab army proceeded on to the upper Ebro, restoring and replenishing Umayyad garrisons in that region.

Despite this, the first major riposte from the Umayyads for nearly forty years, Ordoño II continued his raids unabated. In 921 he launched another one, not reported in the Arab sources, which Sampiro claims nearly reached Córdoba.[8] On his return from this expedition he found that his wife, the Galician Elvira Menéndez, had died. He fairly rapidly married Aragonta González, the daughter of another Galician noble, but gave her up to make a politically more expedient third marriage to Sancha, the daughter of his ally Sancho Garcés I of Pamplona. This occurred within the context of a joint expedition in 923 by the two kings against the principal Arab fortresses in the Rioja: Nájera and Viguera. Both of these were captured. Ordoño II, however, died at Zamora soon after, in the opening months of 924, and was buried in the newly founded cathedral church in León.

His successor was his brother Fruela II (924–5), whose brief reign seems particularly marked by disputes over the succession. He had taken the throne despite the existence of at least three sons of Ordoño, and also faced unspecified difficulties with his cousins, the sons of his father Alfonso III's brother Olmund. The *Chronicle of Sampiro* records that he had them put to death unjustly, and claims that his own subsequent death from leprosy was divine punishment for this deed.[9] His removal led to a brief civil war between the sons of Ordoño II, which is only recorded in the work of Ibn Ḥayyān.[10] The eldest, Sancho Ordoñez, was able to seize León but was expelled by his brother Alfonso, who had the backing of another Alfonso, the son of Fruela II, and of Sancho Garcés I of Pamplona, who was also his father-in-law. Sancho Ordoñez was able instead to establish a kingdom for himself in Galicia, which he held until his death in 929. He was succeeded there by his brother Ramiro. This period of divisions within the ruling dynasty came to a climax with the mysterious events surrounding the abdication and subsequent restoration of the new Leonese king, Alfonso IV (925–31), the second son of Ordoño II.

In 931 the king apparently abdicated voluntarily in favour of his younger brother Ramiro, previously ruler of Galicia, and retired into monastic life. No

---

[8] *Sampiro* (both versions), p. 315.   [9] *Sampiro* (both versions), p. 319.

[10] Ibn Ḥayyān, *Al-Muqtabis*, ed. Chalmeta and Corriente, p. 233.

source, either Christian or Muslim, suggests that this was imposed on Alfonso IV, but if he was inspired by personal piety it proved short-lived. In 932 when the new king Ramiro II was absent campaigning in the vicinity of Toledo, Alfonso left his monastery and tried to raise a revolt in Simancas. He was apparently persuaded to desist by some of his relatives and erstwhile supporters. However, he tried again in 933 and succeeded in making himself master of León. Ramiro II, who was then at Zamora, reacted speedily and crushed his brother's short-lived restoration. At the same time, it seems that three of the sons of Fruela II were attempting to establish an independent kingdom for themselves in the Asturias. They were also rapidly overcome in 933. Ramiro prevented further such revolts by having his brother Alfonso and the sons of Fruela blinded.

Ramiro II (931–51) continued to pursue the military and political objectives of the more successful of his predecessors. These would seem to have been, first, the securing of the frontiers of the kingdom along the valley of the Duero, by means of repopulation and the establishment of new or restored settlements; second, the encouragement of any elements in the marches of al-Andalus opposed to the rule of the Umayyads; and, third, the prosecution of a series of economically valuable raids on the south by royal armies or those raised by the frontier nobility. The almost traditional opposition to centralised rule from Córdoba evinced throughout the Umayyad period by such major cities as Toledo and Zaragoza provided considerable opportunities for the Leonese rulers. Ramiro attempted to succour the rebels in Toledo during ʿAbd al-Raḥmān III's two-year blockade of the city in 930–2, but was unable to prevent its eventual fall to the caliph. This was in part a product of his difficulties in those years with his brother Alfonso IV. From 934 to 937 Ramiro provided aid for the rebel lord of Zaragoza, Muḥammad ibn Hashim. This proved so effective that in 935 ʿAbd al-Raḥmān III negotiated a truce with León to try to stem this assistance, but Ramiro broke the agreement when his ally was besieged in Zaragoza by an Umayyad army in 936. In turn the success of the Leonese intervention that year caused the caliph to lead an expedition in person to force the submission of Zaragoza in 937. Ramiro, however, was then able to give assistance to another rebel, who had made himself master of Santarém in southern Portugal.

It was probably this continuous Leonese involvement in anti-Umayyad revolts, extending over a geographical span that reached from the Atlantic to the Ebro valley that led ʿAbd al-Raḥmān III, once he had eliminated the rebel in Santarém in January 939, to plan a devastating attack on the kingdom of León. The expedition that he led northwards in July of that year led to one of the relatively few large-scale battles between the two parties, and the outcome was a distinct surprise, probably to both sides. ʿAbd al-Raḥmān marched via

Toledo on a direct route towards León, encountering Christian resistance only when he reached the fortress of Simancas on the Pisuerga, a tributary of the Duero. Here on 8 August the caliph's forces suffered a humiliating defeat at the hands of the Leonese army. ʿAbd al-Raḥmān himself was forced to flee, allowing his tent and even his personal copy of the Qurʿān to be captured.

In itself the battle of Simancas was in no sense decisive. In 940 the caliph prepared for another expedition against León, while Ramiro II opened negotiations for peace. Neither side wished to renew the full-scale hostilities of 939, and the peace treaty was finally concluded in October of 941. Amongst other things ʿAbd al-Raḥmān's Qurʿān was returned to him, and the former Zaragozan rebel Muḥammad ibn Ḥashim, who had since become a loyal subject of the caliph, was released from Leonese captivity. The willingness of the Umayyad ruler to make this peace, and the moralising remarks on the episode made by Arab historians, give some sense, however, of the heavy blow that the battle in 939 had inflicted on Islamic morale. The caliph himself avoided leading his armies in person for the rest of his reign. Regrettably, the fifth book of the *Muqtabis* of Ibn Ḥayyān ends with the events of the year 942, and the subsequent book is entirely lost. In the concluding chapters Ibn Ḥayyān claimed that Ramiro was breaking the peace treaty in 942 by allowing Count Vermudo Nuñez of Salamanca to raid the central march and by sending Count Fernán González of Castile to aid King García Sánchez of Pamplona in an attack on Tudela.[11] However, it is possible that these were independent initiatives on the part of the counts. No further royal campaigning is recorded in the *Chronicle of Sampiro* before the last year of Ramiro's life in 950. Then he is stated to have led a raid on Talavera, which resulted in the taking of 7000 captives. He fell ill in Oviedo soon after his return, and died at León in January 951.[12]

If the raids of 942 were made independently of royal authority, it would not be the first time that the frontier counts acted without the consent or indeed in defiance of the king. Amongst the principal backers of Alfonso IV in 932 and 933 had been the Castilian Count Fernando Ansúrez and members of his affinity, who had also been part of a group of comital rebels in this region against Ordoño II in 922. The failure of their candidate, the former Alfonso IV, to re-establish himself on the Leonese throne, led to royal patronage being given instead to their local rival, Fernán González, the recently created count of Lara. The latter also ingratiated himself with the neighbouring Pamplonan monarchy by marrying the royal widow Sancha Sánchez, who had flouted Leonese convention by not entering a convent on the death of her husband, Ordoño II.

---

[11] Ibn Ḥayyān, *Al-Muqtabis*, ed. Chalmeta and Corriente, p. 326.
[12] See Rodríguez (1982), pp. 35–43 for revised dating.

This made Fernán González the brother-in-law of the new king of Pamplona, García Sánchéz I (933–70), and also explains his willingness to aid the latter's attack on Tudela in 942. Fortified both by his own strong military following in Castile and by his ties to Pamplona, Fernán González is reported to have plotted a revolt, in alliance with Count Diego Muñoz of Saldaña. Ramiro II acted rapidly, and both of the rebel counts were imprisoned. It is testimony, however, to the strength of Fernán González's local position that the king in due course found it expedient to restore him to his office, though attempting to secure his loyalty by marrying the count's daughter to his elder son and heir, the future Ordoño III (*c.* 947?).

The problems of the political balancing acts that the Leonese kings needed to perform to satisfy the aspirations of rival sets of regional nobilities became acute in the reigns of Ramiro's two sons: Ordoño III (951–6) and Sancho I the Fat (956–8, 959–66). They themselves were half-brothers, and the history of their father's marriages illustrates the political tensions underlying the apparent stability of the Leonese monarchy. As has been seen, Ramiro II came to power in somewhat mysterious circumstances, with the backing of Galician counts, and replacing the Pamplonan-supported Alfonso IV. His first wife, who was also his cousin, was Adosinda Gutiérrez, the daughter of an important Galician comital dynasty. Between his accession in 931 and 934 Ramiro repudiated her, and in the latter year married Urraca Sánchez, one of the daughters of Sancho Garcés I of Pamplona, and sister of the wives of Alfonso IV and of Fernán González. The pattern here would seem to be identical to that established by the second and third marriages of Ramiro's father Ordoño II: a Galician bride was repudiated in the interests of securing a politically more useful Navarrese marriage.

Not surprisingly, the sons of Ramiro II from his two ventures into matrimony enjoyed the particular support of their respective mothers' peoples. Ordoño III could rely on Galician backing, which proved vital when in 956 he was faced with a confederacy of García Sánchez of Pamplona and Fernán González of Castile, determined to secure the Leonese throne for his half-brother Sancho. In the aftermath, the count of Castile was once more brought back into the Leonese orbit. He was, after all, the king's father-in-law. However, relations may not have been good between Ordoño III and Urraca Fernández, and the king's only known child was a son called Vermudo, who was almost certainly illegitimate and of Galician origin. Although his age cannot be calculated with certainty, Ordoño III probably died before he reached his thirtieth birthday. As a king he seems to have followed his father's military example, and is credited with responsibility for a very profitable raid down the Atlantic seaboard, culminating in the sack, though not the retention, of Lisbon. His memory as a war leader was revered in the Leonese historiographical tradition, as enunciated by Sampiro: 'He was an extremely clever man and in the use and deployment of armies exceedingly wise.'[13]

No such tribute could be paid to his successor. Ordoño III's half-brother Sancho I (956–8, 959–66) had the misfortune not only to be known by later generations as 'the Fat' but also suffered from the consequences during his own lifetime. His inability to mount a horse obviously cast doubts on his credibility as a leader of armies, and this compounded the difficulties he had to face in succeeding a brother with whom he notoriously had not got on, and whose supporters were bound to be disadvantaged under the new regime. Thus, within two years of his accession Sancho had been overthrown by a noble coup which saw him replaced on the Leonese throne by Ordoño IV the Bad (958–9), the son of Alfonso IV and one of the very few surviving male members of the royal line. Apart from any of the blinded sons of Fruela II, the only other candidate would have been Vermudo, the son of Ordoño, but he was both an infant and illegitimate. It was thus the lack of any viable alternative, rather than sentiments of Alfonsine legitimacy, that led to the setting up of Ordoño, whose brief tenure of power has left no memory of deeds that might justify his sinister soubriquet.

Sancho I, in the meantime, took refuge with his uncle García Sánchez I and grandmother Toda Aznárez, the rulers of the kingdom of Pamplona, who had tried to secure the Leonese throne for him against Ordoño III in 951. They advocated an appeal for help to the caliph, and Sancho went south to beg assistance from 'Abd al-Raḥmān III in Córdoba. This was rapidly forthcoming, both in the form of medical treatment for obesity at the hands of the caliph's doctor, and the launching of an expedition to restore Sancho to power in León. By July 959 Ordoño the Bad had been expelled from the city, and although he was able to hold out until 960 in the Asturias, he too was forced to take the road into exile.[14] He appealed to the caliph for military aid, which was not forthcoming, and he died in al-Andalus relatively soon after. His wife Urraca, daughter of Fernán González and previously the widow of Ordoño III, remained with her father until the demise of the unfortunate *rey malo* in 962 left her free to marry her cousin, King Sancho Garcés II of Pamplona.

The second and more extended phase of the reign of Sancho I, from 959 to his death in 966, is better documented, and it is possible to see in these years the appearance of a group of court nobles, mainly of Leonese and of Pamplonan or Navarrese origin, who provided continuity in the conduct of royal administration from the early 960s up to *c.* 980. It is significant that there was rarely more than one Galician noble to be found in this group, and it is not surprising that in general Galicia–Portugal proved to be hostile to the regime in León and

---

[13] *Sampiro*, c. 24, p. 332: 'Vir satis prudens, et in exercendis disponendisque exercitatibus nimis sapiens.'
[14] Rodríguez (1987), pp. 156–85.

the main breeding ground of opposition. Castile, on the contrary, proved at this time more tractable. Fernán González had not proved himself particularly astute in the 950s. Having previously tried to rebel against Ramiro II, he had unsuccessfully supported Sancho against Ordoño III in 951, and then had backed Ordoño the Bad against Sancho in 958/9. However, his own local position was sufficiently entrenched for the kings he had opposed to try to conciliate rather than eliminate him. It is significant, though, that soon after his restoration Sancho married Teresa Ansúrez, a member of the family of the Leonese counts of Monzón, former rivals of Fernán González in Castile.

The recovery of his throne by Sancho the Fat with the assistance of ʿAbd al-Rahmān III inevitably coloured Leonese relations with Córdoba for the rest of the reign. The kingdom became something of a client state of Umayyad al-Andalus, with embassies being despatched regularly, probably annually, to bring presents to the caliphs and to assure them of León's docility. A similar relationship almost certainly developed between the kingdom of Pamplona and Córdoba in the same period. Not until the mid 970s did any form of large-scale conflict break out again, though localised raiding by the marcher lords on both sides of the frontier was undoubtedly endemic even in these otherwise tranquil years. Amongst other benefits that Sancho I sought to obtain from the caliph, by now al-Ḥakām II (961–76), was the return of the body of the Galician noble Pelagius. This youth had volunteered to replace his relative, Bishop Ermogius of Tuy, one of the two bishops captured by ʿAbd al-Rahmān III in 920, and after his arrival in Córdoba he had been put to death, apparently for resisting the amorous advances of the caliph. A *Life of Pelagius* was written by a Cordovan cleric called Raguel.[15] Whatever the truth of the story, Pelagius had come to be regarded as a Christian martyr, and the return of his relics was avidly sought by Sancho and his sister Elvira, who had converted the earlier monastery of St John the Baptist in León into a double house and a suitable repository for this saint's remains.

A more material benefit that Sancho reaped from the pacification of the frontiers was the opportunity of turning his attention to imposing royal authority more effectively on the frontier or peripheral regions of his kingdoms. This meant in particular the marcher districts in the south of the Galicia, between the lower Duero valley and the region around Coimbra. In 966 Sancho led a royal army into Galicia to make himself felt in these territories. As the chronicler Sampiro recorded it, the king made himself master of the region up to the valley of the Duero, but when the dominant noble to the south of the river, Gonzalo Muñoz, realised that Sancho could not be opposed militarily he entered into negotiations over the payment of tribute. In the course of these

---

[15] *Vita Pelagii*, ed. Flórez.

he was able to feed Sancho a poisoned apple, from which the unfortunate king died three days later in December 966, leaving the throne to his five-year-old son Ramiro III (966–85).

The youth of the new king was a problem. Royal minorities had successfully been avoided hitherto in the Asturian and Leonese dynasty, but in 966 the only alternative candidate would have been Ordoño III's illegitimate son Vermudo, who was in the hands of the Galician nobility. A regency, therefore, had to be established for Ramiro III. Interestingly this was exercised by his aunt, the Abbess Elvira Ramírez, rather than his mother, Teresa Ansúrez. The latter, after featuring in some royal charters, disappears entirely from the documentary record by April of 970, and is not found again until December 975. She seems to have been relegated, following Visigothic canonical rules on royal widows, to monastic life and may have become a nun in the newly founded double monastery of San Pelayo (Pelagius) under the authority of her sister-in-law Elvira.[16]

The latter was clearly the dominant figure in the Leonese court in the period 966–75, and is recorded as such in another of the surviving fragments of the great work of Ibn Ḥayyān, this one covering the years 971–5.[17] Behind her were the group of nobles who had provided the court officials and signatories to royal documents throughout the second reign of her brother Sancho the Fat. The continuity with that period also extended to the continued maintenance of good relations with Córdoba and a wary attitude towards the Galician nobility, only one member of which is known to have attended the Leonese court at this time. However, conditions elsewhere were changing. In 970 García Sánchez of Pamplona-Navarre died and was succeeded by his son Sancho Garcés II (970–94), and in the same year the inveterate plotter Count Fernán González of Castile similarly gave way to his son García Fernández (970–95). These two were closely linked, being first cousins, and the Pamplonan king's wife was also the new count's sister. There existed a real danger that the increasingly powerful county of Castile would be drawn into the Navarrese orbit. Also the new rulers were less willing to adhere to the passive policies of their predecessors in their dealings with Córdoba.

These issues came to a head in 975. The Caliph al-Ḥakām II (961–76) had been faced with a revolt by the Berbers in the Umayyad-ruled parts of North Africa. This, mistakenly, was seized upon by García Fernández of Castile as the opportunity to try to take the recently refortified castle of Gormaz on the upper Duero, which was the principal Arab fortress on the southern frontiers of his territories. In this he enjoyed the backing of King Sancho of Pamplona. A siege of Gormaz was undertaken, which initially appeared highly successful,

---

[16] Viñayo (1982). [17] Ibn Ḥayyān, *al-Muqtabis*, trans. García Gómez (1967), pp. 76, 276.

and a relieving army hastily sent north by the caliph failed to force its way across the Duero. It is probably at this point that the regent Elvira came with Ramiro III to take personal charge of the operation, and in consequence to impose Leonese authority on what might otherwise have proved to be a dangerously independent Castilian venture. This turned out to be an unwise decision: the Arab garrison of Gormaz made a sortie that broke the siege and forced the Christian forces to withdraw in disorder. What should have been a triumph turned into a débâcle.

Although the lack of substantial narrative sources makes it impossible to be sure, it is probable that this led to the end of Elvira Ramírez's ascendency in León. Although the evidence of one document proves that she was still living in 982,[18] after July 975 she ceases to feature in the royal charters and would seem to have left the court. In December of that year Ramiro III's mother Teresa makes her first appearance in the documentary record since 970. She thereafter features continuously until 980, when once more she vanishes from the lists of signatories of royal charters. Other texts show that she was still living in the mid-990s, and it is reasonable to suspect that she was again relegated to monastic life by her son. Such a view may be supported by the fact that by October 980 Ramiro III had married Sancha Díaz, of the family of the counts of Saldaña, rivals of his mother's Ansúrez lineage.

The last years of Ramiro's reign thus saw him freed from the influence of both his aunt and his mother. However, by this time the ranks of the court nobility had grown very thin. Death seems to have claimed many of those who had been the principal office holders and attenders of the royal court in León since the early 960s.[19] The royal charters of the opening years of the 980s show that they were replaced by a much smaller number of nobles, a significant number of whom were relatives of the new queen. Thus the power-base upon which Ramiro III based his regime was nothing like as extensive as that of his father or of the regents of the 970s. It must also have seemed clearly factional, and it may be this that prompted the leading Galician noble families to break into open rebellion by October of 982, and to set up a king of their own in the person of Vermudo, the illegitimate son of Ordoño III. An attempt by Ramiro III to put down the rebellion by force in 983 failed, following a drawn battle, and by 984 Vermudo was strong enough to take an army into the plains around León and threaten the capital. Ramiro's regime crumbled and he was forced to leave the city. He died suddenly near Astorga on 26 June 985, probably awaiting the arrival of his supporters with assistance from the south.

---

[18] Mínguez Fernández (ed.), *Colección diplomática del Monasterio de Sahagún (siglos ix y x)*, doc. 313 (18 January 982), pp. 377–8.

[19] See *Colección documental del archivo de la Catedral de León*, ed. Ruiz Asencio and Mínguez Fernández (ed), *Colección* for the documents on which this analysis is based.

The resumption of war with the Arabs by the attack on Gormaz in 975 had not led to serious conflict in the following years, largely because of a power struggle that developed in Córdoba following the death of al-Ḥakām II in 976. In the final phase of this, Ghālib, the general in charge of the central march, called on Count García of Castile and Sancho II of Pamplona for assistance against his son-in-law, Ibn Abī Amr, soon to be called al-Manṣūr ('the Victorious'), who had established himself as the effective ruler of the Umayyad amirate. In a battle fought in July 981 the allies were defeated and Ghālib killed. In the aftermath an army under one of al-Manṣūr's generals invaded the Leonese kingdom and sacked Zamora. This led Ramiro III to join with the king of Pamplona and the count of Castile for a proposed expedition in 982, but al-Manṣūr struck first. He defeated the Christian confederation in battles in 982 and 983 and sacked Simancas in the latter year, killing Count Nepociano Díaz, a brother of the queen and one of the principal props of Ramiro III's regime. It is possible that León was also besieged. These events, representing successive military humiliations for the Leonese king, may have helped to prompt the Galician revolt in the winter of 982 and then to give it wider support throughout the kingdom in 984.

Such an association may have led al-Manṣūr to support Vermudo II's seizure of power in León in 985, and then to turn down the appeals for help from the partisans of Ramiro III. Opposition from some of the noble families, especially that of the late king's wife, seems to have continued for some months after his death, and it seems possible that Vermudo had to rely on troops sent by al-Manṣūr to complete his conquest of the kingdom. Amongst others who at this time turned against the new king were some of his erstwhile Galician supporters who felt ill-rewarded. Some form of Arab garrison may have been established in the principal towns of León, Astorga and Zamora in 985/6, which it took Vermudo a while to get rid of. It is also significant that Leonese documents, other than those of the monastery of Sahagún, do not make the usual reference to a named king ruling in León during the period from April 986 to January 987. By the latter year relations between Vermudo and al-Manṣūr had deteriorated to the point of war. In June of 987 the Arab leader captured Coimbra and established a protectorate over the Portuguese march, with the active cooperation of some of the Christian nobility of the region. In 988 al-Manṣūr invaded the heartlands of the Leonese kingdom, and while Vermudo II took refuge in Zamora the Arab army sacked the capital. In 989 it was the turn of Castile, when al-Manṣūr took the fortress of San Esteban de Gormaz. Although no campaign is known to have been launched in 990, in that year Vermudo seems briefly to have lost control of León, where Count García Gómez, a nephew of Ramiro III's widow, seized power.[20]

[20] Recorded in two charters of March 990: *Colección*, ed. Ruiz Asencio, nos. 534 and 535.

The reorganised Umayyad army, now largely made up of recently imported contingents of Berbers from North Africa, had proved itself to be irresistible, and by 993 if not sooner Vermudo had made peace with al-Manṣūr. This was symbolised by the despatch in that year of a daughter of the king to Córdoba to become one of al-Manṣūr's wives. However, for reasons that are not clear, war was resumed the following year. Al-Manṣūr certainly wished to force the Christian leaders to surrender various Arab rebels who had taken refuge with them, but it is possible that his own political position in Córdoba and his hold over the Berber armies depended on the maintenance of aggressive warfare against the non-Muslims. In 994 al-Manṣūr retook San Esteban de Gormaz and went on to sack Avila, and in 995 he besieged Astorga, whither Vermudo II had transferred his court following the sack of León in 987. The Leonese king was forced to submit and to promise to pay a regular tribute. This did not guarantee the security of his kingdom for long, in that in 997 al-Manṣūr led an expedition into Galicia and in August sacked the shrine of Santiago, destroying the church built under Alfonso III. The church bells and much other loot were carried off and distributed, not least to the Christian nobles from the frontier who had aided him. The supposed body of St James was, however, respected. In 999 al-Manṣūr established a garrison in Zamora. Thus, when Vermudo II the Gouty died in either August or September of 999 his kingdom was little more than a tributary of Córdoba, one that the Arab leader and his Berber troops could pillage at will.

Dismal as in many respects the reign of Vermudo the Gouty had been, he was praised by Sampiro, who admittedly was writing in the reign of either his son or his grandson, for his positive achievements in the field of law. 'He was a very prudent man. He confirmed the laws established by Wamba' (*recte* Egica) 'and ordered the canon laws to be applied. He delighted in mercy and justice. He sought to repress what was evil and to choose what was good.'[21] Unfortunately, no text of the law-codes, either civil or ecclesiastical, has survived that shows signs of deriving from Vermudo's confirmation or reissue. No new legislation was issued, as far as may now be known, in this reign any more than in that of any of the other Leonese kings: there were no Leonese equivalents to Frankish capitularies. Certainly, though, a number of legal documents dating to this period have survived, recording the proceedings of judicial assemblies over which Vermudo presided.[22]

His death, at what for his dynasty was the relatively advanced age of about fifty, left the kingdom facing another minority. His son Alfonso V (999–1028) was only either three or five at the time, and the regency was exercised, at least nominally, by Vermudo's second wife Elvira, the sister of Count Sancho

---

[21] 'Vir satis prudens; leges a Vambano conditas firmavit; canones aperire iussit; dilexit misericordiam et iudicium; reprobare studuit et eligere bonum': *Historia Silense*, p. 172.   [22] Collins (1985).

García of Castile (995–1017). With this reign the original version of the *Chronicle of Sampiro* probably ended, and it is necessary to turn to the twelfth-century continuation by Bishop Pelayo of Oviedo for a brief narrative account of it. This can be supplemented on occasion by some brief regional chronicles, compiled in the same period. Pelayo's statement that Alfonso was brought up under the direction of the Galician Count Menendo González conceals a conflict that developed between the latter and the king's uncle the count of Castile over the exercise of the regency.[23] The earliest royal documents of the reign were issued jointly in the names of the infant king and of his mother Queen Elvira, but in 1003 she disappears from the charters for a period of four years. She may well have been ousted by Menendo González, who in his subscription to one charter entitled himself 'he who under the authority of the aforementioned king ordains and guides all things'.[24] An attempt was made in 1004 by the count of Castile to challenge the ascendancy of Count Menendo. The issue was eventually sent to Córdoba for arbitration in 1004, and a verdict was given in favour of the Galician magnate. The young king was subsequently engaged to Count Menendo's daughter Elvira (d. 1022), strengthening the Galician ties of the dynasty. Menendo's death in 1008, either in battle or by murder, allowed a brief revival of Castilian influence.

Although the military situation of the kingdom may have seemed parlous at the time of Vermudo II's death in 999, surprisingly as it must have seemed to contemporaries it was the Umayyad caliphate of Córdoba rather than the Leonese monarchy whose condition was terminal. This was not immediately apparent, in that after the death of al-Manṣūr in 1002 his eldest surviving son ʿAbd al-Malik continued to direct a series of campaigns against the Christian states. A peace treaty was made in the winter of 1002/3, but this lasted no longer than 1005 when ʿAbd al-Malik led an expedition into Galicia, sacking Zamora once more *en route*. Count Sancho García of Castile, who seems to have made a separate treaty with ʿAbd al-Malik the previous year, accompanied him. By 1007 this Castilian treaty had either lapsed or been broken, and a new Christian alliance was formed between León, Castile and the kingdom of Pamplona. As before, however, this led to a pre-emptive attack from the south. The Arab leader captured and sacked Clunia, the count's principal fortress in southern Castile. While carrying out a similar expedition in the autumn of 1008 ʿAbd al-Malik died, an event which initiated a long period of political confusion and civil war in *al-Andalus*.

The ensuing transformation of the balance of military power in the peninsula enabled the Leonese kingdom to begin the recovery from the devastations of the years 982 to 1007. Internal divisions and factional conflicts between

---

[23] Fernández del Pozo (1984), pp. 31–41.

[24] 'qui sub imperio iam dicti regis hec omnia ordinavit et docuit.': Fernández del Pozo (1984), p. 237.

groups of regionally based nobles remained a problem. As under Vermudo II, the existence of local revolts against Alfonso V can be detected from a number of royal charters in which the monarch redistributes properties confiscated from those who had been unfaithful.[25] The lack of substantial narrative sources makes the dating and delineation of such revolts very difficult, but it has been suggested that one in 1012 involved Munio Fernández, a hitherto loyal supporter of the king and of his father before him, and that another in 1014 was led by Count García Gómez of Saldaña and Alfonso's own uncle, Count Sancho García of Castile.[26] The death of the latter in February 1017, bequeathing the county of Castile to his eight-year-old son García Sánchez (1017–28), left the Leonese king free to reimpose greater royal control over this increasingly independent region and to adjust its boundaries in León's favour.

In 1017 Alfonso V also undertook the reconstruction and repopulation of the city of León, holding a council there of his leading lay and clerical magnates. This was intended as the formal setting for the promulgation of the *Fueros* of León, the constitution of the local government, and the legal privileges and exemptions granted to the inhabitants by their lord. Such *fueros* had been a standard part of the processes of resettlement and repopulation in the Leonese kingdom since the early tenth century. Few early sets of *fueros* survive, however, as they were frequently modified and augmented in the course of successive centuries, and the texts also came to be interpolated to give spurious antiquity to claims for greater liberties.[27] Those of León have given rise to considerable historiographical debate over the development and integrity of the available texts of them.[28]

By the 1020s the Leonese kingdom was in a condition to begin taking the offensive militarily once more, not least to recover fortresses lost on the marches in the time of al-Manṣūr. In the spring of 1027 Alfonso V led an expedition to try to regain Viseu and Lamego, which had been lost in 987. While besieging the first of these, the king was killed by an arrow from the walls, leaving the throne to his only son Vermudo III (1027–37), who was aged less than thirteen at the time. The royal council rapidly arranged a marriage for the new king's sister Sancha to count García Sánchez of Castile, but when he came to León for the betrothal in April 1028 he was murdered by a group of Leonese nobles. The motives behind this are obscure. There existed factional rivalries that stretched back for nearly a century between the family of the counts of Castile and other, less successful lineages, and there may also have been a desire to prevent the count from exercising any influence in the clearly unstable Leonese court. There have also been suggestions made as to the possible involvement of King Sancho Garcés III (1004–35) in the murder. The latter

[25] Ruiz Asencio (1969).   [26] Fernández del Pozo (1984), pp. 61–84.
[27] Martínez Díez (1982 and 1988).   [28] Outlined in Fernández del Pozo (1984), pp. 91–124.

had accompanied the count to León for the wedding and his troops were billeted around the city.[29]

Certainly, it was the dynasty of Pamplona-Navarre rather than that of León which benefited from the murder of Count García. The only heir to the murdered count was his sister Mayor, who was married to King Sancho of Pamplona. Taking over the county in her right, he installed their son Fernando as the new count. Vermudo III's sister Sancha, who was to have married Count García, married Count Fernando instead. This Navarrese domination of Castile led rapidly to serious consequences for the Leonese kingdom. Sancho was able to demand the restoration to the county of various disputed territories that Alfonso V had taken under direct royal authority, and when this was refused he invaded the kingdom in 1033. Many of the leading Leonese nobles and bishops defected to Sancho, and Vermudo III was forced to retreat into Galicia. The unforeseen death of King Sancho in 1035 allowed Vermudo to regain his capital and to expel Fernando from Castile. However, a renewed Navarrese invasion in 1037 proved decisive. The forces of Fernando and his brother, King García III of Navarre (1035–54), together with their Leonese supporters, defeated those of Vermudo III at Tamarón. The king, the last of the Leonese dynasty, fell in the battle, and his throne was taken by his brother-in-law, the victorious Fernando I (1037–65).

THE KINGDOM OF PAMPLONA OR NAVARRE (905–1035)

The kings of Pamplona of the second dynasty, that of the Jiménez, are better known than their ninth-century Arista predecessors, but still appear shadowy in comparison with their Leonese contemporaries. Whereas there is at least Sampiro's work to turn to for León, no narrative history at all was composed in Navarre before the fifteenth century.[30] The collection of royal and comital genealogies compiled at the royal court in Nájera in the late tenth century represents the nearest that the kingdom came to historiography.[31] Even charters, relatively plentiful in León, are scarce before the early eleventh century. Thus, although the kingdom of Pamplona or of Navarre was in many ways a more dynamic force in the wider events in the Iberian peninsula of this period than was its larger Leonese neighbour, especially from the mid-tenth century onwards, most of the details of its internal history are entirely lost.

When the first king of the new dynasty, Sancho Garcés I (905–25), came to power the kingdom still did not possess a foothold in the Ebro valley. The defeat and death in 907, in the course of a raid on Pamplona, of Lubb ibn Moḥammad ibn Mūsā, the principal member of the Banū Qasī, a Muslim

---

[29] Pérez de Urbel (1970), pp. 197–217.   [30] *Crónica de Garci López de Roncesvalles.*
[31] Lacarra (ed.), 'Textos navarros del Códice de Roda'.

lineage of Hispanic origin which had dominated the upper Ebro since the 840s, both removed a threat and opened the way to rapid Navarrese expansion. By 923 Sancho Garcés had acquired Viguera, Nájera, Albelda and Calahorra. This provoked a retaliatory expedition in 924 by ʿAbd al-Raḥmān III, who retook the lost fortresses and went on to sack Pamplona. The substantial account of this expedition given by Ibn Ḥayyān has made it possible to reconstruct this campaign in considerable detail.[32] Despite the severity of these reprisals, Sancho Garcés renewed his challenge in 925, just before his death. Nájera and Viguera were once again taken; this time permanently.

The king having died while his only son was still a minor, the throne passed to his brother Jimeno Garcés (925–33), who took his nephew García Sánchez under his tutelage.[33] At this time far more peaceful relations were established with Córdoba, whose ruler accepted the Navarrese expansion in the Rioja in return for the subservience of the kingdom. Thus, when in 934 ʿAbd al-Raḥmān III led an expedition into the Ebro valley the regent Queen Toda Aznárez brought the young García Sánchez I (933–70) to the caliph for confirmation of his royal title. It has been suggested that this episode represents the Cordovan imposition of García Sánchez against the opposition of his uncle Jimeno or the latter's sons, but the evidence does not support such a view.[34] Following the evidence of the fifth book of the *Muqtabis* of Ibn Ḥayyān, it is clear that the caliph's government regarded Queen Toda as the real ruler of the kingdom of Pamplona in the years from 933/4 up to about 939.[35] As well as being the widow of Sancho Garcés I and the mother of King García, she was also the granddaughter of the last king of the previous dynasty, Fortún Garcés. It is striking that she continued to exercise considerable power even after her son had attained his majority, and several charters record them as ruling jointly. She was still alive and sharing power with her son as late as 958.

In general, the conciliatory attitude towards the Umayyad caliphate that was notable in the 930s was maintained throughout the period up to about 975. In 958, when Sancho the Fat of León was deposed in favour of Ordoño IV the Bad, he fled to his uncle García Sánchez of Pamplona, who in turn sent him on to Córdoba to win the assistance that secured his restoration. The Navarrese monarchs, who from the middle of the century established their court with growing frequency in Nájera in the Rioja, became rather more interested in drawing the Leonese county of Castile into their orbit than in trying to extend their kingdom westward down the Ebro valley towards the Arab-controlled towns of Zaragoza and Huesca. Marriage ties, and perhaps the significant Basque contribution to the repopulation of Castile served to strengthen the links of the county to its eastern neighbour. This culminated, as outlined

[32] Cañada Juste (1976).   [33] *Cartulario de San Juan de la Peña*, ed. Ubieto Arteta, doc. 14 (928).
[34] Ubieto Arteta (1963).   [35] Ibn Ḥayyān, *Al-Muqtabis*, ed. Chalmeta and Corriente, pp. 225–7, 271–5.

above, in the Navarrese acquisition of the county in 1028, and thence in the conquest of the kingdom of León itself in 1033/4 and again, definitively, in 1037.

The greater involvement with Castile did lead to the campaign of Gormaz in 975, and thence to renewed conflict with the caliphate once al-Manṣūr had established his dominance in Córdoba. Sancho II, like his brother-in-law count García Fernández of Castile supported Ghālib in his unsuccessful bid to resist al-Manṣūr in 981. In the ensuing battle Sancho II's half-brother Ramiro, whom he had made subordinate king of Viguera, was killed. This disaster and further reprisals in 982 led the Navarrese king into making peace with Córdoba in 983, and sending one of his daughters to marry al-Manṣūr. A son of this union, nicknamed 'Sanchuelo', made a short-lived attempt to take power in Córdoba in 1008–9. Sancho II himself made a visit to the caliphal court in 992, the protocol for which was designed to reinforce the subordinate status of the Christian king, even in relation to his infant grandson. Under Sancho's son García Sánchez II the Trembler (994–1004) conflict was renewed for reasons that are unknown, and in 999 al-Manṣūr led a devastating raid on the kingdom. In 1006 al-Manṣūr's son 'Abd al-Malik devastated the Aragón valley, as well as occupying parts of the adjacent Christian counties of the central Pyrenees, in the course of an expedition into the Ebro.

To the west of the heartlands of the kingdom surrounding Pamplona lay the county of Aragón, which had been administered for the Navarrese monarchs by a line of hereditary counts since the early ninth century. Around 940 García Sánchez I married Andregoto Galíndez, daughter and heir of Count Galindo Aznárez II, and their son Sancho Garcés is recorded as ruling the county under his father from 948. By this time his parents' marriage had been dissolved, and García Sánchez was remarried (in 943) to a lady called Tarasia, whose family connections are unknown. Sancho Garcés II succeeded his father as king in 970, and the county of Aragón was retained under direct royal rule. In 1035, however, on the death of King Sancho III the Great (1004–35), it was detached, to become the inheritance of one of his sons, Ramiro Sánchez (1035–64), and thus an independent kingdom.

Beyond the eastern frontiers of Aragón the central Pyrenean counties of Pallars and Ribagorza remained in practice self-governing under their indigenous comital dynasties, but were formally subject to the west Frankish kings. This lasted until the reign of Sancho III of Navarre, whose campaigns of 1016–18 to recover territories lost to the Arabs in 1006 established his hegemony over these regions. In 1018/19 he was recognised as ruling over Ribagorza, and in 1020 this was extended to Pallars.[36] The position was

---

[36] Durán Gudiol (1988), pp. 278–85.

regularised in 1025, at least in Ribagorza, when the Countess Mayor (c. 1011–25) resigned her rights over the county to her niece, also called Mayor, the wife of Sancho III. One of their sons, Gonzalo, was invested with the county together with the contiguous one of Sobrarbe, and following Sancho III's death on 18 October 1035 this became an independent kingdom.[37]

The latter part of the reign of Sancho III the Great had seen a quite unprecedented extension of the kingdom. This involved not only the establishment of Navarrese rule over the central Pyrenees and over Castile and León, but also its extension northwards in 1032 to include the duchy of Gascony, following the death of its duke Sancho William, and possibly also the county of Toulouse. In the same period Count Berenguer Ramón I of Barcelona (1017–35), nominally a vassal of the west Frankish king, became a periodic attender at the court of King Sancho. The extent of the latter's dominion is recorded in the eschatocoll to one of his charters of 1033: 'King Sancho Garcés ruling in Aragón, and in Castile and in León, exercising authority from Zamora to Barcelona and over all of Gascony.'[38] This 'empire' fell apart following its creator's death in 1035, not least through its planned quartering amongst his four sons. The influence over the regions north of the Pyrenees and over Catalonia was not regained.

Relatively little is known of the administrative structures of the Navarrese kingdom, at least before the time of Sancho the Great. By the end of the tenth century a distinctive group of nobles had emerged, holding territorial seigneuries. They would appear to have been the equivalents of the counts of the Leonese kingdom, though the territories they administered were probably smaller.[39] Their principal role, especially along the extensive Riojan and Ebro frontiers, was military. A number of fortresses were built at this time, especially under Sancho III, but little evidence survives concerning the existence of public obligations, either by way of construction work on forts, roads and bridges or in garrison duty. Similarly, although a number of forms of tax can be documented from later periods in the history of Navarre, it is not possible to say which of them may have originated at this time.

Where the reign of Sancho the Great marked another important change was in the openness of his court to external cultural influences. In particular in the 1020s the king became interested in the reformed monasticism associated with Cluny.[40] In 1025 he sent Abbot Paternus of the principal Aragonese monastery of San Juan de la Peña to Cluny to study their customs and to introduce them into his house. Monks trained at San Juan were subsequently imposed as abbots on some of the other monasteries in the kingdom to spread this

[37] Galtier Martí (1981).
[38] *Cartulario de San Juan de la Peña*, ed. Ubieto Arteta, doc. 60 (19 March 1033).
[39] Collins (1986), pp. 194–8.   [40] Pérez de Urbel (1950), pp. 297–321.

Cluniac influence. The special relationship that was fostered with Cluny later in the eleventh century by Fernando I of Castile-León thus had its origins in the Navarrese kingdom of his father. Sancho III also was made aware of the ecclesiastical reforms being implemented in many regions of western Europe through the links he forged with the Catalan counties, and one of the letters he received from the principal reformers, Oliba bishop of Vic and abbot of Ripoll and Cuxa, has been preserved in the San Juan de la Peña cartulary.[41]

In the century and a quarter surveyed here, the Christian kingdoms of northern Spain had not increased their territories to any great degree, other than the short-lived imperial florescence of Navarre in the last years of Sancho the Great. They had at least recovered lands lost in the course of the intensive and effective campaigns of al-Manṣūr in the 980s and 990s. They had also clearly enjoyed substantial demographic growth, as the evidence for immigration and the repopulation of many frontier districts indicates. It is possible that such expansion in the quantity of population overall was matched by regional decline in certain areas, such as the Asturias and northern Galicia, that had been of greater political and economic importance in the ninth century. Also, the relative stability of the territorial size of the kingdoms conceals very dramatic shifts in their respective military strength. The dominance of the earlier Leonese kings, such as Ordoño II and Ramiro II, that had extended well beyond the bounds of their realm, was replaced by internal division, factional feuding and military weakness in the time of the last generations of the dynasty. In contrast, the relatively small Navarrese kingdom had grown in military and diplomatic significance throughout the period. In the same time-span the fortunes of the Umayyad regime in al-Andalus had also fluctuated widely, and their caliphate was finally abolished in 1031, to be replaced by a series of independent regional monarchies. The very changed political and cultural circumstances of the Spanish states in 1035 offered the prospect of dramatic developments throughout the peninsula for the rest of the century.

---

[41] *Cartulario de San Juan de la Peña*, ed. Ubieto Arteta, doc. 38 (11 May 1023); d'Abadal i de Vinyals (1948), pp. 208–9.

Table 1 Popes, 885–1024

Stephen V (VI)	*c.* September 885 – 14 September 891
Formosus	*c.* 6 October 891 – 4 April 896
Boniface VI	April/May 896 (15 days)
Stephen VI (VII)	May 896 – August 897 (expelled)
Romanus	August – November 897
Theodore II	November/December 897 (20 days)
John IX	January 898 – January/May 900
Benedict IV	May/June 900 – July/August 903
Leo V	August – September 903 (30 days)
Christopher	September 903 – January 904
Sergius III	29 January 904 – 14 April 911
Anastastius III	*c.* June 911 – *c.* August 913
Lando	*c.* August 913 – *c.* March 914
John X	March/April 914 – May 928 (deposed; d. 929)
Leo VI	May – December 928
Stephen VII (VIII)	December 928 – February 931
John XI	February/March 931 – December 935/January 936
Leo VII	3 January 936 – 13 July 939
Stephen VIII (IX)	14 July 939 – late October 942
Marinus II	30 October 942 – early May 946
Agapitus II	10 May 946 – December 955
John XII	16 December 955 – 4 December 963 (deposed; d. 14 May 964)
Leo VIII	4 December 963 – 1 March 965
Benedict V	22 May 964 – 23 June 964 (deposed; d. 4 July 966)
John XIII	1 October 965 – 6 September 972
Benedict VI	19 January 973 – July 974 (murdered)
Boniface VII	June – July 975 and again August 984 – 20 July 985 (? assassinated)
Benedict VII	October 974 – 10 July 983
John XIV	December 983 – April 984 (deposed; d. 20 August 984)
John XV	August 985 – March 996
Gregory V	3 May 996 – 18 February 999
John XVI	? February 997 – ? May 998 (deposed; d. 26 August)
Silvester II	2 April 999 – 12 May 1003
John XVII	16 May – 6 November 1003
John XVIII	25 December 1003 – June or July 1009
Sergius IV	31 July 1009 – 12 May 1012
Benedict VIII	17 May 1012 – 9 April 1024
Gregory VI	May – December 1012

Antipopes are given in italics.
Many of the dates, especially for the first half of the tenth century, are conjectural and uncertain.

Table 2 Ottonian kings and emperors

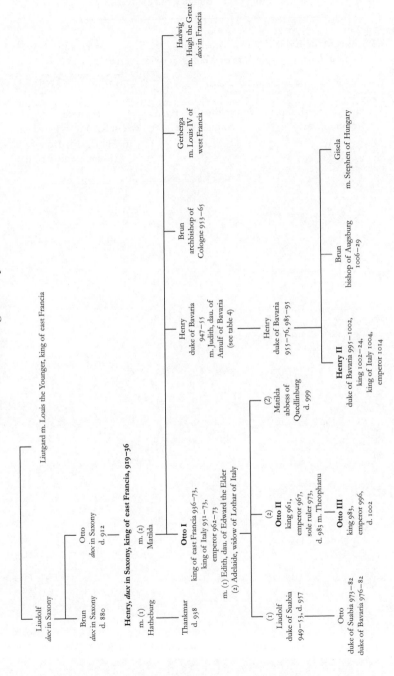

Table 3   The Billungs, dukes in Saxony

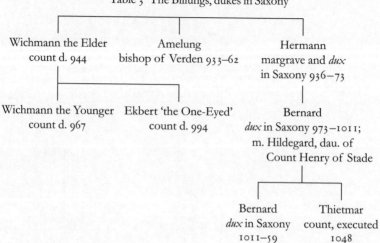

Wichmann the Elder
count d. 944

Amelung
bishop of Verden 933–62

Hermann
margrave and *dux*
in Saxony 936–73

Wichmann the Younger
count d. 967

Ekbert 'the One-Eyed'
count d. 994

Bernard
dux in Saxony 973–1011;
m. Hildegard, dau. of
Count Henry of Stade

Bernard
dux in Saxony
1011–59

Thietmar
count, executed
1048

Table 4 The Luitpoldings, dukes in Bavaria

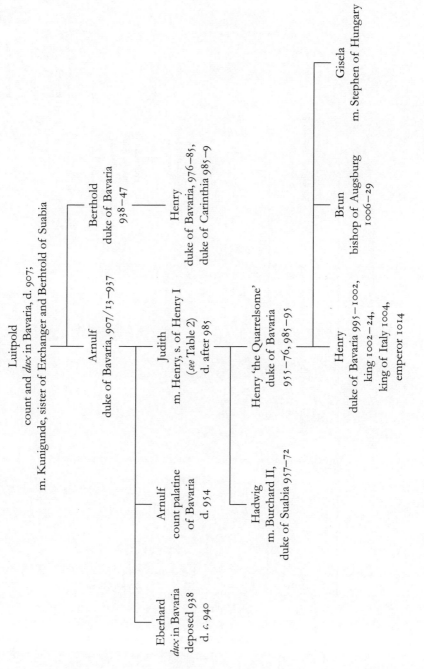

Luitpold
count and *dux* in Bavaria, d. 907;
m. Kunigunde, sister of Erchanger and Berthold of Suabia

Eberhard
dux in Bavaria
deposed 938
d. *c.* 940

Arnulf
count palatine
of Bavaria
d. 954

Arnulf
duke of Bavaria, 907/13–937

Berthold
duke of Bavaria
938–47

Hadwig
m. Burchard II,
duke of Suabia 957–72

Judith
m. Henry, s. of Henry I
(*see* Table 2)
d. after 985

Henry 'the Quarrelsome'
duke of Bavaria
955–76, 985–95

Henry
duke of Bavaria, 976–85,
duke of Carinthia 985–9

Henry
duke of Bavaria 995–1002,
king 1002–24,
king of Italy 1004,
emperor 1014

Brun
bishop of Augsburg
1006–29

Gisela
m. Stephen of Hungary

Table 5 The Conradines, dukes in Franconia and Suabia

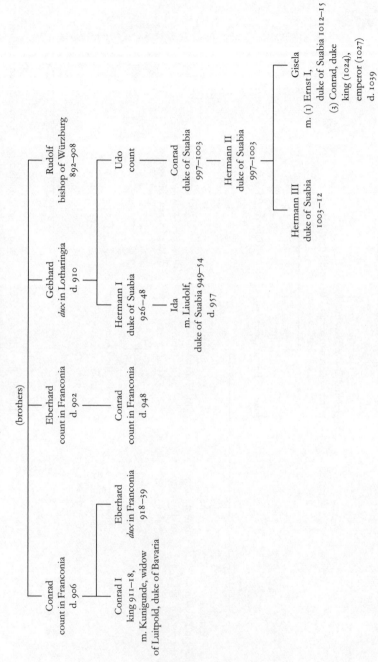

Table 6 Lotharingia: ducal families

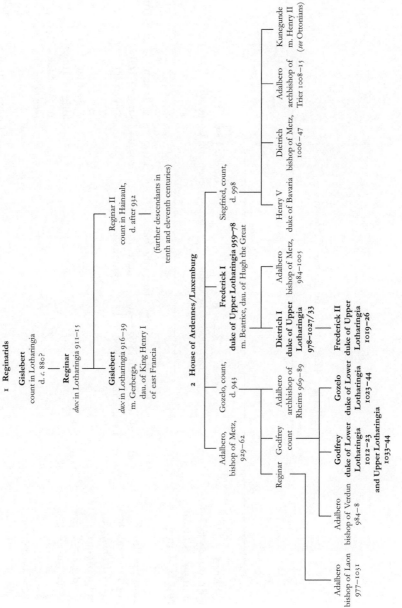

1 Reginarids

Gislebert
count in Lotharingia
d. c. 880?

Reginar
dux in Lotharingia 911–15

Gislebert
dux in Lotharingia 916–39
m. Gerberga,
dau. of King Henry I
of east Francia

Reginar II
count in Hainault,
d. after 932

(further descendants in
tenth and eleventh centuries)

2 House of Ardennes/Luxemburg

Adalbero,
bishop of Metz,
929–62

Gozelo, count,
d. 943

Adalbero
archbishop of
Rheims 969–89

Reginar   Godfrey
count

**Frederick I
duke of Upper Lotharingia 959–78**
m. Beatrice, dau. of Hugh the Great

Siegfried, count,
d. 998

**Godfrey
duke of Lower
Lotharingia
1012–23**

**Gozelo
duke of Lower
Lotharingia
1023–44**

Adalbero
bishop of Verdun
984–8

Adalbero
bishop of Laon
977–1031

**Dietrich I
duke of Upper
Lotharingia
978–1027/33**

Adalbero
bishop of Metz,
984–1005

**Frederick II
duke of Upper
Lotharingia
1019–26**

Henry V
duke of Bavaria

Dietrich
bishop of Metz,
1006–47

Adalbero
archbishop of
Trier 1008–15

Kunegunde
m. Henry II
(*see* Ottonians)

**Godfrey
duke of Lower
Lotharingia
1012–23
and Upper Lotharingia
1033–44**

For dukes of Lower Lotharingia prior to 1012, see Table 12.

Table 7 The family of Boso, king of Provence

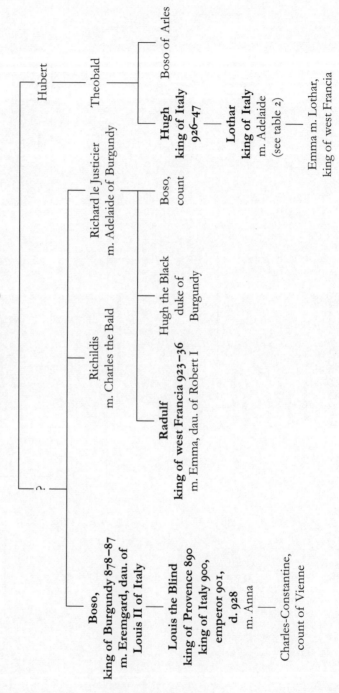

Table 8 The Rudolfing kings of Burgundy and Provence

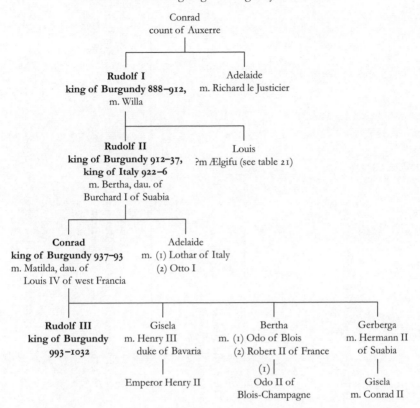

Conrad
count of Auxerre

Rudolf I
king of Burgundy 888–912,
m. Willa

Adelaide
m. Richard le Justicier

Rudolf II
king of Burgundy 912–37,
king of Italy 922–6
m. Bertha, dau. of
Burchard I of Suabia

Louis
?m Ælgifu (see table 21)

Conrad
king of Burgundy 937–93
m. Matilda, dau. of
Louis IV of west Francia

Adelaide
m. (1) Lothar of Italy
(2) Otto I

Rudolf III
king of Burgundy
993–1032

Gisela
m. Henry III
duke of Bavaria

Emperor Henry II

Bertha
m. (1) Odo of Blois
(2) Robert II of France

(1)
Odo II of
Blois-Champagne

Gerberga
m. Hermann II
of Suabia

Gisela
m. Conrad II

Table 9 Dukes of Burgundy in the tenth century

Boso
king of Burgundy
879–87

Richard le Justicier
duke of Burgundy
d. 921

Radulf
duke of Burgundy
king of west Francia 923–36
m. Emma, dau. of
Robert I
king of west Francia

Hugh the Black
duke of Burgundy
936–52

Boso,
count

Gislebert
duke 952–6

Otto
duke of Burgundy
956–65

Henry
duke of Burgundy
965–1002
m. Gerberga

Liutgard   m.

Emma
m. Richard I
of Normandy

Hugh the Great
duke in Francia
d. 956

Hugh Capet
king of France
987–96

Gerberga

Otto-William
count of Burgundy (son of Gerberga)
d. 1026

Table 10 Some tenth-century Burgundian counts

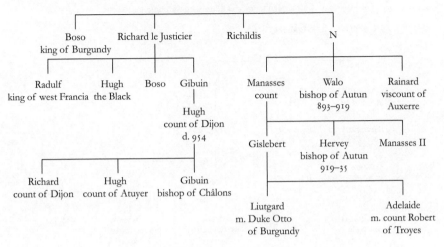

For details of the first two generations, see Table 7.

Table 11   Kings of Italy and margraves of Spoleto and Tuscany

1   Carolingian kings and kings with Carolingian descent

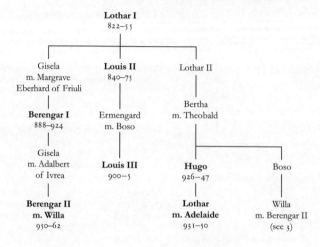

2   The House of Spoleto

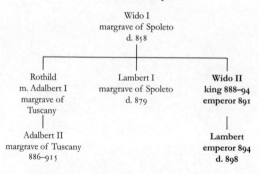

3   The house of Tuscany

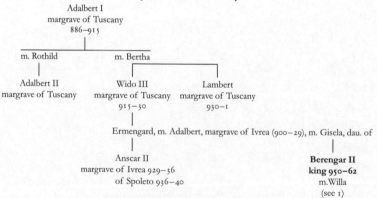

Table 12 West Francia: the Carolingians

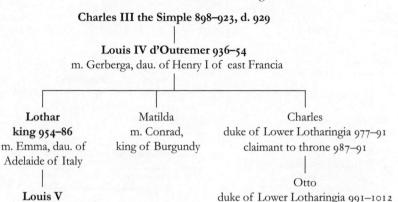

Charles III the Simple 898–923, d. 929

Louis IV d'Outremer 936–54
m. Gerberga, dau. of Henry I of east Francia

Lothar	Matilda	Charles
king 954–86	m. Conrad,	duke of Lower Lotharingia 977–91
m. Emma, dau. of	king of Burgundy	claimant to throne 987–91
Adelaide of Italy		

Louis V
986–7

Otto
duke of Lower Lotharingia 991–1012

Table 13 West Francia: Capetian rulers

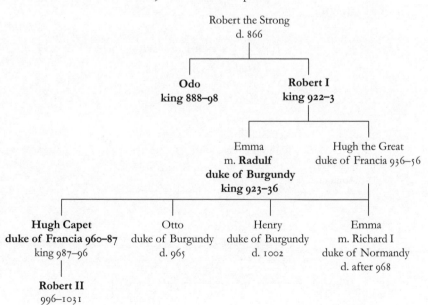

Robert the Strong
d. 866

Odo
king 888–98

Robert I
king 922–3

Emma
m. **Radulf**
duke of Burgundy
king 923–36

Hugh the Great
duke of Francia 936–56

Hugh Capet	Otto	Henry	Emma
duke of Francia 960–87	duke of Burgundy	duke of Burgundy	m. Richard I
king 987–96	d. 965	d. 1002	duke of Normandy
			d. after 968

Robert II
996–1031

Table 14 Dukes of Brittany

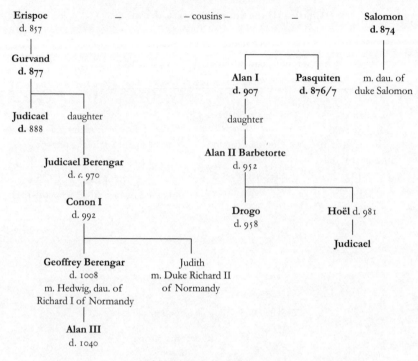

Table 15 Dukes of Normandy

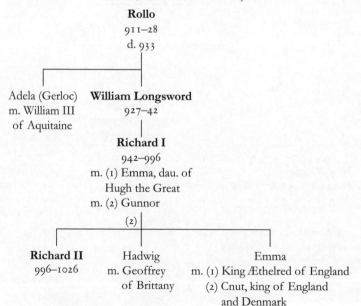

Table 16 Counts of Flanders

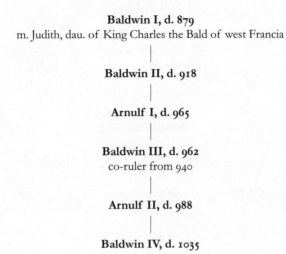

Baldwin I, d. 879
m. Judith, dau. of King Charles the Bald of west Francia
|
Baldwin II, d. 918
|
Arnulf I, d. 965
|
Baldwin III, d. 962
co-ruler from 940
|
Arnulf II, d. 988
|
Baldwin IV, d. 1035

Table 17 Dukes of Aquitaine

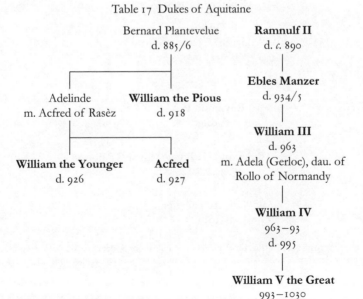

Bernard Plantevelue   **Ramnulf II**
d. 885/6   d. *c.* 890

Adelinde   **William the Pious**   **Ebles Manzer**
m. Acfred of Rasèz   d. 918   d. 934/5

William the Younger   **Acfred**   **William III**
d. 926   d. 927   d. 963
m. Adela (Gerloc), dau. of
Rollo of Normandy

William IV
963–93
d. 995

William V the Great
993–1030

Table 18 Dukes of Gascony

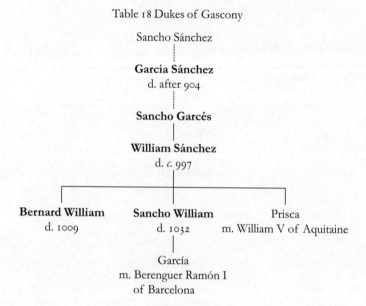

Sancho Sánchez

García Sánchez
d. after 904

Sancho Garcés

William Sánchez
d. *c.* 997

| **Bernard William** | **Sancho William** | Prisca |
| d. 1009 | d. 1032 | m. William V of Aquitaine |

García
m. Berenguer Ramón I
of Barcelona

Table 19 Counts of Toulouse

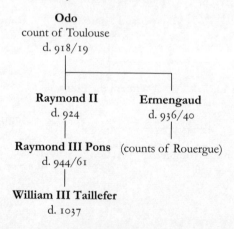

Odo
count of Toulouse
d. 918/19

| **Raymond II** | **Ermengaud** |
| d. 924 | d. 936/40 |

Raymond III Pons (counts of Rouergue)
d. 944/61

William III Taillefer
d. 1037

For an alternative reconstruction of the thin and ambiguous evidence see M. de Framond, ' La succession des comtes de Toulouse autour de l'an mil (940–1030): reconsidérations', *Annales du Midi* 105 (1993), 445–88.

Table 20 Catalonia: counts of Barcelona

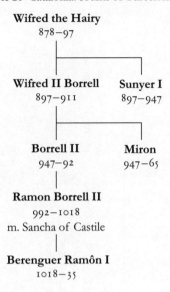

Wifred the Hairy
878–97

Wifred II Borrell   **Sunyer I**
897–911   897–947

Borrell II   **Miron**
947–92   947–65

Ramon Borrell II
992–1018
m. Sancha of Castile

Berenguer Ramôn I
1018–35

The county was ruled jointly for periods in the two generations after that of Wilfred the Hairy. The counties of Urgel, Osona, Gerona and Besalú were often held by younger brothers of the ruling counts in this period.

Table 21 Kings of Wessex and England

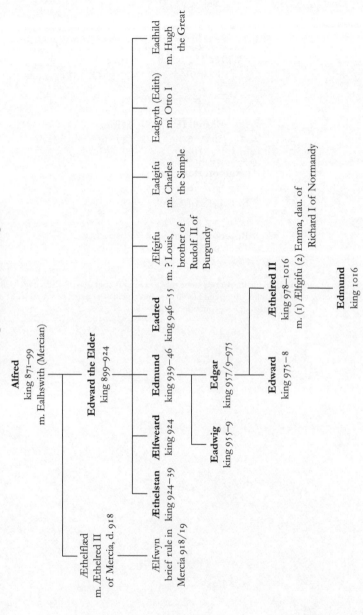

Alfred
king 871–99
m. Ealhswith (Mercian)

Æthelflæd
m. Æthelred II
of Mercia, d. 918

Edward the Elder
king 899–924

Ælfwyn
brief rule in
Mercia 918/19

Æthelstan
king 924–39

Ælfweard
king 924

Edmund
king 939–46

Eadred
king 946–55

Ælfgifu
m. ? Louis,
brother of
Rudolf II of
Burgundy

Eadgifu
m. Charles
the Simple

Eadgyth (Edith)
m. Otto I

Eadhild
m. Hugh
the Great

Eadwig
king 955–9

Edgar
king 957/9–975

Edward
king 975–8

Æthelred II
king 978–1016
m. (1) Ælfgifu (2) Emma, dau. of
Richard I of Normandy

Edmund
king 1016

Table 22　The Ruricovichi rulers of Rus'

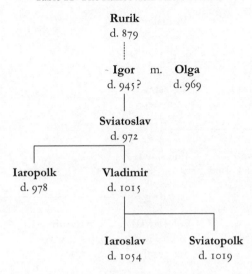

An alternative tradition makes Sviatopolk the son of Iaropolk (d. 978).

Table 23　Piast rulers of Poland

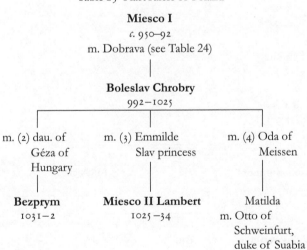

Table 24 Přemyslid rulers of Bohemia

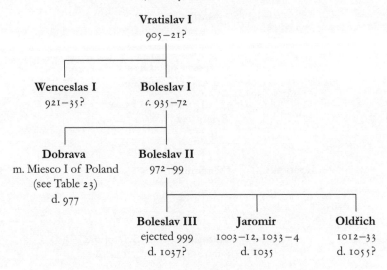

Vratislav I
905–21?

Wenceslas I   **Boleslav I**
921–35?   c. 935–72

Dobrava   **Boleslav II**
m. Miesco I of Poland   972–99
(see Table 23)
d. 977

Boleslav III   **Jaromir**   **Oldřich**
ejected 999   1003–12, 1033–4   1012–33
d. 1037?   d. 1035   d. 1055?

Table 25 Árpád rulers of Hungary

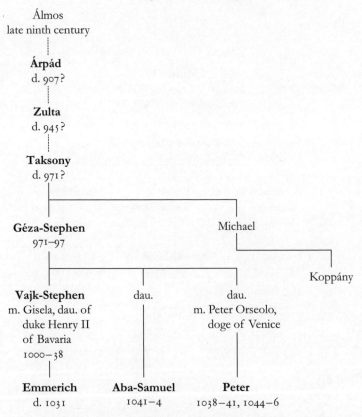

Álmos
late ninth century

Árpád
d. 907?

Zulta
d. 945?

Taksony
d. 971?

Géza-Stephen   Michael
971–97

                                              Koppány

Vajk-Stephen   dau.   dau.
m. Gisela, dau. of   m. Peter Orseolo,
duke Henry II   doge of Venice
of Bavaria
1000–38

Emmerich   **Aba-Samuel**   **Peter**
d. 1031   1041–4   1038–41, 1044–6

Both the genealogy and the dates up to Géza are more than usually uncertain

Table 26 Byzantine emperors

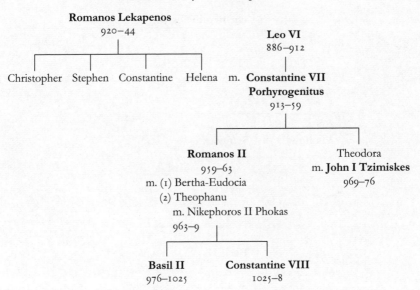

Table 27 Bulgarian rulers

1 The first dynasty

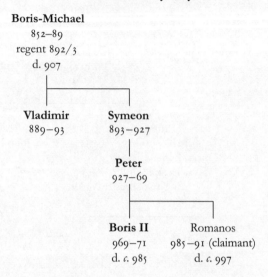

Boris-Michael
852–89
regent 892/3
d. 907

Vladimir
889–93

Symeon
893–927

Peter
927–69

Boris II
969–71
d. *c.* 985

Romanos
985–91 (claimant)
d. *c.* 997

2 The second dynasty
(the Kometopouloi)

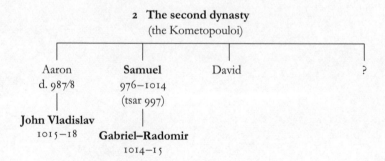

Aaron
d. 987/8

Samuel
976–1014
(tsar 997)

David

?

John Vladislav
1015–18

Gabriel–Radomir
1014–15

Table 28 Princes of Benevento and Capua

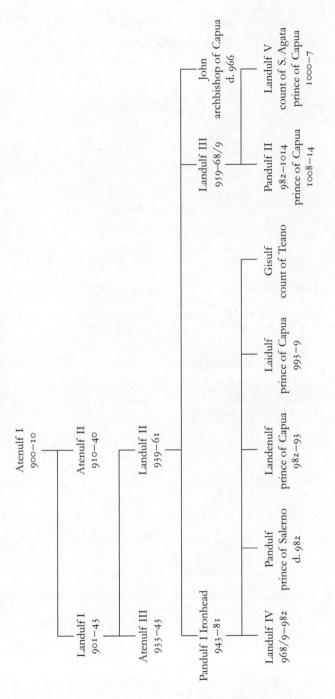

Unless stated otherwise, all of these were princes of both Capua and Benevento.

The regnal years given are those during which they were styled prince, even though this was in association with a father or brother.

Table 29 Princes of Salerno

1 The first dynasty

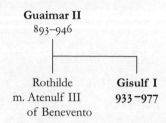

Guaimar II
893–946

Rothilde   **Gisulf I**
m. Atenulf III   **933 –977**
of Benevento

2 The second dynasty

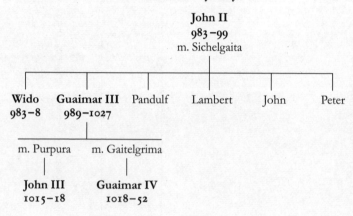

John II
983 –99
m. Sichelgaita

Wido   **Guaimar III** Pandulf   Lambert   John   Peter
983–8   **989–1027**

m. Purpura   m. Gaitelgrima

John III   **Guaimar IV**
1015–18   1018–52

Table 30 Caliphs of Córdoba

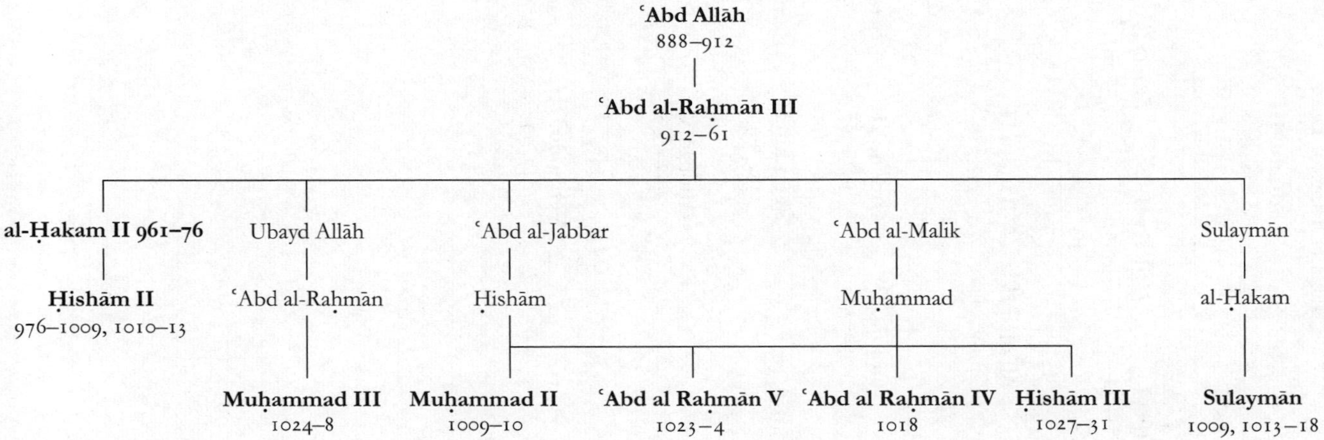

'Abd Allāh
888–912

'Abd al-Raḥmān III
912–61

Sulaymān

al-Ḥakam

'Abd al-Malik

Muḥammad

Hishām III
1027–31

'Abd al Raḥmān IV
1018

Sulaymān
1009, 1013–18

'Abd al-Jabbar

Hishām

Muḥammad II
1009–10

'Abd al Raḥmān V
1023–4

Ubayd Allāh

'Abd al-Raḥmān

Muḥammad III
1024–8

al-Ḥakam II 961–76

Hishām II
976–1009, 1010–13

Table 31 Kings of León

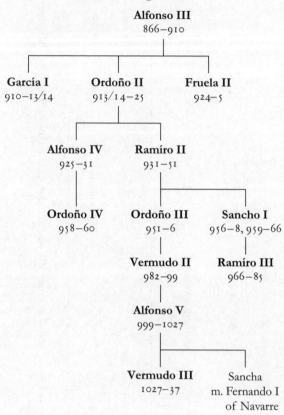

Table 32 Rulers of Navarre, Pamplona and Aragon

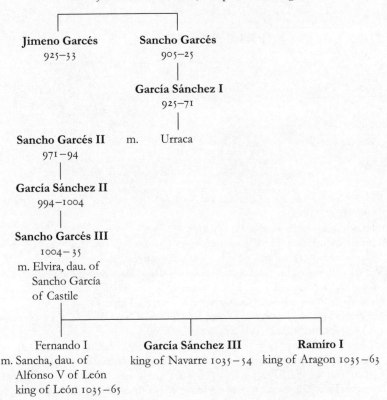

Jimeno Garcés
925–33

Sancho Garcés
905–25

García Sánchez I
925–71

Sancho Garcés II   m.   Urraca
971–94

García Sánchez II
994–1004

Sancho Garcés III
1004–35
m. Elvira, dau. of
Sancho García
of Castile

Fernando I
m. Sancha, dau. of
Alfonso V of León
king of León 1035–65

García Sánchez III
king of Navarre 1035–54

Ramíro I
king of Aragon 1035–63

Table 33 Counts of Castille

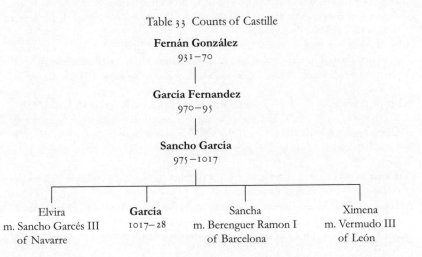

Fernán González
931–70

García Fernandez
970–95

Sancho García
975–1017

Elvira
m. Sancho Garcés III
of Navarre

García
1017–28

Sancha
m. Berenguer Ramon I
of Barcelona

Ximena
m. Vermudo III
of León

PRIMARY SOURCES

A History of Sharvan and Darband in the Tenth and Eleventh Centuries, English trans. V. Minorsky, Cambridge (1958)

Abbo of Fleury, *Liber canonum*, *PL* 139, cols. 473–508

Abbo of Fleury, *Vita Sancti Eadmundi regis Anglorum*, *PL* 139, cols. 507–20; ed. M. Winterbottom, *Three Lives of English Saints*, Toronto (1972)

'Abd Allāh b. Buluggin, *The Tibyan: Memoirs of 'Abd Allāh b. Buluggin, Last Zirid Amir of Granada*, English trans. A. T. Tibi, Leiden (1986)

Accessiones ad historiam abbatiae Casinensis, ed. E. Gattula, Venice (1734)

Acta archiepiscoporum Rotomagensium, ed. J. Mabillon, *Vetera Analecta*, Paris (1723), pp. 222–4, reprinted *PL* 147, cols. 273–80

Acta synodi Atrebatensis a Gerardo Cameracensi et Atrebatensi episcopo celebrata anno 1025, ed. P. Fredericq, *Corpus documentorum inquisitionis haereticae pravitatis Neerlandicae*, 5 vols., Ghent (1899–1902), I, pp. 2–5

Actus Pontificum Cenomannis in urbe degentium, ed. G. Busson and A. Ledru, Le Mans (1902)

Adalbero of Laon, *Carmen ad Robertum regem*, ed. C. Carozzi, *Carmen ad Robertum regum. Poème au roi Robert, Adalbéron de Laon*, Paris (1979); also in G.-A. Hückel, *Les poèmes satiriques d'Adalbéron*, Paris (1901)

Adalbert, king of Italy, *Diplomata*, ed. L. Schiaparelli, *I diplomi di Ugo e di Lotario, di Berengario II e di Adalberto (secolo X)* (Fonti per la Storia d'Italia 38), Rome (1924)

Adalbert of St Maximin, *Reginonis Continuatio*, ed. F. Kurze, Regino of Prüm, *Chronicon*, pp. 154–79

Adam of Bremen, *Gesta Hammaburgensis ecclesiae pontificum*, ed. B. Schmeidler, *MGH SRG* 11, Hanover (1917); ed. W. Trillmich, *Quellen des 9. und 11. Jahrhunderts zur Geschichte der Hamburgischen Kirche und des Reiches* (*AQ* 11), Darmstadt (1961), pp. 137–503; English trans. F. J. Tschan, *The Archbishops of Hamburg-Bremen by Adam of Bremen*, New York (1955)

Adhémar of Chabannes, *Chronicon*, ed. J. Chavanon, *Adémar de Chabannes, Chronique publiée d'après les manuscrits*, Paris (1897)

Adhémar of Chabannes, *Fabulae*, ed. P. Gatti and F. Bertini, *Ademaro di Chabannes, Favole*, Genoa (1988)

Adso of Montier-en-Der, *Epistula ad Gerbergam reginam de ortu et tempore Antichristi*, ed. D.

Verhelst, *De ortu et tempore Antichristi necnon et tractatus qui ab eo dependunt, Adso Dervensis* (CCCM 45), Turnhout (1976)

Ælfric, *Colloquy*, ed. G. N. Garmonsway, 2nd edn, London (1947)

Ælfric of Eynsham, *Lives of the Saints*, ed. W. Skeat (Early English Text Society 82), London (1885)

Æthelweard, *Chronicon*, ed. A. Campbell, *The Chronicle of Æthelweard*, London (1962)

Agnellus of Ravenna, *Liber pontificalis ecclesiae Ravennatis*, ed. G. Waitz, *MGH SRL*, Hanover (1878), pp. 265–391

Aimo of Fleury, *De gestis regum Francorum*, ed. M. Bouquet, *RHF* III, Paris (1869), pp. 21–123

Aimo of Fleury, *Vita S. Abbonis abbatis Floriacensis*, *PL* 139, cols. 387–418 (new edition in preparation by R.-H. Bautier)

Alcuin, *The Bishops, Kings and Saints of York*, ed. P. Godman, Oxford (1983)

Alfred of Wessex, *The Old English Version of Augustine's* Soliloquies, extracts translated into modern English in S. Keynes and M. Lapidge, *Alfred the Great: Asser's Life of King Alfred and Other Contemporary Sources*, Harmondsworth (1983), pp. 138–52

Alfred the Great: Asser's Life of King Alfred and Other Contemporary Sources, ed. and trans. S. Keynes and M. Lapidge, Harmondsworth (1983)

Alpertus Mettensis, *De diversitate temporum et Fragmentum de Deoderico primo episcopo Mettensi*, ed. H. van Rij, Amsterdam (1980)

Amari, M. (ed.), *Biblioteca arabo-sicula*, 2 vols., Leipzig (1857)

Amatus of Monte Cassino, *Storia de'Normanni,* ed. V. de Bartholomeis (Fonti per la Storia d'Italia 76), Rome (1935)

Andrew of Fleury, *Vita Gauzlini abbatis Floriacensis monasterii*, ed. with French trans. R.-H. Bautier and G. Labory, *André de Fleury: Vie de Gauzlin, Abbé de Fleury* (Sources d'histoire médiévale publiées par l'Institut de Recherche et d'Histoire des Textes 3) Paris (1969)

Angilram of Saint-Riquier, *Vita Sancti Richarii abbatis Centulensis primi metrice descripta, PL* 141, cols. 1421–38

Anglo-Saxon Charters, ed. A. J. Robertson (with English trans.), 2nd edn, Cambridge (1956)

Annales Alamannici, ed. G. H. Pertz, *MGH SS* I, Hanover (1826), pp. 22–60

Annales Altahenses maiores, ed. E. von Oefele, *MGH SRG* IV, Hanover (1891)

Annales Bertiniani, ed. F. Grat, J. Vielliard and C. Clémencet, *Annales de Saint-Bertin*, Paris (1964); ed. G. Waitz, *MGH SRG* V, Hanover (1883); English trans. J. L. Nelson, *The Annals of Saint-Bertin*, Manchester (1991)

Annales ex annalibus Iuvavensibus antiquis excerpti, ed. H. Bresslau, *MGH SS* XXX.2, Leipzig (1934), pp. 727–44

Annales Fuldenses, ed. G. H. Pertz, *MGH SS* I, Hanover (1826), pp. 337–415; ed. F. Kurze, *MGH SRG* VII, Hanover (1891); ed. with German trans. R. Rau, *Quellen zur karolingischen Reichsgeschichte* III (*AQ* 7), Darmstadt (1960), pp. 19–117; English trans. T. Reuter, *The Annals of Fulda*, Manchester (1992)

Annales Heremi, ed. G. H. Pertz, *MGH SS* III, Hanover (1839), pp. 138–45

Annales Hildesheimenses, ed. G. Waitz, *MGH SRG* VIII, Hanover (1878)

Annales Kamenzenses, ed. R. Röpell and W. Arndt, *MGH SS* XIX, Hanover (1866), pp. 580–2

Annales Quedlinburgenses, ed. G. H. Pertz, *MGH SS* III, Hanover (1839), pp. 22–90

Annales s. Rudberti Salisburgensis, ed. W. Wattenbach, *MGH SS* IX, Hanover (1851), pp. 758–810

Annales Sangallenses maiores, ed. I von Arx, *MGH SS* I, Hanover (1826), pp. 72–85

Annales Vedastini, ed. B. von Simson, *Annales Xantenses et Vedastini, MGH SRG* XII, Hanover (1909)

Annalista Saxo, ed. G. Waitz, *MGH SS* VI, Hanover (1844), pp. 542–777

Anonymus, *Gesta Hungarorum,* ed. E. Jakubovich and D. Pais, *Scriptores rerum Hungaricarum* I, pp. 13–118; ed. G. Silagi, *Die 'Gesta Hungarorum' des anonymen Notars: Die älteste Darstellung der ungarischen Geschichte,* Sigmaringen (1991)

Anonymus Haserensis, *Liber pontificalis Eichstetensis,* ed. L. C. Bethmann, *MGH SS* VII, Hanover (1846), pp. 253–66; ed. with German trans. S. Weinfurter, *Die Geschichte der Eichstätter Bischöfe des Anonymus Haserensis* (Eichstätter Studien N.F. 24), Regensburg (1987)

Ansegis, *Collectio capitularium,* ed. G. Schmitz (*MGH Cap.,* N.S. 1), Hanover (1996)

Anselm, *Gesta episcoporum Tungrensium, Traiectensium et Leodiensium,* ed. R. Koepke, *MGH SS* VII, Hanover (1846), pp. 189–234

Arabische Berichte von Gesandten an germanische Fürstenhöfe aus dem 9. und 10. Jahrhundert (Quellen zur deutschen Volkskunde 1), Berlin and Leipzig

Arduin, king of Italy, *Diplomata,* ed. H. Bresslau, H. Bloch, R. Holtzmann, M. Meyer and H. Wibel, in *Die Urkunden Heinrichs II. und Arduins, MGH Dip. regum* III, Hanover (1900–3)

Aristakes of Lastivert, *Récit des malheurs de la nation arménienne,* French trans. M. Canard and H. Berberian (Bibliothèque de *Byzantion* 5), Brussels (1973)

Armes Prydein: The Prophecy of Britain, ed. I. Williams with English trans. R. Bromwich (Mediaeval and Modern Welsh Series 6), Dublin (1972)

Arnulf, king of east Francia and emperor, *Diplomata,* ed. P. Kehr, *Arnolfi Diplomata, MGH Dip. Germ.* III, Berlin (1940)

Asser, *Life of King Alfred,* ed. W. Stevenson, Oxford (1904), revised D. Whitelock, Oxford (1959); English trans. S. Keynes and M. Lapidge, *Alfred the Great: Asser's Life of King Alfred and other Contemporary Sources,* Harmondsworth (1983), pp. 67–110

Athanasius, *Contra Arianos,* ed. and trans. A. Vaillant, *Discours contre les Ariens de Saint Athanase,* Sofia (1954)

Attenborough, F. L. (ed. with English trans.), *The Laws of the Earliest English Kings,* Cambridge (1922); see also *Die Gesetze der Angelsachsen*

Atto of Vercelli, *Opera omnia, PL* 134, cols. 27–900

Atto of Vercelli, *Polipticum,* ed. G. Goetz, *Attonis qui fertur Polipticum quod appellatur perpendiculum,* Leipzig (1922)

Auxilius, *De ordinationibus a Formoso papa factis, PL* 129, cols. 1053–1102

Auxilius, *Liber cuiusdam requirentis et respondentis (infensor et defensor), PL* 129, cols. 1101–12

Baronius, C., *Annales ecclesiastici* x, Cologne (1603)

Benedict of Soracte, *Chronicon,* ed. G. Zucchetti, *Il 'Chronicon' di Benedetto monaco di S. Andrea del Soratte* (Fonti per la Storia d'Italia 55), Rome (1920)

Berengar I, king of Italy, *Diplomata,* ed. L. Schiaparelli, *I diplomi di Berengario I (sec. IX–X)* (Fonti per la Storia d'Italia 35), Rome (1903)

Berengar II, king of Italy, *Diplomata,* ed. L. Schiaparelli, *I diplomi di Ugo e di Lotario, di Berengario II e di Adalberto (secolo X)* (Fonti per la Storia d'Italia 38), Rome (1924)

Beševliev, V. (ed.), *Die protobulgarischen Inschriften* (Berliner Byzantinische Arbeiten 23), Berlin (1963)

Böhmer, J. F., *Regesta Imperii* I: *Die Regesten des Kaiserreichs unter den Karolingern 751–918*, revised edn E. Mühlbacher and J. Lechner, Innsbruck (1908); reprinted with additions by C. Brühl and H. H. Kaminsky, Hildesheim (1966)

Böhmer, J. F., *Regesta imperii* II, 1–6: *Die Regesten des Kaiserreichs unter den Herrschern aus dem Sächsischen Haus 919–1024*. II, 1: *Heinrich I. und Otto I.,* revised edn E. von Ottenthal, Innsbruck (1893), reprinted with additions by H. H. Kaminsky, Hildersheim (1967); II, 2: *Otto II.,* revised edn H. J. Mikoltezky, Graz (1950); II, 3: *Otto III.,* revised edn M. Uhlirz, Graz (1956); II, 4: *Heinrich II.,* revised edn T. Graff, Vienna (1971); II, 5: *Papstregesten (911–1024),* ed. H. Zimmermann, Vienna (1969); II, 6: *Register,* ed. H. Zimmermann, Vienna (1982)

Book of the Eparch, ed. and trans. J. Koder, *Das Eparchenbuch Leons des Weisen* (CFHB 33, Series Vindobonensis), Vienna (1991)

Bouquet, M., *Recueil des historiens des Gaules et de France,* 2nd edn ed. L. Delisle, 24 vols., Paris (1869)

Brun of Querfurt, *Epistola ad Heinricum regem,* ed. J. Karwasińska (Monumenta Poloniae Historica Series Nova IV.2), Warsaw (1969)

Brun of Querfurt, *Passio sancti Adalberti,* ed. J. Karwasińska, *Passio sancti Adalberti,* in *Monumenta Poloniae historica,* N.S. IV/2, Warsaw (1969), pp. 3–69

Brun of Querfurt, *S. Adalberti Pragensis episcopi et martyris vita altera,* ed. J. Karwasińska (Monumenta Poloniae Historica Series Nova 4.2), Warsaw (1969)

[Byrhtferth of Ramsey], *Vita Oswaldi archiepiscopi,* ed. M. Raine, *Historians of the Church of York and its Archbishops* (Rolls Series), London (1879), I, pp. 399–475

Cahen, C., 'Un Texte peu connu relatif au commerce oriental d'Amalfi au xe siècle', *Archivio storico per le provincie Napoletane* n.s. 34 (1955), pp. 61–6

Cantera Montenegro, M. (ed.), *Colleción documental de Santa María la Real de Nájera* I: *Siglos X–XIV,* San Sebastián (1991)

Capitula episcoporum, I, ed. P. Brommer, *MGH Cap. episc.* I, Hanover (1984); II, ed. R. Pokorny and M. Stratmann with W.-D. Runge, *MGH Cap. episc.* II, Hanover (1995); III, ed. R. Pokorny, *MGH Cap. episc.* III, Hanover (1995)

Capitularia regum Francorum, ed. A. Boretius and V. Krause, *MGH Cap.,* 2 vols., Hanover (1883–97)

Carloman, king of Bavaria, *Diplomata,* ed. P. Kehr, *MGH Dip. Germ.* I, Berlin (1932–4)

Carloman II, king of west Francia, *Acta,* ed. F. Grat, J. de Font-Réaulx, G. Tessier and R.-H. Bautier, *Recueil des actes de Louis II le Bègue, Louis III et Carloman II, rois de France, 877–884,* Paris (1978)

Carmina Cantabrigiensia, ed. K. Strecker, *Die Cambridger Lieder, MGH SRG XL,* Berlin (1926); ed. Walther Bulst, *Carmina Cantabrigiensia,* (Heidelberger Ausgaben zur Geistes-und Kulturgeschichte 17), Heidelberg (1950)

Cartulaire de Brioude, ed. H. Doniol, Clermont-Ferrand and Paris (1863)

Cartulaire de l'abbaye de Gorze. Ms. 826 de la Bibliothèque de Metz, ed. A. d'Herbomez, 2 vols., Paris (1898–1902)

Cartulaire de l'abbaye de Saint-André-le-Bas de Vienne, suivi d'un appendice de chartes inédites sur la diocèse de Vienne, ed. C. U. J. Chevalier (Collection de Cartulaires Dauphinois 1), Vienne (1869)

Cartulaire de l'abbaye de Saint-Aubin d'Angers, ed. B. de Broussillon, 2 vols., Paris (1903)

Cartulaire de l'abbaye de Saint-Bertin, ed. B. Guérard, Paris (1841)

Cartulaire de l'abbaye de Saint-Père de Chartres, ed. B. Guérard, 2 vols., Paris (1840)

Cartulario de Albelda, ed., A. Ubieto Arteta, Zaragoza (1981)

Cartulario de San Juan de la Peña, ed. A. Ubieto Arteta, 2 vols., Valencia (1962)

Cartulario de San Millán de la Cogolla (759–1076), ed. A. Ubieto Arteta, Valencia (1976)

Cartulario de Santa Cruz de la Serós, ed. A. Ubieto Arteta, Valencia (1966)

Cartulario de Siresa, ed. A. Ubieto Arteta, Zaragoza (1986)

Cartularium Saxonicum, ed. W. de Gray Birch, 3 vols., London (1885–99)

Catalunya carolingia, II: *Els diploms carolingis a Catalunya*, ed. R. d'Abadal i de Vinyals, Barcelona (1926–52)

Cessi, R. (ed.), *Documenti relativi alla storia di Venezia anteriori al mille*, 2 vols., Padua (1940–2)

Charles II (the Bald), king of west Francia, *Acta*, ed. A. Giry, M. Prou and G. Tessier, *Recueil des actes de Charles II le Chauve, roi de France*, 3 vols., Paris (1943–55)

Charles III (the Fat), king of east Francia, *Diplomata*, ed. P. Kehr, *MGH Dip. Germ.* II, Berlin (1937)

Charles the Simple, king of west Francia, *Acta*, ed. P. Lauer, *Recueil des actes de Charles III le Simple, roi de France, 893–923*, 2 vols., Paris (1940–9)

Chronica monasterii Casinensis, ed. H. Hoffmann, *MGH SS* XXXIV, Hanover (1980)

Chronicon episcoporum Hildesheimensium, ed. G. H. Pertz, *MGH SS* VII, Hanover (1846), pp. 845–73

Chronicon Malleacense, ed. with French trans. J. Verdon, *Chronique de Saint-Maixent, 751–1140*, Paris (1979)

Chronicon Mosomense seu Liber fundationis monasterii sancti Mariae O. S. B. apud Mosomum, ed. with French trans. M. Bur, *Chronique ou Livre de fondation du monastère de Mouzon*, Paris (1989)

Chronicon Salernitanum, ed. U. Westerbergh, *Chronicon Salernitanum: A Critical Edition*, Stockholm (1956)

Chronicon Vedastinum, ed. G. Waitz, *MGH SS* XIII, Hanover (1881), pp. 674–709

Chronicon Vulternense del monaco Giovanni, ed. V. Federici, 3 vols. (Fonti per la Storia d'Italia 58–60), Rome (1924–38)

Chronique de l'abbaye de Saint-Bénigne de Dijon, ed. E. Bougard and J. Garnier, Dijon (1875)

Chronique de Nantes, 570 environs–1049, ed. R. Merlet, Paris (1896)

Chroniques Asturiennes, ed. Y. Bonnaz, *Chroniques Asturiennes (fin IXe siècle). Avec édition critique, traduction et commentaire*, Paris (1987); ed. J. Gil Fernández, *Crónicas Asturianas; crónica de Alfonso III (Rorense y 'A Sebastián'); Crónica albedense (y 'profética')*, Oviedo (1985)

Clarius, *Chronicon Sancti Petri Vivi Senonensis*, ed. with French trans. R.-H. Bautier and M. Gilles, Paris (1979)

Codex diplomaticus Caietanus, 2 vols., Monte Cassino (1888–92)

Codex diplomaticus Cavensis, ed. M. Moroldi, OSB, 8 vols., Milan and Naples (1873–1893)

Colección documental del archivo de la Catedral de León, 3 vols., León (1987–90); I: *775–952*, ed. E. Sáez (1987); II: *953–985*, ed. E. Sáez and C. Sáez (1990); III: *986–1031*, ed. J. M. Ruiz Asencio (1987)

Concilia aevi Saxonici 916–1001 I: *916–961*, ed. E.-D. Hehl and H. Fuhrmann, *MGH Conc.* VI, Hanover (1987)

Conrad I, king of east Francia, *Diplomata*, ed. T. Sickel, *Die Urkunden Konrad I., Heinrich I. und Otto I., MGH Dip. regum* I, Hanover (1879–84)

Conrad II, emperor, *Diplomata*, ed. H. Bresslau, *Die Urkunden Konrads II., MGH Dip. regum* IV, Berlin (1909)

Conrad, king of Burgundy, *Diplomata*, ed. T. Schieffer, *Die Urkunden der burgundischen Rudolfinger, MGH Regum Burgundiae e stirpe Rudolfina Diplomata et Acta*, Munich (1977)

Constantine, *Vita Adalberonis II Mettensis episcopi*, ed. G. H. Pertz, *MGH SS* IV, Hanover (1841), pp. 658–72

Constantine Porphyrogenitus, *De administratio imperio*: 1, ed. G. Moravcsik with English trans. R. J. H. Jenkins, Budapest (1949); reprinted (DOT 1/CFHB 1), Washington, DC (1967); II, *Commentary*, ed. R. J. H. Jenkins, London (1962).

Constantine Porphyrogenitus, *De ceremoniis*, ed. I. I. Reiske, *De cerimoniis aulae byzantinae*, 2 vols., Bonn (1829); ed. A. Vogt, *Constantin VII Porphyrogénète: le livre des cérémonies*, 2 vols., Paris (1935–9)

Constantine Porphyrogenitus, *De thematibus*, ed. A. Pertusi (Studi e Testi 160), Rome (1952)

Constantine Porphyrogenitus, *Three Treatises on Imperial Military Expeditions*, ed. J. F. Haldon (CFHB 28), Vienna (1990)

Constitutiones et acta publica imperatorum et regum inde ab a. DCCCCXI usque ad a. MCXCVII (911–1197), ed. L. Weiland, *MGH Const.*, Hanover (1893)

Constitutiones Heinrici ducis Ranshofenses, ed. J. Merkel, in *MGH Leges in folio*, ed. G. H. Pertz, III, Hanover (1863), pp. 484–5

Conventum inter Guillelmum Aquitanorum comitem et Hugonem Chiliarchum, ed. J. Martindale, *EHR* 84 (1969), pp. 528–48

Conversio Bagoariorum et Carantanorum, ed. M. Koš, *Libellus de conversione Bagoariorum et Carantanorum*, Ljubljana (1936); ed. H. Wolfram, *Conversio Bagoariorum et Carantanorum. Das Weissbuch der Salzburger Kirche über die erfolgreiche Mission in Karantanien und Pannonien*, Vienna (1979); ed. F. Lošek, *Die Conversio Bagoariorum et Carantanorum und der Brief des Erzbischofs Theotmar von Salzburg, MGH Studien und Texte* XV, Hanover (1997), pp. 90–137

Corpus Troporum, ed. O. Marcusson, G. Björkvall, G. Iverson, R. Jonsson and E. Odelman (Studia Latina Stockholmiensia 22, 25, 26, 32, 31, 34), Stockholm (1975, 1976, 1982, 1980, 1986, 1986, 1990)

Cosmas of Prague, *Chronica Boemorum*, ed. B. Bretholz, *MGH SRG*, N.S. II, Berlin (1923)

Cosmas the Priest, *Treatise against the Bogomils,* ed. M. G. Popruzhenko, *Kozma Presviter, bolgarskii pisatel' X veka* (B'lgarski Starini 12), Sofia (1936); ed. with French trans. H.-C. Puech and A. Vaillant, *Le Traité contre les Bogomiles de Cosmas le prêtre* (Travaux publiés par l'Institut d'études slaves 21), Paris (1945)

Crónica de Garci López de Roncesvalles, ed. C. Orcastegui Gros, Pamplona (1977)

Darrouzès, J. (ed.), *Epistoliers byzantins du X siècle* (Archives de l'orient chrétien 6), Paris (1960)

Das Martyrolog-Necrolog von St. Emmeram zu Regensburg, ed. E. Freise, D. Geuenich and J. Wollasch, *MGH Lib. Mem., N.S.* III, Hanover (1986)

Das Nekrolog von Möllenbeck, ed. L. Schrader, *Wigands Archiv für Geschichte und Altertumskunde Westfalens* 5 (1832), 342–84

Devic, C. and Vaissette, J. (eds.), *Histoire générale de Languedoc* V, Paris (1745)

Dennis, G. T. (ed. with English trans.), *Three Byzantine Military Treatises* (CFHB 25; DOT 9), Washington, DC (1985)

Die Gesetze der Angelsachsen, ed. F. Liebermann, 3 vols., Halle (1903–16); ed. and trans. F. L. Attenborough as *The Laws of the Earliest English Kings*, Cambridge (1922)

Die 'Honorantie Civitatis Papie', ed. C. Brühl and C. Violante, Cologne and Vienna (1983)

Die Tegernseer Briefsammlung (Froumund), ed. K. Strecker, *MGH Epp. Sel.* III, Berlin (1925)

Die Traditionen des Hochstifts Regensburg und des Klosters S. Emmeram (Quellen und Erörterungen zur bayerischen Geschichte N.F. 8), Munich (1943)

Diplomata Hungariae antiquissima accedunt epistolae et acta ad historiam Hungariae pertinentia I: *1000–1131*, ed. G. Györffy, J. B. Borsa, F. L. Hervay, B. L. Kumorovitz and G. Moravcsik, Budapest (1992)

Diplomatari i escrits literaris de l'abat i bisbe Oliba, ed. E. Junyent ï Subirà, Barcelona (1992)

Duchesne, A., *Histoire généalogique de la maison de Vergy*, Paris (1625)

Dudo of Saint-Quentin, *De moribus et actis primorum Normanniae ducum*, ed. J. A. Lair, Paris (1865); Eng. trans. E. Christiansen, *Dudo of St Quentin, History of the Normans* (Woodbridge, 1998)

Durán Guidol, A. (ed.), *Colección diplomática de la Catedral de Huesca*, 2 vols., Zaragoza (1965–9)

Ecbasis cuiusdam captivi per tropologiam, ed. K. Strecker, *MGH SRG* XXIV, Hanover (1935)

Edmund's Saga, English trans. H. Pálsson and P. Edwards, *Vikings in Russia: Yngvar's Saga and Edmund's Saga*, Edinburgh (1989)

Egils Saga Skallagrímssonar, ed. F. Jónsson, Halle (1924); English trans. H. Pálsson and P. Edwards, Harmondsworth (1976)

Elenchus fontium historiae urbanae II, II, ed. S. Reynolds, W. de Boer and G. MacMiocaill, Leiden (1988)

Erchempert, *Historia Langobardorum Beneventanorum*, ed. G. Waitz, *MGH SRL*, Hanover (1878), pp. 231–64

Ermoldus Nigellus, *Carmen in honorem Hludowici Pii*, ed. E. Faral, *Poème sur Louis le Pieux et Epître au roi Pépin* (Classiques de l'histoire de France au moyen âge 14), Paris (1932, repr. 1964)

Evreisko-khazarskaia perepiska v X veke, ed. P. K. Kokovtsov, Leningrad (1932)

Ex Guimanni libro de possessionibus Sancti Vedasti, ed. G. Waitz, *MGH SS* XIII, Hanover (1881), pp. 710–15.

Excerpta de legationibus, ed. C. de Boor, Berlin (1903)

Flodoard, *Annales*, ed. P. Lauer, *Les annales de Flodoard publiées d'après les manuscrits*, Paris, 1905

Flodoard, *De triumphis Christi*, *PL* 135, cols. 491–886

Flodoard, *Historia Remensis ecclesiae*, ed. J. Heller and G. Waitz, *MGH SS* XIII, Hanover (1881), pp. 405–599; ed. M. Stratmann, *MGH SS* XXXVI, Hanover (1998); ed. with French trans. P. J. F. Lejeune, *Histoire de l'église de Reims par Flodoard*, Rheims (1854); reprinted in *Revue du Moyen Age Latin* 37 (1981), pp. 7–220 (Bk I); 38 (1982), pp. 7–151 (Bk II); 39 (1983), pp. 7–203 (Bk III.i); 40 (1984), pp. 7–212 (Bk III.ii); 41 (1985), pp. 7–238 (Bk IV)

Folcuin, *Gesta abbatum S. Bertini Sithiensium*, O. Holder-Egger, *MGH SS* XIII, Hanover (1881), pp. 600–35

Fontes Byzantini historiae Hungaricae aevo ducum et regum ex stirpe Árpád descendentium, ed. G. Moravcsik, Budapest (1984)

Fontes Graeci historiae Bulgaricae I–XI, Sofia (1954–83)

Fragmentum de Arnolfo duce Bavvariae, ed. P. Jaffé, *MGH SS* xvii, Hanover (1861), p. 570; ed. Reindel, *Die bayerischen Luitpoldinger*, p. 112

Frithegod, *Breuiloquium vitae beati Wilfredi*, ed. A. E. Campbell, *Frithegodi monachi Breuiloquium vitae beati Wilfredi et Wulfstani cantoris narratio metrica de Sancto Swithuno*, Zurich (1950)

Fulbert of Chartres, *The Letters and Poems of Fulbert of Chartres*, ed. with English trans. F. Behrends, Oxford (1976)

Fulk le Réchin, *Fragmentum historiae Andegavensis*, in *Chroniques des comtes d'Anjou et des seigneurs d'Amboise*, ed. L. Halphen and R. Poupardin, Paris (1913), pp. 232–8

Gallus Anonymus, *Chronicae et gesta ducum sive principum Polonorum, Monumenta Poloniae Historica* n. s. ii, ed. K. Maleczyński, Craców (1952)

Gardizi, 'Gardizi's two chapters on the Turks', English trans. A. P. Martinez, *Archivum Eurasiae Medii Aevi* ii (1982), pp. 109–217

George Monachus Continuatus, in Theophanes Continuatus, *Chronographia*, ed. I. Bekker, Bonn (1838)

Gerard of Csanád, *Deliberatio*, ed. G. Silagi, *Gerardi Moresanae aecclesiae seu Csanadiensis episcopi Deliberatio supra hymnum trium puerorum* (CCCM 49), Turnhout (1978)

Gerard of St Medard, *Vita Sancti Romani, PL* 138, cols. 171–84

Gerbert of Aurillac, *Epistolae*, ed. F. Weigle, *Die Briefsammlung Gerberts von Reims, MGH Die Briefe der Deutschen Kaiserzeit* ii, Weimar (1966); ed. J. Havet, *Lettres*, Paris (1889); ed. with French trans. P. Riché and J.-P. Callu, *Gerbert d'Aurillac, Correspondance*, 2 vols. (Classiques de l'histoire de France au moyen âge 35–6), Paris (1993); English trans. H. P. Lattin, *Gerbert, Letters with his Papal Privileges as Sylvester II,* New York (1961)

Gerbert of Aurillac, *Liber de astrolabio*, ed. N. Bubnov, in *Gerberti postea Silvestri II papae Opera mathematica (972–1003)*, Berlin (1899), pp. 109–47

Gerbert of Aurillac, *Opera, PL* 139, cols. 57–350

Gerhard, *Vita sancti Oudalrici episcopi Augustani*, ed. G. Waitz, *MGH SS* iv, Hanover (1841), pp. 377–428; ed. with German trans. H. Kallfelz, *Leben des hl. Ulrich, Bischof von Augsburg verfasst von Gerhard*, in *Lebensbeschreibungen einiger Bischöfe des 10.–12. Jahrhunderts (AQ 22),* Darmstadt (1973), pp. 35–167

Gesta Apollonii, ed. E. Dümmler, in *MGH Poet.* ii, Berlin (1884), pp. 483–506; ed. F. Ermini, *Poeti epici latini del secolo X*, Rome (1920), pp. 109–25

Gesta archiepiscoporum Magdeburgensium, ed. W. Schum, *MGH SS* xiv, Hanover (1883), pp. 374–486

Gesta Berengarii imperatoris, ed. P. von Winterfeld, in *MGH Poetae* iv.1, Berlin (1899), pp. 354–401

Gesta comitum Barcinonensium, ed. L. Barrau Dihigo and J. Massó-Torrents (Chroniques Catalanes 2), Barcelona (1925)

Gesta consulum Andegavorum, ed. L. Halphen and R. Poupardin, *Chroniques des comtes d'Anjou et des seigneurs d'Amboise*, Paris (1913), pp. 25–73

Gesta episcoporum Cameracensium, ed. L. Bethmann, *MGH SS* vii, Hanover (1846), pp. 393–489

Gesta episcoporum Neopolitanorum, ed. G. Waitz, *MGH SRL*, Hanover (1878), pp. 396–439

Gesta episcoporum Virdunensium, ed. G. Waitz, *MGH SS* iv, Hanover (1841), pp. 36–51

Gesta Normannorum Ducum, ed. with English trans. E. Van Houts, *The Gesta*

Normannorum Ducum of William of Jumièges, Orderic Vitalis, and Robert of Torigni, 2 vols., Oxford (1992–5)

Gesta pontificum Autissiodorensium, ed. L.-M. Duru, *Bibliothèque historique de l'Yonne* 1, Auxerre (1850), pp. 309–520

Gombos, A. F., *Catalogus fontium historiae Hungaricae*, 4 vols., Budapest (1937a, 1937b, 1938, 1941)

Gr'tskite zhitiia na Kliment Okhridski, ed. A. Milev, Sofia (1966)

Hagiou Petrou episkopou Argous Bios kai Logoi, ed. K. T. Kyriakopoulos, Athens (1976)

Halphen, L. (ed.), *Recueil d'Annales angevines et vendômoises*, Paris (1903)

Hartwic, *Legenda S. Stephani regis ab Hartvico episcopo conscripta,* ed. E. Bartoniek in *Scriptores rerum Hungaricarum* 11, Budapest (1938), pp. 401–40

Helgaud of Fleury, *Vie de Robert le Pieux; Epitoma vitae regis Rotberti pii*, ed. with French trans. R.-H. Bautier and G. Labory (Sources d'histoire médiévale 1), Paris (1965)

Henry I, king of east Francia, *Diplomata*, ed. T. Sickel, *Die Urkunden Konrad I., Heinrich I. und Otto I., MGH Dip. regum* 1, Hanover (1879–84)

Henry II, king of east Francia and emperor, *Diplomata*, ed. H. Bresslau, H. Bloch, R. Holtzmann, M. Meyer and H. Wibel, *Die Urkunden Heinrichs II. und Arduins, MGH Dip. regum* 111, Hanover (1900–3)

Hermann of the Reichenau, *Chronicon*, ed. G. H. Pertz, *MGH SS* v, Hanover (1844) pp. 67–133

Hill, B. H., *Medieval Monarchy in Action: The German Empire from Henry I to Henry IV* (selected documents in English translation), London (1972)

Historia Francorum Senonensis, ed. G. Waitz, *MGH SS* 1x, Hanover, (1851) pp. 364–9

Historia Salonitana Maior, ed. N. Klaić (Srpska Akademija Nauka i Umetnosti. Posebna Izdanja, Odeljenje Drushchtvenih Nauka 55), Belgrade (1967)

Historia Silense, ed. J. Pérez de Urbel and A. González Ruiz-Zorrilla, Madrid (1959)

Hrotsvitha of Gandersheim, *Gesta Ottonis*, ed. P. Winterfeld, *Hrotsvithae Opera, MGH SRG* xxxiv, Berlin (1903), pp. 201–28

Hrotsvitha of Gandersheim, *Opera*, ed. P. Winterfeld, *MGH SRG* xxxiv, Berlin (1903); ed. K. Strecker, Leipzig (1930); ed. H. Homeyer, Paderborn (1970)

Hudud al-Alam, *'The Regions of the World': A Persian Geography 373 AH–982 AD*, English trans. and comm. V. F. Minorsky (E. J. W. Gibb Memorial Series, n.s. 11), 2nd edn, London (1970)

Hugh, king of Italy, *Diplomata*, ed. L. Schiaparelli, *I diplomi di Ugo e di Lotario, di Berengario II e di Adalberto (secolo X)* (Fonti per la Storia d'Italia 38), Rome (1924)

Hugh of Fleury, *Liber qui modernorum regum Francorum continet actus*, ed. G. Waitz, *MGH SS* 1x, Hanover (1851) pp. 376–95

Hymnarius Severinianus, ed. G. M. Dreves, *Das Hymnar der Abtei S. Severin in Neapel: Nach den Codices Vaticanus 7172 und Parisinus 1092* (Hymnica medii aevi xiv-a), Leipzig (1893)

I placiti cassinesi del secolo X col periodi in volgare, ed. M. Inguanez (4th edn, Miscellanea Cassinese 24), Monte Cassino (1942)

Ibn al-Athīr, *Al-Kamil fi'l-ta'rīkh*, ed. C. J. Tornberg, 12 vols., Leiden (1867–74)

Ibn al-Faradī, *Ta'rīkh 'ulama' al-Andalus*, ed. F. Codera, Madrid (1892)

Ibn Faḍlān, *Risālah*, English trans. J. E. McKeithen, 'The Risālah of Ibn Faḍlān: an annotated translation with introduction', doctoral dissertation, Indiana University (1979)

Ibn Ḥawqal, *Ṣūrat al-anḍ*, ed. J. H. Kramem, Leiden (1939)

Ibn Ḥayyān, *al-Muqtabis*, v (dealing with the first part of ʿAbd al-Raḥmān III's reign, 912–42 AD), ed. P. Chalmeta and F. Corriente, Madrid (1979); Spanish trans. M. J. Viguera and F. Corriente, *Kitab al-Muqtabis fita-'rikh al-Andalus. Crónica de califa ʿAbdarrahman III al-Nasir entre los anos 912 y 942. Ibn Hayyan de Córdoba*, Zaragoza (1981); VII (al-Ḥakam II's reign, 971–75), ed. A. A. al-Hajji, Beirut (1965); Spanish trans. E. Garcia Gomez, *Anales palatinos de califa de Córdoba al-Hakam II*, Madrid (1967)

Ibn Idhārī al-Marrākushī, *Kitāb al-Bayān al-Mughrib* II and III, ed. G. Colin and E. Lévi-Provençal, Leiden (1948–51)

Ibn Rusteh, *Les Autours précieux / Kitāb al-Aclāq an-Nafisa*, trans. G. Wiet, Cairo (1955)

Ibrāhīm ibn Yaʿqūb, *Relatio Ibrahim ibn Jaʿkub de Itinere Slavico, quae traditur apud Al-Bekri*, ed. T. Kowalski, *Monumenta Poloniae Historica* n.s. 1, Cracόw (1946)

Ilarion (Metropolitan), *Das Metropolitan Ilarion Lobrede auf Vladimir der Heiligen und Glaubensbekenntnis*, ed. L. Müller (Slavische Studienbücher 2), Wiesbaden (1962)

Ius graecoromanum, eds. P. and J. Zepos, 8 vols., Athens (1931)

John, Exarch of Bulgaria, *Hexaemeron*, ed. with German trans. R. Aitzetmüller, *Das Hexaemeron des Exarchen Johannes*, 7 vols., Graz (1958, 1960, 1961, 1966, 1968, 1971, 1978)

John VIII, *Epistolae*, ed. E. Caspar, *MGH Epp.* VII, Berlin (1928), pp. 1–272

John VIII, *Fragmenta Registri*, ed. E. Caspar, *MGH Epp.* VII, Berlin (1928), pp. 273–312

John Cinnamus, *Epitome historiarum*, Migne, *PG* 133, cols. 309–677; English trans. by C. M. Brand, *Deeds of John and Manuel Comnenus*, New York (1976)

John Kaminiates, *De expugnatione Thessalonicae*, ed. G. Böhlig (CFHB 4), Berlin and New York (1973)

John of Saint-Arnulf, *Vita Iohannis abbatis Gorziensis auctore Iohanne abbate S. Arnulfi*, ed. G. H. Pertz, *MGH SS* IV, Hanover (1841), pp. 335–77

John of Salerno, *Vita S. Odonis abbatis Cluniacensis*, in Bibliotheca Cluniacensis, ed. M. Marrier and A. Duchesne, Paris (1614) (reprinted Mâcon 1915), 13–56; reprinted *PL* 133, cols. 43–86; English trans. G. Sitwell, *St Odo of Cluny: Being the Life of St Odo of Cluny by John of Salerno and the Life of St Gerald of Aurillac by St Odo*, London (1958), pp. 3–93

John Skylitzes, *Synopsis historiarum*, ed. I. Thurn (CFHB 5, Series Berolinensis), Berlin and New York (1973)

John Zonaras, *Epitome historiarum*, ed. M. Pinder and T. Büttner-Wobst, 3 vols., Bonn (1841, 1844, 1897)

Kallfelz, H. (ed. with German trans.), *Lebensbeschreibungen einiger Bischöfe des 10.-12. Jahrhunderts,* Darmstadt (1973)

Kekaumenos, *Strategikon*, ed. G. G. Litavrin, *Sovety i rasskazy Kekavmena*, Moscow (1972)

Khazarian Hebrew Documents of the Tenth Century, ed. N. Golb, and O. Pritsak, Ithaca (1982)

Kiril and Methodios: Founders of Slavonic Writing, ed. I. Duichev (Dujčev), trans. S. Nikolov (East European Monographs 172), Boulder (1985)

Kitāb al Masālik wa'l-Mamālik, auctore Abū'l Kāsim Obdaillah Ibn Abdallah Ibn Kordādh-beh, accedunt excerpta e Kitāb al-Kharādj auctore Kodāma ibn dja'far, ed. M. J. de Goeje (Bibliotheca Geographorum Arabicorum 6), Leiden (1889)

Lacarra, J. M. (ed.), *Colección diplomática de Irache* I: *958–1222*, Zaragoza (1965)

Lacarra, J. M. (ed.), 'Textos navarros del Códice de Roda', *Estudios de Edad Media de la Corona de Aragón I*, Zaragoza (1945), I, pp. 193–275

Lambert, king of Italy, *Diplomata*, ed. L. Schiaparelli, *I diplomi di Guido e di Lamberto (sec. IX)* (Fonti per la Storia d'Italia 36), Rome (1906)

Lampert of Hersfeld, *Annales*, ed. O. Holder-Egger, *Lampert of Hersfeld Opera, MGH SRG* XXXVIII (1894), pp. 58–304; ed. with German trans. A. Schmidt and W. D. Fritz, *Lampert von Hersfeld, Annalen (AQ* 13) Darmstadt (1962)

Landulf Senior, *Historia Mediolanensis*, ed. A. Cutolo, *Landulphi senioris Mediolanensis historiae libri quatuor (Rerum Italicarum Scriptores*, N.S. IV.), Bologna (1942)

Lapidge, M. (ed.), *The Cult of Saint Swithin* (Winchester Studies 4.2), Oxford (forthcoming)

Laudatio S. Pauli iunioris, ed. H. Delehaye, in *Der Latmos, Milet: Ergebnisse der Ausgrabungen und Untersuchungen seit dem Jahre 1899*, ed. T. Wiegand, Berlin (1913), III.1, pp. 136–57

Laurentius monachus Casinensis archiepiscopus Amalfitanus Opera, ed. F. Newton, *MGH Quellen zur Geistesgeschichte des Mittelalters* VII, Weimar (1973)

Le Carte che si conservano nell'archivio del capitolo metropolitano della città di Trani, ed. A. Prologo, Barletta, (1877)

Le Livre du Préfet, ed. J. Nicole, Geneva (1893)

Le Pergamene di Conversano, ed. G. Coniglio (Codice diplomatico Pugliese 20), Bari (1975)

Legenda s. Emerici ducis, ed. E. Bartoniek, *Scriptores rerum Hungaricarum* II, Budapest (1938), pp. 441–60

Legenda S. Gerhardi, ed. E. Szentpétery, *Scriptores rerum Hungaricarum* II, Budapest (1938), pp. 463–506

Legenda S. Gerhardi episcopi, ed. E. Madzsar, *Scriptores rerum Hungaricarum*, II, Budapest (1938), pp. 461–506

Legenda S. Stephani regis maior, ed. W. Wattenbach, *MGH SS* XI, Hanover (1854), pp. 229–42; ed. E. Bartoniek, *Scriptores rerum Hungaricarum*, II, Budapest (1938) pp. 363–92

Legenda S. Stephani regis minor, ed. W. Wattenbach, *MGH SS* II, Hanover (1854), pp. 226–9; ed. E. Bartoniek, *Scriptores rerum Hungaricarum*, II, Budapest (1938) pp. 392–400

Leo, Metropolitan of Synada, *The correspondence of Leo Metropolitan of Synada and Syncellus*, ed. with English trans. M. P. Vinson (CFHB 23/DOT 8), Washington, DC (1985)

Leo VI, *Novels*, ed. P. Noailles and A. Dain, *Les Nouvelles de Léon le Sage*, Paris (1944)

Leo VI, *Tactica*, *PG* 107, cols. 419–1094

Leo Grammaticus, *Chronographia*, ed. I. Bekker, Bonn (1842)

Leo of Vercelli, *Versus de Ottone et Henrico*, ed. K. Strecker, *MGH Poet.* V, Berlin (1937–9), pp. 480–3

Leo the Deacon, *Historiae*, ed. C. B. Hase, Bonn (1828)

Les Annales de Saint-Pierre de Gand et de Saint-Amand (Annales blandinienses, Annales elmarenses, Annales formoselenses, Annales elnonenses), ed. P. Grierson, Brussels (1937)

Les Documents nécrologiques de l'abbaye Saint Pierre de Solignac, ed. J. L. Lemaître (Recueil des Historiens de la France, Obituaires, sér. in 8°, 1), Paris (1984)

Letald of Micy, *Liber miraculorum Sancti Maximini Miciacensis*, *PL* 137, cols. 795–824

Letald of Micy, *Vita Sancti Iuliani*, *PL* 137, cols. 781–96

Letald of Micy, *Within piscator*, ed. F. Bertini (Fondazione Ezio Franceschini, Biblioteca del Medioevo Latino), Florence (1995)

Letopis popa Dukljanina, ed. F. von Šišić (Srpska Kraljevska Akademija. Posebna izdanja 67, filosofski i filoloshki spisi 18), Belgrade and Zagreb (1928)

Lex Baiwariorum, ed. E. von Schwind, *MGH Leges nat. Germ.* v.2, Hanover (1926)

Li romans de Garin le Loherain, ed. A. Paulin, 2 vols., Paris (1833–5)

Liber Eliensis, ed. E. O. Blake (Camden 3rd Series 92), London (1962)

Liber miracolorum Sanctae Fidis ed. A. Bouillet, Paris (1897); ed. L. Robertini (Biblioteca di 'Medioevo Latino' 10), Spoleto (1994)

Liber tramitis aevi Odilonis abbatis, ed. P. Dinter (CCM 10), Siegburg (1980)

Liber Vitae: Register and Martyrology of the New Minster and Hyde Abbey, Winchester, ed. W. de G. Birch (Hampshire Record Society 5), London and Winchester (1892)

Liudprand of Cremona, *Antapodosis*, ed. J. Becker, *Liudprandi Opera, MGH SRG* XLI, Hanover (1915), pp. 1–158; ed. with German trans. A. Bauer and R. Rau, *Quellen zur Geschichte der sächsischen Kaiserzeit* (*AQ* 8), 2nd edn, Darmstadt (1977), pp. 244–495

Liudprand of Cremona, *Liber de rebus gestis Ottonis magni imperatoris*, ed. J. Becker, *MGH SRG* XLI, Hanover (1915), pp. 159–75; ed. with German trans. A. Bauer and R. Rau, *Quellen zur Geschichte der sächsischen Kaiserzeit* (*AQ* 8), 2nd edn, Darmstadt (1977), pp. 496–523

Liudprand of Cremona, *Relatio de legatione Constantinopolitana*, ed. J. Becker, *MGH SRG* XLI, Hanover (1915), pp. 175–212; ed. with German trans. A. Bauer and R. Rau, *Quellen zur Geschichte der sächsischen Kaiserzeit* (*AQ* 8), 2nd edn, Darmstadt (1977), pp. 524–89; ed. with English trans. B. Scott, London (1993)

Lothar, king of Italy, *Diplomata*, ed. L. Schiaparelli, *I diplomi di Ugo e di Lotario, di Berengario II e di Adalberto (secolo X)* (Fonti per la Storia d'Italia 38), Rome (1924)

Lothar, king of west Francia, *Acta*, ed. L. Halphen and F. Lot, *Recueil des actes de Lothaire et Louis V, rois de France (954–987)*, Paris (1908)

Louis (the German), king of east Francia, *Diplomata*, ed. P. Kehr, *Die Urkunden der deutschen Karolinger* (*MGH Dip. Germ.* 1), Berlin (1932–4)

Louis II (the Stammerer), king of west Francia, *Acta*, ed. F. Grat, J. de Font-Réaulx, G. Tessier and R.-H. Bautier, *Recueil des actes de Louis II le Bègue, Louis III et Carloman II, rois de France, 877–884*, Paris (1978)

Louis III (the Blind), king of Italy, *Diplomata*, ed. L. Schiaparelli, *I diplomi italiani di Lodovico III e di Rodolfo II* (Fonti per la Storia d'Italia 37), Rome (1910)

Louis III, king of west Francia, *Acta*, ed. F. Grat, J. de Font-Réaulx, G. Tessier and R.-H. Bautier, *Recueil des actes de Louis II le Bègue, Louis III et Carloman II, rois de France, 877–884*, Paris (1978)

Louis IV, king of west Francia, *Acta*, ed. P. Lauer, *Recueil des actes de Louis IV, roi de France (936–954)*, Paris (1914)

Louis V, king of west Francia, *Acta*, ed. L. Halphen and F. Lot, *Recueil des actes de Lothaire et Louis V, rois de France (954–987)*, Paris (1908)

Louis the Child, king of east Francia, *Diplomata*, ed. T. Schieffer, *Die Urkunden der deutschen Karolinger* (*MGH Dip. Germ.* IV), Berlin (1960)

Louis the Younger, king of east Francia, *Diplomata*, ed. P. Kehr, *Die Urkunden der deutschen Karolinger* (*MGH Dip. Germ.* 1), Berlin (1932–4)

Lupus, *Vitae Maximini episcopi Trevirensis*, ed. B. Krusch, *MGH SRM* III, Berlin (1896), pp. 71–82

Lupus Protospatharius, *Annales*, ed. G. H. Pertz, *MGH SS* v, Hanover (1844), pp. 52–63

Manaresi, C. (ed.), *I placiti del 'Regnum Italiae'*, 3 vols. (Fonti per la Storia d'Italia 92, 96, 97), Rome (1955–60)

Marchegay, P. and Salmon, A. (eds.), *Chroniques d'Anjou*, Paris (1856)

Matthew of Edessa, *Chronicle*, trans. A. E. Dostourian, *Armenia and the Crusades, Tenth to Twelfth Centuries*, Lanham, New York, and London (1993)

Medieval Trade in the Mediterranean World, ed. and trans. R. S. Lopez and I. Raymond, New York (1955)

Memorials of Saint Dunstan, ed. W. Stubbs (Rolls Series), London (1874)

Michael Psellos, *Chronographia*, French ed. and trans. E. Renauld, *Chronographie*, 2 vols., Paris (1926–8); English trans. E. A. R. Sewter, *Fourteen Byzantine Rulers: The Chronographia of Michael Psellus*, Harmondsworth (1966)

Michael Psellos, *Scripta minora*, ed. E. Kurtz and F. Drexl, 2 vols., Milan (1936–41)

Mínguez Fernández, J. M. (ed.), *Colección diplomática del Monasterio de Sahagún (siglos IX y X)*, León (1976)

Miracula sancti Benedicti, ed. E. de Certain, *Les Miracles de Saint Benôit écrits par Adrevald Aimon, André, Raoul Tortaire et Hugues de Sainte Marie, moines de Fleury*, Paris (1858)

Nikephoros Phokas, *De velitatione*, ed. with French trans. G. Dagron and H. Mihaescu, *Le Traité sur la guérilla (De velitatione) de l'empereur Nicéphore Phocas (963–969)*, Paris (1986)

Nikolaos I Mystikos, *Nicholas I Patriarch of Constantinople: Miscellaneous Writings*, ed. L. G. Westerink (CFHB 20/DOT 6), Washington, DC (1981)

Nikolaos I Mystikos, *Nicholas I Patriarch of Constantinople: Letters*, ed. and trans. L. G. Westerink and R. J. H. Jenkins (CFHB 6/DOT 2), Washington, DC (1973)

Notae necrologiae maioris ecclesiae Frisingensis, ed. F. L. Baumann, *MGH Nec. Germ.* III: *Dioceses Brixinensis, Frisingensis, Ratisbonensis*, Berlin (1905)

Notker the German, *Werke*, ed. E. H. Sehrt and T. Strack, I, Halle (1933)

Notker the Stammerer, *Gesta Karoli*, ed. H. F. Haefele, *MGH SRG* N.S. XII), Munich (1980)

Odilo of Cluny, *Epitaphium Adelhaidae imperatricis*, ed. G. H. Pertz, *MGH SS* IV, Hanover (1841), pp. 633–45; ed. H. Paulhart, *Die Lebensbeschreibung der Kaiserin Adelheid von Abt Odilo von Cluny (MIÖG EB* 20), Graz and Cologne (1962)

Odo of Cluny, *Occupatio*, ed. A. Swoboda, Leipzig (1900)

Odo of Cluny, *Vita Sancti Geraldi Aurilacensis comitis libri quatuor*, PL 133, cols. 639–704; English trans. G. Sitwell, *St Odo of Cluny: Being the Life of St Odo of Cluny by John of Salerno and the Life of St Gerald of Aurillac by St Odo*, London (1958), pp. 94–180

Odo (Eudes) of Saint Maur, *Vie de Bouchard le Vénérable, comte de Vendôme, de Corbeil, de Melun et de Paris (X^e et XIe siècles) par Eudes de Saint Maur*, ed. C. G. Bourel de la Roncière, Paris (1892)

Odorannus of Sens, *Chronica*, ed. with French trans. R.-H. Bautier and M. Gilles, with M.-E. Duchez and M. Huglo, *Odorannus of Sens, Opera omnia* (Sources d'histoire médiévale publiées par l'Institut de Recherche et d'Histoire des Textes 4), Paris (1972), pp. 84–113

Odorannus of Sens, *Opera omnia*, ed. with French trans. R.-H. Bautier and M. Gilles, with M.-E. Duchez and M. Huglo (Sources d'histoire médiévale publiées par l'Institut de Recherche et d'Histoire des Textes 4), Paris (1972)

Oikonomides, N. (ed. with French trans.), *Les Listes de préséance byzantines du IXe et Xe siècles*, Paris (1972)

Otloh, *Vita sancti Wolfkangi episcopi Ratisbonensis*, ed. G. Waitz, *MGH SS* IV, Hanover (1841), pp. 521–42

Otto I, emperor, *Diplomata*, ed. T. Sickel, *Die Urkunden Konrad I., Heinrich I. und Otto I.*, *MGH Dip. regum* I, Hanover (1879–84)

Otto II, emperor, *Diplomata*, ed. T. Sickel, *Die Urkunden Ottos des* II., *MGH Dip. regum* II.1, Hanover (1888)

Otto III, emperor, *Diplomata*, ed. T. Sickel, *Die Urkunden Ottos des III.*, *MGH Dip. regum* II.2, Hanover (1893)

Otto von Freising, *Chronica sive historia de duabus civitatibus*, ed. A. Hofmeister, *MGH SRG* XLV, Hanover (1912); ed. with German trans. A. Schmidt and W. Lammers, *Otto Bischof von Freising: Chronik oder die Geschichte der zwei Staaten (AQ* 16), Darmstadt (1960); English trans. Evans, A. P. and Knapp, C. *The Two Cities: A Chronicle of Universal History to the Year 1146 A.D.*, New York (1928)

Oudalschalk, *Vita Chuonradi episcopi Constantiensis*, ed. G. H. Pertz, *MGH SS* IV, Hanover (1841), pp. 430–6

Pasqual, J., *Sacra Cathaloniae antiquitatis monumenta*, Barcelona, Biblioteca de Catalunya, ms. 729

Paul, bishop of Monemvasia, *Les Récits édifiants de Paul, évêque de Monembasie et d'autres auteurs*, ed. with French trans. J. Wortley, Paris (1987)

Paul the Deacon, *Liber de episcopis Mettensibus*, ed. G. H. Pertz, *MGH SS* II, Hanover (1829), pp. 260–70

Petit, L. (ed.), 'Office inédit en l'honneur de Nicéphore Phocas', *Byzantinische Zeitschrift* 13 (1904), pp. 398–420

Petrus Damiani, *Vita Romualdi*, ed. G. Tabacco (Fonti per la Storia d'Italia 94), Rome (1957)

Photius, *Epistulae et amphilochia*, ed. B. Laourdas and L. G. Westerink, 6 vols. (vol. VI in two parts), Leipzig (1983, 1984, 1985, 1986a, 1986b, 1987, 1988)

Pierre de Marca, *Marca Hispanica sive limes hispanicus, hoc est, geographica et historica descriptio Cataloniæ, Ruscinonis et circumjacentium populorum*, ed. E. Baluze, Paris (1688)

Pontifical Romano-Germanique, ed. C. Vogel and R. Elze, 3 vols. (Studi e Testi 226, 227, 269), Vatican City (1963, 1972)

Poupardin, R. (ed.), *Recueil des actes des rois de Provence, 855–928*, Paris (1920)

Povest' Vremennykh Let ['The Tale of Bygone Years']. *Chast' pervaia: Tekst i perevod*, ed. and trans. V. P. Adrianova-Peretts and D. S. Likhachev, 2 vols., Moscow and Leningrad (1950); English trans. S. H. Cross and O. P. Sherbowitz-Wetzor, *The Russian Primary Chronicle: Laurentian Text* (Mediaeval Academy of America Publication 60), Cambridge, MA (1953)

Pritsak, O. (ed.), *The Origin of Rus'* I: *Old Scandinavian Sources other than the Sagas*, Cambridge, MA (1981)

Provana, L. G., *Studi critici sovra la storia d'Italia a tempi del re Ardoino* (Memorie dell'Accademia delle Scienze di Torino. Classe delle Scienze Morali, Storiche e Filologiche), Turin (1844)

Purchard, *Gesta Witigowonis*, ed. K. Strecker, in *MGH Poet.* V, Berlin (1937–9), pp. 260–79

Radulf (Raoul), king of west Francia, *Acta*, ed. J. Dufour, *Recueil des actes de Robert Ier et de Raoul, rois de France, 922–936*, Paris (1978)

Radulf Glaber, *Historiarum libri quinque*, ed. with English trans. J. France, Oxford (1989)

Raine, J. (ed.), *The Historians of the Church of York and its Archbishops* I (Rolls Series), London (1879)

Rainer, *Miracula S. Gisleni*, ed. O. Holder-Egger, *MGH SS* xv, Hanover (1887–8), pp. 576–85

Rather of Verona, *De Vita Sancti Usmari*, *PL* 136, cols. 345–52; also in *Epistolae*, ed. Weigle, no. 4, pp. 27–9

Rather of Verona, *Epistolae*, ed. F. Weigle, *Die Briefe des Bischofs Rather of Verona, MGH Die Briefe der deutschen Kaiserzeit* I, Weimar (1949); English trans. P. L. D. Reid, *The Complete Works of Rather of Verona*, Binghampton, NY (1991)

Rather of Verona, *Phrenesis*, ed. P. L. D. Reid, in *Ratherii Veronensis Opera, Fragmenta, Glossae*, ed. P. L. D. Reid, F. Dolbeau, B. Bischoff and C. Leonardi (CCCM 46A), Turnhout (1984), pp. 197–218; English trans. P. L. D. Reid, *The Complete Works of Rather of Verona*, Binghampton, NY (1991)

Rather of Verona, *Praeloquia*, ed. P. D. L. Reid, in *Ratherii Veronensis Opera, Fragmenta, Glossae*, ed. P. L. D. Reid, F. Dolbeau, B. Bischoff and C. Leonardi (*CCCM* 46A), Turnhout (1984), pp. 1–196; English trans. P. L. D. Reid, *The Complete Works of Rather of Verona*, Binghampton, NY (1991)

Recueil des actes des ducs de Normandie de 911 à 1066, ed. M. Fauroux, Caen (1961)

Recueil des chartes de l'abbaye de Cluny, ed. A. Bernard and A. Bruel, 6 vols., Paris (1876–1903)

Regino of Prüm, *Chronicon*, ed. F. Kurze, *Reginonis abbatis Prumiensis Chronicon cum continuatione Treverensi, MGH SRG* L, Hanover (1890); ed. with German trans. R. Rau, *Quellen zur karolingischen Reichsgeschichte* III *(AQ* 7), Darmstadt (1969), pp. 182–319

Regularis concordia Anglicae nationis, ed. T. Symons (CCM 7/3), Siegburg (1984), pp. 60–147 (revised edition of *Regularis concordia Anglicae nationis monachorum sanctimonialiumque: The Monastic Agreement of the Monks and Nuns of the English Nation*, ed. with English trans. T. Symons, London (1953))

Reindel, K. (ed.), *Die bayerischen Luitpoldinger, 893–989: Sammlung und Erläuterung der Quellen* (Quellen und Erörterungen zur Bayerischen Geschichte N.F. 11), Munich (1953)

Richer, *Historiae*, ed. and trans. R. Latouche, Richer, *Histoire de France (888–995)* (Classiques de l'Histoire de France au Moyen Âge), 2 vols., Paris (1930, 1937) (reprinted 1960, 1964)

Robert I, king of west Francia, *Acta*, ed. R.-H. Bautier and J. Dufour, *Recueil des actes de Robert Ier et de Raoul, rois de France, 922–936*, Paris (1978)

Robert II, king of west Francia, *Acta*, ed. W. M. Newman, *Catalogue des actes de Robert II roi de France*, Paris (1937)

Rodríguez de Lama, I. (ed.), *Colección diplomática medieval de la Rioja*, II: *Documentos 923–1168*, Logroño (1976)

Rudolf I, king of Burgundy, *Diplomata*, ed. T. Schieffer, *Die Urkunden der burgundischen Rudolfinger, MGH Regum Burgundiae e stirpe Rudolfina Diplomata et Acta*, Munich (1977)

Rudolf II (of Burgundy), king of Italy, *Diplomata*, ed. L. Schiaparelli, *I diplomi italiani di Lodovico III e di Rodolfo II* (Fonti per la Storia d'Italia 37), Rome (1910)

Rudolf II, king of Burgundy, *Diplomata*, ed. T. Schieffer, *Die Urkunden der burgundischen Rudolfinger, MGH Regum Burgundiae e stirpe Rudolfina Diplomata et Acta*, Munich (1977)

Rudolf III, king of Burgundy, *Diplomata*, ed. T. Schieffer, *Die Urkunden der burgundischen Rudolfinger, MGH Regum Burgundiae e stirpe Rudolfina Diplomata et Acta*, Munich (1977)

Ruotger, *Vita sancti Brunonis archiepiscopi Coloniensis*, ed. I. Ott, *MGH SRG N.S.* x, Weimar (1951); reprinted with German trans. H. Kallfelz, *Lebensbeschreibungen*, Darmstadt (1973), pp 169–261

Sacramentarium Fuldense saeculi x., ed. G. Richter and A. Schönfelder, Fulda (1912), reprinted as Henry Bradshaw Society vol. 101 (1972–7)

Sampiro, su crónica y la monarquía leonesa en el siglo X, ed. J. Pérez de Urbel, Madrid (1952)

Sawyer, P., *Anglo-Saxon Charters: An Annotated List and Bibliography* (Royal Historical Society Guides and Handbooks 8), London (1968)

Scriptores rerum Hungaricarum, ed. E. Szentpétery, 2 vols., Budapest 1937–8

Ševčenko, I. (ed.), 'Poems on the deaths of Leo VI and Constantine VII in the Madrid manuscript of Skylitzes', *DOP* 23–4 (1969–70), pp. 185–228

Sharaf al-Zaman Tahir Marvazi, English trans. and comm. V. Minorsky, *Sharaf al-Zaman Tahir Marvazi on China, the Turks and India* (James G. Forlong Fund 22), London (1942)

Sigebert of Gembloux, *Vita Deoderici episcopi Mettensis*, ed. G. H. Pertz, *MGH SS* iv, Hanover (1841), pp. 754–82

Sigehard, *Miracula S. Maximini, AASS Maii* vii, Antwerp (1688), pp. 25–33

Simon de Kéza, *Gesta Hungarorum*, ed. A. Domanovszky, *Scriptores rerum Hungaricarum* i, Budapest (1937), pp. 129–94

Snorri Sturluson, *Heimskringla: History of the Kings of Norway*, English trans. L. M. Hollander, Austin (1964)

Stephen, King of Hungary, *Laws, Szent István törvényeinek XII. századi kézirata az admonti kódexben* [The twelfth-century Admont manuscript of the Laws of Saint Stephen], commentary by G. Györffy, introduction and trans. E. Bartoniek, Budapest (1988); *Laws of the Medieval Kingdom of Hungary 1000–1301*, ed. and trans. J. M. Bak, G. Bónis and J. R. Sweeney, Bakersfield, CA (1989), pp. 1–11.

Stephen, King of Hungary, *Libellus de institutione morum*, ed. J. Balogh, *Scriptores rerum Hungaricarum* ii, pp. 611–27

Stephen of Taron, *Histoire universelle*, trans. F. Macler, Paris (1917)

Sullivan, D. F. (ed. and English trans.), *The Life of Saint Nikon*, Brookline, MA (1987)

Tafel, G. L. F. and Thomas, G. M. (eds.), *Urkunden zur älteren Handels- und Staatsgeschichte der Republik Venedig* (Fontes Rerum Austricarum 12), i, Vienna (1856); reprinted Amsterdam (1964)

Thangmar, *Vita sancti Bernwardi episcopi Hildesheimensis*, ed. G. H. Pertz, *MGH SS* iv, Hanover (1841), pp. 754–82; printed with German trans. H. Kallfelz, *Lebensbeschreibungen*, Darmstadt (1973), pp. 263–361

The Anglo-Saxon Chronicle, English trans. in Whitelock, *English Historical Documents* (1979), pp. 145–261

The Law of Hywel Dda: Law Texts of Medieval Wales, ed. D. Jenkins, Llandysul (1986)

The Old English Orosius, ed. J. Bately (Early English Text Society, Supplementary Series 6), Oxford (1980)

Theodore Daphnopates, *Correspondance*, ed. with French trans. J. Darrouzès and L. G. Westerink, Paris (1978)

Theodosius the Deacon, *De Creta capta*, ed. H. Criscuolo, Leipzig (1979)

Theophanes Continuatus, *Chronographia*, ed. I. Bekker, Bonn (1838)

Thietmar of Merseburg, *Chronicon*, ed. R. Holtzmann, *MGH SRG* N.S. IX, Berlin (1935); ed. with German trans. W. Trillmich, *Thietmar von Merseburg, Chronik* (*AQ* 9), Darmstadt (1957)

Tosti, L. (ed.), *Storia della badia di Montecassino*, 3 vols., Naples (1843)

Ubieto Arteta, A. (ed.), *Jaca: documentos municipales 971–1269*, Valencia (1975)

Udina Martorell, F. *El archivo condal de Barcelona en los siglos IX–X*, Barcelona (1951)

Una cronica anonima de 'Abd al-Rahman III al-Nasir, ed. E. Lévi-Provençal and E. García Gomez, Madrid and Granada (1950)

Vita Adalberti diaconi Egmundae, ed. as *De S. Adalberto diacono Egmundae in Hollandia: Vita a monachis Mediolacensibus descripta*, *AASS Iunii*. V, cols. 97–103; ed. O. Oppermann, *Fontes Egmundenses*, Utrecht (1933), pp. 3–22

Vita Burchardi episcopi, ed. G. Waitz, *MGH SS* IV, Hanover (1841), pp. 829–46

Vita Euthymii Patriarchae CP., ed. with English trans. P. Karlin-Hayter (Bibliothèque de *Byzantion* 3), Brussels (1970)

Vita Gebehardi episcopi, ed. W. Wattenbach, *MGH SS* XI, Hanover (1854), pp. 33–50

Vita Gerardi abbatis Broniensis, *MGH SS* XV, Hanover (1887–8), pp. 654–73

Vita Mathildis reginae antiquior, ed. R. Koepke, *MGH SS* X, Hanover (1852), pp. 573–82; ed. B. Schütte, *Die Lebensbeschreibungen der Königin Mathilde*, *MGH SRG* LXVI, Hanover (1994), pp. 109–42

Vita Mathildis reginae posterior, ed. G. H. Pertz, *MGH SS* IV, Hanover (1841), pp. 282–302; ed. B. Schütte, *Die Lebensbeschreibungen der Königin Mathilde*, *MGH SRG* LXVI, Hanover (1994), pp. 145–202

Vita Meinwerci episcopi Patherbrunnensis, ed. F. Tenckhoff, *MGH SRG* LIX, Hanover (1921)

Vita Pelagii, ed. E. Flórez (España Sagrada 23) Madrid (1765)

Vita prior S. Adalberti Pragensis episcopi, ed. J. Karwasińska, *S. Adalberti Pragensi episcopi et martyris. Vita prior*, in *Monumenta Poloniae historica*, N.S. IV.1, Warsaw (1962)

Vita quinque fratrum, ed. J. Karwasińska, *Vita quinque fratrum eremitarum (seu) vita vel passio Benedicti et Iohannis sociorumque suorum auctore Brunone Querfurtensi; Epistola Brunonis ad Henricum regem*, in *Monumenta Poloniae historica*, N.S. IV.3, Warsaw (1973)

Vita S. Dunstani, see Memorials of Saint Dunstan

Vita S. Eliae Spelaeotae abbatis confessoris, *AASS Septembrii*, III, Antwerp (1750), cols. 848–88

Vita S. Lucae abbatis [of Armento], *AASS Octobrii*, VI, Tongerloo (1794), 337–42

Vita S. Mariae iunioris, *AASS Novembris*, IV, Brussels (1925), cols. 688–705

Vita S. Nili iunioris, *PG* 120, cols. 16–165

Vita S. Pauli iunioris, ed. H. Delehaye, reprinted in *Der Latmos, Milet: Ergebnisse der Ausgrabungen und Untersuchungen seit dem Jahre 1899*, ed. T. Wiegand, Berlin (1913), III.1, pp. 105–35

Vita ss. Cyrilli et Methodii, legenda Pannonica, ed. (excerpts) in Gombos (1938), 2330–1

Vitae sanctae Wiboradae, ed. W. Berschin, *Vitae sanctae Wiboradae: Die ältesten Lebensbeschreibungen der heiligen Wiborada*, St Gallen (1983)

Vogt, A. and Hausherr, I. (eds.), 'Oraison funèbre de Basile I par son fils Léon le sage', *Orientalia Christiana* 26 (1932), pp. 5–79

Waltharius, ed. K. Strecker, in *MGH Poet.* VI.1, Berlin (1951), pp. 1–85

Walther of Speyer, *Libellus scolasticus*, ed. P. Vossen, *Der Libellus Scolasticus des Walther von Speyer: Ein Schulbericht aus dem Jahre 984*, Berlin (1962); ed. K. Strecker, in *MGH Poet.* V.1, Berlin (1937), pp. 1–63

Whitelock, D. (ed.), *English Historical Documents* c. *500–1042*, 2nd edn (EHD 1), London (1979)

Wido, king of Italy, *Diplomata*, ed. L. Schiaparelli, *I diplomi di Guido e di Lamberto (sec. IX)* (Fonti per la Storia d'Italia 36), Rome (1906)

Widric, *Vita Gerardi episcopi Tullensis*, ed. G. Waitz, *MGH SS* IV, Hanover (1841), pp. 490–505

Widukind of Corvey, *Rerum gestarum Saxonicarum libri tres*, ed. P. Hirsch and H.-E. Lohmann, *MGH SRG* LX, Hanover (1935); ed. with German trans. A. Bauer and R. Rau, *Quellen zur Geschichte der sächsischen Kaiserzeit (AQ* 8), 2nd edn, Darmstadt (1977), pp. 1–183

William of Malmesbury, *De gestis regum Anglorum libri quinque*, ed. W. Stubbs, 2 vols. (Rolls Series), London (1887–9); *Gesta Regum Anglorum (The History of the English Kings)*, 1, ed. and trans. R. A. B. Mynors, with R. M. Thomson and M. Winterbottom, Oxford (1998)

Wipo, *Gesta Chuonradi,* ed. H. Breslau, *Wiponis Opera, MGH SRG* LXI, Hanover (1915), pp. 3–62; English trans. T. E. Mommsen and K. F. Morrison, *Imperial Lives and Letters of the Eleventh Century*, New York and London (1967)

Wulfstan of Winchester, *Vita sancti Æthelwoldi*, ed. M. Lapidge and M. Winterbottom, *Wulfstan of Winchester: The Life of St Æthelwold*, Oxford (1991)

Wulfstan the Cantor, *Narratio metrica de Sancto Swithuno*, ed. A. E. Campbell, *Frithegodi monachi Breuiloquium vitae beati Wilfredi et Wulfstani Cantoris Narratio metrica de Sancto Swithuno*, Zurich (1950)

Yaḥyā ibn Saʿid al-Antaki, *The Byzantine-Arab Chronicle (938–1034) of Yaḥyā ibn Saʿid al-Antaki*, ed. J. H. Forsyth (University Microfilms), 2 vols., Ann Arbor (1977)

Yngvar's Saga, English trans. H. Pálsson and P. Edwards, *Vikings in Russia: Yngvar's Saga and Edmund's Saga*, Edinburgh (1989)

Zakon sudnyj ljudem (Court Law for the People), ed. H. W. Dewey and trans. A. M. Kleimola (Michigan Slavic Materials 14), Ann Arbor (1977)

Zimmermann, H. (ed.), *Papsturkunden 896–1046*, 2 vols., Vienna (1985)

Zwentibold, king of Lotharingia, *Diplomata*, ed. T. Schieffer, *Zwentiboldi et Ludowici Infantis Diplomata, MGH Dip. Germ.* IV, Berlin (1960)

BIBLIOGRAPHY OF SECONDARY
WORKS ARRANGED BY CHAPTER

1 INTRODUCTION: READING THE TENTH CENTURY

Althoff, G. (1990), *Verwandte, Freunde und Getreue*, Darmstadt

Althoff, G. (1995), 'Von Fakten zu Motiven. Johannes Frieds Beschreibung der Ursprünge Deutschlands', *HZ* 260: 107–17

Althoff, G. (1997), *Spielregeln der Politik im Mittelalter: Kommunikation in Frieden und Fehde*, Darmstadt

Bak, J. M. (1973), 'Medieval symbology of the state: Percy E. Schramm's contribution', *Viator* 4: 33–63

Barraclough, G. (1976), *The Crucible of Europe*, London

Barthélemy, D. (1992a), 'La Mutation féodale a-t-elle eu lieu?', *Annales ESC* 47: 767–75

Barthélemy, D. (1992b), 'Q'est-ce que le servage, en France, au XI siècle?', *RH* 287: 233–84

Barthélemy, D. (1996), 'Debate: the "Feudal Revolution" I', *Past and Present* 152: 196–205

Barthélemy, D. (1997), 'La Théorie féodale à l'épreuve de l'anthropologie (note critique)', *Annales: Histoire, Sciences Sociales* 52: 321–41

Bartlett, R. (1993), *The Making of Europe: Conquest, Colonization and Cultural Change, 950–1350*, London

Beumann, H. (1950), *Widukind von Korvei: Untersuchungen zur Geschichtsschreibung und Ideengeschichte des 10. Jahrhunderts*, Weimar

Bisson, T. N. (1994), 'The "Feudal Revolution"', *Past and Present* 142: 5–42

Bisson, T. N. (1997), 'Reply', *Past and Present* 157: 208–25

Bloch, M. (1961), *Feudal Society*, trans. C. Postan, London (originally published as *La Société féodale*, Paris (1939))

Böhme, H. W. (ed.) (1991a, 1991b), *Burgen der Salierzeit*, I: *In den nördlichen Landschaften des Reiches*; II: *In den südlichen Landschaften des Reiches* (Monographien des Römisch-Germanischen Zentralmuseum 25–6), Sigmaringen

Bois, G. (1989), *La Mutation de l'an mil*, Paris; English trans. J. Birrell as *The Transformation of the Year One Thousand: The Village of Lournand from Antiquity to Feudalism*, Manchester, 1991

Bonnassie, P. (1975, 1976), *La Catalogne du milieu du Xe à la fin du XIe siècle: croissance et mutations d'une société*, 2 vols., Toulouse

Bonnassie, P. (1991), *From Slavery to Feudalism in South-Western Europe*, Cambridge

Brühl, C. (1990), *Deutschland – Frankreich: Die Geburt zweier Völker*, Cologne and Vienna

Brunner, O. (1968), 'Das Problem einer europäischen Sozialgeschichte', in *Neue Wege der Sozial- und Verfassungsgeschichte*, 2nd edn, Göttingen, pp. 80–102

Calmette, J. (1941), *L'Enfondrement d'un empire et la naissance d'une Europe, IXe–Xe siècles*, Paris

Campbell, J. (1990), 'Was it infancy in England? Some questions of comparison', in M. Jones and M. Vale (eds..), *England and her Neighbours, 1066–1453: Essays in Honour of Pierre Chaplais*, London, pp. 1–17

Campbell, J. (1994), 'The late Old English state: a maximum view', *Proceedings of the British Academy* 87: 39–65

Duby, G. (1953), *La Société aux XIe et XIIe siècles dans la région mâconnaise*, Paris

Duby, G. (1974), *The Early Growth of the European Economy*, London

Duby, G. (1978) *Les trois Ordres ou l'imaginaire du féodalisme*, Paris; English trans. by A. Goldhammer as *The Three Orders: Feudal Society Imagined*, Chicago (1980)

Durliat, J. (1990) *Les Finances publiques, de Diocletien aux Carolingiens (284–889)* (Beihefte der Francia 21), Sigmaringen

Ehlers, J. (1985), 'Die Anfänge der französischen Geschichte', *HZ* 240: 1–44

Ehlers, J. (1994), *Die Entstehung des deutschen Reiches* (Enzyklopädie deutscher Geschichte 31), Munich

Fleckenstein, J. (1966), *Die Hofkapelle der deutschen Könige, 2: Die Hofkapelle im Rahmen der ottonisch-salischen Reichskirche*, Stuttgart

Flori, J. (1979), 'Les Origines de l'adoubement chevaleresque', *Traditio* 35: 209–72

Flori, J. (1983), *L'Idéologie du glaive: préhistoire de la chevalerie*, Geneva

Folz, R. (1950), *La Souvenir et la légende de Charlemagne dans l'empire germanique médiévale*, Paris

Fossier, R. (1982), *Enfance de l'Europe: aspects économiques et sociaux (Xe–XIIe siècles)*, 2 vols. continuously paginated, Paris

Fried, J. (1989), 'Endzeiterwartung um die Jahrtausendwende', *DA* 45: 385–473

Fried, J. (1991), *Die Formierung Europas 840–1046* (Oldenbourg Grundriss der Geschichte 6), Munich

Fried, J. (1994), *Der Weg in die Geschichte bis 1024* (Propyläen Geschichte Deutschlands 1), Berlin

Fried, J. (1995), 'Über das Schreiben von Geschichtswerken und Rezensionen. Eine Erwiderung', *HZ* 260: 119–30

Geary, P. J. (1994), *Phantoms of Remembrance: Memory and Oblivion at the End of the First Millennium*, Princeton

Gelling, M. (1992), *The West Midlands in the Early Middle Ages*, Leicester

Gerhard, D. (1981), *Old Europe: A Study of Continuity, 1000–1800*, New York

Godman, P. (1987), *Poets and Emperors: Frankish Politics and Carolingian Poetry*, Oxford

Hartmann, W. (1989), *Die Synode der Karolingerzeit im Frankreich und Italien*, Paderborn

Head, T. and Landes, R. (eds.) (1993), *The Peace of God: Social Violence and Religious Response in France around the Year 1000*, Ithaca

Hodges, R. (1991), 'Society, power and the first English industrial revolution', *Settimane* 38: 125–57

Hodges, R. and Hobley, B. (eds.) (1988), *The Rebirth of the Town in the West, AD 700–1050*, London

Hoffmann, H. (1964), *Gottesfriede und Treuga Dei* (Schriften der MGH 20), Stuttgart.

Hoffmann, H. and Pokorny, R. (1991), *Das Dekret des Bischofs Burchard von Worms: Textstufen – frühe Verbreitung – Vorlagen* (MGH Hilfsmittel 12), Munich

Kantorowicz, E. H. (1957), *The King's Two Bodies: A Study in Medieval Political Theology*, Princeton

Kelly, S. (1991), 'Anglo-Saxon lay society and the written word', in McKitterick (1991), pp. 36–62

Keynes, S. (1991), 'Royal government and the written word in late Anglo-Saxon England', in McKitterick (1991), pp. 226–57

Kienast, W. (1968), *Der Herzogstitel in Deutschland und Frankreich (9.-12. Jahrhundert): Mit Listen der ältesten deutschen Herzogsurkunden*, Munich

Koziol, G. (1992), *Begging Pardon and Favor*, Ithaca

Landes, R. (1988), ' "Lest the millennium be fulfilled": apocalyptic expectations and the pattern of western chronography, 100–800 C.E.', in W. D. F. Verbeke, D. Verhelst and A. Welkenhysen (eds.) *The Use and Abuse of Eschatology in the Middle Ages* (Medievalia Lovaniensia series 1, studia xv), Louvain, pp. 137–211

Landes, R. (1992), '*Millenarismus absconditus*: l'historiographie augustinienne et l'an mil', *Le Moyen Age* 98: 355–77

Landes, R. (1993), 'Sur les traces du millennium: la via negativa', *Le Moyen Age* 99: 5–26

Landes, R. (1995), *Relics, Apocalypse, and the Deceits of History: Ademar of Chabannes, 989–1034*, Harvard

Lestocquoy, J. (1947), 'The tenth century', *Economic History Review*, second series 17: 1–14

Leyser, K. (1982a), *Medieval Germany and its Neighbours, 900–1250*, London

Leyser, K. (1982b), 'Ottonian government', in Leyser (1982a), pp. 69–101

Leyser, K. (1994a), *Communications and Power in Medieval Europe: The Carolingian and Ottonian Centuries*, ed. T. Reuter, London

Leyser, K. (1994b), '*Theophanu divina gratia imperatrix augusta*: western and eastern emperorship in the later tenth century', in Leyser (1994a), pp. 143–64

Leyser, K. (1994c), 'The ascent of Latin Europe', in Leyser (1994a), pp. 215–32

Leyser, K. (1994d), 'Ritual, ceremony and gesture: Ottonian Germany', in Leyser (1994a), pp. 189–213

Leyser, K. (1994e), 'On the eve of the first European revolution', in Leyser, *Communications and Power in Medieval Europe: The Gregorian Revolution and Beyond*, ed. T. Reuter, London, pp. 1–19

Lifshitz, F. (1994), 'Beyond positivism and genre: "hagiographical" texts as historical narrative', *Viator* 25: 95–113

Lintzel, M. (1956), 'Die Mathilden-Viten und das Wahrheitsproblem in der Überlieferung der Ottonenzeit', *AKG* 38: 152–66

Lopez, R. (1962), *The Tenth Century: How Dark the Dark Ages?*, New York

McKitterick, R. (ed.) (1991), *The Uses of Literacy in Early Medieval Europe*, Cambridge

Magnou-Nortier, E. (1974), *La Société laïque et l'église dans la province ecclésiastique de Narbonne (zone cispyrenéenne) de la fin du VIIIème à la fin du XIème siècle*, Toulouse

Magnou-Nortier, E. (1981, 1982, 1984), 'La Terre, la rente et le pouvoir dans les pays de Languedoc pendant le haut moyen âge', *Francia* 9: 79–115; 10: 21–66; 12: 53–118

Magnou-Nortier, E. (1993), *Aux Sources de la gestion publique*, 1, Lille

Manteuffel, T. (ed.) (1968), *L'Europe aux IXe–XIe siècles: aux origines des états nationaux*, Warsaw

Menand, F. (1993), *Campagnes lombardes au moyen âge*, Rome

Moore, R. I. (1980), 'Family, community and cult on the eve of the Gregorian Reform', *Transactions of the Royal Historical Society*, fifth series 30: 49–69

Mordek, H. (1995), *Bibliotheca capitularium regum Francorum manuscripta: Überlieferung und Traditionszusammenhang der fränkischen Herrschererlasse* (MGH Hilfsmittel 15), Munich

Müller-Mertens, E. (ed.) (1985), *Feudalismus: Entstehung und Wesen*, Berlin

Murray, A. (1978), *Reason and Society in the Middle Ages*, Oxford

Nortier, E. (1996), 'La Féodalité en crise. Propos sur *Fiefs and Vassals* de Susan Reynolds', *Revue Historique* 296: 253–348

Poly, J. and Bournazel, E. (1991), *La Mutation féodale*, 2nd edn, Paris; English trans. C. Higgitt as *The Feudal Transformation, 900–1200*, Chicago (1991)

Poly, J. and Bournazel, E. (1994), 'Que faut-il préférer au "mutationisme". Ou le problème de changement sociale', *Revue d'Histoire de Droit Français et Etranger* 72: 401–12

Remensnyder, A. G. (1995), *Remembering Kings Past: Monastic Foundation Legends in Medieval Southern France*, Ithaca

Reuter, T. (1994), 'Pre-Gregorian mentalities', *JEccH* 45: 465–74

Reuter, T. (1997a), 'The medieval nobility in twentieth-century historiography', in M. Bentley (ed.), *Companion to Historiography*, London, pp. 179–202

Reuter, T. (1997b), 'Debate: the "Feudal Revolution" III', *Past and Present* 157: 177–95

Schröder, I. (1980), *Die westfränkischen Synoden von 888 bis 987 und ihre Überlieferung* (MGH Hilfsmittel 3), Munich

Stafford, P. (1985), *The East Midlands in the Early Middle Ages*, Leicester

Sullivan, R. E. (1989), 'The Carolingian age: reflections on its place in the history of the Middle Ages', *Speculum* 64: 267–306

Taviani-Carozzi, H. (1991) *La Principauté lombarde de Salerne (IXᵉ–XIᵉ siècles): pouvoir et société en Italie lombarde méridionale*, Rome

Tellenbach, G. (1985), '"Gregorianische Reform". Kritische Besinnungen', in K. Schmid (ed.), *Reich und Kirche vor dem Investiturstreit: Gerd Tellenbach zum 80. Geburtstag*, Sigmaringen, pp. 99–114

Tellenbach, G. (1993), *The Church in Western Europe from the Tenth to the Early Twelfth Century*, trans. T. Reuter, Cambridge

Toubert, P. (1973a, 1973b), *Les Structures du Latium médiéval: le Latium méridional et la Sabine du IXᵉ à la fin du XIIᵉ siècle*, 2 vols., Rome

Verhulst, A. E. (1991), 'The decline of slavery and the economic expansion of the early middle ages', *Past and Present* 133: 195–203

Verhulst, A. E. (1993), 'Marchés, marchants et commerce au haut moyen âge dans l'historiographie récent', *Settimane* 40: 23–50

Verhulst, A. E. (1994), 'The origins and early development of medieval towns in northern Europe', *Economic History Review*, second series 47: 362–73

Vollrath, H. (1985), *Die Synoden Englands bis 1066*, Paderborn

White, L. (ed.) (1955), 'Symposium on the tenth century', *Medievalia et Humanistica* 9: 3–29

White, S. D. (1996), 'Debate: the "Feudal Revolution" II', *Past and Present* 152: 205–23

Wickham, C. J. (1984), 'The other transition: from the ancient world to feudalism', *Past and Present* 103: 3–36

Wickham, C. J. (1986), *The Mountains and the City*, Oxford

Wickham, C. J. (1993), 'La Chute de Rome n'aura pas lieu. A propos d'un livre récent', *MA* 99: 107–26

Wickham, C. J. (1997), 'Debate: the "Feudal Revolution" iv', *Past and Present* 157: 195–208

Wolter, H. (1988), *Die Synoden im Reichsgebiet und in Reichsitalien von 916 bis 1056*, Paderborn

Wormald, P. (1977), 'The uses of literacy in Anglo-Saxon England and its neighbours', *Transactions of the Royal Historical Society*, fifth series 27: 95–114

Wormald, P. (1978), 'Æthelred the lawmaker', in D. Hill (ed.), *Ethelred the Unready: Papers from the Millenary Conference* (BAR, British Series 59), Oxford, pp. 47–80

Wormald, P. (1994), '"*Engla Lond*: the making of an allegiance", *Journal of Historical Sociology* 7: 1–24

Yorke, B. (1995), *Wessex in the early Middle Ages*, Leicester

Zimmermann, H. (1971), *Das dunkle Jahrhundert*, Graz

2 RURAL ECONOMY AND COUNTRY LIFE

Abel, W. (1962), *Geschichte der deutschen Landwirtschaft vom frühen Mittelalter bis zum 19. Jahrhundert* (Deutsche Agrargeschichte 2), Stuttgart

Alexandre, P. (1987), *Le Climat en Europe au moyen âge*, Paris

Ariès, P. and Duby, G. (eds.) (1985), *Histoire de la vie privée*, 1: *De l'empire romain à l'an mil*, Paris; English trans. A. Goldhammer as *A History of Private Life*, 1: *From Pagan Rome to Byzantium*, Cambridge, MA (1992)

Arnold, K. (1980), *Kind und Gesellschaft im Mittelalter und Renaissance*, Paderborn

Ashton, T. H. (1987), *Landlords, Peasants and Politics in Medieval England*, Cambridge

Bader, K. S. (1957, 1962, 1973), *Studien zur Rechtsgeschichte des mittelalterlichen Dorfes*, 3 vols., Weimar

Bartmuß, H.-J. (1973), *Deutschland in der Feudalepoche von der Wende des V.–VI. Jahrhunderts bis zur Mitte des XI. Jahrhunderts*, 3rd edn, Berlin

Bertrand, G., Bailloud, G., le Glay, M., and Fourquin, G. (1975), *Histoire de la France rurale*, 1: *Des origines à 1340*, Paris

Bessmertniy, Y. L. (1976), *Histoire du moyen âge*, Moscow

Bloch, M. (1990a), *Les Caractères originaux de l'histoire rurale française*, 3rd edn, Paris; English trans. J. Sondheimer as *French Rural History*, London (1966)

Bloch, M. (1990b), *La Société féodale*, 4th edn, Paris; English trans. C. Postan as *Feudal Society*, London (1961)

Blok, D. P. (ed.) (1985), *Algemene Geschiedenis der Nederlanden*, 1, Haarlem

Bonnassie, P. (1975, 1976), *La Catalogne du milieu du Xème à la fin du XIème siècle*, 2 vols., Toulouse

Bosl, K. (1970), *Die Gesellschaft in der Geschichte des Mittelalters*, Göttingen

Bourin-Derruau, M. (1987a, 1987b), *Villages médiévaux du Bas-Languedoc (XIe–XIVe siècles)*, 2 vols., Paris

Boutruche, R. (1970), *Seigneurie et féodalité*, 1, 2nd edn, Paris

Brooke, C. N. L. (1987), *Europe in the Central Middle Ages, 962–1154*, 4th edn, London

Burguière, A., Klapisch-Zuber, C., Segalen, M. and Zonabend, F. (eds.) (1986), *Histoire de la famille, 1: Mondes lointains, mondes anciens*, Paris; English trans. by S. Hanbury Tenison, R. Morris and A. Wilson as *A History of the Family, 1: Distant World, Ancient World*, Cambridge (1996)

Cantor, L. (ed.) (1982), *The English Medieval Landscape*, London

Chapelot, J. and Fossier, R. (1980), *Le Village et la maison au moyen âge*, Paris

Châteaux et peuplements (1980), *Châteaux et peuplements en Europe occidentale* (Flaran 1), Auch

Cipolla, C. M. (1959), *Storia dell'economia italiana*, II, Turin

Communautés villageoises (1984), *Les Communautés villageoises en Europe occidentale* (Flaran 4), Auch

Contamine, P. (ed.) (1976), *La Noblesse au moyen âge*, Paris

Dollinger, P. (1949), *L'Evolution des classes rurales en Bavière depuis la fin de l'époque carolingienne jusqu'au milieu du XIIIe siècle*, Paris

Donat, P. (1980), *Haus, Hof und Dorf in Mitteleuropa vom 7. bis zum 12. Jahrhundert*, Berlin

Duby, G. (1962), *L'Économie rurale et la vie des campagnes*, Paris; English trans. C. Postan as *Rural Economy and Country Life in the Middle Ages*, London (1968)

Duby, G. (1971), *La Société aux XIe et XIIe siècles dans la région mâconnaise*, 2nd edn, Paris

Duby, G. (1973), *Guerriers et paysans*, Paris; English trans. H. B. Clarke as *The Growth of the Early European Economy*, London (1974)

Ennen, E. (1991), *Frauen im Mittelalter*, 4th edn, Munich; English trans. of 3rd edn E. Jephcott as *The Medieval Woman*, Oxford (1989)

Ennen, E. and Janssen, W. (1979), *Deutsche Agrargeschichte: Vom Neolithikum bis zum Schwelle des Industriezeitalters*, Wiesbaden

Flandrin, J. L. (1984), *Famille, parenté, maison, sexualité dans l'ancienne société*, Paris

Flori, J. (1983), *L'Idéologie du glaive: préhistoire de la chevalerie*, Geneva

Fossier, R. (1968a, 1968b), *La Terre et les hommes en Picardie jusqu'à la fin du XIIIe siècle*, 2 vols., Paris

Fossier, R. (1982a, 1982b), *Le Moyen Age*, I: *Les Mondes nouveaux*; II: *L'Eveil de l'Europe*, Paris

Fossier, R. (1982c), *Enfance de l'Europe: aspects économiques et sociaux (Xe–XIIe siècles)*, 2 vols. continuously paginated, Paris

Fournier, G. (1978), *Le Château dans la France médiévale*, Paris

Franz, G. (1970), *Geschichte des deutschen Bauernstandes vom frühen Mittelalter bis zum 19. Jahrhundert* (Deutsche Agrargeschichte 4), Stuttgart

Fumagalli, V. (1978), *Coloni e signori nell'Italia settentrionale, secoli VI–XI*, Bologna

Ganshof, F.-L. (1955), 'Les Relations féodo-vassaliques aux temps post-carolingiens', *Settimane* 2: 67–114

Gaudemet, J. (1963), *Les Communautés familiales*, Paris

Genicot, L. (1982), *La Noblesse dans l'occident médiéval*, London

Goody, J. (1983), *The Development of Family and Marriage in Europe*, Cambridge

Grand, R. (1951), *L'Agriculture au moyen âge*, Paris

Herlihy, D. (1985), *Medieval Households*, Cambridge, MA.

Hodgkin, H. R. (1953), *A History of the Anglo-Saxons*, 3rd edn, Oxford

Hoskins, W. G. (1970), *The Making of the English Landscape*, London

Latouche, R. (1956), *Les Origines de l'économie occidentale, IVe–XIIe siècles*, Paris; English trans. E. M. Wilkinson as *The Birth of Western Economy*, London (1961)

Lohrmann, D. and Janssen, W. (eds.) (1983), *Villa, curtis, grangia. économie rurale entre Loire et Rhin de l'époque gallo-romaine aux XIIe–XIIIe siècles*, Munich

Lopez, R. S. (1959), *The Tenth Century*, New York

Luzzatto, G. (ed.) (1954), *Problemi communi dell'Europa postcarolingia (Settimane 2)*, Spoleto

Mayer, T. (ed.) (1943), *Adel und Bauern im deutschen Staat des Mittelalters*, Leipzig

Noonan, J. T. (1966), *Contraception: A History of its Treatment by Catholic Theologians and Canonists*, Cambridge, MA

Paysage rural (1980), *Le Paysage rural: réalités et représentations*, Lille

Pitz, E. (1979), *Wirtschafts- und Sozialgeschichte Deustschlands im Mittelalter*, Wiesbaden

Pognon, E. (1981), *La Vie quotidienne en l'an mil*, Paris

Postan, M. M. (ed.) (1966), *The Cambridge Economic History of Europe*, I: *The Agrarian Life of the Middle Ages*, 2nd edn, Cambridge

Pounds, N. J. G. (1994), *An Economic History of Medieval Europe*, 2nd edn, New York

Prinz, F. (1985), *Grundlagen und Anfänge: Deutschland bis 1056* (Deutsche Geschichte 1), Munich

Reuter, T. (ed.) (1979), *The Medieval Nobility: Studies in the Ruling Classes of France and Germany from the Sixth to the Twelfth Centuries*, Amsterdam

Rösener, W. (1985), *Bauern im Mittelalter*, Munich; English trans. A. Stützer as *Peasants in the Middle Ages*, Cambridge (1992)

Russell, J. C. (1969), *Population in Europe, 500–1500*, London

Sanchez-Albornoz, C. (1980), *La España cristiana de los siglos VII al XI* (Historia de España 7), Madrid

Sawyer, P. (ed.) (1976), *Medieval Settlement*, London

Schulze, K. (1963), *Adelsherrschaft und Landesherrschaft* (Mitteldeutsche Forschungen 29), Cologne

Sereni, E. (1961), *Storia del paesaggio agrario italiano*, Bari

Settia, A. (1984), *Castelli e villaggi nell'Italia padana: popolamento, potere e sicurezza fra IX e XII secolo*, Naples

Slicher van Bath, B. H. (1963), *The Agrarian History of Western Europe, AD 500–1850*, London

Structures féodales (1980), *Structures féodales et féodalisme dans l'Occident méditerranéen, Xe–XIIIe siècles*, Rome

Structures sociales (1969), *Les Structures sociales de l'Aquitaine, du Languedoc et de l'Espagne au premier âge féodal*, Paris

Toubert, P. (1973a, 1973b), *Les Structures du Latium médiéval: le Latium méridional et la Sabine du IXᵉ à la fin du XIIᵉ siècle*, 2 vols., Rome

Valdeavellano, L. de (1965), *Historia de España*, Madrid

Wickham, C. (1981), *Early Medieval Italy: Central Power and Society, 400–1000*, London

Wood, M. (1965), *The English Medieval House*, London

Zimmermann, H. (1971), *Das dunkle Jahrhundert*, Graz

3 MERCHANTS, MARKETS AND TOWNS

Agus, I. A. (1965a, 1965b), *Urban Civilization in Pre-Crusade Europe: A Study of Organized Town-Life in Northwestern Europe during the 10th and 11th Centuries Based on the Responsa Literature*, 2 vols., Leiden

Allen, T. and Gaube, H. (1988), *Das Timuridische Herat* (Tübinger Atlas des Vorderen Orient B VII 14: Beispiele islamischer Städte, fasc. 16), Tübingen

Arbman, H. (1939), *Birka. Sveriges äldsta handelsstad: Frå forntid och medeltid I*, Stockholm

Arjona Castro, A. (1982a), *Anales de Córdoba musulmana (711–1008)*, Córdoba

Arjona Castro, A. (1982b), *El reino de Córdoba durante la dominacion musulmana*, Córdoba

Ashtor, E. (1978), 'Aperçus sur les Radhanites', in Ashtor, *Studies on the Levantine Trade in the Middle Ages*, III, London

Austin, D. and Alcock, L. (eds.) (1990), *From the Baltic to the Black Sea: Studies in Medieval Archaeology* (One World Archaeology 18), London

Balbás, L. Torres (1955), 'Extensión y demografía de las ciudades hispano-musulmanas', *Studia Islamica* 3: 35–59

Balbás, L. Torres (1947), 'Plazas, zocos y tiendas de las ciudades hispano-musulmanas', *Al-Andalus: rivista de las escuelas de estudios árabes de Madrid y Granada* 12: 437–76

Barley, M. W. (ed.) (1977), *European Towns: Their Archaeology and Early History*, London, New York and San Francisco

Ben-Sasson, H. H. (ed.) (1976), *A History of the Jewish People*, Cambridge, MA

Biddle, M. (1972), 'The Winton Domesday. Two surveys of an early capital', in W. Besch, K. Fehn, D. Höroldt, F. Irsigler and M. Zender (eds.), *Die Stadt in der europäischen Geschichte: Festschrift Edith Ennen*, Bonn, pp. 36–43

Biddle, M. (1974), 'The development of the Anglo-Saxon town', in *Topografia urbana e vita cittadina nell' alto medioevo in occidente* (Settimane 21/1), Spoleto, pp. 203–30

Biddle, M. (ed.) (1976), *Winchester in the Early Middle Ages: An Edition and Discussion of the Winton Domesday* (Winchester Studies 1), Oxford

Biddle, M. and Hill, D. H. (1971), 'Late Saxon planned towns', *Antiquaries Journal* 51: 70–85

Blake, N. R. (ed.) (1962), *The Saga of the Joms-Vikings*, London

Bocchi, F. (1993), 'Città e mercati nell' Italia Padana', in *Mercati e mercanti*, pp. 139–76

Bordone, R. (1991), 'La città nel X secolo', in *Il secolo di ferro: mito e realtà del secolo X* (Settimane 38), Spoleto, pp. 517–59

Borger, H. (1975), 'Die mittelalterliche Stadt als Abbild des himmlischen Jerusalem', *Symbolon: Jahrbuch für Symbolforschung* N.F. 2: 21–48

Boussard, J. (1976), *Nouvelle Histoire de Paris: de la fin du siège de 885–886 à la mort de Philippe Auguste*, Paris

Brachmann, H. and Herrmann, J. (eds.) (1991), *Frühgeschichte der europäischen Stadt: Voraussetzungen und Grundlagen* (Schriften zur Ur- und Frühgeschichte 44), Berlin

Bradley, J. (1992), 'The topographical development of Scandinavian Dublin', in F. H. A. Aalen and Kevin Whelan (eds.), *Dublin. City and County: From Prehistory to Present. Studies in Honour of J. H. Andrews*, Dublin, pp. 43–56

Brisbane, M. A. (ed.) (1992), *The Archaeology of Novgorod, Russia: Recent Results from the Town and its Hinterland* (The Society for Medieval Archaeology Monograph Series 13), Lincoln

Brown, H. F. (1920), 'The Venetians and the Venetian quarter in Constantinople to the close of the 12th century', *Journal of Hellenic Studies* 40: 68–88

Brühl, C. (1975, 1990), *Palatium und Civitas: Studien zur Profantopographie spätantiker Civitates vom 3. bis zum 13. Jahrhundert*, I: *Gallien*; II: *Belgica I, beide Germanien und Raetia II*, Cologne and Vienna

Callmer, J. (1981), 'The archaeology of Kiev ca A.D. 500–1000. A survey', in R. Zeitler (ed.), *Les Pays du Nord et Byzance (Scandinavie et Byzance): Actes du colloque nordique et international de byzantinologie tenu à Upsal 20–22 avril 1979*, Upsala, pp. 29–62

Carli, F. (1934), *Storia del commercio italiano: il mercato nell' alto medioevo*, Padua

Caune, A. (1992), 'Die Rolle Rigas im Dünamündungsgebiet während des 10.–12. Jahrhunderts', *Zeitschrift für Ostforschung* 41: 489–99

Chalmeta, P. (1993), 'Formation, structure et contrôle du marché arabo-musulman', in *Mercati e mercanti*, pp. 667–713

Chédeville, A. (1980), *La Ville médiévale des Carolingiens à la Renaissance* (Histoire de la France urbaine, ed. G. Duby, 2), Paris

Citarella, A. O. (1977), *Il commercio di Amalfi nell' alto medioevo*, Salerno

Citarella, A. O. (1993), 'Merchants, markets and merchandise in Southern Italy in the high middle ages', in *Mercati e mercanti*, pp. 239–82

Clarke, H. and Ambrosiani, B. (1991), *Towns in the Viking Age*, Leicester and London (2nd edn 1995)

Clarke, H. B. and Simms, A. (eds.) (1985), *The Comparative History of Urban Origins in Non-Roman Europe: Ireland, Wales, Denmark, Germany, Poland and Russia from the 9th to the 13th Century* (BAR International Series 255), 2 vols., Oxford

Constable, O. R. (1994), *Trade and Traders in Muslim Spain: The Commercial Realignment of the Iberian Peninsula, 900–1500*, Cambridge

Dasberg, L. (1958), 'De *Lex familiae Wormatiensis ecclesiae* en de herkomst van de middeleeuwse koopman', *Tijdschrift voor Geschiedenis* 71: 243–9

Despy, G. (1968), 'Villes et campagnes aux IXᵉ et Xᵉ siècles: l'exemple du pays mosan', *Revue du Nord* 50: 145–68

Devroey, J.-P. and Zoller, Ch. (1991), 'Villes, campagnes, croissance agraire dans le pays mosan avant l'an mil', in *Mélanges Georges Despy*, Liège, pp. 223–60

Dilcher, G. (1984), 'Personale und lokale Strukturen kaufmännischen Rechts als Vorformen genossenschaftlichen Stadtrechts', in K. Friedland (ed.), *Gilde und Korporation in den nordeuropäischen Städten des späten Mittelalters* (Quellen und Darstellungen zur hänsischen Geschichte, N.F. 29), Cologne and Vienna, pp. 65–77

Dubov, I. V. (1989), *Velikij Volžkij put'* [The great road of the Volga], Leningrad

Dumas, F. (1991), 'La Monnaie au Xᵉ siècle', in *Il secolo di ferro*, pp. 565–609

Ebrei (1970), *Gli Ebrei nell' alto medioevo* (Settimane 26), Spoleto

Ellmers, D. (1972), *Frühmittelalterliche Handelsschiffahrt in Mittel- und Nordeuropa*, Neumünster

Endemann, T. (1964), *Markturkunde und Markt in Frankreich und Burgund vom 9. bis 11. Jahrhundert* (Vorträge und Forschungen, Sonderband 6), Constance and Stuttgart

Engels, P. (1991), 'Der Reisebericht des Ibrāhīm ibn Yaʿqūb (961–966)', in A. van Euw and P. Schreiner (eds.), *Kaiserin Theophanu. Begegnung des Ostens und Westens um die Wende des ersten Jahrtausends. Gedenkschrift des Kölner-Schütgen-Museums zum 1000. Todesjahr der Kaiserin*, 1, Cologne, pp. 413–22

Ennen, E. (1981), *Frühgeschichte der europäischen Stadt*, 3rd edn, Bonn

Ennen, E. (1987), *Die europäische Stadt des Mittelalters*, 4th edn, Göttingen

Evrard, J.-P. (1990), 'Verdun, au temps de l'évêque Haymon 988–1024', in D. Iogna-Prat and J.-C. Picard (eds.), *Religion et culture autour de l'an mil: royaume capétien et Lotharingie*, Paris, pp. 272–8

Fasoli, G. (1978), 'Navigazione fluviale – porti e navi sul Po', in *Navigazione*, pp. 565–607

Fasoli, G. and Bocchi, F. (eds.) (1975), *La città medievale italiana*, Florence

Ferluga, J. (1993), 'Mercati e mercanti fra Mar Nero e Adriatico: il commercio nei Balcani dal VII all'XI secolo', in *Mercati e mercanti*, pp. 443–89

Fiala, Z. (1967), *Die Anfänge Prags: eine Quellenanalyse zur Ortsterminologie bis zum Jahre 1235*, Wiesbaden

Fichtenau, H. (1994), '"Stadtplanung" im früheren Mittelalter', in K. Brunner and B. Merta (eds.), *Ethnogenese und Überlieferung: angewandte Methoden der Frühmittelalterforschung* (Veröffentlichungen des Instituts für Österreichische Geschichtsforschung 31), Vienna, pp. 232–49

Frojānova, I. Ia. (1992), *Mjatežnyj Novgorod: ocerki istorii gosudarstvennosti social' noj i političeskoj bor'by konca IX – nacala XIII stoletija*, St Petersburg

Ganshof, F.-L. (1943), *Etude sur le développement des villes entre Loire et Rhin au moyen âge*, Paris and Brussels

Garcin, J.-C. (1987), *Espaces, pouvoirs et idéologies de l'Egypte médiévale*, London

Gaube, H. and Haist, A. (1991), *Kairo/Al Qahira. Baubestand* (Tübinger Atlas des Vorderen Orient B VII 14: Beispiele islamischer Städte, fasc. 23), Tübingen

Gaube, H. and Klein, R. (1989), *Das Safavidische Isfahan/Esfahar* (Tübinger Atlas des Vorderen Orient B VII 14: Beispiele islamischer Städte, fasc. 19), Tübingen

Gaube, H. and Wirth, E. (1989), *Aleppo/Hdab, Baubestand* (Tübinger Atlas des Vorderen Orient B VII 14: Beispiele islamischer Städte, fasc. 19), Tübingen

Gieysztor, A. (1993), 'Les Marchés et les marchandises entre le Danube et la Volga aux VIIIᵉ–XIᵉ siècles', in *Mercati e mercanti*, pp. 499–518

Gil, M. (1974), 'The Rhādhānite merchants and the land of Rhadan', *Journal of Economic and Social History of the Orient* 17: 299–328

Goehrke, C. (1980), 'Die Anfänge des mittelalterlichen Städtewesens in eurasischer Perspektive', *Saeculum* 31: 194–239

Goitein, S. D. F. (1971, 1978, 1983, 1988, 1993), *A Mediterranean Society: The Jewish Communities of the Arab World as Portrayed in the Documents of the Cairo Geniza*, 5 vols., Berkeley and Los Angeles

Hall, R. A. (1978), 'The topography of Anglo-Scandinavian York', in R. H. Hall (ed.), *Viking Age York and the North* (CBA Research Report 27), London, pp. 31–6

Halphen, L. (1909), *Paris sous les premiers Capétiens (987–1223): étude de topographie historique*, Paris

Harvey, A. (1989), *Economic Expansion in the Byzantine Empire, 900–1200*, Cambridge

Haslam, J. (ed.) (1984), *Anglo-Saxon Towns in Southern England*, Chichester

Haverkamp, A. (1987), '"Heilige Städte" im hohen Mittelalter', in F. Graus (ed.), *Mentalitäten im Mittelalter: methodische und inhaltliche Probleme* (Vorträge und Forschungen 35), Sigmaringen, pp. 119–56

Hendy, M. F. (1991), 'East and West: divergent models of coinage and its use', in *Il secolo di ferro*, pp. 637–74

Herrmann, J. (ed.) (1989a, 1989b), *Archäologie in der Deutschen Demokratischen Republik: Denkmale und Funde*, 2 vols., Leipzig and Stuttgart

Herzog, E. (1964), *Die ottonische Stadt: die Anfänge der mittelalterlichen Stadtbaukunst in Deutschland* (Frankfurter Forschungen zur Architekturgeschichte 2), Berlin

Hill, D. (1969), 'The Burghal Hidage: the establishment of a text', *Medieval Archaeology* 13: 84–92

Hill, D. (1978), 'Trends in the development of towns in the reign of Ethelred II', in

D. Hill (ed.), *Ethelred the Unready: Papers from the Millenary Conference*, (BAR British Series 59), Oxford, pp. 213–26

Hill, D. (1987), 'The Saxon period', in J. Schofield and R. Leech (eds.), *Urban Archaeology in Britain* (CBA Research Report 61), London, pp. 46–53

Hill, D. (1994), 'An urban policy for Cnut?', in A. R. Rumble (ed.), *The Reign of Cnut: King of England, Denmark and Norway*, Leicester, pp. 101–5

Hodges, R. (1982), *Dark Age Economics: The Origins of Towns and Trade A.D. 600–1000*, London

Hodges, R. and Hobley, B. (eds.) (1988), *The Rebirth of Towns in the West, AD 750–1050* (CBA Research Report 68), London

Hubert, J. (1959), 'Evolution de la topographie et de l'aspect des villes de Gaule du ve aux xe siècle', in *La città nell' alto medioevo* (*Settimane* 6), Spoleto, pp. 529–58

Huml, V. (1990), 'Research in Prague – an historical and archaeological view of the development of Prague from the 9th century to the middle of the 14th century', in Austin and Alcock (1990), pp. 267–84

Ioannisyan, O. M. (1990), 'Archaeological evidence for the development and urbanization of Kiev from the 8th to the 14th centuries', in Austin and Alcock (1990), pp. 285–312

Jakobs, H. (1979), 'Vescovi e città in Germania', in C. G. Mor and H. Schmidinger (eds.), *I poteri temporali dei Vescovi in Italia e in Germania nel Medioevo*, Bologna, pp. 283–328

Janin, V. L. (1992), 'Drevnee slavanstvo i archevlogija Novgoroda', *Voprosy Istorii* 100: 37–65

Jankuhn, H. (1986), *Haithabu: Ein Handelsplatz der Wikingerzeit*, 8th edn, Neumünster

Jankuhn, H., Schietzel, H. and Reichstein, H. (eds.) (1984), *Archäologische und naturwissen-schaftliche Untersuchungen an ländlichen und frühstädtischen Siedlungen im deutschen Küstengebiet vom 5. Jahrhundert v. Chr. bis zum 11. Jahrhundert n. Chr.*, II, Bonn

Jankuhn, H., Schlesinger, W. and Steuer, H. (eds.) (1973, 1974), *Vor- und Frühformen der europäischen Stadt im Mittelalter* (Abhandlungen der Akademie der Wissenschaften in Göttingen, Phil.-hist. Kl., 3. Folge, Nos. 83 and 84), 2 vols., Göttingen

Jarnut, J. (1979), *Bergamo 568–1098: Verfassungs-, Sozial- und Wirtschaftsgeschichte einer lombar-dischen Stadt im Mittelalter* (Vierteljahresschrift für Sozial- und Wirtschaftsgeschichte, Beiheft 67), Wiesbaden

Joris, A. (1988), 'Espagne et Lotharingie autour de l'an mil. Aux origines des franchises urbaines', *Le Moyen Age* 94: 5–19

Keller, H. (1976), 'Die Entstehung der italienischen Stadtkommunen als Problem der Sozialgeschichte', *FmaSt* 10: 169–211

Kirpičnikov, A. N. (1988), 'Ladoga i Ladožskaja zemlja', in *Slavjano-russkie drevnosti vyp. 1*, Leningrad, pp. 38–79

Krautheimer, R. (1983), *Rome: Profile of a City, 312–1308*, 2nd edn, Princeton

Kubiak, W. (1987), *Al-Fustat: Its Foundation and Early Urban Development*, Cairo

Lauda, R. (1984), *Kaufmännische Gewohnheit und Burgrecht bei Notker dem Deutschen: zum Verhältnis von literarischer Tradition und zeitgenössischer Realität in der frühmittelalterlichen Rhetorik* (Rechtshistorische Reihe 34), Frankfurt am Main

Lebecq, S. (1984), 'Aelfric et Alpert. Existe-t-il *un* discours clérical sur les marchands dans l'Europe du Nord à l'aube du xie siècle?', *Cahiers de Civilisation Médiévale* 27: 85–93

Lestocquoy, J. (1947), 'The tenth century', *Economic History Review*, first series 17: 1–14

Lévi-Provençal, E. (1953), *Histoire de l'Espagne musulmane*, III: *Le siècle du califat de Cordoue*, Paris

Lewis, A. R. (1958), *The Northern Seas: Shipping and Commerce in Northern Europe, A.D. 300–1100*, Princeton

Lopez, R. S. (1955), 'Some tenth century towns', *Medievalia et Humanistica*, first series 9: 4–6

Lopez, R. S. (1959), *The Tenth Century: How Dark the Dark Ages?* (Source Problems in World Civilization), New York

Lopez, R. S. (1967), *The Birth of Europe*, London and New York

Lopez, R. S. (1978), *Byzantium and the World Around It: Economic and Institutional Relations*, London

Lot, F. (1945, 1950, 1953), *Recherches sur la population et la superficie des cités remontant à la période gallo-romaine*, 3 vols., Paris

Loyn, H. R. (1971), 'Towns in late Anglo-Saxon England: the evidence and some possible lines of enquiry', in P. Clemoes and K. Hughes (eds.), *England Before the Conquest: Studies in Primary Sources Presented to Dorothy Whitelock*, Cambridge, pp. 115–28

Ludat, H. (1955), *Vorstufen und Entstehung des Städtewesens in Osteuropa*, Cologne

Matheus, M. (1995), 'Zur Romimitation in der Aurea Morguntina', in W. Dotzauer, W. Kleiber, M. Matheus and K.-H. Spiess (eds.), *Landesgeschichte und Reichsgeschichte: Festschrift für Alois Gerlich zum 70. Geburtstag* (Geschichtliche Landeskunde 42), Stuttgart, pp. 35–49

Maurer, H. (1973), *Konstanz als ottonischer Bischofssitz: zum Selbstverständnis geistlichen Fürstentums im 10. Jahrhundert* (Veröffentlichungen des Max-Planck-Instituts für Geschichte 39), Göttingen

Mayer, R. (1943), *Byzantion – Konstantinopolis – Istanbul* (Denkschriften der Akademie Wissenschaften, Phil.-hist. Kl. 71,3), Vienna

Mayr-Harting, H. (1992), 'The church of Magdeburg: its trade and its town in the tenth and eleventh centuries', in D. Abulafia, M. Franklin and M. Rubin (eds.), *Church and City 1000–1500: Essays in Honour of Christopher Brooke*, Cambridge, pp. 129–50

Mercati e mercanti (1993), *Mercati e mercanti nell' alto medioevo: l'area Euroasiatica e l'area Mediterranea* (Settimane 40), Spoleto

Metz, W. (1972), 'Marktrechtsfamilie und Kaufmannsfriede in ottonisch-salischer Zeit', *Blätter für deutsche Landesgeschichte* 108: 28–55

Miquel, A. (1967a, 1967b, 1967c), *La Géographie humaine du monde musulman jusqu'au milieu du 11ᵉ siècle*, 3 vols., Paris and The Hague

Mühle, E. (1988), 'Die topographisch-städtebauliche Entwicklung Kievs vom Ende des 10. bis zum Ende des 12. Jh. im Lichte der archäologischen Forschung', *Jahrbuch für die Geschichte Osteuropas*, N.F. 36: 350–76

Mühle, E. (1991), *Die städtischen Handelszentren der nordwestlichen Rús* (Quellen und Studien zur Geschichte des östlichen Europa 32), Stuttgart

Müller-Boysen, C. (1987), '"stundum i viking e stundum i kaupðertum". Die Rolle der Wikinger im Wirtschaftsleben des mittelalterlichen Europa', *Offa* 44: 248–60

Müller-Boysen, C. (1990), *Kaufmannsschutz und Handelsrecht im frühmittelalterlichen Nordeuropa*, Neumünster

Müller-Mertens, E. (1987), 'Frühformen der mittelalterlichen Stadt oder Städte eigener

Art im Frühmittelalter? Reflexion auf die fränkisch-deutsche Stadtentwicklung vor der Jahrtausendwende', *Zeitschrift für Geschichtswissenschaft* 35: 997–1006

Müter, H. (1955), 'Het onstaan van de stad Tiel', *Bijdragen voor de Geschiedenis der Niederlanden* 9: 161–89

Navigazione (1978), *La navigazione mediterranea nell' alto medioevo* (*Settimane* 25), Spoleto

Neugebauer, W. (1968), 'Truso und Elbing, ein Beitrag zur Frühgeschichte des Weichselmündungsgebietes', in M. Claus, W. Haarnagel, and K. Raddatz (eds.), *Studien zur europäischen Vor- und Frühgeschichte*, Neumünster, pp. 213–34

Nicol, D. M. (1988), *Byzantium and Venice: A Study in Diplomatic and Cultural Relations*, Cambridge

Noonan, T. S. (1988), 'The impact of the silver crisis in Islam upon Novgorod's trade with the Baltic', in *Oldenburg–Wolin–Novgorod–Kiev*, pp. 411–47

Northedge, A. (1990), *Samarra: Entwicklung der Residenzstadt des 'albasidischen Kalifats (221–279/836–892)* (Tübinger Atlas des Vorderen Orient B VII 14: Beispiele islamischer Städte, fasc. 20), Tübingen

Nosov, E. N. (1987), 'New data on the Ryurik Gorodishche near Novgorod', *Fennoscandia Archaeologia* 4: 73–85

Oexle, O. G. (1985), 'Conjuratio und Gilde im frühen Mittelalter. Ein Beitrag zum Problem der sozialgeschichtlichen Kontinuität zwischen Antike und Mittelalter.', in B. Schwineköper (ed.), *Gilden und Zünfte: kaufmännische und gewerbliche Genossenschaften im frühen und hohen Mittelalter* (Vorträge und Forschungen 29), Sigmaringen, pp. 151–214

Oexle, O. G. (1989), 'Die Kaufmannsgilde von Tiel', in *Untersuchungen* (1989b), pp. 173–96

Oikonomides, N. (1993), 'Les Marchands byzantins des provinces (IXᵉ–XIᵉ s.)', in *Mercati e mercanti*, pp. 633–60

Oldenburg–Wolin–Novgorod–Kiev (1988), *Oldenburg–Wolin–Novgorod–Kiev: Handel und Handelsverbindungen im südlichen und östlichen Ostseeraum während des frühen Mittelalters* (Bericht der römisch-germanischen Kommission 69), Mainz

Patlagean, E. (1993), 'Byzance et les marchés du grand commerce vers 830–vers 1030. Entre Pirenne et Polanyi', in *Mercati e mercanti*, pp. 587–629

Pitz, E. (1991), *Europäisches Städtewesen und Bürgertum von der Spätantike bis zum hohen Mittelalter*, Darmstadt

Puhle, M. (1995), *Magdeburg im frühen Mittelalter: vom karolingischen Königshof zur ottonischen Kaiserstadt*, Magdeburg

Renouard, Y. (1969), *Les Villes d'Italie de la fin du Xᵉ siècle au début du XIVᵉ siècle*, vol. 1, Paris

Reynolds, S. (1977), *An Introduction to the History of English Medieval Towns*, Oxford

Roblin, M. (1951), 'Cités ou citadelles? Les enceintes romaines du Bas-Empire d'après l'exemple de Paris', *Revue des Etudes Anciennes* 53: 301–11

Rösch, G. (1982), *Venedig und das Reich: handels- und verkehrspolitische Beziehungen in der deutschen Kaiserzeit* (Bibliothek des Deutschen Historischen Instituts in Rom 53), Tübingen

Rüss, H. (1981a), 'Das Reich von Kiev', in M. Hellmann (ed.), *Handbuch der Geschichte Russlands*, I: *bis 1613. Von der Kiever Reichsbildung bis zum Moskauer Zartum*, Stuttgart, pp. 199–429

Rüss, H. (1981b), 'Gross-Novgorod und Pskov', in M. Hellmann (ed.), *Handbuch der Geschichte Russlands*, 1: *Bis 1613*. *Von der Kiever Reichsbildung bis zum Moskauer Zartum*, Stuttgart, pp. 431–83

Sawyer, P. H. (1983), 'The royal tun in preconquest England', in P. Wormald, D. Bullough and R. Collins (eds.), *Ideal and Reality in Frankish and Anglo-Saxon Society: Studies Presented to J. M. Wallace-Hadrill*, Oxford, pp. 273–99

Schaube, A. (1906), *Handelsgeschichte der romanischen Völker des Mittelmeergebiets bis zum Ende der Kreuzzüge*, Munich and Berlin

Schlesinger, W. (1963), *Beiträge zur deutschen Verfassungsgeschichte des Mittelalters*, 2: *Städte und Territorien*, Göttingen

Schlesinger, W. (1972), 'Vorstufen des Städtewesens im ottonischen Sachsen', in W. Besch, K. Fehn, D. Höroldt, F. Irsigler and M. Jender (eds.), *Die Stadt in der europäischen Geschichte: Festschrift Edith Ennen*, Bonn, pp. 234–58

Schlesinger, W. (1973), 'Der Markt als Frühform der deutschen Stadt', in H. Jahnkuhn, W. Schlesinger and H. Steuer (eds.), *Vor- und Frühformen der europäischen Stadt im Mittelalter, Teil I*, (Abhandlungen der Akademie der Wissenschaften in Göttingen, Phil.-hist. Klasse, 3 Folge, No. 83), Göttingen, pp. 262–93

Schulte, A. (1900a, 1900b), *Geschichte des mittelalterlichen Handels und Verkehrs zwischen Westdeutschland und Italien mit Ausschluss von Venedig*, 2 vols., Leipzig

Schwarz, U. (1978), *Amalfi im frühen MA. (9.–11. Jh.): Untersuchungen zur Amalfitaner Überlieferung* (Bibliothek des Deutschen Historischen Instituts in Rom 49), Tübingen

Secolo di ferro (1991) *Il secolo di ferro: mito e realtá del secolo x* (Settimane 38), Spoleto

Settia, A. A. (1993), '"Per foros Italie". Le aree extraurbane fra Alpi e Appennini', in *Mercati e mercanti*, pp. 187–233

Sláma, J. (1986, 1988, 1989), *Střední Čechy v raném středoveku*, 3 vols., Prague

Slaski, K. (1974), 'Die Schiffe der Ostseeslawen und Polen vom 9.–13. Jahrhundert im Lichte neuer polnischer Forschungen', *Zeitschrift für Archäologie des Mittelalters* 2: 107–19

Šolle, M. (1984), *Staroslovanské hradiško: charakteristika, funkce, vývoj a význam*, Prague

Staffa, S. J. (1977), *Conquest and Fusion: The Social Evolution of Cairo A.D. 642–1850*, Leiden

Steuer, H. (1990), 'Die Handelsstätten des frühen Mittelalters im Nord- und Ostsee-Raum', in *La Genèse et les premiers siècles des villes médiévales dans les Pays-Bas méridionaux*, Brussels, pp. 75–116

Stoob, H. (1962), 'Über Zeitstufen der Marktsiedlung im 10. und 11. Jahrhundert auf sächsischen Boden', *Westfälische Forschungen* 15: 73–80 (reprinted in Stoob, *Forschungen zum Städtewesen in Europa*, 1: *Räume, Formen und Schichten der mitteleuropäischen Städte*, Cologne and Vienna (1970), pp. 43–50)

Studien (1958), *Studien zu den Anfängen des europäischen Städtewesens* (Vorträge und Forschungen 4), Lindau and Constance

Tamari, S. (1966), 'Aspetti principali dell'urbanesimo Musulmano', *Palladio*, n.s. 16: 45–82

Tatton-Brown, T. (1986), 'The topography of Anglo-Saxon London', *Antiquity* 60: 21–8

Teall, J. (1977), 'Byzantine urbanism in the military handbooks', in H. A. Miskimin, D. Herlihy and A. L. Udovitch (eds.), *The Medieval City*, New Haven and London, pp. 201–5

Topografia (1974), *Topografia urbana e vita cittadina nell' alto medioevo in occidente* (*Settimane* 21), Spoleto

Třeštík, D. (1973), 'Trh Moravanů – ústřední trh Staré Moravy', *Československý Časopis Historicky* 21: 869–94

Třeštík, D. (1983), 'Počátky Prahy a českehu státu', *Folia Historica Bohemica* 5: 7–37

Trudy pjatogo (1987), *Trudy pjatogo meždunarodnogo kongressa slavanskoj archeologii* (Publications of the fifth international congress of Slavonic archaeology), I, Moscow

Untersuchungen (1987, 1989a, 1989b), *Untersuchungen zu Handel und Verkehr der vor- und frühgeschichtlichen Zeit in Mittel- und Nordeuropa*, IV: *Der Handel der Karolinger- und Wikingerzeit*, ed. K. Düwel, H. Jankuhn, H. Siems and D. Timpe; V: *Der Verkehr: Verkehrswege, Verkehrsmittel, Organisation*, ed. H. Jankuhn, W. Kimmig and E. Ebel; VI: *Organisationsformen der Kaufmannsvereinigungen in der Spätantike und im frühen Mittelalter*, ed. H. Jankuhn and E. Ebel (Abhandlungen der Akademie der Wissenschaften in Göttingen, Phil.-hist. Kl., 3 Folge, nos. 156, 180, 183), Göttingen

Vdovitch, A. L. (1993), 'Market and society in the medieval Islamic world', in *Mercati e mercanti*, pp. 767–90

Verhulst, A. (1992), *Rural and Urban Aspects of Early Medieval Northwest Europe*, London

Verhulst, A. (1993), 'Marchés, marchands et commerce au haut moyen âge dans l'historiographie récente', in *Mercati e mercanti*, pp. 23–43

Verhulst, A. (1994a), 'The origins and early development of medieval towns in northern Europe', *Economic History Review*, second series 47: 362–73

Verhulst, A. (1994b), 'Le Développement urbain dans le Nord-Ouest de l'Europe du IX au Xᵉ siècle: rupture et continuité', in *Società, Instituzioni, Spiritualità: Studi in onore di Cinzio Violante*, Spoleto, pp. 1037–55

Verhulst, A. (ed.) (1996), *Anfänge des Städtewesens an Schelde, Maas und Rhein bis zum Jahre 1000* (Städteforschung A 40), Cologne, Weimar and Vienna

Vermeesch, A. (1966), *Essai sur les origines et la signification de la France (XIᵉ et XIIᵉ siècles)*, Heule

Violante, C. (1981), *La società milanese nell'età precomunale* (Biblioteca universale Laterza 11), 3rd edn, Rome

Warnke, C. (1965), 'Bemerkungen zur Reise Ibrahim Ibn Jakubs durch die Slawenländer im 10. Jahrhundert', in H. Ludat (ed.), *Agrar-, Wirtschafts- und Sozialprobleme Mittel- und Osteuropas in Geschichte und Gegenwart*, Wiesbaden, pp. 393–415

Wasserstein, D. J. (1993), *The Caliphate of the West*, Oxford

Wiet, G. (1964), *Cairo: City of Art and Commerce*, Normal, ILL

Zug Tucci, H. (1993), 'Negociare in omnibus partibus per terram et per aquam: il mercante Veneziano', in *Mercati e mercanti*, pp. 51–79

4 RULERS AND GOVERNMENT

Airlie, S. (1993), 'After Empire – recent work on the emergence of post-Carolingian kingdoms', *EME* 2: 153–61

Airlie, S. (1994), 'The view from Maastricht', in B. E. Crawford (ed.), *Dark Age Europe*, St Andrews, pp. 33–46

Althoff, G. (1989), 'Königsherrschaft und Konfliktbewältigung im 10. und 11. Jahrhundert', *FmaSt* 23: 265–90

Althoff, G. (1990a), *Verwandte, Freunde und Getreue: zum politischen Stellenwert der Gruppenbindungen im früheren Mittelalter*, Darmstadt

Althoff, G. (1990b), '*Colloquium familiare – colloquium secretum – colloquium publicum*. Beratung im politischen Leben des früheren Mittelalters', *FmaSt* 24: 145–67

Althoff, G. (1991), 'Huld. Überlegungen zu einem Zentralbegriff der mittelalterlichen Herrschaftsordnung', *FmaSt* 25: 259–82

Althoff, G. (1992), *Amicitiae und Pacta: Bündnis, Einung, Politik und Gebetsgedenken im beginnenden 10. Jahrhundert* (Schriften der MGH 32), Munich

Althoff, G. (1997), *Spielregeln der Politik im Mittelalter*, Darmstadt

Bailey, F. (1969), *Stratagems and Spoils: A Social Anthropology of Politics*, Oxford

Bedos Rezak, B. (1992), 'Ritual in the royal chancery: text, image, and the representation of kingship in medieval French diplomas (700–1200)', in H. Duchhardt, R. A. Jackson and D. Sturdy (eds.), *European Monarchy*, Stuttgart, pp. 27–40

Bémont, C. (1884), *Simon de Montfort, comte de Leicester*, Paris

Bernhardt, J. W. (1993), *Itinerant Kingship and Royal Monasteries in Early Medieval Germany, c. 936–1075*, Cambridge

Beumann, H. (1950), *Widukind von Korvei: Untersuchungen zur Geschichtsschreibung und Ideengeschichte des 10. Jahrhunderts*, Weimar

Beumann, H. (1956), 'Zur Entwicklung transpersonaler Staatsvorstellungen', in *Das Königtum* (Vorträge und Forschungen 3), Lindau, pp. 185–204

Bornscheuer, L. (1968), *Miseriae regum: Untersuchungen zum Krisen- und Todesgedanken in der herrschaftstheologischen Vorstellungen der ottonisch-salischen Zeit*, Berlin

Brühl, C. (1990), *Deutschland – Frankreich: die Geburt zweier Völker*, Cologne and Vienna

Byrne, F. (1973), *Irish Kings and High Kings*, London

Campbell, J. (1980), 'The significance of the Anglo-Norman state in the administrative history of western Europe', in W. Paravicini and K.-F. Werner (eds.), *Histoire comparée de l'administration* (Beihefte der Francia 9), Munich, pp. 117–34

Campbell, J. (1986), *Essays in Anglo-Saxon History*, London

Campbell, J. (1989), *Stubbs and the English State* (Stenton Lecture 1987), Reading

Collins, R. (1983), *Early Medieval Spain: Unity in Diversity*, London

Collins, R. (1993), 'Queens-dowager and queens-regent in tenth-century León and Navarre', in J. Parsons (ed.), *Medieval Queenship*, New York and Gloucester, pp. 79–92

Corbet, P. (1986), *Les Saints ottoniens: sainteté royale et sainteté féminine autour de l'an mil*, Sigmaringen

Davies, W. (1982), *Wales in the Early Middle Ages*, Leicester

Davies, W. (1990), *Patterns of Power in Early Wales*, Oxford

Davies, W. (1993), 'Celtic kingships in the early middle ages', in A. Duggan (ed.), *Kings and Kingship in the Middle Ages*, London, pp. 101–24

Deshman, R. (1976), '*Christus rex et magi reges*: kingship and christology in Ottonian and Anglo-Saxon art', *FmaSt* 10: 367–405

Deshman, R. (1988), '*Benedictus Monarcha et Monachus*: early medieval ruler theology and the Anglo-Saxon reform', *FmaSt* 22: 204–40

Dunbabin, J. (1985), 'The Maccabees as exemplars in the tenth and eleventh centuries', in K. Walsh and D. Wood (eds..), *The Bible in the Medieval World: Essays in Memory of Beryl Smalley*, Oxford, pp. 31–41

Ehlers, J. (1985), 'Die Anfänge der französischen Geschichte', *Historische Zeitschrift* 240: 1–44

Fentress, J. and Wickham, C. J. (1993), *Social Memory*, Oxford

Fichtenau, H. (1984) *Lebensordnungen des 10 Jahrhunderts: Studien über Denkart und Existenz im einstigen Karolingerreich*, Stuttgart; English trans. P. Geary as *Living in the Tenth Century: Mentalities and Social Orders*, Chicago (1991)

Fleming, R. (1993) 'Rural elites and urban communities in late-Saxon England', *Past and Present* 141: 3–37

Fletcher, R. (1992), *Moorish Spain*, London

Fried, J. (1989), 'Endzeiterwartung um die Jahrtausendwende', *DA* 45: 381–473

Fried, J. (1990), *Otto III. und Boleslaw Chrobry: das Widmungsbild des Aachenere Evangeliars, der 'Akt von Gnesen' und das frühe polnische und ungarische Königtum*, Stuttgart

Fried, J. (1991), *Die Formierung Europas, 840–1046*, Munich

Fuhrmann, H. (1993), '"Willkommen und Abschied". Über Begrüssungs- und Abschieds-rituale im Mittelalter', in W. Hartmann (ed.), *Mittelalter: Annäherungen an eine fremde Zeit*, Regensburg, pp. 111–39

Geary, P. (1986), 'Vivre en conflit dans une France sans état', *Annales ESC* 41: 1107–33; English trans. in Geary, *Living with the Dead in the Middle Ages*, Ithaca (1994), pp. 125–160

Geertz, C. (1980), *Negara: The Theater-State in Nineteenth-Century Bali*, Princeton

Görich, K. (1993), *Otto III. Romanus, Saxonicus et Italicus: kaiserliche Rompolitik und sächsische Historiographie*, Sigmaringen

Görich, K. (1998), 'Otto III. öffnet das Karlsgrab in Aachen. Überlegungen zu Heiligenverehrung, Heiligsprechung und Traditionsbildung', in G. Althoff and E. Schubert (eds.), *Herrschaftsrepräsentation im Ottonischen Sachsen*, Sigmaringen, pp. 381–430

Head, T. and Landes, R. (eds..) (1993), *The Peace of God: Social Violence and Religious Response in France around the Year 1000*, Ithaca

Heather, P. (1994), 'State formation in Europe in the first millennium A.D.', in B. Crawford (ed.), *Dark Age Europe*, St Andrews, pp. 47–70

Hoffmann, H. (1962), 'Französische Fürstenweihen des Hochmittelalters', *DA* 18:92–119

Iogna-Prat, D. (1990), 'Entre anges et hommes: les moines "doctrinaires" de l'an mil', in R. Delort and D. Iogna-Prat (eds..), *La France de l'an mil*, Paris, pp. 245–63

Keller, H. (1964), 'Das Kaisertum Ottos des Großen im Verständnis seiner Zeit', *DA* 20: 325–88

Keller, H. (1985), 'Herrscherbild und Herrschaftslegitimation', *FmaSt* 19: 290–311

Keller, H. (1989), 'Zum Charakter der "Staatlichkeit" zwischen karolingischer Reichsreform und hochmittelalterlichem Herrschaftsausbau', *FmaSt* 23: 248–64

Keynes, S. (1985), 'King Athelstan's books', in M. Lapidge and H. Gneuss (eds..), *Learning and Literature in Anglo-Saxon England: Studies Presented to Peter Clemoes*, Cambridge, pp. 143–201

Keynes, S. (1990), 'Royal government and the written word in late Anglo-Saxon England', in R. McKitterick (ed.), *The Uses of Literacy in Early Medieval Europe*, Cambridge, pp. 226–57

Keynes, S. (1991), 'Crime and punishment in the reign of Æthelred the Unready', in I. Wood and N. Lund (eds.), *People and Places in Northern Europe, 500–1600: Essays in Honour of Peter Sawyer*, Woodbridge, pp. 67–82

Kienast, W. (1969), 'Der Wirkungsbereich des französischen Königtums von Odo bis Ludwig VI. (888–1137) in Südfrankreich', *HZ* 209: 529–65

Klewitz, H.-W. (1939), 'Die Festkrönungen der deutschen Könige', *ZRG KA* 28: 48–97

Koziol, G. (1992), *Begging Pardon and Favor: Ritual and Political Order in Early Medieval France*, Ithaca

Lanoë, G. (1992), 'Les Ordines de couronnement (930–1050); retour au manuscrit', in M. Parisse and X. Barral i Altet (eds.), *Le Roi de France et son royaume autour de l'an mil. Actes du colloque Hugues Capet 978–1987. La France de l'an mil*, Paris, pp. 65–72

Le Goff, J. (1993), 'Le Roi dans l'Occident médiéval', in A. Duggan (ed.), *Kings and Kingship in the Middle Ages*, London, pp. 1–40

Leyser, K. (1979), *Rule and Conflict in an Early Medieval Society*, London

Leyser, K. (1994), *Communications and Power in Medieval Europe: The Carolingian and Ottonian Centuries*, ed. T. Reuter, London

McKitterick, R. (1992), 'Continuity and innovation in tenth-century Ottonian culture', in L. Smith and B. Ward (eds.), *Intellectual Life in the Middle Ages: Essays Presented to Margaret Gibson*, London, pp. 15–24

Mayr-Harting, H. (1991), *Ottonian Book Illumination*, 2 vols., London

Moore, R. I. (1994), 'Literacy and the making of heresy, *c.* 1000–*c.* 1150', in P. Biller and A. Hudson (eds.), *Heresy and Literacy, 1000–1350*, Cambridge, pp. 19–37

Mostert, M. (1987), *The Political Theology of Abbo of Fleury*, Hilversum

Nelson, J. L. (1988), 'Kingship and empire', in J. H. Burns (ed.), *The Cambridge History of Medieval Political Thought*, Cambridge, pp. 211–51

Ó Corráin, D. (1978), 'Nationality and kingship in pre-Norman Ireland', in T. Moody (ed.), *Nationality and the Pursuit of National Independence*, Belfast, pp. 1–35

Poly, J. and Bournazel, E. (1991), *La Mutation féodale*, 2nd edn, Paris; English trans. as *The Feudal Transformation, 900–1200*, Chicago (1991)

Reuter, T. (1991), *Germany in the Early Middle Ages, 800–1056*, London

Reynolds, S. (1984), *Kingdoms and Communities in Western Europe, 900–1300*, Oxford

Reynolds, S. (1994), *Fiefs and Vassals: The Medieval Evidence Reconsidered*, Oxford

Reynolds, S. (1997), 'The historiography of the medieval state', in M. Bentley (ed.), *The Writing of History: An International Guide to Classical and Current Historiography*, London, pp. 117–38

Sassier, Y. (1987), *Hugues Capet*, Paris

Sawyer, B. and Sawyer, P. (1993), *Medieval Scandinavia*, Minnesota

Schneider, R. (1989), 'Das Königtum als Integrationsfaktor im Reich', in J. Ehlers (ed.), *Ansätze und Diskontinuität deutscher Nationsbildung im Mittelalter* (Nationes 6), Sigmaringen, pp. 59–82

Schneidmüller, B. (1979), *Karolingischer Tradition und frühes französisches Königtum*, Wiesbaden

Schneidmüller, B. (1987), *Nomen patriae: die Entstehung Frankreichs in der politisch-geographischen Terminologie (10.–13. Jh.)* (Nationes 7), Sigmaringen

Schramm, P. E. (1968), 'Anlagen zu 3 A–B: die westfränkischen und die angelsächsischen Krönungsordines', in Schramm, *Kaiser, Könige und Päpste*, 4 vols. in 5 (1968–71), II, pp. 208–48

Smyth, A. P. (1984), *Warlords and Holy Men: Scotland, AD 80–1000*, 2nd edn, London

Sot, M. (1994), *Un Historien et son église: Flodoard de Reims*, Paris

Southern, R. W. (1953), *The Making of the Middle Ages*, London

Stafford, P. (1978), 'The reign of Æthelred II: a study in the limitations on royal policy and action', in D. Hill (ed.), *Ethelred the Unready*, Oxford, pp. 15–46

Stafford, P. (1983), *Queens, Concubines and Dowagers: The King's Wife in the Early Middle Ages*, London

Stafford, P. (1989), *Unification and Conquest: A Political and Social History of England in the Tenth and Eleventh Centuries*, London

Stafford, P. (1993), 'The portrayal of royal women in England, mid-tenth to mid-twelfth centuries', in J. Parsons (ed.), *Medieval Queenship*, New York and Gloucester, pp. 143–68

von Euw, A. and Schreiner, P. (eds..) (1991a, 1991b) *Kaiserin Theophanu: Begegnung des Ostens und Westens um die Wende des ersten Jahrtausends*, 2 vols.., Cologne

Warner, D. A. (1994), 'Henry II at Magdeburg: kingship, ritual and the cult of the saints', *EME* 3: 135–66

Werner, K. F. (1979), *Structures politiques du monde franc (VIe–XIIe siècles)*, London

Werner, K. F. (1987), 'Gott, Herrscher und Historiograph. Der Geschichtsschreiber als Interpret des Wirken Gottes in der Welt und Ratgeber der Könige', in E. D. Hehl, H. Seibert and F. Staab (eds.), *Deus qui mutat tempora. Menschen und Institutionen im Wandel des Mittelalters: Festschrift für Alfons Becker*, Sigmaringen, pp. 1–31

Wickham, C. (1981), *Early Medieval Italy, 400–1000*, London

Wickham, C. (1985), 'Lawyers' time: history and memory in tenth- and eleventh-century Italy', in H. Mayr-Harting and R. I. Moore (eds..), *Studies in Medieval History Presented to R. H. C. Davis*, London, pp. 53–71, reprinted in Wickham (1994), 275–94

Wickham, C. (1994), *Land and Power: Studies in Italian and European Social History, 400–1200*, London

Willmes, P. (1976), *Der Herrscher-'Adventus' im Kloster des Frühmittelalters*, Munich

Wormald, P. (1986) 'Charters, law and the settlement of disputes in Anglo-Saxon England', in W. Davies and P. Fouracre (eds..), *The Settlement of Disputes in Early Medieval Europe*, Cambridge, pp. 149–68

Zotz, T. (1994), 'Carolingian tradition and Ottonian-Salian innovation: comparative observations on palatine policy in the Empire', in A. Duggan (ed.), *Kings and Kingship in Medieval Europe*, London, pp. 69–100

5   THE CHURCH

For fuller bibliography see the bibliographies in Mayeur et al. (1993), Tellenbach (1993) and Wolter (1988)

Aldea Vaquero, Q., Marín Martinez, T. and Vives Gatell, J. (1972–5), *Diccionario de historia eclesiástica de España*, 4 vols., Madrid

Amann, E. and Dumas, A. (1943), *L'Eglise au pouvoir des laïques, 888–1057* (Histoire de l'Eglise 7), Paris

Arnaldi, G. (1991), 'Mito e realtá del secolo X romano e papale', in *Il secolo di ferro: mito e realtá del secolo X* (Settimane 38), Spoleto, pp. 27–53

Aubrun, M. (1981), *L'Ancien Diocèse de Limoges des origines au milieu du XIe siècle*, Clermont-Ferrand

Aubrun, M. (1986), *La Paroisse en France des origins au XVe siècle*, Paris

Barral i Altet, X. (1991), *La Catalogne et la France meridionale autour de l'an mil*, Barcelona

Bautier, R. H. (1951), 'Un Recueil de textes pour servir à l'histoire de l'archévêque de Reims Hervé (Xe siècle)', *Mélanges d'histoire du moyen âge dédiés à la mémoire de Louis Halphen*, Paris, pp. 1–6

Bernhardt, J. H. (1993), *Itinerant Kingship and Royal Monasteries in Early Medieval Germany, c. 936–1075*, Cambridge

Blair, J. (1987), 'Local churches in Domesday Book and before', in J. C. Holt (ed.), *Domesday Studies*, Woodbridge, pp. 265–78

Blair, J. (1988), *Minsters and Local Parishes: The Local Church in Transition, 950–1200*, Oxford

Blair, J. (1995), 'Debate: ecclesiastical organization and pastoral care in Anglo-Saxon England', *EME* 4: 193–212

Blair, J. and Sharpe, R. (eds.) (1992), *Pastoral Care before the Parish* (Studies in the Early History of Britain), Leicester

Borgolte, M. (1992), *Die mittelalterliche Kirche* (Enzyklopädie der deutschen Geschichte 17), Munich

Boshof, E. (1993), *Königtum und Königsherrschaft im 10. und 11. Jahrhundert* (Enzyklopädie der deutschen Geschichte 27), Munich

Bouchard, C. B. (1987), *Sword, Miter, and Cloister: Nobility and the Church in Burgundy, 980–1198*, Ithaca

Brandt, M. and Eggebrecht, A. (eds.) (1993), *Bernward von Hildesheim und das Zeitalter der Ottonen*, 2 vols., Hildesheim

Brooks, N. (1984), *The Early History of the Church of Canterbury* (Studies in the Early History of Britain), Leicester

Bührer-Thierry, G. (1997), *Evêques et pouvoir dans le royaume de Germanie: les églises de Bavière et de Souabe, 876–973*, Paris

Bur, M. (1983), 'Architecture et liturgie à Reims au temps d'Adalbéron', *CCM* 26: 297–302

Bur, M. (1992), 'Adalbéron, archévêque de Reims reconsidéré', in Parisse and Barral i Altet (1992), pp. 55–63

Butler, L. A. S. and Morris, R. K. (1986), *The Anglo-Saxon Church* (CBA Research Report 60), London

Cambridge, E. and Rollason, D. (1995), 'Debate: the pastoral organization of the Anglo-Saxon church: a review of the "minster hypothesis"', *EME* 4: 87–104

Campbell, J. (1986), 'The church in Anglo-Saxon towns', in J. Campbell (ed.), *Essays in Anglo-Saxon History*, London, pp. 139–54

Clayton, M. (1991), *The Cult of the Virgin Mary in Anglo-Saxon England* (Cambridge Studies in Anglo-Saxon England 2), Cambridge

Collins, R. (1989), 'Doubts and certainties on the churches of early medieval Spain', in *God and Man in Medieval Spain: Essays in Honour of J. R. L. Highfield*, Warminster, pp. 1–18

Coolidge, R. T. (1965), 'Adalbero of Laon', *Studies in Medieval and Renaissance History* 2: 1–114

Corbet, P. (1986), *Les Saints ottoniens: sainteté dynastique, sainteté royale et sainteté féminine autour de l'an mil* (Beihefte der Francia 15), Sigmaringen

Crocker, R. and Hiley, D. (eds.) (1990), *The Early Middle Ages to 1300* (The New Oxford History of Music 1), Oxford

Crusius, I. (ed.) (1989), *Beiträge zur Geschichte und Struktur der mittelalterlichen Germania Sacra* (Veröffentlichungen des Max-Planck-Instituts für Geschichte 93), Göttingen

Desportes, P. (1973), 'Les Archévêques de Reims et les droites comtaux du Xe et XIe siècles', in *Economies et sociétés au moyen âge: mélanges offerts à Edouard Perroy*, Paris, pp. 79–89

Devisse, J. (1975–6), *Hincmar, archévêque de Reims, 845–882*, 3 vols., Geneva

Duchesne, L. (1913), 'Serge III et Jean XI', *Mélanges d'Archéologie et d'Histoire* 33: 5–55

Dumas, A. (1944), 'L'Eglise de Reims au temps des luttes entre Carolingiens et Robertiens', *RHEF* 30: 5–38

Dumville, D. N. (1992), *Liturgy and the Ecclesiastical History of Anglo-Saxon England* (Studies in Anglo-Saxon History 5), Woodbridge

Ehlers, J. (1978), 'Die *Historia Francorum Senonensis* und der Aufstieg des Hauses Capet', *JMH* 4: 1–26

Engels, O. (1989), 'Der Reichsbischof in ottonischer und frühsalischer Zeit', in Crusius (1989), pp. 135–75

Fanning, S. (1988), *A Bishop and His World Before the Gregorian Reform: Hubert of Angers, 1006–1047*, Philadelphia

Fernández Conde, F. J. (1972), *La Iglesia de Asturias en la alta Edad Media*, Oviedo

Fichtenau, H. (1984), *Lebensordnungen des 10 Jahrhunderts: Studien über Denkart und Existenz im einstigen Karolingerreich*, Stuttgart; English trans. P. Geary as *Living in the Tenth Century: Mentalities and Social Orders*, Chicago (1991)

Finck von Finckenstein, A. (1989), *Bischof und Reich: Untersuchungen zum Integrationsprozess des ottonisch-frühsalischen Reiches (919–1056)* (Studien zur Mediävistik 1), Sigmaringen

Fleckenstein, J. (1956), 'Königshof und Bischofsschule unter Otto dem Großen', *AKG* 38: 38–62, reprinted in Fleckenstein (1989), pp. 168–92

Fleckenstein, J. (1985), 'Problematik und Gestalt der ottonisch-salischen Reichskirche', in Schmid (1985), pp. 83–98

Fleckenstein, J. (1989), *Ordnungen und formende Kräfte des Mittelalters: Ausgewählte Beiträge*, Göttingen

Fliche, A. (1909), 'Séguin, archévêque de Sens, primat des Gaules et de Germanie (977–999)', *Bulletin de la Société Archéologique de Sens* 24: 149–206

Fliche, A. (1934), 'La Primauté des Gaules depuis l'époque carolingienne jusqu'à la fin de la querelle des investitures (876–1121)', *RH* 173: 349–42

Fonseca, C. D. (1982), 'Particularismo istituzionale e organizzazione ecclesiastica delle campagne nell'alto medioevo nell'Italia meridionale', in *Cristianizzazione ed. organizzazione ecclesiastica delle campagne nell'alto medioevo: espansione e resistenze* (Settimane 29), Spoleto, pp. 1163–1200

Fumagalli, V. (1973), 'Vescovi e conti nell'Emilia occidentale da Berengario I a Ottone I', *SM*, serie terza, 14: 137–204

Gandino, G. (1995), *Il vocabulario politico e sociale di Liutprando di Cremona*, Rome

Garcia Villada, Z. (1929, 1933), *Historia eclesiástica de España*, 2 vols., Madrid

Garcia Villoslada, R. (ed.) (1982), *Historia de la iglesia en España*, II.1, Madrid

Geary, P. J. (1994), *Phantoms of Remembrance: Memory and Oblivion at the End of the First Millennium*, Princeton

Große, R. (1987), *Das Bistum Utrecht und seine Bischöfe im 10. und frühen 11. Jahrhundert*, Cologne

Hannick, C. (1993), 'Les Nouvelles Chrétientés du monde byzantin: Russes, Bulgares et Serbes', in Mayeur et al. (1993), pp. 909–39

Hauck, A. (1920), *Kirchengeschichte Deutschlands*, III, 3rd/4th edn, Leipzig

Head, T. (1991), *Hagiography and the Cult of Saints: The Diocese of Orleans 800–1200* (Cambridge Studies in Medieval Life and Thought 4th series, 14), Cambridge

Head, T. and Landes, R. (1992), *The Peace of God: Social Violence and Religious Response in France around the Year 1000*, Ithaca

Heinzelmann, M. (1979), *Translationsberichte und andere Quellen des Reliquienkultes* (Typologie des sources du moyen âge occidental 33), Turnhout

Hermann, K. J. (1973), *Das Tuskulanerpapsttum, 1012–1046*, Stuttgart

Hoffmann, H. (1986), *Buchkunst und Königtum im ottonischen und frühsalischen reich* (Schriften der MGH 30), 2 vols., Stuttgart

Iogna-Prat, D. and Picard, J.-C. (eds..) (1990), *Religion et culture autour de l'an mil*, Paris

Jaeger, C. S. (1983), 'The courtier bishop in vitae from the tenth to the twelfth century', *Speculum* 58: 291–325

Kaiser, R. (1981), *Bischofsherrschaft zwischen Königtum und Fürstenmacht: Studien zur bischöflichen Stadtherrschaft im westfränkisch-französischen Reich im frühen und hohen Mittelalter* (Pariser Historische Studien 17), Bonn

Karwasińska, J. (1960), *Les Trois Rédactions de la Vita I de S. Adalbert*, Rome

Kehr, P. (1926), *Das Papsttum und der katalanische Prinzipat bi zur Vereinigung mit Aragon* (Abhandlungen der Preussischen Akademie der Wissenschaften, Phil.-hist. Klasse 1), Berlin

Klewitz, H.-W. (1932–3), 'Zur Geschichte der Bistumsorganisation Campaniens und Apuliens im 10. und 11. Jahrhundert', *QFIAB* 24: 1–61

Kloczowski, J. (1993), 'La Nouvelle Chrétienté du monde occidental. La christianisation des Slaves, des Scandinaves et des Hongrois entre le Ixe et le XIe siècles', in Mayeur et al. (1993), pp. 869–908

Kortüm, H.-H. (1985), *Richer von Saint-Rémi: Studien zu einem Geschichtsschreiber des 10. Jahrhunderts*, Stuttgart

Kortüm, H.-H. (1994), *Zur päpstlichen Urkundensprache im frühen Mittelalter*, Sigmaringen

Langres (1986), *Langres et ses évêques, VIIIe–XIe siècles: aux origines d'une seigneurie ecclésiastique. Actes du Colloque Langres-Ellwangen*, Langres

Lotter, F. (1958), *Die Vita Brunonis des Ruotger: ihre historiographische und ideengeschichtliche Stellung*, Bonn

Maccarone, M. (ed.) (1991), *Il primato del vescovo di Roma nel primo millenio: ricerche e testimonianze. Atti del Symposium storico-teologico (Roma, 9–13 ottobre, 1989)* (Pontificio comitato di scienze storiche. Atti e documenti 4), Vatican

McKitterick, R. (1983a), *The Frankish Kingdoms under the Carolingians (751–987)*, London

McKitterick, R. (1983b), 'The Carolingian kings and the see of Rheims, 882–987', in Wormald (1983), pp. 228–49

McLaughlin, M. (1994), *Consorting with Saints: Prayer for the Dead in Early Medieval France*, Ithaca

Mass, J. (1986), *Das Bistum Freising im Mittelalter*, Munich

Mayeur, J. M., Pietri, C. and L., Vauchez, A. and Venard, M. (eds..) (1993), *Histoire du Christianisme*, IV. *Evêques, moines et empereurs (610–1054)*, Paris

Nyberg, T. S. (1986), *Die Kirche in Skandinavien: Mitteleuropäischer und englischer Einfluss im 11. und 12. Jahrhundert. Anfänge der Domkapitel Borglum und Odense in Dänemark* (Beiträge zur Geschichte und Quellenkunde des Mittelalters 10), Sigmaringen

Ortenberg, V. (1990), 'Archbishop Sigeric's journey to Rome in 990', *ASE* 20: 197–246

Parisse, M. (1993), 'L'Eglise en empire (v. 900–1054)', in Mayeur *et al.* (1993), pp. 793–815

Parisse, M. and Barral i Altet, X. (1992), *Le Roi de France et son royaume autour de l'an mil*, Paris

Pokorny, R. (1993), 'Reichsbischof, Kirchenrecht und Diözesanverwaltung um das Jahr 1000', in Brandt and Eggebrecht (1993), pp. 113–19

Prinz, F. (1971), *Klerus und Krieg im früheren Mittelalter*, Stuttgart

Ramsay, N., Sparks, M. and Tatton-Brown, T. (eds.) (1992), *St Dunstan: His Life, Times and Cult*, Woodbridge

Raterio (1973), *Raterio di Verona* (Convegni del centro di studi sulla spiritualitá medievale 10), Todi

Reuter, T. (1982), 'The "imperial church system" of the Ottonian and Salian rulers: a reconsideration', *JEH* 33: 347–74

Riché, P. (1987), *Gerbert d'Aurillac, pape de l'an mil*, Paris

Ridyard, S. (1988), *The Royal Saints of Anglo-Saxon England: A Study of West Saxon and East Anglian Cults* (Cambridge Studies in Medieval Life and Thought, 4th series, 9), Cambridge

Rollason, D. (1989), *Saints and Relics in Anglo-Saxon England*, Oxford

Sansterre, J.-M. (1989), 'Otton III et les saints ascètes de son temps', *RSCI* 43: 376–412

Santifaller, L. (1964), *Zur Geschichte des ottonisch-salischen Reichskirchensystems*, 2nd edn, Vienna

Savigni, R. (1992), 'Sacerdozio e regno in età post-carolingia: l'episcopato di Giovanni X, arcívescovo di Ravenna (905–914) e papa (914–928)', *RSCI* 46: 1–29

Schieffer, R. (1989), 'Der ottonische Reichsepiskopat zwischen Königtum und Adel', *FmaSt* 23: 291–301

Schmid, K. (ed.) (1985), *Reich und Kirche vor dem Investiturstreit: Gerd Tellenbach zum 80. Geburtstag*, Sigmaringen

Schmitz, G. (1977), 'Das Konzil von Trosly (909)', *DA* 33: 341–434

Schmitz, G. (1987), 'Heriveus von Reims (900–922). Zur Geschichte des Erzbistums Reims am Beginn des 10. Jahrhunderts', *Francia* 6: 59–106

Schneider, G. (1973), *Erzbischof Fulco von Reims 883–900 und das Frankenreich*, Munich

Schröder, I. (1980), *Die westfränkischen Synoden von 888 bis 987 und ihre Überlieferung* (MGH Hilfsmittel 3), Munich

Schwarz, U. (1978), *Amalfi im frühen Mittelalter (9–11 Jahrhundert): Untersuchungen zur Amalfitaner Überlieferung* (Bibliothek des Deutschen Historischen Instituts in Rom 49), Tübingen

Sot, M. (1981), *Gesta episcoporum. Gesta abbatum* (Typologie des sources du moyen âge occidental 37), Turnhout

Sot, M. (1985), 'Rhétorique et technique dans les préfaces des "gesta episcoporum" (ixe–xie s.)', *CCM* 28: 181–200

Sot, M. (1993), *Un Historien et son église au Xe siècle: Flodoard de Reims*, Paris

Sutherland, J. N. (1988), *Liudprand of Cremona, Bishop, Diplomat, Historian: Studies of the Man and His Age* (Biblioteca degli 'Studi medievali' 14), Spoleto

Tellenbach, G. (1993), *The Church in Western Europe from the Tenth to the Early Twelfth Century*, trans. T. Reuter, Cambridge

Vescovi (1964), *Vescovi e diocesi in Italia nel Medioevo (sec. IX–XIII)* (Atti del II Convegno di storia della Chiesa in Italia, Roma, 1961 = Italia sacra 5), Padua

Vitolo, G. (1990), 'Vescovi e diocesi', in G. Galasso and R. Romeo (eds.), *Storia del Mezzogiorno*, III: *Alto medioevo*, Naples, pp. 733–51

Vlasto, A. (1974), *The Entry of the Slavs into Christendom*, Cambridge

Vogel, C. (1986), *Medieval Liturgy: An Introduction to the Sources*, revised and translated by W. G. Storey and N. K. Rasmussen, Washington, DC

Vollrath, H. (1985), *Die Synoden Englands bis 1066*, Paderborn

von Euw, A. and Schreiner, P. (eds.) (1991), *Kaiserin Theophanu: Begegnung des Ostens und Westens um die Wende des ersten Jahrtausends*, 2 vols., Cologne

Weinfurter, S. (ed.) (1991), *Die Salier und das Reich*, 3 vols., Sigmaringen

Wemple, S. F. (1979), *Atto of Vercelli: Church, State and Christian Society in Tenth-Century Italy* (Temi e testi a cura di Eugenio Massa 27), Rome

Werner, K.-F. (1989), 'Observations sur le rôle des évêques dans le mouvement de paix aux xe et xie siècles', in C. E. Viola (ed.), *Mediaevalia Christiana XIe–XIIIe siècles: hommage à Raymonde Foreville*, Tournai, pp. 155–95

Williams, P. (1993), *The Organ in Western Culture 750–1250* (Cambridge Studies in Medieval and Renaissance Music), Cambridge

Wolter, H. (1988), *Die Synoden im Reichsgebiet und in Reichsitalien von 916 bis 1056*, Paderborn

Wormald, P. (ed.) (1983), *Ideal and Reality in Frankish and Anglo-Saxon Society*, Oxford

Yorke, B. (ed.) (1988), *Bishop Æthelwold: His Career and Influence*, Woodbridge

Zielinski, H. (1984), *Der Reichsepiskopat in spätottonischer und salischer Zeit, 1002–1125*, I, Stuttgart

6 MONASTICISM: THE FIRST WAVE OF REFORM

European monasticism in the tenth century

Fried, J. (1989), 'Endzeiterwartung um die Jahrtausendwende', *DA* 45: 381–473

Gaussier, P. (ed.) (1991), *Naissance et fonctionnement des réseaux monastiques et canoniaux. Actes du Ier Colloque Internationale du CERCOM Saint-Etienne 16–18 Sept. 1985*, Saint-Etienne

Hallinger, K. (1951a, 1951b), *Gorze – Kluny* (Studia Anselmiana 24/25), 2 vols., Rome

Iogna-Prat, D. and Picard, J.-C. (1990), *Religion et culture autour de l'an mil: royaume capétien et Lotharingie*, Paris

Schmid, K. (ed.) (1985), *Reich und Kirche vor dem Investiturstreit*, Sigmaringen

Il Secolo de Ferro (1991), *Il secolo di ferro: mito e realtà del secolo X* (Settimane 38), Spoleto

Tellenbach, G. (1988), *Die westliche Kirche vom 10. bis zum frühen 12. Jahrhundert* (Die Kirche in ihrer Geschichte. Ein Handbuch, hg. v. B. Moeller, Bd. 2, Lieferung F 1), Göttingen; English trans. T. Reuter as *The Church in Western Europe from the Tenth to the Early Twelfth Century*, Cambridge (1993)

Wollasch, J. (1973) *Mönchtum des Mittelalters zwischen Kirche und Welt* (Münstersche Mittelalter-Schriften 7), Munich

Key groupings within tenth-century reform monasticism

Eremitical monasticism

Gilomen-Schenkel, E. (1986), 'Einsiedeln', in *Lexikon des Mittelalters*, III: *Codex Wintoniensis bis Erziehungs- und Bildungswesen*, Munich and Zürich, cols. 1743–6
Keller, H. (1964), *Kloster Einsiedeln im ottonischen Schwaben* (Forschungen zur Oberrheinischen Landesgeschichte 13), Freiburg im Breisgau
Violante, C. and Fonseca, C. D. (eds.) (1965), *L'eremitismo in occidente nei secoli XI e XII* (Miscellanea del centro di studi medioevali 4), Milan

Cluny

Constable, G *et al.* (eds.) (1998), *Die Cluniazenser in ihrem politisch-sozialen Umfeld*, Münster
Cowdrey, H. E. J. (1970), *The Cluniacs and the Gregorian Reform*, Oxford
Das Martyrolog-Necrolog von St. Emmeram zu Regensburg, ed. E. Freise, D. Geuenich and J. Wollasch (*MGH Lib. Mem.*, NS III) Hanover (1986)
Garand, M.-C. (1978), 'Copistes de Cluny au temps de Saint-Maieul' *BEC* 136: 5–36
Gilomen, H.-J. (ed.) (1991), *Helvetia sacra*, III, 2: *Die Cluniazenser in der Schweiz*, Basel
Hallinger, K (1954), 'Zur geistigen Welt der Anfänge Klunys', *DA* 10: 417–46
Iogna-Prat, D. (1988), *Agni immaculati: recherches sur les sources hagiographiques relatives à Saint Maieul de Cluny (954–994)*, Paris
Iogna-Prat, D. (1992), 'Panorama de l'hagiographie abbatiale clunisienne (v. 940–v. 1140)', in M. Heinzelmann (ed.), *Manuscrits hagiographiques et travail des hagiographes* (Beihefte der Francia 24), Sigmaringen, pp. 77–118
Jakobs, H. (1974), 'Die Cluniazenser und das Papsttum im 10. und 11. Jahrhundert', *Francia* 2: 643–63
Leclercq, J. (1962), 'Pour une histoire de la vie à Cluny', *RHE* 57: 385–408, 783–812
Neiske, F., Poeck, D. and Sandmann, M. (eds.) (1991), *Vinculum societatis: Joachim Wollasch zum 60. Geburtstag*, Sigmaringendorf
Pacaut, M. (1986), *L'Ordre de Cluny*, Paris
Richter, H. (ed.) (1975), *Cluny*, Darmstadt
Rosenwein, B. H. (1982), *Rhinoceros Bound: Cluny in the Tenth Century*, Philadelphia.
Rosenwein, B. H. (1989), *To Be the Neighbor of St Peter: The Social Meaning of Cluny's Property, 909–1049*, Ithaca.
Sackur, E. (1892a, 1892b) *Die Cluniacenser in ihrer kirchlichen und allgemeingeschichtlichen Wirksamkeit bis zur Mitte des elften Jahrhunderts*, 2 vols., Halle an der Saale, reprinted Stuttgart (1971)
Tellenbach, G. (ed.) (1959), *Neue Forschungen über Cluny und die Cluniacenser*, Freiburg im Breisgau
Winzer, U. (1988), 'Zum Einzugsbereich Clunys im 10. Jahrhundert' *FmaSt* 22: 241–65
Winzer, U. (1989), 'Cluny und Mâcon im 10. Jahrhundert', *FmaSt* 23: 154–202
Wollasch, J. (1979), 'Les Obituaires, témoins de la vie clunisienne', *CCM* 22: 139–71
Wollasch, J. (1992), 'Cluny und Deutschland', *StMGBO* 103: 7–32
Wollasch, J. (1996), *Cluny 'Licht der Welt'*, Zurich

Cluny, Italy and Rome in the tenth century

Antonelli, G. (1958), 'L'Opera di Odone di Cluny in Italia', *Benedictina* 4: 19–40
Caraffa, F. (ed.) (1981), *Monasticon Italiae I, Roma e Lazio*, Cesena
Ferrari, G. (1957), *Early Roman Monasteries* (Studi di antichità cristiana 23), Città del Vaticano
Violante, C. (ed.) (1985), *L'Italia nel quadro dell'espansione europea del monachesimo cluniacense* (Italia Benedettina 8), Cesena
Zerbi, P. (ed.) (1979a, 1979b), *Cluny in Lombardia* (Italia Benedettina 1), 2 vols., Cesena

Brogne

Dierkens, A. (1985), *Abbayes et chapîtres entre Sambre et Meuse (VIIᵉ–XIᵉ siècles)* (Beihefte der Francia 14), Sigmaringen
Gérard (1960) *Gérard de Brogne et son œuvre réformatrice, RB* 70: 5–240
Misonne, D. (1983), 'Brogne', in *Lexikon des Mittelalters*, II: *Bettlerwesen bis Codex von Valencia*, Munich and Zurich, cols. 708–9
Misonne, D. (1988), 'L'Histoire des manuscrits de Saint-Denis', *Revue Bénédictine* 98: 21–30
Smet, J. M. M. (1960), 'Recherches critiques sur la Vita Gerardi Abbatis Broniensis', *RB* 70: 5–61

Gorze and other monasteries within the Empire

Parisse, M. (1989), 'Gorze', in *Lexikon des Mittelalters*, IV: *Erzkanzler bis Hiddensee*, Munich and Zurich, cols. 1565–7
Parisse, M. (ed.) (1971), *Le Nécrologe de Gorze* (Annales de l'Est Mém. 40), Nancy
Parisse M. and Oexle, O. G. (eds.) (1993), *L'Abbaye de Gorze au Xᵉ siècle*, Nancy
Schmid, K. (ed.) (1978), *Die Klostergemeinschaft von Fulda im früheren Mittelalter* (Münstersche Mittelalter-Schriften 8,1–3), 3 vols.. in 5, Munich
Wisplinghoff, E. (1970), *Untersuchungen zur frühen Geschichte der Abtei S. Maximin bei Trier von den Anfängen bis etwa 1150* (Quellen und Abhandlungen zur mittelrheinischen Kirchengeschichte 12), Mainz

Saint-Benoît de Fleury-sur-Loire

Berland, J.-M. (1984), 'L'Influence de l'abbaye de Fleury-sur-Loire en Bretagne et dans les Îles Britanniques du xᵉ au xiiᵉ siècle', *Actes du 107ᵉ Congrès national des Sociétés savantes II*, Paris, pp. 275–99
Bulst, N. and Mostert, M. (1989), 'Fleury–Saint-Benoît-sur-Loire', in *Lexikon des Mittelalters*, IV: *Erzkanzler bis Hiddensee*, Munich and Zurich, cols. 547–8
Vidier, A. (1965), *L'Historiographie à S.-Benoît-sur-Loire et les miracles de S. Benoît*, Paris
Wollasch, J. (1959), 'Königtum, Adel und Klöster im Berry während des 10. Jahrhunderts', in G. Tellenbach (ed.), *Neue Forschungen über Cluny und die Cluniacenser*, Freiburg im Breisgau, pp. 107–15
Wollasch, J. (1980), 'Bemerkungen zur Goldenen Altartafel von Basel', in C. Meier and U. Ruberg (eds.), *Text und Bild*, Wiesbaden, pp. 383–407
Wollasch, J. (1982), 'Benedictus abbas Romensis', in N. Kamp and J. Wollasch (eds.),

Tradition als historische Kraft: interdisziplinäre Forschungen zur Geschichte des früheren Mittelalters, Berlin and New York, pp. 119–37

The Regularis concordia

Brooks, N. (1984), *The Early History of the Church of Canterbury*, Leicester
John, E. (1982), 'The age of Edgar', in J. Campbell (ed.), *The Anglo-Saxons*, Oxford, pp. 160–91
Parsons, D. (ed.) (1975), *Tenth-Century Studies: Essays in Commemoration of the Millennium of the Council of Winchester and Regularis concordia*, London and Chichester
Symons, T. (1984), *Regularis concordia Anglicae nationis* (*CCM* VII/1), Siegburg
Vollrath, H. (1985), *Die Synoden Englands bis 1066* (Konziliengeschichte Reihe A) Paderborn

Saint-Bénigne de Dijon

Bulst, N. (1973), *Untersuchungen zu den Klosterreformen Wilhelms von Dijon* (Pariser Historische Studien 11), Bonn
Bulst, N. (1974), 'Rodulfus Glabers Vita domni Willelmi abbatis', *DA* 30: 450–87
Schamper, B. (1989), *S. Bénigne de Dijon: Untersuchungen zum Necrolog der Handschrift Bibl. mun. de Dijon, ms. 634* (Münstersche Mittelalter-Schriften 63), Munich
Schlink, W. (1978), *Saint-Bénigne in Dijon: Untersuchungen zur Abteikirche Wilhelms von Volpiano (962–1031)*, Berlin

7 INTELLECTUAL LIFE

Airlie, S. (1992), 'The anxiety of sanctity: St Gerald of Aurillac and his maker', *JEccH* 43: 372–95
Arlt, W. and Björkvall, G. (eds.) (1993), *Recherches nouvelles sur les tropes liturgiques*, Stockholm
Autenrieth, J. (1985), 'Purchards Gesta Witigowonis im Codex Augiensis CCV', in *Festschrift für Florentine Müterich*, Munich, pp. 101–6
Barone, G. (1991), 'Une Hagiographie sans miracle. Observations en marge de quelques vies du xᵉ siècle', in *Les Fonctions des saints dans le monde occidental (IIIᵉ–XIIIᵉ siècle)* (Collection de l'Ecole française de Rome 149), Rome, pp. 435–46
Bertini, F. (1991), 'Il "Within piscator" di Letaldo di Micy', in *Lateinische Kultur*, pp. 39–48
Beumann, H. (1950), *Widukind von Korvei: Untersuchungen zur Geschichtsschreibung und Ideengeschichte des 10. Jahrhunderts*, Weimar
Bischoff, B. (1984), 'Italienische Handschriften des neunten bis elften Jahrhunderts in frümittelalterlichen Bibliotheken ausserhalb Italiens', in *Il libro e il testo*, ed. C. Questa and R. Raffaelli, Urbino, pp. 171–94
Bozzolo, C. and Ornato, E. (1983), *Pour une Histoire du livre manuscrit au moyen âge: trois essais de codicologie quantitative*, 2nd edn, Paris
Brown, V. (1988), 'Miscellanea beneventana IV. 1: a second new list of Beneventan manuscripts', *Mediaeval Studies* 50: 584–625
Brunhölzl, F. (1992), *Geschichte der lateinischen Literatur des Mittelalters, 2: Die Zwischenzeit von Ausgang des karolingischen Zeitalters bis zur Mitte des elften Jahrhunderts*, Munich

Cavallo, G. (1991), 'Libri scritti, libri letti, libri dimenticati', in *Il secolo di ferro*, pp. 759–94

Chiesa, P. (1991) 'Le traduzioni dal greco. L'evoluzione della scuola napoletana nel X secolo', in *Lateinische Kultur*, pp. 67–83

Chiesa, P. (1994), *Liutprando di Cremona e il codice di Frisinga Clm 6388* (Corpus Christianorum, Autographa Medii Aevi, 1), Turnhout

Chiesa, P. and Pinelli, L. (eds..) (1994), *Gli autografi medievali. Problemi paleografici e filologici* (Atti del Convegno di studio della Fondazione Ezio Franceschini), Spoleto

Constable, G. (1991), 'Cluny in the monastic world of the tenth century', in *Il secolo di ferro*, pp. 391–437

Cremascoli, G. (1991) 'Das hagiographische Werk des Letald von Micy', in *Lateinische Kultur*, pp. 87–93

Daniel, N. (1973), *Handschriften des zehnten Jahrhunderts aus der Freisinger Dombibliothek*, Munich

Davril, A. (1986), 'Johann Drumbl and the origin of the "quem quaeritis". A review article', *Comparative Drama* 20: 65–75

Díaz y Díaz, M. C. (1981), 'Vigilán y Sarracino. Sobre composiciones figurativas en la Rioja del siglo x', in W. Berschin and R. Düchting (eds.), *Lateinische Dichtungen des X. und XI. Jahrhunderts: Festgabe für Walther Bulst*, Heidelberg, pp. 60–92

Díaz y Díaz, M. C. (1991), 'Aspectos léxicos de algunas composiciones del siglo x hispano', in *Lateinische Kultur*, pp. 95–104

Dierkens, A. (1983), 'La Production hagiographique en Lobbes au xe siècle', *Revue Bénédictine* 93: 245–59

Dolbeau, F. (1987), 'Rathier de Vérone', in *Dictionnaire de spiritualité*, Paris, XIII, cols. 135–44

Dronke, P. (1984a), 'Waltharius and the Vita Waltharii', *Beiträge zur Geschichte der deutschen Sprache und Literatur* 106: 390–402

Dronke, P. (1984b), 'Hrotsvitha', in Dronke, *Women Writers of the Middle Ages*, Cambridge, pp. 55–83, 293–7

Drumbl, J. (1981), *Quem quaeritis: teatro sacro dell'alto medioevo* (Biblioteca teatrale 39), Rome

Dunin-Wąsowicz, T. (1972), 'Kulty Świętych w Polsce w x w.', in *Polska w Świecie: szkice z dziejów kultury polskiej*, Warsaw, pp. 61–77

Ferrari, M. (1988), 'La biblioteca del monastero di S. Ambrogio', in *Il monastero di S. Ambrogio: episodi per una storia. Convegno di studi nel XII centenario 784–1984* (Bibliotheca erudita. Studi documenti di storia e Filologia 3), Milan, pp. 82–164

Ferrari, M. (1991), 'Manoscritti e testi fra Lombardia e Germania nel secolo x', in *Lateinische Kultur*, pp. 105–15

Garand, M.-C. (1983), 'Un Manuscrit d'auteur de Raoul Glaber? Observations codicologiques et paléographiques sur le ms. Paris, B.N., lat. 10912', *Scriptorium* 37: 5–28

Gasc, H. (1986), 'Gerbert et la pédagogie des arts libéraux à la fin du dixième siècle', *JMH* 12: 111–21

Gatch, M. (1977), *Preaching and Theology in Anglo-Saxon England: Aelfric and Wulfstan*, Toronto

Gerbert (1985), *Gerberto: scienza, storia e mito*, Bobbio

Gibson, M. (1991), 'Boethius in the tenth century', in *Lateinische Kultur*, pp. 117–24

Golinelli, P. (1991), 'Nota su Raterio agiografo', in *Lateinische Kultur*, pp. 125–31

Gompf, L. (1973), 'Die "Ecbasis cuiusdam captivi" und ihr Publikum', *Mittellateinisches Jahrbuch* 8: 30–42

Haug, A. (1987), *Gesungene und schriftlich dargestellte Sequenzen: Beobachtungen zum Schriftbild der ältesten ostfränkischen Sequenzenhandschriften*, Neuhausen and Stuttgart

Hoffmann, H. (1986), *Buchkunst und Königtum im ottonischen und frühsalischen Reich*, 2 vols.., Stuttgart

Hofmann, H. (1991), 'Profil der lateinischen Historiographie im zehnten Jahrhundert', in *Il secolo di ferro*, pp. 837–902

Holtz, L. (1991), 'Les nouvelles Tendances de la pédagogie grammaticale au xe siècle', in *Lateinische Kultur*, pp. 163–73

Huglo, M. (ed.) (1987), *Musicologie médiévale: notations et séquences*, Paris and Geneva

I, Deug-Su (1983), *L'opera agiografica di Alcuino*, Spoleto

I, Deug-Su (1990), 'La "Vita Rictrudis" di Ubaldo di Saint-Amand: un'agiografia intellettuale e i santi imperfetti', *SM* 31: 545–82

I, Deug-Su (1991), 'L'agiografia del secolo x attraverso le storie d'amore', in *Lateinische Kultur*, pp. 175–84

Il secolo di ferro (1991), *Il secolo di ferro: mito e realtà del secolo X* (*Settimane* 38), Spoleto

Iogna-Prat, D. (1988), *'Agni immaculati': recherches sur les sources hagiographiques relatives à Saint Maieul de Cluny (954–994)*, Paris

Iversen, G. (1987), 'Aspects of the transmission of the "quem quaeritis"', *Text. Transactions of the Society for Textual Scholarship* 3: 155–82

Jacobsen, P. C. (1978), *Flodoard von Reims: sein Leben und seine Dichtung 'De Triumphis Christi'* (Mittellateinische Studien und Texte 10), Leiden

Jacobsen, P. C. (1985), 'Die lateinische Literatur der ottonischen und frühsalischen Zeit', in K. von See (ed.), *Neues Handbuch der Literaturwissenschaft*, Wiesbaden, VI, pp. 437–75

Jacobsen, P. C. (1989), 'Rather von Verona und Lüttich', in K. Ruh, G. Keil, W. Schröder, B. Wachinger and F. J. Worstbrock (eds.), *Die deutsche Literatur des Mittelalters, Verfasserlexikon*, Berlin and New York, VII, cols. 1013–32

Jacobsson, R. M. (1991), 'Les Plus Anciens Tropes des saints. Caractère et fonction', in *Lateinische Kultur*, pp. 203–13

Jacobsson, R. (ed.) (1986), *Pax et sapientia: Studies in Text and Music of Liturgical Tropes and Sequences in Memory of Gordon Anderson* (Studia Latina Stockholmiensia 29), Stockholm

Jeudy, C. (1977), 'Israël le grammarien et la tradition manuscrite du commentaire de Rémi d'Auxerre à l'"Ars minor" de Donat', *SM* 18/2: 185–248

Keynes, S. (1985), 'King Athelstan's books', in M. Lapidge and H. Gneuss (eds.), *Learning and Literature in Anglo-Saxon England: Studies Presented to Peter Clemoes*, Cambridge, pp. 143–201

Kirsch, W. (1991), 'Hrotsvit von Gandersheim als Epikerin', in *Lateinische Kultur*, pp. 215–24

Knowles, D. (1963), *The Monastic Order in England*, 2nd edn, Cambridge

Konrad, R. (1964), *De ortu et tempore Antichristi: Antichristvorstellung und Geschichtsbild des Abtes Adso von Montier-en-Der*, Kallmünz

Kortüm, H.-H. (1985), *Richer von Saint-Remi: Studien zu einem Geschichtsschreiber des 10. Jahrhunderts* (Historische Forschungen 8), Stuttgart

Kratz, D. M. (1991), 'Leo of Naples' Alexander romance', in *Lateinische Kultur*, pp. 225–34

Kürbis B. (1991), 'Slavisch, Lateinisch und Griechisch. An der Schwelle der lateinischen Schriftkultur in Polen', in *Lateinische Kultur*, pp. 235–48

Langosch, K. (1973), *"Waltharius": die Dichtung und die Forschung*, Darmstadt

Lapidge, M. (1988), 'A Frankish scholar in tenth-century England: Frithegod of Canterbury/Fredegaud of Brioude', *ASE* 17: 45–65

Lapidge, M. (1991a), 'Schools, learning and literature in tenth-century England', in *Il secolo di ferro*, pp. 951–98

Lapidge, M. (1991b), 'Tenth-century Anglo-Latin verse hagiography', in *Lateinische Kultur*, pp. 249–60

Lapidge, M. (1992), 'Israel the Grammarian in Anglo-Saxon England', in H. Jan Westra (ed.), *From Athens to Chartres: Neoplatonism and Medieval Thought. Studies in Honour of Edouard Jeauneau*, Leiden and Cologne, pp. 97–114

Lateinische Kultur (1991), *Lateinische Kultur im X. Jahrhundert: Akten des I. Internationalen Mittellateinerkongresses* (Mittellateinisches Jahrbuch 24–5 (1989–90)), ed. W. Berschin, Stuttgart

Le Goff, J. (1957), *Les Intellectuels au moyen âge*, Paris; English trans. T. L. Fagan as *Intellectuals in the Middle Ages*, Oxford (1993)

Leonardi, C. (1960), 'I codici di Marziano Capella', *Aevum* 34: 1–99, 411–524

Leonardi, C. (1967), 'Anastasio Bibliotecario e l'ottavo concilio ecumenico', *SM*, serie terza 8: 59–192

Leonardi, C. (1981), 'S. Gregorio di Spoleto e l'innario umbro-romano dei codici Par. lat. 1092 e Vat. lat. 7172', in W. Berschin and R. Duchting (eds.), *Lateinische Dichtungen des X. und XI. Jahrhundert: Festgabe für Walther Bulst zum 80. Geburtstag*, Heidelberg, pp. 129–48

Leonardi, C. (1987), 'La cultura cassinese al tempo di Bertario', in F. Avagliano (ed.), *Montecassino: dalla prima alla seconda distruzione. Momenti e aspetti di storia cassinese (secc. VI-IX)*, Monte Cassino, pp. 317–29

Leonardi, C. and Menestò, E. (eds..) (1990), *La tradizione dei tropi liturgici*, Spoleto

Lindgren, U. (1991), 'Gerbert von Reims und die Lehre des Quadriviums', in A. von Euw and P. Schreiner (eds.), *Kaiserin Theophanu: Begegnung des Ostens und Westens um die Wende des ersten Jahrtausends*, 2 vols., Cologne, pp. 291–303

Lintzel, M. (1933), *Studien über Liudprand von Cremona*, Berlin

López Pereira, J. E. (1991), 'Continuidad y novedad léxica en las Crónicas Asturianas', in *Lateinische Kultur*, pp. 295–310

Lotter, F. (1983), 'Das Idealbild adliger Laienfrömmigkeit in den Anfängen Clunys: Odos Vita des Grafen Gerald von Aurillac', in W. Lourdaux and D. Verhelst (eds.), *Benedictine Culture 750–1050* (Mediaevalia Lovaniensia series 1, studia 11), Louvain, pp. 79–95

Lowe, E. A. (1980), *The Beneventan Script: A History of the South Italian Minuscule* (Sussidi eruditi 34), II, 2nd edn prepared and enlarged by V. Brown, Rome

McKitterick, R. (1993), 'Ottonian intellectual culture in the tenth century and the role of Theophanu', in *EME* 2: 53–74

Manitius, M. (1923), *Geschichte der lateinischen Literatur des Mittelalters*, II, Munich

Mayr-Harting, H. (1991a, 1991b), *Ottonian Book Illumination: An Historical Study*, 2 vols., London and New York

Mostert, M. (1987), *The Political Theology of Abbo of Fleury: A Study of the Ideas about Society and Law of the Tenth Century Monastic Reform Movement*, Hilversum

Munk Olsen, B. (1991a), *I classici nel canone scolastico altomedievale*, Spoleto

Munk Olsen, B. (1991b), 'Les Classiques au xe siècle', in *Lateinische Kultur*, pp. 341–7

Mütherich, F. (1986), 'The library of Otto III', in P. Ganz (ed.), *The Role of the Book in Medieval Culture* (Bibliologia 3 and 4), 2 vols., Turnhout, II, pp. 11–26

Norberg, D. (1954), *La Poésie latine rythmique du haut moyen âge* (Studia Latina Holmiensia 2), Stockholm

Norberg, D. (1977), *Notes critiques sur l'Hymnarius Severinianus*, Stockholm

Norberg, D. (1988), *Les Vers latins iambiques et trochaïques au moyen âge et leurs répliques rythmiques* (Filologiskt arkiv 35), Stockholm

Oexle, O. G. (1978), 'Die funktionale Dreiteilung der "Gesellschaft" bei Adalbero von Laon', *FmaSt* 12: 1–54

Oldoni, M. (1969), 'Interpretazione del "Chronicon Salernitanum"', *SM*, serie terza 10/2: 3–154

Oldoni, M. (1977), 'Gerberto e la sua storia', *SM*, serie terza 18/2: 629–704

Oldoni, M. (1980, 1983), ' "A fantasia dicitur fantasma" (Gerberto e la sua storia II)', *SM*, serie terza 21/2: 493–622, 24/1: 167–245

Oldoni, M. (1991), ' "Phrenesis" di una letteratura solitaria', in *Il secolo di ferro*, pp. 1034–40

Önnerfors, A. (1988), *Das Waltharius-Epos: Probleme und Hypothesen*, Stockholm

Pittaluga, S. (1991), 'Seneca tragicus nel x secolo. Eugenio Vulgario e la ricezione provocatoria', in *Lateinische Kultur*, pp. 383–91

Poncelet, A. (1908), 'La vie et les œuvres de Thierry de Fleury', *Analecta Bollandiana* 27: 5–27

Ramsay, N., Sparks, M. and Tatton-Brown, T. (eds.) (1992), *St Dunstan: His Life, Times and Cult*, Woodbridge

Riché, P. (1991), 'Les Conditions de la production littéraire: maîtres et écoles', in *Lateinische Kultur*, pp. 413–21

Sansterre, J.-M. (1989), 'Otton III et les saints ascètes de son temps', *Rivista di storia della Chiesa in Italia* 43: 377–412

Schaller, D. (1991), 'Von St. Gallen nach Mainz. Zur Verfasserproblem des Waltharius', in *Lateinische Kultur*, pp. 423–37

Scherbantin, A. (1951), *Satura Menippea. Die Geschichte eines Genos*, Graz

Schleidgen, W.-R. (1977), *Die Überlieferungsgeschichte der Chronik des Regino von Prüm* (Quellen und Abhandlungen zur mittelalterlichen Kirchengeschichte 31), Mainz

Schütze-Pflugk, M. (1972), *Herrscher- und Märtyrerauffassung bei Hrotsvit von Gandersheim*, Wiesbaden

Silagi, G. (ed.) (1985), *Liturgische Tropen: Referate zweier Colloquien des Corpus troporum in München (1983) und Canterbury (1984)*, Munich

Sot, M. (1993), *Un Historien et son église au Xe siècle: Flodoard de Reims*, Paris

Sporbeck, G. (1991), 'Froumund von Tegernsee (um 960–1006/12) als Literat und Lehrer', in G. Wolf (ed.), *Kaiserin Theophanu: Prinzessin aus der Fremde – des Westreichs grosse Kaiserin*, 2 vols., Weimar, I, pp. 369–78

Stafford, P. (1989), *Unification and Conquest: A Political and Social History of England in the Tenth and Eleventh Centuries*, London

Starnawski, J. (1991), 'Über die Anfänge der polnisch-lateinischen Hagiographie', in *Lateinische Kultur*, pp. 457–60

Staubach, N. (1991), 'Historia oder Satira? Zur literarischen Stellung der Antapodosis Liutprands von Cremona', in *Lateinische Kultur*, pp. 461–87

Stella, F. (ed.) (1995), *La poesia carolingia*, with preface by C. Leonardi, Florence

Sutherland, J. N. (1988), *Liudprand of Cremona, Bishop, Diplomat, Historian: Studies of the Man and his Age* (Biblioteca degli 'Studi Medievali' 14), Spoleto

Taviani-Carozzi, H. (1991) *La Principauté lombarde de Salerne (IXe–XIe siècles), pouvoir et société en Italie lombarde méridionale*, Rome

Toubert, P. (1973a, 1973b), *Les Structures du Latium médiéval: le Latium méridional et la Sabine du IXe à la fin du XIIe siècle*, 2 vols., Rome

Traube, L. (1911), *Vorlesungen und Abhandlungen*, II: *Einleitung in die lateinische Philologie des Mittelalters*, ed. P. Lehmann, Munich

van de Vyver, A. (1929), 'Les Etapes du développement philosophique du haut moyen-âge', *Revue Belge de Philologie et d'Histoire* 8: 425–52

Vinay, G. (1978a), 'La "Commedia" di Liutprando', in Vinay, *Alto Medioevo latino*, Naples, pp. 391–432

Vinay, G. (1978b), 'Rosvita: una canonichessa ancora da scoprire?', in Vinay, *Alto Medioevo latino*, Naples, pp. 483–554

Vinay, G. (1978c), 'Haec est Waltharii poesis. Vos salvet Iesus', in Vinay, *Alto Medioevo latino*, Naples, pp. 433–81

Vinay, G. (1989a, 1989b), 'La confessione sdoppiata di Raterio', and 'Una storiografia inattuale', in Vinay, *Peccato che non leggessero Lucrezio: riletture proposte da Claudio Leonardi*, Spoleto, pp. 123–35, 137–50

von den Steinen, W. (1946, 1947), 'Die Anfänge der Sequenzdichtung', *Zeitschrift für schweizerische Kirchengeschichte* 40: 190–212, 241–68; 41: 19–48, 122–62

von den Steinen, W. (1948), *Notker der Dichter und seine geistige Welt*, Berne

von den Steinen, W. (1952), 'Der Waltharius und sein Dichter', *Zeitschrift für deutsches Altertum und deutsche Literatur* 84: 1–47

von den Steinen, W. (1967), *Der Kosmos des Mittelalters*, 2nd edn, Berne and Munich

Wemple, S. F. (1979), *Atto of Vercelli: Church, State and Christian Society in Tenth Century Italy*, Rome

Werner, K. F. (1990), 'Hludovicus Augustus. Gouverner l'empire chrétien. Idées et réalités', in P. Godman and R. Collins (eds.), *Charlemagne's Heir: New Perspectives on the Reign of Louis the Pious (814–40)*, Oxford, pp. 3–123

Werner, K. F. (1991), 'Der Autor der Vita sanctae Chrothildis. Ein Beitrag zur Idee der "heiligen Königin" und des "Römischen Reiches" im x. Jahrhundert', in *Lateinische Kultur*, pp. 517–51

Westerbergh, U. (1957), *Beneventan Ninth Century Poetry* (Studia Latina Stockholmiensia 4), Stockholm

Yorke, B. (ed.) (1988), *Bishop Æthelwold: His Career and Influence*, Woodbridge

Zender, M. (1982), *Die Verehrung des heiligen Maximin von Trier*, Cologne

8 ARTISTS AND PATRONS

Auda, A. (1923), *Etienne de Liège*, Brussels

Belting, H. (1967), 'Probleme der Kunstgeschichte Italiens im Frühmittelalter', *FmaSt* 1: 94–143

Binding, G. (1996), *Der früh- und hochmittelalterliche Bauherr als sapiens architectus*, Darmstadt

Bischoff, B. (1967a), 'Literarisches und künstlerisches Leben in St Emmeram (Regensburg) während des frühen und hohen Mittelalters', in Bischoff, *Mittelalterliche Studien*, Stuttgart, II, pp. 77–115

Bischoff, B. (1967b), *Mittelalterliche Schatzverzeichnisse*, Munich

Boutémy, A. (1950), 'Un Grand Enlumineur du xe siècle, l'abbé Odbert de Saint-Bertin', *Annales de la Fédération Archéologique et Historique de Belge:* 247–54

Brandt, M. (ed.) (1993), *Das Kostbare Evangeliar des Heiligen Bernward*, with contributions by M. Brandt, R. Kahsnitz and H.-J. Schuffels, Munich

Brandt, M. and Eggebrecht, A. (eds.) (1993a, 1993b), *Bernward von Hildesheim und das Zeitalter der Ottonen*, 2 vols., Hildesheim

Buckton, D. (1988), 'Byzantine enamel and the West', in J. D. Howard-Johnston (ed.), *Byzantium and the West c. 850–c. 1200: Proceedings of the XVIII Spring Symposium of Byzantine Studies, Oxford 1984*, Amsterdam, pp. 235–44

Cameron, A. (1987), 'The construction of court ritual: the Byzantine *Book of Ceremonies*', in D. Cannadine and S. Price (eds.), *Rituals of Royalty*, Cambridge, pp. 106–36

Cames, G. (1966), *Byzance et la peinture romane de Germanie*, Paris

Conant, K. J. (1959), *Carolingian and Romanesque Architecture, 800–1200*, Harmondsworth

Demus, O. (1970), *Romanesque Mural Painting*, London

Deshman, R. (1971), 'Otto III and the Warmund Sacramentary: a study in political theology', *Zeitschrift für Kunstgeschichte* 34: 1–20

Deshman, R. (1976), '*Christus rex et magi reges*: kingship and christology in Ottonian and Anglo-Saxon art', *FmaSt* 10: 367–405

Deshman, R. (1995), *The Benedictional of St Ethelwold*, Princeton

Dodwell, C. R. (1971), *Painting in Europe. 800–1200*, Harmondsworth (extensively revised and expanded edition, 1993)

Dodwell, C. R. (1982), *Anglo-Saxon Art: A New Perspective*, Manchester

Dodwell, C. R. and Turner, D. H. (1965), *Reichenau Reconsidered*, London

Dressler, F., Mütherich, F. and Beumann, H. (eds..) (1977, 1978), *Das Evangeliar Ottos III, Clm 4453, der Bayerischen Staatsbibliothek München*, 2 vols., Faksimile- und Textband, Frankfurt

Fillitz, H., Kahsnitz, R. and Kuder, U. (1994), *Zierde für ewige Zeit: das Perikopenbuch Heinrichs II*, Frankfurt am Main

Grabar, A. and Nordenfalk, C. (1957), *Early Medieval Painting*, Lausanne and New York

Hoffmann, H. (1986), *Buchkunst und Königtum im ottonischen und frühsalischen Reich* (Schriften der MGH 30,1/2) 2 vols., Stuttgart

Jantzen, H. (1947), *Ottonische Kunst*, Munich

Keller, H. (1985), 'Herrscherbild und Herrschaftslegitimation: zur Deutung der ottonischen Denkmäler', *FmaSt* 19: 290–311 and plates XXIII–XXIX

Lacarra, J. M. (1950), *Un arancel de aduanas del siglo XI*, Zaragoza

Lasko, P. (1972), *Ars Sacra, 800–1200*, Harmondsworth

Lehmann-Brockhaus, O. (1955), *Die Kunst des X. Jahrhunderts im Lichte der Schriftquellen*, Strasbourg

Magnani, L. (1934), *Le miniature del sacramentario del Ivrea, e di altri codici Warmondiani*, Vatican

Mayr-Harting, H. (1991a, 1991b), *Ottonian Book Illumination: An Historical Study*, 2 vols., London

Mütherich, F. (1973), 'L'Art Ottonien', in L. Grodecki, F. Mütherich, J. Taralon and F. Wormald (eds..), *Le Siècle de l'an Mil*, Paris

Nordenfalk, C. (1972), 'The chronology of the Registrum Master', in A. Rosenauer and G. Weber (eds..), *Kunsthistorische Forschungen für Otto Pächt*, Munich, pp. 62–76

Pevsner, N. (1956), *The Englishness of English Art*, London

Puig i Cadafalch, J. (1935), *La Géographie et les origines du premier art roman*, Paris

Uhlirz, M. (1964), 'Aus dem Kunstleben der Zeit Ottos III', in P. Classen and P. Scheibert (eds..), *Festschrift P. E. Schramm zu seinem siebzigsten Geburtstag*, Wiesbaden, I, pp. 52–6

Wessel, K. (1966), *Die Kreuzigung*, Recklinghausen

Westermann-Angerhausen, H. (1973), *Die Goldschmiedearbeiten der Trierer Egbertwerkstatt*, Trier

Westermann-Angerhausen, H. (1983), 'Blattmasken, Maskenkapitelle, Säulenhäupter', *Boreas* 6: 202–11

Westermann-Angerhausen, H. (1987), 'Spolie und Umfeld in Egberts Trier', *Zeitschrift für Kunstgeschichte* 50: 305–36

Westermann-Angerhausen, H. (1990), 'Das Nagelreliquiar im Trierer Egbertschrein', in H. Krohm and C. Theuerkauf (eds.), *Festschrift für Peter Bloch*, Mainz, pp. 9–23

Williams, J. (1977), *Early Spanish Manuscript Illumination*, London

9 THE OTTONIANS AS KINGS AND EMPERORS

Althoff, G. (1989), 'Königsherrschaft und Konfliktbewältigung im 10. und 11. Jahrhundert', *FmaSt* 23: 265–90

Althoff, G. (1992), *Amicitiae und Pacta: Bündnis, Einung, Politik und Gebetsgedenken im beginnenden 10. Jahrhundert* (Schriften der MGH 32), Munich

Althoff, G. and Keller, H. (1985a, 1985b), *Heinrich I. und Otto der Grosse: Neubeginn auf karolingischen Grundlagen*, 2 vols., Göttingen

Bartmuß, H.-J. (1966), *Die Geburt des ersten deutschen Staates*, Berlin (E)

Bernhardt, J. W. (1993), *Itinerant Kingship and Royal Monasteries in Early Medieval Germany, c. 936–1075*, Cambridge

Beumann, H. (1981), *Der deutsche König als 'Romanorum rex'*, Wiesbaden

Beumann, H. (1987), *Ausgewählte Aufsätze aus den Jahren 1966–1986*, Sigmaringen

Beumann, H. (1991), *Die Ottonen*, 2nd edn, Stuttgart

Brühl, C. (1990), *Deutschland – Frankreich: die Geburt zweier Völker*, Cologne

Corbet, P. (1986), *Les Saints ottoniens*, Sigmaringen

Dümmler, E. (1888), *Geschichte des ostfränkischen Reiches*, III: *Die letzten Karolinger, Konrad I.*, 2nd edn, Leipzig, repr. Darmstadt 1963

Eggert, W. (1970), '919 – Geburts- oder Krisenjahr des mittelalterlichen deutschen Reiches', *Zeitschrift für Geschichtswissenschaft* 17: 46–65

Eggert, W. (1973), *Das ostfränkisch-deutsche Reich in der Auffassung seiner Zeitgenossen*, Berlin (E)

Eggert, W. (1992), 'Ostfränkisch – fränkisch – sächsisch – römisch – deutsch. Zur Benennung des rechtsrheinisch-nordalpinen Reiches bis zum Investiturstreit', *FmaSt* 26: 302–17

Eggert, W. and Pätzold, B. (1984), *Wir-Gefühl und Regnum Saxonum bei frühmittelalterlichen Geschichtsschreibern*, Weimar

Ehlers, J. (1994), *Die Entstehung des deutschen Reiches*, Munich

Eibl, E.-M. (1984), 'Zur Stellung Bayerns und Rheinfrankens im Reiche Arnulfs von Kärnten', *Jahrbuch für die Geschichte des Feudalismus* 8: 73–113

Engels, O. (1989), 'Der Reichsbischof in ottonischer und frühsalischer Zeit', in I. Crusius (ed.), *Beiträge zur Geschichte und Kultur der mittelalterlichen Germania Sacra*, Göttingen, pp. 135–75

Erkens, F.-R. (1982), 'Fürstliche Opposition in ottonisch-salischer Zeit', *AKG* 64: 307–70

Finck von Finckenstein, A. Graf (1989), *Bischof und Reich: Unteruchungen zum Integrationsprozeß des ottonisch-frühsalischen Reiches*, Sigmaringen

Fleckenstein, J. (1966), *Die Hofkapelle der deutschen Könige*, ii: *Die Hofkapelle im Rahmen der ottonisch-salischen Reichskirche*, Stuttgart

Fleckenstein, J. (1980), *Grundlagen und Beginn der deutschen Geschichte*, 2nd edn, Göttingen

Fleckenstein, J. (1985), 'Problematik und Gestalt der ottonisch-salischen Reichskirche', in Schmid (1985b), pp. 83–98

Fleckenstein, J. (1987), *Über die Anfänge der deutschen Geschichte*, Opladen

Fried, J. (1989), *Otto III. und Boleslaw Chrobry*, Stuttgart

Fried J. (1994), *Der Weg in die Geschichte: die Ursprünge Deutschlands bis 1024*, Berlin

Fritze, W. H. (1984), 'Der slawische Aufstand von 983 – eine Schicksalswende in der Geschichte Mitteleuropas', in E. Henning and W. Vogel (eds.), *Festschrift der Landesgeschichtlichen Vereinigung zu ihrem hundertjährigen Bestehen*, Berlin, pp. 9–55

Fuhrmann, H. (1987), 'Die Synode von Hohenaltheim (916) – quellenkritisch betrachtet', *DA* 43: 440–68

Gebhardt, B., ed. (1970), *Handbuch der deutschen Geschichte*, i, 9th edn by H. Grundmann, Stuttgart

Giesebrecht, W. von (1881, 1885), *Geschichte der deutschen Kaiserzeit*, i: *Gründung des Kaiserthums*; ii: *Blüthe des Kaiserthums*, 5th edn, Leipzig

Glocker, W. (1989), *Die Verwandten der Ottonen und ihre Bedeutung in der Politik*, Cologne and Vienna

Hermann, J., Bartmuß, H.-J., Müller-Mertens, E. *et al.* (1982), *Deutsche Geschichte von den Anfängen bis zur Ausbildung des Feudalismus Mitte des 11. Jahrhunderts* (Deutsche Geschichte in zwölf Bänden 1), Berlin (E)

Hirsch, S., Pabst, H., and Bresslau, H. (1862–75), *Jahrbücher des Deutschen Reiches unter Heinrich II.*, 3 vols., Leipzig, repr. Berlin 1975

Hlawitschka, E. (1968), *Lotharingien und das Reich an der Schwelle der deutschen Geschichte*, Stuttgart

Hlawitschka, E. (1986), *Vom Frankenreich zur Formierung der europäischen Staaten- und Völkergemeinschaft 840–1046*, Darmstadt

Hoffmann, H. (1990), 'Grafschaften in Bischofshand', *DA* 46: 375–480

Holtzmann, R. (1943), *Geschichte der sächsischen Kaierzeit*, 2nd edn, Munich, repr. Darmstadt 1967

Karpf, E. (1985), *Herrscherlegitimation und Reichsbegriff in der ottonischen Geschichtsschreibung des 10. Jahrhunderts*, Wiesbaden

Keller, H. (1982), 'Reichsstruktur und Herrschaftsauffassung in ottonisch-frühsalischer Zeit', *FmaSt* 16: 74–128

Keller, H. (1985a), 'Grundlagen ottonischer Königsherrschaft', in Schmid (1985b), pp. 17–34

Keller, H. (1985b), 'Herrscherbild und Herrschaftslegitimation. Zur Deutung der otto-nischen Denkmäler', *FmaSt* 19: 290–311

Keller, H. (1989a), 'Gruppenbildung, Herrschaftsorganisation und Schriftkultur unter den Ottonen', preface by H. Keller, *FmaSt* 23: 245–317

Keller, H. (1989b), 'Zum Charakter der "Staatlichkeit" zwischen karolingischer Reichsreform und hochmittelalterlichem Herrschaftsaufbau', *FmaSt* 23: 248–64

Köpke, R. and Dümmler, E. (1876), *Kaiser Otto der Große*, Leipzig, repr. Darmstadt 1962

Lamprecht, K. (1904), *Deutsche Geschichte*, ii, 3rd edn, Freiburg

Leyser, K. (1968), 'Henry I and the beginnings of the Saxon empire', *EHR* 83: 1–32

Leyser, K. (1979), *Rule and Conflict in an Early Medieval Society: Ottonian Saxony*, London

Ludat, H. (1991), *An Elbe und Oder um das Jahr 1000: Skizzen zur Politik des Ottonenreiches und der slawischen Mächte in Mitteleuropa*, Cologne

Müller-Mertens, E. (1968), 'Die Deutschen. Zur Rolle der politischen Formung bei ihrer Volkwerdung' in *Germanen – Slawen – Deutsche: Forschungen zur ihrer Ethnogenese*, Berlin (E)

Müller-Mertens, E. (1970), *Regnum Teutonicum*, Berlin (E)

Müller-Mertens, E. (1980), *Die Reichsstruktur im Spiegel der Herrschaftspraxis Ottos des Grossen: Mit historiographischen Prolegomena zur Frage Feudalstaat auf deutschem Boden, seit wann deutscher Feudalstaat?*, Berlin (E)

Müller-Mertens, E. (1990), 'Romanum imperium und regnum Teutonicorum. Der hochmittelalterliche Reichsverband im Verhältnis zum Karolingerreich', *Jahrbuch für die Geschichte des Feudalismus* 14: 47–54

Müller-Mertens, E. and Huschner, W. (1992), *Reichsintegration im Spiegel der Herrschafspraxis Kaiser Konrads II.*, Weimar

Pauler, R. (1982), *Das Regnum Italiae in ottonischer Zeit*, Tübingen

Prinz, F. (1985), *Grundlagen und Anfänge: Deutschland bis 1056*, Munich

Reuter, T. (1991), *Germany in the Early Middle Ages, c. 800–1056*, London and New York

Schieffer, R. (1989), 'Der ottonische Reichsepiskopat zwischen Königtum und Adel', *FmaSt* 23: 291–301

Schlesinger, W. (1974), 'Die Königserhebung Heinrichs I., der Beginn der deutschen Geschichte und die deutsche Geschichtswissenschaft', in Magistrat der Stadt Fritzlar (ed.), *Fritzlar im Mittelalter*, Fritzlar, pp. 121–43

Schlesinger, W. (1987), *Ausgewählte Aufsätze von Walter Schlesinger 1965–1979*, ed. H. Patze and F. Schwind, Sigmaringen

Schmid, K. (1964), 'Die Thronfolge der Ottonen', *ZRG GA* 81: 80–163

Schmid, K. (1985a), 'Das Problem der Unteilbarkeit des Reiches', in Schmid (1985b), pp. 1–16

Schmid, K. (ed.) (1985b), *Reich und Kirche vor dem Investiturstreit*, Sigmaringen

Stern, L. and Bartmuss, H.-J. (1973), *Deutschland in der Feudalepoche von der Wende des 5./6. Jahrhunderts bis zur Mitte des 11. Jahrhunderts*, 3rd edn, Berlin (E)

Uhlirz, K. and M. (1902, 1954), *Jahrbücher des Deutschen Reiches unter Otto II. und Otto III.*, Leipzig and Berlin (W)

von Euw, A. and Schreiner, P. (eds.) (1991), *Kaiserin Theophanu: Begegnung des Ostens und Westens um die Wende des ersten Jahrtausends*, 2 vols., Cologne

Waitz, G. (1885), *Jahrbücher des Deutschen Reiches unter König Heinrich I. 919–936*, 3rd edn, Leipzig, repr. Darmstadt 1963

Weinfurter, S. (1986), 'Die Zentralisierung der Herrschaftsgewalt im Reich durch Heinrich II. ', *HJb* 106: 241–97

Zimmermann, H. (1970), *Das dunkle Jahrhundert*, Graz

10 SAXONY AND THE ELBE SLAVS IN THE TENTH CENTURY

Althoff, G. (1982a), 'Das Bett des Königs in Magdeburg. Zu Thietmar II, 28', in H. Maurer and H. Patze (eds.), *Festschrift für B. Schwineköper zu seinem siebzigsten Geburtstag*, Sigmaringen, pp. 141–53

Althoff, G. (1982b), 'Zur Frage nach der Organisation sächsischer *coniurationes* in der Ottonenzeit', *FmaSt* 16: 129–42

Althoff, G. (1984), *Adels- und Königsfamilien im Spiegel ihrer Memorialüberlieferung: Studien zum Totengedenken der Billunger und Ottonen*, Munich

Althoff, G. (1988), 'Causa scribendi und Darstellungsabsicht: Die Lebensbeschreibungen der Königin Mathilde und andere Beispiele', in M. Borgolte and H. Spilling (eds.), *Litterae medii aevi: Festschrift für J. Autenrieth*, Sigmaringen, pp. 117–33

Althoff, G. (1990), *Verwandte, Freunde und Getreue: zum politischen Stellenwert der Gruppenbindungen im früheren Mittelalter*, Darmstadt

Althoff, G. (1991a), 'Die Billunger in der Salierzeit', in S. Weinfurter (ed.), *Die Salier und das Reich*, I: *Salier, Adel und Reichsverfassung*, Sigmaringen, pp. 309–30

Althoff, G. (1991b), 'Gandersheim und Quedlinburg. Ottonische Frauenklöster als Herrschafts- und Überlieferungszentren', *FmaSt* 25: 123–44

Althoff, G., and Keller, H. (1985), *Heinrich I. und Otto der Große: Neubeginn auf karolingischem Erbe*, 2 vols., Göttingen and Zurich

Aubin, H. (1939), *Zur Erforschung der deutschen Ostbewegung*, Leipzig

Aubin, H. (1959), *Die Ostgrenze des alten deutschen Reiches: Entstehung und staatsrechtlicher Charakter*, Darmstadt

Becher, M. (1996), *Rex, Dux und Gens: Untersuchungen zur Entstehung des sächsischen Herzogtums im 9. und 10. Jahrhundert*, Husum

Berges, W. (1963), 'Zur Geschichte des Werla-Goslarer Reichsbezirks vom neunten bis zum elften Jahrhundert', *Deutsche Königspfalzen: Beiträge zu ihrer historischen und archäologischen Erforschung* 1: 113–57

Beumann, H. (1948/1971), 'Die sakrale Legitimierung des Herrschers im Denken der ottonischen Zeit', *ZRG GA* 66: 1–45; also with supplement in E. Hlawitschka (ed.), *Königswahl und Thronfolge in ottonisch-frühdeutscher Zeit*, Darmstadt, 1971, pp. 148–98

Beumann, H. (1950), *Widukind von Korvei: Untersuchungen zur Geschichtsschreibung und Ideengeschichte des 10. Jahrhunderts*, Weimar

Beumann, H. (1969/1972), 'Historiographische Konzeption und politische Ziele Widukinds von Corvey', *Settimane* 17, Spoleto, pp. 875–94; reprinted in H. Beumann, *Wissenschaft vom Mittelalter: Ausgewählte Aufsätze*, Cologne, 1972, pp. 71–108

Beumann, H. (1974/1987), 'Laurentius und Mauritius. Zu den missionspolitischen Folgen des Ungarnsieges Ottos des Grossen', in H. Beumann (ed.), *Festschrift für W. Schlesinger*, Cologne, pp. 238–75; also in H. Beumann, *Ausgewählte Aufsätze aus den Jahren 1966–1986: Festgabe zu seinem 75. Geburtstag*, ed. J. Petersohn and R. Schmidt, Sigmaringen, 1987, pp. 139–76

Beumann, H. (1982/1987), 'Die Hagiographie "bewältigt" Unterwerfung und

Christianisierung der Sachsen durch Karl den Grossen', *Settimane* 28, Spoleto, pp. 129–63; reprinted in H. Beumann, *Ausgewählte Aufsätze aus den Jahren 1966–1986: Festgabe zu seinem 75. Geburtstag*, ed. J. Petersohn and R. Schmidt, Sigmaringen, 1987, pp. 289–323

Beumann, H., and W. Schlesinger (1955/1961), 'Urkundenstudien zur deutschen Ostpolitik unter Otto III. ', *AfD* 1: 132–56; reprinted with additional material in W. Schlesinger, *Mitteldeutsche Beiträge zur deutschen Verfassungsgeschichte des Mittelalters*, Cologne, 1961, pp. 306–412, 479–87

Bohm, E. (1986), 'Elb- und Ostseeslaven', *Lexikon des Mittelalters*, III: *Codex Wintoniensis bis Erziehungs- und Bildungswesen*, Munich and Zurich, cols. 1779–88

Bornscheuer, L. (1968), *Miseriae regum: Untersuchungen zum Krisen- und Todesgedanken in den herrschaftstheologischen Vorstellungen der ottonisch-salischen Zeit*, Berlin

Brackmann, A. (1926/1967), 'Die Ostpolitik Ottos des Großen', *HZ* 134: 242–56; repr. in A. Brackmann, *Gesammelte Aufsätze*, 2nd edn, Darmstadt, 1967, pp. 140–53, together with further articles under the heading 'Reichspolitik und Ostpolitik'

Brüske, W. (1983), *Untersuchungen zur Geschichte des Lutizenbundes: deutsch-wendische Beziehungen des 10.-12. Jahrhunderts*, 2nd edn, Cologne and Vienna

Burleigh, M. (1988), *Germany Turns Eastwards: A Study of* Ostforschung *in the Third Reich*, Cambridge

Büttner, H. (1956), 'Die Burgenbauordnung Heinrichs I.', *Blätter für deutsche Landesgeschichte* 92: 1–17

Claude, D. (1972a, 1972b), *Geschichte des Erzbistums Magdeburg bis in das 12. Jahrhundert*, 2 vols., Cologne

Corbet, P. (1986), *Les Saints ottoniens: sainteté dynastique, sainteté royale et sainteté féminine autour de l'an mil* (Beihefte der Francia 15), Sigmaringen

Engels, O. (1983), 'Mission und Friede an der Reichsgrenze im Hochmittelalter', in H. Mordek (ed.), *Aus Kirche und Reich: Studien zu Theologie, Politik und Recht im Mittelalter. Festschrift für F. Kempf*, Sigmaringen, pp. 201–24

Engels, O. (1991), 'Das Reich der Salier – Entwicklungslinien', in S. Weinfurter (ed.), *Die Salier und das Reich*, III: *Gesellschaftlicher und ideengeschichtlicher Wandel im Reich der Salier*, Sigmaringen, pp. 479–541

Erdmann, C. (1943), 'Die Burgenordnung Heinrichs I. ', *DA* 6: 59–101; also in C. Erdmann, *Ottonische Studien*, Darmstadt, 1968, pp. 131–73

Fischer, F. M. (1938), *Politiker um Otto den Grossen*, Berlin

Fried, J. (1989), *Otto III. und Boleslaw Chrobry: Das Widmungsbild des Aachener Evangeliars, der 'Akt von Gnesen' und das frühe polnische und ungarische Königtum*, Stuttgart

Fritze, W. H. (1984), 'Der slawische Aufstand von 983 – eine Schicksalswende in der Geschichte Mitteleuropas', in E. Henning and W. Vogel (eds.), *Festschrift der Landesgeschichtlichen Vereinigung für die Mark Brandenburg zu ihrem 100–jährigen Bestehen, 1884–1984*, Berlin, pp. 9–55

Giese, W. (1979), *Der Stamm der Sachsen und das Reich in ottonischer und salischer Zeit: Studien zum Einfluß des Sachsenstammes auf die politische Geschichte des deutschen Reiches im 10. und 11. Jahrhundert und zu ihrer Stellung im Reichsgefüge mit einem Ausblick auf das 12. und 13. Jahrhundert*, Wiesbaden

Görich, K. (1991), 'Ein Erzbistum in Prag oder Gnesen?', *Zeitschrift für Ostforschung* 40: 10–27

Hampe, K. (1921), *Der Zug nach dem Osten: die kolonisatorische Großtat des deutschen Volkes im Mittelalter*, Leipzig

Hauck, K. (1954/1965), 'Haus- und sippengebundene Literatur mittelalterlicher Adelsgeschlechter, von den Adelssatiren des 11. und 12. Jahrhunderts her erläutert', *MIÖG* 62: 121–45; revised version in W. Lammers (ed.), *Geschichtsdenken und Geschichtsbild im Mittelalter*, Darmstadt, 1965, pp. 165–99; English trans. in T. Reuter (ed.), *The Medieval Nobility*, Amsterdam, 1979, pp. 61–85

Hermann, J. (ed.) (1985), *Die Slawen in Deutschland: Geschichte und Kultur der slawischen Stämme westlich von der Oder und Neisse vom 6. bis 12. Jahrhundert*, Berlin

Hlawitschka, E. (1987), *Untersuchungen zu den Thronwechseln der ersten Hälfte des 11. Jahrhunderts und zur Adelsgeschichte Süddeutschlands: Zugleich klärende Forschungen um 'Kuno von Öhningen'*, Sigmaringen

Hoffmann, H. (1986a, 1986b), *Buchkunst und Königtum im ottonischen und frühsalischen Reich* (Schriften der MGH 30), 2 vols., Stuttgart

Holtzmann, R. (1925), 'Die Quedlinburger Annalen', *Sachsen und Anhalt* 1: 64–125

Jordan, K. (1958), 'Herzogtum und Stamm in Sachsen während des hohen Mittelalters', *Niedersächsisches Jahrbuch für Landesgeschichte* 30: 1–27

Jordan, K. (1970), 'Sachsen und das deutsche Königtum im hohen Mittelalter', *HZ* 210: 529–59

Karpf, E. (1985), *Herrscherlegitimation und Reichsbegriff in der ottonischen Geschichtsschreibung des 10. Jahrhundert*, Stuttgart

Keller, H. (1964), 'Das Kaisertum Ottos des Großen im Verständnis seiner Zeit', *DA* 20: 325–88

Keller, H. (1985a), 'Grundlagen ottonischer Königsherrschaft', in K. Schmid (ed.), *Reich und Kirche vor dem Investiturstreit: Vorträge beim wissenschaftlichen Kolloquium aus Anlaß des 80. Geburtstags von Gerd Tellenbach*, Sigmaringen, pp. 17–34

Keller, H. (1985b), 'Herrscherbild und Herrschaftslegitimation. Zur Deutung der ottonischen Denkmäler', *FmaSt* 19: 290–311

Keller, H. (1989), 'Zum Charakter der "Staatlichkeit" zwischen karolingischer Reichsreform und hochmittelalterlichem Herrschaftsausbau', *FmaSt* 23: 248–64

Leyser, K. J. (1968a/1982), 'Henry I and the beginnings of the Saxon empire', *EHR* 83: 1–32; also in K. J. Leyser, *Medieval Germany and its Neighbours 900–1250*, London, 1982, pp. 11–42

Leyser, K. J. (1968b/1982), 'The German aristocracy from the ninth to the early twelfth century: a historical and cultural sketch', *Past and Present* 41: 25–53; also in K. J. Leyser, *Medieval Germany and its Neighbours 900–1250*, London, 1982, pp. 161–89

Leyser, K. J. (1979), *Rule and Conflict in an Early Medieval Society: Ottonian Saxony*, Oxford

Lintzel, M. (1933/1961), 'Die Schlacht bei Riade und die Anfänge des deutschen Staates', *Sachsen und Anhalt* 9: 27–51; also in M. Lintzel, *Ausgewählte Schriften*, II: *Zur Karolinger- und Ottonenzeit, zum hohen und späten Mittelalter, zur Literaturgeschichte*, Berlin, 1961, pp. 92–121

Lintzel, M. (1956), 'Die Mathilden-Viten und das Wahrheitsproblem in der Überlieferung der Ottonenzeit', *AKG* 38: 152–66

Lippelt, H. (1973), *Thietmar von Merseburg: Geschichtsschreiber und Chronist*, Cologne

Lübke, C. (1984–8), *Regesten zur Geschichte der Slaven an Elbe und Oder*, 5 vols., Berlin

Ludat, H. (1938/1969), 'Mieszkos Tributpflicht bis zur Warthe', *Deutsches Archiv für*

Landes- und Volksforschung 2: 380–5; also in H. Ludat, *Deutsch-slawische Frühzeit und modernes polnisches Geschichtsbewusstsein. Ausgewählte Aufsätze*, Cologne, 1969, pp. 185–92

Ludat, H. (1968/1982), 'Elbslaven und Elbmarken als Problem der europäischen Geschichte', in W. Schlesinger (ed.), *Festschrift für Friedrich von Zahn*, Cologne, 1, pp. 39–49; also in H. Ludat, *Slaven und Deutsche im Mittelalter: Ausgewählte Aufsätze zu Fragen ihrer politischen, sozialen und kulturellen Beziehungen*, Cologne, 1982, pp. 1–13

Ludat, H. (1971), *An Elbe und Oder um das Jahr 1000: Skizzen zur Politik des Ottonenreiches und der slavischen Mächte in Mitteleuropa*, Cologne and Vienna

Lukas, G. (1940), *Die deutsche Politik gegen die Elbslaven vom Jahre 982 bis zum Ende der Polenkriege Heinrichs II.*, Halle

Lüpke, S. (1937), *Die Markgrafen der sächsischen Ostmark in der Zeit von Gero bis zum Beginn des Investiturstreits*, Halle

Rieckenberg, H.-J. (1941/1965), 'Königsstraße und Königsgut in liudolfingischer und frühsalischer Zeit (919–1056)', *Archiv für Urkundenforschung* 17: 32–154, printed separately, Darmstadt, 1965

Schlesinger, W. (1937/1961), 'Burgen und Burgbezirke. Beobachtungen im mitteldeutschen Osten', in W. Emmerich (ed.), *Von Land und Kultur: Beiträge zur Geschichte des mitteldeutschen Ostens zum 70. Geburtstag R. Kötzsches*, Leipzig, pp. 77–105; repr. with additional material in W. Schlesinger, *Mitteldeutsche Beiträge zur deutschen Verfassungsgeschichte des Mittelalters*, Cologne, 1961, pp. 158–87, 473–7

Schlesinger, W. (1962a, 1962b), *Kirchengeschichte Sachsens*, 2 vols., Cologne

Schlesinger, W. (1974), 'Die sogenannte Nachwahl Heinrichs II. in Merseburg', in F. Prinz, F.-J. Schmale and F. Scheibt (eds.), *Geschichte und Gesellschaft: Festschrift für K. Bosl*, Stuttgart, pp. 350–69

Schneider, R. (1972), 'Die Königserhebung Heinrichs II. im Jahre 1002', *DA* 28: 74–104

Schulze, H. K. (1983), 'Burgward, Burgwardverfassung', *Lexikon des Mittelalters*, 11: *Bettlerwesen bis Codex von Valencia*, Munich and Zurich, cols. 1101–3

von Stetten, W. (1954), 'Der Niederschlag liudolfingischer Hausüberlieferung in den ersten Werken der ottonischen Geschichtsschreibung', typescript dissertation, University of Erlangen

Wattenbach, W., and Holtzmann, R. (1967), *Deutschlands Geschichtsquellen im Mittelalter: die Zeit der Sachsen und Salier*, 1: *Das Zeitalter des ottonischen Staates (900–1050)*, new edn by F.-J. Schmale, Darmstadt

Weinfurter, S. (1986), 'Die Zentralisierung der Herrschaftsgewalt im Reich unter Kaiser Heinrich II. ', *HJb* 106: 241–97

Wilson, K. M. (ed.) (1987), *Hrotsvit of Gandersheim: rara avis in Saxonia?*, Ann Arbor, Michigan

Wippermann, W. (1981), *Der 'deutsche Drang nach Osten': Ideologie und Wirklichkeit eines politischen Schlagwortes*, Darmstadt

11 BAVARIA IN THE TENTH AND EARLY ELEVENTH CENTURIES

Althoff, G. (1990), *Verwandte, Freunde und Getreue: zum politischen Stellenwert der Gruppenbindungen im früheren Mittelalter*, Darmstadt

Althoff, G. and Keller, H. (1985), *Heinrich I. und Otto der Große: Neubeginn auf karolingischem Erbe*, Göttingen.

Bresslau, H. (1958), *Handbuch der Urkundenlehre für Deutschland und Italien*, 3rd edn, 1, Berlin

Brühl, C. (1990), *Deutschland – Frankreich: die Geburt zweier Völker*, Cologne and Vienna

Brunhölzl, F. (1981), 'Die lateinische Literatur', in Spindler (1981), pp. 582–607

Brunner, K. (1973), 'Die fränkischen Fürstentitel im neunten und zehnten Jahrhundert', in H. Wolfram (ed.), *Intitulatio II* (MIÖG EB 24), Vienna, pp. 179–340

Brunner, K. (1979), *Oppositionelle Gruppen im Karolingerreich* (Veröffentlichungen des Instituts für österreichische Geschichtsforschung 25), Vienna

Brunner, K. (1991), 'Der österreichische Donauraum zur Zeit der Magyarenherrschaft', in *Österreich im Hochmittelalter (907 bis 1246)* (Veröffentlichungen der Kommission für die Geschichte Österreichs 17), Vienna, pp. 49–61

Dienst, H. (1978), 'Die Dynastie der Babenberger und ihre Anfänge in Österreich', in *Das babenbergische Österreich* (Schriften des Instituts für Österreichkunde 33), Vienna, pp. 63–102

Dienst, H. (1991), 'Werden und Entwicklung der babenbergischen Mark', in *Österreich im Hochmittelalter (907 bis 1246)* (Veröffentlichungen der Kommission für die Geschichte Österreichs 17), Vienna, pp. 63–102

Dopsch, H. (1981, 1983), *Geschichte Salzburgs*, 1, parts 1 and 2, Salzburg

Eggert, W. (1973), *Das ostfränkisch-deutsche Reich in der Auffassung seiner Zeitgenossen* (Forschungen zur mittelalterlichen Geschichte 21), Vienna, Cologne and Graz

Eibl, E. M. (1984), 'Zur Stellung Bayerns und Rheinfrankens im Reiche Arnulfs von Kärnten', *Jahrbuch für Geschichte des Feudalismus* 8: 73–113

Fichtenau, H. (1971), *Das Urkundenwesen in Österreich* (MIÖG EB 23), Vienna

Fleckenstein, J. (1959), *Die Hofkapelle der deutschen Könige*, 1: *Grundlegung: die karolingische Hofkapelle* (Schriften der MGH 16/1), Stuttgart

Fried, J. (1989a), *Otto III. und Boleslaw Chrobry: das Widmungsbild des Aachener Evangeliars, der 'Akt von Gnesen' und das frühe polnische und ungarische Königtum* (Frankfurter Historische Abhandlungen 33), Stuttgart

Fried, J. (1989b), 'Endzeiterwartung um die Jahrtausendwende', *DA* 45: 381–473

Fuhrmann, H. (1987), 'Die Synode von Hohenaltheim (916) – quellenkundlich betrachtet', *DA* 43: 440–68

Glaser, H. (1981), 'Das geistige Leben. Wissenschaft und Bildung', in Spindler (1981), pp. 519–38

Grönbech, V. (1931), *The Culture of the Teutons*, 2 vols.., London and Copenhagen

Györffy, G. (1988), *König Stephan der Heilige*, Budapest

Hauck, K. (1967), 'Die Ottonen und Aachen, 876 bis 936', in W. Braunfels and P. E. Schramm (eds.), *Karl der Grosse: Lebenswerk und Nachleben*, IV: *Das Nachleben*, Düsseldorf, pp. 39–53

Keller, H. (1966), 'Zum Sturz Karls III. Über die Rolle Liutwards von Vercelli und Liutberts von Mainz, Arnulf von Kärnten und der ostfränkischen Grossen bei der Absetzung des Kaisers', *DA* 22: 333–84

Lechner, K. (1976), *Die Babenberger* (Veröffentlichungen des Instituts für österreichische Geschichtsforschung 23), Vienna

Lhotsky, A. (1963), *Quellenkunde zur mittelalterlichen Geschichte Österreichs* (MIÖG EB 19), Vienna

Mitterauer, M. (1988), '"Senioris sui nomine". Zur Verbreitung von Fürstennamen durch das Lehenswesen', *MIÖG* 96: 275–330

Pohl, W. (1988), *Die Awaren: ein Steppenvolk in Mitteleuropa 587–822 n. Chr.*, Munich

Prinz, F. (1981), 'Die innere Entwicklung: Staat, Gesellschaft, Kirche, Wirtschaft', in Spindler (1981), pp. 352–518

Reiffenstein, I. (1981), 'Das geistige Leben. Die althochdeutsche Literatur', in Spindler (1981), pp. 607–23

Reindel, K. (1953), *Die bayerischen Luitpoldinger, 893–989: Sammlung und Erläuterung der Quellen* (Quellen und Erörterungen zur Bayerischen Geschichte N.F. 11), Munich

Reindel, K. (1956), 'Herzog Arnulf und das Regnum Bavariae', in *Die Entstehung des deutschen Reiches*, ed. H. Kämpf (Wege der Forschung 1), Darmstadt, pp. 213–88

Reindel, K. (1981), 'Das Zeitalter der Agilolfinger (bis 788)', and 'Bayern vom Zeitalter der Karolinger bis zum Ende der Welfenherrschaft (788–1180)', in Spindler (1981), pp. 99–349

Riedmann, J. (1990), 'Mittelalter', in *Geschichte des Landes Tirol*, 2nd edn, Bozen, Innsbruck and Vienna, 1, pp. 267–637

Schmid, A. (1976), *Das Bild des Bayernherzogs Arnulf (907–937) in der deutschen Geschichtsschreibung von seinen Zeitgenossen bis zu Wilhelm von Giesebrecht*, Kallmünz (Opf.)

Schneider, H. (1991), 'Eine Freisinger Synodalpredigt aus der Zeit der Ungarneinfälle (Clm 6245)', in H. Mordek (ed.), *Papsttum, Kirche und Recht im Mittelalter: Festschrift für Horst Fuhrmann*, Tübingen, pp. 95–115

Schneider, R. (1964), *Brüdergemeinde und Schwurfreundschaft* (Historische Studien 388), Lübeck and Hamburg

Schulze, H. K. (1973), *Die Grafschaftsverfassung der Karolingerzeit in den Gebieten östlich des Rheins* (Schriften zur Verfassungsgeschichte 19), Berlin

Schünemann, K. (1923), *Die Deutschen in Ungarn bis zum 12. Jahrhundert* (Ungarische Bibliothek 18), Berlin and Leipzig

Semmler, J. (1990), 'Francia Saxoniaque oder die ostfränkische Reichsteilung von 865/76 und die Folgen', *DA* 46: 337–74

Spindler, M. (ed.) (1981), *Handbuch der bayerischen Geschichte*, 1, 2nd edn, Munich

Störmer, W. (1973), *Früher Adel* (Monographien zur Geschichte des Mittelalters 6, parts 1 und 2), Stuttgart

Störmer, W. (1988), 'Zum Wandel der Herrschaftsverhältnisse und inneren Strukturen Bayerns im 10. Jahrhundert', in F. Seibt (ed.), *Gesellschaftsgeschichte (Festschrift für Karl Bosl zum 80. Geburtstag)*, Munich, 11, pp. 267–85

Störmer, W. (1991), 'Bayern und der bayerische Herzog im 11. Jahrhundert', in S. Weinfurter (ed.), *Die Salier und das Reich*, Sigmaringen, 1, pp. 503–47

Tyroller, F. (1953/4), 'Zu den Säkularisationen des Herzogs Arnulf', *StMGBO* 65: 303–14

Weinfurter, S. (1986), 'Die Zentralisierung der Herrschaftsgewalt im Reich durch Kaiser Heinrich II. ', *HJb* 106: 241–97

Weissensteiner, J. (1983), *Tegernsee, die Bayern und Österreich* (Archiv für österreichische Geschichte 133), Vienna

Wenskus, R. (1976), *Sächsischer Stammesadel und fränkischer Reichsadel* (Abhandlungen der Akademie der Wissenschaften in Göttingen, Phil. hist. Kl., 3 Folge, no. 93), Göttingen

Wolfram, H. (1971), 'The shaping of the early medieval principality as non-royal rulership', *Viator* 2: 33–51

Wolfram, H. (1987), *Die Geburt Mitteleuropas: Geschichte Österreichs vor seiner Entstehung*, Vienna and Berlin

Wolfram, H. (1988), *History of the Goths*, Berkeley, Los Angeles and London
Wolfram, H. (1991), 'Bayern, das ist das Land, genannt die Němci', *Österreichische Osthefte* 33: 598–604

12   LOTHARINGIA

Avouerie (1984), *L'Avouerie en Lotharingie* (Publications de la section historique de l'Institut grand-ducal de Luxembourg 98), Luxembourg
Boshof, E. (1989), 'Kloster und Bischof in Lotharingien', in R. Kottje and H. Maurer (eds.), *Monastische Reformen im 9. und 10. Jahrhundert* (Vorträge und Forschungen 38), Sigmaringen, pp. 197–245
Dierkens, A. (1985), *Abbayes et chapitres entre Sambre et Meuse (VIIe–XIe siècles): contribution à l'histoire religieuse des campagnes du haut moyen âge*, Sigmaringen
Dollinger-Léonard, Y. (1958), 'De la cité romaine à la ville médiévale dans la région de la Moselle et de la Haute-Meuse', in *Studien zu den Anfängen des europäischen Städtewesens* (Vorträge und Forschungen 4), Lindau, pp. 195–226
Génicot, L. (1975), 'Monastères et principautés en Lotharingie du xe au xiiie siècle', in L. Génicot (ed.), *Etudes sur les principautés lotharingiennes*, Louvain, pp. 59–139
Gérard (1960), *Gérard de Brogne et son œuvre réformatrice: études publiées à l'occasion du millénaire de sa mort (959–1959)* (Revue Bénédictine 70), Maredsous
Hlawitschka, E. (1968), *Lotharingien und das Reich an der Schwelle der deutschen Geschichte* (Schriften der MGH 21), Stuttgart
Hlawitschka, E. (1969), *Die Anfänge des Hauses Habsburg-Lothringen: genealogische Untersuchungen zur Geschichte Lothringens und des Reiches im 9., 10. und 11. Jahrhundert*, Saarbrücken
Kupper, J.-L. (1981), *Liège et l'église impériale, XIe–XIIe siècles*, Paris
Kurth, G. (1905), *Notger de Liège et la civilisation au Xe siècle*, 2 vols., Paris, Brussels and Liège
Maison d'Ardenne (1981), *La Maison d'Ardenne, Xe–XIe siècles* (Publications de la section historique de l'Institut grand-ducal de Luxembourg), Luxembourg
Mohr, W. (1974), *Geschichte des Herzogtums Lothringen, I: Geschichte des Herzogtums Gross-Lothringen (900–1048)*, Saarbrücken
Parisot, R. (1898), *Le Royaume de Lorraine sous les Carolingiens (843–923)*, Paris
Parisot, R. (1909), *Les Origines de la Haute-Lorraine et sa première maison ducale (959–1033)*, Paris
Parisse, M. (1990), *Austrasie, Lotharingie, Lorraine* (Encyclopédie illustrée de la Lorraine. Histoire de la Lorraine 2), Nancy
Parisse, M., and Oexle, O. G. (eds..) (1992), *Gorze au Xe siècle*, Nancy
Rousseau, F. (1930), *La Meuse et le pays mosan en Belgique: leur importance historique avant le XIIIe siècle*, Brussels, reprinted Namur 1977
Schieffer, T. (1958), 'Die lothringische Kanzlei um 900', *DA* 14: 16–148
Schneidmüller, B. (1979), 'Französische Lothringenpolitik im 10. Jahrhundert', *Jahrbuch für westdeutsche Landesgeschichte* 5: 1–31
Schneidmüller, B. (1987), 'Regnum und Ducatus. Identität und Integration in der lothringischen Geschichte des 9. bis 11. Jahrhunderts', *Rheinische Vierteljahrsblätter* 51: 81–114

Sproemberg, H. (1941), 'Die lothringische Politik Ottos des Großen', *Rheinische Vierteljahrsblätter* 11: 1–101

Vanderkindere, L. (1902), *La Formation territoriale des principautés belges au moyen âge*, 2 vols., Brussels

Zimmermann, H. (1957), 'Der Streit um das Lütticher Bistum vom Jahre 920/921', *MIÖG* 65: 15–52

13 BURGUNDY AND PROVENCE, 879–1032

Amargier, P.-A. (1963), 'La Capture de Saint Maieul de Cluny et l'expulsion des Sarrasins de Provence', *RB* 73: 316–23

Bautier, R.-H. (1973), 'Aux origines du royaume de Provence: de la sédition avortée de Boson à la royauté légitime de Louis', *Provence Historique* 3: 41–68

Bligny, B. (1965), 'Le Royaume de Bourgogne', in W. Braunfels (ed.), *Karl der Große, Lebenswerk und Nachleben*, 1: *Persönlichkeit und Geschichte*, Düsseldorf, pp. 247–68

Bouchard, C. B. (1979), 'Laymen and church reform around the year 1000: the case of Otto-William, count of Burgundy', *JMH* 5: 1–10

Bouchard, C. B. (1987), *Sword, Miter, and Cloister: Nobility and the Church in Burgundy, 980–1198*, Ithaca

Bouchard, C. B. (1988), 'The Bosonids, or rising to power in the late Carolingian age', *French Historical Studies* 15: 407–31

Bouchard, C. B. (1990), 'Merovingian, Carolingian, and Cluniac monasticism: reform and renewal in Burgundy', *JEccH* 41: 365–88

Chaume, M. (1925, 1927a, 1927b, 1931), *Les Origines du duché de Bourgogne*, 4 vols., Dijon

Dhondt, J. (1941), 'Note sur les deux premiers ducs capétiens de Bourgogne', *Annales de Bourgogne* 13: 30–8

Duby, G. (1971), *La Société aux XIe et XIIe siècles dans la région mâconnaise*, 2nd edn, Paris

Fournial, E. (ed.) (1973), 'Documents inédits des IXe, Xe, XIe et XIIe siècles relatifs à l'histoire de Charlieu', in *Actes des journées d'études d'histoire et d'archéologie organisées à l'occasion du XIe centenaire de la fondation de l'abbaye et de la ville de Charlieu*, Charlieu, pp. 107–21

Fried, J. (1976), 'Boso von Vienne oder Ludwig der Stammler? Der Kaiserkandidat Johanns VIII. ', *DA* 32: 193–208

Geary, P. J. (1994), *Phantoms of Remembrance: Memory and Oblivion at the End of the First Millennium*, Princeton

Hlawitschka, E. (1968), *Lotharingien und das Reich an der Schwelle der deutschen Geschichte* (Schriften der MGH 21), Stuttgart

Jarry, E. (1948), *Formation territoriale de la Bourgogne* (Provinces et pays de France 3), Paris

McKitterick, R. (1983), *The Frankish Kingdoms under the Carolingians, 751–987*, London

Poly, J.-P. (1976), *La Provence et la société féodale (879–1166)*, Paris

Poupardin, R. (1901), *Le Royaume de Provence sous les Carolingiens (855–933?)* (Bibliothèque de l'Ecole des hautes études 131), Paris

Poupardin, R. (1907), *Le Royaume de Bourgogne (888–1038): étude sur les origines du royaume d'Arles* (Bibliothèque de l'Ecole des hautes études 163), Paris

Rosenwein, B. H. (1982), *Rhinoceros Bound: Cluny in the Tenth Century*, Philadelphia

Rosenwein, B. H. (1989), *To Be the Neighbor of Saint Peter: the Social Meaning of Cluny's Property, 909–1049*, Ithaca

Werner, K.-F. (1967), 'Die Nachkommen Karls des Großen bis um das Jahr 1000 (1.-8. Generation)', in W. Braunfels and P. E. Schramm (eds.), *Karl der Große: Lebenswerk und Nachleben*, IV: *Das Nachleben*, Düsseldorf, pp. 402–82

14 THE KINGDOM OF ITALY

Andenna, G., Nobili, M., Sergi, G. and Violante, C. (eds.) (1988), *Formazione e strutture dei ceti dominanti nel medioevo: marchesi, conti e visconti nel regno italico (secc. IX–XII) (Atti del primo convegno di Pisa, 10–11 maggio 1983)*, Rome

Andreolli, B., Bonacini, P., Fumagalli, V. and Montanari, M. (eds.) (1993), *Territori pubblici rurali nell'Italia del medioevo*, S. Marino

Archetti Giampaolini, E. (1987), *Aristocrazia e chiese nella marca del centro-nord tra IX e XI secolo*, Rome

Arnaldi, G. (1987), *Le origini dello Stato della Chiesa*, Turin

Atti (1973), *Atti del 5° Congresso internazionale di studi sull'alto medioevo, Lucca, 3–9 ottobre 1971*, Spoleto

Atti (1986), *Atti del 10° Congresso internazionale di studi sull'alto medioevo, Milano, 26–30 settembre 1983*, Spoleto

Atti (1989), *Atti dell'11° Congresso internazionale di studi sull'alto medioevo, Milano, 26–30 ottobre 1987*, Spoleto

Bazzana, A. (ed.) (1988), *Castrum 3: guerre, fortification et habitat dans le monde méditerranéen au moyen âge (Colloque de Madrid, 24–27 novembre 1985)*, Madrid and Rome

Becker, M. B. (1981), *Medieval Italy: Constraints and Creativity*, Bloomington

Bloch, H. (1897), 'Beiträge zur Geschichte des Bischofs Leo von Vercelli und seiner Zeit', *NA* 22: 13–136

Bonacini, P. (1994), 'Giurisdizione pubblica ed. amministrazione della giustizia nell territorio piacentino altomedievale', *Civiltà Padana. Archeologia e Storia del Territorio* 5: 43–98

Bordone, R. (1980), *Città e territorio nell'alto medioevo: la società astigiana dal dominio dei Franchi all'affermazione comunale* (Biblioteca storica subalpina 200), Turin

Bordone, R. (1987), *La società cittadina del regno d'Italia: formazione e sviluppo delle caratteristiche urbane nei secoli XI e XII* (Biblioteca storica subalpina 202), Turin

Bordone, R., and Jarnut, J. (eds.) (1988), *L'evoluzione delle città italiane nell'XI secolo*, Bologna

Brühl, C. (1968), *Fodrum, Gistum, Servitium Regis: Studien zu den wirtschaftlichen Grundlagen des Königtums im Frankreich und in den fränkischen Nachfolgestaaten Deutschland, Frankreich und Italien vom 6. bis zum Mitte des 14. Jahrhunderts*, Cologne and Graz

Brühl, C. (1975), *Palatium und Civitas: Studien zur Profantopographie spätantiken Civitates vom 3. bis zum 13. Jahrhundert*, vol. 1, Cologne and Vienna

Cammarosano, P. (1974), *La famiglia dei Berardenghi: contributi alla storia della società senese dei secoli XI–XIII*, Spoleto

Cammarosano, P. (1991), *Italia medievale: struttura e geografia delle fonti scritte*, Rome

Cancian, P., Patria, L. and Sergi, G. (eds..) (1992), *La contessa Adelaide e la società del secolo XI (Atti del Convegno di Susa, 14–16 novembre 1991)* (Segusium 32), Susa

Capitani, O. (1966), *Immunità vescovili ed ecclesiologia in età 'pregregoriana' e 'gregoriana': l'avvio all'restaurazione'*, Spoleto

Capitani, O. (1986), *Storia dell'Italia medievale*, Rome and Bari

Capitani, O. (ed.) (1978), *Studi matildici (Atti del III Convegno di studi matildici, Reggio Emilia, 7–9 ottobre 1977)*, Modena

Castagnetti, A. (1979), *L'organizzazione del territorio rurale nel medioevo: circoscrizioni ecclesiastiche e civili nella 'Langobardia' e nella 'Romania'*, Turin

Castagnetti, A. (1981), *I conti di Vicenza e di Padova dall'età ottoniana al comune*, Verona

Castagnetti, A. (1985), *Società e politica a Ferrara dall'età post-carolingia alla signoria estense (sec. X–XIII)*, Bologna

Castagnetti, A. (1986), *La marca veronese-trevigiana*, Turin

Cristiani, E. (1963), 'Note sulla feudalità italica degli ultimi anni del regno di Ugo e di Lotario', *SM* 3rd series, 4: 92–103

Darmstädter, P. (1896), *Das Reichsgut in der Lombardei und Piemont (568–1250)*, Strasbourg

Delogu, P. (1968), 'Vescovi, conti e sovrani nella crisi del regno italico (Ricerche sull'aristocrazia carolingia in Italia, III)', *Annali della scuola speciale per archivisti e bibiotecari dell'Università di Roma* 8: 3–72

Duby, G., and Toubert, P. (eds.) (1980), *Structures féodales et féodalisme dans l'Occident méditerranéen (X^e–XIIIe siècles) (Colloque international organisé par le CNRS et l'Ecole française de Rome, 10–13 octobre 1978)*, Rome

Fasoli, G. (1949), *I re d'Italia (888–962)*, Florence

Fried, J., and Violante, C. (eds..) (1993), *Il secolo XI: una svolta? (XXXII Settimana di studio dell'Istituto storico italo-germanico di Trento, 10–15 settembre 1990)*, Bologna

Fumagalli, V. (1971), *Le origini di una grande dinastia feudale: Adalberto–Atto di Canossa*, Tübingen

Fumagalli, V. (1973), 'Vescovi e conti nell'Emilia occidentale da Berengario I a Ottone I', *SM* 3rd series 14: 137–204

Fumagalli, V. (1976), *Terra e società nell'Italia padana*, Turin

Fumagalli, V. (1978), *Il regno italico*, Turin

Gabba, E. (ed.) (1987), *Storia di Pavia*, II: *L'alto medioevo*, Pavia

Gandino, G. (1988), 'L'imperfezione della società in due lettere di Attone di Vercelli', *Bollettino Storico-Bibliografico Subalpino* 86: 5–38

Gandino, G. (1995), *Il vocabolario politico e sociale di Liutprando di Cremona* (Nuovi studi storici 27), Rome

Golinelli, P. (ed.) (1994), *I poteri dei Canossa: da Reggio Emilia all'Europa* (Atti del convegno internazionale, Reggio Emilia Carpineti, 29–31 ottobre 1992), Bologna

Guglielmotti, P. (1990), *I signori di Morozzo nei secoli X–XIV: un percorso politico del Piemonte meridionale* (Biblioteca storica subalpina 206), Turin

Haverkamp, A. (1982), *Die Städte im Herrschafts- und Sozialgefüge Reichsitaliens* (Historische Zeitschrift, N.S. 7), Munich

Hlawitschka, E. (1969), *Franken, Alemannen, Bayern und Burgunder in Oberitalien (774–962): zum Verständnis der fränkischen Königsherrschaft im Italien*, Freiburg im Breisgau

Il secolo di ferro (1991), *Il secolo di ferro: mito e realtà del secolo X* (Settimane 28), Spoleto

Keller, H. (1969), 'Der Gerichtsort in oberitalienischen und toskanischen Städten. Untersuchungen zur Stellung der Stadt im Herrschaftssystem des Regnum Italicum vom 9. bis 11. Jahrhundert', *Quellen und Forschungen aus italienischen Archiven und Bibliotheken* 49: 1–72

Keller, H. (1979), *Adelsherrschaft und städtische Gesellschaft in Oberitalien. 9–12. Jahrhunderts*, Tübingen

Keller, H. (1982), 'Reichsstruktur und Herrschaftsauffassung in ottonisch-frühsalischer Zeit', *FmaSt* 16: 74–128

Kurze, W. (1989), *Monasteri e nobiltà nel Senese e nella Toscana medievale: studi diplomatici, archeologici, genealogici, giuridici e sociali*, Siena

Leonhard, J.-F. (1983), *Die Seestadt Ancona im Spätmittelalter*, Tübingen

Menant, F. (1992), *Lombardia feudale: studi sull'aristocrazia padana nei secoli X–XIII*, Milan

Merlone, R. (1983), 'Prosopografia aleramica (secolo x e prima metà dell' xi)', *Bollettino Storico-Bibliografico Subalpino* 81: 451–585

Mor, C. G. and Schmidinger, H. (eds..) (1979), *I poteri temporali dei vescovi in Italia e in Germania nel medioevo (Atti della Settimana di studio, Trento, 13–18 settembre 1976)*, Bologna

Padovani, A. (1990), *'Iudiciaria Motinensis': contributo allo studio del territorio Bolognese nel medioevo*, Bologna

Pauler, R. (1982), *Das Regnum Italiae in ottonischer Zeit: Markgrafen, Grafen und Bischöfe als politische Kräfte*, Tübingen

Pavoni, R. (1992), *Liguria medievale: da provincia romana a stato regionale*, Genoa

Piemonte (1985), *Piemonte medievale: forme del potere della società. Studi per Giovanni Tabacco*, Turin

Pivano, S. (1908), *Stato e chiesa da Berengario I ad Arduino (880–1015)*, Turin

Problemi (1955), *I problemi dell'Europa post-carolingia (Settimane 2)*, Spoleto

Racine, P. (1979), *Plaisance du Xe à la fin du XIIIe siècle: essai d'histoire urbaine*, Lille and Paris

Rando, D., and Varanini, G. M. (eds..) (1991), *Storia di Treviso*, II: *Il medioevo*, Venice

Rossetti, G. (1968), *Società e istituzioni nel contado lombardo durante il medioevo: Cologno Monzese*, I, Milan

Schmidinger, H. (1954), *Patriarch und Landesherr: die weltliche Herrschaft der Patriarchen von Aquileia bis zum Ende der Staufer*, Graz and Cologne

Schneider, R. (1987), 'Fränkische Alpenpolitik', in H. Beumann and W. Schröder (eds.), *Die transalpinen Verbindungen der Bayern, Alemannen und Franken bis zum 10. Jahrhundert*, Sigmaringen

Schumann, R. (1973), *Authority and the Commune: Parma 833–1133*, Parma

Schwartz, G. (1913), *Die Besetzung der Bistümer Reichsitaliens unter den sächsischen und salischen Kaisern*, Leipzig and Berlin

Schwarzmaier, H. (1972), *Lucca und das Reich bis zum Ende des 11. Jahrhundert: Studien zur Sozialstruktur einer Herzogstadt in der Toscana*, Tübingen

Sergi, G. (1981), *Potere e territorio lungo la strada di Francia: da Chambéry a Torino fra X e XIII secolo*, Naples

Sergi, G. (1994), *L'aristocrazia della preghiera: politica e scelte religiose nel medioevo italiano*, Rome

Sergi, G. (1995), *I confini del potere: marche e signorie fra due regni medievali*, Turin

Sestan, E. (ed.) (1981), *I ceti dirigenti in Toscana nell'età precomunale (Atti del 1° Convegno del Comitato di studi sulla storia dei ceti dirigenti in Toscana, Firenze, 2 dicembre 1978)*, Pisa

Sestan, E. (ed.) (1982) *Nobiltà e ceti dirigenti in Toscana nei secoli X e XIII: strutture e concetti*, Florence

Settia, A. A. (1983), *Monferrato: strutture di un territorio medievale*, Turin

Settia, A. A. (1984), *Castelli e villaggi nell'Italia padana: popolamento, potere e sicurezza fra IX e XII secolo*, Naples

Settia, A. A. (1989), 'Le frontiere del regno italico nei secoli VI–XI: l'organizzazione delle difesa', *Studi Storici* 1: 155–69

Settia, A. A. (1991), *Chiese, strade e fortezze nell'Italia medievale* (Italia Sacra 46), Rome

Tabacco, G. (1968), 'Il regno italico nei secoli IX–XI', in *Ordinamenti militari in Occidente nell'alto medioevo (Settimane* 15), Spoleto, pp. 763–90

Tabacco, G. (1977), 'Le Rapport de parenté comme instrument de domination consortiale: quelques exemples piémontais', in G. Duby and J. Le Goff (eds..), *Famille et parenté dans l'Occident médiéval* (Collection de l'Ecole française de Rome 30), Rome, pp. 153–8

Tabacco, G. (1979), *Egemonie sociali e strutture del potere nel medioevo italiano*, Turin

Tabacco, G. (1980), 'Alleu et fief considérés au niveau politique dans le royaume d'Italie (X^e–XIIe siècles)', *Cahiers de Civilisation Médiévale* 23: 3–15

Tabacco, G. (1987), 'Vassalli, nobili e cavalieri nell'Italia precomunale', *Rivista Storica Italiana* 99: 247–68

Tabacco, G. (1989), 'La Toscana meridionale nel medioevo', in M. Ascheri and W. Kurze (eds.), *L'Amiata nel medioevo*, Rome, pp. 1–17

Tabacco, G. (1993), *Sperimentazioni del potere nell'alto medioevo*, Turin

Taurino, E. (1970), 'L'organizzazione territoriale della contea di Fermo nei secoli VIII–X', *SM* 3rd series 11: 659–710

Taurino, E. (1973), 'Un distretto minore del ducato di Spoleto nell'alto medioevo: Monte Santo', *Studi Maceratesi* 7: 99–102

Tellenbach, G. (1975), 'L'evoluzione politico-sociale nei paese alpini durante il medioevo', in A. Borst (ed.), *Le Alpi e l'Europa*, IV: *Cultura e politica*, Bari, pp. 27–59

Toubert, P. (1973), *Les Structures du Latium médiéval: le Latium méridional et la Sabine du IXe à la fin du XIIe siècle*, 2 vols., Rome

Vescovi (1964), *Vescovi e diocesi in Italia nel medioevo (sec. IX–XIII) (Atti del II Convegno di storia della chiesa in Italia, Roma, 5–9 settembre 1961)*, Padua

Violante, C. (1953), *La società milanese nell'età precomunale*, Bari

Violante, C. (1975), *Studi sulla cristianità medievale: società, istituzioni, spiritualità*, Milan

Violante, C. (1986), *Ricerche sulle istituzioni ecclesiastiche dell'Italia centro-settentrionale nel medioevo*, Palermo

Werner, K. F. (1979), *Structures politiques du monde franc (VIe–XIIe siècles)*, London

Wickham, C. J. (1981), *Early Medieval Italy: Central Power and Local Society 400–1000*, London and Basingstoke

Wickham, C. J. (1988), *The Mountains and the City: The Tuscan Appennines in the Early Middle Ages*, Oxford

15 WEST FRANCIA: THE KINGDOM

Bates, D. (1982), *Normandy before 1066*, London and New York

Bautier, R.-H. (1961), 'La Régne d'Eudes (888–98) à la lumière des diplômes expédiées par sa chancellerie', *Comptes-rendues de l'Académie des Inscriptions et Belles-Lettres*: 140–57.

Bautier, R.-H. (1990a, 1990b), *Chartes, sceaux et chancelleries: études de diplomatique et de sigillographie médiévales*, 2 vols., Paris

Belaubre, J. (1986), *Histoire numismatique et monétaire de la France médiévale*, Paris

Bonnassie, P. (1975, 1976), *La Catalogne du milieu du Xe à la fin du XIe siècle: croissance et mutations d'une société*, 2 vols., Toulouse

Brühl, C. (1968), *Fodrum, Gistum, Servitium Regis*, 2 vols. continuously paginated, Cologne and Graz

Brühl, C. (1989a, 1989b), *Aus Mittelalter und Diplomatik*, 2 vols., Hildesheim, Munich and Zurich

Brunner, K. (1979), 'Der fränkische Fürstentitel im neunten und zehnten Jahrhundert', in *Intitulatio II*, ed. H. Wolfram, pp. 179–340, Vienna

Bur, M. (1977), *La Formation du comté de Champagne, v. 950–v. 1150*, Nancy

Carozzi, C. (1976), 'Le Dernier des Carolingiens; de l'histoire au mythe', *Le Moyen Age* 82: 453–76

Chaume, M. (1925), *Les Origines du duché de Bourgogne*, Dijon

Chédeville, A. (1973), *Chartres et ses campagnes, XIe–XIIIe siècles*, Paris

Devailly, G. (1973), *Le Berry du Xe siècle au milieu du XIIIe: étude politique, réligieuse, sociale et économique*, Paris

Dhondt, J. (1939), 'Election et hérédité sous les Carolingiens et les premiers Capétiens', *Revue Belge de Philologie et d'Histoire* 18: 913–53

Dhondt, J. (1948), *Etudes sur la naissance des principautés terrritoriales en France (IXe–Xe s.)*, Bruges

Duby, G. (1953), *La Société aux XIe et XIIe siècles dans la région mâconnaise*, Paris

Dumas, F. (1992), 'La Monnaie comme expression du pouvoir (x^e–xiie siècles)', in E. Magnou-Nortier (ed.), *Pouvoirs et libertés au temps des premiers Capétiens*, Paris, pp. 169–94

Dumas-Dubourg, F. (1971), *Le Trésor de Fécamp et le monnayage en Francie occidentale pendant la second moitié du Xe siècle*, Paris

Dunbabin, J. (1985), *France in the Making, 843–1180*, Oxford

Dunbabin, J. (1989), 'The reign of Arnulf II, count of Flanders, and its aftermath', *Francia* 16: 52–65

Ehlers, J. (1978), 'Die *Historia Francorum Senonensis* und der Aufstieg des Hauses Capet', *JMH* 4: 1–25

Fossier, R. (1968a, 1968b), *La Terre et les hommes de Picardie jusqu'à la fin du XIIIe siècle*, 2 vols., Paris

Fournier, G. (1978), *Le Château dans la France médiévale: essai de sociologie monumentale*, Paris

Galliou, P. and Jones, M. (1991) *The Bretons*, Oxford

Ganshof, F.-L. (1949), *La Flandre sous les premiers comtes*, 3rd edn, Brussels

Gerson, P. L. (1986), *Abbot Suger and Saint Denis: A Symposium*, New York

Guillot, O. (1972a, 1972b), *Le Comte d'Anjou et son entourage au XIe siècle*, 2 vols. Paris

Guyotjeannin, O. (1987), *Episcopus et Comes: affirmation et déclin de la seigneurie épiscopale au nord du royaume de France (Beauvais-Noyon, X^e–debut XIIIe siècle)*, Geneva and Paris

Heitz, C., Riché, P. and Héber-Suffrin, F. (1987), *Xème Siècle, recherches nouvelles: contribution au Colloque Hugues Capet 987–1987, 'La France de l'an mil'*, Nanterre

Iogna-Prat, D. and Picard, J.-C. (eds.) (1992), *Religion et culture autour de l'an mil: royaume capétien et Lotharingie*, Paris

Jacobsen, P. C. (1978), 'Die Titel *princeps* und *domnus* bei Flodoard von Reims (893/4–966)', *Mittellateinisches Jahrbuch* 13: 50–72

Kienast, W. (1974), *Deutschland und Frankreich in der Kaiserzeit (900–1270): Weltkaiser und Einzelkonige*, 2nd edn, 2 vols., Stuttgart

Kortum, H. H. (1985), *Richer von Saint-Remi: Studien zu einem Geschichtschreiber der 10. Jahrhunderts*, Stuttgart

Lauranson-Rosaz, C. (1987), *L'Auvergne et ses marges (Velay, Gevaudan) du VIIIe au XIe siècle: la fin du monde antique?*, Le Puy en Velay

Le Patourel, J. (1976), *The Norman Empire*, Oxford

Lemarignier, J.-F. (1955), 'Les Fidèles du roi de France (936–987)', in *Recueil de travaux offerts à M. Clovis Brunel*, 2 vols., Paris, II, pp. 138–62

Lemarignier, J.-F. (1965), *Le Gouvernement royal aux premiers temps capétiens (987–1108)*, Paris

Lemarignier, J.-F. (1970), *La France médiévale, institutions et société*, Paris

Lewis, A. W. (1978), 'Anticipatory association of the heir in early Capetian France', *AHR* 83: 906–27

Lewis, A. W. (1981), *Royal Succession in Capetian France: Studies in Familial Order and the State*, Cambridge, MA and London

Leyser, K. (1994), '987: the Ottonian connection', in *Communications and Power in Medieval Europe: The Carolingian and Ottonian Centuries*, ed. T. Reuter, London and Rio Grande, pp. 165–179

Macdonald, T. (1985), 'Le Ponthieu au xe siècle: en quête de ses origines', *Bulletin de la Société d'Emulation Historique et Littéraire d'Abbeville* 25: 59–70

Magnou-Nortier, E. (ed.) (1992), *Pouvoirs et libertés au temps des premiers Capétiens*, Paris

Martindale, J. (1984), 'The kingdom of Aquitaine and the "dissolution of the Carolingian fisc"', *Francia* 11: 131–91

Media in Francia (1989), *Media in Francia: recueil de mélanges offert à K.-F. Werner à l'occasion de son 65e anniversaire par ses collègues et amis français*, Paris

Mostert, M. (1987), *The Political Theology of Abbo of Fleury*, Hilversum

Nicholas, D. (1992), *Medieval Flanders*, Harlow

Parisse, M. (1989), 'In media Francia: Saint-Mihiel, Salonnes et Saint-Denis (VIIIe–XIIe siècles)', in *Media in Francia*, Paris, pp. 319–43

Parisse, M. and Barral i Altet, X. (eds.) (1992), *Le Roi de France et son royaume autour de l'an mil. Actes du colloque Hugues Capet 987–1987. La France de l'an mil. Paris, Senlis, Juin 1987*, Paris

Poly, J.-P. and Bournazel, B (1991), *La Mutation féodale. X^e–XIIe siècles*, 2nd edn, Paris; English trans. C. Higgitt of 1st edn as *The Feudal Transformation, 900–1200*, Chicago (1991)

Poppe, A. (1976), 'The political background to the baptism of the Rus'', *DOP* 50: 195–244

Rezak, B. R. (1986), 'Suger and the symbolism of royal power: the seal of Louis VII', in P. L. Gerson, (ed.), *Abbot Suger and Saint-Denis: A Symposium*, New York, pp. 95–103

Richard, J. (1954), *Les Ducs de Bourgogne et la formation du duché du XIe au XIVe siècle*, Paris

Sassier, Y. (1980), *Recherches sur le pouvoir comtal en Auxerrois du Xe au début du XIIIe siècle*, Paris

Sassier, Y. (1987), *Hugues Capet*, Paris

Schneider, J. (1986), *Aux Origines d'une seigneurie ecclésiastique: Langres et ses évêques (VIIe–XIe siècles)*, Langres

Schneidmüller, B. (1979), *Karolingische Tradition und frühes französisches Konigtum: Untersuchungen zur Herrschaftslegitimation der westfränkisch-französischen Monarchie im 10 Jahrhundert*, Wiesbaden

Schneidmüller, B. (1987), *Nomen Patriae: die Entstehung Frankreichs in der politisch-geographischen Terminologie (10–13. Jahrhundert)*, Sigmaringen

Sot, M. (1988), 'Hérédité royale et pouvoir sacré avant 987', *Annales ESC* 43: 705–33

Sot, M. (1993), *Un Historien et son église au Xe siècle: Flodoard de Reims*, Paris

Tessier, G. (1962), *Diplomatique royale française*, Paris

Theis, L. (1984), *L'Avènement d'Hugues Capet*, Paris

Werner, K.-F. (1980), 'L'Acquisition par la maison de Blois des comtés de Chartres et de Châteaudun', *Mélanges de numismatique, d'archéologie et d'histoire offerts à Jean Lafaurie*, Paris, pp. 165–72

Werner, K.-F. (1984), *Histoire de France, I: Les Origines*, Paris

16 WEST FRANCIA: THE NORTHERN PRINCIPALITIES

Autrand, F., Barthélemy, D. and Contamine, P. (1991), 'L'Espace français: histoire politique du début du xie siècle à la fin du xve', in *L'Histoire médiévale en France: Bilan et perspectives*, Paris

Bachrach, B. S. (1976), 'A study in feudal politics: relations between Fulk Nerra and William the Great', *Viator* 7: 111–22

Bachrach, B. S. (1983), 'The Angevin strategy of castle-building in the reign of Fulk Nerra, 987–1040', *AHR* 88: 533–60

Bachrach, B. S. (1984), 'The enforcement of the *Forma Fidelitatis*: the techniques used by Fulk Nerra, count of the Angevins (987–1040)', *Speculum* 59: 796–819

Bachrach, B. S. (1985), 'Geoffrey Greymantle, count of the Angevins, 960–987: a study in French politics', *Studies in Medieval and Renaissance History* 17: 3–68

Bachrach, B. S. (1989a), 'Some observations on the origins of the Angevin dynasty', *Medieval Prosopography* 10, no. 2: 1–23

Bachrach, B. S. (1989b), 'Angevin campaign forces in the reign of Fulk Nerra, count of the Angevins (987–1040)', *Francia* 16: 67–84

Bachrach, B. S. (1993), *Fulk Nerra, the Neo-Roman Consul, 987–1040*, Berekley and Los Angeles

Barthélemy, D. (1990), *L'Ordre seigneurial (XIe–XIIe siècle)*, Paris

Barthélemy, D. (1992), 'La Mutation féodale a-t-elle eu lieu? (Note critique)', *Annales ESC* 47: 767–75

Bates, D. (1982), *Normandy before 1066*, London and New York

Bloch, M. (1962), *Feudal Society*, 2 vols. paginated as one, London

Bouchard, C. B. (1981), 'The origins of the French nobility: a reassessment', *AHR* 86: 501–32

Boussard, J. (1968a), 'Les Destinées de la Neustrie du ixe au xie siècle', *Cahiers de Civilisation Médiévale* 11: 15–28

Boussard, J. (1968b), 'Services féodaux, milices et mercenaires dans les armées, en France, aux Xe et XIe siècles', *Settimane* 15, Spoleto, 131–68

Boussard, J. (1970), 'Les Evêques en Neustrie avant la réforme grégorienne (950–1050 environ)', *Journal des Savants*: 161–96

Boussard, J. (1979), 'L'Origine des comtés de Tours, Blois et Chartres', in *103e Congrès national des sociétés savantes, Colloque de Nancy–Metz (1978), Section de philologie et d'histoire*, Paris, pp. 85–112

Bur, M. (1977), *La Formation du comté de Champagne v. 950–v. 1150*, Nancy

Chédeville, A. (1973), *Chartres et ses campagnes (XIe–XIIIe siècles)*, Paris

Chédeville, A. (1974), 'L'Immigration bretonne dans le royaume de France du xiᵉ au début du xivᵉ siècle', *Annales de Bretagne* 81: 301–43

Chédeville, A. and Guillotel, H. (1984), *La Bretagne des saints et des rois, Vᵉ–Xᵉ siècles*, Rennes

Chédeville, A., and Tonnerre, N.-Y. (1987), *La Bretagne féodale, XIᵉ–XIIIᵉ siècle*, Rennes

de Bouard, M. (1955), 'De la Neustrie carolingienne à la Normandie féodale: continuité ou discontinuité?', *Bulletin of the Institute of Historical Research* 28: 1–14

Dhondt, J. (1948), *Etudes sur la naissance des principautés territoriales en France (IXᵉ–Xᵉ siècle)*, Bruges

Dhondt, J. (1967), 'Une Crise du pouvoir capétien (1032–1034)', in *Miscellanea Mediaevalia in memoriam J. F. Niermeyer*, Groningen, pp. 137–48

Duby, G. (1953), *La Société aux XIᵉ et XIIᵉ siècles dans la région mâconnaise*, Paris

Duby, G. (1978), *Les trois Ordres ou l'imaginaire du féodalisme*, Paris; trans. A. Goldhammer as *The Three Orders: Feudal Society Imagined*, Chicago and London, 1980

Dumas-Dubourg, F. (1971), *Le Trésor de Fécamp et le monnayage en Francie occidentale pendant la seconde moitié du Xᵉ siècle*, Paris

Dunbabin, J. (1985), *France in the Making 843–1180*, Oxford

Dunbabin, J. (1989), 'The reign of Arnulf II, count of Flanders, and its aftermath', *Francia* 16: 53–65

Fanning, S. (1985), 'Acts of Henry I of France concerning Anjou', *Speculum* 60: 110–14

Fellows Jensen, G. (1988), 'Scandinavian place-names and Viking settlement in Normandy: a review', *Namn Och Bygd* 76: 113–37

Feuchère, P. (1954), 'Une Tentative manquée de concentration territoriale entre Somme et Seine: la principauté d'Amiens-Valois au xiᵉ siècle', *Le Moyen Age* 60: 1–37

Fossier, R. (1968a, 1968b), *La Terre et les hommes en Picardie*, 2 vols.., Paris

Fossier, R. (1979), 'Sur les principautés médiévales, particulièrement en France', in *Les Principautés au moyen âge: actes des congrès de la société des historiens médiévistes de l'enseignement supérieur public*, Bordeaux, pp. 9–17

France, J. (1992), 'The occasion of the coming of the Normans to southern Italy', *JMH* 17: 185–205

Galliou, P. and Jones, M. (1991), *The Bretons*, Oxford

Ganshof, F. L. (1949), *La Flandre sous les premiers comtes*, Brussels

Ganshof, F. L. (1957), 'La Flandre', in F. Lot and R. Fawtier (eds.), *Histoire des institutions françaises au moyen âge*, vol. 1: *Institutions seigneuriales*, Paris, pp. 343–426

Garnett, G. (1994): '"Ducal" succession in early Normandy', in G. Garnett and J. Hudson (eds.), *Law and Government in Medieval England and Normandy: Essays in Honour of Sir James Holt*, Cambridge, pp. 80–110

Génicot, L. (1962), 'La Noblesse au moyen âge dans l'ancienne France', *Annales ESC* 17: 1–22

Guillot, O. (1972a, 1972b), *Le Comte d'Anjou et son entourage au XIᵉ siècle*, 2 vols.., Paris

Guillotel, H. (1979), 'Le premier siècle du pouvoir ducal breton (936–1040)', in *105ᵉ Congrès national des sociétés savantes, Colloque de Nancy–Metz (1978), Section de philologie et d'histoire*, Paris, pp. 63–84

Guyotjeannin, O. (1987), *Episcopus et Comes: Affirmation et déclin de la seigneurie épiscopale au nord du royaume de France (Beauvais-Noyon, Xᵉ–début XIIIᵉ siècle)*, Geneva and Paris

Guyotjeannin, O. (1989), 'Les Actes établis par la chancellerie royale sous Philippe Iᵉʳ', *BEC* 147: 29–47

Hallam, E. M. (1980), 'The king and the princes in eleventh-century France', *Bulletin of the Institute of Historical Research* 53: 143–56

Halphen, L. (1906), *Le Comté d'Anjou au XIe siècle*, Paris

Hollister, C. W. (1987), 'The greater Domesday tenants-in-chief', in J. C. Holt (ed.), *Domesday Studies*, Woodbridge, pp. 219–41

Houts, E. M. C. van (1984), 'Scandinavian influence in Norman literature of the eleventh century', *Anglo-Norman Studies* 6: 107–21

Jones, M. (1981), 'The defence of medieval Brittany', *The Archaeological Journal* 138: 149–204

Jones, M. (1990), 'The Capetians and Brittany', *Historical Research* 63: 1–16

Keats-Rohan, K. S. B. (1994), 'Ivo fitz Fulcoin, the counts of Maine, the lords of Bellême: a new look at the foundation charter of L'Abbayette', *JMH* 20: 3–25

Keats-Rohan, K. S. B. (1997), '"Un Vassal sans histoire"? Count Hugh II (c. 940/55–992) and the origins of Angevin overlordship in Maine', in K. S. B. Keats-Rohan (ed.), *Family Trees and the Roots of Politics: The Prosopography of Britain and France from the Tenth to the Twelfth Century*, Woodbridge, pp. 189–210

Keynes, S. (1991), 'The æthelings in Normandy', *Anglo-Norman Studies* 13: 173–205

Latouche, R. (1910), *Histoire du comté du Maine pendant le Xe et le XIe siècle*, Paris

Lemarignier, J.-F. (1937), *Étude sur les privilèges d'exemption et de juridiction ecclésiastique des abbayes normandes depuis les origines jusqu'en 1140*, Paris

Lemarignier, J.-F. (1955), 'Les Fidèles du roi de France (936–987)', in *Recueil des travaux offert à M. Clovis Brunel*, 2 vols., Paris, II, pp. 138–62

Lemarignier, J.-F. (1965), *Le Gouvernement royal aux premiers temps capétiens*, Paris

Lemarignier, J.-F. (1968), 'Political and monastic structures in France at the end of the tenth and the beginning of the eleventh century', in F. L. Cheyette (ed.), *Lordship and Community in Medieval Europe*, New York, pp. 100–27

Lewis, A. W. (1978), 'Anticipatory association of the heir in early Capetian France', *AHR* 83: 906–27

Lex, L. (1892), *Eudes, comte de Blois, de Tours, de Chartres, de Troyes et de Meaux (995–1037) et Thibaud son frère (995–1004)*, Troyes

Louise, G. (1992, 1993), *La Seigneurie de Bellême, X^e–XIIe siècles*, 2 vols., Flers

Martindale, J. (1977), 'The French aristocracy in the early middle ages', *Past and Present* 75: 5–45

Martindale, J. (1989), 'Succession and politics in the Romance-speaking world, c. 1000–1140', in M. Jones and M. Vale (eds.), *England and her Neighbours, 1066–1453: Essays in Honour of Pierre Chaplais*, London and Ronceverte, pp. 19–41

Media in Francia (1989), *Media in Francia: recueil de mélanges offert à K.-F. Werner à l'occasion de son 65e anniversaire par ses collègues et amis français*, Paris

Musset, L. (1946), 'Les Domaines de l'époque franque et les destinées du régime domanial du IXe au XIe siècle', *Bulletin de la Société des Antiquaires de Normandie* 49: 7–97

Musset, L. (1954), 'Les Relations extérieures de la Normandie du IXe au XIe siècle, d'après quelques trouvailles monétaires récentes', *Annales de Normandie* 4: 31–8

Musset, L. (1970), 'Naissance de la Normandie (v^e–xie siècles)', in M. de Bouard (ed.), *Histoire de la Normandie*, Toulouse, pp. 96–129

Musset, L. (1976a), 'L'Aristocratie normande au xie siècle', in P. Contamine (ed.), *La Noblesse au moyen âge (XIe au XVe siècles: essais à la mémoire de Robert Boutruche*, Paris, pp. 71–96

Musset, L. (1976b), 'Les Apports scandinaves dans le plus ancien droit normand', in *Droit privé et institutions régionales: études historiques offertes à Jean Yver*, Paris, pp. 559–75

Musset, L. (1979), 'Origines et nature du pouvoir ducal en Normandie jusqu'au milieu du XIe siècle', in *Les Principautés au moyen âge: actes des congrès de la société des historiens médiévistes de l'enseignement supérieur public*, Bordeaux, pp. 47–59

Musset, L. (1989), 'Considérations sur la genèse et le tracé des frontières de la Normandie', in *Media in Francia*, Paris, pp. 309–18

Nelson, J. L. (1992), *Charles the Bald*, London

Potts, C. (1990a), 'The revival of monasticism in Normandy, 911–1066', Ph.D. thesis, University of California at Santa Barbara

Potts, C. (1990b), 'Normandy or Brittany? A conflict of interest at Mont Saint-Michel', *Anglo-Norman Studies* 12: 135–56

Potts, C. (1992), 'The early Norman charters: a new perspective on an old debate', in C. Hicks (ed.), *England in the Eleventh Century: Proceedings of the 1990 Harlaxton Symposium*, Stamford, pp. 25–40

Price, N. S. (1989), *The Vikings in Brittany*, London

Renaud, J. (1989), *Les Vikings et la Normandie*, Rennes

Renoux, A. (1991), *Fécamp: du palais ducal au palais de Dieu*, Paris

Sassier, Y. (1987), *Hugues Capet*, Paris

Searle, E. (1984), 'Fact and pattern in heroic history: Dudo of Saint-Quentin', *Viator* 15: 119–37

Searle, E. (1988), *Predatory Kinship and the Control of Norman Power, 840–1066*, Berkeley and Los Angeles

Shopkow, L. (1989), 'The Carolingian world of Dudo of Saint-Quentin', *JMH* 15: 19–37

Tabuteau, E. Z. (1984), Review of Bates (1982) in *Speculum* 59: 610–15

Tabuteau, E. Z. (1988), *Transfers of Property in Eleventh-Century Norman Law*, Chapel Hill and London

Thompson, K. (1985), 'Family and influence to the south of Normandy in the eleventh century: the lordship of Bellême', *JMH* 11: 215–26

Thompson, K. (1991), 'Robert of Bellême reconsidered', *Anglo-Norman Studies* 13: 263–86

Warlop, E. (1975a, 1975b, 1976a, 1976b), *The Flemish Nobility before 1300*, 2 vols. each in 2 parts, Courtrai

Werner, K. F. (1958–60), 'Untersuchungen zur Frühzeit des französischen Fürstentums (9.–10. Jahrhundert)', *Die Welt als Geschichte* 8: 256–89; 9: 146–93; 10: 87–119

Werner, K. F. (1968), 'Königtum und Fürstentum des französischen 12. Jahrhunderts', in T. Mayer (ed.), *Probleme des 12. Jahrhunderts*, Sigmaringen, pp. 177–225

Werner, K. F. (1976), 'Quelques observations au sujet des débuts du "duché" de Normandie', in *Droit privé et institutions régionales: études historiques offertes à Jean Yver*, Paris, pp. 691–709

Werner, K. F. (1978), 'Kingdom and principality in twelfth-century France', in T. Reuter (ed.), *The Medieval Nobility*, Amsterdam, New York and Oxford, pp. 243–90. This is a translation of Werner (1968)

Yver, J. (1969), 'Les premières institutions du duché de Normandie', *Settimane* 16: 299–366

17 WESTERN FRANCIA: THE SOUTHERN PRINCIPALITIES

Aurell, M. (1994), *Les Noces du comte: mariage et pouvoir en Catalogne (785–1213)*, Paris

Auzias, L. (1937), *L'Aquitaine carolingienne (778–987)*, Toulouse and Paris

Barral i Altet, X. (ed.) (1987), *Le Paysage monumental de la France autour de l'An Mil*, Paris

Barral i Altet, X., Iogna-Prat, D., Mundó, A. M., Salrach, J. M., and Zimmermann, M., (eds.) (1991), *Catalunya i França meridional a l'entorn de l'any mil. La Catalogne et la France meridionale autour de l'an mil*, Barcelona

Biget, J.-L. (1983), *Histoire d'Albi*, Toulouse

Bonnassie, P. (1975, 1976), *La Catalogne du milieu du Xe à la fin du XIe siècle: croissance et mutations d'une société*, 2 vols., Toulouse; abridged edn, *La Catalogue autour de l'an mil*, Paris, 1992

Bonnassie, P. (1978), 'La Monnaie et les échanges en Auvergne et Rouergue aux xe et xie siècles d'après les sources hagiographiques', *Annales du Midi*, 90: 275–88

Bonnassie, P. (1988), 'Le Comté de Toulouse et le comté du Barcelone du début du IXe au début du XIIIe siècle: esquisse d'histoire comparée', in *Vuité Colloqui de llengua i literatura catalana*, Montserrat, 1, pp. 27–45

Bonnassie, P. and Landes, R. (1992), '"Une nouvelle hérésie est née dans le monde"', in M. Zimmermann, (ed.), *Les Sociétés méridionales autour de l'an mil*, Paris, pp. 435–59

Bourin-Derruau, M. (1987a, 1987b), *Villages médiévaux en Bas-Languedoc: genèse d'une sociabilité (X^e–XIVe siècles)*, 2 vols., Paris

Castaldo, A. (1970), *L'Eglise d'Agde (X^e–XIIIe siècles)*, Paris

Clemens, J. (1986), 'La Gascogne est née à Auch au xiie siècle', *Annales du Midi* 98: 165–84

d'Abadal i de Vinyals, R. (1958), *Els primers comtes catalans* (Biografies Catalanes, Sèrie Històrica 1), Barcelona

d'Abadal i de Vinyals, R. (1960), *Com Catalunya s'obri al món mil anys enrera* (Collecció 'Episodis de la història' 3), Barcelona

Debax, H. (1988), 'Les Comtesses de Toulouse: notices biographiques', *Annales du Midi* 100: 215–34

Debord, A. (1984), *La Société laïque dans les pays de la Charente (X^e–XIIe siècle)*, Paris

Dhondt, J. (1948a), *Etudes sur la naissance des principautés territoriales en France (IXe–Xe siècle)*, Bruges

Dhondt, J. (1948b), 'Le Titre du marquis à l'époque Carolingienne', *Archivum Latinitatis Medii Aevi* 19: 407–17

Dufour, J. (1991), 'Obédience respective des Carolingiens et des Capétiens (fin x^e–début xie s.)', in Barral i Altet, *et al.* (1991), pp. 21–44

Duhamel-Amado, C. (1992), 'Poids de l'aristocratie d'origine wisigothique et genèse de la noblesse septimanienne', in *L'Europe héritière de l'Espagne wisigothique, Colloque, Paris*, Madrid, pp. 81–99

Duhamel-Amado, C. (1995), 'La famille aristocratique languedocienne. Parenté et patrimoine dans les vicomtes de Béziers' et d'Agde (900–1170), thèse d'état, Paris

Formació (1985–6), *La formació i expansió del feudalisme català, Colloque, Gérone 1985* (Estudi General 5–6), Girona

Guillemain, B. (1974), *Histoire du diocèse de Bordeaux*, Paris

Higounet, C. (1963), *Histoire de Bordeaux*, II: *Bordeaux pendant le haut moyen âge*, Bordeaux

Higounet, C. (1984), *Le Comté de Comminges de ses origines à son annexion à la Couronne*, 2nd edn, Saint-Gaudens

Iogna-Prat, D. and Delort, R. (ed.) (1990), *La France de l'an mil*, Paris

Kienast, W. (1968), *Der Herzogstitel in Deutschland und Frankreich (9.–12. Jahrhundert). Mit Listen der ältesten deutschen Herzogsurkunden*, Munich

Lauranson-Rosaz, C. (1987), *L'Auvergne et ses marges (Velay, Gevaudan) du VIIIe au XIe siècle: la fin du monde antique?* Le Puy en Velay

Lauranson-Rosaz, C. (1992), 'L'Auvergne', in M. Zimmermann (ed.), *Les Sociétés méridionales autour de l'an mil*, Paris, pp. 13–54

Lemarignier, J.-F. (1951), 'La Dislocation du pagus et le problème des *consuetudines* (x–xie siècles)', in *Mélanges d'histoire du moyen âge dédiés à la mémoire de Louis Halphen*, Paris, pp. 401–10

Lemarignier, J.-F. (1965), *Le Gouvernement royal aux premiers temps capétiens, 987–1108*, Paris

Lewis, A. R. (1965), *The Development of Southern French and Catalan Society (718–1050)*, Austin, Texas

Magnou-Nortier, E. (1964), 'Note sur le sens du mot *fevum* en Septimanie et dans la marche d'Espagne à la fin du xème et au début du xième siècle', *Annales du Midi* 76: 141–52

Magnou-Nortier, E. (1974), *La Société laïque et l'Eglise dans la province ecclésiastique de Narbonne (zone cispyrénéenne) de la fin du VIIIème à la fin du XIème siècle*, Toulouse

Mussot-Goulard, R. (1982), *Les Princes de Gascogne (768–1070)*, Marsolan

Mussot-Goulard, R. (1991), 'Les Rapports de la Gascogne avec la royauté à la fin du xème siècle', in Barral i Altet *et al.* (1991), pp. 96–101

Nadal Farreras, J. and Wolff, P. (1982), *Histoire de la Catalogne*, Toulouse

Ourliac, P. (1988), 'La Pratique et la loi: note sur les actes français et catalans du xème siècle', *Boletín Semestrial de Derecho Privado. . . de la Biblioteca Ferran Vals i Taberner.* 93–118

Poly, J.-P. (1976), *La Provence et la société féodale (879–1166): contribution à l'étude des sociétés dites féodales dans le Midi*, Paris

Saint Victor (1966), *Recueil des actes du Congrès sur l'histoire de l'abbaye Saint Victor de Marseille (29–30 janvier, 1966),* Provence Historique 16, fasc. 65

Salrach, J.-M. (1987), *El procés de feudalització (segles III–XII)* (Història de Catalunya 2), Barcelona

Sobrequés Vidal, S. (1961), *Els grans comtes de Barcelona* (Biografies Catalanes, Série Històrica 2), Barcelona

Structures (1968), *Les Structures sociales de l'Aquitaine, du Languedoc et de l'Espagne au premier âge féodal: colloque, Toulouse 1968*, Annales du Midi 80: 353–624

Structures (1980), *Structures féodales et féodalisme dans l'Occident méditerranéen (X–XIIIème siècles, colloque international organisé par le Centre national de recherche scientifique et l'Ecole française de Rome (Rome, 10–13 octobre 1978. Bilan et perspectives de recherches*, Rome

Wolff, P. (1958), *Histoire de Toulouse*, 2nd edn 1974, Toulouse

Wolff, P. (1967), *Histoire du Languedoc*, Toulouse

Zimmermann, M. (1981), 'La Datation des documents catalans du ixe au xiie siècle: un itinéraire politique', *Annales du Midi* 93: 345–75

Zimmermann, M. (1989), *En els orígens de Catalunya: emancipació política i afirmació cultural*, Barcelona

Zimmermann, M. (1991), 'Naissance d'une principauté. Barcelone et les autres comtés catalans aux alentours de l'an mil', in *Catalunya i França meridional à l'entorn de l'any mil*, Barcelona, pp. 111–35

Zimmermann, M. (ed.) (1992), *Les Sociétés méridionales autour de l'an mil: Répertoire des sources et documents commentés*, Paris.

18 ENGLAND, 900–1016

Blunt, C. E. (1974), 'The coinage of Athelstan, king of England 924–939', *British Numismatic Journal* 42: 35–160

Blunt, C. E. (1985), 'Northumbrian coins in the name of Alwaldus', *British Numismatic Journal* 55: 192–4

Blunt, C. E., Stewart, B. H. I. H. and Lyon, C. S. S. (1989), *Coinage in Tenth-Century England from Edward the Elder to Edgar's Reform*, Oxford

Brooks, N. (1992), 'The career of St Dunstan', in N. Ramsey, M. Sparks and T. Tatton-Brown (eds.), *St Dunstan: His Life, Times and Cult*, Woodbridge, pp. 1–23

Campbell, J. (ed.) (1982), *The Anglo-Saxons*, Oxford

Cooper, J. (ed.) (1993), *The Battle of Maldon: Fiction and Fact*, London

Dumville, D. N. (1983), 'Brittany and "Armes Pridein Vawr"', *Etudes celtiques* 20: 145–88

Dumville, D. N. (1992), *Wessex and England from Alfred to Edgar*, Woodbridge

Fleming, R. (1991), *Kings and Lords in Conquest England*, Cambridge

Hart, C. R. (1992), *The Danelaw*, London

Heighway, C. M. (1984), 'Anglo-Saxon Gloucester to AD 1000', in M. L. Faull (ed.), *Studies in Late Anglo-Saxon Settlement*, Oxford, pp. 35–53

Hill, D. (ed.) (1978), *Ethelred the Unready: Papers from the Millenary Conference* (BAR, British Series 59), Oxford

Keynes, S. (1980), *The Diplomas of King Æthelred 'the Unready' 978–1016: A Study in their Use as Historical Evidence*, Cambridge

Keynes, S. (1986), 'A tale of two kings: Alfred the Great and Æthelred the Unready', *TRHS*, fifth series 36: 195–217

Keynes, S. (1990), 'Royal government and the written word in late Anglo-Saxon England', in R. McKitterick (ed.), *The Uses of Literacy in early Medieval Europe*, Cambridge, pp. 226–57

Keynes, S. (1994), 'The "Dunstan B" charters', *Anglo-Saxon England* 23: 165–93

Keynes, S. (ed.) (1996), *The 'Liber Vitae' of the New Minster and Hyde Abbey, Winchester* (Early English Manuscripts in Facsimile 26), Copenhagen

Lapidge, M. (1993), *Anglo-Latin Literature 900–1066*, London

Loyn, H. (1992), *Society and Peoples: Studies in the History of England and Wales, c. 600–1200*, London

Nelson, J. L. (1986), *Politics and Ritual in Early Medieval Europe*, London

Ridyard, S. J. (1988), *The Royal Saints of Anglo-Saxon England: A Study of West Saxon and East Anglian Cults*, Cambridge

Sawyer, P. (1983), 'The royal *Tun* in pre-conquest England', in P. Wormald, D. Bullough and R. Collins (eds.), *Ideal and Reality in Frankish and Anglo-Saxon Society: Studies Presented to J. M. Wallace-Hadrill*, Oxford, pp. 273–99

Scragg. D. (ed.) (1991), *The Battle of Maldon, AD 991*, Oxford

Smyth, A. P. (1975, 1979), *Scandinavian York and Dublin: The History and Archaeology of Two Related Viking Kingdoms*, 2 vols.., Dublin

Stafford, P. (1989), *Unification and Conquest: A Political and Social History of England in the Tenth and Eleventh Centuries*, London

Stenton, F. M. (1971), *Anglo-Saxon England*, 3rd edn, Oxford

Thacker, A. (1988), 'Æthelwold and Abingdon', in B. Yorke (ed.), *Bishop Æthelwold: His Career and Influence*, Woodbridge, pp. 43–64

Whitelock, D. (1981), 'Wulfstan *Cantor* and Anglo-Saxon Law', in Whitelock, D. *History, Law and Literature in 10th–11th Century England*, London, no. V, pp. 83–92

Williams, A. (1979), 'Some notes and considerations on problems connected with the English succession, 860–1066', in R. A. Brown (ed.), *Proceedings of the Battle Conference on Anglo-Norman Studies, I: 1978*, Ipswich, pp. 144–67, 225–33

Williams, A. (1982), '*Princeps Merciorum gentis*: the family, career and connections of Ælfhere, ealdorman of Mercia 956–83', *Anglo-Saxon England* 10: 143–72

Wormald, P. (1999), *The Making of English Law: King Alfred to the Twelfth Century*, 1: *Legislation and its Limits*, Oxford

Yorke, B. (1988), 'Æthelwold and the politics of the tenth century', in B. Yorke (ed.), *Bishop Æthelwold: His Career and Influence*, Woodbridge, pp. 65–88

19 EUROPEAN RUSSIA, C.500–C.1050

BZ and *Russia Mediaevalis* publish fairly comprehensive and annotated bibliographies of current research on early medieval European Russia.

Arne, T. J. (1914), *La Suède et L'Orient* (Archives d'Etudes Orientales 8), Uppsala

Bálint, C. (1981), 'Some archaeological addenda to Golden's Khazar studies', *Acta Orientalia Academiae Scientiarium Hungaricae* 35: 397–412

Bálint, C. (1989), *Die Archäologie der Steppe: Steppenvölker zwischen Volga und Donau vom 6. bis zum 10. Jahrhundert*, Vienna and Cologne

Blum, J. (1953), ''The beginnings of large-scale landownership in Russia', *Speculum* 28: 776–90

Boba, I. (1967), *Nomads, Northmen and Slavs: Eastern Europe in the Ninth Century*, The Hague and Wiesbaden

Bolin, S. (1953), 'Mohammed, Charlemagne, and Ruric', *Scandinavian Economic History Review* 1: 5–39

Bulkin, V. A., Dubov, I. V. and Lebedev, G. S. (1978), *Arkheologicheskie pamiatniki Drevnei Rusi IX–XI vekov*, Leningrad

Callmer, J. (1981), 'The archaeology of Kiev *ca.* AD 500–1000: a survey', *Figura* 19: 29–52

Callmer, J. (1987), 'The archaeology of Kiev to the end of the earliest urban phase', *Harvard Ukrainian Studies* 11: 323–64

Chadwick, N. (1946), *The Beginnings of Russian History: An Enquiry into Sources*, Cambridge

Chekin, L. S. (1990), 'The rôle of Jews in early Russian civilization in the light of a new discovery and new controversies', *Russian History/Histoire Russe* 17: 379–94

Cross, S. H. (1946), 'The Scandinavian infiltration into early Russia', *Speculum* 21: 505–14

Cross, S. H., and Conant, K. J. (1936), 'The earliest mediaeval churches of Kiev', *Speculum* 11: 477–99

Davidson, H. R. E. (1976), *The Viking Road to Byzantium*, London

Dejevsky, N. J. (1977), 'The Varangians in Soviet archaeology today', *Mediaeval Scandinavia* 10: 7–34

Dubov, I. V. (ed.) (1988), *Istoriko-arkheologicheskoe izuchenie Drevnei Rusi: Itogi i osnovnye problemy* (Slaviano-russkie drevnosti 1), Leningrad

Dunlop, D. M. (1954), *The History of the Jewish Khazars*, Princeton

Dvornik, F. (1956), *The Slavs: Their Early History and Civilization*, Boston

Eck, A. (1933), *Le Moyen Age russe*, Paris, ch. 1

Ericsson, K. (1966), 'The earliest conversion of the Rus' to Christianity', *Slavonic and East European Review* 44: 98–121

Fakhrutdinov, R. G. (1984), *Ocherki po istorii Volzhskoi Bulgarii*, Moscow

Froianov, I. Ia. (1980), *Kievskaia Rus': Ocherki sotsial'no-politicheskoi istorii*, Leningrad

Froianov, I. Ia. (1985–6), 'Large-scale ownership of land and the Russian economy in the tenth to twelfth centuries', *Soviet Studies in History* 24, no. 4: 9–82

Froianov, I. Ia. (1990), *Kievskaia Rus': Ocherki otechestvennoi istoriografii*, Leningrad

Gimbutas, M. (1963), *The Balts* (Ancient Peoples and Places), New York

Gimbutas, M. (1971), *The Slavs* (Ancient Peoples and Places), London

Golb, N., and Pritsak, O. (1982), *Khazarian Hebrew Documents of the Tenth Century*, Ithaca and London

Golden, P. B. (1980), *Khazar Studies: An Historico-Philological Inquiry into the Origins of the Khazars*, 1, Budapest

Golden, P. B. (1982a), 'Imperial ideology and the sources of political unity amongst the pre-Činggisid nomads of Western Eurasia', *Archivum Eurasiae Medii Aevi* 2: 37–76

Golden, P. B. (1982b), 'The question of the Rus' Qaganate', *Archivum Eurasiae Medii Aevi* 2: 77–97

Golden, P. B. (1983), 'Khazaria and Judaism', *Archivum Eurasiae Medii Aevi* 3: 127–56

Golden, P. B. (1990a), 'The peoples of the Russian forest belt', in D. Sinor (ed.), *The Cambridge History of Inner Asia*, Cambridge, pp. 229–55

Golden, P. B. (1990b), 'The peoples of the South Russian steppes', in D. Sinor (ed.), *The Cambridge History of Inner Asia*, Cambridge, pp. 256–84

Goldina, R. D. (1985), *Lomovatovskaia kul'tura v verkhnem Prikam'e*, Irkutsk

Grekov, B. (1959), *Kiev Rus*, Moscow

Hajdú, P. (1975), *Finno-Ugrian Languages and Peoples*, London

Hellie, R. (1971), *Enserfment and Military Change in Muscovy*, Chicago

Hellmann, M. (1962), 'Die Heiratspolitik Jaroslavs des Weisen', *Forschungen zur osteuropäischen Geschichte* 8: 7–25

Hellmann, M. (ed.) (1976), *Handbuch der Geschichte Russlands*, 1, Parts 1–6, Stuttgart, pp. 1–429

Hrbek, I. (1960), 'Bulghār', *Encyclopaedia of Islam*, 2nd edn, 1, Leiden, pp. 1304–8

Ioannisyan, O. M. (1990), 'Archaeological evidence for the development and urbanization of Kiev from the 8th to the 14th centuries', in D. Austin and L. Alcock (eds.), *From the Baltic to the Black Sea: Studies in Medieval Archaeology* (One World Archaeology 18), London, pp. 285–312

Khalikov, A. Kh. (1977–8), 'The culture of the peoples of the middle Volga in the tenth through the thirteenth centuries', *Soviet Anthropology and Archaeology* 16, no. 1: 49–86

Khazanov, A. M. (1984), *Nomads and the Outside World* (Cambridge Studies in Social Anthropology 44), Cambridge

Kipersky, V. (1952), 'The earliest contacts of the Russians with the Finns and Balts', *Oxford Slavonic Papers* 3: 67–80

Kluchevsky, V. O. (1960), *A History of Russia*, 1, New York, pp. 1–100

Kodolányi, J. (1976), 'North Eurasian hunting, fishing, and reindeer-breeding civilizations', in P. Hajdú (ed.), *Ancient Cultures of the Uralian Peoples*, Budapest, pp. 145–71

Liapushkin, I. I. (1968), *Slaviane Vostochnoi Evropy nakanune obrazovaniia Drevnerusskogo gosudarstva* (Materialy i issledovaniia po arkheologii SSSR 152), Leningrad

Macartney, C. A. (1929–30), 'The Petchenegs', *SEER* 8: 342–55

Maenchen-Helfen, O. J. (1973), *The World of the Huns: Studies in their History and Culture*, Berkeley

Magomedov, M. G. (1983), *Obrazovanie khazarskogo kaganata*, Moscow

Martin, J. (1986), *Treasure of the Land of Darkness: The Fur Trade and its Significance for Medieval Russia*, Cambridge

Mezentsev, V. I. (1986), 'The emergence of the Podil and the genesis of the city of Kiev: problems of dating', *Harvard Ukrainian Studies* 10: 48–70

Mezentsev, V. I. (1989), 'The territorial and demographic development of medieval Kiev and other major cities of Rus': a comparative analysis based on recent archaeological research', *Russian Review* 48: 145–70

Mikheev, V. K. (1985), *Podone v sostave Khazarskogo Kaganata*, Khar'kov

Mühle, E. (1987), 'Die Anfänge Kievs (bis *ca.* 980) in archäologischer Sicht: ein Forschungsbericht', *Jahrbücher für Geschichte Osteuropas* 35: 80–101

Mühle, E. (1988), 'Die topographisch-städtebauliche Entwicklung Kievs vom Ende des 10. bis zum Ende des 12. Jh. im Licht archäologischen Forschungen', *Jahrbücher für Geschichte Osteuropas* 36: 350–76

Müller, L. (ed.) (1977–9), *Handbuch der Nestorchronik*, 3 vols.. (Forum Slavicum 48–50), Munich

Noonan, T. S. (1978), 'Cherniakhovo Culture', in *Modern Encyclopedia of Russian and Soviet History* IV, Gulf Breeze, pp. 241–3

Noonan, T. S. (1980), 'When and how dirhams first reached Russia: a numismatic critique of the Pirenne theory', *Cahiers du Monde Russe et Soviétique* 21: 401–69

Noonan, T. S. (1984), 'Why dirhams first reached Russia: the rôle of Arab–Khazar relations in the development of the earliest Islamic trade with Eastern Europe', *Archivum Eurasiae Medii Aevi* 4: 151–282

Noonan, T. S. (1985), 'Furs, fur trade', in *Dictionary of the Middle Ages*, New York, V, pp. 325–35

Noonan, T. S. (1986), 'Why the Vikings first came to Russia', *Jahrbücher für Geschichte Osteuropas* 34: 321–48

Noonan, T. S. (1988), 'Technology transfer between Byzantium and Eastern Europe: a case study of the glass industry in early Russia', in M. J. Chiat and K. L. Reyerson (eds.), *The Medieval Mediterranean: Cross-cultural Contacts*, St Cloud, MN

Noonan, T. S. (1989), *The Millennium of Russia's First Perestroika: The Origins of a Kievan Glass Industry under Prince Vladimir* (Kennan Institute Occasional Paper 233), Washington, DC

Noonan, T. S. (1992), 'Byzantium and the Khazars: a special relationship?', in J. Shepard and S. Franklin (eds.), *Byzantine Diplomacy*, Aldershot, pp. 109–32

Nosov, E. N. (1990), *Novgorodskoe (riurikovo) Gorodishche*, Leningrad

Obolensky, D. (1971), *The Byzantine Commonwealth: Eastern Europe 500–1453*, London

Oborin, V. (1976), *Drevnee iskusstvo narodov Prikam'ia: Permskii zverinyi stil'*, Perm

Paszkiewicz, H. (1954), *The Origin of Russia*, London and New York

Paszkiewicz, H. (1963), *The Making of the Russian Nation*, London

Poppe, A. (1976), 'The political background of the baptism of Rus': Byzantine–Russian relations between 986–89', *DOP* 30: 195–244

Poppe, A. (1980), 'Das Reich der Rus' in 10. und 11. Jahrhundert: Wandel der Ideenwelt', *Jahrbücher für Geschichte Osteuropas* 28: 334–54

Poppe, A. (1982), *The Rise of Christian Russia*, London

Pritsak, O. (1970), 'An Arabic text of the trade route of the corporation of Ar-Rūs in the second half of the ninth century', *Folia Orientalia* 12: 241–59

Pritsak, O. (1975), 'The Pečenegs: a case of social and economic transformation', *Archivum Eurasiae Medii Aevi* 1: 211–35

Pritsak, O. (1978), 'The Khazar kingdom's conversion to Judaism', *Harvard Ukrainian Studies* 2: 261–81

Pritsak, O. (1981), *The Origin of Rus'*, 1: *Old Scandinavian Sources other than the Sagas*, Cambridge, MA

Rispling, G. (1989), 'The Volga-Bulgarian official coinage, AH 338–376 (AD 949–987)', unpublished computer listing of 23 official types

Rispling, G. (1990), 'The Volga-Bulgarian imitative coinage of al-Amir Yaltawar ("Barman") and Mikhail b. Jafar', in K. Jonsson and B. Malmer (eds.), *Sigtuna Papers: Proceedings of the Sigtuna Symposium on Viking-Age Coinage* (Commentationes de Nummis Saeculorum IX–XI in Suecia Repertis. Nova Series 6), Stockholm and London, pp. 275–82

Rybakov, B. (1965), *Early Centuries of Russian History*, Moscow

Sakharov, A. N. (1978–9), 'The "diplomatic recognition" of ancient Rus (AD 860)', *Soviet Studies in History* 17, no. 4: 36–98

Sawyer, P. H. (1982), *Kings and Vikings: Scandinavia and Europe, AD 700–1100*, London and New York

Schramm, G. (1980), 'Die erste Generation der altrussischen Fürstendynastie. Philologische Argumente für die Historizität von Rjurik und seinen Brüdern', *Jahrbücher für Geschichte Osteuropas* 28: 321–33

Sedov, V. V. (1982), *Vostochnye slaviane v VI–XIIIvv.* (Arkheologiia SSSR), Moscow

Sedov, V. V. (ed.) (1985), *Srednevekovaia Ladoga: Novye arkheologischeskie otkrytiia i issledovaniia*, Leningrad

Sedov, V. V. (ed.) (1987), *Finno-ugry i balty v epokhu srednevekhov'ia* (Arkheologiia SSSR), Moscow

Ševčenko. I. (1971), 'The date and author of the so-called fragments of Toparcha Gothicus', *DOP* 25: 115–88

Shepard, J. (1974), 'Some problems of Russo–Byzantine relations *ca.* 860–*ca.* 1050', *SEER* 52: 10–33

Shepard, J. (1978–9), 'Why did the Russians attack Byzantium in 1043?', *Byzantinisch-Neugriechischen Jahrbücher* 22: 147–212

Shepard, J. (1979), 'The Russian-Steppe frontier and the Black Sea zone', *Archeion Pontou* 35: 218–37

Shepard, J., and Franklin, S. (1996), *The Emergence of Rus, 750–1200*, London

Smedley, J. (1979), 'Archaeology and the history of Cherson: a survey of some results and problems', *Archeion Pontou* 35: 172–92

Smith, R. E. F. (1959), *The Origins of Farming in Russia*, Paris and The Hague

Smith, R. E. F. (1977), *Peasant Farming in Muscovy*, Cambridge

Sorlin, I. (1961), 'Les Traités de Byzance avec la Russie au xe siècle', *Cahiers du Monde Russe et Soviétique* 2: 313–60, 447–75

Stalsberg, A. (1982), 'Scandinavian relations with northwestern Russia during the Viking Age: the archaeological evidence', *Journal of Baltic Studies* 13: 267–95

Stokes, A. D. (1961–2), 'The Balkan campaigns of Svyatoslav Igorevich', *SEER* 40: 466–96

Stokes, A. D. (1961–2), 'The background and chronology of the Balkan campaigns of Svyatoslav Igorevich', *SEER* 40: 45–57

Sverdlov, M. B. (1982–3), 'Family and commune in Ancient Rus', *Soviet Studies in History* 21, no. 2: 1–25

Tatishchev, V. N. (1963), *Istoriia Rossiiskaia*, II, Moscow and Leningrad

Thomsen, V. (1877), *The Relations between Ancient Russia and Scandinavia and the Origin of the Russian State*, Oxford and London

Váňa, Z. (1983), *The World of the Ancient Slavs*, Detroit

Varangian (1970), *Varangian Problems* (Scando-Slavica Supplementum 1), Copenhagen

Vasiliev, A. A. (1946), *The Russian Attack on Constantinople in 860*, Cambridge, MA

Vasiliev, A. A. (1951), 'The second Russian attack on Constantinople', *DOP* 6: 161–225

Vernadsky, G. (1948), *Kievan Russia* (A History of Russia, ed. G Vernadsky and M. Karpovich, 2), New Haven

Vlasto, A. P. (1970), *The Entry of the Slavs into Christendom: An Introduction to the Medieval History of the Slavs*, Cambridge

Vodoff, V. (1988), *Naissance de la Chrétienté russe: la conversion du prince Vladimir de Kiev (989) et ses conséquences*, Paris

Vorren, Ø., and Manker, E. (1962), *Lapp Life and Customs*, Oxford

Wozniak, F. (1984), 'Byzantium, the Pechenegs, and the Khazars in the tenth century: the limitations of a great power's influence on its clients', *Archivum Eurasiae Medii Aevi* 4: 299–316

Zakhoder, B. N. (1962–7), *Kaspiiskii svod svedenii o Vostochnoi Evrope*, 2 vols.., Moscow

Zguta, R. (1975), 'Kievan coinage', *SEER* 53: 483–92

20 BOHEMIA AND POLAND

Abraham, W. (1962), *Organizacja Kościoła w Polsce do połowy XII wieku*, 3rd edn, Poznań

Balzer, O. (1895), *Genealogia Piastów*, Cracow

Bosl, K. (ed.) (1966–7, 1971–4, 1967–8, 1969–70), *Handbuch der Geschichte der böhmischen Länder*, I–IV, Stuttgart

Chrystianizacja (1994), *Chrystianizacja Polski południowej*, Cracow

Davies, N. (1982a, 1982b), *God's Playground: A History of Poland*, 2 vols., 2nd edn, Oxford

Dobiáš J. (1964), *Dějiny československého území před vystoupením Slovanů*, Prague

Dowiat, J. (ed.) (1985), *Kultura Polski średniowiecznej X–XIII wieku*, Warsaw

Dvornik, F. (1949), *The Making of Central and Eastern Europe*, London

Fried, J. (1989), *Otto III. und Boleslaw Chrobry: das Widmungsbild des Aachener Evangeliars, der 'Akt von Gnesen' und das frühe polnische und ungarische Königtum*, Stuttgart

Görich, K. (1993), *Otto III. Romanus, Saxonicus et Italicus: kaiserliche Rompolitik und sächsische Historiographie*, Sigmaringen

Grabski, A. F. (1966), *Bolesław Chrobry: Zarys dziejów politycznych i wojskowych*, 2nd edn, Warsaw

Graus, F. and Ludat, H. (eds.) (1967), *Siedlung und Verfassung Böhmens in der Frühzeit*, Wiesbaden

Hellmann, M. (1985), *Daten der polnischen Geschichte*, Munich

Hoensch, J. K. (1983), *Geschichte Polens*, Stuttgart

Hoensch, J. K. (1987), *Geschichte Böhmens: von der slawischen Landnahme bis ins 20. Jahrhundert*, Munich

Jasiński, K. (1992), *Rodowód pierwszych Piastów*, Warsaw and Wrocław

Kętrzyński, S. (1961), *Polska X–XI wieku*, Warsaw

Kłoczowski, J. (ed.) (1966), *Kościół w Polsce*, 1: *Średniowiecze*, Cracow

Krzemieńska, B. (1979), *Boj knížete Břetislava I. o upevnění českého státu (1039–1041)*, Prague

Krzemieńska, B., and Třeštík D. (1979), 'Wirtschaftliche Grundlagen des frühmittelalterlichen Staates in Mitteleuropa (Böhmen, Polen, Ungarn im 10.-11. Jh.)', *Acta Poloniae Historica* 40: 5–31

Labuda, G. (1946, 1988), *Studia nad początkami państwa polskiego*, 2 vols., Poznań (1 2nd edn Poznań 1987)

Labuda, G. (1992), *Mieszko II król polski (1025–1034): czasy przełomu w dziejach państwa polskiego*, Cracow

Leciejewicz, L. (1989), *Słowianie zachodni. Z dziejów tworzenia się średniowiecznej Europy*, Wrocław

Łowmiański, H. (1963a, 1963b, 1967, 1970, 1973, 1985a, 1985b), *Początki Polski*, I–IV (vol. 6 in two parts), Warsaw

Ludat, H. (1971), *An Elbe und Oder um das Jahr 1000: Skizzen zur Politik des Ottonenreiches und der slavischen Mächte in Mitteleuropa*, Cologne and Vienna

Modzelewski, K. (1975), *Organizacja gospodarcza państwa piastowskiego X–XIII wiek*, Wrocław

Modzelewski, K. (1987), *Chłopi w monarchii wczesnopiastowskiej*, Wrocław

Myśliński, K. (1993), *Polska wobec Słowian Połabskich do końca wieku XII*, Lublin

Nasza (1988), *Nasza Przeszłość*, LXIX, Cracow

Niederle, L. (1919), *Slovanské starožitnosti*, III: *Původ a počátky Slovanů západních*, Prague

Początki (1962a, 1962b), *Początki państwa polskiego: Księga Tysiąclecia*, 2 vols., Poznań

Rhode, G. (1966), *Geschichte Polens: ein Überblick*, 2nd edn, Darmstadt

Sedlar, J. W. (1994), *East Central Europe in the Middle Ages* (A History of East Central Europe 3), Seattle and London

Slavi (1983a, 1983b), *Gli Slavi occidentali e meridionali nell'alto medioevo* (Settimane 30), 2 vols., Spoleto

Słownik (1961, 1964, 1967, 1970, 1975, 1977, 1982, 1991, 1996), *Słownik starożytności słowiańskich: encyklopedyczny zarys kultury Słowian od czasów najdawniejszych do schyłku wieku XII* (Lexicon Antiquitatum Slavicarum), 9 vols., Wrocław

Strzelczyk, J. (1999), *Mieszko Pierwszy*, 2nd edn Poznań

Třeštík, D. (1998), *Počátky Přemyslovců*, Prague

Turek, R. (1963), *Čechy na úsvité dějin*, Prague

Tymieniecki, K. (1951), *Ziemie polskie w starożytności: ludy i kultury najdawniejsze*, Poznań

Urbańczyk, P. (ed.) (1997a), *Origins of Central Europe*, Wrocław

Urbańczyk, P. (ed.) (1997b), *Early Christianity in Central and East Europe*, Warsaw

Wattenbach, W. and Holtzmann, R. (1967), *Deutschlands Geschichtsquellen im Mittelalter: die Zeit der Sachsen und Salier*, vols. 2 and 3, new edn by F.-J. Schmale, Weimar

Zernack, K. (1977), *Osteuropa: eine Einführung in seine Geschichte*, Munich

21 HUNGARY

Antonopoulos, P. (1993), 'Byzantium and the Magyar raids', *Byzantinoslavica* 54: 254–67

Bakay, K. (1967), 'Archäologische Studien zur Frage der ungarischen Staatsgründung. Angaben zur Organisierung des fürstlichen Heeres', *Acta Archaeologica Academiae Scientiarum Hungaricae* 19: 105–73

Bakay, K. (ed.) (1994), *Sacra corona Hungariae*, Szombathely

Bálint, C. (1991), *Südungarn im 10. Jahrhundert*, Budapest

Bartha, A (1975), *Hungarian Society in the Ninth and Tenth Centuries*, Budapest

Boba, I. (1967), *Nomads, Northmen and Slavs: Eastern Europe in the Ninth Century*, Wiesbaden

Bogyay, T. (1976), *Stephanus rex*, Munich and Vienna

Bóna, I. (1971), 'Ein Vierteljahrhundert der Völkerwanderungszeitforschung in Ungarn', *Acta Archaeologica Academiae Scientiarum Hungaricae* 23: 265–336

Bowlus, C. (1995), *Franks, Moravians and Magyars: The Struggle for the Middle Danube 788–907*, Philadelphia

Chalmeta, P. (1976), 'La Mediterannée occidentale et El-Andalus de 933 à 941: les données d'Ibn ayyān', *Rivista degli studi orientali* 50: 337–51

Czeglédy, K. (1983), 'From East to West: the age of nomadic migrations in Eurasia', *Archivum Eurasiae Medii Aevi* 3: 25–125

Darkó, J. (1921), 'Zur Frage der urmagyarischen und urbolgarischen Beziehungen', *Kőrösi Csoma Archivum* 1: 292–301

Déer, J. (1965), 'Karl der Grosse und der Untergang des Awarenreiches', in H. Beumann (ed.), *Karl der Grosse, Persönlichkeit und Geschichte*, Düsseldorf, pp. 719–91

Déer, J. (1966), *Die heilige Krone Ungarns* (Osterreichische Akademie der Wissenschaften, Denkschriften, Phil.-Hist. Kl., 91), Graz

di Cave, C (1995), *L'arrivo degli ungheresi in Europa e la conquista della patria: fonti e letteratura critica*, Spoleto

Dienes, I. (1972), *Die Ungarn um die Zeit der Landnahme*, Budapest

Fasoli, G. (1945), *Le incursioni unghare in Europa nel secolo X*, Florence

Göckenjan, H. (1972), *Hilfsvölker und Grenzwächter im mittelalterlichen Ungarn*, Wiesbaden

Golden, P. (1990) 'Peoples of the Russian Forest Belt', in D. Sinor, (ed.), *The Cambridge History of Early Inner Asia*, Cambridge, pp. 229–55

Györffy, G. (1969a), 'Zu den Anfängen der ungarischen Kirchenorganisation auf Grund neuer quellenkritischer Ergebnisse', *Archivum Historiae Pontificiae* 7: 79–113

Györffy, G. (1969b), 'Les Débuts de l'évolution urbaine en Hongrie', *CCM* 12: 127–46, 253–64

Györffy, G. (1971), 'Der Aufstand von Koppány', in L. Ligeti, (ed.), *Studia Turcica*, Budapest, pp. 175–211

Györffy, G. (1975), 'Système des résidences d'hiver et d'été chez les nomades et les chefs hongroises au xᵉ siècle', *Archivum Eurasiae Medii Aevi* 1: 45–153

Györffy, G. (1983), *Wirtschaft und Gesellschaft der Ungarn um die Jahrtausendwende*, Vienna

Györffy, G. (1984), 'Die Anfänge der ungarischen Kanzlei im 11. Jahrhundert', *AfD* 30: 88–96

Györffy, G. (1985) 'Landnahme, Ansiedlung und Streifzüge der Ungarn', *Acta Historica Academiae Scientiarum Ungaricae* 31: 231–70

Györffy, G. (1988a), *König Stephan der Heilige*, Budapest; English trans. as *King Saint Stephen of Hungary*, Boulder, CO, 1994

Györffy, G. (1988b), 'Nomades et sémi-nomades: la naissance de l'état hongrois', *Settimane* 35: 621–35

Hóman, B. (1940), *Geschichte des ungarischen Mittelalters*, 1, Berlin

Innes, M. (1997), 'Franks and Slavs c. 700–1000: the problem of European expansion before the millennium', *Early Medieval Europe* 6: 201–16

Kiss, A. (1985), 'Studien zur Archäologie der Ungarn im 10. und 11. Jh.', in H. Wolfram and A. Scharer, (eds.), *Die Bayern und ihre Nachbarn*, 2 vols., Vienna, II, pp. 217–380

Leyser, K. (1965), 'The battle of the Lech (955). A study in tenth-century warfare', *History* 50: 1–25

Lipták, P. (1957), 'Awaren und Magyaren im Donau-Theiss-Zwischenstromgebiet', *Acta Archaeologica Academiae Scientiarum Hungaricae* 8: 199–268

Lipták, P. (1983), *Avars and Ancient Hungarians*, Budapest

Lüttich, R. (1910), *Ungarnzüge in Europa im 10. Jh.*, Berlin

Macartney, C. A. (1930), *The Magyars in the Ninth Century*, Cambridge

Macartney, C. A. (1940), *Studies on the Early Hungarian Historical Sources*, Budapest

Makk, F. (1989), *The Árpáds and the Comneni: political relations between Hungary and Byzantium in the 12th Century*, Budapest

Moór, E. (1959), 'Die Benennungen der Ungarn in den Quellen des ix. und x. Jahrhunderts', *Ural-Altaische Jahrbücher* 31: 191–229

Moravcsik, G. (1958), *Byzantinoturcica*, 2nd edn, Berlin

Moravcsik, G. (1967), *Studia Byzantina*, Budapest

Moravcsik, G. (1970), *Byzantium and the Magyars*, Budapest

Ostrogorsky, G. (1951) 'Urum-Despotes. Die Anfänge der Despoteswürde in Byzanz', *BZ* 44: 448–60

Róna-Tas, A. (1988), 'Ethnogenese und Staatsgründung. Die türkische Komponente in der Ethnogenese des Ungartums', in *Studien zur Ethnogenese* (Rheinisch-Westfälische Akademie der Wissenschaft, Düsseldorf, Abhandlungen der Phil.-hist. Kl., 78), Opladen, pp. 107–42

Schünemann, K. (1923), *Die Deutschen in Ungarn vom 9. bis 12. Jahrhundert*, Berlin and Leipzig

Silagi, G. (1988), 'Die Ungarnstürme in der ungarischen Geschichtsschreibung', *Settimane* 35: 245–72

Studien (1983), *Studien zur Machtsymbolik des mittelalterlichen Ungarn* (Insignia regni Hungariae 1), Budapest

Szücs, J. (1972), 'König Stephan in der Sicht der modernen ungarischen Geschichtsforschung', *Südost-Forschungen* 31: 17–40

Tagányi, K. (1902), 'Alte Grenzschutzvorrichtungen und Grenzödland: *gyepü* und *gyepüelve*', *Ungarische Jahrbücher* 1: 105–21

Vajay, S. (1962), 'Grossfürst Geysa von Ungarn', *Südost-Forschungen* 21: 45–101

Vajay, S. (1968), *Der Eintritt des ungarischen Stämmebundes in die europäische Geschichte (862–933)*, Mainz

22–5 THE BYZANTINE AND BULGARIAN EMPIRES

Ahrweiler, H. (1975), *L'Idéologie de l'Empire byzantin*, Paris

Althoff, G. (1991), 'Vormundschaft, Erzieher, Lehrer – Einflüsse auf Otto III. ', in A. von Euw and P. Schreiner (1991b), pp. 277–89

Bakalov, G. (1985), *Srednovekovniiat b'lgarski vladetel (titulatura i insignii)*, Sofia

Barbu, D. (1989), 'Monde byzantin ou monde orthodoxe?', *Revue des Etudes Sud-Est Européennes* 27: 259–71

Berschin, W. (1980), *Griechisch-Lateinisches Mittelalter von Hieronymus zu Nikolaus von Kues*, Berne and Munich

Beševliev, V. (1962), 'Souveränitätsansprüche eines bulgarischen Herrschers im 9. Jahrhundert', *BZ* 55: 11–20

Beševliev, V. (1963), *Die protobulgarischen Inschriften* (Berliner Byzantinische Arbeiten 23), Berlin

Beševliev, V. (1979), *P'rvo-B'lgarski nadpisi*, Sofia

Bibikov, M. V. (1991), 'Sravnitel'nyi analiz sostava "Izbornika Sviatoslava 1073 g." i ego vizantiiskikh analogov', *Vizantiiskii Vremennik* 51: 92–102

Bloch, H. (1984), 'Der Autor der "Graphia aureae urbis Romae"', *DA* 40: 55–175

Bloch, H. (1988), 'Peter the Deacon's vision of Byzantium and a rediscovered treatise in his *Acta S. Placidi*', *Settimane* 34.2, Spoleto, pp. 797–847

Boscolo, A. (1978), *La Sardegna bizantina e alto-giudicale* (Storia della Sardegna antica e moderna 4), Sassari

Božilov, I. (1983), *Tsar Simeon Veliki (893–927): Zlatniiat vek na srednovekovna B'lgariia*, Sofia

Božilov, I. (1986a), 'L'Idéologie politique du tsar Syméon: Pax Symeonica', *Byzbulg* 8: 73–88

Božilov, I. (1986b), 'Preslav et Constantinople: dépendance et indépendance culturelles', in *The 17th International Byzantine Congress: Major Papers (Washington, DC. August 3–8 1986)*, New York, pp. 429–54

Brokkar, W. G. (1972), 'Basil Lecapenus', *Byzantina Neerlandica* 3: 199–234

Brown, T. S. (1993), 'Ethnic independence and cultural deference: the attitude of the Lombard principalities to Byzantium c. 876–1077', in Vavřínek (1993), pp. 5–12

Browning, R. (1975), *Byzantium and Bulgaria*, London

Brühl, C. (1968), *Fodrum, Gistum, Servitium Regis* (Kölner Historische Abhandlungen 14), 2 vols. paginated as 1, Cologne and Graz

Brühl, C. (1989a, 1989b), *Aus Mittelalter und Diplomatik. Gesammelte Aufsätze*, 2 vols., Hildesheim, Munich and Zurich

Brühl, C. (1989c), 'Die Kaiserpfalz bei St. Peter und die Pfalz Ottos III. auf dem Palatin (Neufassung 1983)', in Brühl (1989a), pp. 3–31

Burgmann, L., Fögen, M.-T., and Schminck, A. (eds.) (1985), *Cupido Legum*, Frankfurt am Main

Cameron, A. (1987), 'The construction of court ritual: the Byzantine *Book of Ceremonies*', in D. Cannadine and S. Price (eds.), *Rituals of Royalty: Power and Ceremonial in Traditional Societies*, Cambridge, pp. 106–36

Canard, M. (1953), *Histoire de la dynastie des H'amdanides de Jazīra et de Syrie*, Paris

Cheynet, J.-C. (1990), *Pouvoir et contestations à Byzance (963–1210)* (Byzantina Sorbonensia 9), Paris

Chrysos, E. K. (1975), 'Die "Krönung" Symeons in Hebdomon', *Cyrillomethodianum* 3: 169–73

Connor, C. F. (1991), *Art and Miracles in Medieval Byzantium*, Princeton

Cormack, R. (1985), *Writing in Gold: Byzantine Society and its Icons*, London

Cutler, A. (1984), *The Aristocratic Psalters in Byzantium*, Paris

Dagron, G. (1983), 'Byzance et le modèle islamique au X siècle. A propos des *Constitutions tactiques* de l'empereur Léon VI', *Comptes rendus des séances de l'Académie des Inscriptions et Belles-Lettres*, Paris, pp. 219–43

Davids, A. (ed.) (1995), *The Empress Theophano: Byzantium and the West at the Turn of the First Millennium*, Cambridge

Deér, J. (1961), 'Der Globus des spätrömischen und des byzantinischen Kaisers. Symbol oder Insigne?', *BZ* 54: 53–85, 291–318

Denkova, L. (1993), 'Bogomilism and literacy. (An attempt of general analysis of a tradition)', *Etudes Balkaniques* 1: 90–6

Dimitrov, P. (1987), 'Pet'r chernorizets', *Starob'lgarska Literatura* 21: 26–49

Dobschütz E., von (1899), *Christusbilder*, Leipzig

Dölger, F. (1939), 'Der Bulgarenherrscher als geistlicher Sohn des byzantinischen Kaisers', *Izvestiia na B'lgarskoto Istorichesko Druzhestvo* 16–17 (= *Sbornik v pamet na prof. Pet'r Nikov)*, Sofia, pp. 219–32, repr. in Dölger (1976), pp. 183–96

Dölger, F. (1976), *Byzanz und die europäische Staatenwelt*, Darmstadt

Ducellier, A. (1981), *Le Façade maritime de l'Albanie au moyen âge: Durazzo et Valona du XI au XV siècle* (Institute for Balkan Studies 177), Thessalonika

Ducellier, A. (1986), *Byzance et le monde orthodoxe*, Paris

Duichev (Dujčev), I. (ed.) (1985), *Kiril and Methodios: Founders of Slavonic Writing*, trans. S. Nikolov (East European Monographs 172), Boulder, CO

Dujčev, I. (1961), Bibliographical notice on Gerasimov (1960), *BZ* 54: 249

Dujčev, I. (1965, 1968, 1971), *Medioevo Byzantino-Slavo* (Storia e Letteratura. Raccolta di Studi e Testi 102, 113, 119), 3 vols., Rome

Dujčev, I. (1978), 'On the treaty of 927 with the Bulgarians', *DOP* 32: 217–95

Falkenhausen, V. von (1978), *La dominazione bizantina nell'Italia meridionale dal IX all' XI secolo*, Bari

Falkenhausen, V. von (1989a), 'La vita di S. Nilo come fonte storica per la Calabria bizantina', in *Atti del congresso internazionale su S. Nilo di Rossano 28 Settembre – 1 Ottobre 1986*, Rossano-Grottaferrata, pp. 271–305

Falkenhausen, V. von (1989b), 'Die Städte im byzantinischen Italien', *Mélanges de l'Ecole française de Rome: Moyen Age* 101: 401–64

Farag, W. (1977), *The Truce of Safar A.H. 359, December–January 969–970*, Birmingham

Ferluga, J. (1976), *Byzantium on the Balkans*, Amsterdam

Ferluga, J. (1978), *L'amministrazione bizantina in Dalmazia*, Venice

Fine, J. V. A. (1983) *The Early Medieval Balkans: A Critical Survey from the Sixth to the Twelfth Century*, Ann Arbor

Foss, C. (1976), *Byzantine and Turkish Sardis*, Cambridge, MA and London

Foss, C. (1979), *Ephesus after Antiquity: A Late Antique, Byzantine and Turkish City*, Cambridge

France, J. (1991), 'The occasion of the coming of the Normans to southern Italy', *Journal of Medieval History* 17: 185–205

Frolow, A. (1961), *La Relique de la Vraie Croix: recherches sur le développement d'un culte* (Institut français d'études byzantines. Archives de l'Orient chrétien 7), Paris

Frolow, A. (1965), *Les Reliquaires de la Vraie Croix*, Paris

Gay, J. (1904), *L'Italie méridionale et l'Empire byzantin depuis l'avènement de Basile I jusqu'à la prise de Bari par les Normands*, Paris

Gelzer, H. (1893), 'Ungedruckte und wenig bekannte Bistümerverzeichnisse der orientalischen Kirche, II', *BZ* 2: 22–72

Georgiev, E. (1962), *Raztsvet't na b'lgarskata literatura v IX–X v.*, Sofia

Gerasimov, T. (1934), 'Tri starob'lgarski molivdovula', *Izvestiia na B'lgarskiia Arkheologicheski Institut* 8: 350–60

Gerasimov, T. (1938), 'Olovni pechati na b'lgarskite tsare Simeon i Pet'r', *Izvestiia na B'lgarskiia Arkheologicheski Institut* 12: 354–64

Gerasimov, T. (1960), 'Novootkrit oloven pechat na tsar Simeon', *Izvestiia na Arkheologicheskiia Institut* 23: 67–70

Gerasimov, T. (1976), 'B'lgarski i vizantiiski pechati ot Preslav', *Preslav* 2: 125–41

Görich, K. (1993), *Otto III. Romanus Saxonicus et Italicus: kaiserliche Rompolitik und sächsische Historiographie* (Historische Forschungen 18), Sigmaringen

Grégoire, H. (1937), 'Du nouveau sur l'histoire bulgaro-byzantine. Nicétas Pégonitès vainqueur du roi bulgare Jean Vladislav', *Byz* 12: 283–91

Gregory, T. E. (1974), 'The gold coinage of the Emperor Constantine VII', *The American Numismatic Society Museum Notes* 19: 87–118

Gregory, T. E. (1980), 'The political program of Constantine Porphyrogenitus', *Actes du XV Congrès International d'Etudes Byzantines* IV, Athens, pp. 122–30

Grierson, P. (1973a, 1973b), *Catalogue of the Byzantine Coins in the Dumbarton Oaks Collection: Leo III to Nicephorus III, 717–1081*, 2 vols., Washington, DC

Grumel, V. (1936), *Les Regestes des actes du patriarchat de Constantinople*, I.2: *Les Regestes de 715 à 1043*, Chalcedon

Györffy, G. (1988), *König Stephan der Heilige*, Budapest

Haldon, J. (1992), 'The army and the economy: the allocation and redistribution of surplus wealth in the Byzantine state', *Mediterranean Historical Review* 7: 133–53

Haldon, J. (1993), 'Military service, military lands, and the status of soldiers: current problems and interpretations', *DOP* 45: 1–67

Hamilton, B. (1979), *Monastic Reform, Catharism and the Crusades, 900–1300*, London

Harvey, A. (1989), *Economic Expansion in the Byzantine Empire 900–1200*, Cambridge

Hendy, M. (1985), *Studies in the Byzantine Monetary Economy, c. 300–1450*, Cambridge

Hiestand, R. (1964), *Byzanz und das Regnum Italicum im 10. Jahrhundert*, Zurich

Howard-Johnston, J. D. (1983), 'Byzantine Anzitene', in S. Mitchell (ed.), *Armies and*

Frontiers in Roman and Byzantine Anatolia (BAR, International Series 156), Oxford, pp. 239–90

Hunger, H. (1978a, 1978b), *Die hochsprachliche profane Literatur der Byzantiner*, 2 vols., Munich

Hussey, J. M. (1986), *The Orthodox Church in the Byzantine Empire*, Oxford

Ianeva, P. (1987), 'Za izvorite na *Letopis'ts' v'kratse* v Izbornik 1073 g. ', *Palaeobulgarica* 11(3): 98–104

Ivanov, J. (1970), *B'lgarski starini iz Makedoniia*, Sofia

Jenkins, R. J. H. (1966), *Byzantium, the Imperial Centuries, A.D. 610–1071*, London

Jenkins, R. J. H. (1970), *Studies on Byzantine History of the 9th and 10th Centuries*, London

Jolivet-Levy, C. (1987), 'L'Image du pouvoir dans l'art byzantin à l'époque de la dynastie macédonienne (867–1056)', *Byz* 57: 441–70

Jordanov, I. (1984), 'Molybdobulles de Boris-Mihail (865–889) et de Siméon (893–913)', *Etudes Balkaniques* 4: 89–93

Jurukova, J. (1980), 'Sreb'ren pechat na tsar Pet'r (927–968)', *Numizmatika* 14(3): 3–12

Jurukova, J. (1984), 'La Titulature des souverains du premier royaume bulgare d'après les monuments de la sphragistique', in *Sbornik v pamet na Prof. Stancho Vaklinov*, Sofia, pp. 224–30

Jurukova, J. (1985), 'Novi nabliudeniia v'rkhu niakoi redki pametnitsi na sred'novekov-nata b'lgarska sfragistika', *Numizmatika* 19, no. 3: 15–24

Jurukova, J. and Penchev, V. (eds.), (1990), *B'lgarski srednovekovni pechati i moneti*, Sofia

Karlin-Hayter, P. (1981), *Studies in Byzantine Political History*, London

Kazhdan, A. (1983), 'Certain traits of imperial propaganda in the Byzantine empire from the eighth to the fifteenth centuries', in *Prédication et propagande au moyen âge: Islam, Byzance, Occident* (Penn–Paris–Dumbarton Oaks Colloquia 3), Paris, pp. 13–28

Kennedy, H. (1986), *The Prophet and the Age of the Caliphates: The Islamic Near East from the Sixth to the Eleventh Century*, London

Kennedy, H. (1992), 'Byzantine–Arab diplomacy in the Near East from the Islamic conquests to the mid-eleventh century', in Shepard and Franklin (1992), pp. 133–43

Klaić, N. (1971), *Povijest Hrvata u ranom srednjem vijeku*, Zagreb

Kolias, G. (1939), *Léon Choerosphactès, magistre, proconsul et patrice* (Texte und Forschungen zur Byzantinisch-Neugriechischen Philologie 31), Athens

Kravari, V., Lefort, J. and Morrisson, C. (eds.) (1991), *Hommes et richesses dans l'Empire byzantin*, II: *VIII–XV siècle*, Paris

Kuev, K. (1986), 'Pokhvala na tsar Simeon – rekonstruktsiia i razbor', *Palaeobulgarica* 10(2): 3–23

Kusseff, M. (1950), 'St. Nahum', *SEER* 29: 139–52

Lemerle, P. (1967), '"Roga" et rente d'état aux x–xi siècles', *Revue des Etudes Byzantines* 25: 77–100

Lemerle, P. (1979), *The Agrarian History of Byzantium from the Origins to the Twelfth Century*, Galway

Lesńy, J. (1985), 'Państwo Samuel a jego zachodni sąsiedzi', *Balcanica Posnaniensia* 2: 87–112

Leyser, K. (1973), 'The tenth century in Byzantine–Western relationships', in D. Baker (ed.), *Relations between East and West in the Middle Ages*, Edinburgh, pp. 29–63

Leyser, K. (1988), 'Ends and means in Liudprand of Cremona', in J. D. Howard-Johnston (ed.), *Byzantium and the West c. 850–c. 1200*, Amsterdam, pp. 119–43

Leyser, K. (1995), '*Theophanu divina gratia imperatrix augusta*: western and eastern emperorship in the later tenth century', in Davids (1995), pp. 1–27

McCormick, M. (1986), *Eternal Victory: Triumphal Rulership in Late Antiquity, Byzantium and the Early Medieval West*, Cambridge

Macrides, R. (1992), 'Dynastic marriages and political kinship', in Shepard and Franklin (1992), pp. 263–80

Magdalino, P. (1988), 'The bath of Leo the Wise and the "Macedonian Renaissance" revisited: topography, ceremonial, ideology', *DOP* 42: 97–118

Mango, C. (1980), *Byzantium: The Empire of New Rome*, London

Markopoulos, A. (ed.) (1989), *Konstantinos Z' Porphyrogennetos kai e epoche tou* (B' Diethnes Byzantinologike Synantese), Athens

Martin, J.-M. and Noyé, G. (1991), 'Les Villes de l'Italie byzantine (IX–XI siècle)', in Kravari, Lefort and Morrisson (1991), pp. 27–62

Mercati, S. G. (1970), 'Sull' epitafio di Basilio II Bulgaroctonos', repr. in *Collectanea Byzantina*, Bari, II, pp. 226–31

Mikhailov, S. (1990), 'Po razchitaneto na edin oloven pechat na tsar Simeon', *Palaeobulgarica* 14(1): 111–12

Milev, A. (ed.) (1966), *Gr'tskite zhitiia na Kliment Okhridski*, Sofia

Moffatt, A. (1995), 'The Master of Ceremonies' bottom drawer. The unfinished state of the *De cerimoniis* of Constantine Porphyrogennetos', *BSl* 56: 377–88

Morris, R. (1988), 'The two faces of Nikephoros Phokas', *BMGS* 12: 83–115

Morris, R. (1995), *Monks and Laymen in Byzantium, 843–1118*, Cambridge

Nesbitt, J. and Oikonomides, N. (1991–), *Catalogue of Byzantine Seals at Dumbarton Oaks and in the Fogg Museum of Art*, one vol. published so far, Washington, DC

Nicol, D. (1988), *Byzantium and Venice*, Cambridge

Obolensky, D. (1948), *The Bogomils*, Cambridge

Obolensky, D. (1971), *The Byzantine Commonwealth: Eastern Europe, 500–1453*, London

Obolensky, D. (1988), *Six Byzantine Portraits*, Oxford

Obolensky, D. (1993), 'Byzantium, Kiev and Cherson in the tenth century', in Vavřínek (1993), pp. 108–13

Odorico, P. (1987), 'Il calamo d'argento. Un carme inedito in onore di Romano II', *Jahrbuch der österreichischen Byzantinistik* 37: 65–93

Ohnsorge, W. (1958), *Abendland und Byzanz*, Darmstadt

Ohnsorge, W. (1983), *Ost-Rom und der Westen*, Darmstadt

Oikonomides, N. (ed.) (1987, 1990), *Studies in Byzantine Sigillography*, 2 vols., Washington, DC

Pavlova, R. (1991), 'Za tvorchestvoto na Pet'r chernorizets', *Starob'lgarska Literatura* 25–6: 73–84

Petrovskii, N. M. (1913), 'Pis'mo patriarkha Konstantinopol'skogo Feofilakta tsariu Bolgarii Petru', *Izvestiia otdeleniia russkogo iazyka i slovesnosti Imperatorskoi Akademii Nauk* 18(3): 356–72

Popov, G. (1985), *Triodni proizvedeniia na Konstantin Preslavski* (Kirilo-Metodievski Studii 2), Sofia

Prinzing, G. (1993), 'Das Bamberger Gunthertuch in neuer Sicht', in Vavřínek (1993), pp. 218–31

Rentschler, M. (1981), *Liudprand von Cremona* (Frankfurter Wissenschaftliche Beiträge, Kulturwissenschaftliche Reihe 14), Frankfurt am Main

Rodley, L. (1985), *Cave Monasteries of Byzantine Cappadocia*, Cambridge

Runciman, S. (1929), *The Emperor Romanus Lecapenus and his Reign*, Cambridge

Runciman, S. (1930), *A History of the First Bulgarian Empire*, London

Rydén, L. (1984), 'The portrait of the Arab Samonas in Byzantine literature', *Graeco-Arabica* 3: 101-8

Sansterre, J.-M. (1989), 'Otton III et les saints ascètes de son temps', *Rivista di storia della chiesa in Italia* 43: 377-412

Sansterre, J.-M. (1990), 'Le Monastère des Saints-Boniface et Alexis sur l'Aventin et l'expansion du christianisme dans le cadre de la "Renovatio imperii Romanorum"', *Revue Benedictine* 100: 493-506

Schminck, A. (1986), *Studien zu mittelbyzantinischen Rechtsbüchern* (Forschungen zur byzantinischen Rechtsgeschichte 13), Frankfurt am Main

Schramm, G. (1981), *Eroberer und Eingesessene*, Stuttgart

Schramm, P. E. (1929, 1957), *Kaiser, Rom und Renovatio*, 2 vols., vol. 1 2nd edn, Darmstadt

Schramm, P. E. (1954, 1955, 1956), *Herrschaftszeichen und Staatsymbolik* (Schriften der MGH 13/1-3), 3 vols., Stuttgart

Schramm, P. E. (1968a, 1968b, 1969b, 1970, 1971), *Kaiser, Könige und Päpste: Gesammelte Aufsätze zur Geschichte des Mittelalters*, 4 vols. in 5, Stuttgart

Schramm, P. E. (1969a), 'Kaiser Otto III. (*980, †1002), seine Persönlichkeit und sein "byzantinischer Hofstaat"', in Schramm (1969b), pp. 277-97

Schramm, P. E. and Mütherich, F. (1962), *Denkmale der deutschen Könige und Kaiser* (Veröffentlichungen des Zentralinstituts für Kunstgeschichte in München 2), Munich

Segal, J. B. (1970), *Edessa, 'The Blessed City'*, Oxford

Sevčenko, I. (1992), 'Re-reading Constantine Porphyrogenitus', in Shepard and Franklin (1992), pp. 167-95

Shepard, J. (1988), 'Aspects of Byzantine attitudes and policy towards the West in the tenth and eleventh centuries', in J. D. Howard-Johnston (ed.), *Byzantium and the West c. 850-c. 1200*, Amsterdam, pp. 67-118

Shepard, J. (1991), 'Symeon of Bulgaria – peacemaker', *Godishnik na Sofiiskiia universitet "Sv. Kliment Okhridski" Nauchen tsent'r za slaviano-vizantiiski prouchvaniia "Ivan Duichev"*, 83(3): 9-48

Shepard, J. (1995a), 'A marriage too far? Maria Lekapena and Peter of Bulgaria', in A. Davids (ed.), *The Empress Theophano: Byzantium and the West*, Cambridge, pp. 121-49

Shepard, J. (1995b), 'Imperial information and ignorance: a discrepancy', *BSl* 56:107-16

Shepard, J. and Franklin, S. (eds.) (1992), *Byzantine Diplomacy*, Aldershot

Simeonova, L. (1988), 'Vizantiiskata kontseptsiia za izkustvoto da se upravliava spored fotievoto poslanie do kniaz Boris I', *Problemi na Kulturata*, no. 4: 91-104

Simeonova, L. (1993), 'Power in Nicholas Mysticus' letters to Symeon of Bulgaria', in Vavřínek (1993), pp. 89-94

Šišić, F. von (1917), *Geschichte der Kroaten*, I, Zagreb

Soustal, P. (1991), *Thrakien* (Tabula Imperii Byzantini 6: Österreichische Akademie der Wissenschaften, Phil.-hist. Kl., Denkschriften 221), Vienna

Sternbach, L. (1899), 'Christophorea', *Eos* 5: 7-21

Striker, C. L. (1981), *The Myrelaion (Bodrum Camii) in Istanbul*, Princeton

Sutherland, J. (1975), 'The mission to Constantinople in 968 and Liudprand of Cremona', *Traditio* 31: 55-81

Tapkova-Zaimova, V. (1979), *Byzance et les Balkans à partir du VI siècle*, London

Tapkova-Zaimova, V. (1986), 'Les Problèmes du pouvoir dans les relations bulgaro-byzantines (jusqu'au XII s.)', *Byzbulg* 8: 124–30

Tapkova-Zaimova, V. (1993), 'L'Administration byzantine au Bas Danube (fin du X–XI s.)', in Vavřínek (1993), pp. 95–101

Tellenbach, G. (1982), 'Kaiser, Rom und Renovatio. Ein Beitrag zu einem grossen Thema', in N. Kamp and J. Wollasch (eds.), *Tradition als historische Kraft*, Berlin and New York, pp. 231–53

Thierry, N. (1985), 'Un Portrait de Jean Tzimiskès en Cappadoce', *Travaux et Mémoires* 9: 477–84

Thomson, F. J. (1982), 'Chrysostomica Palaeoslavica. A preliminary study of the sources of the Chrysorrhoas (Zlatostruy) collection', *Cyrillomethodianum* 6: 1–65

Thomson, F. J. (1993), 'The Symeonic legium – problems of its origin, content, textology and edition, together with an English translation of the Eulogy of Tsar Symeon', *Palaeobulgarica* 17: 37–53

Tinnefeld, F. (1991), 'Die Braut aus Byzanz – Fragen zu Theophanos Umfeld und Gesellschaftlicher Stellung vor ihrer abendländischen Heirat', in Wolf (1991), pp. 247–61

Totev, T. (1987), 'Les Monastères de Pliska et de Preslav aux IX–X siècles', *BSl* 48: 185–200

Totev, T. (1989), 'Oloven pechat na tsar Pet'r (927–968)', *Numizmatika* 23(2): 40–1

Toynbee, A. J. (1973), *Constantine Porphyrogenitus and his World*, Oxford

Treitinger, O. (1956), *Die oströmische Kaiser- und Reichsidee nach ihrer Gestaltung im höfischen Zeremoniell*, Darmstadt

Tsougarakis, D. (1988), *Byzantine Crete from the 5th Century to the Venetian Conquest*, Athens

Vasiliev, A. A. (1935, 1968, 1950, 1961), *Byzance et les Arabes*, 3 vols., vol. II in 2 parts, Brussels

Vavřínek, V. (ed.) (1993), *Byzantium and its Neighbours from the mid-9th till the 12th Centuries* (= *BSl* 54), Prague

von Euw, A. (1991), 'Ikonologie der Heiratsurkunde der Kaiserin Theophanu', in A. von Euw, and P. Schreiner, (1991b), pp. 175–91

von Euw, A. and Schreiner, P. (eds.) (1991a, 1991b), *Kaiserin Theophanu: Begegnung des Ostens und Westens um die Wende des ersten Jahrtausends*, 2 vols., Cologne

Walker, P. E. (1977), 'The "Crusade" of John Tzimiskes in the light of new Arabic evidence', *Byz* 47: 301–27

Weitzmann, K. (1971), 'The Mandylion and Constantine Porphyrogennetos', repr. in his *Studies in Classical and Byzantine Manuscript Illumination*, Chicago, pp. 224–46

Weitzmann, K. (1972), *Ivories and Steatites, Catalogue of the Byzantine and Early Medieval Antiquities in the Dumbarton Oaks Collection*, III, Washington, DC

Wentzel, H. (1971), 'Das byzantinische Erbe der ottonischen Kaiser: Hypothesen über den Brautschatz der Theophanu', *Aachener Kunstblätter* 40: 11–84

Westermann-Angerhausen, H. (1995), 'Did Theophano leave her mark on the Ottonian sumptuary arts?', in Davids (1995), pp. 244–64

Wolf, G. (ed.) (1991), *Kaiserin Theophanu: Prinzessin aus der Fremde – des Westreichs grosse Kaiserin*, Cologne, Weimar and Vienna

26 SOUTHERN ITALY IN THE TENTH CENTURY

Borsari, S. (1950), 'Monasteri bizantini nell'Italia meridionale longobarda', *Archivio Storico per le Provincie Napoletane* 71: 1–16

Borsari, S. (1959), 'Istituzioni feudali e parafeudali nella Puglia bizantina', *Archivio Storico per le Provincie Napoletane* 77: 123–35

Borsari, S. (1963), *Il monachesimo bizantino nella Sicilia e nell'Italia meridionale prenormanne*, Naples

Borsari, S. (1966/7), 'Aspetti del dominio bizantino in Capitanata', *Atti dell'accademia Pontaniana*, n.s. 16: 55–66

Cassandro, G. (1969), 'Il ducato bizantino', in *Storia di Napoli*, II.1, Naples, pp. 3–408

Cilento, N. (1966), *Le origine della signoria capuana nella Longobardia minore*, Rome

Cilento, N. (1971), *Italia meridionale longobarda*, 2nd edn, Naples

Citarella, A. O. (1967), 'The relations of Amalfi with the Arab world before the Crusades', *Speculum* 42: 299–312

Citarella, A. O. (1968), 'Patterns in medieval trade. The commerce of Amalfi before the Crusades', *Journal of Economic History* 28: 531–55

Del Treppo, M. (1955), 'La vita economica e sociale in una grande abbazia del Mezzogiorno: San Vincenzo al Volturno nell'alto medioevo', *Archivio Storico per le Provincie Napoletane* 74: 31–110

Delogu, P. (1977), *Mito di una città meridionale*, Naples

Falkenhausen, V. von (1967), *Untersuchungen über die byzantinische Herrschaft in Süditalien vom 9. bis ins 11. Jahrhundert*, Wiesbaden

Falkenhausen, V. von (1968), 'Taranto in epoca bizantina', *SM*, 3rd series 9: 133–68

Falkenhausen, V. von (1973), 'Zur byzantinischen Verwaltung Luceras am Ende des 10. Jahrhunderts', *Quellen und Forschungen aus Italienischen Archiven und Bibliotheken* 53: 395–406

Falkenhausen, V. von (1983), 'I longobardi meridionali', in G. Galasso (ed.), *Storia d'Italia*, III: *Il Mezzogiorno dai Bizantini a Federico II*, Turin, pp. 251–364

Falkenhausen, V. von (1989), 'Die Städte im byzantinischen Italien', *Mélanges de l'Ecole française de Rome. Moyen Age* 101: 401–64

Galasso, G. (1959–60), 'Le città campane nell'alto medioevo', *Archivio Storico per le Provincie Napoletane* 77: 9–42 and 78: 9–53

Gay, J. (1904), *L'Italie méridionale et l'empire byzantin depuis l'avènement de Basile Ier jusqu'à la prise de Bari par les Normands (867–1071)*, Paris

Guillou, A. (1965), 'La Lucanie byzantine: étude de géographie historique', *Byz* 35: 119–49; reprinted in Guillou (1970)

Guillou, A. (1970), *Studies on Byzantine Italy*, London

Guillou, A. (1978), *Culture et société en Italie byzantine (VIe–XIe s.)*, London

Guillou, A. (1983), 'L'Italia bizantina dalla caduta di Ravenna all'arrivo dei Normanni', in G. Galasso (ed.), *Storia d'Italia*, III: *Il Mezzogiorno dai Bizantini a Federico II*, Turin, pp. 3–126

Hoffmann, H. (1969), 'Die Anfänge der Normannen in Süditalien', *Quellen und Forschungen aus Italienischen Archiven und Bibliotheken* 49: 95–144

Holtzmann, W. and Guillou, A. (1961), 'Zwei Katepansukunden aus Tricarico', *Quellen und Forschungen aus Italienischen Archiven und Bibliotheken* 41: 1–28; reprinted in Guillou (1970)

Kreutz, B. (1991), *Before the Normans: Southern Italy in the Ninth and Tenth Centuries*, Philadelphia

Loud, G. A. (1994a), 'Montecassino and Byzantium in the tenth and eleventh centuries', in M. Mullett and A. Kirby (eds.), *The Theotokos Evergetis and Eleventh Century Byzantium* (Belfast Byzantine Texts and Translations 6.1), Belfast

Loud, G. A. (1994b), 'The Liri Valley in the Middle Ages', in J. W. Hayes and I. P. Martini (eds.), *Archaeological Survey in the Lower Liri Valley, Central Italy under the Direction of Edith Mary Wightman* (British Archaeological Reports, International Series 595), Oxford, pp. 53–68

Martin, J. M. (1980), 'Eléments préféodaux dans les principautés de Bénévent et de Capoue (fin du VIIIe siècle-début du XIe siècle): modalités de privatisation du pouvoir', in G. Duby and P. Toubert (eds.), *Structures féodales et féodalisme dans l'Occident méditerranéen (X^e–XIIIe siècles) (Colloque international organisé par le CNRS et l'Ecole française de Rome, 10–13 octobre 1978)*, Rome, pp. 553–86

Martin, J. M. (1993), *La Pouille du VIème au XIIème siècle*, Rome

Ménager, L.-R. (1958–9), 'La Byzantinisation religieuse de l'Italie méridionale (IXe–XIIe siècles) et la politique monastique des Normands d'Italie', *Revue d'Histoire Ecclésiastique* 53: 747–74, and 54: 5–40

Mor, C. G. (1951), 'La lotta fra la chiesa greca e la chiesa latina in Puglia nal secolo X', *Archivio Storico Pugliese* 4: 58–64

Mor, C. G. (1952, 1953), *L'età feudale*, 2 vols., Milan

Poupardin, R. (1907), *Les Institutions politiques et administratives des principautés lombards de l'Italie méridionale (IXe–XIe siècles)*, Paris

Schwarz, U. (1978), *Amalfi im frühen Mittelalter (9.–11. Jahrhundert) Untersuchungen zur Amalfitaner Überlieferung*, Tübingen

Skinner, P. (1995), *Family Power in Southern Italy: The Duchy of Gaeta and its Neighbours, 850–1139*, Cambridge

Taviani-Carozzi, H. (1980), 'Pouvoir et solidarités dans la principauté de Salerne à la fin du Xe siècle', in G. Duby and P. Toubert (eds.), *Structures féodales et féodalisme dans l'Occident méditerranéen (X^e–XIIIe siècles) (Colloque international organisé par le CNRS et l'Ecole française de Rome, 10–13 octobre 1978)*, Rome, pp. 587–606

Taviani-Carozzi, H. (1991a), 'Caractères originaux des institutions politiques et administratives dans les principautés lombardes d'Italie méridionale au Xe siècle', *Settimane* 38: 273–328

Taviani-Carozzi, H. (1991b), *La Principauté lombarde de Salerne (IXe–XIe siècle): pouvoir et société en Italie lombarde méridionale*, Rome

Toubert, P. (1976), 'Pour une histoire de l'environnement économique et social du Mont Cassin (IXe–XIIe siècles)', *Comptes Rendus de l'Académie des Inscriptions et Belles-Lettres*: 689–702

Vehse, O. (1927), 'Das Bündnis gegen die Sarazenen vom Jahre 915', *Quellen und Forschungen aus Italienischen Archiven und Bibliotheken* 19: 181–204

Wickham, C. J. (1981), *Early Medieval Italy: Central Power and Local Society 400–1000*, London and Basingstoke

Wickham, C. J. (1985), 'The *Terra* of San Vincenzo al Volturno in the 8th to 12th centuries: the historical framework', in R. Hodges and J. Mitchell (eds.), *San Vincenzo al Volturno: The Archaeology, Art and Territory of an Early Medieval Monastery* (BAR International Series 252), Oxford, pp. 227–58

27 SICILY AND AL-ANDALUS UNDER MUSLIM RULE

Amari, M. (1933, 1935, 1939), *Storia dei Musulmani di Sicilia*, ed. C. Nallino, 3 vols., Catania

Ahmad, A. (1974), *A History of Islamic Sicily*, Edinburgh

Chalmeta, P. (1975), 'Concessiones territoriales en Al-Andalus', *Cuadernos de Historia* 6: 1–90

Glick, T. F. (1979), *Islamic and Christian Spain in the Early Middle Ages*, Princeton

Guichard, P. (1977), *Structures 'orientales' et 'occidentales' dans l'Espagne musulmane*, Paris

Guichard, P. (1991), *L'Espagne et la Sicile musulmane aux XIe et XIe siècles*, Lyons

Lévi-Provençal, E. (1932), *L'Espagne musulmane au Xème siècle*, Paris

Lévi-Provençal, E. (1950a, 1950b, 1951), *Histoire de l'Espagne musulmane*, 3 vols., Paris

Lomax, D. (1978), *The Reconquest of Spain*, London

Manzano Moreno, E. (1991), *La frontera de al-andalus en epoca omeya*, Madrid

Martinez-Gros, G. (1992), *L'Ideologie omeyyade: la construction de la legitimité du Califat de Cordoue*, Madrid

Pavon, B. (1992), *Ciudades Hispanomusulmanas*, Madrid

Scales, P. C. (1994), *The Fall of the Caliphate of Cordoba*, Leiden

Vallve, J. (1992), *El Califato de Cordoba*, Madrid

Vasiliev, A. A. (1935, 1968, 1950, 1961), *Byzance et les Anabes*, 3 vols. vol. II in 2 parts, Brussels

Viguera Molins, M. J. (ed.) (1994), *Los Reinos de Taifas: al-Andalus en el Siglo XI* (Historia de España Menendez Pidal 8), Madrid

Wasserstein, D. (1986), *The Rise and Fall of the Party Kings: Politics and Society in Islamic Spain, 1002–1086*, Princeton

Wasserstein, D. (1993), *The Caliphate in the West*, Oxford

28 THE SPANISH KINGDOM

Arbeloa, J. (1969), *Los orígines del reino de Navarra*, III: *905–925*, San Sebastián

Baliñas Pérez, C. (1988), *Defensores e traditores: un modelo de relación entre poder monárquico e oligarquía na Galicia altomedieval (718–1037)*, Santiago de Compostela

Baliñas Pérez, C. (1992), *Do mito á realidade: a definición social e territorial de Galicia na alta idade media*, Santiago de Compostela

Cañade Juste, A. (1976), *La campaña musulmana de Pamplona (año 924)*, Pamplona

Collins, R. (1985), '*Sicut lex Gothorum continet*: law and charters in ninth- and tenth-century León and Catalonia', *EHR* 100: 489–512

Collins, R. (1986), *The Basques*, Oxford

Collins, R. (1993), 'Queens-dowager and queens-regent in tenth-century León and Navarre', in J. C. Parsons (ed.), *Medieval Queenship*, New York and Gloucester, pp. 79–92

Collins, R. (1995), *Early Medieval Spain, 400–1000*, 2nd edn, London

d'Abadal i de Vinyals, R. (1948), *L'abat Oliba i la seva època*, 2nd edn, Barcelona

de Almeida Fernandes, A. (1982), *Adosinda e Ximeno*, Guimarães

de Oliveira Marques, A. H. (1972), *História de Portugal*, I, Lisbon

Díaz y Díaz, M. C. (1983), *Códices visigóticos en la monarquía leonesa*, León

Díaz y Díaz, M. C. (1979), *Libros y librerías en la Rioja altomedieval*, Logroño

Díez Herrera, C. (1990), *La formación de la sociedad feudal en Cantabria*, Santander

Durán Gudiol, A. (1988), *Los condados de Aragón y Sobrarbe*, Zaragoza

Fernández Conde, F. J. (1971), *El libro de los Testamentos de la Catedral de Oviedo*, Rome

Fernández del Pozo, J. M. (1984), 'Alfonso V, rey de León: estudio histórico-documental', in J. M. Fernández Catón (ed.), *León y su historia*, v, León, pp. 9–262

Galtier Martí, F. (1981), *Ribagorza, condado independiente*, Zaragoza

Goñi Gaztambide, J. (1979), *Historia de los obispos de Pamplona*, i: *s. IV–XIII*, Pamplona

Gros Bitria, E. (1980), *Los límites diocesanos en el Aragón oriental*, Zaragoza

Hitchcock, R. (1978), 'El supuesto mozarabismo andaluz', in *Actas del I Congreso de Historia de Andalucía*, i, Córdoba, pp. 149–51

Isla Frez, A. (1992), *La sociedad gallega en la alta edad media*, Madrid

Lévi-Provençal, E. (1950a, 1950b, 1951), *Histoire de l'Espagne musulmanne*, 3 vols.., Leiden and Paris

Linehan, P. (1993), *History and the Historians of Medieval Spain*, Oxford

Martín Duque, A. J. (ed.) (1983), *Documentación medieval de Leire (siglos IX a XII)*, Pamplona

Martínez Díez, G. (1982), *Fueros locales en el territorio de la provincia de Burgos*, Burgos

Martínez Díez, G. (1988), 'Los fueros leoneses: 1017–1336', in *El reino de León en la edad media*, i: *Cortes, concilios y fueros*, León, pp. 285–352

Mattoso, J. (1981), *A Nobreza medieval portuguesa, a família e o poder*, Lisbon

Mattoso, J. (1982), *Religião e cultura na idade média portuguesa*, Lisbon

Pérez de Urbel, J. (1950), *Sancho el Mayor de Navarra*, Madrid

Pérez de Urbel, J. (1969a, 1969b, 1970), *El condado de Castilla*, 3 vols.., Madrid

Ramos Loscertales, J. M. (1961), *El Reino de Aragón bajo la dinastía pamplonesa*, Salamanca

Rodríguez, J. (1972), *Ramiro II, rey de León*, León

Rodríguez, J. (1982), *Ordoño III*, León

Rodríguez, J. (1987), *Sancho I y Ordoño IV, reyes de León*, León

Sánchez-Albornoz, C. (1965), *Una ciudad de la España cristiana hace mil años*, Madrid

Sánchez-Albornoz, C. (1970), 'El Ejército y la guerra en el reino asturleonés' in Sanchez-Albornoz, *Investigaciones y documentos sobre las instituciones hispanas*, Santiago de Chile, pp. 202–86

Sánchez-Albornoz, C. (1976a), *Vascos y Navarros en su primera historia*, Madrid

Sánchez-Albornoz, C. (1976b, 1976c, 1979), *Viejos y nuevos estudios sobre instituciones medievales españolas*, 3 vols., Madrid

Ubieto Arteta, A. (1989), *Historia de Aragón: orígenes de Aragón*, Zaragoza

Ubieto Arteta, A. (1963), 'Los reyes pamploneses entre 905 y 970: notas cronológicas', *Príncipe de Viana* 24: 77–82

Viñayo, A. (1982), 'Reinas e infantas de León, abadesas y monjas del Monasterio de San Pelayo y San Isidoro', in *Semana de Historia del Monacato Cantabro-Astur-Leonés*, León, pp. 123–35

INDEX